THE INFLUENCE OF MILTON

THE
INFLUENCE OF MILTON
ON ENGLISH POETRY

BY

RAYMOND DEXTER HAVENS
OF THE UNIVERSITY OF ROCHESTER

New York
RUSSELL & RUSSELL
1961

TO

CECILIA BEAUX

WHOSE PAINTINGS ARE BUT ONE ASPECT

OF HER DEVOTION TO THE TRUE

AND THE BEAUTIFUL

Homage to him
His debtor band, innumerable as waves
Running all golden from an eastern sun,
Joyfully render, in deep reverence
Subscribe, and as they speak their Milton's name,
Rays of his glory on their foreheads bear.

GEORGE MEREDITH.

PREFACE

FIFTEEN years ago last spring Mr. C. N. Greenough, now dean of Harvard College, suggested to me Milton's influence in the eighteenth century as one of a number of desirable subjects for a doctor's thesis. Since that time, except for my first three years of teaching and a year and a half during the war, this study has taken all the hours not devoted to professional duties, all my summers, and all of three entire years. I am embarrassingly conscious that this expenditure of time is quite disproportionate to the results; yet, as Michael Wodhull (who had planned to complete his translation of Euripides in "about one year") wrote, a century since, "notwithstanding about eight years have elapsed, during which I cannot charge myself with any gross degree of remissness or inattention, I feel much more inclined to express my fears, lest I should have been too hasty in the publication, than to apologise for my tardiness."

The danger in a study of this kind is that the writer shall be as one who walks in a mist, seeing only what is immediately before him. More time for continuous reading, not alone in the poetry but in the philosophy and criticism of the period, together with more attention to its history, would, I realize, have made the work broader, richer, meatier, and in every way more significant. For the title indicates only the principal subject with which the book is concerned, since I have endeavored not alone to study Milton's influence (touching also on that of his more important followers), but to make some historical and critical evaluation of the works he influenced, to trace the course of blank-verse translations and the development of the principal types of unrimed poetry,—such as the descriptive, the epic, and the technical treatise,—to reach a better understanding of the eighteenth-century lyric awakening, to follow the history of non-dramatic blank verse from its beginnings to the boyhood of Tennyson, and of the sonnet from the restoration of the Stuarts to the accession of Victoria.

My method has been to examine, at least cursorily, all the available English poetry written between 1660 and 1837 regardless of its esthetic value or historical importance, and to reëxamine with more care all that seemed to have any real significance for my purposes. Notwithstanding a constant effort to reduce the bulk of the footnotes, appendices, and bibliographies, such machinery presents an array almost as appalling to read as it was time-consuming to prepare. Yet in a field where assumptions and unsupported assertions have been rife and scholarship is still young, there is need of such dry bones of literary history.

I am grateful to the authorities and attendants of the Harvard Library for the courteous and generous treatment they have given me throughout many years, for their willingness to buy books I suggested, and for their very liberal purchases of other books through which in a relatively few years they have built up a notable collection of eighteenth-century literature. I owe much to my former teachers at Harvard, not only for information but for training and inspiration. To Mr. Greenough, who started me on this study, to Mr. Neilson (now president of Smith College), who read my thesis, chapter by chapter, as it was written and made many helpful suggestions, and to Mr. Kittredge, who gave me letters to various English libraries, ordered books I needed, and otherwise aided me, I am especially indebted. None of these gentlemen, however, are in any way responsible for the pages that follow; for, from the time my thesis was accepted until the rewritten and greatly enlarged work was submitted to the syndics of the Harvard University Press, the only person who has seen any of the manuscript (except Mr. and Mrs. E. H. Hall, who were good enough to read Part I) is my friend and assistant, Miss Addie F. Rowe. Since 1916 Miss Rowe has devoted all her time to the book, bringing to it rare patience and thoroughness, together with experience in preparing manuscripts for publication. She has pointed out and helped to remove infelicities of expression, has called my attention to books that I had not seen as well as to Miltonic phrases that I had not noticed, and in one way or another has improved every page.

Milton's poetry is cited from W. A. Wright's edition, Cambridge, 1903. I shall be glad to receive corrections or additions from any who will be kind enough to send them.

R. D. H.

ROCHESTER, NEW YORK.

CONTENTS

PART I

THE ATTITUDE OF THE EIGHTEENTH CENTURY TOWARDS MILTON

PART II

THE INFLUENCE OF PARADISE LOST

THE INFLUENCE OF PARADISE LOST AS SHOWN IN THE MORE IMPORTANT TYPES OF BLANK-VERSE POETRY

PART III

THE SHORTER POEMS

APPENDICES

BIBLIOGRAPHIES

PART I

THE ATTITUDE OF THE EIGHTEENTH CENTURY TOWARDS MILTON

CHAPTER I

MILTON'S FAME IN THE EIGHTEENTH CENTURY

A FEW years ago one of America's most distinguished citizens wrote, "As to the *Paradise Lost* . . . I have never read it as a whole, and I doubt whether I have known any other person who has ever done so." These words carry weight, for their author was a gentleman of fine culture and of unusually wide acquaintance among cultivated persons both in academic and in diplomatic circles. Nor is his testimony unique. A well-known orator won the smiling approval of a large audience some twenty-five years since, when he referred to Milton's epic as "a poem that every one talks about and no one reads." Conditions may be better in Great Britain and her colonies; yet within the last decade an English author has likened Milton to "the colossal image of some god in a remote and rarely visited shrine." [1] It is to be feared that most persons, though willing to concede the greatness of *Paradise Lost*, regard it as a long, dreary work which no one ever disturbs of his own free will. Of course we are not now concerned with the large class whose reading is confined almost exclusively to newspapers and cheap magazines, but with that fit audience which does turn for inspiration, comfort, and joy to Shakespeare, Wordsworth, Keats, and Tennyson. Even in this select company an admirer of Milton seems to be rare.

Most of us, therefore, have no hesitation in agreeing with the assertion, "Milton has never been a popular poet as Shakespeare is popular, never perhaps even as Scott is popular, or as Byron was in his day and generation." [2] Nor do we question Mr. Saintsbury's dictum that, although the eighteenth century "did not thoroughly understand them, it accepted even Shakespeare and Milton. . . . It regarded Dryden . . . very much as we should regard Shakespeare and Milton rolled into one." [3] Towards the middle of that century, to be sure, Milton and Spenser are known to have played a considerable part in the "romantic revival"; but "by the Augus-

[1] W. M. Dixon, *English Epic and Heroic Poetry* (1912), 201.
[2] H. S. Pancoast, *Some Paraphrasers of Milton*, in *Andover Review*, xv. 53.
[3] *Peace of the Augustans, a Survey of Eighteenth-Century Literature as a Place of Rest and Refreshment* (1916, a work almost as stimulating and unhackneyed as its title leads one to expect), 91.

tans," it is agreed, Milton "was shunned and practically neglected."[1]
Austin Dobson, whose familiarity with the period is unrivalled, says,
in speaking of Mrs. Delany (1700–1788), "During the earlier half of
her lifetime, Pope reigned paramount in poetry, and Milton was
practically forgotten: during the latter half, people were beginning
to forget Pope, and to remember Milton."[2] These views are not
only accepted by most students, but, as they agree with what we
know of Milton and of the age of prose, there would seem to be no
reason for questioning them; yet, since almost any generalization
regarding the eighteenth century needs to be closely scrutinized, it
may be well to discover on what basis they rest.[3]

We naturally turn first of all to the editions of Milton's works,
and, in order to speak with greater certainty on a highly-complicated
matter, we had better confine ourselves to his principal poem. Here
a genuine surprise awaits us, for we find that between 1705 and 1800
Paradise Lost was published over a hundred times.[4] The wonder
grows when we look at the *Faerie Queene*, which, we are accustomed
to think, had approximately the same number of readers as the epic.
If so, they must have borrowed most of their copies, for Spenser's
poem appeared only seven times in the same period. Shakespeare,

[1] W. L. Phelps, *Beginnings of the English Romantic Movement* (Boston, 1893), 87.

[2] *Miscellanies* (2d series, 1902), 110.

[3] Since the present chapter covers much the same ground as J. W. Good's *Studies in
the Milton Tradition* (Univ. of Illinois, Urbana, 1915) and makes use of similar evidence,
it seems only fair to indicate the references to Milton for which I am indebted to Mr.
Good. I have not, however, specified any of the material used in his book which I had
collected before the *Studies* appeared, — not a little of which, indeed, was in my hands
some years before he began his researches. At the same time, the passages to which his
name is attached do not show all my obligations to him; for many suggestions which
it would be impossible to point out definitely, and which were often remote from the
subject he was considering, have come to me as I have read the material that he has so
painstakingly collected.

[4] I have left the number indefinite because without a careful, personal examination
of each edition it is impossible to say how many there are. Several in my bibliography,
which differs considerably from that published by Mr. Good (*Studies*, 25–7), may be
duplicates, while others that should be in it have probably escaped me. A number that
Mr. Good omits I found in English and American libraries which he may not have
consulted, and the same is presumably true of many of those in his list that are not in
mine. But, even if we had a faultless bibliography, there would still be the question as
to how much of it ought to be included under the term "editions" or "publications"
of *Paradise Lost*. Do such categories embrace translations, prose versions, adaptations
(oratorios, for example), issues containing only part of the poem, and Irish, Scottish,
and American editions? Assuming that they do not, and accordingly omitting the six
versions in prose and all other adaptations and translations even when accompanied by
the original text, as well as all publications outside of the British Isles and all selections
(except one of 335 pages devoted exclusively to Milton's epic), and adding thirteen
editions from Mr. Good's list that are not in mine, I have 105 separate publications of
Paradise Lost in the eighteenth century.

to be sure, is in a different category: every family must possess his works even if no one reads them. But what is our astonishment to learn that the eighteenth century was satisfied with fifty editions of his plays! It is true that a number of his dramas appeared separately; but the most popular of these, *Macbeth*, was published by itself only thirteen times, whereas *Comus* in its original form saw three printings and as adapted for the stage over thirty.[1] Furthermore, *Paradise Lost* had the unique honor of being the first poem to be sold by subscription, the first English poem to appear in a critical edition, the first to have a variorum edition, and the first to be made the subject of a detailed critical study.[2] Is it any wonder that when Jacob Tonson, a leading printer of the day, was asked "what poem he ever got the most by," he immediately named *Paradise Lost?* [3]

Obviously, Milton scholarship was active in the eighteenth century; indeed, it was much more active, and aside from Masson's monumental *Life* more fruitful, than it has been since. To prove this, or to give any adequate conception of the extent of the critical attention devoted to Milton, would, however, require not a chapter but a volume. Editions of the poet and essays on his works contain but a fraction of the writings on the subject. Periodicals, histories, biographies, letters, novels, poems, religious tracts, and political pamphlets, as well as discussions of Homer, Longinus, the French Revolution, rhetoric, education, marriage, liberty, and even gardening, all lead to Milton. Francis Blackburne's *Memoirs of Thomas Hollis* and Joseph Warton's *Essay on Pope* are largely devoted to the "mighty-mouthed inventor of harmonies," and for the allusions to him in such writers as John Dennis a proper reference would be, "See works *passim*." Some idea of the unusual attention he was attracting may be gained from an examination of a single periodical

[1] These figures regarding the number of editions of Spenser and Shakespeare are taken from the printed catalogue of the British Museum, which presumably does not list all the issues published. It may be added that *Samson Agonistes*, besides being translated into Greek, was four times adapted for the stage or for music, and that the version made for Handel's oratorio was published at least nine times before 1800.

[2] Tonson's sumptuous folio of 1688 was the second *book* to be published in England by subscription, the first was Walton's Polyglot Bible (see Masson's edition of Milton's poems, 1874, i. 19 n.). Patrick Hume's notes on *Paradise Lost*, which accompanied the 1695 edition, fill 321 closely printed folio pages, and antedate by fourteen years the first critical edition of Shakespeare (Rowe's), which was in comparison a very simple affair. Newton's first variorum edition of the epic appeared in 1749, a second by Marchant was issued in 1751, apparently a third (which I have not seen) by J. H. Rice in 1791, and a fourth by Todd in 1801. There may have been others in 1765 and 1766, — I know only the dubious titles. Addison's *Spectator* papers were published in 1712. Furthermore, Warton's edition of Milton's minor poems (1785) is one of the earliest of the separately-published critical editions of short English pieces.

[3] Spence's *Anecdotes* (ed. Singer, 1820), 344.

like the *Gentleman's Magazine*. This, the leading journal of the day, printed eight pieces dealing with him in both the second and the eighth year of its existence (1732 and 1738), while in the seventeenth (1747) it gave space to twenty and in the twentieth (1750) to eleven.[1] These figures are unusual, to be sure; but from five to seven papers on this supposedly neglected poet frequently appeared in a single year, and the average number was probably greater than any magazine devoted to him on the tercentenary of his birth.

Beyond question, the attitude of the eighteenth century was quite unlike our own, so unlike that it is hardly possible for us to conceive it. Milton's shrine, instead of being, as it is now, "remote and rarely visited," was, like that of Thomas à Becket or of St. James of Compostella in earlier times, closely associated with the life and thought of the day and thronged with persons of all classes, each bearing his gift. In the twentieth century there are few even of Milton's admirers whose feeling for the poet could be characterized as enthusiasm; yet this seems to be the fittest word to describe the attitude of Pope's friend Bishop Atterbury, of Cowper, of Thomas Hollis, of the Wartons, and of many of their contemporaries. For some of them, indeed, the term is not strong enough. Leonard Welsted writes, for example, "I have a fondness" for Waller, but "I pay adoration" to Milton.[2] Warburton, who himself thought the English epic superior to those of Greece and Rome, must have been sneering at more extreme views when he spoke of "all the silly adorers of Milton, who deserve to be laughed at."[3] This recalls the "Gentleman of Oxford" who feared to criticize one whose popularity was so "immeasurably great, and his Reverence little less than divine."[4] "The divine Milton" is Thomas Hollis's favorite phrase

---

[1] These forty-seven pieces include articles bearing on the Lauder controversy, with long extracts from Masenius and from Grotius (of whose *Adamus Exul* ten translations were received in one month, "besides what may come to-morrow"); a prose "apotheosis" of Milton (counted as three pieces, since its parts appeared in three issues); an inscription under Milton's bust; half a dozen poems, including a prologue for *Comus;* and three Latin translations from *Paradise Lost* (counted as one, since in one issue of the magazine).

[2] "Remarks on Longinus," 1712, *Works* (ed. J. Nichols, 1787), 422. Compare an anonymous tribute to Milton (*Verses to the Author,* "by a Divine," in Stephen Duck's *Poems,* 1738, p. 131),

His Lays, inimitably fine,
With Ecstasy each Passion move.

[3] Letter to Richard Hurd, Dec. 23, 1749, in J. Nichols's *Illustrations of Literary History* (1817), ii. 177 n.

[4] *A New Version of the P. L.* (Oxford, 1756), preface. Earlier in the preface we are told that Milton is "the greatest Genius among our *English* Poets," and that "his Poem . . . is generally allowed to exceed all others for Sublimity of Thought and Grandeur of Expression."

for the man whom he also called "my hero, and the guide of my paths."[1] "Idolators" is the expression used by George Hardinge, who adds, "Few, if any, can out-idolize me."[2] Among these "idolators" was Jonathan Richardson the painter, who devoted the "Beloved Retir'd Hours" of many years to the loving study and service of "One to Whom," he declared, "I am Infinitely Oblig'd." "I, even I," Richardson writes in his pleasant, garrulous way, "while a Youth . . . happening to find the First Quarto [of what he elsewhere terms "the Best Poem in the World"] . . . was Dazzled with it, and from that Hour all the rest (*Shakespear* excepted) Faded in my Estimation, or Vanish'd."[3] This recalls the experience of another idolater, Cowper, who "at so ripe an age As twice seven years " "danced for joy" over his discovery of *Paradise Lost*, a work which he too thought "the finest poem in the world" and the author of which he referred to as "this greatest of men, your idol and mine."[4]

This exaggerated estimate was by no means so rare in the "age of reason" as might be expected. It is to be encountered as early as 1704, when the epic was characterized by a leading critic as "the greatest Poem that ever was written by Man,"[5] and as late,as 1796, when it was described as "the noblest poem, perhaps, that ever the wit of man produced."[6] Indeed, John Wesley mentions this as a common opinion. "Of all the Poems which have hitherto appeared in the World, in whatever Age or Nation," he writes, carefully weighing his words, "the Preference has generally been given, by impartial Judges, to *Milton's Paradise Lost*."[7] Richard Bentley, who had little appreciation of the poem, unintentionally confirms this remark when he tries to explain how the work "could pass upon

[1] Francis Blackburne, *Memoirs of Hollis* (1780), 74, 93, 112, and cf. 71, 620.

[2] *Miscellaneous Works* (ed. J. Nichols, 1818), iii. 120. His idolatry was shown in his conduct; for in his first call upon the Swan of Lichfield he "abruptly, and *à propos de rien*, asked her *had she ever heard Milton read?* The *Paradise Lost* was produced, and opened at a venture; the judge jumped upon the table, and read some pages, not to her astonishment only, but to her profound admiration. . . . As abruptly, her visitant closed the volume, descended from the table, made his bow, and without a word disappeared. . . . The next morning a *pacquet* was transmitted to Miss Seward, enclosing an elaborate critique on the English Homer" (*Notes and Queries*, 3d series, i. 26).

[3] *Explanatory Notes on P. L.* (1734), pp. clxxix–clxxxi, cxviii–cxix.

[4] For full quotations and references, see pp. 161–2 below.

[5] John Dennis, *Grounds of Criticism in Poetry* (1704), 54. In the preface to the prose version of *Paradise Lost* (1745) it is characterized as "the finest Poem that ever was wrote."

[6] Life of Milton, prefixed to *Samson Agonistes* (*Bell's British Theatre*, 1797, vol. xxxiv), p. viii.

[7] *Extract from P. L.* (1791), 3. James Paterson, in his *Complete Commentary on P. L.* (1744, p. i), starts with the assumption that it is "the *prime* Poem in the World."

the whole Nation for a perfect, absolute, faultless Composition: The best Pens in the Kingdom contending in its Praises, as eclipsing all modern Essays whatever; and rivaling, if not excelling, both HOMER and VIRGIL." [1] Even Dr. Johnson, who disliked Milton's character, opposed blank verse, and ridiculed *Lycidas* and the sonnets, commended the epic as "a poem which, considered with respect to design, may claim the first place, and with respect to performance the second, among the productions of the human mind." [2] Goldsmith, too, though he shared many of Johnson's prejudices, had a hand in the preparation of a book which exhausts the vocabulary in praise of the English writer who "seems to have rivalled and excelled all other Epic poets." *Paradise Lost*, according to this treatise, is "wonderfully described, painted with such bold and noble strokes, and delivered in such nervous language . . . so original and noble in its plan and contrivance, and wrought up with such wonderful art," that "there is a nobleness and sublimity in the whole . . . which transcends, perhaps, that of any other poem." [3] Still more emphatically Philip Neve declared the "genius" of Milton to be "above example, or comparison. . . . His subject, and his conduct of it, exalt him to a supreme rank . . . with which all other poets compare but as a second class." [4]

Sometimes no specific work is mentioned by an admirer, but Milton is invoked as the "supreme of Verse," [5] or characterized as "an Author of that Excellence of Genius and Learning, that none of any Age or Nation, I think, has excel'd him," or as "perhaps the greatest [genius] that ever appeared among men." [6] Yet it was unquestion-

---

[1] Preface to his edition of *Paradise Lost* (1732).

[2] *Lives of the Poets* (ed. Birkbeck Hill, Oxford, 1905), i. 170. Cf. Johnson's preface to Lauder's *Essay on Milton's Use of the Moderns* (1750): "Mankind . . . have endeavoured to compensate the error of their first neglect [of *Paradise Lost*], by lavish praises and boundless veneration. There seems to have arisen a contest, among men of genius and literature, who should most advance its honour, or best distinguish its beauties."

[3] John Newbery's *Art of Poetry on a New Plan* (1762), ii. 318, 326. Similarly, Daniel Neal, in his *History of the Puritans* (1738, iv. 466–7), speaks of Milton's "incomparable Poem . . . in which he manifested such a wonderful Sublimeness of Thought, as, perhaps, was never exceeded in any Age or Nation in the World" (Good, pp. 122–3).

[4] *Cursory Remarks on English Poets* (1789), 141. Later (p. 144) Neve calls *Paradise Lost* "the greatest work of human genius."

[5] Sneyd Davies, *Rhapsody to Milton* (w. 1740), in John Whaley's *Collection of Poems* (1745), 182. Cf. *Song by Mr. T.* (w. 1767), in J. Nichols's *Collection* (1780), viii. 135:

> But let me with reverence kneel
> O'er the grave of the greatest in verse.

[6] Charles Gildon's continuation of Langbaine's *English Dramatick Poets* (1699), 100; Richard Baron's preface to Milton's *Eikonoklastes* (1756), p. iv. Some of the other references to Milton in Gildon's works contain extravagant praise: see his *Miscellaneous Letters and Essays* (1694), 41–4 ("To Mr. T. S., in Vindication of Mr. Milton's Paradise

ably *Paradise Lost* that such writers had chiefly in mind; for the modern heresy of exalting the shorter poems at the expense of the longer was scarcely known in an age which, whatever its deficiencies, at least appreciated the solid things of literature. The contrary opinion is widely held, to be sure, owing to the attention given to the influence of the 1645 volume upon Gray, Collins, and their contemporaries; but it is quite unwarranted. Even lyric poets, who naturally made more use of the octosyllabics, sonnets, and other short pieces, were as whole-hearted in their admiration of the epic as they were unblushing in adopting its phraseology and diction. During the first forty years of the century, when praise was being lavished upon *Paradise Lost*, the shorter pieces were seldom mentioned, and at no time do they seem to have exerted an influence at all comparable to that of the epic.[1] Evidence of every kind and from a great variety of sources points to the same conclusion, that from the boyhood of Pope to the death of Cowper the preëminence of *Paradise Lost* among the works of its author was never seriously questioned.[2]

But, although the shorter pieces did not receive a tithe of the critical consideration or of the extravagant praise that was showered upon the epic, they were enthusiastically admired. Burke called

---

Lost"); *Examen Miscellaneum* (1702), pp. ii, iii, and first p. 51; *Libertas Triumphans* (1708), 6; *Complete Art of Poetry* (1718), i. 108, 268–9; and *Laws of Poetry* (1721), 34. See also John Duncombe's *Ode to John, Earl of Corke* (1757), in his *Works of Horace*, 1767, ii. 239 (Good, p. 82):

> Though foremost in the Lists of Fame
> We matchless *Milton* place.

[1] The total number of poems which I have found to be significantly influenced by the minor pieces before 1742 is only 41, while in the same period 196 were affected by *Paradise Lost*. The largest number of poems influenced in any decade by any of the shorter pieces was 75 (those affected by the octosyllabics between 1780 and 1790). In this same period 100 poems showed the influence of the epic.

[2] This was pointed out in my *Seventeenth Century Notices of Milton* (*Englische Studien*, xl. 184–5), and has been proved in great detail by Mr. Good, who, indeed, goes too far in the opposite direction. The only exceptions I remember among the hundreds of references to the poems that have come to my attention are in a letter from Lord Monboddo to Sir George Baker, Oct. 2, 1782, and in the *Bee* for 1793 (xvi. 276), where *Comus* is preferred to *Paradise Lost;* in the letters of Miss Seward (see p. 501 below), where the best of Milton's sonnets are thought equal to anything he wrote; and in Goldsmith's *Beauties of English Poesy* (1767, i. 39), where we are told that "a very judicious critic" thought the octosyllabics gave "an higher idea of Milton's stile in poetry" than the epic did. It is interesting to know that Joseph Warton, a great admirer and imitator of the minor poems, arranged Milton's works in the order of their poetic excellence thus, *Paradise Lost, Comus, Samson, Lycidas, Allegro, Penseroso* (T. Warton's edition of the minor poems, 1785, p. 34); and that Ann Yearsley, the Bristol milkwoman, was "well acquainted" with the epic but ignorant of Milton's having written anything else (*Mo. Rev.*, lxxiii. 218).

Penseroso "the finest poem in the English language"; [1] Cowper as a boy was "so charmed" with it and its companion piece that he "was never weary of them"; [2] and Hugh Blair thought them "of all the English Poems in the Descriptive Style, the richest and most remarkable." [3] It was these pieces that Gray had particularly in mind when he mentioned their author as "the best example of an exquisite ear" that he could produce. [4] "If he had written nothing else," said another, apropos of the octosyllabics, he "has displayed such extensive powers of imagination, as would have given him a place among the foremost of the sons of Phoebus." [5] A similar opinion had been expressed more than twenty years earlier: "His *Juvenile Poems* . . . are sufficient to have set him among the most Celebrated of the Poets, even of the Ancients themselves; his *Mask* and *Lycidas* are perhaps Superior to all in their Several Kinds . . . the *Allegro* and *Penseroso* are Exquisite Pictures." [6] Nathan Drake went even farther: "*L'Allegro ed Il Penseroso* are the most exquisite and accurately descriptive poems in his own, or any other, language, and will probably for ever remain unrivalled." [7] John Aikin said much the same, ranking the octosyllabics as "perhaps the most captivating pieces of the descriptive kind that all poetry affords"; [8] while Christopher Smart, in speaking of Dryden's and Pope's odes for St. Cecilia's day, threw all "perhaps's" to the winds and affirmed, "Neither is there to be found two more finished pieces of Lyric Poetry in our Language, L'allegro and Il penseroso of Milton excepted, which are the finest in any." [9] Miss Seward, who "lisped" these companion poems "when only in her third year," and who often delighted herself by repeating *Lycidas* from memory, was "almost" of George Hardinge's opinion, that "the best of Milton's sonnets [are] equal to any thing he has written." [10] As she held that he had but one superior in the world, this is high praise for the sonnets.

[1] Letter to Matthew Smith, *c.* 1750, in Prior's *Burke* (5th ed., 1854), 35.

[2] Letter to William Unwin, Jan. 17, 1782.

[3] *Lectures on Rhetoric* (1783), ii. 375.

[4] *Observations on English Metre* (w. 1760–61), in *Works*, ed. Mitford, 1858, v. 233.

[5] "T. W.," in *Old Maid*, no. 12 (Jan. 31, 1756): Drake's *Gleaner* (1811), ii. 381.

[6] Richardson, *Explanatory Notes* (1734), pp. xv–xvi. The similar praise to be found in Toland's and Fenton's biographies of Milton, published in 1698 and 1725 respectively, is given on p. 424 below.

[7] *Literary Hours* (3d ed., 1804), ii. 89.

[8] *Letters on English Poetry* (2d ed., 1807), 124.

[9] Preface to his *Ode for Musick on St. Cecilia's Day* (*c.* 1755), reprinted in *Poems* (Reading, 1791), i. 39.

[10] See E. V. Lucas, *A Swan and her Friends* (1907), 21; Miss Seward's *Letters* (Edin., 1811), i. 66; and p. 501 below.

But long before Miss Seward and her friends essayed the lyre, in fact while Dryden was still living, the juvenile poems had been declared "incomparable"; before 1728 *Comus* was called "the best [masque] ever written . . . in the Praise of which no Words can be too many"; as early as 1729 there were some who felt for *Lycidas* "the same Veneration, and Partiality, which is paid to the most accomplish'd Works of Antiquity," and in 1756 some who held it "one of the most poetical and moving elegies that ever was wrote."[1] It will be clear later, when we see the great number of poems modelled upon the shorter pieces and the frequency with which phrases were taken from them, that these utterances by no means exaggerate the feelings of a large part of the public. Of course there were not a few who, like Johnson, thought *Lycidas* and the sonnets absurd and were indifferent to the remaining minor poems; but, on the other hand, the commendations that have been quoted fail to give any adequate conception of the widespread, enthusiastic admiration which the poems aroused.

Regarding *Paradise Lost* we have seen that a remarkable unanimity of opinion prevailed. There must have been those who did not care for it, but they either like Chesterfield kept discreetly silent,[2] or else like Bentley made themselves ridiculous in the eyes of their fellows. It is astounding that scarcely one of the innumerable eighteenth-century allusions to the poem speaks of it with the indifference, dislike, or flippancy which are almost the rule to-day. Nor can it be urged that this praise is a perfunctory acceptance of a conventional opinion, for it is usually more enthusiastic and spontaneous than it is judicial. Still less is there warrant for believing that these admirers were willing to pay the epic any tribute save that of reading it; for their familiarity with it — with even the later books — and the frequency with which they quote from it entirely disprove any such charge.[3] "Who has *not* read . . . Paradise lost, and Paradise Regained?" exclaimed a reviewer in 1796,[4] a remark

---

[1] For references and other quotations, see pp. 423, 422, 426 n. 1, 427, below.

[2] See below, p. 24.

[3] Addison, for example, writes, "I have drawn more quotations out of him [Milton] than from any other" (*Spectator*, no. 262); and Lord Monboddo says, "I . . . shall . . . quote him oftener than any other English writer, because I consider him as the best standard for style, and all the ornaments of speech, that we have" (*Origin and Progress of Language*, 2d ed., 1786, iii. 68 n.). John Constable, in his *Reflections upon Accuracy of Style* (1731, pp. 14–16), quotes from *Paradise Lost* four times in three successive pages; Daniel Webb, in *Observations on Poetry and Music* (1769, pp. 14–18), quotes from it six times on five successive pages; and Thomas Sheridan draws almost all the illustrations for his *Lectures on the Art of Reading* (1775) from the same work. Instances of the kind might be multiplied indefinitely.

[4] *Mo. Rev.*, enl. ed., xxi. 226.

that, in contrast to the one with which our chapter opens, mirrors the difference between the twentieth- and the eighteenth-century attitude towards Milton.

Not, of course, that every one thought his epic "the greatest poem in the world." Some modestly claimed for it only a preëminence among English works. Gilbert Burnet, for example, who was entirely out of sympathy with Milton's political activities, qualified his statement that *Paradise Lost* "was esteemed the beautifulest and perfectest poem that ever was writ" by adding, "at least in our language."[1] And such seems to have been the general opinion. The *Spectator* papers, it will be remembered, make no attempt to prove Milton's primacy among British bards; they assume it at the outset in the words, "As the first place among our English poets is due to Milton."[2] So, also, does the *Lay-Monastery*, when it speaks casually of "our great *Milton*, whose Poem, which is justly now acknowledg'd to be the most admirable Production of *British* Genius."[3] Expressions to the same purport, which are to be met with constantly throughout the century and seem to have been rarely questioned,[4] are the more important because it is generally thought to-day that Pope and Dryden were at this time regarded as the greatest English poets. The *Edinburgh Review* was nearer the truth when it declared in 1808, "That he [Pope] is not of the class of Milton and Shakespeare is indisputable; and, notwithstanding the two volumes,

---

[1] *History of my Own Time* (ed. O. Airy, Oxford, 1897), i. 284. This part of the *History* was written about 1700 (*ib.* pp. xxvii, xxxi n.). In *Jure Divino* (1706, book vii, p. 14 n.) Defoe praised the 'Masterly Genius' displayed in *Paradise Lost*, and wrote, " *Milton's Pandemonium*, is allow'd to be the deepest laid Thought, most capacious and extensive that ever appear'd in print." Defoe may have come to know *Paradise Lost* at the dissenting academy he attended four or five years.

[2] No. 262.

[3] No. xxxii, Jan. 27, 1713. Observe that the writer speaks as if Milton had written but one poem. So, too, does William Sewell, in the first version of his *Life of Philips* (1712), p. 3.

[4] Cf. Henry Pemberton's *Observations on Poetry* (1738, p. 80), where Milton is termed "our greatest poet"; the *Muse's Complaint* (by "C," in *Scots Mag.*, 1742, iv. 166), which speaks of him as "chief of modern bards"; Charles Graham's *Eulogium* (*Universal Mag.*, 1785, lxxvii. 98), which declares, "No poet since has equal'd him in song"; the "List of Dramatic Poets" appended to Thomas Whincop's *Scanderbeg* (1747), where *Paradise Lost* is called "the finest Piece in the *English* Language" (noted by Good, pp. 127-8); Catharine Macaulay's *Modest Plea for Copy Right* (1774, p. 23), where it is described as "a Poem, whose merit is of such magnitude, that it is impossible for a genius inferior to his own to do it justice" (Good, pp. 255-6); and the preface to Samuel Woodford's *Paraphrase upon the Canticles* (1679), where Dryden's praise, "one of the greatest . . . Poems . . . this Age . . . has produced," is repeated, and Woodford adds that if the work had been rimed "it had been so absolute a piece, that in spight of whatever the World Heathen, or Christian hitherto has seen, it must have remain'd as the standard to all succeeding Poets."

in which Dr. Warton thought it necessary to prove this truism, we doubt whether any critic, even during the flattery of his own age, ever thought of placing him so high." [1]

What, then, did the Augustans, 'during the flattery of their age,' think as to the relative merits of Waller,[2] Dryden, Pope, Shakespeare, and Milton? In view of the complacency of the neo-classicists, and of the apparent narrowness of esthetic sympathy shown in their remarks about the roughness of English verse before "Mr. Waller refined our numbers," this would seem to be an easy question to answer. Surely the masters of the couplet had little admiration

---

[1] 2d ed., xi. 409. Cf. John Duncombe's ode to the Earl of Corke (see above, p. 8, n. 6), where "matchless Milton" is "foremost in the Lists of Fame," though Pope will long "the Muse's Annals grace." "We still prefer the extravagant beauties of Shakespeare and Milton to the cold and well-disciplined merit of Addison and . . . Pope," remarked Horace Walpole (letter to Élie de Beaumont, March 18, 1765). Even Johnson thought that in the proposed erection of monuments in St. Paul's cathedral Milton's "should have the precedence" over Pope's: "There is more thinking in him and in Butler," he adds, "than in any of our poets" (Boswell's *Johnson*, ed. Hill, ii. 239). Blair, in his *Lectures on Rhetoric*, which were published in 1783 but written much earlier, grants only that "within a certain limited region, he [Pope] has been outdone by no Poet" (ii. 369); and William Belsham writes (*Essays*, 2d ed., 1799, ii. 506), "Though the warmest admirers of Pope have never exalted him to the rank of the greatest poet, he has often been stiled the best versifier in the English language." Belsham allows him to be "the most polished and correct versifier," but not the one "affording the highest degree of delight," since he "does not sufficiently conceal his art." Expressions like that of Lord Middlesex in his poem to Pope (Chalmers's *English Poets*, xii. 135), "Like Milton, then, though in more polish'd strains," or that of A. Betson, who calls Pope "the most perfect Poet we ever had in this Nation" (*Miscellaneous Dissertations*, 1751, p. 86, and cf. pp. 88–91), are apt to be misleading. They do not imply that Pope is the greatest of English poets, but that he is the most regular, the one freest from faults. There were few leading neo-classicists who did not realize that something more than this negative virtue was needed for great poetry.

[2] The question "Whether *Milton* and *Waller* were not the best English Poets? and which the better of the two?" was answered in the *Athenian Mercury* for January 16, 1691/2, as follows: "*Milton* was the *fullest* and *loftiest*, *Waller* the *neatest* and most *correct* Poet we ever had. . . . Mr. *Waller*, tho' a full and noble Writer, yet comes not up in our Judgments to that, — *Mens divinior atque os — Magna Sonaturum*, as *Horace* calls it, which *Milton* has, and wherein we think he was never equalled." When a similar question was raised in the *British Apollo* for 1708 (vol. 1, no. 25), that oracle gave high praise to Waller, but declared,

> *Milton* do's to Nobler Flights aspire,
> With *Virgil's* Beauty and with *Homer's* Fire.
> In Every Image, TRUE SUBLIME, appears,
> And Every Thought, The Stamp of *Phoebus* wears.
> Sprung from the God, Divine are all his Lays,
> And claim by true Desert, the Never DYING BAYS.

William Coward, in his *Licentia Poetica* (1709), discusses "Homer, Horace, Virgil, Milton, Waller, Cowley, Dryden, etc." as "the principal antient and modern Poets." Cf. Addison's *Account of the Greatest English Poets* (1694); A. Betson's *Miscellaneous Dissertations* (1751), 86–90; Defoe's remark quoted on p. 15 below; and the passage from Collins, p. 454 below.

for poetry in every way so unlike their own as was the blank-verse Puritan epic. Yet we have seen the dangers of *a priori* arguments as to what the eighteenth century must have thought, and we remember Addison's *Spectator* papers, and Dryden's famous distichs, which begin,

> Three poets, in three distant ages born.

Indeed, if we are familiar with Dryden, we recall his visit to the blind poet and his dramatization of the epic, which he praised cordially, terming it "one of the greatest, most noble, and most sublime poems which either this age or nation has produced." [1] His friend Nathaniel Lee boldly adapted the following lines from the same poem within thirteen years of its publication:

> They've blown us up with Wild fire in the Air . . .
> Caps, Hats and Cardinals Coats, and Cowls and Hoods
> Are tost about — the sport the sport of winds —
> Indulgences, Dispences, Pardons, Bulls, see yonder!
> Preist, they fly — they're whirl'd aloft. They fly,
> They fly o'er the backside o' th' World,
> Into a Limbo large, and broad, since call'd the Paradise
> Of Fools. [2]

Nor was Addison's praise limited to his celebrated critique. As early as 1694, in his *Account of the Greatest English Poets*, he devoted thirty lines to Milton, and later imitated two of his poems; [3] he had much to say about *Paradise Lost* in his *Discourse on Ancient and Modern Learning*, in the *Tatler*, and in the *Spectator* before and after the publication of his formal criticism; he commended *Allegro* in the *Spectator*, and agreed with a friend that of all masques *Comus* was "the best ever written." [4] What makes his extended examination of the poem particularly significant in the present connection is the fact that it was written by the leading neo-classic critic of the time and was addressed to the neo-classicists. Addison succeeded in proving to his contemporaries that *Paradise Lost* was a correct poem according to Augustan standards, that it conformed to the laws laid done for the epic and lost nothing by comparison with Homer and Virgil. Thanks to the popularity of the *Spectator* and to his own reputation, his papers had a strong influence; they were questioned only by the

---

[1] *Works* (Scott-Saintsbury ed.), v. 112. See also v. 116, 124; xi. 162, 209-10; xii. 300-301; xiii. 17, 18-20, 30, 38, 39, 117; xiv. 143-4, 201-2 ("I dare not condemn so great a genius as Milton"), 214-15.

[2] *Caesar Borgia* (1680), near the end of the last scene; cf. *P. L.*, iii. 487-96. Mr. G. L. Kittredge called my attention to this very early and striking borrowing.

[3] See pp. 104-5, 422, below.

[4] See p. 422 below.

more romantic admirers of Milton, and seem to have been universally accepted as defining the classical attitude towards England's greatest classic poet.

It was not, however, to the *Spectator* that the other leading writers of the time owed their first acquaintance with *Paradise Lost*. Gay's humorous imitation of it, *Wine*, appeared four years before Addison's critique,[1] while Defoe, Prior, Pope, and Swift each gave evidence of a knowledge of the epic before 1709. The biting satire and the distrust of things grand and romantic which one associates with Swift make him almost the last person from whom to expect praise of a lofty and imaginative poem in blank verse; yet he not only declared himself "an admirer of Milton," but annotated an edition of *Paradise Lost* for the use of Stella and "Mrs." Dingley, and in his writings showed familiarity with the entire work.[2] After the Dean himself, the Augustan writer who would seem to have been least likely to appreciate the epic is Daniel Defoe. Yet so early as 1706 Defoe had composed three poems in a verse roughly modelled upon that of *Paradise Lost*, and had asked, "Who can read *Virgil, Horace, Ovid, Milton, Waller,* or *Rochester,* without touching the Strings of his Soul, and finding a Unison of the most charming Influence there?"[3] The company in which Milton is here placed, and the omission from it of Shakespeare, Dryden, and others, should not be overlooked. Pope's frank expressions of admiration and his less frank but more numerous borrowings form too large a subject for discussion here; suffice it to say that he appears to have been more widely acquainted with the complete body of Milton's poems than any other man of his time.[4] As for "Mat" Prior, one would hardly expect to find his light, deft pen employed on the cathedral harmonies of blank verse except in the way of parody. Yet Prior took the unrimed measure very seriously; he imitated it four times, and in his translations of two lofty hymns of Callimachus with some success, while in the preface to his *Solomon* (1718) he attacked rime

---

[1] Another blank-verse burlesque, *Fanscomb Barn* (1713), was composed by the neoclassic poetess Anne, Countess of Winchilsea. It cannot be maintained that these parodies argue a low estimate of Milton, for both were suggested by the similar pieces of John Philips, one of the most ardent admirers of *Paradise Lost*.

[2] See indices to the Bohn editions of his prose and poetry, and that to F. E. Ball's edition of the *Correspondence* (1910–14). Besides these eleven references, there is Swift's part in the *Grub-Street Journal*, in the *Memoirs of Martinus Scriblerus*, and in the satirical commentary that accompanies *The Dunciad*, all of which contain allusions to Milton (see pp. 113 n. 2, 116, below).

[3] *Review of the State of the English Nation*, vol. iii, no. 104. For the poems, see pp. 100–101 below.

[4] See pp. 112–18, 573–83, below.

and declared *Paradise Lost* to be "one of the sublimest Pieces of Invention that was ever yet produced." [1]

Much the same opinion was held by the Duke of Buckingham; for his *Essay on Poetry*, which Dryden and Pope repeatedly praised, ends with a description of the ideal poet, who

> Must above TASSO's lofty flights prevail,
> Succeed where SPENCER, and ev'n MILTON fail. [2]

The Earl of Roscommon's *Essay on Translated Verse*, which the classicists held as a classic, contains a plea for blank verse, a tribute to *Paradise Lost*, and an imitation of it. [3] Congreve mentions an "Immortal Song" which is "As *Spencer* sweet, as *Milton* strong." [4] Lady Mary Montagu, with whom Pope flirted and quarrelled, attacked "the thraldom of monastic rhymes" and praised "the beauties of each living page" of Milton's poem. [5] "The horrid Discord of jingling Rhyme" is also condemned in the celebrated *Characteristics* of the Earl of Shaftesbury, which strongly influenced Pope and many other writers of the time. Shaftesbury's praise of *Paradise Lost* is worth quoting. "Our most approv'd *heroick Poem*," he wrote in 1710, "has neither the Softness of Language, nor the fashionable Turn of Wit; but merely solid Thought, strong Reasoning, noble Passion, and a continu'd Thred of moral Doctrine, Piety, and Virtue to recommend it." [6] Parnell, whose assistance on the *Iliad* Pope requited by editing his friend's posthumous works, wrote two poems on the model of *Allegro* and is said to have been "a careful student of Milton." [7] Curiously enough, Pope's helpers on his *Odyssey*, William Broome and Elijah Fenton, who between them translated half the poem, were likewise Miltonians; for, besides using many words and phrases from *Paradise Lost* in the work they did for Pope, each made an unrimed version of at least one book of Homer, and in addition

---

[1] See also pp. 59-60, 105, below.

[2] This is the latest version; the two earlier forms show less appreciation of Milton. Chalmers (*English Poets*, x. 77-8) quotes Dryden's, Addison's, and Pope's praise of the *Essay*.

[3] See p. 89 below.

[4] *A Pindarique Ode, humbly offer'd to the Queen* (1706), in *Works*, 1710, iii. 1085 (Good, p. 61). In his *Mourning Muse of Alexis* (1695, *ib.* 836) there is a reference to "*Comus* Feast" (Good, p. 141).

[5] *Court of Dulness*, in *Letters and Works* (Bohn ed.), ii. 487-9; cf. *Lines written in a Blank Page of P. L.* (*ib.* 523).

[6] *Characteristics* (3d ed., 1723), i. 276; cf. i. 217-18, and iii. 263-4. To the first of these references my attention was called by C. A. Moore's illuminating paper, *Shaftesbury and the Ethical Poets* (Modern Lang. Assoc., *Publications*, xxxi. 264-325).

[7] *Dict. Nat. Biog.*; and cf. the preface to his *Homer's Battle of the Frogs and Mice* (1717). For the poems, see p. 444 below.

Fenton paraphrased part of a chapter of Isaiah in blank verse, wrote a life of Milton, and 'amended the punctuation' of his principal work.[1]

Another classicist who had a hand in editing the epic was Thomas Tickell, the poet who was the cause of the memorable quarrel between Addison and Pope;[2] while still another of Milton's commentators, Jonathan Richardson, whose extravagant praise of his favorite poet we have already listened to, was for twenty-two years a friend and correspondent of Pope. Not a little of our knowledge of the bard of Twickenham and his circle comes from Spence's *Anecdotes;* yet intimacy with Pope did not prevent the author, Joseph Spence, professor of poetry and later regius professor of modern history at Oxford, from writing two pieces of blank verse that are clearly Miltonic.[3] An earlier occupant of the chair of poetry — an easy-chair in those days — was Joseph Trapp, a man so classical in his tastes that he published his lectures in Latin and found little to admire in poetry written since Roman days. *Paradise Lost*, however, seemed to him a marked exception, for he said of it: "Si Poëma Heroicum proprie dictum non scripsit *Miltonus;* certe Poëma optimum scripsit; omni laude dignus, dicam? imo major: *Homeri*, & *Virgilii*, non servus Imitator, viam aperuit prorsus novam, & suam; Inventionis foecunditate, Ingenii sublimitate, Rerum Vocumque fulgore ac pondere, Judicii denique maturitate, nec *Homero* forsan, nec *Virgilio*, secundus."[4] This is, however, the least of the tributes that Trapp paid to the poet, for he translated all of Virgil into Miltonic blank verse and all of Milton into Virgilian Latin.

One cannot read far in the literature or the history of the early eighteenth century without encountering Bishop Atterbury, the best preacher of the age and according to Addison one of its greatest geniuses, who narrowly escaped execution for his Jacobite activities.

---

[1] See Bibl. I, 1712, 1717, 1727. The 1725 *Paradise Lost* was supervised by Fenton, whose life of Milton was reprinted in many later editions.

[2] Tickell assisted on the 1720 edition. As early as 1707 he had said of John Philips, "Unfetter'd, in great Milton's strain he writes" (*Oxford*, 1707, in *Works*, 1854, p. 171).

[3] See Bibl. I, 1761, 1762.

[4] *Praelectiones Poeticæ* (1711), 3d ed., 1736, ii. 317-18. In the translation entitled *Lectures on Poetry* (1742, p. 351) the passage quoted is rendered thus: "If *Milton* did not write an Heroic Poem, properly so call'd, yet he certainly wrote an excellent one, such as deserves, or rather is above all Commendation. He is no slavish imitator of *Homer* and *Virgil*, he opens a Way entirely new, and entirely his own: In Fruitfulness of Invention, Sublimity of Genius, in the Weight and Lustre of his Thoughts and Words, and, lastly, in the Perfection of his Judgment, he is, perhaps, equal to either of them."

Swift, Prior, Gay, and Addison knew Atterbury well, and Pope proved one of his few faithful friends. "Milton remained to the end of his life his favourite poet," writes his biographer,[1] and from one of the bishop's own letters to Pope we may well believe it. "I protest to you," he wrote, "this last perusal of him [Milton] has given me such new degrees, I will not say of pleasure, but of admiration and astonishment, that I look upon the sublimity of Homer, and the majesty of Virgil, with somewhat less reverence than I used to do. I challenge you, with all your partiality, to show me in the first of these any thing equal to the Allegory of Sin and Death, either as to the greatness and justness of the invention, or the height and beauty of the colouring. What I looked upon as a rant of Barrow's, I now begin to think a serious truth, and could almost venture to set my hand to it."[2] Another of the Anglican clergymen whom Pope, a Catholic, numbered among his intimate friends was Bishop William Warburton, who became his literary executor. Besides writing a commentary on *Paradise Lost* (which he thought superior to the epics of Homer and Virgil), Warburton translated "in imitation of Milton's style" a Latin poem of Addison's, and lauded the minor poems, the *Of Education*, and the *Areopagitica*, a famous sentence from which he appropriated for the conclusion of one of his pamphlets.[3]

Perhaps John Hughes ought not to be included among the Augustans, though he contributed to the *Tatler*, *Spectator*, and *Guardian* and persuaded Addison to put *Cato* on the stage. He was, at any rate, a great admirer of Milton's chief poem and an imitator of his octosyllabics.[4] Young, too, is thought of as romantically inclined because the *Night Thoughts* is in blank verse, but this work did not

---

[1] H. C. Beeching, *Francis Atterbury* (1909), 227.

[2] Nov. 8, 1717, Pope's *Works* (Elwin-Courthope ed.), ix. 9–10. Barrow's "rant" is translated on page 21 below. Atterbury did not care for Shakespeare (Beeching's *Atterbury*, 225). In his inscription on John Philips's tomb in Westminster (see *ib.* 226), and in his preface to the *Second Part of Mr. Waller's Poems* (1690), he praised Milton and blank verse. For his plan that Pope should arrange *Samson Agonistes* for presentation, see p. 117 below.

[3] For the commentary, see *Works of the Learned*, April, 1740, pp. 273–80, and Newton's preface to his edition of the epic (1749, etc.). The poem, *Battle of the Cranes and Pigmies* (1724), and the pamphlet, *A Critical Enquiry into the Causes of Prodigies* (1727), are reprinted in Samuel Parr's *Tracts by Warburton and a Warburtonian* (1789), 56–62, 71–140. For his commendation of Milton, see Nichols's *Illustrations*, ii. 77–82, 177 and n.; and pp. 21, 432, below.

[4] See his edition of Spenser (1715), vol. i, pp. xxvii, xxx, xxxvii, xxxix, xli, lxviii, lxxxiii, etc., and his *Poems* (1735), i. 250, ii. 91, 317–18, 333–4; also the praise of Milton quoted above (page 12) from the *Lay-Monastery*, of which Hughes was one of the editors. For his imitations, see pp. 442–3 below.

begin to appear until its author had by his satires and his *Two Epistles to Mr. Pope* won recognition as a thorough-going classicist. Even
in these heroic couplets he used many phrases from Milton, and in
his greatest work the style and diction are derived from the epic,
which he greatly admired and frequently quoted from. The author
of *The Seasons* is another writer who is commonly ranked among the
romanticists; yet he certainly thought highly of the poetry of his
Twickenham neighbor, with whose circle he was intimate. Thomson's appreciation and imitation of *Paradise Lost* will receive extended treatment later, but it may be noted here that on a single
page of his *Winter* he praises Pope and declares Milton to be equal
to Homer.

Another instance of how the Puritan lion and the Augustan lamb
(as the venomous bard would have liked to be thought) lay down
together occurs in the work of an intimate friend of Thomson and
Pope, Lord Lyttelton. In one of his "Dialogues of the Dead" (1760)
Lyttelton sets Pope and Boileau the interesting task of discussing
Milton. "Longinus," the French critic is made to declare, "perhaps
would prefer him to all other Writers: for he excells even Homer in
the *Sublime*. But other Critics . . . who can endure no Absurdities, no extravagant Fictions, would place him far below Virgil."
To which Pope replies, "His Genius was indeed so vast and sublime,
that his Work seems beyond the Limits of Criticism. . . . The
bright and excessive Blaze of poetical Fire, which shines in so many
Parts of his Poem, will hardly permit one to see its Faults." [1] Lyttelton's intimacy with Pope enabled him to know what that poet
thought of Milton, but we cannot be sure that Boileau held the
opinions which he is here made to express. A far greater French
writer, however, speaks with an enthusiasm that makes the praise
attributed to his countryman seem cold. Writing of "the noblest
Work, which human Imagination hath ever attempted," he says
(the book is in English): "What *Milton* so boldly undertook, he perform'd with a superior Strength of Judgement, and with an Imagination productive of Beauties not dream'd of before him. . . . The
Paradise Lost is the only Poem wherein are to be found in a perfect
Degree that Uniformity which satisfies the Mind and that Variety
which pleases the Imagination. . . . But he hath especially an indisputable Claim to the unanimous Admiration of Mankind, when
he descends from those high Flights to the natural Description of

[1] *Dialogues of the Dead* (3d ed., 1760), 122–3. Lyttelton wrote three pieces in Miltonic blank verse and modelled his best poem upon *Lycidas* (see Bibl. I, 1728, 1762,
c. 1763, and p. 552 below).

human Things." Voltaire is the last person from whom we should expect this praise, yet it is in his *Essay upon Epick Poetry* (1727) that the words occur.[1] True, as he later took back most of his commendation,[2] he may never have meant it; but since he did say it, and may have said something of the kind often while he was in England, there is no escaping the significance or the influence of such a tribute from an eminent foreign poet and critic. Voltaire's opinion tallied so closely with that of the leading Englishmen of the time that he might well have said to them in the significant words which Lyttelton gave to Boileau, "The Taste of your Countrymen is very much changed since the days of Charles the Second, when Dryden was thought a greater Poet than Milton!"[3]

Clearly, then, the maligned Augustans gave Milton his due. They did more, they joined with other writers of the century in classing him with the great poets of antiquity. If a critic of our time says that *Paradise Lost* is equal to the *Iliad* or the *Aeneid*, the comment indicates little more than enthusiasm; but if a contemporary of Dryden or Johnson made the same remark it meant that the English epic had stood the test of being measured by the highest possible standard, — indeed, by the only standard for great poetry. Few persons to-day care particularly whether or not *Paradise Lost* is in accord with Longinus on the sublime; but in Pope's day they cared very much, so much, in fact, that they allowed scarcely any author to be of the first rank who did not in the main conform to the practice of the classical writers and the laws laid down by the classical critics.[4]

That Milton stood this test and was ranked with, if not above, Homer and Virgil, no one can doubt who has read a tithe of the evidence that can be brought forward. It will be recalled that as early as 1688 no less eminent an authority than Dryden had said of the epic poets, Homer, Virgil, and Milton,

> The force of Nature could no farther go;
> To make a third, she join'd the former two.

One doubts whether Dryden really meant this, although he is said to have exclaimed on first reading *Paradise Lost*, "This man cuts us

---

[1] The quotations are from Miss F. D. White's valuable reprint of the *Essay* (Albany, 1915), 131–3.

[2] See *ib.* 68–70, 164–5.

[3] *Dialogues of the Dead*, 123.

[4] This helps explain the indifference or the hostility of many to Shakespeare and Spenser, as well as the reason why long and serious poems like *The Seasons* and *Night Thoughts*, which were liked by almost every one, were not regarded as great.

all out, and the ancients too." [1]   But there is no question that
Cowper, one of the most devoted students of Homer, was sincere
when he repeated Dryden's lines with slight changes a hundred years
later.[2] We have also seen that Atterbury wrote to Pope that he
could almost agree with Barrow's verses,

> *Romans* and *Grecians* yield the bays,
> Yield, all ye bards of old or modern days!
> Who reads this nobler work will own
> *Homer* sung *frogs*, and *Virgil gnats* alone.[3]

It is to be presumed, too, that the learned Bishop Warburton had
weighed his words before he wrote: "Milton . . . found Homer
possessed of the province of MORALITY; Virgil of POLITICS; and
nothing left for him, but that of RELIGION. This he seized . . . and
by means of the superior dignity of his subject, hath gotten to the
head of that Triumvirate, which took so many ages in forming."[4]
We are told that Henry Grove, one of the contributors to the *Spectator*, thought that "for Beauty, Variety, and Grandeur of Descriptions, as well as true Sublime in Sentiments," Milton was "greatly
preferrable" to Homer; "and tho' he allowed *Homer* the Praise of a
very great Genius, he thought the *Iliad* would no more bear a Comparison with *Paradise lost*, than the Pagan Scheme of Theology
with the Christian." [5]   Another writer declared, "It is no Compliment, but a bare Piece of Justice done to *Milton*, when we not only
compare him to *Homer* and *Virgil*, but even prefer him to both those
great Poets; because his Genius evidently appears to have been
superior to theirs, by the frequent Proofs he gives us of that Power
which constitutes a sublime Genius and . . . is more conspicuous

---

[1] Richardson's *Explanatory Notes* (1734), pp. cxix–cxx.

[2] See pp. 162–3 below, where it will be observed that Cowper on several occasions
expressed his belief in the superiority of Milton to Homer and Virgil.

[3] The Latin original was prefixed to the second edition of *Paradise Lost* (1674); this
translation is from the *Gentleman's Magazine*, xxx. 291 (cf. also below, p. 26, n. 5).
Thomas Stratford used almost the same words — probably referring to these lines — in
the preface to his *First Book of Fontenoy* (1784?, see *Mo. Rev.*, lxxi. 95). Sneyd Davies
wrote in 1740 (*Rhapsody to Milton*, in Whaley's *Collection*, 1745, p. 182),

> Such Thought, such Language, that all other Verse
> Seems trifling (not excepting *Greece* and *Rome*)
> So lofty and so sweet, beyond compare,
> Is thine.

Thomas Green remarked in 1800 that the allegory of Sin and Death "renders the
grandest passages in Homer and Virgil comparatively feeble and dwarfish" (*Diary of a
Lover of Literature*, Ipswich, 1810, p. 192).

[4] *Divine Legation of Moses* (1738), in *Works*, ed. R. Hurd, 1811, ii. 95.

[5] *Works of the Learned*, June, 1741, p. 441.

in him than in any other Poet." [1]   Joseph Warton gave poetical expression to the same opinion when he spoke of "those vales of joy"

> Where MARO and MUSAEUS sit
> List'ning to MILTON's loftier song,
> With sacred silent wonder smit;
> While, monarch of the tuneful throng,
> HOMER in rapture throws his trumpet down
> And to the Briton gives his amaranthine crown.[2]

Even the conservative *Critical Review* remarked that the works of Shakespeare and Milton were "superior to all those of antiquity," [3] and one of the editors of *Paradise Lost* declared that its author might "be said to be much superior to *Homer* and *Virgil*." [4]   Richardson, accordingly, had ample grounds not only for asserting that Milton "Excell'd All Ancients and Moderns," but for adding, "I take leave to Say so upon Many Good Authorities." [5]

There can, then, be no question that from the beginning of the century Milton's greatness was recognized by all, that he was, by pretty general consent, at least the equal of Homer and Virgil, that his epic was extravagantly praised by many, and that each of his shorter pieces was regarded by some persons as the greatest of its kind ever written.

The effect upon the public of such an increasing flow of Miltonic adulation must have been very great.   So great indeed was it that — by an impish irony which would have delighted Swift — the most austere and lofty of English poets became, in a notably artificial and prosaic age, the fashion.   There can be no question of the fact.   Even Johnson bears unwilling and scornful witness to it by protesting that Addison "has made Milton an universal favourite, with whom readers of every class think it necessary to be pleased." [6]   Nor was the idea peculiar to Johnson; for some years earlier Cibber had affirmed that as a result of the *Spectator* papers "it became even unfashionable not to have read" Milton.[7]   Warburton also, according to

---

[1] Dodsley's *Museum* (1747), iii. 284.

[2] *To Health*, in *Odes* (1746), 18.   Cf. an anonymous poem entitled *Milton* (*Univ. Mag.*, 1780, lxvii. 375):
> Unenvying Greece and Rome their claims resign,
> And own the palm of Poetry is thine.

Thomas Newcomb said almost the same thing in the second stanza of his *On Milton's Paradice Lost* (*Miscellaneous Poems*, 1740, p. 17).

[3] xviii. 328 (1764).

[4] William Massey, *Remarks upon P. L.* (1761), p. iv.

[5] *Explanatory Notes* (1734), p. xiv.

[6] "Addison," in *Lives* (ed. Hill), ii. 147 (Good, p. 257).

[7] *Lives* (1753), v. 196 n. (Good, pp. 257–8).

Gray, spoke of "the World . . . obliged by fashion to admire" Milton and Shakespeare; and the dilettante Horace Walpole asked a friend to procure him "a print of Vallombrosa," because of the "passion there is for it in England, as Milton has mentioned it." [1]

As late as 1793 John Aikin declared, "A relish for the works of Milton is not only a test of sensibility to the more exquisite beauties of poetry, but a kind of measure of the exaltation of the mind in its moral and religious sentiments." [2] Thomas Warton, though unwilling to go so far as this, anticipated Tennyson's oft-quoted dictum by asserting, "He who wishes to know whether he has a true taste for Poetry or not, should consider, whether he is highly delighted or not with the perusal of Milton's *Lycidas*." [3] "He who professes he has no Taste for *Milton*," remarked still another, "is justly deemed to have no Taste for Polite Literature," [4] a phrase that recalls Steele's surprising reference to Otway, Milton, and Dryden as among "the most polite Writers of the Age." [5] But Steele had previously implied that the loftiest of English poets occupied this anomalous position; for in one of the early numbers of the *Tatler* Mr. Bickerstaff visits Sappho, "a fine lady" who, through breaking a fan "wherein were so admirably drawn our first parents in Paradise asleep in each other's arms," has been led to "reading the same representation in two of our greatest poets. . . . All Milton's thoughts," declares the fair chatterer, "are wonderfully just and natural, in this inimitable description. . . . But now I cannot forgive this odious thing, this Dryden." On a later occasion Sappho repeats to some ladies lines from two poets, Sir John Suckling and Milton, who had said "the tenderest things she had ever read" on the subject of love; and in still another issue of the *Tatler* Milton's lines on wedded love are quoted at a wedding breakfast.[6] No wonder Pope remarked, "Our wives read Milton." [7] But even in 1702, when Steele was just beginning to write, a would-be wit and critic was represented as slight-

---

[1] See Gray's letter to Wharton, Oct. 7, 1757, and Walpole's to Horace Mann, May 13, 1752 (Good, pp. 183, 219).

[2] *Letters from a Father to his Son* (1800), ii. 269 (Good, p. 138).

[3] In his edition of Milton's minor poems (1785), p. 34.

[4] John Marchant, in his edition of *Paradise Lost* (1751), p. viii.

[5] This is the more significant because it occurs in the *Ladies Library* (1714), i. 2–4 (Good, p. 157).

[6] *Tatler*, nos. 6, 40, 79. In the *Student* (1751, ii. 381), "a giddy young girl" named Flirtilla falls into "a rhapsodic vision" while reading Milton's description of Pandemonium (Good, p. 184); and Elizabeth Rowe speaks of a young lady who was so absorbed in reading Milton in the park as not to notice an approaching admirer (*Works*, 1796, i. 115).

[7] *Imitations of Horace*, II. i. 172.

ing Shakespeare, Jonson, Dryden, and Congreve, but as being "a great Admirer of the incomparable *Milton*," whose "*Sublime*" he "fondly endeavours to imitate." [1]

The inevitable result of this homage was that it came to require courage to say anything whatever against "the favourite poet of this nation," as John Jortin called him.[2] "Whoever," remarked the *Monthly Review* in 1760, "at this time ventures to carp at . . . Paradise Lost, must whisper his criticism with caution";[3] and even the great Chesterfield, in admitting to his son, "I cannot possibly read . . . Milton through," was constrained to add, "Keep this secret for me; for if it should be known, I should be abused by every tasteless pedant, and every solid divine, in England." [4]

Presumably there were many who, like Chesterfield, dared not avow their indifference to a work which was regarded not only as "the finest poem in the world" but as a touchstone of poetic taste; yet such persons must have kept their thoughts to themselves, for adverse comments rarely found their way into print. And though some, no doubt, affected a liking for the epic which they did not feel, the genuine enthusiasm of hundreds of writers cannot be questioned. Milton must have been read, for imitations of his style and diction and borrowings from his phraseology are scattered through eighteenth-century literature

> Thick as autumnal leaves that strow the brooks
> In Vallombrosa.

In fact, so many persons really knew the pieces that it was probably not safe to pretend to a knowledge which one did not possess. Even shepherds were observed "poring in the fields" over the epic; [5] and a Bristol milkwoman, Ann Yearsley, whose versifying was encouraged by Hannah More, was "well acquainted" with the *Night Thoughts* and *Paradise Lost* but "was astonished to learn that Young and Milton had written anything else. Of Pope, she had only seen the Eloisa; and Dryden, Spenser, Thomson, and Prior, were quite unknown to her, even by name;" she had read "a few

[1] *The English Theophrastus, or the Manners of the Age* (attributed to Abel Boyer), 10; pointed out in Dowden's *Milton in the Eighteenth Century* (British Acad., *Proceedings*, 1907–8, p. 279).

[2] "Milton," in *Remarks on Spenser's Poems* (1734), 171.

[3] xxii. 119. The same idea is expressed by the "Gentleman of Oxford" in the preface to his *New Version of the P. L.* (see above, p. 6).

[4] Letter, Oct. 4, 1752. "I spoke of . . . *Paradise Lost*," wrote Cowper to Hayley, Feb. 24, 1793, "as every man must, who is worthy to speak of it at all."

[5] Boswell's *Johnson* (ed. Hill), iv. 43 n.

of Shakespeare's plays." [1]   These facts almost make one accept at their face value such assertions as, "*Paradise Lost* . . . is read with Pleasure and Admiration, by Persons of every Degree and Condition;" [2] or, "The . . . *Poem* is in every One's Hand;" [3] or, "Remarkable therefore it is, that *Paradise Lost* and Young's *Night Thoughts* are read by all sorts of people. . . . the common people . . . are fond of Milton's poems." [4]

So general, in fact, did this fondness become that children were early introduced to the poems. It will be remembered that the Swan of Lichfield "lisped" — if a swan may be permitted to lisp — *Allegro* and *Penseroso* "when only in her third year," and that Cowper's enthusiasm dated from his boyhood. [5] Ebenezer Elliott could in his sixteenth year repeat the first, second, and sixth books of *Paradise Lost* "without missing a word"; [6] and a twelve-year-old girl, Caroline Symmons, was so 'passionately attached' to Milton that to have been the author of his octosyllabics she 'would have declined no personal sacrifice of face or form.' [7] In order that children might appreciate the beauties of Milton, editions of his poems were prepared especially for them. The popular clergyman, Dr. Dodd, recommended his *Familiar Explanation of the Poetical Works of Milton* "especially to Parents, and those who have the Care of Youth; if they are desirous that their Children and Trusts should be acquainted with the Graces of the *British Homer*. . . . The fair Sex in particular," he added, "will receive great Advantages from it." [8] As early as 1717 a "Collection of Poems from our most Celebrated English Poets, designed for the Use of Young Gentlemen and

---

[1] *Mo. Rev.*, lxxiii. 218 (1785). The reading of *Paradise Lost* was recommended in John Hill's *Actor* (1755, p. 96) as the ideal training for a player.

[2] William Massey, *Remarks upon P. L.* (1761), p. iii; cf. p. v, "this Book, that is now so universally read."

[3] James Paterson, *Complete Commentary on P. L.* (1744), p. ii.

[4] Robert Potter, *The Art of Criticism, as exemplified in Johnson's Lives of the Poets* (1789), 184–5, 188. It should be observed, however, that William Hayley, in his life of Milton (2d ed., 1796, p. 226), speaks of him as "more admired than beloved," and that Cowper, in a letter to Hayley (May 9, 1792), owns it is "no small disgrace to us English that being natives of a country that has produced the finest poem in the world, so few of us ever look into it. I am acquainted myself," he continues, "with at least a score, who account themselves pretty good judges of poetry too, and persons of taste, who yet know no more of the poem than the mere subject of it." Neither of these men, however, would have been content with much less than idolatry of Milton, and Cowper at least did not have a wide or a representative circle of acquaintances.

[5] See pp. 7, 10, above.

[6] Autobiography, in *Athenaeum*, Jan. 12, 1850, p. 48.

[7] Memoir appended to F. Wrangham's *Raising of Jaïrus' Daughter* (1804), 25.

[8] Preface (dated 1761), pp. vi–vii.

Ladies, at Schools," [1] included eighteen selections from the epic and one from *Samson*, together with Dryden's lines on Milton; and in 1783 appeared *The Beauties of Milton, Thomson, and Young*, for "the rising youth of both sexes." Nearly half of *Poetry Explained for Young People* (1802), by the father of Maria Edgeworth, is devoted to *Allegro* and *Penseroso;* while still later in the century the great actress, Mrs. Siddons, made an abridgment of the epic for her children, because she "was naturally desirous that their minds should be inspired with an early admiration of Milton." This was afterwards published as *The Story of our First Parents, selected from Paradise Lost for the Use of Young Persons* (1822). A similar work, *The Story of Paradise Lost for Children*,[2] a prose dialogue which included some of the original verse, was deemed worthy of republication in New England, where, it is said, "during the greater part of the nineteenth century . . . the *Paradise Lost* was practically a text-book. Children were compelled, as an exercise, to commit long passages of it by heart." [3]

Such tasks were not always so distasteful as one might expect. We are told that the war of the angels was the "favourite of children," and we know that it was on the basis of his own boyhood enthusiasm for the octosyllabics and the epic that Cowper recommended the memorizing of parts of them by another boy.[4] It was natural that Milton should be urged upon children if there were many persons, as there seem to have been, who believed with Dr. Johnson that "in reading *Paradise Lost* we read a book of universal knowledge," [5] and especially if many agreed with a certain editor —

[1] The *Virgin Muse*, compiled by James Greenwood.

[2] By Eliza W. Bradburn, Portland, 1830, "first American, from the London edition." Cf. below, p. 36.

[3] C. F. Adams, in the New York *Nation*, lxxxvii. 600 (1908). According to Mr. Adams, the Puritans of the new world were fifty years behind the mother country in their recognition of the religious epic. "Milton's poems," he writes, "were almost unknown in New England until about the middle of the eighteenth century. There is no well-authenticated case of a copy of *Paradise Lost* on a Massachusetts book-shelf before that period yet brought to light. From about the year 1750 to the beginning of the nineteenth century there is abundant evidence of growing familiarity." Many Americans now living learned grammar by parsing *Paradise Lost*.

[4] Potter, *Art of Criticism*, 13; Cowper to William Unwin, Jan. 17, 1782, and cf. pp. 7, 10, above. "Milton is my favourite," wrote the profligate Lord Lyttelton in the third quarter of the century; ". . . I read him with delight as soon as I could read at all" (quoted in Thomas Frost's life of Lyttelton, 1876, pp. 3–4). Southey tells us that *Paradise Lost* was one of the first books he owned (*Life and Correspondence*, 1849, i. 86); and W. S. Walker was deep in Milton at six years old (i. e., in 1801, see his *Poetical Remains*, ed. Moultrie, 1852, pp. iv–v).

[5] "Milton," in *Lives* (ed. Hill), i. 183. Johnson probably refers to the first lines of

who, to be sure, was recommending a particular edition of the poem as a text-book — that, "as it exhibits a view of every thing great in the whole circle of Being, it would (besides greatly improving them [schoolboys] in their own language) wonderfully open the capacity, improve the judgment, elevate the ideas, refine the imagination, and, finally, infuse a just and noble relish for all that is beautiful and great in the Aeneid and Iliad." [1] Two men, at least, seem to have shared this opinion. Edmund Burke, whose speeches abound with quotations from Milton, "always recommended the study of him to his son, and to all his younger friends, as exhibiting the highest possible range of mind in the English language." [2] And Richard Baron wrote: "MILTON in particular ought to be read and studied by all our young Gentlemen as an *Oracle*. He was a great and noble Genius, perhaps the greatest that ever appeared among men. . . . His works are full of wisdom, a treasure of knowledge." [3]

But, though a boy were brought up in ignorance of Milton, the defect would probably be remedied at the university; for, according to Robert Lloyd, 'Milton-madness' was

an affectation
Glean'd up from college education.[4]

Even at the beginning of the century at least three Oxford professors of poetry, Joseph Trapp, Thomas Warton, and Joseph Spence, were imitators of Milton; Gray and the younger Thomas Warton lived at the universities, and most of the poet's enthusiastic admirers were college men. The extent of their enthusiasm is shown in the volumes of verse written by members of universities in celebration of various public events. These sumptuous folios and quartos are thickly strewn with octosyllabics and blank verse derived from Milton's work, as well as with phrases taken from it; and one of the collec-

Barrow's Latin verses prefixed to the second edition of *Paradise Lost*, which were thus translated in the *Gentleman's Magazine*, xxx. 291 (cf. p. 21 above):

Who reads *Lost Paradise*, the fall
    Of wretched man, what reads he less than all?
All nature's works; from whence they rose;
    Their fates and ends; these lofty lines disclose.

Thomas Marriott says the same thing in his *Female Conduct*, 1759, p. 99 (noted by Good, p. 83); and in the preface to the prose paraphrase of the epic we read, "It comprehends almost every Thing within the Extent of human Knowledge."

[1] James Buchanan, *First Six Books of P. L., rendered into Grammatical Construction* (Edin., 1773), 1–2.
[2] Prior's *Burke* (5th ed., 1854), 30.
[3] Preface to *Eikonoklastes*, 1756 (Good, p. 175).
[4] *On Rhyme* (written *c.*1760), in *Poetical Works*, 1774, ii. 112.

tions contains as many as twenty pieces which employ the meter, style, and diction of *Paradise Lost*.[1]

It may be partly as a result of this early reading that Miltonic allusions rose so naturally to the lips even of "the general" in the eighteenth century. The word "monody," for instance, which is hardly more common to-day than it was before the appearance of *Lycidas*, was much used after 1740.[2] The god Comus, too, became a recognized deity who existed quite apart from Milton's masque;[3] a "busto" of him, erected in a buffet at Hammersmith, attracted considerable attention, and the "temple of Comus" formed one of the most prominent features of Vauxhall.[4] In this same resort, furthermore, was a statue by the much-admired Roubillac which represented Milton "'seated on a rock, in an attitude [of] listening to soft music,' as described by himself, in his *Il Penseroso*."[5] As no place of amusement was more fashionable or popular than Vauxhall, this is as if a likeness of the poet were to face the board walk at Atlantic City. More private tributes are to be found in the facts that ten lines from *Penseroso* were inscribed in a room of the hermitage at Hagley Park,[6] that there was "a beautiful Alcove called *Il Penseroso*" at the end of a garden walk in Surrey,[7] and that Jane Porter and her sister were dubbed "L'Allegro" and "Il Penseroso."

Yet the vogue of the poems was not due entirely to the *reading* of Milton; for *Comus*, with abridged text, additional songs and dances, and attractive new music, came to be one of the most persistently popular musical entertainments of the century. At the same time, *Samson Agonistes*, the octosyllabics, and the version of the Psalms were repeatedly sung in Handel's very popular oratorios; the *Song on May Morning* and the hymn of Adam and Eve were set to music and "performed";[8] *Lycidas* was presented as a "musical entertain-

---

[1] See Bibl. I, 1761 (*Pietas Oxon.*). Two of the other collections of 1761 and 1762 each contain twelve such pieces, and some eighteen or twenty more are listed in Bibliographies I and II under the years 1761, 1762, 1763. Thomas Warton the younger had a good deal to do with several of these volumes. J. Husbands's *Miscellany*, published at Oxford in 1731, contains ten poems that are significantly influenced by *Paradise Lost* and one by *Penseroso*.   [2] See below, pp. 549-55, 680-81.

[3] I have collected over twenty passages in which the god Comus is spoken of with apparently no thought of Milton. The latest is in Byron's *English Bards*, line 650.

[4] Pearch's *Collection* (1783), i. 329; Austin Dobson's "Old Vauxhall," *Eighteenth Century Vignettes* (1st series, 1892), 241.

[5] Dobson, *ib.* 244.

[6] Joseph Heely, *Letters on Hagley*, etc. (1777), i. 193 (Good, p. 211).

[7] *Lond. Mag.*, xxxii. 554 (1763).

[8] Cf. pp. 430-32 below. For the *Song*, with music by M. C. Festing, see *Miscellany of Lyric Poems performed in the Academy of Music* (1740), 61-2; the hymn, "set to musick" by J. E. Galliard, was published in 1728 and 1773.

ment" in memory of the Duke of York;[1] parts of *Allegro* and the *Arcades* were used as songs in Garrick's opera, *The Fairies* (1755); and *Paradise Lost* was arranged for an oratorio at least four times, once by the great Mrs. Delany for Handel and once as the basis of Haydn's *Creation*.[2] Considerable interest was also aroused by Fuseli's "Milton Gallery," where paintings for an edition of the poet were exhibited during parts of two successive years (1799, 1800). But the most curious of these extra-literary evidences of a general interest in the poet is afforded by Philip de Loutherbourg's "Eidophusikon." This precursor of the "Johnstown Flood" and the moving pictures, which consisted of cardboard models skilfully illuminated by colored lights, enjoyed unusual popularity in the years 1781 and 1786 and was warmly commended even by Reynolds and Gainsborough. The culminating scene was "Satan arraying his Troops on the Banks of the Fiery Lake, with the Raising of Pandemonium, from Milton."[3]

The vitality of the enthusiasm for Milton in the eighteenth century is indicated by the storms of protest which broke over the heads of any who dared attack him. Three books in particular roused the fury of the poet's "idolators." The first was the 1732 edition of *Paradise Lost* undertaken at the suggestion of Queen Caroline by the great classical scholar Richard Bentley, who pretended to believe that the blind poet's assistants, besides misunderstanding his dictation and admitting errors through carelessness, had deliberately introduced many changes into the text. "Slashing Bentley," as Pope termed him, accordingly substituted "a transpicuous gloom" for the famous "darkness visible," and bracketed as interpolations the line

> Blind Thamyris and blind Maeonides

and the one that follows it, as well as the superb passage which ends,

> When Charlemain with all his peerage fell
> By Fontarabbia.

These last lines, which were termed "a heap of barbarous Words, without any Ornament or Poetical colouring," Bentley would have

[1] *Lycidas, a Musical Entertainment, the words altered from Milton* [by William Jackson], 1767.

[2] See Mrs. Delany's *Autobiography and Correspondence*, 1861, ii. 280 (letter to Mrs. Dewes, March 10, 1743/4). Mrs. Delany's arrangement and that of Richard Jago (*Adam*, 1784?) were never sung; but Benjamin Stillingfleet's, set to music by Handel's pupil and assistant J. C. Smith, was printed and twice performed in 1760. Haydn, as Mr. Alwin Thaler points out in his *Milton in the Theatre* (Univ. of North Carolina, *Studies in Philology*, xvii. 283–4), used a German rendering of a libretto made by a Mr. Lidley (or Liddell), which was later put back into English.

[3] Austin Dobson, *At Prior Park*, etc. (1912), 114–16, 280.

omitted, because Milton "surely . . . had more Judgment in his old Age, than to clog and sully his Poem with such Romantic Trash." Changes like these — and there are hundreds of them — are to-day simply amusing, or amazing, instances of misapplied ingenuity, but on their first appearance they were regarded as a serious matter and called forth immediate protest. The magazines were filled with essays and verses, the booksellers' windows with pamphlets, satires, and learned refutations of the "sacrilege" to Milton's work. Bentley's name became synonymous with pedantic folly, and is embalmed as such in *The Dunciad* and in the critical essays and notes that accompany it. Sneers and execrations continued to be directed at his work throughout the century, but within fifteen years popular interest was diverted to a new wonder.

This was the charge brought by the Rev. William Lauder that considerable parts of *Paradise Lost* were simply paraphrases of little-known foreign poets. The accusation, first made in the *Gentleman's Magazine* for January, 1747, reached its fullest development in an *Essay on Milton's Use and Imitation of the Moderns*, published towards the close of 1749. If Bentley's emendations had called up a storm of protest, Lauder's writings roused a tempest. Inquiries, protests, denials, reviews, lampoons, and prophecies, in both prose and verse, were poured upon the bloody but unbowed head of Milton's detractor. In the main, however, the charges were not disproved until November, 1750, when the Bishop of Salisbury showed that the passages which Milton was accused of borrowing were not in the works referred to but had been taken by Lauder from William Hog's Latin translation of *Paradise Lost* (1690).[1] The attention attracted by the forgery is indicated not only by the ten books or pamphlets written upon it, and by the articles, nearly forty in number, which a single magazine devoted to the subject, but by many humbler protests, such as "Verses intended to have been spoken at the Breaking-up of the Free Grammar school in Manchester, in . . . 1748, when Lauder's charge of Plagiarism upon Milton engaged the Public Attention."[2]

Upon the detection of the fraud, Dr. Johnson, who had written the preface to Lauder's book, dictated a letter of confession and apology which he compelled the offender to publish over his own

[1] Sir John Douglas, *Milton vindicated from the Charge of Plagiarism* (1751). Oddly enough, Lauder had himself, in his translation of Grotius's *Eucharistia* (1732), made some use of the verse and style of *Paradise Lost.*

[2] John Byrom, *Poems* (Chetham Soc., 1894), i. 178–92. Byrom's loyalty to Milton is the more interesting because he was not an admirer of blank verse (see *ib.* 387–93, and, for his controversy with Roger Comberbach on the subject, 411–28).

name; yet the readiness with which the Doctor believed charges which most persons doubted seems to indicate an antipathy to Milton that is unquestionably present in his life of the poet (1779). In this work, which is marred by gratuitous sneers, misrepresentation of motives, and a willingness to believe the worst things that had been said of its subject, Milton's character, political activities, and prose writings are treated with the intense partisanship of a bigoted Tory. The ire of the poet's admirers was immediately aflame, and the biographer received as rough treatment as he had given. Within a year of the appearance of the *Life*, Archdeacon Francis Blackburne twice published a lengthy arraignment of "the meanness . . . the virulent malignity" exhibited by "the grand exemplar of literary prostitution," in which he thus explained Johnson's reasons for writing the biography: "When the Doctor found, on some late occasions, that his crude abuse and malicious criticisms would not bring down Milton to the degree of contempt with the public which he had assigned him in the scale of prose-writers; he fell upon an expedient which has sometimes succeeded in particular exigencies. In one word, he determined to write his Life." [1] These are harsh words for an archdeacon, and there are harsher in his book; but they are all less surprising than the exclamation of the sweet-spirited recluse of Olney, "Oh! I could thresh his old jacket, till I made his pension jingle in his pocket." [2] Nor was Cowper's wrath short-lived, for thirteen years later he refers to "that literary cossack's strictures" on his idol, and bursts out with, "Oh that Johnson! how does every page of his on the subject, ay, almost every paragraph, kindle my indignation!" [3]

Indeed, anger at Johnson's biography flamed many a year after Cowper was no more. In 1818, almost four decades after the appearance of the offending work, another writer devoted an entire book to attacking it. This critic found the Doctor's "antipathy so marked, so virulent and unrelenting," his "enmity" so "inexorable," that it was "difficult to conjecture into what vehemence of angry reproach it might have hurried him had it not been bridled by his awe of the public." [4]

[1] *Remarks on Johnson's Life of Milton* (1780), 131, 148, 22–3. The *Remarks* first appeared in Blackburne's *Memoirs of Thomas Hollis* (1780), 533*–84*.

[2] Cowper's letter to William Unwin, Oct. 31, 1779; cf. also Jan. 17, 1782, and March 21, 1784.

[3] To William Hayley, Oct. 13 and May 1, 1792; and cf. Nov. 22, 1793. In a letter to Walter Bagot, May 2, 1791 (cf. also March 18, 1791), Cowper promises a "future letter" in which "Johnson gets another slap or two."

[4] T. H. White, *Review of Johnson's Criticism on Milton's Prose* (1818), 29–30.

The bitterness against Johnson — and it was widespread — is the more remarkable because, aside from *Lycidas* and the sonnets, Milton's poems received far more commendation from the Ursa Major of literature than one would expect; to the epic in particular he gave extensive and very high praise. All this approbation, however, was swept aside by the devotees of the poet on the ground that the Doctor dared not do less. "He praises Milton," flared Miss Seward, "under the eye of the public as Pistol eat his leek under that of Fluellen. After all, he endeavours to do away, collectively, all his reluctant praise of that glorious and beautiful poem, by observing, that no person closes its pages with the desire of recurring to them. . . . A self-evident, I could almost say an impudent falsehood." [1] Clearly, Milton's admirers were not easily satisfied. Is it any wonder that Richard Edgeworth feared lest some persons would "deem it a species of literary sacrilege to criticize any part of" the octosyllabics,[2] when Cowper was so displeased with some remarks made by the great Miltonian, Thomas Warton, that he wrote, "Warton in truth is not much better" than Johnson and "deserves . . . to lose his own" ear because he "has dared to say that he [Milton] had a bad one"? [3]

However interesting in itself, such sensitiveness to any criticism of their "idol" would be of little importance if it had been limited to a few persons; what gives these controversies their significance is the large number who took part in them. "The question, whether *Milton* borrow'd from *Masenius*," wrote an Englishman in Louvain to the *Gentleman's Magazine*, "concerns, in my opinion, the whole nation"; [4] and the whole nation seems to have taken the matter as its concern. All of which is inconceivable to-day. When

---

[1] *Letters* (1811), iv. 133. Other criticisms of Johnson's *Life* will be found in the *Gentleman's Magazine*, xlix. 492–3 (1779, two letters), lix. 413–17; *Monthly Review*, lxi. 81–92 (1779), lxii. 479–83; Horace Walpole's letters to William Mason, Oct. 13, 1780, Feb. 5 and 19, 1781, April 14, 1782 (in the last of these he says that Thomas Stratford "cannot bear the name of Johnson, for his paltry acrimony against Milton"); Lord Monboddo's letter to Sir George Baker, Oct. 2, 1782 (William Knight's *Lord Monboddo*, etc., 1900, p. 214); Robert Potter's *Art of Criticism* (1789), 6–19; Philip Neve's *Cursory Remarks on English Poets* (1789), 113, 134; Thomas Twining's letter to his brother, May 3, 1784 (*Country Clergyman of the Eighteenth Century*, 1882, p. 120). Johnson's criticisms of *Samson* (*Rambler*, 1751, nos. 139, 140) were refuted by W. J. Mickle and Richard Cumberland (*Europ. Mag.*, 1788, xiii. 401–6; *Observer*, 1788, no. 111).

[2] *Poetry explained for Young People* (1802), p. ix.

[3] Letters to Hayley, May 1, 1792, and Lady Hesketh, March 6, 1786; and cf. below, p. 57, n. 5. Samuel Darby's pamphlet of forty-one pages, *Letter to T. Warton on his Edition of Milton's Juvenile Poems* (1785), though not hostile in tone, is another illustration of the amount of attention Milton attracted.

[4] xvii. 567 (Good, p. 189).

we remember our perfunctory celebrations of the centenaries of Shakespeare and Milton, we can hardly believe that there ever was a time when for four years the most popular magazine of the day printed article after article regarding an alleged literary plagiarism, and when even schoolboys declaimed upon the subject. It is harder still to realize that any large number of persons ever became deeply interested in revisions of the text of a poet sixty years dead.

These astonishing tributes to the "immeasurably great" popularity of one who expected his audience to be "few" require explanation. How did it happen that poems which are to-day the admiration of a relatively small number excited, a century and a half ago, the enthusiasm of many? One reason immediately suggests itself, — the religious character of the epic. The avowed purpose of *Paradise Lost* is to "justify the ways of God to men," and its persistent and noble prosecution of that purpose has made it the greatest religious poem in English. Nowadays this aspect of the work is either overlooked or remembered with little satisfaction. To most of us the ways of Milton's anthropomorphic God are neither justified nor made attractive; we find little in his two major poems that seems distinctively Christian, little of the patient love for erring men and the yearning to help them that breathe in the parables of the prodigal son and the good shepherd. But in the eighteenth century, when the more tender aspects of Christianity were emphasized much less than they are now, their absence was little felt; then theology was more important, and to most of the orthodox the Puritan justification was satisfactory. The dissenters in particular, who counted Milton peculiarly their own, — as he was, — frequently held his epic second in importance only to the Bible.

Among the earliest of his admirers and imitators, as we shall see later, was a group of writers who seem to have caught their enthusiasm at the nonconformist academy they attended in boyhood; and not a few of his other "adorers," like John Toland, Richard Baron, Thomas Hollis, did not belong to the established church. But all, the orthodox Addison, the deistic Thomson, the Catholic Pope, all agreed as to the importance of the moral and religious, the consciously didactic, element in poetry. A main point in Dennis's criticism was "that Religion is the Basis and Foundation of the greater Poetry," [1] and so late as 1797 the *Monthly Review* spoke of poetry as simply "a happy vehicle for conveying instruction." [2] Addison was

[1] *Grounds of Criticism in Poetry* (1704), 94.
[2] Enlarged ed., xxiv. 460. The preacher's life should correspond with his instruction; hence Pope's anxiety that his life be regarded as "the nobler song." "I much

even willing to mar the perfect conclusion of *Paradise Lost* by omitting the last two lines, in order that the poem might end with the words "and Providence their guide." The religious aspects of the epic unquestionably had much to do with the admiration it awakened in Dennis, Addison, Thomson, Young, Cowper, and even Wordsworth. It was this side of the work that called forth Johnson's highest praise and so deeply impressed Gildon that he censured Addison for discussing the poem as an epic. *Paradise Lost*, he maintained, "is not an heroic poem, but a divine one, and indeed a new species." [1] It must be remembered that a large number of the writers of this period were clergymen, and also that men by no means distinguished for their piety were unanimous in thinking that all great literature teaches religion and morality. For it was at once the weakness and the strength of the eighteenth century that writers and critics of the period did not regard literary beauty as its own excuse for being. Even among the frivolous and the dissipated *Paradise Lost* would never have achieved the reputation it did, if it had not been a moral and religious power. Not, of course, that the genuine liking which many of the fashionable felt for the poem was due primarily to its lofty ethical value; yet without that they might never have read it at all, and would certainly not have held it in that profound respect which was the basis of its popularity.

But, though important even with the frivolous, the religious element loomed large indeed with the more serious of the gentry and with the middle class. There were thousands of readers upon whom the supreme poetic gifts of Milton were practically wasted, devout persons who regarded his richly-colored epic as little more than a religious tract. The humble folk who for a century had been thrilled by Fox's *Book of Martyrs* and had consumed edition after edition of the despised *Pilgrim's Progress*, were also attracted to *Paradise Lost*. To make the poem intelligible to them various devices were employed. Annotation, the most obvious expedient, was of course repeatedly used; and some editions, like the Rev. Dr. Dodd's *Familiar Explanation* (1762), were addressed particularly to the young and the uneducated. [2] Omission of classical allusions, involved similes, and other difficult passages was tried by John

more resent," he wrote to Aaron Hill, Feb. 5, 1730/31, "any attempt against my moral character, which I know to be unjust, than any to lessen my poetical one, which . . . may be very just." See also T. R. Lounsbury's *Text of Shakespeare* (N. Y., 1906), 468–82. The constant advocacy of *Paradise Lost* in the *Tatler* and the *Spectator* may have been part of the campaign of uplift to which those periodicals were devoted.

[1] *Laws of Poetry* (1721), 259.

[2] See above, p. 25.

Wesley,[1] and also, with astonishing results, by "a Gentleman of Oxford." [2] In the last-mentioned product of academic leisure there was an attempt to remove from the poem not only its learning and obscurity but its long sentences and its "roughness," an experiment which led to such nondescript verse as this:

> Of *Adam's* Fall, and the forbidden Tree,
> Whose Fruit brought *Sin* and *Death* into the World,
> With Loss of *Paradise* and Immortality,
> To Him and to his Sons — sing, *heavenly* MUSE!

But the assistance which the less educated readers found most to their taste was more direct and even more astonishing than these makeshifts. It was a prose version, and, what is more, an English translation of a French translation of the original. In 1729 Dupré de St. Maur published in Paris, and in 1743 reissued with corrections, a translation of Milton's epic into French prose, which two years later was put back into English, probably by the same "Gentleman of Oxford." [3] The work was printed ten times, and obviously for religious reasons, since it is made up of this sort of thing:

> Thus SATAN kept talking to BEELZEBUB, with his Head lifted up above the Waves, and glancing his Eyes from Side to Side: As for his other Parts, he lay extended in a melancholy Condition, floating in Length and Breadth over a vast Space of the Abyss.[4]

Another attempt, made in 1773, to render the poem intelligible to "persons of a common Education" was James Buchanan's "First Six Books of Milton's Paradise Lost, rendered into Grammatical Construction; the words of the Text being arranged, at the bottom of each Page, in the same natural Order with the Conceptions of the mind; and the Ellipsis properly supplied, without any Alteration in the Diction of the Poem," — this is but a third of the complete title! John Gillies's edition of the poem, "illustrated with Texts of Scripture," published in 1788 and reprinted in 1793, affords a further indication of the number of readers who associated Milton, not with

---

[1] *Extract from P. L.* (1791). In the first book alone such omissions amount to over 220 lines, and include many of the finest passages. A similar free use of the scissors reduces the first five lines of the second book to "High on a throne, Satan exalted sat."

[2] *A New Version of the P. L., in which the Measure and Versification are corrected and harmonized, the Obscurities elucidated, and the Faults removed* [book i only], Oxford, 1756 (said to be the work of G. S. Green).

[3] *The State of Innocence and Fall of Man, render'd into Prose, with notes from the French of Raymond de St. Maur*, "by a Gentleman of Oxford," 1745. At least two prose versions of *Paradise Regained* were also published, one in 1771 (*The Recovery of Man*) and the other with *Paradise Lost* in 1775.

[4] Page 11; cf. *P. L.*, i. 192–6.

Shakespeare and Spenser, but with Bunyan, Fox, and Watts; for the notes consist simply of passages from the Bible. Even so late as 1830 there appeared in Portland, Maine, the *Story of Paradise Lost for Children*,[1] an innocuous work of the old Sunday-school-library type which has fortunately passed away. The "story," with many quotations from the original, some of considerable length, is drawn from "Mamma," who talks like a rhetoric, by Eliza, Emily, and William, children of awful goodness and wisdom, all under eleven years of age! Through such paraphrases as these Milton reached a class of persons who read little poetry of any sort and none of the rank of an epic, yet some of whom must have been attracted from the prose versions to the original. The extent of the influence exerted in this way cannot be measured, but no doubt it was in part due to these prose renderings that *Paradise Lost* was thought to have "contributed more to support the orthodox creed, than all the *bodies of divinity* that were ever written." [2]

But there were reasons other than the religious why Milton's poetry roused more enthusiasm in the days of Pope and of the Wartons than it does now. For one thing, it was much more of a novelty: the dew of its morning was still upon it. Not, of course, that *Paradise Lost* was new at any time in the eighteenth century; but it was different, people had not become accustomed to it, and in consequence it had not sunk into the position of respected neglect occupied by most classics. Even late in the century a first reading of it often had something of the thrill of discovery.

This difference between Milton's work and that of other poets impressed the neo-classicists strongly because their literature, both what they wrote and what they read, was in almost every respect far less like *Paradise Lost* than ours is. To be sure, Milton's poetry resembles that of the Elizabethans, but about most of this earlier verse his readers knew little and cared less. What struck them as particularly different from their own work was the daring wildness of the epic. It was "read by all sorts of people . . . for its extravagance," we are told.[3] Such terms as "magnificently wild," a "genius

---

[1] By Eliza W. Bradburn.

[2] *Mo. Rev.*, enl. ed., 1792, ix. 5 (Good, p. 220). Cf. Huxley's remark apropos of the notion that the universe was suddenly created from chaos: "I believe it is largely to the influence of that remarkable work [*Paradise Lost*] . . . that this hypothesis owes its general wide diffusion" ("Lectures on Evolution," 1876, in *Science and Hebrew Tradition*, N. Y., 1894, p. 52).

[3] R. Potter, *Art of Criticism* (1789), 185. Philip Neve (*Cursory Remarks on English Poets*, 1789, p. 141) praises "the terror excited by the sublimity" of Milton's "design." The wildness and extravagance of the epic had impressed people from the first; it was on this account that Addison devoted his *Spectator* papers to proving the regularity of the poem.

. . . Astonishing as chaos," [1] were frequently applied to its author, who was regarded as a kind of Michaelangelo of verse, less regular than Homer and Virgil but, in the words of Dennis, "more lofty, more terrible, more vehement, more astonishing," and with "more impetuous and more divine Raptures." [2] Collins pictured him

> High on some cliff, to heaven up-piled,
> Of rude access, of prospect wild,
> Where, tangled round the jealous steep,
> Strange shades o'erbrow the valleys deep.[3]

Gray praised "that enchanting air of freedom and wildness" in his versification; [4] and another poet mentioned "splendid Acts" which "require A MILTON, or a Muse of Fire." [5] It was of Milton that Isaac Watts immediately thought when he invoked the "Adventurous Muse." "Give me," he wrote,

> Give me the Muse whose generous Force
> Impatient of the Reins
> Pursues an unattempted Course,
> Breaks all the Criticks Iron Chains,
> And bears to Paradise the raptur'd Mind.
> There *Milton* dwells: The Mortal sung
> Themes not presum'd by mortal Tongue;
> New Terrors and new Glories shine
> In every Page, and flying Scenes Divine
> Surprize the wond'ring Sense, & draw our Souls along.[6]

The same characteristics were emphasized by the figures of speech under which Milton was described. He is an "Eagle, wonderful in his soarings, [who] shews in his very stoops the power of his wing"; he "pours upon us a torrent of images, great and terrible"; or, to versify the figure,

> MILTON is like a Flood, whose Tide,
> Swell'd with tempestuous Deluge, roars,
> Which from some lofty Mountain's Side
> Resistless foams, and knows no Shores.[7]

---

[1] Robert Merry, *Diversity*, 1788, in *British Album* (Boston, 1793), 231; Thomson, *Summer*, 1569-70.

[2] *Reflections upon an Essay upon Criticism*, 1711, p. 17 (Good, p. 150).

[3] *Ode on the Poetical Character*, 55-8.

[4] *Observations on English Metre*, in *Works* (ed. Mitford), v. 233.

[5] G. T. Ridsdale, *Ode, Congratulatory*, etc. (Dublin, 1799), 14.

[6] *Adventurous Muse*, in *Horae Lyricae* (2d ed., 1709), 212. Half of the piece is devoted to Milton, who is the only poet mentioned.

[7] Daniel Webb, *Remarks on the Beauties of Poetry* (1762), 13; Leonard Welsted, "Remarks on Longinus," 1712, *Works* (1787), 422; *Verses to the Author*, "by a Divine," in Stephen Duck's *Poems* (1738), 129.

"In his most exalted flights," wrote Leonard Welsted, " . . . he appears to me as a vast comet, that for want of room is ready to burst its orb and grow eccentric." [1]

This last comment, like some of the passages previously quoted, hints that *Paradise Lost* was not in complete conformity with the neo-classic rules, a charge that was often made and freely admitted even by Milton's admirers. Dennis, who touched upon nearly all aspects of the work, characterized it as "the most lofty, but most irregular Poem, that has been produc'd by the Mind of Man"; [2] and a writer in the *Bee*, in 1732, declared Milton to be "a prodigious, tho' an irregular Genius." [3]   It may be remembered that when Boileau, in Lyttelton's dialogue, referred to the critics who were disturbed by the "absurdities" and "extravagant fictions" of the poem, Pope replied that Milton's "Genius was indeed so vast and sublime, that his Work seems beyond the Limits of Criticism." [4] This defence, though it sounds strangely romantic, was the one usually offered. Samuel Wesley thought the English Homer "rather above the common Rules of Epic than ignorant of them"; [5] Gray, who was the antithesis of an irregular or formless poet, praised Milton's versification for being "unconfined by any rules but those which his own feeling and the nature of his subject demanded"; [6] and Watts wrote,

> Immortal Bard! Thus thy own *Raphael* sings,
> And knows no Rule but native Fire.[7]

Even to Addison *Paradise Lost* seemed "above the critic's nicer laws," [8] a view that is particularly interesting because the *Spectator* papers were devoted to proving that the poem conformed to the critic's laws.

[1] "Remarks on Longinus," 1712, *Works* (1787), 405.

[2] *Grounds of Criticism in Poetry* (1704), prefatory "Specimen," sign. b1.

[3] i. 449 (1733).

[4] See p. 19 above. An opinion similar to this is to be found in John Newbery's (Goldsmith's?) *Art of Poetry* (1762), ii. 348.

[5] *Life of our Blessed Lord* (1693), preface.

[6] *Observations on English Metre*, in *Works* (ed. Mitford), v. 233–4.

[7] *Adventurous Muse*, in *Horae Lyricae* (1709), 213.

[8] *Account of the Greatest English Poets*, in *Works* (Bohn ed.), i. 24. So, too, William Somervile praises Thomson for being "above the critic's nicer law" (*Epistle to Thomson*, 1730, in Anderson's *British Poets*, viii. 503–4); and Robert Lloyd writes (*On Rhyme*, in *Poetical Works*, 1774, ii. 109),

> But critics (who still judge by rules,
> Transmitted down as guides to fools,
> And howsoe'er they prate about 'em,
> Drawn from wise folks who writ without 'em).

It is probable that Addison and many others really held, in a confused way, to both these opinions. They felt Milton's profound classicism and essential correctness; yet they saw that his work was strangely unlike their own and the French classical productions, and could not be completely reconciled with the letter at least of the rules. It is significant of their unconscious dissatisfaction with their own critical standards that most persons liked the irregularities, that they found the wildness pleasantly disturbing. Presumably a good many felt vaguely what one of them wrote, "Accuracy and Correctness are without doubt Advantages . . . but still they are not Essentials"; [1] and some may have been not far from Dennis's opinion, "The first and grand Rule in the greater Poetry is, that a Poet must every where excite great Passion," or "Enthusiasm." [2] Milton's art was by no means appreciated at this time; his style was thought to be rough, much less finished than Pope's or even Shakespeare's, and he was at times censured for not having "fil'd off his Rust" or "learned to polish some rudeness in his verses." [3] Yet this very rudeness attracted not a few, and by the majority was accepted as a natural drawback of the poet's fascinating irregularity.

It must not be supposed, however, that Milton was thought of as a barbarian. His roughness seemed very different from that of Donne, or of Chaucer and his contemporaries; he was free from the formlessness of Spenser, and his wildness was not the extravagance which many found excessive in the *Faerie Queene* and the *Jerusalem Delivered*. The Augustans enjoyed literary adventures but wished them to be decorous; they liked a certain amount of the unusual but had no taste for roughing it. Their classicism, though not extreme, went deep. Milton could never have held his great body of readers if he also had not been fundamentally classical, if those who read *Paradise Lost* had not felt back of its romantic wildness the standards of Homer and Virgil, of Aristotle and Longinus, just as behind the freedom and apparent irregularity of its verse they were conscious of the regular beat of the iambic pentameter. In the combination of classicism with romanticism lay Milton's strength. It was because his work preserved a balance between these conflicting elements that it was peculiarly adapted to a period of transition; that is what gave it an almost equal appeal not only to readers

---

[1] Dodsley's *Museum* (1747), iii. 284.

[2] *Grounds of Criticism in Poetry* (1704), 15.

[3] Verses prefixed to Dryden's *Absalom and Achitophel* (2d ed., 1681); Hume's *History of England* (new ed., 1762), vi. 126.

of opposing tastes but to the two forces at war in almost all readers. Robert Lloyd has summed up the whole matter in his line,

Thus MILTON, more correctly wild.[1]

To their correct wildness the shorter pieces as well as the epic owed much of their popularity.

This freedom or irregularity which distinguished Milton's poetry was, as his followers and opponents dimly realized, neither superficial nor simply literary, but grew naturally out of his strong love of liberty in all fields. "His political notions," as Johnson informs us, "were those of an acrimonious and surly republican,"[2] which is only the Doctor's Tory way of saying that, next to religion, the deepest feeling of the poet who postponed his chief work in order to write political pamphlets was a passion for liberty, a passion that flamed in the sonnets and in the speeches of Satan, that furnished the subject of practically all his prose and the altar upon which were sacrificed his property, his eyesight, his best years, and almost his life itself. This love of freedom was another reason for the popularity of the poems; for those who shared it (and they were many in the period which culminated in the French Revolution), if they were also lovers of verse, came naturally to look upon Milton as the embodiment of their ideal and almost as the object of their worship.

Thomas Hollis, the motto of whose life might well have been the words he inscribed in one of the books he presented to Harvard College, "Floreat Libertas," was a Milton enthusiast. He collected notes for an edition of the prose of his favorite author, republished Toland's account of his life, presented many editions of his works to libraries, defended him in the public press, acquired relics and portraits of him (one of which was the only thing he attempted to save from a fire), and gave his bed to Akenside in the hope that it might inspire an ode on the one whom he termed "my hero, and the guide of my paths."[3] To Hollis his hero was preëminently the

[1] *A Dialogue,* in *Poetical Works* (1774), ii. 11. It was mainly because *Paradise Regained* was more correctly *tame,* because it lacked the "magnificent images and romantic descriptions" of the earlier poem, that it was less successful: see *Crit. Rev.,* xlv. 74 (Good, p. 218 n.)

[2] "Milton," in *Lives* (ed. Hill), i. 156.

[3] Francis Blackburne, *Memoirs of Hollis* (1780), 365–71; 107; 73, 126, 127–8, 154, 167, 491; 621–7; 86, 95, 106, 167, 513–14, *583*; 111–12. Instances of Hollis's interest are, indeed, to be found on almost every page of the *Memoirs.* In Blackburne's words (p. 526), Hollis "was indefatigable in his researches after every memorial of him [Milton] he could hear of." But, according to Richard Fenton (*Memoirs of an Old Wig,* 1815, p. 127), it was at that time "the rage, not only to write the life of Milton, but to hunt out busts, paintings, prints, nay to trace him through all his different places of residence."

"arch-defender of liberty." "It is to Milton, the divine Milton," he wrote, "and such as he . . . that we are beholden for all the manifold and unexampled blessings which we now every where enjoy." [1] Indeed, it is possible that, like several of his friends, Hollis was less interested in *Comus* and *Paradise Lost* than in the prose writings and the political activities of the Latin secretary of the Commonwealth.[2] It was Johnson's misrepresentation of Milton's love of liberty that called forth the denunciation from Hollis's biographer, Archdeacon Blackburne, who says frankly, "We profess however not to concern ourselves with Milton the poet." [3]

One of the books that Hollis was accustomed to present to libraries in various parts of the world was Thomas Birch's edition of Milton's prose (1738). Birch was a pronounced Whig, and probably expressed his own views when he said in his biography of the poet,[4] "As he look'd upon true and absolute Freedom to be the greatest Happiness of this Life, whether to Societies or single Persons, so he thought Constraint of any sort to be the utmost Misery." A revision of Birch's work was brought out in 1753 by Richard Baron, an extremist as regards both religious and political liberty, who also issued a separate edition of the *Eikonoklastes* (1756). In the preface to the latter book Baron spoke of his author much as Wordsworth did in the sonnet "Milton, thou shouldst be living at this hour." "Many circumstances," he declared, "at present loudly call upon us to exert ourselves. Venality and corruption have well-nigh extinguished all principles of Liberty. . . . One remedy for these evils, is to revive the reading of our old Writers. . . . MILTON in particular ought to be read and studied by all our young Gentlemen as an *Oracle*. He . . . combated Superstition and Tyranny of every form, and in every degree. Against them he employed his mighty Strength." The poet Thomson, who was a great admirer of all Milton's works and who wrote a long poem in praise of liberty, combined his two enthusiasms in a preface to the *Areopagitica* (1738). Another worshipper, Auditor William Benson, who gave Dobson a thousand pounds for a Latin translation of *Paradise Lost*, erected the monument to its author in Westminster Abbey, had a medal

---

[1] *Memoirs*, 236, 93.

[2] At any rate, it was the prose works that he usually presented as gifts (see *ib.* 73, 126, 127-8, 154); and he gave twenty guineas towards the publication of the *Eikonoklastes* (*ib.* 487-8).

[3] *Ib.* 514. For Blackburne's attack on Johnson, see above, p. 31.

[4] Prefixed to his edition of the prose works (1738, p. lix).

struck in his honor, and published a study of his versification,[1] was also a "devoted Whig"; and so was William Roscoe, who praised and imitated Milton.[2] Accordingly, when we find a man of literary tastes, like the elder Nicholas Hardinge, described as a "determined and zealous Whig," we are pretty certain to learn that he was also "a great admirer of Milton."[3] The feelings of all such lovers of liberty are epitomized in Hollis's manuscript note regarding Milton's coat of arms: "Those arms . . . are now in the possession of T. H., & mind him often of Milton & great Actions!"[4]

As the century waned and the love of independence grew, bringing with it revolt and unrest of various kinds, there were many who were inspired, not only by the "great actions" of the "Milton of the commonwealth," but by

the unconquerable will . . .
And courage never to submit or yield

which flame in the speeches and deeds of his arch-rebel. "Give me a spirit," exclaimed Burns, "like my favourite hero, Milton's Satan," and then proceeded to quote four lines beginning "Hail, horrors! hail," which he and many another had doubtless often declaimed to the winds or to tavern companions.[5] Shelley also, attracted by Satan's "courage, and majesty, and firm and patient opposition to omnipotent force," reminded his readers that "the sacred Milton was, let it ever be remembered, a republican and a bold inquirer into morals and religion."[6]

It will be observed that Shelley here connects Milton not only with political but with religious liberty, and in the eighteenth century a great many did the same. Almost all of those who have been mentioned as enthusiasts over Milton and liberty were also liberals in religion, and in many instances were actively engaged in the fight for religious freedom. These men found inspiration not only in the character of Satan but in the life of the poet, in his anti-episcopal

---

[1] *Letters concerning Poetical Translations, and Virgil's and Milton's Arts of Verse* (1739). Benson also gave prizes "at all our great schools" for the best verses on Milton (Warton's edition of the minor poems, 1785, p. 368 n.).

[2] See below, p. 268, n. 5.   [3] Nichols's *Illustrations*, iii. 6–7.

[4] Written in the margin of page lxxvii of the Harvard copy of the 1753 Birch-Baron edition of Milton's prose. On page 62 of the same book Hollis wrote, "Reader, observe, *reverence* this the genuine, full character, of the *matchless* John Milton!"

[5] Letter to James Smith, June 11, 1787. Cf. a letter to William Nicol, June 18, 1787: "I have bought a pocket Milton, which I carry perpetually about with me, in order to study the sentiments — the dauntless magnanimity, the intrepid, unyielding independence, the desperate daring, and noble defiance of hardship, in that great personage, Satan."

[6] Preface to *Prometheus Unbound*.

pamphlets, and in such sonnets as *On the New Forcers of Conscience* and *To Cromwell*. With most of them Milton's words and example had more weight, and could be used more effectively in influencing others, because of his reputation for piety. Conservatives are, however, more numerous than liberals, and some men — Warburton, Johnson, and Thomas Warton, for example — were prejudiced against the poet's character and prose writings by their dislike of his religious and political activities. "Milton's moral character as a member of society," said Warburton, "was certainly the most corrupt of any man's of that age"; yet in the same letter he wrote, "He is the author of three perfect pieces of poetry." [1] It is surprising that persons of such strong prejudices were able to retain their admiration or, as in Thomas Warton's case, their enthusiasm for the verse of a man whom as a man some of them cordially disliked. The strength of Milton's hold upon the public is shown in his ability to rouse the enthusiastic devotion of the radicals and at the same time keep the admiration of the conservatives.

[1] Undated letter to Thomas Birch, *Europ. Mag.*, xi. 439 (1787).

CHAPTER II

BLANK VERSE AND RIME

"THIS neglect then of rime," we read in the note prefixed to *Paradise Lost*, ". . . is to be esteemed an example set, the first in English, of ancient liberty recovered to heroic poem." It was this manifestation of Milton's passion for freedom that attracted far the most attention in the eighteenth century. To us blank verse is an old story, we accept it without question and without enthusiasm; but in Pope's day it was a subject over which men waxed either dithyrambic or violent. No feature of the wildness and irregularity of *Paradise Lost* was so disturbing, pleasantly or otherwise, as its verse. As the laureate Whitehead sang,

> Some hate all RHIME; some *seriously* deplore
> That MILTON wants that one enchantment more.[1]

One poet was moved to "disgust" by rime,[2] whereas many others were of Johnson's opinion that blank verse "seems to be verse only to the eye," and "has neither the easiness of prose nor the melody of numbers." [3]

As might be suspected from the Doctor's partisanship, the movement towards freedom in verse found much the same advocates and opponents as that towards freedom in political and religious matters. It was the progressives or radicals against the conservatives: the one class, dissatisfied with the limitations of contemporary life and poetry, building largely upon theories and hopes, the other, intrenched behind the solid accomplishments of the present and the immediate past, finding literature and life passing comfortable as they were; the one stressing freedom, breadth, and imaginative suggestiveness as the essentials of poetry, the other emphasizing finish,

---

[1] *Charge to the Poets* (1762), in *Plays and Poems*, 1774, ii. 298.

[2] Robert Andrews (or Robert Colvill?), *Eidyllia* (Edin., 1757), 9. As early as 1713 "Jingle" was criticized in Tate's *Monitor* (no. 17, April 6–10) for "always carrying something of Littleness along with it."

[3] "Milton," in *Lives* (ed. Hill), i. 193; Johnson quotes the first phrase from a Mr. Locke. Aaron Hill thought blank verse fit for nothing but the brawls of "Faction": see the last half of his *Cleon to Lycidas* (*Works*, 2d ed., iv. 295–308), which appears to be the "poem in praise of blank verse" to which Joseph Warton refers in his *Essay on Pope*, 1782, ii. 192 n. (cf. *Modern Language Notes*, xxxvi. 247–8).

elegance, and intellectual keenness. Yet these classes were by no means sharply defined or invariably antagonistic; for Gray and some others who admired Milton and agreed with the liberals on most points were opposed to blank verse, whereas many followers of Pope were friendly to it.

As to the relative popularity of blank verse and rime, the evidence is abundant but unfortunately conflicting. Two utterances towards the close of the seventeenth century indicate that unrimed poetry was at that time enjoying some vogue as a novelty,[1] and so late as 1764 Goldsmith wrote in the dedication to *The Traveller* that his poem had "neither abuse, party, nor blank verse to support it." On the other hand, William Mason was "well aware, that by choosing to write blank verse" in 1772 he "should not court popularity," because he "perceived it was growing much out of vogue";[2] and the Swan of Lichfield felt that she was unfashionable in thinking unrimed poetry "much the superior vehicle for the effusions of genius."[3] "It is become a fashion," affirmed W. H. Roberts in 1774, to think that poetry, and blank verse, are inconsistent;[4] or, as Vicesimus Knox, with his eye on Johnson, expressed it, "It is sufficient, in the idea of many, to condemn a poem, that it is written in blank verse."[5] Already, in 1770, the *Critical Review* had asserted with the finality which is the heritage of such publications, "That good rhime, where it can be properly used, is preferable to good blank verse, is now no longer questioned by critics of true taste."[6] Yet

[1] Samuel Woodford, in the preface to his *Paraphrase upon the Canticles* (1679), prophesied that "in the next [age], even Our now cry'd-up Blank Verse will look . . . unfashionable"; and Samuel Wesley, in the preface to his *Life of our Lord* (1693), said that he was "of a different opinion from most others" in not liking blank verse.

[2] Preface to his *English Garden*, in *Works* (1811), i. 206. The preface was written in 1782.

[3] *Letters*, ii. 237 (Feb. 7, 1789).

[4] Preface to his *Judah Restored*.

[5] "On the Prevailing Taste in Poetry" (*Essays*, 2d ed., 1779, no. 127). William Benson, who admired Milton as strongly as he disliked blank verse (see pp. 41–2 above), said that, if *Paradise Lost* had been in rime, "upon the whole it would have been a more agreeable Poem to the Generality of Readers" (*Letters concerning Poetical Translations*, 1739, p. 61); but I have found no one who agreed with him except Samuel Woodford (see above, p. 12, n. 4), and Thomas Shipman, who declared ("To Roger L'Estrange," *Henry III of France*, 1678, prefatory), "*Miltons Paradice* is a work noble, strong and fanciful, but had his humour of contradiction soften'd it into his own sweet *Rhime*, what a *Poem* had it been!"

[6] xxix. 435 (misunderstood by Good, p. 230). Yet in 1800 the same review said that a translator of Lucretius "perhaps would have acted more wisely in employing blank verse. . . . It is more tractable in the discussion of philosophical subjects," declared the reviewer, "and admits a greater variety and beauty of cadence" (new arr., xxviii. 260).

these opinions really represent little more than the prejudices of individuals or the attitude of a small circle; for, judging by them alone, one would conclude that blank verse was popular in the late seventeenth century and lost ground steadily in the eighteenth, whereas the reverse is obviously the truth. Such remarks do, however, confirm the impression, received from other sources, that the general public preferred rime, a preference further indicated by the publication of five rimed paraphrases of parts of *Paradise Lost*, and by versions of Shakespeare, Spenser, and Blair's *Grave* "reduced to couplets." Yet here also there is evidence on the other side, for in 1774 the first canto of the *Faerie Queene* was "attempted in blank verse," and within ten years was republished with the next three cantos.[1] Undoubtedly, however, most readers liked rime, as they do to-day, — no one writes advertisements in blank verse, — and, other things being equal, preferred rimed poetry.

But other things were not equal, they seldom are. Augustan poetry, and in particular that composed in couplets, had never been really popular, and by the time Pope ceased writing the men who reached the people and affected literature vitally were making little use of it. On the other hand, after the first quarter of the century the poems most widely and enthusiastically read were those in blank verse. Not until Scott and Byron swept the public off its feet did any rimed work of length gain a hold upon the people equal to that of *The Seasons, Night Thoughts, The Grave, Pleasures of Imagination*, and *The Task*.[2] These, with *Paradise Lost*, were the poems most read; obviously, then, it is only when a critic restricts himself to such literature as seems to him most significant that he can speak of the heroic couplet as "the normal and habitual form in which poetry,

---

[1] Furthermore, all of James Hervey's prose "Meditations and Contemplations" and one of Young's "moral contemplations" were published in blank verse by Thomas Newcomb between 1757 and 1764; and the same service was done for Elizabeth Rowe's *Devout Exercises of the Heart* by Edward Smyth in 1800(?) and for Ossian by Anthony Davidson in 1812(?).

[2] In the eighteenth century *The Seasons* was probably more popular than any other poem; and *The Grave* (1743), which reached a so-called sixteenth edition in 1786, was reprinted, alone or in collections, at least twenty-nine times more by 1825. Somervile's *Chace* (1735, twelve editions by 1800) and Glover's *Leonidas* (1737, eleven editions by 1810) were also among the more widely-read poems of the time. It was these works that the *Eclectic Review* had in mind when, in commenting on Sir William Drummond's expectation that his *Odin* (1817) would fail because he had written in blank verse, it remarked confidently, at a time when everybody was reading Scott and Byron: "It would, however, be paying the public taste a bad compliment, to imagine that it can prefer the jingling and Hudibrastic rhymes in which our poetical romances, or romantic poems, have been lately written, to that stately and varied march of rhythm, in which our language peculiarly finds itself at ease, and which has been chosen by all our finest poets, as the fittest mode of expressing their feelings" (new series, 1817, viii. 85).

except on the stage, moved in its serious moments." [1] For the un-rimed poems were not only very popular but very numerous. The first half of the eighteenth century saw some 350, and the next fifty years more than twice as many, not a few being works of considerable length. Nor were they limited to forgotten versifiers, for practically every poet of importance from Pope's time to the present has written at least one piece of blank verse. As far as the general public was concerned, the situation was accordingly paradoxical: rime was preferred, but the popular poems were those that did not use it.

It is only natural to suppose that such of the principal critics and poets of the time as did not favor blank verse were, both in theory and in practice, more strongly opposed to it than were "the general." Certainly they would be repelled, as the ordinary reader was not, by the crudity and roughness of contemporary efforts in the measure, many of which were distinguishable from prose only by the capitals at the beginning of the lines. We know there were not a few who would have exclaimed with Dr. Johnson, "When was blank verse without pedantry?" [2] and many who shared the opinion of Robert Lloyd,

> Take it for granted, 'tis by those
> Milton's the model mostly chose,
> Who can't write verse, and won't write prose.[3]

Fastidious writers like Pope and Gray, antagonized by the slovenly and unmelodious imitations of *Paradise Lost*, naturally concluded, as Henry Neele did a hundred years later, that blank verse was another bow of Ulysses, "an instrument which few know how to touch." [4] Realization of the difficulties of the measure came late, however. Adam Smith expressed the common opinion when he sneered, "Even I, who never could find a single rhime in my life, could make blank verse as fast as I could speak." [5] But, whether they thought it difficult or easy to compose, men of taste were not attracted by the general run of pieces written in it by their contemporaries.

---

[1] Gosse, *Eighteenth Century Literature*, 1889, p. 2 (Good, pp. 20–21).

[2] "Akenside," in *Lives* (ed. Hill), iii. 418.

[3] *To . . . about to publish a Volume of Miscellanies* (w. 1755), in *Poetical Works* (1774), i. 106. By those who 'choose Milton as a model' Lloyd seems to mean nothing more than those who write blank verse. Cf. p. 78 below.

[4] Neele's *Lectures on English Poetry*, in *Literary Remains* (N. Y., 1829), 126. Cf. *Crit. Rev.*, 1780, l. 50 ("Blank verse is a weapon which none but the *generals* in our language are able to wield"); *Mo. Rev.*, enl. ed., 1796, xxi. 337 ("To the solemn and dignified tone of blank verse MASTERS only are equal"; see also *ib.* xxii. 86); Drake's *Literary Hours*, 3d ed., 1804, i. 49–50.

[5] *Bee* 1791, iii. 5; see also p. 50, n. 3, below.

Yet to blank verse in the abstract, or when handled by a master, they seem to have been well enough disposed. They could hardly have been insensible to the argument contained in the oft-repeated reminder that Greek and Roman poetry was unrimed, — another instance, it should be observed, of the way in which Milton's resemblances to classical writers gained him admirers. But a greater factor in the popularizing of blank verse was probably the very dominance of rime. Tyranny breeds revolt, and, as the years passed, more and more necks were galled by the yoke of the couplet. Even had there been no great unrimed poetry a reaction must inevitably have set in, but its advance was hastened, and made more conscious and intelligent, by the vogue of *Paradise Lost*.[1] Criticize its verse as they might, if people continued to read and to like the poem they were bound in time to feel the beauty of its freer, more varied measures, as well as the prosodical poverty of their own versification; and when these things were once realized the rigidity as well as the preëminence of the heroic couplet was doomed. It was the men of finer ear, usually the better poets, critics, and writers on prosody, who first became conscious of the deficiencies of neo-classic versification; they had given the most thought to the matter and by writing and reading many thousands of couplets had come to weary of them. This is why such leaders of rimed poetry as Dryden, Pope, and Prior evinced dissatisfaction with it at a time when their followers, the ordinary readers, versifiers, and critics, still remained with deaf and dogged complacency in the rut. For in literature, as in clothes, the leaders are giving over a style just when the rank and file have come to adopt it. The heroic couplet probably reached its widest popularity in the years when most poets worthy of the name were turning to other measures. That men of discernment were supposed, at least by some writers, to be admirers of blank verse is shown by a poem published in 1733, in which the devotees of "rime and rime only" are classed with those who admired Blackmore's epics and preferred Cibber to Pope. Their opinions are ridiculed in this fashion:

> Verse without rhyme I never could endure,
> Uncouth in numbers, and in sense obscure.
> To him as Nature, when he ceas'd to see,
> *Milton's* an *universal Blank* to me.
> Confirm'd and settled by the Nations voice,
> Rhyme is the poet's pride, and peoples choice. . . .

---

[1] Nothing is here said about Shakespeare, for dramatic blank verse, as will be shown later, was regarded as quite distinct from non-dramatic. Even Dr. Johnson's play was unrimed.

Thompson, write blank; but know that for that reason,
These lines shall live, when thine are out of season.
Rhyme binds and beautifies the Poet's lays,
As *London* Ladies owe their shape to stays.[1]

The truth seems to be, therefore, that the general public favored rime but more often read the poems that were without it, whereas more discriminating persons, though well disposed towards blank verse at its best, were disturbed by the crudities of the works written in it; that during the first part of the century blank verse had the advantage of novelty, but after 1745 the leaders of the newer movement in poetry, Gray, Collins, the Wartons, and the rest, made little use of it, although after 1726 it always had the great advantage of being employed in the poems most read by all classes, *Paradise Lost*, *The Seasons*, *Night Thoughts*, and *The Task*.

The obvious fact that rime is better adapted to some purposes and blank verse to others was soon realized by all save extremists. "In *English* Poetry," wrote John Armstrong, "I question whether it is possible, with any Success, to write Odes, Epistles, Elegies, Pastorals or Satires, without Rhime;"[2] and with this opinion, as well as with that of W. H. Roberts, who wished to banish rime entirely from epic, dramatic, and didactic poetry,[3] most persons would apparently have agreed. By universal accord, too, blank verse soon came to be the recognized medium for religious works, and, notwithstanding the vogue of Pope's Homer, for translations of the classics.[4] It was also much used in meditative and philosophical poems, and, owing to the popularity of *The Seasons*, it became the usual vehicle for long descriptions of nature.

Thus it was that rime came to be excluded to a great extent from long, serious poems, and in this way tended to lose the admiration and even the respect of many thoughtful readers. By the more ardent champions of blank verse it was regarded as a somewhat trivial and childish ornament suited only to light songs, satires, and occasional pieces. Such poems "it raises . . . ," said Young, "but sinks the great; as spangles adorn children, but expose men."[5] Hugh Blair, in his pleasantly conventional and hence widely popular *Lectures on Rhetoric*, agrees with "those who think that Rhyme finds

---

[1] James Bramston, *The Man of Taste*, 7-8. The entire poem is ironical.
[2] *Sketches* (1758), 33.
[3] Preface to his *Judah Restored* (1774).
[4] Even Pope and Parnell had to defend themselves for using rime in their translations of Homer: see p. 118, n. 1, below, and Parnell's preface to his *Homer's Battle of the Frogs and Mice* (1717), sign. A 4.
[5] *Conjectures on Original Composition* (2d ed., 1759), 84.

its proper place in the middle, but not in the higher regions of Poetry." [1] There seem to have been many such, particularly in Scotland; for two other leading critics north of the Tweed, Lord Kames and Lord Monboddo, who agreed on little else, united in condemning rime. "Sportive love, mirth, gaiety, humour, and ridicule," said the former, "are the province of rhyme. The boundaries . . . were extended in barbarous and illiterate ages . . . but taste . . . improves daily; and . . . rhyme . . . will in time be forc'd to abandon its unjust conquests." [2] Monboddo regarded the "troublesome bondage" as "no more than a barbarous ornament." [3] Thomas Twining gave expression to a widespread sentiment when he wrote, "To me, a work of length in the rhymed heroic of Pope, etc., is insufferably monotonous and cloying to the ear;" [4] and towards the close of the century William Belsham spoke of the couplet as "unable . . . to stand the comparison with blank verse," which "of all the different kinds of verse known in English poetry . . . is undoubtedly entitled to be first mentioned as first in dignity and importance." [5] As these are not the prejudiced utterances of partisan poets, but the carefully-weighed conclusions of scholars, several of

---

[1] Lecture xxxviii (printed 1783, but first delivered c. 1760). Blair thought rime "unfavourable to the sublime, or to the highly pathetic strain. An Epic Poem, or a Tragedy," he said, "would be fettered and degraded by it."

[2] *Elements of Criticism* (6th ed., Edin., 1785), ii. 176, and cf. 160–63.

[3] *Origin and Progress of Language* (Edin., 1774), ii. 386. On the other hand, Adam Smith, another of the Edinburgh group, "had an invincible contempt and aversion for blank verse, Milton's always excepted" (*Bee*, 1791, iii. 5, and cf. p. 47 above). Johnson, on learning how Smith felt, exclaimed, "Had I known that he loved rhyme as much as you tell me he does, I should have HUGGED him" (Boswell's *Johnson*, ed. Hill, i. 427–8).

[4] *Country Clergyman of the Eighteenth Century* (1882), 120 (letter to his brother, May 3, 1784). In 1752 the *Monthly Review* (vii. 140), declared: "Blank verse is the proper cloathing of the sublime . . . it seems limited and confined if ornamented with this jingle. The battles of gods and speeches of heroes are nobly suited to this form of expression; and as they do not want the gaudy furniture of rhyme, their splendour is in some degree eclipsed by it. It is, on the contrary, just otherwise in subjects in themselves low and mean; which require all the graces and ornaments which can be thrown upon them." Again, in 1758 (xviii. 277), it expresses a similar conviction: "Where the subject of a Poem is extensive, and lofty in its nature, or where the greater passions, as Terror, and Pity, are to be excited . . . Rhime may, with great propriety, be dispensed with." Cf. John Armstrong (*Sketches*, 1758, p. 33), "Blank verse . . . is . . . fittest for works of any considerable Length"; an anonymous writer in the *Bee*, xvi. 272 (Aug. 21, 1793), who regarded it "as the only species of verse, which in our language is suited to works of considerable length;" and Robert Lloyd (*On Rhyme*, in *Poetical Works*, 1774, ii. 114),

> But tho' each couplet has its strength,
> It palls in works of epic length.

[5] *Essays* (2d ed., 1799), ii. 500, 495. The first edition (1789) says substantially the same thing.

whom were men of wide influence, critical opinion appears in this classical century to have been more partial to the use of blank verse for long poems than it is in ours.

At times the partiality seemed likely to be carried farther still, for there were not a few who agreed with Gildon that "rhime is injurious . . . even in the shorter poems."[1] Milton himself may have been their warrant for this view, since in his own sweeping condemnation of "the jingling sound of like endings" he declared "the troublesome and modern bondage of riming" to be "no necessary adjunct or true ornament of poem or good verse, in longer works especially, but the invention of a barbarous age, to set off wretched matter and lame metre. . . . some both Italian and Spanish poets of prime note," he adds, "have rejected rime both in longer and shorter works . . . as a thing of itself, to all judicious ears, trivial and of no true musical delight." Echoes of this preface to *Paradise Lost*, or direct quotations from it, appear so frequently throughout the century as to indicate that it had considerable influence and was adopted literally and in full by many. The idea that rime was unnecessary even for the most airy or trivial pieces not only was accepted but was put into practice. One bard composed several odes, a monody, and a tale in unrimed octosyllabic and pentameter lines,[2] and others wrote sonnets, Pindaric odes, and stanzas in blank verse.[3] Lyrics without rime — usually, like Collins's exquisite *Ode to Evening*, in the meter of Milton's translation of Horace's ode to Pyrrha — were not uncommon after 1740.[4]

Critics and writers on prosody also assailed rime. John Mason,

[1] *Laws of Poetry* (1721), 69. Cf. the *Examen Miscellaneum* (1702, attributed to Gildon), the preface to which is interesting because the poems that follow it are pseudoclassic productions by such men as the Duke of Buckingham, Lord Rochester, and Waller. The editor, who quotes from Milton's attack on rime, holds the "boldness" of using blank verse to be "something necessary in order to reform our vitiated Tast of Poetry, which often palates wretched Stuff dress'd up in Rhime, that it wou'd nauseate if depriv'd of the jingle; which once laid aside, the true Beauties of Poetry wou'd be more our Study." *The Vision*, one of the poems in the volume, employs "that false *jingling Chime*" until the Muse appears and throws aside "barbarous Rhime" (p. 51, first pagination).

[2] Robert Andrews (or Robert Colvill?), *Eidyllia* (Edin., 1757).

[3] See Thomas Fletcher's *Eternity* (*Poems*, 1692, pp. 53–63); James Ralph's *Muses Address to the King* (1728, "a Pindaric ode in blank verse"); Paul Rolli's *Works, consisting of Odes in Blank Verse*, etc. (1735); Roger Comberbach's *Translation of an Ode of Horace* (1754 or 1755); Joseph Strutt's *Elegiac Poem in different Measures, without Rhime* (1779); also below, pp. 560–65, and, for blank-verse sonnets, Bibl. IV, bef. 1715 (Monck), 1767 (Downman, Huddesford), 1774 (Dunster), 1777 (Polwhele), 1778 ("Gentleman of Oxford"), 1784 (Tytler), 1787 (Whitehouse), c. 1790 (Drake), 1802 (White).

[4] For poems in the unrimed stanza of Milton's translation, see Bibl. III c.

minister, teacher of elocution, and able writer on verse, regarded it as "one of the lowest Ornaments and greatest Shackles in modern poesy;" [1] and Johnson's critic, Robert Potter, wrote, "Rhyme . . . has, after I have been reading blank verse, appeared to me trifling, tinkling, and childish . . . and must, I think, in every kind of writing have such an effect on manly ears accustomed to the dignity of blank verse. . . . Rhymes and point are fit only for children." [2] Strangely enough, some of the rimesters themselves shared these extreme opinions. As early as 1691 one wished that he had "broken a barbarous custom and freed [himself] from the troublesome and modern bondage of Rhiming;" [3] while another, in 1775, expressed the belief that "Rhyme rather debases and enervates than gives any real beauty and strength to a Poem. This *Tyranny* of Rhyme . . . hath been the cause of many, not inconsiderable, errors." [4]

But it were a weary, stale, flat, and unprofitable task to try to register all the assaults made upon "jingle" in the century supposed to be devoted to it. One more, however, deserves to be noticed, the *Conjectures on Original Composition* (1759), which is the more interesting because its author also wrote the *Night Thoughts* and in his satires and his *Two Epistles to Mr. Pope* had shown no small skill in handling the heroic couplet. In this work of his old age Young denounced rimes as "childish shackles, and tinkling sounds," declaring blank verse to be "verse unfallen, uncurst; verse reclaim'd, reinthron'd in the true *language of the gods;*" Pope, he asserted, had done Homer an "ignoble wrong" by the "*effeminate* decoration" of rime; it was as if he had "put *Achilles* in petticoats a second time." "Must rhyme then, say you, be banished?" he queried; "I wish the nature of our language could bear its intire expulsion; but our lesser poetry stands in need of a toleration for it." [5]

It may be urged, on the other side, that Dr. Johnson and others were as violently opposed to blank verse as these men were to rime; but such was not the case. There were almost none who denied that the freer measures were better adapted to the stage and, *in the hands of a master*, to a few of the more lofty types of poetry. Even the

[1] *Essay on the Power of Numbers* (1749), 13–14.

[2] *Art of Criticism* (1789), 15–16, 203.

[3] William Wollaston, *The Design of Ecclesiastes,* preface.

[4] The anonymous author of *Bath and it's Environs,* pp. vi–vii. Cf. also Edmund Smith's *Poem on the Death of John Philips* (1708?), 2, 5–7; Lady Mary Montagu's *Court of Dulness;* and Ashley Cowper's *Poetical Epistle to Daniel Wr-y* (*Norfolk Poetical Miscellany,* 1744, i. 166–70; noted by Good, p. 71).

[5] Second ed. (1759), 58–60, 84. Mr. Good (pp. 65, 90, 93, 160–66, 202–7, 230–35, etc.) quotes many other eighteenth-century utterances regarding rime and blank verse, and as many more of equal interest might be gathered.

most dogmatic assertion we have met with as to the superiority of rime is qualified by the clause, "where it can be properly used"; and Johnson himself did not wish *Paradise Lost* changed.[1]

The quarrel between rime and blank verse was long, inconclusive, and apparently futile. Scarcely any of the eighteenth-century discussions of the subject have, for a modern reader, any value save the historical; and, as neither side triumphed or suffered defeat, though each had .to give up certain untenable positions, the whole controversy might seem to have been to no purpose. Yet in reality it was profitable, for it was a campaign of education. Few may have been convinced by the arguments of their opponents, but the discussion was provocative of thought and in the end all were the wiser, for each side came to a better understanding not simply of the meter it opposed but of the one it favored. The greatest accomplishment was, indeed, a gradual clarifying of ideas in regard to prosody, a bringing to the consciousness of both readers and versifiers the existence of problems, difficulties, and possibilities that few had realized at the beginning of the century.

[1] See p. 45 above; and "Milton," in Johnson's *Lives* (ed. Hill), i. 194.

CHAPTER III

PROSODY AND DICTION

"The poets from Dryden to Johnson," writes Mr. Saintsbury, "knocked a real sense of regular rhythm into the English head." [1] Some of the poets and theorists of this period, and many in that which followed, were also knocking into their own and other English heads a sense of irregular rhythm, a realization, to quote the same authority, of "the transcendental union of order and freedom" which makes the versification of Shakespeare and Milton what it is. [2] The undertaking has proved to be an exceedingly difficult one, so much so that there are thousands of English heads into which the idea has not yet penetrated. Besides such minor tasks as reviving the lost art of the lyric and remodelling the sonnet, to the eighteenth century was given the work of adapting the cathedral harmonies of Milton's organ and the crack of Pope's whip-lash to the music of everyday life. Is it any wonder that it staggered and often fell under the load?

So little, however, do we understand the difficulties of others, so slow are we to realize that the heights on which we were born were achieved by our forefathers only after long and painful struggles, that to some the eighteenth century may seem to have had a light burden, a simple, definite task which any one with a fair amount of insight and poetical power could have accomplished easily enough. Most of us see no reason why the blank verse of the *Idylls of the King* and the couplets of *Endymion* should not have been written by Thomson or Pope. As Mr. Saintsbury puts it, "Few people . . . understand what English prosody really is; how entirely it differs from that of every other known language as a result of its blended character; and how very long and difficult the evolution of the new compound was." [3] It seems incredible that for many years most

---

[1] *Peace of the Augustans* (1916), 101; cf. *History of English Prosody* (1908), ii. 458–9.

[2] *Peace of the Augustans*, 101.

[3] *Ib.* What is said about prosody in the pages that follow owes much to T. S. Omond's *English Metrists in the Eighteenth and Nineteenth Centuries* (1907) and to Saintsbury's *English Prosody*. Yet I have depended primarily, not upon these two works or similar studies, but upon the poetry and remarks on versification by eighteenth-century writers.

poets did not realize what constitutes blank verse, "the only difference" between their rimed and unrimed work being, in the words
of one of them, "that the rhyme is wanting; while the verse is constituted in such a manner, that the ear has a right to expect it." [1]
Poets and critics of eminence were alike unconscious, or but vaguely
conscious, that there should be any other difference. The unrimed
translations of Roscommon and Addison and the *Irene* of Johnson
betray no knowledge of other requisites,[2] and as late as 1778 a poet
and essayist of James Beattie's rank assumed that by changing one
riming word in each couplet Pope's Homer could be made into blank
verse![3] According to Bysshe, "Blank verse is where the Measure is
exactly kept without Rhyme," [4] and by "measure" he meant the
strictest neo-classic versification. Many writers published as "imitations of Milton" productions that show no traces of the prosody of
Paradise Lost but are either unrimed couplets or prose cut into ten-
foot lengths; while others, dissatisfied with these pieces but failing
to see where the fault lay, adopted, on the "safety first" principle,
all the distinctive features of the epic, — its style, diction, prosody,
and phrasing.

Furthermore, "the sense of regular rhythm" was so effectively
"knocked into the English head" that scarcely any other rhythm
could get in, with the result that the introduction of hypermetrical
syllables (trisyllabic feet), the inversion or slighting of stresses, and
the shifting of the pause to all parts of the line, features which are
the soul of beauty in verse, came to seem inharmonious, as indeed
they were frequently declared to be. Even poets who were willing to
follow Milton slavishly did not often succeed in maintaining through
many successive lines the fundamental feature of his prosody, the
substitution of the free musical paragraph for the line as the unit of
verse. They had been writing separate lines so long that they could
not rid themselves of the habit. In truth, harmony was confined
within narrow bounds in the days when laws for literature were laid
down by ponderous lawyers, lexicographers, and divines, — heavy
eaters and drinkers and men of excellent sense in the main, but with
little feeling for music or for elusive lyric graces. Instead of "piping

---

[1] W. H. Roberts, *Judah Restored* (1774), p. xx.

[2] Nor does James Ralph's unrimed *Night* (1728), though blank verse receives high
praise in the preface.

[3] *Essays on Poetry and Music*, 382. Samuel Woodford, in the preface to his *Paraphrase upon the Canticles* (1679), printed as poetry a passage from the *Animadversions
upon the Remonstrants Defence*, and asked if it were not as much blank verse as
Paradise Lost was.

[4] *Art of English Poetry* (4th ed., 1710), 35, first pagination.

down the valleys wild," the devotees of unshorn Apollo clicked their high heels on a narrow, straight cement walk, on either side of which bristled a tall hedge of thorn. They occasionally broke through the barriers and wandered for a time in the green pastures that lay beyond, but in the main they kept much to the path in which they expected and were expected to walk. How narrow this path was and how thick the "dont's" bristled on the hedge, we who live in days when poetry seems to have no laws at all can hardly realize. Even Pope was not strict enough to please the self-constituted authorities, who paid little heed to the irregularities actually existing in poetry, but spun their rules, as the spider does his web, out of their own inner consciousness.

These men thought poorly of stanzas of "intermixed rhyme" like the Spenserian, and, for serious poetry, of practically all verse except the octo- and the deca-syllabic. They brought all hypermetrical syllables into line by elisions like "t' admire" and contractions like "vi'let" and "fab'lous"; "lovest," they said, must in verse be "lov'st"; the "ill-sounding Gaping call'd . . . Hiatus" they condemned even in such expressions as "thy Iambicks," and decreed that the e in "the" should always be dropped before a following vowel.[1] The cesural pause, all agreed, should come near the middle of the line, never after the first, second, eighth, or ninth syllable, and there should be another pause at the close of the line. Inversion of accent (the substitution of a trochaic for an iambic foot) was allowed unwillingly and only to a limited extent, even in blank verse. Glover is said to have prided himself on having none at all throughout the weary length of his popular unrimed Leonidas;[2] and Pemberton, who commended this monotony, "corrected" the trochaic lines that he quoted from Paradise Lost.[3] "Heroick measure," according to Dr. Johnson, is "pure . . . when the accent rests upon every second syllable through the whole line. . . . The repetition of this sound or percussion at equal times, is the most complete harmony of which a single verse is capable." On this account the Doctor pronounced some of Milton's finest lines "remarkably unharmonious"; yet, because of the difficulty and monotony of the "pure measure," he was forced to admit the "mixed," in which," as he explained, "some variation of the accents is allowed . . . though it always injures the

---

[1] Bysshe, Art of English Poetry (1710), 10–13, first pagination.

[2] Saintsbury, English Prosody, ii. 493–4; cf. Chalmers, English Poets, xvii. 11.

[3] Observations on Poetry (1738), 130–34. On page 131 he writes, "The emphasis or accent falling upon the foremost of the two syllables in any foot, except the first, . . . or two syllables placed together in the same foot, which must both of necessity be pronounced short, will certainly destroy the harmony of the verse."

harmony of the line considered by itself."[1]   William Mitford, the historian of Greece and also one of the best eighteenth-century prosodists, declared that inversions were rarely found in the third and
fourth feet, even more rarely in the second, and never in the fifth;
the one in the second foot of the line "Of man's first disobedience"
he thought might be "pleasing perhaps to some . . . and not to
all."[2]   "The English heroic [meter] requires the fourth syllable to
be emphatic, and the two concluding feet to be perfect iambics," affirmed the *Monthly Review*.[3]   Even Isaac Watts, who invoked the
"Adventurous Muse" and lauded Milton as "our Deliverer from the
Bondage," was unwilling to accept all the liberty allowed him.
"Scarce any other place in the verse," he wrote, "besides the first
and the third, will well endure a trochee, without endangering the
harmony, spoiling the cadence of the verse, and offending the ear."
To be sure, Milton "has not been so nice an observer of this matter;
but it is granted, even by his admirers, that his numbers are not
always so accurate and tuneful as they should be."   Watts also
agreed to the generally-accepted rule that "a line should never end
with a word which is so closely connected in grammar with the word
following, that it requires a continued voice to unite them; therefore
an adjective ought scarce ever to be divided from its substantive."
One line in ten, he held, should end with a full pause; accordingly he
censured Milton for his "unreasonable run of the sense out of one
line into another," as a result of which "it becomes hardly possible
for the ear to distinguish all the ends and beginnings of his verses,"[4]
a comment which shows that Watts wished each line to be distinct,
as in the heroic couplet. The frequent omission of the initial unaccented foot, which gives much of the charm to *Allegro* and *Penseroso*,
was, in the opinion of Goldsmith, Pemberton, and Scott of Amwell,
"displeasing to a nice ear"; and the poet's ear was frankly pronounced "bad" by his romantically-inclined editor and imitator,
Thomas Warton.[5]   Is it any wonder, then, that "a Gentleman of

[1] *Rambler*, no. 86. Johnson's *Irene*, which is in unrimed couplets, probably represents his conception of blank verse.

[2] *Inquiry into the Principles of Harmony in Language* (2d ed., 1804), 108, 101–2.

[3] Enlarged ed., xxiv. 56 (1797).

[4] *Horae Lyricae* (2d ed., 1709), preface, p. xx; *Miscellaneous Thoughts*, 1734, nos.
lxxii–lxxiii (*Works*, 1810, iv. 618–22).

[5] Goldsmith, *Beauties of English Poesy* (1767), i. 39; Pemberton, *Observations on
Poetry* (1738), 114 n.; Scott, *Critical Essays* (1785), 97; Warton's edition of Milton's
minor poems (1785), 207 (it is significant that the remark does not appear in the second
edition). In the preface to the 1809 edition of *Horae Lyricae* Watts declared: "Some
of his [Milton's] Numbers seem too harsh and uneasy. I could never believe that
Roughness and Obscurity added any thing to the true Grandeur of a Poem."

Oxford" "corrected and harmonized" the "measure and versification" of *Paradise Lost*,[1] that Pope did the same with Shakespeare's plays, and that such a metrical masterpiece as the Spenserian stanza found almost no admirers?

These narrow and unyielding conceptions of prosody were, as has been said, well-nigh universal even among writers of blank verse and admirers of Milton. Nor were they held modestly as mere opinions or as records of the prevailing practice: they were thought to be as certain as truth itself, as changeless as right and wrong. "The foregoing Rules," wrote Bysshe, "ought indispensibly to be follow'd . . . the Observation of them . . . will produce Harmony; the Neglect of them Harshness and Discord." [2] But the rules were not only inflexible and often wrong: they were also harmful in the definiteness and minuteness of their regulations. Even if they had in the main been sound they would have crushed all the freedom and life out of poetry; for to say that a pause or an inversion of accent can come only in a certain part of a line, or that an adjective cannot end a line if its noun immediately follows, is to take the charm and individuality from versification and leave it purely mechanical.[3] That is exactly what Cowper and others accused Pope of having done:

> But he (his musical finesse was such,
> So nice his ear, so delicate his touch)
> Made poetry a mere mechanic art,
> And every warbler has his tune by heart.[4]

"Did he not," asks Henry Headley, "stretch his prerogative too far, by reducing them [poetical numbers] to perfect mechanism? of rhyme has he not made a rattle, and of verse a play-thing?" [5]

---

[1] See p. 35, n. 2, above.

[2] *Art of English Poetry* (4th ed., 1710), 5, first pagination.

[3] To use Mr. Saintsbury's admirable simile, "The Popian line is indeed so thoroughly 'standardised' — its parts are, like those of a cheap watch, made so perfectly interchangeable, that in its mere prosodic influence there is hardly any secret effect left possible (*English Prosody*, ii. 457).

[4] Cowper, *Table Talk*, 652–5.

[5] *Select Beauties of Ancient English Poetry* (1787), introd., p. xxi. A more just statement is that of the *Critical Review* (1788, lxv. 51): "Perhaps, the example of Pope has produced an effect on our poetry, similar to that of Titian in the province of painting. Both were men of undoubted genius, and both possessed the higher excellencies of their art in an eminent degree: but their followers, who had neither so much imagination nor judgment, were captivated with that softness and harmony of colouring, which strikes the observer at first sight; and without giving themselves time to distinguish nobler beauties, made that the immediate object of their pursuit, which is at best but a secondary qualification. The taste, however, of the age is at length gradually recovering itself from this extreme of vicious refinement . . . [and is returning to] the grander and more simple style of Spenser and Milton."

Yet it is doing Pope the flattering injustice of exaggerating his in-fluence to attribute to him all or even the major part of the "stand-ardization" of verse. Bysshe's book, which was published before the "wicked wasp of Twickenham" had shown his sting, and which formulated the belief held by most persons in the century following Milton's death, was far more mechanical and rigid than Pope's practice. The little bard was simply the supreme manifestation of a movement that was flourishing vigorously before his birth. If we are to understand the eighteenth century, we must realize that the neo-classic conception of harmony in versification was not the theory of a few prosodists or the practice of a few poets, but some-thing which in the course of several generations had penetrated so deep into the very blood of Englishmen that they not only believed but felt it; we must see that they had become so accustomed to the regular beat of the heroic couplet that anything else seemed to most of them as dissonant and crude as Wagner and Whitman at first ap-peared to the Victorians. Like the Philipinos, to whom the tom, tom, tom of a drum is music and the mingling and contrasting har-monies of a symphony orchestra are discords, many neo-classicists agreed with Johnson in finding "the most complete" if not the only prosodical harmony in "the repetition of this . . . percussion at equal times." They had grown so accustomed to scanning with their fingers, like schoolboys, to stressing every other syllable and pausing at the end of every line, that Milton's free musical para-graphs naturally left them bewildered and out of breath.[1]

Persons were not all of the same mind, however, in 1721 any more than in 1921. In Pope's day there were not a few, as we have seen, who chafed under the rules and wearied of the monotony, "the brisk insufficiency and commonness," of the heroic couplet. Not only is evidence of this to be found in the increased popularity of blank verse and of the lithe, informal octosyllabic (the favorite meter of Prior and Swift), but there are also frank expressions of dis-satisfaction with the neo-classic prosody. One of the earlier and more interesting of these is in the preface to Prior's *Solomon* (1718), where we read: "*Heroic* [measure] with continued Rhime, as *Donne* and his Contemporaries used it, carrying the Sense of one Verse most commonly into another, was found too dissolute and wild, and came very often too near Prose. As *Davenant* and *Waller* corrected, and *Dryden* perfected it; It is too Confined: It cuts off the Sense at the end of every first Line, . . . produces too frequent an Identity in the Sound, and brings every Couplet to the Point of an Epigram.

[1] Cf. Isaac Watts, quoted below, p. 103.

. . . And as it tires the Writer while he composes, it must do the same to the Reader while he repeats; especially in a Poem of any considerable length. . . . He that writes in Rhimes, dances in Fetters." Blackmore, the author of thousands of couplets, urged run-over lines and varied pauses "to avoid Monotony and Uniformity in finishing the Sense, and giving a Rest at the End of every Couplet, which is tedious and ungrateful to the Reader." [1] Dryden was still alive when the complaint was made that the critics "allow none but *Iambics*, which must by an identity of sound bring a very unpleasing satiety upon the Reader. . . . A great many rough Cadencies, that are to be found in . . . the admirable *Paradise Lost*," continues the anonymous writer, "are so far from Faults that they are Beauties, and contribute by their variety to the prolonging the pleasure of the Readers." [2] Pope had not yet published a poem when Isaac Watts asserted, "It degrades the Excellency of the best Versification when the Lines run on by Couplets, twenty together, just in the same Pace and with the same Pauses. . . . the Reader is tir'd with the tedious Uniformity, or charm'd to sleep with the unmanly Softness of the Numbers, and the perpetual Chime of even Cadences." [3] The idea of Bysshe and other "popular versifiers," that "the chief excellence of poetry" lies in rime and a "flowing smoothness of verse which is now very common," was scouted by Charles Gildon, who held that "a verse composed of five *Iambics* . . . must want, by the uniformity of *cadence*, that variety that produces . . . harmony . . . and therefore *Dryden* and *Milton*, the greatest masters of *English versification*, have frequently given us two or three short quantities together." [4]

But the spread of the rebellion against prosodic regularity is too large a subject to be followed adequately here. Two utterances of unusual interest may, however, be noted. The first is a remark by Gray (who named Milton as "the best example of an exquisite ear" he could produce), that "the more we attend to the composition of Milton's harmony, the more we shall be sensible how he loved to vary his pauses, his measures, and his feet, which gives that enchanting air of freedom and wildness to his versification." [5] Daniel Webb,

---

[1] "Essay upon Epick Poetry," *Essays upon Several Subjects* (1716), 112.

[2] *Poems on Affairs of State* (1697), préface.

[3] Preface to the 1709 edition of *Horae Lyricae*, p. xx; cf. his *Miscellaneous Thoughts* (1734), no. lxxiii.

[4] *Laws of Poetry* (1721), 63; cf. his *Complete Art of Poetry* (1718), i. 292–302.

[5] *Observations on English Metre*, in *Works* (ed. Mitford), v. 233. This was said apropos of *Allegro*. Cf. John Foster's *Essay on Accent and Quantity* (2d ed., Eton, 1763), 67–8: "There is indeed no kind or degree of harmony, of which our language is

though forgotten to-day, made considerable impression upon his own age and is still worth reading because of the vigor of his repeated attacks upon the orthodox prosody. "Of all the modes of versification," he writes, ". . . the Latin distich, and modern couplet are the greatest levellers. There is no liberty, no continuance in their movements."[1] "The perpetual returns of similar impressions," he declares elsewhere, "lie like weights upon our spirits, and oppress the imagination. Strong passions, the warm effusions of the soul, were never destined to creep through monotonous parallels; they call for a more liberal rhythmus; for movements, not balanced by rule, but measured by sentiment, and flowing in ever new yet musical proportions." Webb objected to the regularity of Pope's pauses, and praised the beauty of "those sudden breaks or transitions in . . . verse." He quoted from the *Essay on Man*, with the comment, "Every ear must feel the ill effect of the monotony in these lines;" and in criticising Addison's *Cato* he explained, "The monotony of the couplet does not proceed, as has been imagined, from the repetition of the rhymes, but from a sameness in the movement of the verse. . . . Mr. Addison, accustomed to the secure Monotony of the couplet, had neither the genius to bear him thro', nor courage to attempt the unbounded variety of the Miltonic measures."[2]

There is danger that we may think of these men, and of other objectors to neo-classic regularity, as champions of the fullest prosodic freedom, a conclusion by no means justified. In literary as in religious evolution, there are always those who think themselves emancipated and who do favor great liberty up to a certain point; but beyond that point their minds close and prejudice and conventionality reign. Isaac Watts, who on the same page in which he rejoiced in deliverance from the bondage of rime proceeded to forge new fetters, is an illustration of these half-liberated minds; and so is William Benson, who, though he regarded the varying of the pause as "the Soul of all Versification" and approved of inversion of accent, was yet strongly opposed to blank verse.[3] Nevertheless, even if

capable, which may not be found in numberless instances thro' Milton's writings; the excellency of whose ear seems to have been equal to that of his imagination and learning." "No Poet modern or antient more consulted *Harmony*," affirmed Hesiod Cooke (*Proposals for Perfecting the English Language*, 1729, in *Original Poems*, 1742, p. 305).

[1] *Remarks on the Beauties of Poetry* (1762), 18–19.

[2] *Observations on Poetry and Music* (1769), 113; *Remarks*, etc. (1762), 6, 20, 7, 12–13. According to Omond (*English Metrists*, 31–2), "Webb's ideas seemed upsetting to his contemporaries. . . . The frequent references to his books show that they made their mark on men's minds."

[3] *Letters concerning Poetical Translations* (1739), 39, 45, 50, 72, 78–80. See also the opinions of Mitford, Goldsmith, Scott, and Warton, on p. 57 above.

there were few who either understood or desired the full freedom offered them in *Lycidas* or *Paradise Lost*, many poets, like most writers on versification, feeling the limitations of the heroic couplet and of the orthodox ideas of prosody, strove for greater liberty and variety.

But, some one asks, if these men liked both rime and freedom, why did they not unite the two in a more supple, flowing pentameter couplet? Rime does not necessarily imply end-stopped lines, with a pause near the middle and alternate accents: why not combine Milton with Pope? The answer is probably threefold. In the first place, most writers of that day never thought of combining the two. The eighteenth century was far less eclectic than the twentieth, less likely to take one thing from one poet and another from another. Miltonic blank verse, for example, was not used in plays or Shakespearean in poems; the off-hand style and easy versification of *Hudibras* were frequently imitated in Butler's own meter, but never, so far as I know, in decasyllabics. When Scott of Amwell wrote descriptions of nature in heroic couplets, he took Pope's *Windsor Forest* as his model; when he treated similar themes in blank verse he followed Thomson.

In the second place, most eighteenth-century writers lacked the skill to transfer the Miltonic prosody — which few of them really understood — to the couplet. To us this seems easy enough to do, because it has been done for over a century; but if Thomson, Glover, and the rest could hardly keep their blank verse from slipping back into unrimed couplets, they certainly could not have achieved the prosody of *Paradise Lost* when bound by the fetters of rime. The experiment was made, but — here is the third part of the answer to our question — the results did not please. Isaac Watts "attempted in Rhime the same variety of Cadence, Comma, and Period, which Blank Verse Glories in as its peculiar Elegance," [1] but the world was not interested in his experiments or in any similar ones. Richard Blackmore, "the knight of the burning pestle," held that "the Poet should often run the Second Line into the Third, and after the manner of the *Latines*, and *Milton*, make the Stop in the Beginning or Middle of it; this will vary the Sound . . . [and] relieve the Ear." [2] But there were few who agreed with him. The feeling of the eighteenth century about the matter was expressed by a thoughtful critic in the *Monthly Review:* "In verse where there are rhimes, we naturally expect the pause at the end of the line; when it

---

[1] Preface to *Horae Lyricae* (1706). See below, p. 103.
[2] "Essay upon Epick Poetry," *Essays* (1716), 112.

chances to fall otherwise, the injudicious reader destroys it, and confounds the sentence, by adhering to the jingle; while the reader of more taste sacrifices the rhime to preserve the pause. It is evident they are things quite contrary to one another, and incompatible. The writer therefore who determines on rhime, must be so far a slave to it, as to fetter himself to a sameness of cadence." [1] Even Cowper, who understood prosody as few others of his time did, said that the "breaks and pauses" of blank verse "are graces to which rhyme is not competent; so broken, it loses all its music; of which any person may convince himself by reading a page only of any of our poets anterior to Denham, Waller and Dryden." [2]

But to this as to almost every form of prosodic narrowness Milton's influence was ultimately opposed. As the appreciation of his art grew and ears became accustomed to his constantly-varying cadences, his "transcendental union of order and freedom," these qualities came to be demanded in rimed as well as in blank verse. The end-stopped couplet had to "grow or go," and under the influence of the "mighty-mouthed inventor of harmonies" and his followers it grew until it was transformed. Indeed, the deeper we look into the subject the more are we inclined to agree with its historian:

He [Milton] is one of the very greatest facts of English prosodic history . . . he supplies infallibly, though no doubt undesignedly, all or almost all that is necessary to correct the faults of that time. . . . Moreover, he does something for English prosody at large which had to be done at some time. . . . His blank-verse paragraph, and his audacious and victorious attempt to combine blanks and rhymed verse with paragraphic effect in *Lycidas*, lay down indestructible models and patterns of English verse-*rhythm*, as distinguished from the narrower and more strait-laced forms of English *metre*. . . . It was long before it ['the doctrine and the secret of Milton'] was understood — it is not universally understood or recognised even now. But it was always *there;* and as enjoyment and admiration of the results spread and abode, there was ever the greater chance of the principle being discovered, the greater certainty of its being put into perhaps unconscious operation by imitation.[3]

The diction of the neo-classicists was, both in theory and in practice, almost as restricted as their prosody. We constantly meet the same adjectives attached to the same nouns and followed by the same verbs, a uniformity that was due partly to the narrow field to which poetry had confined itself, but oftener to mere conventionality. The adjectives, which are particularly stereotyped, seem

---

[1] vii. 139–41 (1752).   [2] Preface to his Homer.
[3] Saintsbury, *English Prosody*, ii. 355–6.

commonly to be introduced simply to fill out the lines. Truth, propriety, precision, and inevitability were the most that was sought for in the selection of words. The reader is rarely "stung with the splendor" of an unexpected word, and color and imaginative suggestiveness in diction were so long ignored that the language of poetry became as thin as it was sharp.

As a result of this and other causes, many words frequently employed by Milton and the Elizabethans had dropped so completely not only from poetry but from all other usage that their meaning was no longer understood. No criticism of Spenser and Milton was so often made as that of employing unusual and obsolete words,[1] and unquestionably such words did furnish the most serious hindrance to the understanding and enjoyment of these poets. Yet this very strangeness of diction fascinated as well as repelled, and was often a source of subconscious pleasure to many who sensed only annoyance; it was, indeed, another element in that wildness which formed an important part of Milton's attractiveness. We feel it much less than the Augustans did, because, owing largely to the reading of Shakespeare, Milton, and Spenser for the past two hundred years, our vocabulary has come to be far richer than theirs and actually nearer to that of the sixteenth and seventeenth centuries. In 1742, for example, Gray mentions "beverage," "mood," "array," "wayward," and "smouldring" as obsolete words in Dryden.[2] About the same time Peck names among Milton's "old" words "minstrelsy," "murky," "carol," "chaunt," and among his 'naturalized' Latin words "humid," "orient," "hostil," "facil," "fervid," "jubilant," "ire," "bland," "reluctant," "palpable," "fragil," and "ornate."[3] "Self-same" and "hue" seem to have been rare;[4] and in 1778 "bridal," "gleam," "hurl," "plod," "ruthless," "wail," "wayward," and "woo" were declared to be "now almost peculiar to poetry," though "once no doubt in common use."[5]

That most of Milton's admirers found his "quaint Uncouthness

---

[1] Leonard Welsted, for instance, in his *Dissertation concerning the Perfection of the English Language*, 1724 (*Works*, 1787, p. 123), speaks of "an uncouth unnatural jargon, like the phrase and style of Milton, which is a second Babel, or confusion of all languages; a fault that can never be enough regretted in that immortal Poet, and which if he had wanted, he had perhaps wanted a Superior"; and the great lexicographer, who rejoiced in his own sesquipedalian locutions, says that Milton "wrote no language" but "a Babylonish Dialect" (*Lives*, ed. Hill, i. 190–1; Johnson borrows these phrases). Cf. Isaac Watts's criticism, p. 103 below.

[2] Letter to Richard West, April 8(?), 1742.

[3] *New Memoirs of Milton* (1740), 107, 110–111.

[4] John Scott, *Critical Essays* (1785), 63; *Mo. Rev.*, enl. ed., x. 276 (1793).

[5] James Beattie, *Essays on Poetry and Music*, 237; see also p. 116 below.

of Speech" pleasing is proved by the frequency with which they copied his diction in their own poems. "In order to write like Milton," it was said, "little more is required than to select certain peculiar, now exploded, words . . . as *nathless, caitiff, erst, ken, governance, &c.*"[1] "Without abundance of such words as these [dulcet, gelid, umbrageous, redolent], a friend of Pope's wrote satirically, "a poem will never be esteemed truly Miltonic."[2] Yet Pope himself confessed to making use of the diction of *Paradise Lost* in his Homer, and he might well have extended his confession to include the other poems in which he borrowed from the 1645 volume.[3] The truth is that poets who really admired Milton could hardly help feeling, as they read his richly-colored lines, the tameness, the dearth of picturesqueness and individuality, of their own language. Nor was it the epic alone that impressed them as unusual in diction; for the vocabulary of the minor poems was in a different way quite as unlike their own, and from the time of Pope's earliest pieces left an unmistakable mark on English verse. So frequent, indeed, are the echoes of Milton's minor poems in the work of the Wartons and Mason that at times one can hear little else. As a result, the criticism most often made of these men, as of Gray, Collins, the sonneteers, and most of the poets of the lyric awakening that began about 1740, was concerning their use of "obsolete words out of Spenser and Milton."

It is no mere coincidence that the men who turned from satire, wit, and the artificial pastoral to the lyric and the poetry of real nature were the men who were seeking for fresher and less hackneyed words. A new art requires new tools as well as a new spirit. Not that all artists are at first conscious of this requirement. Many poets employed Milton's diction, as they did his style and meters, from the habit of slavish imitation so general in the eighteenth century; yet if they had taste and penetration they realized as soon as they donned the new garment how drab and shabby the old one had been. The debt to Milton and Spenser was, of course, not limited to bits of gold lace or embroidery clearly taken from their gorgeous vestments. When a man who has always worn the Quaker costume adopts a colored tie or a derby hat, the step to a striped suit and pointed shoes is an easy one; and, similarly, when a writer or a reader has once become accustomed to unusual phraseology, he is likely to develop a sensitiveness to the imaginative and sonorous

---

[1] *Mo. Rev.*, xii. 159 (1755).

[2] *Grub-Street Journal*, Feb. 5, 1730 (*Memoirs of the Society of Grub-Street*, no. 5). Cf. the *Guardian*, no. 78 (by Pope); and James Ralph's *Night* (1728), p. vii.

[3] See below, pp. 115–16, and Appendix A.

value of language, and to seek increasingly for an expression of his meaning which will be not only adequate but picturesque, haunting, magic, exquisite, magnificent, or otherwise memorable.   English poetry from Pope to Keats shows a steadily-increasing attention to the connotative, the imaginative and poetic, value of words, a change that is due largely to the influence of Spenser, Shakespeare, and Milton.[1]

It would, however, be misleading to represent Milton's influence upon diction as entirely beneficial. The strongly Latinic, learned, and grandiloquent vocabulary of his epic, though admirably adapted to Pandemonic councils and the rebellion of archangels, was a dangerous model for mediocre bards who were dealing with prosaic themes. Unfortunately, also, the most influential of his early followers exaggerated his lofty and unusual Latinisms, or at least did not modify them when dealing with very different subject-matter. As a result, bombast and blank verse became almost synonymous, and most renouncers of rime made themselves ridiculous in their attempts to walk upon stilts.[2] Nor can it be denied that Thomas Warton and some of the other imitators of the minor poems often showed less poetic discrimination than boyish delight over a new toy, in their use of

> Phrase that time has flung away;
> Uncouth words in disarray,
> Trick'd in antique ruff and bonnet,
> Ode, and elegy, and sonnet.[3]

[1] Since Spenser was read less than the other two poets and seemed more antiquated and remote, his diction was used more consciously than theirs, by fewer writers, and in more definite imitations of his manner. Shakespeare's language seems to have attracted a still smaller degree of attention and, until the beginning of the nineteenth century, to have had less influence than one would expect. Yet no one can speak with anything like certainty in these matters until extensive researches have been made into the entire subject of poetic diction, a neglected field in which the many recent concordances are of invaluable service.

[2] The *Monthly Review*, for example, maintained in 1804 (enl. ed., xliv. 428, 425)that "blank verse requires a certain majesty of diction, and is debased by low and vulgar expressions," and that "'incomprehensible' is not a word so proper for this measure [the Spenserian stanza] as for Miltonic blank verse." "I am no great friend to blank-verse for subjects which are to be treated of with simplicity," Fox wrote Wordsworth (May 25, 1801, Harper's *Wordsworth*, i. 418). And so late as 1810 Chalmers (*English Poets*, xvii. 12) regarded words like "forestall, uncomfortable, acquiescence, obtuse, exemplified, meritorious, absurdity, superfluous, timber, assiduity, elegantly, authoritative, supercede, convalescence, circumscription," as " too familiar" for an unrimed epic. Yet Lord Lyttelton rejoiced in Glover's discovery that "hard Words, and affected Phrases, are no more necessary in this sort of Metre [blank verse], than in Rhime, and that if *Milton* himself had been more sparing of them, he would not . . . have spoil'd the Style of so many of his Successors, who have chose to imitate him chiefly in this Point" (*Common Sense*, April 9, 1737).

[3] Johnson, quoted in Boswell's *Johnson* (ed. Hill), iii. 158 n.

Milton's numerous followers in the sonnet were, indeed, widely and justly criticized for what Coleridge termed "their quaint phrases, and incongruous mixture of obsolete and Spenserian words," [1] language which undoubtedly injured the popularity of the *genre*.

An especially undesirable feature of this tumid diction was the use of periphrases, such as "glossy kind" or "plumy race" for "birds," or "the sable rock inflammable" for "coal," or "frequent the gelid cistern" for "take a cold bath." These objectionable and often absurd circumlocutions were generally admired and used, by writers of blank verse in particular. Indirectly they owed much to Milton, not because he was addicted to them himself, but because his followers employed them in the hope of capturing the sonorous grandeur and aloofness from common things to which his epic owes much of its beauty. The influence of *Paradise Lost* was unquestionably away from simple directness and towards the high-sounding and the elaborate. Yet the relish for inflated Latinisms and periphrases which Milton's usage fostered, if it did not originate, would never have fastened itself upon poetry if there had not been in the air a genuine and general love of grandiloquence, a love which is plainly revealed in the Swan of Lichfield's letters and the prose of Johnson, Burke, and Gibbon.

Still another force that made strongly for unnaturalness of diction was the constant dread of being prosaic.[2] Nothing shows the unpoetic nature of the eighteenth century more clearly than this fear, which, based as it was on the realization that there was no essential difference between the prose and much of the verse of the period, led to the creation of mechanical and adventitious differences. In consequence, writers who had courage to give up the most obvious of

[1] "Introduction to the Sonnets," *Poems*, 2d ed., 1797, p. 73. Cf. *Crit. Rev.*, new arr., xxi. 151 (1797), where contemporary sonnets were assailed for not using "the genuine language of simple . . . nature."

[2] Parnell asked (in a dialogue prefixed to his *Homer's Battle of the Frogs and Mice*, 1717, A 4) if a blank-verse translation of Homer would be "remov'd enough from Prose, without greater Inconveniences "; and Alexander Kellet wrote in 1778 (see *Crit. Rev.*, xlvi. 457), "In an age of ignorance an expedient turned up, that so obviously distinguished prose and poetry, as to lay claim for a time to constitute the essential of the last; and this was the Gothic invention of rhyme." The general understanding of the matter was voiced in the preface to James Buchanan's *First Six Books of P. L.* (Edin., 1773, p. 4), where we read, "Rhime, without any other assistance, throws the language off from prose; but, in blank verse, the poet is obliged to use inversion, as well as pomp of sound, and energy of expression, in order to give harmony and variety to his numbers, and keep his stile from falling into the flatness of prose." The same idea is expressed in John Aikin's *Letters on English Poetry* (2d ed., 1807, p. 118), and in Sir William Jones's *Design of an Epic Poem* (*Works*, 1807, ii. 433). On the entire subject, see my *Poetic Diction of the English Classicists* (*Kittredge Anniversary Papers*, Boston, 1913, pp. 435-44).

these distinctions, rime, felt constrained to substitute for it a style stiffened with strange words arranged in an unusual order. The widespread conviction that, if an unrimed work was made sufficiently unlike prose, it would be good blank verse illustrates again how completely the measure was misunderstood.

This vicious diction, "the Miltonic dialect" as it was called, is to be found as late as *The Task* (1785), and occasionally in the work of Tennyson's early contemporaries, or even in our own day; [1] but its force was largely spent by the middle of the century. As more blank verse was written and read, people came to understand it better and to distinguish what was essential from what was peculiar to Milton; at the same time poets were gaining greater mastery of it, making it more and more supple in style and natural in language, till in *Tintern Abbey* no trace of evil influence from *Paradise Lost* is to be found. Yet Milton had by no means ceased to affect the language of poets. Wordsworth quoted his practice as authoritative in diction, and often copied it, while Keats, a lover of words, appropriated not a few from the epic, the masque, and the monody.

The usage of these men may well remind us that in diction, as in all other matters, Milton's example, notwithstanding its undesirable aspects, was on the side of freedom. It would certainly have gratified him to know that much of his popularity was due to the inspiration which lovers of liberty of every kind found in his life and works, that his influence was a potent force towards enfranchisement in political, religious, and literary fields.

But any assertion as to Milton's influence must be taken partly on faith until more evidence for it has been offered. Even the testimony which has been presented regarding his popularity is of the more external sort, consisting largely in an enumeration of editions and in opinions and controversies about the poems. The great proof of his vogue, as well as of his influence, will be found in the succeeding chapters, which will trace through the poetry of the eighteenth and nineteenth centuries the unmistakable evidences of his style, diction, prosody, and subject-matter. For the closeness with which his various poems were copied is almost incredible: no one to-day would think of writing a serious poem modelled obviously and in detail after the *Blessed Damosel* or the *Hound of Heaven*, much less after *Allegro*. But it was not so in the days of our forefathers. With them imitation flourished openly and universally. They liked it, and referred frankly to Mason's and Warton's "imitations of Milton" without a thought of disparagement, just as Gray compli-

---

[1] A familiar instance is the "reeking tube and iron shard" of Kipling's *Recessional*.

mented West on his "very picturesque, Miltonic, and musical" *Ode to May*.[1] Reviewers referred to the "happy imitation of the Miltonic style" in Crowe's *Lewesdon Hill;* they were pleased with Drummond's *Odin* for its general resemblance to *Paradise Lost*, and praised Cowper as "perhaps the most successful" imitator of Milton.[2] One popular writer even maintained that imitation was a higher art than original writing: "'Tis easier to strike out a new Course of Thought, than to equal old Originals, and therefore it is more Honour to surpass, than to invent anew. *Verrio* is a great Man from his own Designs, but if he had attempted upon the *Cartons*, and outdone *Raphael Urbin* in Life and Colours, he had been acknowledged greater than that celebrated Master, but now we must think him less."[3] Every successful poem was imitated, — Dryden's *Ode for St. Cecilia's Day*, Pope's *Dunciad*, Philips's *Cyder*, Gray's *Elegy*, Collins's *Ode to Evening*, and many others; while the *Faerie Queene* alone furnished the model for hundreds of pieces. Even the greatest writers in some of their highest flights were clearly imitating. The eighteenth century produced few finer poems than Thomson's *Castle of Indolence*, yet even in language it is an imitation. William Mason, besides following *L'Allegro* and *Il Penseroso* about as closely as he could in his *Il Bellicoso* and *Il Pacifico*, wrote *Musaeus, a Monody, in imitation of Milton's Lycidas*, and apparently no one objected, not even his intimate friend the fastidious Gray, who revised all three poems for him.[4] Indeed, the detecting of imitations seems to have been one of the pleasures our ancestors derived from reading verse.

The additional testimony of the following chapters is, however, not needed to show that only by gross self-righteousness and ignorance can we accuse the eighteenth century of neglecting Milton. On the contrary, its enthusiasm for him was something that we can hardly understand. His life and his works furnished reading and topics of discussion as inexhaustible and as unescapable as the weather. In truth, a contemporary of Johnson or Cowper would have found it exceedingly difficult to avoid the poet whom he is

---

[1] Letter to West, May 8, 1742.

[2] See *Mo. Rev.*, lxxviii. 308; and below, pp. 170, 307. In 1790 the *Critical Review* (lxix. 156) praised John Roberts's *Deluge* for being "no unhappy imitation of Milton's forcible and classic style."

[3] Henry Felton, *Dissertation on Reading the Classics* (5th ed., 1753), 15–16; quoted in R. S. Crane's *Imitation of Spenser and Milton* (Univ. of North Carolina, *Studies in Philology*, 1918, xv. 195–206), where the whole subject is discussed.

[4] See an undated and unaddressed letter "from Mason," in Gray's *Letters* (ed. Tovey), i. 187, n. 3; also one from Gray to Mason, June 7, 1760, *ib.* ii. 140, n. 5.

charged with slighting. If he went to the theater, he was likely to witness a production of *Comus*, or at least to pass a "busto" of the god in the lobby, and he might hear Sheridan recite from *Paradise Lost;* if he preferred music, there were several popular oratorios drawn from Milton's poems; if he fled to the "movies" of the day, Pandemonium confronted him; if he chose to wander through Vauxhall, he passed under the "temple of Comus" and encountered a statue of the blind bard as Il Penseroso. He went to church only to hear the religious epic quoted, and returned to find his children committing passages of it to memory. His son had probably caught the Miltonic madness at college; at any rate, the "Pietas et Gratulatio " volume, which the fond parent preserved in full leather binding because of his offspring's academic verses, contained little English poetry that was not Miltonic. If his friends were clergymen or lawyers, they were likely to be literary and have ideas on blank verse or be writing letters to the *Gentleman's Magazine* on *Paradise Lost;* if they were ardent republicans, they made him listen to passages from the *Areopagitica,* if dilettantes they spouted *Allegro.* If he picked up a magazine, Miltonic blank verse stared him in the face, and he would turn the page only to encounter Miltonic sonnets and octosyllabics or an essay on the indebtedness of *Paradise Lost* to the *Iliad;* the letters to the editor were likely to deal with some Miltonic controversy then raging, and the reviews discussed poems "in imitation of Milton" and editions of the poet's works. If he turned to books it was no better, even though he chose his reading carefully; for poetry, essays, biographies, volumes of letters, works on theology, language, and literature, were sure to quote, imitate, or discuss "the greatest writer the world has ever seen."

If he fled London for Edinburgh, he ran into a "nest of ninnies" on the subject of Milton among both poets and critics; if he turned to Bath, there was Lady Miller's coterie prattling phrases from the minor poems, if to Lichfield, he encountered its famous Swan

> Between her white wings mantling proudly

and rowing her state with Miltonic feet. In remote Devonshire and Cornwall there were Richard Polwhele and his group of sonneteers and scribblers of blank verse, while in remoter Wales lurked Milton's follower John Dyer. No village was free from the contagion; and if he sought peace in the country, he came upon Il Penseroso alcoves, upon travellers reading *Paradise Lost* by the roadside, ploughboys with copies of it in their pockets, and shepherds, real shepherds, 'poring upon it in the fields.' Even among the poor and the uneducated it was the same: not only ploughboys and shepherds, but threshers, cotters, cobblers, and milkwomen read and imitated the poet who expected his audience to be "few."

If he finally crossed the Channel in search of a refuge, he would do well to avoid Italy; for at Vallombrosa and Fiesole travellers were declaiming "Of man's first disobedience," and at Florence the English colony was publishing volumes of patent imitations of the poet whom he was trying to escape. Nor would he be better off in other countries, for cultivated Frenchmen and Germans would be sure to speak to him of his nation's epic and its influence upon their own poetry, and would probably quote from Addison's critique. There were, of course, many parts of the continent and some remote places in Great Britain where Milton's voice was not heard, but the only Englishmen who were certain of getting beyond its reach were the Alexander Selkirks lost on "some unremembered isle in far-off seas."

Other writers may have dominated, or have seemed to dominate, English literature more completely than Milton did, but on closer scrutiny their influence will be found to have been limited to relatively short periods of time and to comparatively small, though it may be very important, fractions of the public. More than this, most of them failed to rouse at the same time the profound admiration and the enthusiastic devotion which were felt for the author of *Paradise Lost, Comus, Penseroso*, and the *Areopagitica*. It is hardly an exaggeration to say that from Pope's day to Wordsworth's Milton occupied a place, not only in English literature but in the thought and life of Englishmen of all classes, which no poet has held since and none is likely to hold again.

PART II

THE INFLUENCE OF PARADISE LOST

CHAPTER IV

THE CHARACTERISTICS OF PARADISE LOST AND THEIR RELATION TO EIGHTEENTH-CENTURY BLANK VERSE

BLANK-VERSE poems have long since become so much a matter of course that we accept them as we do matches, telephones, trains, or religious liberty, without much thought. It does not ordinarily occur to us that these things ever had a beginning or that they were once subjects of wonder, doubt, and strife. To-day, when blank verse is the recognized medium for long poems, the one in which many of the pieces we like best are written, we have difficulty in realizing that as late as 1785 men of the ability and position of Johnson and Goldsmith could hardly speak about it calmly.

But, though it is generally assumed that this kind of verse has always existed, the average lover of poetry would be put to it to name half a dozen examples that he has read which were published before *Tintern Abbey*. He knows of *The Seasons, The Task, Night Thoughts*, and perhaps a few others; but he knows very little of them, and is obliged to confess that to him blank-verse poetry means the nineteenth century and Milton. Nor is this all; for of the half-dozen poems he can mention not one was written before *Paradise Lost*. Did Milton compose the first unrimed poem? Most of us are quite sure he did not; we assume that blank verse is as old as the couplet, which, as we know, goes back to Chaucer. When, however, we are asked to name some early blank verse we hesitate. A scholar will remember that Surrey's translation of parts of the *Aeneid* (1557) is supposed to be the first unrimed English poem, and he may recall Gascoigne's *Steele Glas* (1576); but if he can name any other blank verse off-hand he will do well.[1] The pieces that he does remember, moreover, he may never have read; and even if he has gone through them it is unlikely that they have left any definite impression on his mind, — they mean little or nothing to him. In other words, there are few persons living to-day who really know any non-dramatic

[1] For a list of blank-verse poems published before *Paradise Lost*, with some account of them, see J. P. Collier's *Poetical Decameron* (1820), i. 54–8, 88–145, ii. 231.

blank verse written before 1667. *Paradise Lost* is, to all intents and purposes, our earliest unrimed poem.

If such is the case now, when the literature which flourished from the fourteenth century to the seventeenth has so many admirers, what must have been the situation in an age that was in Cimmerian darkness regarding nearly every English work written before its own time? Very few of the contemporaries of Dryden had ever read or even heard of any blank-verse poem in English except *Paradise Lost;* and Milton himself had written, "This neglect then of rime . . . is to be esteemed an example set, the *first in English*, of ancient liberty recovered to heroic poem." [1] Isaac Watts had the same idea in 1734, when he said, "Mr. Milton is esteemed the parent and author of blank verse among us;" [2] and Johnson, when writing his life of Milton forty-five years later, could remember but two unrimed poems before *Paradise Lost*, and one of those he had only heard about.[3] Undoubtedly the critic who wrote in 1793, "Milton introduced a new species of verse into the English language which he called blank verse," [4] expressed the all-but-universal opinion.

But, it will be objected, these men had the drama, — Shakespeare, Ben Jonson, Lee, Otway, Dryden, and plenty of others; blank verse was perfectly familiar to them. True, blank verse was perfectly familiar to them, and it would seem to have been a simple matter to transfer this verse from the plays to poems. Yet no one did it; indeed, no one seems even to have thought of doing it. The fact is that to the eighteenth century dramatic blank verse was one thing and poetic blank verse an entirely different thing. Even so late as 1814 C. A. Elton declared, "Of blank verse there are two species. . . . The Epic and Dramatic measure have little more in common than the absence of rhyme;" [5] and William Crowe's *Treatise on English Versification* (1827) has a chapter "Of Blank Verse" and another "Of Dramatic Verse." Many of the greatest and most popular plays of the later seventeenth century were unrimed, — Lee's *Rival Queens, Mithridates*, and *Caesar Borgia*, Otway's *Orphan* and *Venice Preserved*, the tragedies of Southern and Rowe, as well as Dryden's *All for Love* and most of his *Spanish Friar* and *Don Sebastian;* yet I have found only nine poems written between 1605 and 1700 that

---

[1] "The Verse," prefixed to the fifth issue of the first edition of *Paradise Lost*. The italics are mine.

[2] *Miscellaneous Thoughts*, no. lxxiii (*Works*, 1810, iv. 619).

[3] *Lives* (ed. Hill), i. 192.

[4] *Bee*, xvi. 272 (Aug. 21, 1793). So Thomson spoke of Philips as "the second" who "nobly durst" to sing "in rhyme-unfettered verse" (*Autumn*, 645–6).

[5] *Specimens of the Classic Poets*, vol. i, p. xiii.

follow Milton's example. Dryden, at the very time he urged abandoning the couplet on the stage, apparently thought that *Paradise Lost* would be much better 'tagged.'[1] I have examined hundreds of blank-verse plays of the seventeenth and eighteenth centuries, and have yet to find one that is at all Miltonic; but, as will be shown later, there are comparatively few unrimed poems of these centuries that are not influenced by *Paradise Lost*. The dramatic blank verse was, so far as it was imitative at all, Shakespearean or Jonsonian,[2] the non-dramatic was usually Miltonic. Almost the only poem that is likely to have derived its style and prosody from the drama is Blair's *Grave*, and this was also influenced by *Paradise Lost*.[3] The most striking instances of the absolute separation between the two kinds of verse are to be found in the works of such men as Thomson, Glover, Mason, and Mallet, who wrote both kinds. By way of illustration, here is a typical passage from Glover's drama *Boadicia* (1753) and one from his epic *Leonidas* (1737):

> Go, and report this answer to Suetonius.
> Too long have parents sighs, the cries of orphans,
> And tears of widows, signaliz'd your sway,
> Since your ambitious Julius first advanc'd
> His murd'rous standard on our peaceful shores.
> At length unfetter'd from his patient sloth,
> The British genius lifts his pond'rous hands
> To hurl with ruin his collected wrath
> For all the wrongs, a century hath borne,
> In one black period on the Roman race.[4]

> He said. His seeming virtue all deceiv'd.
> The camp not long had Epialtes join'd,
> By race a Malian. Eloquent his tongue,
> But false his heart, and abject. He was skill'd
> To grace perfidious counsels, and to cloath
> In swelling phrase the baseness of his soul,
> Foul nurse of treasons. To the tents of Greece,
> Himself a Greek, a faithless spy he came.
> Soon to the friends of Xerxes he repair'd,
> The Theban chiefs, and nightly consult held.[5]

[1] Aside from turning parts of it into rime in his *State of Innocence and Fall of Man*, he says in the "Essay on Satire" prefixed to his translations from Juvenal (*Works*, ed. Scott-Saintsbury, xiii. 20), "Neither will I justify Milton for his blank verse . . . for . . . his own particular reason is plainly this, that rhyme was not his talent."

[2] The use of Miltonic blank verse in translations of Greek tragedies and other classic dramas is a not unnatural exception (see pp. 346–51 below).

[3] See pp. 383–5 below.

[4] *Boadicia*, act i.

[5] *Leonidas*, ii. 224–33.

If we realize that to the seventeenth- and eighteenth-century poets blank verse in a drama was an entirely different thing from blank verse in a poem, and that to them there was but one unrimed poem, *Paradise Lost*, we shall better understand the powerful influence which this work exerted. Blank verse meant verse that was Miltonic, and "Miltonic verse" usually meant little more than blank verse. Two poems published in the *London Magazine* in 1738, for example, are said to be "attempted in Miltonic verse," [1] which must mean blank verse, for the pieces have no more suggestion of *Paradise Lost* than has Addison's translation, *Milton's Style Imitated*, where the imitation is limited to the absence of rime. [2] In the following lines by Edmund Smith "Miltonian verse" means simply blank verse:

> Oh! might I paint him in *Miltonian* verse. . . .
> But with the meaner Tribe I'm forc'd to chime,
> And wanting Strength to rise, descend to Rhyme. [3]

If a writer grew tired of the couplet or desired a freer measure, there was, accordingly, but one thing for him to do, — follow *Paradise Lost*. And it is not to be wondered at that, in following his model, he usually copied many characteristics which were merely the personal peculiarities of Milton and hence had no necessary connection with blank verse. He did not distinguish between the two things. As a result, blank-verse poems usually stood by themselves, with their style, diction, and prosody little affected by those of either the drama or the couplet. This curious state of affairs led the same man to write Popean couplets on one day and Miltonic blank verse containing no suggestion of Pope on the next. [4] To us such a complete separation is hard to understand. Why should not a poet merely have taken a hint from Milton and written his own blank verse? Why not have combined the diction of Pope with the prosody of Milton? It seems perfectly easy. But we forget that the truisms of to-day are the discoveries of yesterday; we forget how slowly and painfully the world came to ideas which we imbibed naturally in childhood; we forget Columbus and the egg.

Yet even when a man did think of writing poems in blank verse of

---

[1] vii. 44: *Hymn to the Morning* and *Hymn to Night*.   [2] See pp. 104–5 below.

[3] *Poem on the Death of John Philips* (1708?), 2. So John Nichols (*Illustrations*, 1817, i. 664) speaks of one who "has left the *Miltonic* measure, and falls with graceful ease into rhyme." See also p. 47 above.

[4] Compare, for example, Fenton's riming of the first, fourth, nineteenth, and twentieth books of Pope's Homer, with his translation of the eleventh book of the *Odyssey* "in Milton's style"; or Prior's rimed paraphrase of the thirteenth chapter of 1 Corinthians with his unrimed version of the two hymns of Callimachus.

his own he was unable to do it well.   There were not many who tried
it in Dryden's or Pope's day,[1] and those who did produced unrimed
couplets like these:

> Unpolish'd Verses pass with many Men,
> And *Rome* is too Indulgent in that Point;
> But then, to write at a loose rambling rate,
> In hope the World will wink at all our faults,
> Is such a rash, ill-grounded confidence,
> As men may pardon, but will never praise.
> Consider well the Greek Originals,
> Read them by day, and think of them by night.[2]

If Wentworth Dillon, Earl of Roscommon, author of the famous
Essay on Translated Verse, could do no better than this, is it any
wonder that the ordinary, struggling poet made no attempt to strike
out for himself, but slavishly followed in Milton's tracks?

To break away from *Paradise Lost* and yet not at the same time
fall to the dead level of Roscommon's translation, that is, to write
what we may think of as everyday blank verse, was a task so difficult that English writers were one hundred and fifty years in ac-
complishing it.   One thing which held them back was their fear of
being prosaic.[3]   If even at this late day we are not entirely free from
the impression that poetry and rime are almost synonymous, how
much more strongly must this feeling have been with those who were
bred under the dominance of the heroic couplet.   Most blank verse
seemed hardly more like poetry to hundreds of the contemporaries
of Dryden, Pope, and even Johnson than do the measures of Walt
Whitman or Amy Lowell to many readers of to-day.   Yet Milton's
unrimed lines did impress nearly everybody as poetry.   They were
made so, it was commonly supposed, by certain original characteristics or devices which lifted them above prose and separated them
sharply from stanzaic or couplet verse.   Without the stiffening of
these characteristics, it was thought, blank verse could not stand.
Many versifiers therefore copied them blindly, others scattered
them through their prosaic lines as a cook may mix raisins and sugar
into bread dough to make it seem like cake, and still others adopted
them almost unconsciously.

[1] Such pieces of non-Miltonic blank verse published between 1667 and 1750 as I
have come upon are listed in Appendix B, below.

[2] Roscommon's translation, *Horace's Art of Poetry* (1680), p. 18.   Most of Milton's
predecessors in non-dramatic blank verse did no better; nor did Walter Pope (see
below, p. 90, n. 3), or the "Gentleman of Oxford," whose original blank-verse "argument" is even worse than his unrimed *New Version of P. L.* (cf. p. 35 above).

[3] See pp. 67-8 above.

To trace the influence of *Paradise Lost*, therefore, we have only to discover these outstanding characteristics which were thought to distinguish it alike from other poetry and from prose, and to search for them in later poetry. They seem to me to fall into nine main classes: —[1]

1. DIGNITY, RESERVE, and STATELINESS. *Paradise Lost* is as far removed from conversational familiarity in style or language as any poem could well be:

> Of Man's first disobedience, and the fruit
> Of that forbidden Tree, whose mortal taste
> Brought death into the world, and all our woe,
> With loss of Eden, till one greater Man
> Restore us, and regain the blissful seat,
> Sing, Heavenly Muse.

2. The ORGAN TONE, the sonorous orotund which is always associated with Milton's name:[2]

> Against the throne and monarchy of God.

> Who durst defy the Omnipotent to arms.

> O Prince, O Chief of many throned powers,
> That led the embattled Seraphim to war.

> O thou that, with surpassing glory crown'd,
> Look'st from thy sole dominion like the god
> Of this new World.[3]

3. INVERSION OF THE NATURAL ORDER OF WORDS AND PHRASES, one of Milton's many Latinisms:

> Them thus employ'd beheld
> With pity Heaven's high King.

> Ten paces huge
> He back recoil'd.

> Me, of these
> Nor skill'd nor studious, higher argument
> Remains.[4]

---

[1] There is a somewhat similar list in Francis Peck's *New Memoirs of Milton* (1740, pp. 105–32), a curious hodge-podge that contains a good deal of valuable information. A brief examination of Milton's style will be found in the *Spectator*, no. 285.

[2] Cf. Bowles's

> Great Milton's solemn harmonies . . .
> Their long-commingling diapason roll,
> In varied sweetness

(*Monody on Warton*, 121–5); Tennyson's "God-gifted organ-voice of England" (*Milton*, 3); and Wordsworth's "Thou hadst a voice whose sound was like the sea" (sonnet on Milton, 10).

[3] i. 42, 49, 128–9; iv. 32–4.   [4] v. 219–20; vi. 193–4; ix. 41–3.

a. An inversion that is particularly Miltonic is the placing of a word between two others which depend upon it or upon which it depends, as a noun between two adjectives, a noun between two verbs, a verb between two nouns, etc. For example, " temperate vapours bland," "heavenly form Angelic," "unvoyageable gulf obscure," "gather'd aught of evil, or conceal'd";

> Firm peace recover'd soon, and wonted calm.

> Strange horror seize thee, and pangs unfelt before.[1]

4. The OMISSION OF WORDS NOT NECESSARY TO THE SENSE, one feature of the condensation that marks Milton's style:

> Though all our glory extinct, and happy state
> Here swallow'd up in endless misery.

> And where their weakness, how attempted best,
> By force or subtlety.

> Extended wide
> In circuit, undetermined square or round.[2]

5. PARENTHESIS AND APPOSITION. These two devices, similar in character, — since apposition is a kind of parenthesis, — were also probably due in a considerable degree to Milton's fondness for condensed expression. Familiar examples are:

> Of Abbana and Pharphar, lucid streams.

> Ahaz, his sottish conqueror, whom he drew.

> Their song was partial, but the harmony
> (What could it less when Spirits immortal sing?)
> Suspended Hell, and took with ravishment
> The thronging audience. In discourse more sweet
> (For eloquence the soul, song charms the sense)
> Others apart sat on a hill retired.

> Thus saying, from her side the fatal key,
> Sad instrument of all our woe, she took.

> Where eldest Night
> And Chaos, ancestors of Nature, hold.

> Sable-vested Night, eldest of things,
> The consort of his reign.

> The neighbouring moon
> (So call that opposite fair star).[3]

---

[1] v. 5; ix. 457–8; x. 366; v. 207, 210; ii. 703.

[2] i. 141–2; ii. 357–8, 1047–8

[3] i. 469, 472; ii. 552–7, 871–2, 894–5, 962–3; iii. 726–7. Cf. also ii. 769, 790–91, 921–2; iii. 372–84; iv. 321–4.

6. The USE OF ONE PART OF SPEECH FOR ANOTHER. Other poets have resorted to this practice, but none so often as Milton.[1]

a. Sometimes a verb or an adjective is employed in a participial sense, as

> Yet oft his heart, *divine* of something ill.[2]

b. Now and then an adjective is used as a verb:

> May serve to better us and *worse* our foes.[3]

c. Occasionally a substantive is made to take the place of a verb, as when trees "*gemmed*" their blossoms, or sea-monsters "*tempest*" the ocean, or Satan "*voyaged*" the deep.[4] Participles from such noun-verbs appear in the expressions "*fuell'd* entrails," "his *consorted* Eve," "roses *bushing* round." [5]

d. More frequently verbs seem to be used as nouns, though it is often hard to say whether the word in question is a verb or a clipped form of substantive: "the great *consult* began"; Satan "began . . . his *roam*"; "without *disturb* they took alarm"; "the place of her *retire*." [6]

e. One interchange of the parts of speech that was a favorite with Milton and his followers is the use of an adjective where an adverb would ordinarily be employed. Because of the distorted order it is often impossible to tell whether the word in question is intended to be an adjective or an adverb; but at any rate ordinary prose usage would employ adverbs in such cases as these, "with gems . . . *rich* emblazed," "grinned *horrible*," "his grieved look he fixes *sad*," "his proud step he *scornful* turn'd." [7]

f. As common, if not more so, is the use of an adjective for a noun. This device is sometimes very effective, the vague suggestiveness of a general expression being far better for Milton's purposes than the more definite word with its human associations would be, — when, for example, he speaks of chaos as "the palpable *obscure*" or "the vast *abrupt*," of a trumpet as "the sounding *alchemy*," of the sky as "Heaven's *azure*" or "the *vast* of Heaven." [8] Other instances are "this huge *convex* of fire," "dark with excessive *bright*," "Satan with

---

[1] It is hard to say how much of this is due to his fondness for the shortened forms of words. For example, in "made so *adorn* for thy delight" (viii. 576), does he mean "adorned" or does he intend to use the verb as an adjective?

[2] ix. 845.   [3] vi. 440.

[4] vii. 325, 412; x. 471.

[5] i. 234; vii. 50; ix. 426.

[6] i. 798; iv. 536–8; vi. 549; xi. 267.

[7] i. 538; ii. 846; iv. 28, 536.

[8] ii. 406, 409 (cf. Raleigh's *Milton* 1915, pp. 228–9), 517; i. 297; vi. 203.

his *rebellious*," "on *smooth* the seal" plays, "quit The *dank*," "tending to *wild*," "putting off *Human*, to put on Gods."[1]

7. VOCABULARY. Through his wide and constant reading, his
unusual familiarity with the classics, his admiration for Chaucer and
for Spenser, Shakespeare, and other Elizabethans, Milton had acquired an unusual vocabulary, which shows itself even in his prose
works. In *Paradise Lost* he naturally made frequent use of still other
unfamiliar words to describe the exceptional persons and places
with which he dealt; for ordinary language is not only inadequate
but too definite and too connotative of commonplace things to picture archangels, chaos, hell, and heaven. These persons and places
Milton with great art *suggests* to us through the atmosphere and
sound of the poem, and in order to create this atmosphere and
to obtain harmonies that produce this sound he had to depart from
the ordinary vocabulary. For these reasons his diction would be
marked in any age; but in the time of Pope and Johnson, when the
poetic vocabulary was unusually limited and when many old words
that are common to-day were obsolete, it must have seemed strange
enough.[2]

The words in *Paradise Lost* that would have sounded unusual to
the average intelligent reader of the late seventeenth or early eighteenth century fall into four main classes, the general effect of each
of which, it will be observed, is to give splendor, as well as a certain
strangeness or aloofness, to the poem:

a. Archaic words found in Chaucer, Spenser, Shakespeare, or their
contemporaries, but obsolete in the eighteenth century, such as
"erst," "grunsel," "welkin," "frore," "lore," "grisly," "ken,"
"areed," "avaunt," "behests," "wons," "emprise."[3] Since, however, any eighteenth-century writer who uses such words may have
derived them from Spenser or Shakespeare or possibly Chaucer, they
count for little in tracing Milton's influence.

b. Unusual words from the Greek or Latin. Under this head
Peck, in 1740, noted "dulcet," "panoplie," "sapience," "nocent,"
"congratulant," "attrite," "insanguin'd," "sequent."[4] Latin
words, whether common or uncommon, appealed strongly to Milton.

c. Words in general use but employed by Milton in senses obsolete in the eighteenth century. To such words he usually gives

[1] ii. 434; iii. 380; vi. 414 (cf. i. 71); vii. 409, 440–1; ix. 212, 713–14.
[2] We know that it did: see above, p. 64.
[3] i. 360, 460; ii. 538, 595, 815; iii. 622; iv. 821, 962 (two); vi. 185; vii. 457; xi. 642.
[4] *New Memoirs of Milton*, 110–111. Cf. *P.L.*, i. 712; vi. 527 (and 760); vii. 195;
ix. 186; x. 458, 1073; xi. 654; xii. 165.

the meanings they had in Latin or Anglo Saxon. For example, "the *secret* top Of Oreb" (L., retired); "a singèd bottom all *involved* With stench" (L., wrapped in); "*tempt*" an abyss (L., attempt); "his *uncouth* way" (A. S., unknown); "the *buxom* air" (A. S., yielding); "habit fit for speed *succinct*" (L., girt up); "*unessential* Night" (L., unsubstantial); "comes *unprevented*" (L., unanticipated); "*argument*" (L., theme); "*sagacious* of his quarry" (L., keen-scented); "turn My *obvious* breast" (L., in front of).[1]

d. Words required or suggested by the subject, as ambrosial, chaos, adamant or adamantine, ethereal, void, abyss, umbrageous, embattled, amarant or amaranthine.[2]

8. The introduction into a comparatively short passage of a CONSIDERABLE NUMBER OF PROPER NAMES that are not necessary to the sense but add richness, color, and imaginative suggestiveness:

> And what resounds
> In fable or romance of Uther's son,
> Begirt with British and Armoric knights;
> And all who since, baptized or infidel,
> Jousted in Aspramont, or Montalban,
> Damasco, or Marocco, or Trebisond;
> Or whom Biserta sent from Afric shore
> When Charlemain with all his peerage fell
> By Fontarabbia.

> Of Cambalu, seat of Cathaian Can,
> And Samarchand by Oxus, Temir's throne,
> To Paquin of Sinaean kings, and thence
> To Agra and Lahor of Great Mogul,
> Down to the golden Chersonese, or where
> The Persian in Ecbatan sat, or since
> In Hispahan, or where the Russian Ksar
> In Mosco, or the Sultan in Bizance.[3]

9. UNUSUAL COMPOUND EPITHETS, formations probably borrowed from Homer, and much more frequent in *Comus* than in the later poems. Typical examples are "sail-broad vans," "high-climbing hill," "arch-chemic sun," "half-rounding guards," "night-warbling bird," "love-labour'd song," "seven-times-wedded maid," "sky-tinctured grain," "three-bolted thunder," "Heaven-banish'd host,"

---

[1] i. 6–7, 236–7; ii. 404–5, 407, 842; iii. 643; ii. 439; iii. 231; ix. 28; x. 281; xi. 373–4.

[2] Milton has "ambrosial" 13 times, "chaos" 25, "adamant" or "adamantine" 11, "ethereal" 25, "void" 15, "abyss" 19, "umbrageous" 1, "embattled" 5, "amarant" or "amaranthine" 2.

[3] i. 579–87; xi. 388–95 (this roll of names continues for sixteen more lines). Cf. also i. 392–521, 576–9; ix. 77–82, 505–10; x. 431–6, 695–706, etc.

"shape star-bright," "joint-racking rheums," "double-founted stream." [1]

Three other characteristics of *Paradise Lost*, though worth mentioning because they are generally overlooked, are so common in earlier poetry as to be, in my opinion, of no value in determining influence. One of them, which must have pleased Milton's ear (since it occurs frequently in all his poems) and which may have had something to do with his puns,[2] is the INTENTIONAL REPETITION of a word or a phrase:

> And feel by turns the bitter change
> Of fierce extremes, extremes by change more fierce.

> So he with difficulty and labour hard
> Moved on: with difficulty and labour he.[3]

A second feature of Milton's style which is also to be found in the work of his predecessors is the use of an UNINTERRUPTED SERIES OF WORDS in the same construction, — participles, adjectives, verbs, substantives, etc.:

> Unrespited, unpitied, unreprieved.

> Exhausted, spiritless, afflicted, fall'n.

> But apparent guilt,
> And shame, and perturbation, and despair,
> Anger, and obstinacy, and hate, and guile.[4]

Such series are not frequent in *Paradise Lost*, however, and might be used independently of Milton.

A third characteristic of *Paradise Lost* which might perhaps appear in any writer whether he knew the epic or not, but which is apt to gives lines a Miltonic ring, is the use of ADJECTIVES IN -EAN OR -IAN from proper nouns. Some examples are Memphian, Ausonian, Atlantean, Serbonian, Cerberean, Trinacrian, Ammonian, Philistean, Cronian, Cathaian, Memnonian, Bactrian, Plutonian, Dictaean, Thyestean.

---

[1] ii. 927; iii. 546, 609; iv. 862; v. 40, 41, 223, 285; vi. 764; x. 437, 450; xi. 488; xii. 144. Laura E. Lockwood's *Milton Lexicon* (N. Y., 1907), pp. 667–71, lists all the words hyphenated in the original text.

[2] See, for example, iv. 181 ("at one slight bound high overleap'd all bound"), v. 583–4 ("the empyreal host Of Angels, by imperial summons call'd"), vi. 383–4 ("to glory aspires, Vain-glorious").

[3] ii. 598–9, 1021–2. Cf. also ii. 618–25; iii. 188–93, 446–8, 645–6; v. 146, 791–2; vi. 244–5. In iv. 639–58 and x. 1086–1104 passages of some length are repeated.

[4] ii. 185 (cf. iii. 372–5, v. 898–9); vi. 852; x. 112–14. Cf. also ii. 618–28, 947–50; iii. 489–93; iv. 344; v. 772; vii. 502–3.

It is not through oversight that nothing has been said of Milton's prosody. Master as he was of all the resources of verse, he was less an innovator in "numbers" than in other things. Every important characteristic of his versification which is capable of being defined, isolated, and catalogued is to be found in the plays of Shakespeare and the lesser Elizabethans. Peculiarities of *Paradise Lost* that seem to be due to its prosody will, when examined more closely, be seen to lie in other categories. True, Milton's verse is in general less flowing, less conversational, and more exalted than that of the dramatists, but does not this difference spring from the nine qualities we have just been examining? The remarkable freedom, flexibility, and variety that characterize his prosody he secured by constantly using run-over lines, by moving the cesural pause from one part of the line to another, by inverting the metrical accent through the substitution of trochaic for iambic feet, by slighting one or more of the metrical accents in nearly every line, and by shifting the location of those he slighted. Yet, as all these devices are used by Shakespeare, they are of no assistance in tracing Milton's influence.

The features of *Paradise Lost* that have been listed include by no means all of its characteristics, but they are all I have found to be useful in detecting the influence of the poem. In fact, a number of them are by themselves of no account. A work may be dignified and reserved, may contain unusual Greek or Latin words or unusual compound epithets and make frequent use of parentheses and appositives, and yet not be Miltonic; but if we are sure on other grounds that it has been influenced by *Paradise Lost* the presence of these qualities will show the extent of the influence, and if we are doubtful their presence will help settle the matter. The frequency with which they occur is naturally an all-important matter. An occasional inversion, an adjective used now and then for an adverb or a noun, a few words employed in obsolete senses, these may be found in almost any poem and hence are of no significance. To give a piece the Miltonic ring they must be fairly common.

But does the presence of these qualities, however frequently they occur, necessarily prove the influence of *Paradise Lost?* May they not have been derived from other poems or have been hit upon by some writers quite independently? Some of them may have been, and are therefore, as has been said, of slight value in establishing influence. A considerable number, however, — and it is upon these that the burden of proof rests, — cannot in the eighteenth century very well have been derived from any source but *Paradise Lost*. True, the same qualities may occasionally be found in the other poetry with which the Augustans were familiar, but they are not so common as to make any impression or have any influence. Besides, since rimed and unrimed poetry were so far apart, Miltonic characteristics when they occur in blank verse were probably derived from blank verse, that is, from the writings of Milton or his imitators; and what likelier source could there be than the widely-read and universally-admired work which every one regarded as the model for all unrimed poetry?

It must always be remembered that many earlier writers who are familiar enough to us, poets who have furnished inspiration and guidance to nearly every singer from Keats to Bridges, were in the eighteenth century either unknown or unregarded. Aside from Sidney, Spenser, Shakespeare, and Milton, most English writers before Dryden meant little or nothing to the contemporaries of Pope and Johnson.[1] Chaucer and Donne they knew to some extent, but mainly as curiosities; Ben Jonson they talked about, and Beaumont and Fletcher they occasionally read; but the work of none of these men made much impression on them, for in order to exert an influence a poem must be both familiar and popular. Furthermore, much of the literature they really knew they made very little use of, for in Augustan times poetry ran in a narrow groove which few cared either to widen or to get out of. Writers did not seek the strange and unusual, they did not like novel effects. They had much to say of Homer and Pindar, but copied them very little; when it came to writing they followed one another or contemporary Frenchmen. Horace and Virgil, to be sure, they did admire and follow; but they did not imitate Pindar, they imitated Cowley's imitation of Pindar. True, during the latter half of the century interest in the life and literatures of earlier times and other peoples greatly increased; yet even then the models upon which poetry was written remained much the same,—there was still the school of Pope, the school of Milton, the school of Spenser. The relative importance of these groups had changed, but there were no new names. Thomas Warton, for example, notwithstanding his familiarity with literature ranging from the twelfth century to the seventeenth, wrote verses little affected by any one who lived in this long period except Spenser. One might expect to find lyrics modelled after those of Carew, Suckling, or Herrick, sonnets that copied those of the Elizabethans, fantastic conceits from Donne, a new Canterbury tale, a medieval debate or romance. Instead, we have poems usually more romantic in subject and treatment than those of the Augustans, but still following the

[1] See below, pp. 480–82.

same models and still scarcely touched by any work of Shakespeare's contemporaries or predecessors except the *Faerie Queene*.

Fortunately for our present purposes, the eighteenth-century writers show little of the complexity and subtlety of influence which mark more recent literature. If the broad knowledge, the eclectic tastes, the love of unusual effects, that belong to the nineteenth century had been equally characteristic of the eighteenth, the present study would have been vastly more difficult and its results far more vague, unsatisfactory, and inconclusive.

CHAPTER V

THE INFLUENCE BEFORE THOMSON, 1667–1720

It was thirteen years after the appearance of *Paradise Lost* before the publication of another poem without rime.[1] Except for being in blank verse, this piece gives no evidence of Milton's influence, but five years later, in 1685, some lines which do show it appeared from the same pen. Milton was fortunate in his first follower, who was no other than the Earl of Roscommon, nephew of the Earl of Strafford. Roscommon was not only a person of rank, but a poet highly esteemed in Augustan circles; his life was written by Johnson and his verse appeared in all the great collections of English poetry published in the eighteenth and early nineteenth centuries. His reputation, however, always rested largely upon one work, a poetical *Essay on Translated Verse* (1684). This famous piece, though written in couplets, contains a strong plea for discarding rime, and in the second edition (1685) concludes with twenty-seven lines in acknowledged imitation of *Paradise Lost*. Here are the first ten:

> Have we forgot how *Raphaels* Num'rous Prose
> Led our exalted Souls through heavenly Camps,
> And mark'd the ground where proud Apostate Thrones,
> Defy'd *Jehovah!* Here, 'twixt Host and Host,
> (A narrow but a dreadful Interval)
> Portentous sight! before the Cloudy van,
> Satan with vast and haughty Strides advanc'd,
> Came tow'ring arm'd in Adamant and Gold.
> There Bellowing Engines, with their fiery Tubes,
> Dispers'd Æthereal forms.

The contents and diction of this passage were undoubtedly derived from *Paradise Lost*, but the style was not, nor was the prosody, for in most of the lines one expects rime and is somewhat disturbed by its absence. This means ti.at Roscommon had freed himself but slightly from the end-stopped lines, the regular, equal stresses, the few internal pauses (and most of those near the middle of the lines), which mark the heroic couplet.

---

[1] This work, *Horace's Art of Poetry* (1680), was quoted on p. 79 above. The idea of discarding rime was undoubtedly derived from *Paradise Lost*.

On the other hand, Milton's unusual versification was what particularly attracted one of Roscommon's contemporaries, Samuel Say, and led him to some unusual ideas of prosody which he exemplified in blank-verse translations of four of Horace's epistles (1698) and later set forth in two essays, one *On the Numbers of Paradise Lost*.[1] Most of Say's pieces are, like this passage, comparatively simple and natural in style:

> Or in some Grove retir'd
> Thou walk'st Unseen; in Contemplation high
> Rais'd up above the World, and seest beneath,
> Compassionate, the Cares and fond Designs
> Of restless Mortals, always in pursuit
> Of what they always have; still heaping up
> Stores to be us'd, yet never use their Stores.[2]

Occasionally, however, there will be a line as Miltonic as,

> But if Behind
> You loiter far, or strenuous run Before.[3]

The early influence of *Paradise Lost* was, however, by no means limited to blank-verse poetry; it was, indeed, more obvious in the interminable rimed epics of Sir Richard Blackmore. Of this writer it may be said that few men of so little consequence have been abused by so many illustrious pens. Dryden, Pope, Swift, Gay, Garth, Sedley, Steele, and many lesser men each had his fling at the physician-poet, who long remained a target for the shafts of his literary brethren.[4] As late as 1762 Robert Lloyd referred to his

> Heroic poems without number,
> Long, lifeless, leaden, lulling lumber,[5]

[1] This essay, the earliest work of its kind (written in 1737), is published with one *On the Harmony, Variety, and Power of Numbers, whether in Prose or Verse*, and with some unrimed lyrics suggested by Milton's translations from Horace (see pp. 563-4 below), in *Poems and Two Critical Essays* (written in 1698, but not printed till 1745), 139-71, 95-136, 1-26.

[2] *To Thomas Godfrey* (*ib.* 24).

[3] *Epistles of Horace*, i. 2 (*ib.* 17). It was in 1698 that the astronomer, Walter Pope, published his *Moral and Political Fables, done into Measured Prose intermixed with Ryme*. I have not seen the work; but, according to Mr. Saintsbury (*English Prosody*, ii. 499), "the quality of its blank verse appears to be pretty accurately designated in the title," a remark that certainly applies to *The Wish*, which Pope issued the year before.

[4] Many of these poetical tributes are quoted in Birkbeck Hill's notes to Johnson's life of Blackmore, or are referred to in the *Dictionary of National Biography*. An entire volume of satirical "Commendatory Verses" appeared in 1700 and was reprinted in 1702. The most amusing of the Blackmore squibs is Gay's rimed catalog of the works of "England's arch-poet" (*Verses under the Picture of Blackmore*), which is erroneously included among Swift's poems (cf. Pope to Jervas, Nov. 14, 1716).

[5] *On Rhyme*, in *Poetical Works* (1774), ii. 114. Cf. the elder Thomas Warton's *Poems* (1748), 20.

lines that contain more truth than satire, for Blackmore had neither
inspiration nor taste, but jingled along with complete self-confidence
in the monotonous jog-trot of an overworked cab-horse. He was
capable not only of writing an epic with the title *Eliza*, but of putting
into it lines like these:

> The *Spaniard's* Nose receiv'd the Fauchion's Edge,
> Which did in sunder cut the rising Bridge.
> The Blood that follow'd part distain'd his Breast,
> And trickling down his Throat ran inwardly the rest.[1]

A partial excuse for such deficiencies is to be found in the circumstances under which the poems were composed, their author being a
busy, middle-aged London doctor, the physician to King William,
with little time for literature. "For the greatest part," so he informed his readers, his first epic ". . . was written in *Coffee-
houses*, and in passing up and down the Streets," because he had
"little leisure elsewhere to apply to it."[2] This work, *Prince Arthur,
an Heroick Poem in ten Books* (1695), was followed by three others,
King Arthur (1697) in twelve books, *Eliza* (1705) in ten, and *Alfred*
(1723) in twelve, besides many pieces of a less heroic character, some
in prose, some in verse. In the preface to *King Arthur* Blackmore
terms Milton "a very Extraordinary *Genius*" and acknowledges
having made "a few allusions" to some of his "*Inventions*,"[3] — a
very modest confession of many unmistakable plagiarisms.

As a matter of fact, the first three epics (which differ little except
in the names of the characters) are under a considerable debt to
Paradise Lost, since they employ Satan and his followers, together
with the archangels of heaven, for their supernatural machinery.
The plan of each poem is much like that of the *Aeneid*. At the beginning, Satan, jealous of the prosperity of the hero (or the heroine),
summons a council in hell and lays the matter before the peers.
After various spirits have made speeches, it is agreed to send one of
the number to stir up trouble for the principal character of the poem,
who, however, by the aid of Uriel and other angels passes victori-
ously through all the plots and gory battles. These councils in hell
form the most Miltonic feature of the epics, for, although there may
be several of them in a single poem, the characteristics of the speakers and of their proposals are invariably taken almost without

---

[1] Page 106.

[2] *King Arthur*, p. v.

[3] *Ib*. xiii. Blackmore praised Milton in his *Nature of Man* (*Collection of Poems*, 1718,
p. 193; cf. Good, p. 63). His Pindaric *Hymn to the Light of the World* seems, particularly at the beginning, to attempt the lofty style and diction of *Paradise Lost*.

change from the great assembly in Pandemonium. In *Eliza*, for example, the principal debate of the fiends proceeds as follows:

> *Chemosh* arose, a Prince of great Renown,
> No bolder Chief assail'd th' Almighty's Throne;
> Scarce greater Deeds by *Satan's* Arms were done.
> Deform'd with Seams and Ignominious Scars,
> From ghastly Wounds receiv'd in Heav'nly Wars;
> Above the Demons that compos'd the Crowd,
> The Potentate, Majestick Ruin, stood. . .
> He ceas'd: Then *Baal* did with Choler swell,
> A fiercer Spirit was not found in Hell . . .
> And thus th' Infernal Dyet he address'd. . . .
> Tho' disappointed oft, I still declare
> For bold Attempts in Arms, and glorious War. . . .
> He ceas'd, and *Dagon* rose, a Prince serene,
> Of Aspect mild, and of a winning Mein. . . .
> He still preserv'd a wond'rous pleasing Air,
> Graceful in Torment, in Perdition, fair. . . .
> Thus he began, *Seraphs*, I speak my Mind
> With Deference due to Spirits more refin'd;
> Of clearer Judgment, and of greater Weight,
> More able in the Business of the State. . . .
> Why should we fruitless War and Strife repeat?
> Can all our Force Omnipotence defeat? [1]

But these Stygian councils are only one of Blackmore's many borrowings from Milton. In *King Arthur* there is an account of Satan's flight through chaos to the earth; [2] in *Eliza* the entire history of his revolt and of the battles in heaven is given, and there are allusions, in other connections, to the use of cannon in the celestial warfare and to the wounds inflicted by "Victorious Michael's Steel"; [3] while in *Prince Arthur* Christ appears in a triumphal chariot to end the war of the angels, Satan's "faded Splendor and illustrious Scars" and the storm of fire that pursued him to hell are mentioned, there is another description of the Miltonic chaos with an account of the strife between the atoms, a reference to angels' crowns wreathed with gold and amarant, and one to Sin and Death, as well as other borrowings.[4] Furthermore, when Blackmore deals with supernatural characters his diction is decidedly Miltonic. Empyreal, adamant, adamantine, massy, refulgent, cerulean, tartarean, are words that occur frequently, and the use of adjectives in *-ean* or *-ian* derived

---

[1] Pages 12–16 *passim.*   [2] Page 150.   [3] Pages 205–8, 11, 2.

[4] Pages 5, 8 (cf. *King Arthur*, 152), 36–7, 43, 47. Note also page 22, where a huge fury suddenly contracts her size, as do the demons in Pandemonium; and page 243, where Satan assumes the appearance of a beautiful young angel. The names of Blackmore's angels are taken from *Paradise Lost.*

from proper nouns becomes almost a mannerism with him. In one place he has six in seven lines,[1] and he is never long without one. Not only do we have Cyclopian, Herculean, Bolerian, Dobunian, Catuclanian, Ottadenian, Durotrigian, and hundreds more of the same kind, but we meet such unexpected manufactures as Vulcanian, Ætnean, Ithacian, Arragonian, Nassovian (from Nassau), Pightlandian, and Laplandian. Although Blackmore wrote too rapidly and knew too little of *Paradise Lost* to follow it closely,[2] a careful reading of his works would probably reveal a number of verbal borrowings. The few I have noticed are dubious.[3] On the whole, however, when it is remembered that the epics are in rime, that they began to appear only twenty-eight years after the publication of *Paradise Lost*, and that they are anything but dignified or sublime in style, it will be seen that their debt to Milton is considerable.

The first great protagonist of *Paradise Lost* was not Addison but the forgotten John Dennis. As the enthusiasm which the poem roused in this sturdy inventor of stage thunder cropped out in all his critical writing, one is not surprised to find it affecting his verse. That it did so he was himself the first to point out; for he explained in the preface to his *Court of Death* (1695, an irregular ode on the death of Queen Mary), "In the writing these Pindarick Verses, I had still *Milton* in my Eye, and was resolv'd to imitate him as far as it could be done without receeding from *Pindar's* manner." The attempt to combine Milton and Pindar as models probably arose from Dennis's desire for sublimity, the quality in poetry that he admired above all others and the one for which he persistently but vainly strove in his own productions. As the style and prosody of *Paradise Lost* are hardly transferable to a rimed ode, he could borrow only words, phrases, and ideas, but all of these he took. The *Court of Death* describes a visit to the lower world and to a Stygian assembly much like that held in Pandemonium, over which Death, who shakes "a dreadful Dart," presides.[4] Such expressions as "Empyrean Lyre," "Adamantine Chains," "Silence was ravish'd as she sung," "their formidable King the great Consult began," "the

---

[1] *King Arthur*, pp. 56–7.

[2] The invention of cannon, for example, he attributes (*Eliza*, p. 11) to the celestial angels instead of to Satan's forces.

[3] "The Eternal's Co-eternal Son" (*Eliza*, p. 4, cf. *P. L.*, iii. 2); the picture of God's throne shining "with excessive Brightness" (*Prince Arthur*, p. 43, cf. *P. L.*, iii. 380); and the account of filling the sun, originally a "spungy globe," with light, — "The thirsty Orb drinks in the liquid Beams" (*ib.* 38, cf. *P. L.*, vii. 361–2).

[4] Section vii.

griesly Terror spoke," "Discord . . . Thro all her thousand Mouths," show the debt to Milton's phrasing.[1]

"Through the reigns of William and Anne," observes Johnson, "no prosperous event passed undignified by poetry." [2] Dennis had already broken into song on three public occasions, and four others were to arise to call forth his efforts. Between his earlier and his later productions, however, there is one significant difference, — the earlier are pindaric odes, the later are without rime. It is convenient to speak of these last pieces as written in blank verse, although the meter of none of Dennis's work really deserves that name. Like Roscommon, he either disregarded or did not understand the fundamental principles of Milton's prosody, and in consequence most of his lines are nothing but heroic couplets without the rime. It is not improbable, indeed, that one reason for his discarding rime was to save himself trouble. There seems to be nothing Miltonic about his earliest attempt at blank verse, *The Monument* (1702), in which the death of King William is lamented through sixty pages, or about his last unrimed eulogy, *On the Accession of King George* (1714). Between these panegyrics came his poems on Blenheim and Ramellies (1704, 1706), which together fill nearly one hundred and seventy pages with bombastic platitude, and recall Dryden's regret over another English victory because of the amount of bad verse it would call forth. In style, language, syntax, and prosody neither of these efforts shows much Miltonic influence, though inversions are frequent, adjectives are occasionally used for adverbs, and some unusual words and borrowed phrases are to be found.[3] Few passages are even so much like *Paradise Lost* as this:

> The *French* were all of *Gallick* Troops the Flow'r,
> Experienc'd and Victorious were their Chiefs,
> Soldiers and Chiefs inur'd to vast Success:
> And claiming Right to Conquest and Renown,

---

[1] Sections ii, vi, ii (cf. *P. L.*, iv. 504, and *Comus*, 557–60), v (cf. *P. L.*, i. 798), vii (cf. *P. L.*, ii. 704), x (cf. *P. L.*, ii. 967).

[2] "Prior," in *Lives* (ed. Hill), ii. 186.

[3] A few of his obvious borrowings from Milton are: "swinging slow with hoarse and sullen Roar" (*Blenheim*, in *Works*, 1718, i. 160, cf. *Penseroso*, 76); "Italia! Ah how fall'n, how chang'd from her, Who" (*ib.* 176, cf. *P. L.*, i. 84–5); "raise my advent'rous Song" (*ib.* 196; cf. *P. L.*, i. 13); "Instruct me, Goddess, for Thou only know'st" (*ib.* 196, cf. *P. L.*, i. 17–19); "Collected in himself, a while he stood" (*Ramellies*, *ib.* 235, cf. *P. L.*, ix. 673); "as a Flock of tim'rous Fowl" (*ib.* 245, cf. *P. L.*, vi. 856–7); "the midmost Regions of the Air" (*ib.* 245, 256, cf. *P. R.*, ii. 117); "the stedfast Empyrean" (*ib.* 255, cf. also 299, and *P. L.*, vi. 833, iii. 57); "Down tow'rds the Earth she wheel'd her airy Flight" (*ib.* 256, cf. *P. L.*, iii. 739–41). Four lines of *Blenheim* (*ib.* 213) are devoted to the praise of Milton.

From long Possession; with their dearest Blood
Resolv'd their lofty Title to defend.
By long Success presumptuous grown and vain.[1]

The *Battle of Ramillia* not only is in blank verse but makes use of the Miltonic machinery. It opens with a council of infernal spirits summoned by Satan to his palace (hung between the moon and the earth) to devise means of thwarting the progress of Goodness and Queen Anne. The long and insulting speech of "Hell's black Tyrant" is roundly answered by Discord, who offers to go to the aid of King Louis; her plan is accepted and the assembly dismissed. This gathering recalls the council in Pandemonium, but is closer to the one described in the second book of *Paradise Regained*, where the meeting-place is similar. Still more like Milton is the scene in heaven with which Dennis's fourth book opens, for here the Eternal Father calls the attention of the Son to the machinations of the evil one and sends an angel to thwart them.[2]

It is doubtful whether these poems were ever much read; certainly they are quite unreadable to-day, — dull, tumid, false, lacking in grace and fluency as well as in the Augustan virtues of wit and finish. Yet Dennis was the most extensive writer of blank verse between Milton and Thomson, and, with the exception of Addison, probably did more than any other one man to establish the reputation of *Paradise Lost*.

The councils of fallen spirits that found favor with Blackmore and Dennis also play an important part in two pieces which were published the same year, 1702, under the same name, *The Vision*. One of these is in rime till the appearance of Urania, who, casting aside "that false *jingling Chime*," describes an assembly in Pandemonium of the fallen angels mentioned in *Paradise Lost*, at which Belial proposes, as he does in *Paradise Regained*, to ruin man through lust.[3] This *Vision* is anonymous, as the second might about as well be, for the poet's name is given as "M. Smith." The author imagines that he is carried through the Miltonic chaos (where he observes the

---

[1] *Blenheim, ib.* 190–91.

[2] Cf. *P. L.,* iii. 56–415, v. 219–90. The fourth and ninth books of the *Gierusalemme Liberata*, which Dennis admired, describe scenes in heaven and hell, but his work is not so close to them as to the similar passages in *Paradise Lost*. Furthermore, his diction when he deals with the supernatural is decidedly Miltonic. Translations from the *Gierusalemme* into Miltonic blank verse, with inversions not in the original, are introduced into his *Grounds of Criticism in Poetry,* 1704 (*Works,* ii. 436, 448–50; and compare the translation from Homer on 453 with *P. L.,* vii. 410–12).

[3] Charles Gildon, *Examen Miscellaneum* (1702), 51 ff., first pagination; cf. *P. R.,* ii. 150 ff. See above, p. 51, n. 1, where an attack on rime is quoted from the same volume.

war of the atoms), past the gates of hell "of nine-fold Adamant" (guarded by Sin, the 'offspring of Satan's brain'), to a great palace where the evil spirits are assembled. After "Silence was bid,"

> The awful Monarch from his Seat did rise,
> And having roul'd about his Baleful Eyes,
> He said
> Great Princes, Virtues, Dominations, Pow'rs;
> Once Potentates of Heav'n; no longer ours:
> Such the Almighty's Thunder prov'd, unknown,
> Till we attempted the Imperial Throne
> Of Heav'n. Tho great, yet Glorious was our Fall . . .
> But more, Ambitious Minds like mine 'twill please
> To Reign in Torment, then to serve in Ease.[1]

Is it any wonder that Mr. Smith feared he should be called "a Plagiary, for taking some Hints from Milton"? [2]

The first Milton enthusiast seems to have been John Philips, who when still a schoolboy liked to sit and read *Paradise Lost* while his long hair was being combed.[3] At Oxford he "studied" his favorite poet "with Application, and trac'd him in all his successful Translations from the Ancients. There was not an Allusion in his *Poem*, drawn from the Thoughts, or Expressions of HOMER or VIRGIL, which he could not immediately refer to." [4] The fruits of this devotion are to be seen in a parody which was published anonymously in 1701 with the title *Imitation of Milton*,[5] but which four years later appeared over the author's name as the *Splendid Shilling*. This short piece quickly became popular and long remained so. By 1720 it had been printed, either by itself or in miscellanies, as many as nine times, and had been lauded in the *Tatler* by Addison as "the finest burlesque poem in the British language." [6] Later in the century Goldsmith wrote of it, "This is reckoned the best parody of Milton in our language: it has been an hundred times imitated, without success." [7] It was also praised by Cowper and Crabbe, and was twice translated into Latin.[8] This is the beginning:

---

[1] Pages 23–49. The author — who proves to be the Rev. Matthew Smith, a nonconformist minister of Mixenden, Yorkshire — uses such words as "appetency," "adamantine," "lucid," "orient," "refulgent."

[2] "To the Reader." A council of devils in William Shippen's rimed *Moderation Display'd* (1704) may also owe something to Milton.

[3] *Dict. Nat. Biog.*   [4] *Life* [by George Sewell], 1712, p. 3.

[5] Charles Gildon, *New Miscellany of Original Poems* (1701), 212–21. The *Imitation* is also somewhat like Horace's second epode.

[6] No. 249, Nov. 11, 1710.

[7] *Beauties of English Poesy* (1767), i. 255.

[8] *The Task*, iii. 455–6; *The Borough*, xi. 9. The Latin versions are Thomas Tyrwhitt's *Splendens Solidus* (in his *Translations in Verse*, Oxford, 1747, the text being

Happy the Man, who void of Cares and Strife,
In Silken or in Leathern Purse retains
A Splendid Shilling; he nor hears with Pain
New Oysters cry'd, nor sighs for chearful Ale;
But with his Friends, when Night[l]y Mists arise,
To *Juniper's*, or *Magpye*, or *Town-Hall* repairs.

An idea of how Miltonic the style is may be gathered from these
lines near the end:

My *Galligaskins* that have long withstood
The Winter's Fury, and encroaching Frosts,
By time subdu'd, (what will not time subdue!)
A Horrid Chasm disclose, with Orifice
Wide, discontinuous; at which the Winds
Eurus and *Auster*, and the dreadful Force
Of *Boreas*, that congeals the *Cronian* Waves,
Tumultuous enter with dire chilling Blasts.

It must not be thought that any slight upon *Paradise Lost* was
intended by the parody; Philips's humor was simply the playfulness
of an admiring friend. His attitude towards "his darling Milton"[1]
is expressed in no uncertain terms in a later poem:

Oh, had but He that first ennobled Song
With holy Raptures, like his *Abdiel* been,
'Mong many faithless, strictly faithful found;
Unpity'd, he should not have wail'd his Orbs,
That roll'd in vain to find the piercing Ray,
And found no Dawn, by dim Suffusion veil'd!
But He — However, let the Muse abstain,
Nor blast his Fame, from whom she learnt to sing
In much inferior Strains, grov'ling beneath
Th' *Olympian* Hill, on Plains, and Vales intent,
Mean Follower.[2]

All of his poems, furthermore, as he himself points out in every case
but one, are "in imitation of Milton."[3] They include a tumid piece
on the battle of Blenheim (1705), which is no worse than such poems
usually are; *Cerealia* (1706), a Miltonic parody devoted to the
praise of ale, which, though published anonymously and not printed
over Philips's name until 1780, is in all probability his;[4] and *Cyder*

almost identical with that of the *Splendens Nummus* in Edward Popham's *Selecta
Poemata*, Bath, 1776, iii. 101–7), and an anonymous *Nummus Splendidus* appended to
the Latin translation of Gray's elegy made by Christopher Anstey and W. H. Roberts
in 1778.
[1] Sewell's *Life*, 3.   [2] *Cyder*, i. 785–95.
[3] See the full titles of the *Splendid Shilling* and *Cerealia*, and the third line of *Cyder*.
[4] John Nichols (*Collection of Poems*, 1780, iv. 274 n.) refers to a copy of the 1706
edition in the Lambeth library "in which the name of Philips was inserted in the hand-

(January, 1707/8), a georgic in two books, which treats in detail of the care of orchards and the making of cider.[1] In style and diction all his works are alike, for the exaggerated Miltonisms which he introduced into the *Splendid Shilling* for the sake of humor Philips never shook off. Indeed, he probably regarded them as beauties, or at least as essentials to blank verse, although to the modern ear they make all his verse sound like parody. The following description of the making of cider, which is typical of his principal work, will show how grotesque some of his "imitations" are:

> Now exhort
> Thy Hinds to exercise the pointed Steel
> On the hard Rock, and give a wheely Form
> To the expected Grinder: Now prepare
> Materials for thy Mill, a sturdy Post
> *Cylindric*, to support the Grinder's Weight
> Excessive, and a flexile Sallow' entrench'd,
> Rounding, capacious of the juicy Hord.
> Nor must thou not be mindful of thy Press
> Long e'er the Vintage; but with timely Care
> Shave the Goat's shaggy Beard, least thou too late
> In vain should'st seek a Strainer, to dispart
> The husky, terrene Dregs, from purer Must.[2]

Philips's debt to his "darling" was not limited to style and diction. The opening of *Cerealia* is clearly based on that of *Paradise Lost*, and there are many phrases, like "buxom air," "impresses quaint emblazon'd," "bedropt with gold," "with speed succinct," and "bold emprise," taken from the same source.[3] In *Cyder*, Miltonic borrowing begins with the fourth line and riots throughout the poem. Besides saying that a river "drew her humid Train," and speaking of the "volant Touch" of a musician and of "Pearl and Barbaric Gold," [4] Philips introduces whole lines from *Paradise Lost*:

writing of Abp. Tennison," and adds, "It was published by T. Bennet, the Bookseller for whom *Blenheim* was printed." The style, diction, and prosody are Philips's, the subject-matter suggests the *Splendid Shilling* and *Cyder*, and the poem reveals a familiarity with Milton unusual at that time.

[1] To Philips have also been attributed *The Fall of Chloe's Piss-pot* [*Jordan*], first printed in the *London Magazine* for February, 1754; and *Ramelies*, published anonymously in 1706 and reprinted as Philips's in Alexander Harrach's *John Philips* (Kreuznach, 1906, pp. 111–21). Neither piece, however, shows the prosody, the language, or the style of Philips. Dr. Harrach also reprints (pp. 96–110, and see 64–71) *The Sylvan Dream, or the Mourning Muses* (1701), because on the title-page of the British Museum copy the name "John Philips" is written. But there is no other reason (except a possible borrowing from *Comus*, see below, p. 429, n. 1) for thinking that this dull, conventional work, partly in heroic couplets and partly in Pindarics, is from the pen that wrote the *Splendid Shilling* and *Cyder*.   [2] *Cyder*, ii. 78–90.

[3] Cf. *P. L.*, ii. 842, v. 270; ix. 34–5; vii. 406, x. 527; iii. 643; xi. 642.

[4] i. 205 (cf. *P. L.*, vii. 306); ii. 424 (cf. *P. L.*, xi. 561); ii. 657 (cf. *P. L.*, ii. 4).

Adventrous I presume to sing; of Verse
Nor skill'd, nor studious.

Till, with a writhen Mouth, and spattering Noise,
He tastes the bitter Morsel, and rejects
Disrelisht.

If no Retinue . . .
Dazle the Croud, and set them all agape.

Berries, and Sky-dy'd Plums, and what in Coat
Rough, or soft Rind, or bearded Husk, or Shell.

Maladies, that lead to Death's grim Cave,
Wrought by Intemperance, joint-racking Gout,
Intestine Stone, and pining Atrophy.[1]

There were some who did not relish the Philipian variety of Miltonic language and style. Blackmore assailed the 'harsh numbers,' "uncouth Strains," and 'tortured language' of *Bleinheim*;[2] while Pope declared, "Philips, in his Cyder, has succeeded extremely well in his imitation of it [Milton's style], but was quite wrong in endeavouring to imitate it on such a subject."[3] Johnson, who admired the *Splendid Shilling*, wrote, "Whatever there is in Milton which the reader wishes away, all that is obsolete, peculiar, or licentious is accumulated with great care by Philips."[4]

Yet such adverse judgments were rare. The poet's biographer had "never heard but of One" faultfinder;[5] and even Johnson inserted into his life of Edmund Smith a quotation which speaks of Philips as "that second Milton, whose writings will last as long as the English language, generosity, and valour."[6] His acknowledged works were, indeed, very popular. Not only did the *Splendid Shilling* have an unusual vogue, but *Bleinheim* reached its sixth edition in 1720, *Cyder* its fourth in 1728, and the three together saw what was called the tenth edition in 1744.[7] If they have not fulfilled a contemporary

---

[1] i. 4–5 (cf. *P. L.*, i. 13, and ix. 41–2); i. 447–9 (cf. *P. L.*, x. 566–9, said of eating fruit in each case); i. 741–4 (cf. *P. L.*, v. 355–7); ii. 53–4 (cf. *P. L.*, v. 341–2); ii. 471–3 (cf. *P. L.*, xi. 467–88).

[2] *Advice to the Poets* (2d ed., 1706), 10. Note that Philips's title is *Bleinheim*, not *Blenheim*.

[3] Spence's *Anecdotes* (ed. Singer, 1820), 174.

[4] "Philips," in *Lives* (ed. Hill), i. 318. Charles Gildon declared (*Laws of Poetry*, 1721, p. 321) that, except for the *Splendid Shilling*, Philips "never did any thing . . . worth looking on."

[5] Sewell's *Life*, 27 (the one critic was Blackmore). *Cyder* is criticized, though perhaps humorously, in a passage in Gay's *Wine*, 1708 (lines 114–20 of the Muses' Library edition), which praises *Bleinheim*.

[6] *Lives* (ed. Hill), ii. 7.

[7] Some of these editions were not entirely new; the first issue of *Cyder*, for example, formed part of the *Whole Works* (1720). Within four months of the publication of

prediction that they would "live . . . as long as *Blenheim* is remember'd, or *Cyder* drunk in *England*," [1] two of them, *Cyder* and the
Splendid Shilling, continued to be read at least to the end of the century. The *Critical Review* declared in 1762 that the two poems were
"sufficient to eternize the memory" of their author; [2] and on the
appearance of *The Task* the *Gentleman's Magazine* hailed Cowper as
"perhaps, without excepting even Philips, the most successful of the
imitators of Milton." [3] Not only did an Italian translation of *Cyder*
go through two editions (1749, 1752), but the original poem was
edited with an imposing array of "notes provincial, historical, and
classical" in 1791, and as late as 1804 a critic of good standing wrote
that it still maintained "a respectable place among compositions of
its class." [4] This popularity makes Philips a much more important
writer than has been realized. Although far from being a great poet,
he was influential: to his example are to be referred most of the unrimed burlesques, the technical treatises, and the humorous poems
on liquor that were popular in the eighteenth century. Furthermore, as the only widely-read writer of blank verse before Thomson,
he helped to endow the new measure with what none of his contemporaries were able to give it, popularity. Milton, Roscommon, and
Dennis had gained respect for it, and lesser men had made the public
somewhat accustomed to it, but most of their productions found few
readers and fewer admirers. Philips did much to bring blank verse
"out of closets and libraries, schools and colleges, to dwell in clubs
and assemblies, at tea-tables and in coffee-houses," and through his
influence on Thomson he became a figure of unquestionable significance in the development of English poetry.

The blank verse produced by Daniel Defoe fell as far short of

---

Cyder, Gay's imitation of it, *Wine*, appeared (see pp. 107–8 below); and during the
following year, 1709, some unknown bard put forth *Milton's Sublimity asserted in a
Poem occasion'd by a late celebrated Piece entituled Cyder*. This curious and confused
production criticises Philips for debasing Milton's verse, the writer (whose sanity is
open to question) apparently not realizing that, since his poem also is in Miltonic blank
verse and his theme far from exalted, he is doing the very thing for which he blames
Philips. He refers in the preface to "the fam'd Author of that idoliz'd piece, *Cyder*,"
and adds, "I do not think there is any Work extant, that hath alarm'd the World more
than his; and bin I may say, some years so much the talk and hopes of the Publick."

[1] Henry Felton, *Dissertation on Reading the Classics* (5th ed., 1753), 225.

[2] xiv. 154; see also *ib.* xxxv. 54 (quoting from W. H. Roberts's *Poetical Epistle to
Christopher Anstey*, 1773), and *Mo. Rev.*, enl. ed., vii. 22 (1792), x. 272 (1793), xxx. 393
(quoting from Lady Manners's *Review of Poetry*, 1799). Henry Baker in 1723 termed
Philips a "celestial bard" who sang of cider "in lines immortal" (*Invocation of Health*,
in *Anthologia Hibernica*, 1793, i. 226).

[3] lvi. 235.

[4] John Aikin, *Letters on English Poetry* (2d ed., 1807), 144.

exemplifying that harmony for which he praised poetry [1] as his life failed to embody the truth which he fervently invoked in song; yet it is of greater interest than are many more melodious productions. Its significance lies not so much in its author's reputation as in affording an instance of an essentially journalistic and unpoetic writer who, so early as 1705, admired the cathedral harmonies of blank verse sufficiently to imitate them to some extent, and in the fact that his crude poems were written not for a small circle or as a private experiment but for publication in a newspaper, *The Review*. The necessity of providing copy quickly for his periodical may have been Defoe's reason for abandoning the troublesome bondage of riming; for, though he sneers at those who "will miss the Jingle, and like the Pack-Horse that tires without his Bells, be weary of the Lines for Want of the Rhyme," he admits that one of his pieces, which fills three pages, was 'the birth of as many hours.' [2] Many of his lines are hardly verse at all; but it will be seen from those quoted below that he tried, by clipping past participles ("contaminate"), by using verbs for nouns ("dispose"), and particularly by inverting the word-order, to get something of a Miltonic effect:

> Immortal Truth, thou Counterpart of God,
> Immense, and like him Bright, tho' Undiscern'd
> *Tell us, Why Mortal Frauds assault thy Throne,*
> *Assume thy Likness,* and thy Face Sublime
> So aptly Counterfeit? Why *mask'd* they strive
> To pass for thy bright Self? *How Crime* and *Guilt*
> Of Hell conceiv'd, and from the Place *Surnam'd*
> *Contaminate,* can Heaven it self Invade. . . .
> Not *high assembl'd Crowds of Tyrant Men,*
> Who boast the vast Dispose of *Mortal Power,*
> Shall thy Unbyass'd Resolutions fright.[3]

[1] See his *Review*, vol. iii, no. 104 (Aug. 31, 1706). It is in this connection that he commends Milton (see p. 15 above).

[2] *Ib.* no. 61. The poem *On the Fight at Ramellies* is in the same number; the last sixteen lines of it are rimed.

[3] *Hymn to Truth*, in the *Review*, vol. ii, no. 1 (Feb. 27, 1705). See also the lines in Supplement, no. 5 (January, 1705), appended to volume i of the *Review*. My attention was called to these poems, and to the reference to Milton, by Mr. A. L. Bouton of New York University, to whose knowledge of seventeenth- and eighteenth-century prose I am otherwise indebted. Through C. A. Moore's *Shaftesbury and the Ethical Poets* (Modern Lang. Assoc., *Publications*, xxxi. 277–8) I have learned of two wretched unrimed poems published in 1711 by Henry Needler, "the first actual literary follower of Shaftesbury." The more important of these pieces is a deistic attempt to prove the existence of God from the works of creation, the other is entitled *To the Memory of Favonia* (*Works*, 2d ed., 1728, pp. 135–9, 198–200). Needler quotes from *Paradise Lost* on pages 66 n., 67, 70–71 n., 73 n.

Defoe's *Review* was not the only periodical in the early eighteenth century to publish blank verse, for between 1708 and 1711 more than sixty examples of it appeared in the *British Apollo*.[1] Many of the questions and answers which make up this prototype of *Notes and Queries* are in verse, the style and meter of the questions being copied in the answers. The *Apollo* contains a few references to *Paradise Lost*, as well as several phrases borrowed from it,[2] and practically all the unrimed questions and replies have some echoes of the Miltonic style and diction, the sublimity of which the contributors often made painful efforts to copy. Apparently the writers were convinced that to escape being prosaic it was necessary to get as far as possible from ordinary speech, for one bard actually referred so grandiosely to making malt that he was understood to mean farming![3] Yet, although the pieces are written in the sorriest doggerel, the frequent use of blank verse for such purposes in a periodical so popular that it went through four editions is of considerable significance.

Although Isaac Watts is known to-day only as a writer of hymns, his collected works fill six huge tomes. Among the most popular of his productions was the *Horae Lyricae*, originally published in 1706 and reprinted for the sixteenth time in 1793. This volume contains eight poems in an easy, flowing blank verse which as a rule shows little influence from *Paradise Lost*. A few lines from *True Courage* will show what Watts's unrimed poetry is like:

> He that unshrinking and without a Groan
> Bears the first Wound may finish all the War
> With meer couragious Silence, and come off
> Conqueror: for the Man that well conceals
> The heavy Strokes of Fate he bears 'em well.[4]

Frequently, however, the style stiffens and becomes more formal and heroic, with the result that we have passages like this:

> And his Throne
> Mortal Access forbids, projecting far
> Splendors unsufferable and radiant Death.
> With Reverence and Abasement deep they fall
> Before his Sovereign Majesty, to pay
> Due Worship.[5]

---

[1] See below, Bibl. I and Appendix B, 1708–11.

[2] For two references, see vol. i, nos. 25, 113. The phrase "ever during Dark" (from *P. L.*, iii. 45) is in vol. i, quarterly paper no. 1; "Disastrous Influence shed" (cf. *P. L.*, i. 597) is in vol. i, supernumerary paper no. 8; "Earth, self-ballanced in Ambient Air" (from *P. L.*, vii. 242, 89) and "massy" (*P. L.*, i. 285, 703, etc.) occur in vol. ii, no. 104.

[3] Vol. ii, no. 18, and supernumerary paper no. 4.   [4] *Horae Lyricae* (2d ed., 1709), 191.

[5] *To Mitio* (*ib.* 270). The heroic poem, *The Celebrated Victory of the Poles over Osman*

Here are the inverted word-order, the diction, and something of the sonorous pomp which distinguish *Paradise Lost*. Another poem in the same volume [1] shows the "vast Reverence" Watts had for Milton, though he declares, "The Length of his Periods, and sometimes of his Parentheses runs me out of Breath. . . . I could never believe that Roughness and Obscurity added any thing to the true Grandeur of a Poem; nor will I ever affect Archaisms, Exoticisms, and a quaint Uncouthness of Speech, in order to become perfectly *Miltonian*. 'Tis my Opinion that Blank Verse may be written with all due Elevation of Thought in a modern Stile." [2] It is to Watts's credit, indeed, that he dropped many Miltonic characteristics that were not suited to his purpose, but kept the run-over lines and the constant shifting of the pauses which many of his contemporaries disregarded. So partial was he to these features of Milton's prosody that he even introduced them into the heroic couplet. "I have attempted in Rhime," he announced, "the same variety of Cadence, Comma and Period, which Blank Verse Glories in as its peculiar Elegance." [3] The result was poetry like the following, an ugly duckling that gave little promise of the suppleness and grace the freer couplet was to develop:

> Then our Zeal
> Blaz'd and burnt high to reach th' Ethereal Hill,
> And Love refin'd like that above the Poles
> Threw both our Arms round one another's Souls
> In Rapture and Embraces. Oh forbear,
> Forbear, my Song! this is too much to hear,
> Too dreadful to repeat; such Joys as these
> Fled from the Earth for ever! [4]

Watts was one of a group of men and women who admired *Paradise Lost*. Prefixed to the third edition of his *Horae Lyricae* (1715) are two unrimed poems, both written in 1706, one of which, by Joseph Standen, speaks thus of the rebellious angels:

> Incarnate Fiends! outragious they defy'd
> Th' Eternal's Thunder, and Almighty Wrath
> Fearless provok'd, which all the other Devils
> Would dread to meet.

The other prefatory poem is by Watts's first cousin and life-long friend, Henry Grove, one of the contributors to the *Spectator*. This

---

(*ib.* 229–38), is more Miltonic; but, as it is the only piece of the kind that Watts wrote, the passage given above is more typical.

[1] Quoted above, p. 37; and see pp. 38, 425.
[2] *Horae*, 1709, preface, pp. xx–xxi.   [3] *Horae*, 1706, preface, p. [x].
[4] *Funeral Poem on Thomas Gunston* (composed 1701), *Horae*, 1709, p. 327.

piece is not Miltonic, but another of its author's short productions is.[1] Grove and Watts received their early education at a nonconformist academy kept by Thomas Rowe, where they had as schoolmates Samuel Say, whose essays on Milton and imitations of him we have already noticed, and John Hughes, one of the first poets to copy the minor poems.[2] Furthermore, another Thomas Rowe, a nephew of the teacher and a friend of Watts, translated one of Horace's odes into the verse of *Paradise Lost*, and his wife, "the famous, ingenious, and justly admir'd Mrs. Singer," wrote one confessed imitation of Milton, two others in which the indebtedness is equally clear, and considerable non-Miltonic blank verse.[3] It should be noticed that this group was made up of dissenters, that all but two of the men were ministers, all but one of unusual piety, and that the only one of the seven who was not particularly interested in religious matters, John Hughes, was the only one who did not write blank verse. There can be no question that in these cases, as in many others, Milton's Puritanism and the religious nature of his principal poem had not a little to do with the admiration he received.

In the first sixty years after the publication of *Paradise Lost* blank verse was most often employed (outside of the drama) for translations of the classics. This is not to be wondered at, since the English epic was obviously patterned after those in Greek and Latin, which were themselves unrimed. In these early metrical paraphrases, however, Milton's style and prosody frequently had little or no place. They do not, as we have seen, enter into the first unrimed poem published after his epic (Roscommon's version of the *Ars Poetica*, 1680), nor are they to be found in Thomas Fletcher's brief translations from the *Aeneid*, which came twelve years later.[4] But they do appear in the adaptations of Horace made by Samuel Say and by Thomas Rowe, and they are frankly acknowledged in a piece which Addison brought out in 1704, *Milton's Stile Imitated, in a Translation out of the Third Aeneid*. This poem, which shows a de-

---

[1] See Bibl. I, 1709.   [2] See pp. 90 above and 442-3 below.
[3] See Bibl. I, 1708 w., 1704 ?, bef. 1710 ?, and App. B, 1729-39. Mrs. Rowe's devotional books had a remarkable sale throughout the eighteenth century.
[4] See below, Appendix B, 1692. Fletcher had previously translated the first book into heroic couplets (*Poems*, 1692, pp. 65-119), a performance which he afterwards deeply regretted. "There is nothing which I can so hardly forgive my self," he wrote in the preface, "as that I took such pains to make it worse than I needed. I mean, by confining my self to Rhime, when blank Verse, as it would have been more easie, so I am perswaded it would have been more natural. . . . Rhimes . . . do but emasculate Heroick Verse, and give it an unnatural Softness. In Songs, Pastorals, and the softer sorts of Poetry, Rhimes may perhaps be not unelegantly retain'd; but an Heroe drest up in them looks like *Hercules* with a Distaff."

cided tendency to fall into couplets, is a poor imitation, but verbal borrowings at times bring it close to its model.[1] It is nearest "Milton's stile" in the following passage:

> 'Tis said, that thunder-struck Enceladus
> Groveling beneath the incumbent mountain's weight,
> Lies stretched supine, eternal prey of flames;
> And, when he heaves against the burning load,
> Reluctant, to invert his broiling limbs,
> A sudden earthquake shoots through all the isle,
> And Aetna thunders dreadful under-ground.

In view of the admiration for *Paradise Lost* which Addison later expressed in the *Spectator* papers, it seems only natural that he should have imitated it; but we are surprised to find "Mat" Prior, "the earliest, as he was one of the most consummate, masters of English familiar verse," doing the same thing. Prior's versions of two of the lofty hymns of Callimachus are so highly condensed as to be abrupt, but his blank verse is much better than what Addison or most other men of the time wrote. Prosodically it is marked by a large proportion of the weak endings that distinguish Shakespeare's later manner but are rare in *Paradise Lost*. His use of blank verse was not limited to translations, for three of the poems recently discovered at Longleat are without rime, — a brief, crudely-expressed prophecy, a six-line paraphrase from Virgil's fourth Georgic, and a "Prelude" with the beginning of a tale from Boccaccio. In the first two of these far from successful ventures there is little if any trace of Milton's style, but in the last one there are marked signs of it, as the following interesting assault upon neo-classic rules will show:

> Of the noblest Heights and best Examples,
> Ambitious, I in English Verse attempt.
> But not as heretofore, the line prescrib'd
> To equal cadence, and with semblant Sounds
> Pointed, (so Modern Harmony advises)
> But in the Ancient Guise, free, uncontroll'd,
> The Verse, compress'd the Period, or dilated,
> As close discourse requires, or fine description.
> Such Homer wrote; such Milton imitated.[2]

---

[1] Compare, for example, the description of Mt. Etna in eruption,

> The bottom works with smothered fire involved
> In pestilential vapours, stench, and smoke,

with Milton's lines (*P. L.*, i. 236–7); and note the use of "orient beams" (cf. *P. L.*, ii. 399, iv. 644, vi. 15), "he back recoiled" (cf. *P. L.*, vi. 194), "on the grundsil edge" (cf. *P. L.*, i. 460).

[2] *Prelude to a Tale from Boccace*, in Waller's edition of Prior's *Writings* (Camb., 1907), ii. 339. For the other two pieces, see pp. 318, 334, of the same volume. Another

We have already made the acquaintance of the critical Oxford professor of poetry, Joseph Trapp, who, not content with championing *Paradise Lost*, turned it into Latin.[1] In 1703 Trapp began a translation of the complete works of Virgil, the first to be made in blank verse. The character of this decidedly Miltonic version — which was not finished till 1731, and which, strangely enough, enjoyed a considerable popularity, reaching its fourth edition in 1755 — may be judged by comparison of the following lines with Addison's rendering of the same passage:

> 'Tis said, the Bulk of huge *Enceladus*
> Blasted with Light'ning, by This pond'rous Mount
> Is crush'd; and *Ætna*, o'er him whelm'd, expires
> Flame from it's burst Volcano's: And whene'er
> He shifts his weary Side, *Trinacria* all
> Groans trembling, and with Smoke obscures the Sky.[2]

The first part of Trapp's *Aeneid* was not published till 1718, four years after Nicholas Brady, author of a famous metrical version of the Psalms, had brought out the first book of his translation.[3] "When dragged into the world, [it] did not live long enough to cry," Johnson said of this work,[4] which neither he nor the writer on Brady in the *Dictionary of National Biography* had ever seen. Theirs was no great loss; for Brady's version is inferior to Trapp's, and is interesting principally for its many lines with weak endings, for such offhand phrases as "Peace Let's rather make," "two of our Gang," Andromache "the Relict" of Hector,[5] as well as for being generally conversational and hence on the whole but slightly Miltonic. An anonymous *Verbal Translation of Part of the First Aeneid*, which came out in 1726 (the year Brady finished his rendering) and extended to only two pages, is more literal and still less Miltonic.[6]

To the unrimed and uninspired versions of parts of the *Odyssey* and *Iliad* which Elijah Fenton and William Broome published in 1717 and 1727 respectively a special interest attaches, not only because these are the earliest renderings of Homer into blank verse, but because their authors also turned half of the *Odyssey* into couplets

of the poet's expressions of dissatisfaction with the closed couplet is given on pp. 59–60 above.

[1] See p. 17 above. His Latin version appeared in two volumes (1741, 1744).
[2] *Aeneis*, iii. 728–33; cf. above, p. 105.
[3] A year before, in 1713, he had published as a "specimen" the first hundred lines of book i, as *Proposals for Publishing a Translation of Virgil's Aeneids in Blank Verse*.
[4] "Dryden," in *Lives* (ed. Hill), i. 453.
[5] iv. 132–3, iii. 809, 422.
[6] *Miscellaneous Poems by Several Hands*, published by D. Lewis, 1726, pp. 307–9.

for Pope. Their rimed and unrimed translations are entirely unlike,
the one being as unmistakably pseudo-classic as the other is Miltonic; yet in the books that Fenton rimed for Pope there are not a
few words and phrases taken from *Paradise Lost*, a circumstance
which will surprise no one who knows that he wrote a life of Milton,
edited his epic, and used its meter and style in a paraphrase of a
chapter from Isaiah.[1]

The first poem to popularize blank verse was, as we have already
observed, a parody, the *Splendid Shilling* (1701), the success of which
naturally led other writers to attempt the same easy path through
humor to fame. The only unexpected thing about these imitations,
eight of which appeared before 1725, is that they came so slowly.
The first one, Gay's *Wine* (1708), does not mention the *Splendid
Shilling*, but refers to Philips's *Cyder* as if that alone were its source.[2]
There can be no question, however, of its indebtedness to the earlier
burlesque, and, as will be seen from the following lines, to the epic
which both poems parody:

> Bacchus divine, aid my advent'rous song,
> That with no middle flight intends to soar:
> Inspir'd, sublime, on Pegasean wing,
> By thee upborne, I draw Miltonic air.[3]

The poem exhibits not only the obvious indications of "Miltonic
air," — inverted word-order, parentheses, and the use of adjectives
for adverbs, — but also a fondness for unusual words in *-ean* or *-ian*.[4]
Like Philips, Gay seems to have thought well of the work he parodied, for the number of verbal borrowings from widely separated
parts of *Paradise Lost* indicate a familiarity with that poem which
could hardly have resulted from indifference or dislike.[5] *Wine* is a

[1] See Bibl. I, 1712. For the use Broome made of *Lycidas* and the octosyllabics, see
pp. 426, 445-6, below.

[2] See lines 114-20 (Muses' Library ed.), where *Bleinheim* also is mentioned.

[3] Lines 12-15; cf. *P. L.*, i. 13-14.

[4] For example, Pegasean, Titanian, Celtiberian, Heliconian, Lenæan, Oxonian,
Ariconian, Phœbean, sylvestrian, Croatian, Centaurian, scymmetrian, Dircean.

[5] Here are a few of them:

> So mists and exhalations that arise
> From hills or steamy lake dusky or grey
> Prevail, till Phoebus sheds Titanian rays,
> And paints their fleecy skirts with shining gold.
>> The upheaved oak,
> With beaked prow, rides tilting o'er the waves.
> Drive hence the rude and barbarous dissonance
> Of savage Thracians.

(Lines 50-53, 67-8, 171-2; cf. *P. L.*, v. 185-7, xi. 745-7, vii. 32-4.) Compare also the
passage quoted in the text with *P. L.*, i. 13-14.

jovial piece and, although the humor is somewhat heavy, can still be enjoyed; it certainly furnished a suitable entrance into the world of letters for its lazy and lovable author, who owed his reputation to a burlesque pastoral and a comic opera and who jested even in his own epitaph.

The other parodies that followed in the wake of the *Splendid Shilling* are of little importance and of less worth. One which resembles Philips's work in confessing its burlesque imitation of Milton and in being devoted to the joys of drinking, is by the Countess of Winchilsea;[1] three others belong with the large body of indecent literature published at the time. Some slight interest, however, attaches to translations of two mock-heroic Latin poems of that period. The first of these, Edward Holdsworth's *Muscipula* (1709), which describes "with the purity of Virgil and the pleasantry of Lucian" a plague of rats and the invention of a mouse-trap, was a favorite in the eighteenth century, appearing alone or in collections some thirteen times (four the first year) and apparently being turned into English eight or nine times. At least three of these translations are unrimed burlesques of *Paradise Lost*, — those published in 1709 (by Daniel Bellamy), 1715 (by an unknown writer), and 1749 (by John Hoadly); the last two are really amusing. The translation, "in imitation of Milton's style," of Addison's Latin battle of the cranes and the pigmies, made in 1724 by Bishop Warburton, Pope's friend and literary executor, is significant as a concrete illustration of the friendly relationship existing between the two supposedly hostile schools of poetry; for Warburton, who often expressed his admiration for *Paradise Lost*, no more showed a poor opinion of blank verse by making humorous use of it than did the author of the *Splendid Shilling*.[2]

If these parodies have lost much of the humor they once had, it is in part because the epics, translations of the classics, and other even loftier flights which they burlesqued no longer attract the attention they once did. It will be remembered that these were years when Blenheim and Ramillies, Oudenarde and Malplaquet, were furnishing bards with lofty themes, when pseudo-sublime Pindaric odes were in great favor, when Blackmore was busy penning "heroic poems," when Dryden was translating Virgil, Pope Homer, and Prior Callimachus. And there were even more ambitious attempts

[1] Bibl. I, 1713.

[2] Warburton's poem contains a number of phrases borrowed from *Paradise Lost*. For the burlesques and mock heroics noticed above, and many later parodies, see pp. 315–22 below.

than these, for between 1714 and 1726 a number of writers chose the most exalted of all subjects, making heaven, hell, and chaos their scenes of action and the Almighty himself one of their characters. Their success is considerably greater than would be expected, probably because the poems are all frank and close imitations of *Paradise Lost;* for obviously many difficulties and dangers connected with the Miltonic manner are avoided when it is employed on Miltonic matter.

The first of these essays in the sublime [1] seems to have been *Praeexistence, a Poem in Imitation of Milton*, which, originally published in 1714, was reprinted in 1740 and 1800 and obtained a wide circulation through being included in "Dodsley's Miscellany." [2] Even if it is, as Gray declared, "nonsense in all her altitudes," [3] yet the "nonsense" is couched in some of the best blank verse written during the period. The poem opens with the return of the angels from victory over Satan, and describes their reception by Milton's schoolmaster Deity, who tells them of the world that is to be created. The earth, curiously enough, is to be a place of punishment, where the less sinful of Satan's followers may have a second chance. In style and diction the piece is quite as Miltonic as in subject-matter; yet it escapes the pitfalls of tumidity and dull prose into one or the other of which most contemporary blank verse fell, and at its best is not without dignity and nobility of utterance. The coming of the Deity is thus described:

> Out flows a Blaze of Glory; for on high
> Tow'ring advanc'd the moving Throne of God,
> Vast and Majestick; on each radiant side

[1] Unless we include Samuel Wesley's rimed *Hymn on Peace to the Prince of Peace* (1713), because of such verbal borrowings as

> Th' Etherial Mold
> Purg'd off its *Dross*, and Shone with Native Gold,

> The Father's *Co-eternal* Son,

> Or Mantling *Vine's*, on Mossy Couches laid,
> Near the soft *Murmur* of some bubling Spring
> With Angel-Guests *Discourse*

(lines 31–2, 42, 66–8; cf. *P. L.*, ii. 139–41, iii. 2, iv. 258–60, and *Comus*, 276, 294). Wesley quotes three lines from *Paradise Lost* on his title-page. See also pp. 38, 45 n. 1, above, and p. 429, n. 1, below.

[2] Edition of 1748, i. 164–78. A poem with the same title — presumably the same work — was printed at Newcastle in 1768, with the note that it was "written in the last century, and now carefully revised by D. Mountfort."

[3] *Correspondence of Gray, Walpole, West*, etc. (ed. P. Toynbee, Oxford, 1915), ii. 91. Although Gray was writing about the first edition of the "Miscellany" (1748), Mr. Toynbee's notes seem to refer to some other issue, and hence are confusing.

> The pointed Rays slope glittering, at the foot
> Glides a full Tide of Day, that onward pours
> In liquid Torrents through the black Abyss.[1]

The other end of the story of our universe, the *terminus ad quem* which loomed large in the thought and reading of religious persons in the eighteenth century, is taken up in an anonymous and undated piece, *The Last Day*, which must have appeared about the same time as *Prae-existence*.[2] It seems to be a production which its few readers were not unwilling to let die, for apparently only the first book was published. In this book the Deity summons his angels about him to announce the destruction of the world and sends Elijah to warn mankind to repent. Here is part of the description of the heavenly assembly:

> Full of himself, amidst
> The ample Concave, the Almighty sate,
> Sate unapproach'd; below the Hierarchal States,
> Ten thousand thousand Demigods await
> His Motion, he his Scepter gently bowing
> In Signal of Permission, strait assume
> The immortal States with Reverence due, their Thrones
> Order above Order, in bright Array
> Like radiant Constellations.[3]

A similar work, *The Last Judgment of Men and Angels*, brought out in 1723 by Thomas Newcomb, is of importance solely because of its size; for until 1787, when Glover's *Athenaid* like a wounded snake dragged its slow length through thirty dreary books, it seems to have been the longest unrimed poem in English. Yet this splendid folio, with its 12,350 lines, dropped into oblivion without causing a ripple to reach the shores of literary history; and no wonder, for, since Newcomb makes every character declaim a vague, lofty speech several pages in length on every possible occasion, the work is both tiresome and hard to follow. The long opening scene in heaven, in which a Puritan Deity commands his angels to destroy the world, is followed by various councils to which Satan summons Belial, Moloch, and their peers in order to thwart this design. A war be-

---

[1] Lines 42–7. Such expressions as "the vast Obscure," "th' *Empyræum* vast," "th' impyral Mould," "th' *Æthereal Mould*" (lines 15, 80, 113, 204), are characteristic of the diction of the poem.

[2] Another anonymous work on the same subject, which I have not seen, *Description of the Four Last Things, viz., Death, Judgment, Hell, and Heaven, in Blank Verse*, appeared in a second edition in 1719.

[3] Page 9. On page 19 is a not unpleasing description of "the delightful Banks of the River Mola, near Bansteed in Surrey," part of which recalls *Paradise Lost*, i. 781–8, iv. 680–88.

tween the two forces is ended, as in *Paradise Lost*, by the coming of
Messiah, who from a flaming chariot hurls thunderbolts upon the
rebel angels. Then follows the destruction and renovation of the
world, after which, again as in Milton, an angel shows Adam a
lengthy vision. As if this were not enough, the prosody, diction,
and style of the work are frankly Miltonic, and a large number of
phrases are unblushingly transferred from the earlier work.[1] Although the following passage is not so close to *Paradise Lost* as are
most others, it will give some idea of the verse, — which is far better
than one would expect, — as well as of Newcomb's feeling for the
broad aspects of nature:

> Thus spoke our common Parent! while the Eve
> Hasting apace all down the *Western* Sky
> Led on the Twilight; that, a browner Veil
> Of Darkness shadowing all the Vales below,
> Parent of downy Slumbers![2]

[1] Here are a few instances. After casting their chaplets on the pavement before the
Deity (i. 120–21, cf. *P. L.*, iii. 349–52), the angels sing: "Thee, Father, first they name,
Immense, Supreme" (i. 181, cf. *P. L.*, iii. 372–3). The assembly of heathen deities that
convenes at Satan's call (vii. 404–533) is closely modelled on Milton's enumeration of
the same evil spirits as they rise from the lake of fire (*P. L.*, i. 392–521); the description
of Satan's "faded Majesty" (ii. 603–46) is from Milton (*P. L.*, i. 589–608); so is the
scene in which Satan casts his "baleful Eye" upon his followers and thus addresses
them,

> Warriors, Thrones,
> Angels, the Boast so late of yonder Skies;
> Chuse ye these Billows then, whereon to lay
> Your weary'd Limbs after the cruel Toil
> Of Battel?

(viii. 604–6, 619–23, cf. *P. L.*, i. 56, 315–21); and so are his reference to Azazel (whom
he mentions by name in vi. 348),

> A Cherub (who by right that Station claim'd)
> Unfurl'd the heav'nly Ensign

(ii. 257–8, cf. *P. L.*, i. 533–6), his apostrophe to light,

> Hail sacred Light! whose fair and beauteous Beam
> More gladly I revisit, wandring long
> Beneath the nether Shades

(iv. 1–3, cf. *P. L.*, iii. 1, 13–15), and his description of hell as a place

> Just serving thro' the Darkness to reveal
> Sad Scenes of Sorrow

(xii. 518–19, cf. *P. L.*, i. 63–5). Some of the shorter phrases borrowed are "the Lapse
of murmuring Streams" (i. 803. cf. *P. L.*, viii. 263); "from Morn to Eve, from Eve to
dewy Morn" (ii. 381, cf. *P. L.*, i. 742–3); "pensive Steps, and slow" (x. 875, cf. *P. L.*,
xii. 648); "dark thro' Excess of Light" (xii. 144, cf. *P. L.*, iii. 380); "varied alone with
soft or solid Fires" (xii. 508, cf. *P. L.*, i. 228–9, said of hell in each case).

[2] x. 915–19; cf. x. 775– xi. 35 *passim*. Some years later Newcomb published four
other works in Miltonic blank verse: *Part of Psalm cxlviii after the Manner of Milton*
(pp. 339–42 of his *Miscellaneous Collection of Poems*, 1740; see also *ib*. 17–20, 218–19,

Still another religious work that not only makes use of the language and style of *Paradise Lost*, but borrows many phrases from it, is William Thompson's *Poetical Paraphrase on Part of the Book of Job, in Imitation of the Style of Milton* (1726).[1] About the time this work appeared Thomas Curteis (1690–1747) published some fifteen pages of verse, which he reissued in 1728 as *Eirenodia*, a vague, ecstatic performance for which "the great Milton" furnished the "pattern." It describes scenes in heaven, portrays the earthly life of the

> Prince of Peace! from the Jessaean stem
> Self-infinite descended!

and, after enlarging on the greatness of

> Fair Albion, compend of the wondrous globe
> Terrene,

ends with a picture of the last judgment. Curteis has unqualified praise for Milton, the "brightness" of whose "diction" he particularly admired and, as may be seen from the following lines, closely imitated:

> Massy globes,
> Continuous or excav'd, annoy no more
> The serried ranks compact, with havoc dire.[2]

Most of the writers we have thus far considered are minor, almost minus, poets who are deservedly forgotten. If the reader feels that it matters little by whom they were influenced, he should at

On Milton's P. L. and *On Milton's Bust in Westminster-Abbey*); *Mr. Hervey's Meditations and Contemplations* (1764, but two of the six pieces had appeared in 1757); *The Retired Penitent, a Poetical Version of one of Young's Moral Contemplations* (1760); *The Death of Abel* (from Salomon Gessner, "attempted in the stile of Milton," 1763).

[1] Some of Thompson's pilferings are from Milton's minor poems, as "dapple dawn" (p. 3, cf. *Allegro*, 44), "the Eye-lids of the Morn Opening" (p. 16, cf. *Lycidas*, 26). A few of his other borrowings are, "shedding soft Influence, with orient Beams" (p. 2, cf. p. 6, and *P. L.*, vi. 15, vii. 375); "with choral Symphonies" (p. 2, cf. *P. L.*, v. 162); "sure Pledge of rising Day (p. 3, cf. *P. L.*, v. 168); "scowls o'er the bleak Landskip Snow or Hail" (p. 6, cf. *P. L.*, ii. 491); a description of the ostrich "fledg'd with Pens," whose eggs "burst"

> With kindly Rupture, and disclos'd put forth
> The callow Brood

(p. 10, cf. *P. L.*, vii. 419–21); or of the huge creature that

> Wallowing unweildy, enormous in his Gate
> . . . . to his Mind
> Firm Peace recover'd soon and wonted Calm

(p. 18, cf. *P. L.*, vii. 411, v. 209–10). The preface expresses profound veneration for Milton and violent antipathy to rime.

[2] R. Freeman's *Kentish Poets* (Canterbury, 1821), ii. 126, 134, 127. Curteis's praise of Milton and his attack upon rime are on pages 120, 129–30.

least think of them as straws that reveal a breeze from a new quarter, which, gathering in volume, was about to strike the keen and glittering spars on which Alexander Pope stretched his sails. To be sure, the artificiality of Pope's verse suggests not so much a winged boat as a swift, sharp-prowed launch, with the "put, put" of its exhaust corresponding to the incisive regularity of the heroic couplet; hence one may argue that this particular craft would scarcely have felt the wind at all. It would, indeed, be hard to find any poetry more unlike *Paradise Lost* and *Lycidas* than *The Dunciad* and the *Epistle to Arbuthnot*. The differences are not limited to style, prosody, diction, and the like, but extend to verse-form, subject-matter, types of poetry used, and even to the men themselves and their conceptions of literature and life. As a result, admirers of the one are seldom able to do justice to the poetry of the other, and it is naturally assumed that Pope himself did not appreciate the work of Milton. This assumption may be correct, for the real thoughts and tastes of "the wicked wasp of Twickenham" are hard to fathom;[1] but at least he had read the earlier poet carefully. Indeed, many a person who has prided himself on his enjoyment of *Paradise Lost* and thought Pope had no conception of what true poetry is, has not possessed a tithe of the scorned bard's knowledge of Milton.

Evidence of this knowledge is of many kinds and is found in every possible place. First of all, explicit references to Milton abound in Pope's poems, letters, prefaces, footnotes, and in the record of his conversations.[2] One of the most interesting of these references is in

[1] For instance, though he translated Homer and edited Shakespeare, one cannot be certain that he cared particularly for either poet.

[2] Besides writing an epigram on Bentley's edition of *Paradise Lost* (which, according to the preface of Newton's edition, he had examined throughout with care), Pope mentioned Milton ten times in his poetry (see Abbott's *Concordance*), the best-known passage being in his *Imitations of Horace* (II. i. 99–102):

> Milton's strong pinion now not Heaven can bound,
> Now, serpent-like, in prose he sweeps the ground;
> In quibbles, angel and archangel join,
> And God the Father turns a school-divine.

There are also references to Milton in *Windsor Forest*, 7–10, the *Epistle to Arbuthnot*, 319–20, the satirical essays prefixed to *The Dunciad* (*Works*, Elwin-Courthope ed., iv. 73, 85), and in Pope's footnotes to the same poem (e. g., ii. 92, iv. 4, 112, 247, and the note to the appended "Declaration," *Works*, iv. 227; in many of these notes borrowings from Milton are pointed out). *Paradise Lost* is quoted appreciatively in letters to Caryll, Blount, and Digby (*Works*, vi. 177, Dec. 21, 1712; vi. 380–81, Oct. 21, 1723; ix. 75, July 20, 1720); and *Lycidas* in a letter to Trumbull (*ib.* vi. 6, March 12, 1713). Particularly interesting is Pope's correspondence with Jonathan Richardson, the Milton enthusiast, who consulted him about the *Explanatory Notes on Paradise Lost* which he was preparing (*Works*, ix. 492–509), and to whom Pope sent a sonnet beginning "Fair mirror of foul times," which had been discovered in Chalfont and attributed

a letter to Caryll, to whom he writes, "I keep the pictures of Dryden, Milton, Shakspeare, &c., in my chamber, round about me, that the constant remembrance of them may keep me always humble." [1] Much more convincing than this dubious humility, however, is the indisputable evidence from the words, phrases, and lines which Pope transferred from Milton's verse to his own. In *The Dunciad* alone he used such expressions no fewer than thirty times and in the *Iliad* fifty-six times. The extent of these borrowings — there are over one hundred and ninety of them [2] — is surprising in view of the differences not only between the two men but between the meters they employed. Poets who admired *Paradise Lost* commonly took phrases from it, but they used them almost exclusively in their blank verse. Not until we reach Thomas Warton do we find a writer who introduced Miltonic phrases into rimed poetry so frequently as Pope did, and perhaps no one else has ever employed so many in the heroic couplet. Furthermore, Pope's borrowings are not crowded into a

to Milton (*History of the Works of the Learned*, 1739, ii. 107–8). In the course of the acquaintanceship indicated by these letters, which extended over a period of twenty-two years (1722–44), there must have been considerable discussion of Richardson's favorite poet. From Pope's conversation as recorded in Spence's *Anecdotes* (ed. Singer, 1820, index and pp. 197–8) nine references to Milton have been preserved, of which the following is the most interesting: "Milton's style, in his *Paradise Lost*, is not natural; 'tis an exotic style. As his subject lies a good deal out of our world, it has a particular propriety in those parts of the poem: and, when he is on earth, wherever he is describing our parents in Paradise, you see he uses a more easy and natural way of writing. Though his formal style may fit the higher parts of his own poem, it does very ill for others who write on natural and pastoral subjects" (*ib.* 174). In the notes to the *Iliad*, *Paradise Lost* is either quoted from or referred to thirty-two times (i. 9, 97, 478; ii. 255, 440, 552, 939, 950, and "Observations on the Catalogue"; v. 164, 422, 517, 928, 971; vi. 245; vii. 48, 526; viii. 16, 88, 364; xiii. 384; xiv. 296, 395; xv. 17, 86, 252; xvi. 194, 354, 904; xvii. 564; xxii. 114; xxiv. 417); and there is one citation from *Samson Agonistes* (vi. 329). In one of the notes (xiv. 395) thirty lines from three books of the epic are introduced. The notes to the *Odyssey* are by Broome and, it is interesting to observe, contain few references to *Paradise Lost*. Pope's own postscript to the *Odyssey*, however, has a paragraph on Milton, who is also mentioned three times in the preface to the *Iliad*. In the last of these passages, "any one who translates Homer" is urged "to consider him attentively in comparison with Virgil above all the ancients, and with Milton above all the moderns." Finally, it is probable that Pope had a hand in some of the twenty or more pieces in the *Grub-Street Journal* that deal with Milton. These pieces are either reprinted or referred to in *Memoirs of the Society of Grub-Street* (1737), i. 19–24, 42–5, 129, 167, 168; ii. 96–9, 102–3, 133, 182–3 (4 pieces), 222, 245, 254–5 (2 pieces), 257–62 (2 pieces), 292, 308, 323; those merely referred to in the *Memoirs* may be read in the *Gentleman's Magazine*, i. 377–8, ii. 571–2, 658–9, 690–1, 753–4, 840–1, 905–6. The *Journal*, to quote Mr. Elwin, "was set up in Pope's interest, and . . . he was 'suspected of having projected it, and was at least a frequent contributor'" (Pope's *Works*, viii. 268, n. 1). See below also, p. 115, n. 5.

[1] *Works*, vi. 145, June 25, 1711. In a letter to Richardson he speaks of himself as "a worse writer by far than Milton" (*ib.* ix. 506, June 17, 1737).

[2] See below, Appendix A.

few pieces, but are scattered throughout his work, being found in at least twenty-five poems. It is also significant that, while practically all of the early pilferers from Milton made use of his epic only (few persons at that time having any appreciation of the minor poems[1]), yet Pope used the shorter pieces in his early and later work, and, except in *The Dunciad* and the Homer, borrowed from them quite as much as he did from the epic. Lines or phrases from nearly all of them appear in his verse, — from *Allegro, Penseroso, Comus* (there are nineteen from *Comus*), *Lycidas*, the *Nativity*, from three of the sonnets, and even from *Arcades* and the *Vacation Exercise*. Nor is it fair to suggest, as Thomas Warton did, that he was "conscious that he might borrow from a book then scarcely remembered, without the hazard of a discovery, or the imputation of plagiarism."[2] On the contrary, Pope praised the volume and lent it to at least one of his friends.[3] It is striking that a poet so deficient in lyric power should be found among the earliest admirers of these lyric masterpieces, and should be the first writer to make much use of them,[4] as well as the first to show familiarity with the great body of Milton's work.[5]

In the preface to his *Iliad* Pope wrote, "Perhaps the mixture of some Graecisms and old words after the manner of Milton, if done without too much affectation, might not have an ill effect in a version of this particular work, which most of any other seems to require a venerable antique cast." He does not say here that such words have been introduced, but in the postscript to the *Odyssey* he frankly acknowledges that "in order to dignify and solemnize these plainer parts . . . some use has been made . . . of the style of *Milton*. A just and moderate mixture of old words," he adds, "may have an

---

[1] Even Dennis, who borrowed freely from *Paradise Lost*, appears to have quoted from them only once, and Philips not at all (cf. below, p. 423, notes 5, 6).

[2] In his edition of Milton's minor poems (1785), p. ix. Warton says it was through his father, the elder Thomas Warton, that Pope came to know the poems, and adds, "We find him soon afterwards sprinkling his *Eloisa to Abelard* with epithets and phrases of a new form and sound, pilfered from *Comus* and the *Penseroso*." As a matter of fact, Pope knew these poems long before 1717, when his *Eloisa* appeared; and the "sprinkling" that Warton observed is to be found in the *Pastorals* and *Windsor Forest*, which were published the one eight and the other four years before the *Eloisa* epistles.

[3] Sir William Trumbull (see his letter to Pope, Oct. 19, 1705, Pope's *Works*, vi. 1–2).

[4] Except, to be sure, Robert Baron, whose work was of no consequence (see pp. 427–8 below).

[5] He borrowed not only from ten of the minor poems and from the epic, but from *Paradise Regained* and *Samson*. Every book of *Paradise Lost* yielded one or more contributions to his work, and one book gave as many as 25. Pope's copy of Bentley's edition of the epic showed that he had carefully considered the suggested textual emendations and marked such as appealed to him (Newton's ed., preface).

effect like the working old abbey stones into a building . . . to give a kind of venerable air." From these remarks the reader might expect to find considerable Miltonic diction in the translation, but he would be doomed to disappointment. To be sure, such words as "refulgent," "refluent," "resplendent," "translucent," "adamantine," "massy," "ethereal," do occur, though infrequently;[1] and there are unusual words like "circumfusile," "intorted," "oraculous," "obtend,"[2] besides common words employed in their original meanings, as "th' effusive wave" (poured out), "the narrative old man" (fond of telling stories), "stoops incumbent" (bending or resting over), "implicit" (entwined), "depending vines" (hanging).[3] Yet these are not "old words," and to us, at least, have nothing of the effect of "old abbey stones." We should remember, however, that a large number of words which are perfectly familiar to-day, and many of which were common in Shakespeare's time, seemed to the Augustans strange and antiquated. "Bridal," "gleam," "host" (in the sense of army), "hurl," "ruthless," "wail," and "woo" were spoken of as late as 1778 as "once no doubt in common use."[4] This shows how difficult it is to determine what Pope meant by "old words after the manner of Milton." We may get light, however, from a satirical article contributed to the *Grub-Street Journal*, which says that "another method of imitating MILTON is to make use of antiquated words, scarce any where else to be met with, such as *dulcet, gelid, umbrageous, redolent*, &c."[5] As these adjectives are all from the Latin, it may be that by "antiquated" Pope meant "antique." In any case, his language was probably loose and his thought somewhat vague; but he seems to have had in mind words,

---

[1] For example, v. 2, 348, vii. 128, x. 350, 534, etc.; v. 51; v. 549, ix. 570, 634; x. 434, xvii. 105; x. 473; vii. 112, ix. 287, 567, etc.; v. 150, 351, etc.

[2] iii. 541, 555, x. 642, xxii. 88. "Disparted," "discumbers," "adherent," "welters" (v. 468, 474, 547, xiv. 155), and many more might be added.

[3] xxii. 490 (cf. v. 412, "from his . . . mouth effus'd the briny tide"); iii. 80 (also *Iliad*, iii. 200); v. 63; ix. 514 (also *Iliad*, xxiii. 823); v. 88 (and cf. xiii. 131). Note also "decent hand" (xiii. 273), and "vest succinct" (xiv. 83). As the concordance to Pope's works does not include his translations of Homer, it is difficult to say how many of these unusual, Miltonic words there are or how often they occur, but the total number is considerable. They are scattered, however, through thousands of lines, so that they produce scarcely any effect. In the part of the *Odyssey* entrusted to Fenton, on the other hand, one is distinctly conscious of the loftier, more formal, and more Miltonic diction.

[4] James Beattie's *Essays on Poetry and Music*, 237; cf. 238, and p. 64 above.

[5] *Memoirs of the Society of Grub-Street* (1737), i. 22. Two of the words are mentioned in the same connection in the *Art of Sinking in Poetry* (Pope's *Works*, x. 372), and similar advice is given in the *Guardian*, no. 78 (which is by Pope), although the section in question was omitted when the essay was reprinted as the fifteenth chapter of the *Art of Sinking*.

derived in the main from Greek or Latin, which were unusual at the time and which nowadays, if we noticed them at all, we should term poetic. Some of them were probably not taken from Milton, but were merely of the kind that his usage had sanctioned. However it was, the employment of these uncommon words by so conservative a writer as Pope shows how appreciably Milton was enlarging the poetic vocabulary.

While the bard who "lisp'd in numbers" was still a child of twelve or thirteen he composed four thousand lines of an epic on the puissant Alcander, prince of Rhodes. "There was Milton's style," he told Spence, "in one part" of this poem; but, as the remaining parts were modélled upon Spenser, Cowley, Homer, and others, the work was presumably rimed and was affected by *Paradise Lost* only in subject-matter, diction, phrasing, and possibly "machinery." [1] This juvenile performance, which was later destroyed, is of no great significance except as showing at how early an age Pope began to admire Milton. Nor can much stress be laid upon Atterbury's plan (to which his imprisonment put an end) of having Pope adapt *Samson Agonistes* for the stage. [2] There is, however, another of Pope's unfinished projects that deserves more attention than it has yet received. This work, undertaken when its author was at the height of his powers, was, like the boyish piece, to have been an epic. It was to deal with Brutus, the mythical founder of Britain, and was, he told Spence, "more than half" done because "all exactly planned." Yet only these few lines seem to have been composed, and until recently even these were lost:

> The Patient Chief, who lab'ring long arriv'd
> On Britain's coast and brought with fav'ring Gods
> Arts Arms & Honour to her Ancient sons:
> Daughter of Memory! from Time
> Recall; and me wth Britains Glory fir'd,
> Me far from meaner Care or meaner Song,
> Snatch to the Holy Hill of spotless Bay,
> My Countrys Poet, to record her Fame
> Say first w[t] Cause? that Pow'r h . . . [3]

This blank verse is not specially Miltonic. There are some inversions, to be sure, particularly in the first, fifth, and sixth lines; but

---

[1] See Spence's *Anecdotes*, 24–5, 276–9, and Ruffhead's *Life of Pope* (1769), 25–7.

[2] We are told that it was to have been divided into acts and scenes and presented by the king's scholars at Westminster. See Atterbury's letter referring to an earlier conversation (Pope's *Works*, ix. 49, June 15, 1722), and Newton's *Paradise Lost* (2d ed., 1750), vol. i, p. lxii.

[3] Discovered by E. D. Snyder and quoted with variant readings in his note on "Pope's Blank Verse Epic," *Journal of English and Germanic Philology*, xviii. 583.

the passage is too brief to admit of any certainty regarding such points (about which Pope himself was doubtless far from clear) as the prosody, diction, and style of the work and their probable indebtedness to Milton. But was an unrimed epic written early in the eighteenth century by a poet who had already made extensive use of *Paradise Lost* likely to have escaped such indebtedness, particularly when, in direct violation of Boileau's dictum, its author had taken for his "machinery" not pagan gods but the Almighty and the good and bad angels of the Puritan work? If, therefore, the deformed, sickly body could have retained its equally deformed though resolute spirit for a few years more, — 'much less than ten' would have been enough, he told Spence, — we might have had the supreme tribute from the leader of the Augustans to the last of the Elizabethans.[1]

In view of the surprising extent of the influence Milton exerted on Pope, one turns expectantly back to Dryden, but only to find a totally different state of affairs. Dryden's admiration for *Paradise Lost* was frequently and generously expressed,[2] but it had slight effect upon his work. He never wrote an unrimed poem, and he borrowed but a phrase or two from Milton;[3] yet he did what has never been attempted since, he turned the loftiest of epics into a spectacular play. It was this undertaking that led to the meeting between the last of the giants of the Renaissance, old, blind, and "fallen on evil days," and the brilliant and highly successful leader of the new literary school. To Dryden's request for permission to make a rimed drama of the epic Milton replied, "It seems you have a mind to *Tagg* my Points, and you have my Leave to *Tagg* 'em." [4]

---

[1] Before the appearance of Mr. Snyder's article our knowledge of Pope's plan came from two sources, Spence's *Anecdotes* (pp. 288–9, from a conversation with Pope in 1743), and Ruffhead's *Life* (1769, pp. 409–23), which was compiled from the poet's own papers now in the British Museum. This projected epic gives interest to Percival Stockdale's story (*Memoirs*, 1809, ii. 44) that, when Pope was asked why he had not made a blank-verse translation of Homer, he replied that "he could translate it more easily into rhyme." Had he experimented with blank verse? The passages in *The Seasons* which have been attributed to him are probably Lyttelton's (see G. C. Macaulay in the *Athenaeum*, Oct. 1, 1904, p. 446, and in *James Thomson*, 1908, pp. 243–4).

[2] See above, p. 14 and n. 1.

[3] Langbaine's *Account of the English Dramatick Poets* (Oxford, 1691, p. 157) points out the similarity of these lines to a passage in *Samson Agonistes:*

> Unmoved she stood, and deaf to all my prayers,
> As seas and winds to sinking mariners.
> But seas grow calm, and winds are reconciled

(*Aureng-Zebe*, act i, in *Works*, Scott-Saintsbury ed., v. 212; cf. *Samson*, 960–62). The seventh line of *Veni, Creator Spiritus*, "O source of uncreated light" (*ib.* xi. 193), recalls the opening of the third book of *Paradise Lost*.

[4] See my note in *The Review* (later *The Weekly Review*), New York, June 14, 1919.

The result of the tagging, *The State of Innocence and Fall of Man,
an Opera* (1677), is a very curious production, such a line as

> O Prince, O Chief of many throned powers,

for example, appearing as

> Prince of the thrones, who in the fields of light.[1]

Great condensation was necessary on Dryden's part, since he
crowded into his five brief acts considerable new as well as much of
the old conversation, besides all the important happenings of the
epic. In consequence the great Vallombrosa simile is reduced to

> Our troops, like scattered leaves in autumn, lie.[2]

The sophistication, the conventionality of expression, the "points"
and antitheses of which the bewigged Restoration wits were fond,
characterize the inhabitants of Dryden's hell and of his Eden. The
fallen angels, for instance, in leaving the lake of fire,

> Shake off their slumber first, and next their fear;[3]

Eve replies to Adam's wooing,

> Some restraining thought, I know not why,
> Tells me, you long should beg, I long deny;[4]

while Adam, assuring her that he expects to live "still desiring"
what he still possesses (her love), declares that at their union "roses
unbid"

> Flew from their stalks, to strew [the] nuptial bower . . .
> And fishes leaped above the streams, the passing pomp to view.[5]

Such grotesque features are obvious enough and have been noticed
by most readers, with the result that admirers of Dryden have been
at a loss to explain how that appreciative and skilful artist came to
make such a feeble and absurd adaptation of a great work. The difficulty has been increased by the plausible remark of Sir Walter
Scott, whose comment prefixed to the standard edition of the play
has been read more often than the work itself: "The *costume* of
our first parents, had there been no other objection, must have excluded the *State of Innocence* from the stage, and accordingly it was
certainly never intended for representation."[6] Yet, in view of the
prominence which Dryden gives to scenery and mechanical devices,

---

[1] Act i (*Works*, v. 126; cf. *P. L.*, i. 128).   [4] Act ii, scene ii (*ib.* 140).
[2] *Ib.* (cf. *P. L.*, i. 302–3).   [5] Act iii (*ib.* 142–3).
[3] *Ib.* 127.   [6] *Ib.* 95.

it will be clear that the situation is exactly the reverse of what Scott thought it, and that Milton's 'tagged verses' really serve as little more than a frame-work for an elaborate musical spectacle. With Dryden the action and verse are subordinated to mechanical contrivances, and many of the lines may have no other function than to carry the story and gain time for the scene-shifters.[1] But either no one cared to spend the large sum necessary to stage the piece, or possibly Milton's political activities were not yet forgotten; at any rate, it was never given. It it had been, the honor which fell to Addison of being the popularizer of England's greatest poem might, though in less measure, have been Dryden's.

We have now followed the influence of *Paradise Lost* up to 1726. We have found several rimed poems, notably those of Blackmore, which employ the supernatural machinery of the epic; some others, like those of Pope, which take words and phrases from it; and approximately one hundred and fifty-five pieces in blank verse, all but about sixty-six of which make use of its style. For an age that delighted in imitation and held an exalted opinion of Milton, this is

---

[1] The frequent and detailed stage directions indicate many changes of scene, and, in the opportunity they afford for producing striking effects through costly mechanical contrivances, recall the elaborate masques of the period, upon one of which £2400 was expended. Here are some of the directions: "Betwixt the first Act and the second, while the Chiefs sit in the palace, may be expressed the sports of the Devils; as flights, and dancing in grotesque figures: And a song, expressing the change of their condition" (end of act i, *ib.* 133). — "Raphael descends to Adam, in a cloud. . . . They ascend to soft music, and a song is sung. The Scene changes, and represents, above, a Sun gloriously rising and moving orbicularly. . . . A black Cloud comes whirling from the adverse part of the Heavens, bearing Lucifer in it; at his nearer approach the body of the Sun is darkened" (act ii, scene i, *ib.* 133, 136). — "A Night-piece of a pleasant Bower: Adam and Eve asleep in it. . . . A Vision, where a tree rises loaden with fruits; four Spirits rise with it, and draw a canopy out of the tree; other Spirits dance about the tree in deformed shapes" (act iii, *ib.* 146–7). — "The Cloud descends with six Angels in it, and when it is near the ground, breaks, and on each side discovers six more" (act iv, *ib.* 151). — "The Scene shifts, and discovers deaths of several sorts. A Battle at Land, and a Naval Fight. . . . Here a Heaven descends, full of Angels and blessed Spirits, with soft Music, a Song and Chorus" (act v, *ib.* 175–6).

Intended stage presentation is also indicated by the attention which Dryden gives to music, dancing, and songs, and by his plan of omitting the transformation — impossible in the theater — which Lucifer makes in his appearance before meeting Uriel (see *P. L.*, iii. 634–44; Dryden's Lucifer simply puts on "a smooth, submissive face," act ii, scene i, *ib.* 136). Furthermore, in the *State of Innocence* it is not, as in the Bible and in Milton, the serpent who tempts Eve, since in the theater this idea would be hard to carry out and probably ludicrous; it is Lucifer in his own shape. The "costume" of our first parents, which to Scott presented an insurmountable difficulty, could easily have been managed, as it has been to-day in moving pictures of the story. Clearly, Dryden did not intend the characters to appear *in puris naturalibus*, for, besides having them exhibit no consciousness of nudity after the fall, he introduces into a vision in the third act a woman who is "habited like Eve."

not extensive borrowing. Besides, although we have encountered a number of eminent writers in this survey, we have found very few Miltonic poems with which even scholars are familiar, and, except for the *Splendid Shilling* and *Cyder*, none that appear to have attracted much of any attention even in their own day. Thomson, for example, refers to *Cyder* as the first poem after *Paradise Lost* to discard rime.[1] Furthermore, few of these early followers of Milton exhibit whole-hearted allegiance to his measure. Their productions seem as a rule to have been experiments, and not entirely satisfactory ones at that, for they were seldom repeated more than once or twice. Writers like Dennis or the editors of the *British Apollo*, who return frequently to the new meter, appear to have done so to avoid the trouble of riming.

It was not the hostility of the Augustans to blank verse in the abstract that stood in the way, for we have seen that even Pope used the measure and that most of his friends were favorably inclined towards it. To what, then, was the neglect due? To the poems themselves which Milton's followers wrote. These almost without exception lack inspiration and interest of any kind. Most of them are translations, hollow panegyrics, religious moralizings, or burlesques, and their verse, usually colorless and dull, falls either into unrimed couplets or into sheer prose. We find them unreadable and leave them unread, and there is every indication that the contemporaries of Pope and Addison did the same. In point of expression they are at their best when their subjects are most exalted, that is, when farthest from ordinary life; for the ablest verse is to be found in translations of the classics, and in pieces like *Prae-existence* and the *Last Day*, which have practically the same subject-matter as *Paradise Lost*. The *Splendid Shilling*, to be sure, had shown how effectively Milton's style and diction might be employed for humorous purposes; but this knowledge was of little account, for most writers had even less occasion to use the burlesque than the epic. Up to 1726 *Cyder* afforded almost the only instance of the serious treatment of an unpretentious topic in blank verse; and yet, though its success might be expected to have inspired imitation, it seems in the first seventeen years after its publication to have influenced only two pieces, one an attack upon it and the other a parody. That is, no one appears to have been willing to follow Philips in using blank

---

[1] *Autumn*, 645-7. At the end of the century even so good a scholar as Thomas Warton was ignorant not only of Philips's predecessors but of his contemporaries and immediate successors; for he tells us in his edition of Milton's minor poems (1785, p. x) that blank verse "after its revival by Philips had been long neglected."

verse seriously for everyday subjects. Most writers, rolling tamely in the rut of neo-classicism, never thought of doing so, others may have agreed with Pope that it was "quite wrong" to employ Milton's style for such themes, and many presumably doubted their ability to handle topics of the kind in a measure not yet domesticated.

For Milton's example, together with the praise of Roscommon, Dennis, Addison, and similar critics of rank, had made blank verse respected, admired, — and shunned. *Paradise Lost* was so remote, so unlike other poetry, that men stood in awe of it; they did not know how to adapt its lofty language, involved style, and strange irregular prosody to their humbler and less imaginative themes. In a word, blank verse seems to have been regarded in 1725 much as the telephone was in 1875, as a remarkable toy which it was interesting to experiment with but of which only a few enthusiasts expected to make any real use; or, to choose an illustration from the field of literature, its position in 1725 was similar to that of *vers libre* in 1900, — it could no longer be called a novelty but was by no means a popular meter. Cordially disliked and vigorously assailed by many, warmly admired and eloquently defended by others, Milton's measure, like Whitman's, seemed so ill adapted to the purposes and methods of most poetry that there was apparently little prospect of its coming into general use. Very few, to be sure, had so high an opinion of *Leaves of Grass* as Pope's contemporaries had of *Paradise Lost*, but in each case there was general doubt whether the new meter could be effectively employed by any save the master who invented it.

There was certainly no reason why the partisans of the couplet should be alarmed if a period of sixty years produced only one hundred and fifty unrimed poems, nearly half of which did not extend beyond a few lines. Indeed, at the end of the first quarter of the eighteenth century neo-classicism was seated firmly on the throne of public opinion with the closed couplet as its scepter; English numbers were being, if they had not already been, refined to the highest possible point, and sacrifices were constantly offered before the altars of Reason, Propriety, and Elegance, whose supremacy no one seemed seriously to question.

CHAPTER VI

THOMSON [1]

WHEN the fortunes of English verse seemed to be thus comfortably settled for some time to come, there appeared in the London bookshops a thin shilling folio of sixteen pages, one of which announced in large type, "Winter, a Poem, by James Thomson, A.M." The work gave rise to little comment, but must have found not a few readers, since it was reprinted within three months and passed through two more editions before the year was out. Encouraged by this reception, the author issued in the following year, 1727, a companion poem, *Summer*, in 1728 a third, *Spring*, and in 1730 the completed *Seasons*. The work came eventually to include 5,541 lines, but the germ of the whole and all its significant features are to be found in the 405 lines of the original *Winter*, which may fairly be termed "an epoch-marking work." Yet, as is often the case, the marking was done so quietly that no one seems to have been conscious of anything unusual about the poem. Even Thomson himself, a few months before composing it, wrote to a friend, "I firmly resolve to pursue divinity as the only thing now I am fit for," and after it was partly finished referred to it as "only a present amusement," which he should probably drop before long.[2]

Nor is the real significance of *Winter* generally understood at the present time. The poem is supposed to be one of the earliest and most important manifestations of what has unfortunately been termed the "beginnings of the romantic movement"; but such "beginnings" may be found at almost any time and place one chooses to look for them, and all who know Thomson best are agreed as to his essential classicism. The importance of the use of blank verse in *The Seasons* has often been emphasized, but without sufficient realization of the number of unrimed poems that preceded it or of its differences from them. As regards nature poetry also Thomson's

---

[1] Since 1907, when this chapter was first written, a number of what seemed to be its more novel points of view have appeared in G. C. Macaulay's *James Thomson* (*English Men of Letters*, 1908). The delay has, however, enabled me to take advantage of various suggestions in that sound and discriminating study.

[2] Letters to Dr. Cranston, April 3, and September, 1725, *Poetical Works* (Aldine ed. 1847), vol. i, pp. xvi, xxiii.

contribution has frequently been misunderstood; for, though he is a figure of the first importance in this field, he did not create the taste by which he was appreciated. The feeling for the beauty of the external world revealed in Lady Winchilsea's *Nocturnal Reverie*, Gay's *Rural Sports*, Shaftesbury's *Characteristics*, and other works published before 1726 has been pointed out by various scholars; and it is noteworthy that a genuine love of nature is apparent in Ramsay's *Gentle Shepherd*, Dyer's *Grongar Hill*, and John Armstrong's description of winter, all of them published, or composed, in the years 1725 and 1726, when *Winter* was being written. Accordingly, while Thomson is the most important nature poet before Wordsworth, he was by no means the first writer of his time to feel, or the first to give effective expression to the feeling, that 'night and day, sun, moon, and stars, likewise a wind on the heath, are all sweet things.'

The principal significance of *The Seasons* lies in its popularity. Blank verse as good as Thomson's had been written before *Winter* appeared; Philips had employed it for familiar themes, and Watts had arrived at a style, diction, and prosody much nearer to those in vogue to-day than what the Scottish poet made use of. Yet English literature went on unchanged. Poetry far more romantic, with a finer feeling for nature expressed in nobler, more lyric verse, — pieces, that is, not unlike the "Songs of Innocence" or the best of the "Lyrical Ballads," — might conceivably have been written in 1725; but they would almost certainly have left as few traces on the century which gave them birth as did Blake's work and Thomson's own *Castle of Indolence*. *The Seasons* accomplished two things of the highest importance. It showed how real nature could be dealt with effectively in poetry, and how blank verse could be successfully devoted to the treatment of everyday subjects; but it did both by virtue of its popularity, by being enjoyed by all, the people as well as the poets. It might have contained twice as many faults and half as many excellences as it did and still, had it remained equally popular, have lost none of its historical significance. What was needed was success, and Thomson's success was due in part to his limitations and in part even to his very faults.[1] It was only a road which "got somewhere" that would have been followed, one that seemed both to readers and to poets clearly to lead well up towards the summit of

---

[1] Wordsworth held that what the eighteenth century principally admired in Thomson was "his false ornaments," which "are exactly of that kind . . . most likely to strike the undiscerning" (*Prose Works*, ed. Grosart, 1876, ii. 119). Miss Reynolds's remark is better, "A touch more of subtlety, of vision, of mystery, of the faculty divine, and Thomson might have waited for recognition as Wordsworth did" (*Nature in English Poetry*, 2d ed., Chicago, 1909, p. 101).

Parnassus. Less obvious ways, that wound past shyer flowers, or through valleys overflowing with a more haunting melody of birds, or by cliffs affording wider views of the might and mystery of "old ocean's gray and melancholy waste," would to us be more alluring; but in Pope's day their beauty would have been seen by few, and without the sanction of popular approval they would have been little used. For the eighteenth century did not share our interest in lovely by-ways that lose themselves in woods. The cult of the minor poet had not yet risen; revivals of perverse but powerful writers, or of rapturous but formless and obscure ones, were unknown. It was a period when bards were unusually willing to follow a leader, and this was true not only of the Augustans but of those who were stirred by vague feelings which they hardly understood and to which they were unable to give poetic voice.

The enthusiasm and rapidity with which Thomson's example was followed illustrates how ready poets were for a clear path into new fields. In the sixty years before *Winter* appeared there were only some hundred and fifty unrimed pieces, whereas over a hundred were printed in the fifteen years (1731–45) that followed the completion of *The Seasons* and about seventy in the next five years. Among the poems that came after 1726 were a number of the most widely-read works of the century, Somervile's *Chace* (1735), Glover's *Leonidas* (1737), Young's *Night Thoughts* (1742–6), Armstrong's *Art of Preserving Health* (1744), and Akenside's *Pleasures of Imagination* (1744). Thomson is, of course, not responsible for all the blank verse published between 1731 and 1750, but he had some effect on most of it, and without his example many of the pieces that employed it, particularly the longer works, would never have been written. Furthermore, his influence had only begun to make itself felt by 1750, for it persisted well into the nineteenth century, even after the shores of England had slipped forever from the straining eyes of Byron and Keats and the bay of Spezzia had closed over the restless heart of Shelley.

The vogue of *The Seasons* was far greater than is generally realized. *Winter* went through four editions the year it was published, and was reprinted in 1728, 1730, and 1734; *Summer* reached five separate editions, *Spring* three, *Autumn* one; the collected *Seasons* was printed three times in 1730 and forty-seven times more before the end of the century, besides being included in twenty-two editions of the poet's works: that is, it was published in whole or in part no less than eighty-eight times in the seventy-four years after it was first printed. Nor did its popularity cease then. Four editions appeared in each of the years 1802 and 1803, five in 1805, and, counting those included in the works and the three printed in America, there were forty-four in the first two decades of the century.[1] It was some seventy years after the first of the "Seasons" was written that Coleridge, seeing a much-worn copy of the poem lying on the window-seat of an obscure inn, exclaimed, "That is true fame!"[2]

Tributes to the poem are so embarrassingly abundant that there is room to quote only a few of the later ones. In 1774 the author of the *Sentimental Sailor* declared that Thomson's "matchless song" would last as long as "the circling seasons still appear."[3] In 1781 the *Critical Review* remarked, "The *beauties of spring* have already been so amply described, and so nobly treated by Thomson, that few readers will bring themselves to imagine that any other writer can treat this subject with equal force, elegance, and propriety."[4] This comment occurs in a review of an anonymous poem on spring, the author of which "adores" the "amazing heights, by thee [Thomson] alone attain'd."[5] The *Monthly Review* asserted in 1793 that, to be effective, descriptive poetry needed to be "written by a master hand, little inferior to Thomson himself," and six years later mentioned certain requisites without which "the finest passages in Homer, Virgil, Milton, and Thomson, would excite no emotion."[6] In view of these commendations and the opinion of James Grahame—himself no mean nature poet — that Thomson's descriptions have "a genius and felicity which none of his followers need ever hope to equal,"[7] it is not strange that John Aikin affirmed in 1804, "*The Seasons . . .* yields, perhaps, to no other English poem in popularity."[8] One is somewhat surprised, however, to find Hazlitt remarking fourteen years later that Thomson was "perhaps, the most popular of all our poets, treating of a subject that all can understand, and in a way that

---

[1] These figures are taken mainly from the Caxton Head sale catalogue (No. 556, Feb. 19, 1912, which lists "nearly 150 different editions " of *The Seasons*), with additions from the British Museum catalogue, and some from the *Cambridge History of English Literature* (English ed., x. 446–7). An episode in *Autumn* was developed into "a legendary tale" (*Philemon and Lavinia*) by David Mountfort in 1783; *Gleanings from Thomson, or the Village Muse*, appeared about 1800 (see *Mo. Rev.*, enl. ed., xxxi. 323), and a professed imitation so late as 1808 (see *Europ. Mag.*, liv. 218).

[2] Hazlitt, *Lectures on the English Poets*, 1818 (*Works*, 1902, v. 88).

[3] Quoted, *Mo. Rev.*, li. 342.

[4] lii. 201.

[5] Quoted, *ib.* 203.

[6] Enlarged ed., xii. 222, xxix. 337; cf. vi. 455.

[7] Preface to his *British Georgics* (Edin., 1809).

[8] *Letters on English Poetry* (2d ed., 1807), 164. In the *Cabinet of Poetry* (ed. S. J. Pratt, 1808), which professes to include "only the best and most exquisite pieces," Milton occupies one whole volume (351 pages), Thomson 184 pages, and Pope 144.

is interesting to all alike." [1] Mr. Dennis's assertion that *The Seasons* "was to be found in every cottage, and passages from the poem were familiar to every school-boy," [2] is borne out by the facts that in 1761 Michael Bruce "employed himself at leisure hours in transcribing large portions of Milton and of Thomson," [3] that Burns declared his fellow-countryman to be one of his "favourite authors," [4] and that a certain H. I. Johns, who was born in 1780, "while quite a lad . . . committed to memory nearly the whole of Thomson's *Seasons*," for "Thomson was his idol, and to his impassioned and glowing descriptions of Nature he ascribed, in no small degree, his love of the country and his taste for elevating studies." [5] It is accordingly no more than the truth to say, with Mr. Seccombe, "From 1750 to 1850 Thomson was in England the poet, *par excellence*, not of the eclectic and literary few, but of the large and increasing cultivated middle class"; [6] or with Mr. Saintsbury, "No poet has given the special pleasure which poetry is capable of giving to so large a number of persons in so large a measure as Thomson." [7]

Such a popularity as this must have had far-reaching effects, which can be estimated only in a general way and many of which are hardly to be traced. In the field of poetry this influence was all the more marked because *The Seasons* appeared before either blank-verse or descriptive pieces had established themselves. Had it been published twenty-five years later, its vogue might possibly have been as great but its influence on literature would not have been a tithe of what it was. Furthermore, to quote again from Mr. Saintsbury, Thomson "has the peculiar merit of choosing a subject which appeals to and is comprehensible by everybody; which no one can scorn as trivial and yet which no one can feel to be too fine or too esoteric for him. And though he treats this in the true poetical spirit of making the common as though it were uncommon, he does not make it too uncommon for the general taste to relish." [8] In conse-

---

[1] *Lectures on the English Poets*, 1818 (*Works*, 1902, v. 87). About the same time one William Wight prophesied, in his lines for the anniversary of Thomson's birth (*Cottage Poems*, Edin., 1820, pp. 8–9), that the "warblings" of his "heaven-taught lyre" would "but with Nature's self expire."

[2] *Age of Pope* (1894), 91.

[3] Memoir, in *Works* (ed. Grosart, Edin., 1865), 16–17.

[4] Letter to John Murdoch, Jan. 15, 1783.

[5] W. H. K. Wright, *West-Country Poets* (1896), 275. So late as 1827 Henry Neele declared in his *Lectures on English Poetry* (*Literary Remains*, N. Y., 1829, p. 123), "Thomson is the first of our descriptive poets; I had almost said, the first in the world."

[6] *Dict. Nat. Biog.*

[7] Ward's *English Poets*, iii. 169.   [8] *Ib.* 170.

quence he was eagerly read by the simple cottager, the prosperous merchant, the fashionable lady, and the college don, while poets of all kinds paid tribute to him, — the sophisticated and artificial Pope, the spontaneous Burns, the delicate Collins, and the massive Wordsworth.

It may be interesting and not altogether profitless to speculate as to what would have been the development of blank verse without *The Seasons*. No later work could have taken its place, since both in subject-matter and in treatment it pleased all sorts and conditions of men better than any other poem of its century did, and since, aside from *Paradise Lost*, the only other unrimed work that enjoyed an extensive popularity was the *Night Thoughts*, which did not begin to appear till 1742, and in which even at this late time Young might not have relinquished his lifelong devotion to the couplet had it not been for the influence of the Scottish poet. Of course Thomson did not work alone. Enthusiasm for *Paradise Lost*, which was increasing rapidly between 1712 and 1745, could not fail to affect poetry, and Thomson's immediate predecessors had done no slight service in familiarizing both writers and readers with the new measure. Twenty-five years earlier such a work as *Winter* could hardly have been composed at all, nor would the English public have been ready to receive it. The probabilities are, therefore, that without *The Seasons* unrimed poems would have increased slowly in number and that now and then one of length would, like *Cyder*, have achieved some popularity. Yet it is hard to tell how far-reaching would have been the effect if the general use of blank verse had been delayed twenty years.

How is it that Thomson came to do what none of his contemporaries seemed capable of? The explanation is probably that *Winter*, which determined the character of all the "Seasons," was a Scottish work, was hardly more an expression of the literary England of its day or a product of the normal evolution of English poetry than was *Leaves of Grass* one hundred and twenty-five years later. It is Scottish throughout, it was written by a Scot, it was suggested by Scottish verses, it pictures Scottish scenes.[1] Like the American work, it was the outcome of a different environment, of a somewhat different race and literary tradition, from that which found expression in the

---

[1] While composing the poem Thomson wrote to his friend Cranston (September, 1725?): "There [in Scotland] I walk in spirit, and disport in its beloved gloom. This country I am in, is not very entertaining; no variety but that of woods, and them we have in abundance; but where is the living stream? the airy mountain? and the hanging rock? with twenty other things that elegantly please the lover of nature?" (*Poetical Works*, 1847, vol. i, p. xxii).

London literature of its time. Thomson had been reared in a wild Scottish country. He had, to be sure, spent ten years at the University of Edinburgh; but the northern capital was then separated from the southern by a long, arduous journey and by marked divergences in almost every aspect of life and thought. "Broad Scots," which Thomson never lost, was then universal in Edinburgh; men were less formal and finished but sturdier as well as more natural than in London; and pieces like the *Gentle Shepherd* and the winter poems of Riccaltoun, Thomson, and Armstrong (all written between 1724 and 1726) show, when contrasted with the satires of Pope, Swift, and Young, or with the lighter verse of Prior and Gay, that poetry was closer to life in the northern metropolis than in the southern.

Since the days of the Stuarts, English literature had been drawing more and more away from the people. By attaching itself to the court circle and, like the court, becoming dominated by artificial French standards, it had to a great extent come to be the diversion of a leisured coterie that set an exaggerated value upon regularity, precision, elegance, and wit. These qualities, it goes without saying, did not then, as they do not now, particularly interest the average reader, who, though he may well have enjoyed the clever satire and the shrewd, tersely-expressed observations on life that mark neoclassic verse, nevertheless missed many things which his forefathers had found in poetry. That such was the true state of affairs is shown by the eagerness with which he turned to the periodicals, sentimental drama, and fiction of the day, to the redactions of old romances, and to Milton. The attitude of the people is strikingly illustrated in the enthusiasm with which they greeted *The Seasons*. Here at last was contemporary poetry adapted to their taste, something that appealed to their imagination, their love of the real country, as well as to their national pride and their sentimentality. Hitherto there had been a great gulf not only between blank verse and the fashionable poetry of the day, but between both kinds of verse and the taste of the large body of readers. Something had been done towards filling this gulf, but the process promised to be a slow one; when suddenly an outsider, following his natural bent with little realization of its divergence from the habit of his new neighbors, bridged the chasm.

But though scarcely more of a revolutionist than Johnson, — for he loved his ease and in general, even on most literary subjects, thought much like other men, — the bard "more fat than bard beseems" did in some matters raise a banner of mild revolt. He looked forward to finding at Hagley, his friend Lyttelton's estate, "the muses of the great simple country, not the little, fine-lady muses of Richmond Hill." [1]   To the second edition of *Winter* he added a vigorous preface assailing the literature of his time as a "wintry world of letters, . . . the reigning fopperies of a tasteless age" made up of "forced unaffecting fancies, little glittering prettinesses, mixed turns of wit and expression, which are as widely different from native poetry as buffoonery is from the perfection of human thinking." He urged poetry to "exchange her low, venal, trifling, subjects for such as are fair, useful, and *magnificent*," and to "execute these so as at once to please, instruct, *surprise*, and *astonish*." This "choosing of great and serious subjects" was, he thought, a first step towards a much-needed "revival of poetry," and in his opinion nature afforded the best of themes because of its "magnificence" and "inspiring" qualities, because it "enlarges and transports the soul." Hence, he concluded, "the best . . . Poets have been passionately fond of retirement, and solitude. The wild romantic country was their delight." [2]   These were vigorous words to pen when Pope, Swift, and Gay were at the height of their powers. They were probably called forth by adverse criticisms of the first edition of *Winter;* for there is every indication that Thomson had no idea of reforming English taste when he wrote the poem, since he said of it, "Being only a present amusement, it is ten to one but I drop it whenever another fancy comes across." [3]

In this same preface he spoke of nature's putting on "the crimson robes of the morning, the strong effulgence of noon, the sober suit of the evening, or the deep sables of blackness and tempest." Clearly, a poet who flamed thus in the cooler element of prose loved the florid and exuberant, the grand and vague. No wonder he was fond of Hakluyt's *Voyages,*[4] the *Faerie Queene*, and of works which "up the lofty diapason roll," [5] or that he desired his "numbers" and his theme to be "wildly great." [6] He had a strong and instinctive dislike for limitations of almost every kind. His fervent imagination was not definite, like Dante's; it delighted, as did Milton's, in large, general effects. It demanded a wide sweep. Such a line as

> Infinite splendour! wide-investing all [7]

is typical of him.

---

[1] Letter to Lyttelton, July, 1743, *Works* (1847), vol. i, p. lxxxvii.

[2] I quote from the reprint in J. L. Robertson's admirable Oxford edition of Thomson (pp. 240–41), to which all my references are made. The italics are mine.

[3] Letter to Cranston, September, 1725?, *Works* (1847), vol. i, p. xxiii.

[4] See his letter to Mallet, Aug. 9, 1745 (Philobiblon Soc., *Miscellanies*, 1857–8, iv. 39, first pagination).

[5] *Castle of Indolence*, I. xli. 362.   [6] *Winter*, 27.

[7] *Autumn*, 1210. Miss Reynolds has an excellent paragraph on Thomson's "dislike of boundaries," in her *Nature in English Poetry* (1909), 92–3.

It was inevitable that a poet with these tastes should be deeply stirred by the most sublime and sonorous of English poets. Thomson has high praise for Milton in the first edition of *Winter:*

> Great *Homer* too appears, of *daring* Wing!
> *Parent* of Song! and *equal*, by his Side,
> The *British Muse*, join'd Hand in Hand, they walk,
> *Darkling*, nor miss their Way to Fame's Ascent.[1]

In the second of the "Seasons," *Summer*, he expressed his feelings with still greater warmth:

> And every greatly amiable *Muse*
> Of elder Ages in thy *Milton* met!
> His was the treasure of Two Thousand Years,
> Seldom indulg'd to Man, a God-like Mind,
> Unlimited, and various, as his Theme;
> Astonishing as *Chaos;* as the Bloom
> Of blowing *Eden* fair; soft as the Talk
> Of our *grand Parents*, and as *Heaven* sublime.[2]

Thomson also wrote a preface to the *Areopagitica*, imitated both *Allegro* and *Penseroso*, referred to their author several times in his letters, and borrowed not only words and phrases but whole passages from him.[3] Since nearly half of these numerous borrowings are from the minor poems, they reveal a close acquaintance, very unusual at the time, with the shorter as well as the longer works; and, as some of them occur in Thomson's juvenilia, it is clear that his familiarity with Milton dates from an early and impressionable age.

The language and style of *The Seasons* also, as one would expect, give abundant evidence of admiration for *Paradise Lost*. They do more: they indicate an essential kinship between the two poets on many vital matters. For example, the author of *The Seasons* liked the grand style and strove to write in it. Part of his admiration for *Paradise Lost* must have been due to its lofty aloofness of expression, to the organ tone which he apparently tried to catch in the orotund and often splendidly impressive climaxes to which he was fond of working up. Milton's largeness of utterance will be heard in single lines, like

> Had slumbered on the vast Atlantic deep;

or in such passages as these:

---

[1] Lines 289–92.

[2] Quoted from the first edition (1727), pages 47–8; the passage corresponds to lines 1567–71 of the latest text.

[3] See below, Appendix A. For passages in Thomson's letters which refer to Milton, see Macaulay's *Thomson*, 24 ("Evil is their good," cf. *P. L.*, iv. 110), 54 (Milton's

The vegetable world is also thine,
Parent of Seasons! who the pomp precede
That waits thy throne, as through thy vast domain,
Annual, along the bright ecliptic road
In world-rejoicing state it moves sublime.

Hence, in old dusky time, a deluge came:
When the deep-cleft disparting orb, that arched
The central waters round, impetuous rushed
With universal burst into the gulf,
And o'er the high-piled hills of fractured earth
Wide-dashed the waves in undulation vast,
Till, from the centre to the streaming clouds,
A shoreless ocean tumbled round the globe.[1]

The sonorousness of such resounding lines is sometimes increased by the Miltonic device of introducing unusual proper names which have an imaginative appeal:

Whence with annual pomp,
Rich king of floods! o'erflows the swelling Nile.
From his two springs in Gojam's sunny realm
Pure-welling out, he through the lucid lake
Of fair Dambea rolls his infant stream. . . .
. . . . and all that from the tract
Of woody mountains stretched thro' gorgeous Ind
Fall on Cormandel's coast or Malabar;
From Menam's orient stream.[2]

One passage of the kind is of particular interest because the first part of it was clearly suggested by a purple patch in *Paradise Lost:*

The huge incumbrance of horrific woods
From Asian Taurus, from Imaus stretched
Athwart the roving Tartar's sullen bounds;
Give opening Hemus to my searching eye,
And high Olympus pouring many a stream!
Oh, from the sounding summits of the north,
The Dofrine Hills, through Scandinavia rolled

"Hail, wedded love," is quoted), 55 ("the mind is its own place" is cited, without quotation-marks, from *P. L.*, i. 254). In the preface to the second edition of *Winter* Milton is mentioned and the expression "the sober Suit of the Evening" (cf. "civil-suited Morn, *Penseroso,* 122) is used.

[1] *Summer,* 1008, 112–116; *Spring,* 309–16. See also *Spring,* 70–77; *Summer,* 175–84, 651–2; *Winter,* 94–117. The following lines (*Summer,* 90–94) illustrate how Thomson, owing partly to the jerkiness of his style, sometimes failed in his attempts at the orotund:

Prime cheerer, Light!
Of all material beings first and best!
Efflux divine! Nature's resplendent robe,
Without whose vesting beauty all were wrapt
In unessential gloom!

[2] *Summer,* 804–27.

To farthest Lapland and the frozen main;
From lofty Caucasus, far seen by those
Who in the Caspian and black Euxine toil;
From cold Riphaean rocks, which the wild Russ
Believes the stony girdle of the world.[1]

There are some respects in which the Scottish bard even outdid his master, what was with the earlier poet a native manner frequently becoming with the later one an exaggerated mannerism. In the following typical passage, for instance, naturalness of expression, as well as the flow of the verse, has been lost through excessive and inartistic inversions and the use of adjectives for adverbs:

Here wandering oft, fired with the restless thirst
Of thy applause, I solitary court
The inspiring breeze, and meditate the book
Of Nature, ever open, aiming thence
Warm from the heart to learn the moral song.
And, as I steal along the sunny wall,
Where Autumn basks, with fruit empurpled deep,
My pleasing theme continual prompts my thought.[2]

There may be as many distortions of the normal word-order in *Paradise Lost* as in *The Seasons*, but they seem less frequent because they are better adapted to the epic style and because Milton introduces them more skilfully. It will be observed that in the passage quoted the adjectives which take the places of adverbs are likely to be out of their normal order, and that some of them, like "solitary" in the second line, are used not so much adverbially as appositively. Except in such instances appositives are not common in Thomson, nor are parenthetical expressions.[3]

Thomson's use of words is no less Miltonic than his style. Adjectives, besides being, as we have seen, constantly employed as adverbs, are occasionally used as nouns. We find, for instance, "the blue profound," "that full complex," "the pure cerulean," "the blue immense," "the blue serene," "the breezy void," "the solitary vast," "the . . . licentious proud," and "whatever fair [i. e., beauty]

---

[1] *Autumn*, 782–93; cf. *P. L.*, iii. 431–2. A passage in Thomson's *Liberty* (iii. 226–56), from which the following lines are taken, contains many proper names:

To where the frozen Tanais scarcely stirs
The dead Maeotic pool, or the long Rha
In the black Scythian sea his torrent throws.

[2] *Autumn*, 668–75. Note such chiasmic inversions as "To the quire celestial Thee resound" (*Summer*, 190).

[3] I have noticed parenthetical expressions in *Summer*, 1627 (cf. line 995 of the 1730 edition); *Autumn*, 732, 889–91, 900–901, 1204; *Winter*, 410, 667, 926.

High fancy forms." [1]   Adjectives are made into verbs in such expressions as "Spring . . . Greened all the year," "whatever greens the spring," "to . . . serene his soul," "savaged by woe," "truth . . . Elates his being," "the . . . ray Russets the plain." [2] Verbs and substantives interchange places in the phrases "in sad presage," "a sweep of rivers," "the chide of streams," "one wide waft," "oaks . . . tuft the . . . mounts," "by hardship sinewed," "a . . . calm Fleeces unbounded ether," "the swain Disastered stands," "tempest the . . . brine." [3] In *The Seasons*, as in *Paradise Lost*, intransitive verbs are sometimes made transitive, and vice versa. The Nile, for instance, "devolves his maze," and a tongue is described as "devolving . . . A roll of periods"; similarly, we have "dejects his . . . eye," "gazing the inverted landscape," "meditate the blue profound," "meditate the book," "protrudes the bursting gems," and, as examples of transitive verbs used intransitively, "insect armies waft Keen in the . . . breeze," and lightning "discloses wide." [4]

In this matter of interchanging the parts of speech Thomson is, except in using adjectives for adverbs, more conservative than his master, but in the number of his unusual compound words he leaves him far behind. He makes these in almost every conceivable way: by combining adverbs with participles, as in "idly-butting," "idly-tortured," "seldom-meeting," "soon-descending," "ever-cheating," "ill-submitting"; [5] adverbs (or adjectives used as adverbs) with adjectives, as in "wildly-devious," "fair-diffusive," "richly-gorgeous," or with verbs, as in "full-exerts," "wide-hover," "thick-urge," "gay-twinkle"; [6] nouns with participles, as in "woodbine-wrought," "fever-cooling," "life-sufficing," "jargon-teaching," "stench-involved," "forest-rustling," "wisdom-tempered," "folly-painting,"

---

[1] *Summer*, 1248 (cf. *P. L.*, ii. 980), 1785; *Autumn*, 1097, 1356; *Winter*, 693; *Autumn*, 126; *Winter*, 804 (cf. *P. L.*, vi. 203), 322; *Spring*, 1139–40 (cf. *P. L.*, ix. 608, xi. 717, etc.).

[2] *Spring*, 320–21; *Autumn*, 1260; *Spring*, 870; *Summer*, 1081; *Autumn*, 1336–7; *Hymn*, 95–6.

[3] *Summer*, 1050 (cf. *P. L.*, vi. 201, *P. R.*, i. 394, etc.); *Autumn*, 712, 1267; *Winter*, 271; *Spring*, 915; *Summer*, 1468; *Autumn*, 958; *Winter*, 278–9, 1016 (cf. *Liberty*, iv. 142, and *P. L.*, vii. 412).

[4] *Summer*, 816; *Autumn*, 16–17; *Summer*, 1066, 1247 (cf. *P. L.*, viii. 258, etc.), 1248 (cf. *Comus*, 547, and *Lycidas*, 66); *Autumn*, 670, 1311; *Spring*, 121–2 (cf. *P. L.*, ii. 1042); *Summer*, 1138. Somewhat similar is the use of "preys," instead of "preys upon" with an object, in "The . . . eagle . . . preys in distant isles" (*Spring*, 759–65).

[5] *Spring*, 801, 1044; *Summer*, 26; *Winter*, 50, 210, 957.

[6] *Summer*, 80, 851, 1622; *Spring*, 1120; *Autumn*, 173; *Winter*, 141, 788.

"snow-fed," or with adjectives, as in "dew-bright," "blood-happy," "plume-dark," or even with other nouns, as in "household-kind," "torrent-softness," "monarch-swain," "Parent-Power," "reaper-train," "labourer-ox." [1] Most common of all is the combination of an adjective (as a rule used adverbially) with a participle (commonly the present), as in "white-empurpled," "fresh-expanded," "various-blossomed," "mellow-tasted," "sad-dispersed," "mute-imploring," "nice-judging," "white-dashing," "dire-clinging," "deep-fermenting," "fierce-conflicting," "swift-gliding," "new-moulding," "hollow-blustering," "new-creating." [2] As both present and past participles are used in these words, and as the adjectives are related to the participles in different ways, there is greater variety in such compounds than is at first realized; yet their number can hardly fail to impress even the casual reader, for a single line sometimes contains two, and five successive lines occasionally have as many as four.[3]

But the feature of Thomson's diction that is likely to attract most attention is his use of uncommon words derived from the Latin. He has, for example, "vernant," "clamant," "prelusive," "amusive," "infusive," "diffusive," "effulgent," "effulged," "effulgence," "detruded," "sublimed," "convolved," "convolution," "exanimate," "efflux," "distent," "emergent," "relucent," "turgent," "luculent," "conjunctive," "incomposed," "effused," "infracted," "auriferous," "sequacious," "ovarious," "innoxious," "flexile," "illapse," "magnific," "concoctive," "empurpled," "agglomerating," "incult," "relumed," "constringent." [4] Thomson also follows Milton in giving to a word a meaning or an application which it had in Latin or Greek but has lost in English. Thus we find such expressions as the farmer "incumbent o'er" the plough, "the liberal

---

[1] *Summer*, 461, 668, 836, 1544; *Autumn*, 1206; Winter, 151, 377, 615, 995; *Summer*, 86; *Autumn*, 456, 869; *Spring*, 772, 985; *Summer*, 494, 546; *Autumn*, 225; *Winter*, 240.

[2] *Spring*, 110; *Summer*, 477; *Autumn*, 5, 705; *Winter*, 263; *Spring*, 163, 408, 912; *Autumn*, 875; *Winter*, 13, 159, 196, 951, 989, 1044.

[3] See, for example, *Spring*, 1059; *Winter*, 210, 437; *Spring*, 381-5.

[4] *Spring*, 82 (cf. *P. L.*, x. 679); *Autumn*, 350; *Spring*, 175, 216 (also *Summer*, 1660), 868; *Summer*, 1229 (also *Autumn*, 657, 882); *Spring*, 190 (also *Summer*, 135, 635, *Autumn*, 38, etc.); *Summer*, 1519 (the *New English Dictionary* gives no instance of "effulge" before 1729, — Thomson's *Britannia* and Savage's *Wanderer*); *Autumn*, 25 (also *Winter*, 643, etc.; cf. *P. L.*, iii. 388, v. 458, vi. 680); *Spring*, 568, 827 (also *Summer*, 110), 837 (also *Summer*, 343, *Autumn*, 1183, cf. *P. L.*, vi. 328); *Autumn*, 839; *Spring*, 1052; *Summer*, 92; *Spring*, 145, 263; *Summer*, 162; *Autumn*, 693; *Winter*, 710; *Summer*, 1776, 491 (cf. *P. L.*, ii. 989), 509 (also 1256), 604, 648, 1713; *Autumn*, 875, 1161; *Summer*, 980, 1262; *Autumn*, 134 (cf. *P. L.*, v. 773, x. 354), 408, 674, 766, 884; *Winter*, 491 (also 838), 699. See also Macaulay's *Thomson*, 157-9.

air" (abundant), "the crude unripened year," "the effusive South," the "lapse" of a stream, the "horrid heart" of a lion, a pool "reverted" by its bank, "the latent rill," "Essential Presence" (God), "unessential gloom," "the opponent bank" (opposite), eaglets "ardent with paternal fire," "the informing Author" (God, who works within), "the outrageous flood" (violent), "will preventing will" (anticipating), "the sordid stream" (muddy), "bounteous" milk, "diffused" (of a person), walking "in cheerful error," storks "in congregation full," mountains "invested with a keen . . . sky," "frequent foot," a river "constrained" between two hills, "the inflated wave," "frost-concocted glebe" (cooked or solidified), "obsequious" reindeer (obedient).[1] It will be seen that these peculiarities of diction not only are of the same kind that Milton employed, but are frequently the same words put to the same uncommon uses. Other words which Thomson seems to have borrowed from the master are "mossy-tinctured," "low-thoughted," "massy," "shagged," "dappled," "weltering," "darkling."[2]

Any such analysis as this must, however, fall far short of giving an adequate impression of the language and style of *The Seasons*. It cannot show how frequently the characteristics occur, and it must overlook much that cannot be tabulated but that materially affects the general impression. The fact is that, if there is a pompous, contorted way of saying a thing, Thomson is likely to hit upon it; that of two words he prefers the one of Latin origin and of two Latin words that which is less common. Calling things by their right names and speaking simply, directly, and naturally, as in conversation, seems to have been his abhorrence. The stories of Musidora and "the lovely young Lavinia" are closer to real country life than the language and style in which they are told are to ordinary speech;

[1] *Spring*, 41 (cf. the . . . beech that o'er the stream Incumbent hung," *Summer*, 1363–4, "night incumbent o'er their heads," *Winter*, 924, and *P. L.*, i. 226), 98, 142 (cf. *Lycidas*, 3), 144 (cf. "effusive source," *Summer*, 1732, "large effusion" of rain, *Spring*, 176, and *P. L.*, vi. 765), 160 (cf. *P. L.*, viii. 263), 265 (cf. the "horrid loves" of animals, 830, and *P. L.*, ix. 185, etc.), 407, 496, 557 (cf. *P. L.*, v. 841); *Summer*, 94 (cf. *P. L.*, ii. 439); *Spring*, 666, 760, 860 (cf. "Informer of the planetary train," i. e. God, and "Poetry . . . informs the page With music," *Summer*, 104, 1753–5), 1071 (cf. *P. L.*, ii. 435, vii. 212, x. 232), 1123 (cf. *Nativity*, 24); *Summer*, 386, 679; *Autumn*, 517 (cf. *Samson*, 118), 626 (cf. with *P. L.*, iv. 239, vii. 302, and cf. "erroneous race," *Isaac Newton*, 199, with *P. L.*, vi. 146), 859, 882 (cf. *P. L.*, i. 208, iii. 10, vii. 372); *Winter*, 6, 101, 166, 706 (also *Autumn*, 7), 854 (cf. *P. L.*, vi. 783).

[2] *Spring*, 381 (cf. *P. L.*, v. 285, *Comus*, 752); *Autumn*, 967 (cf. *Comus*, 6); *Spring*, 840 (also *Summer*, 669, *Autumn*, 1244, etc., and cf. *P. L.*, i. 285, ii. 878, etc., eleven times in all), 910 (cf. *Winter*, 281, and *Comus*, 429); *Summer*, 48 (cf. *Allegro*, 44, of the dawn in each case), 265 (cf. *P. L.*, i. 78, *Lycidas*, 13); *Autumn*, 753 (also *Winter*, 536, and cf. *P. L.*, iii. 39).

and, widely as these artificial pastorals differ from the homely tale of Michael's sheepfold, Thomson is nearer to Wordsworth in what he says than in how he says it. Instead of "You steal silently along the dale overhung with woods," he writes,

> There along the dale
> With woods o'erhung . . .
> You silent steal.[1]

Such a sentence, and contortions of English like

> The winding vale its lavish stores,
> Irriguous, spreads,[2]

would not be objectionable now and then; but what can be said in defense of passages like these?

> A voice, than human more, the abstracted ear
> Of fancy strikes.

> Then too the pillared dome magnific heaved
> Its ample roof; and luxury within
> Poured out her glittering stores. The canvas smooth,
> With glowing life protuberant, to the view
> Embodied rose.[3]

Furthermore, Thomson has a penchant for words which are to-day particularly disliked, such as "swain," "glebe," "gelid," "lucid," "vernal," "verdant," "umbrage," "mead," "verdure," "the fair," "the muse." He also delighted in unnatural and inflated circumlocutions, like "the household feathery people" (hens); "the copious fry" or "the finny race" or "the glittering finny swarms" (fish); "the furry nations," which include "the docile tribe" (reindeer) that live amid "the heapy wreath" or "the white abyss" commonly called snow.[4] For birds he had more than fifteen periphrases, speaking of them in one place as "the plumy burden" that "winnow the waving element." [5] His masterpiece in circumlocution, however, he reserved for the volcano,

> The infuriate hill that shoots the pillared flame.[6]

---

[1] *Spring*, 909–14. [2] *Ib*. 494–5.

[3] *Summer*, 543–4; *Autumn*, 134–8.

[4] *Winter*, 87, 877; *Spring*, 395; *Autumn*, 922; *Winter*, 811, 854, 818, 819.

[5] *Spring*, 747–8. The other names I have noticed are "the plumy people," "the gay troops," "the tuneful nations," "the coy quiristers," "the glossy kind," "the fearful race," the muse's "brothers of the grove," "the soft tribes," "the feathered youth," "the aërial tribes," "the weak tribes," "the wanderers of heaven," "the plumy race," "the tenants of the sky" (*Spring*, 165, 584, 594, 597, 617, 689, 703, 711, 729; *Summer*, 1121; *Autumn*, 986; *Winter*, 80, 137, 138). See also *Spring*, 753, 772, 789; *Winter*, 242.

[6] *Summer*, 1096.

This is all bad, very bad.   Indeed, the turgid diction and the distorted, pompous style of *The Seasons* are largely responsible for the current underestimate of the poem.   These qualities are the more objectionable because they are used in picturing simple country life; for, according to our twentieth-century feeling, nature poetry ought above all other kinds to be natural.   Our ancestors, however, held quite the opposite opinion.   They used nature in poetry, as in painting and architecture, for purely decorative purposes; as they conventionalized leaves and flowers for ornamental borders and the capitals of columns, so they conventionalized the landscapes with which they adorned their poems.   It was chiefly in nature poetry, whether rimed or not, whether written before 1726 or after, that "poetic diction" flourished.   One would expect, therefore, to find it in *The Seasons*.

What makes this the more likely is that Thomson wrote in blank verse. The new measure, which was not yet established, still seemed to many mere prose; hence to be acceptable it needed every possible enrichment. The "swellings" of style and luxuriance of language in which Philips and Thomson indulged are in part, therefore, a kind of paste jewels used to offset the severity of their unadorned measure.   Much like this motive is that to which John Aikin called attention in 1804.   "The writers of blank verse," he remarked, "have been so sensible of their near approach to prose in the versification, that they have been solicitous to give their language a character as different as possible from that of common speech.   This purpose, while it has favoured loftiness and splendour of diction, has also too much promoted a turgid and artificial style, stiffened by quaint phrases, obsolete words, and perversions of the natural order of sentences." [1]

Another reason why "loftiness and splendour of diction" were, in the minds of Thomson and his contemporaries, inseparable from good blank verse is that these qualities were strongly marked in the only unrimed poetry for which they had any regard, that of Milton and Philips.   From Milton, as we have seen, Thomson not only took many of the actual words and phrases that he employed, but acquired the habit of using inversions, pompous Latinisms, strange compounds, and other uncommon expressions that lay at the bottom of his turgidity.   But his debt was even greater than this, for in general he came under the spell of the luxuriance, splendor, and sonorous vagueness of *Paradise Lost*.   Milton had naturally much of the Elizabethan gorgeousness, and it stood him in good stead

[1] *Letters on English Poetry* (2d ed., 1807), 118–19.

when dealing with a subject in which definiteness was often impossible and usually undesirable. By means of sound, by the "long-commingling diapason" of his lines (obtained mainly through the use of Latin words), and in part through a style and diction as lofty and as remote from everyday life as was his theme, he conveyed a vivid impression of persons, things, places, and acts that are beyond description. This manner of Milton's Thomson adopted without realizing that what was fitting, necessary even, in picturing the wars of archangels and the creation of the solar system became ridiculous when applied to Musidora's bathing or to the shearing of sheep. To write of Vulcan,

> And in Ausonian land
> Men call'd him Mulciber,

is poetry, but to describe a visit to Italy by saying,

> The muse gay roved the glad Hesperian round,

is absurdity.[1] To speak of the angel Raphael as "the winged Hierarch," Satan as a "mighty Paramount," and the trumpets used by seraphim as "the sounding alchymy" is both suitable and impressive; but to call birds "the glossy kind" and frozen earth "the frost-concocted glebe," or to say that streams "lead the humid maze" instead of "wind," is neither.[2] Satan may well have "writhed him to and fro convolved," but why should lambs be

> This way and that convolved in friskful glee?[3]

But, even if the subject of *The Seasons* had been similar to that of *Paradise Lost*, Thomson, like others, would almost certainly have brought many discords out of Milton's mighty but complicated instrument. The exquisite ear and supreme art of its inventor enabled him to do things with it which, if attempted by almost any one else, would have resulted in failure. Latinisms appear to come naturally to him, his inversions do not seem distorted or his unusual words far-fetched. Many phrases that sound absurd when transferred to the writings of his imitators are harmonious and beautiful in their original settings. The expression "vernal bloom," for example, is not good, but who has objected to it in Milton's great lament over his blindness? Much of the tumidity of *The Seasons*, therefore, arises

---

[1] *P. L.*, i. 739–40; *Liberty*, i. 2.

[2] *P. L.*, v. 468, ii. 508, 517; *Spring*, 617, *Winter*, 706, *Hymn*, 51.

[3] *P. L.*, vi. 328; *Spring*, 837 (cf. *Summer*, 343, and *Autumn*, 1183, where bees, overcome by sulphur fumes, are said to be "convolved and agonizing in the dust"). This paragraph and the preceding one repeat some things said on pages 66–8, 78–9, 83, above.

from the attempt of a Phaëthon to drive the chariot of the sun. A great deal of Thomson's tumidity came from his adopting without sufficiently adapting Milton's practice. It is not a matter of this or that word, of a few stylistic devices or syntactical peculiarities; it is a question of the general character of the words employed, of the way in which they are used, the order in which they are placed, and the kind of sentences made from them. Thomson's entire conception of the language and style of poetry seems, indeed, to have been moulded by *Paradise Lost*.

There is no evidence that Thomson knew *Cyder* until 1730, when in *Autumn*, the last of the "Seasons" to be written, he referred to

> *Phillips*, facetious bard, the second thou
> Who nobly durst, in rhyme-unfetter'd verse,
> With *British* freedom sing the *British* song.[1]

This particular "British song" was, however, widely read, and in the eighteen years between its publication and the appearance of *Winter* would almost inevitably have come to the attention of one who cared for poetry of the kind. Furthermore, the similarities between the two works make it practically certain that there is some connection between them. Each discards rime, although at the time rime was the rule; each deals with homely country life; each owes much to Virgil's *Georgics* and to *Paradise Lost;*[2] but, most of all, each makes use of the exaggerated, tumid Miltonisms which Philips had introduced into the *Splendid Shilling* for the sake of parody. *The Seasons* is more flowing than its predecessor and less stilted and bombastic; but the resemblances to *Cyder* are sufficiently marked to make it difficult to determine how much Thomson derived from Milton and how much from Philips. In his first two unrimed pieces, and in the few lines we have of an early draft of *Winter*,[3] the style is simpler and more direct and the language more natural than in *The Seasons*. This would indicate that Thomson deliberately stiffened his later verse; and, as he certainly knew Milton before writing any of these pieces but seems not to have been familiar with the *Splendid Shilling* when composing his juvenile burlesque,[4] it appears likely that in making over the gorgeous Miltonic garment for work-a-day purposes he consciously followed Philips's practice. It may even be that he

---

[1] *Autumn*, 639–41 (text of 1730). Most later editions substitute "Pomona's" for "facetious."

[2] For the influence of Virgil on Thomson, see Macaulay's life, 146–7 n. In the 1750 edition of Thomson's works Lyttelton removed the description of the orgy of food and drink from *Autumn* (482–569 of the later texts) and printed it as a separate poem, *The Return from the Fox-Chace, a Burlesque Poem, in the Manner of Mr. Philips*.

[3] Letter to Dr. Cranston, September, 1725?, *Poetical Works* (1847), vol. i, p. xxiii.

[4] *Lisy's Parting with her Cat*, written about 1718.

did not so much adapt this apparel himself as modify Philips's adaptation.

Obviously, *Paradise Lost* and *Cyder* would not have exerted such an influence upon Thomson if they had not fallen in with his natural tendencies. He turned to these poems and to the *Faerie Queene* as inevitably as a flower turns to the sun; [1] yet the use which the flower makes of the sun's rays depends upon its own nature and environment. The same Miltonic light that awakened Thomson fell upon Landor, Keats, and Wordsworth, but in them it produced very different results. Thomson used inversions and other Latinisms not simply because Milton did so but because he liked them; these characteristics or similar ones would have marked his poetry had *Paradise Lost* never been written. The English epic inspired him, brought out what was latent in him, opened his eyes to many things he would otherwise have overlooked, and showed him how to get effects he desired; but it did not originate his turgidity, it only accentuated and directed it. He was, as we have seen, impatient with the "wintry world of letters" of his own day; he wanted the color, the feeling, and the richness of summer. He wished to banish the drab uniformity of neo-classic poetry, to substitute imagination for wit, feeling for brilliance, luxuriance for precision, to appeal to the emotions rather than the intellect, to the heart rather than the head. His defects sprang from lack of fineness of taste and from want of skill in handling a strange medium. He failed to distinguish dignity from stiltedness, grandeur from turgidity, loftiness from pomposity; he failed to see that one is not always nearer to poetry by being farther from prose.

These limitations were not peculiar to Thomson. Other men of the time, Mallet, Dyer, and Akenside, for example, had them too, though usually to a less degree; for dignity, splendor, and pomp of writing were admired then far more than they are now. In poetry as in dress it was a time of velvet coats, tight neck-bands, and flowing, powdered wigs. Henry Pemberton, in 1738, praised Glover's *Leonidas* for not naming such utilitarian objects as hay and straw, but for describing "the magazines of them in the camp of Xerxes . . . by periphrasis, as follows:

> There at his word devouring Vulcan feasts
> On all the tribute, which Thessalia's meads
> Yield to the scythe, and riots on the heaps
> Of Ceres emptied of the ripen'd grain. . . .

[1] Spenser seems to have had little direct influence upon *The Seasons;* but his example, like Milton's, undoubtedly strengthened Thomson's tendencies away from the things for which Pope stood and in general towards ornament and profusion.

This is a refinement," adds Pemberton, "which seems to have arisen by time. In Homer we often find the commonest things expressed by their plain names."[1] "The style of a didactic poem," Joseph Warton asserted a few years later, " . . . ought certainly to abound in the most bold and forcible metaphors, the most glowing and picturesque epithets; it ought to be elevated and enlivened by pomp of numbers, and majesty of words, and by every figure that can lift a language above the vulgar and current expressions."[2] As late as 1785 John Scott, himself a pleasing poet, criticized Thomson for using such a "wretched prosaism" as "to tempt the trout" or "stealing from the barn a straw," and for speaking of birds' "streaking their wings with oil" instead of "moistening their plumage with an oleaginous matter."[3] Even Johnson, who hated blank verse and all its works, praised the diction of *The Seasons*, though he regarded it as "too exuberant."[4] But how could he have condemned it in view of his own pompous Latinisms and the "relaxation of his gravity" caused by Shakespeare's use of the words "peep," "blanket," "dun," and "knife" in a tragedy?[5] One contemporary reviewer asserted that Thomson excelled "in the real sublime, in a strength and justness both of thought and *expression*";[6] and the critical Swift, though "not over fond of " *The Seasons* "because . . . nothing is doing," did not mention its turgidity.[7] Many, to be sure, who approved of Thomson's general practice censured some of his expressions or thought he went too far.[8] Thus we read in Cibber's *Lives* (1753), "Mr. Thomson's poetical diction in the Seasons is very peculiar to him. . . . He has introduced a number of compound words; converted substantives into verbs, and in short has created a kind of new language for himself. His stile has been blamed for its singularity and stiffness . . . yet is it admirably fitted for description," since, "though its exterior form should not be comely," it enables him to paint nature "in all its lustre."[9]

---

[1] *Observations on Poetry*, 86–7.   [3] *Critical Essays*, 316, 309, 316, 301.

[2] *Works of Virgil* (1753), i. 403–4.   [4] *Lives* (ed. Hill), iii. 300.   [5] *Rambler*, no. 168.

[6] Andrew Reid, *Present State of the Republick of Letters* (1728), i. 430. The italics are mine.

[7] Letter to Charles Wogan, Aug. 2, 1732.

[8] Joseph Warton, for example, granted that "the diction of the *Seasons* is sometimes . . . turgid and obscure," but added immediately, "yet is this poem on the whole . . . one of the most captivating . . . in our language (*Essay on Pope*, 4th ed., 1782, i. 43). In his blank-verse *Enthusiast*, which is itself not without turgidity, he praises Thomson as one "who strongly painted what he boldly thought" (Wooll's *Biographical Memoirs of Warton*, 1806, p. 117; cf. *Autumn*, 57–64).

[9] v. 202–3. In the same paragraph there is a reference to "the tow'ring sublimity of Mr. Thomson's stile."

At this time, as we know, it was an accepted principle that the language of poetry should be widely separated from that of prose, that homely words like "blanket" or "knife," and 'terms appropriated to particular arts,' like "seam" or "mallet," "should be sunk in general expressions." [1] Pope and his contemporaries found Homer and the Bible much too simple and matter-of-fact, and therefore adorned them with tinsel and "raised" them with vague, high-sounding, inappropriate words. Even prose, under the guidance of Johnson, Gibbon, Burke, and their followers, returned to the traditions of rhetorical elaboration, becoming Latinic and structurally involved. The Swan of Lichfield thought liberty "a thousand times preferable to the dispiriting fetters of an unimpassioned connexion," and referred to language which "had every happiness of perspicuity, and always expressed rectitude of heart and susceptibility of taste." [2] That any human being, much less an important literary personage, could habitually express herself after this fashion, is far more difficult to understand than is the turgidity of *The Seasons*.

Even among Thomson's contemporaries, however, there were those who objected to his style and diction. Johnson, as we have seen, remarked mildly that it was "too exuberant," and Cibber acknowledged that it had been "blamed for its singularity and stiffness." Curiously enough, John Scott — he who favored "moistening their plumage with an oleaginous matter" — wrote that Thomson, "in attempting energy and dignity, produces bombast and obscurity; and in avoiding meanness, becomes guilty of affectation." [3] Lyttelton and his friends were so much disturbed by the diction of *The Seasons* that in the edition of the poem which his lordship, as Thomson's literary executor, brought out in 1750 "great corrections" were made and "many redundancies . . . cut off." [4] The world, however, preferring the original with its redundancies, justified Patrick Murdoch, the poet's friend and biographer, in declaring, "Certain it is, that T[homson]'s language has been well receiv'd by the publick." [5]

[1] Johnson, *Rambler*, no. 168; "Dryden," in *Lives* (ed. Hill), i. 433.

[2] *Letters*, iv. 179; *Memoirs of Dr. Darwin* (1804), 110.

[3] *Critical Essays* (1785), 296.

[4] Lyttelton's letter to Dr. Doddridge, quoted in Macaulay's *Thomson*, 75. See also above, p. 140, n. 2.

[5] From an undated letter to Andrew Millar, in Wooll's *Biographical Memoirs of Joseph Warton*, 256–7. Murdoch recommended "my Lord's acquaintances . . . to read Milton with care, and the greatest part of their objections would vanish." So late as 1821 Rowland Freeman (*Kentish Poets*, Canterbury, 1821, ii. 113) quoted the whole of Thomas Curteis's egregiously stilted and distorted *Eirenodia* (see p. 112 above), because it "has in many parts great merit, and is a very good specimen of the Miltonic style."

The truth of this assertion is borne out not only by the remarkable vogue of the poem, but by the adoption, with little conscious modification, of the language, diction, and style of *The Seasons* on the part of most contemporary writers of blank verse. Even the cold, fastidious Akenside made use of them, and in the unrimed work of Shenstone, who lacked neither taste nor discernment, their peculiarities are far more conspicuous than in *The Seasons* itself. To most writers of the time these mannerisms appeared attractive in themselves as well as an essential feature of all pleasing blank verse, since they solved a difficulty which had previously seemed insurmountable, — how to beat into ploughshare and pruning-hook the mighty sword and spear that had been forged for the combats of archangels. Previous writers, it was felt, had not done this, or, if they had, the results were uninteresting, which came to the same thing. Most of these adventurers had been wrecked either in the Charybdis of flat prose, near which protruded the rocks of the couplet prosody, or on the Scylla of epic bombast; the few who escaped had, with the exception of Philips, been lost in the great deep of oblivion. Before 1726, therefore, authors did not know what kind of blank verse to write, or if they did they were unable to write it effectively and for that reason usually left it alone. But as soon as it was generally recognized that Thomson had discovered a good course they promptly followed him, with the result that his vices came to be so firmly fastened upon blank verse that they persisted almost to the end of the century. Indeed, the development of the poetry written in the measure from his time to Wordsworth's is in the main a record of its gradual emancipation from the faults which *The Seasons* brought into vogue.

But it is a mistake to attribute all that is objectionable in Thomson to the influence of the poetry of his day, since in point of fact his language and style are related to that poetry less as a result than as a cause. They are, as we have seen, in large part the outgrowth of his own natural predilections (which, it must not be forgotten, were of Scottish not English origin) and of the example of Milton. Something much like them, to be sure, is to be found in the work of his predecessors, — in *Cyder*, the *Splendid Shilling*, and other burlesques, in translations of the classics, in epics, and in works in which the Deity is a character; but, aside from *Cyder*, such productions obviously form a class by themselves apart from most literature, and many of even these pieces are comparatively free from the exaggerated Miltonisms of later unrimed poems. It is possible, therefore, that if Thomson had adopted a simpler method of expression other writers would have done the same and eighteenth-century blank verse would have developed along quite different lines. Such a supposition, however, proceeds on the very dubious assumptions that a more natural blank verse could have been written effectively in 1726, and that, if written, it would have been popular. If Wordsworth's simplicity seemed stupidity in 1798, what would it have been thought in 1726? If the strains of *Tintern Abbey, Michael*, and *Alastor* fell on deaf ears in the first quarter of the nineteenth century, what chance would *Winter*, in equally unadorned verse, have had a hundred years earlier? Furthermore, Thomson himself used a more direct and natural form of expression in his first efforts, but apparently saw, as every one has seen since, that it was not a success. Who, then, shall say he was not right in deliberately adopting a more ornate manner?

"The blank verse of *The Seasons*," writes Mr. Beers, " . . . has been passed through the strainer of the heroic couplet." [1] Admirers of the poem may at first resent this criticism, but they will find more and more evidence of its truth as they examine the prosody of Thomson. He did not have a delicate ear, and probably missed many of the finer harmonies of Milton's verse, which, it will be remembered, was in 1725 admired far more than it was understood. He repeatedly uses lines of the same marked cadence,[2] has pauses in the same places in successive lines, and seems to have given no heed to inversions of accent, if indeed he was conscious of them. At the beginning of a line he, like Pope and the other classicists, frequently has a trochee, but with this exception there are only eleven inversions of the stress in the first three hundred lines of *Summer*.[3] In the same passage there are, as I read it, but eighty run-over lines,[4] or less

---

[1] *English Romanticism in the Eighteenth Century* (N. Y., 1899), 111.

[2] The oft-noted examples of this habit,

> And Cancer reddens with the solar blaze,
> And Egypt joys beneath the spreading wave,
> And Ocean trembles for his green domain,
> And Mecca saddens at the long delay,
> And Thulè bellows through her utmost isles,
> And the sky saddens with the gathered storm

(*Summer*, 44, 821, 859, 979, 1168, *Winter*, 228), can hardly be used, as Mr. Saintsbury suggests (*English Prosody*, ii. 479), to emphasize the ends of paragraphs, since the first and last instances quoted occur near the beginnings of paragraphs. Cf. also *Summer*, 833, and Mr. Macaulay's discussion of the subject in his *Thomson*, 166–7.

[3] So, at least, says Léon Morel in his *James Thomson* (Paris, 1895), 470. I find even fewer.

[4] According to Robertson's edition, 108 lines are without punctuation at the end.

than twenty-seven per cent, as against forty-five per cent in *Para-dise Lost* and about six per cent in the *Essay on Man*. Much of the prosodic variety of *The Seasons* comes from a slighting of the stresses, one of which is passed over in nearly every line. The cesura is not managed so well; for, though it falls in or after the first foot more often than it does in *Paradise Lost*, it is usually near the middle of the line.[1] Occasionally Thomson has such a line as

or
> Flames through the nerves, and boils along the veins,
>
> Bright as the skies, and as the season keen,[2]

which might have come from Pope's *Essay on Criticism*. Much more common, however, are two or three lines that fall into unrimed couplets or triplets, a number of which now and then come together to form a passage like the following:

> Yet found no times, in all the long research,
> So glorious, or so base, as those he proved,
> In which he conquered, and in which he bled.
> Nor can the muse the gallant Sidney pass,
> The plume of war! with early laurels crowned,
> The lover's myrtle and the poet's bay.
> A Hampden too is thine, illustrious land!
> Wise, strenuous, firm, of unsubmitting soul.[3]

The truth seems to be that when off his guard Thomson relapsed into writing not metrical paragraphs but separate lines, and that he had to exert himself to vary his pauses and to avoid a slight break after every tenth syllable. The freer prosody was unquestionably what he preferred, but the end-stopped line with a medial cesura and rare trochaic substitutions was, so to speak, in his blood and inevitably showed itself. How well he succeeded in freeing himself from it we may see by comparing his juvenile blank verse, in which almost every line stands by itself, with his later work. He did much better than most writers of the time, because he had a clearer understanding of Milton's prosody and a heartier liking for it.

Thomson's six or eight other unrimed poems — one of which, *Liberty*, contains nearly thirty-four hundred lines — need not detain

[1] In the first fifty lines of *Summer* I find the cesuras occurring as follows: 1–5 (i. e. five times after the first syllable), 2–5, 3–3, 4–11, 5–12, 6–11, 7–5, 8–2, 9–0. Compare their distribution in the first fifty lines of the *Essay on Man:* 1–3, 2–7, 3–2, 4–11, 5–18, 6–7, 7–4, 8–4, 9–0.

[2] *Spring*, 1104; *Winter*, 703 (cf. 485, 677, 836–7, and *Liberty*, ii. 24, 26, 31, 37, 40, etc.).

[3] *Summer*, 1508–15. The prosody of the preceding forty lines is much the same.

us long.[1] They attracted few readers when they appeared and have
had no willing ones since. Historians of literature and biographers
of the poet have felt constrained to say something about the pieces
and have tried to find something good to say, but it has been wasted
labor. Johnson records that he attempted to read *Liberty* when it
came out, but "soon desisted" and "never tried again."[2] Those
who have tried again have usually desisted as soon. When Thomson
left nature inspiration left him, and in *Liberty* even the descriptions
are tame. Of course the poems contain a number of excellent lines
and some good passages; but on the whole they have very few of the
virtues of *The Seasons* and all of its vices, — the roaring of the British lion, the obvious moralizing, the shallow pessimism, the fulsome
commendation of friends, the tumidity, and the contorted word-
order. They tend towards flattery and didacticism, and even when
they spring in part from a worthy impulse the impulse has not been
so deeply felt by their author as to give rise to poetry. Thomson's
mind may have been in them, but his heart was not; and his mind,
like that of many another bard, was by no means remarkable. It is
to be regretted that he did not rise above his fellow-mortals by recog-
nizing this fact and by realizing the questionable efficacy of moralizing in verse; but if he had done so he would not have been James
Thomson.

It is easy to find fault with Thomson's work. His painting of nature is never ennobled by intensity of spiritual feeling; he has many
tedious passages and more errors of taste both in subject-matter and
in expression, and a hasty reading brings these defects into prominence. The poem (or extracts from it) is frequently studied for one
purpose or another; but since large portions are seldom read for
their own sake, and since those who judge it are often more fastidious
than robust in their taste and rarely are so familiar with it that the
faults no longer obscure the virtues, Thomson suffers much from
being damned with faint, patronizing praise. One may even be tol-
erably well acquainted with his work and yet remember little save
its obvious merits and defects, and consequently may think that the

---

[1] See Bibl. I, 1713 w., *c.* 1718 w., 1727, 1729, 1734, 1737; App. B, 1726. The first
two are juveniles, the second being an unsuccessful attempt at the mock-heroic. That
to James Delacour, which is omitted from most editions of the poet's works, was first
printed in the *London Magazine* for November, 1734, over the signature "J. Thompson," and was attributed in Delacour's *Poems* (Cork, 1778, p. 54) to "J. Thomson,
author of the *Seasons*." Mr. Robertson (Oxford edition of Thomson, pp. 457, 462)
gives several reasons for thinking that the *Poem to the Memory of Mr. Congreve*, which
has on slender grounds been attributed to Thomson, is not really his. The abrupt,
ejaculatory style seems to me not that of *The Seasons*.

[2] *Lives* (ed. Hill), iii. 301.

author always paints with a broad brush and only the beauties which every one sees. But let such a reader return to *The Seasons* with a fresh and open mind and he will be struck with the closeness of observation it frequently exhibits, its fine feeling for shy loveliness in nature and for the "beauty, which, as Milton sings, hath terror in it." He can hardly fail to admire the poet's healthy manliness and human sympathy, the excellence of many of his single lines, and the sonorous pomp, breadth, and Byronic power of his larger pictures. He will have a far better understanding of the eighteenth century after he has come to see these qualities in Thomson and to realize that they are features of a piece which, from the days of Pope and Young, through the dictatorship of Johnson and the increasingly romantic times of Gray, Cowper, and Burns, and even to the stirring years of Wordsworth, Shelley, Lamb, and Hazlitt, was the most popular and perhaps the most influential poem in English.

CHAPTER VII

YOUNG

ONE of the earliest and most important results of Thomson's popularizing blank verse was the appearance, in 1742, of the first part of *The Complaint, or Night Thoughts*, by Edward Young. There is, to be sure, no proof that it was Thomson's example which led his fellow-poet to use the new measure; but since *The Seasons* was at the time in the flush of its first popularity, and since *The Complaint* is very different in character from anything its author had written before, there must have been some connection, and perhaps not a slight one, between the two works.

It is Young's good fortune that he is little read. Most lovers of poetry who know the eighteenth century only through anthologies think of *The Seasons*, the *Night Thoughts*, and *The Task* as esthetically on the same low plane, an estimate that does great injustice to Thomson and Cowper, who, notwithstanding their defects, had genuine inspiration. Young lacked this and had little to offer in its place. The *Night Thoughts* is one of the dullest and falsest poems that ever achieved fame. It is rhetorical and declamatory in style, unpoetic in both conception and expression, commonplace in thought, sentimental, insincere, and lugubrious in its insistent religion. To the modern reader the hollow theatricality of its parade of gloom is particularly repellent because of the smug piety which is supposed to inspire it. The poem excites no admiration for its author, who, one is not surprised to learn, spent the best part of his life seeking those tinsel trappings which it belittles. The gross flattery contained in the dedications of his works and in his poetic references to persons of influence prepare us to hear that for years he danced attendance on two of the most profligate and unscrupulous noblemen of the time, and that he even stooped to beg aid of the king's mistress for advancement in the church![1] There can be no question that the gloom of his poetry is in part due to disappointed

---

[1] For an admirable analysis of Young's character, see George Eliot's essay, *Worldliness and Other-worldliness*. H. C. Shelley's brief for Young (*Life and Letters*, 1914) seems to me to avoid, or to touch lightly, on everything in the poet's life or writings that would produce an unfavorable impression.

ambition, and that his scorn of worldly pleasures and honors rings hollow from a man who strove hard to obtain them.

Young's first published volume appeared when he was thirty, and from that time until he was fifty-nine he issued a book of verse nearly every year. With the exception of a few stanzaic odes and three tragedies, all these poems are written in couplets of the most pronounced pseudo-classic type. The best of them, and in some respects the best of all his work, is *Love of Fame, the Universal Passion* (1725-8). The seven satires that make up this volume possess a finish, brilliance, and epigrammatic point which render them at times but little inferior to those of the "wasp of Twickenham," which they antedate.[1] Quite fittingly, therefore, Young's last work in the couplet consisted of two laudatory "Epistles to Mr. Pope" (1730).

Between the satires and his later writings lies "a gulf profound as that Serbonian bog"; for, after fifty-nine years of life and thirty in the service of the couplet, Young suddenly threw in his lot with the poetical insurgents by renouncing "childish shackles and tinkling sounds"[2] and all that went with them. The *Night Thoughts*, his most famous production, is in blank verse. No mere change of theme was responsible for his transferred allegiance, but a real change of heart. "What we mean by 'blank verse,'" he wrote at the age of seventy-six, "is, verse unfallen, uncursed; verse reclaimed, reenthroned in the true language of the gods: who never thundered, nor suffered their Homer to thunder, in rime. . . . Must rime, then, say you, be banished? I wish the nature of our language could bear its entire expulsion; but our lesser poetry stands in need of a toleration for it."[3]

Few men of sixty undertake new things, still fewer gain a mastery of them. No wonder, then, that Young never learned to write good blank verse. In his thirty years of practice he had acquired admirable dexterity in handling the heroic couplet, but his fingers had become so adapted to the material with which they worked that they involuntarily shaped the new product with the old touch. In the early eighteenth century, good blank verse and good couplets stood leagues apart and generally implied quite dissimilar conceptions of poetry, much as the tango and the court minuet are not merely

---

[1] According to Pope's editor (*Works*, Elwin-Courthope ed., vi. 340 n.), the *Essay on Man*, which was published anonymously, was thought to be by Young, and the Dublin reprint was advertised with his name.

[2] *Conjectures on Original Composition* (1759, reprinted by M. W. Steinke, 1917), 58.

[3] *Ib.* 58-9, 65.

different dances but expressions of different civilizations. Young was too old to gain facility in the free, new measure; his verse always tends to be choppy and ejaculatory,[1] to fall into a series of individual lines or to read like prose. The following is a fair example:

> Each night we die,
> Each morn are born anew: Each day, a life!
> And shall we kill each day? If trifling kills;
> Sure vice must butcher. O what heaps of slain
> Cry out for vengeance on us! Time destroy'd
> Is suicide, where more than blood is spilt.
> Time flies, death urges, knells call, heaven invites,
> Hell threatens: All exerts; in effort, all.[2]

Surely there is nothing of Milton here, or in hundreds of similar lines in the *Night Thoughts*. Yet there can be no question of Young's familiarity with *Paradise Lost* or of his willingness to borrow phrases from it.[3] "Milton! thee," he exclaimed, "ah could I reach your strain!"[4] But there was the trouble, — he couldn't. Even if he had wanted to copy the style and versification of *Paradise Lost*, he could not have freed himself from the shackles of the couplet. He had written lines and pairs of lines too long to roll on "in full flow, through the various modulations of masculine melody";[5] he had been brilliant and incisive too long to become sonorous and majestic. Besides, since the *Night Thoughts* is a series of versified sermons, its style is probably similar to that Young employed in the pulpit. Declamatory, ejaculatory, abounding in short rhetorical questions, direct appeals, and exclamatory words and phrases, it is quite unlike the stately involutions of the Miltonic sentence. Hence the influence of the epic upon the *Night Thoughts* may have been greater than appears at first sight. The extent of a change depends not so much

[1] This is due in part to the punctuation. In forty lines of book ix there are 33 marks of exclamation, and in thirteen lines 15 marks of interrogation; in eight lines of book vii there are 10 marks of interrogation and one of exclamation; and spots no less bristling may be opened to almost anywhere in the work.

[2] *Night Thoughts*, p. 24. As no edition of Young with numbered lines is easily accessible, the references will be to the pages in the Aldine edition of the *Poetical Works* (1852).

[3] This is shown in his epigram on Voltaire in defense of the allegory of Sin and Death in *Paradise Lost* (see *Works*, Aldine ed., vol. i, p. xxxiv, n.); in his remark that "these *violent* and *tumultuous* authors put him in mind of a passage of Milton, ii. 539" (*ib.* pp. xxxvii–xxxviii, n.); in his prefixing an extract from *Paradise Lost* (ix. 896–900) to the fifth satire of his *Love of Fame*, and in definitely referring to an incident in the epic at the close of the sixth satire and again in the *Night Thoughts* (*Works*, ii. 95, 132–3, i. 124); but most of all in his numerous borrowings from Milton (see Appendix A, below).

[4] *Night Thoughts*, p. 15.

[5] *Conjectures on Original Composition* (reprint of 1917), 58.

upon where one is as upon how far one has come, and Young had covered no small distance. Remote from *Paradise Lost* as is much of his lugubrious preachment, it is leagues away from his previous poems and from his blank-verse dramas.

Furthermore, although the passages which do not recall Milton constitute the larger part of the *Night Thoughts*, they are by no means the whole of it. Indeed, it would be as difficult to find ten consecutive lines in the poem that have no echo of *Paradise Lost* as not to find the hundreds of places where that echo is unmistakable. Yet even in these last the resemblance soon fades or disappears, for not many passages of any length are dominated by the Miltonic style and diction. That is, although many passages show the influence of *Paradise Lost* as plainly as this one, few show it for so many lines:

> In grandeur terrible, all heaven descends!
> And gods, ambitious, triumph in his train.
> A swift archangel, with his golden wing,
> As blots and clouds, that darken and disgrace
> The scene divine, sweeps stars and suns aside.
> And now, all dross remov'd, heaven's own pure day,
> Full on the confines of our ether, flames.
> While (dreadful contrast!) far, how far beneath!
> Hell, bursting, belches forth her blazing seas,
> And storms sulphureous; her voracious jaws
> Expanding wide, and roaring for her prey.[1]

Here are obvious Miltonisms and plenty of them, but they come out more clearly in contrast with what we may assume to have been Young's natural, uncontaminated blank verse, — the colorless, rhetorical prose which he cut up into five-foot lengths for his tragedies:

> He can't persuade his heart to wed the maid,
> Without your leave; and that he fears to ask
> In perfect tenderness: I urg'd him to it,
> Knowing the deadly sickness of his heart,
> Your overflowing goodness to your friend,
> Your wisdom, and despair yourself to wed her;
> I wrung a promise from him he would try;
> And now I come a mutual friend to both.[2]

A comparison of these two quotations shows that the differences between them are due mainly to the presence, in the first passage, of many characteristics distinctive of *Paradise Lost*. The most obvious of these, inversion, though common throughout the *Night Thoughts*, is less frequent and much less noticeable than in most blank verse of the time, for the sentences are so short and so broken

---

[1] Page 230.   [2] *The Revenge* (1721), II. i (*Works*, 1762, ii. 131).

that elaborate inversion is impossible.[1] But Young seldom writes many lines without involving his words in some kind of knot, to the confusion of the reader. Next to inversion, the most fruitful source of difficulties is the omission of words that are usually expressed. He says, for example, "Enthusiastic this?" instead of "Is this enthusiastic?", and "All exerts, in effort, all," which seems to mean "Everything exerts itself." How frequent such omissions are at times, and how much obscurity they cause, may be seen from this passage:

> Because, in man, the glorious dreadful power,
> Extremely to be pain'd, or blest, for ever.
> Duration gives importance; swells the price.
> An angel, if a creature of a day,
> What would he be? A trifle of no weight;
> Or stand, or fall; no matter which; he's gone.[2]

Very often it is parenthetical expressions that impede the reader's progress. Such phrases, whether within marks of parenthesis or not, have an unmistakably Miltonic effect, although they are far more common with Young than with Milton:

> Or, spider-like, spin out our precious all,
> Our more than vitals spin (if no regard
> To great futurity) in curious webs
> Of subtle thought, and exquisite design;
> (Fine net-work of the brain!) to catch a fly!
> The momentary buzz of vain renown!
> A name! a mortal immortality!
> Or (meaner still!) instead of grasping air. . . .[3]

Two stylistic features of the *Night Thoughts* have less significance because they also occur in the work of Milton's predecessors. One is the use of a series of words in the same construction:

> War, famine, pest, volcano, storm, and fire.

> Rocks, desarts, frozen seas, and burning sands:
> Wild haunts of monsters, poisons, stings, and death.

> Unraptur'd, unexalted, uninflam'd.

> Triune, unutterable, unconceiv'd.

> All regions, revolutions, fortunes, fates.[4]

[1] It is rare, for example, to find an inversion so long and elaborate as that in the fourth and fifth lines of the first extract, — "As blots . . . divine," which belongs after "aside."

[2] Page 170.

[3] Page 117. On page 27 there are three in six lines, and on page 212 two in three.

[4] Pages 8, 10 (cf. 252, "Seas, rivers, mountains," etc., and *P. L.*, ii. 621–2), 129, 293, 293.

The other trait, repetition of a word or a phrase, is much more frequent in Young than in Milton, and, as will be seen from these instances, is often more elaborate:

> What pleads Lorenzo for his high-priz'd sports?
> He pleads time's num'rous blanks; he loudly pleads.

> For why should souls immortal, made for bliss,
> E'er wish (and wish in vain!) that souls could die?
> What ne'er can die, Oh! grant to live; and crown
> The wish.[1]

The respects in which the language of the *Night Thoughts* departs from ordinary usage are noted in M. Thomas's admirable study of the poet.[2] It may be interesting, as an illustration of how much Young's diction owes to Milton's, to know that every one of these differences is included in the list of characteristics of *Paradise Lost* which I had compiled before making any study of Young, and before even knowing of the existence of the French work.[3] The similarity in language cannot be accidental, for the resemblance does not exist in the poet's earlier writings. "Tant qu' il se rattacha à l'école néoclassique anglaise," writes M. Thomas,[4] "Young suivit l'exemple des chefs de cette école, ainsi que le prouve une étude attentive de ses premières oeuvres. Comme Dryden et Pope, il redoute le néologisme ou du moins en use peu. . . . Mais quand on passe aux Nuits, les conditions changent sensiblement . . . il s'octroie une liberté de plus en plus grande à mesure qu'il avance dans son travail."

The language of the *Night Thoughts* diverges most strikingly from that of the poetry of the day in employing unusual words from the Greek and Latin, many of which Young borrowed directly.[5] "He seems to think with apothecaries," remarked Pope, "that *Album Graecum* is better than an ordinary stool."[6] M. Thomas gives "terraqueous," "optics" (eyes), "defecate," "feculence," "manumit," "indagators," "conglobed," "fucus," "concertion";[7] I have noticed "fuliginous," "gnomons," "plausive," "obliquities," "ebullient," "elance," "tenebrious," "turbant," "intervolv'd."[8] Young

---

[1] Pages 17, 179.
[2] *Le Poète Edward Young, Étude sur sa Vie et ses Oeuvres* (Paris, 1901).
[3] See above, chapter iv.
[4] Pages 390–91.
[5] Some of them he may have taken from Milton, as "ethereal," "nectareous," "oozy," "magnific": pp. 173 (also 198, 222, 225, 247, etc.), 206, 229, 250.
[6] Quoted by Thomas, p. 391, n. 5.
[7] Thomas, pp. 391–2; Young, pp. 10, 19, 30 (cf. 261, "defecate from sense"), 32 (and 69), 72, 100, 166 (cf. *P. L.* vii. 239), 196, 267.
[8] Pages 25, 28, 62, 191, 221, 244, 254, 261, 264 (cf. *P. L.*, v. 623).

also follows Thomson and Milton in using some words in their original but obsolete meanings: "flow redundant, like Meander," "incumbent weight," "each option" in the human heart, "obnoxious" to storm, an "animal ovation" (animal joy), "eliminate my spirit, give it range," "ardours" of soul, "ardent with gems," planets "without error rove," the "tacit doctrine" of God's works, "erect thine eye," "night's radiant scale" (ladder).[1] Like them, too, he makes new words out of those in common use, as "entenders," "bestorms," "re-thundered," "resorbed," "necromantics," "uncoift," "rationality," "displosion," and "prelibation." [2] M. Thomas calls attention to Young's habit of manufacturing negative words, like "uncreate" and "disinvolve," and especially negative adjectives, like "unabsurd," "unadept," "insuppressive; [3] I have noticed "unrefunding," "unprecarious," "unbottomed," "insalubrious," "unanxious," "unarrived," "unupbraided," "unlost," "unmysterious," "un-terrestrial," [4] and a dozen similar formations. Another characteristic of *Paradise Lost* frequently met with is what appears to be a clipt form of the participle, particularly from verbs in -*ate*: "souls elevate," "satiate of his journey," the mind's "corrugate, expansive make," God's works "how complicate," Scripture "uncorrupt by man." [5]

Not the least conspicuous of Young's Miltonisms is his interchange of the parts of speech. Sometimes he forces a verb into service as a noun, as "give thy thoughts a ply," "appall'd with one amaze," "thy nocturnal rove," "an overwhelm Of wonderful," "nature . . . gave A make to man . . . A make set upright," "the deep disclose Of . . . nature." [6] Sometimes he reverses the process, as when he speaks of a night "that glooms us," of passions that "tempest human life," of "unprecarious flows of vital joy"; or when he says that "heaven's dark concave" shall "urn all human race," or the shades of night "antidote the pestilential earth." [7] Participles from such noun-verbs appear in "this escutcheon'd world," "starr'd and plan-

---

[1] Pages 63 (cf. 256, a garden "redundant" in fruit), 174 (cf. 259), 183 (and 184), 187 (cf. *P. L.*, ix. 170, 1094), 220, 243, 244, 256, 258, 264, 267, 276. Cf. Thomas, pp. 392-3.

[2] Pages 31, 69, 170, 187, 192, 200, 203, 249, 296.

[3] Thomas, p. 394; Young, pp. 174, 233, 153, 244, 149.

[4] Pages 162, 202 (and 211), 206, 212, 217, 234, 246, 249, 250, 277. On one page I found four such adjectives in four lines.

[5] Pages 25 (cf. 250, "things more elevate," 261, "minds elevate," 59, "minds create "), 240, 266, 267, 244.

[6] Pages 27, 234 (cf. 167, "redouble this amaze"), 245, 245, 251 (cf. 27, "Man's make incloses the sure seeds of death"), 272.

[7] Pages 26, 140, 202, 162, 265.

eted inhabitants," "basin'd rivers." [1] Occasionally an adjective is raised to the dignity of a verb, as when hope "serenes" man's heart, a face "consummates bliss," a thought "shallows thy profound," or footsteps are "foul'd in hell"; [2] and once in a while a noun sinks into an adjective, as when man is called "the tale of narrative old time." [3] Adjectives sometimes serve as adverbs: "muffled deep," "flow redundant," "spontaneous rise," "tumultuous rise," "impetuous pour," "let loose, alternate . . . rush Swift and tempestuous," "new awak'd," "deeply stamps . . . Indelible," "if man hears obedient," "refining gradual," "rich endow'd." [4]

But it is by turning adjectives into nouns that Young most frequently 'confounds grammatical functions.' Almost every page has instances as ridiculous as these: "that awful independent on tomorrow," "subtilize the gross into refin'd," "trifle with tremendous" and "yawn o'er the fate of infinite," "th' irrationals," "reason is man's peculiar," "much Of amiable," "the world's no neuter," "the moist of human frame," "the dark profound," "this obscure terrestrial," "the steep of heaven," "the more of wonderful," "the grand of nature," "mind, For which alone inanimate was made," "what of vast," "the sublime of things," "deity breaks forth In inconceivables to men," "the dark of matter,"

> Thy lofty sinks, and shallows thy profound,
> And straitens thy diffusive.[5]

As to the compound epithets that are common in *Paradise Lost* but rare in Young's rimed pieces, "l'on remarque sans peine que notre auteur en est relativement prodigue dans ses Nuits." [6] Here are a few that he uses: "hair-hung," "breeze-shaken," "dark-prison'd," "heart-buried," "high-flusht," "heaven-lighted," "soft-suspended," "heaven-labour'd," "heaven-assum'd," "wide-consuming," "all-prolific," "all-providential," "freighted-rich," "sure-returning," "earth-created," "high-bloom'd," "far-travell'd," "hundred-gated," "new-blazing." [7]

---

[1] Pages 26, 248, 252.   [2] Pages 181, 242, 248, 279 (cf. 266, "foul'd with self").
[3] Page 185.
[4] Pages 41, 63, 83, 140 (cf. 165, "tumultuous driven"), 211, 229, 264, 282, 284, 288, 292.
[5] Pages 25 (cf. 287, "all of awful, night presents . . . of awful much, to both"), 78, 98 (cf. 245, "that infinite of space, With infinite of lucid orbs replete"), 173, 180 (cf. *P. L.*, vii. 368), 186, 193, 228, 235 (also 263, and cf. 267, "emerge from thy profound," 280, "the more profound of God," and *P. L.*, ii. 980), 243, 247, 250, 250, 251–2, 252 (cf. 273, "the vast of being"), 255, 283, 292, 248.
[6] Thomas, p. 401.
[7] Pages 24, 24, 25, 25, 27 (and 196), 36, 41, 42, 42, 42, 56, 130, 151, 161, 231, 236, 244, 252, 297.

In his prosody, as might be expected from his long experience with the couplet, Young departs widely from Milton's usage. Instead of sweeping his readers along with the "long-commingling diapason" of *Paradise Lost*, he jolts them over series of exclamations and ejaculations. On a page of thirty-four lines, only five or six on an average are run-over, and in some cases only two or three; usually not more than seven lines end even with commas, the remaining twenty-two being cut off from their fellows by semicolons, colons, periods, or marks of exclamation or interrogation. The *Night Thoughts* is over-punctuated, to be sure; some of its points might be dispensed with and commas substituted for fully a third of the rest, to the clarification of its meaning and the elimination of part of its jerkiness. Yet the punctuation is not altogether to blame; for on the first pages that I open to very few of the full stops (periods and question- or exclamation-marks), with which exactly half the lines end, could be omitted or changed so as to let the sense run over. One feature of Milton's prosody Young did adopt, — the extensive use of those strong pauses within the line which were anathema to the Augustans, and to Young himself so long as he wrote in rime.[1] Yet, as these pauses usually occur near the middle of the line, where (as in the couplets of the day) most of his cesuras fall, and as his lines are usually not run-over, the effect of his prosody is rarely Miltonic.

What determined his versification was not the desire for flow, for beauty or variety of rhythm, but his staccato style and his penchant for aphorisms. The *Night Thoughts* is unusually quotable, and for nearly a century its gnomic lines were in everybody's mouth:

> Tir'd Nature's sweet restorer, balmy sleep.
>
> Procrastination is the thief of time.
>
> All men think all men mortal, but themselves.
>
> Blessings brighten as they take their flight.
>
> Wishing, of all employments, is the worst.
>
> By night an atheist half-believes a God.
>
> Death loves a shining mark.
>
> A man of pleasure is a man of pains.[2]

In thus transferring to blank verse the epigrammatic terseness of the couplet, Young was making more of an innovation than is commonly

---

[1] Instances of these strong internal pauses, which often make a separate sentence of each half-line, will be found on page 151 above. The *Monthly Review* (1776, liv. 309) declared that in point of versification the *Night Thoughts* was "more faulty than any other composition of acknowledged merit in the class of English poetry."

[2] Pages 1, 13, 14, 33, 54, 83, 107, 206.

realized; for, from the very nature of Milton's prosody and the character of his epic, there are few quotable *lines* in *Paradise Lost*, and the same is true of *Cyder*, *The Seasons*, and the other unrimed poems of the period. Now quotability, always an asset, was a real step forward at a time when readers had been trained by Augustan poetry to expect it; and writers of blank verse were not slow in taking the hint. Even the conversational Cowper (who likewise had a long preliminary training in rime) introduced many sententious lines into *The Task*. But it is not through quotability alone that Young helped to bring the couplet and blank verse closer together. His more direct style, his short sentences, his strong medial cesuras and end-stopped lines, his freedom from the elaborate Miltonic involutions and inversions, — his very defects, it should be noticed, — were all away from Milton and towards Pope. Little as we may like these features of the *Night Thoughts*, they were of service in the development of blank verse. The task of the eighteenth century was to hammer down Milton's style, which, like Lucifer's shield, was of "ethereal temper, massy, large, and round," into something less glorious but more usable, something better adapted to human nature's daily needs. In this cause no one did more than Young.

For the vogue of the *Night Thoughts* was tremendous. At least thirty-four editions, published either separately or in Young's works, appeared in the second half of the eighteenth century, and the poem made something of a sensation when translated into French (Robespierre is said to have carried a copy in his pocket during the Revolution), besides having a triumphal progress through Germany.[1] Dr. Johnson, who preferred Young's description of night to either Shakespeare's or Dryden's, agreed that the *Night Thoughts* was "one of the few poems in which blank verse could not be changed for rhyme but with disadvantage." [2] Burke committed many passages of it to memory,[3] and even the fastidious Horace Walpole thought that in the author's "most frantic rhapsodies" there were "innumerable fine things." [4]

What heav'n-born Seraph gave thy Muse its fire?

queried one bard; [5] another declared,

---

[1] See Thomas's *Young*, p. 539; and J. L. Kind's *Young in Germany* (N. Y., 1906).
[2] "Young," in *Lives* (ed. Hill), iii. 395; Boswell's *Johnson* (ed. Hill), iv. 42–3, n. 7 (and cf. v. 269–70); cf. also Mrs. Piozzi's *Anecdotes* (1786), 58–9.
[3] Moulton's *Library of Literary Criticism*, iii. 489.
[4] Letter to the Earl of Strafford, July 5, 1757.
[5] C. Graham, in *Univ. Mag.* (1785), lxxvii. 98; cf. William Thompson's *Sickness*, iii. 412–16.

The starry host put back the dawn,
Aside their harps ev'n Seraphs flung
To hear thy sweet Complaint, O Young; [1]

and many shared this admiration who were unable to express it, —
devout souls like Bowles's mother, who revered the *Night Thoughts*
"next to God's own Word." [2] Considerable evidence could, in
truth, be adduced in support of Samuel J. Pratt's assertion that "no
composition can . . . boast a greater number of readers." [3] Numerous readers implied some imitators, and these Young had. Even
before the last books of the poem had been published, other *Night
Thoughts*, *Day Thoughts*, and pieces "after the manner of Dr.
Young" or "in imitation of" him or "occasioned by" his work were
being composed.[4] Most of his followers, to be sure, did not acknowledge their indebtedness so frankly as this, but writers continued
even into the nineteenth century to copy the poem or to be influenced by it.

These pieces that are patterned more or less after the *Night
Thoughts* do not sound particularly Miltonic, as, for that matter,
their original usually does not. Yet Young was far more influenced
by *Paradise Lost* than were most of the men who wrote verse like his,
for he had more to unlearn. The author of *Conjectures on Original
Composition* was hardly the man to copy any one. Had he not asserted as early as 1730, "No Man can be like *Pindar*, by imitating
any of his *particular* Works; any more than like *Raphael*, by copying
the *Chartoons*. The Genius and Spirit of such great Men must be
collected from the *whole;* and when thus we are possess'd of it, we
must exert its Energy in *Subjects* and *Designs* of our own. . . .
Nothing so unlike as a *Close Copy*, and a *Noble Original*"? [5] And

---

[1] James Grainger, *Solitude*, in "Dodsley's Miscellany," 1755, iv. 235.

[2] Bowles, *Banwell Hill*, ii. 80–89.

[3] *Observations on the Night Thoughts* (1776), quoted in *Crit. Rev.* xli. 65. "He was
indeed a favourite author from my childhood," Pratt said of Young (*ib.*); and
Samuel Rogers, who was born in 1763, remarked, "In my youthful days Young's
Night-Thoughts was a very favourite book, especially with ladies" (*Table-Talk*, ed.
Dyce, 1856, p. 35).

[4] See Bibl. I, 1745 (Davies), 1752 (anon.), 1753 n., 1754 n., 1755 (anon.), 1757–64,
1760 (Newcomb), 1765 ("T. L." and Letchworth), 1775 (anon.), 1791 (Philpot). Two
of these are curious, — a stupid blank-verse rendering of James Hervey's prose *Meditations and Contemplations*, and a "poetical version" of one of Young's prose "moral
contemplations " (cf. above, p. 111, n. 2). James Foot (*Penseroso*, 1771, preface) says
that he used blank verse because Young and "most of the celebrated writers of the
present times" used it. Young is cleverly parodied by William Whitehead (see
Young's *Works*, 1854 vol. i, pp. lxi–lxii) and by John Kidgell (*The Card*, 1755, i.
241–2).

[5] Preface to his *Imperium Pelagi*.

twenty-nine years later, in his *Conjectures*, had he not again declared, "It is by a sort of noble contagion, from a general familiarity with their writings, and not by any particular sordid theft, that we can be the better for those who went before us"? [1] We have seen that Young knew *Paradise Lost* well, and in view of the wide gulf between his early and his late verse there can be little doubt as to the "noble contagion" he caught from it; but the "particular thefts" are so few in comparison with those in the blank verse of his contemporaries (in *The Seasons*, for example) that he may have been unconscious, or almost unconscious, of them. What Milton did for him was to rouse him, to free him from the shackles of rime, to get him out of the neo-classic rut. Young was wise enough not to slip from one rut into another, not to become a slave to his new guide. The vehicle he hacked out for himself, though perhaps a poor thing, was his own, and it was of no little help to those who came later.

[1] Reprint of 1917, p. 49.

CHAPTER VIII

COWPER

THERE were many men in the eighteenth century who knew their Milton as well as our grandmothers knew their Bible, — Gray, Thomas Warton, Philips, and perhaps Pope, besides such minor notables, now forgotten, as Jonathan Richardson, Thomas Hollis, Leonard Welsted, and George Hardinge.[1] Yet it is doubtful if any of these men were better acquainted with Milton's writings than was the poet Cowper. His editor, Canon Benham, asserts, "He appears to have known Milton nearly by heart";[2] and he himself wrote, "Few people have studied Milton more, or are more familiar with his poetry, than myself."[3] This familiarity, as we learn from *The Task*, began in his early years:

> Then Milton had indeed a poet's charms:
> New to my taste, his Paradise surpassed
> The struggling efforts of my boyish tongue
> To speak its excellence; I danced for joy.
> I marvelled much that, at so ripe an age
> As twice seven years, his beauties had then first
> Engaged my wonder, and, admiring still
> And still admiring, with regret supposed
> The joy half lost because not sooner found.[4]

And of *Allegro* and *Penseroso* he said, "I remember being so charmed with [them] when I was a boy that I was never weary of them."[5] It was this early love for Milton, combined with an extraordinary verbal memory,[6] that made him know the poems so well.

[1] On the minor writers, see above, pp. 6–7.
[2] Globe ed., p. xxv.
[3] To Clotworthy Rowley, Oct. 22, 1791.
[4] iv. 709–17.
[5] Letter to William Unwin, Jan. 17, 1782.
[6] See, for example, his letter to Unwin, May 1, 1779, "Not having the poem, and not having seen it these twenty years, I had much ado to recollect it"; he then quotes from memory the four stanzas of his Latin translation of Prior's *Chloe and Euphelia*. Later he tells the same friend (presumably in August, 1786, see Wright's edition of the *Correspondence*, iii. 89), "I did not indeed read many of Johnson's Classics; those of established reputation are so fresh in my memory, though many years have intervened since I made them my companions, that it was like reading what I read yesterday over again. In a letter to John Newton, Dec. 13, 1784, he recalls Cleopatra's use of "worm" for "asp," though he has not read the play "these five-and twenty years."

Nor was his feeling the cool, intellectual appreciation that is commonly given to Milton to-day, but a warm, personal devotion that led him even at sixty to burst out: "I would beat Warton if he were living, for supposing that Milton ever repented of his compliment to the memory of Bishop Andrews. I neither do, nor can, nor will believe it. Milton's mind could not be narrowed by any thing." [1] He was still more incensed by the harsh treatment his favorite received at Johnson's hands. "Oh! I could thresh his old jacket," he raged, "till I made his pension jingle in his pocket," [2] — strong words for an author of the *Olney Hymns*. "I abominate Nat. Lee," he wrote to Hayley, "for his unjust compliment to Dryden so much at the expense of a much greater poet." [3] He even dreamed of meeting his "idol" and being graciously received by him.[4] Such a strong, personal admiration was due in no small degree to the religious character of *Paradise Lost* and the lofty principles and noble life of its author. Even some of the defects of what he termed "the finest poem in the world," [5] — its narrow Puritanism, its literal interpretation of the Bible, and its Hebraic conception of God,— probably seemed to him virtues.

Cowper's devotion was lifelong. Beginning at fourteen, it gave birth to the first of his poems that has been preserved; and when the shades of melancholy settled over him never again to rise they found him editing and dreaming of his favorite poet. Between the two periods is scattered many a Miltonic item. The well-known hymn, "Jesus, where'er thy people meet," which appeared in his first volume, *Olney Hymns* (1779), contains a line,

> And bring all heaven before our eyes,

taken with the change of only a pronoun from *Penseroso*. The next year came his Latin translations of a simile from *Paradise Lost*,[6] and of Dryden's couplets on Milton (a modified form of these couplets he afterwards introduced into his *Table Talk*);[7] and three years later followed his tribute in *The Task*,

---

[1] Letter to Walter Bagot, Oct. 25, 1791.

[2] See letters to Unwin, Oct. 31, 1779, and March 21, 1784; to Walter Bagot, May 2, 1791 (in which Johnson is threatened with "another slap or two"); to William Hayley, May 1, 1792 ("Oh that Johnson! how does every page of his on the subject [Milton], ay, almost every paragraph, kindle my indignation!"), and Oct. 13, 1792.

[3] Nov. 25, 1792.   [4] Letter to Hayley, Feb. 24, 1793.

[5] Letter to Hayley, May 9, 1792.

[6] See his letter to Unwin, June 8, 1780; cf. *P. L.*, ii. 488 ff.

[7] Lines 556–9:   Ages elapsed ere Homer's lamp appeared,
And ages ere the Mantuan swan was heard;
To carry nature lengths unknown before,
To give a Milton birth, asked ages more.

Milton, whose genius had angelic wings,
And fed on manna.[1]

In 1790 the supposed disinterment of Milton's body called from his
pen some "Stanzas," two of which are translated from Milton's
Mansus.[2] The following year appeared the preface to his Homer,
containing, along with a number of other references, the words, "So
long as Milton's works, whether his prose or his verse, shall exist, so
long there will be abundant proof that no subject, however important, however sublime, can demand greater force of expression than
is within the compass of the English language;" and six months later
he wrote to a friend, "My veneration for our great countryman is
equal to what I feel for the Grecian; and consequently I am happy,
and feel myself honourably employed whatever I do for Milton. I
am now translating his *Epitaphium Damonis*, a pastoral in my judgment equal to any of Virgil's *Bucolics*." [3] The translation he refers
to was part of a new edition of Milton, for which he was to turn the
Latin and Italian poems into English and furnish notes. Through
this work he came to know Milton's biographer, William Hayley,
with whom he translated the *Adamo* of Andreini, a poem important
only because of its possible influence on *Paradise Lost;* and he was
engaged upon the editing when his dreaded melancholia and hal-
lucinations returned for the last time. Thus from youth to old age
there were never many months when he was not occupied in parody-
ing or praising or translating or imitating or editing "this first of
poets." [4]

The earliest work of Cowper's that we have is a travesty of *Paradise Lost* which was probably struck in the mint of the *Splendid
Shilling:*

> For neither meed
> Of early breakfast, to dispel the fumes
> And bowel-racking pains of emptiness,
> Nor noontide feast, nor evening's cool repast,
> Hopes she from this, presumptuous, — though perhaps
> The cobbler, leather-carving artist, might.[5]

Strange to say, his masterpiece, *The Task*, was also begun as a kind
of parody on Milton's epic. "The Sofa," which Lady Austen had
jestingly proposed to him as a subject, could hardly be the theme of
a serious poem; yet he seems to have thought that he might do

---

[1] iii. 255–6.   [2] Lines 91–3.
[3] To James Hurdis, Dec. 10, 1791.
[4] Letter to Hurdis, Nov. 24, 1793.
[5] *Verses written in his 17th year, on Finding the Heel of a Shoe* (1748), 4–9.

something amusing by handling it in the involved and dignified style of *Paradise Lost*. The beginning of *The Task* certainly recalls passages in Milton's two long poems:

> I sing the Sofa. I who lately sang
> Truth, Hope, and Charity, and touched with awe
> The solemn chords, and with a trembling hand
> Escaped with pain from that adventurous flight,
> Now seek repose upon an humbler theme.

This appears to be an adaptation of the opening lines of *Paradise Regained*,

> I, who erewhile the happy Garden sung
> By one man's disobedience lost, now sing . . . ,

with a jocose reference to the "advent'rous song" and to another famous passage in *Paradise Lost*,

> Thee I revisit now with bolder wing,
> Escaped the Stygian pool, though long detain'd.[1]

A little farther on, in the humorous description of the evolution of the chair,

> With here and there a tuft of crimson yarn,
> Or scarlet crewel in the cushion fixed:
> If cushion might be called what harder seemed . . . ,[2]

the last line seems to parody the language in which Milton pictures Death,

> The other Shape,
> If shape it might be call'd that shape had none.[3]

There can be no question of the parody in the following passage:

> The nurse sleeps sweetly, hired to watch the sick,
> Whom snoring she disturbs. As sweetly he
> Who quits the coach-box at the midnight hour
> To sleep within the carriage more secure,
> His legs depending at the open door.
> Sweet sleep enjoys the curate in his desk,
> The tedious rector drawling o'er his head,
> And sweet the clerk below: but neither sleep
> Of lazy nurse, who snores the sick man dead,
> Nor his who quits the box at midnight hour
> To slumber in the carriage more secure,
> Nor sleep enjoyed by curate in his desk,
> Nor yet the dozings of the clerk, are sweet,
> Compared with the repose the Sofa yields.[4]

---

[1] *P. L.*, i. 13, iii. 13–14.   [2] *Task*, i. 53–5.
[3] *P. L.*, ii. 666–7, and cf. i. 227–8. Possibly "as yet black breeches were not" (*Task*, i. 10) was intended to recall Milton's "as yet this world was not" (*P. L.*, v. 577).
[4] *Task*, i. 89–102. Compare Eve's words to Adam, "Sweet is the breath of Morn,"

The burlesque is not continued beyond these lines, and reappears but once, in the third book, in a good-natured parody of Philips or Thomson.[1] For, after a hundred lines of jesting, the poet slips off the sofa for a walk, and rambles on till the work that started upon "any subject" comes to include almost every subject, and the sofa is forgotten.

Cowper's enthusiasm for *Paradise Lost* inevitably made itself felt in his blank verse; yet Milton exerted less influence on *The Task* than on the work of many men — Thomson, for instance — who cared less for him. For this there are several reasons. In the first place, Cowper's native abilities and inclinations did not lie in stately periods but in easy, flowing, conversational verse, in the description not of sublime but of domestic scenes. The qualities that give charm to his poetry are those which made him a delightful letter-writer and by no means those which produced the lofty and austere beauties of *Paradise Lost*. These natural aptitudes, furthermore, he had developed in the volume of rimed poems he had just published, the first of which is, characteristically enough, called *Table Talk*. Then, too, a work undertaken to please a sprightly lady and dispel its author's gloom, a work which deals with tame hares, tea-drinking, winter-morning walks, and the pleasures of the garden and the fireside, is hardly one to employ the style and diction consecrated to the rebellion of archangels. To be sure, Philips, Grainger, and even Thomson had used the stately periods of *Paradise Lost* in the treatment of lowly themes; but Cowper's finer taste and far more delicate literary feeling would never have permitted the enormities these men were guilty of. Such topics as liberty, religion, war, and slavery, with which the poem has much to do, might properly enough have been discussed in a Miltonic style if the tone of the poem had not been fixed by the quiet pictures of nature and the homely subjects that receive most of the attention, and if Cowper had not preferred to treat even weighty matters in an incidental, conversational manner rather than with the formality required by a loftier strain.

For these reasons it is not surprising that *The Task* contains many passages like the following, which show no influence from *Paradise Lost:*

etc., "But neither breath of Morn . . . nor rising Sun . . . nor grateful Evening . . . without thee is sweet" (*P. L.*, iv. 641–56). Other passages in Cowper that seem to be derived from Milton are noted in Appendix A, below. In lines 14–16 of *Yardley Oak* there is a reference to *Paradise Lost*, ix. 1084–1100; and in a letter to Lady Hesketh, Oct. 13, 1798, there is one to Milton's sonnet on his blindness.

[1] iii. 446–543 (directions for raising cucumbers).

He is the happy man, whose life even now
Shows somewhat of that happier life to come;
Who, doomed to an obscure but tranquil state,
Is pleased with it, and, were he free to choose,
Would make his fate his choice; whom peace, the fruit
Of virtue, and whom virtue, fruit of faith,
Prepare for happiness; bespeak him one
Content indeed to sojourn while he must
Below the skies, but having there his home.[1]

Verse so easy and flowing, so natural and conversational as this, is rare even near the end of the eighteenth century. It anticipates Wordsworth, and seems to belong to an entirely different age from that which produced *Leonidas*, the *Sugar-Cane*, and *The Fleece*. With Cowper, indeed, we reach the most supple blank verse, the kind best adapted to the ordinary uses of poetry, that was written before *Tintern Abbey* and *Michael*.[2]

Although the passage just quoted is typical of much of *The Task*, rarely are so many consecutive lines free from any suggestion of *Paradise Lost*. Ordinarily in this poem, as in the *Night Thoughts*, one or another feature of Milton's style or diction occurs in almost every paragraph. Yet such characteristics do not usually become marked throughout a number of consecutive lines, but only in short passages like these:

Hard fare! but such as boyish appetite,
Disdains not, nor the palate, undepraved
By culinary arts, unsavoury deems.

Ocean . . . invades the shore
Resistless. Never such a sudden flood,
Upridged so high, and sent on such a charge,
Possessed an inland scene. Where now the throng
That pressed the beach, and hasty to depart
Looked to the sea for safety? They are gone,
Gone with the refluent wave into the deep.

Immortal Hale! for deep discernment praised,
And sound integrity, not more than famed
For sanctity of manners undefiled.

Those Ausonia claims,
Levantine regions these; the Azores send
Their jessamine, her jessamine remote
Caffraria.

[1] vi. 906–14.

[2] Besides making blank verse more supple and flowing, Cowper, like Young, helped to give it some of the epigrammatic crispness of the couplet.

> Thy rams are there,
> Nebaioth, and the flocks of Kedar there;
> The looms of Ormus, and the mines of Ind,
> And Saba's spicy groves, pay tribute there.[1]

It will be noticed that what most frequently gives these lines their Miltonic ring is the inversion of the normal word-order, from which few sentences in *The Task* are free. When the inversion is accompanied by the omission of an auxiliary in a negative sentence, as in "disdains not," "nor conversant," "nor wanted aught within," "nor suspends," "proved He not plainly," "he seeks not," "not slothful he," [2] there is a strong suggestion of *Paradise Lost*. That particularly Miltonic inversion, a word placed between two dependent words or phrases, — "devious course uncertain," "feathered tribes domestic," "a sordid mind Bestial," "for deep discernment praised And sound integrity," [3]—was as attractive to Cowper as to his predecessor. By no means so common, but perhaps as frequent as in Milton (an instance on nearly every page), is his use of an adjective where an adverb would ordinarily be employed, as "spring spontaneous," "invades the shore Resistless," "cherups brisk," "sedulous I seek," "sipping calm," "disposes neat," "breathe mild," "wheeling slow," "impeded sore," "blazing clear," "sheepish he doffs his hat," "now creeps he slow, and now . . . Wide scampering." [4]

The diction of *The Task*, as might be expected in a poem published half a century later than *Winter* and but two years before Wordsworth entered college, is more simple and natural than was usual in eighteenth-century blank verse. Cowper's language is, indeed, more conversational than that of many authors who came after him. What makes us think of *The Task* with *The Seasons* rather than with *The Prelude* is its style and contents, not its diction. The strongly Latinized vocabulary that is largely responsible for the turgidity of Thomson and his followers is not a characteristic of Cowper. Occasionally, however, he does make use of such unusual words from the Greek or Latin as "vermicular," "recumbency," "arthritic," "revolvency," "feculence," "peccancy," "vortiginous," "refluent," "sempiternal," "oscitancy," "meliorate," "stercoraceous," "agglomerated," "ebriety," "tramontane," "introverted," "indu-

---

[1] i. 123–5; ii. 111–20; iii. 258–60, 582–5; vi. 804–7.

[2] i. 124; iii. 24; v. 156; vi. 308, 447, 920, 928.

[3] iii. 3; v. 62, 453–4; iii. 258–9; cf. also v. 119–20, 153, 164 (three instances on one page).

[4] i. 603; ii. 114–15; iii. 9, 367, 391, 423, 443, 499; iv. 343, 381, 628; v. 48–9. For other instances, see i. 20, 110–11, 266, 347, 510–11; ii. 103, 374; iii. 563, 579; iv. 291, 293, 343–4, 478–9, 541; v. 7, 24–6 (two instances), 359–60, 426; vi. 79, 375–6, 723, etc.

rated," "vitreous," "lubricity," "terraqueous," "confutation," "prelibation," "propense," "ostent." [1] Now and then he employs words in their original though obsolete meanings or applications, as "speculative height" (affording an extensive view), "devotes" (vows to destruction), "obnoxious" (exposed to), "coincident" (agreeing), "soliciting" (trying to draw out, as darts in the side of a deer), "congenial" (kindred), "assimilate" (make similar), "admire" (wonder), "invest" (clothe the branch of a tree), "involved" (enveloped, as in tobacco-smoke), "induced" (drew on, of a chair-cover), "reprieve" (said of preserving shade-trees), "lapse" (said of snowflakes), "ardent" (said of clouds).[2]

The most vicious of the many varieties of poetic diction that cursed the eighteenth century, the periphrasis, is so infrequent in *The Task* as to be negligible. Yet such phrases as "the sprightly chord" (harp?), "the sylvan scene" (fields), "philosophic tube" (telescope), "the fragrant lymph" (tea), "clouds Of Indian fume" (tobacco-smoke), "the feathered tribes domestic" (hens), "the fleecy flood" (snow), "the prickly and green-coated gourd" (cucumber), "the fragrant charge of a short tube That fumes beneath his nose" (tobacco),[3] show a kinship between the poet of Olney and the writers of the first half of his century.

"Compound epithets," Cowper wrote in the preface for a second edition of his Homer, "have obtained so long in the poetical language of our country, that I employed them without fear or scruple." Even in *The Task* they are quite as common as in *The Seasons*, but, being more "happily combined,"[4] are far less noticeable. The first page I open to has three instances (an average number), all in the Thomson vein, — "card-devoted," "homely-featured," "bird-alluring." [5]

Save for his frequent use of adjectives for adverbs, Cowper does not often make one part of speech do service for another. Yet in phrases like "all-essenced o'er With odours," "basket up the family," "well equipaged," "filleted about with hoops," "to buckram

---

[1] i. 30, 82, 105, 372, 684; ii. 72, 102, 120, 499, 774; iii. 304, 463, 472; iv. 460, 533, 633; v. 98, 161, 165, 281, 567, 574, 585; vi. 486.

[2] i. 289 (cf. *P. L.*, xii. 588–9, *P. R.*, iv. 236); ii. 20, 156, 374; iii. 115, 205; iv. 329; vi. 128; iii. 666 (and vi. 169); iv. 472; i. 32, 264; iv. 327; v. 4.

[3] ii. 78, 107; iii. 229, 391; iv. 472–3; v. 62, 63; iii. 446; v. 55–6. The last two examples may be intended humorously, as those in iii. 463–543 certainly are. These are all the periphrases I have noted, but there are probably others.

[4] Preface for a second edition of his Homer.

[5] iv. 229, 252, 263; some editions hyphenate "slow moving" (246). "Spectacle-bestrid," "ear-erecting," "truth-tried," and "cheek-distending" (ii. 439, iii. 9, 56, iv. 488) are instances of Cowper's more marked and less successful combinations.

out the memory,"[1] he uses substantives as verbs; while in "garnish
your profuse regales," and "the employs of rural life,"[2] he turns the
tables. In "deluging the dry," "I am no proficient," "spare the
soft And succulent," "no powdered pert," "the first and only fair"
(meaning God), "in the vast and the minute,"[3] adjectives appear as
nouns; in "saturate with dew," "emancipate and loosed," "unadul-
terate air,"[4] we have the clipt form of participle that Milton liked.

Since Cowper's natural, easy, and somewhat diffuse style is in
marked contrast to the brevity and condensation of *Paradise Lost*,
his poem might be expected to contain comparatively few of the
parenthetical or appositional expressions that served Milton so well.
Appositives, like "he of Gath, Goliath," and

> No works indeed
> That ask robust tough sinews bred to toil,
> Servile employ,[5]

are rare; but parenthetical expressions are thick as autumnal leaves
in Vallombrosa. "There's a parenthesis for you!" he exclaimed on
one occasion, after quoting (for another purpose) four lines from
Paradise Lost. "The parenthesis it seems is out of fashion, and perhaps the moderns are in the right to proscribe what they cannot
attain to. I will answer for it that, had we the art at this day of insinuating a sentiment in this graceful manner, no reader of taste
would quarrel with the practice."[6] Many of the parentheses in *The
Task* involve too little condensation to seem Miltonic, but a considerable number do recall *Paradise Lost;* for example,

> The rest, no portion left
> That may disgrace his art, or disappoint
> Large expectation, he disposes neat.

> Often urged,
> (As often as, libidinous discourse
> Exhausted, he resorts to solemn themes
> Of theological and grave import,)
> They gain at last his unreserved assent;
> Till hardened his heart's temper in the forge
> Of lust, and on the anvil of despair,
> He slights the strokes of conscience.

---

[1] ii. 227–8, 667; iii. 98; v. 402; vi. 652.
[2] iii. 551 (cf. his *Odyssey*, i. 177, ii. 25), 625 (cf. 406).
[3] ii. 56; iii. 210, 417–18; iv. 145; v. 675, 811.
[4] i. 494; ii. 39; iv. 750 (cf. v. 465).
[5] iv. 269–70; iii. 404–6.
[6] Letter to Bagot, Oct. 25, 1791.

> And now, his prowess proved, and his sincere
> Incurable obduracy evinced,
> His rage grew cool.[1]

Cowper's tendency to diffuseness also kept him, as a rule, from omitting words that would be expressed in prose. Yet there are not a few instances like these: "what can they less," "nor this to feed his own," "the gods themselves had made," "happy who walks with Him," "so little mercy shows who needs so much," "who . . . forgets, Or can, the more than Homer," "who will may preach, And what they will," "not slothful he, though seeming unemployed,"

> Was honoured, loved, and wept
> By more than one, themselves conspicuous there.

> Moral truth
> How lovely, and the moral sense how sure,
> Consulted and obeyed, to guide his steps.[2]

The result of these various departures from ordinary usage is that a reader who is attentive to the matter catches reverberations from *Paradise Lost* on every page of *The Task*. These echoes were heard and admired at the time; for the *Gentleman's Magazine* lauded Cowper as "perhaps, without excepting even Philips, the most successful of the imitators of Milton." [3] A curious, back-handed compliment this seems to us, but the writer probably meant that the blank verse of *The Task* was among the very best of the century and that it was essentially Miltonic. And these things are true.

With the completion of *The Task*, Cowper, whose mind "abhorred a vacuum as its chief bane," [4] was already sinking into a fit of his old depression, when one day, happening to take up a copy of the *Iliad*, he translated a few lines by way of diversion. The experiment succeeded so well that he tried it again, and eventually, in 1791, published the whole of Homer in blank verse. One would expect the translation to be as much more Miltonic than *The Task* as its subject-matter is more heroic and exalted: the epic demanded "heigh style," and what example of lofty blank verse was there to compare with *Paradise Lost?* Nevertheless, it is with something of a shock that a reader of *The Task* opens the Homer. For the conversational ease and natural, flowing charm of the early work have given place

---

[1] iii. 421–3; v. 659–66; vi. 531–3.
[2] ii. 644; iv. 452; v. 292; vi. 247, 431, 645–7, 889–90, 928; ii. 786–7; v. 672–4. Note also p. 167 above.
[3] lvi. 235 (March, 1786).
[4] Letter to Newton, Dec. 3, 1785.

to a distorted word-order, an involved, jerky style, to inversions within inversions, parentheses crowding appositives, and to adjectives, torn from their natural positions, regularly performing the functions of adverbs. It is hard to see how Homer could be made any more Miltonic. My own first thought was that the inversions and the rest were introduced to preserve the word-order and other features of the original; but, on comparing with the Greek the passages that had struck me as most Miltonic, I found this was not the case. The line, "These things pondering in his mind, which were not to be fulfilled," [1] for example, Cowper translates,

> In false hopes occupied and musings vain. [2]

"If quickly had not perceived [him] great crest-tossing Hector. He went then through the van armed in shining brass," he renders,

> Had not crest-tossing Hector huge perceived
> The havoc; radiant to the van he flew. [3]

"'For the dearest men are under my roof.' Thus he spoke, and Patroclus obeyed his dear companion," is changed to,

> For dearer friends than these who now arrive
> My roof beneath, or worthier, have I none.
> He ended, and Patroclus quick obey'd
> Whom much he loved. [4]

"So I spoke, and the soul of swift-footed Æacides withdrew with great strides along the asphodel meadow, glad that I had said his son was famous," is contorted into

> So I; then striding large, the spirit thence
> Withdrew of swift Æacides, along
> The hoary mead pacing with joy elate
> That I had blazon'd bright his son's renown. [5]

"He knew [me] immediately when he saw me with his eyes, and me he, sorrowing, with winged words addressed," appears as

> Me his eye
> No sooner mark'd, than knowing me, in words
> By sorrow quick suggested, he began. [6]

[1] In my translations everything else has been sacrificed to literalness and a close adherence to the word-order of the original.
[2] *Iliad*, ii. 36; Cowper, ii. 44.
[3] *Iliad*, v. 680–81; Cowper, v. 807–8.
[4] *Iliad*, ix. 204–5; Cowper, ix. 252–5.
[5] *Odyssey*, xi. 538–40; Cowper, xi. 658–61.
[6] *Odyssey*, xi. 615–16; Cowper, xi. 749–51.

Is even Pope's version farther from the spirit of Homer than these
verses? It may be, of course, that Cowper, while not trying to reproduce the original word-order of any particular passage, felt that the
general use of inversions and of adjectives for adverbs would give the
effect of the Greek; but in reality they produce an impression entirely unlike Homer's by destroying his simple directness, naturalness, and rapidity.[1] The explanation is probably to be found in
Cowper's desire to give his translation epic dignity, in his love for
Paradise Lost, and in the false taste of the period with which he was
inevitably tainted.

When the poet's friends, and the reviewers (who were of a younger
generation), objected strongly to these excessive Miltonisms, the
translator himself insisted they were not there. "With respect to
inversions in particular," he wrote, "I know that they do not
abound. Once they did, and I had Milton's example for it. . . .
But on Fuseli's remonstrance against them, I expunged the most,
and in my new edition have fewer still. I know that they give dignity, and am sorry to part with them." [2] In the "new edition" to
which he refers, though he introduced some additional inversions
and other Miltonisms, he undoubtedly did remove many of the old
ones, and thus made the translation more simple and flowing if less
spirited. In that version, published two years after his death, two
of the passages given above run thus:

> I spake, whose praises of his son, the ghost
> Of swift Æacides exulting heard,
> And measuring with larger strides, for joy,
> The meadow gray with asphodel, retir'd.

> Soon as he beheld
> He knew me, and in sorrow thus began.[3]

The Task and the translation of Homer had done so much to dispel
the gloom which was never far from the unfortunate poet that as

---

[1] The diction is often equally objectionable: e. g., "coëtaneous," "stridulous," "dismissed" (of a spear), "salutiferous," "expressed" (of juice), "retracting" (of a cord),
"impressed" (of wounds), "in peculiar," "promulge," "revulsed," "conflicted" (as a
verb), "acuminated," "afflictive," "necessitous," "chode," "grumous" (*Iliad*, i. 315;
ii. 268; iii. 422, and vii. 320, xi. 459, 685, etc.; v. 469, 1074; viii. 374, 472; ix. 119; ix.
123 and x. 356; xii. 481; xiii. 830; xv. 585; xvi. 15, 1021; xvii. 520; xxiii. 872).

[2] Letter to Samuel Rose, Feb. 17, 1793.

[3] *Odyssey*, xi. 657–60, 746–7. It is the first edition that Southey reprinted, following
the advice of all with whom he consulted; likewise it is the first edition of Cowper's
Odyssey that appears in Everyman's library. Cowper also translated some of the *Aeneid*
and a few of Milton's Latin poems into blank verse. As might be expected, these translations show more influence from *Paradise Lost* than does *The Task*. The humorous
unrimed skit, *To the Immortal Memory of the Halibut* (written 1784), is also slightly
Miltonic.

soon as the *Odyssey* was finished he and his friends cast about for a subject of a new poem to occupy his attention. Some one suggested *The Four Ages of Man*, and he seems himself to have thought of *Yardley Oak;* but, although he began each poem (both, it should be observed, in blank verse), he carried neither beyond a few pages. The *Four Ages* is not unlike the dull parts of *The Task;* but *Yardley Oak* achieves a much loftier strain, "a combination of massiveness and 'atmosphere'" which Mr. Saintsbury finds unmatched, outside of Spenser and Shakespeare, by any earlier English poet.[1] At any rate, no writer of the century composed any nobler piece of blank verse. Nor did the giants of the following age often do better, for *Yardley Oak* is not unworthy of Wordsworth, whose *Yew-Trees* it prefigures. Superficial Miltonisms, such as "excoriate forks deform," "fostering propitious," "I wou d not curious ask," "the heat Transmitting cloudless," "by the tooth Pulverized of venality,"[2] are less marked in *Yardley Oak* than in the Homer; but there is a full-toned largeness of utterance in such lines as these that make them more profoundly Miltonic than any others Cowper wrote:

> Time made thee what thou wast, king of the woods,
> And Time hath made thee what thou art — a cave
> For owls to roost in. Once thy spreading boughs
> O'erhung the champaign; and the numerous flocks
> That grazed it stood beneath that ample cope
> Uncrowded, yet safe-sheltered from the storm. . . .
> While thus through all the stages thou hast pushed
> Of treeship, first a seedling, hid in grass;
> Then twig; then sapling; and, as century rolled
> Slow after century, a giant-bulk
> Of girth enormous, with moss-cushioned root
> Upheaved above the soil, and sides embossed
> With prominent wens globose, till at the last
> The rottenness, which time is charged to inflict
> On other mighty ones, found also thee.[3]

[1] *Peace of the Augustans*, 341. I cannot, however, agree with this eminent critic when he says (*ib.* 339) that "what Cowper might have been as a poet is perhaps only shown" in this piece and *The Castaway;* for, short as *Yardley Oak* is, it is not sustained. There are dull passages (e. g., lines 29–32, 45–9, 120–24, 137–61), unrhythmical lines (57, 94, 123), and objectionable diction (5, 66, 110). The latter part, and particularly the concluding lines, show such a decided falling-off both in contents and in expression that it looks as if Cowper abandoned the poem because his inspiration had fled, because he found he had nothing to say and could not sustain the lofty tone with which he began.

[2] Lines 5, 39, 42, 74, 123.

[3] Lines 50–68. Lines 14–16 contain a reference to *Paradise Lost*, ix. 1084–1100; and some of the diction is perhaps Miltonic, — e. g., "meed" (13, cf. Lycidas, 14), "with vegetative force instinct" (34, cf. *P. L.*, ii. 937, vi. 752), "globose" (66, cf. *P. L.*, vii. 357, etc.), and such Latinisms as "latitude of boughs" (21) and "impulse" of the wind (84). Strangely enough, J. C. Bailey, in his excellent edition of Cowper (1905, p. lvi),

In 1791, while Cowper was visiting William Hayley, the two men, one of whom was editing Milton and the other writing a life of him, translated the *Adamo* of Andreini, a probable source of *Paradise Lost*. Like the original, the translation (by no means a masterpiece) is in short lines, generally of irregular length and without rime. The diction and style, as might be expected of a poem in which God, Satan, angels, Adam and Eve, are the characters, frequently though never strongly recall *Paradise Lost*. Some idea of the work may be gathered from these lines:

> Adam, awake! and cease
> To meditate in rapturous trance profound
> Things holy and abstruse,
> And the deep secrets of the Trinal Lord.[1]

This brief examination of Cowper's writings shows that both in the bulk and in the importance of the poems affected the influence of Milton looms large. The *Verses on Finding the Heel of a Shoe*, *The Task*, the poem to the halibut, the *Four Ages*, *Yardley Oak*, the sonnets, the translations of Homer, Virgil, Andreini, and of Milton's Italian and Latin poems, — these pieces, which make up the most considerable and the most important part of Cowper's work, are all unmistakably Miltonic.[2] Yet in one of his letters he speaks of "having imitated no man," and continues: "Milton's manner was peculiar. So is Thomson's. He that should write like either of them, would, in my judgment, deserve the name of a copyist, but not of a poet."[3] Cowper was no copyist. *The Task* and *Yardley Oak* are entirely his own in style no less than in subject-matter; no one else could have written them. His relations to Milton were like those we bear to our father and mother. We do not deliberately imitate our parents; we love them, and are in constant close association with them through the years when we receive our deepest impressions, and thus our ideals, our opinions, our acts, are affected by them in a hundred ways of which we are not conscious. So Cowper, who had read the elder poet enthusiastically since his fourteenth year and re-

remarks that the poem "stands alone among his works in being rather akin to Shakespeare than to Milton"!

[1] Cowper's *Works* (ed. Southey), x. 251. The Italian is,

> Sueglisi Adamo, e lasci
> Di fruir in bel rapto alte, e Diuine
> Occultissime cose,
> E del Trino Signor profondi arcani.

Not a little of the diction which seems to be Miltonic is derived from the original.

[2] For the influence of Milton on Cowper's sonnets, see p. 510 below.

[3] To John Newton, Dec. 13, 1784.

garded him as "this great man, this greatest of men, your idol and mine,"[1] came to feel that blank verse and *Paradise Lost* were inseparable, that non-Miltonic blank verse was a contradiction in terms. Among the requisites of blank verse he mentions "a style in general more elaborate than rhime requires, farther removed from the vernacular idiom both in the language itself and in the arrangement of it."[2] Since these qualities are neither distinctive of blank verse nor essential to it, is not this equivalent to declaring that good blank verse must be Miltonic?

Another requirement that Cowper repeatedly stressed as a *sine qua non* of unrimed poetry was the pause, or pauses, within the line and the necessity of constantly shifting them about, a device to which, as he pointed out, Milton's "numbers" were "so much indebted both for their dignity and variety." These pauses were to be commended, he held, even when they produced an occasional rough line, because such roughness "saves the ear the pain of an irksome monotony. . . . Milton," he continued, "whose ear and taste were exquisite, has exemplified in his Paradise Lost the effect of this practice frequently."[3] In these matters, and indeed in his entire theory and practice of prosody, Cowper seems to have been strongly influenced by his favorite poem. He wrote to a friend, "The unacquaintedness of modern ears with the divine harmony of Milton's numbers, and the principles upon which he constructed them, is the cause of the quarrel that they have with elisions in blank verse."[4] And a little earlier he had said: "The practice of cutting short a *The* is warranted by Milton, who of all English poets that ever lived, had certainly the finest ear. Dr. Warton, indeed, has dared to say that he had a bad one; for which he deserves, as far as critical demerit can deserve it, to lose his own."[5]

Yet it was not simply in prosody but in diction as well that Milton was the final authority. Seven times in the course of his Homer Cowper justifies his use of a word by quoting from Milton,[6] whereas to the language of all other English poets he acknowledges but four

---

[1] Letter to Hayley, Nov. 22, 1793.

[2] Preface to his Homer. If the *Thunder Storm* — which first appeared in Wright's *Life* (1892, p. 177) but which Bailey rejects both because of insufficient external evidence and because, as he justly observes, it does not sound like Cowper — is really by the poet of Olney, it shows that even his unpremeditated and unrevised verse was clearly Miltonic.

[3] Preface to his Homer.

[4] To Walter Bagot, Aug. 31, 1786.

[5] Letter to Lady Hesketh, March 6, 1786.

[6] *Iliad*, v. 641, xv. 168, xxiii. 195; *Odyssey*, i. 178, xi. 19, 139, xxiv. 43.

obligations.[1] Indeed, he had come to regard *Paradise Lost* as a well-nigh perfect poem, one that furnished in all matters the model of good taste and the standard of good usage. "I am filled with wonder," he wrote to Lady Hesketh when he decided to drop from his Homer "the quaintness that belonged to our writers of the fifteenth century," "I am filled with wonder at my own backwardness to assent to the necessity of it, and the more when I consider that Milton, with whose manner I account myself intimately acquainted, is never quaint, never twangs through the nose, but is every where grand and elegant, without resorting to musty antiquity for his beauties." [2] With Cowper, as with Wordsworth, the first and last question was usually, "What was Milton's usage?" To employ his own words, "The Author of the Paradise Lost [furnishes] an example inimitable indeed, but which no writer of English heroic verse without rhyme can neglect with impunity." [3] He intended neither to neglect nor servilely to follow this inimitable example, and he did neither; but he little realized how subtly, how variously, and how extensively his admiration for his "idol" had affected his writings.

[1] *Iliad*, vii. 167 (Dryden); *Odyssey*, viii. 324 (Gray); x. 161, xxiv. 5, 11 (Shakespeare).

[2] March 22, 1790. "Borrowing," he wrote to Thomas Park, Feb. 19, 1792, "seems to imply poverty, and of poverty I can rather suspect any man than Milton."

[3] Preface for a second edition of his Homer.

CHAPTER IX

WORDSWORTH

THE influence of *Paradise Lost* as we have seen it thus far has been almost exclusively literary. Writers have been attracted not by Milton's message but by his art, not by his character and opinions but by his versification and diction, not by what he said but by how he said it. His admirers have used his tools and tried to imitate his method of handling them, but for the most part they have been indifferent to his personality, as well as to his conceptions of poetry and life. The Miltonism of Milton is, therefore, exactly what they have lacked. They could copy his diction, mimic his style, and at times catch something of the roll of his lines; but the character behind all this, the spirit which animated and the purpose which consecrated it, they did not even strive for. It was not necessary, in most cases it was not desirable, that they should; if Thomson and Cowper, for example, had done so they would have written poems quite unlike *The Seasons* and *The Task*. Yet the fact remains that the admirers of Pope, Keats, Tennyson, and Whitman have caught much of the spirit and message as well as the form of their favorites, whereas Milton's followers have found him so unlike other poets that as a rule they have been content with merely reproducing his manner.

In one writer, however, these conditions are reversed, and with most significant results. For the familiar evidences of the influence of *Paradise Lost* — adjectives employed as adverbs or substantives, unusual compound epithets, parentheses, appositives, omitted words, and the rest — indicate very inadequately the extent of that influence on the poetry of Wordsworth. Such peculiarities of style and diction do occur here and there, but they are not sufficiently marked to give a noticeable Miltonic ring to any large number of lines. Yet there sounds throughout Wordsworth's verse a note, scarcely heard in the simpler pieces but often unmistakable in the profounder ones, which at times rises till it becomes the dominant tone, almost drowning all others, a note which recalls the lofty severity, the intensity of moral purpose, and the organ tone of the most exalted of English poets. To be sure, this note was natural to Wordsworth, and it is impossible to say where temperamental similarity ends and influence begins; yet similarity of this sort obviously furnishes the best possible ground for influence to work upon. It is because Wordsworth was in essentials so much like the earlier Puritan that he admired him so highly, was so susceptible to his influence and so capable of profiting by it.[1]

The two men were, indeed, as regards the fundamentals of life and poetry, much more alike than is at first apparent. Both were Puritans, deeply religious men with high ideals, strong convictions, and a tendency towards narrowness and intolerance. Both were somewhat austere and aloof, believers in "plain living and high thinking," absolutely sincere, confident of their powers, and unswayed by popular opinion. Neither possessed a sense of humor or the grace of doing little things with ease, and neither was what is commonly known as "a good fellow"; yet both were fond of romances, tales of impossible adventure, and the poetry of Spenser. Each was devoted heart and soul to the cause of liberty and to England's political welfare, each took a profoundly serious view of poetry, each regarded his life as dedicated to the service of God and his fellow-men. Wordsworth declared, "Every great poet is a teacher; I wish either to be considered as a teacher or as nothing."[2] And the purpose of Milton's epic was: "Whatsoever in religion is holy and sublime, in vertu amiable, or grave, whatsoever hath passion or admiration in all the changes of that which is call'd fortune from without, or the wily suttleties and refluxes of mans thoughts from within, all these things with a solid and treatable smoothnesse to paint out and describe. Teaching over the whole book of sanctity and vertu. . . ."[3] The two men were alike, it should be noticed, in their defects no less than in their virtues. Wordsworth was not repelled, as many have been, by the elder poet's egotism, his exacting nature, or his lack of easy geniality, for he had the same faults himself and thought lightly of them. He regarded Milton as an "awful soul" and admired him on that account.

Externally, of course, there were great differences between the two. The lake poet was a kind of Milton in homespun. Milton was an aristocrat with an air of distinction, and in a way a man of the

---

[1] Conversely, it is because Wordsworth was so unlike Spenser that the *Faerie Queene*, for which he had a great admiration, exerted only a slight influence upon him.

[2] Letter to Sir George Beaumont, 1807? (*Letters of the Wordsworth Family*, ed. Knight, Boston, 1907, i. 331). To Landor's remark that he was "disgusted with all books that treat of religion," Wordsworth replied (Jan. 21, 1824): "I have little relish for any other. Even in poetry it is the imagination only, viz., that which is conversant with, or turns upon infinity, that powerfully affects me."

[3] *Reason of Church-Government*, 1641, in *Works* (Pickering ed., 1851), iii. 147.

world, whereas in Wordsworth there was something of the rustic. Milton's great learning, wide culture, and intellectual curiosity caused him to be sought after, and, together with his strong though well-controlled passions, gave vigor, variety, and brilliance to his conversation. Wordsworth, on the other hand, was — at least in his later years — slow, ponderous, and introspective, and perhaps to most persons never a particularly interesting companion. In their verse the two men seem at first glance even farther apart than in their social qualities. The earlier poet chose the sublimest of themes and handled it in the loftiest of styles; the later one usually dealt in a simple way with wild-flowers, birds, his own quiet life and that of the peasants about him. Not only as a poet but as a man each had much in common with the period in which he spent his youth, Milton with the renaissance, Wordsworth with the eighteenth century. Yet the differences are not essential; for the purposes, the ideals of life, and the conceptions of poetry of the two were surprisingly alike. In fundamentals Wordsworth was closer to the author of *Paradise Lost* than any other English poet has been.

This basic similarity was largely responsible for the profound veneration that Wordsworth felt for his predecessor. As the resemblances between the two men were no less personal than literary, it was natural that the devotion of the later poet to the earlier should be quite as much to the man as to his works. At times, indeed, it would seem as if he revered the man above the poet, for in the sonnet "Milton, thou shouldst be living at this hour," he devoted twelve lines to his favorite's character and two to his verse. We may well pause for a moment over the circumstances that gave rise to this sonnet. Wordsworth had been in France, deeply concerned for the cause of liberty. Returning to his own country, he was depressed by its lack of heroism, by its wealth, its smug ease, its "vanity and parade." In this state of mind he thought of whom? the Greek and Roman patriots? Alfred? Hampden? Cromwell? No, of Milton, — not the poet, but the man among men, the pamphleteer who had given his eyes in liberty's defense. Stirred to his depths, the young patriot cried out:

> Milton! thou should'st be living at this hour:
> England hath need of thee: she is a fen
> Of stagnant waters: altar, sword, and pen,
> Fireside, the heroic wealth of hall and bower
> Have forfeited their ancient English dower
> Of inward happiness. We are selfish men;
> Oh! raise us up, return to us again;

And give us manners, virtue, freedom, power.
Thy soul was like a Star, and dwelt apart:
Thou hadst a voice whose sound was like the sea:
Pure as the naked heavens, majestic, free,
So didst thou travel on life's common way,
In cheerful godliness; and yet thy heart
The lowliest duties on herself did lay.

Nor was this a passing mood. In the same month he wrote,

Great men have been among us; hands that penned
And tongues that uttered widsom — better none:
The later Sidney, Marvel, Harrington,
Young Vane, and others who called Milton friend;

and in still another sonnet of that month he exclaimed,

We must be free or die, who speak the tongue
That Shakespeare spake; the faith and morals hold
Which Milton held.[1]

These are significant lines: it is the "tongue," or poetry, of Shakespeare and the "faith and morals" of Milton of which England should be proud. A year later, when fearing the Napoleonic invasion, Wordsworth summoned those who,

like the Pyms and Miltons of that day,
Think that a State would live in sounder health
If Kingship bowed its head to Commonwealth.[2]

Similarly, in his prose *Convention of Cintra* he refers to England's "long train of deliverers and defenders, her Alfred, her Sidneys, and her Milton." [3]

Long before 1802, however, Wordsworth had felt the appeal of Milton's personality. Even in his idle Cambridge days it had impressed him; for he wrote in *The Prelude*,

Yea, our blind Poet, who, in his later day,
Stood almost single; uttering odious truth —
Darkness before, and danger's voice behind,
Soul awful — if the earth has ever lodged
An awful soul — I seemed to see him here
Familiarly, and in his scholar's dress
Bounding before me, yet a stripling youth —
A boy, no better, with his rosy cheeks
Angelical, keen eye, courageous look,
And conscious step of purity and pride.[4]

[1] "Great men," 1–4; "It is not to be thought of," 11–13.
[2] *Lines on the Expected Invasion*, 7–9.
[3] *Prose Works* (ed. Grosart, 1876), i. 112.
[4] iii. 283–92.

In the lines following these, Wordsworth confessed that the only time he was affected by liquor was when he "poured out Libations" to the "temperate Bard" in the room the latter had occupied as a student. On another occasion, in speaking of the degenerate days of Charles II, he recalled Milton's fearless service to truth:

> Yet Truth is keenly sought for, and the wind
> Charged with rich words poured out in thought's defence. . . .
> And One there is who builds immortal lays,
> Though doomed to tread in solitary ways,
> Darkness before and danger's voice behind;
> Yet not alone, nor helpless to repel
> Sad thoughts; for from above the starry sphere
> Come secrets, whispered nightly to his ear;
> And the pure spirit of celestial light
> Shines through his soul — "that he may see and tell
> Of things invisible to mortal sight." [1]

He contrasted Milton's unselfish heroism with the conduct of Goethe, who, in Wordsworth's opinion, "was amusing himself with fine fancies when his country was invaded; how unlike Milton, who only asked himself whether he could best serve his country as a soldier or a statesman, and decided that he could fight no better than others, but he might govern them better." [2] Finally, in one of his prefaces he goes out of his way to make "a public acknowledgment of one of the innumerable obligations, which," he declares, "as a Poet *and a Man*, I am under to our great fellow-countryman." [3] Wordsworth was, in truth, inspired as no other writer has been by the life and character of this "great fellow-countryman," and it was such inspiration, together with the admiration lying back of it, that made possible the influence which Milton's work exerted upon his own.

It is a matter of some importance that Wordsworth's delight in *Paradise Lost* and the other works of its author began in boyhood days. "The Poet's father," we are informed, "set him very early to learn portions of the works of the best English poets by heart, so that at an early age he could repeat large portions of Shakespeare, Milton, and Spenser;" [4] and Wordsworth himself told Mrs. Davy that Milton's poetry "was earlier a favourite with him than that of Shakespeare." [5] Nor is there any question as to the permanence of

[1] *Ecclesiastical Sonnets*, III. iv ("Latitudinarianism").
[2] Caroline Fox, *Memories of Old Friends* (3d ed., 1882), ii. 41, Oct. 6, 1844.
[3] "Advertisement" to the first edition of his *Sonnets* (1838). The italics are mine.
[4] Christopher Wordsworth, *Memoirs of Wordsworth* (ed. Henry Reed, Boston, 1851), i. 34.
[5] "Conversations," etc., *Prose Works* (ed. Grosart), iii. 457.

this enthusiasm.   One of his friends wrote in 1826, "Spenser, Shake-speare, and Milton are his favourites among the English poets, especially the latter, whom he almost idolizes." [1]   And after his death another said, "Wordsworth's favourite poet was Milton. . . .   It is curious to observe how Milton's genius triumphed over political prejudices in a mind so strongly imbued with them as that of Words-worth. . . .   Perhaps he was almost as much attached to Milton as he was to his own lakes and mountains." [2]

A lifelong admiration like this resulted, of course, in an unusual familiarity with Milton's poetry.   Not only could he ' repeat large portions of it at an early age,' but when he was thirty-two, so he wrote Landor, he knew all the sonnets by heart.[3]   Accordingly, Charles Lamb, in giving him a first edition of *Paradise Regained* inscribed "To the best Knower of Milton," [4] was merely express-ing what is clear enough from Wordsworth's own poems and letters and the reports of his conversation.   Crabb Robinson, for example, has left an account of a walk in which "Wordsworth was remarkably eloquent and felicitous in his praise of Milton":

He spoke of the *Paradise Regained* as surpassing even the *Paradise Lost* in perfection of execution, though the theme is far below it, and demand-ing less power.   He spoke of the description of the storm in it as the finest in all poetry; and he pointed out some of the artifices of versification by which Milton produces so great an effect, — as in passages like this: —

> "Pining atrophy,
> Marasmus, and wide-wasting pestilence,
> Dropsies, and asthmas, and joint-racking rheums."

In which the power of the final *rheums* is heightened by the *atrophy* and *pestilence*.   Wordsworth also praised, but not equally, *Samson Agonistes*. He concurred, he said, with Johnson in this, that it had *no middle*, but the beginning and end are equally sublime.[5]

Another conversation is recorded by the poet's nephew:

Milton is falsely represented by some as a democrat.   He was an aristo-crat in the truest sense of the word. . . . Indeed, he spoke in very proud and contemptuous terms of the populace.   *Comus* is rich in beautiful and sweet flowers, and in exuberant leaves of genius; but the ripe and mellow fruit is in *Samson Agonistes*.   When he wrote that, his mind was Hebraized.

---

[1] J. J. Tayler, *Letters* (1872), i. 72.
[2] Edward Whately, *Personal Recollections of the Lake Poets*, in *Leisure Hour*, Oct. 1, 1870, p. 653.
[3] See below, p. 529, n. 2.
[4] *Works* (ed. Lucas, 1905), vii. 912.
[5] *Diary*, etc. (ed. T. Sadler, 1869), Jan. 7, 1836, and see Jan. 26.

Indeed, his genius fed on the writings of the Hebrew prophets. . . . One of the noblest things in Milton is the description of that sweet, quiet morning in the *Paradise Regained* after that terrible night of howling wind and storm. The contrast is divine.[1]

In one of his letters Wordsworth noted that Milton's tractate *Of Education* "never loses sight of the means of making man perfect, both for contemplation and action, for civil and military duties." [2] To Lord Lonsdale he wrote, "I have long been persuaded that Milton formed his blank verse upon the model of the *Georgics* and the *Aeneid*, and I am so much struck with this resemblance that I should have attempted Virgil in blank verse, had I not been persuaded that no ancient author can be with advantage so rendered." [3] "Milton says of pouring ' easy his unpremeditated verse,' " he remarked to W. R. Hamilton. "It would be harsh, untrue, and odious to say there is anything like cant in this; but it is not *true* to the letter, and tends to mislead. I could point out to you five hundred passages in Milton, upon which labour has been bestowed, and twice five hundred more to which additional labour would have been serviceable; not that I regret the absence of such labour, because no poem contains more proof of skill acquired by practice." [4] How naturally Miltonic phrases rose to his mind is shown by his writing to Sir George Beaumont, "My creed rises up of itself with the ease of an exhalation, yet a fabric of adamant." [5]

But all these evidences of Wordsworth's familiarity with his favorite pale before the testimony offered by his poems. These contain at least one hundred fifty-eight borrowings from Milton, a larger number than has been found in the work of any other poet, with the exception, strangely enough, of Pope.[6] It is worth noting that these borrowings are scattered through more than seventy poems, and that they are taken not simply from *Paradise Lost*, *Allegro*, and *Penseroso*, but from *Comus*, *Lycidas*, *Samson*, *Paradise Regained*, the *Nativity*, and the sonnets. They leave no doubt as to

---

[1] "Conversations," etc., *Prose Works* (ed. Grosart), iii. 461. Cf. *P.R.*, iv. 432–8.
[2] To John Scott, June 11, 1816.
[3] Feb. 5, 1819.
[4] Letter of Nov. 22, 1831.
[5] May 28, 1825; cf. *P.L.*, i. 710–11,

> Anon out of the earth a fabric huge
> Rose like an exhalation.

[6] This number does not include references to Milton or quotations from his works prefixed to several of Wordsworth's poems. The most comprehensive printed list of such references, quotations, etc., is in Kurt Lienemann's *Die Belesenheit von William Wordsworth*, [Weimar], 1908.

Wordsworth's familiarity with all the more important poetry of his predecessor, and not merely the poetry, for *Artegal and Elidure*, which "was written . . . as a token of affectionate respect for the memory of Milton," [1] is based upon the latter's *History of Britain*. More than this, many of the phrases that Wordsworth takes are so inconspicuous as to have escaped the notice of his editors. Such expressions as "sober certainty," "teachers . . . Of moral prudence," "my genial spirits droop," "the . . . vessel . . . Rode tilting o'er the waves," "the vine . . . with her brings Her dower, the adopted clusters, to adorn" the elm, "reason is her [the soul's] being, Discursive, or intuitive," [2] can have been impressed upon his mind only by many careful readings. Some of the most interesting of his borrowings occur, singularly enough, in one of his prose works, the *Convention of Cintra*. Besides mentioning Milton among England's "deliverers and defenders," this piece contains five quotations from his poetry and four references to it, and closes with an extract from his prose.[3] Few would expect to recognize this last borrowing, since it is from the *History of Britain;* [4] but how many would detect a Miltonic phrase in "the central orb to which, as to a fountain, the nations of the earth ' ought to repair, and in their golden urns draw light ' "? [5] There are certainly not many who would notice anything from *Paradise Lost* in the sentence, "Wisdom is the hidden root which thrusts forth the stalk of prudence; and these uniting feed and uphold ' the bright consummate flower ' — National Happiness." [6]

Wordsworth wrote fifty-five poems in blank verse. Most of these, it must be confessed, belong to that desert, unwatered by the springs of imagination and unshaded by the foliage of beauty, which

---

[1] Fenwick note prefixed to the poem.

[2] For Wordsworth's use of these phrases, see below, Appendix A.

[3] *Prose Works* (ed. Grosart), i. 49, 50, 93, 109, 112 (see p. 180 above), 126, 128, 149, 171, 174.

[4] *Works* (Pickering ed.), v. 100. Grosart's note (i. 359) is incorrect.

[5] *Ib.* (Grosart), 112; cf. *P.L.*, vii. 361-5,

> The sun's orb. . . .
> Hither, as to their fountain, other stars
> Repairing, in their golden urns draw light.

[6] *Ib.* 171; cf. *P.L.*, v. 479-81,

> So from the root
> Springs lighter the green stalk, from thence the leaves
> More aery, last the bright consummate flower.

Neither this borrowing nor the preceding one is pointed out by Grosart or Knight. I owe them, and several other references and quotations, to Mrs. Alice M. Dunbar, of Wilmington, Delaware, who has generously placed at my disposal the extensive collection of material on Wordsworth's indebtedness to Milton which she made at Cornell University under the direction of Mr. Lane Cooper.

stretches its dreary expanse through a large part of his verse. Of these fifty-five pieces there are few that do not show some influence from *Paradise Lost*, and fourteen are sufficiently Miltonic to be included in the appended bibliography. Less than half of the fourteen, however, have enough beauty or other importance to detain us. One of this number, one that deserves a much wider circle of readers than it seems to have gained, is the *Address to Kilchurn Castle*, a poem of only forty-three lines, but nobly conceived and expressed in its author's loftiest Miltonic manner. The organ tone is certainly here:

> Child of loud-throated War! the mountain Stream
> Roars in thy hearing; but thy hour of rest
> Is come, and thou art silent in thy age . . .
> Cast off — abandoned by thy rugged Sire,
> Nor by soft Peace adopted; though, in place
> And in dimension, such that thou might'st seem
> But a mere footstool to yon sovereign Lord,
> Hugh Cruachan, (a thing that meaner hills
> Might crush, nor know that it had suffered harm;)
> Yet he, not loth, in favour of thy claims
> To reverence, suspends his own; submitting
> All that the God of Nature hath conferred,
> All that he holds in common with the stars,
> To the memorial majesty of Time
> Impersonated in thy calm decay!

Yew-Trees, though even shorter, is much better known. It is similar to the *Address* in dignity and largeness of utterance, as well as in the subordination of the object seen to the feelings and pictures of the past which it calls up to the imagination. The diction, it will be observed, is decidedly Miltonic, and at the same time, because of the dignity of the theme, eminently suitable:

> Of vast circumference and gloom profound
> This solitary Tree! a living thing
> Produced too slowly ever to decay;
> Of form and aspect too magnificent
> To be destroyed. But worthier still of note
> Are those fraternal Four of Borrowdale,
> Joined in one solemn and capacious grove;
> Huge trunks! and each particular trunk a growth
> Of intertwisted fibres serpentine
> Up-coiling, and inveterately convolved;
> Nor uninformed with Phantasy, and looks
> That threaten the profane; — a pillared shade.

Of the remaining poems of Wordsworth that call for consideration, two, *Home at Grasmere* and *The Excursion*, are parts of a long, unfinished work, *The Recluse*, "a philosophical Poem, containing views of Man, Nature, and Society," [1] to which a third, *The Prelude*, is the prolog. The significance and implications of these well-known facts are apt to be overlooked, since we are bent on regarding Wordsworth as a poet of nature and of the quiet lives of simple country folk, and since the passages that we remember from *The Prelude* are the descriptions of the out-of-doors and of boyish sports and adventures. Yet these descriptions and brief narratives exist not for their own sake, but to help us understand the "growth of a poet's mind": they are illustrations of philosophic truths. The conviction that Wordsworth's true province was the English lakes should not make us forget his own emphatic declaration that "the Mind of Man" was his "haunt and the main region" of his "song." [2] Certainly this was the field of his longest and, to him, most important poems. Such pieces, it goes without saying, would be very different from simple narratives like *Michael;* they would naturally be learned in diction, dignified and somewhat formal in style, and, if written in blank verse at the close of the eighteenth or the beginning of the nineteenth century, they would almost inevitably be Miltonic. [3] *The Recluse* and its prefatory poem are not spontaneous warblings, but monumental literary works deliberately built up, with definite purposes and conscious art.

One would expect works dealing largely with nature to be affected by the descriptive poetry of Thomson, the Wartons, Cowper, Hurdis, Grahame, and others; yet Wordsworth seldom referred to these writers and, except for Thomson, was apparently little influenced by any one of them. [4] Their collective influence, however, and that of their contemporaries was doubtless powerful, as the force of early reading and of the tastes and ideals with which one is surrounded in the formative years must always be. Yet it was unconscious, for

---

[1] "Advertisement" to *The Prelude*.

[2] Lines 40–41 of the extract from *The Recluse* prefixed to *The Excursion*.

[3] The theories of poetry which Wordsworth exemplified in the *Lyrical Ballads* and formulated in the preface to the second edition of that work had not a little to do with the simplicity of language and style of *Tinturn Abbey* and other pieces written at the time. In most of the poems composed after 1800, whether rimed or not, there is a tendency towards a more literary diction and a more formal style, which was in part a return to Wordsworth's natural method of expression (see Whately's remarks on the poet's conversation, quoted below, p. 190 n. 1, 196 n. 1).

[4] Much is said in *The Prelude* about books, but nothing that I remember about eighteenth-century poems in blank verse. The "Essay supplementary to the Preface" (*Poems*, Oxford ed., 948–9), the sonnet "Bard of the Fleece," and the correspondence with Lady Beaumont, Allan Cunningham, and Alexander Dyce (*Letters*, i. 273, 539, ii. 210, 358–9) do, however, reveal a warm admiration for Thomson and Dyer. At one time Wordsworth even thought of editing some of Thomson's works (*ib.* ii. 393).

Wordsworth did not regard Thomson, Young, and Cowper as suitable literary models. "When I began to give myself up to the profession of a poet for life," he said to Crabb Robinson, "I was impressed with a conviction, that there were four English poets whom I must have continually before me as examples — Chaucer, Shakspeare, Spenser, and Milton. These I must study, and equal *if I could;* and I need not think of the rest." [1] Of these four the first three were not of a kind seriously to affect blank-verse philosophic works such as Wordsworth planned. Nor, it may be, would Milton have exerted much influence had not his style and diction come to be recognized as the most suitable for poems of the sort; but in view of the course of English poetry in the eighteenth century, and of Wordsworth's admiration for the star-like soul that dwelt apart, the strongest single influence upon this part of his work would normally be that of *Paradise Lost.*

With these things in mind, we shall not be surprised to find the style of the long unrimed pieces very different from that of the short ones and from what we may think of as Wordsworthian. Of course, written, as they were, not at the beginning but at the end of the eighteenth century, they will not show the pompous language and contorted style of 1726, for between them and *The Seasons* lay a long development of blank verse.

Most of the stylistic peculiarities of *Paradise Lost*, though present in *The Prelude* and *The Excursion*, are not marked. Condensation is frequently gained by the omission of words, parenthetical expressions are fairly common, and occasionally a Miltonic apposition such as "Romorentin, home of ancient kings," is encountered; but one may read whole books of either work without meeting a clipped form of participle or a single adjective used for an adverb or a substantive. Inversion, however, the great mark of the Miltonic style, abounds. Not only is it on every page and in every paragraph, but seldom are five consecutive lines free from it. Furthermore, the inversions are often meaningless; that is, they add nothing to the beauty or effectiveness of the passage, but appear to be used merely for the sake of the meter or to make the verse seem less like prose. [2]

---

[1] "Conversations," etc., *Prose Works* (ed. Grosart), iii. 459–60. In a letter to Alaric Watts, Nov. 16, 1824, he quoted a passage in the same vein: "I am disposed strenuously to recommend to your habitual perusal the great poets of our own country, who have stood the test of ages. Shakespeare I need not name, nor Milton, but Chaucer and Spenser are apt to be overlooked. It is almost painful to think how far these surpass all others."

[2] A characteristic which *The Excursion* and *The Prelude* share with *Paradise Lost* but which may not be derived from the earlier work — which might, indeed, so nat-

As a result of these inversions, of the many learned words, and of the condensation caused by the omission of words ordinarily expressed, — notably auxiliaries, — Wordsworth's long poems, and particularly *The Prelude*, are marked by a formality which at its best rises to dignity and at its worst degenerates into stiffness. Here is what may be termed a neutral passage, neither the best nor the worst that might be found:

> We were framed
> To bend at last to the same discipline,
> Predestined, if two beings ever were,
> To seek the same delights, and have one health,
> One happiness. Throughout this narrative,
> Else sooner ended, I have borne in mind
> For whom it registers the birth, and marks the growth,
> Of gentleness, simplicity, and truth,
> And joyous loves, that hallow innocent days
> Of peace and self-command. Of rivers, fields,
> And groves I speak to thee, my Friend! to thee,
> Who, yet a liveried schoolboy, in the depths
> Of the huge city, on the leaded roof
> Of that wide edifice, thy school and home,
> Wert used to lie and gaze upon the clouds
> Moving in heaven; or, of that pleasure tired,
> To shut thine eyes.[1]

The influence of *Paradise Lost* is by no means so marked throughout the long poems as it is in these lines. Yet it is clearly, though not unpleasantly, evident in the style in which a large part of *The Prelude* and some of *The Excursion* are written, a style easier and more attractive than that of the extract just quoted, as the following passage will show:

> Oh, sweet it is, in academic groves,
> Or such retirement, Friend! as we have known
> In the green dales beside our Rotha's stream,
> Greta, or Derwent, or some nameless rill,
> To ruminate, with interchange of talk,
> On rational liberty, and hope in man,
> Justice and peace.[2]

urally belong to any poet that, except for Wordsworth's unusual familiarity with Milton, it would not be worth noticing — is the use of a series of adjectives, participles, or nouns in the same construction. Here are a few of the many instances: "Abject, depressed, forlorn, disconsolate" (*Prelude*, v. 28); "Fierce, moody, patient, venturous, modest, shy" (v. 415); "Unbiassed, unbewildered, and unawed" (vi. 41); "Unchastened, unsubdued, unawed, unraised" (vi. 505); "Great, universal, irresistible" (xi. 17, and see ix. 373, xii. 64); "Self-reviewed, Self-catechised, self-punished" (*Excursion*, vi. 386–7).

[1] *Prelude*, vi. 255–71.   [2] *Ib.* ix. 390–96.

Unfortunately, Wordsworth's inspiration did not keep pace with his desire to write. Often, like a soldier marking time who goes through the motions of walking without getting anywhere, he produced work of the stuffed-bird variety, that has every characteristic of the living thing but one, life. At other times he composed verses which, though awkward, might have been wrought into excellent poetry if they had undergone the laborious revision that some of his best pieces received. The blank verse produced at such times has much in common with the pseudo-Miltonic work of minor eighteenth-century writers. Passages like the following, for example, abound in *The Excursion:*

> A pomp
> Leaving behind of yellow radiance spread
> Over the mountain sides, in contrast bold
> With ample shadows, seemingly, no less
> Than those resplendent lights, his rich bequest.
>
> Those services, whereby attempt is made
> To lift the creature toward that eminence
> On which, now fallen, erewhile in majesty
> He stood; or if not so, whose top serene
> At least he feels 'tis given him to descry;
> Not without aspirations, evermore
> Returning, and injunctions from within
> Doubt to cast off and weariness; in trust
> That what the Soul perceives, if glory lost,
> May be, through pains and persevering hope,
> Recovered.[1]

Most of Wordsworth's shorter unrimed pieces that are Miltonic are of this type. A single illustration will probably more than satisfy the reader:

> And yet more gladly thee would I conduct
> Through woods and spacious forests, — to behold
> There, how the Original of human art,
> Heaven-prompted Nature, measures and erects
> Her temples, fearless for the stately work,
> Though waves, to every breeze, its high-arched roof,
> And storms the pillars rock. But we such schools
> Of reverential awe will chiefly seek.[2]

Matthew Arnold's comment that Wordsworth "has no assured poetic style of his own," that "when he seeks to have a style he falls into ponderosity and pomposity," [3] may be the explanation of this kind of verse. Certainly it is true of many eighteenth-century poets

---

[1] iv. 1301–5; v. 297–307.
[2] "A little onward lend thy guiding hand," 33–40.
[3] *Essays in Criticism*, 2d series (1889), 155–6.

that when they exerted themselves to write well they grew turgid. But was not Wordsworth's trouble rather that "ponderosity and pomposity" were natural to him and became evident whenever he *failed* to exert himself, when he wrote without being in the mood for writing, when he handled subjects that had not fired his imagination or about which he did not feel with sufficient intensity? We know that two of his finest things, *Michael* and *Laodamia*, cost him a great deal of trouble, and that he wrote excellent sonnets so long as he found them difficult to write; we also know that his conversation was apt to degenerate into long didactic monologues, and to contain such formal, bookish words that once when he was talking his grandson exclaimed, "Grandpapa is reading without a book!"[1] The faults of *The Excursion* may, therefore, be the most natural things in it, the defects that impressed all who talked with the poet and that only deep feeling and hard labor removed.

Admirers of Wordsworth are likely to regard as his most characteristic blank verse one that shows practically no traces of Milton's influence, — the kind found in *Tintern Abbey*, *Michael*, and in most of the nature passages in *The Prelude*. It is easy, simple, and direct, but considered merely as style it usually lacks richness, distinction, variety, as well as the finer subtleties of cadence and flow; hence Arnold's complaint that Wordsworth "has no style." Illustrations of it need hardly be quoted, for any one can have them before him by recalling the descriptive passages he likes best in the lake poet's unrimed pieces. It is our familiarity with these descriptions that leads us to think of the style in which they are written as characteristic of the poems as a whole.

This non-Miltonic blank verse suffers just as the Miltonic does when the poet in Wordsworth goes to sleep and the pedagog or the preacher takes his pen. What then results is a quantity of prosaic, matter-of-fact lines, sometimes good enough as to thought, but lacking the imagination, the intensity of feeling, and the finality of phrasing which would lift them into poetry. Verse of this sort led Tennyson to remark that a typical Wordsworthian line would be "A Mr. Wilkinson, a clergyman."[2] But it is impossible to parody a poet who himself wrote,

> And at the *Hoop* alighted, famous Inn.

> That rural castle, name now slipped
> From my remembrance, where a lady lodged.

---

[1] Whately, in *Leisure Hour*, Oct. 1, 1870, p. 652. "His mode of talking," says Whately, "sometimes resembled a moral declamation." Cf. below, p. 196, n. 1.

[2] Hallam Tennyson, *Tennyson and his Friends* (1911), 264.

As a preparatory act
Of reverence done to the spirit of the place.[1]

A longer extract will show still better how close to prose Wordsworth's blank verse often comes:

Yet for the general purposes of faith
In Providence, for solace and support,
We may not doubt that who can best subject
The will to reason's law, can strictliest live
And act in that obedience, he shall gain
The clearest apprehension of those truths,
Which unassisted reason's utmost power
Is too infirm to reach. But, waiving this,
And our regards confining within bounds
Of less exalted consciousness, through which
The very multitude are free to range,
We safely may affirm that human life —

But *we*, I think, may safely affirm with Arnold and Jeffrey that, "as a work of poetic style, ' This will never do.' " [2]

It is the preponderance of such blank verse, or of the pseudo-Miltonic variety which prevailed in the eighteenth century, that makes *The Excursion* as a whole unread and unreadable. One reason why Wordsworth slipped into these prosaic styles is that the later, inferior books of *The Prelude*, all but the admirable first two books of *The Excursion*, and nearly all of the poorer short pieces in blank verse were written after the fire of his poetic inspiration had died down, only to reappear fitfully and at long intervals. Furthermore, *The Excursion* has but little to do with nature, Wordsworth's most certain source of inspiration, but is largely taken up with argument. Now, Wordsworth was not, like Goethe, a great thinker,[3] or, like Emerson, a great seer, nor did he possess Dryden's power of reasoning in verse. The few essential things of life he saw with great clearness and felt with unusual intensity, and because these things possessed a grandeur that touched his imagination and reached to the center of his being he could be deeply poetic when he dealt with them. They were the distilled essence of many hours of quiet reflection, something very different from the philosophical system that he worked out with his reason.

Wordsworth wrote one other type of blank verse, as rare in quality as in occurrence. This includes a few hundred lines of his noblest

---

[1] *Prelude*, iii. 17, ix. 483–4; *Excursion*, vi. 89–90.

[2] *Essays in Criticism*, 2d series, 156. The Wordsworth passage is from *The Excursion*, v. 515–26.

[3] Unless it be in his prose discussions of the poet's art.

utterance, his sublimest description, and his loftiest thought. Here are to be found his most Miltonic passages, and it is here that we best realize how deeply he had drunk at the fountain-head of English poetic blank verse and with what insistence the "voice whose sound was like the sea" kept ringing in his ears. Yet, for the very reason that these passages are imbued with the spirit of *Paradise Lost*, they are far from being slavish copies of its manner. The following lines, for example, are almost free from the inversions, parentheses, appositives, the use of one part of speech for another, and the similar mannerisms that disfigure most eighteenth-century unrimed poems:

> A single step, that freed me from the skirts
> Of the blind vapour, opened to my view
> Glory beyond all glory ever seen
> By waking sense or by the dreaming soul!
> The appearance, instantaneously disclosed,
> Was of a mighty city — boldly say
> A wilderness of building, sinking far
> And self-withdrawn into a boundless depth,
> Far sinking into splendour — without end!
> Fabric it seemed of diamond and of gold,
> With alabaster domes, and silver spires,
> And blazing terrace upon terrace, high
> Uplifted; here, serene pavilions bright,
> In avenues disposed; there, towers begirt
> With battlements that on their restless fronts
> Bore stars — illumination of all gems!
>
> Wisdom and Spirit of the universe!
> Thou Soul that art the eternity of thought,
> That givest to forms and images a breath
> And everlasting motion.[1]

The organ tone in some of Wordsworth's loftier passages, as in those quoted below, is due partly to the Miltonic practice of introducing proper names for their imaginative suggestiveness and sonorous pomp:

> They — who had come elate as eastern hunters
> Banded beneath the Great Mogul, when he
> Erewhile went forth from Agra or Lahore,
> Rajahs and Omrahs in his train, intent
> To drive their prey enclosed within a ring
> Wide as a province.

[1] *Excursion*, ii. 830–45; *Prelude*, i. 401–4. To this class also belongs most of *Yew-Trees*, of *Kilchurn Castle*, and of the extract from *Home at Grasmere* prefixed to *The Excursion*.

> Tract more exquisitely fair
> Than that famed paradise of ten thousand trees,
> Or Gehol's matchless gardens, for delight
> Of the Tartarian dynasty composed
> (Beyond that mighty wall, not fabulous,
> China's stupendous mound) by patient toil
> Of myriads and boon nature's lavish help.[1]

It will be noticed that the second extract exhibits less of the manner and more of the mannerisms of *Paradise Lost*. These mannerisms creep not infrequently into Wordsworth's more exalted, just as they do into his more prosaic, blank verse, and for the same reasons. Either his imagination did not glow sufficiently to fuse his materials and get rid of the dross, or he did not hammer the lines long enough to work out the blemishes and perfect the form. Sometimes, as in this passage, the Miltonic largeness of utterance is combined with touches of the Miltonic diction and style in a way surprisingly close to that of *Paradise Lost*:

> This is our high argument.
> — Such grateful haunts foregoing, if I oft
> Must turn elsewhere — to travel near the tribes
> And fellowships of men, and see ill sights
> Of madding passions mutually inflamed;
> Must hear Humanity in fields and groves
> Pipe solitary anguish; or must hang
> Brooding above the fierce confederate storm
> Of sorrow, barricadoed evermore
> Within the walls of cities — may these sounds
> Have their authentic comment; that even these
> Hearing, I be not downcast or forlorn![2]

The Miltonic element in Wordsworth's diction is considerable, yet it is easily overlooked. For one thing, it is not expected: we think of the author of *The Daffodils*, *Michael*, and *Tintern Abbey* as a writer of simple, direct poems, often profound and sometimes magical, but dealing in the main with nature and the quiet lives of humble people. The style usually impresses us as natural and flowing, so that we assume the language — which we rarely notice — to be equally simple. Then, too, we remember the poet's own declaration, "My purpose was to imitate, and, as far as possible, to adopt

---

[1] *Prelude*, x. 17–22; viii. 75–81.

[2] Lines 71–82 of the passage prefixed to *The Excursion* (which constitute lines 824–35 of *The Recluse*, book i, *Home at Grasmere*). The extract is not typical, since the fragmentary *Recluse*, though less pedestrian in style than *The Excursion*, is on the whole less formal than *The Prelude*. Traces of *Paradise Lost* are slight, but seldom long absent.

the very language of men." [1] Yet, so far as his blank verse and other more serious work is concerned, this conception of Wordsworth's diction is quite mistaken, since, except in his earlier and simpler poems, his language is distinctly literary and often unduly learned. His *Old Cumberland Beggar*, for instance, although dealing in a simple way with a commonplace subject, contains language like this:

> All behold in him
> A silent monitor, which on their minds
> Must needs impress a transitory thought
> Of self-congratulation, to the heart
> Of each recalling his peculiar boons,
> His charters and exemptions; and, perchance,
> Though he to no one give the fortitude
> And circumspection needful to preserve
> His present blessings, and to husband up
> The respite of the season, he, at least,
> And 'tis no vulgar service, makes them felt.[2]

True, this passage is not typical of all Wordsworth's poetry, but it is characteristic of a large part of his blank verse, particularly of the more formal and philosophical works like *The Excursion* and *The Prelude*. In these poems we are continually meeting such words as "abstrusest," "disjoin," "innocuously," "conglobated," "extrinsic," "intervenient," "succedaneum," "admonishment," "presage," "prelibation," "extravagate," "colloquies," "arbitrement," "patrimony," "subversion," "perturbation"; [3] and expressions like "preclude conviction," "erewhile my tuneful haunt," "monitory sound," "domestic carnage," "kindred mutations," "inveterately convolved." [4] There would be little objection to these words and phrases if they were merely unusual; the trouble is that they are with difficulty assimilated in poetry and that Wordsworth rarely succeeds in assimilating them.[5] Many poets, Swinburne and Francis

---

[1] Preface to the second edition of *Lyrical Ballads* (*Poems*, Oxford ed., 936).

[2] Lines 122-32.

[3] *Excursion*, i. 65 (also iii. 702, ix. 234, and *Prelude*, i. 44, vi. 297, ix. 397, xii. 132); iii. 58 (also *Prelude*, viii. 436, xii. 232, and in one other poem), 516, 974; *Prelude*, i. 545 (and viii. 624, xiii. 218); ii. 201, 214; iv. 125 (also vii. 546, x. 77, and in two other poems); v. 36 ("presageful" occurs in the poem beginning "Pastor and Patriot," 4), 245, 503; ix. 470; x. 127, 157, 268 ("subvert" is used in six places); xi. 373 (and in eight other places).

[4] *Prelude*, x. 165 (there are seven similar instances of the use of "preclude"), 244, 324 (there are four similar instances), 356, xiv. 94; *Yew-Trees*, 18 (see the whole passage quoted on p. 185 above).

[5] "Words in themselves," as Mr. J. L. Lowes has shown (*Convention and Revolt in Poetry*, Boston, 1919, p. 193), ". . . are neither poetic nor unpoetic. They become poetic, or they remain unassimilated prose, according as the poet's imaginative energy is or is not sufficiently powerful to absorb them." Wordsworth usually employed words like those mentioned above when his imaginative energy was low.

Thompson, for example, use stranger words than these and more of them, and of course Shakespeare and Milton employ a much wider vocabulary than Wordsworth did; but these writers introduce unfamiliar expressions for poetical effect, whereas Wordsworth's diction is stiff, bookish, and lacking in imaginative or emotional appeal. Words like those given above attract attention by being uncommon, but serve no good purpose.

Worse still, the language of *The Excursion* and *The Prelude* is often absurdly ill adapted to the persons who are supposed to be speaking it or to the subjects with which it deals. This is what makes the picnic described in *The Excursion* such a lugubrious festivity. The party consisted of the Solitary, the Wanderer, the Poet, and the Pastor, — a kind of later Job with his three friends; the Pastor's wife, "graceful was her port"; their daughter, a "gladsome child"; their son and "his shy compeer," boys of "jocund hearts" and with "animation" in their "mien." [1] We know little of what was said at the picnic, but on the previous day "grateful converse" of the following variety was carried on:

> "In your retired domain,
> Perchance you not unfrequently have marked
> A Visitor." . . .
> The Solitary answered: "Such a Form
> Full well I recollect."

The supper, we are told, was merry, but the description of it does not sound exhilarating. All

> partook
> A choice repast — served by our young companions
> With rival earnestness and kindred glee;

after which

> Launched from our hands the smooth stone skimmed the lake,

and

> Rapaciously we gathered flowery spoils.

In view of these solemn relaxations, we are not surprised to learn that the abode of the Pastor and his gamesome family was approached by a path of "pure cerulean gravel," and to read of the edifice itself,

> Like image of solemnity, conjoined
> With feminine allurement soft and fair,
> The mansion's self displayed.[2]

[1] viii. 501, 496; ix. 431, 475; viii. 572.
[2] viii. 58; vi. 95–7, 102–3; ix. 529–31, 532, 538; viii. 452, 459–61.

Yet the author of these lines wished that his poetry might "keep the Reader in the company of flesh and blood"![1]

But this is not the worst. Wordsworth is capable of employing language not only unsuitable but at times even bad. Although he said concerning "what is usually called poetic diction," "As much pains has been taken to avoid it as is ordinarily taken to produce it; this has been done . . . to bring my language near to the language of men," he used hundreds of phrases that not only were never heard in the language of men but had become extremely hackneyed even in poetry.[2] Much better illustrations of the vicious poetic diction of the eighteenth century can be found in his own later work than in the sonnet by Gray which he quotes for the purpose. He speaks, for instance, of an actor as "a proficient of the tragic scene"; the stars he calls "heaven's ethereal orbs," sunshine "the solar beam," eyes "these visual orbs," birds "the feathered kinds," a lake a "crystal mere," a stage-coach an "itinerant vehicle," a gun "the deadly tube," an ass "the brute In Scripture sanctified."[3] Even the unobjectionable words Wales and Welsh he never uses, but employs Cambria and Cambrian in their places seven times; Albion he mentions five and Caledonia (or Caledon) three times. Occasionally he makes use of elaborate periphrases, as in his account of a sore throat,

> The winds of March, smiting insidiously,
> Raised in the tender passage of the throat
> Viewless obstruction;

or when he says the "soil endured a transfer in the mart Of dire rapacity," meaning the land was sold, or

> We beheld
> The shining giver of the day diffuse
> His brightness,

meaning we saw the sun shine; or when he tells us that an old man "had clomb aloft to delve the moorland turf For winter fuel" instead

---

[1] Preface to *Lyrical Ballads* (*Poems*, Oxford ed., 936). The pompous absurdity of much of Wordsworth's diction is equally characteristic of his prose and was a marked feature of his conversation. According to Edward Whately, who saw a good deal of him at one time, "Both his sentences and his words were too long and too high-flown to suit the subject he was discussing . . . he used the most high-flown language in speaking of the most common-place, ordinary affairs of life" (*Leisure Hour*, Oct. 1, 1870, p. 652).

[2] Preface to *Lyrical Ballads* (*Poems*, Oxford ed., 936). Blake commented, "I do not know who wrote these Prefaces; they are very mischievous, and direct contrary to Wordsworth's own practice" (Crabb Robinson's "Reminiscences," quoted in Arthur Symons's *William Blake*, 1907, p. 300).

[3] *Excursion*, iii. 466, 662 (and cf. *Pilgrim's Dream*, 23); iv. 447 (also *Evening Walk*, 203), 180, 450 (cf. *Home at Grasmere*, 203, MS.); v. 82 (and ix. 701); *Prelude*, viii. 544; *Home at Grasmere*, 266 ("sentient tube" occurs in the *Italian Itinerant*, 23), 506-7.

of saying he had gone to dig peat, or speaks of "the impediment of rural cares" when he means farm-work.[1] From the conventional, hackneyed expressions common in eighteenth-century poetry, the crystal-font-purple-bloom-vernal-breeze sort of thing, Wordsworth is almost entirely free, but he does annoy us by his fondness for "yon," "haply," "albeit," "erewhile," "corse" (for corpse), and the like.

All that is objectionable in Wordsworth's diction — the use of learned and grandiose words and of pompous circumlocutions in place of familiar terms—is marked in the blank verse of the eighteenth century. It is such phraseology that irritates the reader of Thomson, Young, and Cowper and is even more noticeable in the work of their less gifted contemporaries. That Wordsworth should take some features of his diction, as well as of his style and versification, from the writers who immediately preceded him was only natural. It is easy to forget that he was nearer to these men than we are to him or to Shelley or Byron, nearer to most of them than we are to Tennyson, Browning, and Arnold. He was born in 1770, the year in which the *Deserted Village* was published; he was fifteen when *The Task* and Boswell's *Tour to the Hebrides* appeared, and throughout the period in which he was forming his taste and producing his best work it was principally eighteenth-century writings that people read. Indeed, aside from Spenser, Shakespeare, and Milton, hardly any other English poetry was accessible to them. Only the force of Wordsworth's personality and the depth of his convictions kept him from being dominated by his immediate predecessors.

Is it likely that the older poets affected his diction, except occasionally through the borrowing of single words? He was familiar with Chaucer, Spenser, and Shakespeare, as well as with many of the seventeenth- and most of the leading eighteenth-century verse and prose writers, and may have taken from one of several sources any of his uncommon words or peculiar uses of words. Yet the matter is not so difficult as it seems; for, since Milton's poetry was more familiar to him than anything else in English literature (except possibly Shakespeare's plays), Milton's use of a word would be the one to linger in his memory. Furthermore, Chaucer, Spenser, and Shakespeare, the other poets most likely to influence him, would certainly not have turned him towards learned and grandiose terms of Latin origin, but Milton would lead him in precisely this direction. When Wordsworth speaks of an "edifice" or a "habitation," or of "the embowered abode — our chosen seat," or of "striplings . . .

[1] *Excursion*, vii. 683–5; iii. 917–18, 540–42; ii. 787–8; vii. 736.

graced with shining weapons," [1] is he not doing just what was done, what had to be done, in the epic of the fall of man? Many words that are quite unobjectionable in *Paradise Lost* would sound pompous and absurd in *The Excursion*.

But we are not left to surmises in the matter, for one of Wordsworth's acquaintances wrote, "His veneration for Milton was so great, that if that poet used a particular word in a particular sense, he would quote his authority to justify himself when his wife or daughter objected to its employment in his own poems." [2] Instances of this habit are to be found in his letters. Writing to Sir George Beaumont, he remarked that, although Bowles disapproved of the word "ravishment," "yet it has the authority of all the first-rate poets, for instance, Milton." [3] In another letter he justified the use of "immediately" in verse by noting that it appeared "to have sufficient poetical authority, even the highest," and then quoted from *Paradise Lost*.[4] It is probable, therefore, that "adamantine," "compeers," "darkling," "begirt," "empyrean," "encincture," "fulgent," "effulgence," "refulgent," "gratulant," "griesly," "massy," "ministrant," "panoply," "Tartarean," "terrene," "unapparent," "vermeil," "welter," and the like were derived from *Paradise Lost*. Many words employed in a peculiar sense or in an unusual way he seems also to have taken from Milton: "audience" (of readers), "commerce" (intercourse), "covert" (shelter), "descant" (of a bird's song), "essential" (having substance), "incumbent" (resting on or bending over), "inform" (form within), "instinct with" (impelled or animated by), "lapse" (of a stream), "oblivious" (used actively), "paramount" (as a substantive), "principalities" (order of angels), "profound" (as a substantive), "punctual" (like a point), "rout" (a disorderly crowd), "sagacious" (keen-scented), "use" (as an intransitive verb), "vast" (as a substantive), "viewless" (invisible).[5]

It would, of course, be folly to explain Wordsworth's language altogether by reference to eighteenth-century writers and Milton, that is, to overlook the importance of his own personality. Any poet who is fond of abstract speculation, who is inclined to be formal and impersonal, who has little sensuous richness in his nature,

---

[1] *Ib.* iii. 521; vii. 766-7. He uses "edifice" seven times and "habitation" twenty-two.

[2] E. Whately, as above, p. 182, n. 2.

[3] Nov. 16, 1811.

[4] To Francis Wrangham, July 12, 1807.

[5] For the occurrence of these words, see pp. 618-20 below, and Lane Cooper's *Concordance to Wordsworth* (1911).

and who "wishes to be regarded as a teacher or as nothing," will not employ the vocabulary of Keats; and if he composes works

On man, on Nature, and on Human Life,

he will probably use language that is somewhat learned and stately. It would have been so even if the author of *The Excursion* had never read *Paradise Lost;* his knowledge of the epic only strengthened his natural tendencies. Not that Wordsworth intentionally imitated the diction of Milton and his followers, but that he adopted more of it than he realized. He was so accustomed to a formal style stiffened with words from the Greek and Latin that he easily slipped into it when he was not on his guard. Except when he was dealing with nature or with simple, narrative subjects, he preferred the sound of lines that contained learned words and somewhat pompous phrases; but was it not because of his familiarity with the stately periods and the formal, Latinic diction of Milton and his imitators that such lines pleased him?

Wordsworth would himself have been the last person to deny that he was influenced by Milton. He tells us that he was inspired to write his first sonnets by the "soul-animating strains" of his predecessor, and we have seen that he tooks pains to make "public acknowledgment of . . . the innumerable obligations which," he said, "as a Poet and a Man, I am under to our great fellow-countryman."[1] He seems, indeed, to have felt that every poet should look to Milton for guidance. At the beginning of his career, it may be remembered, he had been impressed with the conviction that there were four English poets whom he must continually have before him as examples, Chaucer, Shakespeare, Spenser, and Milton; and in the preface to the 1815 edition of his poems he wrote, "The grand store-house of enthusiastic and meditative Imagination, of poetical, as contradistinguished from human and dramatic Imagination, is the prophetic and lyrical parts of the holy Scriptures, and the works of Milton, to which I cannot forbear to add those of Spenser."

Yet he was almost certainly unconscious of the extent to which Milton influenced him. If he thought of the matter at all, he may have reflected that his verse was free from those peculiarities of *Paradise Lost* which marred eighteenth-century unrimed poetry, — as, indeed, to a large extent it was. Inversion he and his contemporaries doubtless regarded not as a trait peculiar to *Paradise Lost*, but as a characteristic of all good blank verse. Then, too, his very resemblance to Milton would have blinded him to his indebtedness,

[1] See below, p. 529, and above, p. 181.

for it is hard to realize how much one owes to a lifelong friend of similar views but greater powers. To be sure, though he may not have known how numerous they were, he must have been aware of the many phrases and of some of the more unusual words that he borrowed; but such things would not have troubled him. He regarded Milton's authority as supreme, at least in diction, and accordingly may have thought that borrowing from him was like taking words from the dictionary. The similarity between his own exalted, orotund passages and those of *Paradise Lost* he undoubtedly felt and felt with pride.

Nor need those of us who look upon Wordsworth as one of the chief glories of English literature be disturbed to learn that he derived from another some of the materials and methods he used in the lofty building he erected. Surely one of the uses, and one of the best uses, of great poets is to furnish inspiration and guidance for those who come after them. This is not the least of the important functions that *Paradise Lost* has been performing for the last two and a half centuries. In Wordsworth's case it accomplished its purpose the more easily and effectively because what it offered was similar to what he himself had. Its influence on his poetry does not seem, for example, like Gothic vaulting in a Greek temple, for it did not tend to deflect him from his course, but merely strengthened him in it by showing him how to pursue it. That is why the last of the great Elizabethans became a power with one of the first of the great romanticists, why Wordsworth is the most Miltonic poet since Milton.

CHAPTER X

KEATS

IT is generally agreed that Spenser and Leigh Hunt made Keats a poet, but it is not so generally understood that they failed to complete their task, that they left him a rather formless, languorous, saccharine, and at times silly poet. He was naturally romantic, delighting in color rather than form, in richness rather than restraint, in ideal beauty rather than reality, and craving "a life of sensations rather than of thoughts." These traits were exaggerated by his youth, his admiration for Spenser, and his intimacy with Hunt, and as a result his first volume contains a number of rambling and rather pointless poems, with many rimes of the kisses-blisses sort and but one piece of real distinction. Likewise the second publication, *Endymion*, is a luxuriant wilderness, "the author's intention appearing to be," as even the generous Shelley wrote, "that no person should possibly get to the end of it." [1] Fortunately Keats had himself come to realize these defects, and in the preface to *Endymion* had acknowledged that the reader of his romance "must soon perceive great inexperience, immaturity, and every error denoting a feverish attempt, rather than a deed accomplished."

In this same preface the poet expressed the hope of writing another work that should deal with "the beautiful mythology of Greece." This was *Hyperion*, which was originally conceived as a romance,[2] probably rimed and otherwise similar to *Endymion*, though "more naked and Grecian." But, before he came to write, a new planet swam into his ken which not only changed his plans but affected all his subsequent poetry. This transforming power was *Paradise Lost*. Keats had known Milton's poetry from boyhood, and had borrowed from the minor pieces and even from the epic; but the latter had meant little to him.[3] He ' had heard of it by the hearing of the

---

[1] To Charles and James Ollier, Sept. 6, 1819.

[2] "The time would be better spent in writing a new Romance I have in my eye for next summer" (letter to Haydon, Sept. 28, 1817). Colvin, in his life of Keats (1918, p. 334), suggests that this "romance" may possibly have been the *Eve of St. Agnes*.

[3] His lines,

> You first taught me all the sweets of song . . .
> Miltonian storms, and more, Miltonian tenderness;
> Michael in arms, and more, meek Eve's fair slenderness

(*Epistle to Charles Cowden Clarke*, 53, 58-9, written in September, 1816, but referring to a period several years earlier), show little appreciation of Milton's real greatness.

ear but now his eye saw it.' Blinded by the beauty of the Spen-
serians, he had not possessed sufficient maturity to appreciate the
consummate art and "severe magnificence of *Paradise Lost*" until
his attention was called to it by his friends Severn and Bailey, both
ardent Miltonians. If, as Mr. de Sélincourt thinks, the admiration
for *Paradise Lost* began in the summer of 1817, when Keats was but
half through *Endymion*,[1] the epic may have been an important element in bringing him to a realization of the "mawkishness" of his
early work. It seems quite as likely, however, that he had himself
begun to feel the weakness of his verse and was half consciously
looking for help before writing his second long piece, when at the
suggestion of his friends he took up *Paradise Lost* and found there
what he needed. He could hardly have done better. The poem
possesses the color, the richness, the imaginative appeal, and the
prosodic beauty that he craved, as well as the vigor, the classic restraint, and the sublimity that his own verse had lacked.

He plunged into Milton's work with characteristic enthusiasm
and, to use his own word, ' feasted ' upon it.[2] "When I see you," he
wrote to Bailey, "the first thing I shall do will be to read that about
Milton and Ceres, and Proserpine";[3] and later he exclaimed, "I am
convinced more and more, every day, that fine writing is, next to
fine doing, the top thing in the world; the *Paradise Lost* becomes a
greater wonder."[4] "It is unique," he declared, ". . . the most remarkable production of the world."[5] Milton became to him the
standard in poetry; for, when weighing Wordsworth's genius, he
thought it would be "a help, in the manner of gold being the meridian
Line of worldly wealth," to consider "how he differs from Milton."[6]

---

[1] Keats's *Poems* (2d ed., 1907), 489, 437. This very thorough and admirable edition
of Keats contains the best discussion we have of the influence of Milton upon any
English poet. Though I differ from Mr. de Sélincourt on many points, I am under
great obligations to him. So far as I can discover, the only basis for the opinion mentioned above is that in September, 1817, Keats visited Bailey at Oxford and while
there worked on the third book of *Endymion*, which, according to Mr. de Sélincourt,
contains phrases that imply a recent study of *Paradise Lost* (see pp. 437, 439, 440, of his
edition). It seems to me, however, that the expressions mentioned are either dubious
or unimportant, and that passages which recall the epic quite as strongly as these may
be found in Keats's earlier work. The reference to Adam's dream (in a letter to Bailey,
Nov. 22, 1817, not mentioned by De Sélincourt) certainly suggests a recent reading of
Milton's poem, with which, to be sure, we know that Keats was familiar before 1816.

[2] Letter to Reynolds, April 27, 1818.

[3] July 18, 1818. Later in the same letter he quoted from *Comus*.

[4] To Reynolds, Aug. 25, 1819. Ten days before he had used almost the same words
in a letter to Bailey. There is another reference to Milton in the letter to Reynolds,
and a letter to James Rice of March 24, 1818, is filled with humorous remarks about
Milton, Salmasius, and others.

[5] Letter to George Keats, Sept. 17–27, 1819 (this part probably written on the 21st).

[6] Letter to Reynolds, May 3, 1818. Earlier in this letter he quoted a line and a half
from *Paradise Lost* (see note 1, p. 203, below).

This "feast" upon Milton, which lasted for a year and a half or two years, profoundly affected the young and unusually sensitive poet. It gave him an admirable familiarity with the work of his predecessor,[1] as well as a rare understanding of its spirit,[2] and left him, so far as poetry was concerned, another man. The first fruits of the change were shown in the transformation of *Hyperion*, which was composed while the feast was at its height. For the romance which Keats planned developed into an austere epic, obviously modelled upon *Paradise Lost*.[3] He himself acknowledged the indebtedness, as we shall see later; but in any case there could be no doubt about it, for the poem is fundamentally Miltonic. Nor is it a question merely of certain stylistic qualities, of some unusual words and a few borrowed phrases, but of the entire conception, tone, and handling of the work. Instead of copying Milton's peculiarities, Keats, one might almost say, tried to write a poem as Milton would have written it, and as a result *Hyperion* is more like *Paradise Lost* than is any other great poem we have. The debt of *The Seasons*, great as it is, is limited to expression,— Milton would never have written anything like it; nor is it conceivable that he should have produced *The Task* or *The Prelude*. He might have composed *Hyperion*.

To realize how Miltonic the poem is we have only to compare it with other epics. Keats is not at all Homeric; his gods, for example, have almost nothing in common with the very human deities of the *Iliad* and the *Odyssey*, nor has he the action, the swiftness and buoyancy, of the Grecian. He leaves an impression, as Milton does in the main, of characters, places, and scenes rather than of events; and he is concerned entirely, as Milton is largely, not with mortals, as are other epic poets, but with gods and demigods. This is of course one reason why both poems lack human interest. The entire action of *Hyperion*, furthermore, raised as it is above human passions, has the

---

[1] This appears in the words and phrases he borrowed from Milton: see Appendix A, below. His familiarity with passages that do not usually attract attention is significant. In the letter to Reynolds just referred to (May 3, 1818) he quotes, quite casually,

> Notus and Afer, black with thundrous clouds
> From Serraliona

(*P. L.*, x. 702–3); and in one to Dilke (Sept. 21, 1818) he writes, "Imagine 'the hateful siege of contraries' — if I think of fame . . . it seems a crime to me" (cf. *P. L.*, ix. 119–22).

[2] As shown by his penetrating comments on *Paradise Lost* and its author (see the "Notes" in Forman's edition of his works, iii. 17–30).

[3] Any one who thinks that Keats would not consciously have patterned his work after another poem should remember that the versification of *Lamia* is, in Mr. de Sélincourt's words (p. 453), "closely modelled upon the *Fables* of Dryden."

largeness, the exalted dignity, the solemnity, the aloofness, which are particularly associated with *Paradise Lost*. Here are the pictures of Saturn and Thea:

> Along the margin-sand large foot-marks went,
> No further than to where his feet had stray'd,
> And slept there since. Upon the sodden ground
> His old right hand lay nerveless, listless, dead,
> Unsceptred; and his realmless eyes were closed. . . .
>
> She was a Goddess of the infant world;
> By her in stature the tall Amazon
> Had stood a pigmy's height: she would have ta'en
> Achilles by the hair and bent his neck;
> Or with a finger stay'd Ixion's wheel.
> Her face was large as that of Memphian sphinx,
> Pedestal'd haply in a palace court,
> When sages look'd to Egypt for their lore.[1]

These are figures worthy to have sat at the great council in Pandemonium.

Keats's style, as may be seen from the passages just quoted, is marked by the absence of prettiness; it has the stately dignity and the condensation that distinguish *Paradise Lost*. Yet these lines are by no means so Miltonic as many others; in fact, except for the phrase "pedestal'd haply," the more technical marks of Milton's influence do not appear at all. Nor are they anywhere prominent in the poem. The contorted style which eighteenth-century writers regarded as Miltonic, Keats saw to be a cheap imitation and instinctively avoided. Yet two of the most obvious characteristics of *Paradise Lost*, those without which Miltonic blank verse can hardly be written, inversion of the word-order and the use of adjectives for adverbs, he employed. In fact, he said himself that "there were too many Miltonic inversions" in his epic.[2] Here are six in the first twenty-five lines I open to: "influence benign on planets pale," "Deity supreme," "thine eyes eterne," "chariot fierce," "triumph calm," "gold clouds metropolitan."[3] Of the use of adjectives where one would expect adverbs there are over twenty cases like "rumbles reluctant," "crept gradual," "I here idle listen";[4] and occasionally other parts of speech are shifted about.[5] *Hyperion* also gets a Mil-

---

[1] i. 15–19, 26–33.   [2] Letter to Reynolds, Sept. 22, 1819.   [3] i. 108–29.
[4] i. 61, 260; iii. 106. See also i. 11, 94, 222, 308, 357; ii. 51, 74, 144, 164, 250, 284, 324, 329, 377, 388; iii. 15, 49, 52, 53, 74.
[5] As in "sphere them round" (i. 117), "space region'd" (i. 119), "made . . . His eyes to fever out" (i. 138, cf. ii. 102), "how engine our wrath" (ii. 161), "antheming a lonely grief" (iii. 6), "Apollo anguish'd" (iii. 130), "voices of soft proclaim" (i. 130), "with fierce convulse" (iii. 129), "stubborn'd with iron" (ii. 17). In "foam'd along

tonic ring from the presence of condensed or elliptical expressions like "thus brief," "uncertain where," "though feminine," "all prostrate else," "neighbour'd close," "what can I?", "all calm," "this too indulged tongue,"[1] and from constructions like these,

> Save what solemn tubes,
> Blown by the serious Zephyrs, gave of sweet
> And wandering sounds.[2]
>> At whose joys . . .
> I, Coelus, wonder, how they came and whence;
> And at the fruits thereof what shapes they be.[3]

At times, also, one is reminded of Milton by an unbroken series of adjectives, as "nerveless, listless, dead, Unsceptred"; or by a list of proper names like

> Cœus, and Gyges, and Briareüs,
> Typhon, and Dolor, and Porphyrion.[4]

Words and phrases from the "Chief of organic numbers" will be found throughout Keats's work,[5] but borrowings from *Paradise Lost* are naturally much more common in *Hyperion* than in the other poems. Except in such borrowings, the vocabulary of Keats's epic, though of course less conversational and more classic than that of his lyric and romantic pieces, is less affected by Milton's than might be expected. What would be the most important influence upon it, if we could be sure the practice was derived from Milton, is that in *Hyperion* Keats for the first time makes extensive use of adjectives formed by adding -*ed* to nouns.[6] Whether or not such adjectives — "orbed," "lion-thoughted," "mountained," "mouthed," etc. — come from Milton, with whom they are common, they are at least a great improvement over those in -*y*, "orby," "gulfy," "foody," "flamy," and the like, which are unpleasantly frequent in Keats's early work.[7]

By . . . winged creatures " (ii. 234-5) an intransitive verb is used transitively. Note also the adjectives formed from nouns by the addition of -*ed* (see text above).

[1] i. 153; ii. 9, 55, 65, 74, 160, 204, 298.
[2] i. 206-8; cf. *P. L.*, i. 182-3, ii. 20-21,

> Save what the glimmering of these livid flames
> Casts pale and dreadful.

> With what besides, in counsel or in fight,
> Hath been achieved of merit.

[3] i. 312-16; cf. *P. L.*, ii. 990, "I know thee, stranger, who thou art."
[4] i. 18-19; ii. 19-20.
[5] They have been carefully noted by his editors, and have for convenience been collected below in Appendix A.
[6] This obligation is pointed out in W. T. Arnold's edition of Keats's works (1884), pp. xxxiv–xxxvi, where a large number of Milton's adjectives in -*ed* are also quoted.
[7] Mr. de Sélincourt is undoubtedly right in believing that Milton's influence "is

One other possible relation between the two poems, to which all writers on the subject have called attention, is the similarity of the assembly of the Titans to the council in Pandemonium. It seems to me, however, that the resemblances are so superficial that they would never have been noticed if the conception of the Titans and the general tone and style of the poem had not been decidedly Miltonic. To be sure, each is an assembly of fallen immortals, at which, as might be expected, there are several speeches and some differences of opinion; but the two gatherings are otherwise quite unlike. The meeting of the Titans is not pre-arranged, no one calls it or presides over it, no plans are discussed and no action is decided on; the account simply stops at the arrival of the sun-god. It is hard to see wherein Keats could have made his assembly any less like Milton's if he had tried.

Hyperion is unfinished. Although it is one of Keats's greatest works, and probably the noblest fragment in English poetry, it was abandoned.

"There were too many Miltonic inversions in it," he complained to Reynolds; "Miltonic verse cannot be written but in an artful, or, rather, artist's humour. I wish to give myself up to other sensations. English ought to be kept up. It may be interesting to you to pick out some lines from Hyperion, and put a mark + to the false beauty proceeding from art, and one || to the true voice of feeling. Upon my soul, 'twas imagina-

---

shown far more in allusion and . . . cadence, than by the borrowing of definitely Miltonic words" (p. 582). Indeed, while the words in his valuable "Glossary" do in general point to this influence and to that of the Elizabethans, only the few given on page 624 below are, in my opinion, likely to have had their origin in definite passages of the epic or the 1645 volume. It is probable, however, as he suggests, that "adorant," "aspirant," "penetrant," "cirque-couchant," and "ministrant" were formed in imitation of "congratulant," "volant," "couchant," "ministrant," and the like in *Paradise Lost*, and that Milton's practice may have led to the use of an adjective for a noun in "the hollow vast" (*Endymion*, iii. 120, cf. ii. 240, iii. 593, etc., and *P. L.*, vi. 203); to the use of verbs as nouns in "there was . . . fear in her regard" (*Hyperion*, i. 37, cf. *P. L.*, iv. 877, x. 866, etc.), "he made retire From his companions" (*Lamia*, i. 230–31, cf. "bowers of soft retire," *Song of Four Fairies*, 6, and *P. L.*, xi. 267), "at shut of eve" (*Hyperion*, ii. 36, and "The day is gone," 5, cf. *P. L.*, ix. 278); and to the turning of nouns into verbs or participles in "who could paragon The . . . choir" (*Sleep and Poetry*, 172-3, cf. *P. L.*, x. 426), "a . . . tree Pavilions him in bloom" (*Endymion*, ii. 55-6, cf. *P. L.*, xi. 215), "her enemies havock'd at her feet" (*King Stephen*, I. ii. 23, cf. *P. L.*, x. 617), "lackeying my counsel" (*Otho*, I. i. 97, cf. *Comus*, 455), "like legioned soldiers" (*Endymion*, ii. 43, cf. "legion'd fairies," *Eve of St. Agnes*, xix. 6), "orbing along" (*Otho*, IV. i. 79, cf. "orbed brow," etc., *Endymion*, i. 616, etc., and *P. L.*, vi. 543), "pedestal'd . . . in a palace court" (*Hyperion*, i. 32, cf. "image pedestall'd so high," *Fall of Hyperion*, i. 299). In the case of "argent," "disparted," "drear," "dulcet," "empty of," "freshet," "lucent," "parle," "ramping," "slumberous," "spume," and some other words, for most of which Mr. de Sélincourt gives several possible sources, it seems to me impossible to be certain of any single origin.

tion — I cannot make the distinction — Every now and then there is a Miltonic intonation."[1] To his brother he expressed it thus: "The *Paradise Lost*, though so fine in itself, is a corruption of our language. It should be kept as it is, unique, a curiosity, a beautiful and grand curiosity, the most remarkable production of the world; a northern dialect accommodating itself to Greek and Latin inversions and intonations. The purest English, I think — or what ought to be the purest — is Chatterton's. . . . I prefer the native music of it to Milton's, cut by feet. I have but lately stood on my guard against Milton. Life to him would be death to me. Miltonic verse cannot be written, but is the verse of art. I wish to devote myself to another verse alone."[2]

The difficulty in determining just what Keats meant by these utterances, with their failure to discriminate between style and language and their curious praise for the purity of Chatterton's manufactured language, is probably due to a vagueness in his own mind. It must be remembered that he wrote them, not in a carefully-worded preface, but in familiar letters presumably composed carelessly and in haste and in the mood that happened to be dominant at the time. By taking simply the parts that are clear and interpreting them literally, we arrive at the easy, definite, and commonly-accepted idea that the poem was abandoned because of its excessive use of such external Miltonisms as inversion. But so great a poem could hardly have been laid aside merely on account of a number of "Greek and Latin inversions and intonations," which as a matter of fact were not particularly numerous and might easily have been removed. Besides, such Latinisms are quite as characteristic of Wordsworth's best work — which Keats sincerely admired — as of *Hyperion*, and are indeed to be found in the noblest English blank verse.

Why, then, was it discontinued? Clearly, because of some feeling of constraint begotten by its Miltonic character. Yet it may be that Keats confused the fundamental similarity to *Paradise Lost* with some of the superficial marks of that similarity.[3] The pith of his remarks is contained in the clause, "Miltonic verse cannot be written but in an artful, or, rather, artist's humour," that is, with self-

---

[1] Letter of Sept. 22, 1819. The reason alleged in the publishers' advertisement, that the reception given to *Endymion* "discouraged the author from proceeding," Keats himself branded as a "lie" (see De Sélincourt's edition, p. 487).

[2] To George Keats, Sept. 17-27, 1819, the part quoted presumably being written on the 21st. In the letter to Reynolds noticed above he praised Chatterton's "genuine English Idiom in English words."

[3] As Robert Bridges remarks (*Keats*, 32-5), Keats "attributes his dissatisfaction to the style; but one cannot read to the end without a conviction that the real hindrance lay deeper. . . . he had not abused inversion in *Hyperion*."

conscious effort as distinguished from natural self-expression, from
the poet's "easy unpremeditated verse." As a result, "the true
voice of feeling" seemed to him to be killed by "the false beauty
proceeding from art"; he felt constrained and the poem seemed artificial. This "artful, or, rather, artist's humour" he attributed to
the lack of "genuine English Idiom in English words"; but if he had
removed the foreign idiom and words could he have completed the
work? Apparently not. He seems to have gone over it marking its
superficial Miltonisms, and was baffled by the result. "I cannot
make the distinction," he exclaimed — "Every now and then there
is a Miltonic intonation — But I cannot make the division properly.
The fact is, I must take a walk." Does not this indicate that he
failed to find the root of the difficulty, that he was troubled because
removing the foreign words, idioms, and inversions did not remove
the "false beauty proceeding from art" or the general Miltonic impression the poem produces? He was right in standing on his guard
against Milton, and in thinking, "Life to him would be death to
me"; but he apparently saw later that an influence so portentous to
originality must go deeper than words and idioms. He might have
inverted the inversions, changed the classical constructions, and
dropped the foreign words if he had wished, but there would have
remained the austere restraint, the impersonality and aloofness, the
lack of color, warmth, and human interest, which deadened "the
true voice of feeling." These qualities were not natural to him; he
could assume them for a time, but the farther he proceeded in the
poem the more conscious he grew of their constraint, until at last he
found it intolerable. He came to feel that his enthusiasm for *Paradise Lost* had carried him out of his natural bent and led him to
attempt a kind of work not suited to his powers.[1]

And he was right. For the greatness of *Hyperion* should not blind
us, any more than it did him, to its defects. Nothing really happens
in it; the central incident, the assembly of the Titans, to which the
meeting of Thea and Saturn and in a way the account of Hyperion
lead up, comes to nothing. No course of action is even discussed.
So far as one can see, the intention is simply to introduce more characters and give a further picture of the fallen gods. To be sure, each
of these scenes, as well as the deification of Apollo, does prepare for
later action, but in what other epic is so little accomplished or even

---

[1] The theory that Keats's ill health and hopeless love for Fanny Brawne made it
impossible for him to go on with *Hyperion* fails to take account of the reason the poet
himself gave, or to explain how, after abandoning his epic, he was able to compose most
of his best work, including a piece as long as *Lamia*.

planned in the first nine hundred lines? [1] Much noble description,
many lofty speeches, Keats has certainly given us, but *Hyperion* is
supposed to be a *narrative* poem. In reality it is nothing of the kind;
it is distinctly static and sculpturesque, with a tone, style, and manner admirably adapted to depicting the colossal deities of an elder
world, but to Keats at least hampering and cumbersome when it
came to making them move. When he tried narrative, as in describing Apollo's metamorphosis into a god, he was unsuccessful. A careful study of the poem leaves one with the feeling that Keats did not
know just what to do with his characters or how to get them to doing
anything, that he could create gods but could not make them act.
He was himself too good a critic of his own work not to be conscious
of this defect, and at the beginning of the third book turns from the
Titans with the words:

> O leave them, Muse!   O leave them to their woes;
> For thou art weak to sing such tumults dire:
> A solitary sorrow best befits
> Thy lips, and antheming a lonely grief.

That is, he felt unequal to the epic action that the poem required,
and after writing one hundred and thirty lines more gave up the task.

But the fragment was too good to be lightly discarded, and a few
months later he tried recasting it. This later version, *The Fall of
Hyperion*, was, be it remembered, his last important work and was
probably laid aside because of failing strength. The clouds that
hung low over the last sixteen months of Keats's life so dimmed his
poetic powers and blurred his judgment that the second form of
Hyperion is clearly inferior to the first. Furthermore, as the revision
covers only a third of the original fragment, and as Keats said
nothing of his plans concerning it, we have little idea what the
later work was to have been. For these reasons a comparison of the
two versions is sure to be perplexing and but partly satisfactory; yet
the second does show an attempt on Keats's part to free himself
from the aloofness and impersonality which had previously hampered him. The most important difference between the two versions
is that to the second is prefixed an entirely new beginning in which
the poem becomes a vision or dream. This change from an epic to a
vision is significant, for it indicates the difference in tone and manner
between the two forms of the work. As the story may now be inter-
rupted at any time, there is much more freedom in the manner of

---

[1] In the words of Mr. Bridges (*Keats*, 33–4), "The subject lacks the solid basis of
outward event, by which epic maintains its interest: like *Endymion*, it is all imagination . . . a languor . . . lingers in the main design."

telling it; and, as the events are shown to the poet by Moneta, the last of the Titans, they come to us colored by the impressions of the two, Moneta and the poet, each of whom comments on them. Consequently the poem is less formal, less objective and impersonal; it is, to use Keats's own expression, "humanized." [1] Even when the words of the first version remain, they gain a tenderness and pathos when spoken by the mourning Moneta of her fellow-Titans that they do not possess in their original form. [2] Usually, however, there are omissions and slight changes which make the characters more human and moving, though less impressive. Compare, for instance, the following lines with the earlier form of them given on page 204 above:

> Along the margin sand large footmarks went
> No farther than to where old Saturn's feet
> Had rested, and there slept, how long a sleep!
> Degraded, cold, upon the sodden ground
> His old right hand lay nerveless, listless, dead. [3]

Often the insertion of new passages of comment, interpretation, or description between the old ones tends to break the severity of the earlier fragment. For example, the fine line with which it opened,

> Deep in the shady sadness of a vale,

though unchanged in the revised work, takes on an entirely different character:

> Side by side we stood
> (Like a stunt bramble by a solemn pine)
> Deep in the shady sadness of a vale
> Far sunken from the healthy breath of morn. [4]

It will also be seen how the tender beauty of a passage like the following, introduced just before Saturn's first speech, softens the fallen Titan's lament:

> As the moist scent of flowers, and grass, and leaves
> Fills forest-dells with a pervading air,
> Known to the woodland nostril, so the words
> Of Saturn fill'd the mossy glooms around . . .
> With sad, low tones, while thus he spake, and sent
> Strange musings to the solitary Pan. [5]

[1] *The Fall*, ii. 2.

[2] To feel this, one has but to compare the opening lines of the second canto of *The Fall* with the corresponding passage in *Hyperion* (i. 158–68).

[3] *The Fall*, i. 319–23. A better illustration, but one too long to quote, will be found in the two descriptions of Thea: *ib.* i. 332–40; *Hyperion*, i. 26–37.

[4] *The Fall*, i. 292–5; cf. also 319–40, 389–417, with *Hyperion*, i. 15–37, 83–112.

[5] *The Fall*, i. 404–11.

It might be expected that in the revision Keats not only would have "humanized" the poem in these various ways, but would have eliminated those Miltonisms of style and diction which had formerly troubled him. Strange to say, he did nothing of the kind.[1] Before recasting it he evidently came to realize how much deeper than these matters of expression the real trouble lay, and seems to have become quite indifferent to them. He certainly retained a number of external Miltonisms in the new version, — "influence benign on planets pale," "Deity supreme," "of triumph calm," "voices of soft proclaim," "for rest divine," "with strides colossal." [2] Likewise in the new lines that he wrote for *The Fall* he used freely such "Greek and Latin inversions and intonations" as "roof august," "with act adorant," "the faulture of decrepit things," and

> "That I am favour'd for unworthiness,
> By such propitious parley medicin'd
> In sickness not ignoble, I rejoice,
> Aye, and could weep for love of such award."
> So answer'd I, continuing.[3]

The use of adjectives for adverbs is more noticeable in *The Fall* than in the earlier version. Here, for example, are two instances within two lines:

> Soft mitigated by divinest lids
> Half closed, and visionless entire they seem'd.[4]

New Miltonic constructions, such as "me thoughtless," "Moneta silent," [5] are introduced, as well as no fewer than five borrowings from Milton.[6] It is true that some of the *changes* Keats made do leave the poem less Miltonic, but these can be explained on grounds not connected with *Paradise Lost*.[7] It is also true that the most Mil-

---

[1] None of the critics or editors seem quite clear as to why Keats abandoned the original poem or just what his purpose was in revising it, but all agree with Mr. Bridges (*Keats*, 41) that "the effect of an imitation of Milton is fairly got rid of from the *Revision*, and whole passages are excluded because they were too Miltonic, yet inversions and classicisms are used" (so, too, Hoops's edition of *Hyperion*, Berlin, 1899, pp. 29–30, 37; De Sélincourt, pp. 493, 516, 519–24; and L. Wolff's *Keats*, Paris, 1910, pp. 400–407, 568 n. 2). The following pages contain my reasons for thinking otherwise.

[2] *The Fall*, i. 414, 416, 433, 435, ii. 36, 39 (*Hyperion*, i. 108, 111, 128, 130, 192, 195).

[3] i. 62, 283, 70, 182–6.

[4] i. 266–7. See also i. 27, 76, 124, 146, 159, 217, 245, 301, 393, 397, 447, ii. 52.

[5] i. 368, 388.   [6] See below, Appendix A.

[7] The only changes that might conceivably have been made in order to avoid the "excessive Miltonisms" of the first version are the following:

a. The lines in *Hyperion* (i. 83–4),

> One moon, with alteration slow, had shed
> Her silver seasons four upon the night,

tonic passages in the first version are not found in the second; but this is either because they had to be dropped to fit the change of plan, or, as is more often the case, because they were not reached in the second version, which covers only a third of the original fragment.[1]

---

become in the new version (i. 389–97),

> I bore
> The load of this eternal quietude . . .
> Ponderous upon my senses, a whole moon;
> For by my burning brain I measured sure
> Her silver seasons shedded on the night. . . .
> . . . . Oftentimes I pray'd
> Intense, that death would take me.

Here, to be sure, Keats has eliminated two inversions; but is not this simply an incidental result of the presence of "I bore," of the change necessitated by making the poet a character in the poem? The lines could not have remained as they were; and the second form, with such diction as "eternal quietude . . . Ponderous upon my senses," and with "sure" and "intense" used as adverbs, is if anything more Miltonic than the first.

b. In the line "The frozen God still couchant on the earth" (*Hyperion* i. 87), the expression "couchant on," which is misleading (since gray-haired Saturn "sat," not "lay"), is changed in *The Fall* to the more accurate term "bending to" (i. 386).

c. The line "Upon the gold clouds metropolitan" (*Hyperion*, i. 129) Keats expanded into "From the gold peaks of heaven's high-piled clouds" (*The Fall*, i. 434), possibly for the sake of clearness, or, as Mr. de Sélincourt suggests (p. 524), because the latter expression is "more natural and perhaps more highly poetical." If it was the inversion that troubled Keats, why did he leave "Of triumph calm" in the preceding line?

d. In the revision, "For as among us mortals omens drear" (*Hyperion*, i. 169) becomes "For as upon the earth dire prodigies" (ii. 18), obviously because in the second version Moneta is speaking and cannot use the words "us mortals." When these words had been altered the meter required further changes.

e. For "oft made Hyperion ache" (*Hyperion*, i. 176) we have in *The Fall* the less Miltonic "make great Hyperion ache" (ii. 24), because in the revision the portents are represented as continuous occurrences.

f. The expression "came slope upon the threshold of the west" (*Hyperion*, i. 204, where "slope" is probably derived from *P. L.*, iv. 261, 591) is changed to "is sloping to" (*The Fall*, ii. 48), possibly because "slope" seemed too unusual to be entirely pleasant or clear. At any rate, on the preceding page the Miltonic verb "snuff" (in "still snuff'd the incense," *Hyperion*, i. 167, cf. *P. L.*, x. 272), which is not open to the same objection, is kept.

1 Two omissions need to be considered. The first is the "essentially Miltonic" passage,

> While sometimes eagle's wings,
> Unseen before by Gods or wondering men,
> Darken'd the place; and neighing steeds were heard,
> Not heard before by Gods or wondering men

(i. 182–5). This recalls *Paradise Lost* to Mr. de Sélincourt (p. 524) because of the repetition. Repetition is certainly common in Milton, but it is used so generally by poets that particular instances of it cannot safely be attributed to the influence of any one man. To me the lines are less Miltonic than those just before them, which are retained in the second version,

> And all its curtains of Aurorian clouds
> Flush'd angerly.

Yet the "humanizing" of the poem was not the sole, perhaps not even the main, purpose of the revision. Keats may well have had several objects in view. He certainly wished to bring out the allegory or "meaning," and to express his ideas about the functions of a poet as he was not free to do in an epic. Perhaps it was the influence of Dante that led him to change to a vision and to introduce a guide and interpreter (in the person of Moneta) who should perform a part similar to that of Virgil in the *Divina Commedia*.[1] But it must be frankly acknowledged that, since we know very little as to what he intended to do with the poem either in the original or in the revised form, we can know still less about his reasons for changing it. The only thing clear is that the elimination of Miltonic phraseology formed no part of his plan, whereas the removal of what was to him the unnatural aloofness and austerity of the Miltonic epic he did attempt.

Keats once wrote, with fine insight into the character and temperament of Milton:

He had an exquisite passion for what is properly, in the sense of ease and pleasure, poetical Luxury; and with that it appears to me he would fain have been content, if he could, so doing, have preserved his self-respect and feel of duty performed; but there was working in him as it were that same sort of thing as operates in the great world to the end of a Prophecy's being accomplish'd: therefore he devoted himself rather to the ardours than the pleasures of Song.[2]

In view of Keats's own "exquisite passion for poetical luxury," he may have thought he resembled the youthful Milton, and may have hoped, when working on *Hyperion*, to become a poet not unlike the mature author of *Paradise Lost*. For unquestionably he had a good

Keats may have discarded the passage because he was dissatisfied with eagles' wings and the neighing of horses; perhaps he felt that they were too earthy and not sufficiently dignified to serve as omens to the god of the sun.

The other passage which is thought to have been omitted because of its Miltonic character is the description of the opening of Hyperion's palace-door at his approach (i. 205–12). The only words in these splendid lines that recall *Paradise Lost* are "ope" for "open" and "save what solemn tubes . . . gave of sweet And wandering sounds," which might easily have been changed had it been the Miltonisms that troubled Keats. The difficulty seems to have been that in the revision the poet could not himself describe the opening of the door for the Titan to enter, since he did not see it but had his first view of Hyperion after the god was within the palace. If, then, the passage were to be kept, it had to be put into Moneta's mouth; but, as her account is everywhere comparatively direct, and as she is here concerned simply with impressing upon the poet Hyperion's distraught state of mind, she would never have taken eight lines to say — what might, indeed, be assumed — that the door opened for the god to enter. It may be that Keats planned to use the lines later in the poem.

[1] See Bridges, *Keats*, 40–41; Hoops, *Keats*, 31–3.

[2] "Notes on Paradise Lost" (*Works*, ed. Forman, iii. 19).

deal in common with the author of *Comus*. Milton belonged in many respects with the Elizabethans, the writers from whom Keats derived a large part of his inspiration; and both men were the poetical sons of Spenser. "Keats probably borrowed more from *Comus*," says Mr. de Sélincourt, "than from any other poem (or part of a poem) of the same length"; [1] and the last work he planned, the one he talked about on his voyage to Italy, was to have been on Sabrina,[2] a subject admirably adapted to his powers, as it combined his love of mythology with his devotion to Milton and offered a fine scope for his imagination and his passion for sensuous beauty.

In this projected work, in his letters, and in his poems modelled more or less upon *Allegro* and *Penseroso* we seem to have evidences, not of a waning admiration for Milton, but of a realization that if he was to follow him at all closely it must be in the minor poems and not in the epic. For on one side, and an important side, Keats was quite unlike the author of *Paradise Lost*. The natural loftiness of character, the strong moral purpose, the deep concern over political affairs, the devotion to liberty, the scholarly interests, these were qualities quite alien to him who summed up all human knowledge in the words, "Beauty is truth, truth beauty." Furthermore, Keats was very young, he lacked the nobility that comes from great sacrifice, the discipline of close study, the "years that bring the philosophic mind." He had the richness of Milton but not the intensity or the restraint.[3] The reason why he could carry *Isabella*, the *Eve of St. Agnes*, and *Lamia* to triumphant conclusions but could not finish *Hyperion* was that the former were Elizabethan or Renaissance in spirit and the latter classic. His venture on the epic heights was in the nature of a *tour de force:* he could sustain it for a short time, but he could not breathe freely in the cold thin air, and soon turned back to the rich lowlands that he loved. Yet his apprenticeship to Milton made a different poet of him. He did not return to the "mawkishness" of *Endymion* and the earlier volume, but pushed forward to his masterpieces, the *Eve of St. Agnes*, *Lamia*, and the odes. These poems, which with *Hyperion* constitute Keats's greatest heritage to English literature, are the result of his study of Milton.[4]

[1] Page 582, n. 2.

[2] Joseph Severn to C. Brown, Sept. 19, 1821, in Sharp's *Life and Letters of Severn* (1892), 110.

[3] The fundamental difference between the two is illustrated by Milton's kinship with the prophets and poets of Palestine and the tragedians of Greece, whose utterances constituted his favorite reading and exerted the most powerful influence upon his mature work but had no effect upon Keats.

[4] Pointed out by Bridges (*Keats*, 32–7, 48–9, 54, 94).

CHAPTER XI

THE INFLUENCE OUTSIDE OF BLANK VERSE

Ossian, Blake, Shelley, Byron

THERE remain to be considered several writers who, notwithstanding their importance, require comparatively brief treatment because Milton's influence upon them is either slight or not capable of detailed proof. The first of these is the young Scotsman, James Macpherson, who long shrouded his unquestionable poetic gifts under the assumed character of a translator. In 1762 and 1763 he published *Fingal* and *Temora*, 'ancient epic poems, composed by Ossian and translated from the Galic by James Macpherson.' The triumphant progress of these pieces through Scotland, England, and across the continent, the impression they made even upon such men as Goethe, and the long dispute regarding their authorship are matters too well known to need retelling here. Though nominally epics, it was not for their narrative qualities that they became famous, but for their supposed antiquity, their vague, shadowy grandeur, and their sonorous, rhythmic prose.

In order, presumably, to give his work dignity and to gain for it consideration among the world's greatest poems, Macpherson called attention in the notes of *Fingal* to many passages in which Ossian resembled Homer, Virgil, and Milton. He seems, however, to have realized later that in so doing he was furnishing weapons to his opponents, for in *Temora*, published the following year, he did not mention similarities to other epics.

But the harm had been done. In a "Dissertation on the Authenticity of Ossian's Poems" which Malcolm Laing printed as an appendix to his *History of Scotland* (1800), one argument advanced for Macpherson's authorship of the pieces was their many borrowings from the Bible, Homer, Virgil, Pope, Milton, and others. Although most of the parallels were very far-fetched, their number was greatly increased in the edition of Ossian that Laing brought out in 1805. Of the one hundred and twenty-six mentioned in this work, not more than twenty-five seem to me worth calling attention to, and of these only the following should, in my opinion, be taken seriously:

"Their chief . . . tall as a glittering rock. His spear is a blasted pine. His shield the rising moon."[1] — "The heroes . . . stood on the heath, like oaks, with all their branches round them; when . . . their withered leaves are rustling to the wind."[2] — "Like the darkened moon . . . when she moves, a dun circle, through heaven; and dreadful change is expected by men."[3] — "Thy voice shall remain in their ears."[4] — "Like the noise of a cave; when the sea of Togorma rolls before it: and its trees meet the roaring winds."[5] — "A thousand swords, at once unsheathed, gleam on the waving heath."[6] — "O thou that rollest above, round as the shield of my fathers! Whence are thy beams, O sun! thy everlasting light? Thou comest forth, in thy awful beauty; the stars hide themselves in the sky. . . . But thou thyself movest alone."[7] — "Where have ye been, ye southern winds! when the sons of my love were deceived? Bu have yet been sporting on plains. . . . O that ye had been rustling, in the sails of Nathos!"[8] — "Long-streaming beam of light."[9] — "Rustling wing."[10]— "His words are mixed with sighs."[11] —"Now would they have mixed in horrid fray, had not the wrath of Cathmor burned."[12]— "Years roll on, seasons return, but he is still unknown."[13]

Borrowings much more numerous and striking than these have been noted in many writers of the time, and, in view of Milton's extraordinary vogue, it would be strange if the Ossianic epics did not take some phrases from *Paradise Lost*. Seven of those given above Macpherson himself mentioned, but he also pointed out a

---

[1] *Fingal*, i (Laing, i. 9, "tall as a rock of ice" in 1st ed.); cf. *P. L.*, i. 283–92.

[2] *Fingal*, ii (Laing, i. 64); cf. *P. L.*, i. 611–15. Cf. also *Fingal*, ii (Laing i. 76), "Stood Erin's . . . sons; like a grove through which the flame had rushed, hurried on by the winds of the stormy night; distant, withered, dark they stand"; *Fingal*, iv (Laing, i. 138–9), "Silent and tall he seemed as an oak on the banks of Lubar, which had its branches blasted of old by the lightning of heaven"; *Calthon and Colmal* (Laing, i. 481), "He stood . . . with his host. They were like rocks broken with thunder, when their bent trees are singed and bare."

[3] *Fingal*, ii (Laing, i. 75); cf. *P. L.*, i. 596–9. Cf. also *War of Caros* (Laing, i. 237), "dim, like the darkened moon behind the mist of night"; *Carric-Thura* (Laing, i. 415–16), "like a light cloud on the sun, when he moves in his robes of mist, and shews but half his beams"; *Temora*, viii (Laing, ii. 254), "they are darkened moons in heaven"; *Cath-Loda* (Laing, ii. 316), "like Cruth-loda fiery-eyed, when he looks from behind the darkened moon, and strews his signs on night."

[4] *Comala* (Laing, i. 227); cf. *P. L.*, viii. 1–2.

[5] *War of Caros* (Laing, i. 235); cf. *P. L.*, ii. 284–7. Cf. also *Dar-Thula* (Laing, i. 386–7), "His voice was like hollow wind in a cave."

[6] *Battle of Lora* (Laing, i. 286); cf. *P. L.*, i. 663–4.

[7] *Carthon* (Laing, i. 342–4); cf. *P. L.*, iv. 32–5.

[8] *Dar-Thula* (Laing, i. 381–2); cf. *Lycidas*, 50–57.

[9] *Oithona* (Laing, i. 519); cf. *Comus*, 340.

[10] *Croma* (Laing, i. 539); cf. *P. L.*, i. 768.

[11] *Temora*, i (Laing, ii. 29); cf. *P. L.*, i. 621.

[12] Ib. iv (Laing, ii. 126); cf. *P. L.*, iv. 990–96.

[13] Ib. (Laing, ii. 131–2); cf. *P. L.*, iii. 40–41.

number of other parallels in which there is so little similarity that he could hardly have had them in mind while making his "translation." Compare, for example, his "rustling winds roar in the distant wood" with Milton's

> As when hollow rocks retain
> The sound of blustering winds; [1]

or his "the gloom of battle poured along; as mist that is rolled on a valley," with the picture of the cherubim descending a hill in Eden,

> As evening mist
> Risen from a river o'er the marish glides,
> And gathers ground fast at the labourer's heel
> Homeward returning. [2]

Macpherson must have read Milton, — his notes alone show that, — and his imagination may well have been stimulated by the reading; yet he can hardly have been influenced in any vital way by a poem so remote from the vague, romantic rhapsodies or the short, simple declarative sentences he put into the mouth of Ossian.

About the time the vogue of *Fingal* and *Temora* was nearing its height, their influence touched a young man whose work was destined to have none of the immediate, meteoric popularity of Macpherson's, but to gain steadily in favor long after the Scottish forgeries had ceased to be read. William Blake, who painted, engraved, saw visions, consorted with revolutionists, piped songs of innocence, and thundered prophetic books, offers many a troublesome problem to the student over whom he casts his spell, for the majority of persons find his "definition of the most sublime poetry" — "allegory . . . altogether hidden from the corporeal understanding" [3] — only too applicable to all his longer works. One of the most interesting of the problems which the corporeal understanding finds baffling in Blake is that of his debt to *Paradise Lost*.

As to his knowledge of Milton's poetry and the importance of the part it played in his thoughts, there can be no question. Over ninety of his paintings and engravings deal with the work of the earlier poet, some forty-two with *Paradise Lost*, twelve with *Paradise Regained*,

---

[1] *Fingal*, i (Laing, i. 29); *P. L.*, ii. 285–6. The previous line of each work contains the word "murmur," to which Macpherson does not call attention. In Ossian, however, the murmur "rolls along the hill" and is actually caused by the "rustling winds"; in Milton it fills Pandemonium and is *like* "the sound of *blustering* winds."

[2] *Fingal*, ii (Laing, i. 69); *P. L.*, xii. 629–32. In the first edition "poured" and "rolled" change places.

[3] Letter to Thomas Butts, July 6, 1803.

thirteen with *Allegro* and *Penseroso*, seventeen with *Comus*, seven with the *Nativity;* one is a portrait of the poet himself, and one was suggested by a line in the *Death of a Fair Infant*.[1] His published writings, his letters, and the records of his conversations also contain numerous references to Milton, who came to him frequently in visions and who furnished the title and principal character for one of his most important prophetic books. Three times in the course of his prose *Public Address* he refers enthusiastically to the author of *Paradise Lost*,[2] and in his vigorous and astonishing *Marriage of Heaven and Hell* he gives his interpretation of the poem. Satan, he tells us, represents desire, and the Messiah reason or "the restrainer" — really the Evil One, for "those who restrain desire, do so because theirs is weak enough to be restrained; and the restrainer or reason usurps its place and governs the unwilling." In a characteristic note there is the added information, "The reason Milton wrote in fetters when he wrote of Angels and God, and at liberty when of Devils and Hell, is because he was a true Poet and of the Devil's party without knowing it."

In speaking of the things for which he was particularly grateful, Blake said,

Flaxman hath given me Hayley his friend to be mine, such my lot upon Earth. Now my lot in the Heavens is this, Milton lov'd me in childhood and shew'd me his face.[3]

A little later he wrote Hayley, "In the meantime I have the happiness of seeing the Divine countenance in such men as Cowper and Milton more distinctly than in any prince or hero."[4] In *Vala* (or

---

[1] These figures are taken from W. M. Rossetti's "Descriptive Catalogue" (appended to the second volume of Gilchrist's *Life of William Blake*, new ed., 1880) and from the Grolier Club catalogue of Blake's works (1905). While not exact, they are probably not far wrong and err through understatement. Of some of the pictures, such as the frontispiece to *Europe* (suggested by *Paradise Lost*, vii. 224–31, as the British Museum copy indicates), Blake made a number of replicas.

[2] Gilchrist, ii. 168, 172.

[3] Letter to Flaxman, Sept. 12, 1800. Ezra, Isaiah, Shakespeare, Paracelsus, and Jacob Böhme are mentioned in the lines that follow.

[4] Letter of May 28, 1804. He also referred to Milton in letters to Dr. Trusler, Aug. 16 and 23, 1799 (see p. 222 below), and to Thomas Butts, Nov. 22, 1802, first letter ("Perhaps *picturesque* is somewhat synonymous to the word taste, which we should think improperly applied to Homer or Milton, but very well to Prior or Pope"), April 25 and July 6, 1803. It will be remembered that, when Butts surprised Blake and his wife sitting unclad in their summer-house, they "had been reciting passages from *Paradise Lost*" (Gilchrist i. 112). In the "Descriptive Catalogue," no. v (Gilchrist, ii. 155), Blake writes (speaking of himself in the third person), "The stories of Arthur are the acts of Albion. . . . In this Picture, believing with Milton the ancient British History, Mr. B. has," etc. According to M. Denis Saurat (*Blake and Milton*,

The Four Zoas) there is a sort of genealogy which "represents the whole history of the human race beginning with Los, the spirit of poetry, descending through various spiritual forms to Adam, the materialized 'natural man,' and ascending through Solomon, Charlemagne, Luther, and others to Milton, the last named and hence intended to be the greatest man who has yet appeared on earth." [1]

Of the references that Crabb Robinson noted down from Blake's conversation, the most interesting is this:

As he spoke of frequently seeing Milton, I ventured to ask . . . which of the . . . portraits . . . is the most like. He answered, "They are all like, at different ages. I have seen him as a youth and as an old man with a long flowing beard. He came lately as an old man — he said he came to ask a favour of me. He said he had committed an error in his Paradise Lost, which he wanted me to correct, in a poem or picture; but I declined. I said I had my own duties to perform. . . . He wished me to expose the falsehood of his doctrine, taught in the Paradise Lost, that sexual intercourse arose out of the Fall." [2]

Such an inexplicable misunderstanding of *Paradise Lost* shows how subjective, how indifferent to details, was Blake's manner of reading,

Bordeaux, 1920, p. 36), he here "refers to Milton's History of Britain as his covering authority"; but is the reference not rather to Milton's plan for an epic on Arthur? In the *Island in the Moon*, chap. vii (pp. 73-4 of E. J. Ellis's *Real Blake*, 1907), Blake gives as the remark of the complacently imbecile Quid, "Homer is bombast, and Shakespeare is too wild, and Milton has no feelings." In his marginal notes to Reynolds's *Discourses* he refers four times to Milton (pp. 372, 376, 381, 392, of the *Real Blake*), quoting from the *Reason of Church Government* in one place, and writing in another, "The Neglect of such as Milton in a Country pretending to the Encouragement of Art is Sufficient Apology for my Vigorous Indignation." In the climax of *Jerusalem* (98: 9) "Bacon & Newton & Locke" (the three scientists) and "Milton & Shakspear & Chaucer" (the three poets) appear in heaven along with "innumerable Chariots of the Almighty."

[1] In the list of women's names that follows this genealogy, the last is "Mary," the greatest of women (see *Vala*, viii. 357-9). The quotation in the text is from a manuscript note furnished me by Mr. S. Foster Damon of Newton, Massachusetts, who has generously given me the advantage of his extensive study of Blake and allowed me to read a chapter in his forthcoming book, *The Philosophy and Symbols of William Blake*.

[2] Robinson's "Reminiscences," under the date "26/2/52", as quoted in Arthur Symons's *William Blake* (1907), 295-6. This is the fuller but later account and may contain recollections of other talks with Blake. Robinson's original notes on this conversation (which are also given by Symons, pp. 263-4, Dec. 17, 1825) do not differ materially. Instead of "sexual intercourse," the original diary has "the pleasures of sex"; but either is inconsistent with *Paradise Lost*, iv. 741-70, viii. 510-20, 579-600. Blake probably had in mind the distinction (which he thought false) made in the epic between love and lust. The other references to Milton that Robinson noted are on pages 262, 265, 273, 274, 294, of Symons's book. Gilchrist (i. 362) cites as typical of Blake's "familiar conversations with Mr. Palmer and other disciples": "'Milton the other day was saying to me' so and so. 'I tried to convince him he was wrong, but I could not succeed.' 'His tastes are Pagan; his house is Palladian, not Gothic.'"

a point that comes out still more clearly in his *Imitation of Spenser*, where no two stanzas use the same meter, none follow Spenser exactly, and where the number of lines in a stanza varies from eight to ten. Whatever his powerful imagination seized upon was likely to be so transformed as to be scarcely recognizable. He presumably read with his mind's eye, paying relatively little heed to words, phrasing, or style. "I do not behold the outward creation," he asserted, ". . . to me it is hindrance. . . . I question not my corporeal eye any more than I would question a window concerning a sight. I look through it and not with it." [1]

Such a man, even without the intense originality which is averse to borrowings of any kind, was not likely to take many words or expressions from the authors he read. Blake's frequent use of Biblical language is a not unnatural exception, but he also adopted more phrases from Shakespeare and Milton than would be anticipated. Some of these may have slipped from his pen without thought of their source, but hardly these opening lines of *Europe*, which are indebted to the stanza, the phrasing, and the subject-matter of the *Nativity:*

> The deep of winter came;
> What time the secret child
> Descended thro' the orient gates of the eternal day:
> War ceas'd, & all the troops like shadows fled to their abodes.[2]

Perhaps in writing "when early morn walks forth in sober grey," "human form divine," "when vocal May comes dancing from the East," "effluence Divine," "Eternity expands Its ever during doors," [3] Blake did not think of Milton; possibly he did not even in saying "a cavern shagged with horrid shades," and "englobing, in a

---

[1] Sequel to his description of the "Last Judgment" (Ellis's *Real Blake*, 327). Mr. Damon mentions as an example of his indifference to details his six spellings of the name of a soldier with whom he quarrelled, — Scofield, Schofield, Skofeld, Skofield, Scofeld, and Scholfield (*Jerusalem*, 5:27, 7:25, 8:41, 17:59, 43:51; and letter to Butts, Aug. 16, 1803).

[2] Cf. *Nativity*, 29–30, 48, 53–4, 232–3. Note also how many of the heathen deities mentioned in *Milton*, 37: 20–29, are found in lines 197–213 of the *Nativity*. For Blake's enthusiasm for the poem, see below, p. 228, n. 1.

[3] *Song*, "When early morn," 1 (cf. *Lycidas*, 187, *P. R.*, iv. 426–7); *Divine Image*, 15, also *Milton*, extra page 32, line 13 (cf. *P. L.*, iii. 44); *Vala*, ix. 193 (cf. *May Morning*, 2–3); *Milton*, 31:35 (cf. *P. L.*, iii. 6); *ib.* 48–9 (cf. *P. L.*, vii. 205–6). One of these parallels and several of those given later were called to my attention by Mr. Damon, who feels that the names of the twelve daughters of Albion, in *Vala*, ii. 61–2, and *Jerusalem*, 5: 41–4, together with the way some of these names are spelled, indicate a familiarity with Milton's *History of Britain*. He likewise believes that the exaltation of the Bible at the expense of Greek and Latin writers in the preface to *Milton*, may have been suggested by *Paradise Regained*, iv. 331–42.

mighty globe self-balanced;"[1] but he must have had *Paradise Lost* in mind when he referred to Satan as "the father of Sin and Death," and when he wrote,

> I came forth from the head of Satan: back the Gnomes recoil'd
> And called me Sin, and for a sign portentous held me;

and,

> In pits & dens & shades of death: in shapes of torment & woe.
> The plates & screws & wracks & saws & cords & fires & cisterns.[2]

[1] *Vala*, iii. 124 (cf. *Comus*, 429), i. 123 (cf. *P. L.*, vii. 239–42).

[2] *Milton*, 10:38–9 (cf. *P. L.*, ii. 755–61); 24:33–4 (cf. *P. L.*, ii. 621). Other passages that may owe something to Milton are: "the pendulous earth" (*Urizen*, ix. 8, cf. *P. L.*, iv. 1000); "collected in himself in awful pride (*Vala*, i. 322, cf. vi. 298, "collected, dark, the spectre stood," and *P. L.*, ix. 673, iv. 986); "spirits of flaming fire on high governed the mighty song" (*ib.* i. 368, cf. *P. L.*, vii. 30, to which Blake refers in a letter quoted on p. 222 below); "pangs smote me unknown before" (*ib.* iv. 93, cf. *P. L.*, ii. 703); "threw his flight" (*ib.* vi. 2, 161, vii. 3, cf. *P. L.*, iii. 741, of an angel in each case); "redounding smoke" (*ib.* vii. 9, cf. "cast forth red smoke and fire" eight lines farther on, also 601, and *P. L.*, ii. 889); "chaos & ancient night" (*Milton*, 10:21, 15:24–5, 18:33, cf. *P. L.*, ii. 970, etc.);

> He formed golden compasses,
> And began to explore the Abyss

(*Urizen*, vii. 8, cf. *Vala*, ii. 29, 142, and *P. L.*, vii. 225–9);

> Ten thousand thousand were his hosts of spirits on the wind,
> Ten thousand thousand glittering chariots shining in the sky

(*Vala*, i. 328–9, cf. *P. L.*, vi. 767–70);

> The Harrow cast thick flames, & orb'd us round in concave fire,
> A Hell of our own making

(*Milton*, 10:22–3, cf. *P. L.*, ii. 635, vi. 750–51);

> Loud Satan thunder'd . . .
> Coming in a Cloud with Trumpets and with Fiery Flame,
> An awful Form eastward from midst of a bright Paved-work
> Of precious stones, by Cherubim surrounded: so permitted
> . . . . to imitate
> The Eternal Great Humanity Divine (*ib.* 40:22–7, cf. *P. L.*, ii. 508–15).

The similarities in the following are more dubious: "the Prince of Light with splendour faded" (*Vala*, iii. 46, and *Jerusalem*, 29:35, cf. *P. L.*, iv. 870–71); "the Prince of thunders . . . Fell down rushing, ruining" (*Vala*, iii. 141–3, cf. *P. L.*, vi. 868); "warping upon the winds" (*ib.* iv. 186, cf. *P. L.*, i. 341); "in serpents and in worms stretched out enormous length" (*ib.* vi. 114, cf. *P. L.*, i. 209); "the Chariot Wheels filled with Eyes rage along" (*Jerusalem*, 63:11, cf. *P. L.*, vi. 749–55);

> But infinitely beautiful the wondrous work arose
> In sorrow and care, a golden world whose porches round the heaven,
> And pillar'd halls and rooms received the eternal wandering stars.
> A wondrous golden building, many a window, many a door,
> And many a division let in and out the vast unknown. . . .
> . . . Thence arose soft clouds and exhalations

(*Vala*, ii. 240–53, cf. *P. L.*, i. 710–30). Another possible borrowing is given on p. 224 below. The expressions "adamantine doors" (*To Winter*, 1), "adamantine chains"

Even in the prose preface to *Jerusalem* Blake adopted the phraseology of the preface to *Paradise Lost:*

When this Verse was first dictated to me I consider'd a Monotonous Cadence like that used by Milton & Shakspeare & all writers of English Blank Verse, derived from the modern bondage of Rhyming, to be a necessary and indispensable part of Verse. But I soon found that in the mouth of a true Orator such monotony was not only awkward, but as much a bondage as rhyme itself.[1]

How naturally ideas and words of the earlier poet came to him is shown by his explaining in a letter that he was "of the same opinion with Milton when he says that the Muse visits his slumbers and awakes and governs his song when morn purples the east."[2] There is probably an unconscious reference to another passage from *Paradise Lost*, of similar import, in his remark to Butts, "I have written this poem from immediate dictation, twelve or sometimes twenty or thirty lines at a time, without premeditation."[3] He seems to have taken Milton's allusions to the visits of the muse more seriously and to have interpreted them more literally than most persons do, for he wrote: "The Ancients did not mean to Impose when they affirmed their belief in Vision and Revelation. Plato was in earnest. Milton was in earnest. They believed that God did visit Man really and Truly."[4] It is also not unlikely that the phrase "the Daughters of Memory," which he uses several times when scornfully contrasting

---

(*Vala*, ii. 66), "adamantine leaves" (*ib*. vi. 171), "the vast of Nature" (*Song of Los*, 42), suggest *Paradise Lost*, i. 48, ii. 645-6, etc., vi. 203, as do the words "englobed," "englobing," "conglobing" (*Urizen*, ix. 9, *Vala*, i. 123, iii. 87, iv. 95, vi. 120, etc., cf. *P. L.*, vii. 239), and "petrific" (*Vala*, iv. 168, cf. *P. L.*, x. 294). M. Paul Berger (*William Blake, Mysticisme et Poésie*, Paris, 1907, p. 329) regards *Blind-man's Buff* as "inspiré par un passage de l'*Allegro* de Milton," but only five lines (8-12) in Blake's octosyllabics have for me any suggestion of Milton's. *Samson*, which was originally published as prose, Mr. E. J. Ellis, following W. M. Rossetti, prints as blank verse and considers Blake's "most Miltonic fragment" (*Poetical Works*, 1906, i. 539-40). M. Berger (pp. 328-9) says of it, "Les expressions de Milton et celles de la Bible sont copiées presque mot à mot." I find but one such expression, — the very dubious description of the angel, "His form was manhood in the prime" (cf. *P. L.*, xi. 245-6), — and, except possibly in the fourth and fifth sentences, no evidence of Milton's influence. The piece, in my opinion, was intended as poetry but not as blank verse.

[1] Compare Milton's "rime being no necessary adjunct . . . of . . . good verse . . . a fault avoided . . . in . . . all good oratory . . . the troublesome and modern bondage of riming."

[2] To Dr. Trusler, Aug. 16, 1799; cf. *P. L.*, vii. 28-31.

[3] Letter of April 25, 1803; cf. *P. L.*, ix. 20-24, "my celestial patroness . . . dictates to me . . . my unpremeditated verse." Milton likewise dictated "Ten, Twenty, or Thirty Verses at a Time" to his amanuenses (see Phillips's life, p. xxxvi, in Milton's *Letters of State*, 1694).

[4] Note in Reynolds's *Discourses* (Ellis's *Real Blake*, 392).

the classical muses with "the Daughters of Inspiration," [1] was suggested by the noble words in the *Reason of Church Government*, where Milton refers to his epic as a work "not to be obtained by the invocation of dame Memory and her siren daughters." We know that this passage impressed Blake, since he wrote it in a copy of Reynolds's *Discourses*.[2]

The style and diction of *Paradise Lost* he would seem no more likely to adopt than he was to borrow phrases. The "Monotonous Cadence" of blank verse he felt to be "as much a bondage as rhyme," and discarded it for a loose, half-prose measure of his own with long lines that fall into six, seven, or eight feet, usually seven. Yet, just as he did not escape borrowed expressions, he could not rid himself entirely from the qualities with which he had always been familiar in unrimed poetry. He may not have tried; at any rate, he has many inversions that are marked and unnatural, as well as many adjectives used as adverbs which frequently sound more Miltonic from being taken out of their normal positions. Sometimes, as in *Paradise Lost*, a noun is placed between two of its qualifying adjectives, as "heavy clouds confused," "ornamented pillars square Of fire," "hard iron petrific," "flakey locks terrific," "a mighty sound articulate," "in white linen pure he hovered," "fluxile eyes englob'd roll." [3] When there are several adjectives after the noun and but one or none before it, there is a Miltonic effect something like that of apposition: "a crack across from immense to immense, Loud, strong"; "panting in sobs, Thick, short, incessant"; "dire flames, Quenchless, unceasing"; "a lovely form, inspired, divine, human";

> He approached the East,
> Void, pathless, beaten with eternal sleet, and eternal hail and rain.

> Thirty of Tiriel's sons remained, to wither in the palace —
> Desolate, loathed, dumb, astonished.[4]

The following passages will show that at times the prophetic books are clearly influenced by the style of *Paradise Lost*:

> I hear the screech of Childbirth loud pealing, & the groans
> Of Death, in Albion's clouds dreadful utter'd over all the Earth.

---

[1] For example, at the beginning of his account of his picture the "Last Judgment," and in *Milton*, preface, and 12:29.

[2] See Ellis's *Real Blake*, 381.

[3] *Tiriel*, v. 14; *Vala*, ii. 275–6, iv. 168, vi. 238, ix. 12; *Jerusalem*, 29:38 (also *Vala*, iii. 51), 29:68.

[4] *Vala*, iii. 151–2, 157–8; vi. 263–4; vii. 465; vi. 144–5; *Tiriel*, v. 33–4. M. Berger, who calls attention to this Miltonism of Blake's (pp. 426–7), notes similar instances in *Paradise Lost*, i. 52–3, 60. Though not unusual in *Vala*, it is very rare in the other prophetic books.

The Twelve Daughters of Albion attentive listen in secret shades
On Cambridge and Oxford beaming soft, uniting with Rahab's cloud,
While Gwendolen spoke to Cambel, turning soft the spinning reel.

Henceforth, Palamabron, let each his own station
Keep: nor in pity false, nor in officious brotherhood, where
None needs, be active. Mean time Palamabron's horses
Rag'd with thick flames redundant, & the Harrow madden'd with fury.

They Plow'd in tears! incessant pour'd Jehovah's rain & Molech's
Thick fires, contending with the rain, thunder'd above rolling
Terrible over their heads.

Suddenly around Milton on my Path, the Starry Seven
Burn'd terrible: my Path became a solid fire, as bright
As the clear Sun & Milton silent came down on my Path.
And there went forth from the Starry limbs of the Seven, Forms
Human, with Trumpets innumerable, sounding articulate
As the Seven spake.[1]

The lines given below not only illustrate the style of *Vala* but may
show indebtedness to the subject-matter of *Paradise Lost*, particularly to that part of the fifth book in which Satan first plots rebellion
with Beelzebub:

                                        His family
Slept round on hills and valleys in the region of his love.
But Urizen awoke, and Luvah awoke, and they conferred thus.
Thou Luvah, said the Prince of Light, behold our sons and daughters
Repose on beds. Let them sleep on, do thou alone depart
Into thy wished kingdom, where in Majesty and Power
We may create a throne. Deep in the North I place my lot,
Thou in the South. Listen attentive. In silence of this night
I will infold the universal tent in clouds opaque, while thou
Seizest the chariots of the morning. Go; outfleeting ride
Afar into the Zenith high. . . .
Luvah replied: Dictate thou to thy equals, am not I
The Prince of all the hosts of men, nor equal know in Heaven? . . .
But Urizen with darkness overspreading all the armies
Sent round his heralds secretly, commanding to depart
Into the North. . . .
Sudden, down fell they all together into an unknown space,
Deep, horrible, without end, from Beulah separate, far beneath.[2]

[1] *Jerusalem*, 34:23–4, 82:10–12; *Milton*, 5:42–5, 6:27–9, 40:3–8.
[2] *Vala*, i. 457–514; cf. *P. L.*, v. 647–701, vi. 864–70. This similarity and one or two
others that I have called attention to were pointed out by M. Saurat (*Blake and Milton*,
15–23, 35). Perhaps M. Saurat is justified in asserting (p. 17), "The journeys of
Urizen in the sixth Night of *Vala*, his explorations through the dark world of Urthona
are strongly reminiscent of Satan's travels through outer Hell and Chaos." Urizen's
journey, particularly the part described in *Vala*, vi. 72–176, is vaguely suggestive of
Satan's, and his encounter with the "three terrific women" who are his daughters
(*Vala* vi. 1–23) is somewhat like Satan's meeting with his offspring Sin and Death;

Blake's supreme tribute is the poem *Milton*, which not only contains a larger proportion of phrases from *Paradise Lost* than do the other books, makes as much use of its style, and prints its line,

To Justify the Ways of God to Men,

on the title-page, but introduces its author as a principal character. Yet, since the only connections between this title-character and the man John Milton are the references to his "sixty" (really sixty-six) years of life, to his death a "hundred" (really one hundred thirty) years before this poem was begun, and to his three wives and three daughters, it seems as if Blake intended him to represent not so much the author of *Paradise Lost* as "the poet" in general. For, in the words of M. Berger, "Milton était pour lui le Poète par excellence." [1] The work pictures Milton as "unhappy tho' in heav'n" because his "Sixfold Emanation" (his three wives and three daughters, his separation from whom represents his errors) is "scatter'd thro' the deep In torment." Through the song of a bard — an allegorical account of Blake's quarrel with Hayley which represents the subjection of genius to inferiority — he is roused to 'give up Selfhood' and redeem this "Sixfold Emanation" by descending once more into the world and by entering into Blake. The remainder of the poem is taken up with the acts of the strange mythological beings who people the other prophetic books.

Milton's entrance into Blake may mean simply the descent of poetic inspiration and the divine commission; it may also signify that the spirit of the elder writer prompted the younger to compose a poem intended to correct, among other things, the errors taught in *Paradise Lost* regarding sex; [2] or it may mean that in general Milton's spirit had taken possession of his admirer. There are several reasons why Blake might have regarded himself as a kind of reincarnation or poetic son of the earlier writer. The emphasis in *Paradise Lost* upon the nudity of our first parents would have met with his hearty approval, for he seems to have had a decided preference for the undraped figure in life as well as in art; the frank treatment of Adam's relations with Eve must have pleased him still more, since the doctrine on which he insisted most often was that of com-

but the similarities are so few and general that there is no certainty that the Milton passages were even unconsciously in Blake's mind when he wrote.

[1] Berger, p. 426.

[2] Blake, it will be remembered, told Crabb Robinson that Milton asked him to "correct, *in a poem* or picture," an error he had made in *Paradise Lost* (see above, p. 219; the italics are mine). Allan Cunningham asserts (*Lives of the most Eminent Painters*, etc., 1830, ii. 157) that Milton "entrusted him with a whole poem of his, which the world had never seen," — that is, *Milton*.

plete freedom in matters of sex; and the teachings of the epic as to
the superiority of the male and the absolute authority to be exercised over the female were in entire accord with his own theory and
practice. Milton's vigorous, dynamic, positive personality was also
very much to the taste of one who even on his death-bed sang so
powerfully as to 'make the rafters ring,' who regarded negative
virtues as vices, and scorned the mild insipidity of Hayley, whose
"mother on his father him begot." [1] Furthermore, the lofty nobility
that marks all of Milton's work would be neither overlooked nor
unappreciated by one who was deeply religious in his own way, who
worshipped the Bible, took a profoundly serious and spiritual view
of life, and was intolerant of the mean, the low, and the trivial. The
verse of *Paradise Lost* likewise appealed to Blake, for he tells us that
he at first considered using something like it in *Jerusalem*. Milton
did not go far enough, to be sure; but he was the recognized leader of
the free-verse movement, and Blake's meter was closer to his than
to that of any other English poem. The extensive use of run-over
lines in *Paradise Lost*, and the substitution of free musical paragraphs for lines as the basis of prosody, must also have pleased and
probably have influenced the author of *Jerusalem*. Then, too, Milton's feeling that his unpremeditated verse was dictated to him by
a heavenly messenger coincided with Blake's conception of the
origin of his own work and may have strengthened him in the idea.[2]

Besides, Blake was a revolutionist, one who associated with radicals like Tom Paine, Godwin, Mary Wollstonecraft, and Priestley,
and hailed the American and French republics with enthusiasm.
Although he disapproved of the political activities of the Latin
secretary of the Commonwealth, his highly-strung nature must have
vibrated in deep sympathy with Milton's passion for liberty of every
kind. As he read his life and works, talked with his biographer Hayley, or considered his independence in religion, literature, politics,
and divorce, he may well have thought that the spirit which did
these things had indeed entered into him. Satan, the arch-rebel of
all poetry, must have thrilled him with unusual joy. At least, he
once declared him to be the true Saviour, and gave his name to an

---

[1] "Of H——'s birth," Ellis's edition of *Works*, i. 170. In *Vala*, iii. 116–20, Urizen
contrasts "feminine indolent bliss" and "passive idle sleep" with "active masculine
virtue," and exclaims,

Thy passivity, thy laws of obedience and insincerity
Are my abhorrence.

"The Weak Man may be Virtuous Enough, but will Never be an Artist," Blake wrote
in Reynolds's *Discourses* (Ellis's *Real Blake*, 378).

[2] See p. 222 above.

important character (a very different one, to be sure) in the prophetic books and his spirit and some of his deeds to other characters. It may be that, like Burns during these very years, Blake held the apostate angel as his "favourite hero"; and perhaps, like Landor, another kindred spirit of the time, he sometimes 'recited aloud in solitary walks the haughty appeal of Satan and the deep penitence of Eve.' [1]

It was not alone Satan's rebellious spirit that attracted the rebel poet, but the power which the ruined archangel and his peers have over the imagination. Beelzebub, Moloch, Belial, Azazel, Abdiel, Michael, Raphael, and Uriel were beings after his own heart and must have influenced him not a little in the creation of the mythological personages who throng his poetic universe. For Blake's imagination, like Milton's, was cosmic. The vastness, the shadowy grandeur, of the countless cherubim and seraphim, their tremendous battles that shook heaven to its base, the coming of the Messiah, his Blakesque chariot covered with eyes and

> Flashing thick flames, wheel within wheel, undrawn,
> Itself instinct with spirit,

the fall from heaven, the flames and sombre glories of hell, the wondrous temple that "rose like an exhalation," Satan's daring journey through the infernal world and across chaos, his encounters with his monstrous offspring Sin and Death, their immense bridge, the shadowy throne of Chaos and ancient Night, the golden compasses and the creation of our universe, — these pictures and many like them stirred Blake profoundly. Some of them he actually copied (with important modifications of his own), for they were the kind of work he wanted to do. He disliked limits of all kinds; he scorned things "smoothed up and niggled and poco-pen'd, and all the beauties paled out, blurred, and blotted"; he decried Pope and Dryden and exalted "Michael Angelo, Shakespeare, and Milton." [2] Such men fed his imagination, stimulated him, peopled his world of visions, helped him to be himself and to bring out what was in him; and these were the things he sought in art.

We have seen that from the one whom he regarded as "the poet *par excellence*" Blake borrowed what was for him a considerable number of phrases, lines, and incidents, some stylistic features of which he made no little use, as well as the name and perhaps a few of the deeds of Satan. This is all that can be proved, although it is highly probable that in his prosody and in the general freedom

---

[1] See p. 294 below.   [2] "Public Address," Gilchrist, ii. 168.

of his verse he was influenced by the example of *Paradise Lost* and possibly by the choruses of *Samson*. Yet tangible, demonstrable matters like these are not sufficiently numerous or important to express his debt, a debt which better knowledge of the prophetic books, the paintings, ·and the engravings serves only to magnify.[1] All students of Blake feel this indebtedness, and most will probably agree that Milton's greatest service to his disciple was through encouragement and stimulus in matters wherein the two were akin, and through the titanic figures, the tremendous deeds, the vast spaces and wondrous worlds, which he opened to the strange and preternaturally-active imagination of the artist-mystic and which appear transformed in *Vala, Jerusalem, Milton*, and the minor prophetic books.

> I dreamed that Milton's spirit rose, and took
>   From life's green tree his Uranian lute;
> And from his touch sweet thunder flowed, and shook
> All human things built in contempt of man, —
> And sanguine thrones and impious altars quaked,
> Prisons and citadels. . . .[2]

This fragment of Shelley's — I have quoted all of it — is of little esthetic value, but it helps us to understand the poet's attitude towards Milton. For few things lay closer to Shelley's heart than the shaking down of "sanguine thrones," "impious altars," "prisons and citadels," and other "things built in contempt of man." It was far more important to him than it would be to most poets that Milton was not only the "Sire of an immortal strain," but one who, like Shelley himself, had suffered persecution from

> The priest, the slave, and the liberticide.[3]

"Let it ever be remembered," he reminds us, that "the sacred Milton" was "a republican, and a bold inquirer into morals and religion." [4] This republicanism, the passionate devotion Milton felt

---

[1] Blake's quarrel with Hayley and with the soldier Scofield stirred him profoundly and left no slight marks upon his work; but, were it not for our knowledge of the facts, we should be unable to trace the influence of either event. There is no such key to the impress Milton may have left; but a remark of Blake's about his picture, the "Riposo," shows how his mind may have worked. "It represents," he explains, "the Holy Family in Egypt, guarded in their repose from those fiends the Egyptian gods. And though not directly taken from a poem of Milton's (for till I had designed it Milton's poem did not come into my thoughts), yet it is very similar to his *Hymn on the Nativity*, which you will find among his smaller poems, and will read with great delight" (letter to Butts, July 6, 1803). Is it not likely that the poem was in the background of his consciousness while he was making the picture?

[2] *Milton's Spirit.*   [3] *Adonais*, 30, 32.   [4] Preface to *Prometheus Unbound*.

for freedom in marriage, religion, and government, may have had
almost as much weight as the greatness of his poetry in gaining for
him the high praise,

> His clear Sprite
> Yet reigns o'er earth; the third among the sons of light.[1]

For the same reason, it was almost inevitable that Shelley should
be drawn to Milton's hero, the rebellious Satan. In the preface to
Prometheus Unbound he wrote, "The only imaginary being resem-
bling in any degree Prometheus, is Satan; and Prometheus is, in my
judgement, a more poetical character than Satan, because, in addition to courage, and majesty, and firm and patient opposition to
omnipotent force, he is susceptible of being described as exempt
from the taints of ambition, envy, revenge, and a desire for personal
aggrandisement." May not Shelley have come to think later that
Satan also was "susceptible of being described" as a disinterested
rebel against tyranny? At least the character attracted him, for he
left two short fragments (which have been named *Satan Broken
Loose* and *Pater Omnipotens*) that deal with it. The first of these is
in rime, the second is so admirably Miltonic in both diction and
style that it should be quoted entire:

> Serene in his unconquerable might
> Endued, the Almighty King, his steadfast throne
> Encompassed unapproachably with power
> And darkness and deep solitude and awe
> Stood like a black cloud on some aëry cliff
> Embosoming its lightning — in his sight
> Unnumbered glorious spirits trembling stood
> Like slaves before their Lord — prostrate around
> Heaven's multitudes hymned everlasting praise.

Shelley's only completed poem that shows appreciable influence
from *Paradise Lost* is his earlier work, that pageant of wild natural
scenery, *Alastor, or the Spirit of Solitude* (1816). The slender thread
of story that connects the descriptions tells of the wanderings of a
young poet through vast forests and ruined cities of old, over the
sea, and down a subterranean river until he finds a quiet death. In
this there is nothing epic or grandiose, nothing to call for the sonorous dignity, the lofty aloofness, of Milton's style. And most of the
poem is not Miltonic; it has too much of Shelley's vague allegory
and dreamy loveliness, too little restraint and condensation, to be
that. Yet when we read such phrases as "sudden she rose," "calm,

[1] *Adonais*, 35-6.

he still pursued," "vast Aornos seen from Petra's steep," or lines
like

> And mighty Earth
> From sea and mountain, city and wilderness,
> In vesper low or joyous orison,
> Lifts still its solemn voice,[1]

we are certainly reminded of *Paradise Lost.* In other passages the
similarity is even more marked:

> The fountains of divine philosophy
> Fled not his thirsting lips, and all of great,
> Or good, or lovely, which the sacred past
> In truth or fable consecrates, he felt
> And knew.
>
> The Poet wandering on, through Arabie
> And Persia, and the wild Carmanian waste,
> And o'er the aërial mountains which pour down
> Indus and Oxus from their icy caves
> In joy and exultation held his way.[2]

But the larger utterance, the restraint and grandeur, of Milton are
best caught in these lines:

> His wandering step
> Obedient to high thoughts, has visited
> The awful ruins of the days of old:
> Athens, and Tyre, and Balbec, and the waste
> Where stood Jerusalem, the fallen towers
> Of Babylon, the eternal pyramids,
> Memphis and Thebes, and whatsoe'er of strange
> Sculptured on alabaster obelisk,
> Or jasper tomb, or mutilated sphynx,
> Dark Æthiopia in her desert hills
> Conceals.[3]

---

[1] Lines 172, 539, 240, 692–5.   [2] Lines 71–5, 140–44.

[3] Lines 106–16. Shelley seems to have borrowed from Milton's "chariot of Paternal
Deity" (*P. L.*, vi. 750–66) the passage,

> The restless wheels of being on their way,
> Whose flashing spokes, instinct with infinite life,
> Bicker and burn to gain their destined goal

(*Queen Mab*, ix. 152–4, repeated in the *Daemon of the World*, ii. 536–8). His "wings of
skiey grain" (*Prometheus*, i. 760) recall Raphael's "feather'd mail, Sky-tinctured
grain" (*P. L.*, v. 284–5); his "quips and cranks" (*Witch of Atlas*, 453) is certainly from
Allegro, 27; and his "mighty legions . . . each troop emblazoning its merits On meteor
flags" (*Witch*, 460–62) seems to have been suggested by "the imperial ensign, which . . .
Shone like a meteor . . . With . . . golden lustre rich emblazed, Seraphic . . . trophies"
(*P. L.*, i. 536–9). "Though fallen — and fallen on evil times" and "low-thoughted
care" (*Letter to Maria Gisborne*, 198, 294) must have been suggested by Milton (*P. L.*,
vii. 25–6, *Comus*, 6), particularly since the last line of the poem in which they occur is
the last line of *Lycidas*. It is likely also that the "vultures frighted from Imaus"

It may be that the superb versification of *Alastor*, which probably owes not a little to Wordsworth, was also affected by *Paradise
Lost*. We cannot be sure. Yet the total influence of Milton, even
when we include his octosyllabics and sonnets, was not profound.
Shelley took from all sources, but he assimilated so thoroughly that
what he produced was almost always distinctly his own. Yet if he
had gone on with Satan's second revolt, using the verse, style, and
diction of *Pater Omnipotens*, he might have left us the great Miltonic
monument of the nineteenth century.

The attraction Satan exerted upon Shelley he likewise exercised
for the same reasons, and at about the same time, on Byron. The
Lucifer that Byron introduced into his blank-verse drama, *Cain, a
Mystery* (1821), is not, however, the Satan of *Paradise Lost*. Byron's
fallen angel is more complex, more modern, far less admirable and
impressive. He is the spirit of negation and doubt; he does not fight,
he sneers. There is little of the archangel ruined about him, no excess of glory obscured, no

> dauntless courage, and considerate pride
> Waiting revenge.

He has, however, the dignity, the pride, the love of freedom, the
scorn of homage to the Almighty, which distinguish Milton's Satan.[1]
The resemblance is strongest in this first description of him:

> If I shrink not from these, the fire-armed angels,
> Why should I quail from him who now approaches?
> Yet — he seems mightier far than them, nor less
> Beauteous, and yet not all as beautiful
> As he hath been, and might be: sorrow seems
> Half of his immortality.[2]

It will be remembered that Byron's poetical commandments
began,

> Thou shalt believe in Milton, Dryden, Pope,[3]

(*Hellas*, 50) sprang from the famous one in *Paradise Lost* (iii. 431–9). The passage
in *Prometheus*, iv. 135–7,

> Our spoil is won,
> Our task is done,
> We are free to dive, or soar, or run,

recalls *Comus*, 1012–13, and in each case the lines that follow contain similar ideas.
One of the choruses in *Hellas* (197–238) seems to employ part of the stanza of the
Nativity (see p. 567 below), and the address *To Harriet* prefixed to *Queen Mab* is in the
measure of the translation from Horace. For Shelley's use of the meter and plan of
Allegro, see pp. 474–5 below.

[1] Cf. *Cain*, I. i. 237–9, 305–8, 383–90, 552–4, II. i. 5–12, ii. 425–46, with *P. L.*, i.
94–124, 589–606, iv. 970–90.

[2] I. i. 91–6.   [3] *Don Juan*, I. ccv.

and that he wrote in the preface to *Cain*, "Since I was twenty I have never read Milton; but I had read him so frequently before, that this may make little difference." The most important effect of these repeated readings lies in the entire conception of the supernatural parts of *Cain*,—the character of Lucifer, the picture of hell, and the vague grandeur and immensity of the unknown worlds which are shown to the rebellious mortal. Something of this will be felt in the following passage, in which as usual the similarity to *Paradise Lost* is heightened by the Miltonic diction and lessened by the loose-jointed flabbiness of Byron's blank verse:

> How silent and how vast are these dim worlds!
> For they seem more than one, and yet more peopled
> Than the huge brilliant luminous orbs which swung
> So thickly in the upper air, that I
> Had deem'd them rather the bright populace
> Of some all unimaginable Heaven,
> Than things to be inhabited themselves,
> But that on drawing near them I beheld
> Their swelling into palpable immensity.[1]

The appeal which Milton's Satan had for Burns, Blake, Shelley, and Byron has not been felt in the same force by the less romantic and revolutionary poets of later times. To be sure, the once-popular *Festus* (1839), which Philip James Bailey began as an imitation of Goethe but made increasingly Miltonic in style and diction through extensive additions, has a Lucifer who recalls the hero of

---

[1] *Cain*, II. ii. 1–9. The following passages from *Cain* recall lines in *Paradise Lost:*

> If he has made,
> As he saith — which I know not, nor believe —
> But, if he made us — he cannot unmake

(I. i. 140–42; cf. *P. L.*, ix. 718–20, and v. 850–66);

> But let him [God]
> Sit on his vast and solitary throne —
> Creating worlds, to make eternity
> Less burthensome to his immense existence
> And unparticipated solitude;
> Let him crowd orb on orb: he is alone

(I. i. 147–52; cf. 471–7, and *P. L.*, viii. 364–5, 404–7);

> All the stars of heaven,
> The deep blue moon of night, lit by an orb
> Which looks a spirit, or a spirit's world —
> The hues of twilight — the Sun's gorgeous coming —
> His setting indescribable . . .
> The forest shade, the green bough, the bird's voice . . .
> All these are nothing, to my eyes and heart,
> Like Adah's face (II. ii. 255–68; cf. *P. L.*, iv. 641–56).

Manfred also was somewhat influenced by *Paradise Lost*. Note especially II. ii. 185–8, III. iv. 336–8, 389–92 (cf. *P. L.*, i. 600–603, 252–5).

Paradise Lost in certain scenes near the end.[1] Indirectly Milton may also be somewhat responsible for the conception of Satan in Meredith's splendid sonnet *Lucifer in Starlight* (1883), George Santayana's nobly-conceived and finely-executed "theological tragedy" *Lucifer* (1899), and similar works. Decidedly inferior to these poems but interesting because of its date, 1915, and its frank plagiarism is the *Armageddon* of Stephen Phillips. The prolog and epilog of this "modern epic drama" are laid in hell, and the first rising of the curtain discloses a kind of pandemonic council with Satan on "a shadowy throne," whence he rules with despotic sway. In the addresses of Beelzebub, Moloch, and Belial that follow, each fallen angel preserves the character given him in *Paradise Lost*, and the lines Belial speaks even have the old deferential oily style. As in Milton, the sentiments of this sensuous, ease-loving spirit are delivered immediately after Moloch's eulogy on war, to which they are somewhat opposed. He begins thus:

> O Lords, I scarcely know, if now I rise
> In order, to address this full conclave,
> I, Lord of Lies; nor would I seem to slight
> The ancient, grand prerogative of Force.

If the style of the poem owes anything to *Paradise Lost*, it is in these lines:

> Spirit, to me alone inferior.

> Inaction is the bread of mutiny.

> But the main field and region of grand war
> Disputed lies, an indecisive plain.

> Splendid is Force, but solitary, falls
> And self-defeated, unrelieved by lies.

[1] Note particularly section L of the fiftieth-anniversary edition, and compare A. D. McKillop's thesis (Harvard, 1920), *The Spasmodic School in Victorian Poetry*. Bailey's *Angel World*, *The Mystic*, and *Spiritual Legend* are, in diction and in the extensive use of strange proper nouns, astonishingly Miltonic for poems published so late as 1850 and 1855.

THE INFLUENCE OF PARADISE LOST AS SHOWN
IN THE MORE IMPORTANT TYPES OF
BLANK–VERSE POETRY

THE influence of *Paradise Lost* upon its early admirers and upon the principal later writers who were affected by it has now been studied in considerable detail. In order that the reader might understand the method of determining this influence and be able to test for himself the validity of the conclusions reached, numerous passages have been quoted and long lists of words, phrases, references, and borrowings have been introduced. Dull as much of this matter is, its importance in the present connection, together with the significance of the authors studied, has, it is to be hoped, given a certain interest to many a tedious page. To continue this process, however, through John Duncan's dreary *Essay on Happiness*, W. H. Drummond's dull *Pleasures of Benevolence*, or the anonymous stupid *Wisdom*, through the twenty-five books of Cottle's absurd *Cambria* or the thirty of Glover's unreadable *Athenaid*, were to plant brambles in the thorny path of learning. The limits both of patience and of space require that only the more important of these minor works be considered at all, and they but briefly; for, even after the hundreds of still-born or forgotten short pieces have been passed over, there remains a mass of blank verse that looms before us like a huge purgatorial mountain. Few of the works that enter into this pile can be made to take on any of the fascination of romance if they are to keep much of their own character; yet, by arranging the poems according to types and following the development of each type, we may learn not a little literary history and gain some much-needed insight into what our forefathers thought and liked. In the following chapters, accordingly, the longer of the remaining poems that show the influence of *Paradise Lost* will be studied along with other pieces that belong to the same class.

Obviously, no sharp line can be drawn between philosophical, religious, technical, reflective, and descriptive poems. Intellectual speculation, religious emotion, comment on human life, and description of natural scenery abound in all literature and sometimes form the most significant parts of works into which they are introduced incidentally; yet if we ask ourselves whether a work is primarily concerned with religious teaching, technical instruction, or philosophical speculation, we can usually determine under what class it falls. To continue this separating process, however, so as to collect all the philosophical, didactic, technical, or descriptive passages of any length to be found in the poetry of the time, would be an interminable task that would defeat its own end. This has not been attempted, but it is hoped that no important poem or part of a poem has been overlooked.

CHAPTER XII

MEDITATIVE AND DESCRIPTIVE POETRY

On the whole, the most interesting of all the forgotten verse of this neglected century, the most readable and from the standpoint of literary development the most significant, is to be found among descriptive poems. These include, it should be observed, the greatest unrimed pieces of the period, *The Seasons, The Task*, and *The Prelude;* and in them may be traced the course of two of the more notable movements in modern life and literature, — the development of the love of nature and of the power to express that love in poetry. These two things we commonly think of as synonymous, and thus do serious injustice to our earlier writers. Yet we know that even to-day, when nature-worship has become a fad, there are many mute, inglorious Wordsworths, as well as writers who give very inadequate expression to their love of the out-of-doors. How much more difficult must the writing of descriptive verse have been at a time when the leading poets of the day could find no better words for the miracle of spring than "Blushing Flora paints th' enamelled ground"![1]

There is no warrant for thinking that, because an author employs conventional phraseology and a turgid style, he does not feel the beauties of which he writes. Who would guess from the poems alone the intense love of nature which lay behind Wordsworth's *Descriptive Sketches* and the odes of Gray? Yet much had been done before these men wrote. Wordsworth, like Burns, was the culmination of a long line of development, of unconscious divergence from accepted forms, of experimentation, failure, and partial success. What would either of them have done had he been born a century earlier? What might *The Seasons* have been had it come at the end instead of the beginning of its century? The world will never be sufficiently grateful for the forgotten men who drained bogs, felled trees, removed stumps and boulders, ploughed, harrowed, and fertilized the soil, to add new fields to the pleasant land of poesie, — fields which Wordsworth, Shelley, and Tennyson found ready for their use. If we keep in mind the great cause which these unknown men were helping to advance, if we look for it behind what they said to what they prob-

[1] Pope, *Windsor Forest*, 38; Thomson, *Lines on Marlefield*, 20.

ably felt, and if we are on the watch for the growth of the faculty of close observation and of true and fluent expression, we shall find not a little to interest us in their productions, faulty and dull as they are.

Thomson's *Seasons* is almost the first long descriptive poem in English. There had, to be sure, been many pastorals and a few pieces like *Coopers Hill* and *Windsor Forest;* but in them nature, instead of being the center of interest, was little more than a pleasant background or setting for man and his works. Furthermore, they did not attempt to picture the real country, but dealt with artificial nature in a conventionalized way.[1] Thomson, on the contrary, showed a real enthusiasm for the out-of-doors and for country life, and described them with more reality and at much greater length than had any previous poet. Since, then, *The Seasons* was practically the first and for a time the only important descriptive poem, and since it remained throughout the century not merely the greatest work of its kind but the most popular of any kind, it naturally became the most potent influence in this style of writing. The best evidence of such influence is that Thomson made blank verse the accepted vehicle for nature poetry, and even fastened upon that poetry his own turgid diction and contorted style. This was a particularly unfortunate legacy, for, to be effective, nature poetry must be natural. In epic and didactic works a certain amount of bombast is tolerable, and even in descriptions of floods, storms, and other unusual phenomena a heightened style is not unsuitable; but a view from a hill-top or a twilight walk along a river loses its charm when described in the manner of Dr. Johnson.

As a matter of fact, turgidity of style and diction forms the principal defect of the nature poetry of the century, and on this account particular attention will be paid to its gradual elimination. The process was for several reasons more gradual than might be expected. In the first place, the time was anything but revolutionary; poets were conservative and usually conventional, they did what others had done and the public was pleased. Then, too, pomposity and stylistic contortions gave a kind of poetic covering to what was really prose. But even a poetic conception would hardly have seemed poetic if expressed with the simplicity of *Tintern Abbey.* For any such plainness the poets and the public were alike unready. The development was, to be sure, towards a more natural and more conversa-

[1] This is probably the reason why the heroic couplet was little used by the best descriptive poets of the eighteenth century. It had been developed only along the line of terseness and brilliance, and in this field connoted work such as Pope did. To picture the country truly and movingly in couplets, either the ability or the courage was lacking.

tional style, that is, towards prose; yet the timid versifiers of the time were so anxious not to be prosaic that they adopted what they regarded as poetic manner. Besides, love of the country was by no means so common in the days of Pope and Johnson as it is to-day, and men often wrote about nature without much enthusiasm or much knowledge of the subject. Under these conditions conventionality flourished and the contorted and grandiose expressions sanctioned by *The Seasons*, and in a way by *Paradise Lost*, yielded very slowly before the advances of simplicity.

The influence of Thomson made itself felt almost immediately. Within a few months of the publication of his *Winter* (1726), David Mallet — or Malloch, as his name had been in Scotland — composed an unrimed piece of a thousand lines which he called *The Excursion*, a misleading title, for Mallet meant by it "a short excursive survey of the Earth and Heavens," including descriptions of storms, earthquakes, volcanic eruptions, and the like.[1] The poem was undoubtedly suggested by Thomson's work, which had been written while the two young Scots were rooming together. It is destitute of inspiration and is weighed down by exaggerated Miltonisms of style and language. For these, however, Mallet did not have to go to Thomson, since he had already employed them five years before in a short piece which confessedly imitated "the greatest of all the English poets."[2] Furthermore, many of the phrases in *The Excursion* testify to a considerable familiarity with Milton.[3]

Some years later, in 1747, Mallet published a second unrimed poem, *Amyntor and Theodora, or the Hermit*, a variation of the old story of the hermit who saves the life of a young man only to find that the youth is the son of his greatest enemy and the beloved of his own lost daughter. Later the daughter is recovered and all ends happily. The best passages, like this one (which gives far too favor-

---

[1] See the summary prefixed to the poem in the "corrected" edition of his works (1759), i. 66. About the same time another of Thomson's fellow-countrymen, Dr. John Armstrong, was busying himself with a winter-piece in imitation of Shakespeare, which, however, was not printed until 1770 (in his *Miscellanies*, i. 147–58). It contains realistic pictures of the season, but has slight value as poetry.

[2] See Mallet's letter to John Ker, Dec. 21, 1721 (*Europ. Mag.*, 1793, xxiii. 413), which also settles the date of the poem. For the piece itself, *The Transfiguration*, see *ib.* xxv. 52.

[3] For example, "hoar Hill" (1st ed., 1728, p. 13, cf. *Allegro*, 55), "quick-glancing" (p. 17, cf. *P. L.*, vii. 405), "void profound" (p. 35, cf. *P. L.*, ii. 438), "prime Orb" (p. 60, cf. *P. L.*, iv. 592, of the sun in each case), "Star amid the Train of Night" (p. 64, cf. *P. L.*, v. 166). The later edition, which is considerably enlarged, contains "the clouds assume Their gayest liveries" (*Works*, 1759, i. 70, cf. *Allegro*, 62), "by winds sublim'd" (*ib.* 85, cf. *P. L.*, i. 235, of a volcano in each case), etc.

able an impression of the poem as a whole), are those that describe
the wild scenery of the Hebrides, where the story is laid:

> From this steep,
> Diffus'd immense in rowling prospect lay
> The northern deep. Amidst, from space to space,
> Her numerous isles, rich gems of *Albion's* crown,
> As slow th' ascending mists disperse in air,
> Shoot gradual from her bosom: and beyond,
> Like distant clouds blue-floating on the verge
> Of evening skies, break forth the dawning hills.
> A thousand landschapes! barren some and bare,
> Rock pil'd on rock amazing up to heaven,
> Of horrid grandeur: some with sounding ash,
> Or oak broad-shadowing, or the spiry growth
> Of waving pine high-plum'd, and all beheld
> More lovely in the sun's adorning beam;
> Who now, fair-rising o'er yon eastern cliff
> The vernal verdure tinctures gay with gold.[1]

Thomson's influence also made itself felt in the four books of
James Ralph's *Night* (1728), each of which is a nocturnal picture, in
conventional style and language, of the more obvious features of
one of the seasons. Ralph inclines to couplet prosody and to a
style but slightly Miltonic. He had been somewhat closer to *Paradise Lost* the year before in his *Tempest, or the Terrors of Death*, an
uninspired moralized description of a storm at sea.[2]

Formal description of nature plays practically no part in Somervile's *Chace* (1735), but many incidental touches reveal the keen eye
and the hearty love for the out-of-doors which might be expected of
a country gentleman devoted to hunting. We are shown the hares,
for instance, "'mong Beds of Rushes hid," sitting "wary, and close"
near the "matted Blade," listening "intent . . . with one Ear erect";
or we watch them as

> In the long Grass they skulk, or shrinking creep
> Among the wither'd Leaves.

We follow the hounds as they range "in the rough bristly Stubbles,"
or in the copse,

> Thick with entangling Grass, or prickly Furze;

---

[1] ii. 76–91; see also iii. 359–69. The references are to the revised version of the
poem as published in his *Works*, i. 141–2, 173.

[2] In the preface to *Night* he discusses *Paradise Lost* and its verse at some length, and
on the title-page of *The Tempest* quotes four lines from it. For his epic *Zeuma*, see
p. 280 below.

and, "where ancient Alders shade The deep still Pool," we see them
sweep the "Morning Dews"

> that from their Feet besprinkling drop
> Dispers'd, and leave a Track oblique behind.[1]

That the inability to write simple, fluent blank verse makes
eighteenth-century poetry a very inadequate representation of the
feelings of its authors is illustrated in the work of John Dyer. Dyer
was a true poet, not great or particularly virile, but a man of fine
sensitiveness to the beauties of the external world, and of considerable
skill in verse. The following lines record the impression that the
Roman ruins made in 1740 upon an earlier Childe Harold:

> Fall'n, fall'n, a silent Heap; her Heroes all
> Sunk in their Urns; behold the Pride of Pomp,
> The Throne of Nations fall'n; obscur'd in dust;
> Ev'n yet Majestical: The solemn Scene
> Elates the soul, while now the rising Sun
> Flames on the Ruins, in the purer air
> Tow'ring aloft, upon the glitt'ring plain,
> Like broken Rocks, a vast circumference;
> Rent Palaces, crush'd Columns, rifted Moles,
> Fanes roll'd on Fanes, and Tombs on buried Tombs.[2]

These lines are from a forgotten poem. Their author's *Grongar Hill*
has preserved him a place in the anthologies, and his *Fleece* is known,
at least by name, to many. Why, then, has this unwarranted neglect
fallen upon *The Ruins of Rome?* The explanation is in part to be
found in lines like these:

> Swift is the Flight of Wealth; unnumber'd Wants,
> Brood of voluptousness, cry out aloud
> Necessity, and seek the splendid Bribe;
> The citron Board; the Bowl emboss'd with Gems,
> And tender Foliage, wildly wreath'd around,
> Of seeming Ivy, by that artful Hand,
> *Corinthian Thericles;* whate'er is known
> Of rarest acquisition; *Tyrian* Garbs,
> *Neptunian Albion's* high testaceous Food.[3]

"How could the author of the previous passage have written this
one?" we exclaim. But how could he, living when he did and not
being a great poet, have done otherwise? He admired the blank

---

[1] The *Chace*, ii. 32, 30, 213, 41-2, 58; iii. 41-2; iv. 380-81, 416-18. On Somervile,
see pp. 361-3 below.

[2] *Ruins of Rome* (1740), p. 2.

[3] *Ib.* 26. The lines that immediately follow the first passage quoted are almost as
bad as these.

verse of *Paradise Lost* and tried to imitate it, and the only other unrimed poems that he knew, *Cyder* and *The Seasons*, had the same
defects as his own. Although his taste was in the main excellent, he,
like most of his contemporaries, undoubtedly enjoyed an inflated
style and a turgid diction and found little to object to in the lines
just quoted.

Dyer possessed a genuine though slender vein of poetry, and
might, had he been born fifty years later, have produced something
of 'power to live and serve the future hour'; but he had fallen on evil
days for a writer of blank verse. Like other descriptive poets, he is
best when he is least Miltonic, — but he is usually Miltonic. Practically every characteristic that distinguishes *Paradise Lost* is annoy-
ingly in evidence in his verse, — inversion, apposition, the use of an
adjective for an adverb or a substantive or of words in their original
but obsolete senses, and a fondness for series of proper names or for
adjectives made from such names by the addition of *-ean*.[1]

Another cultivated Englishman who sought to record in blank
verse the impressions made upon him by travels on the continent
was George Keate. The title of Keate's first unrimed poem, *Ancient
and Modern Rome* (written in 1755), recalls that of the first part of
Thomson's *Liberty*, "Ancient and Modern Italy compared," but in
contents it is much nearer to the *Ruins of Rome*. Like Dyer's work,
it is a descriptive poem interspersed with reflections, but here the
similarity ends, for the oft-invoked "Muse" was deaf to Keate's
call. Nor does his epic fragment *The Helvetiad* (written in 1756),
which Voltaire dissuaded him from finishing, give any evidence of
her visitations. Yet she seems to have taken some interest in his
nature poem, *The Alps* (1763), an inflated, formal, stilted work, but
one that does reveal a knowledge and love of the mountains among
which Keate lived for many years. It may be that few modern
readers will derive much pleasure from the piece; but any one who
goes through it attentively can hardly help feeling that its author
wrote with his heart in the subject and his eye on the object, and
that the defects of expression were to be expected at a time when
writers were inexperienced in describing the wild and sublime in
nature. Keate's work is notable for its observation rather than for
its poetry; yet it contains somewhat impressive pictures of Alpine
forests, rivers, avalanches, snow-storms, and thunder-storms. This
is one of his best passages:

[1] Dyer's octosyllabics, *Grongar Hill* and *The Country Walk*, are almost entirely
descriptive; and his blank verse, *The Fleece*, shows in many single lines and in a few
long passages an appreciation of romantic scenery, of the ocean, and particularly of the
English landscape that is much like Thomson's. See below, pp. 446–7, 367–72.

> These as they glide along survey their banks
> With mountains circled that appear to bend
> Beneath the woods they bear. The mournful Larch
> Its drooping foliage hangs: the stately Pines,
> Their boughs together mix'd, in close array
> (Wedg'd like the ancient Phalanx), from the axe
> Rear their tall heads secure; on craggy cliffs
> Rooted, or over Precipices dread
> Waving their umbrage broad.[1]

It is unnecessary to dwell on the Miltonic character of these lines, but it should be remembered that we have no means of determining how much of this character may have been derived from *Paradise Lost* and how much from *The Seasons*. There seems to be no debt to the *Night Thoughts*, though Keate was an intimate friend and correspondent of Young's. One other matter should be noticed, — Keate was fortunate in his subject: the Miltonic style is much better adapted to describing the Alps than to teaching the care of sheep. We have every reason to believe that, if he had chosen to picture a pastoral English scene, he would have used the same language and style which he employed in describing an avalanche, and would thereby have become ridiculous.

Yet there was at least one writer who used simple language to describe simple things. Towards the middle of the century Dr. John Brown wrote an enthusiastic letter about a visit to Keswick and a twenty-line description of a moonlight scene there. For conveying a sense of the hushed awe and magic of a moonlight night, this fragment is unsurpassed in the unrimed verse of the century; indeed, as a rendering of a mood of nature it stands quite by itself. I therefore quote it all:

> Now sunk the Sun, now Twilight sunk, and Night
> Rode in her zenith; nor a passing breeze
> Sigh'd to the groves, which in the midnight air
> Stood motionless, and in the peaceful floods
> Inverted hung: For now the billow slept
> Along the shore, nor heav'd the deep, but spread
> A shining mirror to the Moon's pale orb,
> Which, dim and waining, o'er the shadowy clifts,
> The solemn woods and spiry mountain-tops
> Her glimmering faintness threw: Now every eye,
> Oppress'd with toil, was drown'd in deep repose;
> Save that the unseen shepherd in his watch,

---

[1] *Poetical Works* (1781), ii. 63–4. *The Alps* was praised by the *Critical Review* (xv. 390–91). Keate's romanticism is also seen in his descriptive elegy on Netley Abbey (1764). His two volumes of prose *Sketches from Nature* (1779) reached a fifth edition by 1802, besides being reprinted in America and translated into French.

> Propt on his crook, stood list'ning by the fold,
> And gaz'd the starry vault and pendant moon;
> Nor voice nor sound broke on the deep serene,
> But the soft murmur of swift-gushing rills,
> Forth-issuing from the mountain's distant steep,
> (Unheard till now, and now scarce heard) proclaim'd
> All things at rest, and imag'd the still voice
> Of quiet whispering to the ear of Night.[1]

Except for the sound of streams unheard by day, these lines reveal no unusual closeness of observation, but in expression they are surprisingly simple and direct without being prosaic. Yet they are not quite free from what seem to be Miltonisms, — "inverted hung," "nor heav'd the deep," "gaz'd the starry vault," "the deep serene"; and there is one probable borrowing, "her glimmering faintness threw." [2]

We have, however, been anticipating somewhat, for between the work of Dyer and Keate came the blank verse of the Warton brothers. The Warton family, the father and his two sons, played no small part in spreading the enthusiasm for Milton which characterized the middle of the eighteenth century. They admired *Paradise Lost* and borrowed many phrases from it, but they belonged to a group of poets who were attracted to lyric measures and made slight use of the couplet or of blank verse (with which the most distinguished of them, Gray, was not in sympathy[3]). It is noteworthy, in view of the Wartons' enthusiasm for Milton, that the father wrote only four short pieces of blank verse, and that his sons produced but a few hundred lines of it, composing most of these in their schooldays. Indeed, the only unrimed poem of any length that the elder brother, Joseph, published was practically his first poetic venture, *The Enthusiast, or the Lover of Nature*, which he wrote in 1740. The title excites hopes that are not satisfied, for the poem is mainly a polemic on the superiority of nature to art. The descriptive passages are nearly all conventional and bookish, indicating little close observation and almost none of the love of the out-of-doors which the author undoubtedly felt. Perhaps the following lines are an exception; at least, they reveal unusual interest in wild scenery:

> Ye green-rob'd Dryads, oft at dusky eve
> By wondering shepherds seen, to forests brown,
> To unfrequented meads, and pathless wilds,

---

[1] Richard Cumberland, *Odes* (1776), prefatory, 5; reprinted in Anderson's *British Poets* (1795), x. 887.
[2] Cf. *P. L.*, iv. 609 (of the moon in each case).
[3] Norton Nicholls's "Reminiscences," in Gray's *Letters* (ed. Tovey), ii. 280.

> Lead me from gardens deck'd with art's vain pomps. . .
> . . . . let me choose some pine-topt precipice
> Abrupt and shaggy, whence a foamy stream,
> Like Anio, tumbling roars; or some bleak heath,
> Where straggling stands the mournful juniper,
> Or yew-tree scath'd; while in clear prospect round,
> From the grove's bosom spires emerge, and smoke
> In bluish wreaths ascends, ripe harvests wave,
> Low, lonely cottages, and ruin'd tops
> Of Gothic battlements appear, and streams
> Beneath the sun-beams twinkle.[1]

This love for the wild and bleak aspects of nature is carried to an absurd extreme in the *Pleasures of Melancholy*, which Thomas Warton, author of the *History of English Poetry*, composed in his seventeenth year, 1745. The young bard is perversely determined not to be comfortable. He shuns "ambrosial blooms," "broider'd meads," and "Mirth's mad shouts," preferring, he declares, to go with Contemplation

> to solemn glooms
> Congenial with my soul; to cheerless shades,
> To ruin'd seats, to twilight cells and bow'rs.[2]

In his love of horrors he anticipates Ann Radcliffe and "Monk" Lewis:

> But when the world
> Is clad in Midnight's raven-colour'd robe,
> 'Mid hollow charnel let me watch the flame
> Of taper dim, shedding a livid glare
> O'er the wan heaps; while airy voices talk
> Along the glimm'ring walls.[3]

All this comes as a surprise from the genial author of *Oxford Ale*, who was notoriously fond of his ease and of the good things of life. Indeed, he protests too much. Like most eighteenth-century poets of melancholy, he was toying with a feeling of which he knew little. Then, as always, there were of course persons, like Gray and Young, who were inclined to depression; but most of the literature of gloom is conventional and has no more basis in actual experience than had the sonnet sequences of the Elizabethans. A large number of the odes addressed to Despair, Horror, Night, and their sister spirits

---

[1] Lines 1–4, 29–38. Joseph Warton's four other blank-verse pieces seem Miltonic, but the only interest attaching to them is that three are occasional, one having been recited to the king when he was on a visit to Winchester College.

[2] Lines 25, 27, 77, 17–19. The references are to the revised version of the poem as published in the *Poetical Works* (Oxford, 1802, i. 68–95).

[3] Lines 42–7.

were the products of normal and what are termed "reasonably happy" individuals, who wrote them as a society girl tries roughing it or slumming, — partly to be in the fashion and partly to vary the monotony of ease and comfort with some of the thrills of distress. No one who has actually faced horrors, or knows what real depression is, talks about the *pleasures* of melancholy or writes as Warton did:

> Few know that elegance of soul refin'd,
> Whose soft sensation feels a quicker joy
> From Melancholy's scenes, than the dull pride
> Of tasteless splendor and magnificence
> Can e'er afford.[1]

There are not many unusual words in the *Pleasures of Melancholy*, and the style, though stilted, is less inflated than that of most blank verse of the time. The influence of Milton appears chiefly in the numerous phrases borrowed from his works (most of them from his minor poems),[2] a feature that is also noticeable though less striking in Joseph Warton's *Enthusiast*. Each piece reveals some of the framework of *Allegro* and *Penseroso*.

We know from his other poems that Thomas Warton really cared for nature, but from his treatise on melancholy we should hardly suspect as much. Of its three hundred and fifteen lines, these eight sound the least conventional and the most like personal observation:

> Yet not ungrateful is the morn's approach,
> When dropping wet she comes, and clad in clouds,
> While thro' the damp air scowls the louring south,
> Blackening the landscape's face, that grove and hill
> In formless vapours undistinguish'd swim. . . .
>   . . . . the waving elms . . .
> Are mute, nor echo with the clamors hoarse
> Of rooks rejoicing on their airy boughs;
> While to the shed the dripping poultry crowd.[3]

But just before this passage is one which shows how imperfectly Warton distinguished between the conventional and the true:

> Blooming morn's approach,
> Ev'n then, in youthful pride of opening May,
> When from the portals of the saffron east
> She sheds fresh roses, and ambrosial dews.

To Thomas Warton has been ascribed *Five Pastoral Eclogues*, in Miltonic blank verse, dealing with the horrors of war. If anything

---

[1] Lines 92–6. There were many eighteenth-century writers who, like Warton, enjoyed their melancholy and plumed themselves on it.

[2] See below, Appendix A.   [3] Lines 135–46.

can be more intolerably trite, conventional, and dull than this work, which appeared in 1745, it is the *Four Pastoral Essays* of Thomas Stratford, "written chiefly in the year 1756" and published at Dublin in 1770. From the preface to the *Eclogues* we learn that the author "endeavour'd to imitate the simplicity of the ancients," and it must be admitted that both in style and in language the poems are much simpler than most of those published at the time. Stratford's trite "Essays" have not even this virtue, for their language is often pompous; yet on one account the reader may prefer them to the "Eclogues," — there is one less of them.[1] These volumes illustrate the difficulty poets had in freeing themselves from the conventions associated with a type of literature like the pastoral. When the poems were rimed the task was all the harder, as any one may see by contrasting the admirably simple, natural blank verse of John Scott's descriptive poem, *Amwell*, with the couplets of his Moral and of his Amoebaean "Eclogues," in which close observation is concealed by the stilted poetic diction, the frigid conventionality, and the monotonous cadences that went with the rimed pastoral.

Until the publication of *Amwell* in 1776, the pleasantest descriptive blank verse written by any of Thomson's followers came from the pen of the gentle Michael Bruce. One may doubt whether Bruce would ever have become a great poet, but there can be no question as to the beauty of his character or the love for the Scottish country that his poems reveal. As the young school-teacher, not yet of age, lay dying of consumption, he composed a narrative and descriptive work of some six hundred lines which he called *Lochleven*. Marred though it is by the constant use of conventional poetic diction,[2] the style is, for the time, unusually natural and flowing. Bruce usually dwells upon the more obvious beauties of the landscape, but he also sees

> The patient heron, and the bittern dull,
> Deep-sounding in the base.[3]

Lines like the following, when composed as early as 1766, are notable for several reasons:

---

[1] Stratford showed his admiration for Milton by translating the first book of *Paradise Lost* (which he thought greater than Homer or Virgil, see p. 21, n. 3, above) into Greek in 1770, and by using in his blank-verse *Fontenoy* (1784?) the involved style and "bloated kind of diction" which mark the *Essays*. Only one of the nine books of this last work appears to have been published (see *Mo. Rev.*, 1784, lxxi. 95-8), and this I have not seen.

[2] The diction is seldom learned or Miltonic, however. It is language like this that is objectionable: "To obvious swain . . . She'd bring the beauteous spoils [flowers] . . . ev'ry herb . . . That paints the robe of Spring . . . every warbler in the vernal wood" (*Works*, Edin., 1865, p. 182).   [3] *Ib.* 193.

> While twilight meek,
> Enrob'd in mist, slow-sailing thro' the air,
> Silent and still, on ev'ry closéd flow'r
> Shed drops nectareous; and around the fields
> No noise was heard, save where the whisp'ring reeds
> Wav'd to the breeze, or in the dusky air
> The slow-wing'd crane mov'd heav'ly o'er the lee,
> And shrilly clamour'd as he sought his nest.[1]

Three or four years earlier Bruce had written for a college literary society another unrimed piece, *The Last Day*, which was clearly inspired by "Night's seraphic bard, immortal Young."[2] It is more formal and Miltonic than *Lochleven* and by no means so good.

The volume which Joseph Sympson, a follower of Thomson, had the courage to issue in 1781, with the title *The Beauties of Spring*, though it furnished two lines for one of Wordsworth's Duddon sonnets,[3] seems to have been no more significant than the forty pages of vague, conventional, sentimentalized descriptions that make up S. J. Pratt's *Landscapes in Verse* (1785). There is also much of the uninspired and conventional, as well as much of the hackneyed machinery of gloom, in Henry Headley's *Invocation to Melancholy* (1786), although genuine imaginative power appears in many of Headley's sombre, sonorous lines, — these, for example:

> Lo, at her call New Zealand's wastes arise!
> Casting their shadows far along the main,
> Whose brows, cloud-cap'd in joyless majesty,
> No human foot hath trod since time began;
> Here deathlike silence ever-brooding dwells,
> Save when the watching sailor startled hears,
> Far from his native land at darksome night,
> The shrill-ton'd petrel, or the penguin's voice,
> That skim their trackless flight on lonely wing,
> Through the bleak regions of a nameless main.[4]

In the days of Gray and Cowper several types of literature flourished which have since either fallen into disuse or wholly disappeared. One of these is the topographical poem, in which the reader is taken to the top of a hill, shown the surrounding country, and entertained with an account of such country-seats as are visible and of historical or legendary events connected with the neighborhood. Among the

---

[1] *Ib.* 191.   [2] *Ib.* 196.

[3] No. vi. Wordsworth, in his note to this sonnet, says that Sympson "was educated . . . at Hawkeshead school: his poems are little known, but they contain passages of splendid description." Knight identifies him with the "Pastor" of *The Excursion*. I know the *Beauties* only from the *Critical Review*, lii. 201–3.

[4] *Poetical Works* (in T. Park's *British Poets*, 1808, vol. xli), p. 15.

best things in *The Task* are some two hundred lines in the first book which might easily be detached from the rest to form a poem of this kind.[1] The first and most notable example of the type, however, seems to have been the delightful *Coopers Hill* (1642) of Sir John Denham, which was much admired in the period we are studying. The second in point of time and of importance was Dyer's octo-syllabic *Grongar Hill* (1726), which, however, is lyric rather than descriptive. These two pieces are in rime;[2] and, as they are much earlier, rather different in plan, and in other respects unlike the blank-verse loco-descriptive works, they had little apparent influ-ence on the type or on its popularity.

For in the forty years following 1767 the unrimed topographical poem enjoyed such a vogue that for a considerable period in the latter part of the century practically all the descriptive blank verse written was of this kind. The *Gentleman's Magazine* complained in 1788 that readers "have been used to see the Muses labouring up . . . many hills since Cooper's and Grongar, and some gentle Bard reclin-ing on almost every mole-hill."[3] One thing, at least, may be said of the form, — it was not artificial. Persons who live near a hill are constantly climbing it for the sake of the view; and what is more natural, if one writes verses, than to attempt to picture a favorite scene? Now, since naturalness was what descriptive poetry most needed, the spontaneity of these pictures may explain why they con-stitute the most pleasing of the early descriptions of rural scenery. It is also worth noting that such pieces are typical of their time in dwelling upon the larger and more obvious beauties of rural scenery. Many persons enjoy the view from a hill who see no charm in the winding country road that takes them thither, in weeds blossom-ing by crumbling stone-walls, or in a lonely marsh at twilight. We have heard very little thus far about the quieter beauties of nature; it is the sweet and pretty or the grand and sublime that have been dwelt on. This does not mean that no one felt the simpler beauties, but that poets had not thought of writing about them.

Although the vogue of the topographical poem seems to have begun in 1767,[4] there is nothing about the work which was published

---

[1] i. 141–366.   [3] lviii. 151.

[2] For later rimed poems of this class, see below, Appendix C A.

[4] On some accounts W. H. Draper's *Morning Walk, or City Encompass'd* (1751), belongs in this class and is thus the earliest unrimed poem of the kind; yet, as there is no hill and practically no description of nature in the piece, which is devoted mainly to the evils of gin, it hardly belongs here. It is, rather, a pedestrian survey — extremely pedestrian from the esthetic point of view — of the outskirts of London, described in the blank verse of one of Draper's favorite works, *Paradise Lost* (see the *Morning Walk,* pp. xi–xiii, 14, 27, 34, 39, 69, 72–3). James Fortescue's *Pomery-Hill,* 1754 (see *Gent.*

on that date to invite imitation. It is, in truth, a stilted, dreary production, Richard Jago's *Edge-Hill*, in which, as its sub-title announces, "the Rural Prospect" is "delineated and moralized" through four books![1] Of moralizing there is certainly no lack, but the rural prospect is hardly Jago's chief concern. He is interested rather in picturing country estates, in complimenting the gentry, and in describing the mines and manufactures of the region.

The "Muse," he writes, cannot

> Forget her Shenstone, in the youthful Toil
> Associate; whose bright Dawn of Genius oft
> Smooth'd my incondite Verse;[2]

yet she seems to have no memory of Somervile, who performed the same function, and who through this assistance, as well as through his example in *The Chace*, may have had some effect upon the blank verse of *Edge-Hill*. Jago's pompous style and language are ill adapted to his subject and are manifestly influenced by *Paradise Lost*. Proof of this influence will be found in his borrowings from Milton's work,[3] and in his oratorio, *Adam, or the Fatal Disobedience*,

Mag., xxiv. 245), and the anonymous *Cooper's Hill*, 1766? (see *Crit. Rev.*, xxii. 380–81), I have not seen. *Clackshugh, a Poem in Miltonic Verse* (1755), by an exciseman named Daniel, is a tumid, conventional hill-poem of two hundred lines which gives some account of mining.

[1] This sub-title might well serve for almost all the descriptive pieces of the century; for not only were the bards of the day, like their descendants in America a few generations later, consumed with a desire to "moralize their song," but critics and readers were practically unanimous in emphasizing the necessity of obvious didacticism in all serious poetry. As a result, *The Seasons* is "moralized" throughout, and *The Task*, though remembered chiefly for its descriptive passages, is at least three-quarters didactic. Perhaps most writers felt with Ogilvie, when he "indulged himself very freely in the vein of moral sentiment arising naturally from the subject," that it was a difficult matter "to give a sensible mind entertainment, in the perusal of a descriptive poem of any length" (*Paradise*, 1769, advertisement).

[2] iii. 351–3. The references are all to the first edition, which differs considerably from the one published by Chalmers, presumably the last.

[3] For example, "Guardian Spirits, which round *Paradise* Perform'd their nightly Watch" (i. 3–4, cf. *P. L.*, ii. 412–13, iv. 684–5, 778–80, etc.); rivers that "further still their humid Train . . . drew . . . And in the tender Ooze . . . Fretted" their "winding Track" (i. 102–6, cf. *P. L.*, vii. 302–6); references to Uriel, who upon the sun's "Evening-Beam to *Paradise* Came gliding down" and "on its sloping Ray To his bright Charge return'd"(i. 507–10, cf. *P. L.*, iv. 555–6, 589–91), and to Michael, who "on Eden's Hill" removed the "film" from Adam's eyes "and purg'd his visual Nerve To see Things yet unform'd" (i. 510–13, cf. *P. L.*, xi. 377–8, 411–15). The lines,

> Hence fabling Poets feign'd
> Th' enchanted Castle, and its cursed Train
> Of Goblins, Furies, and Chimeras dire!

(i. 406–8), recall *Comus*, 513–17, and *P. L.*, ii. 628. At iii. 43–4 Jago has put within quotation-marks "But Cloud instead and ever-during Night Surround it" (cf. *P. L.*, iii. 45–6), and at iv. 13 "With Song of early Birds" (cf. *P. L.*, iv. 651).

compiled from the Paradise Lost (1784). Conventional poetic diction abounds in *Edge-Hill:* "richly-painted Flow'rs," in "Flora's Liv'ry gaily dight," form an "embroider'd Verge of various Dyes"; a nunnery is a "chaste Asylum to the female Train," and coal "the crumbly Rock" or (in later editions) "the sable rock inflammable." [1] Yet, dull as the poem is, refreshing breezes occasionally blow across its arid wastes fraught with the fragrance of such unconscious humor as,

> The Scissars' double Shaft,
> Useless apart, in social Union join'd,
> Each aiding each! Emblem how beautiful
> Of happy nuptial Leagues! [2]

More typical of Jago at his best is a picture like this:

> There, white with Flocks, and, in her num'rous Herds
> Exulting, CHADSUNT's Pastures, large, and fair
> Salute the Sight, and witness to the Fame
> Of LICHFIELD's mitred Saint. The furzy Heaths
> Succeed; close Refuge of the tim'rous Hare,
> Or prowling Fox, but Refuge insecure!
> From their dark Covert oft the Hunter-Train
> Rouse them unwilling, and, o'er Hill, and Dale,
> With wild, tumultuous Joy, their Steps pursue. [3]

This passage might well have been taken from among the poorer of the four hundred and forty-six lines of *Amwell*, which John Scott published the year the American colonies declared their independence. Nothing could be less suggestive of "war, or battle's sound," or even of "the busy hum of men," than this quiet, simple pastoral which breathes of the Quaker faith, the pensiveness, and the abundant leisure of its lovable author. Scott finds his joy in gazing upon "smooth vales by winding streams Divided,"

> romantic farms,
> And humble cots of happy shepherd swains;
> Delightful habitations! with the song
> Of birds melodious charm'd, and bleat of flocks
> From upland pastures heard, and low of kine
> Grazing the rushy mead, and mingled sounds
> Of falling waters and of whisp'ring winds. [4]

His "roving sight" loves to range

> Where frequent hedge-rows intersect rich fields
> Of many a different form and different hue,
> Bright with ripe corn, or green with grass, or dark
> With clover's purple bloom. [5]

---

[1] ii. 40, i. 547, ii. 28; ii. 382, iii. 502. [2] iii. 551-4.
[3] ii. 94-102.   [4] Lines 255-6, 259-65.   [5] Lines 173-6.

These last lines show that, although he usually dwells upon the broad, obvious aspects of the familiar English landscape so dear to him, he also feels some of its shyer, more evanescent beauties. Elsewhere he mentions the "slender group of airy elm," the "walnut's gloomy breadth of boughs," the "willow groves . . . with trembling tufts Of osier intermix'd," the "linden pale, and blossom'd thorn Breathing mild fragrance," and the "rich perfume" of "blooming beans." [1]

In such pictures of nature and in most other respects *Amwell* is far better than *Edge-Hill*, and yet the two are much alike. Both, for example, are hill-poems. Scott takes us,

> By winding pathways thro' the waving corn,

to "the airy point that prospect yields," shows us the view in one direction and then in another, tells us about the legends and the historical or literary associations of the region, muses, moralizes, and at length, "oft looking back, and lingering," leads us down.[2] He also makes liberal use of the artificial, hackneyed diction that disfigures Jago's work. We wander with him

> In verdant meads, by Lee's cerulean stream,

by "flowery meads And shining silver rills," through the "verdant maze" or beside the "irriguous marge" or up "th' acclivious steep" where "Favonius' wing . . . Wafts balmy redolence"; we see the "swain" guiding the "shining share" as he tills the "glebe"; we are told that, as the "circulating sanguine fluid" extends through the "arterial tubes," so the "limpid store" or "purchas'd wave" of "mercenary" streams is brought to cities.[3] Scott thoroughly approved of expressions like these, and censured Thomson for such "prosaisms" as "stealing from the barn a straw," "clean and complete," and "to tempt the trout."[4] Yet it was principally from Thomson and his followers that he derived his diction as well as his style, an indebtedness he frankly acknowledged by invoking the "Descriptive Muse" who had inspired "the Seasons . . . Grongar Hill, the Ruins of Rome, and that excellent neglected poem, the Fleece," and who had "to Shenstone's ear" brought "sweet strains of rural melody." [5]

---

[1] Lines 293, 295, 290–92, 82–3, 308–9.   [2] Lines 39, 40, 379.
[3] Lines 50 (cf. 180, 272), 237 (cf. 104), 92, 270, 383, 405–7; 408–12; 129, 127, 112, 131, 123.
[4] See p. 142 above.
[5] Lines 11–19, and notes. In the note to line 443 he mentions "the sublime Collins." Though a friend of Johnson's, Scott wrote sonnets (see Bibl. IV, 1766–70), an ode mod-

How much Scott owed to the original father of blank-verse poetry it would be hard to say. He used a number of Miltonic phrases, — "pleasant interchange of soft ascent And level plain," "tufted trees," "rustling leaves, The sound of water murmuring . . . and music soft Of distant bells . . . In slow sad measure mov'd," "mantling vines," "blissful seat." [1] Lines like

> Not for these, or aught
> Beside, wish I in hyperbolic strains
> Of vain applause to elevate your fame,[2]

recall *Paradise Lost* rather than *The Seasons*, and there is something of the sonorous Miltonic pomp in the reference to the aqueduct,

> suppos'd a work
> Of matchless skill, by those who ne'er had heard
> How, from PRENESTE's heights and ANIO's banks
> By TIVOLI, to ROME's imperial walls,
> On marble arches came the limpid store,
> And out of jasper rocks in bright cascades
> With never ceasing murmur gush'd; or how,
> To LUSITANIAN ULYSIPPO's towers,
> The silver current o'er ALCANT'RA's vale
> Roll'd high in air, as ancient poets feign'd
> ERIDANUS to roll thro' Heaven.[3]

But in general, as must be clear from the first two passages quoted above, Scott is much more simple, direct, and natural than his predecessors. As compared with theirs, his style is neither pompous nor involved, and his diction, though conventional, is not learned or Latinic. In these respects, as in his genuine love for the milder, more familiar aspects of nature and in his charming expression of that love, he takes a distinct step forward.

Very different from *Amwell* is *Leith Hill*, a work given to the world, apparently by Peter Cunningham, in 1779, which was thus sum-

---

elled upon Milton's octosyllabics (Bibl. II, 1762 w.), and an interesting volume of "Critical Essays" (1785) on *Coopers Hill, Lycidas, Windsor Forest, Grongar Hill, Ruins of Rome, Oriental Eclogues,* Gray's *Elegy, The Deserted Village,* and *The Seasons.*

[1] Lines 44–5 (cf. *P. L.,* ix. 115–16), 186 (cf. *Allegro,* 78), 197–201 (cf. *Penseroso,* 129, 144, 74–6), 303 (cf. *Comus,* 294), 438 (cf. *P. L.,* i. 5, iii. 527).

> The marge
> Of smooth translucent pools, where willows green . . .

(428–9), was perhaps suggested by *Comus,* 232, 861.

[2] Lines 418–20.

[3] Lines 108–18. These passages might, however, have been suggested by Thomson. Scott uses a number of sonorous names again in lines 246–51, 267–74. Inversions abound in his poem, and there are many adjectives used as adverbs, as in "streamers gay Triumphant fluttering" (62–3), "her iron reign Ruthless extends" (205–6), "jocund chants" (324), "annual ye resound . . . as he . . . Guides slow his shining share; ye annual hear The shouts" (410–13).

marily disposed of by the *Gentleman's Magazine*, "In blank verse, high-sounding language, without clear ideas," [1] an admirable characterization of many of the poems we have been considering. Can there be any doubt that it is Miltonic? George Wallace's *Prospects from Hills in Fife*, published in 1796 but written "many years ago," certainly is. It likewise uses "blank verse, high-sounding language," and, though evidently more poetical than *Leith Hill*, seems to contain more digressions than prospects.[2]

By no means all loco-descriptive pieces are like these. William Crowe's *Lewesdon Hill* (1788), which at one time had many readers, went through several editions, and was praised by Wordsworth, Coleridge, Moore, Rogers, and Bowles,[3] only to be forgotten soon after its sturdy author's death, is still enjoyable. Its descriptions, though few, are of excellent quality. This is one of the best:

> How changed is thy appearance, beauteous hill!
> Thou hast put off thy wintry garb, brown heath
> And russet fern, thy seemly-colour'd cloak
> To bide the hoary frosts and dripping rains
> Of chill December, and art gaily robed
> In livery of the spring: upon thy brow
> A cap of flowery hawthorn, and thy neck
> Mantled with new-sprung furze and spangles thick
> Of golden bloom: nor lack thee tufted woods
> Adown thy sides: Tall oaks of lusty green,
> The darker fir, light ash, and the nesh tops
> Of the young hazel join, to form thy skirts.[4]

Most of the work is concerned with dignified and rather sombre reflections expressed with something of the large Miltonic utterance found in these lines:

> Nor yet that elder work (if work it were,
> Not fable) raised upon the Phrygian shore,
> (Where lay the fleet confederate against Troy,
> A thousand ships behind the vasty mole
> All shelter'd) could with this compare, though built
> It seem'd, of greatness worthy to create
> Envy in the immortals. . . .
>
> But what is yonder Hill, whose dusky brow
> Wears, like a regal diadem, the round
> Of antient battlements and ramparts high;
> And frowns upon the vales? I know thee not.[5]

---

[1] lix. 1019 (1789).

[2] See *Scots Mag.*, lviii. 623–7. I know these two poems only from the reviews.

[3] See Wordsworth's postscript to the Duddon sonnets (1820); Coleridge's *Watchman*, April 2, 1796, and *Biographia Literaria* (Bohn ed.), 8; Moore's *Memoirs* (1853), ii. 180; Rogers's *Table-Talk* (ed. Dyce, 2d ed., 1856), 225–9; *Notes and Queries*, 2d series, vi. 42–3. [4] Page 2. [5] Pages 17, 20.

Crowe's style, it will be observed, though formal and Miltonic, is not grandiose, nor is his language of the popular Philips-Thomson variety. This virtue may be due in part to the example of *Amwell*, but more probably it is derived from *The Task*, which appeared three years before Crowe's poem.[1]

At the time of their publication, the *Lyrical Ballads* and *Gebir* seemed to many readers and critics no more significant than did two topographical poems on Malvern Hills which appeared the same year, 1798. In fact, while the puzzled reviewers spoke of the *Ancient Mariner* as "the strangest story of a cock and bull that we ever saw,"[2] they said that one of the hill-pieces "bids fair to live as long as the language in which it is written, or the mountains which it celebrates shall stand."[3] In reality both Malvern poems are dull affairs, containing much obvious moralizing, many commonplace reflections on life, and a small amount of description. Both are unmistakably Miltonic. One was from the prolific but uninspired pen of Joseph Cottle, the publisher-friend of Southey and Coleridge; the other was by a clergyman, Luke Booker. Cottle's work, which Wordsworth liked well enough to quote from,[4] is not unnatural in style and at its best is pleasing in a mild, pastoral way. Most of Booker's struts so absurdly that it might easily be taken for a parody; but a few passages are surprisingly good, and the following lines, unusual both in observation and in expression, are among the very best that we have thus far met:

> The slender stems
> Of hare-bells blue are motionless and still:
> The thistle-down assumes its silvery wing,
> As if to wanton with the morning breeze,
> But to the ground, unboyant, soon descends.
> Tranquillity the elements pervades,
> And Harmony the woods. No cloud obscures
> The wide horizon's undulating line,
> Where join'd seem earth and sky, — where azure mist
> Veils the soft landscape melting into light.[5]

---

[1] Crowe's admiration for Cowper is expressed in his *Treatise on English Versification* (1727), 72, 306, 310. His knowledge of Milton appears throughout the same volume, especially at pages 26-8, 318-34, as well as in such phrases in his *Lewesdon Hill* as "above the noise and stir of yonder fields" (p. 4, cf. *Comus*, 5), "won from the straiten'd main" (p. 16, cf. *P. L.*, iii. 12), "arches massy proof" (p. 16, cf. *Penseroso*, 158), "hazardous emprize" (p. 16, cf. *P. L.*, xi. 642), and possibly "villages Half-hid in tufted orchards" (p. 1, cf. *Allegro*, 78).   [2] *Mo. Rev.*, enl. ed., xxix. 204.

[3] *Gent. Mag.*, lxxii. 16 (letter by "J. W." concerning Booker's *Malvern*).

[4] *Prelude*, viii. 48-52. Lamb laughed at the piece in a letter to Manning (November, 1802), but said it was "very popular."

[5] *Malvern* (Dudley, 1798), p. 9; see also pp. 7-8. Booker's other unrimed topo-

In the decade between the publication of Crowe's work and the Malvern pieces but one unrimed hill-poem seems to have appeared, the two pages of tame, conventional, but decidedly Miltonic verse which H. F. Cary, the translator of Dante, published in 1794 as *The Mountain Seat*.[1] Nor did the number increase, for the next thirty years apparently saw only four more. In the first of these, *Beachy Head* (1807), the "stupendous summit" is little more than a starting-point from which Charlotte Smith, the sonneteer and novelist, wanders at will. Mrs. Smith, "an early worshipper" of nature and of its "rudest scenes — warrens, and heaths, And yellow commons,"[2] had also a sharp eye for many things overlooked by her contemporaries. She saw, for example, the frightened rooks "rising slow on whispering wings"; she noticed

> in the breeze
> That wafts the thistle's plumed seed along,
> Blue bells wave tremulous. The mountain thyme
> Purples the hassock of the heaving mole,
> And the short turf is gay with tormentil,
> And bird's foot trefoil, and the lesser tribes
> Of hawkweed; spangling it with fringed stars.[3]

No such vivid details give life to the forty-five pages of tumid Miltonic blank verse which make up William Hamilton Drummond's *Clontarf* (1822), but instead "roves th' excursive glance" o'er "perennial verdure," "crystal rills," and "finny tribes."[4]

Meanwhile Thomas Noble had shown in his *Blackheath* (1808) how slowly the human race learns, for the grandiose diction and pompous yet crabbed style of its two thousand lines have most of the defects of Philips's *Cyder*, which appeared a hundred years before. Had John Scott, Cowper, and even Wordsworth written to no purpose? The trouble is not that the poem is perfunctory, not that

---

graphical poem, *Knowle Hill* (1789), which I have not seen, is reviewed in the *Critical Review* (new arr., x. 41).

[1] *Gent. Mag.*, lxiv. 161–2. The similarity to Milton is not limited to the style, but includes such borrowings as "cornfield and pasture, pleasing interchange" (cf. *P. L.*, ix. 115–16), "in close covert of immuring shades" (cf. *Penseroso*, 139, *Comus*, 521, *P. L.*, iv. 693), "boon Nature" (cf. *P. L.*, iv. 242), "if chance a parting gleam, shot from the West" (cf. *P. L.*, ii. 492), "palmer's weeds of amice grey" (cf. *Comus*, 189, *P. R.*, iv. 427).

[2] *Beachy Head*, etc. (1807), p. 24.

[3] *Ib.* 32, 31.

[4] The Irish Unitarian clergyman who composed *Clontarf* (and also the *Pleasures of Benevolence*, see below, p. 393) should not be confused with other William Drummonds, some of whom were writing at the same time. Clontarf, a village near Dublin, was the scene of a battle with the Danes which figures prominently in the poem. Pages xiii and xiv of the preface are devoted to a discussion of "Loco-descriptive Poetry."

it merely repeats what has been said before, but that, like many others, Noble was unable to give adequate expression to what he felt. His love of the country was genuine and his power of observation unusual, but they were submerged under the turgid pomposity which had been so long associated with blank verse that most readers failed to recognize it as pomposity. In the following passages, however, which are among the best in the poem, Noble's defects are not glaring;

> There, the plover skims,
> With wailful cry, along the sedgy dykes;
> And water-locusts, on pellucid wings
> Azure or green, flit, circling, o'er the stream,
> Or, lightly settling on the tremulous reeds,
> Spread their cerulean vans.

> And the thrush,
> Whirring thro' every coppice, pours his note
> With wilder cadence: — then, each object round,
> In soft succession, seems to fade away,
> And tender shadows, deepening as they blend,
> Roll slowly upward from the darkened vales,
> Cling to the hills, and on the cloudless air
> Steam, mantling, 'mid the lingering flush of day.[1]

The last topographical poem [2] seems to be *Banwell Hill*, which William Lisle Bowles brought out in 1828, a year after Alfred and Charles Tennyson published their first volume. The late date is not significant, however, as the *genre* had long been dead. Bowles, who was sixty-six when he composed this, almost his last piece, was only reverting to a disused form which had been in vogue in his boyhood.[3] He himself calls it a "local descriptive poem," and it clearly belongs to the class: the hill and the prospect from it, the moralizing, even the distant villages and country estates, are all there. The pleasing, pensive descriptions of scenery that give a quiet beauty to Bowles's sonnets lend charm to parts of this piece also; but as a whole it is tiresome and unreadable, like his other long works. It is seen at its best in such lines as these:

---

[1] v. 89–94, 208–15. *Blackheath* differs from other loco-descriptive poems in that it includes the views from a number of hills located on the same heath.

[2] Except W. S. Roscoe's fragmentary *Contemplative Day*, "suggested by scenery in the neighbourhood of Allerton, and Woolton Hill" (*Poems*, 1834, pp. 128–58), a pleasing, somewhat wistful and desultory production in the manner of Bowles. Like Roscoe's translation from *The Messiah* (see below, pp. 351–2), it is decidedly Miltonic in its style and in some of its phrasing, more so than would be expected in a descriptive poem of its date.

[3] Similarly, Mrs. Smith was fifty-seven when she wrote *Beachy Head* and Drummond forty-four when he published *Clontarf*.

But I view
Brean Down beyond; and there thy winding sands,
Weston; and, far away, one wandering ship,
Where stretches into mist the Severn sea.

Along this solitary ridge,
Where smiles, but rare, the blue campanula,
Among the thistles and gray stones that peep
Through the thin herbage, to the highest point
Of elevation, o'er the vale below,
Slow let us climb.[1]

The Miltonic element in these descriptions has almost reached the vanishing point, but in passages like the following, which attempt a loftier strain, it is unmistakable:

With sober splendour, yet not gorgeous,
Her mitred brow tempered with lenity
And apostolic mildness — in her mien
No dark defeature, beautiful as mild,
And gentle as the smile of charity, —
Thus on the Rock of Ages may uplift
Her brow majestic.[2]

Bowles was the author of three shorter hill-poems, — *Coombe-Ellen* (1798), *St. Michael's Mount* (1798, which is rimed and owes something to *Lycidas*),[3] and *Sketch from Bowden Hill after Sickness* (1809); he also wrote a number of other pieces in the blank verse of *Paradise Lost*, three of which, the *Spirit of Discovery by Sea* (1804), the *Grave of the Last Saxon* (1822), and *St. John in Patmos* (1833), are of considerable length. Nearly all make frequent use of Milton's words and phrases,[4] are somewhat plaintive in tone, contain numerous descriptive passages, are "subservient to that which alone can give dignity to poetry, — the cause of moral and religious truth,"[5] — and, though tame and diffuse, are otherwise unobjectionable. Bowles needed the restrictions of the sonnet form and the stimulus of youthful emotion.

Not all loco-descriptive poems deal with hills. There is a group, for instance, that pictures the West Indies, — Nathaniel Weekes's *Barbados* (1754), John Singleton's *General Description of the West-Indian Islands* (1767), and George Heriot's *Descriptive Poem,*

---

[1] i. 75-8, 183-8.   [2] v. 178-84.   [3] See lines 247-72.
[4] A striking instance occurs in these lines from *Coombe-Ellen* (241-2; cf. *Lycidas*, 132, and *Samson*, 1):

Return, my Muse! the fearful sound is past;
And now a little onward.

[5] Introduction to *Grave of the Last Saxon.*

written in the West Indies (1781). Any one who wishes an account in Miltonic verse of the customs, climate, fauna, and flora of these islands will find it here, but if he asks for poetry he will be given instead lines like these:

> For *pickles, sweetmeats, cordials,* and *preserves,*
> The world resounds thy praise; without these gifts,
> What figure would a *British* side-board make? [1]

There is also John Fitchett's "little descriptive poem," which celebrates country life and "the ancient mansion of *Bewsey* . . . in that kind of style which is formed by reading Thomson and similar authors." [2] Nathaniel Howard's tumid, highly-colored *Bickleigh Vale* (1804) has not even the merit which Dr. Johnson allowed to Gray, — that of being "dull in a new way"; and the praise it receives in N. T. Carrington's *Dartmoor* (1826) [3] would carry more weight if Carrington himself exhibited greater poetic gifts. Both pieces gain some interest from their subject (for "Bickleigh's vale romantic" is on Dartmoor), [4] and from the genuine love for nature even in her grander aspects which their authors display. As might be expected, the sombre, epic beauty of the general appearance of the moors so impressively described and interpreted in the *Return of the Native* is scarcely, if at all, touched upon by either Howard or Carrington. Both writers make free use of inversions, of adjectives in place of adverbs, and of other Miltonisms, and both spoil the naturalness of their poems by conventional and inflated diction. [5] Francis Webb's *Somerset* (1811) is in part suggested by the view from a hill. Its cold, stiff, rhetorical style — which, like some of its ideas, reminds one of Akenside — effectively conceals any feeling for the out-of-doors that Webb may have had, but not his admiration for Milton. He writes, for example,

> Now dubious Twilight sheds a glimm'ring beam;
> And sober Evening, clad in amice grey,
> Silent and soft her step, comes slowly on. [6]

---

[1] Weekes, *Barbados* (see *Mo. Rev.*, xi. 328). I have seen only reviews of this work and of Heriot's *Descriptive Poem* (see *Crit. Rev.*, lii. 147). Weekes is ridiculed, together with Ogilvie, Mason, and others who decried imitation of the ancients, in A. C. Schomberg's empty, confusing satire, *Bagley, a Descriptive Poem* (Oxford, 1777).

[2] *Crit. Rev.*, new arr., xvii. 353. The extract in the *New Annual Register*, 1796, pp. [167–8], shows that the poem (which I have not seen) is decidedly Miltonic, as is Fitchett's long epic *King Alfred* (see p. 312 below).

[3] Second ed., p. 19.

[4] Felicia Hemans in 1821, and Joseph Cottle in 1823, also published poems on Dartmoor. The first is rimed; I have not seen the second.

[5] For Howard's other poems that show the influence of Milton, see below, p. 354, and Bibls. I, II, III c, under the year 1804.

[6] Page 38; cf. *P. L.*, iv. 598–9, and *P. R.*, iv. 426–7.

When we leave the topographical poem and return to the other forms of descriptive verse, we must retrace our steps to 1788. At this time, it may be remembered, Scott's *Amwell* had been in circulation only twelve years and *The Task* only three. These facts are important, for they point to a new era in blank verse: the Philips-Thomson type was giving way before the simpler, more natural variety that Cowper used. For this turn of the tide *The Task* was of course not solely, perhaps not even chiefly, responsible, for we have seen the change coming through the work of Brown, Bruce, and Scott. Even if Cowper had never written, it must have come quite as inevitably, though more slowly. *The Task* did, however, by its popularity help to crystallize taste. It apparently furnished a model to unoriginal poets and gave courage to timid ones; for, with one exception, every important descriptive poem published after this time is much nearer to Cowper's verse than to Thomson's. This by no means implies that the popularity or the influence of *The Seasons* was over, — far from it; it is only that forward-looking writers of finer taste felt the advantages of the more natural and supple manner.

The most conversational style produced in the eighteenth century, one that at times skirts dangerously near, if it does not reach, the baldness of prose, is that of James Hurdis. Lines like these come as a surprise from an Oxford professor of poetry:

> 'Come,' said the careful father, 'weep no more.
> Go to the cot, ere chilly ev'ning come,
> And the damp wood affect thee. Where's my daughter?' [1]

Yet Hurdis held his professorship eight years (1793–1801). His first work, the *Village Curate*, appeared in 1788, the year in which Crowe, who was public orator of the university, published *Lewesdon Hill*. The two poems enjoyed almost equal popularity, the *Village Curate* going through four editions by 1797, besides being reprinted in America. Yet they are very different in style, as may be seen by contrasting the following lines (among the best in Hurdis's work) with those previously quoted from Crowe's:

> One labour more the cheerful hand awaits;
> Then the glad year is done. We seize with joy
> The precious interval, and shape our walk
> At early ev'ning down the meadow path;
> Till sunk into the vale, fast by the brook
> We spy the blooming hop, and with light heart
> The glorious garden enter. . . .

[1] *Adriano* (1790), p. 63.

> . . . . Long let us stray,
> Enjoy the grateful covert, and admire
> The one continued cluster over-head
> Of blossoms interwoven, and depending
> E'en to the touch and smell. Long let us stray,
> And ever as we come to the flat mead
> And quit the garden with reluctance. . . .[1]

This is not great poetry, but it *is* pleasing, and the easy, natural flow of the lines comes as a welcome change from what we have been reading. Hurdis undoubtedly owed much to Cowper, with whom he corresponded and whom he twice mentions in this work; [2] and, though he was temperamentally lacking in vigor, it may be in part due to *The Task* that the *Village Curate* is thin, invertebrate, and ultra-conversational.

Yet, chatty, pleasant sentimentalist though he was, he was not able to free himself entirely from the conventional diction and grandiose style which had become fastened upon blank verse and which give his work an old-fashioned sound. He speaks, for example, of "Philomel," the "fair," "the flexile path," the "long beloiter'd day," "the azure canopy of heav'n," "the azure covert of these veins," "matters strangely complicate," and addresses "ye thoughtless young" with the counsel,

> Deem it not hard
> If old experience check your wild career.[3]

It is in phrases and lines like these — and there are many of them — that the *Village Curate* is most Miltonic; the descriptive passages, as may be seen in that quoted above, do not often produce a Miltonic impression. Yet Hurdis leaves no one in doubt as to his familiarity with *Paradise Lost*, for his first three and a half lines are taken verbatim from the opening of it, and there are a number of other Miltonic borrowings scattered through the *Village Curate*.[4]

---

[1] First ed. (1788), pp. 92–3.

[2] *Ib.* 2, 118. "It was the chief ambition of Hurdis to be like Cowper," remarked H. F. Cary (*Memoir*, by Henry Cary, 1847, ii. 295).

[3] *Ib.* 38 (and 56, 116, etc.), 59 (and 76, 86, 88, 116, etc.), 50, 59 (cf. 115), 38, 59, 37, 82 (cf. *Penseroso*, 173).

[4] "Veil'd in a show'r of roses and perfumes" (p. 1, cf. *P. L.*, ix. 425–6); "the forehead of the morning" (p. 16, cf. *Lycidas*, 171); "come and aid my song . . . Dip my advent' rous pen" (p. 22, cf. *P. L.*, i. 13); "the thick maze Of movements intricate, confus'd" (p. 29, cf. *P. L.*, v. 622–3); "his axle cools" (p. 51, cf. *Comus*, 96, of the sun in each case); "the wealth of Ind" (p. 52, cf. *P. L.*, ii. 2); "the deep artillery of heav'n" pp. 53, 85, cf. *P. L.*, ii. 715); "when day His garish eye has veil'd" (p. 77, cf. *Penseroso*, 141); "pent up in city stench" (p. 92, cf. *P. L.*, ix. 445); "with awful reverence" (p. 105, cf. *P. L.*, ii. 478); "Confusion reigns, uproar and loud mis-rule" (p. 112, cf. *P. L.*, iii. 710, vii. 271); "holds attention mute" (p. 119, cf. *P. L.*, i. 618); "half flying,

In 1790, two years after the publication of his first work, Hurdis brought out a sentimental Sunday-School story in blank verse to which he gave the romantic title *Adriano*. The bald, prosaic lines quoted a few pages above [1] are typical of the poem, except in being quite free from inversions and other characteristics of *Paradise Lost*, of which it makes some use. A similar versified story, *Elmer and Ophelia*, which Hurdis published later in the same year, shows little influence from Milton but impresses upon women a moral of which he would have heartily approved:

> Come then and learn, thou lovely friend of Man,
> Main-spring of all his actions good and bad,
> Learn all thy duty in one word, *obey*.[2]

From these two poems it would seem that Hurdis had largely emancipated himself from the inflated style and language that are so ill adapted to rural descriptions. In reality he had done nothing of the kind, for in his remaining works he becomes increasingly Miltonic.[3] *Tears of Affection* (1794), a lugubrious piece similar to the *Night Thoughts* in its enjoyment of grief,[4] is written in a more formal style than that of its predecessors, and the *Favorite Village*, which appeared in 1800, a year before its author's death, is decidedly Thomsonian.[5] Struggling through the turgidity of expression in this last

half on foot" (p. 133, cf. *P. L.*, ii. 941–2); "hide your diminish'd heads" (p. 139, cf. *P.L.*, iv. 35); "the adamantine gates Of treble-bolted Hell" (p. 142, cf. *P. L.*, ii. 645–6);

> Like the vanquish'd fiend,
> Out-cast of heav'n, oft thro' their armed files
> Darts an experienc'd eye, and feels his heart
> Distend with pride (p. 7, cf. *P. L.*, i. 567–72);

> Things unattempted yet in prose or rhyme,
> A shilling, breeches, and chimaeras dire

(p. 135, cf. *P. L.*, i. 16, ii. 628). On page 106 Hurdis himself points out an allusion to Milton's Satan, while two lines on page 120 and ten on pages 130–31 contain references to Milton in terms adapted from his epic (*P. L.*, vii. 12–14, iii. 26–44).

[1] Page 259.　　　　　　　　　　　　[2] *Poems* (1790), p. 57.

[3] An earlier piece, *Panthea* (in great part written several years before 1790, when it was published), is taken from Xenophon's *Cyropaedia*, and in its narrative portions uses a more condensed, epic style than does Hurdis's other work. The extensive dialogues are non-Miltonic, probably because *Panthea* was first conceived as a play.

[4] Note particularly pp. 32–4, 58–9. The appeals to Alcanor, and the declamatory, fault-finding tone of the smug minister, which mar parts of the *Village Curate*, also remind one of the *Night Thoughts*.

[5] The account of the robin's visit to a house in winter (pp. 123–6) recalls that in Thomson (*Winter*, 245–56); and expressions like these are common,—"the bright egress of effulgent day" (p. 27), "the minor fly, chirurgeon keen, . . . The small phlebotomist" (p. 70), "the lunar orb renewed or at its hour Of plentitude arrived" (p. 77), "the sportsman's tube, disglutted o'er the lake" (p. 100), "the lazy cloud . . . Lambent . . . of the . . . hill" (p. 110). The influence of Cowper is unmistakable in the descriptions of the winter evening at home (pp. 101–2) and the winter-morning walks (pp. 105–21).

work are a deep love of nature, a keen eye for her less obvious beauties, and an enjoyment of the characteristic though unimportant sights about the farm which light up every page. Some idea of Hurdis's close observation of country life, closer perhaps in this poem than in any that preceded it, may be gained from a few extracts:

> Yet not devoid of *pleasure* is the field,
> Howe'er the gale may buffet, nature still
> Some grateful objects yielding to the sight.
> Though brown the common with its withered fern,
> And sad the valley with its leafless wood,
> Yet crimson haws, and hips of ruddy hue,
> And cluster'd privet-berries, dark as jet,
> The cheerful hedgerow sprinkle.

> With folded feet inverted slumbers puss
> The livelong evening on the quilted hearth,
> Or warmer knee, caressed and often stroked.

> Now breaks, in vapour wrapt, the piercing dawn.
> Unusual light upon the cieling thrown
> Wakes from its slumber the suspicious eye,
> And bids it look abroad on hill, and dale,
> Cottage, and steeple, in the niveous stole
> Of Winter trimly dressed. The silent shower,
> Precipitated still, no breeze disturbs,
> While fine as dust it falls.[1]

This tendency to "number the streaks of the tulip, or describe the different shades in the verdure of the forest," which, according to Dr. Johnson and other classicists, is not "the business of a poet," [2] also distinguishes Hurdis's earlier work. The *Village Curate*, for example, has such touches as "the glossy raven . . . waddles"; "the fern Unclenching all her fingers"; the chimney-swallow's song "twitter'd to young-eyed day"; "the tough and sinewy furze . . . With golden baskets hung"; "the sky-blue periwinkle climbs Up to the cottage eaves, and hides the . . . dairy lattice with a thousand eyes"; and the curate's joy in seeing "the little goldfinch pluck The groundsil's feather'd seed, and twit and twit." [3]

Apparently few of these evidences of sharp eyes mark the description of the country near London which William Fox, Jr., published in 1801 as *La Bagatella, or Delineations of Home Scenery*. The poem seems, however, to have the diffuseness, the sentimentality, and the

---

[1] Pages 96, 102, 112–13.   [2] *Rasselas*, ch. x.

[3] Pages 43–4, 40, 44, 38, 40, 44, and cf. 115–16. Southey had warm praise for Hurdis, but noted that even so early as 1827 his name was "little remembered" (*Quart. Rev.*, xxxv. 201).

conversational style of Hurdis and, fortunately, also his ability to draw pleasant and natural pictures of familiar scenes. This is one:

> The common grass here scents
> As pure as in the unfrequented vale.
> The gently rippling stream here runs as clear
> As other streams — the birds as sweetly sing
> As forest birds, where no one lists to hear.
> And this our homely well, and bubbling brook,
> Tho' never honour'd yet by poet's song,
> To me more grateful flow than stranger rills,
> Whose sides no friend hath trod.[1]

Little poetic merit is discoverable in the forty pages of William Sotheby's *Tour through Parts of Wales* (1790), but its appreciation of the lonely mountain scenery of a country seldom mentioned by poets gives it some interest. The language is simple, but the style is that of the middle of the century:

> With rapture wild I gaze
> On the rude grandeur of the mountain view. . . .
> Tremendous Snowdon! while I gradual climb
> Thy craggy heights, though intermingled clouds
> Various of watery grey, and sable hue,
> Obscure the uncertain prospect, from thy brow
> His wildest views the mountain genius flings.[2]

Another dull work, interesting only for what it fails to do with an admirable subject, is John Bidlake's *Sea* (1796). Any appreciation of

> the beauty and mystery of the ships,
> And the magic of the sea,

that Bidlake may have had is obscured by his wearisome, stereotyped phraseology and grandiose, Thomsonian style; but it is doubtful if he or many of his contemporaries felt any such beauty and magic. Falconer expresses none of it in his *Shipwreck*, and it is very rare in any poetry written before *Childe Harold*.

In the development of the powers of observation and expression which we have been following, it may have been noticed that the same poem rarely displays both excellences. *Lochleven*, *Amwell*, and *Lewesdon Hill* treat of little more than the broad, general aspects of nature, but describe these in pleasing verse, whereas *Blackheath* reveals unusual knowledge of the country but no skill in expression. In the case of Hurdis the same phenomenon is illustrated in the dif-

---

[1] *Crit. Rev.*, new arr., xxxv. 108. I have not seen the book.

[2] Edition of 1794, pp. 33-4. There are pleasant pictures of the obvious beauties of nature, conventionally expressed, in Sotheby's epic *Saul* (see below, p. 304, n. 2) and also in his sonnets.

ferent works of a single author: the *Village Curate* is notable for its fluent, natural style rather than for the sharpness of its author's eyes, while the *Favorite Village* is unnatural in style but shows close observation. Another poem that possesses one of these qualities to an unusual degree but lacks the other is Thomas Gisborne's *Walks in a Forest* (1794). This work enjoyed considerable popularity in its day, going through eight editions in nineteen years; but it has been so completely forgotten by later generations that the copy in the Harvard Library lay for a hundred years uncut. "The scenes and incidents," the preface explains, ". . . are such . . . as occur in the Forests of Great Britain. The Author has endeavoured to delineate them with such a degree of particularity as might mark the characteristic features of each." This shows that Gisborne was not unconscious of what he was doing, yet it is doubtful if he realized how significantly his poem differed from those that preceded it. In exteriors it is much the same, — stilted, grandiose, and unceasingly moralizing. As in the work of Thomson and his followers, historical, sentimental, and tragic episodes are inserted, together with descriptions of deserts, snow-storms, forest fires, and volcanic eruptions. These digressions, however, have little interest for the twentieth-century reader. What arrests his attention is the minute detail of the pictures and the appreciation of beauties which most men fail to see: touches that show the horse in winter, "on indurated balls Of snow upraised," with "quivering ears now forward bent, Now backward swiftly thrown"; the snow "tinging with thin-spread white the frozen brook"; the cows "breathing loud," as "with fastidious nose" they snuff at the frozen pool; "the marly cliff, Its base by oozing springs with frostwork glazed"; or a picture like this,

> With shrill and oft-repeated cry,
> Her angular course, alternate rise and fall,
> The woodpecker prolongs.[1]

Such details and bits of unobstrusive beauty abound in the *Walks* as perhaps in no other English poem. Here is another of the numerous sketches of birds:

> Oft the heron,
> Posted in Dove's rich meads, with patient guile
> And pale grey plumes with watery blue suffused
> Stands like a shadow: then with out-strech'd neck,
> While near with sidelong gait the fowler creeps,
> Rises, and, steering to the distant fen,
> Shrieks from on high, and flaps her solemn wing.[2]

---

[1] *Walks*, etc. (8th ed., 1813), pp. 114, 109, 146, 128, 13.   [2] *Ib.* 94.

A rain-storm on a ridge of hills is thus described:

> The torrent rain
> Smokes on their deluged sides. The shower drives on:
> Hill after hill successive disappears
> Before the encroaching vapour. Lost awhile,
> They mingle with the sky: now far behind
> Gradual emerge, obscurely through the rear
> Of the spent storm discern'd: now glimmer faint
> With watery beams; now through the freshen'd air
> Swell on the sight, and laugh in cloudless day.[1]

These passages, which are as good as any in the *Walks*, show that Gisborne had sharp eyes and poetic feeling, but that he was not a poet.

It is probable that the plan of the work — walks in a forest at different seasons of the year — was suggested by the "Winter Morning Walk" and "Winter Walk at Noon" of *The Task*. Gisborne was a "most warm and Enthusiastic admirer" of Cowper,[2] whom he praised highly in the *Walks* and made the subject of two odes;[3] yet, since what he particularly admired in the bard of Olney was the combination of the "faithful monitor's and poet's care," [4] the influence was almost wholly on the didactic side. The two poets were really quite different. Gisborne's appreciation of the wild and rugged in nature was as far beyond Cowper's timid clinging to the fireside, to "trim gardens" and rolling meadows, as the delicate art of *The Task* was beyond the stilted turgidity of the *Walks*. The style and diction of the later poem certainly remind one of Thomson much more than of Cowper, no doubt because Gisborne was temperamentally inclined to the more formal and massive type of verse and wrote it more easily. There was probably some direct influence from *Paradise Lost*, four lines of which are quoted in the *Walks*;[5] but from

---

[1] *Ib.* 94–5.

[2] See *Letters of Lady Hesketh to the Rev. John Johnson concerning Cowper* (1901), under dates of April 21 and May 9, 1799. Lady Hesketh adds that Gisborne ranked Cowper's works "next to his Bible," and cherished them as his "pocket companions" and "bosom friends."

[3] "To the Harp of Cowper" and "Ode to the Memory of Cowper," *Walks*, etc., 201–8.

[4] *Ib.* 102. According to the preface, one of Gisborne's objects in writing the poem was "to inculcate . . . those moral truths, which the contemplation of the works of God in the natural world suggests." This may have had something to do with the *Critical Review's* praise (new arr., xvi. 42–5).

[5] Pages 104–5, 153 n. Gisborne has a number of unusual words that occur in Milton, — "ever-during," "sable-vested," "massy," "mazy," "sapient," "umbrageous," "lucid," "plumy," "nectarean," "ethereal," "empyreal," "empyrean," "refulgent," "horrent," "shag" (as a verb), "fabric" (a building), — as well as some phrases that probably came from him, "his radiant files" (p. 82, cf. *P. L.*, iv. 797), "contiguous

whatever sources Gisborne's Miltonisms were derived they are as unmistakable as they are omnipresent.

It is a comforting reflection that most forgotten things deserve to be forgotten, a truth that holds in literature as in everything else, though, as the world never knew a large number of the volumes in print, it could not forget them. Yet occasionally one picks from the dust-heap of oblivion something that impresses one as a living book, something that one wishes the busy world could still find a little time for. Such a book, it seems to me, was written by the Scottish lawyer and minister, James Grahame. Vigor and richness are lacking, to be sure, and there is no lofty flight; but the poems are pleasant reading and reveal a knowledge and whole-hearted love of the rough Scottish country that few other writings of the time can equal. Grahame's first work, *The Rural Calendar* (1797), consists of twelve short descriptions, one for each month of the year. The pictures, though disconnected, are sympathetic and true and often contain unusual details; but the style is so colorless and the language inclined to be so conventional and turgid that most readers will agree with the author's wife in thinking poorly of the work. Seven years later, in 1804, Grahame sprang into something like fame with his *Sabbath*, a poem of less than nine hundred lines breathing the peace and quiet, the love of God and nature, that one feels on a Sunday in rural Scotland.[1] Religion rather than nature was Grahame's chief interest in *The Sabbath*, and it is the more obvious beauties of the country that he describes; yet he pictures these with a simple sincerity and affection that bring them home to us as earlier poetry does not. His sensitiveness to the sounds and silences of the country will be seen from such lines as these,

> The wheeling plover ceas'd
> Her plaint; the solitary place was glad,
> And on the distant cairns, the watcher's ear
> Caught doubtfully at times the breeze-borne note;

shade" (p. 84, cf. *P. L.*, vi. 828), "tufted . . . woods" (p. 93, cf. *Allegro*, 78, *Comus*, 225), "arrowy sleet" (p. 121, cf. "arrowy storm," p. 97, and *P. R.*, iii. 324, but note Gray's *Fatal Sisters*, 3). He may also have been affected by the *English Garden* (1772-82) and some of the rimed poems of William Mason, on whom he wrote an elegy and an epitaph (*Poems*, 3d ed., 1803, pp. 139, 151).

[1] *The Sabbath* went through four editions within a year and in a few months was published in America. By 1821 it had reached a ninth edition, and by 1863 had been reprinted at least six times more. Byron's sneer (*English Bards*, 319-26, 924) counts for little in view of Scott's praise (Lockhart's *Scott*, 1900, i. 389), and of Southey's remark that *The Sabbath* "had found its way from one end of Great Britain to the other; — it was in the mouths of the young, and in the hearts of the aged" (*Quart. Rev.*, 1810, iii. 457). In 1816 "Professor" Wilson published some "Lines" to the "author of *The Sabbath*" (*Poetical Works*, 1874, pp. 410-18).

or these,

> Far in moors, remote from house or hut . . .
> Where ev'n the hum of wand'ring bee ne'er breaks
> The quiet slumber of the level waste; [1]

or these from the opening of the poem,

> How still the morning of the hallow'd day!
> Mute is the voice of rural labour, hush'd
> The ploughboy's whistle, and the milkmaid's song.
> The scythe lies glitt'ring in the dewy wreath
> Of tedded grass, mingled with fading flowers,
> That yester-morn bloom'd waving in the breeze:
> Sounds the most faint attract the ear, — the hum
> Of early bee, the trickling of the dew,
> The distant bleating, midway up the hill.

More unusual is the picture of the partridge with her young:

> Close nestling 'neath her breast
> They cherish'd cow'r amid the purple blooms.[2]

To the second edition of *The Sabbath* Grahame added four brief "Sabbath Walks," which suggest Thomson in that there is one for each of the seasons. They are similar to their predecessor and, like it, give evidence not only of sharp eyes and keen ears but of some powers of imagination and expression. The title *Sabbath Walks* recalls Gisborne's *Walks in a Forest*, which Grahame presumably had read; yet all his verse is closer to that of Hurdis than to other unrimed descriptions.

Grahame's piety, which is apparent in everything he wrote, completely dominates the short accounts of Bible scenes — esthetically of slight value — which he published in 1806 as *Biblical Pictures*. The same year, however, he took a long step forward in his *Birds of Scotland*, the most significant and to me the most enjoyable of his poems. It is almost a treatise on ornithology, and as such belongs in a way with the *Sugar-Cane* and the *Hop-Garden*. But Grahame's purpose was different from Grainger's and Booker's; for in the preface he explained, "I have studied not so much to convey knowledge, as to please the imagination, and warm the heart," words which mark their author as belonging to the new century. The poem contains a good deal of information regarding the haunts and habits of Scottish birds, their food, the materials, form, and location of their nests, the number and color of their eggs, and so on; but, instead of being the labored, pedantic work that it would probably have proved had it been written thirty years earlier, it is fresh,

---

[1] First American ed. (N. Y., 1805), pp. 17-18, 22.   [2] *Ib.* 18.

sincere, and poetic. It takes us away from the gardens where "Philomel pours her plaint," away from the rolling meadows and cultivated fields in which the English "Muse" had so long wandered, to
"the thorny dingle," the "bosky cleugh," "the blooming vetchy
ridge," to the "whinny braes . . . garlanded with gold" and the
brook "wimpling through hazelly shaw, and broomy glen." [1] For
perhaps the first time in English poetry we watch a real lark as he
sings his "downward-veering song" to his mate:

> Slow the descent at first, then, by degrees,
> Quick, and more quick, till suddenly the note
> Ceases; and, like an arrow-fledge, he darts,
> And, softly lighting, perches by her side.[2]

In the ideal country-place of which Grahame dreams he wants "no
gravelled paths, pared from the smooth-shaved turf," such as Cowper loved, but "the simple unmade road." [3] The temptation to
quote extensively from the *Birds of Scotland* is strong, but one more
passage must suffice, one that seems to me to catch something of the
dewy freshness of the Scottish wilds:

> With earliest spring, while yet in mountain cleughs
> Lingers the frozen wreath, when yeanling lambs,
> Upon the little heath-encircled patch
> Of smoothest sward, totter, — the GORCOCK's call
> Is heard from out the mist, high on the hill;
> But not till when the tiny heather bud
> Appears, are struck the spring-time leagues of love.
> Remote from shepherd's hut, or trampled fold,
> The new joined pair their lowly mansion pitch,
> Perhaps beneath the juniper's rough shoots;
> Or castled on some plat of tufted heath,
> Surrounded by a narrow sable moat
> Of swampy moss.[4]

Grahame could never write long without touching on the cruelty
of hunting, of robbing nests and imprisoning song-birds, or on the
horrors of child-labor, the press-gang, or slavery. His interest in this
last evil led him to join with James Montgomery and Elizabeth Benger in a volume of *Poems on the Abolition of the Slave Trade* (1809); [5]

---

[1] *Birds*, etc. (Edin., 1806), pp. 20, 60 (cf. 20), 26, 43, 22.   [2] *Ib.* 4.
[3] *Ib.* 60 (cf. *The Task*, i. 351–2).   [4] *Ib.* 13–14.
[5] The African slave-trade, which was discussed in Parliament from 1788 to 1807,
when it was abolished, is the subject of at least four other blank-verse poems of length
that I have not seen: Mrs. Ann Yearsley's *On the Inhumanity of the Slave-Trade* (1788);
John Jamieson's *Sorrows of Slavery, containing a Faithful Statement of Facts respecting
the African Slave Trade* (1789); the anonymous *Address to every Briton on the Slave
Trade, being an effectual Plan to abolish this Disgrace to our Country* (1791); and "an

but his contribution, *Africa Delivered*, is naturally enough sentimental and unimpressive, since it deals with a subject unsuited to
his quiet, descriptive talents and one about which he could have
known little at first hand. In his longest poem, *British Georgics*
(1809), he returns to his own heath and to the one subject that inspired him, nature; yet, since his primary object is not to describe
the country but to furnish suggestions about agriculture for gentlemen farmers, much of the work belongs with the technical treatises
that are to be considered later. The pictures of wild nature in which
Grahame excels are rare, but the many incidental descriptions,
though disfigured by wretched poetic diction, reveal his keen observation and love of the country, and the best of them have the quiet
charm of *The Sabbath:*

> No more at dewy dawn, or setting sun,
> The blackbird's song floats mellow down the dale;
> Mute is the lark, or soars a shorter flight,
> With carol briefly trilled, and soon descends.[1]

The *Georgics* is in every respect more tame, formal, and unoriginal
than the earlier pieces, perhaps because Grahame was here for
the first time making use of a conventional literary form and thus
was to some extent consciously modelling his work on that of others.
For the *British Georgics* owes not only its name but its purpose and
method to the *Georgics* of Virgil, and probably derives something
from English works of the same kind — *Cyder, Agriculture*, the *Hop-
Garden*, and the *Sugar-Cane*. It is also under no small debt, which
Grahame did not attempt to conceal,[2] to the father of blank-verse
descriptive poetry. The influence of *The Seasons* is shown principally in a greater formality of style and a tendency to grandiose

Under Graduate's" *Dictates of Indignation* (1791). To judge from the reviews, the first
is emotional and declamatory, the second is based on the reports of investigators and is
free from exaggeration, the third is an enthusiastic, highly-colored invective, and the
fourth is romantic, sentimental heroics. The second and fourth are clearly Miltonic,
as is the vague, rhetorical, and inflated *Wrongs of Africa* which William Roscoe (the
biographer of Lorenzo de' Medici and the subject of a paper in the *Sketch Book*) published in 1787–88.

[1] Page 129. The poem is divided into twelve parts, one for each month; it treats
chiefly of "Scottish husbandry, scenery, and manners" (p. v).

[2] Five of the twelve quotations prefixed to the several "Georgics" he took from
The Seasons, and in the preface he wrote: "That I have been preceded by Thomson,
is a consideration of a more serious kind. He, no doubt, with a genius and felicity
which none of his followers need ever hope to equal, has described many of the most
striking appearances of Nature, and many of the most poetical processes, so to speak,
of husbandry. But though he has reaped, why may not others be permitted to glean?"
Coming so late as 1809, after most of Wordsworth's significant work was done, this
remark is an impressive tribute to Thomson's popularity.

diction. Expressions like "such flights to hinder, nought conduces more," "hyacinthine rods Enwreathed with azure bells," "each gaudy chaliced bloom," "surpassing far the medicated cup,"[1] sound more like 1726 than 1809. It is probably from Thomson, also, that Grahame took the unusual compound epithets which are sprinkled copiously through his last three volumes.[2] Along with such compounds, the absurd periphrases that deface *The Seasons* find their way not only into the *British Georgics* but into the genuinely poetic passages of the *Birds of Scotland*. To the words "powder," "gun," and "shot" Grahame seems to have had a real aversion, using instead "the explosive grain," "the murderous tube," "the two-fold tube, formed for a double death," "the leaden viewless shower, Vollied from flashing tube," and "the leaden bolt, Slung from the mimic lightning's nitrous wing."[3]

The influence of Milton on Grahame's work may be inferred from what has been said of the several pieces. In the nature passages and in the earlier, simpler poems — the *Rural Calendar, The Sabbath,* and *Sabbath Walks* — there is little, often nothing, to remind one of *Paradise Lost*, although *The Sabbath* does contain such expressions as "in peace they home resort," "be pictur'd bright To latest times," "had pow'rless struck Th' infatuate monarch";[4] and the *Rural Calendar* opens with the lines,

> Long ere the snow-veiled dawn, the bird of morn
> His wings quick claps, and sounds his cheering call.

The later works, however, which are more formal in manner, recall Milton clearly though never strongly. Even the descriptive parts often show his influence:

> Long ere the wintry gusts, with chilly sweep,
> Sigh through the leafless groves, the swallow tribes,
> Heaven-warned, in airy bevies congregate,
> Or clustering sit, as if in deep consult
> What time to launch; but, lingering, they wait,
> Until the feeble of the latest broods
> Have gathered strength, the sea-ward path to brave.

---

[1] Pages 133, 134, 135, 141. Similar expressions which recall Thomson and his followers are to be found in the *Birds of Scotland* and *Africa Delivered*. In the former, for example, we have "clinging supine, to deal the air-gleaned food" (p. 65), and "single drops, Prelusive of the shower" (p. 66).

[2] Here are five that occur within twelve lines, — "cassia-perfumed," "deep-logged," "stern-emblazoned," "carnage-freighted," "ocean-buried" (*Birds of Scotland*, p. 80).

[3] *British Georgics*, p. 159; *Rural Calendar* (September); *Birds of Scotland*, pp. 12, 40, 84.

[4] Pages 15, 17.

Amid November's gloom, a morn serene
Will sometimes intervene, o'er cottage roof,
And grassy blade, spreading the hoarfrost bright,
That crackles crisp when marked by early foot.[1]

Although the unusual compound epithets, the grandiose diction
into which, as we have seen, Grahame occasionally slipped, and the
parenthetical expressions of which he is fond were of course derived
ultimately from *Paradise Lost*, he may have adopted them unconsciously from other eighteenth-century poets. For, though he borrowed several of Milton's very phrases,[2] it is doubtful if he was
directly influenced by him to any appreciable extent.

We have now followed the long blank-verse descriptive poem from
its birth in *Cyder* and *The Seasons* through the first decade of the
nineteenth century.[3] Here, singularly enough, it disappears. No
important long poem, rimed or unrimed, the main purpose of which
is to describe nature, seems to have been published since 1810.
Scattered survivals there undoubtedly are, like the few green leaves
that may struggle from the trunk of an old tree; but these do not
indicate any real vitality. The type is dead, or rather it has been
absorbed into other types and broken up into shorter poems. Wordsworth's verse illustrates the change; for, while it includes many sonnets and other short pieces that picture the out-of-doors, and while

---

[1] *Birds of Scotland*, p. 67; *British Georgics*, p. 213.

[2] For example, "the . . . plough-boy singing, blythe" (*Rural Calendar*, March, cf.
Allegro, 63–5); "from morn to dewy eve" (*Birds of Scotland*, p. 65, cf. *P. L.*, i. 742–3);
"bloomy sprays" (*Sabbath*, p. 27, cf. sonnet to the nightingale, line 1).

[3] Five other descriptive pieces that I have seen should be mentioned, although they
make little or no attempt to picture the out-of-doors: E. Cooper's *Bewdley* (1759, a
rambling, tedious piece concerned chiefly with "the harmless, charming fair," which
borrows several phrases from Milton), Charles Dunster's *St. James's Street* (1790),
Charles Lucas's *Old Serpentine Temple of the Druids* (1795), R. C. Dallas's *Kirkstall
Abbey* (1797), and William Holloway's *Scenes of Youth* (1803). There is also considerable description (usually of obvious beauties expressed in stilted language) in blank-
verse poems that will be considered in subsequent chapters, — for example, in Blair's
Grave (1743), J. G. Cooper's *Power of Harmony* (1745), and James Foot's *Penseroso*
(1771), which are noticed below under Philosophical Poetry. A number of later pieces
of some length in Miltonic blank verse I have passed over, because, as they seem to be
dull, conventional, and without a strong love of nature, they apparently contributed
nothing to the development of descriptive poetry, but knowing them only from reviews I may not do them justice: an anonymous *Ride and Walk through Stourhead*
(1779); "Mr." Robinson's *Prize of Venus, or Killarney Lake* (1786); William Greenwood's *Poem written during a Shooting Excursion on the Moors* (1787); the anonymous
Address to Loch Lomond (1788, perhaps by James Cririe) and *Morning Walk* (1792);
Thomas Cole's *Life of Hubert* (1795–7,"a narrative, descriptive, and didactic poem");
John Jackson's *Gils-land Wells* (1797); Brian Broughton's *Six Picturesque Views in
North Wales* (1801); James Cririe's *Scottish Scenery* (1803). For the reviews in which
they are noticed, see Bibliography I, under the several dates.

there are many descriptive passages in *The Prelude* and *The Excursion*, the main purpose of all his longer works is philosophical. Two of the earliest pieces, it is true, the *Evening Walk* and *Descriptive Sketches*, belong, except that they are in rime, to the class we have been considering; but it is significant of the changing order that none of the mature poems do.

The form had served its purpose and there is no reason to regret its passing. Admirable as was much of the descriptive verse, a long poem cannot be made up entirely of pictures of nature, and the episodes, moralizings, and accounts of famous persons and places with which Thomson and his successors diversified their works are hardly successful. In previous and subsequent poetry descriptions are introduced incidentally, or, better still, as with Wordsworth and Hardy, are made an integral part of a narrative or philosophical work. The inevitable formlessness and digressiveness of the long nature poem brought it into disrepute among more critical readers.[1] Pope sneered at his own early work, in which "pure Description held the place of Sense," and, like many of his contemporaries, seems to have regarded pictures of the country as purely decorative, for he thought a poem made up of them "as absurd as a feast made up of sauces." [2] The *Monthly Review* held that this kind of verse "is doubtless inferior, both in dignity and utility, to ethic compositions," and questioned whether it were not "in itself a bad species of poetry." "More descriptive poetry!" it exclaimed on the appearance of Wordsworth's second volume, "Have we not yet enough? Must eternal changes be rung on uplands and lowlands, and nodding forests, and brooding clouds, and cells, and dells, and dingles?" [3] Yet there can be no doubt as to the popularity of most pieces of the class. "The cultivators of the higher species of the poetic art," declared the *Critical Review*, "must be contented with the applause of the learned and discerning few: but the poet who pourtrays the appearances of nature . . . provides a feast for the public, and will not fail to obtain the reward to which he is entitled. — Hence, while the

---

[1] These qualities, together with the inflated language and contorted style of many poems of the class, are amusingly parodied in Samuel Wesley's piece, *The Descriptive, a Miltonick, after the Manner of the Moderns* (*Poems*, 1736, pp. 151–6).

[2] See Joseph Warton's edition of Pope (1797), iv. 22 n.

[3] xviii. 278 (1758); enl. ed., xii. 166, 216–17 (1793). In 1798 it referred to "the ill success of most adventurers in this province of poetry" (enl. ed., xxvii. 106), while twelve years earlier it had remarked, "In poems merely descriptive, it requires no common command of language, as well as strength of fancy, to support the simple majesty of blank verse, as many unsuccessful attempts have sufficiently proved" (lxxiv. 70). Chalmers in 1810 (*English Poets*, xvii. 451) thought Scott's *Amwell* "liable to all the objections attached to descriptive poetry."

odes of Gray are read by few and relished by fewer still, the Seasons of Thomson are in the hands of every one." [1]

What light, we may well ask before leaving the subject, does this survey of unrimed descriptive verse throw upon the work of the greater men who wrote it, Thomson, Cowper, and Wordsworth? As to Thomson there can be no question. Not only is *The Seasons* the first extensive picture of the out-of-doors, but until the publication of *The Task* it dominated poetry of the kind no less in style and diction than in plan and in the aspects of nature presented, and even in Wordsworth's day its influence was still considerable.

With Cowper the case is different. He was not so much an innovator as a perfecter. He did not begin things, but encouraged them in a direction they were already taking. It is doubtful if the course of English literature would have been noticeably different if he had never written; at the most he but strengthened tendencies already started. His work is largely didactic and religious, like that of his contemporaries; and, like most of them, he seldom loses sight of a house and never strays from the peaceful, cultivated country to the wild moors or the lonely mountain lakes. In observation, and in drawing finely detailed pictures of actual scenes, Cowper made no notable advance. It is his humor, taste, and sensitiveness, his delicate, deft art, that make *The Task* what it is; and these his admirers rarely caught. Yet he undoubtedly was a strong force in the development of simple, fluent expression, and by strengthening the tendencies of men like Hurdis and Grahame in the same direction he probably helped prepare the way for *Michael* and *Tintern Abbey*.

Wordsworth's greatness becomes more apparent when his work is compared with that of his predecessors, for it is then seen to be as important historically as it is esthetically. He was not the first, to be sure, to make nature the center of the picture; that had been done in the *Walks in a Forest*, the *Birds of Scotland*, and some other poems; and, so far as closeness of observation and the use of details go, he really falls behind Gisborne and Grahame.[2] But with Wordsworth

---

[1] New arrangement, xxxi. 83 (1801).

[2] It is commonly supposed that Wordsworth, if he did not actually discover the English lakes, was at least practically the first to make them known to literature. Miss Reynolds, in her *Treatment of Nature in English Poetry*, has discussed the poems of Brown and Dalton, as well as the prose of Amory, Arthur Young, Gray, Gilpin, Hutchinson, and others who deal with the region, and may have thought it unnecessary to mention the numerous more obscure works of the same kind that were published before 1800. Yet few of us realize that so early as 1792 the public had "reason to be almost sated" with "those admired lakes" (*Crit. Rev.*, new arr., vi. 545), that the trip through them was "the *fashionable* tour of the times" (*Mo. Rev.*, enl. ed., xii. 342–3), and that even in noticing Wordsworth's *Evening Walk* the *Critical Review* (new arr.,

there is something greater than details, something that lies behind them, that is perceived not with the eyes but with the imagination, something that is, so far as poetry is concerned, the very heart of nature. It is the depth of his insight into this inner spirit, the intensity with which he felt its power, that is the new and invaluable element in his poetry. His landscapes are no more real than those of his predecessors, but they are flooded with a new light,

> The light that never was, on sea or land,
> The consecration, and the Poet's dream.

He dwelt upon aspects of nature unmentioned in earlier poetry, on

> The silence that is in the starry sky,
> The sleep that is among the lonely hills.

Again, eighteenth-century writers, however beautiful and interesting they found the out-of-doors, thought of it not as closely related to man but as a thing apart. To Wordsworth the two seemed vitally connected:

> One impulse from a vernal wood
> May teach you more of man,
> Of moral evil and of good,
> Than all the sages can.

"The round ocean and the living air, And the blue sky," spoke to him not of God alone but of man; he heard in them "the still, sad music of humanity." Shaftesbury, Akenside, and the other deists had realized the spiritual ministry that nature may perform, but with them it was largely an intellectual perception that played a small part in their lives and was by no means the center of interest in their work. Wordsworth, on the other hand, exemplified it in his life and insisted upon it in his poetry to an extent undreamed of by previous writers. Indeed, he went farther than all but a very few have cared to follow him. "Therefore am I still," he wrote, in words so familiar that their full meaning is apt to be overlooked,

> well pleased to recognise
> In nature and the language of the sense,
> The anchor of my purest thoughts, the nurse,
> The guide, the guardian of my heart, and soul
> Of all my moral being.

viii. 347) remarked, "Our northern lakes have of late years attracted the attention of the public in a variety of ways. They have been visited by the idle, described by the curious, and delineated by the artist." Richard Cumberland's *Ode to the Sun* (*Odes*, 1776, with an important preface), the anonymous *Ode to the Genius of the Lakes in the North of England* (1781, see *Crit. Rev.*, lii. 234), Joseph Budworth's *Windermere* (1798), and William Taylor's *Topographical Ode* (Southey's *Annual Anthology*, 1799, i. 1–9) all deal with the region.

It is these things, and not any supposed beginnings of romanticism or of nature poetry, that make Wordsworth's part in the *Lyrical Ballads,* aside from its esthetic value, a memorable contribution to English literature.

CHAPTER XIII

EPIC AND BURLESQUE POETRY

The Epic

"A CORRESPONDENT wrote us lately," declared the *Edinburgh Review* in 1808, "an account of a tea-drinking in the west of England, at which there assisted no fewer than six epic poets — a host of Parnassian strength, certainly equal to six-and-thirty ordinary bards." [1] Although this noteworthy encounter took place in the days of Wordsworth and Coleridge, there must have been similar occasions attended by quite as many rivals of Homer and Virgil when Queen Anne 'sometimes counsel took and sometimes tea,' or when Cowper and Johnson were votaries of "the bubbling and loud hissing urn."

For the epic ferment was unusually active in the eighteenth century. From 1695 to 1723, it will be remembered, Blackmore was pouring out

> Héroic poems without number,
> Long, lifeless, leaden, lulling lumber; [2]

and Pope's earliest and latest works were epics. The impulse towards heroic poetry seems to have grown rather than abated as the century advanced.

> Oft do I burn to snatch the Epic Lyre,

declared H. F. Cary in 1788; and, though his ambition was dampened by his less than sixteen years, he urged his friend the Swan of Lichfield to "proceed, the Epic wire Awake." [3] "By the sacred energies of Milton," Lamb wrote to Coleridge, ". . . I adjure you to attempt the Epic." [4] "Young poets," said Southey, "are, or at least used to be, as ambitious of producing an epic poem, as stage-stricken youths of figuring in Romeo or Hamlet. It had been the earliest of my daydreams. I had begun many such." [5]

---

[1] xi. 362.   [2] See p. 90 above.   [3] *Sonnets and Odes* (1788), 33, 9.

[4] Jan. 10, 1797. Further evidences of the interest in this kind of writing are seen in Voltaire's *Essay on Epic Poetry* (1727, with Rolli's *Remarks* upon it, 1728) and his epic *La Henriade* (1723, with John Lockman's translation of it into blank verse, 1732), and William Hayley's rimed *Essay on Epic Poetry* (1782, "in five epistles" with elaborate notes).

[5] Preface to the 1837 edition of *Joan of Arc* (*Works*, 1837, vol. i. p. xvii); see also his *Life and Correspondence* (1849), i. 118-19. Southey completed *Joan* when he was only nineteen; Pope began an epic called *Alcander* when he was thirteen, and James Montgomery one on Alfred when he was two years older; Glover published nine books of his

Although most of these juvenile efforts were never completed, or if finished were never published, so many of them did get into print that the *Monthly Review* declared in 1802, "Epic poems are become 'as plenty as blackberries '"; [1] and the young Byron exclaimed,

> Another Epic! Who inflicts again
> More books of blank upon the sons of men? [2]

If these ambitious attempts had been warranted by considerable success in verse, or by evidences of unusual powers of poetical narration on the part of their authors, there would be less cause to wonder at their number; but as a rule they appear to have sprung only from the wish to join the ranks of the "bright celestial choir Of bards" by writing

> such potent lays
> As may the wide world fill with dumb amaze. [3]

Not that any of them succeeded in amazing the world; for we are told that they seldom lived longer "than the constitution of a republic, or the celebrity of a German drama," [4] and it is certain that few eighteenth-century Iliads reached a second edition, and that only one, Glover's *Leonidas*, was really popular. [5]

Epic-writing was not, however, an isolated phenomenon; it was an expression of that love of the heroic — of mouth-filling words, long speeches, and noble sentiments, of self-conscious but incredibly brave princes — which struts through the tragedy of the time. If even in that day such things did not attract readers, no wonder they now appear as absurd as drum-majors and showy uniforms in real war, no wonder they have been relegated to the melodrama, to the speeches of demagogues, and to Fourth-of-July orations. The epic seems to us, as indeed it did to Horace Walpole, [6] to belong, with the

Leonidas at the age of twenty-five; Sir William Jones was twenty-three when he formed the "design" and composed at least part of *Britain Discovered*, "an heroic poem in twelve books"; Richard Cumberland wrote part of an epic on India soon after he left college, and Landor composed the Phocaeans while at college; Henry Milman began *Samor* at Eton and nearly finished it before leaving Oxford; Macaulay wrote three cantos of *Olaus the Great* when he was only eight years old, and parts of at least three more epic poems before he was fourteen; and John Fitchett cannot have been much over twenty when he began his lifelong struggle with *King Alfred*.

[1] Enlarged ed., xxxvii. 359.   [2] *English Bards*, 385–6.

[3] Cary, *Sonnets*, etc. (1788), 33.

[4] *Mo. Rev.*, enl. ed., xxxvii. 359 (1802). The year previous the *Critical Review*, after a long discussion of Ogilvie's epic, concluded somewhat wearily (new arr., xxxii. 403), "It is saying little to add, that the Britannia is not inferior to any one of the numerous works of the same class which have lately made their appearance."

[5] The indifference of the public may also be deduced from the number of epic poems that were published in part but never completed.

[6] See his letter to William Mason, June 25, 1782.

popular ballad and the chronicle play, to the past. Keats and Arnold are the only notable English poets of the last century who attempted it, and *Hyperion* remained but a fragment and *Sohrab and Rustum* but an episode. The chief heroic story of the British, in which Milton saw another *Aeneid*, became in Victorian hands the *Idylls of the King*, and one that suggests the *Odyssey* emerged from even the saga-loving mind of William Morris as the *Earthly Paradise*.

On one point we should probably agree with the writers of eighteenth-century epics, that if there is to be heroic poetry the proper vehicle for it is blank verse.[1] There were several reasons for the prevalence of such an opinion in the days of Thomson and Cowper,— the difficulty of writing a long work in heroic couplets, the monotony of it when written, the examples of Homer and Virgil, which carried great weight, and that of Milton, which in this instance probably carried even greater. For, as we have seen, by 1730 it was commonly agreed that *Paradise Lost* was the greatest epic in any modern language and for loftiness and grandeur the supreme English work. The matter of grandeur was of no small importance, inasmuch as poets accepted the epic conventions and, worrying very little about naturalness of expression, sought for the sublime. In order to do this they frankly copied Milton's style, diction, and at times even his "machinery," with the result that in no other field was his influence so marked and in no other was it of so little value.

Since these epics did not appeal to the reading public but remained exotics fostered only by the ambitions of poets, and since they had slight influence on one another, they show little development. To be sure, those composed after 1800 are usually free from many of the vices which disfigure those written a hundred years

---

[1] The following rimed epics (of which only the *Epigoniad* is of any importance) are all I have noticed: Edward Howard's *Caroloiades, or the Rebellion of Forty One* (1689); Richard Blackmore's *Prince Arthur* (1695), *King Arthur* (1697), *Eliza* (1705), and *Alfred* (1723); Thomas Ken's *Edmund* and *Hymnotheo* (written before 1711); John Henley's *Esther* (1714); Aaron Hill's *Gideon* (c. 1716-49) and *Fanciad* (1743); an anonymous *Britannia, a Poem of the Epic Kind* (Canterbury, 1723; not seen, may be in blank verse); John Harvey's *Life of Robert Bruce* (Edin., 1729, reprinted as *The Bruciad*, 1769); William Wilkie's *Epigoniad* (Edin., 1757); George Cockings's *War* (1760), *Paoliad* (1769), and *American War* (1781); James Ogden's *British Lion Rous'd* (1762), *Revolution* (1790), and *Emanuel, or Paradise Regained* (Manchester, 1797; not seen, may be in blank verse); Hannah Cowley's *Siege of Acre* (1799); Sir James Bland Burges's *Richard the First* (1801); H. J. Pye's *Alfred* (1801); W. H. Drummond's *Battle of Trafalgar* (Belfast, 1806), and Thomas Adams's poem with the same title (*Poetical Works*, Alnwick, 1811, pp. 14-114); Joseph Cottle's *Messiah* (1815). The American epics, Timothy Dwight's *Conquest of Canaan* (Hartford, 1785) and Joel Barlow's *Columbiad* (Hartford, 1787), are worth noting. *Washington, or Liberty Restored* (1809), by Thomas Northmore, also an American, follows Milton in verse, style, phrasing, and "machinery."

earlier, they exhibit better taste and a better understanding of blank verse; but anything approaching epic power is still as much to seek as in Blackmore's days. The later pieces are more readable, but, except for those of Southey, Landor, and Keats, there is no more reason for their being read. The earlier efforts, it has been said. constitute "the most desolate region of English poetry, a dreary '*No man's land*,' forbidding desert, without sign of human occupation or interest . . . through which few, if any, living travellers have ever forced their way." [1] And it must be owned that eighteenth-century epics do not possess the interest many duller works have by virtue of dealing with the times in which their authors lived, and that they rarely entice the reader to continue to the end or leave any definite impression on his mind. The truth is that, with the possible exception of Southey's *Madoc* and *Roderick*, even the best want that quality indispensable in an epic but usually lacking in all English poetry, narrative power. They are largely given over to speeches, soliloquies, descriptions, and comments; they are without action, their story never hurries one along, and their men and women are lifeless types. As Walpole said, "Epic poetry is the art of being as long as possible in telling an uninteresting story." [2]

What makes the poems tiresome is in part the lack of suppleness and swiftness in the blank verse of the period, which had not yet been made a good narrative medium, and in part the desire to be impressive, which led writers to stiffen their style with inversions and other Miltonisms until rapid movement was impossible; but to a considerable extent it is because men who possessed any power of sustained narration were then turning to the newest, most popular, and most remunerative of literary forms, the novel. Indeed, it may be urged with considerable justice that *Tom Jones* is a truer epic than any of its ponderous verse-contemporaries that claimed the title. Only after a course of penitential reading in the narrative poems of the eighteenth and early nineteenth centuries can the *Lay of the Last Minstrel* and *Marmion*, *The Giaour* and *Mazeppa*, be appreciated and their immediate and remarkable vogue be understood. They are, of course, romances not epics, and they have many obvious faults; but they are unquestionably good stories, swift, vivid, well told, and full of movement, which is more than can be said of their predecessors for a century preceding. *Gebir* and *Hyperion* atone as poems for what they lack as stories; but the eighteenth-century epic-writers were neither story-tellers nor poets, and for such there

[1] W. M. Dixon, *English Epic and Heroic Poetry* (1912), 241.
[2] Letter to Mason, June 25, 1782.

is no hope. There was but one thing for them to do, — laboriously to copy Homer, Virgil, and Milton, employing the plan and many of the details of the Greek or the Roman writer and the language and style of the English one, together with a goodly number of the long similes and classical allusions with which all three abound. In the matter of "machinery" they found Pope's advice useful, "If you have need of devils, draw them out of Milton's Paradise." [1]

Milton's influence on heroic poetry was first seen in the works that have already been noticed, — the rimed productions of Blackmore, such quasi-religious epics as the anonymous *Prae-existence* (1714) and *Last Day* (c. 1720) or Thomas Newcomb's *Last Judgment of Men and Angels* (1723), and the poems on the battles of Blenheim and Ramillies. [2] A little later James Ralph, who had sailed from America in the company of Benjamin Franklin, published his *Zeuma, or the Love of Liberty* (1729), the story of a king of Chili who dies resisting the Spanish invaders. For this romantic and grandiose picture of a noble savage passionately devoted to freedom and to his sweetheart, Ralph used a more Miltonic style, diction, and kind of versification than he had employed in his earlier blank verse. These lines are typical:

> At first the *Hero* gave unbounded loose
> To anger and revenge; then, calmly sad,
> His fury ebb'd in silent tears away;
> Strait, prompted by despair, he rav'd anew. [3]

Zeuma is too romantic and too brief to be termed an epic. The first unrimed poem after *Paradise Lost* which can lay any claim to that title is the only one that ever enjoyed any real popularity, Richard Glover's *Leonidas* (1737). This work reached a fourth edition within two years, and even after 1800 was three times reprinted, once in America; [4] it was immediately translated into French, while in Germany it had considerable vogue and no little influence. Lyttelton devoted an issue of *Common Sense* to its

---

[1] *Art of Sinking in Poetry*, ch. xv (*Works*, Elwin-Courthope ed., x. 403).

[2] See pp. 90–95, 97, 101 n. 2, 109–11, above.

[3] Page 47. For Ralph's other Miltonic blank verse, see p. 239 above.

[4] No editions were published in London between 1739 and 1798, except the enlarged one that Glover brought out in 1770, which, though reprinted at Dublin two years later, seems to have attracted little attention. It is hard to understand how it came to be reissued in 1804, 1810, and 1814, since the references to the poem show that the first enthusiasm had soon waned (see, e. g., *Europ. Mag.*, 1786, ix. 2, 4; *Mo. Rev.*, 1788, lxxix. 515, and enl. ed., 1797, xxiv. 455; Chalmers, *English Poets*, 1810, xvii. 9–10; Boaden's *Memoirs of Kemble*, 1825, i. 303). Within ten years of its publication, indeed, Horace Walpole wrote (to H. S. Conway, Oct. 24, 1746) that *Leonidas* was already forgotten.

praise, as "*one of those few* [poems] of distinguish'd Worth and Excellence, which will be handed down with Respect to all Posterity,
and which, in the long Revolution of past Centuries, but *two or three
Countries* have been able to produce"; [1] Matthew Green, in his witty
poem *The Spleen* (1737), gave more than twenty lines to Glover, —

> But there's a youth, that you can name,
> Who needs no leading-strings to fame,
> Whose quick maturity of brain
> The birth of Pallas may explain . . . ;[2]

and William Thompson declared in a poem *To the Author of Leonidas*,

> Promiscuous Beauties dignify thy Breast,
> By Nature happy, as by Study blest,
> Thou, Wit's *Columbus!* from the Epick-Throne
> New Worlds descry'd, and made Them all our own. [3]

Yet the thirty books of the "stupendous and terrible" *Athenaid*
(1787), in which Glover sought to repeat his success by continuing
the story of the Persian invasion to its end, seem to have been an
utter failure.[4] To be sure, no one in recent years has become sufficiently interested in either work to determine whether *Leonidas* is
really superior to its sequel; but at least it is shorter (there were only
nine books until 1770, when three more were added), it had the
advantage of coming fifty years earlier, and it is apparently richer
in lofty sentiments and paeans on liberty. These last are said to
have been largely responsible for its immediate popularity, since

[1] April 9, 1737. Robert Phillimore (*Memoirs of Lyttelton*, 1845, i. 100) says that
"Fielding and Pitt were scarcely behind Lyttelton in extolling" the merits of *Leonidas*.

[2] Lines 556–77.

[3] *Poems on Several Occasions* (Oxford, 1757), 33. Striking testimony to Glover's
immediate vogue is afforded by the publication, within a year, of Henry Pemberton's
Observations on Poetry, especially the Epic, occasioned by Leonidas (1738). "Pray who
is that Mr. Glover," asked Swift, writing from Ireland to Pope, May 31, 1737, "who
writ the epic poem called Leonidas, which is reprinting here, and has great vogue?"
"Nothing else," according to Joseph Warton (in his edition of Pope's *Works*, 1797, ix.
297 n.), "was read or talked of at Leicester-house." Some of this popularity is undoubtedly due to the subject-matter; for Southey wrote to Bedford, Nov. 13, 1793,
"Leonidas . . . has ever been a favourite poem with me; I have read it, perhaps more
frequently than any other composition, and always with renewed pleasure . . . perhaps,
chiefly owing to the subject."

[4] They "fell plumb into the water of oblivion," declares Dowden (*Life of Southey*,
1879, p. 51). Cowper, who had to read the first book twice before he could understand
it, concluded finally, "It does not deserve to be cast aside as lumber, the treatment
which I am told it has generally met with" (letters to Samuel Rose and Lady Hesketh,
Jan. 19 and Feb. 4. 1789). Southey thought that if published nearer to *Leonidas* it
might have "partaken the gale, for its merits are not inferior" (*Life and Works of
Cowper*, 1836, ii. 319).

the Prince of Wales's party, who thought themselves the guardians of freedom, treated it as an attack on Walpole.[1]

As "Leonidas Glover" was but twenty-five years old when he published his first epic, he naturally exhibits in it the faults typical of youth, — rant, pose, sentimentality, a self-conscious, romantic idealism, and a lack of understanding of real men and women. His characters shine with so many virtues that it is difficult to see them. The "god-like presence" of Leonidas, for example, is pictured thus:

> Dignity and grace
> Adorn his frame, and manly beauty join'd
> With strength Herculean. On his aspect shines
> Sublimest virtue, and desire of fame,
> Where justice gives the laurel; in his eye
> The inextinguishable spark, which fires
> The souls of patriots: while his brow supports
> Undaunted valour, and contempt of death.[2]

He moves like a tragic hero:

> Now from th' assembly with majestic steps
> Forth moves their godlike king, with conscious worth
> His gen'rous bosom glowing.[3]

Even when with his family he is the same:

> Great in woe
> Amid his children, who inclose him round,
> He stands indulging tenderness and love
> In graceful tears.[4]

Between personages of this sort there can be no conversation. Instead, each delivers orations at the others, and, though the interstices between their speeches are filled with prodigies of valor, it is the harangues that claim the chief interest.

It is hard to see how any one who really appreciated the direct simplicity and naturalness of Homer or the native dignity of Milton's style could have failed to detect the theatrical pose and buckram stiffening of Glover's work. But the eighteenth century was too fond of swelling phrases, lofty sentiments, heroic characters, and striking attitudes to be over-particular as to whether they were sensible and true. They were impressive, and that was enough. Modern readers who share these tastes — and there are not a few — may likewise find the two epics interesting, may be moved by the heroic actions depicted in them and by their expression of scorn for

---

[1] Lyttelton's poem on *Leonidas* (*Poetical Works*, 1801, pp. 136–8) deals with it not from the esthetic but entirely from the political point of view.

[2] i. 117–24.   [3] i. 174–6; cf. ii. 67–9.   [4] i. 369–72.

what is low, may see beauty in their many long similes and splendor in the roll of their lines, or may, like earlier generations, enjoy declaiming their sounding speeches and learning their quotable passages; but most persons will, like Mr. Saintsbury, find them "impossible."

When Lyttelton wrote, "If the Diction of *Leonidas* be softer, and the general Flow of the Numbers more harmonious than that of *Milton* himself, it may, in part, be ascrib'd to Mr. *Pope*, as the great Polisher and Improver of our Verse," [1] he called attention to the two main influences at work on Glover's epic, — Pope's Homer and *Paradise Lost*. Although there is no mythological machinery in *Leonidas*, the subject-matter of the work, the numerous battles and speeches, and the long similes are undoubtedly patterned after the *Iliad;* the characterization, spirit, and atmosphere, the self-consciousness and artificiality which pervade the whole, suggest Pope; the style is obviously Miltonic, and the diction that of Milton conventionalized by Pope. The prosody also reveals a strange union of Puritan and Augustan conceptions, for it is blank verse fettered by the regularity and end-stopped lines of the heroic couplet. A few men of discernment, like Samuel Say, [2] must have been annoyed by these bastard Miltonisms; but the majority failed, as did Lyttelton and Pemberton, to perceive the tawdry glitter of *Leonidas* or the monotony of its "softer" and "more harmonious" versification. [3] Part of its popularity was unquestionably due to these very defects, to its combining in what seems to us an absurd manner the three principal literary forces of the day, classicism, Popeism, and Miltonism. [4]

Between 1737 and 1792 Glover had the field of the blank-verse epic practically to himself. In 1756, to be sure, George Keate began his *Helvetiad*, but was dissuaded by Voltaire from continuing it; [5] and though in 1759 Alexander Gordon, "a volunteer in the Prussian service," presented to Frederick the Great his *Prussiad*, which deals with the Silesian war, yet a piece of less than six hundred lines can hardly be termed an epic. [6] Joseph Hazard's still briefer *Conquest of*

---

[1] *Common Sense*, April 9, 1737.   [2] See above, p. 90.   [3] See above, p. 56.

[4] For Glover's Miltonic *Poem on Sir Isaac Newton* (1728), and his *London, or the Progress of Commerce* (1739), see p. 383 below.

[5] This same year appeared the anonymous *Sophronia*, one of the very few unrimed narrative poems of the period that are not epic. It contains five books of extremely moral, extremely dull, and extremely Miltonic blank verse.

[6] *The Prussiad* pictures Frederick as a very pious but crafty prince who

> From motives justify'd, and self-defence,
> Urg'd, tho' reluctant, drew his legions forth (lines 2–3).

It is pompous, uninspired, and obviously Miltonic. The same may be said of the *Prussian Campaign*, "a Poem celebrating the Atchievements of Frederick the Great in

Quebec (1769) and Charles Crawford's *First Canto of the Revolution* (1776) are negligible for the same reason.[1] Crawford, it is true, planned a mighty effort in twelve parts dealing with the revolution of 1688, but he apparently never published more than one book, which does not finish Monmouth's rebellion.[2] Sir William Jones seems not to have got even so far as this with his *Britain Discovered* (which was to be "an heroic poem in twelve books"), perhaps because he could not determine whether to use blank verse or rime.[3]

The one heroic work of epic proportions to be published between Glover's *Leonidas* (1737) and his *Athenaid* (1787) was an account of the fall of Babylon and the return of the Israelites to Jerusalem which the Rev. William H. Roberts brought out in 1774 as *Judah Restored*. It is not an important contribution. There is nothing objectionable about it, to be sure; Roberts does not rant and is never ridiculous or sentimental, but his book is monotonous and uninteresting and there seems to be no adequate excuse for its existence. Its author undoubtedly thought it would be of value religiously, like his dull, pompous *Poetical Epistle on the Existence, Attributes, and Providence of God* (published in three parts in 1771), for biblical references are spattered over the foot of nearly every page. Perhaps, since he was for many years one of the king's chaplains, he may have intended *Judah* to edify royalty. At least it has the pomp befitting so august an audience, and is in keeping with what we know about the writer, "a portly man and of much pride and state," — "parading" is Fanny Burney's word.[4] Yet for eighteenth-century blank verse, particularly as used for heroic purposes, his style, though

1756-7," which William Dobson (who had translated *Paradise Lost* into Latin and who used its verse in two translations from the Latin, see p. 328, n. 2, below) issued in 1758.

[1] Note also *Quebec* (1760), "a Poetical Essay in imitation of the Miltonic Stile: being a regular Narrative of the . . . Transactions performed by the British Forces . . . in the glorious Expedition against Canada, in the year 1759; the Performance of a Volunteer." The American war, the "low and almost desperate state" in which it left England, together with "her sudden and unexpected recovery, under Mr. Pitt's administration," forms the subject of the seven dull books of James Brown's *Britain Preserved* (Edin., 1800). The year previous William Hildreth had poured out a quantity of unusually heroic blank verse which he termed *The Niliad*, "an Epic Poem written in honour of the glorious Victory off the Mouth of the Nile."

[2] Although Crawford commends Milton highly in the opening lines, and makes unblushing use of his style and language, it is the muse of the "still greater" Voltaire that he invokes (see *Crit. Rev.*, xli. 475-8).

[3] For the "design" of his poem, with one passage in heroic couplets and two longer ones without rime (written in 1770), see his *Works*, 1807, ii. 429-54.

[4] Cole (Addit. MS. 5879, f. 38 *b*), quoted in *Dict. Nat. Biog.*; Madame D'Arblay's *Diary*, Nov. 23, 1786.

hardly natural enough to warrant Southey's praise for its "plain dignity," [1] is comparatively free from distortion and pomposity.

Roberts was one of those ardent admirers of blank verse who wished to banish rime entirely from serious poetry; yet he understood his favorite measure sufficiently to see that few who wrote it had "learnt the secret of relieving the ear by a proper variation of the cadence" or by the use of run-over lines. He avoided these mistakes himself by patterning his work after "that wonderful monument of human Genius, Paradise lost." [2] He made no secret of this indebtedness; how could he, indeed, in view of the style, the strange proper names, and the verbal borrowings of a passage like this?

> That throne, where conscious of superior worth
> Cyrus exalted sits. Around him stand
> . . . . Carmanian chiefs,
> And Arachosian, Ctesias, and the son
> Of old Orontes, and that dreaded name
> Tigranes. Near the throne on either side
> Stands Gadatas, and Gobryas.[3]

The first attempt after *Paradise Lost* to write a *Christian* epic seems to be Richard Cumberland's *Calvary, or the Death of Christ* (1792). Its debt to Milton is, as the author frankly acknowledged, very great.[4] The first of the eight books is devoted to a council,

---

[1] "I read it often," he says, "and can still recur to it with satisfaction: and perhaps I owe something to the plain dignity of its style, which is suited to the subject, and everywhere bears the stamp of good sense and careful erudition" (*Life and Works of Cowper*, 1836, iii. 32 n.). G. I. Huntingford, in his *Introduction to the Writing of Greek* (pt. ii, 3d ed., Oxford, 1791, p. 119), remarks of *Judah Restored*, "It is impossible to mention this Work, without adding, that it contains many Sublime and Pathetic strokes."

[2] *Judah*, preface, pp. xx, xvi (but Roberts does not say he patterned his work after Milton's). His *Poetical Epistle to Christopher Anstey, on the English Poets, chiefly those who have written in Blank Verse* (1773), begins with attacking rime and praising Milton (quoted in *Crit. Rev.*, xxxv. 53).

[3] iii. 442–51; cf. *P. L.*, ii. 1–5, 959–67. Even the last line of the poem,
> Sonorous trumpets join their martial sound,

is adapted from *Paradise Lost*, i. 540,
> Sonorous metal blowing martial sounds.

Other borrowings that I have noticed are: "streams, like a meteor" (ii. 163, cf. *P. L.*, i. 537); "thrice his colour chang'd" (iii. 460, cf. *P. L.*, iv. 114–15); "sees, or thinks he sees" (iii. 464, cf. *P. L.*, i. 783–4, part of a simile in each case; see also *Judah*, vi. 162); "flies diverse" (v. 41, cf. *P. L.*, x. 284); "draws his train" (vi. 158, cf. *P. L.*, vii. 306, of a river in each case); "for speed succinct" (vi. 368, cf. *P. L.*, iii. 643); "comes mantling o'er his arms" (vi. 456, cf. *P. L.*, v. 279); "uncreated light" (vi. 490, cf. *P. L.*, iii. 4–6, ii. 150);
> Long the way,
> And perilous, which from Chaldea leads
> To Salem's ruin'd walls (iii. 173–5, cf. *P. L.*, ii. 432–3).

[4] "It was not till I had taken up Milton's immortal poem of *Paradise Lost*, and read

summoned by Satan, in which various plans for defeating the Christ are discussed. After several of the fallen angels have given their opinions it is decided that Moloch shall tempt Judas. The entire deliberation is modelled closely on that held in Pandemonium: the speakers are the same, their natures are the same, and so is the trend of their several suggestions. Throughout the poem, which deals with the life of Christ from the last supper to the resurrection, Satan and his angels play an important part. Gabriel is also a character, and in the harrying of hell, which strongly suggests *Paradise Lost*, he is the one who executes Christ's commands. Verbal borrowings are everywhere,[1] and, as this passage will show, the diction, style, and constructions could hardly be more Miltonic:

> His princes thus review'd, from the hill top
> SATAN swift-glancing flew, and in the midst
> Rose like a meteor; whereat all the host
> Sent up a general shout: he with his hand
> Gave sign, and wheel'd the Stygian phalanx round. . . .
> Tho' in his heart, by mut'nous passions torn,
> Thought clash'd with thought, and all was anarchy,
> Yet with assum'd composure beck'ning forth
> His princes, whilst th' inferior throng stood off,
> And mute attention reign'd, in few thus spake.[2]

Calvary was at first neglected; but Nathan Drake's commendation in his *Literary Hours* (1798) brought it "out of . . . obscurity, and," in the opinion of the author, "obtained for it a place amongst our British classics." [3] As a result it went through seven editions in eleven years and was reprinted at least three times in America. It is

it studiously and completely through," he says in his *Memoirs* (1807, ii. 264), "that I brought the plan of *Calvary* to a consistency, and resolved to venture on the attempt."

[1] For example: "fuel'd clouds" (i. 76, cf. *P. L.*, i. 234); "bold emprize" (i. 245, cf. *P. L.*, xi. 642, and *Comus*, 610); "Chemos, the sin of Moab; power obscene" (i. 281, cf. *P. L.*, i. 406); "In me is . . . no delay" (i. 716, cf. *P. L.*, xii. 615); "pow'rs and dominions" (iii. 690, cf. *P. L.*, ii. 11, the opening of Satan's address in each case); "Mammon exalted sate" (iii. 762, cf. *P. L.*, ii. 5); "of adamantine proof" (iii. 845, cf. *Samson*, 134); "the grisly monarch" (iv. 169, cf. *P. L.*, ii. 704, iv. 821); "Chaos and old Night" (iv. 787, cf. *P. L.*, i. 543); "golden panoply" (vi. 244, cf. *P. L.*, vi. 527), etc., etc. An idea is often borrowed from Milton but expressed in somewhat different words, as in i. 212–14:

> Satan thus
> Stood eminent, and call'd his dark compeers;
> So loud he call'd that to the farthest bounds . . .

(cf. *P. L.*, i. 589–91, 314–15).

[2] i. 352–66; cf. *P. L.*, i. 533–621.

[3] Cumberland's *Memoirs*, ii. 377. Drake's analysis of the poem (*Literary Hours*, 3d ed., 1804, nos. 18–21) seems to be based upon Addison's *Spectator* papers on *Paradise Lost*.

much the best piece of religious blank verse produced in the eighteenth century.[1]

Encouraged by the success of *Calvary*, Cumberland contemplated a second heroic work, to be based on the Old Testament. "Whilst these thoughts were in my mind," he tells us, " . . . my friend Sir James Burges suggested to me the history of Moses . . . and . . . imparted to me a plan deliberately and minutely methodized, and apportioned into books . . . with the argument of each correctly drawn up; a work . . . which seemed to leave little to the pen, that followed him, except the task of filling up the outline," [2] which the two men undertook jointly. Not much could be expected of a poem composed in this fashion, even if it had borne a less benumbing title than *The Exodiad*. Accordingly, although the first four books (published in 1807) took the Israelites only to the wilderness, the public seemed so content to leave them there that the remainder of the work never appeared.[3] Cumberland's *Retrospection, a Poem in Familiar Verse* (1811), written in his eightieth year, deals with his grandfather (Richard Bentley, the famous scholar) and his friends Johnson, Burke, Reynolds, and Garrick. The style, which has only a suggestion of Milton, is much the most direct and natural that he wrote.[4]

Judah Restored was soon forgotten, *The Athenaid* had been still born, and *Calvary* did not become known until after 1798; so that Southey had some reason for attributing part of the success of his *Joan of Arc* (1796) to the dearth of new English epics in the sixty years following the publication of *Leonidas*. This lack the young republican felt born to remedy. "Producing an epic poem," he wrote, ". . . had been the earliest of my day-dreams. I had begun

[1] At least one line of *Calvary* (vii. 179) is worthy to live:

Like the slow swell of seas without a wind.

The rising of Death from his pit in response to Satan's summons is also impressively described (vii. 397–413).

[2] *Memoirs*, ii. 377–8.

[3] Another work on the same subject, of the same calibre, and published the same year is Charles Hoyle's *Exodus*, of which I have seen only extracts. In the thirteen books of this poem, which apparently uses the Miltonic machinery, the *Edinburgh Review* (xi. 363, 369) found "no ray of interest or entertainment. . . . All is comfort and tranquillity in the calm creation of Mr. Hoyle; and the excellent treatise on Whist by his illustrious synonim, is fully as likely to betray the reader into unbecoming emotions." Presumably the same Rev. Charles Hoyle wrote sonnets on Scottish scenery which were praised by his friend W. L. Bowles (*Scenes and Shadows of Days Departed*, 1837, p. xlii, n.).

[4] Cumberland made a translation of part of Virgil's third *Georgic* in Miltonic blank verse when he was a boy of thirteen, and undertook an epic on the history of India soon after leaving college. Specimens of each work are given in his *Memoirs* (i. 82–7, 168–74).

many such." [1] Nor was it long before he brought one to completion, for he was just entering his twentieth year when, in the mornings of six short weeks, he composed his *Joan of Arc.*

This astonishing work had the still more astonishing good fortune of being accepted by a bookseller, Southey's friend and fellow-townsman, Joseph Cottle, — himself destined to wake the epic lyre, — who recompensed the author as handsomely as he printed his poem. The first proof-sheet, however, somewhat dampened the self-complacency of the young bard, who for six months "re-cast and re-composed" the work "while the printing went on." Before the second edition appeared he made other extensive changes, omitting all that remained of the allegorical machinery (in part the work of Coleridge) which he had originally introduced throughout the poem, and writing an entirely new and much better beginning.[2] As other alterations were made in 1806, 1812, and 1837, the poem that we now have is much more simple and natural, less crudely Miltonic and absurd, than what the boy of nineteen wrote. "Pity's crystal gem," for instance, no longer hangs on Joan's "rubied cheek"; she does not in her first speech address the Bastard of Orleans ("adown" whose "batter'd arms the tide of life Roll'd purpling") as if he were a child, or mention a wolf "horrid with brumal ice"; [3] but she is still "the delegated Maid," and at times she still speaks in words like these, almost unchanged from those that appeared in the first edition:

> "Do thou, Dunois,
> Announce my mission to the royal ear.
> I on the river's winding bank the while
> Will roam, collecting for the interview
> My thoughts, though firm, yet troubled. Who essays
> Achievements of great import will perforce
> Feel the heart heave; and in my breast I own
> Such perturbation."
> On the banks of Vienne
> Devious the Damsel turn'd.[4]

The epic heroine who delivers this address is, of course, not the simple peasant girl to whom, as she was abiding in the field keeping watch over her flocks, the angel of the Lord appeared as he had to

---

[1] See above, p. 276. For an account of some of these boyish epics, the earliest of which, composed when he was between nine and ten, was an imitation of Ariosto in heroic couplets, see his *Life and Correspondence* (1849), i. 118–19.

[2] See prefaces to *Joan of Arc* and *Vision of the Maid of Orleans*, in *Poetical Works* (1837), vol. i, pp. xv–xx, 304.

[3] First ed., i. 27–8, 18–19, 49.

[4] Edition of 1837, iii. 125–33 (first ed., iii. 101–9).

other shepherds centuries before. Yet for his melodramatic misrepresentation Southey was not to blame, since the facts regarding Joan's life and character were not known in 1796; and at least he did not picture her as a witch, a maniac, or a charlatan. Indeed, the fault with "the missioned Maid" is that she has little character of any kind; she is simply a heroic personage.

In this respect, as in its style, diction, and sentimentality, its fondness for rhetoric and noble sentiments, the poem is obviously of the eighteenth century. Its model was *Leonidas*, which Southey, as we have seen, thought he had read "more frequently than any other composition, and always with renewed pleasure . . . perhaps, chiefly owing to the subject." [1] The subject, the defence of liberty against despotism, was unquestionably a principal source of the attraction that *Leonidas* had for the enthusiastic young republican, and it was because Joan of Arc had fought for this same cause that he chose her as the heroine of his poem. She was also French and therefore doubly interesting, for those were the wondrous days of the French Revolution, when the world's great age seemed to begin anew. "Few persons but those who have lived in it," the poet wrote long afterwards, "can conceive or comprehend what the memory of the French Revolution was, nor what a visionary world seemed to open upon those who were just entering it. Old things seemed passing away, and nothing was dreamt of but the regeneration of the human race."[2] And, just as Wordsworth and Coleridge hoped for a French victory when England attacked the young republic, so Southey, acting "in direct opposition" to the rule that an epic should be national, chose for his subject the defeat of his country. "If among my readers," he announced, "there be one who can wish success to injustice, because his countrymen supported it, I desire not that man's approbation." [3] Consistently enough, therefore, he makes Joan internationally-minded, —

> To England friendly as to all the world,
> Foe only to the great blood-guilty ones,
> The masters and the murderers of mankind.

[1] See above, p. 281, n. 3. He wrote these words a few weeks after completing *Joan*. William Haller, in his admirable *Early Life of Southey* (N. Y., 1917, p. 107), thinks that Lucan's *Pharsalia*, "a great favorite with all the young romantic revolutionists," was the other chief influence on *Joan*.

[2] Letter to Caroline Bowles, Feb. 13, 1824.

[3] Preface to the first edition of *Joan*, p. vii. What Southey reprinted as this preface in the collected edition of his *Poetical Works* contains so many omissions, additions, and changes that it is much nearer to the preface of the second edition.

"May the God of Peace and Love," she prays,

> Be merciful to those blood-guilty men
> Who came to desolate the realm of France,
> To make us bow the knee, and crouch like slaves,
> Before a tyrant's footstool! . . .
> 　　　　. . . . Wretched men,
> Forced or inveigled from their homes, or driven
> By Need and Hunger to the trade of blood.[1]

Southey, accordingly, had grounds for attributing the "chief cause" of the poem's "favourable reception" to its voicing the "republican spirit" which was then sweeping across England.[2] But this was not the only cause, for even in its original form, with all its absurdities on its head, the piece is effective in a rhetorical way; it contains pleasing nature-pictures, and is more spontaneous, interesting, and rapid in its action, as well as more vigorous and condensed in its expression, than are Southey's later epics.

Even before his first heroic poem was published the industrious bard was occupied with a second, which he thought "would probably be the greatest" he should ever produce.[3] This work, *Madoc*, though completed four years later, was not published till 1805, when six more years had elapsed, one of which was "diligently employed in reconstructing" the poem.[4] In its first form it was probably not unlike its predecessor, but as finally published it differs markedly from *Joan* in style and versification, a change due not alone to the careful revision it received, but to Southey's increased maturity and conservatism. The crimson glow that had flushed the heavens and had seemed to the author of *Joan* the dawn of a new era had faded into the light of common day. The enthusiastic college boy who dreamed of an ideal commonwealth on the shores of the Susquehanna had become the busy, travelled man struggling to support a family, who was shortly to accept a pension from the crown, and to whom the beauty of regularity and propriety, the advantages of a settled and well-ordered life, appealed more and more. The change is reflected in the subject-matter of the two works; for, while Joan fights the oppressors of her country for the preservation of liberty, Madoc sails away from the oppression and injustice of his native land to seek freedom in the New World, as the

---

[1] viii. 642–4, x. 82–91. These extracts are taken from the poem as it was first printed, because their vehemence is somewhat toned down in later editions.

[2] Preface to *Joan*, in *Poetical Works* (1837), vol. i, p. xxix.

[3] See preface to the first edition of *Joan*, p. ix; and preface to *Madoc*, in *Poetical Works*, vol. v, p. xi.

[4] Preface to *Madoc* (*ib.* p. xii).

poet himself had withdrawn to the solitudes of the lake country. Yet it is easy to exaggerate the contrast, and not to recognize in the colony Madoc established in America a kind of epic pantisocracy, a realization in verse of the dreams of the young Coleridge and Southey.

Readers of *Madoc* were told, "It assumes not the degraded title of Epic";[1] and indeed such a title would have been more of an unwarranted assumption than its author realized, for the work is really a romantic tale. Though far from exhibiting the oriental strangeness of *Thalaba* or the *Curse of Kehama*, it is the production of one who as a boy read and reread the *Jerusalem Delivered* and the *Orlando Furioso* and who 'took Spenser for his master.'[2] Madoc's voyage across the Atlantic, his battles with the Aztecs, their human sacrifices, snake gods, and the rest, might, to be sure, furnish the material for an epic, but they naturally suggest the romantic treatment that Southey gave them. His emphasis on the tender emotions, his frequent pictures of nature, and above all his diffuseness make his pleasant meanderings too sentimental and familiar, too deficient in austerity, condensation, and vigor, too "soft," for an epic. These lines are typical:

> The affection of his voice,
> So mild and solemn, soften'd David's heart,
> He saw his brother's eyes, suffused with tears,
> Shine in the moon-beam as he spake; the King
> Remembered his departure, and he felt
> Feelings, which long from his disnatured breast
> Ambition had expell'd: he could almost
> Have follow'd their strong impulse.[3]

The "softness," it will be observed, makes itself felt in the style and language, which in general are simple, natural, and conversational, too much so to be epic. It had been said of *Joan*, "The language is, for the most part, modelled on that of Milton,"[4] and, "The style of the first book seems to waver in its choice of a model between Milton and Cowper. In the greatly superior second it becomes wholly Miltonic."[5] No such comment was passed on *Madoc*. Yet it would have been well-nigh impossible at the close of the eighteenth century to write a blank-verse epic, or what aspired to be one, that was uninfluenced by *Paradise Lost*. Accordingly, there is no part of this work or of its successor that does not contain lines as Miltonic as these:

[1] Preface to the first edition. Yet the preface to *Joan* had announced "*Madoc*, an Epic Poem."
[2] *Poetical Works* (1837), vol. i, preface, p. viii.
[3] *Ib.* v. 129–30.
[4] *Mo. Rev.*, enl. ed., xix. 363.
[5] Miss Seward's *Letters*, iv. 295.

> But other doom was his, more arduous toil
> Yet to achieve, worse danger to endure,
> Worse evil to be quell'd, and higher good
> Which passeth not away educed from ill;
> Whereof all unforeseeing, yet for all
> Prepared at heart, he over ocean sails.[1]

Southey's final long poem, the first volume he issued after becoming poet laureate, was *Roderick, the Last of the Goths*, which he began in 1809 and published five years later. It is much like its predecessor, cumbered with hundreds of pages of learned historical and illustrative notes, and without the "machinery" or the long similes of the epic, which it neither claims to be nor is. But it is better than *Madoc*, more condensed and closely knit, of tougher fibre, less sentimental, and seventy-five pages shorter. Religion and liberty, always prominent in Southey's poems, are here again the mainspring of the action; for Roderick, the last of the Gothic kings of Spain, who has dishonored the daughter of one of his nobles, after a long penance returns disguised as a priest to help save his country from the Moors. Sometimes, though not as a rule, the style and language are as Miltonic as in this passage:

> Cautious with course circuitous they shunn'd
> The embattled city, which in eldest time
> Thrice-greatest Hermes built, so fables say,
> Now subjugate, but fated to behold
> Ere long the heroic Prince (who passing now
> Unknown and silently the dangerous track,
> Turns thither his regardant eye) come down
> Victorious from the heights.[2]

Nobody now reads or even talks about the long narrative poems upon which Southey confidently built his expectations of literary immortality. On the contrary, they receive much less than their due, and their author is remembered, if remembered at all, as the friend of Wordsworth and Coleridge who wrote a poem on a famous battle and some tinkling lines about a waterfall.

During his college days or soon afterwards, Southey began to compose the short blank-verse *Inscriptions* which he turned out at intervals throughout his long life. These poems — fifty-two in all — make some use of the style of *Paradise Lost*, but were, in the beginning at least, confessedly patterned after the similar productions of Akenside.[3] It may be, indeed, that all Southey's Miltonisms were de-

---

[1] *Poetical Works*, v. 204.
[2] *Ib.* ix. 102. Southey also planned an epic on Noah, in hexameters: see his *Commonplace Book*, 4th series (1850), 2–3.   [3] *Poetical Works*, vol. iii, p. xi.

rived second-hand from Glover, Akenside, Cowper, Bowles, and other eighteenth-century blank-verse poets. He does not mention Milton among the twenty writers by whom he felt that his work had been affected,[1] and from the nature of his infrequent references to him it is pretty clear that he had no real love for his poetry.[2] It is an indication of the passing of Milton's vogue that a poet so preoccupied with religion and ordered freedom as was Southey should be indifferent to *Paradise Lost*. Doubtless it seemed cold and austere to the romantic author of *Thalaba*, the domestic, sentimental editor of Kirke White's *Remains*.. He admired it and left it alone, as have a host of his successors. We have arrived at the nineteenth century.

Very unlike Southey's attitude is that of his friend and admirer, Walter Savage Landor, for Landor is Milton's most ardent eulogist. Two lines in *Paradise Lost* he calls "the richest jewel that Poetry ever wore," which he "would rather have written . . . than all the poetry that has been written since Milton's time in all the regions of the earth." [3] Later he says, "My ear, I confess it, is dissatisfied with everything, for days and weeks after the harmony of *Paradise Lost*."[4] In one of his poems he speaks of

> The mighty man who open'd Paradise,
> Harmonious far above Homerick song,
> Or any song that human ears shall hear;[5]

and he wrote, "Never will I concede that he [Dante] has written so grand a poem as *Paradise Lost;* no, nor any man else. The *Iliad* in

---

[1] See *ib.*, vol. i, general preface. But neither does he mention Glover, whom, as we know, he read repeatedly (see p. 281, n. 3, above).

[2] See letters to Miss Barker, Feb. 17 and March 3, 1804, in *Selections from Letters* (1856), i. 160, 168; and below, pp. 559 n. 4, 565 n. 1. There are more favorable comments in his *Life and Correspondence* (1849), i. 86, 187, 191, iii. 204, and in his inscription for Henry Marten's apartment (*Poems*, 1797, p. 60). The only book he carried with him on a tramp in 1793 was Milton's *Defence*. In his *Hymn to the Penates* (*Poetical Works*, ii. 277) he points out a borrowing from *Paradise Lost*. In *Madoc*, "the griding steel Shall sheer its mortal way" (*ib.* v. 54) was certainly suggested by Satan's first wound (*P. L.*, vi. 325–30); a "crystal Ark, instinct with life" (*ib.* 84), recalls God's chariot "instinct with spirit" and its "crystal firmament" (*P. L.*, vi. 752, 757); "bedeck'd with gems and gold" (*ib.* 336) may be from *Paradise Lost*, i. 538, vi. 474–5. So, too, "rolling round his angry eyes" and "collected in himself" (*Joan*, first ed., viii. 454, x. 280) are like *Paradise Lost*, i. 56, ix. 673. For other poems of Southey's that show the influence of Milton, see below, pp. 473 n., 518–19, 564–5, and Bibl. I, 1794 w., 1797, 1797 w., 1828 w.

[3] *Imaginary Conversations*, "Southey and Landor" (*Works and Life*, ed. Forster, 1876, iv. 445–6). The two lines are from *Paradise Lost*, iv. 310–11,

> Yielded with coy submission, modest pride,
> And sweet, reluctant, amorous delay.

[4] *Conversations* (*ib.* 471).

[5] *To the Author of "Festus"* (*ib.* viii. 238).

comparison is Ida to the Andes. The odes of Pindar to Milton's lyrics, that is, the sonnets, Allegro, Penseroso, &c. are Epsom race-course to the New Forest." [1] These utterances might seem like the impulsive superlatives of one who did not weigh his words, were it not that Landor expressed himself to this effect frequently throughout his life. He is constantly referring to Milton. Two of the "Imaginary Conversations" are devoted to him, [2] in three more he is one of the speakers, [3] and in several others he is discussed. [4] Even in Landor's verse, where direct references would scarcely be expected, Milton is made the subject of several poems and is mentioned in many others, especially in those written during old age. [5]

Landor came under the spell of the man 'great above all other men' [6] in his twentieth year, when after his rustication from college he was spending his time in lonely rambles along the Welsh coast and in extensive reading. At first it was the classics, and particularly Pindar, that stirred him; but later, as he tells us, "My prejudices in favour of ancient literature began to wear away on *Paradise Lost;* and even the great hexameter sounded to me tinkling when I had recited aloud in my solitary walks on the seashore the haughty appeal of Satan and the deep penitence of Eve." [7]

The most important fruit of this period was the poem *Gebir*, which appeared in that *annus mirabilis* 1798, the year that saw the publication of the *Lyrical Ballads*, of Malthus's far-reaching *Essay on Population*, of the first significant American novel (Brockden Brown's *Wieland*), and of Schiller's *Wallensteins Lager;* that witnessed the completion of *Sense and Sensibility*, the birth of Leopardi, the check to Napoleon's power at the battle of the Nile, and the composition of the first great sonata produced by the revolutionary genius of Beethoven. None of the morning stars of that new day attracted less attention than did *Gebir*, but among its few readers was a reviewer who accused the author of "the common error of those who aspire to the composition of blank-verse, by borrowing too many phrases and epithets from our incomparable Milton." [8] "I challenge

---

[1] Letter of Jan. 8, 1850, quoted in Forster's *Landor* (1869), ii. 524.

[2] The two between Southey and Landor.

[3] In the two between Milton and Andrew Marvel, and the one between Galileo, Milton, and a Dominican.

[4] In those between Abbé Delille and Landor, Andrew Marvel and Bishop Parker, and most of the modern "Conversations."

[5] See, for example, *Works*, etc. (ed. Forster), viii. 137, 144, 202, 203, 215, 220, 229, 232, 239, 250, 258, 282, 285, 322, 326, 339, 341.

[6] *Last Fruit*, "Various," xxix.

[7] *Conversations*, "Abbé Delille and Landor" (*Works*, etc., iv. 101–2).

[8] *Mo. Rev.*, enl. ed., xxxi. 206–7.

him to produce them," Landor fulminated in an unpublished re-
joinder. ". . . For the language of *Paradise Lost* ought not to be the
language of *Gebir*. . . . I devoutly offer up my incense at the shrine
of Milton. Woe betide the intruder that would steal its jewels! It
requires no miracle to detect the sacrilege. The crime will be found
its punishment." [1] Several later critics have, however, maintained
that the poem is Miltonic,[2] an opinion the more natural because
Landor's enthusiasm for *Paradise Lost* began shortly before he wrote
Gebir, and because his earlier pieces were composed in heroic couplets of the pronouncedly neo-classic type. But the fact is that, as
Southey's blank verse ought not to be Miltonic but is, so Landor's
ought to be but is not. Undoubtedly the rebellious Oxford boy received stimulus, inspiration, and guidance from his reading of the
epic; undoubtedly his change from the couplet to blank verse was
due to that reading, and naturally enough there are some borrowed
phrases and occasionally a line or two that have something of a
Miltonic sound. Inversions are frequent, as they are in Greek and
Roman poetry, and adjectives are at times used for adverbs; but the
abruptness of the style prevents anything like the organ tone or the
sonorous pomp of *Paradise Lost*. If the effect of Landor's poetry is
ever Miltonic, it is in these lines:

> "Than Rhine
> What river from the mountains ever came
> More stately? most the simple crown adorns
> Of rushes and of willows intertwined
> With here and there a flower: his lofty brow
> Shaded with vines and mistletoe and oak
> He rears, and mystic bards his fame resound. . . ."
> She toucht his eyelashes with libant lip
> And breath'd ambrosial odours, o'er his cheek
> Celestial warmth suffusing.[3]

What may at first seem to be Miltonic in *Gebir* will usually prove
to be classic; in fact, parts of it were originally written in Latin. The
real model for its style is explained in one of its author's letters:
"When I began to write *Gebir*, I had just read Pindar a second time.

---

[1] Quoted in Forster's *Landor*, i. 130.

[2] Notably William Bradley (*Early Poems of Landor*, 1914), who gives a large number
of passages supposed to be taken from Milton or to be in his manner. It seems to me
that none of these are certain, and that only six of Landor's possible borrowings from
Milton are worth considering: *Gebir*, ii. 174 (cf. *Lycidas*, 165), 233–4 (cf. *P. L.*, i. 222–3),
iii. 201–2 (cf. *P. L.*, i. 177), vi. 2 (cf. *P. L.*, iv. 238); *Chrysaor*, 200–201 (cf. *P. L.*, i. 45,
49). Apparently Mr. Bradley did not notice "robe succinct" (*Gebir*, i. 176, cf. *P. L.*,
iii. 643), but he very properly mentions Landor's use of the Miltonic series of nouns
or adjectives (*ib.* iv. 22, 59, 228).

[3] *Gebir*, vi. 121–32.

. . . What I admired was what nobody else had ever noticed — his proud complacency and scornful strength. . . . I was resolved to be as compendious and exclusive." [1] "Compendious and exclusive" the piece certainly is, — it has excluded most readers, — but not otherwise Pindaric. Landor's classicism is, indeed, not that of the best Greek period; it is not Homeric or Sophoclean, but Hellenistic, Virgilian, or even Ovidian. [2] Restrained and extremely condensed as most of the poem is, it has not a few passages, like luxuriant flowers sprouting in rocky crannies, that are merely decorative, rich in color and warm with tender emotion.

Gebir is a strange, wild Arabian tale of war, magic, love, the lower world, and death; it makes no claim to be an epic. An unfinished earlier work, however, *The Phocaeans*, was intended as heroic poetry. If *Gebir* is a series of fine passages connected by "flea-skips of association," [3] *The Phocaeans* lacks even the flea-skips. It is neither more nor less Miltonic than its successor, and is interesting chiefly as one of the most obscure poems in English and as an expression of its author's enthusiasm for Liberty, to whom it is dedicated. [4]

Landor's "finest piece of narrative writing in blank verse," [5] *Chrysaor*, is a brief epic episode similar to *The Phocaeans* and of about the same date. Most of the numerous unrimed pieces that he composed in later life are Greek love-stories (Hellenistic again), more conversational, less cryptic and abrupt in style, than are his youthful verses. Except for their condensed expressions, omitted words, their occasional inversions and appositives, they do not suggest Milton at all. [6] Yet this does not prove that the enthusiastic,

---

[1] *Works*, etc. (ed. Forster), i. 49.

[2] This is strikingly shown, as Mr. J. H. Hanford remarked to me, in the two lines from *Paradise Lost* that Landor praised as "the richest jewel that Poetry ever wore" (see above, p. 293, n. 3).

[3] A remark by William Taylor, quoted in Forster's *Landor*, i. 182 n.

[4] See lines 5–6. "*Gebir* and *From the Phocaeans*," Landor observed, "were written . . . when our young English heads were turned towards the French Revolution, and were deluded by a phantom of Liberty" (*Letters*, etc., ed. Stephen Wheeler, 1897, p. 135). Wheeler (*ib.* 136, 236–8) prints two fragments of *The Phocaeans* that are not in Crump's version, and William Bradley (*Early Poems of Landor*, 1914, pp. 26–58, 113–21) gives a helpful analysis and prints an otherwise inaccessible portion of it. Forster omits it altogether.   [5] Colvin's *Landor* (1881), 37.

[6] The most Miltonic passage in Landor's shorter poems is this one from his lines *To John Forster:*

> From Eliot's cell
> Death-dark, from Hampden's sadder battle-field,
> From steadfast Cromwell's tribunitian throne,
> Loftier than kings' supported knees could mount,
> Hast thou departed from me, and hast climbed
> Cecropian highths, and ploughed Aegean waves.

lifelong devotion of the younger to the older Hellenist bore no fruit. Milton gave Landor stimulus and inspiration; he furnished a model to which the unusual temperament of the young writer responded as it did to no other.

"I should not think," declared Coleridge, "of devoting less than twenty years to an Epic Poem. Ten years to collect materials and warm my mind with universal science . . . the next five in the composition of the Poem, and the five last in the correction of it."[1] This plan, characteristic of the originator of large projects which remained only projects, was not the one followed by the Homers of the day, certainly not by the bard to whom it was mentioned, Joseph Cottle. That enterprising and amiable publisher composed three epics, aggregating seventy-seven books, in a quarter less time than Coleridge allotted to one. It is difficult to take such a writer seriously, and indeed none of the readers who have "taken" him at all in recent years seem to have done so. Most have been content, with Byron, to pass him by as "Mr. Cottle, Amos, Joseph, I don't know which, but one or both,"[2] and let it go at that. Richard Garnett has disposed of him with the comment. "Even Cottle's poems would have given a very inadequate idea of his stupidity without his memoirs."[3] These "memoirs," indeed, entitled *Early Recollections, chiefly relating to Samuel Taylor Coleridge* (1837), recount their author's chief title to fame, — his friendship with Southey, Coleridge, and Wordsworth, whose early volumes, including the *Lyrical Ballads*, he published.

With a fine impartiality, Cottle, after composing two epics in blank verse, wrote one in couplets which employs the Miltonic machinery. This wretched paraphrase of parts of the Old Testament narrative, *The Messiah* (1815), pictures the fallen angels lying on the burning lake, Satan rising to urge that they win over the beings recently created to fill their former places in heaven, Beelzebub and Belial speaking against Satan's leadership, but Mammon standing by his chief and flying with him through hell and past its gate to earth, then the fall, the expulsion from Eden, Satan's return

---

[1] In a letter to Cottle printed in the latter's *Early Recollections* (1837), i. 192. Even Milton, who devoted much more than twenty years to the preparation of his epic, never dreamed of the equipment Coleridge outlined: "I would thoroughly understand Mechanics; Hydrostatics; Optics, and Astronomy; Botany; Metallurgy; Fossilism; Chemistry; Geology; Anatomy; Medicine; then the mind of man; then the minds of men; in all Travels, Voyages, and Histories" (*ib.*).

[2] *English Bards*, 406 n.

[3] *Dict. Nat. Biog.* It was Cottle who, by promising to buy all the verse that Coleridge wrote, enabled him to marry, and who conveyed to him De Quincey's gift of three hundred pounds.

to hell, and a scene in heaven in which Messiah promises to assume the sins of mankind, — all strongly reminiscent of *Paradise Lost*.[1] Many of Cottle's couplets are of the rigid neo-classic type, but he has numerous run-over lines and strong internal pauses, while occasionally he makes use of a style and prosody as Miltonic as

> One burst of universal joyance rose,
> Stupendous.[2]

Had the world been more appreciative of the twenty-eight books of *The Messiah*, the narrative, which extends from the creation to the death of David, might have been continued through the New Testament;[3] but, since this third epic was issued before the author's two preceding ones were assimilated, its reception was such that Cottle did not again attempt the heroic strain.

The two in blank verse had, however, been greeted more favorably. *Alfred* (1800), besides being reissued in America, reached a fourth English edition and the *Fall of Cambria* (1808) a second. *Alfred* was praised in the *Critical Review* for its "rapid, various, and interesting" action and its "many passages which . . . display those fine touches which designate the hand of a master."[4] The *Monthly Review*, less favorably impressed,[5] criticized particularly "the bad consequences resulting from some hasty opinions lately promulgated, respecting simplicity of diction," — an interesting reference to Wordsworth's famous utterance. "We have opposed," the reviewer continues, "the recent attempts to despoil poetry of her proper language; and we regret that we are again called to assert the distinction between simplicity and meanness. . . . The greater part of it [*Alfred*] is really written in measured prose, which is void

---

[1] There are also minor similarities, and the borrowing of many words and of some expressions (such as the departure from Eden "with trembling step and slow," iii. 362, cf. *P. L.*, xii. 648). In his preface Cottle explains that his plan put him "under the unfortunate necessity of coming in contact with our Greatest Bard. . . . I am satisfied," he adds, "to become a *foil* to one, with whom competition is impossible."

[2] viii. 448-9.

[3] The remainder of the Old Testament was, however, to be omitted (preface, p. x). Over a third of the part published is devoted to the life of David, but Cottle's handling of the story is quite different from Sotheby's or Pennie's (see pp. 304-5 below).

[4] New arrangement, xxxi. 171.

[5] As was Southey, who had "laboured hard and honestly to suppress its birth" and was "thrown into a cold sweat by recollecting it" (letter to William Taylor, Nov. 26, 1800, in J. W. Robberds's *Memoir of Taylor*, 1843, i. 363); while Lamb expressed his opinion in two delicious letters to Coleridge (Aug. 26 and Oct. 9, 1800). "Poor Alfred! Pye has been at him too!" lamented Byron (*English Bards*, 406 n.); and, indeed, not only Cottle and Pye, but Blackmore in 1723, James Montgomery about 1786, John Fitchett between 1808 and 1834, R. P. Knight in 1823, and M. T. Sadler in 1842, tried their hands at epics on Alfred.

of every requisite for sublime poetry." [1] A vigorous reply to this
criticism makes the long preface to the second edition of the poem
(1804) more interesting and important than the work itself. [2] Cottle's
chief concern was the 'impress on the heart.' "My primary desire,"
he explained, "has been, to please . . . him, or her, who seeks not to
repress every spontaneous emotion, and who deems it no degrada-
tion, to obey the impulse which prompts the glowing cheek, or the
falling tear." [3] For one of this bias, and particularly if he has only
the humble gifts of a Cottle, heroic poetry is hardly a suitable medium. In simple narrative, descriptive, and domestic scenes *Alfred*
is often pleasing, but its epic flights usually end in the sentimentality
and ridiculous rant of melodrama:

> "Monsters, lie there! " he cried, as thro' their hearts
> He plunged his crimson blade. [4]

These contrasting aspects of *Alfred*, which are equally marked in
the *Fall of Cambria* (a story of the conquest of Wales by Edward I), [5]
show that Cottle is a transition figure, that he combines the defects
of Glover with some of the virtues of the lake poets. He was probably influenced more by the blank-verse epics of Southey — the
first of which he himself published — than by the *Lyrical Ballads* or
the other early pieces of Wordsworth, few of which are unrimed. [6]

---

[1] Enlarged ed., xxxv. 2, 9.

[2] Cottle censured those who "erroneously supposed that sublimity consisted more
in the expression than in the thought," and cleverly rewrote one of the speeches in his
poem as it would appear in the typical epic of the period. Of the rewritten passage —
which is not exaggerated — he said justly: "There is not one appeal to the breast. It
is the language of imbecility, not of passion. The images are far-fetched, and such as
would never occur to a man, in the situation . . . nor be adopted by any one who either
felt himself, or expected to make his Reader feel. The ideas are wholly of a cold and
general nature, without being, in the slightest degree, calculated to arrest the attention
or impress the heart." "For my own part," he declared, "I have endeavoured to express the language of Nature, and in every dubious point, have consulted alone my own
heart." These quotations are taken from the American reprint of the second edition
(Newburyport, 1814, pp. 16–19 *passim*).

[3] *Ib.* 32. Or, in the words of the *Critical Review* (new arr., xxxi. 161), Cottle "strives
rather to melt the heart, than to nerve the arm of heroism."

[4] vi. 36–7 (of the American reprint; the first edition has no "Monsters").

[5] More than half a century earlier, in 1749, Richard Rolt had exclaimed,

> CAMBRIA, thou! unnoted pass
> By the PIERIAN train? Forbid it heav'n!

and in order to avoid such a calamity had written the three books of his *Cambria*, in
which "the MUSE . . . fondly . . . assay'd To rove the flow'ry HELICONIAN round (i. 3–4,
iii. 448–50). This atrocious performance, which reached a second edition the same
year, is lost in an "amfractuous maze" (iii. 62) of the history and description of Wales.
Rolt also published in 1749 the 385 lines of his slightly less Miltonic *Poem to the Memory
of Sir W. W. Wynne.*

[6] It would seem as if the author of *Alfred* must also have known and have been in-

Southey was certainly much better known to the publisher-poet than was Wordsworth, and his *Madoc* has a number of things in common with the *Fall of Cambria* other than the fact that it deals with Wales in the early days. He would also have been more in sympathy with Cottle's deliberate preaching of morality and religion,[1] and with his external Miltonisms, which, particularly in the heroic passages, are more marked than in Wordsworth's work.[2]

Another friend of Coleridge, Wordsworth, and Southey, as well-meaning as Cottle and much abler, but in some respects as ridiculous, likewise mistook himself for a poet. This was John Thelwall, whose enthusiasm for the French Revolution and for liberty of all kinds resulted in his imprisonment and made him a source of anxiety to the friends of the lake poets. "But neither the grated chambers of the Tower, nor the noxious dungeons of Newgate," their prisoner informs us, "were unconscious to the visitations of the Muse,"[3] with the result that freedom received the additional tribute of a "National and . . . Constitutional Epic," *The Hope of Albion, or Edwin of Northumbria* (1801). The work was apparently never completed, and, as the parts that were written failed to satisfy even their complacent author's easy standards, only the plan and some specimens of the verse reached the public. The "action," we learn, is "heroic; the form Epic — after the models of classical antiquity — tho approaching more to the plan of the Odyssey than of the Iliad. . . . The consummation of the action is the establishment of the English Constitution on the broad bases of civil and religious Liberty."[4] In his egotistic and pompous autobiography Thelwall says of himself,

fluenced by Romaine Joseph Thorn, who at the time when Southey, Coleridge, and Cottle were living at Bristol sang the praises of his city in a poem entitled *Bristolia* (1794). Cottle would have liked Thorn's sentimental but simply-expressed pastoral tale, *Lodon and Miranda* (1799), and the praise of religion and virtue in his *Retirement* (1793). One cannot be sure, however, that he would have approved of his *Howe Triumphant! an Heroic Poem* (1794), in which, according to the *Critical Review* (new arr., xiii. 112), "Mr. Thorn mounts upon heroic stilts, and sings the glories of the naval victory of the first of June, in what, we suppose, he himself calls blank verse."

[1] "I have endeavoured," declares Cottle in the preface to the first edition of *Alfred*, "to support the cause of Religion and Virtue, in comparison of which, all other commendation I esteem of little value."

[2] In the preface to the second edition of the *Fall of Cambria* he affirms, — what is obviously the truth, — "I have not aimed at the stately march of Milton"; and it is probable he did not realize that his inversions, parentheses, and his use of adjectives for adverbs were derived ultimately if not directly from *Paradise Lost*. For his *Malvern*, see above, p. 254.

[3] Memoir prefixed to his *Poems chiefly written in Retirement* (1801), p. xxix.

[4] Thelwall's *Poetical Recreations of the Champion* (1822), 235. Several pages of extracts from the *Hope of Albion* which do not appear in the *Poems in Retirement* are given in the *Recreations*.

that he sought his "accustomed solace in the exuberant descriptions of Thomson, or the sublime pathos of the Bard, who

Into the Heaven of Heavens presum'd to soar." [1]

In Milton, however, he found more than solace, for he borrowed from *Comus* and *Allegro* in his *Fairy of the Lake,* and introduced the style, language, and some of the phrases of *Paradise Lost* into his epic. His use of "the demon gods Of Scandinavia," who make up the "machinery" of the *Hope of Albion,* also shows the influence of Milton; for he pictures them as "that rebel rout" which fell with Satan

> when, ambition-fir'd, he sought
> To quell the omnipotent.[2]

An extract, though not sufficient, as Thelwall said of another passage, "to illustrate in any degree the conduct and texture of the Poem, as an epic whole," [3] will at least give an idea of its style, and especially of its use of northern mythology, one of its few interesting features:

> Thee, Frea! thee they praise, embrothel'd queen
> Of wanton dalliance! and thy warrior spouse,
> Asgardian Woden, in his Hall of Shields,
> Horrid with blood; and cloud compelling Thor
> (Fruit of your loves connubial) and the rest
> Who, with septemviral sway, with magic rites,
> And impious festivals, alternate shar'd
> Diurnal homage.[4]

The rant and sentimentality of George Skene's not uninteresting legendary tale of the Scottish islands, *Donald Bane* (1796), "an Heroic Poem in three books," should have secured it some popularity, particularly as the work was praised and quoted at length in the *Monthly Review.*[5] Its markedly Miltonic style, too, though it was

---

[1] *Poems in Retirement,* p. xii. On page ix we are told that he "devoured with insatiable avidity Pope's translation of Homer, and committed several hundred verses to memory," — which shows that Thelwall, like many others, belonged both to the "school of Milton" and to the "school of Pope."

[2] ii. 153-4, 95, 100-101 (*ib.* pp. 189, 187).

[3] *Poetical Recreations,* 240.

[4] ii. 162-9. Thelwall wrote a number of other blank-verse poems, more conversational than his epic but somewhat influenced by *Paradise Lost,* particularly in the frequent use of parentheses. The 246 lines of Miltonic blank verse which he published in 1805 as the *Trident of Albion, an Epic Effusion,* undoubtedly form an effusion, but as they tell no story their sole epic quality seems to be pomposity. Four lines from Milton appear on the title-page of his *Poems written in Close Confinement* (1795), and some years later he had the inmates of his school for stammerers recite *Comus* (see Crabb Robinson's *Diary,* Dec. 27, 1815).

[5] Enlarged ed., xxiv. 49-56.

sharply criticized for being, "like that of Cowper [!] . . . often affectedly stately, studiously inverted, and habitually inharmonious," should have found favor, especially if it describes many heroes like this one:

> On his polished brow
> The shield of valour shone; his eye contained
> Benevolence, and seemed to swim in tears
> Of pity for the sorrows of mankind,
> Save in the rage of battle when he fought,
> Heroic ardour breathing.

Yet Skene's ambitious effort appears to have attracted no more attention than did Samuel Wilcocke's *Britannia*,[1] which was issued a few months later and was so little known that within four years another epic was published with the same title.

This far better poem, one of the best of its kind that the century gave birth to, came from the pen of John Ogilvie in 1801. It is a sumptuous folio of six hundred and thirty pages, and is equally grand if not grandiose in its style, which, owing to frequent inversions and the omission of many words that would normally be expressed, is apt to be jerky. Though it is too long and deals with a subject too difficult for Ogilvie's limited powers, though it follows the epic conventions and makes no pretence to realism either of action or of expression, yet it is as free from rant, pose, and bombast as could be expected, and succeeds in being extremely Miltonic without being absurd. Both the characters and the action show largeness and nobility of conception, and the poem as a whole is dignified, restrained, and often admirably expressed. The influence of *Paradise Lost* is quite as apparent in the diction as in the style, a state of affairs which might be expected in view of Ogilvie's ideas on the subject. In his opinion, a writer of blank verse "ought to give particular attention" to "preventing the language of the *Poet* from degenerating into the tameness of prose." Yet he admitted that "to maintain the poetic idiom at all times, in executing so comprehensive a plan as that of the Epopoea," was "almost impossible."[2] How hard he tried may be judged from this passage:

[1] Wilcocke seems to have intended to write a "poetical heroic history of his country" (*ib.* 454), but the eighty-three pages that he published did not finish the Roman period. Both his style and diction are unmistakably Miltonic, and he borrows at least one passage from *Paradise Lost* (see *ib.* 457). This work and *Donald Bane* I know only from the review.

[2] "A Critical Dissertation on Epic Machinery," *Britannia*, 43–4. In the fifty-two closely printed pages of this "Dissertation," Ogilvie defended the use of "machinery" against Lord Kames and William Hayley.

> Some emanation from the orb of day,
> Fraught with his purest radiance, seem'd to float
> Along the empyrean; but the fiend
> Mark'd, on th' effulgence, spreading, as it moved
> Onward in majesty serene, the sons
> Of heaven enthroned; and nearer as it came,
> Beheld the light of panoply divine.[1]

Ogilvie's debt to *Paradise Lost*, which is clear enough from these lines, was not limited to matters of expression. His subject, the establishment by Brutus of a Trojan colony in Britain, may well have been suggested to him by Milton's plan to compose a work on the same theme, and his "machinery" is frankly derived from the Christian epic.[2] In his second, third, and fourth books (which are laid in hell), Satan, a commanding figure with a "deeply scarred" front, assumes his throne and hears a fallen spirit recount his unsuccessful attempts to keep Brutus from Britain. In the other sixteen books Satan stirs up the giant inhabitants of the island to resist the Trojans (who are assisted by Milton's Ithuriel and other good angels), with the result that, in the many battles which follow, the powers of good and evil figure in much the same way as do the Greek deities in the *Iliad*. The bulkiness of the work, its publication in remote Aberdeen, the reputation of its author's other poems (which was deservedly poor[3]), all stood in the way of its becoming widely known; yet it is hard to see why a piece that maintains a high level throughout, and that has passages as good as the following, should have been utterly disregarded by its own and by later ages:

> Oblivious Lethe slowly winds
> His tide in silence onwards. — On its bank
> Glimmer the flitting lights that in the stream
> Shine dim, and mournful; glides the sleepy wave
> Stirr'd by no breath, save when remote, the wail
> Of Spirits pent within the gulph of fire,
> Comes lingering o'er the waste.[4]

[1] Page 606. Ogilvie probably took from *Paradise Lost* a number of his unusual words, like "massy," "adamantine," "compeers," "panoply," etc., as he almost certainly did the expressions "world of waters" (pp. 54, 59, cf. *P. L.*, iii. 11), "to rest Your wearied virtue" (p. 61, cf. *P. L.*, i. 319–20), "a solitary void . . . received us" (p. 153, cf. *P. L.*, ii. 438–9), "horrent arms" (p. 622, cf. *P.L.*, ii. 513), as well as the reference to Uriel throned in the sun (p. 149, cf. *P. L.*, iii. 621–53).

[2] See above, p. 302, n. 2.   [3] See pp. 395–7 below.

[4] Pages 90–91. Most of the critics spoke slightingly of it, and the *Monthly Review* (enl. ed., xxxvii. 361, 364) boldly declared: "The machinery and classical allusions of Dr. Ogilvie have the same resemblance to the verse of Homer and Milton, which a leaden statue, fresh from Piccadilly, bears to the sculpture of Phidias or Praxiteles. . . . We have found it much too long; and we apprehend that few persons will be able to accomplish a progress through the whole."

The diffuseness and fondness for long speeches which mark most epics of the early nineteenth century are particularly wearisome in the heavy contribution that John Fitzgerald Pennie made to the form. Pennie's quasi-autobiographic *Tale of a Modern Genius* (1827) shows that he was poor, precocious, ambitious, and vain, and his epics make it equally clear that, although he had gifts, he was no poet but mistook the desire to write for the power. As his taste was none of the best, he ornamented his works with such pretentious expressions as "the gem-wreath of regality" (the crown), "the colossean thunderbolt of war," and with such conventional pictures of nature — for which he shows no real love — as

> While the sun
> Gilds with refulgence sweet the azure vault,
> And paints the landscape with a thousand flow'rs.[1]

The first of his two epics, the *Royal Minstrel* (1817), narrates the life of David from his shepherd boyhood to his coronation.[2] Satan, Moloch, Belial, and the witch of Endor, who constitute the "machinery," hold councils much like those in *Paradise Lost*, and in one of these Belial suggests, as in *Paradise Regained*, that they "set women in the eye of" their intended victim.[3] If there remains any doubt as to the author's debt to Milton, it will be dispelled by the numerous verbal borrowings scattered through the twelve books of this poem and the twelve of his next epic, *Rogvald*, which appeared six years later.[4] The plot of this second work is complicated; for

[1] *Rogvald*, p. 266; *Royal Minstrel*, pp. 87, 89. Another of the jewels that grace *Rogvald* is the line, "With pity's tear-drop, gemmed the iron gyves" (p. 89). Though Pennie's diction is often pompous and amusing, it shows that he sought for unhackneyed expressions which have color and connotative value. Many of his unusual words either come direct from Milton or are of the Miltonic kind. He is particularly fond of compound epithets.

[2] It is likely that Pennie was acquainted with William Sotheby's *Saul* (1807), an unrimed epic shorter and better than his own, which covers the same ground. There is nothing striking about this poem (which, in spite of Byron's sneer that it went only "from Stationer's Hall to Grocer's Stall," was reprinted in America); yet, aside from a style as jerky and unmistakably Miltonic as this (p. 46), it is not bad:

> Seen afar, amidst the pomp,
> Gorgeously mail'd, but more by pride of port
> Known, and superiour stature, than rich trim
> Of war and regal ornament, the King,
> Thron'd in triumphal car, with trophies grac'd,
> Stood eminent.

For Sotheby's *Tour through Wales*, see p. 263 above.

[3] Argument of book viii; cf. *P. R.*, ii. 153.

[4] A few of these may be quoted. From the *Royal Minstrel:* "Sabaean odours" (p. 32, cf. *P. L.*, iv. 162), "bank damask'd with flow'rs" (p. 33, cf. *P. L.*, iv. 334), "oaten reed" (p. 60, cf. *Comus*, 345), "flaunting woodbine" (p. 316, cf. *Comus*, 545);

Rogvald, the leader of the forces that dethrone the English king Ethelred, is the accepted lover of Elburga (whom the king seeks to marry) and in the end proves to be the son of the neglected queen. Rhetorical, melodramatic, and even absurd as the poem often is, it has a kind of splendor and is more interesting and unusual than most of the works we have been examining. It also gains picturesqueness by describing barbaric scenes like the immolation of wife, children, and horses on the funeral pyre of a great prince, and by using Scandinavian deities as "machinery." Pennie draws from the elder Edda and from Mallet's *Northern Antiquities*, but he fails to catch the Norse spirit, as may be judged from the following description of the gods going forth to battle:

> Chariots of chrysolite and gleaming steel,
> With barbed horse and rider sheathed in mail,
> Stood with terrific grandeur flame-involved.
> Above the glittering files, in pomp, was seen
> Intrepid Tyr, the bravest of the gods;
> Towering in radiant panoply, he seemed
> A moving rock of diamond! — Vali too,
> The son of Rinda, and that lovely god
> Uller, were seen all glorious on the plain.[1]

> By some whom storms had haply on its shores
> Night-founder'd

(p. 3, cf. *Comus*, 483, and *P. L.*, i. 204);

> Beam'd like a meteor waving on the winds

(p. 4, cf. *P. L.*, i. 537);

>   Others apart
> In calmer consultation sat retir'd

(p. 7, cf. *P. L.*, ii. 557);

> Nor orator of ancient Greece, nor Rome,
> The seat of eloquence, when in her height
> Of pow'r and wide dominion, could compare

(p. 17, cf. *P. L.*, ix. 670–72);

>   Myrrh and cassia, nard and balm,
> Flung the blest odours of Arabia's gales

(p. 107, cf. *P. L.*, iv. 162–3, v. 292–3);

> Compos'd of lovelier flow'rs than Proserpine
> Let fall from Dis's iron-shafted car
> When Ceres sought her through the world in vain

(p. 317, cf. *P. L.*, iv. 269–72). In two other cases (see pp. 435, 438) the author himself points out Miltonic parallels, and in the fifth line of book iii he refers to Milton.

From *Rogvald:* "arched window, dight With storied pane" (p. 51, cf.*Penseroso*, 159); "irriguous vale" (pp. 56, 167, cf. *P. L.*, iv. 255); "eyelids of the morn"(p. 104, cf. *Lycidas*, 26); "bedropped with" (p. 120, cf. *P. L.*, vii. 406, x. 527); "Hymen, saffron-robed" (p. 154, cf. *Allegro*, 125–6); "fleecy skirts" of a cloud (p. 250, cf. *P. L.*, v. 187); "giant brood" (p. 251, cf. *P. L.*, i. 576); "bold emprize" (p. 283, *Comus*, 610, and *P. L.*, xi. 642); "spicy woods Of Araby the blest" (p. 323, cf. *P. L.*, iv. 162–3).

[1] Page 249.

In this use of Scandinavian deities for "machinery" Pennie may have been influenced by Thelwall's *Hope of Albion*, or by two later works, the Earl of Carysfort's *Revenge of Guendolen* (1810, privately printed 1786) and Sir William Drummond's *Odin* (1817). All four writers were pretty certainly stimulated by Gray's two Norse odes, and at least one, Carysfort, was "led by the notes to the last Canto of Mr. Hayley's Essay on Epic Poetry, to try the effect of the northern mythology in a composition of the narrative kind." [1] The Earl's story, however, which deals with the successful revolt of Queen Guendolen, divorced by the mythical English king Locrine in order that he might marry his captive Estrildis (their child is Sabra, the Sabrina of *Comus*), seems to have been taken from Milton's *History of Britain*.[2] The poem was probably thought too short — it contains less than 2600 lines — to be termed an epic, but, as the following passage will show, it has all the heroics and Miltonisms that were regarded as necessary in such a work:

> And now two chiefs of force immense, whose spears
> Wide-wasting had with many an inroad gor'd
> The front of battle, in their sanguine course,
> Approach, and adverse stand with threat'ning arms.[3]

Some of the scenes in the *Revenge of Guendolen* — an incantation, for example, and a picture of the hall of Odin — are striking but reveal only slight familiarity with Scandinavian mythology. In this they differ widely from the pictures in Sir William Drummond's poem, which tells how Pharnaces, the son of Mithridates, after being defeated with his father by the Romans, moved northward and, in the guise of their deity Odin, became the ruler of the Germanic tribes. Drummond's work may have been suggested by a remark in the *Decline and Fall of the Roman Empire*, that the legend of the historical Odin (which is found in the prose Edda, the *Heimskringla*, and in earlier works), "by deducing the enmity of the Goths and Romans from so memorable a cause, might supply the noble groundwork of an Epic Poem." [4] If so, Gibbon would have taken some satisfaction in the Latinic diction and the lofty, rhetorical style in which *Odin* is written, — in such a passage as this, for example:

---

[1] *Dramatic and Narrative Poems* (1810), ii. 4.

[2] *Ib.*

[3] Page 113. The battle "with many an inroad gor'd" is from *Paradise Lost*, vi. 386–7, and "the pond'rous spear Seems like a pine ... on Norweyan hills" (p. 123) is from the first book (lines 284–93) of the same epic.

[4] Second ed. (1776), vol. i, ch. x, n. 12. My attention was called to this reference by Mr. F. E. Farley's admirable *Scandinavian Influences in the English Romantic Movement* (Boston, 1903).

> Now on the verge they stood of a broad sea
> Tempestuous. In the midst the snake-like God
> Of slimy Mignard, (his lithe body coil'd
> In many a spiral fold voluminous,)
> Uplifted o'er the wave his crested head
> Majestic. Serpent old! believed of yore,
> Where Nile and Ganges flow, to circulate
> The ocean-stream that girts the universe.[1]

The reader will probably agree with the *Eclectic Review* that Drummond's style "is obviously formed upon the model of the *Paradise Lost*"; and if he turns to the work itself he may add with the critic, "We are better pleased, however, with the general resemblance to Milton, which his [Drummond's] learning and classical taste enable him to keep up, in erudite allusion, and richness of ornament, than with his close imitation of particular passages."[2] It is doubtful whether, so late as 1817, any large part of the public shared the critic's pleasure in a style "obviously formed upon the model of the Paradise Lost." At any rate, though Drummond was a diplomat and scholar of repute, and though he had the first four books of his epic sumptuously printed, they found so little favor that he pub-

[1] Page 103. This extract gives far too favorable an impression of the poem, which is monotonous and devoid of poetic power. Much of it reads as if each line were composed without reference to any other.

[2] New series, viii. 87. Among these "close imitations" are the speeches at the council (pp. 60–72, cf. *P. L.*, ii. 1–467); the reference to "the King of shades . . . With sin and death, his Hell-born offspring" (p. 111, cf. *P. L.*, ii. 746–89); the list of heathen deities (pp. 111–12, cf. *P. L.*, i. 376–522); the phrases "clad with vines" (p. 123, from *P. L.*, i. 410, of a valley in each case), "sea-girt isles" (p. 131, from *Comus*, 21), "Nature, best instructress" (p. 135, cf. *Comus*, 377), "sky-tinctured plumage" (p. 160, cf. *P. L.*, v. 285, of wings in each case); and the following passages:

> For now the rebel Satraps hemm'd him round;
> Their serried ranks drawn up in close array,
> An iron front, horrent with bristling spears

(p. 59, cf. *P. L.*, i. 547–8, ii. 511–13, iv. 979–80);

> Distinct he shone in radiant panoply,
> Refulgent mail, gorgeous, inlaid with gold

(p. 59, see also p. 160, and cf. *P. L.*, vi. 526–7, 760–61);

> When purple to the sea her fountains ran
> Ensanguined

(p. 73, cf. *P. L.*, i. 450–52);

> Knit with Spring and Autumn, hand in hand,
> Danced round the smiling Year

(p. 116, cf. *P. L.*, iv. 267–8, v. 394–5);

> The blear illusions of her magic spells

(p. 150, cf. *Comus*, 154–5). As for diction, Drummond has words like "mortiferous," "refulgent," "relucent," "panoply," "colorific," "insentient," "darkling," "hirsute," "tauriform," "malefic," "monarchal" (the last seven are on two pages, 83 and 112).

lished no more. By most readers and critics this tiresome first part was ignored; but the *Eclectic Review*, which could spare only five pages of the same number to condemn *Manfred* as "scarcely worth being transmitted from the Continent" and as not likely to "raise Lord Byron's reputation," gave *Odin* thirteen pages of commendation![1]

Teutonic mythology is also employed to some extent in H. H. Milman's *Samor, Lord of the Bright City* (1818), which contains a scene with the Valkyrie and a human sacrifice but which as a whole is far from suggesting the strangeness or the terse vigor of the Old Norse. Instead, it reminds one of Southey, particularly of his *Madoc*, since its hero wanders about England in the days of Vortigern rousing the British against the Saxon invaders. Milman termed his piece "an heroic poem," but the dominant note is not epic, for we hear more of Samor's piety, his sufferings, his feelings for his murdered family, than of his heroism; furthermore, several love-stories are introduced as episodes and there are frequent moralizings and descriptions of nature. Although begun when its author was a schoolboy of eighteen and practically finished during his undergraduate years at Oxford, the poem has none of the fire or abandon of youth, but is rather what might be expected from the mature Milman who won merited laurels as the historian of the Jews and of Latin Christianity, as the editor of Gibbon, and as the dean of St. Paul's. It is dignified without being bombastic, often impressive, generally pleasing, and it reveals a love of the quieter aspects of nature; but it lacks freshness and life, is too long, contains too much talk and too little action, and such action as it has is episodic rather than progressive. To Southey it was "a work of great power," but charged with "a perpetual stretch and strain of feeling. . . . With less poetry," he declared, "Samor would have been a better poem."[2]

Although within a year of its publication it not only reached a second edition but was reprinted in America, and though it is undoubtedly better than most of its predecessors, more natural, less pompous and rhetorical, yet it has a curious stiltedness and conventionality of expression that give it an academic air. Later Milman made some attempt to correct these faults, which he attributed in part to "the ambition of creating that which . . . the language still

[1] New series, viii. 66, 90.

[2] Letter to C. H. Townshend, April 12, 1818; see also his letter to Scott, March 11, 1819. *Samor* was harshly criticized in the *North American Review*, ix. 26–35, and the *Quarterly Review*, xix. 328–47. Milman later became so frequent a contributor to the *Quarterly* that Byron, who said "The fellow has poesy in him" (letter to J. Murray, Sept. 12, 1821), mentioned him in the squib "Who killed John Keats?"

wants — narrative blank verse. The Miltonic versification," he goes
on to say, "is the triumph of poetic art; but . . . it is too solemn,
stately, and august for subjects of less grave interest." [1] Inasmuch
as considerable blank verse less "solemn, stately, and august" and
better adapted to narration than that of *Samor* had been written
before 1818, this is a somewhat singular defense. How Miltonic the
poem often is will appear from these lines:

> Him delighted more
> Helvellyn's cloud-wrapt brow to climb, and share
> The eagle's stormy solitude; 'mid wreck
> Of whirlwinds and dire lightnings, huge he stood,
> Where his own Gods he deem'd on volleying clouds
> Abroad were riding, and black hurricane.[2]

One of the most striking instances of the persistence in the nineteenth century of the tastes and methods of the eighteenth is to be
found in *Christ Crucified*, "an epic poem in twelve books," by W. E.
Wall. There is nothing about this ponderous work, whether in
style, diction, plan, or contents, to indicate that its five hundred and
fifteen pages were written later than Glover's *Leonidas* (1737); yet it
appeared in 1833 and stands in the Harvard Library next to *In Me-
moriam!* Like many eighteenth-century epics, it employs the "machinery" of *Paradise Lost*,—Satan and the fallen angels, councils
in hell at which various evil spirits propose plans, a Miltonic Deity
justifying himself in Miltonic but unchristian speeches to a host of
angels who chant his praises, etc., etc. Innumerable details and
phrases are also taken from Milton, as are the turgid style and the
absurd diction. But let the poem speak for itself:

> Beneath, upon a throne of awful height,
> (As 'twere to emulate the Heaven of God,)
> Fram'd as of solid darkness, Satan sate
> Resplendent!

> In the realms
> Ethereal, above th' empyrean high,
> Thron'd in sun-dazzling glory, compass'd bright
> With Seraphim, saw the Almighty Sire,
> (From his high optic hill of Providence
> Foreseeing secrets deep of hoary time,)
> His Son belov'd advancing to his death.
> Immediate from heav'n's argent clouds proceeds
> The voice of God.[3]

---

[1] *Works* (1839), vol. ii, p. xii. These "introductory observations" are contradictory,
confused, and confusing, and imply a much more thorough revision of the poem than
Milman actually made.

[2] *Ib.* 25.   [3] i. 682–5; iii. 1324–32.

The Miltonic garb in which Wall clothed his poem seems even stranger when it appears in the far better work, *Attila, King of the Huns*, which the distinguished dean of Manchester, William Herbert, published as late as 1838.[1] Herbert was a scholar of wide reading in several literatures; he wrote considerable Latin, besides some Greek, Italian, and Norwegian verse, made translations from the Greek, Spanish, German, and Icelandic,[2] and was an eminent naturalist. With his epic he published a long "historical treatise" on the same subject, which, together with his numerous notes, indicates that he could have quoted chapter and verse for every detail in the poem. As a result of the years of close but varied study that had preceded it, *Attila* is stiffened throughout with learned allusions and with names famed in history or romance, features which give it much of its Miltonic character. Yet, just as he took over the character of Satan, Herbert must have deliberately adopted the manner of *Paradise Lost* in order to gain the grandeur and impressiveness for which he strove. He could be simple when he wished, but for his epic his models were not Wordsworth or Tennyson, since his ear was "cloy'd Unto satiety" with the "honied strains" and "meretricious gauds of modern song."[3] He "walk'd" rather with "Melesigenes and Maro," and with "British Milton," who drew from his "vocal shell"

> Numbers sonorous, fraught with science deep;
> Such as majestic Greece had wondering heard,
> Nor Freedom's proudest sons disdain'd to own.[4]

It was undoubtedly from "British Milton" that he learned to use such words as "besprent," "darkling," "meteorous," "panoply," "adamant," "irascent," "ingulph'd," "glebe," "confusive," "egression," "battailous," "piation," "minaciously," "Riphaean," "Vul-

---

[1] In his *Works* (1842) the title is *Attila, or the Triumph of Christianity*.

[2] Interest in the myths and customs of the early Teutonic peoples influenced Herbert, as it had Cottle, Thelwall, Pennie, Carysfort, and Drummond, in choosing the subject of his epic; but his knowledge of the field was far more profound that theirs. His *Select Icelandic Poetry, translated, with notes* (1804–06), is said to contain "the first adequate illustration of ancient Scandinavian literature which had appeared in England" (*Dict. Nat. Biog.*), and his *Hedin, Helga* (which shows the influence of Scott and Byron), *Brynhilda*, and *Sir Ebba* are all based on the Old Norse.

[3] *Farewell* (appended to *Attila*), 93–4, 117.

[4] *Farewell*, 119–20; *Written in Somersetshire* (1801), 81–4. It seems to have been his admiration for Milton that led him to make Satan show Attila a vision of the world similar to that with which, in *Paradise Regained*, he tempted Christ (*Attila*, ii. 285–696, *P. R.*, iii. 267–346); to introduce Sin as she is pictured in *Paradise Lost* (ii. 245–7, cf. *P. L.*, ii. 648–54, 746–67); to refer to one of Milton's Latin poems (in a note to ii. 315); and to borrow the phrases "arrowy sleet" (i. 236, cf. *P. R.*, iii. 324), "odours . . . From blest Arabia" (ii. 62–3, cf. "Sabaean sweets," iii. 457, and *P. L.*, iv. 162–3), "hurl'd headlong from the etherial cope" (ii. 242, cf. *P. L.*, i. 45, of Satan in each case), "no

canian," "Cimmerian," "Erecthean," and expressions like "empyreal concave," "celestial fulgor radiated." How much the style owes to *Paradise Lost* may be judged from the account of Attila's tomb:

> Nigh that marmorean dwelling of the dead,
> Kaiazo, where revered Cadica lies
> Entomb'd with Cheva and Balamber old,
> At dead of night the monarch was inhumed
> With secret rites mysteriously; and he,
> Who lived in darkness, was in darkness given
> Dust unto dust. Within his vault they placed
> Arms of the slain, by him in battle won,
> Trappings o'erlaid with gems, and plumed casques,
> And standards manifold, from Greece and Rome,
> From the famed Avars torn, or those who tread
> Far Thule, and the sons of gloomy Dis
> In Druid Gaul.[1]

It should be apparent from this extract that Herbert is no ordinary versifier. Although his epic was 'wafted' far sooner than he dreamed

> To that Lethean pool, where earthly toils
> Sink unregarded in forgetfulness,[2]

it is by no means lacking in imaginative and poetic power. Original or inspired it is not, for Herbert's strength lay in the direction of translation and imitation; and in this instance the imitation is too palpable. Yet *Attila* is dignified, restrained, always in good taste, and usually both rich and impressive. It has too little story, and that little moves too slowly; but for a heroic work in the grand style it is both readable and enjoyable, and must be regarded as one of the best, as it is one of the last, blank-verse epics in English.[3]

other deem Than" (ii. 257–8, cf. *P. R.*, iv., 44–5), "self-balanced spheres" (ii. 345, cf. *P. L.*, vii. 242), "high advanced" (iv. 35, cf. *P. L.*, i. 536, v. 588, of a banner in each case), "that Sirbonian swamp" (iv. 175, cf. *P. L.*, ii. 592), "flew diverse" (iv. 315, cf. *P. L.*, x. 284)," "smit with love Of" (v. 203–4, cf. *P. L.*, iii. 29), "barbaric silks and gold" (x. 90, cf. *P. L.*, ii. 4), "panoply of gold" (xii. 356, cf. *P. L.*, vi. 527, 760–61), "umbrage never sere" (*Farewell*, 118, cf. *Lycidas*, 2), and the lines,

> O for the voice of him,
> Who drew the curtain of apocalypse

(i. 269–70, cf. *P. L.*, iv. 1–2),

> Distance seem'd
> Annihilate, and each minutest shape
> As view'd thro' optic lens. So angels see

(ii. 293–5, cf. *P. L.*, i. 288, 59).

[1] xii. 314–26. The Miltonic use of proper names in this passage is a favorite device with Herbert.

[2] *Farewell*, 132–4.

[3] Herbert wrote six shorter pieces of blank verse (see Bibl. I, 1801 w., 1804 w.,1822, 1838 w., 1846), which, with the exception of *The Christian* (1846), are less Miltonic than *Attila*.

Others have, to be sure, been written since. Indeed, the *Quarterly Review*, in an article published in 1852 under the alarming title "Recent Epics," remarks, "The course of these stars of the first magnitude (we class them by size) is seldom observed, or the world would be astonished at the host which keep rising in mist to set in darkness."[1] Two of the epics published between 1840 and 1845 that the *Quarterly* discusses use the style and diction of *Paradise Lost*, and two even copy its angels and devils.[2] In John Fitchett's *King Alfred*, for example, there are many infernal councils at which Satan addresses the

> Powers deathless, progeny of heaven, once slaves;[3]

and the fourth book, which "into the Heaven of Heavens presumes," pictures Michael with many angels approaching the "sovereign throne" to ask a favor and gives the answer of the Almighty. Such scenes are brought still closer to *Paradise Lost* by the decidedly Miltonic style in which they are described. Here is a sample:

> High in the midst upon his sable throne
> Satan majestic sat. His lofty form
> None might discern, save when the sudden gleam
> Of some dark-flaming billow, surging vast,
> Through sinking clouds with momentary flash
> Half shew'd him terrible, and swift-display'd
> A range immense of hideous crowded forms
> Silent awaiting round. The fearful sight
> Seem'd, (if with earthly scene it holds compare)
> As when a traveller. . . .[4]

King Alfred is an astonishing production in other respects, since its forty-eight books include 131,238 lines, which make it "the longest poem in the English, or perhaps any other language . . . twice as long as the Iliad, the Aeneid, the Divine Comedy, *Jerusalem Delivered*, and *Paradise Lost*, all added together!"[5]

The geologist Thomas Hawkins makes no use of the style of *Paradise Lost* for the nine books of his *Wars of Jehovah, in Heaven, Earth, and Hell* (1844), but, according to the *Quarterly*, he does not

---

[1] xc. 334.

[2] This does not include Cottle's *Alfred* and Montgomery's *Luther* (see pp. 298 above and 412 below), which are also considered in the article.

[3] iii. 460.   [4] iii. 429–38.

[5] *Palatine Note-Book* (1882, ii. 169), where other information regarding the poem is given. It seems that Fitchett was a highly-successful attorney who, after laboring forty years over his epic and printing a first version privately between 1808 and 1834, left it unfinished. His clerk, Robert Roscoe (son of the biographer of Lorenzo de' Medici), "edited" it, added over 2500 lines in bringing it to 'a brief and rapid termination,' and published it in 1841–2. For Fitchett's *Bewsey*, see above, p. 258.

hesitate to borrow freely from its subject-matter. W. R. Harris, on the contrary, in his *Napoleon, an Epic Poem in twelve cantos* (1845), discards the devils but keeps the style of the Puritan work. No secret is made of the indebtedness, for he tells us frankly,

> He who now adventurous tardy pours
> Heroic lay, from *earliest infancy*
> Courted, *enamour'd, Milton's flowing strain:*
> Mute — till a *heavenly* theme his fancy fired![1]

Harris was, however, no servile imitator, for by a happy inspiration he introduced "sudden bursts of rhyme, varying in length from a couplet to a hundred lines," whenever the humor seized him. In consequence of many such idiosyncrasies, *Napoleon*, like the *Wars of Jehovah* and one of the other "recent epics" discussed in the article, seems like the work of a somewhat unbalanced mind.

Aside from the sneers of the *Quarterly*, these productions apparently attracted no attention whatever, and, though similar poems have doubtless appeared since, the surprising vitality of the epic tradition must have been almost exhausted by 1850. It may be significant that in 1855, when Susannah Henderson published her *Olga* (the life of a Russian empress of the tenth century) she did not term it an epic, as she probably would have done fifty years earlier.[2] Certainly Milman, who composed *Samor* as a schoolboy, attempted nothing of the kind again, and Herbert's *Attila*, though published as late as 1838, was begun much earlier, perhaps, like Fitchett's *Alfred*, soon after 1800. The later epics of Southey, like the work of Pennie, Drummond, Hawkins, and Harris, are the last manifestations of a force almost spent; and *Hyperion*, though written in 1818–19 and in Miltonic blank verse, was not a part of the literary movement that produced the others.

The epic may, therefore, be said to have been moribund throughout the second quarter of the nineteenth century and to have died soon after. It has never revived. Occasionally, to be sure, epic fragments and even complete poems have been written in subsequent years, and in the case of *Sohrab and Rustum* with no small success; but these are "sports" of literary evolution which do not prove any

---

[1] *Quart. Rev.*, xc. 345. I have not seen this epic or Hawkins's. Hawkins wrote at least two other poems, of which I know only the titles, *The Lost Angel and the History of the Old Adamites* (1840) and *Prometheus* (1850).

[2] In most respects her poem belongs to the preceding century; for it employs conventional poetic diction, with words like "decidence," "congelations," "appetence," "perturbated," and "bold emprize," as well as many other Miltonisms, and jogs along in unmistakable though unrimed heroic couplets which have none of the condensed brilliance of Pope and make little effort to conceal their lack of inspiration under loftiness of style.

vitality for the form. Arnold's episode is unique in that it is composed in a blank verse which is heroic without being Miltonic. This is not true of Ernest Myers's noble *Judgment of Prometheus* (1886), as the opening lines will show:

> Now through the royal hall, for Heaven's dread Lord
> Wrought by the Fire-king's hand, the assembled Gods,
> Upon the morn appointed, thronging ranged
> Expectant; mute they moved, and took their thrones,
> Gloom on their brows, though Gods; so dark the dread
> Of huge impending battle held their hearts,
> Battle of brother Kings, Heaven and the Sea
> In duel dire, convulsive war of worlds.[1]

Classical influences undoubtedly entered strongly into Myers's writings, but the fine insight into the character of the earlier poet shown in his sonnet on Milton must have borne fruit when he came to write the epic fragment.[2]

Another short poem of recent years, more romantic or Hellenistic than the *Judgment of Prometheus* but one that, like it, might well be part of an extended epic, is Alfred Noyes's *Last of the Titans* (1908). The style of this rich, dignified narrative occasionally recalls that of *Paradise Lost*, as when the chariots rolled

> Their flaming wheels remote, so that they seemed,
> E'en Alioth and Fomalhaut, no more
> Than dust of diamonds in the abysmal gloom;

or when

> two monstrous bulks arose,
> Mountainous,

with eyes

> as of wild crimson torches
> Far-sunken in a thick and savage wood,
> Yet imminent;

or when, as in the opening lines,

> Over what seemed a gulf of glimmering sea,
> Huger than hugest Himalay arose
> Atlas, on weary shoulders heaving dark
> The burden of the heavens.[3]

In view of these recent heroic episodes and fragments, it cannot be denied that impressive and interesting epic poetry may still be

---

[1] *Gathered Poems* (1904), 3.

[2] For the sonnet, see *ib.* 120; notice also 61 (*Vallombrosa*). The *Olympic Hermes* (*ib.* 41–6) and some of Myers's other brief pieces of blank verse on classical subjects recall *Paradise Lost* in their lofty utterance and their occasional inversions. In his drama on the Greek model, *The Puritans* (1869), Milton is a principal character.

[3] *Golden Hynde*, etc. (N. Y. 1908), 56, 64, 65, 54.

written. But this is not to say that impressive and interesting *epics* may be written, for all these pieces are short. Would twelve books of *Sohrab and Rustum* be popular? How many persons would read the completed *Hyperion* — or, for that matter, how many read the incomplete? Should we enjoy three hundred pages of the *Judgment of Prometheus* or the *Last of the Titans?* On this last question some light might be expected from the twelve books of Mr. Noyes's *Drake, an English Epic* (1906–8), were not this work romantic rather than heroic. The difference does not, of course, lie in the dropping of supernatural machinery and classical subjects, for such changes are likely to be made if the form is ever to awake to renewed vitality. It is rather that *Drake* suggests a medieval romance rewritten by Tennyson, is descriptive and reflective, and lacks the directness, the objectivity, and the interest in action which mark the *Iliad* and *Paradise Lost*.

Is there, then, no future for the epic? May not another Milton arise and give us a work differing perhaps from the poetry of our time as much as *Paradise Lost* did from that of the Restoration? It may be. At least such a work, if it is ever written, is likely to violate many of our preconceptions.[1] There is no certainty that it will be in blank verse; it may resemble *Don Juan* more than it does *Hyperion;* it may even be in prose; perhaps it will follow the lines of Thomas Hardy's *Dynasts*, a drama partly in prose but with more of the epic sweep than any other English work of our time. Homers and Miltons have never been numerous or predicable, and the non-appearance of one of the "giant brood" for two and a half centuries does not warrant the belief that they are no more, or prove that a mightier Whitman or Masefield may not some day, with a theme like the discovery and settlement of the western United States, show us that the race of heroic poets still lives.

THE BURLESQUE

The sublimity and distinctive style of *Paradise Lost* invite parody, and at a time when the poem was widely read and imitated the invitation was frequently accepted. Some seventy-five humorous poems in blank verse have come to my attention, most of which probably go back, directly or indirectly, to the first, the *Splendid Shilling* (1701). If Philips's humor is somewhat obvious and deliberate, that of his successors is rarely so good, and in consequence has long been forgotten; for "the merit of such performances," as Dr. Johnson

[1] As does Mickiewicz's Polish epic, *Pan Tadeusz* (1834, translated by G. R. Noyes, 1917).

said, "begins and ends with the first author." [1] The poems were too easy to write to be well written: they are funny, but not funny enough. Furthermore, the pentameter and tetrameter couplets had developed a terse brilliance that the slower, heavier, and more diffuse blank verse of the day could not rival; consequently, men whose bent was towards wit or humor usually followed Pope, Swift, and Churchill in devoting their energies exclusively to rime. Certainly very few flowers of genius were wasted upon the desert air of the eighteenth-century burlesque.

But not much could be expected of works that make so little attempt at originality as these humorous pieces in blank verse. Practically all of them do the obvious thing, — apply a pompous exaggeration of the style of *Paradise Lost* to humble themes. In execution many are passable, but none show anything like the cleverness of conception that marks the *Rape of the Lock*, or "Whistlecraft's" *King Arthur*, or *Don Juan*, or the best things in the *Anti-Jacobin*. The extent to which they openly copy Philips is astonishing. Many acknowledge either in the titles or in the poems themselves that they are "in imitation of the *Splendid Shilling*," and several begin as it does, "Happy the man ... who." Rarely is there so refreshingly unexpected a turn to this hackneyed opening as in the lines,

> Happy the man! whose well-stor'd shelf contains,
> In various piles, for the whole year compos'd,
> A set of goodly sermons. He nor fears
> Returning Saturday, or next day's toil.[2]

Even the choice of subject was usually suggested by Philips. The *Splendid Shilling* laments not only poverty but the "eternal drought" which accompanies it; for the pots of ale which the poet "tipples" are, alas, imaginary! This hint was enough to call forth at least eight paeans on liquor from the heavy-drinking bards of the day,[3] *Wine* (1708), *Gin* (1734), *A Bacchanalian Rhapsody* (1746), *Small-beer* (1746), *Oxford Ale* (1750), *A Tankard of Porter* (1760), *The Corkscrew* (1760), and *Punch* (1769). Nor should the solemnly ludicrous picture of the orgy after the fox-chase, in Thomson's *Autumn* (1730),[4] be forgotten, or two poems on the gout (1756, 1768). Philips's "warming Puff ... from Tube as black As Winters Chimney" may have suggested the unrimed humorous *Verses on Bad Tobacco* (1738) and *The Tobacco-stopper* (1760). He had little to say about food, but his

[1] "Philips," in *Lives* (ed. Hill), i. 317.
[2] *The Curate's Caution* (1794), in *Gent. Mag.*, lxiv. 365–6.
[3] Philips's *Cerealia* and *Cyder*, which also deal with drink, probably had some influence. [4] Lines 492–569.

followers praised *Pudding* (1759), *Apple Dumpling* (1774), *Potatoes* (1786), and *Good Eating* in general (1772). Money is the theme not only of the *Splendid Shilling*, but of the *Sick-bed Soliloquy to an Empty Purse* (1735), the *Empty Purse, a poem in Miltonics* (1750),[1] the *Crooked Sixpence* (two poems, 1743 and 1802), the *Birmingham Halpenny* (1757), the *Copper Farthing* (1763), and the *Soliloquy on the Last Shilling* (1773).

With Philips are also connected several of the humorous pictures of school and college life: *An Epistle from Oxon* (1731), *A Day in Vacation at College* (written in 1750 by the notorious Dr. Dodd), Woty's *Campanalogia* (1761), Mrs. Pennington's *Copper Farthing* (1763), Maurice's *School-boy* (1775) and *Oxonian* (1778),[2] Lardner's *College Gibb* (1801), and the none-too-exhilarating *Panegyric on Oxford Ale* (composed in 1748) in which Thomas Warton follows, "in verse Miltonic,"

> the matchless bard, whose lay resounds
> The SPLENDID SHILLING'S praise.

Philips is likewise partly responsible for the marked tendency of these poems to avoid the elegant society pictured in the *Rape of the Lock* and to condescend to men and things of low estate, a tendency noticeable in the pieces already mentioned, as well as in *Poverty* (1748), *A Louse* (1749), *The Street* (1764), *The Old Shoe* (1770), *The Bugs* (1773), *The Sweepers* (1774), *The Cat* (1796), *Washing-day* (1797), and *An Old Pair of Boots* (1797). The humor is often broad and sometimes vulgar; but in only three instances is it, like so much of the facetious rimed verse of the day, really indecent.

The *Splendid Shilling* is not really mock-heroic, nor are any of the other pieces that have been considered; for, although they use the grand style in treating lowly themes, they do not, like the Homeric *Battle of the Frogs and the Mice*, Boileau's *Lutrin*, and Pope's *Rape of the Lock*, parody epic action, speech, or characters. There is, accordingly, no reason why the unrimed mock-heroics, all but one of which are translations,[3] should owe anything to Philips. Three are renderings of Edward Holdsworth's popular *Muscipula* (1709),[4] which tells

---

[1] I know nothing of these two pieces except their titles; they may be under no debt to Philips, and the first may not even be in blank verse.

[2] *Campanalogia* is dedicated "to the Society of College-Youths," and seems to deal with life at one of the universities. The *Copper Farthing*, and the *School-boy* (which Johnson praised, see Maurice's *Poems*, 1800, p. 23 n.), both sing of the joys and sorrows of a schoolboy, and both are closely patterned after the *Splendid Shilling*.

[3] Dr. Frank Sayers's amusing Homeric parody, *Jack the Giant-Killer* (1803), though in blank verse, is not Miltonic. [4] See p. 108 above.

of the invention of the mouse-trap. The first, published by Daniel
Bellamy in 1709, is frankly "in imitation of Milton," and at times
travesties *Paradise Lost* as closely as this:

> He ended frowning. . . .
> But ONE *Ycleped* TAFFY, soon up rose,
> Great CAMBRIA's chiefest Pride, who seem'd alone
> For Dignity compos'd, and high Exploit;
> Both *Vulcan* and a *Senator*, whose Tongue
> Dropping down *Manna*, charming to the Ear,
> With soft, persuasive Accent thus began.
> "If CHEESE, most NOBLE PEERS, our Nation's Boast,
> Should be by this *intestine* Foe destroy'd,
> I dread the Consequence." [1]

The second, which appeared anonymously six years later, is likewise
"done in Milton's stile," but follows *Paradise Lost* no more closely
than does the third (the work of John Hoadly) in this passage:

> He spake, and strait the fragments, mouldy scraps,
> Reliques of rapine, monuments of theft,
> High in their sight uprearing, rous'd their rage;
> Now thirst of dire revenge, now lust of fame
> Burns emulous, and fires each Patriot breast;
> Each meditates to Mouse unheard-of fate,
> And ev'ry brain is hamm'ring on a TRAP. [2]

If Hoadly's poem does not call up the figure of "Laughter holding
both his sides," the heavy humor of Bishop Warburton's version of
Addison's Latin *Battle of the Cranes and Pigmies* (1724) certainly
will not. The announcement in the title that the translation is "in
imitation of Milton's style" is scarcely necessary in view of such
borrowings as these: "collected in their might;" "*Briarius, Titanian,*
or Earth-born;" "involv'd in Smoak;"

> Hurl'd to, and fro, with Jaculation dire.
>
> Above the rest,
> In Shape and Gesture proudly eminent,
> Stood like a Giant. . . .
> . . . . his honest Face
> Deep Scars of hostile Tallons had intrench'd. [3]

Less savoury but more amusing than any of these translations is
a description of the war between Pulex and Pediculus (a flea and a

---

[1] Bellamy's *Dramatic Pieces*, etc. (1739), 21, third pagination; cf. *P. L.*, ii. 106–20.

[2] "Dodsley's Miscellany" (1758), v. 262. The translation was made in 1737.

[3] *Tracts by Warburton*, etc. (ed. Samuel Parr, 1789), 60 (cf. *P. L.*, ix. 673), 61 (cf.
P. L., i. 198–9, of the Titans' war against Jove in each case), 61 (cf. *P. L.*, i. 236–7),
61 (cf. *P. L.*, vi. 665), 59 (cf. *P. L.*, i. 589–91, 600–601).

louse), which William Woty published in 1770 as *The Pediculaiad, or Buckram Triumphant*. Although Woty disclaims the muse

> Who from the *Aonian* mount . . .
> Bore our great *Milton* with advent'rous wing,

invoking instead the "great *Sartoria*, cross-legg'd Goddess" of his tailor-hero Buckram, he travesties *Paradise Lost* in these lines:

> High on his shop-board in exalted state
> Pre-eminent sat *Buckram*, full of thought,
> And wan with care. Upon his faded brow,
> Entrench'd with many a frown, pale Discontent
> Hung lowring. Inward anguish tore his soul
> And deep despair. Thrice he essay'd to speak,
> And thrice his words fell inward, unpronounc'd.[1]

It is in the head of Buckram that "sage Pediculus," who deigns not "to inhabit other seat Than the imperial Capitol," has his home, although another "citadel . . . *galligaskins* hight " is the scene of his mortal combat with Pulex. *The Pediculaiad*, like its author's other humorous pieces in blank verse, is better than most poems of the kind; and, as Woty published a greater number than any one else (fourteen in all), he is entitled to the modest distinction of being, after Philips, the leading writer in the field.[2] To be sure, poets who are in general of far more importance composed humorous blank verse, — Lady Winchilsea, Gay, Thomson, Somervile, Akenside, Cowper, and the laureates Whitehead and Thomas Warton;[3] but none of their productions live or deserve to live, none are even so good as the forgotten pieces that parodied the *Allegro-Penseroso* movement.[4] For humor, like other things that sparkle, is apt to become flat with the passing of time.

One of Woty's productions, *The Spouting-Club*, was stolen by a certain Richard Lewis and published in 1758 as his own work. Apparently Lewis did write *The Robin Hood Society* (1756), "a Satire, with notes Variorum, by Peter Pounce," — stupid doggerel designed

---

[1] *Works* (1770), i. 142–4; cf. *P. L.*, ii. 1–5, i. 600–605, 619–21. This piece and several others by Woty have no suggestion of Philips. Nor has Francis Fawkes's *Parody on a Passage in Paradise Lost* (1761), R. Jephson's *Extempore Ludicrous Miltonic Verses* (1776) or his *Burlesque Miltonic* (1778), Thomas Maurice's *Oxonian* (1778, which contains several borrowings from *Paradise Lost*), W. O. Lardner's *College Gibb* (1801), or A. C. Schomberg's *Bagley* (1777, see above, p. 258, n. 1). For two parodies of the *Night Thoughts*, see above, p. 159, n. 4.

[2] Woty was joint-editor of the *Poetical Calendar* (12 vols., 1763), and author of at least eight pieces of serious Miltonic blank verse, three of the *Allegro-Penseroso* type, and four in the meter of the translation from Horace.

[3] See above and below, pp. 15 n. 1, 107–8, 140, 363, 392 n. 1, 163, 159 n. 4, 317.

[4] See below, p. 467.

to represent "the Weekly Society for free Enquiry, &c. who meet at the sign of the Robin Hood without Temple-Bar, as an assembly of illiterate, deistical mechanics, and profligate persons; who indulge themselves in an unwarrantable, illegal, abuse of the liberty we enjoy, of freely debating upon sacred subjects." [1] The only un-rimed political satire of the period seems to be the anonymous *Paradise Regain'd, or the Battle of Adam and the Fox* (1780), an imag-inative if not a poetic treatment of the duel between William Adam and Charles James Fox, ironically dedicated to Lord North in recog-nition of his powers of "invention." It relates how Adam, banished from Eden to Scotland (where William Adam lived), is tempted by the serpent to undertake a duel with its enemy, the Fox, who is wounded by Adam. After "endeavouring to flounder through this chaos of half-formed ideas," [2] expressed in a wretched adaptation of the verse of *Paradise Lost*, the reader will hardly be in the mood for Nathaniel Lancaster's *Methodism Triumphant, or the Decisive Battle between the Old Serpent and the Modern Saint* (1767); for, according to the *Critical Review*, Lancaster "writes in Miltonic verse, and his manner is so formal, that in five books he hardly excites one emotion of pleasantry." [3] These three pieces, together with Gascoigne's *Steele Glas* (1576), seem to be the only satires of any length writ-ten in blank verse before 1800 and presumably for a considerable time thereafter. There were, however, several long enough to be published by themselves, and perhaps, like John Carr's *Filial Piety* (1764), in handsome folio sheets. Carr invokes

> HER, whose Hand divine
> Pats the sleek Brain of many a mighty Bard;
> Whose Names I fain wou'd write, but fear the Worst.
> All hail, propitious DULNESS! (who, but yawns
> And stretches with congenial Sympathy?). [4]

A curious kind of burlesque, curious because for fully half the poem the author seems not to have quite made up his mind whether to be quizzically in earnest or good-humoredly to poke fun, is William Shenstone's *Œconomy, a Rhapsody, addressed to Young Poets* (1764). Funny the rhapsody rarely is; besides, seven hundred lines of burlesque is too much. Like the *Splendid Shilling*, it pictures the shifts and privations of impecunious poets, who are urged, in

---

[1] *Mo. Rev.*, xv. 86.

[2] *Ib.* lxii. 323. Regarding the duel, see the *Dictionary of National Biography*, under "William Adam."

[3] xxv. 66–7 (1768). I know the poem only through this review.

[4] Page 3.

order that the wherewithal necessary for their lavish temperamental natures may be forthcoming, to devote some of the dregs of their time to their accounts and to

> Œconomy! thou good old-aunt! whose mien
> Furrow'd with age and care the wise adore.[1]

Shenstone must have had Philips's original in mind, for some of his phrases clearly burlesque *Paradise Lost*,[2] a fact the more interesting because, notwithstanding his romantic tastes, his ode-writing, and his imitation of Spenser, Shenstone never wrote sonnets or copied *Allegro* and *Penseroso*. Yet he did write two more unrimed poems of some three or four hundred lines each, *Love and Honour* (a stilted tale of a Spanish captive and a British hero), and *The Ruin'd Abby, or the Effects of Superstition*, in which his passion for landscape gardening is strangely combined with a chronological survey of the evils brought upon England by Catholicism. "His blank verses," wrote Johnson, "those that can read them may probably find to be like the blank verses of his neighbours,"[3] an utterance which is equally applicable to nearly all unrimed humorous poems, and under which, as under an epitaph, they may be allowed to rest.

Yet there is one which, though no better than many others, has unusual contemporary interest because of its date (1914) and because of its appearance in that remarkable production of twentieth-century America, the *Spoon River Anthology* (1915). The last piece in Mr. Masters's volume is *The Spooniad*, a mock-heroic which in three passages parodies Milton. It begins,

---

[1] *Works* (1764), i. 293. Akenside's *Poet* (1737) also describes the poverty of hack-writers.

[2] For example, "broom never comes, That comes to all" (p. 303, cf. *P. L.*, i. 66–7); "seas of bliss! Seas without shore!" (p. 291, cf. *P. L.*, xi. 749–50); "ballanc'd with friendship . . . The rival scale of interest kicks the beam" (p. 287, cf. *P. L.*, iv. 997–1004);

> Sweet interchange
> Of river, valley, mountain, woods, and plains!

(p. 301, cf. *P. L.*, ix. 115–16);

> Of sweet refreshment, ease without annoy,
> Or luscious noon-day nap. Ah much deceiv'd,
> Much suff'ring pilgrim! thou nor noon-day nap,
> Nor sweet repose shalt find

(p. 304, cf. *P. L.*, ix. 403–7);

> His delighted eye,
> Tho' wrapt in thought, commercing with the sky

(p. 304, cf. *Penseroso*, 39–40).

[3] "Shenstone," in *Lives* (ed. Hill), iii. 358.

> Of John Cabanis' wrath . . .
> . . . . and the fall
> Of Rhodes' bank that brought unnumbered woes
> And loss to many, with engendered hate.

A little later come the lines,

> Say first,
> Thou son of night, called Momus, from whose eyes
> No secret hides. . . .

and, two pages farther on, this patent burlesque of the opening of the second book of *Paradise Lost,*

> High on a stage that overlooked the chairs . . .
> Sat Harmon Whitney, to that eminence,
> By merit raised in ribaldry and guile,
> And to the assembled rebels thus he spake.[1]

[1] Cf. *P. L.*, i. 1-4, 27; ii. 1-10.

CHAPTER XIV

TRANSLATIONS OF THE CLASSICS [1]

BLANK verse was first employed, outside of the drama, in Surrey's translation of two books of the *Aeneid* (1557). The use to which the new measure was put was not due entirely to chance; for to Englishmen who have loved the literature of Greece and Rome, who have grown up with it at school, have escaped to it from the pressure of affairs, and have mellowed their old age with its serenity, — to such men, and they have fortunately been many, the impulse to translate their favorite authors has been strangely potent. It has led to the making of hundreds of translations that have never appeared, and of hundreds of others the printing of which has been a costly luxury to their authors or publishers; yet published a large number of them are, notwithstanding the few purchasers or readers they find. Even the feverish life and scholarship of America have in recent years felt this impulse (which is the reverse of utilitarian) to no slight degree.

But the significance of Surrey's work lies not so much in its being a translation as in its being written in blank verse; and, the more we think of it, the more fitting it seems that our first unrimed poem should be a rendering of one of the great poems of antiquity. For, notwithstanding the merited popularity of Dryden's Virgil and Pope's Homer, lovers of Greek and Latin have never been entirely satisfied with the heroic couplet as an English equivalent of the classical hexameter. Even in Pope's day there were many who thought with Bentley, "The verses are good verses, but the work is not Homer." [2] Indeed, far more serious objections could be urged against rime in the eighteenth century than at present; for the couplet had become a highly-finished, brilliant medium associated

---

[1] This chapter I would gladly have left unwritten, for to do it justice one ought to have experience in verse translation and a wide and thorough knowledge of Greek and Latin literature, of Dante, and of various modern writers. Even then the amount of time required might prove disproportionate to the results. Yet blank-verse translations are so numerous and important, and they are under such a heavy debt to Milton, that in a study of his influence they cannot be ignored. I hope that what I have written, unsatisfactory as it is, may give some idea of this extensive but neglected field of eighteenth- and nineteenth-century poetry. The inaccuracy with which the originals are rendered is stressed in J. W. Draper's *Theory of Translation in the Eighteenth Century* (*Neophilologus*, Groningen, Holland, vi. 241-54).

[2] Pope's *Works* (ed. J. Warton, 1797), iv. 23 n.

in every one's mind with argument, wit, satire, and artificiality, with such works as *Absalom and Achitophel*, the *Essay on Criticism*, the *Rape of the Lock*, and *The Dunciad*.

Yet in any age the difficulties of rimed translation are very great. It is hard enough to reproduce accurately, simply, and pleasantly the mere meaning of a poem written in a notably-condensed foreign language; it is far harder to render the manner and spirit of the original, to give approximately the same impression that it gives, — of robust vigor, for example, or natural ease, or exquisite art; but it is most difficult of all to make the work not simply faithful but fresh, natural, and interesting, to make it read well a hundred pages at a time, like an original production. To achieve these three things will test the mettle of the ablest writer; and, if the fetters of rime be added, which are much heavier in translation than in an original work, where the thought can be modified to fit the meter, the task becomes almost impossible. In the words of a well-known translator, "The exigencies of rhyme positively forbid faithfulness."[1] It is like a woman's undertaking to act Hamlet, an exceedingly difficult part at the best: In a rimed translation the thought or the spirit or the verse usually suffers, and sometimes all three. J. S. Blackie makes light of the difficulties of rime, and later translators in general have less to say about them than did the earlier. But the opposition has not so much decreased as shifted its ground: modern poets feel more subtle objections. Rime seems to them, in the words of E. H. Plumptre, "to introduce an element more or less incongruous, to fetter the free flow of thought by the periodicity of the same sound recurring at fixed intervals, to present a temptation, very difficult to guard against, to expansion and over-ornamentation for the sake of it."[2]

Even the Augustans, practically all of whom tried their hands at translation, of course felt "the troublesome and modern bondage of riming," but accepted it in the main as a necessary evil. Yet Dryden is said to have declared, "Nor would I have done my *Virgil* in rime if I was to begin it again";[3] and, when Lyttelton expressed surprise that Pope had not used blank verse for his *Iliad*, the master of the heroic couplet did not defend his measure but answered that rime was easier for him.[4] The Augustans also felt that riming was a *modern* bondage and thus misrepresented the original, just as the

---

[1] F. W. Newman, *The Iliad, faithfully translated* (1856), preface, p. vii.
[2] *Tragedies of Sophocles* (2d ed., 1867), p. xi.
[3] Joseph Richardson, *Explanatory Notes on P. L.* (1734), p. cxx.
[4] Percival Stockdale, *Memoirs* (1809), ii. 44.

actress's sex would misrepresent the Prince of Denmark. Even so early as 1766 one writer anticipated Matthew Arnold's chief objection to the couplet. "Rhyme," he wrote, "besides obliging you to end the line with a good sound, serves also as a barrier between each in a couplet."[1]

Opposition to rime increased through the eighteenth and nineteenth centuries as greater control was gained over blank verse and as a more scrupulous faithfulness came to be demanded of the translator. But the most important development since Pope's time is the growth in popularity of prose translations, which the Augustans apparently did not consider at all but which to-day are probably read more than any others. Yet, though the average reader may prefer prose, poets and men of learning as a rule do not. To them the *Iliad*, the *Aeneid*, and the *Divine Comedy* are first of all poems, and no other aspect of such works is it so important to convey to the reader as the poetic. Prose versions of these masterpieces, they object, are like black-and-white reproductions of a Turner or a Monet, in which no attempt is made to render the artist's supreme excellence, color. To the retort that no color is better than bad color, they reply that the color, though of course far short of the original, need not be bad. But it is not simply the loss of beauty that poets complain of; it is something more fundamental. A great poem, they remind us, is conceived as a poem and expressed in the language and figures of poetry; if it had been conceived and expressed as prose it would be something entirely different. Prose, they insist, misrepresents it as much as French Alexandrine verse would misrepresent Bacon's *Essays*,[2] for the language and style of poetry seem unnatural in a prose work.[3] Certain it is that the production of new poetic translations is, if anything, on the increase in recent years and that the older verse translations are frequently reissued. Pope's Homer, Cary's and Longfellow's Dante, all have a steady sale, and cheap reprints of the Earl of Derby's *Iliad* and Cowper's *Odyssey* have recently appeared.

Almost every possible and some impossible meters have been employed for translation of the classic epics, — the Spenserian and

[1] That is, between each pair of lines in a couplet and those that precede or follow it. The comment is Robert Andrews's (*Works of Virgil*, 1766, p. 2). Cf. Arnold, *On Translating Homer* (1861), lecture i, p. 15: "Rhyme inevitably tends to pair lines which in the original are independent, and thus the movement of the poem is changed."

[2] This simile is H. D. Sedgwick's (*Dante*, New Haven, Conn., 1918, p. 173).

[3] It is illuminating to learn that Lewis Campbell began his version of Sophocles in prose, "but soon found that, for tragic dialogue in English, blank verse appeared a more natural and effective vehicle than any prose style which he could hope to frame" (*Sophocles, the Seven Plays*, 1883, prefatory note, p. xxvi).

other stanzas, the octosyllabics of *Marmion*, a ballad meter consisting of a tetrameter and a trimeter half-line, the quatrains of Omar, rimed or unrimed pentameter or hexameter, hendecasyllabics, and fourteeners. The unrimed dactylic hexameter, which theoretically would appear to be the best medium for rendering the Greek and Latin hexameter, has been strongly urged by so sympathetic and discriminating a classicist and so eminent a critic as Matthew Arnold. Yet there are grave difficulties. It would seem obvious that a great translation of Homer or Virgil must be in a meter which has domesticated itself in English, as the hexameter had in Greek and Latin; otherwise, however excellent in itself, it would sound academic and strange and thus false to the original. Furthermore, good hexameters such as Arnold describes are even more difficult than rimes,[1] and to employ them in a poem as long as the *Iliad*, without sacrificing any of its spirit or meaning, is a task to which no one as yet seems to have been equal. Arnold himself acknowledges that "a good model, on any considerable scale, of this metre, the English translator will nowhere find"; but he sweeps aside the difficulty in his most Olympian manner by declaring, "This is an objection which can best be met by *producing* good English hexameters." [2]

Well, sixty more years have passed and they have not yet been produced! Except for Southey's far from successful *Vision of Judgement*, Clough's humorous *Bothie of Tober-na-Vuolich*, and the much-criticized meter of *Evangeline* and the *Courtship of Miles Standish*, in which no one wishes to read Homer, they remain academic exercises.

These lame hexameters the strong-wing'd music of Homer!
No — but a most burlesque barbarous experiment,

Tennyson exclaimed of some of them;[3] and in a matter of this kind his opinion, particularly when it is reinforced by that of Swinburne and of Landor,[4] carries no less weight than Arnold's.

[1] One reason for this is suggested by Cranch in the preface to his translation of the *Aeneid* (Boston, 1872, pp. v–vi): "To say nothing of the greater advantage the Latin has in its winged and airy vowel-syllables, the trouble is to find in English pure spondaic words enough, without which the lines must be overloaded with dactyls; the result being . . . fatiguing and monotonous. . . . I cannot but think that the hexameter belongs exclusively to the costume of the antique ages, and that the less the epic muse has to do with it, the better."

[2] *On Translating Homer*, lecture iii, pp. 80, 76.

[3] *In Quantity: On Translations of Homer*. "Some," he remarked on another occasion, ". . . have endeavoured to give us the *Iliad* in English hexameters, and by what appears to me their failure have gone far to prove the impossibility of the task. I have long held by our blank verse in this matter" (note to his *Specimen of a Translation of the Iliad*, in *Works*, ed. Hallam Tennyson, N. Y., 1913, p. 925).

[4] "At best what ugly bastards of verse are these self-styled hexameters," wrote Swinburne (*Essays and Studies*, 1875, p. 163); and Landor, who felt,

Like Tennyson and Landor, an ever-increasing number are coming to regard blank verse as the proper medium for rendering the classics. It has the variety which is essential to works of length and which English hexameters and couplets usually lack. It is "freighted with all the authority of the greatest tradition in English literature; in it Shakespeare, Milton, Wordsworth wrote;" [1] and from the time of *Paradise Lost* to that of *Hyperion* and to our own day it has been indisputably the English epic meter. For these reasons it is generally considered our equivalent for the meter of the *Iliad* and the *Aeneid*.

Yet owing principally to the difficulty in writing blank verse that is heroic but not Miltonic, it is not the ideal verse-form for the classics of other tongues that some have thought it. Milton's manner is his own, something so different from Homer's or Virgil's or Dante's that his learned diction and the involutions of his style, when transferred to these poets, entirely misrepresent them. Perhaps it is due to his influence that blank verse lacks the rapidity, lightness, and suppleness necessary for an adequate rendering of Homer and Virgil. This is not to say that it *need* lack these qualities and may not become an ideal medium for the purpose. A great poet whose genius lay in this direction could probably bend the heroic couplet, the hexameter, or the blank verse to his will and give us a masterpiece of translation; but such poets are rare, and it is unlikely that any of them would undertake the task.

It will be noticed that part of the *Aeneid* was translated into blank verse before any of the *Iliad*, and that Dryden's Virgil preceded Pope's Homer by eighteen years. This precedence of the Roman work over the Grecian continued throughout the eighteenth and, to a lesser degree, the nineteenth century, probably because Virgil is briefer than Homer and is studied more generally. After the renderings of two short passages of the *Aeneid* by Addison (1704) and an anonymous translator (1726), of the whole poem by Brady (1713–26), and of all Virgil by Trapp (1703–31), [2] the next translation of the

> We have a measure
> Fashion'd by Milton's own hand, a fuller, a deeper, a louder,

parodied the hexameter thus:

> Afar be ambition to follow the Roman,
> Led by the German uncomb'd and jigging in dactyl and spondee,
> Lumbering shapeless jackboots which nothing can polish or supple

(*English Hexameters*, in *Last Fruit*).　　　[1] Sedgwick, *Dante*, 174.
　　[2] See pp. 104–6 above. In the preface to the second edition of *Winter* (1726) Thomson translated twelve lines of the *Georgics* into blank verse.

Latin epic was that which Alexander Strahan began to publish in 1739 and completed in 1767. "Mr. Strahan," remarked the *Monthly Review*, — which gave the first six books the dubious praise of being "not inferior to the former translations of *Virgil* into blank verse," — "Mr. Strahan endeavours to imitate *Milton's* manner, as thinking it the only true method of succeeding in a translation of *Virgil*: he keeps close to his author, in respect to his sense." [1] Here are some typical lines:

> From hence to *Acheron's Tartarean* stream
> The way: a turbid gulph, with whirlpool vast,
> Boils over here, disgorging all its sand
> Into *Cocytus*.[2]

Bad as this is, it is no worse and not a great deal more Miltonic than may be found in other versions of the time, — that, for example, made in 1764 by the Oxford professor of poetry, William Hawkins, which the *Critical Review* declared to be "the worst garb he [Virgil] ever appeared in." [3] William Mills had even shorter shrift:

> Read the commandments, MILLS, *translate* no further,
> For there 'tis written — *Thou shalt do no murther*.[4]

Yet Mills's rendering of the *Georgics* (1780) is too dull and feeble to be called murder. There is more vigor and more stilted Miltonic inversion (Mills has none at all), but no more poetry or interest, in Capel Lofft's *First and Second Georgic, attempted in Blank Verse* (1784). The version of the complete *Georgics* which James R. Deare issued in 1808 seems, on the contrary, to be pleasant if not vigorous or inspired, and is the better for making but little use of Milton's style.[5]

---

[1] ix. 1 (1753). The complete *Aeneid* is noticed in the *Review* for November, 1767, where it is called dull. I have not seen Strahan's work.

[2] *Ib*. 2. The tenth and twelfth books of Strahan's version were contributed by William Dobson, who had turned *Paradise Lost* into Latin and who afterwards put the first book into Greek. In 1757 Dobson translated the first book of Cardinal de Polignac's Latin *Anti-Lucretius* into stiff, decidedly Miltonic blank verse.

[3] xvii. 425. I have not seen the work (which included the entire *Aeneid*, though only half of it was published), but from the extracts in the review it appears to be little if any below the average. The reviewer objected particularly to the expressions "shalt *joy* thy shrine" and "matter for *hereafter joy*"; but the other Miltonisms are inoffensive, — "gods . . . Auspicious drave the blasts," "the queen . . . her fame Unheeding," "thus fair Venus she bespeaks," "exploit Egregious this."

[4] *Crit. Rev.*, l. 55; an adaptation of Abel Evans's epigram on Trapp.

[5] I know these three translations of the *Georgics* only from the extracts and reviews in the magazines: for Mills, see *Crit. Rev.*, l. 50–55 (1780); for Lofft, *Mo. Rev.*, lxxii. 345–8 (1785); for Deare, *Quart. Rev.*, i. 69, 76–7 (1809). James Mason's translation of the entire *Georgics* into blank verse in 1810, and Robert Hoblyn's of the first book in

Aside from Trapp's work, the only blank-verse rendering of all Virgil to appear in the eighteenth century was that of Robert Andrews, which Baskerville printed for the author in 1766. It is a singular affair, vigorous, abrupt, condensed, formal, often racy, but tending to fall into a series of separate lines, probably because it is a line-for-line translation. Such a jerky style does not permit elaborate inversions; yet the poem constantly, though only for a few words or phrases at a time, recalls *Paradise Lost:*

> Accept, O Sire! whom the Olympic king
> Thus proclaims worthy the prime meed select.
> This old Anchise's present, hence be thine,
> This embost goblet; which the Thracian Cisseus
> Erst on my sire magnificent confer'd,
> His friendship's dear and monumental pledge.[1]

It was almost thirty years before Virgil again appeared in blank verse, this time at the hands of James Beresford, whose *Aeneid* (1794) seems to be no worse than the average, though rather more Miltonic. It is such wearisome reading, however, that one turns with relief to the eccentricities of James Henry's *Eneis* (1845). A successful physician, Henry left his practice in Dublin to walk with his wife and daughter back and forth across Europe, writing strange poems in stranger meters and examining manuscripts and editions of Virgil. He was one of the greatest of Virgilian scholars, notwithstanding his many peculiarities, such as translating his favorite into a jargon like this:

> The compaginate
> Dire, of war's iron portals, shall be closed. . . .
> He says, and Maia's son demits from high,
> The lands of Carthage, and young towers to open
> Hospitious to the Teucrian; lest, of fate
> Unweeting, Dido from her bounds off-warn.[2]

At the opposite extreme in many respects stands the blank-verse translation of Virgil's works begun by Rann Kennedy and finished

1825, I know only by title. Prior's Miltonic rendering of part of the fourth *Georgic* (written before 1721), and Richard Cumberland's of part of the third (written about 1745), should also be mentioned.

[1] v. 533–8. Andrews went mad soon after his Virgil was published. For his hatred of rime, see p. 325 above.

[2] i. 358–66. As if to remove all doubts of his indebtedness to *Paradise Lost*, he quotes two lines from it on his title-page. The *Eneis* includes only books one and two. Henry's rendering of the first six books, curiously entitled *Six Photographs of the Heroic Times* (c. 1850?), I have not seen. Conington (*English Translators of Virgil*, in *Quarterly Review*, cx. 109) says it is "not metrical, but rhythmical . . . the rhythm is changed from time to time . . . pages of trochaic time being succeeded by others where anapaests are predominant, and these again by ordinary blank verse, a measure which is preserved through the whole of the Fourth Book."

in 1849 by his son Charles, who in 1861 brought out a complete version of his own.   The Kennedy translations are readable, clearly Miltonic, but stiff, tame, and prosaic.[1]

The *Works of Virgil, closely rendered into English Rhythm, and illustrated from English Poets* (1855–59), by R. C. Singleton, is a curious performance, — not a poem, we are warned, but "a mere translation, such as . . . should be required from the schoolboy."[2] One of its principal objects, indeed, was "to help in giving a more poetic turn to the translation of the classical poets by the schoolboy."[3]   A preference for Anglo-Saxon words, which is one of Singleton's announced principles, results in bastard Spenserio-Miltonisms like "grunsel," "eyne," "steepy," "engrasped," "turmoiled," "eld," "armature," "haught," "eke," "prideful," and "hugeous." Such language, and a stilted, involved style, — the result in part of another of his principles, "adherence to the Latin order," — make the work sound as Miltonic as if it had been published a century earlier.   This is how Andromache speaks of Pyrrhus:

> Who then, on following Leda-sprung Hermione,
> And Spartan nuptials, me, his handmaid e'en,
> Unto his lacquey Helenus transferred,
> To be possessed. But him, by mighty love
> Of his betrothèd reft away, enfired,
> And hounded by the Furies of his crimes,
> Orestes doth surprise when off his guard
> And butchers at the altars of his sire.[4]

Similar to Singleton's work in its marked Miltonisms and its strange diction is the free translation of the *Aeneid* that W. J. Thornhill brought out in 1886.   The linguistic eccentricities (which include "hight," "steepy," "eld," "shagged with," "eke," "be-mad," "holpen," "the reboant cave reverbs") seem, like the frequent abruptness and undue brevity of style, to be due to a desire for vigor and raciness, but they quite destroy the ease and charm of the Roman poet.   One curious feature of this version is the occasional use of Alexandrines; another is the frank introduction of "expressions,

---

[1] The blank-verse translations of the *Aeneid* by John Miller (1863) and T. S. Burt (1883) I have not seen.

[2] Preface, p. i.

[3] *Ib.* vi.   The same purpose animated William Sewell (Singleton's successor at Radley school) in the blank-verse rendering of the *Georgics* which he brought out in 1846 and (after entirely rewriting it) republished in 1854.   To judge from the specimen Conington gives (*Quart. Rev.*, cx. 107), it is too Miltonic to be easy or flowing.   Sewell's *Agamemnon* (1846) and his *Odes and Epodes of Horace* (1850), translated like his *Georgics* "literally and rhythmically," I have not seen.

[4] *Aeneid*, iii. 465–72.

and in some few cases even whole lines, from Milton, Shakspeare, etc.," [1] as in this passage:

> He spake; and straight the duteus Power prepares
> His sire's behest to speed: first to his feet
> His wingèd shoon he ties of downy gold. . . .
> Here first, hovering on balanced wings, down dropt
> Cyllene's god; thence to the flood full swoop
> Throws his steep flight.[2]

G. K. Rickards's rendering of the first six books of the *Aeneid* (1871) is abler, more concise, and less Miltonic than Singleton's or Thornhill's; yet in avoiding the "debilitating expansion of the sense" he lost what he himself thought "the highest merit of a poetical translation," that it should "read like an original" and "preserve . . . the manner and spirit of the author." To whom do the following typical lines "read like an original" or suggest the Virgilian ease and grace?

> 'Tis famed that Daedalus, from Minos' realm
> Escaping, on aerial pinions borne,
> Far to the chilly north his flight pursued,
> Till, resting on Chalcidian heights at last,
> He vowed, in homage to the Delian God,
> Where first he touched the earth, his oar-like wings.[4]

Rickards's work was completed in 1872, when Lord Ravensworth published the latter half of the *Aeneid* (the eleventh book being done by Rickards). The first six books were again translated in 1893 by James Rhoades, who, holding that nothing "savours so much of Vergil as parts of the Blank Verse of Milton and of Cowper," followed all too closely the style and diction of *Paradise Lost:*

> Daedalus, flying from Minos' realm, 'tis said,
> Dared on swift wings to trust him to the sky,
> Upon his uncouth journey floated forth
> Toward the chill Bears, and stood light-poised at last
> On the Chalcidian hill. Here first to earth
> Restored, he dedicated to thy name,
> Phoebus, the oarage of his wings.[4]

Two years later Sir Theodore Martin printed for private circulation his translation of the sixth book in a blank verse intended to be

---

[1] Preface, p. xvii. Thornhill gives some examples on page xviii; others may be found on pages 195 (line 2), 237 (line 8), etc.

[2] Page 129 (book iv). "Downy gold" and "throws his steep flight" are from *Paradise Lost*, v. 282 (of wings in each case) and iii. 741.

[3] vi. 15–20. The passages quoted in the text above are from the preface.

[4] vi. 16–22. Rhoades's *Georgics translated into English Verse* (1881) I have not seen.

Shakespearean rather than Miltonic. The work has distinction, but falls far short of its author's wish that it should "read as an English poem." [1] Equally distinguished and equally un-Miltonic is the line-for-line version of the whole *Aeneid* which Charles J. Billson brought out in two volumes in 1906. It is a dignified, admirable piece of work that moves easily within its narrow bounds, but it impresses me as prose, not verse.

Apparently the first unrimed version of the *Aeneid* to be made in the United States was the one issued by C. P. Cranch in 1872. Though uninspired, it is easy, pleasant reading, and though Miltonic it is fairly natural, often conversational, with the result that it was reprinted in 1886 and 1897. Lines so good as

> Flashing with tremulous splendor on the sea [2]

are rare; but, as an hour spent with the book fortunately leaves a better impression than ten minutes do, no extract so short as these words of Andromache's can do it justice:

> While we, — our country burned, o'er many seas
> Conveyed, having in servitude brought forth
> Our children, — we were forced to bear the pride
> And contumely of the Achillean race,
> And of a haughty youth, who seeking then
> Hermione in Spartan nuptial bonds,
> Transferred me, slave to him, to be possessed
> By Helenus, who also was his slave. [3]

Seven years after the publication of these lines, J. D. Long, then lieutenant-governor of Massachusetts and later governor, Congress-man, and secretary of the United States navy, brought out his *Aeneid*, "the snatch and pastime of the last year," a work so pro-saic and off-hand, so deficient in Virgilian finish and grace, that, notwithstanding its vigor, it is interesting principally as one of the all-too-rare products of American statesmen in the field of letters. The line,

> No sooner said, than Mercury sets out, [4]

represents one extreme of Long's style. The other extreme — short passages stately and Miltonic in character — may be seen here:

> Now sweeping full and free along these banks . . .
> Parting the teeming fields, where my proud home,
> Mistress of haughty states, shall one day rise. [5]

---

[1] See his "L'envoi," pp. xi–xii.   [2] vii. 11.   [3] iii. 417–24.
[4] iv. 316. Compare Atlas's head "frowsy with pines" (iv. 329), "instructing him Anent the inhabitants" (vi. 1165–6), "day done meantime, the," etc. (viii. 343).
[5] viii. 76–9.

The war gave a pause to translating, as to other occupations of leisure; yet a blank-verse rendering of Virgil, the latest that has come to my attention, was completed in America by Theodore C. Williams during the second year of the conflict.[1] Though not one of our few great translations, and perhaps not the best Virgil in English (if such a thing exists), it is the one that I should prefer to read. It aims to be popular and "at the same time . . . really exact and scholarly."[2] Some of the principles announced in the admirable introduction, — the desire to bring out the "dramatic and argumentative force" of the speeches and the "religious suggestiveness" of the language,[3] — though novel, appear to be carefully thought out and sound. But what especially commends the translation is that as a rule it is finely poetic in a Virgilian way, and that it is readable: we are enticed on from page to page as in very few other versions. Yet it is surprisingly Miltonic, too much so indeed, for it abounds in such expressions as "This admonition given Latinus hid not."[4] As Williams's work, like its original, is not a poem of striking passages, any brief extract will be unsatisfactory:

> Now Sleep has portals twain, whereof the one
> Is horn, they say, and easy exit gives
> To visions true; the other, gleaming white
> With polished ivory, the dead employ
> To people night with unsubstantial dreams.[5]

The most successful blank-verse translation of Virgil, or perhaps of any classic poet, does not, however, come from America, but properly enough from the British aristocracy. It is Lord Burghclere's *Georgics* (1904). This highly poetic but not ornate version is equally happy in the noble prayer with which the first book ends; in such "signs of cloudless calms and sunny skies" as these (lines which are dreary prose in most renderings),

> The rooks in bated tones
> Thrice and again repeat a softened note,
> And you shall hear them in their roost above
> Chattering to one another in the leaves,
> Thrilled with I know not what mysterious charm;[6]

in the pathetic final separation of Orpheus and Eurydice;[7] and in pictures like this,

---

[1] The *Aeneid* appeared in 1908, the *Georgics* and *Eclogues* in 1915.

[2] *Aeneid*, introd., p. xxvi.

[3] *Ib.* xxviii.

[4] vii. 105–6.

[5] vi. 894–8.

[6] Pages 41, 42.

[7] Page 189.

And arbute flings him largess in the woods.
Or golden autumn lays its varied store
Down at his feet, whilst on the cliffs above
The vintage basks and mellows in the sun.
Ay, and sweet little ones shall climb and cling
Close to his lips; and spotless virtue guard
The innocence of home.[1]

Burghclere was wise enough not to imitate Milton.

The translations of Lord Burghclere and T. C. Williams are for
the present our latest unrimed versions of the Latin poet; but others
are doubtless preparing, for there are no indications that interest in
either Virgil or blank verse is falling off. Renderings of Homer, on
the other hand, are neither so recent nor so numerous; in fact, there
have been only three in blank verse that are complete. Unrimed
Homeric translation also began much later, for Virgil had been rendered in part by Surrey, Addison, Trapp, and Brady before 1717,
when Fenton Englished the eleventh *Odyssey*. But what is more surprising is that, with four exceptions (apart from a few translations
of short passages), the unrimed versions of Homer were all published
in the thirteen years from 1859 to 1871.[2] Perhaps the dearth before
1859 may be due to the extraordinary vogue of Pope's version and
the popularity of Pope and Cowper as poets, for other writers would
naturally have shrunk from the inevitable comparison with these
masters. The passing of their popularity towards the middle of the
century would also help to account for the number of unrimed
translations of Homer made at that time, just as to the admirable
prose versions of Butcher and Lang (1879) and Lang, Leaf, and
Myers (1883), and to the success, in America at least, of Bryant's
rendering in blank verse (1870–71) and Palmer's in rhythmical prose
(1891), may be attributed the decline of blank-verse translations in
recent years. Some versions in rime and some in dactylic hexameter
have appeared, to be sure; but, except for those of Maginn, Sotheby,
Alford, Newman, Morris, Way, Mackail, Cummings, and Cotterill,
most of them have been limited to a book or two, and even these
would hardly bring the number up to what might be expected.

Between the experiments of Fenton and Broome [3] and the completion of Cowper's monumental task there seem to be only five frag-

[1] Page 95.

[2] It was in 1861, just before most of these translations appeared, that Matthew
Arnold published the three lectures "On Translating Homer" which he had delivered
the year before.

[3] See pp. 106–7 above.

ments of Homer in blank verse. The first of these is a creditable rendering of the parting of Hector and Andromache, made about 1750 by William Hamilton of Bangour.[1] Though clearly Miltonic, it is more natural and pleasing than the work of Fenton or Broome, or than the *Essay towards a Translation of Homer's Works, in Blank Verse*, which J. N. Scott brought out in 1755. Pope's errors, which Scott dwelt upon, formed the excuse for this version; yet, as the critics pointed out, Scott himself exhibits most of the faults of the Augustan but produces scarcely any lines that are "excellent or poetical in themselves," except "those he has taken *verbatim* from *Milton*, without the slightest acknowledgment."[2] The thirteen passages he rendered into English were intended as specimens of a complete Homer, which the reviewers' castigations seem to have dissuaded him from finishing. A more virulent assailant of Pope, the Rev. Samuel Langley, met with the same fate when, in 1767, he issued his blank-verse translation of the first book of the *Iliad* as "a Specimen of the Whole, which is to follow." The whole had, indeed, "lain long finished by him," probably distorted after the fashion of the "Specimen":

> Shouted the Greeks applause, and all agreed
> The priest was to be rev'renc'd, and his gifts
> Receiv'd so splendid.

Curiously enough, the prose of the conceited author's preface is as pompous and involved as his verse.[3]

Cowper's version, which came out in 1791, appears to have neither discouraged nor stimulated Homeric translation. His picture of the shield of Hercules seemed "flat and prosaic" to a certain Thomas Vivian, who thought Pope's rendering of the same passage "a burlesque." Inasmuch as Vivian criticized Cowper for not keeping "a steady eye on Milton," it is no wonder that his own version of the lines, though condensed, is pompous, ornate, and involved, that he writes "frequent was the sound Of Hymenæal song," and "rapid

[1] *Poems on Several Occasions* (1760), 190–94. For Hamilton's Miltonic translation of part of *Philoctetes*, and his other blank verse, see Bibl. I, 1748, *c.*1750 w., 1760; for his imitations of *Allegro* and *Penseroso*, see below, pp. 451–3.

[2] See the *Monthly Review*, xii. 369, where two of these thefts from *Paradise Lost* are given. I have seen only criticisms of the work,—in this review (pp. 355–70) and in the *Scots Magazine*, xvii. 165–6.

[3] I have seen only extracts from the work (*Crit. Rev.*, xxiii. 36–41). Another fragmentary version is listed below, Bibl. I, 1786. I have not seen the translation of part of the *Iliad* made by Edward Capell sometime before 1781 (see Lofft's *Laura*, no. 861, n.), or another sample of the *Iliad* (running to only three hundred lines) which appeared anonymously in 1807 as *Specimen of an English Homer, in Blank Verse*.

mid it's numerous reeds a stream Sonorous flow'd." [1] Gilbert Thompson's *Select Translations from Homer and Horace* (1801), though, in the words of the reviewer, "accurate and plain," makes considerable use of Miltonic inversions and has lines as creditable as

> For neither the great Acheloian king,
> Omnipotence itself, can equalise;
> Nor the vast strength of the resounding main.[2]

But far more poetic and pleasing than any of these versions, and more natural than Cowper's, are the forty-seven pages that C. A. Elton published in 1814. As usual, the best passages, like this one, are the least Miltonic:

> Upon the hearth glow'd bright
> A fire wide-blazing; and the curl'd perfume
> Of the cleft cedar and the cypress-tree,
> Red in the flame, far off the island fill'd
> With fragrant smoke. She, trilling her sweet voice,
> Within the grotto sate, and cross'd the web
> With golden shuttle.[3]

Even short passages of Homer in blank verse must have been rare in the first half of the nineteenth century, for no others made in England have come to my attention. Far away in Virginia, however, a busy lawyer and statesman, William Munford (1775–1825) was occupying his spare time in turning the *Iliad* into blank verse. His work, which was not published till 1846, has attracted little attention, probably because, although less Miltonic (but scarcely less pleasing, it would seem), it differs too little from Cowper's version to justify its existence.[4] For, although Augustine Birrell says that Cowper's rendering "has many merits, and remains unread," [5] and

---

[1] "Some Observations on Hesiod and Homer, and the Shields of Hercules and Achilles," with translations, in *Essays by a Society of Gentlemen at Exeter* (1796), 443, 436, 444, 467, 471:

[2] *Crit. Rev.*, new arr., xxxvi. 108. I have seen only this review of the work. The extract from Charles Dunster's *Specimen of an English Homer in Blank Verse* (1807), which Egerton Brydges prints in his *Censura Literaria* (2d ed., 1815, ii. 401–3), is literal, crabbed, and un-Miltonic. James Morrice's translation of the entire *Iliad* into blank verse (1809) I know only by title.

[3] *Specimens of the Classic Poets*, i. 38 (from the *Odyssey*).

[4] I know Munford's work only from the article upon it in the *North American Review*, lxiii. 149–65. These lines, quoted there, seem to be typical:

> Them their chiefs
> With ease distinguish'd, and in order plac'd,
> As skilful herdsmen readily select
> From hundreds mingled in their pastures wide,
> Each his own flock of goats.

[5] *Res Judicatae* (1892), 102.

A. H. Clough queried, "Where is the man who has ever read it?,"[1] the *North American Review*, in discussing Munford's work, remarked that "the two most popular" translations of Homer were Pope's and Cowper's;[2] and much similar testimony might be adduced.[3] Indeed, for half a century the only blank-verse translation, and except for Pope's the only version of any kind that was at all satisfactory, was that by the poet of Olney. Even to-day, when if not forgotten it is talked about rather than read, his *Odyssey* has been reprinted in a cheap, popular form. Much can be said in defence of his work, and not a little has been said by so eminent a Homeric scholar and translator as J. S. Blackie, who, agreeing with "Professor" Wilson that it is "only dunces who think Cowper dull," insists that "his excellences are such as require a cultivated taste to appreciate them." What Blackie particularly objects to is the poet's "tameness and a want of perception of the minstrel character of Homer . . . the more quiet and rural domain of the *Odyssey*" being better suited to his talents.[4] Bookish, formal, involved, pompous, and excessively Miltonic the translation certainly is;[5] but its greatest defect is a lack of the spontaneous, easy charm that has endeared Cowper's original verse to thousands of readers.

Thus far the unrimed renderings of Homer have been few, but between 1859 and 1870 they come thick and fast. The first Englishman after Cowper to turn any large part of the Greek epics into blank verse seems to have been I. C. Wright, who brought out his rendering of the *Iliad* between 1859 and 1864. It is an admirable work, noble, flowing, rapid, and in the main direct and fairly natural. Some of the most beautiful passages in the original, with which most translators fail, Wright rendered effectively and simply. Yet objection might be made to expressions like "whilom," "hight," "what time," to the use of adjectives for adverbs, and to the frequent inversions which make most of the poem unmistakably Miltonic. These lines, neither the simplest and best, nor, on the other hand, the closest to *Paradise Lost*, are perhaps typical:

---

[1] Quoted in the preface to the Globe edition of Cowper, p. lxvii.

[2] lxiii. 156.

[3] "I delight in Cowper's *Homer;* I have read it again and again," said Samuel Rogers (*Table-Talk*, 2d ed. 1856, p. 29); and Rogers's editor adds in a footnote, "Thomas Campbell once told me how greatly he admired Cowper's *Homer:* he said that he used to read it to his wife, who was moved even to tears by some passages of it."

[4] "On Poetical Translation, and the English Translations of Homer," in his *Homer and the Iliad* (Edin., 1866), i. 437, 440.

[5] See pp. 170–72 above.

> This said, illustrious Hector stretch'd his arms
> To clasp the child; but with a cry of fear
> Back drew the infant to the nurse's breast,
> Scared at the brazen mail and horse-hair plume
> That waved terrific o'er the crested helm.
> Out laughed the father, and the noble mother.
> Instant the hero from his brow removed
> The glittering helm, and placed it on the ground.[1]

Before Wright's *Iliad* was completed a similar version appeared, in 1864, which was destined to be more popular than his and to be reprinted in cheap form half a century later. The rank and political prominence of the translator, the Earl of Derby, may have had something to do with his success, which is somewhat remarkable since his work is less rapid and flowing, and above all less poetic, than Wright's. It contains wretched lines like

> Pollux, unmatch'd in pugilistic skill,

and, as in Hector's words to his wife,

> Haply in Argos, at a mistress' beck,
> Condemn'd to ply the loom, or water draw
> From Hypereia's or Messëis' fount,
> Heart-wrung, by stern necessity constrain'd,[2]

has the "elaborate and self-retarding . . . Miltonic movement of Cowper,"[3] whom the earl often follows closely and from whom he adapts many lines.

When, in 1863, the Rev. T. S. Norgate brought out his translation of the *Odyssey*, Cowper was the only writer who had printed more than a single book of the poem without rime. Norgate published his version of the Homeric *Batrachomyomachia* the same year and of the *Iliad* in 1864, thus becoming one of the three poets who have translated all of Homer into English blank verse. Yet so little attention did his work attract that I have been able to learn only that it "appears to have the merit of general accuracy . . . the language is simple and vigorous, but the verse lacks music and rhythm."[4] George Musgrave was ignorant of its existence when in 1865 he published his own *Odyssey* in blank verse. In this translation the ocean is "the beauteous lake saline," Minerva the "goddess of light-gleaming eye," one of "the immortal deities eterne"; indeed, so pompous is the language, so inverted and involved the style, that the poem reads like a burlesque of *Paradise Lost*. Here is a sample:

[1] vi. 503-10.   [3] Arnold, *On Translating Homer*, lecture i.
[2] iii. 277, vi. 531-4.   [4] *Westminster Rev.*, new series, xxvi. 554 (1864).

> Nor did Calypso, of the goddess race
> True goddess prov'd, when now approaching near
> His form she hail'd, her visitant ignore.[1]

This in the year of grace 1865!

Three unrimed translations of the *Odyssey* appeared in 1869. That by Lovelace Bigg-Wither, in "accentuated dramatic verse," I have been unable to find anything further about.[2] G. W. Edginton's was condemned by the *Westminster Review* as "bald, spiritless, and monotonous," since the blank verse, which "is almost never varied, . . . becomes very wearisome" and the style is "pedestrian, and even slipshod." [3] E. E. Witt's rendering of the fifth and ninth books is pleasing and poetic, similar to Wright's *Iliad* but more attractive. Edginton's work seems to be but slightly Miltonic, and Witt's, as may be seen from these lines, is far less so than Cowper's:

> Him fairy-footed goddess Ino saw,
> Leucothöe, child of Cadmus, who of old
> A mortal was of voice articulate,
> But now within the chambers of the deep
> A mermaid dwelt with rank of deity.[4]

The next year saw two American translations of Homer. Such lines as,

> I fear it will be hard to find a man
> To go on such an errand, all alone,

reveal the conversational and prosaic character of W. G. Caldcleugh's *Iliad*, while a passage on the same page shows that each line tends to stand apart from the others and that Miltonic inversions are introduced in order to make prose appear verse, —

> If to the guards
> He will consent to go, and orders give;
> His son and Merion their captains are, —
> Charge of the watch to them intrusted is.[5]

The other rendering of Homer that appeared in 1870 was the *Iliad* of William Cullen Bryant, who supplemented it the following year by the publication of the *Odyssey*. Although these widely-read

---

[1] v. 120–122. Strangely enough, Musgrave's work reached a second edition in 1869. Meantime E. L. Swifte had in 1868 translated the first book of the *Iliad* and extracts from other books into "Early-English blank verse." I have not seen his work.

[2] R. F. Bigg-Wither, *Materials for a History of the Wither Family* (Winchester, 1907), 64. The author says that his father also translated the *Iliad* "into verse" but did not publish it.

[3] New series, xxxvi. 644 (1869). The brief quotation given in the *Review* bears out the criticism.

[4] Page 29.   [5] Page 174.

translations have undoubtedly owed part of their vogue to the popularity of Bryant's original poems, they deserve the reputation they have enjoyed. Made on principles almost as different from Cowper's as from Pope's, they are as unlike either of these versions as they can well be. For Bryant "endeavored to be strictly faithful," to preserve "the natural order of the words" and the Homeric "simplicity of style," to "attain what belongs to the original, — a fluent narrative style, which shall carry the reader forward without the impediment of unexpected inversions and capricious phrases."[1] And he achieved these objects: his rendering is easy, rapid, and direct. Yet one reason why it is so natural and readable is that it does not strive for the sonorous splendor and the stateliness of verse which constitute much of the beauty and greatness of Homer. Bryant's version is not "pre-eminently noble," it is not "in the grand style." Most earlier translators had intended that theirs should be; it was their desire to reproduce these qualities that led them to employ the language and manner of *Paradise Lost*, of which Bryant makes no use. They went too far in one direction and he in another, with the result that a satisfactory blank-verse rendering of Homer is still to seek.[2]

For the subsequent translations are of little account, — appear to be, I should say, for there are probably a number, like that issued by J. B. Rose in 1874, which I have not seen. Mordaunt Barnard's *Odyssey* (1876) had as its object "to assist backward students in mastering the original, and to give . . . a simple and unambitious version, often differing little from mere prose." This humble purpose it achieves; it is also rapid, readable, and much nearer being poetic and inspired than is the version of the first twelve books of the same poem which General G. A. Schomberg brought out in 1879. Schomberg has a large proportion of end-stopped lines, and, like Barnard, follows Bryant in not attempting the grand style. These men found it easy not to be Miltonic; but the Earl of Carnarvon accomplished a far more difficult task in giving his version of the first half of the *Odyssey* (1886) considerable distinction and nobility without employing the style of *Paradise Lost*.[3] Meanwhile, in his *Similes of Homer's Iliad* (1877), W. C. Green had published transla-

---

[1] Preface to his *Iliad*.

[2] Temperamentally Bryant was not adapted to the translation of Homer: he was punctilious, ascetic, and rather cold; he lacked spontaneity, he was too much of an "indoor man."

[3] Carnarvon had rendered books v and xi separately in 1880. In 1879 he had also translated the *Agamemnon* of Aeschylus into blank verse. I do not see that this work is at all Miltonic.

tions that are Miltonic in the best sense, rich, dignified, and lofty but not pompous. Yet, when he went on to the narrative passages, though his Miltonisms remained his inspiration deserted him, with the result that his careful translation of the first half of the *Iliad*, which appeared along with the original text in 1884, is pedestrian and somewhat awkward. William Cudworth's blank-verse renderings of eight books of the *Odyssey* and three of the *Iliad* (1891–5) I have not seen. The complete *Iliad*, published in 1911 by A. G. Lewis, an American, confessedly owes something to Bryant's version, but is less poetic and less effective; indeed, it is the extreme of non-Miltonic, conversational translation.

Odysseus's son, Telemachus, received from eighteenth-century translators more attention, considering his importance, than the much-enduring hero himself. Fénelon's *Télémaque* (1699) has, in whole or in part, been rendered into English over thirty times, and some of these translations have seen six or even twelve editions. Most of them are, like the original, in prose; but, as the work is a kind of epic, at least six are not unnaturally in blank verse. I have seen none of them; but, to judge from extracts of the one issued by John Youde between 1775 and 1793, they can hardly have raised the standard of English poetic translations. This is what Youde called blank verse:

> Almost all men to marriage are inclin'd;
> There's nothing hinders it but poverty.
> If you oppress them not with taxes, they
> Their wives and children will with ease maintain;
> For still the earth, the ever-grateful earth,
> On those who cultivate her with due care,
> Largely bestows her fruits.[1]

"To represent the 'Ovidian graces,'" remarked the *Monthly Review* with some little truth, ". . . the couplet, the language, and the manner of Dryden and Pope appear to us peculiarly adapted."[2] J. J. Howard was not of this opinion, however, for in 1807 he published the two volumes of his *Metamorphoses* in a dull, stiff, unpoetic adaptation of the verse and style of *Paradise Lost:*

---

[1] *Mo. Rev.*, enl. ed., xi. 105 (1793). For the other eighteenth-century blank-verse renderings that I have noticed, see Bibl. I, 1729 n. (anon.), 1742 n. (Hinchliffe), 1773 n. (Clarke), 1787 (Whitehouse), 1788 n. (Canton). Clarke's version was received with curt disapproval by the reviewer. John Lockman's translation of Voltaire's *Henriade* (which I have not seen) is of interest because of its early date, 1732.

[2] Enlarged ed., liv. 426.

> Their neighbouring scite,
> Acquaintance first encourag'd, — *primal* step
> To further intimacy: love, in time,
> Grew from this chance connection; and they long'd
> To join by lawful rites; but harsh forbade
> Their rigid sires the union fate had doom'd.[1]

Howard's failure cannot be laid to the meter; for Ovid's stories, if not all his "graces," were interestingly rendered into blank verse in 1871 by Henry King, whose version, though Miltonic, is rapid, pleasing, and thoroughly readable, as may perhaps be seen in this picture of Perseus:

> When now the Youth, to either ankle bound
> His feathery wings resumed, and on his thigh
> The moony falchion girt, and cleaving light
> With oary foot the liquid air, afar
> O'er many a realm and many a people flew,
> Till down upon the Æthiopian shores,
> Of Cepheus ruled, he looked; — where Ammon's wrath
> Unjust had doomed Andromeda.[2]

Lucretius, greatest of didactic poets, might have exerted considerable influence in so didactic a century as the eighteenth if he had been a popular writer; but, as his arguments are not easy reading and his ideas and point of view were not attractive to most Englishmen of the period, his impress on literature was slight. Creech's rimed translation of the *De Rerum Natura*, which went through six editions in forty years (1682–1722), seems to have held the field alone till an anonymous prose version appeared in 1743, a rimed one of the first book in 1799, and a rendering of the whole poem in blank verse by J. M. Good in 1805. This last is a dignified work in the Thomsonian style and diction marked by nearly all the Miltonic devices, which render it sonorously effective in the more poetic passages, though stiff and inflated in those devoted to argument. Among the more successful lines are these:

> Far, far from mortals, and their vain concerns,
> In peace perpetual dwell th' immortal Gods:
> Each self-dependent, and from human wants
> Estrang'd for ever. There, nor pain pervades,
> Nor danger threatens; every passion sleeps;
> Vice no revenge, no rapture virtue prompts.[3]

---

[1] Quoted, *Mo. Rev.*, enl. ed., liv. 427. I have not seen the work itself.

[2] iv. 786–93. George Turberville translated six "Heroycall Epistles" of Ovid into blank verse (1567), and Nicholas Breton is said to have done something "of the same kind" (J. P. Collier, *Poetical Decameron*, 1820, i. 117–18).

[3] i. 57–62. Unusual interest in Lucretius was manifested during the two decades following 1795. In 1796 R. P. Knight produced his rimed *Progress of Civil Society*, the

In view of the comparative excellence of Good's translation, it is hard to see why C. F. Johnson, an American, should have brought out another blank-verse Lucretius in 1872, particularly since his version is less easy and poetic than the earlier one and nearly as Miltonic.

De Arte Graphica, or the Art of Painting, translated from the Latin of C. A. Dufresnoy, is the title of a work published in 1754 by James Wills. Dufresnoy's poem must have had many admirers in England; for it was also translated by Dryden and by William Mason, and even Wills's bald, line-for-line version, which though unrimed is but slightly Miltonic, was reprinted in 1765. Another blank-verse rendering of a Franco-Latin work (*The Temple of Gnidus*, 1763) has a more curious history, for it was derived from Montesquieu's French prose through a Latin translation made by an Englishman. Here is a specimen:

> He stays his tardy lapse! The sequent streams
> Find waves that move not, while the am'rous God
> Pleas'd in his placid channel rests supine.[1]

The year in which Wills's work first appeared Isaac Hawkins Browne published his Latin prose essay *De Animi Immortalitate*, which was immediately turned into dull Miltonic verse by Richard Grey. Two other English versions, besides one of the first book, were printed the same year, two more in 1765 and 1766,[2] and a sixth (with the Latin text, an elaborate commentary, and notes) in 1795. This last, the work of John Lettice, though like Grey's in blank verse, is more stilted, not so close to the original or so clear. It distorts the style of *Paradise Lost* in this fashion:

> Doubt'st thou still this? Then say, what reas'ning proves
> A God supreme, in equity, who rules,
> Or wisdom infinite? [3]

"general design" of which was "taken from the latter part of the fifth book" of *De Rerum Natura*. Besides that published in 1799, another rimed version of book one was brought out in 1808 by W. H. Drummond; in 1813 Thomas Busby issued his rendering of the entire poem into rime. Good's work had the honor of being praised by Nathan Drake before it appeared (*Literary Hours*, 1798, no. 1), and of being reprinted several times, along with a new prose version, in the Bohn library (1848, etc.).

[1] *Crit. Rev.*, xv. 389. I have not seen the poem itself, which is anonymous. The Latin version was by Michael Clancy.

[2] Soame Jenyns, William Hay, and John Byrom published rimed versions in 1754 (Byrom of book i only). I do not know what meter John Cranwell used in the translation he issued at Cambridge in 1765; Joseph Highmore's prose rendering appeared in 1766.

[3] ii. 498–500. Lettice points out (p. 193) that lines 19–21 of his first book are "imitated from" *Lycidas*, 67–8, and the same borrowing in Byrom's version is noted by his editor. On pages 309–10 Lettice translates a passage from Claudian into equally Miltonic blank verse.

Such unrimed translations from other Greek and Latin poets as have come to my attention are unimportant,—the forgotten, and as a rule fragmentary, efforts of minor writers. Prior's rendering of the two hymns of Callimachus, already noticed, is an exception.[1] Horace, one of the last poets most persons would think of putting into blank verse, was among the first to be so rendered. As early as 1698 four of the epistles were translated into the Miltonic measure by that discerning champion of *Paradise Lost*, Samuel Say; and in the mid-eighteenth century Roger Comberbach defended blank verse against the attacks of John Byrom by translating one of the odes into it.[2] Gilbert Thompson's attempts, "Select Translations from Homer and Horace" (1801), are unrimed,[3] and so is the "imitation" of "Integer vitae" made some time before 1846 by W. S. Walker.[4] *Ditis Chorus, or Hell Broke Loose* (1781), is the winsome title of an anonymous version of Petronius Arbiter's *Satyricon*, which was "faithfully adapted to the times" in this fashion:

> I curse the height to which myself have rais'd
> Britannia's name, and my own gifts repent.

The disgusted author even rejoices in "Bunker's fatal hill" and "Lexington heap'd high with double slaughter."[5] Bits of Lucan's *Pharsalia* were put into Miltonic dress in the first quarter of the nineteenth century,[6] but not until 1896 was the whole poem rendered into blank verse. This translation, the work of Edward Ridley (who reprinted it in 1905), has some of the color and youthful vigor as well as some of the faults of its original, facts that may explain how a work published almost in our own day comes to be so strangely formal, stilted, and abrupt. These characteristic lines, for example, might well occur in an eighteenth-century imitation of *Paradise Lost:*

> Darkness unbroken, save by chanted spells,
> Reigns ever. Not where gape the misty jaws
> Of caverned Taenarus, the gloomy bound
> Of either world, through which the nether kings

[1] See p. 105 above. A Miltonic version of the "Hymn on the Bath of Minerva" appeared in C. A. Elton's *Specimens of the Classic Poets* (1814), i. 283-91.

[2] See pp. 90, 30 n. 2, above.

[3] See p. 336 above.

[4] *Poetical Remains* (ed. J. Moultrie, 1852), 157-8. Walker also translated into decidedly Miltonic blank verse three short pages of fragments from Ennius and a page from the *Persae* of Aeschylus (*ib.* 167-72). See also p. 351 below.

[5] *Crit. Rev.*, liii. 67-8. I have not seen the poem.

[6] See Bibl. I, 1808 (Noble), 1814 (Elton), 1821 ("A. S."). One of the earliest pieces of blank verse was Marlowe's line-for-line translation of Lucan's first book (1600).

> Permit the passage of the dead to earth,
> So poisonous, mephitic, hangs the air.[1]

Hesiod seems to have been first put into blank verse in 1796, when Thomas Vivian rendered the descriptive part of the *Shield of Hercules* and a passage from the *Works and Days*.[2] In 1812 Elton ran the entire *Shield of Hercules* into a decidedly Miltonic mould,[3] and at the same time translated the *Theogony* in this fashion:

> First Chaos was: next ample-bosom'd Earth,
> The seat eternal and immoveable
> Of deathless Gods, who still th' Olympian heights
> Snow-topt inhabit.[4]

These lines, as well as the whole poem, are far closer to the style of *Paradise Lost* than are the renderings from Homer or from such of the fifty-nine other Greeks and Romans as Elton turned into blank verse for his *Specimens of the Classic Poets*.[5] Though he was a stout defender of Milton's measure, he used rime in most of his translations. Similar to the *Specimens* in that it contains a number of short passages from various Greek poets rendered in the style and verse of *Paradise Lost*, is Jacob Bryant's *New System, or an Analysis of Antient Mythology* (1774–6). According to the *Critical Review*, E. B. Greene's unrimed *Hero and Leander, from Musaeus* (1773), "is executed in a style of mediocrity," [6] which probably means it is tame. That is hardly the fault to be found with these typical lines from the pompous Miltonic version of the *Cassandra* of Lycophron which Philip Yorke, Viscount Royston, published in 1806:

> Which erst the King
> Of Waters, Amoebéan architect,
> Piled to the clouds, but in the piny womb
> Of some great ammiral the massy bulk
> Flew lightly o'er the waves.[7]

Lady Sophia Burrell's *Thymbriad, from Xenophon's Cyropædia* (1794), is by no means a translation but a greatly enlarged, sentimentalized version of the story of Panthea and of Cyrus's war

---

[1] vi. 764–9.

[2] "Observations on Hesiod," etc., in *Essays by a Society of Gentlemen at Exeter* (1796), 455–65, 432–3 n.

[3] Hesiod's *Remains* (1812), 199–233.

[4] Lines 166–9 (*ib.* 75). In later editions of the *Theogony* Elton's phraseology is considerably changed.

[5] See above, p. 336.

[6] xxxvii. 315 (1774). Thomas Gibbons appended to his *Christian Minister* (1772) short translations from Cleanthes, Pythagoras, Casimir, and Watts.

[7] Lines 708–12; cf. *P. L.*, i. 292–4.

against Croesus. A few lines will give some idea of the Miltonic style and the couplet prosody which mark the hundred and fifty-four pages of Lady Burrell's diffuse work:

> From his pavilion, negligent of rest,
> The prince unto Araspes' tent repair'd. . . .
> With looks feroce, and tongue that spake severe.[1]

Few distinctions built upon what is apparently so slight a foundation were so carefully preserved in the eighteenth century as that between dramatic and non-dramatic blank verse. Yet, although the style and diction of *Paradise Lost* were rarely if ever employed in the many English verse-plays of the time, they were generally used in translations of Greek drama, which might, not unnaturally, have followed the lofty passages in Shakespeare. Milton, however, was more classic, he stood pre-eminently for noble dignity; and, too, the writings of Aeschylus, Sophocles, and Euripides were thought of as poems almost more than as plays. Furthermore, in most aspects Milton's genius was closer to the Greek drama than to Homer; if, therefore, his style and diction were suitable for an English *Iliad*, they should be for an English *Antigone*. Milton had borrowed from Sophocles: let him repay the debt! Strangely enough, his own drama, *Samson Agonistes*, seems to have exerted no influence whatever on these translations of the very works on which it was modelled.

Aside from the fragment of *Philoctetes* put into blank verse by Hamilton of Bangour about 1750, the influence of Milton in this field was first seen in Amyas Bushe's *Socrates, a Dramatic Poem* (1758). This was not made from a Greek drama, however, but was a rendering, "and, in most parts, a literal one, of *Plato's* dialogues . . . digested . . . into five regular acts," with rimed choruses. Although "on the whole not ill executed . . . ," comments the reviewer, it is "in many parts very dull, languid, and prosaical," — notwithstanding its decidedly Miltonic style, he might have added, as these lines will show:

> Must you not confess
> That realms and cities, which have foremost stood
> In the records of fame, for arts polite
> And wisdom's lore renown'd, have ever held
> The gods in veneration high?[2]

---

[1] Pages 21, 36. For James Hurdis's treatment of the same story, in his *Panthea* (1790), see above, p. 261, n. 3. Lady Burrell also follows Milton in her *L'Allegro* (*Poems*, 1793, ii. 239).

[2] *Crit. Rev.*, vi. 89–94. I have not seen the poem itself.

The year in which *Socrates* appeared Thomas Francklin brought out the first part of what was long to remain the best English rendering of Sophocles. The splendid march of the hexameter and the lyric beauty of the choruses Francklin does not reproduce at all, but he does convey impressively if not brilliantly the nobility and simple grandeur of his great original. He has tried to be natural, — an unusual aim in any translation of the classics made at that time, — and accordingly has many passages as conversational as this:

> Let me hear the sound
> Of your long-wish'd for voices; do not look
> With horror on me, but in kind compassion
> Pity a wretch deserted and forlorn
> In this sad place.[1]

True, he often carries this laudable purpose too far, to the detriment of his verse, as when he writes,

> The man thou seek'st is not far from thee . . .
>   . . . . cease then thy search, and tell me
> Wherefore thou com'st; [2]

yet there is not a page, or hardly a speech, in his entire volume that does not bear the stamp of *Paradise Lost*. Here is an example:

> Behold before thee Paean's wretched son,
> With whom, a chance but thou hast heard, remain
> The dreadful arrows of renown'd Alcides,
> Ev'n the unhappy Philoctetes, him
> Whom the Atridae and the vile Ulysses
> Inhuman left, distemper'd as I was
> By the envenom'd serpent's deep-felt wound.[3]

The latter part of this passage was thus rendered in 1788 by Robert Potter, the next writer to put Sophocles into blank verse:

> Philoctetes; whom the Chiefs,
> And Cephallene's king, here basely left
> An outcast, and alone, with dire disease
> Consumed, and tortured with this gnawing wound
> By the fell serpent's venom'd tooth impress'd.[4]

This extract may be too brief to show that it is from a more diffuse, but more formal and Miltonic and hence less spirited, translation than Francklin's. It also does scant justice to Potter, the best of whose versions — he rendered all the dramas of the Greek triumvirate into blank verse — was his first, Aeschylus, which he brought out in 1777. "As most things have been said, and well said in our

[1] *Philoctetes*, II. i. 7–11.
[2] *Ajax*, I. i. 8–11.
[3] *Philoctetes*, II. i. 40–46.
[4] New ed., 1820, p. 306.

language," remarked William Taylor, "it is often necessary to plagiarize; Potter could not translate Aeschylus without stealing from Milton and Gray." [1] Here are some of the thefts:

> I heard his thund'ring voice, I saw his form
> In bulk and stature proudly eminent;
> I saw him roll his shield, large, massy, round,
> Of broad circumference: it struck my soul
> With terror. On its orb no vulgar artist
> Express'd this image, A Typhæus huge,
> Disgorging from his foul enfoulder'd jaws,
> In fierce effusion, wreaths of dusky smoke,
> Signal of kindling flames. [2]

Between 1781 and 1783, when Potter published the two volumes of his Euripides, Michael Wodhull's rendering of the same dramatist appeared (1782). Less formal and Miltonic than Potter's, it is also less interesting and less impressive, — duller, more diffuse, and more prosaic. There are too many lines like that with which several of the plays close,

> And thus does this important business end.

As a rule, the style is not so close to *Paradise Lost* as in this passage:

> As on our turrets
> We stood exalted, and o'erlook'd the plain,
> The Argive host we saw, with silver shields
> Conspicuous, from Teumessus' mount descend:
> Over their trenches in their rapid march
> Soon vaulting, to the city they drew near. [3]

These were the great eighteenth-century translations of the Greek drama. With all their shortcomings they were the best to be had, and in some cases almost the only ones accessible. As they were better than most versions of the classics made at the time, edition after edition of them was called for, and they held undisputed sway till past the middle of the nineteenth century. Indeed, over a hundred years after they first appeared, all three were in whole or in part reprinted in cheap popular form. Not until the appearance of Gilbert Murray's finely poetic free renderings have any later translations of these dramas attained such vogue as those of Francklin,

---

[1] J. W. Robberds, *Memoir of Taylor* (1843), i. 329.

[2] *Seven against Thebes*, Potter's Aeschylus (Norwich, 1777), p. 169; cf. *P. L.*, i. 590, 284–6, vi. 765–6. *The Choephorae* has the phrase "Around his gloomy eyeballs throw" (*ib.* 364, cf. *P. L.*, i. 56); also the two lines quoted on page 471 below (the suggestion of *Allegro* is not in the original), and probably other borrowings. For Potter's imitation of *Lycidas*, see Bibl. III A, 1759.

[3] *Phoenician Damsels*, in *Nineteen Tragedies*, etc. (new ed., 1809), i. 214.

Potter, and Wodhull enjoyed. Strange to say, except for a few single plays no further blank-verse translations seem to have been published till 1865, when E. H. Plumptre brought out his excellent Sophocles; but since that time the number has steadily increased. The best of these later renderings are far more poetic than the earlier, more noble and simple, and much more successful in their handling of the lyric choruses. Their blank verse has, of course, like that of other poems of the time, come to be less Miltonic than that written in 1777; yet a suggestion of *Paradise Lost* still clings to a large number of them. In many speeches it does not appear at all, while in some it is marked; but usually it is seen in only one or two lines out of five, ten, or even twenty. It is therefore difficult to illustrate, but a passage in which it is fairly clear may be quoted from Plumptre's *Philoctetes:*

> A son of Priam, Helenos his name,
> There was, whom this man, going forth alone
> By night (I mean Odysseus, full of craft,
> On whom all words of shame and baseness fall)
> As prisoner took, and where the Achaeans meet
> As goodly spoil displayed him.[1]

Plumptre's renderings of both Sophocles (1865) and Aeschylus (1868) are distinguished by having the lyric choruses unrimed, a practice that was also followed by Robert Whitelaw in his Sophocles (1883). Passages as Miltonic as this occur throughout Whitelaw's able but somewhat stiff work:

> I see within the eyes of all of you
> Some fear of my intrusion, fresh portrayed;
> But shun me not, nor blame with hasty speech:
> For hither, charged with words, not deeds, I come,
> I who am old, and know that ye are strong,
> Ye and your city — in Hellas stronger none. . . .
> All with one voice insistent, since to me
> To mourn a kinsman's sufferings most belonged.[2]

The year in which Plumptre issued his Sophocles saw the publication of the first part of Anna Swanwick's Aeschylus (completed in 1872), which, though its literary merits are slight, has often been reprinted in the Bohn library. The style is more Miltonic than that of most translations of the period, yet each line, as the following extract shows, tends to stand apart from its fellows:

> She of her roaming hath the limit heard,
> That she not vainly to have heard may know,

---

[1] Lines 604-9. [2] *Oedipus at Colonus*, 729-39.

> Her woes ere coming here I will relate,
> Sure pledge thus giving that my tale is true.
> Tedious array of words I shall omit,
> And of thy roamings reach at once the goal.[1]

The version of the same dramatist by E. D. A. Morshead, which began to appear in 1877, is as much more poetic than Miss Swanwick's as it is less Miltonic, but many passages, like the admirable opening of *The Furies*, certainly recall *Paradise Lost:*

> First in this prayer of all the gods I name
> The prophet-mother Earth; and Themis next,
> Second who sat — for so with truth is said —
> On this her mother's shrine oracular.
> Then by her grace, who unconstrained allowed,
> There sat thereon another child of Earth —
> Titanian Phoebe.[2]

Lewis Campbell's vigorous, noble renderings of Sophocles (1883) and Aeschylus (1890) are much like Morshead's work. Often they do not seem at all Miltonic, and probably their debt is never greater than in these lines:

> Earth-born Palaechthon was my sire; I am named
> Pelasgus, and bear rule o'er all this land.
> Whence, rightly named from me their sovereign,
> Pelasgian are they called who reap these fields.
> Of all the region Strymon's holy stream
> Divides, the westward portion owns my power.[3]

Meanwhile translations of single dramas, or extracts from them, were appearing. Sometime before 1846 W. S. Walker rendered a scene from the *Persae* of Aeschylus,[4] and in 1849 George Burges published a version of the *Ajax* as stiltedly Miltonic as this:

> Dare not
> Unfeeling thus to cast away this man
> Without a burial; nor let violence urge thee
> So much to hate, as justice to tread down.[5]

This passage is typical of C. C. Clifford's *Prometheus Chained* (1852):

> Titan, give ear. Thee to thy mischief wise,
> Thee of the bitter spirit, that didst sin
> Against the Gods, to creatures of a day
> Bestowing honours, and the fire from heaven
> Stolen, thee the betrayer, I address.[6]

[1] *Prometheus Bound*, 842–7.
[2] *House of Atreus* (2d ed., 1889), p. 137. I have not seen Morshead's translation of Sophocles's *Oedipus*, 1885.
[3] Aeschylus's *Suppliants*, in *Seven Plays* (new ed., 1906), p. 10.
[4] See above, p. 344, n. 4.   [5] Lines 1314–17.   [6] Page 41.

Another version of the *Prometheus* (together with one of the *Agamemnon*) almost if not quite as Miltonic as Clifford's had been issued in America three years earlier by H. W. Herbert; and in 1873 J. G. Brincklé published in Philadelphia a translation of the *Electra* which follows *Paradise Lost* as closely as this:

> He sought of Hellas' games the illustrious pageant,
> To win the Delphic prize; and when he heard
> The loud proclaim of him that heralded
> The foot-race first in order, forth he stepped,
> Magnificent, — of all to be revered.[1]

Milton's influence on the style and diction of these later translations is not vital or even important, but it affords an unconscious tribute to the supreme excellence of his manner for the purposes of lofty poetry.

If a Greek drama that uses the verse and style of *Paradise Lost* is unexpected, a German play that follows the same course is even more so, particularly when it comes from the flippant pen with which Robert Lloyd had poked fun at Milton's followers. Yet Klopstock's *Death of Adam*, which Lloyd turned into English in 1763, is on the Greek model and in subject suggests the Christian epic. More was needed, however, than the occasional use of an adjective for an adverb, like "my breath Labours incessant," or of an inversion like "I have, of import, much to talk with Seth,"[2] to make this decidedly conversational translation at all impressive. Klopstock, "the Milton of Germany," owed so much to *Paradise Lost* that English versions of his works, even though made in the nineteenth century, might very naturally be Miltonic. The four of the *Messiah* in blank verse that I have seen certainly are: that of the first book issued in 1810 at Georgetown, South Carolina (the work of Solomon Halling), the brief passage from the ninth book which W. S. Walker translated about the same time, the anonymous rendering of all fifteen books that appeared in 1826, and the fragment published by W. S. Roscoe in 1834.[3] From the last part of the anonymous version many hundred lines of the original are omitted; yet, since the piece extends to over six hundred pages, it is surely long enough. As a rule, it is less condensed and rather less effective than in this passage:

> Tow'rd th' Asphaltic sea,
> Meantime, Obaddon, minister of Death,
> Spread his broad wing; and soon, envelop'd thick

---

[1] Lines 681–5.   [2] Pages 20, 14.   [3] See below, Bibl. I, 1813, 1826, 1834.

> In sable clouds, upon its shore he stood,
> And call'd th' apostate angels.[1]

Roscoe's paraphrase of a small part of the same work, which is far more impressive, not only uses the style of *Paradise Lost* but takes words and phrases from it:

> Him saw no eye,
> Their eyes so dimm'd by sorrow and despair,
> Save Zophiel's, herald he of hell. . . .
> From Satan sudden the dim vapour fled,
> And rob'd in terrors sate the grisly chief.[2]

At least two other German poets have appeared in an English dress that owes something to *Paradise Lost*. Salomon Gessner's *Death of Abel* was turned into "a charming poem" in "truly Miltonic" blank verse by Thomas Newcomb in 1763;[3] a part was translated in the same measure, from the prose rendering of Mrs. Collyer, by William Woty in 1770; and the whole poem was versified from the same prose work by W. C. Oulton in 1811 or 1814 and by "M. B. C." in 1840."[4] In 1800 Stolberg's *Hymn to the Earth* and other poems were Englished by John Whitehouse, whose version called forth this interesting comment from the *Critical Review*: "His imitation of Milton's manner has, however, betrayed him into the admission of some harsh lines, which, although not only tolerable, but ornamental, in so long a poem as the *Paradise Lost*, are altogether insufferable in so short a composition as the Hymn to the Earth."[5] The "imitation" is not marked.

"The first translation from Dante . . . produced avowedly as a translation, in English," appeared in 1719,[6] four centuries after his death, and, strange to say, it was in blank verse and by our old friend

---

[1] xii. 666–70.

[2] *Poems* (1834), 162. The phrases "dimmed by sorrow and despair" and "terrors . . . the grisly chief" are from *Paradise Lost*, iv. 114–15, ii. 704. Cf. also "in the dun air" (p. 167) with *P. L.*, iii. 72; "girt with omnipotence" (p. 174) with vii. 194; "bold emprise" (p. 176) with xi. 642, etc.; "golden panoply" (p. 178) with vi. 527, 760; "with lingering feet And sad" (p. 188) with xii. 648; "tears such as . . . angels weep" (p. 188) with i. 620; and many more. Roscoe published only part of the second book, but from his note on page 159 he would seem to have translated the entire work.

[3] *Crit. Rev.*, xvi. 50–55. I know the poem only from the extracts given there. For Newcomb's other work in blank verse, see pp. 110–12 above.

[4] I have seen nothing but the titles of these works.

[5] New arrangement, xxxi. 348.

[6] Paget Toynbee, in his admirable and exhaustive *Dante in English Literature* (1909), i. 197. The first rendering of Dante in blank verse was by Milton himself; it consisted of three lines introduced into his *Of Reformation*, 1641 (see Toynbee, vol. i, p. xxvii).

Jonathan Richardson.[1] It was undoubtedly his enthusiasm for *Paradise Lost* that led Richardson to discard rime, but his version of the Ugolino episode is not otherwise Miltonic. Nor is the next rendering of Dante, which is of the same episode, in the same meter, and by none other than Thomas Gray. If Richardson's translation is "not a brilliant performance,"[2] Gray's is so little better that he never published it himself. Doubtless it is a youthful exercise, for it is his one attempt at non-dramatic blank verse, and surely the mature poet would have produced lines farther removed from prose than these:

> From his dire Food the griesly Fellon raised
> His Gore-dyed Lips, which on the clotter'd Locks
> Of th' half devour'd Head he wiped, and thus
> Began.[3]

The first complete translation of the *Inferno* to be printed in English, that issued in 1782 by Charles Rogers, also uses blank verse. "Entirely devoid of any spark of poetry," and lacking "even the merit of being faithful,"[4] it is too bald and prosaic to produce anything of the effect of Milton's style; yet such inversions as these do recall *Paradise Lost:*

> Whene'er a guilty Soul before him comes
> It all confesses: He the proper place,
> Well knowing, that of Hell's to be their due,
> So many times his Tail around him twists,
> As the Degrees to which he'd have it cast.
> Many before him always ready stand,
> Who forward come, and are in order tried.[5]

"Shocked to think that so elegant a Poet should have so wantonly" given Minos a tail "and of such enormous Length," H. C. Jennings omitted this passage from the very free and eccentric rendering of the Paolo and Francesca and the Ugolino episodes that he printed privately in 1794.[6] Jennings's blank verse, though too slightly removed from prose to be Miltonic, is better than that of Joseph Hume, whose lines frequently end with "the," "and," "of," or "to." Yet Hume's *Inferno* (1812), "the worst translation of any portion

---

[1] In his pleasantly-entitled "Discourse on the Dignity, Certainty, Pleasure, and Advantage of the Science of a Connoisseur" (*Works*, new ed., 1792, pp. 184–6). On Richardson, see pp. 7, 10, above.

[2] Toynbee, vol. i, p. xxxi.

[3] Gray's *Works* (ed. Gosse, 1884), i. 157–60, where the translation as a whole was first printed. The last fifteen lines had appeared in the *Gentleman's Magazine* for October, 1849.

[4] Toynbee, i. 383.   [5] Canto v. 7–13.

[6] Toynbee, i. 517–22. I have not seen the work itself.

of Dante's works ever published," [1] has some suggestion of *Paradise Lost*, as this passage shows:

> Complying; I, tight round MY GUARDIAN's neck
> Clung instantly. He, fit moment chusing,
> And a spot, when mov'd the monster's wing, grasp'd
> Hard his shaggy cov'ring: thence down his side,
> Clotted with ice, he slowly, the labor
> Great, descended.[2]

"National custom," asserted Nathaniel Howard in 1807, "obliged Dante to confine his great genius to the shackles of rhyme. Blank-verse seems more analogous to his sublime manner." [3] If Howard did not reproduce that "sublime manner" and totally failed to capture the poetic beauty of the original, he did give an idea of Dante's earnestness, the power of his sombre imagination, and the terse, austere vigor of his style. These lines are a fair sample:

> From arch to arch, by various converse led,
> Which now, my Muse intends not to record,
> We mov'd. Climbing the frontier-rock, we saw
> Another vast of MALEBOLGE.[4]

Howard's illuminating comment, "Dante . . . composed also a work entitled Vita Nuova, a singular narrative of his amours with Beatrice," [5] is on a par with his reason for not translating the *Purgatorio* and *Paradiso*, — they "are certainly too much tinctured with the philosophy and scholastic theology of the age, to be understood and relished by modern readers." [6]

Yet there was truth in the remark; for when Cary's Dante appeared "it was noticed with praise by the *Gentleman's Magazine*, and with contempt by the *Critical Review*, and then for several years lay dead and forgotten." [7] And this was the version that Wordsworth regarded as "a great national work," [8] and of which Ruskin said, "If no poet ever was liable to lose more in translation, none was ever so

---

[1] Toynbee, ii. 80.   [2] Quoted by Toynbee, ii. 81. I have not seen Hume's book.
[3] Preface to his translation of the *Inferno* (1807).
[4] Canto xxi. 1–4. I have noticed a few borrowings from Milton: "bedropp'd With vivid hues" (p. 2, cf. *P. L.*, vii. 406, x. 527); "everduring night" (p. 16, cf. *P. L.*, iii. 45); "high-climbing" (p. 42, cf. *P. L.*, iii. 546); "with mazy error" (p. 87, cf. *P. L.*, iv. 239); "liquid lapse" (p. 181, cf. *P. L.*, viii. 263, of a stream in each case); "grisly king" (p. 205, cf. *P. L.*, iv. 821); "wonderous fabric" (p. 205, cf. *P. L.*, i. 710, of a building in each case); "his sail-spread vans" (p. 207, cf. *P. L.*, ii. 927, of wings in each case); "hurl'd headlong from the battlements of heav'n" (p. 209, cf. *P. L.*, i. 45, 742).
[5] Page xxiii.
[6] Page viii. For Howard's *Bickleigh Vale* and other Miltonic poems, see above, p. 258 and n. 5.
[7] Toynbee's edition of Cary's Dante, 1900, vol. i., p. lix.
[8] Samuel Rogers, *Table-Talk* (2d ed., 1856), 284 n.

carefully translated; and I hardly know whether most to admire the rigid fidelity, or the sweet and solemn harmony, of Cary's verse." [1] This great translation, the greatest and most influential that had appeared since Pope's Homer, was begun in 1797 and published, at its author's expense, between 1805 and 1814. To appreciate its originality and its faithfulness to the spirit of Dante, one should come to it after examining versions of the Greek and Latin classics, for it is, as it should be, quite unlike these. The terseness, the restraint, the concentrated power, of the *Divina Commedia* are admirably reproduced in a style that achieves dignity with ease and without pomposity. The liquid beauty of Dante's verse Cary did not strive for, but his lines have a "sweet and solemn harmony" of their own. Miltonic they certainly are, but so unobtrusively, so naturally, does he use his Miltonisms that he may have been almost as unconscious of them as is the average reader. Yet they are not so much occasional as pervasive, woven into the very fibre of the style, so that scarcely five successive lines are free from them, — inversions, parentheses, the use of strange words from the Latin and of adjectives in place of adverbs, as well as the omission of words that are normally expressed. Traces of Milton are surely obvious enough in this passage:

> As to ascend
> That steep, upon whose brow the chapel stands,
> (O'er Rubaconte, looking lordly down
> On the well-guided city,) up the right
> The impetuous rise is broken by the steps
> Carved in that old and simple age, when still
> The registry and label rested safe;
> Thus is the acclivity relieved, which here,
> Precipitous, from the other circuit falls:
> But, on each hand, the tall cliff presses close. [2]

Since the appearance of Cary's work there have been over twenty renderings of Dante, and in almost every meter. Longfellow's remarkable line-for-line version (1867), in a sort of unrimed terzarima, has enjoyed a great vogue in America; but in the mother country, at least, "the popularity attained by Cary's translation in his lifetime has been maintained unimpaired down to the present day, and . . . it still remains the translation which . . . first occurs

---

[1] *Stones of Venice*, vol. ii, ch. vii, § xli, note. "If I could only read English," he adds, "and had to choose . . . between Cary's Dante and our own original Milton, I should choose Cary without an instant's pause."

[2] *Purgatory*, xii. 93–102. I have noticed but one borrowing from Milton, "fledge with wings" (*Hell*, xiii. 16, cf. *P. L.*, iii. 627); but there are probably others.

to the mind of an Englishman on the mention of the name of Dante. Cary, in fact, once and for all made Dante an English possession." [1]

It must be admitted that this survey of unrimed translations has furnished little exhilarating reading. Nor would there have been much more if the rimed versions had been included, for the impression left by most renderings of the classics, whatever their meter, is that voiced over a century and a half ago by the *Monthly Review* apropos of Strahan's *Aeneid:* "We have perused it without either much pleasure or much pain . . . while we were deceived from page to page with a faint prospect of the genius and invention of the poet, we bore with the languor of the English verse." [2] It is depressing to contrast the time and mental effort that have gone into making translations with the pitiful results achieved. Most are still-born, some have a temporary vogue, and a few are reprinted, but in a short time almost all, good and bad alike, are not only unread but unknown.

Many of the early translators would have been more successful if they had never read Milton. Unconsciously, or through an imperfect understanding of their originals, they transferred to the *Iliad* and the *Aeneid* the "elaborate and self-retarding movement" of the English epic. It was not simply a matter of Miltonisms of style and diction, for these permeated nearly all of the earlier blank verse. The trouble was that, under the influence of *Paradise Lost*, the translators stressed unduly the dignity and sonority of Greek and Latin heroic poetry to the neglect of other qualities. They overlooked the minstrel character of Homer, his swiftness and naturalness, as well as the tender grace, the exquisite ease and art, of Virgil. Then, too, most men who have undertaken to turn the greatest poetry of the past into English have not possessed the requisite poetic endowment. The standards were, and still are, too low. People deluded themselves into believing that merely respectable or passable translations were of value, as probably they were in Trapp's and Brady's day, when even the contents of the classic poems were inaccessible; but that was long ago.

---

[1] Toynbee, *Dante in English Literature*, vol. i, pp. l–li. The only other translations of Italian writers into Miltonic blank verse that I have noticed are the fragments of Tasso's *Jerusalem Delivered* rendered by John Dennis (1704), Elizabeth Rowe (probably before 1710), and Nathan Drake (1820), and the version of Andreini's *Adam* made by Cowper and Hayley in 1791. Mrs. Monck's rendering of a fragment from Tasso (1716) is not Miltonic; Philip Doyne's blank-verse translation of the whole *Jerusalem* (Dublin, 1761) I have not seen.

[2] xxxvii. 323 (1767).

Since 1750 the only reason — aside from obtaining greater accuracy — for translating Homer or Virgil has been to make us feel the power and beauty of the poems. This few writers have done. Most versions of the classics are unread because they are unreadable, because they are neither poetic in themselves nor capable of suggesting the poetry of their originals. Whoever reads one for any length of time usually does so, not because he is held by the poem, but because he wishes to know what the Greek or the Roman author had to say; and, since this can as a rule be learned more easily, more accurately, and quite as pleasantly through a prose translation, he generally prefers prose. Perhaps he is right; certainly most of the men who in the past have undertaken to put Virgil, Homer, or Sophocles into English were far more likely to write vigorous, interesting prose than to overcome the many difficulties of rime, hexameter, or blank verse in addition to those of translation. Since Pope's day our best poets either have not attempted anything beyond brief experiments in translation or, like Cowper, have not succeeded. For of course not every good poet is a good translator; in fact, several of the best modern renderings in verse are by men not otherwise distinguished as poets. Wordsworth, who wrote so fine a classic poem as *Laodamia*, could not translate Virgil or Chaucer effectively. Tennyson, in the opinion of many, might have given us a great rendering of Virgil, but he preferred more rewarding and possibly less arduous tasks; and unless the unexpected happens his successors will do the same. Undoubtedly the ideal medium for translating poetry is verse, not prose; but as yet few verse translations have possessed the advantage which theoretically they should have. They are so mediocre as poetry that they leave the reader wondering what there is that is great about Homer, Virgil, and Dante.

Unfortunately, the percentage of English-speaking persons who can read the Greek tragedians or Homer in the original with sufficient ease to make the reading enjoyable is becoming perilously small, and the proportion even of those who can make their way comfortably through Virgil and Dante is relatively insignificant. If these master-poets are to continue a power in England and America, if they are to feed our civilization as they might and as it deeply needs, they must do it increasingly through translations, but translations that we shall read *through* and not *at*, poems that will hold us much as the originals hold those who can enjoy them, that will be read not alone for what their originals say but for what they themselves give. And happily the long development through respectable but mediocre work seems to have been of some value. Writers have gradually learned to be faithful to the original, at first to the letter and more recently to the spirit and manner. They have long since ceased to allow themselves such liberties as Chapman and Pope took, or to be content with such crudely prosaic versions as the early ones of Dante. Translations are becoming more and more worth while in themselves.

What form will be used in the great renderings that we hope are to come it is idle to conjecture. G. H. Palmer has been successful with rhythmical prose; Gilbert Murray, who has done some of the finest and most popular contemporary work in this field, uses rime, as does A. S. Way in his many admirable translations; while C. H. Grandgent has recently shown how effective the difficult terza-rima can be made for rendering Dante. Yet both Cary's and Bryant's very popular works, like the recent versions of Burghclere and Williams, discard rime. Logically, perhaps, the development should be in the direction of blank verse. If that form can be made more supple and rapid and kept relatively free from Miltonisms, it may well prove what so great a metrical master as Tennyson held it to be, the best of all meters for translations from the classics.

CHAPTER XV

TECHNICAL TREATISES IN VERSE

POETRY was a far more common vehicle of expression in the eighteenth century than it has been since. For, although almost every one occasionally drops into rime, amateur verses are to-day regarded simply as verses and do not place their authors among the poets. But in the days of Robert and Horace Walpole any person interested in literature was likely to publish a long, ambitious poem, — an epic, a satire, or a treatise on religion, gardening, or the art of doing something that the author himself had never done. Nor were such works confined to men who made writing their chief occupation; there were a great many from the pens of clergymen, lawyers, physicians, university fellows, or country gentlemen, and a considerable number were produced by cobblers, tailors, carpenters, by threshers like Stephen Duck and milkwomen like Ann Yearsley, and even by children of thirteen or fifteen years. Chatterton and Burns showed what boys and ploughmen might do, while Southey's *Lives of Uneducated Poets* indicates that there were many others who won temporary success in a field where to-day they would probably not venture. The position of verse is further exemplified in the many sermons, novels, and essays that were rewritten in it, and in the number of long versified attacks on the slave-trade. As Mr. Saintsbury remarks, "Poetry has hardly ever received more, and rarely so much, honour," and "for anybody who would give it [the eighteenth century] verse after its own manner it had not unfrequent rewards, dignities . . . and almost always praise, if not pudding, given in the most liberal fashion." [1]

This state of affairs resulted from and led to a pedestrian conception of poetry. The distinction between prose and verse was certain to be obscured in an age when there were no great poets, when the didactic impulse had almost supplanted the lyric, when literary leaders were interested in sophisticated city life rather than in nature and valued elegance and satirical power above imagination. Throughout the period there was little understanding of what subjects are suitable for poetry, of how rare is the muse's gift and how

---

[1] *Peace of the Augustans* (1916), 90–91.

vast the difference between it and the humbler powers of the average person. Consequently, such distinctions as were made between poetry and prose were apt to be the artificial ones of rime or of peculiar word-order and diction, and any scribbler was likely to attempt the most difficult of literary types, the epic, and perhaps a little later to present the public in all gravity with a rimed cookbook or with metrical directions for the raising of hops or children.

The last-mentioned poems, which may be termed "technical treatises in verse," are among the neo-classic phenomena that we find most difficult to understand. Obviously they owe their origin, and often much more, to Hesiod's *Works and Days*, Horace's *Art of Poetry*, and particularly to Virgil's widely-read and admired *Georgics*. Their authors also received stimulus and sanction from numerous works of the kind, many of them in Latin, composed by French and Italian writers of the sixteenth, seventeenth, and eighteenth centuries.[1] Much of their vogue, however, was due to the feeling that verse forms a sugar-coating for the pill of information, to the belief, apparently warranted, that "the same thoughts which might lie neglected, if published in prose, may be read with some degree of avidity, when a little ornamented with the graces and imagery of poetical diction."[2] Apparently most persons agreed with the *Critical Review* in "thinking that didactic poetry is susceptible of all the beauties of the epic, when properly introduced, and may be improved to more exalted purposes"[3]; for some seventy of these versified technical treatises appeared between 1680 and 1820, and several

---

[1] There is evidence that the following works found some readers among eighteenth-century Englishmen: Oppian's *Halieutica* and *Cynegetica* (*c.* 180 A.D.), Vida's *De Arte Poetica* and *De Bombyce* (1527), G. Fracastoro's *Syphilis* (1530), Scévole de Sainte-Marthe's *Paedotrophia* (1584, very popular), J. A. de Thou's *Hieracosophion sive De Re Accipitraria* (1584), Castore Durante's *Il Tesoro della Sanità* (1586), Claude Quillet's *Callipaedia* (1655), René Rapin's *Hortorum Libri IV et Cultura Hortensis* (1665), Charles A. Dufresnoy's *De Arte Graphica* (1668), Boileau's *L'Art Poétique* (1674), Jacques Vanière's *Praedium Rusticum* (1696, popular), Gouge de Cessières's *L'Art d'Aimer* (1745), the anonymous *L'Art de Plaire* and *L'Inoculation* (both 1758), E. L. Geoffroy's *Hygieine sive Ars Sanitatem Conservandi* (1771), Roffet's *L'Agriculture* and l'Abbé Romans's *L'Inoculation* (both 1774), Père André de Rouen's *L'Art de Converser* (1777), Jacques Delille's *Les Jardins* (1782). Three such works appeared after 1800: J. E. Despréaux's *L'Art de la Danse* (1806), Colnet du Ravel's *L'Art de Dîner en Ville* (1810), L. Hayois's *L'Art Épistolaire* (1842). For English translations of many of these treatises, see Appendix D, below. On the whole subject, see M. L. Lilly, *The Georgic* (Baltimore, 1919).

[2] Preface to James Foot's *Penseroso* (1771). Similarly, Richard Rolt, in order to render a historical description of Wales "the more amusing, . . . made choice of the poetical diction, as that alone," he writes, "may possibly invite a great number of British subjects to gather a little information" on the subject (*Cambria*, 2d ed., 1749, p. 25 n.).

[3] xviii. 475 (1764).

were often reprinted. Two-thirds of them are rimed;[1] yet, except for the two earliest, Buckingham's *Essay on Poetry* (1682) and Roscommon's *Essay on Translated Verse* (1684), only those in the Miltonic measure were widely read. The first of the treatises to discard rime was Philips's *Cyder* (1708),[2] which on account of its priority and its popularity throughout the century became, together with *The Seasons*, the model after which most works of the kind were patterned. Their exaggerated Miltonic style and diction, the introduction of episodes, the preference for subjects connected with country life, all point to Philips and Thomson.

Indeed, the writer who next entered the field, William Somervile, said frankly, "I shall not be asham'd to follow the Example of *Milton*, *Philips*, *Thomson*," and referred to

> *Silurian* Cyder . . . by that great Bard
> Ennobled, who first taught my groveling Muse
> To mount aerial. O! cou'd I but raise
> My feeble Voice to his exalted Strains.[3]

Somervile was an acquaintance of Thomson's and, being twenty-five years his senior, took the liberty of criticizing his diction and of giving him the advice (which he himself sedulously followed),

> Read Philips much, consider Milton more.[4]

Somervile also read and considered Thomson; in fact, it is more likely to have been the success of the recently-completed *Seasons* than that of the far less popular *Cyder* (which had been twenty-seven years in print) that led him, when already past middle life, to essay blank verse for the first time.

His earliest unrimed poem, *The Chace* (1735), is a technical treatise only in so far as parts of its four books are devoted to the breeding, training, and care of hounds and to some directions for their use. The popularity which it immediately won, and has never entirely lost,[5] must have been due principally to its spirited descriptions of hunting the hare, the deer, and the otter, as well as (though in a less

---

[1] See Appendix D, below. The *Monthly Review* declared in 1752 (vii. 139-41) that works of the kind should not be written in blank verse.

[2] See above, pp. 97-100.

[3] *The Chace* (1735), preface; *Hobbinol* (1740), pp. 48-9, cf. 3-4. Somervile's name is spelled with one "l" in his autograph letters and in all the editions of his works published during his lifetime.

[4] *Epistle to Thomson, on his Seasons*, in Anderson's *British Poets*, viii. 504.

[5] Three editions were published the first year and at least eight others before the close of the century, besides the six that had been issued by 1801 with Somervile's other poems. There have been five printings since 1850, the last of which, with illustrations by Hugh Thomson, appeared as recently as 1896.

degree) to its picturesque accounts of lion-trapping, of "the magnificent Manner of the Great Mogul, and other *Tartarian* Princes . . .
and the History of *Gengiskan* the Great."[1] The author of *The Chace*
was an educated country squire, with little delicacy of taste or of ear;
his style is pompous, his verse lacks variety and frequently consists
of end-stopped lines with medial cesuras. Yet he has the excellences
as well as the defects of his class: his principal work is vigorous,
fresh, and readable; it often breathes of the out-of-doors and exhibits
a quality all too rare in poetry of the period, — gusto. Somervile
writes about what he loves, and when at his best, as in the following
picture of hunting the hare, succeeds in imparting his enthusiasm to
his readers:

> They [the horses] strain to lead the Field, top the barr'd Gate,
> O'er the deep Ditch exulting Bound, and brush
> The thorny-twining Hedge: The Riders bend
> O'er their arch'd Necks; with steady Hands, by turns
> Indulge their Speed, or moderate their Rage.
> Where are their Sorrows, Disappointments, Wrongs,
> Vexations, Sickness, Cares? All, all are gone,
> And with the panting Winds lag far behind. . . .
> Hark! from yon Covert, where those tow'ring Oaks
> Above the humble Copse aspiring rise,
> What glorious Triumphs burst in ev'ry Gale
> Upon our ravish'd Ears! The Hunters shout,
> The clanging Horns swell their sweet-winding Notes,
> The Pack wide-op'ning load the trembling Air
> With various Melody; from Tree to Tree
> The propagated Cry, redoubling Bounds. . . .
> And ardent we pursue; our lab'ring Steeds
> We press, we gore; till once the Summit gain'd,
> Painfully panting, there we breath awhile;
> Then like a foaming Torrent, pouring down
> Precipitant, we smoke along the Vale. . . .
> They're check'd, — hold back with Speed — on either Hand
> They flourish round — ev'n yet persist — 'Tis Right,
> Away they Spring; the rustling Stubbles bend
> Beneath the driving Storm.[2]

As a rule, Somervile's language is more natural than that of Thomson or of other contemporary writers; yet in the lines just before this
passage he writes, "Coursers . . . fleet the verdant Carpet skim";
elsewhere he calls an arrow a "feather'd Death," speaks of "the
bright scaly Kind" that inhabit "the whelming Element," and has
such expressions as "to Arms devote," "submiss attend," "with

---

[1] Argument of book ii.   [2] ii. 164-258.

Eyes deject," "th' incumbent Earth." [1] He frequently introduces compound epithets, uses adjectives for adverbs, and constantly inverts the order of his words. That he derived these Miltonisms not alone from Philips and Thomson but in part directly from their fountain-head, is made probable by his many verbal borrowings from *Paradise Lost*,[2] and by his lines,

> Majestick *Milton* stands alone
> Inimitably great!
> Bow low, ye Bards, at his exalted Throne,
> And lay your Labours at his Feet.[3]

Furthermore, he wrote a short piece, *Hudibras and Milton Reconciled*, and in *Hobbinol, or the Rural Games* (1740), frankly burlesqued "Milton's Style." [4]

---

[1] ii. 160–61; iii. 328; iv. 354 (cf. 436, 463), 447; i. 73; ii. 112 (cf. iii. 350); iii. 394, 288.

[2] For example, "nor skill'd nor studious" (i. 74, cf. *P. L.*, ix. 42); "fly diverse" (iii. 543, cf. *P. L.*, x. 284); "with oary Feet" (iii. 557, cf. *P. L.*, vii. 440); "Nature boon" (iv. 470, cf. *P. L.*, iv. 242); "veil'd in clouded Majesty" (iv. 522, cf. *P. L.*, iv. 607–8);

> Now high in Air, th' Imperial Standard waves,
> Emblazon'd rich with Gold, and glitt'ring Gems . . .
> Streaming Meteorous (ii. 384–7, cf. *P. L.*, i. 536–8);

> From File to File he darts
> His sharp experienc'd Eye; their Order marks

(ii. 345–6, cf. *P. L.*, i. 567–9). See also note 4 below.

[3] *Imitation of Horace*, in *Occasional Poems* (1727), 34; quoted in Good's *Studies*, 63.

[4] Preface, p. iii. This work, which runs to over twelve hundred lines, describes in heavy, mock-heroic style the dancing, wrestling (with a free-for-all fight thrown in), cudgel-playing, and smock-racing of some villagers. Although it is too long and is seldom really amusing, it reached a third printing the year it was published and a ninth by 1813. Some of the following borrowings from *Paradise Lost* are introduced with humorous effect: "heav'nly Fragrance fills The Circuit wide" (1st ed., p. 11, cf. *P. L.*, v. 286–7); a "Front entrench'd with many a glorious Scar" (p. 13, cf. *P. L.*, i. 601); arms wielded "with huge two handed Sway" (p. 25, cf. *P. L.*, vi. 251); "ever-during Hate" (p. 38, cf. *P. L.*, iii. 45);

> Like some grave Orator
> In *Athens*, or free *Rome*, when Eloquence . . .

(p. 30, cf. *P. L.*, ix. 670–71);

> Gorgonius now with haughty Strides advanc'd

(p. 33, cf. *P. L.*, vi. 109);

> Others apart, in the cool Shade retir'd

(p. 48, cf. *P. L.*, ii. 557);

> Or to the Height of this great Argument

(p. 49, cf. *P. L.*, i. 24);

> *Oread*, or *Dryad*, or of *Delia's* Train . . .
> And Goddess-like Deport

(p. 52, cf. *P. L.*, ix. 387–9);

The Chace can hardly have been responsible for the lascivious treatise on sexual matters which Dr. John Armstrong, a fellow-countryman of Thomson's, published anonymously the following year as *The Œconomy of Love* (1736). As such a production could scarcely have helped the reputation of a physician of note who was the friend of ladies like Fanny Burney, Armstrong tried in later editions to excuse it as a "juvenile Performance . . . chiefly intended as a Parody upon some of the didactic poets"; and "that it might be still the more ludicrous," he added, "the Author in some places affected the stately Language of MILTON." About the language there can be no question; but the burlesque element is dubious, particularly as Armstrong's next work, *The Art of Preserving Health* (1744), is exactly the sort of piece he professed to parody. This oft-reprinted "prophylactic lay," which Lord Monboddo declared to be "the best didactic poem, without dispute, in our language,"[1] reads to-day quite as much like a burlesque of *Paradise Lost* as does its predecessor. Besides making use of a few Miltonic phrases,[2] and of such expressions as "adust," "profuses," "obnoxious" to change, "extravagant" branches of a tree, fogs "involve" a hill, Euphrates "devolves" a flood,[3] it is "replete" with words like "glebe," "swains," "meads," "humid," "tumid," "turgid," "gelid," and with periphrases like "venous tubes" (pores), "recremental fume" (blood), "Pomona's store" (apples), "fleecy race" (sheep), "Muscovy's warm spoils" (furs), "dun fuliginous abyss" (smoky air), "essay Their flexible vibrations" (breathe), and — his *chefs d'oeuvre* — "frequent The gelid cistern" (take cold baths) and "th' attenuated lymph Which, by the surface, from the blood exhales" (perspiration).[4] Armstrong, who was sufficiently intimate with his fellow-

---

Know'st thou not me? false Man! not to know me
Argues thyself unknowing. . . .
Thou knew'st me once

(p. 62, cf. *P. L.*, iv. 827–30). Somervile's *Field Sports* (1742), an unrimed poem of about three hundred lines devoted principally to hawking, is virtually a supplement to *The Chace*.

[1] *Origin and Progress of Language* (2d ed., 1786), iii. 166. Armstrong's *Art* contains some two thousand lines divided into four books, which treat of air, diet, exercise, and the passions.

[2] For example, "cold and hot, or moist and dry" (i. 26, cf. *P. L.*, ii. 898), "the chearful haunts Of men" (iv. 152–3, cf. *Comus*, 388). The *Œconomy of Love* has "and without Thorn the Rose," and

The Sapient King . . .
Held Dalliance with his fair *Ægyptian* Spouse

(pp. 22–3, cf. *P. L.*, iv. 256, ix. 442–3).

[3] i. 182 (also ii. 322); ii. 344, 193, 370; i. 311; ii. 361.

[4] i. 93; iii. 254 (cf. 276), 476, 84, 485; i. 86, 171–2; iii. 292–3; i. 168–9. Even the

Scot to have been the subject of one and the author of three stanzas in the *Castle of Indolence*, was probably not a little influenced in his Miltonisms by Thomson's usage. Such lines as these inevitably recall *The Seasons:*

> I burn to view th' enthusiastic wilds
> By mortal else untrod. I hear the din
> Of waters thundering o'er the ruin'd cliffs.
> With holy rev'rence I approach the rocks
> Whence glide the streams renown'd in ancient song.
> Here from the desart down the rumbling steep
> First springs the Nile; here bursts the sounding Po
> In angry waves; Euphrates hence devolves
> A mighty flood to water half the East;
> And there, in Gothic solitude reclin'd,
> The chearless Tanais pours his hoary urn.
> What solemn twilight! What stupendous shades
> Enwarp these infant floods! Thro' every nerve
> A sacred horror thrills, a pleasing fear
> Glides o'er my frame. The forest deepens round;
> And more gigantic still th' impending trees
> Stretch their extravagant arms athwart the gloom.[1]

The prosody of this passage is not typical of the *Art of Preserving Health,* fully a third of which is made up of single lines that have clearly been "passed through the strainer of the heroic couplet." A number of these are somewhat sententious and quotable, and occasionally there is one as good as

> While the soft evening saddens into night;[2]

but such verses, like the passage previously quoted, give too favorable an impression of their author's work.

If Armstrong's productions are not exactly what he would have termed "Pegasean flights," they seem such in comparison with the heavy cavorting and lumbering tread of the cobs with which Christopher Smart and Luke Booker cultivated their Hop-Gardens. The poems on the Eternity, Immensity, Omniscience, Power, and Goodness of the Supreme Being, with which Smart five times won the Seatonian prize,[3] are turgid and absurd enough; but his georgic, which was probably written earlier, is much worse and renders still

---

short passage which describes the scenes of his boyhood (iii. 75–96) has "love-sick swains," "meads," "the fleecy race," "painted meadows," "blooming sons," "vernal clouds," "I lav'd" instead of "I swam," and "sollicite to the shore The . . . prey" instead of "catch fish." Such diction is the harder to understand in view of Armstrong's own vigorous attacks upon it in his essays "Of Language" and "Of Turgid Writing" (*Sketches or Essays on Various Subjects,* 1758), which are themselves admirably simple and natural.

[1] ii. 354–70.   [2] iii. 380.   [3] See below, p. 404.

more inexplicable the lyric power that sweeps through his *Song to David*. The defects of the *Hop-Garden* (1752) arise partly from Smart's imitation of *Cyder*, the "graceful ease," "art," and "fire" of which impressed him far more than they do us.[1] Instead of invoking the muses, he summons Philips to his aid:

> Thou, O Hesiod! Virgil of our land,
> Or hear'st thou rather, Milton, bard divine,
> Whose greatness who shall imitate, save thee?

As a result, we read of "Vulcanian fires," of "meads Enrich'd by Flora's daedal hand," of "egregious shepherds" who

> plough Tunbridgia's salutiferous hills
> Industrious, and with draughts chalybiate heal'd,
> Confess divine Hygeia's blissful seat,

and are told that, after "Eurus comes"

> To hyemate, and monarchize o'er all,

"Tellus' facile bosom" may be "meliorated with warm compost."[2] On his title-page Smart printed an extract from Vanière's *Praedium Rusticum;* at the beginning of the second book he quotes from Virgil's *Georgics*, from which, as his notes indicate, a number of his lines are taken;[3] while his frank declaration, "I teach in verse Miltonian,"[4] makes clear his imitation of *Paradise Lost* even to those who overlook his verbal borrowings,[5] the character of his other work in blank verse, and his three imitations of the octosyllabics, which he thought 'the finest pieces of lyric poetry in any language.'[6]

The *Hop-Garden* won no prizes; in fact, it did not even prevent an indefatigable versifier and imitator of Milton, Luke Booker,[7] from publishing another poem on the same subject and with the same title forty-seven years later. As a practical treatise Booker's georgic may conceivably have had some value; at least it sticks to its subject, which is more than can be said in Smart's favor. But it is no less dull, and in the matter of simple, natural expression, though

---

[1] i. 278–80. [3] i. 32–3, 156–68, 329; ii. 106–27, 209.

[2] i. 269–71, 133, 104–5, 36, 41–3, 72, 74, 284, 87. [4] i. 7.

[5] Compare, for example, i. 99–129 with *P. L.*, iv. 641–56, and i. 270–76 with *P. L.*, ii. 1–2, iii. 7–8; "smiling June in jocund dance leads on Long days (i. 331–2) recalls *P. L.*, iv. 267–8; "bright emblazonry" (i. 364) is from *P. L.*, ii. 513, "the vast abrupt" (i. 397) from *P. L.*, ii. 409, "panoply divine" (i. 416) from *P. L.*, vi. 760–61, "hold dalliance" (ii. 266) from *P. L.*, ix. 443.

[6] See above, p. 10; below, p. 404, and Bibl. II, 1752; and *Poems on Several Occasions* (1752), 179–93, where his Latin translation of *Allegro* is given.

[7] See above, p. 254; below, Bibls. I, 1785, 1787, 1789 n., 1798, 1799, 1805, and III c, 1785.

issued as late as 1799, it stands almost at the nadir of eighteenth-century blank verse.[1]

It is a significant tribute to the vogue this extinct *genre* once enjoyed that the leading publisher of the day and the editor of a very popular miscellany, who should have known what the public liked, himself composed a technical treatise in verse. This ambitious project, Robert Dodsley's *Public Virtue*, was to have consisted of three long books, one on "Agriculture," a second on "Commerce," and a third on "Arts"; but, as the fifteen hundred lines of the first book (1753) were coldly received, the busy and modest publisher decided to "stick to his last," a forbearance that will be appreciated by any one who exercises his ingenuity in discovering to what process the following description applies:

> Continu'd agitation separates soon
> The unctuous particles; with gentler strokes
> And artful, soon they coalesce: at length,
> Cool water pouring from the limpid spring
> Into a smooth-glaz'd vessel, deep and wide,
> She gathers the loose fragments to an heap.[2]

Though so eminent a critic as Leslie Stephen has declared, "Dyer's longer poems are now unreadable,"[3] there are "a grateful few" who, like Wordsworth, think of John Dyer as one "of our minor poets — minor as to quantity — of whom one would wish to know more,"[4] and who recognize "that excellent neglected poem, the Fleece,"[5] as the most successful example of a once-popular literary type. Yet as a whole the work probably is unreadable, for a great many of its

[1] An advertisement printed at the back of Booker's *Malvern* announced that the *Hop-Garden* was "intended as a counterpart to Philips's *Cyder*"; there is a quotation from *Cyder* on the title-page, and the opening invokes the muse who inspired Philips's work. To the 1200 lines of his original poem Booker appended a "Sequel" of 457 lines, dealing principally with ale.

[2] iii. 391–6. *Agriculture* is divided into three cantos, the first of which is introductory, the second treats of soils and trees, and the third of the harvest, minerals, and the care of animals. Yet no "young Agricolist" would have derived much assistance from this vague, rambling, rhapsodic effort. Dodsley also wrote a rimed *Beauty, or the Art of Charming* (1735), and a rimed *Art of Preaching, in Imitation of Horace* (1738).

[3] *Dict. Nat. Biog.*

[4] See his sonnet to the "Bard of the Fleece," and his letter to Alexander Dyce, Jan. 12, 1829. One would particularly like to know more of the years Dyer spent in a wild and romantic part of South Wales, of his rambling through the neighboring country as an itinerant artist, and of his trip to Italy to study painting.

[5] John Scott, *Amwell*, 16 n. *The Fleece* received extended and very favorable notices in both the *Monthly Review* and the *Critical* (xvi. 328–40, iii. 402–15) and was highly praised in Drake's *Literary Hours* (1798, nos. 10, 11). Johnson's severe strictures in his *Lives of the Poets* are, on the whole, sound.

twenty-seven hundred lines are prosaic and wearisome and not a few are absurd. To enjoy it one must overlook serious and frequently-recurring faults and read only for the touches of natural beauty and for the phrases, lines, and occasional passages that reveal the vision and the voice of a true poet.

Dyer is a curious compound of one of his earlier and one of his later contemporaries, — Thomson, who knew him, and Gray, who thought he had "more of poetry in his imagination, than almost any of our number." [1] *The Fleece* (1757) has much the same subject-matter as *The Seasons* and is marked by the same breadth, sonorous pomp, and love of the country; while *Grongar Hill*, in its restrained and somewhat fastidious lyricism of the semi-romantic classicist, recalls Gray. All Dyer's poems exhibit a fineness and distinction which Gray possessed but which Philips, Thomson, Somervile, Armstrong, Young, and most of their successors lacked. These qualities were native to him and would have characterized his verse if, like *Grongar Hill*, it had all appeared the same year as *Winter;* but, inasmuch as *The Fleece* was published as late as 1757, it was inevitably influenced by a poem so similar and so highly successful as *The Seasons*. Such lines as these are Thomson through and through:

> The fluctuating world of waters wide,
> In boundless magnitude, around them swells;
> O'er whose imaginary brim, nor towns,
> Nor woods, nor mountain tops, nor aught appears,
> But Phoebus' orb, refulgent lamp of light,
> Millions of leagues aloft: heav'n's azure vault
> Bends over-head, majestic, to its base,
> Uninterrupted clear circumference.[2]

Yet Dyer must have derived a good deal directly from Thomson's original. As a young man he studied painting under Jonathan Richardson, whose enthusiasm for *Paradise Lost* knew no bounds;[3] he modelled his octosyllabics upon those of Milton at a time when the 1645 volume was little appreciated; he introduced into *The Fleece* phrases from *Allegro, Comus, Lycidas*, and *Paradise Lost;*[4] and

---

[1] See Thomson's letters to Mallet, June 13 and Aug. 2, 1726 (Philobiblon Soc., *Miscellanies*, 1857–8, iv. 12, 32, first pagination); Gray's letter to Walpole, 1748 (*Correspondence of Gray, Walpole*, etc., Oxford, 1915, ii. 91).

[2] iv. 29–36.

[3] See pp. 7, 10, 22 above, and 424 below.

[4] For example: "dews impearl'd" (i. 363, cf. *P. L.*, v. 746–7); "liquid lapse" (i. 532, cf. *P. L.*, viii. 263, of a stream in each case); "the soothest shepherd" (i. 631, cf. *Comus*, 823); "honours due" (i. 678, cf. *Allegro*, 37); "Nor taint-worm shall infect the yeaning herds" (i. 690, cf. *Lycidas*, 46); "light fantastic toe" (i. 692, cf. *Allegro*, 34); "the

he adopted most of the peculiarities of Milton's style and diction, including some that play little or no part in *The Seasons*. For example, he carried inversion, apposition, the use of compound epithets and of adjectives for adverbs or nouns, much farther than did most writers of blank verse;[1] and he may have derived from Milton his fondness for repetitions like

> The little smiling cottage warm embow'r'd,
> The little smiling cottage, where at eve,

or

> Wisdom, wit, and strength,
> Wisdom, and wit, and strength, in sweet accord;

and for such lists of things as

> Woods, tow'rs, vales, caves, dells, cliffs, and torrent floods,

or

> Beast, bird, air, fire, the heav'ns, and rolling worlds.[2]

When the lists are made up of proper names that stir the imagination and add to the sonorous roll of the lines, they are almost certainly influenced by *Paradise Lost*, as will be felt in passages like these, with which *The Fleece* abounds:

> Darwent's naked peaks,
> Snowden and blue Plynlymmon, and the wide
> Aerial sides of Cader-yddris huge.

> The cloudy isles,
> Scyros, and Scopelos, and Icos, rise,
> And Halonesos: soon huge Lemnos.

> Caria, and Doris, and Iönia's coast,
> And fam'd Tarentum, where Galesus' tide,
> Rolling by ruins hoar of ancient towns,

level brine" (ii. 246, cf. *Lycidas*, 98); "inwrought with mystic forms" (ii. 607, cf. *Lycidas*, 105); "audience pure . . . Though few" (iii. 4–5, cf. *P. L.*, vii. 31); "usefully succinct" (iii. 41, cf. *P. L.*, iii. 643, of garments in each case); "dropping gum" (iv. 106, cf. *P. L.*, iv. 630); "Sabean frankincense" (iv. 122, cf. *P. L.*, iv. 162); "world of waters" (iv. 606, cf. *P. L.*, iii. 11);

> Early fruits,
> And those of frugal store, in husk or rind;
> Steep'd grain, and curdled milk with dulcet cream
> Soft temper'd

(i. 706–9; cf. i. 35, iv. 237–8, and *P. L.*, v. 341–2, 347). There are references to Sabrina in i. 679, iii. 587; and in i. 162–3, where England's great men are mentioned, Milton is the only poet named.

[1] There are six compound epithets in the first forty-five lines of *The Fleece* and eight in twenty-four lines of book ii (151–74).

[2] i. 120–21; ii. 487–8 (see also i. 569–70, 703–4, iii. 104–7, iv. 255–8—quoted p. 371 below); i. 657; iii. 23 (see also i. 180–81, iii. 580, iv. 458–61, 614, etc.).

> Through solitary vallies seeks the sea.
> Or green Altinum.
>
> Pactolus, Simoïs, or Meander slow.
>
> Oby, and Irtis, and Jenisca, swift.[1]

This fondness for proper nouns led Dyer to make many adjectives from them, as Dorchestrian, Herculanean, Biscaian, Segovian, Ammonian, Tripontian, Hinclean, Hyperborean, Lappian, Silurian, Cambrian, Apulian, Turdetanian, Salopian, Dimetian, Menapian.

Yet he did not, like many writers of the time, adopt these Miltonisms blindly, through ignorance of how to write blank verse without them. To be sure, he had by no means assimilated them completely, and, as both his inspiration and his taste were uncertain, he is frequently wooden, mechanical, even absurd. But, just as he had instinctively adopted the verse of *Paradise Lost*, he fell naturally into its style and diction because they were congenial to him and because he saw that through them he could secure certain results which he greatly desired. Like Thomson and not a few other writers of the day, Dyer was fond of large effects, of splendor and magnificence; he disliked limitations and loved sonorous, rolling lines, of which he wrote not a few. His earliest blank verse, *The Ruins of Rome*, which is grandiose throughout and really impressive at times, showed unmistakably his leaning in this direction;[2] and, though the subject of *The Fleece* demands a humbler strain, he repeatedly rises out of it in passages like this:

> Hail noble Albion! where no golden mines,
> No soft perfumes, nor oils, nor myrtle bow'rs,
> The vig'rous frame and lofty heart of man
> Enervate: round whose stern cerulean brows
> White-winged snow, and cloud, and pearly rain,
> Frequent attend, with solemn majesty:
> Rich queen of mists and vapours![3]

The entire fourth book, which, though poetically the best part of the work, seems to have been overlooked by the majority of readers, is given over to a subject that has little direct connection with fleece, to a highly romantic and imaginative picture of the extent of English commerce. The progress of English wool round the world to strange ports and coasts famed in story,

> Bukor, Cabul, and the Bactrian vales,
> And Cassimere, and Atoc, on the stream
> Of old Hydaspes, Porus' hardy realm,

---

[1] i. 193–5; ii. 243–5, 316–20; iv. 110, 469.   [2] See the extract given on p. 240 above.
[3] i. 153–9. The seventeen lines that follow are in much the same strain.

is described as if it were the voyage of Cleopatra's barge. Here is
one of the best passages:

> The flat sea shines like yellow gold,
> Fus'd in the fire; or like the marble floor
> Of some old temple wide. But where so wide,
> In old or later time, its marble floor
> Did ever temple boast as this, which here
> Spreads its bright level many a league around?
> At solemn distances its pillars rise,
> Sofal's blue rocks, Mozambic's palmy steeps,
> And lofty Madagascar's glittering shores.[1]

This love of the grand and stately, strengthened by an admiration
for Milton and Thomson, led in *The Fleece*, as it had in *The Seasons*,
to turgidity and absurd periphrases, to what Johnson called "cloathing small images in great words."[2] Dyer spoke of sheep as the "bleat-
ing kind," the "fleecy tribe," and the "frail breed"; of wool as
"their yearly tribute," "the costly burden," "the downy vesture,"
"our fleecy wealth," "our spungy stores"; and he urged the "jolly
swains" to "seek the sounding caves Of high Brigantium" and receive from "Vulcan's strong sons"

> The sharpen'd instrument, that from the flock
> Severs the fleece.[3]

But at other times no one can be more bald and prosaic. For "gouty
ails, by shepherds term'd the halt," he urges to "salt again, th' utility of salt Teach thy slow swains," and a few lines beyond discusses
"th' infectious scab" and says that

> Sheep also pleurisies and dropsies know.[4]

Frankness and ornate diction are combined somewhat amusingly in
the suggestion that "wise custom,"

> Or ere they've past the twelfth of orient morn,
> Castrates the lambkins: necessary rite.[5]

Yet the greater part of these absurdities are the fault, not of
Dyer's treatment, but of the kind of work he was writing. A technical treatise in verse must inevitably fail either as a treatise or as a
poem; it must be so general as to be of little practical value or so detailed as to be dull and unpoetic. Dyer constantly adorned and
"lifted" his subject, but he did not, like Luke Booker, omit such

---

[1] iv. 345–7, 254–62.   [2] "Dyer," in *Lives* (ed. Hill), iii. 346.
[3] i. 285, 380, 393, 582, 240, 584, 635, ii. 134; i. 555–63 (he explains in a note that he
refers to "the forges of Sheffield . . . where the shepherds shears . . . are made").
[4] i. 276, 283–4, 286, 294.   [5] i. 347–9.

"circumstances" as were "either not very important, or unsusceptible of poetical ornament." [1] He was deeply interested in the wool industry, and, feeling that much of his country's greatness depended on it, desired to make his work of real service. Hence it was that he wrote what has been termed "the most extensive industrial poem of the eighteenth century, if not of English literature." [2] His practical suggestions are by no means confined to sheep-raising; for he discusses intemperance, smuggling, the digging of canals (including one through Panama), the relation of machinery to the laborer's welfare, the encouragement of foreign artisans to settle in England, and the erection of county houses in which the poor should be compelled to work on wool. As Wordsworth pointed out,

The character of Dyer, as a patriot, a citizen, and a tender-hearted friend of humanity, was, in some respects, injurious to him as a poet; and has induced him to dwell in his poem upon processes which, however important in themselves, were unsusceptible of being poetically treated. Accordingly, his poem is in several places, dry and heavy; but its beauties are innumerable, and of a high order. In point of *imagination*, and purity of style, I am not sure that he is not superior to any writer in verse since the time of Milton. [3]

This last is going too far; yet the

> Bard of the Fleece, whose skilful genius made
> That work a living landscape fair and bright,

does at least deserve that

> pure and powerful minds, hearts meek and still,
> A grateful few, should love his modest Lay,
> Long as the shepherd's bleating flock shall stray
> O'er naked Snowdon's wide aërial waste;
> Long as the thrush shall pipe on Grongar Hill! [4]

Such a treatise as *The Fleece* may well have served some useful purposes; but no such justification can be found for the thirty-seven pages of Robert Shiells's *Marriage* (1748), which ceases to be dull only when it becomes lascivious, or for the eighty-six pages of Richard Shepherd's *Nuptials* (1761), in which the dreariness of fatuous, sentimental advice concerning matrimony is unrelieved.

[1] Preface to his *Hop-Garden*.

[2] C. A. Moore, *Humanitarianism in the Periodical Essay and Poetry, 1700–1760* (doctor's thesis, Harvard, 1913), 227. Mr. Moore points out that Dyer emphasized the dignity and importance of trade and sought to remove the social stigma attached to it (see *The Fleece*, ii. 611–59 and the whole of book iv).

[3] Letter to Lady Beaumont, Nov. 20, 1811. See also Wordsworth's postscript to his Duddon sonnets, and Knight's *Life of Wordsworth* (Edin., 1889), ii. 324.

[4] Wordsworth's sonnet to Dyer. In the fourth line from the end I have changed "shall" to "should" and "thy" to "his."

Shiells quotes from *Paradise Lost* on his title-page, and praises its author as "the lawful Prince of Song," one "possess'd of all the Wit Which lavish Nature grants."[1] Shepherd also alludes to Milton, but there could in any case be no question as to the source of a style like this:

> In Quest of Happiness, attractive Spring
> And Soul of Action, see the motley Tribe
> The nuptial Bark with Foot adventurous climb.[2]

A later *Ars Amoris*, given to the world in 1807, is Martin Kedgwin Masters's *Progress of Love*. It is as harmless as Shepherd's, and like it abounds in comments and advice on many aspects of love and marriage. Masters had very little education,[3] but neither Oxford nor Cambridge could have given him a less natural style and diction:

> Again to wake the monitory strain
> And charm to mute attention heedless youth,
> My theme imperious bids.[4]

In the *Sugar-Cane*, which Dr. James Grainger published in 1764, information is "pour'd abundant," though unfortunately his theme is now, as before he visited the West Indies, one

> Whence never poet cropt one bloomy wreath.[5]

Some few leaves of laurel might possibly have decked Grainger's brow if he had possessed even a rudimentary sense of humor; but what hope is there of a man who uses the blank verse of *Paradise Lost* for a solemn treatment of "rats and other vermin," of weeds (including the "cow-itch"), of "the greasy fly," of the "care of mules" and the "diseases to which they are subject," as well as for a discussion as to whether, in planting, "dung should be buried in each hole, or scattered over the piece"?[6] The bard himself when he came to some of these subjects and was trying to "adorn" them "in poetic garb," exclaimed, "Task how difficult!" and queried,

> Of composts shall the Muse descend to sing,
> Nor soil her heavenly plumes?

Yet he not only answered in the affirmative and concluded the subject with

> Enough of composts, Muse; of soils, enough,

---

[1] Page 33.

[2] i. 284–6; the reference to Milton is two lines earlier. Shepherd was a voluminous writer, but only three of his other poems show the influence of Milton (see Bibls. I and II, 1761).

[3] See the preface, p. viii.

[4] ii. 423–5. In iii. 20 he quotes "cheerful haunts of men" (cf. *Comus*, 388).

[5] i. 301. [6] See the arguments prefixed to the first three books; and ii. 123.

but later said of negroes, "Worms lurk in all!"[1] This willingness to call a spade a spade would indicate a dislike of periphrases, were it not for expressions like "lave . . . with the gelid stream," "Raleigh's land" (Virginia), "the chlorotic fair; "

> Tho' coction bid
> The aqueous particles to mount in air;

> Bristol, without thy marble, by the flame
> Calcin'd to whiteness, vain the stately reed
> Would swell with juice mellifluent.[2]

Grainger has, in fact, practically all the vices of his frankly-acknowledged models, "pastoral Dyer, . . . Pomona's bard, And Smart and Sommerville." "In their steps," he wrote, "I shall always be proud to tread," and added, "Vos sequor . . . Quod vos imitari aveo."[3] He also wished to imitate Hesiod and

> lofty Maro (whose immortal muse
> Distant I follow, and, submiss, adore).[4]

Obviously, the style and diction of these lines and of those previously quoted are derived from Milton or his followers, and the numerous verbal borrowings indicate that the direct influence of *Paradise Lost* was not slight.[5]

---

[1] i. 297-9 (the word "adorn" is significant), 218-19, 255; iv. 103.

[2] iii. 321-2, 259; iv. 150; iii. 347-8, 381-3. Grainger uses such words as "fugacious," "endemial," "depurated," "perflation," "vermifuge" (i. 368; ii. 120; iii. 253, 340; iv. 312). The influence of the couplet prosody upon the *Sugar-Cane* is unmistakable: in the first passage to which I open (ii. 440-47) eight successive lines end with semicolons or periods, while within the lines there are only commas. The most interesting passage in the poem is that which pictures a hurricane, a calm, and an earthquake (ii. 270-426). In iii. 539-42, 566-7, Grainger expresses an appreciation of the beauty of the ocean which was unusual at the time.

[3] i. 12-13; preface, vi-vii.

[4] ii. 132-3.

[5] For example: "Pan, Knit with the Graces" (i. 61-2, cf. *P. L.*, iv. 266-7); "draw her humid train" (i. 147, cf. *P. L.*, vii. 306); "hold amorous dalliance" (i. 387, cf. *P. L.*, ix. 443); "fruit of vegetable gold" (i. 429, cf. *P. L.*, iv. 219-20); "shed genial influence" (i. 437, cf. *P. L.*, vii. 375, of the heavens in each case); "at shut of eve" (ii. 11, cf. *P. L.*, ix. 278); "scales bedropt with . . . gold" (ii. 142, cf. *P. L.*, vii. 406, of fishes in each case); "in her interlunar palace hid" (ii. 311, cf. *Samson*, 89); "to gratulate . . . the beginning year" (iii. 10-11, cf. *P. R.*, iv. 438); "Fountain of being" (iii. 212, cf. *P. L.*, iii. 375, of God in each case);

> Tho' no herald-lark
> Here leave his couch, high-towering to descry
> The approach of dawn, and hail her with his song

(iii. 558-60, cf. *P. R.*, ii. 279-81). For other borrowings, see iii. 256-7 (cf. *Comus*, 95-7), 274 (cf. *P. L.*, xi. 484, 488), 372-3 (cf. *Allegro*, 133-4); iv. 8 (cf. *P. L.*, iii. 7, invocation in each case), 554-81 (cf. *P. L.*, iv. 641-56); and the following, which are indicated by quotation-marks, i. 90-92 (from *Comus*, 21-3), 132 n. (from *P. L.*, ix. 1101-10), iv. 500 (from *P. L.*, iv. 138). Grainger's *Solitude* is modelled upon *Penseroso*.

Grainger knew a good deal about his subject and evidently tried to make both the poem and the notes to it useful; but he did not go so far as William Mason, who asserted that, since "to amuse was only a secondary motive" with him in writing his *English Garden*, he thought the 'copious and complete Commentary, which the partiality of a friend had induced him to write upon it, would be of more utility than the poem itself would be of entertainment.'[1] It is very doubtful, however, if the vain and much-flattered "Scroddles" really thought anything of the kind, for he embellished his treatise with two long episodes and devoted more attention to nature descriptions and other adornments than did his fellows. Such a subject as fence-making, for example, which he found an "ingrateful" task, he was not content to expound "in clear preceptive notes," but tried

> by modulation meet
> Of varied cadence, and selected phrase,
> Exact yet free, without inflation bold,
> To dignify.[2]

As regards both varying the cadence and writing without inflation Mason succeeded better than most writers did,[3] although if the "Simplicity" whom he twice summoned to preside over his poem [4] had really responded he would probably have been not a little discomfited. But in his subject-matter, landscape architecture, he did vigorously uphold simplicity and naturalness against regularity or formality, and on this account, as well as because of his imitation of Milton's monody, octosyllabics, and sonnets, he is of some significance in the romantic movement. His romanticism and his poetic powers are seen at their best in lines like these:

[1] Preface.   [2] ii. 247–55.

[3] He has, to be sure, a good deal of the "verdant mead" and "crystal stream" sort of thing, and occasional enormities like the reference to an ice-house (iv. 95–8) as

> the structure rude where Winter pounds
> In conic pit his congelations hoar,
> That Summer may his tepid beverage cool
> With the chill luxury.

Yet neither this passage, nor that which describes the "thundering death" from the "fell tube"

> Whose iron entrails hide the sulphurous blast,
> Satanic engine!

(ii. 215–18), is typical of the poem. Mr. Beers is, therefore, hardly fair to Mason's georgic (by no means the most absurd of its class), when he quotes these two passages to bear out his remark, "The influence of Thomson's inflated diction is here seen at its worst" (*English Romanticism in the Eighteenth Century*, 124–5).

[4] At the beginning of the first and fourth books.

Happy art thou if thou can'st call thine own
Such scenes as these: where Nature and where Time
Have work'd congenial; where a scatter'd host
Of antique oaks darken thy sidelong hills;
While, rushing through their branches, rifted cliffs
Dart their white heads, and glitter through the gloom.
More happy still, if one superior rock
Bear on its brow the shiver'd fragment huge
Of some old Norman fortress; happier far,
Ah, then most happy, if thy vale below
Wash, with the crystal coolness of its rills,
Some mould'ring abbey's ivy-vested wall.[1]

The influence of the style, prosody, and perhaps diction of *Paradise Lost* upon this passage will surprise no one who is familiar with Mason's slavish imitation of Milton's early works. Phrases from these works, as well as from the epic, are introduced into the *English Garden*,[2] together with references to their author and a tribute to "Milton's inimitable description of . . . Eden" as a prototype of the English garden.[3]

Mason divided his work into four parts (published separately in 1772, 1777, 1779, and 1782), devoting the first book to general principles and the later ones to their practical application, — to sunken fences, the arrangement of shrubbery, and the like. A similar plan was adopted by Richard Polwhele, the Devonshire clergyman who flitted industriously, but without either genius or that "infinite capacity for taking pains" which is allied to it, between poetry, topography, literary history, and theology. Polwhele regarded the *English Garden* as "the faultless Model of Didactic Poetry,"[4] and in imitation of it divided his *English Orator* into four books, in the first of which he considered "general Precepts" and in the other three

[1] i. 374–85. Unfortunately, Mason favored the erection of "old Norman fortresses" for barns and of "mould'ring abbeys" as screens for ice-houses, etc. (iv. 79–109). His grotto (iv. 118–31) also reminds one unpleasantly of Pope's; but he at least appreciated the ocean (iv. 110–14).

[2] For example, "Contemplation imp Her eagle plumes" (i. 152–3, cf. *Comus*, 377–8, and the sonnet to Fairfax, line 8); "the gadding woodbine" (i. 433, cf. *Lycidas*, 40); "airs of Dorian mood" (iii. 502, cf. *P. L.*, i. 550); "huddling brooks" (iii. 522, cf. *Comus*, 495); "glimm'ring glade" (iv. 656, cf. *Penseroso*, 27);

> The spicy tribes from Afric's shore,
> Or Ind, or Araby, Sabaean plants
> Weeping with nard, and balsam

(iv. 234–6, cf. *P. L.*, iv. 162–3, v. 293, and *Comus*, 991). The following borrowings are indicated by quotation-marks: i. 239 (*Allegro*, 133), 453–9 (*P. L.*, iv. 240–63), iii. 370 (*P. L.*, ii. 628), iv. 458–62 (*P. L.*, iv. 248–51).

[3] i. 448–66, and note v. (p. 392).

[4] *English Orator*, iv. 334 n. (on p. 6 of the "Notes").

applied these precepts to the eloquence of the bar, the senate, and the pulpit. He also followed Mason in issuing his work in parts (1785-9) and in adopting the style, diction, and prosody of *Paradise Lost*.[1] Here, however, the similarity ends, for the *English Orator* affords no relief from the pompous dulness of such lines as these:

> Hence the Strength
> Of Argument, whate'er its destin'd End,
> Educe; and to the litigated Point
> Apply, not careless of forensic Forms.[2]

Hartley Coleridge could, therefore, hardly have been familiar with Polwhele's work when he wrote of the *English Garden*, "We will not . . . say that it is the dullest poem we ever read, but it is assuredly one of the dullest we ever attempted to read."[3] Much less could he have known the twelve hundred lines which Thomas Gibbons, the author of some forty or fifty works, issued in 1772 under the title *The Christian Minister*. The following bare, prosaic passage from Gibbons's tract is in marked contrast to Polwhele's turgidity:

> Let ev'ry Action, ev'ry Look arise
> From what you feel within. Address your Flock
> Much as you would address a Friend, who ask'd
> Your sentiments on some momentous Point.[4]

The Essex literary society of which Polwhele was a contentious member also included a literary physician, Hugh Downman, who wrote Miltonic blank verse, octosyllabics, and sonnets, and discussed the sonnet form with the author of the *English Orator*.[5] This work may, indeed, have been influenced by Downman's *Infancy, or the Management of Children*, which, as it appeared in three parts in

---

[1] In his notes to i. 65 and iv. 654 Polwhele quotes from Milton's *Of Education* and *Paradise Lost*, and at the opening of his fourth book takes a line from the latter (*P. L.*, i. 10-11), refers to Ithuriel's spear, and summons the "Muse of Fire"

> whom God's own Bard
> Sounding to epic Notes his Harp, invok'd.

For other poems of Polwhele's that show the influence of Milton, see Bibls. I, 1787, 1787 w., 1794-6 w., 1798, and III c, 1790 w.; for his sonnets, Bibl. IV, 1777– w.

[2] ii. 37-40.

[3] *Northern Worthies* (1852), ii. 348. It seems to me that, although the *English Garden* is far from being a joy forever, it is not particularly *dull* for those who are interested in its subject.

[4] i. 291-4. Gibbons was a dissenting minister whom Johnson "took to" (Boswell's *Life*, ed. Hill, iv. 126). For his brief translations and original pieces in Miltonic blank verse, see Bibl. I, 1745 w., 1750, 1772.

[5] Some of the letters that passed between the two men are printed in Polwhele's *Traditions and Recollections* (1826) and *Reminiscences* (1836). For Downman, see below, pp. 471, 495 n. 2; Bibls. I, 1760 w., 1774-6, 1787 w., 1803; II, 1761 w., 1767 w., 1792; IV, 1767–.

1774, 1775, and 1776, preceded Polwhele's treatise by ten years. *Infancy* is a versified *Care and Feeding of Children*, and seems to have occupied much the same position in the eighteenth century that Dr. Holt's work does in the twentieth. To-day no physician would think of composing a *poem* on the subject, and no mother of buying such a production if it were composed; yet seven editions were called for by the mothers of that time. Downman's popularity must have been due principally to his detailed, sensible, and somewhat advanced treatment of a subject that has wide appeal.[1] He divided his poem into six books, which discuss the early care of the child, its diet, clothing, exercise, and diseases. Like the author of the *English Garden*, he invoked

> Simplicity, who hates
> The swelling phrase bombast, the insipid term
> Pompously introduced;

but his conception of this lady was even more curious than Mason's, for he commonly wrote after this fashion,

> Nice, and perhaps erroneous in their plan,
> The younger animals as yielding less
> Of due nutrition, and digested slow,
> Some disallow. That, food prepared from those
> Of growth mature, thro the intestinal maze
> Less tardily proceeds, we not deny.[2]

This style, vicious in itself and quite unsuited to the subject, probably owed not a little to Akenside, whose elegant but frigid dignity seems particularly to have attracted Downman.[3] Yet the poem is not without interest, for the defects of expression cannot entirely obscure the author's enthusiasm, good sense, and poetic feeling.

Infancy was reprinted as late as 1809, when the vogue of the versified technical treatise was about over. Apparently but eight works of the kind were written in the nineteenth century, and three of these, including T. P. Lathy's *Angler* (1819), are in rime, while a fourth, Jerome Alley's *Judge* (1803), is taken up principally with fulsome praise of an Irish chancellor.[4] Of another *Angler*, which W. H.

---

[1] For example, he urges light, loose clothing for infants, says their legs and feet should be uncovered until they can walk, and condemns "the cradle's most absurd Pernicious motion" (iv. 99 ff., 303–7; v. 201–2).

[2] ii. 14–16; iii. 267–72. He recognized some of his themes as "unanimating," and "strove to adorn" them (iv. 100, 103). An amusing attempt at such adornment is his "descant" on pinning the baby's "vesture" (iv. 149–59). In iii. 526–8 he praises the "polisht taste," "art," "rural wildness, and simplicity" of the *English Garden*, and in the lines immediately preceding commends Armstrong.

[3] See iii. 518–21; iv. 505–14.

[4] Lord Clare, who had recently died. The 1558 lines of this dull work contain such

Ireland published in 1804 over the name "Charles Clifford," and of T. F. Dibdin's *Bibliography* (1812), only the first books were issued; but Dibdin's poem was privately printed, and the failure of Ireland's dull piece largely given over to digressions proves nothing as to the popularity of the literary type to which it belongs. John Vincent's *Fowling*, for example, met with no such indifference when it appeared four years later, although it may have owed its second edition to pleasant descriptive passages like the following:

> As up the rugged path I press, how wide
> The prospect opens, but not here bedeck'd
> From Summer's varied and fantastic loom,
> But clad in mantle coarse of sober brown
> And dusky purple mix'd; one homely hue
> Stretches unvaried round, save where some rock
> Lifts its gray forehead.[1]

Except for Grahame's *British Georgics* (1809),[2] *Fowling* seems to have been the last technical treatise of any importance. For over a hundred years this form in which our great-grandfathers found pleasure has been extinct, and for obvious reasons. Verse is no longer a means of attracting us to a dull subject, and for practical purposes we now demand a direct, scientific, accurate treatment of a matter such as is possible only in prose. More than this, we are now agreed that poetry is not adapted to handbooks of agriculture or of hygiene, and we realize that the ornament and buckram with which eighteenth-century bards tried to make such works seem poetic only render them ridiculous. "Familiar images in laboured language have," as Johnson said, "nothing to recommend them but absurd novelty," and, as most of these artless treatises on the arts are written in verse which "seems to be verse only to the eye,"[3] they constitute a dreary waste profitable only for a better understanding of the period and refreshing only in their incidental descriptions.

From the number of these didactic poems and the frequency with which some of them were reprinted, it might appear that their dullness and absurdity were not felt at the time. But the age of Fielding,

gems of expression as "plausive cherubs" (i. 305), "if she not find within her procreant glebe" (i. 37), "by pure comments sage, meantime, illumes" (iii. 703).

[1] *Fowling: a Poem in five books, descriptive of Grouse, Partridge, Pheasant, Woodcock, Duck, and Snipe Shooting* (1808, 2d ed. 1812). I know of the poem only from W. H. K. Wright's *West-Country Poets* (1896, pp. 459–60), and from the *Monthly Review* (enl. ed., lx. 320), which speaks well of it. Vincent was an Oxford man who died in Bengal in 1818 as chaplain of the East India Company.

[2] See above, pp. 269–70.

[3] See "Somervile" and "Milton," in *Lives* (ed. Hill), ii. 320, i. 193.

Goldsmith, and Sterne was far from lacking a sense of humor, and was by no means so blind as it is sometimes pictured. "All the assembled wits burst into a laugh," we are told, when Grainger (who was reading his *Sugar-Cane* at Sir Joshua Reynolds's), "after much blank-verse pomp . . . began a new paragraph thus: —

'Now, Muse, let's sing of *rats*.' . . .

'What could he make of a sugar-cane?'" exclaimed Johnson, on hearing the story. "'One might as well write the *Parsley-bed, a Poem;* or *The Cabbage-garden, a Poem.*'"[1] Of *The Fleece* the same apostle of common sense remarked, "The subject, Sir, cannot be made poetical. How can a man write poetically of serges and druggets?"[2] Nor were such criticisms unusual. The letters and diaries of the period record opinions of contemporary verse that are often no more flattering than our own, and the critical reviews could hardly have been more caustic than they were or more unsparing in their condemnation of literary mediocrity. The reviewers seem, indeed, to have felt that most of the poetry and fiction published in the latter half of the eighteenth century was not worth reading.[3]

Even the more popular periodicals found amusement in the rambling bombast of the versified tractates, for in 1802 the *European Magazine* parodied them in what was alleged to be a fragment of the *Art of Candle-Making, a Didactic Poem, in twenty books*. The author had certainly felt the absurdity of imitating *Paradise Lost* in such a treatise:

> Inspir'd by Hops, a bard has sung its praise,
> And prov'd its influence in narcotic strains:
> The Cyder-making and Wool-combing arts
> Have both found bards their secrets to explain. . . .
> Say, why should Candles be alone unsung?
> No! I shall sooner seize th' advent'rous pen;
> And, though unequal to so great a task,
> Shall, in Miltonic numbers, nobly dare
> To paint the labours of a Melting day.

He had also noticed, as the "argument of book i" shows, the discursiveness, the fondness for moralizing and for classical allusion, that mars these preceptive lays:

---

[1] Boswell's *Johnson*(ed. Hill), ii. 453–4.   [2] *Ib.* 453.

[3] The defects of Smart's *Hop-Garden*, for example, are admirably pointed out and traced to their causes in the *Monthly Review*, vii. 139–42. Perhaps the greatest fault of the eighteenth-century reviewers was their tendency to speak well of a mediocre work if it taught morality and religion. Here is a typical comment: "If this work has but a slight claim to praise for its poetical or philosophical merit, it yet challenges our approbation for being the zealous advocate of religion and virtue' (*ib.*, enl. ed., 1800, xxxii. 438).

Subject proposed — Invocation — The subject proved to be of great importance to Poets — To Lovers — The tale of Hero and Leander — To Moralists — The resemblance a Candle bears to the life of Man — The story of Prometheus, the inventor of Candles — Remarks on the Mythology of the Ancients — Ovid — Hesiod — Homer — Of Machinery — The early ages fond of it, and why? — The story of Theseus and Ariadne — Light-houses, the great benefit of — Eddystone Light house — Candles probably made use of on this occasion among the Ancients — Light — Sir Isaac Newton — Optics — Astronomy — Chronology — Age of the World not known — Moses — Bonaparte — Friar Bacon — Conclusion.[1]

[1] *Europ. Mag.*, xlii. 424–6. The extensive notes, another feature of the piece, make it clear that Smart, Philips, and Dyer are the writers parodied.

CHAPTER XVI

PHILOSOPHICAL AND RELIGIOUS POETRY

Philosophical Poetry

If the regions through which we have just passed have seemed a rugged waste, those that lie before us form no land of dreams, rather

> a darkling plain
> Swept with confused alarms of struggle and flight,
> Where ignorant armies clash by night.

In the realms of epic and descriptive poetry and of the technical treatise there are sometimes noble prospects, and, though rocks lie everywhere, they are often picturesquely piled and hold in their crannies fragrant herbs and flowers. Besides, often when the country is not beautiful it gains a certain interest from being unusual. No such interest attaches to eighteenth-century philosophical and religious poetry; for whoever advances into that flat and sandy desert is likely to feel, with Satan,

> In the lowest deep, a lower deep
> Still threatening to devour me opens wide,
> To which the Hell I suffer seems a Heaven.

Passing by for the present poems that are in the main not simply ethical but distinctively Christian, we have a group of versified reflections or moral harangues which, though almost as destitute of real philosophy as of real poetry, may for want of a better term be dubbed "philosophical poems." The title of one of Coleridge's pieces, *Religious Musings, a Desultory Poem*, would fit most of them; for, if they are not devoted to the exposition of deistic doctrines or the defense of orthodox beliefs, they consist of vague disquisitions on the benevolence of God or the greatness of England, thickly larded with moral platitudes. That shallow but triumphant refutation of heresy, Young's *Night Thoughts* (which began to appear in 1742), was among the earliest of these works, and in its rambling, rhetorical treatment of serious subjects is typical of many of them. Pope's *Essay on Man*, the supreme example of the type, though it is rimed and is unique in the compact brilliance of its expression, resembles the rest in its lack of sustained thought. As a rule these versified reflections are not even amusing, much less novel or stimulating, and the obviousness of their thought is unrelieved by any poetic beauty or power. In general they are like old sermons, and quite as tiresome, for the authors have mistaken their *cacoëthes scribendi* for a message.

What may perhaps be called the earliest of these poems in blank verse, although of course not really philosophical, are Thomson's *To the Memory of Sir Isaac Newton* and *Britannia*, both written in 1727. More typical of the later works of the class, and not much better than they, is his long, dull, inflated *Liberty* (1734-6), which says little that is worth the saying.

The death of Newton also called forth nearly five hundred lines of tumid blank verse from "Leonidas" Glover, then only sixteen years old. This effusion Glover followed with one that is no better,[1] in which he sought to rouse the nation against the Spanish and in favor of a large army, — *London, or the Progress of Commerce* (1739). In another poem entitled *Commerce* (1751), Cornelius Arnold devotes two hundred and eighty-seven lines of pompous Miltonic blank verse to a rambling panegyric on trade. One of its few oases is this delightfully mixed figure:

> When thro' your Western Tour, with lib'ral Hand,
> In Pleasure's Cup, Humanity You mixt,
> And serv'd it round — All was tumultuous Joy![2]

The year before, Arnold had brought out some eight pages of unrimed couplets aptly entitled *Distress*, which is filled with platitudes about benevolence and the sufferings caused by loss of money.

Just as the *Night Thoughts* was beginning to appear, a little-known clergyman in a small Scottish parish, Robert Blair, was putting the final touches on an unrimed poem similar to Young's in its gloomy subject-matter, its exclamations and rhetorical questions, and its general style, as well as in the popularity it was destined to achieve.[3] Prosodically *The Grave* is far closer to *Paradise Lost* than is Young's work, but otherwise it bears little resemblance to the epic. It contains, to be sure, a number of compound epithets, as "black-plaster'd," "smooth-complexion'd," "high-fed," "heavy-halting," "lawn-rob'd," "hell-scap'd," "big-swoln";[4] occasional adjectives used as adverbs, as in "sudden! he starts," "frolick . . . unapprehensive," "stalk'd off reluctant," "smil'd so sweet," "expire so soft";[5]

---

[1] Yet Fielding praised it extravagantly in the *Champion*, Nov. 24, 1739.
[2] Lines 266-8.
[3] Published in 1743, it reached a sixteenth edition in 1786, and was reprinted alone or in collections at least thirteen times more before 1800, besides being turned into rime in 1790.
[4] Lines 36, 235, 246, 316, 513, 590, 610.   [5] Lines 63, 476-7, 587, 706, 715.

and some verbal borrowings, as "low-brow'd," "spectres . . . Grin horrible," and

> The fierce *Volcano*, from his burning Entrails
> That belches molten Stone and Globes of Fire,
> Involv'd in pitchy Clouds of Smoke and Stench.[1]

Yet very few passages are as Miltonic as these:

> The big-swoln *Inundation*,
> Of Mischief more diffusive, raving loud.

> THE SON OF GOD thee foil'd. Him in thy Pow'r
> Thou couldst not hold: Self-vigorous he rose.[2]

On the other hand, there are plenty of matter-of-fact lines:

> Sure! 'tis a serious Thing *to Die!* My Soul!
> What a strange Moment must it be, when near
> Thy Journey's End, thou hast the Gulf in View? . . .
> To tell what's doing on the other Side! . . .
> Tell us what 'tis *to Die?* Do the strict Laws
> Of your Society forbid your speaking . . . ?
> Never to think of *Death*, and of *Ourselves*
> At the same Time? As if to learn *to Die*
> Were no Concern of ours.[3]

Inasmuch as *The Grave* is often reminiscent of Shakespeare and seldom recalls Milton or his followers, it may present one of the very few instances of an eighteenth-century unrimed poem that derived its style, diction, and prosody (for it has many hypermetrical lines) from the drama. At any rate, its influence—which in subject-matter at least was considerable since it had much to do with the epidemic of graveyard literature — was away from the excessive Miltonisms of the period. Yet its vigorous but often homely diction, and its style, which at times is strangely conversational, were not likely to be copied often at a time when poets were haunted by the fear of being prosaic. Nor would it have been a safe model. If Blair, a writer of some ability and power who elaborated very slowly his work of less than eight hundred lines, is himself often tame and flat, most of his contemporaries, had they followed his example, would probably have produced only colorless, commonplace prose. The English literary public was not yet ready to write or to appreciate *Michael*, and, until it was, Milton, Thomson, and later Cowper were the safest guides for writers of blank verse.

---

[1] Lines 17 (cf. *Allegro*, 8), 40–41 (cf. *P. L.*, ii. 845–6), 606–8 (cf. *P. L.*, i. 233–7).
[2] Lines 610–11, 669–70.
[3] Lines 369–71, 373, 440–1, 472–4.

The Grave was extravagantly praised as late as the nineteenth century, and in expression it is frequently effective, even impressive; but a greater master than Blair was needed to give vitality to its obvious, gloomy moralizings. To-day no one reads it voluntarily or desires to reread it; if it is known at all except by name, it is through Blake's remarkable illustrations. To me its most attractive lines are these, at the close:

> 'Tis but a Night, a long and moonless Night,
> We make the *Grave* our Bed, and then are gone.
> Thus at the Shut of Ev'n, the weary Bird
> Leaves the wide Air, and in some lonely Brake
> Cow'rs down, and dozes till the Dawn of Day.

Another lugubrious theme was undertaken about this time by William Thompson, a great admirer of

> gentle Edmund, hight
> Spenser! the sweetest of the tuneful throng,
> Or recent, or of eld.[1]

Thompson diversified his long poem, *Sickness* (1745), with an extended account of the palace of Disease, in imitation of the palace of Pride and the procession of the seven deadly sins in the *Faerie Queene*. Yet this passage has nothing of the style, the language (except in the lines quoted above), or the peculiar charm of Spenser, but is stiff with Miltonisms and patched with phrases from *Paradise Lost*. Even in his figurative visits to Spenser's tomb Thompson employs the expression "with reverent Steps and slow."[2] It was so with most poets. The tangible influence of the *Faerie Queene* was practically restricted to pieces in the Spenserian stanza and to occasional borrowings of words and subject-matter. Even writers who would have liked to take more found — or believed — that, whereas they could adapt Milton for every occasion, the gorgeous Elizabethan allegory offered little they could use in most of their verse.

If their adaptations of the style of *Paradise Lost* were not often happy, they seemed so to many eighteenth-century readers. It is not unlikely, for example, that Thompson's flamboyant descriptions of various diseases and his account of the patients' sufferings (written after his own recovery from small-pox) were at the time they were composed thought vivid and impressive and his turgid style not far

---

[1] See his *Sickness*, i. 276–8. Unless otherwise designated, the references are to the first edition, the only one with numbered lines. In the second edition (*Poems on Several Occasions*, Oxford, 1751, ii. 195–317) there are marked changes, for two of which see below, p. 642, n. 2.

[2] Second ed., v. 2; cf. *P. L.*, xii. 648. Instead of this phrase, the first edition (iii. 407) has "who knows *not* Spenser's tomb?" (cf. *Comus*, 50).

from the sublime. A reading of the entire twenty-one hundred lines (and a rereading of many of them) leaves me, however, with the conviction that *Sickness*, though better than many of its contemporaries, is uninteresting and uninspired. The influence of Milton (whom Thompson 'preferred to Virgil himself'[1]) is unmistakable, as these lines, descriptive of the Spenserian palace of Disease, will show:

> In sad magnificence the palace rears
> Its mouldering columns; from thy quarries, Nile,
> Of sable marble, and Egyptian mines
> Embowel'd.[2]

Aside from the *Essay on Man* and the *Night Thoughts*, the greatest and most admired philosophical poem of the century was Mark Akenside's *Pleasures of Imagination*, which, published in 1744, when its author was just entering upon his twenty-third year, reached a thirteenth edition in 1795. Akenside was the Landor of his day, sensitive and passionate, widely read, enthusiastic over Greek and Latin literature, and sedulous to catch its fine restraint in his highly-finished verses. Yet both the man and his poems show a taint of neo-classicism from which Landor was free. He had, for example, "a pomp and stiffness of *manner*. . . . He looked as if he never could be undressed . . . and the laboured primness of a powdered wig in stiff curl, made his appearance altogether unpromising, if not grotesque."[3] There was a good deal of "the laboured primness of a powdered wig in stiff curl" about his *Pleasures of Imagination*, a poem in which "there is so much to admire . . . and so little to enjoy,"[4] which has height without lift and splendor without warmth, and which, though it may be studied, can no longer be read. An

---

[1] Note to i. 405. Other references to Milton or to his work occur in i. 266 n., 359–68 and n., 531 n.; ii. 253–4; iii. 109–111, 275 n., 514–16. Two lines from *Paradise Lost* are prefixed to book ii in the second edition; two more are quoted in i. 335–6 of the first edition, and there are a number of phrases borrowed from the epic and the minor poems, — "the spicy beds Of Araby the blest" (i. 313–14, cf. *P. L.*, iv. 162–3), "irreconcil'd in ruinous design" (i. 332, cf. *P. R.*, iv. 413), the strife of "hot, and cold, and moist, and dry" (i. 341, cf. *P. L.*, ii. 898), "a low-brow'd cave" (i. 434, cf. *Allegro*, 8), "at their visual entrance quite shut out" (ii. 229, cf. *P. L.*, iii. 50), "white-handed Hope" (ii. 636, cf. *Comus*, 213), "a dewy-skirted cloud Fleecy with gold" (iii. 122–3, cf. *P. L.*, v. 187), "flowry-footed May Leads on the jocund hours" (iii. 125–6, cf. *P. L.*, iv. 267–8), "cedar allies" (iii. 158, cf. *Comus*, 990, of fragrance in each case). Thompson is fond of parentheses and appositives, and of such words as "horizon'd," "ignipotent," "inundant," "stonied," "flammivomous," "detrude," "effulging" and "effusing" (i. 6, 175, 179, 437; ii. 284, 638; i. 546; iii. 127). The paraphrase of Job mentioned on page 112 above is by another William Thompson.

[2] i. 324–7.

[3] George Hardinge to John Nichols, June 19, 1813, in Nichols's *Literary Anecdotes*, viii. 522.

[4] Saintsbury, *English Prosody*, ii. 491.

illuminating comment upon it is its author's remark that "poetry was only true eloquence in metre";[1] for the reader seems throughout to be listening (not always attentively) to an oration of bygone days, vague, flowery, learned, and, though he is not sure just what it is all about, undoubtedly able.

Akenside's language is decidedly Latinized and grandiose. His pages "effuse" such words as effulgence, effluence, empyreal, empyrean, disparting, educing, brede, adamantine, illapse, preventing (anticipating), and phrases like "essential pleasure," "lucid orb," "the cerulean convex," "the wide complex Of coexistent orders," "attend His will, obsequious"; with him a cloud is "obvious to" the sun, planets "absolve The . . . rounds of Time," Ilissus "devolv'd" his stream, a task "impends," a pavilion "diffus'd Its floating umbrage."[2]

Such diction was probably due in Akenside's case, as in Thomson's, to a fondness for the boundless and the vast. For we get no details and little that is definite in the *Pleasures of Imagination;* everything is vague, general, and abstract; "actual existencies," "human interests," and experiences play almost no part.[3] Akenside was, for example, unusually fond of the out-of-doors, and has a great deal to say about it in his poem; yet he does not picture nature, he only talks about it. He never tells us what flowers are at his feet or what soft incense hangs upon the boughs. Very likely he did not know; his mind may have been indifferent to such details. At any rate, he mentions only the "perennial sweets" of the "balmy walks of May," "the rosy mead," "autumnal spoils," "the generous glebe Whose bosom smiles with verdure," or "the gay verdure of the painted plain";[4] that is, he employs the vague, vicious poetic diction of Thomson and his contemporaries.

As a result of this inflated language and involved style, of the abstract subject and the way in which it is treated, the course of Akenside's thought is hard to follow. "His images," declared Johnson, himself no stickler for simplicity, "are displayed with such luxuriance of expression that they are hidden, . . . lost under superfluity of dress. . . . The words are multiplied till the sense is hardly perceived; attention deserts the mind and settles in the ear. The reader wanders through the gay diffusion, sometimes amazed and sometimes delighted; but after many turnings in the flowery laby-

[1] Mason, *Memoirs of Gray* (prefixed to Gray's *Poems*, York, 1775), 261 n.

[2] ii. 158, 226, iii. 465 (cf. ii. 110), ii. 320–21, iii. 544–5; iii. 429 (cf. ii. 225, and second version, i. 90), i. 194–5, 594, ii. 68, 293–4.

[3] Dyce, in Aldine edition of Akenside, p. lxxxix.

[4] iii. 368–9, i. 426, ii. 288, i. 364–5, iii. 495.

rinth comes out as he went in." [1] Even if a particular passage is
understood, its connection with what goes before and what follows
is likely not to be clear. Akenside intended to depict the pleasures of
imagination, to show how they arise from the perception of greatness,
novelty, and beauty in the natural world and the fine arts; but he
was particularly anxious, "by exhibiting the most engaging prospects of nature, to enlarge and harmonize the imagination." [2] Yet
instead of putting his readers in tune with the infinite he only gets
them out of touch with the definite, with the result that few of them
carry away from the book any clear ideas. Take these lines, for
example:

> We hasten to recount the various springs
> Of adventitious pleasure, which adjoin
> Their grateful influence to the prime effect
> Of objects grand or beauteous, and enlarge
> The complicated joy. The sweets of sense,
> Do they not oft with kind accession flow,
> To raise harmonious Fancy's native charm? [3]

If the gentle reader is vague as to what this is all about, let him
imagine his state of mind after reading fifty such passages!

The parts of the poem most likely to impress him are those that
prefigure Keats's doctrine as to the identity of truth and beauty and
Wordsworth's as to the moral and spiritual power to be derived
from nature. Mr. C. A. Moore has shown that these ideas are derived from Shaftesbury and are common to the deistic poetry of the
time; [4] but Akenside's expression of them is memorable and, in view
of the popularity of his work and the admiration the lake poets had
for it, [5] may well have been influential. He asserts that from the
contemplation of natural beauty man derives more than beauty:

---

[1] "Akenside," in *Lives* (ed. Hill), iii. 417. "Sir, I could not read it through," he declared to Boswell (Boswell's *Life*, ed. Hill, ii. 164). Gray also thought poorly of it and
of the *Hymn to the Naiads* (see his letters to Wharton, April 26, 1744, and March 8, 1758,
and Mason, March 24, 1758).

[2] From the "Design" prefixed to the poem. "And by that means," he continued,
"insensibly dispose the minds of men to a similar taste and habit of thinking in
religion, morals, and civil life." Hence he emphasized "the benevolent intention of
the author of nature in every principle of the human constitution," and was careful to
"unite . . . in the same point of view" morality and good taste.

[3] ii. 69–75.

[4] *The Return to Nature in English Poetry* (Univ. of North Carolina, *Studies in Philology*, xiv. 273–8). According to Mr. Moore, Akenside "undertook to versify almost the
entire *corpus* of Shaftesbury's speculation. He included, for example, the doctrine
that the perfect harmony of Nature is the only revelation of the Deity required by a
reasonable creature, a spirited attack on orthodox superstition, a defense of ridicule as
a legitimate weapon in religious debate."

[5] In the preface to the third volume of his *Works*, Southey acknowledges that his

> For the attentive mind,
> By this harmonious action on her powers,
> Becomes herself harmonious. . . .
>   . . . . Thus the men
> Whom Nature's works can charm, with God himself
> Hold converse; grow familiar, day by day,
> With his conceptions, act upon his plan;
> And form to his, the relish of their souls.[1]

These ideas receive their highest expression in that part of the poem (composed over a quarter of a century after the original work was published) which Mr. Saintsbury declares to be "not only almost alongside of Cowper, but very nearly in presence of Wordsworth." [2] In this fragmentary fourth book of the rewritten *Pleasures of the Imagination*, Akenside refers to

> Those studies which possess'd me in the dawn
> Of life, and fix'd the colour of my mind,

to the "dales of Tyne," the "most ancient woodlands, where . . . the giant flood obliquely strides," and to

> The rocky pavement and the mossy falls
> Of solitary Wensbeck's limpid stream . . .
> Belov'd of old, and that delightful time
> When all alone, for many a summer's day,
> I wander'd through your calm recesses, led
> In silence by some powerful hand unseen.[3]

This passage is hardly closer to Wordsworth's conception of the spiritual functions of nature than is this other to the general character of his blank verse:

inscriptions and his *Hymn to thePenates* were inspired by Akenside; and William Haller (*Early Life of Southey*, N. Y., 1917, p. 108 n.) points out that the mottoes prefixed to Southey's *Poems* (1797) and to Coleridge's *Moral and Political Lecture* (1795) and *Religious Musings* (1796) are all taken from Akenside. Note also Coleridge's *Elegy imitated from one of Akenside's Blank-Verse Inscriptions*, his *Destiny of Nations*, and lines 48–64 of Wordsworth's *Lines left upon a Seat*, which recall the *Pleasures of Imagination*. Akenside had several interesting connections with romanticism. He helped Dyer on *The Fleece* (see Aldine ed. of Akenside, p. lxxi), he had "long been intimately acquainted with" Thomas Edwards, one of the revivers of the sonnet (*ib.* lxxviii), and he was "a great admirer of Gothic architecture" (*ib.* lxix). His odes, the subject of his principal poem, his Spenserian imitation *The Virtuoso*, his use of blank verse, all point towards the milder classicism of Gray, Mason, and the Wartons. Yet he has several poems, including the classical satire *An Epistle to Curio*, in heroic couplets; and he based the *Pleasures* itself upon some of Addison's *Spectator* papers.

[1] iii. 599–633.

[2] *English Prosody*, ii. 491.

[3] iv. 49–50, 31–45.

> For thus far
> On general habits, and on arts which grow
> Spontaneous in the minds of all mankind,
> Hath dwelt our argument.[1]

Akenside's debt to *Paradise Lost* must be clear from the extracts that have been given. Parentheses and appositives, to be sure, are rare, and inversions, though numerous, are neither so frequent nor so elaborate as in most blank verse of the day. But the inflated Thomsonian diction shows all the Miltonic peculiarities, — unusual words from the Greek and Latin, words employed in their original but obsolete senses, uncommon hyphenated epithets, adjectives used as adverbs or as nouns, nouns used as verbs, and so on. The most objectionable of these idiosyncrasies, which are to be attributed to youth and to the influence of *The Seasons*, are in large part purged from the later version written between 1757 and 1770.[2] The admiration for Milton implied in the use of his style and language Akenside expressed frankly. In his ode *On the Absence of the Poetic Inclination*, he asks if he shall seek the "soul of Milton" in order to win back the muse, and immediately breaks out,

> O mighty mind! O sacred flame!
> My spirit kindles at his name;
> Again my lab'ring bosom burns;
> The Muse, th' inspiring Muse returns![3]

Later he wrote:

> Mark, how the dread Pantheon stands,
> Amid the domes of modern hands:
> Amid the toys of idle state,
> How simply, how severely great!
> Then turn, and, while each western clime
> Presents her tuneful sons to Time,
>   So mark thou Milton's name;
> And add, "Thus differs from the throng
> The spirit which inform'd thy awful song,
> Which bade thy potent voice protect thy country's fame."[4]

Clearly it was Milton's character and patriotism, as well as his poetry, that Akenside admired. Nor was his admiration for the

---

[1] iv. 58–61. Wordsworth's title, *Influence of Natural Objects in calling forth and strengthening the Imagination*, might serve for Akenside's work.

[2] Compare, for example, i. 185–211 with i. 243–69 in the later version.

[3] In the first edition of his *Odes* (1745) this was ode vi; in later editions it became ode x of book i, *To the Muse*, and the lines were changed.

[4] *To Francis, Earl of Huntingdon*, iii. 2. Section iii. 3 of this ode is largely devoted to Milton, other references to whom will be found in the tenth and seventeenth odes of book i, the second, fourth, and tenth of book ii, and in i. 168 of the second version of the *Pleasures*.

poetry confined to the epic; for he borrowed from *Lycidas*,[1] and was one of the first imitators of *Allegro* and *Penseroso*.[2]

The influence of Milton should not be confused with the similar influence of the classics, in which Akenside was steeped. The *Pleasures of Imagination* undoubtedly derives in the main from the English Homer and his imitators, whereas the more direct and severe inscriptions (which influenced Southey and perhaps, through him, Landor) suggest Greece and Rome. Yet even in them there are lines as Miltonic as these:

> Thus at length
> Expert in laws divine, I know the paths
> Of wisdom, and erroneous folly's end
> Have oft presag'd: and now well-pleas'd I wait.[3]

The noble *Hymn to the Naiads* (written in 1746), which has the coolness and impersonality of the brooks and springs themselves, together with something of the aloofness of the Epicurean gods, is confessedly an imitation of the hymns of Callimachus.[4] It is of Greece rather than of Milton that we are reminded in these, the best lines:

> Ye Nymphs, ye blue-ey'd progeny of Thames,
> Who now the mazes of this rugged heath
> Trace with your fleeting steps; who all night long
> Repeat, amid the cool and tranquil air,
> Your lonely murmurs, tarry: and receive
> My offer'd lay. To pay you homage due,
> I leave the gates of sleep; nor shall my lyre
> Too far into the splendid hours of morn
> Engage your audience.[5]

---

[1] "Hill and dale with all their echoes mourn" (iii. 566, cf. *Lycidas*, 39–41). I have noted a few other Miltonic borrowings in the *Pleasures:* "the enamel'd green" (ii. 434, cf. *Arcades*, 84), "flew diverse" (ii. 640, cf. *P. L.*, x. 284),

> Whose unfading light
> Has travell'd the profound six thousand years,
> Nor yet arrives

(i. 204–6, cf. *P. L.*, ii. 979–80),

> The sable woods
> That shade sublime yon mountain's nodding brow

(iii. 286–7, cf. *Comus*, 37–8). There are, besides, a number of phrases, like "congregated floods" (ii. 282, cf. *P. L.*, vii. 308) and "of each peculiar" (iii. 6, cf. *P. L.*, vii. 368), that may have been suggested by the epic.

[2] See pp. 449–50 below. The first paragraph of the *Pleasures* makes some use of the *Allegro-Penseroso* structure (see p. 471 below).

[3] Inscription vii, *The Wood Nymph*.

[4] Note to line 327. Dyce declares (Aldine ed. of Akenside, p. xc) that English literature contains "nothing more deeply imbued with the spirit of the ancient world."

[5] Lines 5–13.

Yet in a note to the *Hymn* Akenside refers to Milton as "the only modern poet (unless perhaps . . . Spenser) who, in these mysterious traditions of the poetic story, had a heart to feel, and words to express, the simple and solitary genius of antiquity"; [1] furthermore, the poem contains not a few lines as Miltonic, in everything but diction, as any in the *Pleasures of Imagination*.

The *Hymn* recalls Collins's best odes, and, had it been no longer than they, might have been almost as good. The two poets, who were born the same year, seem to have drawn more of their classicism from Greece than from Rome (whence contemporary writers derived most of theirs); and each published within twelve months of the other a volume of odes which were unusual for the time and which reveal a fondness for personified abstractions and for Milton's octosyllabics. But, except at rare intervals, Akenside's verse falls far short of Collins's; it is seldom simple, never sensuous or passionate, and, notwithstanding its distinction and elegance, is almost always rhetoric or "eloquence" rather than poetry.

The *Hymn to the Naiads*, though not published till 1758, was written twelve years earlier and circulated somewhat in manuscript. In this form it came to the attention of William Whitehead shortly before he was made poet laureate, and seems to have inspired his only serious effort in blank verse, a *Hymn to the Nymph of Bristol Spring* (1751). Whitehead's *Hymn* reminds one of Akenside's (which it mentions) not only in title but in style and diction. Its four hundred and seventy lines praise the salubrious properties of Bristol waters in as stiltedly Miltonic a fashion as this:

> Thee the sable Wretch,
> To ease whose burning Entrails swells in vain
> The Citron's dewy moisture, thee he hails;
> And oft from some steep Cliff at early dawn
> In Seas, in Winds, or the vast Void of Heaven
> Thy Power unknown adores.[2]

[1] Note to line 83. Lines 82–6 are obviously derived from a passage in *Paradise Lost* (iv. 275–9) which is quoted in this same note; there is also a quotation from Milton in the note to line 25. Akenside wrote two other pieces of blank verse, *The Poet* (1737, a parody), and *A British Philippic*, "occasioned by the Insults of the Spaniards, and the present Preparations for War" (1738, cf. Glover's *London*, written on the same occasion), which is more direct, simple, and vigorous, and hence less Miltonic, than most of his later blank verse. He also "had made some progress in an Epic poem . . . *Timoleon*" (*Gent. Mag.*, lxiii. 885), in which he would almost certainly have employed the style, diction, and prosody of *Paradise Lost*.

[2] Lines 54–9. The *Hymn to the Naiads* is commended in lines 103–6 and note. Whitehead's *Lyric Muse to Mr. Mason* ("Dodsley's Miscellany," 1758, vi. 58–60) suggests Milton's octosyllabics in meter and in the movement of the lines.

The influence of the *Pleasures of Imagination* is most obviously seen in the imitation of its title by other poets. Warton used it for his *Pleasures of Melancholy* (written in 1745), Rogers for his *Pleasures of Memory* (1792), Courtier for his *Pleasures of Solitude* (1796), Campbell for his *Pleasures of Hope* (1799), and William Hamilton Drummond for his *Pleasures of Benevolence* (1835). Rogers's and Campbell's pieces are rimed, but Drummond's thirty-four hundred lines are in the kind of unmistakably Miltonic blank verse that was in vogue a century before he wrote. They touch on almost every aspect of human life, while inculcating the joy and duty of kindness to all creatures, animals as well as men, and insisting on the goodness of God at work through all the evils of the world. To what extent a reading of the poem is one of the pleasures of benevolence may be surmised from these typical lines,

> How richly dight with thy magnificence,
> Yon star-bespangled concave! Wide expands
> Th' immeasurable ether; streams of light,
> Bright coruscations of the boreal morn. . . . [1]

or from the fact that the copy in the Harvard Library has stood on the shelves for eighty-five years uncut!

The deistic philosophy which inspired the *Pleasures of Imagination*, as it did much of *The Seasons* and of the *Essay on Man*, played no small part in other eighteenth-century poetry. One aspect of it furnished John Gilbert Cooper with the theme of his *Power of Harmony* (1745), in which he attempted "to shew that a constant attention to what is perfect and beautiful in nature, will by degrees harmonize the soul to a responsive regularity and sympathetic order"; or, as he expressed it in verse,

> From these sweet meditations on the charms
> Of things external [nature, art, music] . . .
> The soul, and all the intellectual train
> Of fond Desires, gay Hopes, or threat'ning Fears,
> Through this habitual intercourse of sense
> Is harmoniz'd within, till all is fair

---

[1] Pages 9-10. I have noticed these Miltonic borrowings: "Siloa's brook" (p. 25, from *P. L.*, i. 11); "Araby the blest" (p. 33, from *P. L.*, iv. 163, in connection with odors in each case); "thro' unfathomed seas, Tempests leviathan" (p. 41, cf. *P. L.*, vii. 412); "the den of loud misrule" (p. 57, cf. *P. L.*, vii. 271-2); "hyacinthine locks" (p. 106, cf. *P. L.*, iv. 301); "winglets of downy gold . . . Maia's son" (p. 107, cf. *P. L.*, v. 282-5, of an angel in each case);

> Sabbaths return, but not to him returns
> Rest, or sweet respite

(p. 37, cf. *P. L.*, iii. 41-2). On page 86 is quoted "the drop serene That quenched his orbs" (cf. *P. L.*, iii. 25).

And perfect; till each moral pow'r perceives
Its own resemblance, with fraternal joy,
In ev'ry form compleat, and smiling feels
Beauty and Good the same.[1]

These lines are simpler, less suggestive of Thomson, than are most of
the others; for the poem abounds in compound epithets, in a Latinized vocabulary, — "effuse," "effulgence," "relumes," "obsequious" (prompt to follow), "præenjoy," "tepefying," "invests the
boughs," "devolves his . . . stream," "obvious" pebbles,[2]—and in
other objectionable forms of poetic diction. These features, as well
as the use of adjectives for adverbs and the elaborate and frequent
inversions, Cooper may have derived from Milton, whose octosyllabics he copied a year later[3] and whose phrasing he borrowed
several times in this poem.[4]

Why natural beauty has the power of harmonizing the soul was
explained in 1751 by Shaftesbury's nephew, James Harris, in the one
hundred and seventy Miltonic lines of his *Concord*. The universal
Mind, who is also Beauty, "Himself pour'd forth" through all
matter, animate and inanimate:

Hence man, allied to all, in all things meets
Congenial being, effluence of mind.
And as the tuneful spring spontaneous sounds
In answer to his kindred note; so he
The secret harmony within him feels,
When aught of beauty offers.[5]

Many of these deistic ideas were accepted by persons who in
general remained orthodox, — like John Duncan, for example,
chaplain of the king's own regiment and author of a joy-dispelling
Essay on Happiness (1762). Duncan maintains through nearly sixteen hundred lines that the world was originally perfect and completely happy, that it is still better and happier than is commonly

---

[1] *Poems on Several Subjects* (1764), 83, 119. Cooper may have been influenced by
Akenside, to whom he addressed a rimed panegyric, *The Call of Aristippus* (1758), and
whom he praised in his *Letters concerning Taste* (1754, letter xv).

[2] *Poems*, etc., 97 (cf. 118), 107, 102, 90, 90, 94, 96, 109, 109.

[3] See below, p. 451.

[4] For example, "th' Aonian mount" (p. 88, cf. *P. L.*, i. 15); "Chaos reign'd, And
elemental Discord; in the womb Of ancient Night, the war of atoms . . . Anarchy, Confusion . . . Dissonance, and Uproar" (p. 88, cf. *P. L.*, ii. 150, 894–7, 960–67); "congregated clouds"(p. 110, cf. *P. L.*, vii. 308); "Euphrosyne, heart-easing" (p. 112, cf.
Allegro, 12–13); "the flow'ry field Of Enna (p. 113, cf. *P. L.*, iv. 268–9). "The first
man . . . in the flood A godlike image saw," etc. (pp. 119–20), seems to be derived
from Eve's first view of herself (*P. L.*, iv. 455–65). Something of the *Allegro-Penseroso* structure appears three times in the poem (pp. 87–8, 105–6, 111–12).

[5] *Poetical Calendar* (1763), xii. 55–6.

conceived, that all evil arises from false self-love, that the happiness and rank of the various orders of beings — God, angels, men — depends upon the degree to which they partake of true love (benevolence), and that happiness is promoted by reason and virtue and is finally established in the love of God. These ideas are, however, derived much more easily from the summaries that precede the four books of the *Essay* than from the poetry itself, which, perhaps "dark through excessive bright," devolves its maze in this fashion:

> Not thus eludes th' angelic eye the grace
> On lapsed man residing. Unobscur'd
> By low-born mist his comprehensive view
> In thy sole essence lost, all-seeing God,
> O'er all creation's charms expatiates free.[1]

The Miltonic character of these lines requires no comment; but attention should be called to a definite mention of *Paradise Lost*,[2] to such borrowings from it as "the gloom of unessential night," "human face divine," "the . . . wealth of *Ind*," "love-notes wild,"[3] to the description of Eden (where "with sprightly glee Gambol'd the fiery pard" and "the smiling hours and seasons led The circling dance" to the songs of the birds),[4] as well as to the effect on nature of the fall of man.[5]

Deistic writings like these, including as they did many of the leading productions of the time in prose as well as in verse, caused no small disturbance among the narrowly orthodox. One of the pens wielded as a cudgel in defence of the older theology was that of the Presbyterian divine, John Ogilvie, who entitled his last work *The Triumphs of Christianity over Deism* (1805). Forty years earlier he had, to his own satisfaction at least, established the faith of all doubting Thomases and crushed the skepticism of such bolder spirits as his fellow-Scotsman Hume, in the three thousand lines of his inflated, blank-verse *Providence, an Allegorical Poem* (1764). Only persons already convinced, or those with feeble doubts, could have been impressed by the work; men of real thought, like Hume, must have sneered at Ogilvie's solemn elucidation of the obvious, as well as at

[1] Pages 72–3. On page 12 Duncan refers with approval to the deists Shaftesbury and Hutcheson.

[2] Page 40, and note.

[3] Pages 24 (cf. *P. L.*, ii. 438–9, of chaos in each case), 31 (cf. *P. L.*, iii. 44), 51 (cf. *P. L.*, ii. 2), 45 (cf. *Allegro*, 134).

[4] Pages 30–31 (cf. *P. L.*, iv. 340–50, 264–8).

[5] Pages 40 (earth "groan'd . . . with grief" at the picking of the forbidden fruit, cf. *P. L.*, iv. 780–84), 43–4 (cf. *P. L.*, x. 651–714, and note that in each poem the animals "glared" on Adam).

the anthropomorphism of his selfish, petty deity who delayed the coming of Christ lest man should arrogate to himself the discovery of His teachings, and who revealed the true religion to "a favour'd Few" in order that they might be properly grateful.[1]

The poem attempts to prove, through a series of visions expounded by allegorical personages, that without divine revelation the human mind is incapable of evolving a satisfactory religion, that there is a beneficent Providence behind floods, droughts, volcanic eruptions, excessive heat and cold, and the like, as well as behind the prosperity of the wicked and the afflictions of the righteous. To elucidate these matters would have been sufficiently difficult even if Ogilvie had not hampered himself with "the vain stiffness of a letter'd Scot," [2] with a style and diction often more absurdly Miltonic than in these lines:

> Rash alike thou deem'st
> Of wisdom or injustice. — Grant that Heav'n
> Submiss, to Nature's glimmering search had lent
> Internal light . . .
> Then had thy thought elate disdain'd to own
> The boon conferr'd; thine all the work had been.[3]

But it is unnecessary to comment on a poem that was so well characterized by a brilliant and merciless contemporary:

> Under dark allegory's flimsy veil
> Let them with Ogilvie spin out a tale
> Of rueful length; let them plain things obscure,
> Debase what's truly rich, and what is poor
> Make poorer still by jargon most uncouth . . .
> With bloated style, by affectation taught,
> With much false colouring, and little thought . . .
> With words, which nature meant each other's foe,

---

[1] See ii. 813–48, 931–42.   [2] Charles Churchill, *The Journey*, 148.

[3] ii. 814–22. A more interesting but less typical passage is i. 653–65, which pictures "the romantic wild . . . mountains piled Sublime in horrid grandeur to the sky." It was to Ogilvie that Johnson said, "The noblest prospect which a Scotchman ever sees, is the high road that leads him to England" (Boswell's *Life*, ed. Hill, i. 425, and see 421). There appear to be some borrowings from Milton, such as "shagg'd with . . . hills, Rocks, desarts, woods, dales," etc. (i. 58–9, cf. *Comus*, 429, and *P. L.*, ii. 621), "with contiguous shades" (i. 245, cf. *P. L.*, vi. 828), "with downy gold" (i. 258, cf. *P. L.*, v. 282), "the griesly shape" (i. 326, cf. *P. L.*, ii. 704), "floats on the gale redundant" (i. 1022, cf. *P. L.*, ix. 502–3), "face That glow'd celestial" (ii. 240–1, cf. *P. L.*, viii. 618–19), "hurl'd them headlong" (ii. 617, cf. *P. L.*, i. 45), "back th' astonish'd thought Recoil'd" (ii. 681–2, cf. *P. L.*, ii. 759, vi. 194), "smit with the dust of earth" (ii. 690, cf. *P. L.*, iii. 29), "bedrop'd with" (ii. 720, cf. *P. L.*, x. 527, of the ground in each case), "mazes intricate" (iii. 178, cf. *P. L.*, v. 622), "balmy as the citron grove" (iii. 787, cf. *P. L.*, v. 22–3), "tinctured with the dies Of heav'n " (iii. 912–13, cf. *P. L.*, v. 283–5)," innumerable wings . . . fann'd the undulating air" (iii. 916–17, cf. *P. L.*, vii. 431–2). Four of Ogilvie's odes are Miltonic (see Bibl. II, 1762, 1769), as is his epic *Britannia* (see pp. 302–3 above).

Forced to compound whether they will or no;
With such materials, let them, if they will,
To prove at once their pleasantry and skill,
Build up a bard to war 'gainst common sense,
By way of compliment to Providence.[1]

There are many similarities between Ogilvie's work and James Foot's *Penseroso, or the Pensive Philosopher in his Solitudes* (1771), only a small part of which is of the graveyard variety. Though 'embellished with pastoral description' (which, stilted and unpoetic as it is, shows that Foot had his eye on the object), the *Pensive Philosopher* is not concerned primarily with nature, but rather is designed "to recommend piety, the social virtues, and a love of liberty. It introduces . . . Penseroso," as Foot goes on to explain, "reflecting in his solitudes . . . upon the state of the moral and natural, the religious and civil world." [2] Nothing could be more typical of the late eighteenth century, since the problems that have perplexed mankind throughout the ages are disposed of with the complacent ease of narrow, insular orthodoxy. The six books are devoted respectively to "the State of Man"; worldly disasters and "the Wisdom of the Divine Government"; death and immortality; the wickedness of heathenism and the excellence of Christianity as shown through "the wisdom, power, and goodness of God in the visible creation"; the evils of Romanism, together with "the Benefits of Liberty, Charity, and Moderation"; and, finally, "Civil Government and the Glory of the English Nation."

Foot employed blank verse because it "admits of a greater variety in . . . its numbers," and because "it is for the most part adopted by Young, Mallet, Glover, Akenside, Armstrong, Ogilvie, and in short, by most of the celebrated writers of the present times." [3] Thomson, whom he does not mention, seems to have influenced him not a little; and Milton, who

plucks the palm from Maro's head;
And far the bard of Greece or Rome exceeds,[4]

gave him much more than his title. For not only are the style and diction clearly Miltonic, but there are many such expressions as "enchantments drear," the "curfew sends its swinging roar," "th' oblivious pool," "stores Of nitrous spume, bitumen, sulphur,"

---

[1] Churchill, *The Journey*, 125–42. The unusual compound epithets that Churchill ridiculed are very common in *Providence*.

[2] Preface, p. iii.

[3] Preface, p. vi. "The elegant Mr. Mason" is mentioned on the preceding page.

[4] Page 294.

"floating redundant," "far as an angel sees," "with horror plum'd';[1] and a scene in hell is unblushingly copied from *Paradise Lost* even in its phraseology.[2]

Abraham Portal's *Innocence* (1762) need not detain us long, for there have probably been very few readers whom it has detained at all. It consists of thirteen hundred lines of jerky, turgid, decidedly Miltonic blank verse, the confused maunderings of a very second-rate mind.[3] The author, an unsuccessful tradesman and dramatist who ended his career as a box-keeper at Drury Lane theater, seems to have been the embodiment of the innocence he lauds. His love episode is surely naïve enough; for the maid, on seeing

> A Man stand guardant, all confus'd arose,
> Blushing inimitable,

and "curtsied silent" her acceptance when the "guardant" male proposed in his first speech to her![4]

Some years later an equally innocent author asked his readers to

> Permit the muse to dictate; she means well.

This was a Welsh farmer's son, David Lloyd, who by teaching himself Latin and Greek had become a clergyman and felt equal to writing a poem on the *Voyage of Life*.[5] Lloyd invokes the muse of

> the plaintive bard immortal YOUNG,
> Whom at an humble distance I pursue,
> So might I haply catch some vital spark
> Of his celestial fire to warm my strain.[6]

---

[1] Pages 12 (and 252, cf. *Penseroso*, 119), 23 (cf. *Penseroso*, 74–6), 36 (cf. *P. L.*, i. 266), 78 (cf. *P. L.*, vi. 479, 512, 515, of explosives in each case), 138 (cf. *P. L.*, ix. 503), 138 (cf. *P. L.*, i. 59), 138 (cf. *P. L.*, iv. 989).

[2] Pages 140–144. The anonymous *Nature* (book i, Bristol, 1786, to be completed in five more books), which I know only by the extract and comment in the *Monthly Review* (lxxiv. 564), seems to be a philosophical poem on the nature of things, on motion, attraction, repulsion, and the like. It is expressed in crabbed Miltonic blank verse and was probably suggested by the *De Rerum Natura*.

[3] The effect of the fall of man on nature—plants, animals, the climate, etc. (pp. 14–16)—is the same as in *Paradise Lost*, x. 651–714; the line "High in the middle Regions of the Air" (p. 17) seems to be an adaptation of *Paradise Regained*, ii. 117 (said of a meeting-place of evil spirits in each case); "Smit with the Love of Science" (p. 61) is reminiscent of *Paradise Lost*, iii. 29; while

> There Love his golden Shafts employs, there lights
> His brightest Fires (p. 55),

is certainly derived from *Paradise Lost*, iv. 763–4.

[4] Pages 65–74.

[5] First ed., 1792; enlarged, 1812. For the line quoted, see first ed., iv. 551.

[6] i. 81–4. Young is also referred to in the notes to i. 238, iv. 373, vi. 415, ix. 355; and an imaginary "Eugenio" is addressed after Young's fashion in iv. 276, 325.

Yet the expression "so might I haply catch" in this extract, as well as the phrase "this advent'rous task" a few lines later, recalls another poet whom he frequently mentions or borrows from and to whom, directly or indirectly, he seems far more indebted than he is to Young.[1] There is certainly little of the staccato style, the sententiousness, or the couplet prosody that mark the *Night Thoughts* in the forty-eight hundred lines of stilted preaching that make up the *Voyage of Life*.

In 1794 fifty-four pages of dull, unrimed couplets were published anonymously under the title *War*. To judge from the specimen in the *Monthly Review*, the critic is well within the bounds of truth when he suggests that "of highly-wrought pathos or impressive sublimity there is not enough to stamp the writer a poet." [2] The platitudinous, invertebrate character of this work is what might be expected; yet one writer of the time really had something to say on so hackneyed but so vital a theme. For Joseph Fawcett's *Art of War* (1795) is a vigorous and thoughtful indictment of civilization for its approval of scientific butchery. Fawcett is concerned not so much with painting the horrors of war as with showing that we praise nations for the very crimes which we punish in individuals. He strips off the trappings, the empty courtesies, and the scientific methods under which the essential barbarism of so-called "civilized warfare" is concealed, and lays the blame squarely upon us all — cheering crowds as well as statesmen and officers. The *Art of War* is not an attractive poem. Its argument is pursued relentlessly without the usual digressions, episodes, or decorative passages; yet it is not easy to follow, and would gain if its twelve hundred and fifty lines were considerably condensed, if the distraction of its marked allitera-

[1] Milton is referred to in the notes to ii. 144, 292, v. 59; he is praised in v. 25–7 as "Britain's glorious bard, of equal fate, And equal majesty," with "old Maeonides"; and the phrases "kicks the beam" (ii. 299, cf. *P. L*, iv. 1004), "Ganges, or Hydaspes, far famed streams" (ii. 361, cf. *P. L.*, iii. 436), "trace . . . 'Eternal Providence,' and vindicate God's righteous ways to man" (vi. 4–7, cf. *P. L.*, i. 25–6), and "raise my . . . muse, to soar . . . Above the middle regions" (vii. 13–14, cf. *P. L.*, i. 6, 14) are taken from his epic.

[2] *Mo. Rev.*, enl. ed., xvi. 107–8 (1795). I have not seen this poem, or the anonymous *War, in Blank Verse,* which was announced in August, 1745. The *Essay on War, in Blank Verse*, which Nathaniel Bloomfield, a tailor, published in 1803, owes nothing to *Paradise Lost;* but Peter L. Courtier's *Revolutions* (1796), in which a youthful lover of liberty attacks war and pictures the evils of the French Revolution, contains 940 lines of the emptiest pseudo-Miltonic rant wearisomely enhanced with personifications. It seems significant that Courtier's unrimed *Pleasures of Solitude* (*Poems*, 1796, pp. 97–114), which is quite as rambling and pointless but less objectionable in style, is followed by some lines *To the Memory of Thomson*.

tion were removed,[1] and if its exuberant, decidedly Miltonic style
and diction (which obscure the thought) were pruned. Yet there are
a number of passages, like the one given below or the appeal to reason with which the poem closes, that, notwithstanding their stylistic
contortions and obscurities, are admirably direct, vigorous, and even
impressive:

> A single culprit, hark! the hounds of Law
> Hunt in full cry: but where's the custody,
> On culpable communities can shoot
> The bulky bolt? for culprit empires where
> The huge colossal constable, to whom
> Such criminals will crouch? Where stands the court,
> Of ample area, like the arch of heaven,
> Within whose walls wide-swelling, plaintiff states
> Offending states may sue, and nations wait
> Their sentence, meek submitted to the mouth
> Of so sublime a bench? [2]

Is the answer the League of Nations?

If the *Art of War* is not easy reading, what shall be said of a work
that pursues through three cantos a style as amazing as this:

> Th' ideas receiv'd thro' sense
> *Perfection* souls; these wide with age augment,
> And thro' eternal time new wisdom blooms. . . .
> I see the first form'd *beings*, not born, on leaves
> Of roses *lay;* complete their frames, I see
> The hand divine around their *craniums* move! [3]

The comment of the *Monthly Review* on the piece—George Nason's
Aphono and Ethina, including the Science of Ethics (1799)—was,
"Whoever wishes to peruse dissertations on the most abstruse and
incomprehensible subjects, on the nature and attributes of God and
of the soul, on the connection between matter and spirit, on the
origin of thought, on the essence of moral virtue, &c. enveloped

---

[1] Such lines — and there are hundreds of them — as

> Supreme that sways
> The swallow'd soul, and drives to deeds of death

(p. 29), would be strange at any time, but are doubly so in the eighteenth century.

[2] Pages 48-9. Fawcett, who had been a popular dissenting minister, reprinted this piece and his rimed *Art of Poetry* in his *Poems* in 1798 and issued some *War Elegies* in 1801. I have noticed only two Miltonic borrowings in the *Art of War*, — "round she rapid rolls Her beauteous eyes" (p. 15, cf. *P. L.*, i. 56) and "sportive becks, And wanton nods, and smiles" (p. 32, cf. *Allegro*, 27-8); but the war of fiends in mid-air (p. 30) recalls the battles in heaven. Mr. Arthur Beatty, in his essay on Fawcett (Univ. of Wisconsin, *Studies in Language*, etc., No. 2, 1918, pp. 224-69), which reached me after this chapter was written, points out the influence of Fawcett's preaching and conversation on Godwin, Hazlitt, and Wordsworth.

[3] *Mo. Rev.*, enl. ed., xxxii. 437-8. I have not seen the poem.

in all the profound and sublime beauties of *blank-verse*, may here by gratified. The *story* . . . does not occupy three pages of the 118."

This may be as good a place as any to notice a number of works which, though not really philosophical, are closer to the poems we are considering than to any other type. There is, for example, the *Sketches of Beauty*, "two hundred and thirty-eight pages, involved in mist and obscurity," which "Vicarius" published in 1787. The beauty of the *Sketches* may be judged from this extract:

> Along the vegetative, soul-sequester'd vale,
> Where beauty courts the silent soft recess;
> Twice pleased, modestly shines, it comes and goes
> Unmark'd: a turn will take.[1]

There is also the *Progress of Liberty*, in which the famous "Perdita" Robinson endeavored by frequent exclamations and rhetorical questions to make some fifteen hundred lines of dull, sentimental commonplaces seem the inspiration of poetic frenzy:

> Shall the poor AFRICAN, the passive slave,
> Born in the bland effulgence of broad day,
> Cherish'd by torrid splendours, while around
> The plains prolific teem with honey'd stores . . .
> . . . . shall such a wretch
> Sink prematurely to a grave obscure,
> No tear to grace his ashes? Or suspire,
> To wear submission's long and goading chain? [2]

"O Liberty! Liberty! how many crimes are committed in thy name!"

Another work that may be mentioned here is the *Renovation of India* (1808), written in competition for a prize offered by the University of Edinburgh, where its author, Thomas Brown, was later a famous professor of moral philosophy. The six hundred and thirty lines of this piece present a lurid picture of Indian rites and massacres and a prediction of the blessings that are to be wrought by Christianity. In his oft-reprinted *Lectures on the Philosophy of the Human Mind* (1820) Brown quoted extensively from the English poets, particularly Pope, Young, and, most of all, Akenside, whose luxuriant style probably affected his own. The closing lines of his poem will show that it is less Miltonic and more impressive than many of its contemporaries:

---

[1] *Mo. Rev.*, lxxviii. 80. I have not seen the poem.

[2] *Works* (1806), iii. 30. The poem, which was written about 1795, contains high praise of Milton (*ib.* 17).

When rushing worlds,
The comets of the infinite, shall flash
Loose thro' the gloom, and the last thundering shock
Of Earths and Suns still shout their worshipp'd God.[1]

"How charming is divine philosophy!" is not the first exclamation that rises to the lips after reading the poems we have been considering. Nor could their authors claim, with Addison, that they
"brought philosophy out of closets and libraries, schools and colleges, to dwell in clubs and assemblies, at tea-tables and in coffee-
houses." Many of the pieces are so destitute of real thought that
they could have had but little influence, and almost none present
their ideas in a way that is attractive or easy to follow. They lack
Dryden's rare faculty of reasoning in verse, they are far too abstract, their arguments are not presented simply enough and do not
follow naturally from one to another; digressions are numerous and
not easily distinguished from the main thought, and too often the
ideas are confused by an inflated, involved style and exuberant
diction that are entirely unsuited to the purpose. The eighteenth
century produced any number of versified treatises on Knowledge,
Beauty, Concord, Grace, Distress, Wisdom, Commerce, Poverty,
Truth, Money, Gratitude, Humility, Genius, Society, Reason,
Benevolence, Conscience, and the like, in which high-sounding language and an ornate, involved style were used as a kind of alembic
for converting dull prose into inspired verse. Such themes can be
vitalized and poetized only by an unusual writer, and great poets
were lacking. Vigorous and acute thinking was no rarity in the
days of Berkeley, Hume, Adam Smith, Johnson, and Burke, but
it did not get into poetry. The *Essay on Man*, *Night Thoughts*, and
Pleasures of Imagination are typical of the philosophical poems of
the time, which might be shrewd and clever, dull and platitudinous,
or vague and rhapsodical, but which were pretty sure not to be well
arranged, closely reasoned, or profound.

RELIGIOUS POETRY

Most persons who read poetry to-day think of the rebellion of
Satan as a myth and the story of Adam and Eve as an allegory. A
large number, to be sure, still believe or profess to believe in the
literal truth of the early chapters of Genesis, but they do not hold
the events narrated in that part of the Bible as a vital part of their

[1] Brown also wrote some blank-verse "Musings during a Night-walk" (see his
Wanderer in Norway, 2d ed., 1816, pp. 145–60).

creed. It was not so in the eighteenth century. Then the fall of man, the personality of the devil, the terrors of a real hell-fire, and the joys of heaven not only were believed in but were thought matters of prime importance; they were preached from the pulpit and talked of at the hearth. Particularly was this the case among the dissenters, who proudly counted Milton as one of their number. With the Puritans, and to a less extent with the Methodists, Baptists, and other nonconformists, a large part of whose leisure thinking, talking, and reading was occupied with religious matters, the next world was an ever-present reality.

By this class novels and plays were severely frowned upon and most secular literature was looked at askance, with the result that such religious books as were allowed were eagerly seized upon. Little is said about most of these works in our histories of literature, since, although no popularity is so great as that of the religious book, none is usually so ephemeral. Who has ever heard of Elizabeth Rowe, whom Johnson, Klopstock, and Wieland praised? of her *Friendship in Death*, which was twice translated into French? or of her *Devout Exercises of the Heart*, which, after going through editions without number, was turned into blank verse? How many persons know that Isaac Watts wrote a book of poems that was reprinted at least twenty-five times? [1] Who but the student of American beginnings ever heard of Wigglesworth's *Day of Doom*, the most widely-read book, after the Bible, in colonial New England? Or, turning to our own day, who now reads the thousands of volumes of Spurgeon's or Talmage's sermons, or the millions of copies of *Titus, Comrade of the Cross?* Second-hand bookstores always have Young's *Night Thoughts*, Pollok's *Course of Time*, and Ingraham's *Prince of the House of David* in stock, but seldom find purchasers for them. Yet these are the books that have gone to the people's hearts, the sources from which the young have derived their ideals and the old received their consolation. They are the works that shaped popular taste to an extent that we do not realize, and, if literary history ever takes account of what is really read, they must receive attention. Of course, they rarely have any esthetic value. Their appeal is, in the main, to uncultivated readers whose taste in all the arts must necessarily be undeveloped; and their success is often due to their very faults, to sentimentality or morbidity, to a declamatory, rhetorical style or a fluent expression of platitudes.

[1] *Horae Lyricae* (1706). Watts's *Hymns* (1707) have few readers to-day; yet fifty thousand copies were printed annually one hundred years after their first publication. In America alone his songs for children were published 25 times at Hartford, 64 times at Haverhill, and 97 times at Boston before 1797 (W. M. Stone, *Divine and Moral Songs of Isaac Watts*, N. Y., privately printed, 1918, pp. 74-81).

It is hard to realize that *Paradise Lost* could ever have been thought of in the same class as these melancholy moralizings long since forgotten; yet such was unquestionably the position it held in the minds of hundreds of religious persons who were largely indifferent to its esthetic qualities. Even among the educated, the religious aspect of Milton's work gained it no few readers and imitators in a century that laid preponderant stress on the moral and spiritual side of literature.[1] Thus it was that among the earliest uses to which the verse and style of the Christian epic were put was the religious, and that among the writers most ready to follow Milton were dissenting clergymen (like Isaac Watts and his friends), some of whose poems enjoyed great popularity and probably had considerable influence.[2] As blank verse came to be more generally adopted, those who employed it for religious poetry naturally became more numerous; yet for a long time they confined most of their efforts to short pieces, principally to paraphrases of chapters in the Bible.[3] About the middle of the century their number was considerably augmented through the bequest of the Rev. Thomas Seaton, who in 1741 left his estate to the University of Cambridge on condition that the income should be given annually to the master of arts who wrote the best poem on "the Perfections or Attributes of the Supreme Being," or some similar subject. It was further stipulated that the successful piece should be printed.

The prize was first won in 1750 by the erratic and unfortunate Christopher Smart, whose poem *On the Eternity of the Supreme Being* begins thus:

> Hail, wond'rous Being, who in pow'r supreme
> Exists from everlasting, whose great name
> Deep in the human heart, and every atom
> The Air, the Earth or azure Main contains
> In undecypher'd characters is wrote —
> INCOMPREHENSIBLE! — O what can words,
> The weak interpreters of mortal thoughts,
> Or what can thoughts (tho' wild of wing they rove
> Thro' the vast concave of th' aetherial round). . . .

As Smart received the prize the three following years, and again in 1755, and as his poems are all in the same style as the first, he not only pointed out the path which the winners of Seatonian laurels should take but gave them a good start on it.[4] His example was sedulously followed; for of the forty-six successful poems published

---

[1] See pp. 33–6 above.   [2] See pp. 102–4, 109–12, above.
[3] I have noticed nineteen paraphrases, mainly of Psalms, from 1712 to 1751.
[4] For Smart's other poems, see pp. 365–6 above.

between 1750 and 1806 all but seven copy *Paradise Lost* in their verse and style,[1] many of them keeping closer to it than Smart does, besides often borrowing its words, phrases, and ideas. These thirty-nine poetical exercises by no means represent all the verse of the kind that was written in the competition, for some of the efforts published by unsuccessful aspirants are quite as Miltonic as those which won the prize.[2]

These Seaton pieces, which were very numerous and fairly regular in their appearance, must have had not a little influence upon the religious verse of the time. One unrimed religious poem of some length had, however, been written several years before the prize was awarded, Thomas Hobson's *Christianity the Light of the Moral World*, an attempt to prove that morality needs the light of revealed religion.[3] Hobson copies the verse of *Paradise Lost* in this fashion:

> The palpable obscure
> Of antient *Chaos* and her *Sister-Night*
> Confounded fled. All nature smil'd serene. . . .
> At thy approach, if philosophic minds
> Conjecture truth, the vegetable race
> Spontaneous kindled into fragrant life.[4]

The versified sermons, like many other eighteenth-century publications, were often issued without the names of their authors, — an indication, it may be hoped, of some doubt in the writers' minds as to their inspiration. Such self-distrust would certainly have been

---

[1] All but those for 1760, 1761, 1762 (these three by the same man), 1781, 1783, 1785, 1790. Some years the prize seems not to have been awarded, for the *Cambridge Prize Poems* (2 vols., 1808), which professes to be complete to 1806, gives but forty-six in fifty-seven years; and occasionally, as in 1775, two prizes were given in the same year. One of the pieces that does not employ Milton's blank verse, the poem for 1762, is clearly influenced by his octosyllabics.

[2] See Bibl. I, 1757 (Bally), 1804 (Wrangham), and perhaps 1771 (Roberts). *The Redemption, a Monody*, by James Scott, which failed to receive the prize in 1763 but is printed in the *Cambridge Prize Poems* volumes (i. 323-32), is modelled on *Lycidas*.

[3] Hobson's work, published in 1745, was composed "above eight years" earlier (see p. 15).

[4] Page 22 ("the palpable obscure" is from *P. L.*, ii. 406). A few of the other phrases borrowed directly from Milton are: "darkness spread Her black pavilion" (p. 18, cf. *P. L.*, ii. 960); "sin-born Death" (p. 34, cf. *P. L.*, x. 596); "orient beam" (p. 34, cf. *P. L.*, iv. 644, of the sun in each case); "universal frame" (p. 37, cf. *P. L.*, v. 154, of the universe in each case); "optic tube" (p. 46, cf. *P. L.*, iii. 590, of the telescope in each case); "self-balanc'd . . . hangs" (p. 56, cf. *P. L.*, vii. 242);

> Whate'er is dark
> Illuminates, whate'er is low, exalts . . .
> Enlightens all the ways of God to man

(pp. 50-51, cf. *P. L.*, i. 22-6). Between the title and the first line of the poem a passage from *Paradise Lost* is quoted.

warranted in the case of four long religious poems that appeared anonymously during the first two decades after Thomas Seaton endowed the religious muse. The first of these, *The Great Shepherd, a Sacred Pastoral* (1757), consists of three dialogues that relate to the creation of man, his fall, and his restoration through the coming of Christ. Presumably it is under some debt to *Paradise Lost* for its subject-matter, as it certainly is for its style in expressions like "rocks th' astonish'd earth" and "descending dreadful to the dark abyss." [1]

The *Great Shepherd* was termed by the *Monthly Review* a "sublime pastoral," an "uncommon and elegant poem"; but most religious verse did not fare so well. The author of the *Visitations of the Almighty, Part the First* (1759), seems, indeed, to have received so little encouragement that the visitations ceased. This first part employs Miltonic blank verse to portray famines and pestilences; the three subsequent ones were to present a veritable orgy of disasters, "Insurrections, War, Land-Hurricanes, Sea-Storms, Inundations, fiery Eruptions from Volcanoes, Earthquakes and Conflagrations"! [2] Is it any wonder that reviewers of the first book of the anonymous *Messiah* (1763) shuddered, "Another sacred poem! dear good religious gentlemen, why must we so often repeat to you, that poetry and Christianity will never mingle properly together?" The "good and pious sentiments" of the author, continued the critic, if "thrown into honest prose, might furnish . . . a tolerable . . . sermon, though, as a poem, it is altogether contemptible." [3] As to the justice of this opinion, and as to the model after which the unknown author patterned his style, the reader may judge for himself:

> In being *frail*,
> To *Adam*, justly, we impute the cause;
> But for *Damnation*, thine, not *Adam's* guilt,
> Incurs the punishment, and gives a hell.
> Offended wrath, cease, therefore, to arraign. [4]

If these lines are not a sufficient illustration of the dearth of literary feeling and power in most of the religious bards, one has

---

[1] *Mo. Rev.*, xvi. 400–402. I have not seen the poem. Another anonymous piece, *Wisdom*, which was published six years earlier (1751), consists of some 250 lines of tumid Miltonic blank verse devoted to religious platitudes.

[2] *Mo. Rev.*, xx. 17–20. I have not seen the piece. Of James Ogden's poem, *On the Crucifixion and Resurrection* (1762), I know nothing except that it is unrimed and that it did not impress the *Critical Review* (xiii. 363–4).

[3] *Crit. Rev.*, xvii. 318. The poem, which I have not seen, consists of four parts, published separately, *The Nativity, The Temptation, The Crucifixion,* and *The Resurrection* (*ib.* 318–20, 472, and xviii. 320).

[4] *Ib.* xvii. 319.

only to turn to the long, anonymous paraphrase of Ecclesiastes published in 1768 as *Choheleth, or the Royal Preacher*. In the tedious circumlocutions of this work, the haunting verse, "Or ever . . . the golden bowl be broken, or the pitcher be broken at the fountain, or the wheel broken at the cistern," reappears as,

> The precious Golden Bowl itself, of frame
> Stupendous, or shrunk up, or overstretch'd,
> No longer can, with fresh recruit, supply
> Th' exhausted spirits. Gasping Nature sighs
> In vain for succour. At the Fountain-head,
> The shatter'd Pitcher can no more receive
> The vital Fluid; nor the circling Wheel
> Raise from its Reservoir, and swift repell
> The purple Current thence to parts remote.[1]

After moralizings like this, the reader may be glad to see eddies or ripples of any kind in the sluggish stream of eighteenth-century religious verse; and, if he is curious as to how the clergymen of the day practised what they preached, he may derive unhallowed satisfaction from the career of the Rev. William Dodd.[2] Dodd was known as the editor of a very popular *Beauties of Shakspere* (1752),[3] as the author of a volume of poems (1767), and as a king's chaplain whom Cambridge had made a doctor of laws; but he was most commonly thought of as the "macaroni parson," whose affecting sermons drew large audiences. He dressed elaborately, lived extravagantly, and kept fast company; there were stories afloat of tavern dinners, gambling, and intrigues with women; and he was known to have tried to get a rich living through bribery, but after a short absence in France he returned to undiminished popularity. The extravagance, with its resulting debts, which had brought him into this last difficulty led him afterwards to forge the name of his pupil, Lord Chesterfield, to a bond for £4,200. His crime was immediately detected, he was arrested and condemned to be hanged, and, though Dr. Johnson wrote a number of addresses and prayers for him and Earl Percy presented the king with a petition for clemency signed by twenty-three thousand persons, the sentence was carried out. Notoriety had only increased his popularity, and his execution was one of the famous sights of the time.

[1] Pages 121–2 (Ecclesiastes, xii. 6).
[2] Dodd might well have formed the subject of one of the "Moral Tales in Verse" which Thomas Hull of the Covent Garden theater published in 1797, and which included a blank-verse poem on the *Advantages of Repentance*, that had first appeared in 1776.
[3] Often reprinted up to 1880, and still in print. It is said to have been through this volume that Goethe became acquainted with Shakespeare.

While in Newgate awaiting death Dodd wrote a long blank-verse poem, *Thoughts in Prison* (1777), which from its character and the circumstances attending its composition naturally found many readers. Written as it was by a vain sentimentalist, weak-willed but kind-hearted, fond of theatrical effects and craving publicity even in his private affairs, the book is filled with gloomy reflections on the weakness of mankind, with the culprit's forgiveness of his enemies, and with his Christian resignation, with everything, in short, but an adequate realization of his own remissness and folly. From a literary standpoint it is worthless, — "vapid, stilted, unprofitable," his biographer calls it.[1] In subject-matter and tone, as well as in title, its debt to the *Night Thoughts* is apparent; but the style is less ejaculatory and more Miltonic, as will be seen from this description of prison life:

> Hear how those veterans clank, — even jovial clank,
> Such is obduracy in vice, their chains! . . .
>   . . . . Not exulting more
> Heroes or chiefs for noble acts renown'd,
> Holding high converse, mutually relate
> Gallant atchievements worthy; than the sons
> Of Plunder and of Rapine *here* recount
> On peaceful life their devastations wild;
> Their dangers, hair-breadth 'scapes, atrocious feats,
> Confederate.[2]

This book was not Dodd's first tribute to Milton. More than twenty-five years before, when a young Oxonian, he had published an unrimed, mock-heroic *Day in Vacation at College* (1751), and in 1758 had followed this with eleven hundred lines of blank verse which he termed *Thoughts on the Glorious Epiphany of the Lord Jesus Christ*. The aim of this rambling, diffuse, tedious preachment, Miltonic in diction and in such inversions as "a squadron to behold of port divine," was to arouse a desire for the second advent of Christ by painting "the glories of his coming, and the happiness of it to believers."[3] In a volume of his poems published nine years later Dodd had included two more pieces of Miltonic blank verse, four odes modelled on *Allegro* and *Penseroso* (one of them in the meter and style of *Paradise Lost*), and a prologue to *Comus*.[4] Mean-

---

[1] Percy Fitzgerald, *A Famous Forgery* (1865), 123. On Dodd, see also Boswell's *Johnson* (ed. Hill), iii. 120–22, 139–48, 270–71. The *Critical Review* (xliv. 218–21) was both impressed and moved by the *Thoughts*, finding "in almost every page . . . an appearance of the author's unfeigned contrition, piety, and benevolence."

[2] Part iii, pp. 54–5, of the edition printed at Exeter, New Hampshire, 1794.

[3] See line 580, and page vii.

[4] See below, Bibl. I, 1760 w., 1767; II, 1759 w., 1760 w., 1767; and *Poems* (1767), 88.

while he had prepared his *Familiar Explanation* of Milton's works (1762),[1] and, as if this were not enough, he later quoted five lines from the epic on the title-page of his *Thoughts in Prison*. Yet, as his poems seem to contain none of the usual references to Milton and no phrases borrowed from his works, it is doubtful if the flashy, fashionable preacher was well acquainted with the writings of the stern Puritan, if his use of the style or the plan of Milton's poems meant anything more than that these were the models then in vogue.

Dodd was but one of a host of eighteenth-century clergymen who were given to versifying. Many of them doubtless got their effusions into print, as the Rev. Charles Billinge did his *Poems on Christian Charity, Contentment, and Melancholy* (1784), "by the concurrence of a very respectable and numerous List of Subscribers"[2] who admired the author and perhaps knew little about poetry. Billinge's work, though quite as dull and even more stiltedly Miltonic in style and diction than are the other pieces of its class, has at least the virtue of being short, whereas William Gilbank's *Day of Pentecost* (1789) contains twelve books. The title is a misnomer; for the piece is not particularly concerned with the gift of tongues, but aims to give a "comprehensive view of our religion, as it is supported by a long chain of extraordinary facts, and striking interpositions of Providence, recorded in the sacred histories." The scenes in heaven are modelled after Milton, "whose style and manner," the reviewer observes, "Mr. Gilbank not improperly, but feebly imitates," and without concealing the imitation, since he "apologises in his preface for introducing some well-known lines from Milton and Shakspeare."[3]

The year that favored the world with Gilbank's lengthy lucubrations also gave it another work of the same kind, and, notwithstanding its seven editions, of the same negative excellence, — the Rev. Joseph Swain's *Redemption*. Its first book, "The Primitive State and Fall of Man," owes something to the contents of *Paradise Lost*, and the style and language of the entire work, though commonplace enough, are frequently as Miltonic as in these lines:

> Satan perhaps exulted. He might think
> God's ancient purpose frustrate; all the fruit
> Of his high counsel in creating man
> Abortive rendered, and this embryo world
> His own dominion, where to range at large.[4]

---

[1] See above, p. 25.   [2] Preface, p. iv.

[3] *Crit. Rev.*, lxvii. 351–4. I have not seen the poem.

[4] First American ed. (Boston, 1812), p. 66. The poem originally consisted of five books, but in the second edition was extended to eight. The *Monthly Review* thought poorly of it, giving Swain the dubious title, "a middling poet" (enl. ed., ii. 459–61).

On a granite obelisk near Southampton are the words, "The grave of Robert Pollok, author of *The Course of Time:* His immortal Poem is his monument," [1] — an interesting contrast to that other inscription, carved about the same time, "Here lies one whose name was writ in water." No one reads the *Course of Time* to-day, nor is there any reason for reading it. It is a long work of three hundred pages, purporting to be an account of life on earth related in heaven to spirits from other worlds. There is a great deal of diffuse moralizing of an obvious kind, but little apparent system. Hell and heaven are described, and almost every aspect of earthly existence is reviewed from a narrowly religious standpoint; nature descriptions and illustrative episodes are introduced; and the closing books picture the last ages of the world, its final destruction, and the day of judgment. An undertaking of this kind is typical of the eighteenth century, and the appearance of such a work in 1827 shows how slowly the influence of the romantic poets made itself felt. The poem is, indeed, a later *Night Thoughts* in the style and manner of *The Task;* for, aside from Milton, Pollok's literary enthusiasms were Young and Cowper, poets representative of the age that was past. If we miss the homelike charm and the incisive, vigorous expression which mark Cowper at his best, we are at least spared the hollow, declamatory pessimism of Young and the pompous involutions of eighteenth-century blank verse. The influence of the newer poetry was at work, but it had not gone far. The *Course of Time* is easy reading, and pleasant if one skips the moralizing and does not read too long. It is sincere,

Another writer who "of Redemption made damned work" was William Williams, a young law-student, who planned to issue a book of his *Redemption, with Notes, Doctrinal, Moral, and Philosophical,* every three months; but fortunately only the first book of his dull discourse, which is slightly Miltonic in style, seems to have got into print (see *Mo. Rev.,* 1796, enl. ed., xxi. 226–7). I have not seen this poem, or the three which Mason Chamberlin published in 1800 and 1801 as *Equanimity, Harvest,* and *Ocean,* and of which the *Monthly Review* said (enl. ed., xxxiii. 429–30, xxxvi. 437–8, and cf. *Crit. Rev.,* new arr., xxxi. 112): "The first of these poems is in fact a sermon in blank verse, on the text *In patience possess your souls;* and the latter may be considered as a composition of the same description, on the subject of *grateful piety and trust in God.* . . . texts of scripture are very liberally interwoven, which often produce a prosaic effect. . . . We cannot compliment Mr. C. as manifesting the fervid glow of poetic sentiment," — which, to judge from the extracts given, is putting it mildly. The style shows some influence from *Paradise Lost.* George Townsend's *Armageddon,* in twelve books, eight of which were published in 1815, is called extravagant and absurd by the *Eclectic Review* (new series, iv. 392–5). God and Christ are characters and the style is patterned on Milton's.

[1] The inscription was of course none of his doing. Four editions of the *Course of Time* were sold within a year, and the seventy-eighth thousand was published in 1868. A striking testimony to the high repute in which Pollok was held is the fifty-page essay, "Sacred Poetry, Milton and Pollok," which was published as late as 1861 in T. McNicoll's *Essays on English Literature.*

comparatively natural in expression, and at times impressive, but it lacks vigor, is diffuse, and soon becomes monotonous. It has not proved "immortal," for it has no spark of the divine fire. Yet, when one learns that it was written by a high-minded youth of twenty-seven who died of overwork the year it was published, one hesitates to mention anything but the unusual talents that the poem certainly exhibits.

Pollok's style, though similar to Cowper's, is much more Miltonic. It is, indeed, strangely so for a work that appeared the same year as Tennyson's first volume; but here again it belongs with the eighteenth century. Inversions occur in almost every line, adjectives are commonly used for adverbs, and words that would be expressed in prose are frequently omitted. The diction, however, recalls Milton's only in the scenes in heaven, which are among Pollok's best and, as might be expected, are closely modelled on those in *Paradise Lost*. I shall quote not from any of these passages, but from a more characteristic one devoted to Byron:

> As some fierce comet of tremendous size,
> To which the stars did reverence as it passed,
> So he, through learning and through fancy, took
> His flight sublime, and on the loftiest top
> Of Fame's dread mountain sat; not soiled and worn,
> As if he from the earth had laboured up;
> But as some bird of heavenly plumage fair,
> He looked, which down from higher regions came,
> And perched it there, to see what lay beneath.[1]

We who think of the first third of the nineteenth century as the period of Byron, Wordsworth, Shelley, and Keats are likely to be disconcerted when we find what the people of the time actually read and wrote, when we learn that after these men were dead or had ceased composing, and even after two of Tennyson's volumes had appeared, verses quite as inflated and absurdly Miltonic in expression as Philips's *Cyder* were still being composed. One of these works was indeed by a later Phillips, who, however, spelled his name with two *l*'s and was called William instead of John. His poem, *Mount Sinai*, which appeared in 1830 with a dedication accepted by the king, narrates in four books the giving of the ten commandments, the making of the golden calf, and the building of the ark of the

---

[1] iv. 720–28. Pollok refers to Milton in vi. 68–72, ix. 500–511. His brother writes that Robert first read *Paradise Lost* when he was in his eighteenth year, and was immediately "captivated with it . . . from that time Milton became his favourite author and, . . . next to the Bible, his chief companion. Henceforward, he read more or less of him almost every day" (*Life*, by David Pollok, 1843, p. 19).

covenant. In the preface he announces, "I have adhered to the metrical economy of Milton, as preferable to that of numbers of more modern extraction." But "metrical economy" and "numbers" must have been elastic terms to Phillips, covering style and diction no less than prosody, as will appear from these lines, by no means the most inflated in the poem:

> In robes of living light,
> Before Jehovah, so effulgent he [Moses]
> That mortal sense had fancied him resolved
> As 'twere to featured empyrèan fire.
> His glowing hands the Tables of the Law
> Tenacious held, and from his upward eye
> Flash'd pious ecstacy. Replete arose
> The fragrant sweets of calamus, and stacte . . .
> Effused in ether.[1]

Mount Sinai was not the last religious poem to employ the excessive and objectionable Miltonisms that distinguish eighteenth-century blank verse. These are almost as marked in some of the numerous effusions of Robert Montgomery, the natural son of a professional clown and a schoolmistress, who shot like a comet across the heaven of popular favor. When but twenty-one Montgomery published a piece in heroic couplets, *The Omnipresence of the Deity* (1828), which ran through "eight editions in as many months" and by 1855 reached the twenty-eighth separate reprinting. Thereafter work followed work in rapid succession, until in the collected editions of 1840 and 1841 his complete poems filled six volumes. Many of these pieces are short and not a few of them are rimed; but several are long works in blank verse, *Satan, or Intellect without God* (1830, tenth edition 1842), *The Messiah* (1832, eighth edition 1842), *Luther* (1842, sixth edition 1852). Very likely the reader has never heard of any of these productions and would be unable to obtain them in either bookstores or libraries; yet their author receives more space in Allibone's *Dictionary of Authors* than is allotted to Coleridge, and his *Satan*, we are told, "ran through more editions, and suddenly elicited more contemporary fame than the publication of any poet since the death of Byron." [2]

In Macaulay's remorseless exposure of the emptiness of Montgomery's poems,[3] their vogue is attributed to "the modern practice

---

[1] Pages 131-2. A year after the appearance of Phillips's narrative another unrimed poem with a similar title, *Mount Sion*, was published by John Newby Mosby (*Fall of Algiers*, Doncaster, 1831, pp. 359-418). This production, which fills sixty pages with a vision of the day of judgment, is a dull enough copy of the style and particularly the diction of *Paradise Lost*, though less absurdly Miltonic than its predecessor.

[2] *Dict. Nat. Biog.*   [3] *Edin. Rev.*, li. 193-210.

of puffing," but it was probably due quite as much to the fluency of their grandiloquent expression of sentimental religious platitudes. For, with the exception of *The Messiah*, which recounts the life of Christ, nearly all of Montgomery's effusions are really sermons, with considerably more of nature but no less of rambling verbosity than such productions often manifest. Much of Macaulay's characterization of *Satan* is applicable to the other poems, — "a long soliloquy . . . concerning geography, politics, newspapers, fashionable society, theatrical amusements, Sir Walter Scott's novels, Lord Byron's poetry, and Mr. Martin's pictures," which "always returns" to the "preaching tone." [1]

Some of Montgomery's blank verse is colorless and conversational; but as a rule, since he was quite without originality, he naturally copied the unrimed religious poetry of the preceding hundred and fifty years, stiffening his style freely with inversions, adjectives used for adverbs, and other Miltonisms, though, unlike most imitators of *Paradise Lost*, borrowing no words or phrases from it. Lines like these are typical:

> Inaudibly, along a darken'd stage
> Of wonders, moves the lone Almighty now,
> Himself evolving what His love decrees
> Inscrutable, by boasting man unshared.
> And e'en like Philip to Azotus rapt,
> Sightless, or lost, shall Luther for a while
> Appear; and safe in castled shade retire.[2]

So unblushing an imitation might have been expected a hundred years earlier, but to find such lines not only written but widely admired in Tennyson's day is surprising. Still more curious is it that a popular religious poet should copy and even try to look like that antichrist of his time, Lord Byron! Doubtless it was the desire to be grand and impressive that led him to choose such models; but, whatever the cause, there can be little question of the influence of *Manfred* on the opening lines of *Satan*, which represent Montgomery at his best:

> Awake, ye thunders! — and with gloomy roar
> Deepen around me, while a darkness shrouds
> The air, as once again this World I greet
> Here on the haughty mountain, where of old
> The God Incarnate, in the heavens re-throned,
> Was tempted and withstood me. Lo! the powers

---

[1] *Ib.* 209–10. The work receives its title from Satan, who utters the soliloquy; but, as Macaulay suggests (*ib.* 210), if "about a hundred lines in different parts of this large volume" were omitted or altered, it might be republished "under the name of *Gabriel.*"

[2] *Luther*, section on "Moral Results," *Poetical Works* (1854), 217–18.

Of Nature, by my dread command sublimed,
Mount into rage, and magnify the storm
To elemental grandeur; while as Prince
By whom the spirit-peopled air is bound
In bondage, from my viewless throne I gaze,
Prompting the Tempest.

Montgomery's blaze of popularity was the most brilliant, if not the last,[1] flare from the feeble torch held up for the guidance of benighted mankind in unrimed religious verse.[2] The extinction of the beacon, or of what essayed to be one, attracted no attention, and even had it been observed would have called forth only rejoicings from most readers. For, we are assured, "the extreme difficulty of exhibiting religious subjects in a poetical dress" had "long been seen and confessed."[3] The critics certainly confessed their feelings frankly enough. "We do not object to the piety, but poetry of the author," they said of one "sacred poem";[4] and against another they turned Pope's lines,

To laugh, were want of goodness and of grace;
But to be grave, exceeds all power of face.[5]

And they were right. The religious poetry written in blank verse during the eighteenth and the first part of the nineteenth centuries consisted almost entirely of the tedious moralizings of uninspired clergymen who had either no message to deliver or no ability to deliver it in verse.

It is easy to throw the blame on the low state of religion or of poetry in the eighteenth century, and unquestionably both were responsible. Yet it was during this century that the great Wesleyan revival shook England, and surely Cowper, Smart, Pollok, and Grahame were genuinely religious men. During what period, indeed, except Milton's own, has religion been "married to immortal verse," and particularly to verse of considerable length? The truth is that the religious muse, though often invoked, has seldom responded, and

[1] So late as 1866 E. H. Bickersteth, Bishop of Exeter, frankly used both the substance and the style of *Paradise Lost* in the twelve books of his *Yesterday, To-day, and For Ever*.

[2] In the United States, where literary and other styles began and ended later, poems of this kind appeared occasionally throughout the nineteenth century. A few that I have chanced upon (all published in New York) are *Abaddon, the Spirit of Destruction*, by Sumner L. Fairfield, 1830; *Anastasis*, and *The Temptation of the Wilderness*, by Thomas Curtis, 1850; *Christ in Hades*, by W. W. Lord, 1851; *Satan Chain'd*, by Nathaniel Dunn, 1875.

[3] *Mo. Rev.*, enl. ed., xxi. 226 (1796).

[4] *Crit. Rev.*, lxvii. 352 (1789).

[5] *Mo. Rev.*, xliv. 90 (1771); *Epistle to Arbuthnot*, 35–6.

then usually for "short swallow flights of song." In the eighteenth century she was not so often summoned for long unrimed works as would be expected from the vogue of Milton, Mrs. Rowe, and Young, and from the large number of versifying clergymen. Even counting the *Night Thoughts*, *The Task*, and the religious epics, I find only forty or fifty pieces of the kind issued in the first two hundred years after the publication of *Paradise Lost*.

The failure of the greater part of these can be attributed only in part to the use of blank verse, for their authors' rimed pieces are no better.[1] In many cases, to be sure, rime may have been discarded in order to save trouble, — a boomerang policy, since blank verse, though one of the easiest mediums to use, is perhaps the hardest to use effectively; and during the eighteenth century, when so few of its difficulties had been mastered, the freedom it offered was, like that of the irregular Pindaric, fatal to mediocrity. There was in the meter of *Paradise Lost* the additional disadvantage that, when mediocre bards adopted it, they also adopted many if not most of the peculiarities of style and diction that went with it, and these involved Miltonisms made their work seem forced and artificial, rather than the simple, direct expression of deep conviction.

[1] A notable exception is Smart's *Song to David*, which is a religious lyric.

PART III

THE SHORTER POEMS

CHAPTER XVII

LATE VOGUE OF THE SHORTER POEMS

THE Augustans were essentially non-lyric. Their lack of imagination, the emphasis they laid upon reason, propriety, and form, and their avoidance, in verse, of any expression, of ecstasy or tender personal feeling, all these were fatal to song. For over a century, in consequence, the lyric impulse was dead in England. Lyrics there were, to be sure, and some good ones, but hardly so many as a single year produced in the spacious times of Elizabeth and James. Even the beauty of the Restoration songs is the beauty of decay; and years before Pope began to lisp in numbers the impulse to sing and the power of song were practically gone, not to reappear until the eve of the nineteenth century.[1]

It must not be thought that the disappearance of song was due merely to a mistaken theory of what poetry is; the causes were deeper than that. The qualities that lie at the heart of the lyric — spontaneity, intensity, subjectivity — were gone from verse and with them had departed the singing voice. Interest in lyric poetry had likewise ceased, for the Augustans were apparently as little inclined to listen to outpourings from the hearts of others as to pour themselves out in song. Most lyrics probably seemed to them a bit silly, bordering on bad taste, or lacking in reserve, if not, like Shakespeare's sonnets, actually dull. Real ecstasy they disliked, hence the failure of Smart's superb *Song to David* to find an audience; fine poetic feeling and delicacy of fancy were beyond most of them, hence Collins's *Odes* did not sell and so late as 1789 Blake's *Songs of Innocence* fell on deaf ears; hence, too, what is more to our purpose, for many years Milton's minor poems found almost no admirers.

If *Lycidas* is, as Tennyson once asserted, "a touchstone of poetic taste,"[2] there must have been little sensitiveness to the finer qualities

---

[1] If conservative dates are desired, 1687 (the death of Waller, the completion of Locke's *Essay concerning Human Understanding*, and the publication of Newton's *Principia*) or 1688 (the Revolution and the birth of Pope), and 1786 (the Kilmarnock Burns) or 1783 (Blake's *Poetical Sketches*) may be taken; but the period could with safety be extended ten years at each end, particularly at the latter, since Burns's songs were in no respect the product of the English literature of his time and Blake's found no readers.

[2] See a letter from Edward Fitzgerald to Fanny Kemble, March 26, 1880. The same idea had been expressed by Thomas Warton in his edition of Milton's minor poems (1785, p. 34), and by Miss Seward (*Letters*, 1811, i. 191).

in verse throughout the century following the Restoration; for Milton's monody, though published in 1638 and reissued along with his other short poems in 1645, was rarely mentioned before 1740. Nor were any of its companions generally appreciated until they had been at least a hundred years in print. This neglect is the more surprising because by 1740 the pieces had appeared in at least ten editions of Milton's complete poems,[1] and had been published by themselves twice in English (1645, 1673) and once in French (1730). Moreover, *Paradise Regained, Samson, Lycidas*, and *Comus* had been turned into Latin by William Hog (1690–98), and *Allegro, Penseroso*, and *Lycidas* had been included in two editions of Dryden's popular *Miscellany* (1716, 1727). Much has been made, too much, of the failure of *Paradise Lost* to win immediate recognition; yet little surprise has been expressed that the minor poems, though published twenty-two years before the epic, attracted slight attention for as many years after it had achieved popularity.[2] In the numerous early references to Milton it is almost always *Paradise Lost* that is mentioned,[3] and even such writers as allude to the shorter pieces usually seem not to expect their readers to be familiar with them.

It is not strange, therefore, that in the period of approximately a century between their publication and 1742 the total number of pieces thus far discovered which show any influence from the various minor poems,[4] except in borrowed phrases, is only forty-two, and that of these only two, Parnell's *Hymn on Contentment* and Dyer's *Grongar Hill*, were generally known or of much importance. Yet there was no prejudice like that against blank verse to stand in the way of these lyrics, nor would their general character lead one to expect such neglect; for they are not mysterious or dithyrambic, but deal with universal feelings and have the restraint, the impersonality, the quiet, and the careful workmanship which are the delight of the true classicist. One can see that the Augustans might not have cared for the ecstatic *Song to David* or the strange, childlike *Songs of Innocence;* but their indifference to *Allegro, Penseroso, Comus*, and *Ly-*

---

[1] It is impossible without examining each edition (which I have been unable to do) to say just how many were published. The "Poetical Works" usually appeared in two volumes, which were sold separately; and, as there was more demand for the first volume, *Paradise Lost*, a single issue of the remaining poems seems often to have sufficed for two or more editions of the "Works." I can find evidence for only nine printings of the complete minor poems before 1740.

[2] That is, after the publication of the *Spectator* papers in 1712.

[3] See pp. 8–9 above.

[4] Except the poem *To Aristus*, the sonnet in the *London Magazine* for July, 1738, and that by Philip Yorke, which were influenced by Milton's sonnets (see below, pp. 489–90).

cidas gives rise to the suspicion that most of them were deaf to the subtler harmonies of poetry. No doubt there were many readers whose attention had never been called to the lyrics, but, as thousands of copies were sold, a large number of persons must at one time or another at least have glanced them over. In the first half of the eighteenth century there were probably many who agreed with what Johnson said of *Lycidas:* "The diction is harsh, the rhymes uncertain, and the numbers unpleasing. What beauty there is we must therefore seek in the sentiments and images. . . . In this poem there is no nature, for there is no truth; there is no art, for there is nothing new. Its form is that of a pastoral, easy, vulgar, and therefore disgusting."[1] In 1783 an admirer of the poem acknowledged its "incorrectness" and doubted if it "should be considered as a model of composition."[2] Even the open-minded Dryden seems not to have cared for Milton's minor poems. "Rhyme was not his talent," he declares; "he had neither the ease of doing it, nor the graces of it; which is manifest in his *Juvenilia*, or verses written in his youth, where his rhyme is always constrained and forced, and comes hardly from him."[3]

In this matter Pope had broader sympathies than his predecessor, for he praised the "Juvenilia," lent them to a friend, and even in his earliest publications used many phrases from them.[4] His opponent, Lewis Theobald, the original hero of *The Dunciad*, explained that "the general Beauties of those two Poems of MILTON, intitled, *L'Allegro* and *Il Penseroso*, are obvious to all Readers, because the Descriptions are the most poetical in the World."[5] The poet laureate Nahum Tate, who was also pilloried in *The Dunciad*, seems to have taken a phrase from *Allegro* and the suggestion for an entire poem

---

[1] "Milton," in *Lives* (ed. Hill), i. 163. This was no chance utterance; he told Miss Seward "he would hang a dog that read the Lycidas twice" (see her *Letters*, i. 66).

[2] John Scott, *Critical Essays* (1785), 63–4. Scott says, however (p. 38), that Johnson in his account of *Lycidas* 'widely dissented from the *vox populi*.' As late as 1804 John Aikin, a critic of good standing, wrote that it was "a poem of a peculiar cast, concerning which you will probably find it difficult to fix your judgment. . . . The constructions are . . . occasionally harsh, and the language obscure . . . yet there are passages in which I think you cannot fail to recognise the master-hand of a true poet" (*Letters on English Poetry*, 2d ed., 1807, pp. 125–6).

[3] *Essay on Satire* (*Works*, Scott-Saintsbury ed., xiii. 20). Dryden may, to be sure, have liked the poems apart from their rimes.

[4] See above, p. 115; and below, Appendix A.

[5] Preface to his edition of Shakespeare (1733), pp. xix–xx. Pointed out by George Sherburn in his *Early Popularity of Milton's Minor Poems* (*Modern Philology*, xvii. 259–78, 515–40). I am indebted to Mr. Sherburn's articles (which appeared after this chapter was finished) for some ten or fifteen references that are acknowledged in my notes.

from the little-known *Nativity* ode.[1] Nor was Addison's devotion restricted to the epic. Allan Ramsay's correspondent, who thought
Milton's masque "the best ever written . . . in the Praise of which no
Words can be too many," remembered to have heard "the late excellent Mr. Addison" agree with him in that opinion.[2] To *Allegro*
Addison gave the tribute of imitation, for his *Ode for St. Cecilia's Day*,
which was sung at Oxford in 1699, has the lines,

> Next let the solemn organ join
> Religious airs and strains divine,
> Such as may lift us to the skies,
> And set all heaven before our eyes.[3]

Later he wrote in the *Spectator:* "Milton, in a joyous assembly of
imaginary persons, has given us a very poetical figure of laughter.
His whole band of mirth is so finely described, that I shall set down
the passage at length."[4] The way in which *Allegro* is here referred
to seems to indicate that the poem was not well known, an inference
certainly warranted by another passage in the same periodical. "In
this sweet retirement," writes the unknown contributor, "I naturally
fell into the repetition of some lines out of a poem of Milton's, which
he entitles Il Penseroso, the ideas of which were exquisitely suited
to my present wanderings of thought."[5] A similar conclusion in
regard to *Comus* may be drawn from Steele's remark about "a passage in a mask writ by *Milton*, where two brothers are introduced
seeking after their sister, whom they had lost in a dark night and
thick wood";[6] and from Francis Peck's reference, ten years later, to
"the immortal Milton['s] . . . *Circe*, a beautiful Piece of *Doric* or
Pastoral Poetry, most of it written in Blank Verse, wrought into a
Mask, and presented at *Ludlow* Castle . . . [which] is printed in the
Second Volume of his Poetical Works."[7] In much the same way
John Hughes, who praised and copied the companion pieces, referred
in 1715 to the "Poem call'd *Il Penseroso*" and "a Mask, by our
famous *Milton;* the whole Plan of which is Allegorical, and is written
with a very Poetical Spirit."[8] So, too, Zachary Pearce alluded to an
expression "us'd by *M.* in his Poem call'd *L'Allegro*."[9] These re-

---

[1] The phrase "Wood-wild Notes," in his poem prefixed to Gildon's *History of the
Athenian Society* (1693?), may be, as Mr. Sherburn points out (p. 522), from *Allegro*,
134. For the debt to the *Nativity*, see pp. 566–7 below.

[2] See note to Ramsay's *Nuptials* (*Poems*, 1728, ii. 143).

[3] *Works* (Bohn ed.), vi. 534.   [5] No. 425.

[4] No. 249.   [6] *Tatler*, no. 98.

[7] *Sighs upon the Death of Queen Anne* (1719), p. xiv.

[8] In his edition of Spenser (1715), vol. i, pp. xxxvii, xxxix. Cf. pp. 442–3 below.

[9] *Review of the Text of P. L.* (1733), 93. In support of the received text of the epic,
Pearce quotes Milton's usage in his other works, referring to *Lycidas* once, to the octo-

marks, and the fact that Thomas Parnell, who died in 1718, named a character in one of his songs Comus and twice imitated *Allegro*,[1] indicate that the leading classicists knew the 1645 volume but the people in general did not.

Yet the early pieces were not entirely without admirers among less cultivated readers. In 1691, for example, the *Athenian Mercury* declared the "Poems . . . on Mirth and Melancholly, an Elegy on his Friend that was drown'd, and especially a Fragment of the Passion [!]" to be "incomparable"; [2] and so early as 1657, in Joshua Poole's *English Parnassus*, "nearly the whole of the Ode on the Nativity is inserted in different extracts; the quotations from L'Allegro are copious; and lines are given from Lycidas and other pieces." [3] These infrequent instances of justice to the poems,[4] however, only accentuate the general indifference and render it harder to understand. Other books of extracts, like Cotgrave's *English Treasury of Wit and Language* (1655) and Bysshe's *Art of English Poetry* (1702), contain nothing from Milton's early writings, although the latter quotes extensively from *Paradise Lost*. It was not till 1733 that commentators used the "Juvenilia" to throw light upon the epic; before 1730 very few of the many enthusiastic admirers and imitators of that work give evidence of knowing anything whatever about *Allegro, Penseroso, Comus*, or *Lycidas*. John Philips, for instance, never borrows from these pieces,[5] and Dennis and Watts do so but once.[6]

The early biographers of Milton of course mention his shorter poems; but they usually give more attention to *Comus* and *Lycidas*, because these pieces, having been published separately, require

syllabics twice, to the sonnets three and to *Comus* four times; but there is no evidence that he admired the poems, and reference to them in a scholarly work of this kind is no indication that they were popular.

[1] See his second *Anacreontick* ("Gay Bacchus "); and p. 444 below.

[2] Vol. v, no. 14. No reference is made to *Comus*.

[3] William Godwin, *Lives of Edward and John Philips* (1815), 286. I do not doubt that the statement is substantially true, for I have found quotations on pages 265, 400–401, 477, 483, 519, 553, 554 (*Nativity*); 432, 445, 449, 450, 491, 556 (*Allegro*); 430 (*May Morning*); 351, 444, 445, 577 (*Lycidas*).

[4] Some others for the period 1735–40 are given on pp. 425–6, 432, below.

[5] Philips has the phrase, "Bacchus, author of heart-cheering mirth" (*Cyder*, ii. 366), which may possibly have been suggested by *Allegro*, 13–16.

[6] In *Blenheim*, Dennis has "swinging slow with hoarse and sullen Roar" (*Select Works*, 1718, i. 160; cf. *Penseroso*, 76). The line "Silence was ravish'd as she sung," which occurs in section ii of his *Court of Death* (1695), he probably took from *Paradise Lost*, iv. 604, not from *Comus*, 557–60. In a letter written about 1705 defending the stage (*Original Letters*, 1721, i. 236, noted by Sherburn, p. 273), Dennis refers to Milton's *Samson*, to his "fine Encomium on *Shakespear*," as well as to his "extraordinary Esteem for *Johnson*" (in *Allegro*, 131–2?); but singularly enough he makes no mention of *Comus*. For Watts, see p. 425 below.

separate notice in a chronological survey, and because in accounts devoted principally to facts the occasions that called forth these two works would naturally be mentioned. Even so late as 1753, however, many of the biographies which laud *Paradise Lost* to the skies either have no praise at all for the earlier poems or simply repeat some earlier, undiscriminating comment. Usually they give the 1645 volume a brief, blanket commendation, so vague as to make no impression on the reader and not even to convince him that the writer knew the pieces he praised. To be sure, Edward Phillips mentions "that most excellent Monody . . . Intituled *Lycidas,*" and adds, "Never was the loss of Friend so Elegantly lamented"; [1] but Milton's nephew and pupil could hardly have said less.[2] Toland in 1698 refers to only two of the poems, but he exhibits a real appreciation for them. Of *Comus* he writes, "Like which Piece in the peculiar disposition of the Story, the sweetness of the Numbers, the justness of the Expression, and the Moral it teaches, there is nothing extant in any Language"; and "the Monody wherin he bewails his Learned Friend Mr. *King* drown'd in the *Irish* Seas" he characterizes as "one of the finest he ever wrote." [3] Fenton speaks, in 1725, not only of these two works but of the octosyllabics as well; yet his praise is too vague to mean much.[4] Nine years later Richardson, in addition to general commendation, declares *Allegro* and *Penseroso* to be "Exquisite Pictures," *Comus* and *Lycidas* "perhaps Superior to all in their Several Kinds," and, after quoting Toland's opinion of the masque, remarks, "As great an Encomium have I heard of *Lycidas* as a Pastoral, and That when *Theocritus* was not forgot." [5] But Richardson, as his readers all knew, was addicted to superlatives. Peck, in 1740, analyzes the principal short poems (including the

[1] Milton's *Letters of State* (1694), p. ix. "Among the rest of his Juvenile Poems," Phillips goes on to say, "some he wrote at the Age of 15, which contain a Poetical Genius scarce to be parallel'd by any *English* Writer."

[2] Similarly, the few borrowings from these early pieces that Grosart points out in his notes to the poems of Andrew Marvell (who died in 1678) prove nothing, since they are rather less than might be expected from a man who was Milton's friend and assistant. Two are dubious, "gadding vines" (*Upon Appleton House*, 610, cf. *Lycidas*, 40) and "the last distemper of the sober brain" (*Fleckno*, 28, cf. *Lycidas*, 71); but this one (from the *First Anniversary under the Protector*, 151-2, cf. *Nativity*, 172) is striking:

And still the dragon's tail
Swinges the volumes of its horrid flail.

[3] Pages 16, 44, of the life prefixed to the 1698 edition of Milton's prose works.

[4] All he says is that the four pieces are "of such an exquisite strain! that though He had left no other monuments of his Genius behind him, his name had been immortal" (pp. xix-xx of his edition of *P. L.*). Fenton seems not to have cared for *Lycidas;* at least, he makes no mention of it in his *Florelio*, "a Pastoral lamenting the Death of the Marquis of Blandford" (Feb., 1702/3), in which he does refer to Spenser's *Astrophel*.

[5] *Explanatory Notes on P. L.* (1734), pp. xv-xvi.

Nativity), gives their sources and the occasions for which they were composed, and comments on sundry passages, but except in his discussion of the rimes of *Lycidas* says nothing to indicate appreciation. Giles Jacob in 1720, Birch in 1738, Newton in 1749, and Theophilus Cibber in 1753 give only the facts regarding the poems and repeat briefly the comments of others.[1] On the whole, therefore, the attitude of Milton's biographers, from whom undue partiality for all his works might be expected, reflects the general indifference to his shorter pieces.

Yet as regards one of the poems these writers exhibit an appreciation which seems not to have been common, for the passages that have been quoted contain a goodly part of the few allusions to *Lycidas* made in the Augustan age. Joseph Trapp says nothing about the poem in his *Praelectiones Poeticae* (1711–22), though he has warm praise for *Paradise Lost*, discusses both the elegiac and the pastoral form, and alludes to the *Shepherd's Calendar*. Walsh wrote to Pope in 1706, "I am sure there is nothing of this kind [the pastoral] in English worth mentioning." [2] In the course of examining hundreds of books of the period in which one would expect Milton's elegy to be referred to, I have found, up to 1756, only thirteen such references besides those mentioned above and but seven pieces that were at all influenced by it.[3] Yet in *Lycidas*, as Mark Pattison tells us, "we have reached the high-water mark of English poesy"!

After 1698 I find no mention of the monody — except Fenton's general commendation of the minor poems, a quotation in one of Pope's letters and one in a poem by William Hinchliffe,[4] a borrowing by Isaac Watts,[5] and the expression "*Lycidas*, the Friend," in Thomson's *Winter* [6] — until 1727, when Moses Browne, the editor of

---

[1] Birch compared the Cambridge manuscripts with the printed versions of *Comus*, *Lycidas*, and some of the sonnets, and devoted several pages to variant readings; but it seems to have been scholarly thoroughness rather than admiration of the poems that led him to do this. He may have had a special interest in *Comus* because of the recent presentation of Dalton's version of the masque, to which he refers.

[2] Pope's *Works* (Elwin-Courthope ed.), vi. 50–51.

[3] See Bibl. III A, below. The extracts in Poole's *English Parnassus* (see above, p. 423, n. 3), and Pope's verbal borrowings (below, Appendix A), should not, however, be forgotten.

[4] "For fame, though it be, as Milton finely calls it, *the last infirmity of noble minds*" (Pope to Trumbull, March 12, 1713), and "Flames in the Forehead of the Eastern Sky" (Hinchliffe, *To Sylvia*); cf. *Lycidas*, 71, 171.

[5] In his *Funeral Poem on Thomas Gunston* (*Horae Lyricae*, 1709, p. 330):

> So shines thy GUNSTON's Soul above the Spheres
> *Raphael* replies, and wipes away my Tears.

Cf. *Lycidas*, 168, 77, 181; note also Watts's three preceding lines, and the general similarity in idea between the last parts of the two poems.

[6] First ed. (1726), 298. The name Lycidas is not, so far as I know, particularly

Walton, spoke of it as a neglected work and used it as the model for
one of his eclogues.[1] This piece the *Gentleman's Magazine* reprinted
in May and June, 1740, with the comment, "The following Poem . . .
is reckon'd the best Imitation of MILTON's *Lycidas* that has yet
appear'd." Since there seem to have been no other poems in print
at the time that would normally be termed imitations of *Lycidas*, it
may be that the writer in the magazine had in mind not whole pieces,
but passages like this in William Broome's verses on the death of
Elijah Fenton:

> Where were ye, Muses, by what Fountain side,
> What River sporting when your Fav'rite dy'd? . . .
> Unlike those Bards, who uninform'd to play,
> Grate on their jarring Pipes a flashy Lay.[2]

In 1731 Elizabeth Rowe spoke of "reading Milton's elegy on *Lycidas*";[3] three years later Warburton answered some questions of
Theobald's regarding a passage in it,[4] and John Jortin quoted four
of its lines;[5] the following year William Duncombe printed seven
lines of it in a life of John Hughes;[6] while two more lines appear in
an essay on prosody written about the same time by that great admirer of *Paradise Lost*, Samuel Say, who refers to *Lycidas* as "a

associated with friendship outside of Milton. In the second line of the *Morning in the
Country*, which he wrote about 1720, Thomson borrowed from *Allegro* the phrase "in
thousand liveries drest."

[1] "It has a long Time been Matter of wonder to me," he wrote (*Piscatory Eclogues*,
1729, p. 31), "that among so many *Admirers* and *Imitators* of that *great Man*, none have
taken Notice of this Poem, so *perfectly Original*, which I can never read, for my own
part, without the same Veneration, and Partiality, which is paid to the most accomplish'd Works of *Antiquity*." Browne believed it was Phineas Fletcher's death that
called forth *Lycidas*, a mistake which he corrected in his second edition. The rivers
passage in his "Strife" eclogue is, as Mr. Sherburn points out (p. 537), clearly based
upon that in Milton's *Vacation Exercise*, 91-100 (to which Browne refers in his note);
the phrases "Trent to clasp her stretch'd out all his Arms" and "sedgy Lea" (*Eclogues*,
96, 97) are from the same poem, and perhaps the river that "drew along his humid
Train" is from *Paradise Lost*, vii. 306; one of the characters in the piece is named
Comus. Towards the end of the "Sea Swains" eclogue Browne introduces the "admit
him to their train" of *Allegro*, 38, the "oozy locks" and "level brine" of *Lycidas*, 175,
98, and the "birds of calm" of the *Nativity*, 68. Near the beginning of "The Nocturnal"
he has the "hedgerow elms" of *Allegro*, 58, and towards the end he compresses *Allegro*,
63-6, into two lines (noted by Sherburn, p. 521), which in the third edition he encloses
in quotation-marks.

[2] *Poems on Several Occasions* (2d ed., 1750), 210-11. This poem (noted by Sherburn,
p. 535) was written in 1730. The four lines are close together in a work of some length.
For a piece in the same volume influenced by *Penseroso*, see pp. 445-6 below.

[3] *Letters Moral and Entertaining*, II. viii (*Works*, 1796, i. 240; Sherburn, p. 275).

[4] Nichols, *Illustrations*, ii. 634, 648 (Sherburn, p. 276).

[5] "Samson Agonistes," in *Remarks on Spenser's Poems* (1734), 185-6.

[6] Hughes, *Poems* (1735), vol. i, p. iii. Duncombe introduces the quotation with the
remark, "So just is the Reflexion of *Milton* in his *Lycidas*."

Pastoral Ode so remarkable for the Variety and Power of Numbers, as well as for every other Beauty." [1] By 1755, moreover, Milton is invoked as the author, not only of the epic and the octosyllabics, but of the monody; [2] and in the following year the *London Magazine* published a letter devoted entirely to the piece, which was termed "one of the most poetical and moving elegies that ever was wrote," the passage that begins "Return, Alpheus, the dread voice is past," being praised in particular as "extremely striking and beautiful, superior to anything of the kind I ever read." [3] Yet this same year another periodical said, "As to the structure of the verse, and the irregular succession of the rhimes, we must confess, they do not greatly delight us; but some, perhaps, will see grace and beauty in that wildness and disorder, which to others may afford only perplexity and disgust." [4] Johnson's strictures appeared in 1779, and as late as 1793 the poem was characterized as "a stiff unnatural performance." [5] It was not until 1785, one hundred and forty-seven years after its publication, that anything like John Scott's twenty-eight-page critique of it appeared. [6] Was a great poem ever so long in coming to its own!

The earliest appreciation of *Lycidas* of which we have any record has been omitted from the foregoing account because it contained a still warmer tribute to the other minor poems. This work is the curious jumble known as the *Cyprian Academy*, which came from the pen of Robert Baron two years after the appearance of the 1645 volume. Though "imitation is the sincerest flattery," plagiarism may be regarded as the most complete, and from this point of view Baron's work is "the perfect tribute." There are many lines as close to Milton as

Flame in the forehead of the azure skie, [7]

and many passages much longer than the following and quite as untainted by originality, —

---

[1] *Poems and Two Critical Essays* (1745), 118. This comment, like Duncombe's (p. 426, n. 6, above), sounds as if it were uncertain that readers would be familiar with the poem. Say also quotes from *Comus* (*ib.* 127).

[2] H. Kiddell, *Genius of Milton* (see *Gent. Mag.*, xxv. 518; noted by Good, p. 81).

[3] xxv. 235–6.   [4] *Mo. Rev.*, xiv. 352.

[5] *Bee*, Aug. 21, 1793. Two years earlier (May 11, 1791) a writer in the same journal said that Adam Smith praised the octosyllabics but thought "all the rest of Milton's short poems were trash."

[6] See above, p. 251, n. 5.

[7] ii. 28; cf. *Lycidas*, 171. Baron's plagiarisms, as well as a number of the other matters mentioned in this chapter, were pointed out by that great Miltonian, Thomas Warton, in his edition of Milton's minor poems (2d ed., 1791, pp. 403–7), where many illustrations are given. Warton (*ib.* p.v) also discovered among Archbishop Sancroft's papers in the Bodleian a transcript of the *Nativity* made about 1648, and one of Milton's paraphrase of the fifty-third Psalm.

> *Sol* has quencht his glowing beame
> In the coole Atlantick streame,
> Now their shines no tell-tale sun
> *Hymens* rites are to be done,
> Now Loves revells 'gin to keepe,
> What have you to doe with sleepe?
> You have sweeter sweets to prove,
> Lovely *Venus* wakes, and love,
> Goddesse of Nocturnall sport
> Alwaies keep thy jocond court.[1]

As Baron borrowed from most of Milton's early pieces, it is not surprising that he took a phrase from one of the sonnets.[2] He seems to have been one of the few, however, who read those "soul-animating strains" before 1738. Philip Ayres, to be sure, mentioned them in 1687 as unsuccessful;[3] Phillips appended four of them to his life of the poet and Toland quoted six in his, but in each case it was merely for biographical purposes; Zachary Pearce referred to three;[4] John Hughes borrowed from one,[5] Pope from three,[6] his assistant Elijah Fenton quoted one,[7] and phrases and ideas taken from three make up the lines *To Aristus, in Imitation of a Sonnet of Milton*.[8] But the general attitude was probably that of John Hughes, an admirer and imitator of the octosyllabics, who, after discussing Spenser's sonnets, adds baldly enough, "*Milton* has writ some, both in *Italian* and *English*." [9]

The references given in this chapter to the various minor poems cannot, of course, pretend to include every mention of the pieces in the first hundred years after their collective publication. Yet they represent more than the findings of one man: they include not only everything I have discovered, but everything that seems to me significant in what a century and a half of English and American scholarship has pointed out. Accordingly, though other references to these poems will undoubtedly come to light, it is not likely that they

---

[1] i. 59; cf. *Comus*, 95–7, 141, 122–8. In the first line the original reads "have" instead of "has," probably a misprint.

[2] Not, however, for the *Cyprian Academy*, but for the *Pocula Castalia* (1650, p. 27). Todd called attention to this borrowing in his note to Milton's sonnet, "How soon hath Time"; cf. also his appendix on Baron's imitations, at the end of his last volume (1801 ed.). On page A2 *verso* of the *Pocula* a number of lines from Milton's poem on Shakespeare are introduced.

[3] See below, p. 488, n. 7.   [5] See below, p. 443, n. 4.

[4] See above, p. 422, n. 9.   [6] See Appendix A, below.

[7] Fenton, in speaking of Waller's lines on Lawes, quotes the sonnet to Lawes. See "Observations" appended to his edition of Waller's *Works*, 1730, p. c (noted by Sherburn, p. 275).   [8] See below, p. 489.

[9] In his edition of Spenser (1715), vol. i, p. cx. On the widespread indifference to sonnets in the eighteenth century, see pp. 480–82, 488 n. 7, 521–3, below.

will be numerous or enthusiastic enough to change the conclusions based upon the testimony we have now. Verbal parallels will continue to be adduced, as they have been hitherto; but, unless there is other evidence that an author probably knew Milton's early work, such parallels are usually worthless.[1] Phrases from the 1645 volume are most frequent and striking in Pope and Thomson, who made use of them in their earliest pieces and (except in Pope's Homer) borrowed from them about as often as from the epic.[2] One important source of information as to the popularity of the poems — the number of pieces influenced by them — will be examined in detail a little later. The conclusions to be drawn from such an examination will,

[1] This is why little weight can be attached to the only parallel which seems to me significant that Alexander Harrach gives in his attempt to prove the anonymous *Sylvan Dream* (1701) to be the work of John Philips:

> Hear me, Sweet Echo, hear, and bless
> One that like thy Narcissus is

(*John Philips*, 1906, p. 100; cf. *Comus*, 230, 237). Nor does the phrase "sooth'd with soft *Lydian* Airs," in Samuel Wesley's *Hymn on Peace to the Prince of Peace* (1713, p. 8), prove that Wesley (who certainly was familiar with *Paradise Lost*, see pp. 38, 45 n. 1, 109 n. 1, above) knew *Allegro*, 136, any more than the line, "Thro' the long levell'd Tube, our stretching Sight," makes it certain that the author of an *Epistle from a Gentleman to his Friend in the Country* (*Bee*, 1733, i. 543) knew *Comus*, 340. Yet there can hardly be any question as to the source of the "wanton Wile, And Nod, and secret Beck, and amorous Leer" which N. Brown introduced into the Miltonic blank verse of his *North-Country Wedding* (*Miscellaneous Poems*, published by M. Concanen, 1724, p. 9). Of Mr. Sherburn's parallels, aside from those in poems that have been or will be referred to, the following seem to me striking, though hardly sufficient by themselves to establish a case: "Warble . . . the wild-wood Notes" (William Thompson, *Nativity*, 1736, in *Poems*, Oxford, 1757, i. 62, cf. *Allegro*, 134; the early borrowings from *Allegro* and *Lycidas* given above, p. 112, n. 1, are from the work of another William Thompson);

> Fly, rigid Winter, with thy horid face,
> And let the soft and lovely Spring take place;
> Oh! come thou fairest season of the year,
> With garlands deck'd and verdant robes appear

(Elizabeth Rowe, *On our Saviour's Nativity*, 1733, in *Letters Moral and Entertaining*, III. xii, *Works*, 1796, ii. 56, and cf. her *To Mrs. Arabella Marrow*, in *Works*, iii. 116–17);

> Onward *she* comes with silent step and slow,
> In her brown mantle wrapt, and brings along
> The still, the mild, the melancholy *Hour*,
> And *Meditation*, with his eye on heaven

(David Mallet, *Excursion*, in *Works*, 1759, i. 77; and note "hoar hill," p. 71, cf. *Allegro*, 55). Mallet certainly knew *Penseroso* later (see p. 451 below). Yet in the first edition of *The Excursion* (1728, the only one published before 1740), the last two lines quoted above appear as one,

> The serious *Hour*, and solemn *Thoughtfulness;*

and, since the latter part of the first line is pretty clearly adapted from the last but one of *Paradise Lost* (with which Mallet was familiar), there is little left in the passage to suggest *Penseroso*.   [2] See Appendix A, below.

however, be found to be in line with what we have already learned; for, aside from *Allegro* and *Penseroso*, the minor poems had almost no influence before 1740, and even the number of pieces modelled on the companion poems (thirty) was decidedly small as compared either with the number that copied *Paradise Lost* in the same period or with the number that imitated the octosyllabics themselves a decade or two later.[1]

Yet, if up to 1740 Milton's early productions had little of the vogue which his epic enjoyed, it is clear that they were known to many and were warmly admired by some. That is, the evidence would show that Joseph Warton went altogether too far in saying that *Allegro* and *Penseroso* "lay in a sort of obscurity, the private enjoyment of a few curious readers, till they were set to admirable music by Mr. Handel." [2] Warton refers to Handel's oratorio, *L'Allegro, Il Pensieroso, ed Il Moderato*, which was first sung in 1740 and was popular enough to require two printings of the libretto that year and five others before 1802.[3] The success of this oratorio encouraged Handel to undertake immediately another composition with a Miltonic libretto, drawn this time from *Samson Agonistes* (1742), and by 1746 to complete his *Occasional Oratorio*, the words of which are taken mainly from Milton's translations of the Psalms. Since these last are among the minor poems, this use of them, wretched perversions of the Scriptures though they be, is interesting in the present connection; yet it is less significant than the interpolation into the *Samson* of a number of lines from the *Nativity, On Time, At a Solemn Music*, and the *Epitaph on the Marchioness of Winchester*.[4] Handel's music undoubtedly did much to make people familiar with Milton's work outside of the epic field, and in particular with the companion pieces; but those who admired the octosyllabics before 1740, like those who cared for *Paradise Lost* before 1712, were by no means limited to "a few curious readers." Such off-hand remarks as Warton's regarding contemporary conditions are apt to carry more weight than they should; [5] and, as the author of this one

---

[1] These figures are summarized above, p. 9, n. 1, and below, p. 469.

[2] *Essay on Pope* (1756), 4th ed., 1782, i. 40.

[3] Mr. Alwin Thaler (*Milton in the Theatre*, Univ. of North Carolina, *Studies in Philology*, xvii. 286) records three performances in London the first season, three in Dublin the following year, and six more by 1822.

[4] The last twelve lines of act i are adapted from *On Time;* four of the last six of act ii, and six of act iii, scene i, from the *Nativity*, stanzas vi, xvii, xxvi; six lines of act iii, scene iii, from the *Marchioness of Winchester*, 47–50, 67–8; and the last six lines of act iii from *At a Solemn Music*. Mr. Thaler notes (p. 278) eight performances in 1743 and twenty-two more by 1829, besides at least twelve editions of the text (by Newburgh Hamilton) before 1840.

[5] In the same volume, for example, he wrote (p. 154), "When Thomson published

was a schoolboy at Winchester from 1736 to 1740 and at Oxford from 1740 to 1744, he could have known very little about literary conditions at the capital. Certainly men who were to become the chief poets of the mid-century and were to give Milton's pieces their great vogue did not become acquainted with them through Handel's work. Gray was on the continent when the oratorio was given; besides, he had referred to *Penseroso* in a letter to Walpole in 1736, and the same year two of his intimate friends exhibited familiarity with other of the minor poems.[1] The Warton brothers undoubtedly gained their enthusiasm for Milton from their father, one of the earliest of the eighteenth-century admirers and imitators of the 1645 volume; and Joseph Warton, in turn, probably made the poems known to his schoolmate and college friend Collins, the first of whose "Oriental Eclogues," written about 1738, shows the influence of *Allegro*. Nor could the popular Scottish poet, Hamilton of Bangour, have been attracted to the Puritan lyrics by Handel, as his Miltonic octosyllabics were composed at least a year before the oratorio was given.

In fact, it seems highly probable that Warton had the cart before the horse, and that Handel came to use *Allegro* and *Penseroso* through the influence of some discriminating friends upon whom the beauty of the poems had recently dawned. For there are signs on every side, about this time, of an awakening, among more intelligent readers, to an interest in Milton's early work. Evidence of this new appreciation is to be found in the rapid increase in the number of poems influenced otherwise than verbally by the octosyllabics. Before 1700 there are only three such poems, between 1700 and 1715 three, from 1716 to 1725 seven, from 1726 to 1735 seven, from 1736 to 1740 (five years only) eleven, from 1741 to 1745 (five years) sixteen, and in 1746 alone, an unusual year, sixteen. That is, the companion pieces seem to have exerted almost as much influence in the one year 1746 as they did in the ninety years before 1736, which is approximately

his *Winter* . . . it lay a long time neglected"; yet the second edition of *Winter* appeared within three months of the first. Thomas Warton, in his edition of Milton's minor poems (1785, p. x), remarked that blank verse "after its revival by Philips had been long neglected"; and H. J. Todd said in his edition of *Comus* (Canterbury, 1798, preface, p. xvi), "It was not till late in the present century, that *Comus* emerged from the obscurity in which it had long been buried," an assertion that will be shown to be absolutely false. Even the truth-loving Wordsworth wrote in 1815 (*Prose Works*, ed. Grosart, ii. 114) that Milton's minor poems were "little heard of till more than 150 years after their publication," that is, not until 1800!

[1] *Correspondence of Gray, Walpole*, etc. (ed. Toynbee, Oxford, 1915), i. 94, 79, 96. West's octosyllabic, *The View from the Thatcht House*, written in 1738, also shows unmistakably the influence of Milton's companion poems (see p. 453 below).

the state of affairs as regards all of Milton's early poems. Furthermore, between 1728 and 1730 Pope referred to the "famous Allegro
and Penseroso," and the *Grub-Street Journal* praised the latter poem
while sneering at Dennis's adaptation of a line from it.[1] In 1735
appeared Hughes's new conclusion for what his editor termed "*Mr.
Milton's* Incomparable Poem, entitled, *Il Penseroso*."[2] Readers of
the *Gentleman's Magazine* for April, 1737, would have come upon
the phrase, "Or, as *Milton* elegantly expresses it, *Music was married
to Poetry*."[3] During the same month they might have witnessed
Paul Rolli's opera *Sabrina*, based upon *Comus*, and at about the
same time might have seen an elaborate performance of Milton's
Song on May Morning, which in 1740 was printed in a collection of
songs and cantatas.[4] It was about 1738 that Say praised *Lycidas*,[5]
and probably a year or so earlier that Warburton declared *Comus* to
be one of Milton's "three perfect pieces" and the companion poems
"certainly master-pieces in their kind."[6] In 1739 Richard Barton
put on the title-page of his *Farrago* ten lines from *Penseroso*, while in
1740 the *Gentleman's Magazine* printed Browne's eclogue as "the
best Imitation" of *Lycidas*,[7] and Francis Peck brought out his *Memoirs* of Milton, in which are numerous references to the minor poems.
A circumstance that may have awakened interest in the early as
well as the later writings was the placing of a bust of the poet in
Westminster Abbey in 1737.

More important than any of these things, however, was the presentation of *Comus* at Drury Lane the next year. The masque was
given, not as Milton wrote it, but with additional dances and songs
(one of them, significantly enough, being twenty-six lines from the
beginning of *Allegro*), for which the celebrated Dr. Thomas Arne
wrote the music. As thus adapted, it was an immediate success.
"Every Night that it has been perform'd," we are told, "the Audience have receiv'd it with the utmost Satisfaction and Delight."[8]
Four editions of this arrangement of the masque (by John Dalton)
were printed in 1738 and two more by 1741; and in abbreviated,
debased versions (made in 1772 by George Colman and 1815 by
Thomas J. Dibdin, and constantly changed through the introduction
of new songs and dances) it enlisted the services of the chief English

---

[1] Spence's *Anecdotes* (ed. Singer, 1820), 21; *Memoirs of the Society of Grub-Street*,
no. 5 (Feb. 5, 1730).
[2] *Poems* (1735), vol. i, p. lviii.   [4] See p. 28 above.
[3] vii. 195; cf. *Allegro*, 136–7.   [5] See pp. 426–7 above.
[6] Letter to Thomas Birch, Nov. 24, 1737, Nichols's *Illustrations*, ii. 79, 81.
[7] See p. 426 above.
[8] *Universal Spectator*, March 25, 1738, quoted in *Gent. Mag.*, viii. 152.

actors and actresses until 1843.[1] Yet the writer who gave an account of the first production thought it necessary to tell his readers that the work was "a *Pastoral* kind of Poem" and was "wrote by *Milton.*" [2]

Too much time has perhaps been taken up with these quotations and figures, yet they throw light on a matter of considerable interest and importance. What the eighteenth century thought of *Lycidas*, for example, is in itself of no particular significance; the question becomes important only because *Lycidas* is a touchstone of poetic appreciation. The gradual awakening to the beauty of Milton's minor poems meant the passing of the monopoly which translations, pastorals, satires, and other forms of "wit" had held in the field of verse. It meant the quickening of the imagination, the renaissance of the lyric, and the bringing back into English poetry of the color, music, fragrance, and freedom which spell romanticism.

There is, however, no need of following the career of the 1645 volume through the remarkable vogue which lasted until the end of the century and affected almost every writer of lyrics between Gray and Keats, for this later popularity has already been touched upon and will receive abundant illustration in the chapters that follow. Instead, we may well ask ourselves how the rapid shift from ignorance and indifference to widespread enthusiasm is to be explained if it is not due to Handel's oratorio. How is it that men, unacquainted with one another and living in different parts of England, began about the same time to pay attention to the poems?

Aside from chance and the natural increase in the number of admirers, the explanation is to be found principally in the change which was coming over English thought and life and which in literature was marked by the passing of the dominance of Pope and his school. Not that pseudo-classicism was dead in England; on the contrary, at least fifty years of robust health lay ahead of it. But the extreme form, as manifested by Pope, Swift, Addison, and their contemporaries, had lost its hold on English poetry. Pope's last work (except for the fourth book of *The Dunciad*) appeared in 1738, when the mind of Swift was well-nigh gone and Arbuthnot, Gay, Congreve, Prior, Addison, and Parnell had been dead from three to twenty years. The great figures that had ruled English taste and dominated English literature for half a century were no more; younger men were coming to the front with tastes and ideals of their own. They

[1] A full account of the stage history of *Comus* is given by Mr. Thaler (North Carolina *Studies*, xvii. 289–308), who notes "one or more" productions almost every year down to 1820, with 11 in 1760, 21 in 1777, 10 in 1780, 15 in 1815 (a gorgeous spectacle, with a company of fifty), 18 in 1842, and 11 in 1843 (with Macready in the title-rôle).

[2] Same as note 8 on p. 432 above.

also were classicists, but of a broader, less rigorous type than Pope or Addison, and by natural development and the strength they derived from one another they came in time to have many points of difference from the poets who had immediately preceded them. The most marked of these differences lay in their abandonment of the couplet and their preference for the stanzaic, octosyllabic, true Pindaric, and sonnet verse-forms. Mason, for instance, until he was nearly fifty, when his taste seems to have changed, had used the heroic couplet but twice; Collins employed it only twice in his earliest works, Gray devoted less than one page in thirteen to it,[1] Joseph Warton but one in twenty, and his brother Thomas about one in five. Yet the father of the Wartons, though an imitator of Milton and Spenser as well as a writer of runic odes, had been sufficiently of the earlier generation to use it in over a third of his work.

The rapidity with which the public taste thus swung away from the favorite meter of the neo-classicists is shown in the differences between the earlier and the later volumes of Dodsley's *Collection of Poems*. In the first three volumes (published in 1748) there are 57 pages devoted to blank verse, 132 to octosyllabics, 205 to stanzas, and 404, or nearly half, to couplets; in the last three (the fourth published in 1755, the fifth and sixth in 1758) 73 pages are given to blank verse, 146 to octosyllabics, 427 to stanzas, and 246 (practically a quarter) to couplets.[2] It will be noticed that in the ten-year interval the stanzaic poems have exchanged places with those in couplets. If either of these sets of figures be compared with those derived from typical miscellanies of the beginning of the century, it will be seen how great a change was coming over English meter. In the *New Miscellany of Original Poems* edited by Charles Gildon (1701) blank verse has 9 pages, octosyllabics have 11, stanzas 29, and couplets 204; in the *Poetical Miscellanies* edited by Steele (1714) blank verse has 2, octosyllabics have 12, stanzas 26, and couplets 217, in each case fully three-quarters of the volume being taken up by couplets.

Coincident with this change in meter, and springing from the same cause, came the passing of the long poem. Until the close of

---

[1] That is, in his original poems. His translations from Statius, Tasso, Propertius, and Dante, which he never published, are all in heroic couplets.

[2] These figures take no account of the fourteen sonnets in volume ii and the two in volume iv, of the epigrams in volumes ii and v, of pieces in anapestic tetrameter couplets, or of irregular or dramatic works that do not fall into any of the classes named. If we count the number of poems rather than the number of pages they occupy, we shall likewise find that blank-verse and octosyllabic poetry gained greatly in popularity; for in the first three volumes there are 7 poems in blank verse, 34 in octosyllabics, 77 in stanzas, and 83 in couplets; in the last three, 18 in blank verse, 58 in octosyllabics, 173 in stanzas, and 69 in couplets.

the century, when Mason in his old age produced three poems of length, the men of the new school had written only five pieces longer than *Penseroso*, and Gray, Collins, and the elder Warton never published any that are so long.[1] The younger men were weary of satires and arguments in verse: they wanted songs, they sought in poetry not reason but imagination. It is surprising, too, to find how clearly some of them realized and expressed their wants. Joseph Warton prefaced the *Odes* which he published in 1746 with the declaration:

The Public has been so much accustom'd of late to didactic Poetry alone, and Essays on moral Subjects, that any work where the imagination is much indulged, will perhaps not be relished or regarded. The author therefore of these pieces is in some pain least certain austere critics should think them too fanciful and descriptive. But as he is convinced that the fashion of moralizing in verse has been carried too far, and as he looks upon Invention and Imagination to be the chief faculties of a Poet, so he will be happy if the following Odes may be look'd upon as an attempt to bring back Poetry into its right channel.[2]

Similarly, in the preface to a volume of 1761 Richard Shepherd tells his readers that the ode, the favorite species of verse with the new school, "is built intirely upon Fancy, and Ease and Simplicity of Diction are its peculiar Characteristicks."

When men held these ideas regarding reason and imagination in verse, it is not strange that the dominant influence in poetry passed from Pope to Spenser and Milton. We have seen that there is good reason for thinking Spenser attracted by no means so many readers as Milton; it might also be shown that his influence was practically confined to the *Faerie Queene* and did not affect his admirers so profoundly as that of the later poet did his. At any rate, no characteristic of the men of the new school is more marked than their admiration for Milton.[3] They praised him, imitated each of his poems in turn, borrowed words, phrases, or lines from him, and were so saturated with his works that many of their imitations and borrow-

---

[1] Collins's *Ode on the Popular Superstitions of Scotland*, which is forty-six lines longer, was not printed until 1788, many years after his death.

[2] Warton's discursive *Essay on Pope* (1756–82) is an examination of the poetry of Pope and his contemporaries in the light of these principles. The gist of it is expressed in the dedication: "In that species of poetry wherein POPE excelled, he is superior to all mankind: and I only say, that this species of poetry is not the most excellent one of the art." "A stroke of passion," he remarked in his *Reflections on Didactic Poetry* (appended to his translation of Virgil, 1753), "is worth a hundred of the most lively and glowing descriptions. Men love to be moved, much better than to be instructed."

[3] They have, accordingly, come to be spoken of as "the Miltonic group," an unfortunate designation, since they were in reality less Miltonic than Philips, Thomson, Cowper, and others.

ings were undoubtedly unconscious. Large numbers of their verbal pilferings are from *Paradise Lost*, a circumstance which should be a sufficient answer to the charge that they did not care for the epic. As a matter of fact, the popularity of the octosyllabics and the monody received no little help from the much greater vogue of the loftier work. Few unrimed poems, to be sure, were written by the new school. Collins composed none, Gray but one (a translation), the three Wartons and Mason only fourteen altogether, and most of those less than one hundred lines in length; but their neglect of blank verse was due to a preference for lyric measures and for short pieces in which the epic meter is less likely to be used. The widespread enthusiasm for Milton's early productions and the frequent use made of them seem strange to most of us, who enjoy the poems, but without rapture or thought of imitating them. In 1740, however, they swam like a new planet into the ken of those who were tired of gazing upon the more familiar constellations. The star, to be sure, was old, older than those they had been gazing upon, but it was new to them and possessed the strangeness in which lies much of the fascination of beauty.

The vogue of the poems was also due in no small measure to their being peculiarly adapted to the transitional character of the times. So much emphasis has been laid on the romanticism of the poets of the mid-eighteenth century that their fundamental classicism is apt to be overlooked. They unquestionably grew more romantic, but their classicism was so dyed in the grain that it could not be washed out, and colored almost every poem they wrote. It is vain to listen for notes which

> Charm magic casements, opening on the foam
> Of perilous seas, in faery lands forlorn;

one hears only "Philomela's voice." Of revolt there was very little. Conventionality continued to abound, propriety and decorum were always observed, and the personal note was rarely struck. Yet these men did have romantic yearnings; they seem, indeed, to have wanted to be romanticists but to have lacked the courage or not to have known how. They were interested in romantic things — ruins, superstitions, Gothic architecture, early Celtic and Germanic poetry, and other remains of the picturesque past; they liked suggestions of the strange and the mysterious, but for full-fledged romanticism they were not ready. Most Elizabethan literature, including Shakespeare's sonnets, left the greater part of them indifferent, and even

Warton regarded the stanza of his beloved Spenser as "so injudiciously chosen" that it "led our author into many absurdities." [1] It was not merely by chance that they ignored the *Song to David* and the *Poetical Sketches*, for they wrote nothing of the same kind themselves. Curiosity and antiquarian interest were strongly developed in many of them, but the "renaissance of wonder," so marked in Blake, had not yet begun. It may be remembered that in 1798 Jane Austen made her Marianne, who represents excessive "sensibility," exclaim,

"To hear those beautiful lines which have frequently almost driven me wild, pronounced with such impenetrable calmness, such dreadful indifference!"

" . . . But you *would* give him Cowper," objects Mrs. Dashwood.

"Nay, mamma," the young lady replies, "if he is not to be animated by Cowper!" [2]

It was poetry like *The Task*, — quiet, contemplative descriptions of nature and country life,—or odes to abstractions, that the so-called romanticists of the eighteenth century enjoyed. For *Christabel*, the *Solitary Reaper*, *The Cloud*, and the *Ode to a Nightingale* they were not ready. They turned to Milton because to them, brought up under the neo-classic régime, his work seemed romantic in spirit and form and yet had the exquisite finish, the restraint, the reserve and impersonality, to which they were accustomed. It possessed for them the fascination of the strange without the shock of the inelegant, the thrill of adventure without its dangers and discomforts.

Milton's early pieces were thus peculiarly adapted to the awakening lyricism of the romantically-inclined classicists of the mideighteenth century. *Allegro* and *Penseroso*, the most popular of all, are easy, friendly, yet dignified poems which convey the charm of the out-of-doors and of life in the country with a simplicity, a freshness, and a joy that are entirely lacking in the pseudo-classic pastorals. Yet they are not Wordsworthian: they mention only the obvious things, and those but briefly. They warm our hearts by their references to familiar sights and sounds, — the smoke from the cottage chimney, the distant bell, the rooster and hens, the nut-brown ale, the walks under arching trees and along the brook; yet, though real, the poems are not realistic, though homelike and familiar, they

---

[1] *Observations on the Fairy Queen* (2d ed., 1762), i. 115, 114.
[2] *Sense and Sensibility*, ch. iii; cf. ch. x.

are not personal. They give us pictures of the contemplative, scholarly leisure so attractive to the eighteenth century, and hints

> Of turneys, and of trophies hung,
> Of forests, and enchantments drear;

but there is no romantic extravagance or excess, all is beautifully finished with delicate reserve and quiet loveliness. This is exactly what the poets of the time liked, what they sought to do in their own work. To realize this, one has only to recall two of the greatest and most admired short poems of the century, Gray's *Elegy* and Collins's *Ode to Evening*. Except for the melancholy tinge of the *Elegy*, which may be matched in *Lycidas*, the tone of these pieces is that of Milton's early poems; they have similar descriptions of nature and of country life, and are marked by the same quiet refinement and careful but unobtrusive finish. Is it any wonder, then, that classicists with romantic leanings who wished to write short reflective or descriptive pieces of a kind that had not recently been in vogue, took as models the newly-discovered minor poems of Milton?

CHAPTER XVIII

THE INFLUENCE OF L'ALLEGRO
AND IL PENSEROSO

If we are to follow the influence of Milton's shorter poems without confusion, we must not attempt to jump back and forth from one to another, from octosyllabics to *Lycidas*, from sonnets to *Comus;* we must separate the several types and study each by itself. The octosyllabics will naturally come first, since they were the first to make themselves felt, and in order to trace their influence it will be necessary to have their salient characteristics clearly in mind. These are:

1. Doublets. In form the two poems are parallel throughout, though diametrically opposed to each other in meaning.

2. Title. The titles are in Italian.

3. Meter. The regular meter is iambic tetrameter; but fifty-six lines of *Allegro* and twenty-eight of *Penseroso* are, like the nine-syllable lines in Chaucer, without the initial unaccented foot, and thus may be regarded as catalectic iambics or trochaics.[1]

4. Cadence. There is a peculiar airy, lilting movement to the lines that distinguishes the poems from practically all other octosyllabics, including Milton's own *Epitaph on the Marchioness of Winchester*. This cadence, particularly tripping and delicate in *Allegro*, more subdued and gentle in *Penseroso*, is never heavy, jerky, or abrupt, never falls into the jog-trot of Swift or Butler.[2]

5. Opening. The first ten lines differ from the rest in length and in rime-scheme. The old-numbered lines have six syllables each, the even ones ten. The rimes are *a b b a c d d e e c.*

---

[1] Some critics deny that these lines are iambic, on the ground that such pause as there is comes after the second syllable rather than after the first. This is true of some lines, but by no means of all.

[2] The impression appears to be general that the alternation of catalectic and normal lines is alone responsible for this cadence. Such alternation probably does help, but it will be found also in the *Epitaph on the Marchioness of Winchester* and in many other pieces which are entirely without this peculiar lilt. To me the secret of the tripping movement seems to lie in the choice of words that give to each metrical accent practically the same amount of stress, — for example, "quíps, and cránks, and wánton wíles." Such a choice practically implies the elimination of the slighted stresses that are almost universal in poetry, and, since a word can have but one strong accent, the elimination of long words. It is also necessary for the lilting effect that the unaccented syllables shall be such as are lightly and quickly pronounced. Spondees make a line heavy.

6. PERSONIFICATIONS. Personified abstractions, such as Melancholy, Mirth, Jest, Jollity, Contemplation, Peace, and many more, play an important part.

7. "HENCE." An execrated personified quality (or qualities) is described by implication and bidden to flee.

8. "COME." A desired personified quality is described and invoked.

9. MANNER. The manner in which the invoked quality is requested to come is mentioned: for example, "Keep thy wonted state." Under this head may also be included the dress of the invoked quality, which is given only in *Penseroso*.

10. PARENTAGE. The parents of both the invoked and the execrated qualities are named and characterized.

11. BIRTH. The circumstances attending the courtship of the parents of the invoked quality and those incident on her own birth are detailed.

12. TRAIN. The invoked quality is asked to bring with her an attendant train of personified abstractions similar to herself. These companions are also characterized.

13. OCCUPATIONS. The occupations of the thoughtful and of the light-hearted man are given. The latter, for example, walks out into the country, watches the milkmaid and the mower, goes to the city, witnesses pageants, attends the theater, reads, listens to music, etc.

14. ENDING. The speaker desires to live with the invoked quality if she can furnish such pleasures as he has mentioned.

Must an eighteenth-century poet whose work shows a number of these characteristics necessarily have derived them from Milton? This question, it should be noted, is not equivalent to "Are these characteristics found in pre-Miltonic poetry?" but rather to "Are these characteristics found in pre-Miltonic poems which eighteenth-century poets are likely to have known and copied?" The former query it is difficult to answer, the latter can be answered easily and emphatically, "No." Aside from meter and personification, the features that have been enumerated were rare, and occurred only in pieces practically unknown and not likely to be imitated by the few who did know them. There was, of course, nothing new about iambic tetrameter: it was perhaps the commonest middle-English romance meter; it was used in *Hudibras*, and was a favorite verse-form of Swift and Gay. Yet it was not *popular* in the Augustan period any more than it is to-day; hence its vogue in the third quarter of the eighteenth century is almost certainly due to Milton. Personified abstractions, too, are nearly as old as conscious thought and were no novelty in English poetry; they abound, for example, in Cowley. Poems devoted to such abstractions, like the middle-English *Patience* or Chaucer's *Truth* and *Gentilesse*, are frequently met with, and in a few of them the qualities are personified. But odes addressed to personified abstractions, which rioted through English verse of the later eighteenth century and of which Wordsworth's *Ode to Duty* is a survival, are rare before 1730. Their popularity was apparently not the gradual development that might be expected; for an examination of the miscellanies from 1673 to 1731 in the Harvard Library (some sixty volumes, including several thousand pieces) has failed to bring to light any poems of this kind except two that are manifestly based on *Allegro* or *Penseroso*. Not more than six of the whole number are concerned with abstract qualities. As there is no better way of getting at the poetical temper of the time than through its miscellanies. which vary greatly in character, this testimony seems to be conclusive, particularly as a search through the magazines shows that even so late as 1760 there were practically no poems addressed to abstractions.[1]

The use of such impersonal personified qualities is in keeping with the neo-classic fondness for universal truths, with its preference for the general rather than the particular, for the abstract rather than the concrete. Yet abstractions seem, in a way, to have taken the place occupied in the earlier and more strictly neo-classic verse by Greek and Roman deities.[2] The poems that employ them are distinguished from most other lyrics by a lack of individual experience or feeling, a defect that is largely responsible for their barrenness. Their vogue appears to have begun about 1742 with the elder Warton, Gray, and Collins, who wrote many of them; indeed, the first volumes of Collins and Joseph Warton contain little else. Other young poets, vaguely dissatisfied and half-consciously wishing for more lyric forms, turned eagerly to this one to furnish the wings for their flight. The fuel was, therefore, ready for the fire. The spark almost certainly came from *Allegro* and *Penseroso*, for the odes to personified qualities were under a very heavy debt to the structure, phraseology, and content of Milton's octosyllabics.

Without doubt all the rest of the "fourteen points" are to be found in earlier verse, and several of them presumably occur now

[1] There were, of course, the comparatively few modelled on *Allegro* and *Penseroso* which are noted below in Bibliography II.

[2] "The proper substitute for this servile and unlawful use of mythology," says George Dyer (*Poetics*, 1812, ii. 148-9), ". . . is, in my opinion, personification, a modest use of which gives grace and dignity to poetry."

and then in the same piece; yet it is safe to say that very few English or American poets of to-day are familiar with any poems except Milton's written before 1700 which have these features. If this be true of the twentieth century, how much truer must it be of the eighteenth, a period notorious for its ignorance of preceding literature! Only an antiquary of the time is likely to have known any poems similar to *Allegro.* "But," some one objects, "at least two of the leading poets of the time, Gray and Thomas Warton, were very learned in the field of letters, and Collins and Joseph Warton had no little interest in antiquarian matters." True enough; but even if these men were familiar, as they probably were, with the lines by Burton, Fletcher, and Marston which are thought to have influenced Milton in composing his octosyllabics, if they had come upon the delicate, lilting octosyllabics of Wither's *Shepherd's Hunting,*[1] or had read the chorus in Kyd's translation of Garnier's *Cornelia,*[2] or had noticed the personifications tripping lightly through Cowley's tetrameter, yet, saturated as they were with Milton, would they have been likely in their own writing to turn from their favorite author to copy a neglected minor poet? To-day this might be done, for we seek the unusual and the out-of-the-way, we cherish the element of strangeness in beauty; but eighteenth-century bards did not.

The influence of Milton's octosyllabics was at first confined to an occasional phrase, a few lines, or a stanza, and throughout the century many pieces were affected no more deeply than this. Yet along with these poems there came, before a great while, to be others in which the influence was not external and occasional but structural and vital, poems cut, so to speak, after the *Allegro-Penseroso* pattern. Halfway between such imitations and the merely phrasal borrowings (early instances of which have already been given [3]) stands the work of John Hughes. Though Swift and Pope agreed that Hughes was "among the *mediocribus,*"[4] he is of considerable interest to a student of the lyric awakening. He was very fond of music, played himself, and composed a large number of cantatas and other poems for music, as well as one of the first operas given in English. Scattered through these pieces are brief songs (written in short lines and obviously intended to be sung), which, though otherwise uninteresting, show an attempt to be lyric. These facts, together with the love for nature and descriptive poetry and the preference for

[1] Eclogue iv.

[2] IV. ii. 188–95. Mr. H. M. Ayres called my attention to this chorus.

[3] See above, pp. 422–9 *passim.*

[4] Letter from Swift to Pope, Sept. 3, 1735; and one from Pope to Swift, Sept. or Nov., 1735.

country life apparent in his work,[1] make Hughes seem like one of the Gray-Collins-Warton group born out of due time. He certainly possessed in common with these men a love for Spenser, whom he edited, and for Milton, whom he imitated. As early as 1697 he began a poem with this obvious borrowing from the opening of *Allegro*:

> Hence slavish Fear! thy *Stygian* Wings display!
> Thou ugly Fiend of Hell, away!
> Wrapp'd in thick Clouds, and Shades of Night,
> To conscious Souls direct thy Flight!
> There brood on Guilt, fix there a loath'd Embrace,
> And propagate vain Terrors, Frights,
> Dreams, Goblins, and imagin'd Sprights,
> Thy visionary Tribe, thy black and monstrous Race.[2]

These lines are from one of Hughes's two paraphrases of odes of Horace, each of which begins with a stanza not in the original but derived from Milton. In his *Court of Neptune* (1699), moreover, he has the phrase "your little Tridents wield," and in his *Ode in Praise of Musick* (1703) the line "Let the deep-mouth'd *Organ* blow."[3] Hughes also wrote a "Supplement and Conclusion" to *Penseroso*, and two octosyllabics which recall Milton's poems in that meter. One, *A Thought in a Garden*, written in 1704, begins:

> Delightful Mansion! Blest Retreat!
> Where all is Silent, all is Sweet!
> Here Contemplation prunes her Wings,
> The raptur'd Muse more tuneful Sings,
> While *May* leads on the Chearful Hours.[4]

The other, *The Picture*, is closer to *Allegro*:

> Queen of Fancy! hither bring
> On thy gaudy-feather'd Wing
> All the Beauties of the Spring.
> Like the Bee's industrious Pains
> To collect his Golden Gains,
> So from ev'ry Flow'r and Plant
> Gather first ih' immortal Paint.
> Fetch me Lilies, fetch me Roses,
> Daisies, Vi'lets, Cowslip-Posies.[5]

---

[1] See his essay *On Descriptions in Poetry* (*Poems*, 1735, ii. 329–35), and his poem *A Letter to a Friend in the Country* (*ib.* i. 111–13), both written before 1720.

[2] *Horace, Book i, Ode xxii* (*ib.* i. 113).

[3] *Poems*, i. 35 (cf. *Comus*, 27), 165 (cf. *Penseroso*, 161).

[4] Cf. *Comus*, 377–8; and the sonnet to the nightingale, 4.

[5] For Hughes's other references to Milton, see his *Poems*, i. 250, and ii. 91, 317–18, 333–4; his edition of Spenser (1715), vol. i. pp. xxvii, xxx, xxxvii, xxxix, xli, lxviii, lxxvii, ci, cx; and cf. p. 422 above.

Far greater powers than Hughes possessed were displayed by the accomplished Latinist, pleasing poet, and intimate friend of Pope, Swift, and Gay, — Thomas Parnell. One of Parnell's several octosyllabics is a *Hymn to Contentment* (1714), which has a Miltonic lilt quite unlike the cadence of the others:

> Lovely, lasting Peace of Mind!
> Sweet Delight of human kind!
> Heavenly born, and bred on high,
> To crown the Fav'rites of the Sky. . . .
> Whither, O whither art thou fled,
> To lay thy meek, contented Head? . . .
> Ambition searches all its Sphere
> Of Pomp and State, to meet thee there. . . .
> Lovely, lasting Peace appear!
> This World it self, if thou art here,
> Is once again with *Eden* bless'd,
> And Man contains it in his Breast.

More use of the structure of *Allegro* is made in his *Health, an Eclogue,* which is written in heroic couplets:

> Come, Country *Goddess*, come, nor thou suffice,
> But bring thy Mountain-Sister, *Exercise.* . . .
> Oh come, thou *Goddess* of my rural Song,
> And bring thy Daughter, calm *Content*, along,
> Dame of the ruddy Cheek and laughing Eye.[1]

Much of the dull Pindaric *Ode for the New Year* MDCCXVI, in which Nicholas Rowe flattered the king, is in lines of four feet, and, besides other borrowings from Milton's companion poems, contains this passage:

> Hence then with ev'ry anxious Care!
> Begone pale Envy, and thou cold Despair!
> Seek ye out a moody Cell,
> Where Deceit and Treason dwell. . . .
> But thou Hope, with smiling Chear,
> Do thou bring the ready Year.

In 1718 William Hinchliffe published in his *Poems, Amorous, Moral, and Divine,* some four hundred octosyllabic lines entitled *The Seasons,* divided into four poems, *Spring, Summer, Autumn,* and *Winter*. The movement of Hinchliffe's lines reminds one of *Allegro,*

---

[1] Parnell's *Hermit*, which is also in heroic couplets, has the phrase "the dappled Morn arose" (line 149, cf. *Allegro*, 44), and the lines,

> Now sunk the Sun; the closing Hour of Day
> Came onward, mantled o'er with sober gray

(lines 43–4, cf. *P. L.*, iv. 598–9, 609).

as do the personified abstractions, the description of their attire, and the pictures of nature; but the similarity is principally metrical, as will be seen from these, the most Miltonic passages in the poem:

> And now sweet *Flora* doth appear,
> The Nymph for ever young and fair.
> Lightly around her slender Waste
> A party-colour'd Mantle's cast;
> Enrich'd with ev'ry Flow'r that grows. . . .
> She comes! the lovely graceful Queen!
> Wrap'd in a Robe of brightest Green.
> *Phoebus*, the gallant Goddess leads
> O'er the smooth Lawns and yellow Meads. . . .
> *Summer* by Mortals, but above
> She's call'd the *Nut-brown Maid of* Jove. . . .
> . . . glowing *August* bears her Train.
> In one Hand golden Ears of Corn,
> Poppies, and Lavender are born.[1]

The *Allegro-Penseroso* structure is combined with decidedly Miltonic blank verse in the *Invocation of Health* which Henry Baker, a naturalist of importance who married Defoe's daughter, published in 1723. Baker describes "lovely Hygeia," and then invokes her in the grand style:

> Vouchsafe thy presence! nor yet leave behind
> Thy fair companions, sprightly exercise,
> Smiling good nature, hearty cheerfulness. . . .[2]

Most of the piece, however, is given over to "Disease (thine opposite)" and her "dire train" of personifications.

It may be remembered that William Broome, the translator of a third of Pope's *Odyssey* and author of all the notes, also turned parts of Homer into the style and meter of *Paradise Lost*.[3] In the dull tetrameter ode, *Melancholy*, that he composed in 1723 on the death of his daughter he made some use of the companion poems:

---

[1] Pages 45, 47, 49, 50. *Summer*, like *Allegro*, ends with a reference to the rescue of Eurydice by Orpheus. My attention was called to the poem by C. A. Moore's *Predecessor of Thomson's Seasons* (*Modern Language Notes*, 1919, xxxiv. 278-81). Cibber (*Lives*, 1753, v. 25-6) prints a lyric of Hinchliffe's, *The Invitation*, which ends thus:

> Haste, nymph, nor let me sigh in vain,
> Each grace attends on thee . . .
> For love and truth are of thy train. . . .

[2] *Anthologia Hibernica* (Dublin, 1793), i. 226. The phrase "her baleful eyes around Rolling" is from *Paradise Lost* (i. 56); and so are "unwieldy . . . A bulk enormous" (cf. *P. L.*, vii. 410-11) and "monsters dire! Centaurs, chimeras, gorgons" (cf. *P.L.*, ii. 625-8).

[3] See above, pp. 106-7. For the lines Broome borrowed from *Lycidas*, see above, p. 426.

> Adieu vain Mirth, and noisy Joys! . . .
> Thou thoughtful Melancholy deign
> To hide me in thy pensive Train! . . .
> Come, blissful Mourner, wisely sad,
> In Sorrow's Garb, in Sable clad. . . .
> With solemn Pace, demure, and slow.

The *Hymn on Solitude* which Thomson wrote the year he began *The Seasons* is simple, natural, and in one part charming. Unfortunately these, its most Miltonic lines, are not the best:

> Hail, mildly pleasing Solitude,
> Companion of the wise and good . . .
> The herd of fools and villains fly. . . .
> Descending angels bless thy train,
> The virtues of the sage, and swain —
> Plain Innocence in white arrayed . . .
> Religion's beams around thee shine . . .
> About thee sports sweet Liberty. . . .
> Oh, let me pierce thy secret cell,
> And in thy deep recesses dwell! . . .
> When meditation has her fill.

The debt to *Allegro* is equally marked in the brief lyric, "Come, gentle god of soft desire," that Thomson sent to the *Gentleman's Magazine* in 1736.[1]

But, when it comes to pleasing octosyllabics, the almost-forgotten bard of the *Fleece*, John Dyer, whose blank verse is a none-too-successful copy of *The Seasons*, far outstrips Thomson and all his contemporaries. His *Country Walk*, to be sure, is in no way remarkable, though it contains such pleasant lines as,

> I am resolv'd, this charming Day,
> In the open Field to stray,
> And have no Roof above my Head,
> But that whereon the Gods do tread.

But *Grongar Hill* is as delightful in its fresh love of nature as in its lilting meter:

> Grass and flowers Quiet treads,
> On the meads, and mountain-heads . . .
> And often, by the murm'ring rill,
> Hears the thrush, while all is still,
> Within the groves of Grongar Hill.

Rarely did the eighteenth century moralize so charmingly as in the passage,

---

[1] For the numerous phrases from Milton's minor poems in Thomson's other works (some of them composed before either of these), see below, Appendix A.

A little rule, a little sway,
A sun beam in a winter's day,
Is all the proud and mighty have
Between the cradle and the grave.

And see the rivers how they run,
Thro' woods and meads, in shade and sun,
Sometimes swift, sometimes slow,
Wave succeeding wave, they go
A various journey to the deep,
Like human life to endless sleep!

The cadence of these octosyllabics certainly recalls *Allegro*, as does the plan of the earlier part of the poem:

Silent Nymph, with curious eye! . . .
Come with all thy various hues,
Come, and aid thy sister Muse. . . .
Grongar, in whose mossy cells
Sweetly-musing Quiet dwells. . . .
So oft I have, the evening still . . .
'Till Contemplation had her fill.[1]

Dyer's handling of his meter, his love of nature, and his pensive strain all indicate that a new current was moving in English verse. As yet it was not romanticism, but classicism turning in a new direction. Dyer faced towards Shelley and Wordsworth, but he was nearer to Thomson and Gray, or even to Pope. *Grongar Hill* shows this, for as first published it was an irregular Pindaric ode and scarcely better than the rest of that wretched species. It contained some lines of eight syllables, and was presumably followed a little later by the *Country Walk*, entirely in octosyllabics. At any rate, the two pieces appeared in the same miscellany, which was edited in 1726 by Johnson's friend, the unfortunate Richard Savage.[2] Apparently Dyer was told by his friends, or soon saw for himself, how much better were his octosyllabics than his Pindarics; for that same year he published *Grongar Hill* as we now have it,[3] an interesting example of a work of art made in the reworking.

Imitation of Milton's companion poems was by no means confined to octosyllabics or even to rime. In 1731 appeared anonymously

[1] The phrase "mossy cells" in this last extract may be from *Penseroso*, 169, and "gardens trim" in the *Country Walk*, 115, from *Penseroso*, 50 (George Sherburn, in *Modern Philology*, xvii. 528, 525, cf. 520).

[2] *Miscellaneous Poems and Translations*, 48–57, 60–66. Another piece in Dyer's characteristic octosyllabics, *An Epistle to a Famous Painter*, may be seen in Chalmers's *English Poets*, xiii. 251.

[3] *Miscellaneous Poems, published by D. Lewis* (1726), 223–31. *Grongar Hill* influenced not a few eighteenth-century poems. In 1785 it was made the subject of one of John Scott's "Critical Essays."

eight pages of very Miltonic blank verse with the title *Il Penseroso* and the motto (from *Paradise Lost*) "Solitude sometimes is best Society." [1] In the first half of the poem, which pictures the life of a solitary nature-lover, much the same things are done as in *Allegro*. Two rather similar poems adopted Milton's title to emphasize their own melancholy strain, James Foot's blank-verse *Penseroso* (1771),[2] and an anonymous *Il Penseroso, an Evening's Contemplation in St. John's Church-yard, Chester, a Rhapsody, written more than twenty years ago* (1767), of which the *Monthly Review* remarked, "If this poem hath any merit at all, it is entirely local, from the objects it describes, and therefore we cannot recommend it beyond the precincts of St. John's church-yard in Chester, where it was born, and where it was buried, in the year of our Lord 1767; aged twenty years." [3]

Another unexpected use of the *Allegro-Penseroso* structure appears in the opening of *Constantia*, a very free and highly-sophisticated rendering of the *Man of Law's Tale*, which Henry Brooke, author of *Gustavus Vasa* and the *Fool of Quality*, contributed to Ogle's *Canterbury Tales of Chaucer Modernis'd* (1741). The poem begins,

> Hence, *Want*, ungrateful Visitant, adieu,
> Pale Empress hence, with all thy meager Crew,
> Sour Discontent, and mortify'd Chagrin;
> Lean hollow Care, and self-corroding Spleen.

After twelve more lines of evil spirits, Virtue is introduced with her long train of personified abstractions; then come more vices until the capital letters are well-nigh exhausted, then Virtue again, and finally the story, tilting on nicely-balanced heroic couplets.

Truly, features of the companion poems were appearing in strange places and being put to strange uses! Their plan and meter will be found in the verses under the second plate of Hogarth's "Rake's Progress" (1735),[4] in the wedding entertainment which the poet-

---

[1] *Miscellany of Poems, publish'd by J. Husbands* (Oxford, 1731), 161-9. The closest verbal similarity to Milton is "divine Philosophy, Here [let me] ever dwell with Thee" (p. 164). A few lines (1-49, 363-94) of the unrimed *Death* which James Macpherson of Ossianic fame composed about 1750 show the influence of Milton's octosyllabics.

[2] See pp. 397-8 above.

[3] xxxvi. 409. The poem proves to have been written by Dr. William Cowper, a physician of Chester, who died in 1767. Another physician, "Dr. G. P. . . ." of Baltimore, used this same title of Milton's for a brief stanzaic piece on the sadness of winter and the gladness of spring (*Europ. Mag.*, 1788, xiii. 222).

[4] Dr. John Hoadly, who translated Holdsworth's burlesque *Muscipula* into the verse of *Paradise Lost* (see pp. 108, 318, above), wrote a few tetrameter couplets for each plate of the series. Those under the third print contain the line (from *Comus*, 47), "Sweet poison of misused wine." The verses are all reprinted in "Dodsley's Miscellany" (1758,

publisher Robert Dodsley wrote in 1732, and in the pantomime he composed in 1745.[1] Sir William Blackstone (author of the *Commentaries*) employed them in 1744 to bid farewell to his muse and welcome to his new profession,[2] while in 1746 Benjamin Hoadly unblushingly put them into a cantata which was sung in honor of the Duke of Cumberland's victory at Culloden.[3]

Early in 1745, a year after he published the *Pleasures of Imagination*, Mark Akenside brought out his *Odes on Several Subjects*. In the words of the "advertisement," the author "pretends chiefly . . . to be correct," and this goal — a curious one for a lyric poet — is all he achieves. Yet the odes (which were subsequently increased from ten to thirty-three), though quite free from inspiration, move slowly with the new current in poetry; for, besides being stanzaic and often octosyllabic, they deal with nature and with personifications. One of the tetrameters, the *Hymn to Cheerfulness*, is in part clearly modelled on the companion poems:

> Come, Cheerfulness, triumphant fair,
> Shine through the hovering cloud of care:
> O sweet of language, mild of mien,
> O Virtue's friend and Pleasure's queen. . . .
> Thy lenient influence hither bring.

The courtship of the parents of Cheerfulness and the account of her birth are patently taken from *Allegro:*

> As once ('twas in Astraea's reign) . . .
> It happen'd that immortal Love
> Was ranging through the spheres above. . . .
> When Health majestic mov'd along . . .
> And, known from that auspicious morn,
> The pleasing Cheerfulness was born.

Nearly six years before the publication of his *Odes* Akenside had contributed to the *Gentleman's Magazine* a *Hymn to Science*, which

---

v. 269–74), in the volume that contains *The Grotto* ("printed in . . . 1732 but never published," *ib.* 159) by Matthew Green, author of *The Spleen*. A page and a half, perhaps, of the ten pages of Green's easy, pleasant octosyllabics seem pretty clearly suggested by Milton's work in the same measure. Both Hoadly's and Green's borrowings are pointed out by Sherburn, pp. 519, 530, 520, 524.

[1] See Bibl. II, below.

[2] In *The Lawyer's Farewel to his Muse* ("Dodsley's Miscellany," 1755, iv. 228–32). The lines that are closest to Milton's are,

> Yet let my setting sun, at last,
> Find out the still, the rural cell,
> Where sage Retirement loves to dwell!

[3] See Bibl. II. This occasion also called forth an anonymous octosyllabic ode in which the "goddess of immortal song" is asked to "descend, and bring along Fame, Concord," etc. (*Gent. Mag.*, xvi. 267).

he wisely never republished.[1] These lines show the debt to Milton:

> Science! thou fair effusive ray . . .
> Descend with all thy treasures fraught. . . .
> Disperse those phantoms from my sight . . .
> The scholiast's learning, sophist's cant. . . .
> Her secret stores let Memory tell,
> Bid Fancy quit her fairy cell,
> In all her colours drest. . . .
> While, undeluded, happier I
> From the vain tumult timely fly,
> And sit in peace with thee.

This piece may have been in Swift's mind when he wrote his burlesque *Ode on Science*, which is similar in title and structure, has the same meter, and was composed about the same time, though perhaps earlier. Swift's *Ode* seems to ridicule the commonplaces of poetry, — which characterize Akenside's *Hymn* but become much more obnoxious later in the century, — as well as the use of vague language that sounds impressive but means little or nothing. It was certainly directed at some of Milton's imitators:

> O, HEAVENLY born! in deepest dells
> If fairest science ever dwells
> Beneath the mossy cave. . . .
> Come, fairest princess of the throng,
> Bring sweet philosophy along,
> In metaphysic dreams. . . .
> Drive Thraldom with malignant hand . . .
> Iërne bear on azure wing;
> Energic let her soar, and sing
> Thy universal sway.

The Dean was himself the subject of a good-natured parody in Isaac Hawkins Browne's *Pipe of Tobacco* (1735–6). The last of the six "imitations" that make up this volume burlesques Swift; yet it makes some use of the *Allegro-Penseroso* structure, which Swift employed only in the *Ode on Science:*

> Come jovial Pipe, and bring along
> Midnight, Revelry and Song;
> The merry Catch, the Madrigal,
> That echoes sweet in City Hall. . . .
> *Britons*, if undone, can go,
> Where TOBACCO loves to grow.

Probably Browne did not intend the "come" and "bring" and other Miltonisms as part of the imitation, but introduced them because

[1] *Gent. Mag.*, ix. 544 (1739); reprinted in the Aldine edition of his *Works* (1835), 293–6. See also p. 471 below.

they were associated in his mind with the octosyllabic, Swift's favorite meter.[1]

Contentment, which "E. L." contributed to the *Gentleman's Magazine* for October, 1736, begins,

> Descend, celestial *Peace of Mind!* . . .
> Hence, *murmurs, sighs,* and *Fears*, exclude!

and David Mallet's octosyllabic *Fragment* (1743?), though it does not make use of the "hence" or "come," has the Miltonic cadence and personifications and mentions a number of the things that are done in *Penseroso*. Health is first invoked:

> Thou oft art seen, at early dawn,
> Slow-pacing o'er the breezy lawn. . . .
> But when the sun, with noontide ray,
> Flames forth intolerable day;
> While *Heat* sits fervent on the plain,
> With *Thirst* and *Languor* in his train;

then, "amid the shadows brown," Imagination listens to "every murmur of the wood," to the brook, the bee among the flowers, the "woodman's echoing stroke," and "the thunder of the falling oak."[2]

After 1740 the number of these imitations increased so rapidly that it would be both impracticable and unprofitable to consider them all. One that should be mentioned, however, not only for its length but because it illustrates the influence of Handel's oratorio *L'Allegro, Il Pensieroso, ed Il Moderato* (1740), is *The Estimate of Life* (1746), which, like Handel's work, consists of three parts, *The Melancholy, The Cheerful, The Moderate*.[3] John Gilbert Cooper, the author, who had used the verse and style of *Paradise Lost* the preceding year in his *Power of Harmony*,[4] did not hesitate to follow the companion poems as closely as this:

> Grim Superstition, hence away,
> To native Night, and leave the Day;
> Nor let thy hellish Brood appear,
> Begot on Ignorance and Fear!
> Come gentle Mirth and Gaiety,
> Sweet Daughters of Society.

An earlier, pleasanter, and more important writer of octosyllabics, but one who likewise belongs to the "minor orders," is William Hamilton of Bangour, follower of the Pretender and author of *The Braes of Yarrow*. Though a mild classicist, Hamilton furnishes one

---

[1] Browne's *Ode to Health*, presumably written later than his *Pipe of Tobacco*, is also patently Miltonic.
[2] Cf. *Penseroso*, 122–44.   [3] See below, Bibl. II.   [4] See above, pp. 393–4.

of the many points of connection between Milton's work and the reappearance of romanticism in English poetry, for he was a contributor to Ramsay's *Tea-Table Miscellany* and a frequent imitator of *Paradise Lost* and of *Allegro*. Dr. Johnson, who scented romantic tendencies from afar, said that the verses of the young Scotsman were "nothing better than what you generally find in magazines; and that the highest praise they deserved was, that they were very well for a gentleman to hand about among his friends." The crushing truth of this criticism Boswell did not accept. "I comforted myself," he tells us, "with thinking that the beauties were too delicate for his robust perceptions." [1]

Four of Hamilton's octosyllabics, written in 1739 or somewhat earlier, have the cadence of *Allegro*, as well as the "hence," "come," the personifications, a number of verbal borrowings,[2] and in one place something of the parentage and birth,[3] — pretty good evidence that he derived the meter, which he used extensively, from Milton. The structure of his second ode, which consists of four paragraphs, the first and third devoted to "hence," the second and fourth to "come," may help to account for the later vogue of the companion poems, for any one can write verses of this kind on any occasion or without occasion:

> Begone, pursuits so vain and light,
> Knowledge, fruitless of delight;
> Lean Study, sire of sallow Doubt. . . .

---

[1] Boswell's *Life* (ed. Hill), iii. 150–51. Hamilton shows some love of nature (see his *Contemplation*, in *Poems*, ed. Paterson, Edin., 1850, p. 39), which was probably stimulated by Dyer, for the line "Now on the flow'ring turf I lie" is borrowed from *Grongar Hill*, 138.

[2] *Contemplation* has the rimes "aged oak . . . woodsman's stroke," "pellucid stream . . . mystic dream" (*Poems*, 36, cf. *Penseroso*, 135–6, 147–8); and the phrases "sober-suited maid" (*ib.* 37, cf. *Pen.*, 122), "the decent nun fair Peace of Mind" (*ib.*, cf. *Pen.*, 31, 36), and "above, below, and all around" (*ib.* 39, cf. *Pen.*, 152, of sound in each case). *Ode I, To Fancy*, has "meek-ey'd Peace" (*ib.* 49, cf. *Nativity*, 46), "fickle troop of Morpheus' train" (*ib.*, cf. *Pen.*, 10), and

> In a gown of stainless lawn,
> O'er each manly shoulder drawn?
> Who, clad in robe of scarlet grain
> The boy that bears her flowing train?

(*ib.* 48, cf. *Pen.*, 33–6); the manuscript version has "clouds . . . skirts of gold" (*ib.* 56, cf. *P. L.*, v. 187), and

> Or view the honey-making bee
> Load with sweets her amber thigh

(*ib.*, cf. *Pen.*, 142, and cf. the whole passage with *Pen.*, 131–48). *Ode II* has "Nods, and wreaths, and becks and tips" (*ib.* 53, cf. *Allegro*, 28). *Miss and the Butterfly* and *On a Summer-House*, which owe little else to Milton, have the expressions "as sages sing" (*ib.* 53, cf. *All.*, 17) and "Here chaste Calliope, I live with thee" (*ib.* 115, cf. *All.*, 152, *Pen.*, 176).

[3] *Contemplation*, *ib.* 37.

I come, nor single, but along
Youthful sports a jolly throng!
Thoughtless joke, and infant wiles;
Harmless wit, and virgin smiles. . . .

But, anxious Care, be far from hence;
Vain surmise, and alter'd sense;
Mishapen doubts, the woes they bring;
And Jealousy, of fiercest sting. . . .

But come, all ye who know to please;
Inviting glance, and downy ease . . .
Nods, and wreaths, and becks and tips;
Meaning winks, and roguish trips.

In August, 1738, Richard West, Gray's friend, while visiting
Horace Walpole at Richmond Park, was asked to "write something"
upon the "Thatcht House" there. Accordingly, he sent Walpole
over one hundred and twenty-five not unpleasant octosyllabic lines,
of which the following and some others reveal a familiarity with
Allegro:

Fallows grey, and pastures green,
Where herds and flocks are grazing seen,
With many a woody park, & hill
Hanging o'er some shadowy rill. . . .
There oft, ere yet the grey-eyed Dawn
Has visited the dewy lawn,
The early chace with cheerful yell
Calls sleepy Echo from her cell. . . .
Observe the reapers' tawny band,
Each with his sickle in his hand.[1]

Four years afterwards Gray received from him an octosyllabic ode
divided into stanzas, which uses the "come" and the train of personifications:

Come, fairest Nymph, resume thy reign!
Bring all the Graces in thy train!
With balmy breath, and flowery tread,
Rise from thy soft ambrosial bed. . . .
Come then, with Pleasure at thy side.[2]

About the time West wrote his lines on the "Thatcht House"
another Miltonic piece was being composed, the earliest we have

[1] *Correspondence of Gray, Walpole, West,* etc. (ed. Toynbee, Oxford, 1915), i. 191–3.

[2] These lines are from the version given by Mason in the "Memoirs" prefixed to
Gray's *Poems,* 1775, pp. 147–8. D. C. Tovey (*Gray and his Friends,* Camb., 1890, pp.
165–6) publishes a form that differs considerably and is rather less Miltonic. It has the
lines,

Oh, come with that enchanting Face
That lively Look, that youthful Grace!

For another passage reminiscent of *Allegro,* see West's monody (below, pp. 550–51.)

from the pen of the most inspired and possibly the most nearly romantic poet produced in the first eighty years of the century, William Collins, who like Smart and Clare paid dearly for his gifts by spending some of his last years in an insane asylum. The disordered minds of these three men, the peculiarities of Blake, and the tragic lives of Burns, Coleridge, Keats, Shelley, and Byron give some basis for thinking romanticism a disease. Yet there is nothing diseased or morbid in Collins's clean-cut work, nothing ecstatic or violent even; rather it is delicate, reserved, and, what is more surprising in view of the rare beauty of the best of it, not really lyric. Collins seems not to have had the singing voice, and his fondness for abstractions was opposed to the concreteness of the lyric.[1] Yet in lacking the singing quality, in being descriptive and contemplative rather than emotional, and in employing many personified abstractions, his poems are typical of their time.

It is surely significant that in his *Ode on the Poetical Character*, although he refers to the " school " of Spenser and to an episode in the *Faerie Queene*, Collins mentions no poet but Milton, and that he devotes twenty-two lines to him, more space than he gives to any other English writer except Shakespeare in all the rest of his work put together. The description of the cliff, which symbolizes Milton in the passage, shows how the romantic classicists of the day looked upon him:

> High on some cliff, to heav'n up-pil'd,
> Of rude access, of prospect wild,
> Where, tangled round the jealous steep,
> Strange shades o'er-brow the valleys deep,
> And holy genii guard the rock,
> Its glooms embrown, its springs unlock,
> While on its rich ambitious head
> An Eden, like his own, lies spread. . . .
>   Thither oft, his glory greeting,
>   From Waller's myrtle shades retreating,
> With many a vow from Hope's aspiring tongue,
> My trembling feet his guiding steps pursue;
> In vain — such bliss to one alone
> Of all the sons of soul was known.

As the "his" in these lines means "Milton's," we have in the concluding lines a frank avowal of Collins's attempt to follow the earlier poet. There is, to be sure, nothing to indicate a knowledge of *Allegro* or the other minor poems, but such knowledge is abundantly attested by the verbal borrowings and the structure of this and other

---

[1] One would not, of course, expect anything impassioned or ecstatic from him; but songs of the type of "Hark, hark, the lark" or "Who is Sylvia?" he might have written.

odes. Of words and phrases taken from Milton there are in all something over twenty, a fair number considering how little Collins wrote; yet few of them are obvious, and as a rule they consist of only a word or two. Occasionally one finds as patent a borrowing as "round him rolls his sullen eyes; [1] but more typical are "nature boon," "love-darting eye," "the meeting soul," or such dubious cases as "upland fallows," "buskin'd Muse," or the use of "decent" in the sense of "decorous." [2]

Milton's influence upon the meter and plan of Collins's odes is of the same elusive kind. It is most clearly seen in *The Manners:*

> Farewell, for clearer ken design'd,
> The dim-discover'd tracts of Mind. . . .
> Where Science, prank'd in tissu'd vest,
> By Reason, Pride, and Fancy drest,
> Comes like a bride so trim array'd,
> To wed with Doubt in Plato's shade! . . .
> Thy walks, Observance, more invite! . . .
> Retiring hence to thoughtful cell,
> As Fancy breathes her potent spell . . .
> In pageant quaint, in motley mask. . . .
> O Humour, thou whose name is known . . .
> Me too amidst thy band admit,
> There where the young-ey'd healthful Wit . . .
> In laughter loos'd attends thy side! . . .
> The Sports and I this hour agree
> To rove thy scene-full world with thee!

Here we have the meter, personifications, train, manner, and dress, a kind of "hence" and "come," verbal borrowings, and the ending. Most of these characteristics may also be discovered in the *Ode to Fear:*

> Ah Fear! ah frantic Fear!
> I see, I see thee near!
> I know thy hurried step, thy haggard eye! . . .
> For lo what monsters in thy train appear!
> Danger, whose limbs of giant mold . . .
> And with him thousand phantoms join'd . . .
> Whilst Vengeance, in the lurid air,
> Lifts her red arms, expos'd and bare . . .
> Who, Fear, this ghastly train can see,
> And look not madly wild, like thee? . . .
> Say, wilt thou shroud in haunted cell,
> Where gloomy Rape and Murder dwell?

---

[1] *Popular Superstitions*, 102; cf. *P. L.*, i. 56.
[2] *Manners*, 71 (cf. *P. L.*, iv. 242); *Poetical Character*, 8 (cf. *Comus*, 753); *Simplicity*, 48 (cf. *Allegro*, 138); *Evening*, 31 (cf. *Allegro*, 92); *Pity*, 34 (cf. *Penseroso*, 102); *Simplicity*, 10 (cf. *Penseroso*, 36).

> Or in some hollow'd seat. . . .
> Ne'er be I found, by thee o'eraw'd,
> In that thrice-hallow'd eve abroad
> When ghosts, as cottage maids believe,
> Their pebbled beds permitted leave,
> And goblins haunt, from fire, or fen,
> Or mine, or flood, the walks of men! . . .
> Hither again thy fury deal! . . .
> And I, O Fear, will dwell with thee! [1]

Milton's accounts of the wooing of the parents of Mirth and Melancholy are reflected in the *Ode on the Poetical Character*, where Collins, through his fondness for the *Allegro-Penseroso* structure, is led into obscurity and the bad taste of representing the Creator as courted by Fancy, who gives birth to the sun!

> Long by the lov'd enthusiast woo'd,
> Himself in some diviner mood,
> Retiring, sate with her alone . . .
> And thou, thou rich-hair'd Youth of Morn,
> And all thy subject life, was born!
> The dang'rous Passions kept aloof . . .
> But near it sate ecstatic Wonder,
> List'ning the deep applauding thunder;
> And Truth, in sunny vest array'd.

These similarities to Milton in Collins's various poems can hardly be due to chance, for he wrote slowly and revised carefully. A few lines from three other odes will show how the structure of the companion pieces repeatedly crops out in his work:

> Come, Pity, come! By Fancy's aid. . . .
> There Picture's toils shall well relate . . .
> The buskin'd Muse shall near her stand. . . .
> There let me oft, retir'd by day,
> In dreams of passion melt away,
> Allow'd with thee to dwell. [2]

> O Peace, thy injur'd robes up-bind!
> O rise, and leave not one behind
> Of all thy beamy train! . . .
> But come to grace thy western isle,
> By warlike Honour led! [3]

---

[1] Line 58, "Ne'er be I found, by thee o'eraw'd," forms a kind of "hence." The two lines beginning "And goblins haunt" (62-3) are to me more suggestive of *Penseroso*, 93-4, than are any of the parallels given by W. C. Bronson on page 99 of his excellent edition of Collins.

[2] *Pity*, 25-39.   [3] *Peace*, 13-21.

> O Music, sphere-descended maid,
> Friend of Pleasure, Wisdom's aid. . . .
> O bid our vain endeavours cease,
> Revive the just designs of Greece,
> Return in all thy simple state.[1]

The last extract also gives an idea of the poet's tetrameter, a meter he uses considerably but never throughout a poem. This passage is his nearest approach to Milton's cadence.

Collins began copying *Allegro* when he was about seventeen, in what seems to be the first poem we have from his pen. As the piece in question, the first "Oriental Eclogue," is a conventional, pseudo-classic pastoral in heroic couplets, it is the last place where one would think of looking for the *Allegro* structure. Yet here it is unmistakably:

> Come thou, whose thoughts as limpid springs are clear,
> To lead the train; sweet Modesty, appear. . . .
> With thee be Chastity, of all afraid,
> Distrusting all, a wise suspicious maid. . . .
> No wild Desires amidst thy train be known,
> But Faith, whose heart is fix'd on one alone;
> Desponding Meekness with her down-cast eyes;
> And friendly Pity full of tender sighs.[2]

Six of Collins's fourteen odes and one of his ten remaining pieces are therefore affected by the plan of the octosyllabics, a greater percentage than is found in any other English writer. Inasmuch as his finest work, the *Ode to Evening*, is in the unrimed stanza of Milton's translation from Horace and his *Ode to Simplicity* seems to employ a modification of the *Nativity* stanza,[3] and as he borrowed a number of phrases, he was under no small debt to Milton's earlier poems.

If the patient reader of this volume were to stroll through the glorious but sadly-disfigured aisles of Westminster Abbey until he reached the transept which is paved and lined with the tombstones of illustrious poets, his eye in the course of its wanderings might chance to light on the monument to Gray. If so, he would notice a female figure holding in one hand a medallion of the poet and with the other pointing upward to the bust of Milton. On the base of the statue he would read,

> No more the Grecian Muse unrivall'd reigns,
> To Britain let the nations homage pay;
> She felt a Homer's fire in Milton's strains,
> A Pindar's rapture from the lyre of GRAY.

---

[1] *The Passions*, 95–117.   [3] For these two poems, see below, pp. 561–2, 565–6.
[2] Lines 53–66.

If the sight of this memorial should lead him on his return home to open a volume of the poet, he might notice that the first line on the first page and the last line but five on the last page contain phrases from Milton. If he were to glance up this last page he might observe three other borrowings from the same source, and were he to continue his readings he would find many more of the same kind. A number of them, like "margent green," "starry fronts," "vermeil-cheek," "not obvious, not obtrusive," [1] are so slight that he would dismiss them, did he not remember Gray's slow, painstaking, self-conscious method of composition. [2] There are in all about fifty verbal borrowings from Milton, or almost one to a page. [3] Yet Gray's fine taste taught him how to borrow, for every phrase he takes he assimilates so that it seems his own. A typical instance is the line

> Right against the eastern gate,

which he transfers from the joyous sunrise of *Allegro* to the grim nether-world of the *Descent of Odin*, fitting it so perfectly into its new surroundings that the average reader does not suspect any indebtedness. Although originality is not a striking characteristic of Gray's work, his fastidiousness did not allow him to compose the patent imitations that were common in his day. Accordingly, much as he admired the "voice as of the cherub-choir" he modelled none of his poems upon those of Milton. Parts of two of them do, however, show a decided influence from the 1645 volume. There can, for example, be no question as to the source of these stanzas from one of his earliest pieces, the *Hymn to Adversity:*

> Scared at thy frown terrific, fly
> Self-pleasing Folly's idle brood,
> Wild Laughter, Noise, and thoughtless Joy,
> And leave us leisure to be good.
> Light they disperse, and with them go
> The summer Friend, the flatt'ring Foe;
> By vain Prosperity received. . . .
>
> Wisdom in sable garb array'd
> Immers'd in rapt'rous thought profound,

---

[1] *Eton College*, 23 (cf. *Comus*, 232); *The Bard*, 112 (cf. *Passion*, 18); *Pleasure arising from Vicissitude*, 3 (cf. *Comus*, 752); *Ode for Music*, 78 (cf. *P. L.*, viii. 504).

[2] "No poetry is less spontaneous than Gray's; of *him* it is emphatically true that there is 'not a line of his, but he could tell us very well how it came there'" (Tovey, *Gray's English Poems*, Camb., 1898, p. 123).

[3] Gray also dropped into Miltonic language in his letters, — as when he wrote to Walpole (Sept., 1737), "At the foot of one of these [trees] squats ME I (il penseroso)"; or to James Brown (Dec. ?, 1759), "I am glad to find you are so lapt in music at Cambridge" (cf. *Allegro*, 136).

>And Melancholy, silent maid
>>With leaden eye, that loves the ground,
>Still on thy solemn steps attend:
>Warm Charity, the general Friend,
>>With Justice to herself severe,
>And Pity, dropping soft the sadly-pleasing tear.

Here we have the personifications, the train, the manner, a modified form of the "hence" and "come," and several Miltonic phrases.

None of Gray's octosyllabics have Milton's cadence; the nearest approach to it is to be found in these more abrupt lines:

>Where he points his purple spear,
>Hasty, hasty Rout is there,
>Marking with indignant eye
>Fear to stop, and shame to fly:
>There Confusion, Terror's child,
>Conflict fierce, and Ruin wild.[1]

Gray's last poem was the perfunctory *Ode for Music*, written for the installation of the Duke of Grafton as chancellor of Cambridge University. It is a stilted, dreary piece, for Gray's heart was not in it; even Mr. Tovey's praise, "good as it is amongst Installation Odes," [2] is not reassuring. Yet in the present connection the poem is of interest, for it begins with the "hence," the personifications, and the meter of *Allegro*:

>Hence, avaunt, ('tis holy ground)
>>Comus, and his midnight crew,
>And Ignorance with looks profound,
>>And dreaming Sloth of pallid hue,
>Mad Sedition's cry profane,
>Servitude that hugs her chain,
>Nor in these consecrated bowers
>Let painted Flatt'ry hide her serpent-train in flowers.

After as much more of this sort of thing, Milton appears and speaks in the stanza of his *Nativity*, using a number of his own phrases. Outside of these passages, the *Ode* contains at least six Miltonic borrowings. It appears, therefore, that when Gray had a poem to write and did not know what to say he turned to Milton to furnish him a kind of form which he might fill out. Most versifiers of the later eighteenth century did the same, only with them it was the rule to have nothing to say.

Typical of such writers is the uninspired but indefatigable William Mason. It speaks ill for the judgment of the time that Mason was

---

[1] *Triumphs of Owen*, 33–8.　　　[2] *Gray's English Poems*, 281.

taken very seriously as a poet. As a friend and biographer of Gray
he is still known, but no one thinks of reading his verses, which are
significant merely because they embody with unusual clearness certain tendencies of the time. The better taste of his friends usually
kept them from flagrant imitation, but Mason was not one to do
things by halves. Since he had started to imitate Milton, he carried
the matter to its logical conclusion. Beginning with a slavish copy of
Allegro and then one of *Penseroso*, he followed them with a professed
imitation of *Lycidas;* later he composed Miltonic sonnets, wrote a
long poem on the English garden in Miltonic blank verse, borrowed
a scene from Milton's masque, and even proposed to Dodsley to edit
the minor poems.[1]

Mason's *Il Bellicoso* and *Il Pacifico* show to what extremes the
copying of Milton often went: they have every characteristic of
L'Allegro and *Il Penseroso* save the essential one, beauty. They are
companion poems, parallel in structure and opposed in meaning; the
titles, the irregular opening, the "hence," the "come," the movement of the lines, the contents, the phrasing, the ending, — everything is slavishly copied. But *Il Pacifico* may speak for itself:

> Hence, pestilential MARS,
>> Of sable-vested Night and Chaos bred,
>> On matter's formless bed,
> Mid the harsh din of elemental jars:
>> Hence with thy frantic crowd,
> Wing'd Flight, pale Terror, Discord cloth'd in fire. . . .
>> But hail, fair PEACE, so mild and meek,
> With polish'd brow and rosy cheek . . .
> For Saturn's first-born daughter thou;
> Unless, as later bards avow,
> The youthful God with spangled hair
> Closely clasp'd Harmonia fair. . . .
> Then to the city's social walls. . . .
> And ev'ry man and ev'ry boy
> Briskly join in warm employ. . . .
> And joys like these, if PEACE inspire,
> PEACE with thee I string the lyre.

There is some influence from Milton's octosyllabics in parts of
three of Mason's odes, none of which preserve either the iambic

---

[1] Ralph Straus, *Robert Dodsley* (1910), 114. On Mason's poems, see above, pp.
375–7, and below, pp. 496, 551–2, 557. His classical tragedies may owe something to
Samson Agonistes (but see p. 559 below), as they certainly do to the epic and octosyllabics. In one of the choruses of his *Caractacus*, for example, he uses "the descant
bold" (*Works*, 1811, ii. 110, cf. *P. L.*, iv. 603), and "lapt . . . in ecstasy" (*ib.* 111, cf.
Allegro, 136, of music in each case), besides employing bits of the *Allegro-Penseroso*
structure.

tetrameter or the *Allegro-Penseroso* structure throughout.   The first extract is from the fifth ode, *For Music:*

> Come, imperial Queen of Song;
> Come with all that free-born grace . . .
> That glance of dignity divine,
> Which speaks thee of celestial line;
> Proclaims thee inmate of the sky,
> Daughter of Jove and Liberty. . . .
> Still may'st thou keep thy wonted state
> In unaffected grandeur great.

The second stanza of the sixth ode, *To Independency*, begins,

> Come to thy vot'ry's ardent prayer,
> In all thy graceful plainness drest:
> No knot confines thy waving hair,
> No zone, thy floating vest;
> Unsullied Honour decks thine open brow,
> And Candour brightens in thy modest eye.

The twelfth ode, *To the Naval Officers of Great Britain*, opens as follows:

> Hence to thy Hell! thou Fiend accurst,
>   Of Sin's incestuous brood, the worst
>   Whom to pale Death the spectre bore: [1]
> DETRACTION hence! 'tis Truth's command. . . .
> Old ENGLAND's Genius leads her on . . .
> The Goddess comes, and all the isle
> Feels the warm influence of her heav'nly flame.

The verses of the elder Thomas Warton (1688?–1745) contain in the germ most of the things that were to make his sons' work distinctive. They show a love for nature, ruins, and solitude, a fondness for Chaucer, Spenser, and Milton, for Greek and Scandinavian poetry, and for odes to abstractions, along with other evidences of romantic leanings that are of unusual interest when they occur in verse written between 1705 and 1745 by a professor of poetry at Oxford. Warton's devotion to Milton (whose minor poems he thought he had brought to Pope's attention [2]) was, like that of his sons, unusual. He wrote three odes modelled on *Allegro* and *Penseroso* and one in the meter of the translation from Horace, an invocation to a water-nymph which recalls *Comus*, besides four pieces in a blank verse that owes something to *Paradise Lost*. Here is a sample of his octosyllabics:

---

[1] "Alluding to the well-known allegory of SIN and DEATH, in the second Book of *Paradise Lost*" (Mason's note, *Works*, 1811, i. 59).

[2] See above, p. 115, n. 2.

> O Gentle, feather-footed *Sleep*,
> In drowsy Dews my Temples steep . . .
> O leave thy Bed of balmy Flow'rs,
> And waken all thy dewy Pow'rs,
> And wafted on the silent Wing,
> The Dreams, thy little People bring!
> Let sobbing Grief, and midnight Feast,
> *Comus*, and loudly-laughing *Jest*,
> Never near my Couch appear,
> Nor whistling Whirlwinds wound my Ear . . .
> But whispering Show'rs from off the Eaves,
> Softly dripping on the Leaves.[1]

Joseph Warton, the older and less gifted son of Thomas Warton, was for many years principal of Winchester College, where he encouraged the poetical efforts of his pupil, William Lisle Bowles. He is best known by his rambling, two-volume *Essay on the Genius and Writings of Pope* (1756–82), the first important attempt to point out the deficiencies of pseudo-classic poetry, and therefore one of the more noteworthy critical documents of the eighteenth century. Milton is mentioned, quoted from, or discussed on almost every page. Warton intended to publish his first poems, *Odes on Various Subjects*, with those of his schoolmate Collins, but the plan failed and the two volumes of odes appeared separately in the same month, December, 1746. Warton was a dull, uninspired Collins, yet his odes reached a second edition the next year, while his friend's far more distinguished work fell flat. In his preface Warton attacks didactic verse and asserts that imagination and invention are the "chief faculties" of a poet.[2] Seven of his eighteen odes are modelled on *Allegro* or *Penseroso*.[3] The most Miltonic is the tetrameter *Ode to Fancy*, which is much like the pieces we have been examining; but the *Ode to Health*, though influenced in only four of the seven stanzas, shows a more interesting adaptation of the Miltonic formula:

> O Whether with laborious clowns
> In meads and woods thou lov'st to dwell,
> In noisy merchant-crouded towns,
> Or in the temperate Brachman's cell. . . .
>
> O lovely queen of mirth and ease. . . .
>
> To aid a languid wretch repair,
> Let pale-ey'd Grief thy presence fly,

---

[1] *Ode to Sleep.*   [2] See above, p. 435.

[3] Wooll's *Memoirs* (1806) contains four not included in the 1746 volume, which in turn has four that are not in Wooll. For Warton's other Miltonic pieces, see pp. 243–4 above and 561, 566, below.

The restless demon gloomy Care,
And meagre Melancholy die;
Drive to some lonely rock the giant Pain,
And bind him howling with a triple chain!

O come, restore my aking sight.

In the brief *Ode to Music* the movement of *Allegro* is happily caught,

Queen of every moving measure,
Sweetest source of purest pleasure,
Music! why thy powers employ
Only for the sons of Joy?

but there is no further resemblance, nor are any of Warton's other poems in tetrameter, except his *Temple of Love*, influenced by Milton other than in the verbal borrowings which are characteristic of all his work.

The younger Thomas Warton was high priest of the eighteenth-century Milton cult. Others may have imitated the master more closely and in more poems, and a few may have admired him as deeply, but none were so saturated with his work and none followed him so constantly and so variously. The very slavishness of Mason's imitations shows them to have been external, things that any one might have done; whereas only close familiarity with a poet would lead one to borrow steadily from him, as Warton did from Milton, now a word, now a phrase, now a meter, now an idea or perhaps a bit of structure. Warton is also distinguished as being much the best poet of the men who followed Milton closely. His devotion seems to have been lifelong. Starting as it probably did under his father's direction in boyhood, it caused him to employ in his earliest piece, written when he was seventeen, the verse of *Paradise Lost* and something of the plan of *Penseroso;* it brought four Miltonic borrowings into the first eight lines of his second poem, led him to write a monody similar to *Lycidas*, one ode closely modelled on *Allegro* and two in which the resemblance is less striking, two translations in Milton's unrimed Horatian stanza, and nine Miltonic sonnets, besides keeping him busy up to the end of his life editing the 1645 volume. For this last work, a learned compilation from which all subsequent editors have quarried, particularly for its parallel passages, he must have been gathering material during many years.[1] First published in 1785, it did not appear in its final form till 1791, after Warton's death.

Such a devotion as this, lasting from childhood to old age, pro-

---

[1] Mant, in his edition of Warton (Oxford, 1802, vol. i, p. xxviii), speaks of "a copy of Fenton's edition of Milton's smaller Poems, which was in his [Warton's] possession in 1745, his 17th year, and abounds in MS. notes and references" made about that time.

duces a remarkable familiarity with a writer. Its effect upon Warton's poetry is seen most clearly in Miltonic words and phrases, of which he uses a larger proportion than does any other English poet, which indeed make of some passages in his poems little else than Miltonic mosaics.[1] As most of these borrowings are from the 1645 volume, it would appear that Warton was more familiar with the minor poems and probably preferred them to *Paradise Lost*. How pervasive, and often how unexpected and probably unconscious, was the influence of these shorter pieces is shown in his blank-verse *Pleasures of Melancholy;* for scattered through its lines are phrases and bits of structure from Milton's octosyllabics which, when put together, make a fairly complete piece of the *Penseroso* type:

> O come then, Melancholy, queen of thought!
> O come with saintly look, and steadfast step . . .
> Where ever to the curfeu's solemn sound
> List'ning thou sitt'st. . . .
> But never let Euphrosyne beguile
> With toys of wanton mirth my fixed mind. . . .
> Tho' 'mid her train the dimpled Hebe. . . .
> Yet are these joys that Melancholy gives,
> Than all her witless revels happier far. . . .
> Then ever, beauteous Contemplation, hail! . . .
> Hail, queen divine! whom, as tradition tells,
> Once in his evening walk a Druid found.
>
> The taper'd choir, at the late hour of pray'r,
> Oft let me tread, while to th' according voice
> The many-sounding organ peals on high,
> The clear slow-dittied chaunt, or varied hymn,
> Till all my soul is bath'd in ecstasies,
> And lapp'd in Paradise.[2]

Fond as Warton was of the octosyllabic measure, he modelled but one of his poems, the *Ode on the Approach of Summer*, upon Milton's tetrameters. But in this ode he did what was characteristic of himself and often of his age, though a feat that seems impossible to us, — he wrote a very close imitation (of *Allegro* in this case) and an attractive poem. Unfortunately, even an extended quotation from a work some fourteen pages long must be given up largely to isolated lines which show the Miltonic structure of the ode but give little idea of its charm:

[1] Cf. Appendix A, below.

[2] Lines 279–307, 196–201. Furthermore, lines 209, 211–225, are clearly based on *Penseroso*, 76, 97–120. In the passages quoted above we have the "come," the personifications, the manner, a sort of "hence," the train, ending, birth, some of the occupations, and a number of verbal borrowings.

Hence, iron-scepter'd WINTER, haste
  To bleak Siberian waste!
Haste to thy polar solitude;
  Mid cataracts of ice,
Whose torrents dumb are stretch'd in fragments rude. . . .
But come thou rose-cheek'd cherub mild,
Sweetest SUMMER! haste thee here,
Once more to crown the gladden'd year.
Thee APRIL blithe, as long of yore,
Bermudas' lawns he frolick'd o'er . . .
Thee, as he skim'd with pinions fleet,
He found an infant, smiling sweet. . . .
Haste thee, nymph! and hand in hand,
With thee lead a buxom band;
Bring fantastic-footed Joy,
With Sport, that yellow-tressed boy:
Leisure, that through the balmy sky
Chases a crimson butterfly. . . .
But when the Sun, at noon-tide hour,
Sits throned in his highest tow'r;
Me, heart-rejoicing Goddess, lead
To the tann'd haycock in the mead. . . .
But ever against restless heat,
Bear me to the rock-arch'd seat,
O'er whose dim mouth an ivy'd oak
Hangs nodding from the low-brow'd rock. . . .
Or bear me to yon antique wood,
Dim temple of sage Solitude! . . .
Yet still the sultry noon t'appease,
Some more romantic scene might please. . . .
But when mild Morn in saffron stole
First issues from her eastern goal,
Let not my due feet fail to climb
Some breezy summit's brow sublime. . . .
But when life's busier scene is o'er,
And Age shall give the tresses hoar,
I'd fly soft Luxury's marble dome,
And make an humble thatch my home.

Although this is the only poem of Warton's that follows *Allegro* or *Penseroso* closely, the tone, content, or phrasing of the others constantly recall Milton, as in these lines:

Oft upon the twilight plain,
Circled with thy shadowy train,
While the dove at distance coo'd,
Have I met thee, Solitude!
Then was loneliness to me
Best and true society.

The tufted pines, whose umbrage tall
Darkens the long-deserted hall:
The veteran beech, that on the plain
Collects at eve the playful train:
The cot that smokes with early fire,
The low-roof'd fane's embosom'd spire! [1]

Warton's chief merits lie in his descriptions of the more quiet, obvious beauties of English landscape and rural life. He has many charming poems of the meditative-descriptive type, in the spirit as well as in the meter, form, and diction of *Allegro* and *Penseroso*. He also catches admirably the romantic, pensive glamour of ruined abbeys and castles, and the pomp and daring of the days of chivalry. Here, of course, he is much influenced by Gray and Spenser, though, in view of his great admiration for the latter and of his two volumes of *Observations on the Faerie Queene*, it is surprising to note how little Colin Clout affected his verse. Even Gray is more in evidence; while, as compared with Milton, Spenser touched the form, meter, diction, and content of Warton's work but slightly.[2] The reason is that already suggested: the meter and form of Milton's minor poems were adapted to Warton's needs, their tone suited his ear, and their subject-matter, particularly in the octosyllabics, was of the kind that he naturally chose himself.

Warton had an engaging personality and is still an attractive figure, though his importance has waned sadly in the last hundred and thirty years. In his time he was a man of note, — a learned antiquary, a scholarly editor, an important poet, professor of poetry at Oxford, and laureate. Besides editing Milton's early pieces, Theocritus, and a volume of Latin and Greek inscriptions, and writing his *Observations on the Faerie Queene*, he worked for many years at his monumental but incomplete *History of English Poetry*. He was a man of wide and curious information, which appears in all his works and adds greatly to their value. In his medieval learning, his few genuinely attractive poems, and his passion for Gothic architecture, early English literature, and other things deemed romantic at a time when few shared his enthusiasm, lies his significance. Yet with many the figure that his name calls first to mind is not the learned romanticist of our text-books, but the burly poet playing pranks with the pupils of his dignified brother, or issuing in soiled

---

[1] *Ode IV, Solitude at an Inn*, 1–6; *Ode V, Sent to a Friend*, 13–18.
[2] "The effect of his medieval researches," as W. P. Ker well says (*Camb. Hist. Eng. Lit.*, English ed., x. 239), "was not to make him an imitator of the Middle Ages, but to give him a wider range in modern poetry. Study of the Middle Ages implied freedom from many common literary prejudices."

gown from some resort of the Oxford watermen to follow the lure of a drum.

The influence of the Wartons, Mason, Collins, and particularly of Gray was very strong from 1745 to 1800. Although ridiculed and parodied by men of the Johnson-Goldsmith school, who still vigorously maintained the entire pseudo-classic tradition, they were the guides of such writers as were turning towards newer things. Eighteenth-century poets usually followed the fashion, and these men said what the fashion was to be. They admired, praised, and imitated *Allegro* and *Penseroso*, and their friends, admirers, and imitators did the same. As a result, the poems that had lain "in a sort of obscurity " for nearly a century sprang into a popularity which they have never since attained. They became the vogue, and for a time shared with the Miltonic sonnet the distinction of furnishing the models most generally used for occasional verse. They enjoyed to the full the flattering ridicule of parody, — as, for instance, in the *Garrulous Man, a Parody upon L'Allegro* (1777), in Barron Field's *La Ciriegia, an Austere Imitation of L'Allegro* (1807), and Horace Twiss's *Fashion, a Paraphrase of L'Allegro* (1814). An *Ode to Horror*, "in the Allegoric, Descriptive, Alliterative, Epithetical, Fantastic, Hyperbolical, and Diabolical Style of our modern Ode-wrights, and Monody-mongers" (1751),[1] which employs the meter and structure of the companion pieces and invokes the "mild *Miltonic* maid," is directed principally at the Wartons. Colman and Lloyd's joint odes *To Obscurity* and *To Oblivion* (1759) laugh at the work of Gray and Mason; Mason and others are burlesqued in five poems of the same type in the *Probationary Odes* (1785), and fun is made of Gray's work in the *Anti-Jacobin* (1798).[2] All these pieces belong to the *Allegro-Penseroso* type, and therefore ridicule the extensive use which the poets in question made of Milton's octosyllabics.

For us the most significant of such burlesques are those contained in two widely-read satires of the day. The second book of Churchill's *Ghost* (1762) begins with an attack upon the custom of invocation in poetry, which, however, since it is the fashion, the satirist himself follows:

> TRUTH, GODDESS of celestial birth,
> But little lov'd, or known on earth . . .
> Where *Fraud* and *Falshood* scorn thy sway . . .
> With LOVE and VIRTUE by thy side . . .
> Amongst the Children of CONTENT . . .

[1] *Student*, ii. 313–15.
[2] See Bibl. II below, under the dates given.

Hither, O hither, condescend,
ETERNAL TRUTH, thy steps to bend. . . .
But come not with that easy mien
By which you won the *lively* DEAN . . .
But come in sacred vesture clad,
Solemnly dull, and truly sad!
Far from thy seemly Matron train
Be Idiot MIRTH, and LAUGHTER vain! . . .
Of Noblest *City Parents* born,
Whom Wealth and Dignities adorn,
Who still one constant tenor keep,
Not quite awake, nor quite asleep,
With THEE let formal DULNESS come,
And deep ATTENTION, ever dumb.

The other satire, called *The Birth of Fashion, a Specimen of a Modern Ode*, forms the third "letter" in Christopher Anstey's amusing *New Bath Guide* (1766). The closeness with which Anstey follows *Allegro* indicates that he realized how much the "modern ode" derived from Milton:

Come then, Nymph of various Mien. . . .
MORIA Thee, in Times of Yore,
To the motley PROTEUS bore;
He, in Bishop's Robes array'd,
Went one Night to Masquerade,
Where thy simple Mother stray'd.
She was clad like harmless Quaker. . . .
There mid Dress of various Hue,
Crimson, yellow, green, and blue,
All on Furbelows and Laces,
Slipt into her chaste Embraces. . . .
Bring, O bring thy Essence Pot,
Amber, Musk, and Bergamot. . . .
Come, but don't forget the Gloves. . . .
Then, O sweet Goddess, bring with Thee
Thy boon Attendant Gaiety,
Laughter, Freedom, Mirth, and Ease,
And all the smiling Deities.

Such parodies must have been more numerous than has been realized; for in 1780 the *Critical Review* spoke of one "apparently designed, as a hundred others have been before it, to ridicule *ode-writing*," [1] and this hundred does not include the twenty-three "Probationary Odes" (supposed to have been submitted in competition for the laureateship) which make fun of the would-be lyricists of the day. One of these burlesques has the lines,

[1] xlix. 396.

Geography, terraqueous maid,
Descend from globes to statesmen's aid!
Again to heedless crowds unfold
Truths unheard, tho' not untold:
Come, and once more unlock this vasty world.[1]

In the same volume a "Table of Instructions for the Rev. Thomas Warton," the successful candidate, suggests that, as invocations "have of late years been considered by the Muses as mere cards of compliment, and of course have been but rarely accepted, you must not waste more than twenty lines in invoking the Nine, nor repeat the word Hail more than fifteen times at farthest."[2] As early as 1758 the *Critical Review* had remarked that the "mixture of new-fangled and unintelligible epithets, wild thoughts, and affected phrases" which it found in the anonymous *Fancy, an Irregular Ode* "must mean (if they mean any thing) to ridicule the fashionable species of poetry, called ode-writing";[3] and in 1797, after condemning the "prettyism," "tinsel," and "imbecillity" of a volume of contemporary *English Lyricks*, it observed, "Gray and Collins . . . have produced such tribes of imitators, that we are weary of this species of composition. . . . Avaunt such frippery!"[4] Meanwhile, in 1782 the *Monthly Review* had declared: "No species of composition appears to be more at enmity with common sense than the modern ode. The Pindars of the present hour seem to think that the personification of a few abstract ideas, no matter whether they are brought together in any order or connection, completes the whole of what is expected from them."[5] Apparently, contemporary readers saw quite as clearly as we do to-day the failure of the lyric efforts of the later eighteenth century.

To follow the subsequent course of the *Allegro-Penseroso* movement in the same detail as we have studied its beginnings would be tiresome and profitless. The poems affected do not differ materially from those we have examined, and from a literary standpoint they are usually not so good. The rise and fall of the fad — for fad it became — can be traced in the number of pieces that show the influence of the companion pieces. From 1740 to 1750 I have found 41; from 1750 to 1760, 46; 1760 to 1770, 71; 1770 to 1780, 68; 1780 to 1790, 75; 1790 to 1800, 61; 1800 to 1810, 40; 1810 to 1820, 6. That is, their popularity was at its height from 1760 to 1790, declined rapidly after 1800, and by 1810 had practically disappeared. These

---

[1] *Ode IX* (by Richard Tickell?), in *Probationary Odes for the Laureatship* (1785), 39.
[2] *Ib.* 130.
[3] v. 162.
[4] New arrangement, xxi. 340.
[5] lxvii. 387.

figures, it should be understood, are conservative; they by no means include every piece that shows any influence from *Allegro* or *Penseroso;* if they did, if they took into account every production that belongs in a general way to the type or that borrows a few expressions from Milton's octosyllabics, they would embrace, along with many miscellaneous poems, nearly every ode to an abstraction published in the latter half of the century. In the work of Mrs. Mary Robinson, for example, — the "Perdita" who still smiles on us from the canvases of Reynolds, Romney, and Gainsborough with the charm that brought the Prince of Wales to her feet, — nearly one hundred and forty pages are devoted to odes on subjects like The Muse, Della Crusca, Genius, Reflection, Envy, Health, Vanity, Melancholy, Despair, Beauty, Eloquence, the Moon, Meditation, Valour, Night, Hope, Humanity, Winter, Peace, Apathy.[1] Nearly all of these odes are affected by the companion pieces in one way or another, but only a third of them seem to me close enough to Milton to belong in the appended bibliography.

Likewise, in other eighteenth-century poems almost every conceivable kind and degree of influence from the octosyllabics may be found. Often it is limited to a phrase or two; frequently only the first few lines or a single stanza or a short passage are Miltonic; perhaps the influence extends throughout the piece but is confined to the meter and cadence. Many poems do not employ tetrameter at all but show their indebtedness in the "hence" or "come," the personification, the train, the occupations, or other points. There are some doublets and even some triplets, and a few pieces are as slavish copies as Mason's *Il Bellicoso* and *Il Pacifico.* So great, indeed, was the vogue of Milton's octosyllabics that traces of their influence crept into the most unexpected places. A dramatic pastoral of Robert Lloyd's, for instance, which shows no other connection with Milton, has the couplet,

> Hither haste, and bring along
> Merry Tale and jocund Song.[2]

A humorous blank-verse piece, *Upon a Birmingham Halpenny,* begins,

> Hence! false, designing cheat, from garret vile,
> Or murky cellar sprung! [3]

In another unrimed production we come suddenly on the lines,

> Come then, O Night! and with thee, by the hand,
> Thy younger sister, Melancholy, bring,
> In sable vestment clad;

[1] *Poetical Works* (1806), i. 81–218.   [3] *Gent. Mag.*, xxvii. 325 (1757).
[2] *Arcadia* (1761), act i.

and a page farther on,

> Then let me still with Melancholy live,
> And haunt the hermit Contemplation's cell.[1]

There is no other suggestion of Milton's octosyllabics in the poems, or, until we read these lines near the end, in the eight pages that Sneyd Davies addressed to the Rev. Timothy Thomas in 1744:

> But chiefly thou, divine Philosophy,
> Shed thy blest Influence; with thy Train appear
> Of Graces mild; far be the Stoick boast,
> The Cynick's Snarl, and churlish Pedantry.
> Bright Visitant, if not too high my Wish,
> Come in the lovely Dress you wore, a Guest
> At *Plato's* Table; or at *Tusculum.* . . .
> See crouching Insolence, Spleen and Revenge
> Before thy shining Taper disappear.[2]

The most distinguished piece of blank verse into which the *Allegro* structure penetrated is the *Pleasures of Imagination*, in the tenth line of which Akenside invokes "Indulgent Fancy" and, as her companion,

> Let Fiction come, upon her vagrant wings
> Wafting ten thousand colours through the air. . . .
> Wilt thou, eternal Harmony, descend
> And join this festive train? for with thee comes . . .
> Majestic Truth; and where Truth deigns to come,
> Her sister Liberty will not be far.

Sonnets likewise were affected, for the first of those "written in the Highlands of Scotland" by Hugh Downman begins, "Hence Sickness . . . where the Night-raven sings." Even Greek tragedy was not exempt: in a chorus of his translation of Aeschylus Robert Potter introduces the lines,

> Thou, son of Maia, come, and with thee lead
> Success, that crowns the daring deed;[3]

[1] Mrs. Hampden Pye, *Philanthe* (written 1758; in *Poems*, 2d ed., 1772, pp. 42, 43).

[2] John Whaley, *Collection of Original Poems* (1745), 334-5. Cf. also Crabbe's *Borough*, beginning of letter xi; J. G. Cooper's *Power of Harmony*, beginning of the first and second books; Christopher Smart's *Hop-Garden*, i. 257-69; William Woty's *Tankard of Porter*, near the end, and *Chimney-Corner*, 49-50; Robert Fergusson's *Good Eating* (*Works*, 1851, p. 215); S. J. Pratt's *Landscapes in Verse* (*Sympathy*, etc., 1807, pp. 81, 117); James Hurdis's *Elmer and Ophelia* (*Poems*, 1790, pp. 57-9); Henry Moore's *Private Life* (1795?), 15-17.

[3] *The Choephorae* (*Tragedies of Aeschylus*, Norwich, 1777, p. 365). Potter's *Ode to Sympathy* is slightly, and his *Ode to Health* decidedly, influenced by *Allegro* (see *Poetical Amusements near Bath*, 1781, iv. 112-23). His *Farewell Hymne to the Country, in the manner of Spenser's Epithalamion* (1749, reprinted in *Bell's Classical Arrangement*, 1790, xi. 105-19), contains at least four borrowings from Milton, and his *Kymber* (1759) is a close imitation of *Lycidas*.

and Andrew Becket writes in one of his choruses,

> O haste along;
> Come, O come and bring with thee,
> Truth and bright Humanity.[1]

These lines and many others like them may owe nothing *directly* to Milton. For without doubt some authors merely followed the latest mode in versifying without being conscious of its origin, and so familiar did the "hence," the "come," the train of personifications, and the tripping octosyllabics become that their source was probably overlooked or forgotten by many who knew and loved the 1645 volume.

It has often been thought that *Penseroso* had not a little to do with the rise of the "graveyard school" of poetry that flourished in the eighteenth century, a natural assumption that is not borne out by the facts. The most important and most popular representatives of the literature of melancholy, Young's *Night Thoughts* (1742–6), Blair's *Grave* (1743), and James Hervey's prose *Meditations among the Tombs* (1746), were quite uninfluenced by *Penseroso*. Moreover, the vogue of this literature began before that of Milton's 1645 volume, and few of the poems that imitated the octosyllabics are of the graveyard variety or show any preference for the less lively of the companion pieces. Milton's poem, furthermore, is not *Il Melancholio*, but *Il Penseroso*, the praise of a retired, studious life such as the poet led in his happy years at Horton. The love of gloom which characterized much of the literature of the middle and latter part of the eighteenth century belongs with the fondness for the Middle Ages, for ruins, and for wild nature. It was a part of the romantic and rather sentimental tendency of the time; it is alien to the mood of *Penseroso*, and would have been quite the same if Milton's poem had never been written.[2]

Among the more important writers who used the *Allegro-Penseroso* form and who used it most frequently are Thomas Blacklock, the blind versifier whose kind letter sent Burns to Edinburgh instead of to Jamaica; John Langhorne, the translator of Plutarch and of some of Milton's Italian and Latin poems; Tobias Smollett and Charles Brockden Brown, the novelists; Mrs. Barbauld, the poetess and writer for children; William Richardson, the Shakespearean scholar; and Henry Kirke White, the pathetic, overrated consumptive upon whom Southey tried to confer immortality. There is no reason for

---

[1] *Socrates*, "a drama on the model of the ancient Greek tragedy" (1806, reprinted in *Dramatic and Prose Miscellanies*, ed. W. Beattie, 1838, i. 272, cf. 209).

[2] See my *Literature of Melancholy*, 1909 (*Modern Language Notes*, xxiv. 226–7).

pausing on the work of these men and women, but there are survivals of the *Allegro-Penseroso* movement in a few later poets that
have unusual interest.

Coleridge, who, when uninspired seems to belong wholly to the
eighteenth century, has three pieces of the type we have been studying. Two of them, *Music*, and *Inside the Coach*, —

> Slumbrous God of half-shut eye!
> Who lovest with limbs supine to lie, —

are humorous and are affected for only a few lines, but the third is
an out-and-out imitation:

> Hence! thou fiend of gloomy sway,
> That lov'st on withering blast to ride
> O'er fond Illusion's air-built pride.
> Sullen Spirit! Hence! Away!
>
> Where Avarice lurks in sordid cell,
> Or mad Ambition builds the dream,
> Or Pleasure plots th' unholy scheme
> There with Guilt and Folly dwell! . . .
>
> Then haste thee, Nymph of balmy gales!
> Thy poet's prayer, sweet May! attend! . . .
>
> Peace, that lists the woodlark's strains,
> Health, that breathes divinest treasures,
> Laughing Hours, and Social Pleasures
> Wait my friend in Cambria's plains.[1]

Coleridge employed the *Allegro-Penseroso* form in 1792, when it
was still popular; Wordsworth dropped into it for a few lines some
years after its vogue had passed. In an irregular ode *To Enterprise*
that he composed in 1820, the personifications, the parentage, the
circumstances attending the birth and early training of the abstraction, all suggest Milton, as do a borrowing from *Comus* and a reference to *Penseroso;* yet, as the similarities are limited to thirty of the
one hundred and sixty-one lines of the poem, they may be accidental:

> Bold Spirit! who art free to rove
> Among the starry courts of Jove,
> And oft in splendour dost appear . . .
> Where Mortals call thee ENTERPRISE.

---

[1] *To Disappointment* (*Poetical Works*, ed. E. H. Coleridge, Oxford, 1912, i. 34).
Southey's irregular odes, *To Horror* and *To Contemplation* (written 1791-2, *Poetical
Works*, 1837, ii. 129-34), are somewhat Miltonic in style, and the latter has a few distinct borrowings: "high-tufted trees" (cf. *Allegro*, 78), "slow-moving on the surges
hoar Meet with deep hollow roar" (cf. *Penseroso*, 75-6), "Far from all the haunts of
men" (cf. *Comus*, 388, and *Pen.*, 81). This last line is in the midst of a passage (beginning "But sweeter 'tis to wander") probably suggested by *Penseroso*, 139-47.

Daughter of Hope! her favourite Child,
Whom she to young Ambition bore. . . .
Thee wingèd Fancy took, and nursed
On broad Euphrates' palmy shore. . . .
She wrapped thee in a panther's skin . . .
And thou (if rightly I rehearse
What wondering Shepherds told in verse)
From rocky fortress in mid air
(The food which pleased thee best to win)
Did'st oft the flame-eyed Eagle scare.[1]

One hardly expects to find a source for Shelley's shorter poems.
They are too spontaneous and ethereal, too much the children of the
wind and the cloud, the rainbow and the sun, to be fathered upon
any mortal. Yet one of his lyrics, *To Jane, the Invitation*, written in
1822, only a few weeks before he was drowned, comes strikingly near
to the *Allegro-Penseroso* type:

Best and brightest, come away!
Fairer far than this fair Day,
Which, like thee to those in sorrow,
Comes to bid a sweet good-morrow. . . .
The brightest hour of unborn Spring,
Through the winter wandering,
Found, it seems, the halcyon Morn
To hoar February born. . . .
Reflection, you may come to-morrow,
Sit by the fireside with Sorrow. —
You with the unpaid bill, Despair, —
You, tiresome verse-reciter, Care. . . .
Expectation too, be off! . . .
Hope, in pity mock not Woe. . . .
Radiant Sister of the Day,
Awake! arise! and come away!

Shelley would not consciously have adopted a hackneyed eighteenth-
century verse-form, or have taken directly from one of Milton's
poems "machinery" which, as he must have known, had previously
been borrowed by hundreds of poetasters; yet here we have the
meter and movement, the "come," the "hence," the personified
abstractions (together with the parentage and the circumstances
attending the finding of one of them), and a clear verbal borrowing.[2]
There is nothing strange in his employing the meter and movement

---

[1] Compare the first two lines of the quotation with the first line of *Comus* (spoken, it
should be observed, by the attendant "spirit"), "Before the starry threshold of Jove's
court." The reference to *Penseroso* is at line 145. I have taken the last five lines from
the first edition because of the Miltonic ring of the parenthetical clauses, particularly
the first, which recalls *Allegro*, 17. These clauses were afterwards omitted or changed.

[2] Compare the third and fourth lines with *Allegro*, 45–6. For Shelley's other borrowings from Milton's minor poems, see pp. 228–31 above and 567 below.

of *Allegro*, for he had probably borrowed them before in his *Lines written among the Euganean Hills* (1818),[1] much as in other poems he had used the Spenserian stanza and the sonnet form. Nor can the other similarities in *To Jane* be brushed aside as mere coincidences, for the empty personified abstractions and the parentage and birth of Morning are not the sort of thing one expects in Shelley. Perhaps he was led into them unconsciously by the "come away" and the verbal borrowing of his beginning.

Keats wrote eleven poems in iambic tetrameter, most of which catch, at least for a time, the lilt of Milton's octosyllabics. They differ, however, in that almost every line lacks the initial unaccented syllable. Two quotations, the first from *Fancy*, the second from the *Song of Four Fairies*, will serve to show the metrical similarity:

> Sit thee there, and send abroad,
> With a mind self-overaw'd,
> Fancy, high-commission'd: — send her!
> She has vassals to attend her:
> She will bring, in spite of frost,
> Beauties that the earth hath lost;
> She will bring thee, all together,
> All delights of summer weather.

> Happy, happy glowing fire!
> Dazzling bowers of soft retire,
> Ever let my nourish'd wing,
> Like a bat's, still wandering,
> Faintless fan your fiery spaces,
> Spirit sole in deadly places.
> In unhaunted roar and blaze,
> Open eyes that never daze.[2]

It is hazardous to base a claim of influence on meter and cadence alone, and in *Fancy* there is, indeed, more; there is the sitting by the fireside at night, the harvesting, the early lark, the personified abstraction who will bring various things, and the ending,

> And such joys as these she'll bring.

Moreover, Keats could compose tetrameter that has none of the *Allegro* lilt, and it must be remembered that he said of Milton,

> Thy spirit never slumbers,
> But rolls about our ears
> For ever and for ever![3]

---

[1] Besides *To Jane, the Invitation*, and its earlier form *The Pine Forest of the Cascine near Pisa*, he also wrote (in 1822) two other octosyllabics with the Miltonic lilt, *With a Guitar, to Jane*, and *Lines written in the Bay of Lerici*.

[2] Keats's octosyllabic *To Fanny*, first published in 1909 by the Bibliophile Society of Boston, Massachusetts, has much the same lilt.

[3] *On a Lock of Milton's Hair*, 3–5.

Perhaps the music of *Allegro* was rolling about his ears when he composed his octosyllabics. It seems to have been when he wrote his recently-discovered sonnet *On Peace.* "O Peace!" he writes,

> Joyful I hail thy presence; and I hail
> The sweet companions that await on thee,

one of whom is "the sweet mountain nymph . . . Liberty." [1]

The delightful octosyllabic *Solitude* (1821) of John Clare also "suggests" Milton (as Mr. de Sélincourt says of *Fancy*), but the resemblance is much slighter than in Keats's poem. The similarity to *Penseroso* of William Motherwell's *Melancholye* (1832) may be merely accidental, notwithstanding the "hence," the "come," the manner, and the personifications; yet it is pleasant to think of these lines, with their fresh fragrance, as the last and one of the loveliest flowers which the rather thorny octosyllabic movement put forth: [2]

> Adieu! al vaine delightes
> Of calm and moonshine nightes. . . .
> Adieu! the fragrant smel
> Of flowres in boskye dell;
> And all the merrie notes
> That tril from smal birdes' throates. . . .
> And welcome gloomy Nighte,
>   When not one star is seene. . . .
>
> Come with me, Melancholye,
> We'll live like eremites holie,
> In some deepe uncouthe wild
> Where sunbeame never smylde:
> Come with me, pale of hue,
>   To some lone silent spot,
> Where blossom never grewe,
>   Which man hath quyte forgot.
>
> Come, with thy thought-filled eye,
> That notes no passer by,
> And drouping solemne heade,
> Where phansyes strange are bred.

The *Allegro-Penseroso* vogue belonged, not only in time but in kind, to the second half of the eighteenth century. When the fresh breath of the true lyric began to sweep again across the fields of English verse, the odes to abstractions withered away and died. They had long since fulfilled their function and no one mourned their passing. The later eighteenth century was a period of many petty

---

[1] Note the personification, the invocation, the train, and the borrowing from *Allegro*, 36.

[2] Coventry Patmore's *L'Allegro* (1878) has practically no resemblance to Milton's except in title.

and rather silly versifiers who really expressed themselves in the trite stupidities of their pseudo-lyrics. They wanted to be "bards" but did not know how, and Milton's octosyllabics furnished a way out of the difficulty by affording a mould in which their banalities could quickly and easily be turned into something that looked like poetry, something they thought was poetry. A ludicrous picture of the way some of their effusions were composed is drawn in Horace Walpole's account of the Batheaston vase.

Near Bath is erected a new Parnassus, composed of three laurels, a myrtle-tree, a weeping-willow, and a view of the Avon, which has been new christened Helicon. . . . They hold a Parnassus fair every Thursday, give out rhymes and themes, and all the flux of quality at Bath contend for the prizes. A Roman vase dressed with pink ribbons and myrtles receives the poetry, which is drawn out every festival; six judges of these Olympic games retire and select the brightest compositions, which the respective successful acknowledge, kneel to Mrs. Calliope Miller, kiss her fair hand, and are crowned by it with myrtle, with — I don't know what. You may think this is fiction, or exaggeration. Be dumb, unbelievers! The collection is printed, published. — Yes, on my faith![1]

The collection to which Walpole referred, *Poetical Amusements at a Villa near Bath*, eventually consisted of four volumes (1775–81), one of which actually reached a third edition. They are filled with octosyllabics and personified abstractions, with "avaunt's" and "come's" and other bits of the *Allegro-Penseroso* recipe for producing a poem at short notice on any subject.[2] It was persons who belonged to literary circles like this and indited poetical effusions upon the slightest provocation, that gave Milton's octosyllabics much of their vogue. But obviously such popularity could not last. It passed away soon after the passing of the century, whereas the influence of *Paradise Lost* and of the sonnets remains.

Yet *Allegro* and *Penseroso* were of considerable assistance to Parnell, Dyer, Collins, Gray, the Wartons, and other true if minor poets, men who had something to say and ability to say it but who were timid and inexperienced. To such men, who were feeling towards the lyric, Milton's shorter poems furnished an inspiration and a guide. If the guide could not take them all the way into the land of wonder, mystery, and rapture, it did lead them as far as they were ready to go.

[1] Letter to H. S. Conway and the Countess of Ailesbury, Jan. 15, 1775.
[2] One of the poems (see below, Bibl. II, 1775, Burgess) could hardly be closer to *Allegro* than it is.

CHAPTER XIX

MILTON AND THE SONNET

WITH A HISTORY OF THE SONNET IN THE EIGHTEENTH
AND EARLY NINETEENTH CENTURIES

In taking up the study of the eighteenth-century sonnet we enter *terra incognita*. A few scholastic explorers, to be sure, have viewed the region from afar, but even had theirs been the Pisgah vision we should have needed others to spy out the land. Such, however, there have not been, principally, it would seem, because those who have scanned the country from the neighboring summits have reported no Canaan flowing with milk and honey, but a small and desert waste. And so it is that the rich fields of the Elizabethan sonnet with their monotonously fantastic vegetation have been repeatedly traversed, but not a few of the deserts, quiet valleys, and sunny meadows of this demesne — a far wider one than has been suspected — have these many years scarcely felt the print of a human foot. The last four decades of the eighteenth century are probably the most neglected period of English literature, and within this period the greatest neglect has befallen the sonnet.

Before we can understand the eighteenth-century sonnet we must know what preceded it, that is, what antecedent influences were at work upon it. These influences were, in the main, three — the Elizabethan, the Miltonic, and the Italian sonnets. The quatorzain of the Elizabethans is, as a rule, made up of three elegiac quatrains followed by a couplet, riming *a b a b c d c d e f e f g g;* but this, the Shakespearean form, is by no means the only one. Spenser's *Amoretti* have the linked rimes *a b a b b c b c c d c d e e;* and some writers even dispense at times with the couplet-ending, perhaps the most universal and distinctive feature of the Elizabethan sonnet.[1] Yet few even approximate the strict Italian arrangement and very rarely does any one achieve it. This matter of rime-scheme is not the slight, external affair that it is commonly regarded, for it often determines the structure and modifies the idea of the sonnet. Each quatrain, for example, is usually more or less separated from what follows by a pause and a slight change in thought; and the final couplet is likely to be isolated from the rest of the poem, because

---

[1] Sidney has twenty-five quatorzains that do not end with a couplet, and, like Wyatt, he uses the Petrarchan arrangement of the octave more than any other.

ordinarily it is preceded by a strong pause and is devoted to an epigrammatic turn or a sententious summing up of the whole subject.

As to contents, the outstanding feature of the Elizabethan quatorzain is the presence of exaggerations and conceits. Samuel Daniel asks Delia to

> Yield Cytherea's son those arcs of love;
> Bequeath the heavens the stars that I adore,
> And to the Orient do thy pearls remove; [1]

and Sidney queries,

> When Nature made her chief work, Stella's eyes,
> In colour black why wrapt she beams so bright? [2]

To be effective, conceits must be novel. Unfortunately, those in Elizabethan sonnets are repeated until they become mannerisms: the lady's eyes are always stars, her breast always ice or marble, her teeth always pearls, and we are usually asked to believe that her beauties will live eternally in her lover's verse. The unoriginal character of these figures and hyperboles (the greater part of which were borrowed from the French or the Italian) has no bearing on the present discussion, for it was not realized by eighteenth-century writers. They must, however, have felt the lack of originality manifest in the subjects chosen, — one is tempted to say the subject, for the poems recall the daisy oracle, "He loves me, loves me not, he loves me, loves me not." A number of quatorzains, to be sure, are on sleep, on the moon, on abstract or religious themes, and there are some in commendation of books or addressed to friends or patrons; but in comparison with the poems on love the others are few.

Although the Elizabethan sonnets furnished the key with which Shakespeare is said to have unlocked his heart, and although in his day they concerned themselves mainly with the heart, they are not, as a rule, moving. On the whole, they belong to the poetry of ingenuity rather than of feeling. The greatest of them, of course, Shakespeare's, Sidney's, and such noble ones as that attributed to Sylvester, are for us the most tender of love-poems, the most perfect expressions of feeling. But we are accustomed to Elizabethan literature; its vocabulary, its ornate style, its point of view, are so familiar to us that we can ignore the conceits and see only the beauty. Even to-day it is not so with the untrained reader, — with the average undergraduate, for instance; and it was not so with the cultivated in Pope's and Johnson's time, when lyric beauty fell on rather dull ears and far-fetched figures and other exaggerations met with little favor.

---

[1] *Delia*, xix. 2–4.   [2] *Astrophel and Stella*, vii. 1–2.

In style the Elizabethan sonnet is marked by elaboration and adornment, by rich sweetness, grace, delicate loveliness and charm, and a copious, slow-moving flow of pleasing words. Shakespeare's work has also a stateliness and a splendor rarely met with in the quatorzains of his contemporaries; yet, when contrasted with the sonnets of Milton and Wordsworth, Shakespeare's are seen to have a sweeter, richer, more graceful beauty which stamps them as indubitably Elizabethan.

Such, in general, was the English sonnet up to 1630. Of course the description here given does not fit all Elizabethan quatorzains; nor is it necessary that it should, for, so far as influence upon the eighteenth century is concerned, little counts except the work of Sidney, Spenser, and Shakespeare, and only the best that even these men wrote. It is very difficult for us of the twentieth century to realize the ignorance and indifference of our ancestors towards earlier English literature. Striking instances of how little they knew or cared to know may be found in the absurd mistakes that writers of the standing of Pope and Warburton made in their editions of Shakespeare. Theobald and Steevens were among the few men of the time who were familiar with Elizabethan prose and poetry; the rest gloried in their ignorance and sneered at what they held to be stupid and profitless grubbing. Of Steevens and Dr. Grey (the editor of *Hudibras*) John Pinkerton wrote, "Both are fellow labourers in the congenial mines of dulness; where no man of taste or science ever dirtied himself." [1] In 1764 a critic in a leading English review had never heard of Spenser's *Epithalamium*, and nine years later the *Gentleman's Magazine* printed Herrick's famous *Corinna's Going a Maying* as an unknown poem by an unknown author.[2] But most astonishing of all is an opinion expressed in the *Monthly Review* of 1797, "Milton . . . was, we believe, the first Englishman that was induced to attempt the sonnet in the language of our island." [3]

The principal reason for such gross ignorance was that eighteenth-century readers did not like most of the early literature they knew. It seemed to them Gothic and uncouth, it did not square with the rules of Aristotle and Boileau, it lacked the elegance and refinement introduced by Waller and perfected by Pope. Strange as it may appear, even the sonnets of the greatest Elizabethan did not meet with their approval. As late as 1793 Steevens omitted from his edition of Shakespeare all the sonnets and other poems because, as he was good enough to tell us, "the strongest act of Parliament that

---

[1] Robert Heron [i. e., Pinkerton], *Letters of Literature* (1785), 315.
[2] *Crit. Rev.*, xvii. 79; *Gent. Mag.*, xliii. 243.   [3] Enlarged ed., xxiv. 17.

could be framed, would fail to compel readers into their service." [1]
About all Malone can say in their favor in 1790 is that he thinks
"they have been somewhat under-rated," [2] and Boswell is very
cautious in his praise even in 1821, when Tennyson and Browning
were schoolboys.[3] Inasmuch as these editors of the poet might be
expected to have an undue partiality for his works, their remarks
indicate an astounding attitude on the part of the public at large.
No publisher, moreover, would have left out the poems if there had
been any demand for them. How little the demand was may be surmised from Nathan Drake's comment in his popular *Literary Hours*
(1798). "The sonnets of Shakspeare," he writes, "are buried beneath a load of obscurity and quaintness; nor does there issue a
single ray of light to quicken, or to warm the heavy mass. . . . his
last Editor has, I think, acted with greater judgment, in forbearing
to obtrude such crude efforts upon the public eye: for where is the
utility of propagating compositions which no one can endure to
read?" And so with Spenser. "It is scarcely necessary to say,"
Drake remarks, "that he has completely failed. In his long series of
sonnets, the critic will recognise many of the trifling conceits of the
Italian, but find little to recompense the trouble of research." [4] As
late as 1803 George Henderson wrote that the Elizabethan quatorzains included in his sonnet anthology were inserted not because of
their excellence, for "few" of them "could be found agreeable to
modern taste," but "to illustrate the progressive refinement of this
species of versification. . . . Until the time of Drummond," he continues, "we can advance slender claim to any degree of elegance in
this species of versification . . . in too many instances . . . our early
Sonnets abound with sentiments so hyperbolically uttered, and resemblances so extravagantly and uncouthly drawn, as must necessarily render them disgusting to any but a rude or uncultivated
taste." [5]

---

[1] "Advertisement," p. vii. For Steevens's dislike of the sonnet form, see p. 521
below.

[2] See his edition, x. 296.

[3] Boswell's Malone (1821), xx. 222. "The poetical merits of Shakspeare's Sonnets,"
he writes, "are now, *I believe, almost* universally acknowledged. . . . *Whatever may be the
reader's decision*, he has here an opportunity . . . of judging for himself." The italics are
mine.

[4] Third ed. (1804), i. 107–8. Yet for Milton's sonnets Drake has high praise.

[5] *Petrarca*, pp. vii, viii, xxi, xxii. It is by no means a mere coincidence that the first
person in the eighteenth century to care for Shakespeare's sonnets seems to have been
William Blake, the first poet of the century with a real gift for song. In 1806 B. H.
Malkin (*A Father's Memoirs of his Child*, p. xxxiv) mentioned "Shakspeare's Venus
and Adonis, Tarquin and Lucrece, and his Sonnets " as "poems, now little read, [which]
were favourite studies of Mr. Blake's early days."

Negative evidence quite as important as these outspoken criticisms is to be found in the striking absence of references to Shakespeare's quatorzains in the literature of the period, even in the many poems and essays that laud his plays. Miss Seward, for example, in her numerous discussions of sonnets, apparently mentions those of Shakespeare and Spenser but once, and then only to speak of their conceits, their "quaintness" and "quibbling." Yet she thought Shakespeare's dramas the highest productions of human genius.[1] If Englishmen of the eighteenth century held so poor an opinion of the poems of the greatest writer of their past, is it any wonder that they neither knew nor cared to know those of his contemporaries?

The sonnets of Milton differ in almost every respect from those of the Elizabethans. Most of them are stamped with the Puritanism of their author, than which nothing can be more alien to the sonnet sequences of the sixteenth and seventeenth centuries. Instead of showing the light grace, the richness and ornate beauty, of the earlier type, they are distinguished by vigor, dignity, and exaltation. They are more sonorous and direct, they have what Wordsworth termed "republican austerity," [2] they are restrained and classic; in a word, they are Miltonic, for they are marked by the characteristics that distinguish Milton the man and the poet. Yet, notwithstanding the greatness of many lines, they lack the grace, loveliness, and sheer beauty of Shakespeare's quatorzains, of *Comus*, *Lycidas*, and the octosyllabics, a deficiency which was strongly but not unpleasantly felt by the eighteenth century. Miss Seward, a profound admirer of the poems, praises their "hardnesses," their "energetic plainness," and compares them to "the pointed and craggy rock, the grace of which is its roughness." [3] The elegance of the more intimate ones, the suggestion of Horace in that to Lawrence and the first to Cyriack Skinner, and the somewhat stately grace of the one to Lawes and that to "a virtuous young lady" seem to have left no trace upon the eighteenth-century quatorzain.

The changes which Milton made in subject-matter have received final phrasing from the pen of Landor:

> He caught the sonnet from the dainty hand
> Of Love, who cried to lose it; and he gave
> The notes to Glory.[4]

---

[1] *Letters* (1811), v. 159, 188-9. Henry White's remarks on the sonnet, in the *Gentleman's Magazine* for 1786 (lvi. 1110), mention neither Shakespeare nor Spenser.

[2] Letter to Landor, April 20, 1822.

[3] *Letters*, i. 201, ii. 257-8. Sir Egerton Brydges (*Censura Literaria*, 1808, vi. 415) says that people spoke of the "harsh and bald deformities" of Milton's sonnets.

[4] *To Lamartine*, in *Last Fruit*.

Of his "Petrarchian stanzas"[1] in English, only the one to the nightingale deals with love, and that but briefly. Half of them are addressed to friends, an important point as regards influence; the rest
are devoted to an attack on the Presbyterians, an appeal for pro-
tection, the defense of a pamphlet, the author's birthday, his blindness, his dead wife, and the Piemontese martyrs. It is this widening
and ennobling of its theme that constitutes Milton's greatest service
to the sonnet. Obviously, with subjects like these the elaborate
trifling, the conceits and exaggerations, of the Elizabethans could
have no place. Instead we find seriousness and directness, simplicity
and truth. The poems plunge immediately into the subject, eleven
of them beginning with vocatives, a feature borrowed by many later
writers.[2] They impress us not with their author's cleverness but with
his sincerity; they do not savor of art for art's sake, of something
written to while away an idle hour, to fill out a sequence, or to follow
a fad. Each, we feel, was called forth by some actual event or strong
emotion without which it would not have been written. Hence,
though spread over a period of twenty-five or thirty years, they are
but nineteen in all. Those on the writer's blindness and his dead
wife reveal a deep pathos; while the one entitled *On the New Forcers
of Conscience* and the second on *Tetrachordon* flame with the indignation which in the nobler cause of the Piemontese martyrs glows
like a deep fire. In several, indeed, intensity is a distinguishing feature.

Structurally Milton's sonnets mark a return to the Petrarchan
form. Aside from three of those in Italian, — which from the point
of view of influence are almost negligible, — only one concludes with
a couplet, the rest having a legitimate rime-scheme throughout.[3]
Oddly enough, the two respects in which Milton departs from the
structure of his Italian models are among the very few in which his
English predecessors almost always followed it. Thus, in most
Elizabethan sonnets the pauses at the end of the first quatrain and
the octave are preserved, whereas in six of Milton's English sonnets
the first of these pauses is omitted and in nine the second. More
than this, in six cases, instead of a pause at the end of the octave,

---

[1] Milton uses this phrase regarding his sonnet, *On his being Arrived at the Age of
Twenty-three*, in a letter quoted in Masson's *Life* (1881), i. 325.

[2] One other has a vocative after the first word. In seven cases, as usually with Milton's followers, the vocative is a proper name.

[3] That is, they rime in the octave *a b b a a b b a*, and in the sestet *c d c d c d*, or *c d e
c d e*, or *c d e d c e*, or *c d d c d c*, or *c d c e e d*, or *c d d c e e*. Milton has one tailed
sonnet (an Italian form of twenty lines), *On the New Forcers of Conscience*, the 13th
and 14th lines of which do not form a couplet but the 19th and 20th do.

Milton has a run-over line. Such lines occur so frequently in all parts of all his sonnets as to furnish another difference between his work and that of his predecessors. Still further, the Italians and Elizabethans — though the latter are less rigorous in this particular — avoided strong pauses within the line, a principle which Milton disregarded entirely. According to the punctuation of Wright's edition, the nineteen English sonnets have twenty-eight strong pauses (indicated by semicolons, colons, periods, or interrogation-points) within the line, eleven of which mark the ends of sentences. In other words, the prosody of Milton's sonnets is much like that of his blank verse. With this prosody goes, not unnaturally, that inversion of the normal word-order which is a marked feature of *Paradise Lost*.[1]

It is important to bear in mind that Milton ended one of his English sonnets, the famous one to Cromwell, with a couplet. Any later sonnet which has this form cannot, therefore, be said to follow the Elizabethans rather than Milton. The difficulties of the Petrarchan form loomed so large in the eighteenth century, a period of little metrical facility, that many of the poets who regarded Milton's usage as authoritative were glad to avail themselves of his sanction of the couplet-ending. We read in the *Gentleman's Magazine* for 1786: "Of Milton's English sonnets, only that to Oliver Cromwell ends with a couplet; but that single instance is a sufficient precedent. However, in three out of his five Italian ones, the two concluding lines rhime to each other."[2] Many persons regarded the Petrarchan rime-scheme as the ideal and made an effort to conform to it,[3] their

---

[1] These innovations are probably undesirable in a poem so brief, and therefore so highly finished, as the sonnet.

[2] lvi. 1110. The article is by the Rev. Henry White, a cousin of Miss Seward, whose ideas it represents and who, though an uncompromising devotee of the Miltonic sonnet and of what she regarded as the legitimate form, ended approximately half of her own effusions with couplets. "Little elegies, consisting of four stanzas and a couplet," added White, "are no more sonnets than they are epic poems."

[3] Charlotte Smith wrote in the preface to her "Elegiac Sonnets" (1784), most of which are Shakespearean or nearly so, "The little poems which are here called Sonnets, have, I believe, no very just claim to that title." She held that the Petrarchan structure was too difficult for any but poets of "uncommon powers" to handle in English. Capel Lofft urged Kirke White to use the legitimate form and not to call quatorzains sonnets (see White's *Remains*, ii. 57). The *Critical Review* held in 1786 (lxi. 467) that, so far as rimes were concerned, Mrs. Smith's poems were not sonnets at all, and in 1793 (new arr., ix. 383) agreed with William Kendall that only poems written "according to the strict rules of that species of versification" were entitled to be called sonnets. Charles Lloyd, the friend of Lamb and Coleridge, thought the same (see his *Nugae Canorae*, 1819, pp. 167–74). For the decided opinions of Miss Seward and her circle, see the preceding note, and pp. 500–502 below. George Henderson quoted Miss Seward's utterances with approval in his *Petrarca* (1803, pp. xxvii, xxix, xxx), as the *Monthly Review* (enl. ed., xxix. 361–4) had previously done. There were many, on the other hand, who heartily disliked the Petrarchan form.

irregularities being not intentional variations but attempts at the legitimate scheme which fell wide of the mark. The order of their rimes is as near Petrarch's as writers with a feeble sense of form, little metrical skill, less inspiration, and almost no literary fastidiousness would be likely to get.

The influence from Italy has been left to the last, because for the present purposes Italian sonnets may be regarded as Elizabethan quatorzains with the Miltonic rime-scheme.[1] This does not imply that they are distinguishable from the work of Shakespeare and his contemporaries merely by their language and their arrangement of rimes; it means that so far as their influence goes this is the case, that it is hardly possible by internal evidence alone to decide whether the style, subject-matter, or method of treatment of a poem is derived from the Elizabethans or the Italians. Fortunately there is no need of making this distinction, for English poets of the eighteenth century knew little about Italian sonnets and did not like what they knew. To be sure, Laura, "Vaucluse's vale," and the poet who celebrated them are frequently mentioned; but, as the *Gentleman's Magazine* observed, "the strains of Petrarch" were "more talked of than imitated."[2] From Miss Seward's letters and poems, for example, one would surmise that the Swan of Lichfield often floated on the waters of the Arno; yet she wrote of Petrarch's sonnets, "Judging of them by the translations and imitations of them, which I have seen, they want . . . pathetic simplicity."[3] That is, from her slight knowledge of them she had an unfavorable impression. Coleridge seems to have voiced the general ignorance and the general prejudice when, though he "did not understand a word of Italian" and knew Petrarch "only by bald translations of some half-dozen of his Sonnets," he wrote, "I have never yet been able to discover either sense, nature, or poetic fancy in Petrarch's poems; they appear to me all one cold glitter of heavy conceits and metaphysical abstractions."[4]

Translations of about twenty Italian sonnets were printed between 1690 and 1776; and between 1777 and 1790, outside of magazines and of two books which apparently no one read, about thirty

[1] J. S. Smart, in his valuable *Sonnets of Milton* (Glasgow, 1921, pp. 19–34), points out that there was considerable freedom as to the rime-scheme in Italian sonnets, that a number of Elizabethan quatorzains approach the less rigid Italian arrangements, and that run-over lines, internal pauses, and disregard of regular pauses characterize the work of Giovanni della Casa (d. 1556), a copy of whose sonnets Milton owned.

[2] lvi. 334 (1786).

[3] *Letters*, v. 58; cf. i. 261, ii. 304, and *Sonnets*, nos. 25, 64, 86.

[4] "Introduction to the Sonnets," *Poems* (2d ed., 1797), 71.

seem to have appeared.[1] When it is remembered that over one hundred and thirty persons were composing quatorzains at this time, and that a single writer sometimes produced between fifty and a hundred, it will be seen how ridiculously few the translations were. There were more in the last decade of the century, but the number was still small. I know of some sixty-five; but, as the dates of many sonnets are uncertain, the number outside of magazines may be between one and two hundred. Furthermore, eighteenth-century bards who translated Italian sonnets usually did only one or two, and apparently worked those up for the occasion in order to make an impression upon their readers, for the translating rarely left any mark on the author's original productions.[2] The truth is, the Englishmen of the time missed in Petrarch and his countrymen the things for which they cared most, and they cared little for many of the qualities which the Italian poems possess. The latter seem to have affected the English quatorzain principally by strengthening the influence of Milton towards the legitimate form.

One feature of the Italian sonnet which seems not to have been understood in England until the nineteenth century is the bipartite structure, or the turn in thought which should come at the beginning of the sestet. Such a turn, though frequent in Elizabethan quatorzains, is apparently accidental. Any short, non-stanzaic poem is likely to fall into two parts, — Goethe's "Ueber allen Gipfeln," for example, where the first six lines describe the peace of nature, the last two the peace to which man looks forward. There is, accordingly, no warrant for concluding that, because Coleridge devoted the first eight of his lines To the Autumnal Moon to describing the moon and

---

[1] I know of but seventeen before 1777, but I did not record those that appeared in magazines after 1742. The two books referred to — which I have been unable to see and to which later writers do not refer — are an anonymous Sonnets and Odes (1777) and W. Lipscomb's Poems (Oxford, 1784).

[2] A surprising feature of these translations is that they are rarely from Dante, and that many of them are from little-known Italian poets of the sixteenth, seventeenth, and eighteenth centuries. Lofft's Laura (1813–14) contains translations of sonnets — many of them previously published — by 118 Italian writers. A Dublin dramatist and slave of the pen, William Preston, who died of overwork in 1807, included twenty-seven dull, stilted sonnets in the two volumes of Poetical Works which he published in 1793. Five of these are translations from Petrarch, and almost all the rest deal with the poet's love for a young lady whose death several of them lament. None have the couplet-ending, and all but two use the legitimate octave. Prefixed to the sonnets is a preface (to which Coleridge took violent exceptions, see Poetical Works, Globe ed., pp. 542–3), that does not mention the quatorzains of Shakespeare, Milton, or any eighteenth-century writers, but contains a strong defence of Petrarch. It seems clear, therefore, that Preston drew his inspiration mainly from the great Italian poet. I am indebted to the Boston Athenaeum for the use of the copy which the author presented, with a glowing tribute, to George Washington.

the last six to the thoughts it suggested, he therefore consciously heeded the rules of the legitimate sonnet. If there is a turn in the thought, it is most likely, apart from any rule, to come at the end of the second quatrain, particularly if there are no run-over lines and if the rime-sequence of the sestet differs from that of the octave.[1] That the frequent observance of the strict bipartite structure in the Elizabethan and the eighteenth-century quatorzains is to be regarded either as chance or as an unconscious conformity to an esthetic law, is shown by the numerous instances in which the rule is disregarded even by writers who in the main observe it, and by the absence of any mention of such a requirement in the definitions and discussions of the sonnet which abound in the eighteenth century.[2] In some of the Elizabethan quatorzains, and in one or two of Milton's, such turn as there is seems to come before the last two lines; but in most of Milton's either there is no turn at all or it falls earlier or later than it should, sometimes in the middle of a line.[3] In these particulars the eighteenth century often followed him.

But the bipartite structure was not the only aspect of the sonnet regarding which the eighteenth century was ignorant. The first six editions of the *Encyclopaedia Britannica* (1771–1824) explained that the sonnet consisted of "two stanzas . . . of four verses each; and two of three; the eight first verses being all in three rhimes." Chambers's *Cyclopaedia* said the same in 1728 and 1752, except that it corrected the three rimes in the octave to two and added, "It is to end with some pretty, ingenious thought: the close must be particularly beautiful, or the *sonnet* is naught."[4] Nothing, it should be observed, is said here regarding the bipartite structure or the *order* of the rimes. It was apparently these articles that led Miss Seward astray and caused her irregular quatorzains to be accepted as legiti-

---

[1] This is explained more fully on pp. 533–4 below. Mr. Smart maintains (*Sonnets of Milton*, 34–8) that in many of the sonnets of Petrarch or of other Italians there is no turn, and that it was first mentioned as a requisite of the form in 1880. But Wordsworth discussed it in 1833 (see p. 532 below).

[2] Miss Seward wrote in 1795, "The legitimate sonnet generally consists of one thought, regularly pursued to the close" (*Letters*, iv. 144–5). In a quatorzain of Capel Lofft's, urging Kirke White to use the legitimate form (see White's *Remains*, ii. 57), the eighth line is run over!

[3] Milton's failure to fit his form to his thought has seldom been criticized; but surely little is gained by avoiding the couplet-ending if the last two lines of the poem stand apart from the others in sense, as they do in seven of Milton's sonnets. Similarly, there may be no important reason why the thought should not move forward without a break; but, if it does, the rimes and their relation to one another ought not to change suddenly at the beginning of the ninth line. On the other hand, if the poem falls into two parts the rimes should change where the thought does.

[4] Edition of 1752; the 1728 edition stops at "beautiful."

mate. She disputed the remark regarding the close (which the *Monthly Review* repeated in 1795 [1]), but otherwise the encyclopaedia articles seem to have gone unquestioned. Still more surprising is Coleridge's misconception of the sonnet, which will be noticed later. But strangest of all is the reproof addressed by Capel Lofft — who edited an anthology of sonnets and translated many from the Italian — to Kirke White on account of the irregularity of the latter's fourteen-line poems. This stickler for regularity couched his objections in the form of a quatorzain, presumably a model, in which the rimes have the astonishing arrangement *a b b a a b a b c d d c e e*.[2]

The eighteenth-century sonnet, as has been said, is *terra incognita*. There are few subjects that have been so inadequately treated by distinguished writers and few about which so much misinformation is available. The received opinion seems to be that "from Milton to William Lisle Bowles . . . few sonnets of any kind and hardly one of note can be found." [3] Charles Tomlinson, in his book on the subject, says that "Milton's sonnets . . . made but little impression on the course of English literature; for in the long interval between Milton and Cowper . . . the sonnet was neglected." He mentions Gray, Mason, and Warton, to be sure, but he regards Bowles as "the reviver of the sonnet in recent literature." [4] One critic of fine taste declares that in the eighteenth century "very few essayed the sonnet, and still fewer . . . succeeded in writing sonnets of worth"; and another asserts that "of the best" between Milton and Wordsworth "it can only be said . . . that they are 'not bad.'" [5] Mr. Gosse is responsible for the extraordinary remark, which with slight modifications has often been repeated, that Walsh is "the author of the only sonnet written in English between Milton's, in 1658, and Warton's, about 1750." [6] It is true that, if we omit "Warton's," if we say 1740 instead of 1750 and "published" instead of "written," — which may be what Mr. Gosse meant, — the remark is not particularly misleading; for, even including translators, only thirteen persons are known to have used the form between 1660 and 1740.[7] All

---

[1] Enlarged ed., xvi. 463. For Miss Seward's views, see below, p. 500.

[2] White's *Remains*, ii. 57.

[3] Norman Hepple, *Lyrical Forms in English* (Camb., 1911), 97–8. Cf. *Dublin Rev.*, xxvii. 423 (1876).

[4] *The Sonnet, its Origin, Structure*, etc. (1874), 79.

[5] L. E. Lockwood, *Sonnets Selected*, etc. (Boston, 1916), p. xiii; J. A. Noble, *The Sonnet in England* (1893), 37.

[6] Ward's *English Poets*, iii. 7. Cf. the books on romanticism by H. A. Beers and W. L. Phelps (pp. 53 and 44 respectively), and John Dennis's *Age of Pope*, p. 247.

[7] I have come upon only five or six between 1660 and 1700. Matthew Stevenson's *Poems, or a Miscellany of Sonnets, Satyrs*, etc. (1673), I know only by title. Samuel

their productions are on either the Elizabethan or the Italian model, and none of them seem to have had any connection with those that followed.

The course of the sonnet between 1740 and 1750 resembles the progress of a strange infectious disease which appears here and there, no one knows how or why, and spreads at first slowly and then with increasing rapidity. The earliest appearance of the new form seems to have been in the *London Magazine* for July, 1738, *A Sonnet, in Imitation of Milton's Sonnets*. This anonymous piece is typical of most of the eighteenth-century quatorzains that succeeded it, — simple, direct, and dignified in style, noble in sentiment, Petrarchesque in the arrangement of its rimes, addressed to a person (with whose name, in the vocative, it begins), and yet clearly uninspired.[1]

Apparently the second example of the new type was that addressed by Philip Yorke, second earl of Hardwicke, to his brother Charles, June 8, 1741. It seems to have been first printed in 1806.[2] As it is earlier by a year than Gray's well-known sonnet, and has hitherto escaped the notice of writers on the subject, it may well be quoted here:

> O Charles! replete with learning's various store;
> Howe'er attentive to th' historic page,
> The poet's lay, or philosophic lore,
> Thy thoughts from these high studies disengage.

Woodford's *Paraphrase upon the Canticles* (1679) includes in an appendix nine quatorzains, four of which are translations. Philip Ayres's *Lyric Poems, made in Imitation of the Italians* (1687), contains thirty sonnets, of which twenty-four deal with love, eleven are translations, seven have the Shakespearean and two the Petrarchan arrangement; the preface mentions Spenser, Sidney, Fanshaw, and Milton, "the success of all which," adds Ayres, "cannot much be boasted of." Jane Barker's *Poetical Recreations* (1688) has one poem in seven couplets that is not called a sonnet, and one in four quatrains that is. In Charles Cotton's *Poems on Several Occasions* (1689) there are four sonnets on four young ladies and one translation(all riming *a b b a c d d c e e f g g f*), besides a number of fourteen-line octosyllabics called sonnets; all are on love. William Walsh's sonnet on death (in his *Letters and Poems*, 1692), has a Spenserian octave, with *d d c e e c* in the sestet. In 1715 John Hughes spoke of the sonnet as "a Species of Poetry so entirely disus'd, that it seems to be scarce known among us at this time. . . . *Milton* . . . is, I think, the last who has given us any Example of them in our own Language" ("Remarks," etc., in his *Spenser*, vol. i. pp. cviii, cx). For sonnets published after 1700, see Bibl. IV, below.

[1] An anonymous stanzaic poem of forty-two lines, *To Aristus, in Imitation of a Sonnet of Milton* (Steele's *Poetical Miscellanies*, 1714, pp. 116–19), which adapts, with omissions and some changes, Milton's sonnets *To a Virtuous Young Lady, To Mr. Lawrence,* and the first to Cyriack Skinner, is of interest because of its early date. There may be some importance in two sonnets by "Signior Nenci, an Italian poet now in London," which were published and translated in the *London Magazine* for 1740 and 1741 (ix. 555–6, x. 47).

[2] Thomas Park's enlargement of Walpole's *Catalogue of Royal and Noble Authors* (1806), iv. 400.

Let Horace rest and Locke, and quick repair
To Wrest, that ancient honourable seat!
In its wide garden breathe a purer air,
And pass the fleeting hours in converse sweet.
From this short respite shall thy mind renew
(Whose spirit by the midnight lamp decays)
Her native strength, its labours to pursue,
And in thy bloom of age outstrip the praise.
Each studious vigil thou shalt pleas'd review,
When honours crown thy well-spent early days.

Notwithstanding its irregular rime-scheme, the general Miltonic character of this poem is as unmistakable as is its specific debt to the first of the sonnets to Cyriack Skinner.[1] If there were any doubt about the matter, it would be dispelled by the two similar quatorzains, frankly entitled "in Imitation of Milton," which Charles Yorke (to whom the one quoted above is addressed) wrote to his brothers in 1743, and by his explanation in a postscript to one of them, "Colonel is to be pronounced as a word of three syllables on the authority of Milton. . . . A scripture allusion, as that of the Leviathan, is in Milton's manner, as you will readily recollect." [2] All three poems are addressed to persons, all begin with vocatives, all are direct, dignified, serious, and somewhat stiff, and none of them deal with love; all make free use of run-over lines and internal pauses, and all are irregular in rime-scheme.

Gray's admiration for Dante and Petrarch was probably responsible for his use of the sonnet to lament the death of his friend Richard West, as well as for the particular rime-scheme he employed.[3] The absence of run-over lines in his poem, the preservation of the pauses at the end of the first and second quatrains and of the turn at the beginning of the sestet, also seem to point to an Italian model;

---

[1] Compare the fourth and fifth lines given above with Milton's fifth, sixth, and seventh:

> To-day deep thoughts resolve with me to drench
> In mirth that after no repenting draws;
> Let Euclid rest, and Archimedes pause.

The general idea of the two sonnets is also the same, — that one works better for having some play.

[2] P. C. Yorke, *Life and Correspondence of Philip Yorke* (Camb., 1913), i. 292-3, ii. 147.

[3] I find that Mr. Gosse (*Gray*, 60) is of the same opinion. For Gray's knowledge of Italian literature and his love of Dante, see Paget Toynbee's *Dante in English Literature* (1909), vol. i, pp. xxxvii, 231-2. Gray had but recently returned from Italy and had "run over" Petrarch only a few months before composing his poem (letter to West, May 8, 1742). I do not remember finding the rime-scheme *a b a b a b a b c d c d c d* in preceding English sonnets. It is common in the early Italian poets, and is also that of Dante's 29th, and of the 13th, 39th, and 42d of Petrarch's *Morte*.

yet, as Gray certainly knew some Elizabethan quartorzains and presumably had read a good many,[1] the richness of his opening lines and their embroidery of the idea they express may be due to Shakespeare, Spenser, or their contemporaries. On the other hand, there may be some influence from Milton, whom Gray strongly admired and by whom his other pieces were affected. This seems the more probable because the poem was written about a person and was called forth by a definite occasion, because it contains three verbal borrowings from *Paradise Lost*,[2] and because certain lines exhibit a simple sincerity and depth of feeling which even the stilted phraseology of the eighteenth century cannot conceal. Yet the main influence was certainly Italian. The poem was not published, or apparently even shown to friends, until 1775, after Gray's death; and therefore it had no influence upon the *revival* of the sonnet. In structure and language it is quite different from any of the quartorzains that succeeded it.

The sonnets that seem to come next in chronological order met with a fate singularly like that of their predecessors: remaining for many years unpublished, they appear to have been practically unknown and so to have had no traceable influence. These pieces were the work of Benjamin Stillingfleet, the *littérateur* who is best known for having given rise to the term "blue-stocking." H. J. Todd, who examined the manuscripts, tells us that one of the sonnets was dated 1746.[3] As Stillingfleet edited Milton's poems and arranged an oratorio from *Paradise Lost*, one might expect him to have been influenced by the elder poet. On this point his biographer leaves no doubt, for he writes: "The study of Milton and the preparations for an edition of his works, led Mr. Stillingfleet to an imitation of his style; and soon after this period, copying the example of his favourite bard, he addressed to his beloved friends and companions of the common room, a Series of Sonnets."[4] But even without these facts there could be little question as to the "truly Miltonick"[5] character of poems like the following:

> Grandson to that good man, who bravely dared
> Withstand a Monarch's will, when crowds around
> Of noble serving men stoop'd to the ground

[1] See his *Observations on English Metre*, in *Works* (ed. Mitford), v. 249–50.

[2] "Smileing mornings," "amorous descant," "attire" (for a covering of the fields); cf. *P. L.*, v. 168, iv. 603, vii. 501.

[3] In his edition of Milton (1801), v. 446. Internal evidence gives approximately the same date.

[4] *Literary Life and Select Works* [by William Coxe], 1811, i. 94.

[5] Todd's Milton, preface.

Whene'er Corruption's guilty face appear'd;
Thou nobly firm, like him, hast ever rear'd
Thy front sublime; thou, with the giddy found
Steady and wise, hast kept thyself unbound
By glittering chains that others have ensnar'd;
So shall thy virtue due reward obtain,
While they, like Greeks and Trojans heretofore,
Fright holy Virtue from her peaceful seat;
Destroying each his rival, but to gain
A phantom Helen; thou shalt her adore,
Her real, and enjoy in thy retreat.

Lofty in sentiment and dignified in style as this is, it is not great; but in these respects, as well as in dealing not with love but with the friend to whom it is addressed, in beginning with a vocative, in using run-over lines and internal pauses, in adhering to the Petrarchan rime-scheme and the pauses at the end of the first and second quatrains, it is typical of its fellows. The preservation of the pauses may be due to Italian or to Elizabethan influences, though in every other respect in which Milton differs from his predecessors Stillingfleet follows him.

It is important to bear in mind that none of these sonnets — those of the two Yorkes, Gray, and Stillingfleet — were published or generally known until many years after they were written. They are significant only as showing that the sonnet ferment was working and how it was working. As for influence, they had apparently none whatever.

The real father of the eighteenth-century sonnet, "the only begetter" whom his contemporaries knew as such, and accordingly the one who may have done much to settle the kind of poem it was to be, was Thomas Edwards. In the second volume of "Dodsley's Miscellany" (1748), that important collection through which many of the new impulses in English poetry found expression, there appeared fourteen sonnets, all by Edwards except the first, which was probably an imitation of the others.[1] Thirty-nine more quatorzains of Edwards's were published, but none appeared until ten years later, after his death. The qualities that marked the first ones are present in all the rest: they are, as their editor described them, "correct, simple, not aiming at points or turns, in the phrase and structure rather ancient, for the most part of a grave, or even of a melancholy cast; formed in short upon the model of the Italians of the good age,

---

[1] It is an "imitation" from Lope de Vega, by Richard Roderick, the friend of Edwards and his follower in other literary activities. See the 1782 edition of the "Miscellany," ii. 336, 324.

and of their Imitators among us, Spenser and Milton." [1] This one
is typical:

> Harvy, dear Kinsman, who in prime of youth
> (When Passions rule, or proud Ambition's call
> Too oft misleads our heedless steps to fall
> From the fair paths of Virtue, Peace, and Truth,)
> For erring Souls touch'd with a generous ruth,
> Did'st vow thy service to the God of All;
> Anxious to rescue free the captive thrall
> From the old Serpent's deadly poisonous tooth;
> Great is the weight, important is the care,
> Of that high office which thou made'st thy choice;
> Be strong, be faithful therefore to thy best,
> Nor pains, nor pray'ers, nor fair example spare;
> So thou shalt hear at least that chearing voice,
> "Well done, good Servant, enter into rest."

That this sonnet is formed upon the model of Milton's seems clear
enough, and not alone because of the obvious similarity in the first
line, in three of the rime-words, and in the general idea to Milton's
"Lady, that in the prime of earliest youth." In these respects it is
unlike most of Edwards's poems; but in tone, style, and structure,
in beginning with a proper name in the vocative, and in having a
person as the subject, it is typical of its author, and, save for its lack
of genius, it is typically Miltonic. There would seem, then, to be
little doubt that Edwards patterned his sonnets on Milton's. Unfortunately, he himself declared he did not. In a letter to the novelist
Richardson he said:

The reading of Spenser's Sonnets was the first occasion of my writing
that species of little poems, and my first six were written in the same sort
of stanza as all his and Shakespeare's are. But after that Mr. Wray
brought me acquainted with the Italian authors ... I wrote in that stanza;
drawing from the same fountains as Milton drew from; — so that I was
complimented with having well imitated Milton when I was not acquainted with his Sonnets. I hope I shall never be ashamed of imitating
such great originals as Shakespeare, Spenser and Milton, whom to imitate
with any degree of success is no small praise. But why is my writing of
sonnets, imitation any more than theirs? At least, it is not imitating
them, but the same authors whom they imitated. .... I have only to add
that the impulse was that way; and to borrow an expression of Mr. Pope's,

I wrote in sonnet, *for the numbers came.* [2]

---

[1] "Advertisement" prefixed to the sixth edition (1758) of Edwards's *Canons of Criticism,* in which fifty of his sonnets are printed.

[2] Richardson's *Correspondence* (ed. A. L. Barbauld, 1804), iii. 91–2, July 18, 1754.

At a first reading this is certainly baffling, and yet it may prove to be illuminating. It is to be noted that Edwards does not distinguish between Shakespearean and Spenserian sonnets, that his published work contains none on the Shakespearean and but four on the Spenserian model, and that these four recall the Elizabethan productions only in their rime-scheme and in the fact that one of them touches on love. The influence of the Italians is equally dubious, for there is no trace of it save in the Petrarchan structure and rime-sequence, which are used in all but the four Spenserian poems. Clearly Edwards's memory was at fault, or else some of his sonnets were not published. He was a pious, good man, who would not intentionally deceive; but a desire to assert his originality may have affected his recollection somewhat, or have caused him to overstate the case, particularly if he had been accused of imitating Milton. What makes this conjecture the more probable is his friendship with the Yorke brothers, whose Miltonic quatorzains, composed in 1741 and 1743, he must have known, since he addressed three of his earliest sonnets to them and their father, and since Daniel Wray, who 'brought him acquainted with the Italian authors,' knew the Yorkes well and bantered them on their intimacy with both Edwards and his opponent Warburton.[1] Very likely Mr. Wray explained to Edwards the general structure of the legitimate sonnet (saying nothing about run-over lines or internal pauses) and read him a few translations from the Italian. Thereafter Edwards undoubtedly tried to follow the rules that had been given him, but there is no evidence of his getting anything else "from the same fountains as Milton drew from." If, then, the character of his sonnets is neither Elizabethan nor Italian, and if we attach any significance to his declaration that they were not derived from Milton, whence are they?

Perhaps his concluding sentence will give us a clue, — "the impulse was that way." It must be remembered that the continuity of sonnet development had been entirely broken. Edwards presumably knew but few sonnets of any kind, and had only vague and incorrect notions of those the Elizabethans and Italians had written. More than this, he had neither inherited nor unconsciously assimilated any preconceptions in the matter. The sonnet was dead. If

[1] The 18th sonnet (as numbered in the *Canons of Criticism*) is addressed to the Lord Chancellor himself, the 7th and 15th to his sons Philip and Charles Yorke. In Nichols's *Collection*, vi. 106, the 18th is dated 1746 and the 15th 1747; but, as these follow neither the Spenserian nor the Shakespearean model, they ought not, according to Edwards's letter just quoted, to be his earliest sonnets. Inasmuch as the 7th, that to Philip Yorke, *is* Spenserian and also comes first in the first group printed (in "Dodsley's Miscellany," 1748), it is likely to be the first one he wrote. For Wray's remarks, see George Hardinge's *Biographical Anecdotes of Daniel Wray* (1815), 54.

Edwards chose to revive it he might, and probably would, instinctively turn it to purposes entirely different from those to which it had previously been devoted. An Elizabethan would naturally have written as his friends were writing; but since, aside from the Yorkes, Edwards's friends were not writing sonnets, he followed his own bent. It is all-important to realize that the eighteenth-century sonneteers, in their ignorance of what lay on the other side of the deep gulf stretching between them and their forefathers, were free to do whatever they chose, and that they naturally did something quite different from what the Elizabethans or the Italians had done. Milton's poems, however, were so generally known and liked that their influence could hardly be avoided. It was so in Edwards's case. However he came to write sonnets, he must have known and admired Milton's before composing most of those he published, although some of the characteristics which the earlier poet first brought into the English sonnet Edwards may well have reintroduced independently.[1]

Since, except for the "imitation" in the *London Magazine*, Edwards's sonnets were the first of the new type to be published, and since those that followed are much like his, it is natural to inquire what influence he exerted. "Dodsley's Miscellany" was often reprinted, and it is fair to suppose that, among the many hundred sonnets published in the latter part of the eighteenth century, a number were affected by the considerable body of Edwards's work and that some authors owed their initial impulse to it.[2] But, as his

[1] Thirty-six of Edwards's sonnets — nearly seventy per cent — begin with vocatives, which in sixteen cases are proper names; four others have proper names in the vocative later in their first lines. Almost every one of them has to do with some friend and is addressed to him. The usual pauses are nearly always observed, but in the 23d and the 26th there is a run-over line at the end of the first quatrain, and in the 33d one at the end of the second, the turn coming at the beginning of the tenth line. In the fifty-two sonnets there are nineteen internal pauses and 178 lines without final punctuation, nearly half of them being very closely connected with the lines that follow. These figures seem to point to a structure derived through Mr. Wray from the Italian but modified by familiarity with Milton. The subjects, style, and opening lines certainly suggest Milton. "Sabrina's flood" is mentioned in the first sonnet, and Milton is referred to in the 17th, 32d, and 45th; in the 45th, a line and a half are devoted to *Paradise Lost*, the phrase "warbling tunes his Doric lays" is borrowed from *Lycidas*, 189, and "Fancie's Child" is applied to "sweet Shakespear," as it is in *Allegro*. In the 39th the lines,

While jolly spring

In frolic dance leads-up the blooming May,

are from Milton's sonnet *To the Nightingale;* and there are also the similarities in the 30th, quoted above, p. 493.

[2] There is a marked similarity between Edwards's sonnets and the thirty-two that Hugh Downman "presented with the first impression of *Poems to Thespia*" in 1781. All of these are addressed to persons and twenty begin with vocatives; internal pauses abound, as do run-over lines, which often come at the end of the octave, but the order

poems closely resemble those of men who wrote independently of him, — Stillingfleet's, for example, — it is only by external evidence that one can be certain of his influence. Of such evidence there is very little; in fact, so rare are references to Edwards in the sonnets of the period and in the critical writings upon them that his prestige can hardly have been great.[1] Only three persons can be definitely shown to have been his followers, and two of these, Susannah Highmore and Hester Mulso Chapone, belonged to the bevy of ladies who fluttered about the novelist Richardson and thus knew Edwards personally. The third, Gray's friend and biographer, William Mason, is of more consequence.

Mason's debt to Edwards may be inferred from the title of his first sonnet, *Sent to a Young Lady with Dodsley's Miscellanies*, and from its date, 1748, the year Edwards's poems appeared in these same "Miscellanies." His thirteen other quatorzains were written at rather wide intervals until the close of the century; yet, singularly enough, only two were published before 1797. All have the Petrarchan octave, and but one ends with a couplet; six of the fourteen are concerned with the friends to whom they were addressed, two are in defence of the English garden, and three are anniversary poems. In seriousness, as well as in the absence of conceits, the arrangement of rimes, the presence of run-over lines and internal pauses, and the frequent omission of the pauses at the end of the first and second quatrains, they are clearly on the Miltonic model.[2] To be sure, Mason, like Edwards, may not have intended to follow Milton; but that is improbable, since four years before writing his first sonnet he had composed flagrant copies of *Lycidas*, *Allegro*, and *Penseroso*, and before a third of his quatorzains were penned had begun a long poem in the style of *Paradise Lost* and made some use of *Comus* in one of his dramas. His sonnets thus seem to round out the circle of his conscious imitations of the master.

In 1755,[3] seven years after the publication of the first three volumes of "Dodsley's Miscellany," a fourth volume was added. In this were

of rimes is usually haphazard. Most of Downman's twenty-three other quatorzains are conventional nature-poems. Five are in blank verse.

[1] In 1799, however, the *Monthly Review* (enl. ed., xxix. 362) declared, "Perhaps the best modern sonnets are those of Edwards." They are also well spoken of, though not enthusiastically, in *Petrarca* (1803), p. cxcvi.

[2] A footnote to one of them (*Works*, i. 133) indicates that the phrase "plain in its neatness" is from Milton's translation of Horace; but "smit with the love of Song" in another (*ib.* prefatory) is unacknowledged. One of the sonnets (*ib.* 130) is occasioned by one of Milton's.

[3] An early Miltonic sonnet that long remained unpublished was written about 1750 by William Hall, urging Nicholas Hardinge to defend Milton from Lauder's attacks (see p. 686 below). It is Petrarchan, and begins with a proper name in the vocative.

two sonnets by that delightful personage, large of girth and larger of heart, who was at once laureate of the king and of Oxford ale, as well as boon companion of watermen, professor of poetry, and one of the best scholars of his day, — Thomas Warton. The two sonnets, one on the absence of his brother, the other on bathing, are Petrarchan in arrangement of rimes, but have six run-over lines and each observes only one pause; in the second the turn comes at the end of the sixth instead of the eighth line. Warton's seven other sonnets, in structure, subjects, and style of the same type as the first two, were not published till 1777. Those written in Dugdale's *Monasticon*, at Stonehenge, and to the river Lodon live at least in our anthologies; but the others are also good, containing here and there lines of such quiet beauty as,

> Or Evening glimmer'd o'er the folded train.[1]

Warton's sonnets are significant not only because they are among the best the century produced, if not, as Hazlitt termed them, "some of the finest . . . in the language," [2] but because in several respects they marked out paths that were afterwards to be much trodden. They were the first to turn for their subjects from persons to nature and to places of legendary or historic interest. That to the river Lodon, furthermore, strikes apparently for the first time the note of pensive wistfulness in the presence of nature which a little later was dominant in the sonnet. Accordingly, though it probably is not Warton's best and does not represent the medievalism or the Miltonic stateliness of some of his quatorzains, it will be quoted as the one that perhaps exerted the most influence:

> Ah! what a weary race my feet have run,
> Since first I trod thy banks with alders crown'd,
> And thought my way was all thro' fairy ground,
> Beneath thy azure sky, and golden sun:
> Where first my Muse to lisp her notes begun!
> While pensive Memory traces back the round,
> Which fills the varied interval between;
> Much pleasure, more of sorrow, marks the scene.
> Sweet native stream! those skies and suns so pure
> No more return, to cheer my evening road!
> Yet still one joy remains, that not obscure,
> Nor useless, all my vacant days have flow'd,
> From youth's gay dawn to manhood's prime mature;
> Nor with the Muse's laurel unbestow'd.

[1] Fifth line of the first sonnet, in its final form.

[2] *Lectures on the English Poets*, 1818 (*Works*, 1902, v. 120). Oliver Elton remarks (*Survey of English Literature*, 1912, i. 73) that in his sonnets Warton "aims at resonance and rich historical colouring. . . . He has that sense of an antiquity, half-ruined by time and half rescued by scholarship and piety, which goes back to the Renaissance."

The more one studies eighteenth-century sonnets, the deeper grows the conviction of Warton's importance in their development. Although it was 1777 before most of those he wrote got into print, they probably circulated in manuscript among his friends, his brother's pupils at Winchester, and various poetically-inclined students and fellows at Oxford. Owing to his position as laureate, scholar, and professor of poetry, owing also to the inherent worth of the verses themselves, they were sure to attract considerable attention. We shall find evidence of their influence on Russell and Bowles, and a strong likelihood of their effect on Bampfylde, Holmes, Warwick, and Brydges, a group which, with Warton himself, includes the best sonneteers of the period. It is noteworthy that in 1803, when George Henderson made the selections for his *Petrarca*, a moderate-sized anthology of sonnets intended to represent the public taste, he included all of Warton's.[1]

Warton, it will be remembered, was a great admirer of Milton's minor poems, which he not only edited but constantly imitated and borrowed from in his own verse.[2] His sonnets may well have been suggested by those of Edwards; yet it is possible that, like the Yorkes, Gray, Stillingfleet, and Edwards himself, he turned to the quatorzain without any thought of his contemporaries, though moved by the same *zeitgeist* that stirred them.[3] But, from whatever source the impulse came, it is highly probable from the nature of the poems, their marked inversions of word-order, and the character of their author's other productions, that his conception of the *genre*, as well as his model for the poems he wrote in it, was derived from the "organ voice of England," to which he, together with his father and brother, paid lifelong devotion.

After the sonnet had received a start from these men it was taken up by others and slowly grew into popularity. Almost every one who wrote after 1750 experimented with it now and then, — Boswell, "Peter Pindar," Hannah More, James Montgomery, Dr. Dodd (the clergyman who was hanged for forgery), Charles Burney (Fanny's father), Bishop Percy, Anna Seward, William Roscoe (the biographer

---

[1] Warton's influence is also seen in Thelwall's sonnet to Warwick Castle (*Poetical Recreations*, 1822, p. 44), and in Thomas Park's sonnets (1797), particularly the 19th. It is impossible to say just how much he affected other writers after 1789, when his influence blended with that of Bowles; but, according to the *Monthly Review* (enl. ed., xviii. 430), Warton's sonnets were widely read in 1795.

[2] See above, pp. 243–5, 463–7, and below, p. 561.

[3] Warton may have become interested in sonnets through his father (see pp. 461–2 above and 560–61 below), particularly since the elder poet has a fourteen-line piece in couplets which almost certainly suggested one of his son's quatorzains (see Mant's edition of the son's poems, Oxford, 1802, ii. 154 n.).

of Lorenzo de' Medici), "Perdita" Robinson, Cowper, Burns, Lamb, Southey, Thelwall, Leigh Hunt, Kirke White, Byron, and all the other romanticists, including those who wrote novels, Horace Walpole, William Beckford, Ann Radcliffe, Charlotte Smith, Helen Maria Williams, Amelia Opie, and Thomas Holcroft. Yet authors were so slow in publishing their productions that it was long before the sonnet came into anything like general use. Of the quatorzains we have thus far considered, only fifty-five — the one in the *London Magazine*, Richard Roderick's, fifty of Edwards's, one of Mason's, and two of Warton's — were printed before 1775, and most of these were little known and not of a kind to inspire imitation. Brydges gives us to understand that in 1782, when he began to write sonnets, he knew of none published since Elizabethan days except Milton's, Warton's, and Bampfylde's.[1] How slowly the form gained favor is revealed by the periodicals; for the total number of quatorzains I have found in them all until 1777 is under twenty, whereas in 1789 the *Gentleman's Magazine* alone printed fifteen in a single issue and fifty-nine in the course of the year.[2] In the last two decades of the century the same periodical and the *European Magazine* published between them nearly six hundred, the sonnet having by that time become perhaps the most popular kind of magazine verse. As some fifteen hundred or two thousand appeared in books during the same decades, the oft-repeated remark as to the scarcity of sonnets in the latter half of the eighteenth century must be another of those imaginative touches with which scholarship has adorned this arid age.[3]

The most prolific writer of sonnets that the times produced was that Britomart of eighteenth-century poetry who has gone down to posterity as "the Swan of Lichfield." Anna Seward, to use her baptismal name, has enriched the world with three volumes of poetical effusions and six of selections from her epistolary recreations. She took herself so seriously that she exhausted the seriousness of the subject, and thus has furnished a deal of amusement(particularly

---

[1] *Poems* (4th ed., 1807), 213–14.

[2] The *European Magazine* published 17 in 1789, 24 in 1790, 34 in 1797, and on an average something over one a month. The average of the *Gentleman's Magazine* for the last quarter of the century was a trifle less than one a month, of the *Scots* and the *London* it was two a year.

[3] In 1793 the *Critical Review* (new arr., x. 114) affirmed, "The Sonnet . . . has been so much cultivated of late years, and especially since Mr. Bowles and Mrs. Charlotte Smith have gratified the public ear with their elegant productions . . . that, to say the truth, we begin to be almost satiated with *sonnets*." Cf. *ib*. xxvii. 135 (1799); *Mo. Rev.*, enl. ed., xxiv. 17 (1797), "Sonnets have of late been a very prevalent form of composition"; and the reference in Henderson's *Petrarca* (p. xxxv) to "the multiplicity of attempts which the world has been lately accustomed to behold in this species of poetry." Over a thousand sonnets were published in Capel Lofft's *Laura* (1813–14).

since the appearance of E. V. Lucas's delightful book, *A Swan and her Friends*) for those whom she expected to edify. Our concern, unfortunately, is not with Miss Seward's sentimental but decided personality, or with the unfailing though unintended amusement to be found in her letters, but with her one hundred and five quatorzains. She began to write these in 1770, but published only a few before 1799. On the sonnet, as on almost everything else, Miss Seward had ideas of her own. The rhythm, she held, should be that of blank verse, the pauses coming within rather than at the end of the line.[1] To the *order* of the rimes she paid no attention, but she held their *number* to be important, maintaining firmly that the octave should have but two.[2] The concluding couplet she allowed, using it in nearly half of her own sonnets; yet she wrote, "Nothing can be . . . more improper, than a new or detached thought for the conclusion . . . brilliance, epigrammatic turn or point, belong not to that species of composition."[3] On the contrary, she held that "dignity and energetic plainness were its most indispensable characteristics," that it should be "grave and severe," should have "strength and majesty," and "rather an elevated simplicity than that Popean smoothness and polish."[4] This was what Miss Seward regarded as a legitimate sonnet; it was the kind she wrote, and therefore the kind that every one else should write. Such a conception could have been

---

[1] "Your objection to the monotonous chime of the legitimate sonnet . . . would be just," she wrote in 1786, "if the sense were carried on, as in the couplet, to the end of each line. But that jingling effect is entirely done away where the verses run into each other with undulating flow, and varied pause, after the manner of blank verse, as in the sublime anathema of Milton on the massacre of Piedmont (*Letters*, i. 186)." In ii. 303 she speaks of "the characteristic grace of the legitimate sonnet, the floating pause"; and in ii. 256 she regrets that her friend "should not love the varying pause, undulating through the lines of the Miltonic sonnet."

[2] Thus in the preface to her *Original Sonnets* (1799) she says that all but nine of the hundred are "strictly Sonnets. Those nine," she adds, "vary only from the rules of the legitimate Sonnet in that they rhime *three*, instead of *four* times in the *first* part." By this she means that nine, instead of having two rimes occurring four times, as in the legitimate form, have three rimes, one occurring twice, the others three times each. In reality, 62 of the sonnets are not legitimate; 26 of them would be if it were not for the final couplet, and so would six more but for irregularities in the order of rimes in the sestet, while the remaining 30 have irregular octaves. Twenty of these last she considered legitimate, because she disregarded the order in which the rimes occur; that is, such arrangements as *a b b a a b a b* (in sonnets 3, 12, 18, 20, etc.) and *a b b a b b a a* (in 50, 53, 57, etc.) seemed to her regular. The five sonnets not printed in her "centenary" (see below, Bibl. IV, 1770) are all irregular.

[3] *Letters*, iv. 145. See also above, p. 487, n. 2.

[4] *Ib.* ii. 257–8, iv. 145. Cf. i. 201: "I am surprised at your idea, that Milton's sonnets have a singular flow of numbers, and that their author thought smoothness an essential perfection in that order of verse. The best of Milton's have certain hardnesses, though there is a majesty, perhaps, in that very hardness, which, besides producing an enchanting effect . . . seems to mark the peculiarity of the composition."

derived from but one source, — of that we should be certain even
if there were no external evidence. But Miss Seward has left posterity no doubt in the matter. Milton she regarded as "the superior
of Virgil, and the equal of Homer," though not so great as Shakespeare; she spoke of him as "that poet, who has but two equals in the
world," [1] and she "almost" agreed with George Hardinge in thinking
"the best of Milton's sonnets equal to any thing he has written." [2]
"A few of them," she declared a little later, "are the best-possible
models for that order of verse . . . and . . . should, I think, be
kept in view by sonnet writers, as the painters of ideal beauty keep
the Phidian statues in their galleries." [3] If this "should" be done,
Miss Seward of course did it. We are therefore not surprised that
she wrote of her "centenary" of quatorzains, "I dare assert . . .
the regularity of their construction, after rules deduced from the
Miltonic sonnet." [4]

Her productions "ensued from time to time, as various circumstances impressed the heart, or the imagination of their Author." [5]
They accordingly show considerable variety in subject-matter, being
devoted to friends, passing events, literary criticism, Contemplation,
Ingratitude, and so on; but nature is the most frequent theme and
melancholy the dominant tone. Most of them are commonplace in
thought and harsh in expression; yet a few are really pleasing. This
is one of the best:

> Now on hills, rocks, and streams, and vales, and plains,
> Full looks the shining Day. — Our gardens wear
> The gorgeous robes of the consummate Year.
> With laugh, and shout, and song, stout Maids and Swains
> Heap high the fragrant hay, as thro' rough lanes
> Rings the yet empty waggon. — See in air
> The pendent cherries, red with tempting stains,

[1] *Ib.* iv. 225, iii. 318; cf. i. 239, ii. 52. Notwithstanding her high opinion of Shakespeare, she could see in his sonnets, as in those of Spenser, only "quaintness" and
"quibbling" (v. 159). Petrarch, whom she mentioned frequently but knew only in
translation, she also thought poorly of for the same reason (ii. 304; cf. v. 58).

[2] *Ib.* i. 239. This eccentric friend of Miss Seward's, who mounted a table to read
Paradise Lost to her (see p. 7, n. 2, above), was, like his father, a Milton enthusiast.
"Few, if any," he wrote, "can out-idolize me." His sonnets are not unlike Edwards's:
they are addressed to persons, are Petrarchan in rime-scheme, and half of them begin
with vocatives. As the one that seems to have been written first was composed at
Vaucluse in 1776, it is not surprising to find that twenty-four are translations from
the Italian.

[3] *Ib.* ii. 303–4.

[4] *Ib.* v. 60. In numbers 5, 23, 51, 64, 67 n., 74, 75, and 78 of her *Sonnets* she
either borrows from Milton or refers to him; number 77 seems to be based on Shakespeare's "Full many a glorious morning."

[5] Preface to her *Sonnets.*

Gleam thro' their boughs. — Summer, thy bright career
Must slacken soon in Autumn's milder sway;
Then thy now heapt and jocund meads shall stand
Smooth, — vacant, — silent, — thro' th' exulting Land
As wave thy Rival's golden fields, and gay
Her Reapers throng. She smiles, and binds the sheaves;
Then bends her parting step o'er fall'n and rustling leaves.[1]

"The tenth Muse, the all-accomplished Seward," [2] was a person of no little reputation in her day; yet, as most of her poems were not published till the last years of the century, when sonneteers had plenty of other models, it is hard to say how much influence she exerted. At least her sonnets are typical of a considerable number of those written at the time. Henry F. Cary, the translator of Dante, who as a youth was an adopted cygnet of the Lichfield Swan, wrote to her in June, 1789:

A distinction should be made between the Miltonic and Spenseric sonnet; the first may be used on grave and sublime, the latter on tender subjects; the diction of the former ought to be elevated yet simple, and should require a sort of majesty by the pauses and breaks peculiar to blank verse; that of the latter should be neat, polished, and smooth throughout.[3]

By "Spenseric," Cary presumably meant no more than tender and flowing; for he seems to have been quite uninfluenced by the *Amoretti* and probably shared Miss Seward's dislike for what little he knew of them. Yet, misleading as is the name he gave it, he was right in distinguishing a non-Miltonic type of contemporary sonnet. His own work, like that of his patroness and of William Hayley, whom both admired, like the effusions of Charlotte Smith, Helen Williams,[4] Mrs. Robinson, Richard Polwhele, and many more whose names on earth are dark, differs in many ways from the poems hitherto considered. These later quatorzains are looser in structure, more careless in rime-scheme (inclining to the couplet-ending), more sentimental, melancholy, fluent, and trivial, hence less condensed and dignified; yet practically none of them deal with love, or intro-

---

[1] Sonnet 36.

[2] Dedication of R. F. Cheetham's *Odes*, etc. (Stockport, 1796?): see *Crit. Rev.*, new arr., xxii. 84. Cf. *ib.* xvii. 154, xxxvi. 413; *Gent. Mag.*, liv. 778, lix. 71; *Univ. Mag.*, lxxix. 43; etc.

[3] Henry Cary, *Memoir of H. F. Cary* (1847), i. 34.

[4] Miss Williams, who led an adventurous life in Paris during the Revolution, was in 1789 the recipient of a letter from Burns and was the subject of Wordsworth's earliest quatorzain. Her sonnet *To Twilight*, published in 1783, is good. She was one of the first to introduce sonnets into novels, and went so far as to scatter eight of her own through her translation of *Paul and Virginia* (1795).

duce conceits, or give any other evidence of Italian or Elizabethan influences.[1] Indeed, their composers were often, like Miss Seward, enthusiastic admirers of Milton and his professed followers in the field of the sonnet. Hayley wrote a sympathetic life of him, Polwhele imitated him frequently, and Cary, whose great translation shows the influence of *Paradise Lost*, scattered its author's phrases through his own quatorzains. Yet the work of these poetasters, though more like Milton's than any one's else, is not Miltonic. It is, indeed, like nothing before and fortunately like very little since, but is distinctly of the second half of the eighteenth century.

Just who began writing these invertebrate, fourteen-line occasional poems it would be hard to say; several favorite sons and daughters of Apollo may have slipped easily and unconsciously into them at about the same time. At any rate, their vogue was due, not to the influence of Hayley or Miss Seward, but to their being the kind of poem that bards who were tired of composing mechanical imitations of *Allegro* and *Penseroso* found most to their taste. The tendency of the poems to deal with nature, and to be pensive or even melancholy in tone, reached its orbed fulfilment in the "Elegiac Sonnets" of Charlotte Smith. These doleful ditties, which came finally to number ninety-four, enjoyed a remarkable popularity: they went through eleven English editions and were reprinted in America; they were praised by Wordsworth and Scott and were regarded as models by Coleridge.[2] One periodical spoke of them as "the most popular in the language, and deservedly so"; another declared that Milton's did not compare with them; and a third asserted, "A very trifling compliment is paid to Mrs. Smith, when it is observed how much her Sonnets exceed those of *Shakspeare* and *Milton*. She has undoubtedly conferred honour on a species of poetry which most of her predecessors in this country have disgraced."[3] Yet twentieth-century readers of her verses, if there be any such, will agree rather with the writer who termed her "a puny poet, puling to the moon";[4]

---

[1] Mrs. Mary Robinson ("Perdita") wrote the only eighteenth-century sonnet-sequence that I know. It consists of forty-three poems which deal with Sappho's unfortunate love for Phaon, and which, strangely enough, are in every respect legitimate sonnets. Mrs. Robinson, like others of her kind, is fond of such lines as

Night's dewy orb, that o'er yon limpid stream.

[2] Wordsworth, *Prose Works* (ed. Grosart, 1876), iii. 151; Scott, *Prose Works* (1827), iv. 49–50; Coleridge, *Poetical Works* (Globe ed.), 543.

[3] *Crit. Rev.*, new arr., xxxiv. 393 (1802); *Univ. Mag.*, xci. 414 (1792); *Gent. Mag.*, lvi. 334 (1786). Cf. *New London Mag.*, v. 212 (1789); *Crit. Rev.*, new arr., xxxvi. 413 (1802), and xxi. 149–51 (1797, an unfavorable comment).

[4] Quoted by Miss Seward (who heartily agreed) in *Letters*, vi. 43; and cf. ii. 287, where she speaks of Mrs. Smith's "everlasting lamentables, which she calls sonnets,

for most of her elegies are quite impossible, — diffuse, self-conscious, sentimental, written in a conventional, stilted diction, and, notwithstanding the genuineness of their author's sorrows, apt to leave an impression of rhetoric and declamation rather than of real feeling. Nearly half of them employ the Shakespearean rime-scheme, and the irregularity of the remainder seems to be due to Mrs. Smith's unwillingness — which she shared with most writers of this kind of sonnet — to work hard over her productions. In encouraging the use of these easier arrangements of rimes, in introducing quatorzains into her popular novels (a practice quickly adopted by Ann Radcliffe, Beckford, and others), and in fastening the elegiac mood upon the *genre* so firmly that it remained throughout the century and was regarded by many as indispensable,— in these things she is a force to be reckoned with.

Mrs. Smith dedicated her "everlasting duns on pity" [1] to William Hayley, the fluent, pretty emptiness of whose sonnets and other poems seems to have had not a little influence upon writers of her kind. In 1780 his brow seemed wreathed with unfading laurel, but if he is known at all to-day it is as the friend of Blake, Cowper, and Romney. Byron erred in describing his verse as

> For ever feeble and for ever tame,[2]

for some of his sonnets to persons have sufficient dignity to recall faintly those of Milton, whom he greatly admired; but as a rule they tinkle along as aimlessly as water in a drawing-room fountain. Like many of the fourteen-line effusions written during the last quarter of the century, they are not bad but futile. In expression they are conventional and far from vigorous. There is usually no particular fault to be found with any single line, but after reading many lines we remember none, because they contain nothing but empty compliments and obvious ideas, because they leave only the impression that their author is a well-meaning, sentimental person who desires to write but has nothing to say. The attitude of such poetasters towards the form was thus expressed by Richard Polwhele in 1785: "The sonnet seems peculiarly turned to the beautiful; and . . . the more picturesque objects of still life. But the sublime . . . is obviously incompatible with such miniature-painting . . . the

made up of hackneyed scraps of dismality, with which her memory furnished her from our various poets." Mrs. Smith's genuine and often pleasantly-expressed love of nature is more clearly seen in her descriptive poem, *Beachy Head* (see p. 255 above), than in her sonnets.

[1] Miss Seward, *Letters*, vi. 43.
[2] *English Bards*, 314.

Italian method, perhaps, needs not in all cases be abandoned; though
... it often gives the sonnet an air of formality and constraint." [1]

The diffuse, pretty, melancholy type of quatorzain was gladly
received and made the most of by the lesser luminaries, who rejoiced
in the ease with which it could be written. As a result,

> Reams of outrageous sonnets, thick as snow,[2]

descended upon the press, and amateur versifiers who lacked both
skill and ideas turned to the sonnet and the ode as fit vehicles for
their saccharine imbecilities. The most popular of these triflers were
known as the Della Cruscans, from a famous Florentine academy to
which one of them belonged. After publishing two volumes of miscellanies — one unmistakably Miltonic — during a residence in
Italy, some of them transferred their activities to an English daily,
The World, where "Della Crusca" "announced himself by a sonnet to
Love," which was taken up by "Anna Matilda," "Laura Maria,"
"Benedict," "the Bard," and others, until "from one end of the
kingdom to the other, all was nonsense and Della Crusca." These
silly prattlers and others like them had greatly injured the reputation of the quatorzain before Gifford silenced them with his slashing
satires.[3] Fortunately, there were always some persons who continued the tradition of the serious, dignified, Miltonic sonnet, and it
is to these that we now return, interposing a little ease in our survey
of commonplace, conventional verse by pausing over some neglected
flowers of true poetry.

[1] *Traditions and Recollections* (1826), i. 174-5.
[2] William Gifford, *The Maeviad*, 272.
[3] *The Baviad* (1791), and *The Maeviad* (1795). The introduction to the collected
(1797) edition of these two works — the best account we have of the movement — is
the source of the quotations given above. The Della Cruscans were no more a definite
body than were the New England transcendentalists. Mrs. Piozzi (Dr. Johnson's
Mrs. Thrale) was the center of the group in Florence; but, except for a piece by Bertie
Greatheed and one by William Parsons, Robert Merry appears to have been the only
one of the number who contributed to the *World*. As the poems published in this paper
were anonymous, apparently any one — even Sheridan — who fell in with the fad and
had his verses accepted was a Della Cruscan. Merry and "Perdita" Robinson were,
however, the principal offenders. It was not by a "sonnet," but by a piece of forty-
four lines that Merry "announced himself." Gifford's mis-statement illustrates the
close connection in the popular mind between the Della Cruscans and sonneteering.
So far as the professedly incomplete *Poetry of the World* shows, only fourteen quatorzains were published in the *World* (see Bibl. IV, 1778 w., 1786-90 w., 1787-8, and 1790);
yet Mrs. Robinson wrote many sonnets, and Gifford quotes and refers to others in
his satires on the movement. The few volumes of verse composed by the Della
Cruscans are in themselves negligible, but as a symptom of the times, as a crystallization
of vague, floating tendencies, they are of some importance. Della Cruscanism was in
the air before Merry began to write, and was exhibited by many who never read the
Florence Miscellany or the *World*. I shall accordingly use the term in its larger and
looser signification, not restricting it to verse by members of the group.

Of these, "the rathe primrose that forsaken dies" is represented by the work of John Bampfylde, a poet whose character, unfortunate career, and fresh, hearty verses in praise of country life recall the forgotten John Clare and the Scottish peasant, contemporary with both, who

> walked in glory and in joy,
> Following his plough, along the mountain-side.

Those who would learn what little is known of the strange rustic of noble birth who, when taken from the farm and the free out-of-doors which he loved, fell into dissipation and lost his mind, recovering it only to die of consumption, must read Southey's letter to Sir Egerton Brydges.[1] Not all of Bampfylde's sonnets have been published, and the sixteen that he printed in 1778 are practically unknown; yet their love of nature and of rustic life, their close observation, their healthy, happy genuineness and poetic feeling, entitle them to remembrance. They are historically important as the earliest printed sonnets to deal almost exclusively with nature, and except for Warton's (most of which were published the year before) the earliest to be in themselves really attractive.[2] In their rime-scheme, their use of run-over lines, their disregard of the pauses and the turn, their dignity and slight stiffness, they suggest Milton, from whom they borrow a number of phrases. Here is a typical sonnet:

> As when, to one who long hath watch'd, the Morn
> Advancing, slow fore-warns th' approach of day,
> (What time the young and flowery-kirtled May
> Decks the green hedge and dewy grass unshorn
> With cowslips pale, and many a whitening thorn;)
> And now the Sun comes forth with level ray,
> Gilding the high-wood top and mountain grey;
> And as he climbs, the Meadows 'gins adorn:
> The Rivers glisten to the dancing beam,
> Th' awaken'd Birds begin their amorous strain,
> And Hill and Vale with joy and fragrance teem;
> Such is the sight of thee; thy wish'd return
> To eyes, like mine, that long have wak'd to mourn,
> That long have watch'd for light, and wept in vain.[3]

---

[1] Brydges, *Autobiography* (1834), ii. 257–61.

[2] Bampfylde's sonnets were probably influenced, if not suggested, by those of the laureate; for the tenth is "To Mr. Warton, on reading his History of English Poetry," and the second "On having Dined at Trinity College, Oxford," an occasion on which, as Mr. Saintsbury suggests (*Camb. Hist. Eng. Lit.*, English ed., xii. 133), Warton, who lived at Trinity, may well have been the host. The younger poet's "I ween," "erst," "sprent," etc., also recall Warton. Six sonnets by Robert Holmes, which were published the same year as Bampfylde's, likewise deal with nature, though in a conventional way, and show the same influence.

[3] *Sixteen Sonnets* (1778), no. iii. Lines 6–9 are perhaps indebted to Shakespeare's

Equal with Bampfylde in fate as well as in renown is the gifted young Oxford don, Thomas Russell, who did not live to see the publication of his poems in 1789. Southey termed him "the best English sonnet-writer," Wordsworth transferred four of his lines to one of his own sonnets, and Landor, with characteristic exaggeration, said that the following lines on Philoctetes at Lemnos would "authorise" Russell "to join the shades of Sophocles and Euripides":[1]

> On this lone Isle, whose rugged rocks affright
> The cautious pilot, ten revolving years
> Great Paean's Son, unwonted erst to tears,
> Wept o'er his wound: alike each rolling light
> Of heaven he watch'd, and blam'd it's lingering flight,
> By day the sea-mew screaming round his cave
> Drove slumber from his eyes, the chiding wave,
> And savage howlings chas'd his dreams by night.
> Hope still was his: in each low breeze, that sigh'd
> Thro' his rude grot, he heard a coming oar,
> In each white cloud a coming sail he spied;
> Nor seldom listen'd to the fancied roar
> Of Oeta's torrents, or the hoarser tide
> That parts fam'd Trachis from th' Euboic shore.

This is by no means Russell's only notable sonnet; in fact, nearly all of the seventeen that are original are so good that it is hard to understand why they are not better known. The one on Philoctetes is unrepresentative only in being more classic in subject than the rest; for Russell often joined the band which

> On Cherwell's sedgy banks with Warton stray'd
> And woo'd the Muse in gothic stole array'd.[2]

"Full many a glorious morning," and the first line to *P. L.*, ix. 445. Here are a few of the fifteen or twenty other phrases he took from Milton: "meads with slime are sprent and ways with mire" (i. 5, cf. Milton's sonnet to Lawrence, 2); "Voice, and Verse Divine, and Tuscan Air" (ii. 11, cf. also 12 and *P. L.*, vii. 2); "ere the lawns . . . appear" (iv. 4, cf. *Lycidas*, 25); "rocking winds" and "winds are piping loud" (v. 9, vi. 2, cf. *Penseroso*, 126); "secure rode tilting o'er the placid wave" (vi. 9, cf. *P. L.*, xi. 746–7); "other climes, and other shades among" (x. 13, cf. *Lyc.*, 174); "Lycid, 'bright Genius of the sounding shore'" (xi. 9, cf. *Lyc.*, 183); "Myrtle never-sear, and gadding Vine . . . mossy cell" (xii. 2, 9; cf. *Lyc.*, 2, 40, and *Pen.*, 169). Bampfylde's observation and poetic power are shown in such touches as "The glow-worm's kindling ray . . . The long moist grass with greenish Light illumes" (from the Harvard manuscript); or in his description of a wet summer (sonnet xvi. 11–14),

> Mute is the mournful plain,
> Silent the swallow sits beneath the thatch,
> And vacant hind hangs pensive o'er his hatch,
> Counting the frequent drop from reeded eaves.

[1] For these and other references, see D. M. Main's *Treasury of English Sonnets* (Manchester, 1880), 363–5. I am much indebted to Mr. Main's admirable notes.

[2] Henry Kett, *Verses on the Death of Mr. Headley,* in Park's edition of Henry Head-

He sang of minstrels and chivalry, of the owl, the curfew, "towers of antique fame," "Gothic fanes, dim isles, and cloysters hoar," of the *Arabian Nights*, and of Boccaccio's Ghismonda.[1] It was natural that he should take the Oxford professor of poetry somewhat as his model; for their literary tastes were similar, he had been a pupil of the elder Warton at Winchester when the younger brother published his sonnets, and, as he came to the defence of the *History of English Poetry*,[2] he must have known its likable author in the eight years that both were at Oxford. Russell's poems have the fondness for nature and the melancholy — though of a darker hue — that mark Warton's work, but almost none of its savor of quaintness. They move with greater ease, sometimes softening the dignity of the elder poet into pity and tenderness, and again lifting it to a nobility of utterance that the sonnet had not known since Milton's day. This last trait is seen not only in the account of Philoctetes, but in such lines as

> Not for thy Gothic Trumpet's martial rage . . .
> The Bard sublime of Terrour, and of Tears.[3]

Indeed, in their vigor, compactness, and dignified reserve, as well as in their loftiness of thought and expression, some of Russell's sonnets are not only the most Miltonic but probably the best that the eighteenth century produced.

"It was, while at Cambridge, in my twentieth year [1781]," wrote Sir Egerton Brydges, "that constantly poring over Milton, and increasing in my admiration of his early poems, from the impotent attempt of Johnson to decry them, I proceeded from that admiration to a rash effort to imitate those simply-majestic productions in this way," [4] — that is, in writing sonnets. This information is of the

---

ley's *Poems* (1808), p. 8. Headley, a friend of Russell and Bowles and author of one uninteresting sonnet, was strongly influenced by Thomas Warton, particularly by his blank verse.

[1] Three of his sonnets are from the Italian, one from the German, and two from the Portuguese; he has a fourteen-line "imitation" from the Greek (in couplets), an ode "imitated" from the Spanish, and an interesting address to Cervantes in which he laments that reason has banished romance. He refers to the *Philoctetes* of Sophocles as "that romantic . . . tragedy." One of the sonnets is on love. Russell was an admirer of Spenser, but neither his style nor his diction is influenced by the *Faerie Queene*, and there is no evidence that he even knew the *Amoretti*. The first stanza of his ode *To Silence* is modelled upon *Allegro* and *Penseroso*.

[2] *Gent. Mag.*, lii. 574–5, liii. 123–4 (1782–3).

[3] Sonnet vi, *To Boccaccio*, 1, 14. Mr. J. H. Hanford, to whom I am indebted for many excellent suggestions, remarks that the nobility of the Philoctetes sonnet is due in part to the greatness of Sophocles's tragedy from which it is derived, and particularly to the chorus that begins at line 676.

[4] *Poems* (4th ed., 1807), 213–14. Brydges called attention (*ib.* 215–19) to the similarity of his first, twelfth, seventeenth, and twenty-first sonnets to some of Milton's,

more value because the poems do not seem particularly Miltonic. To be sure, the legitimate arrangement of rimes is found in the early ones, the pauses are often disregarded, and run-over lines are common; but the poems all lack the intensity, austerity, and condensation which mark those of Brydges's master. They deal with nature, — somewhat pensively, as a rule, — and, though neither magical nor profound, are far more pleasing than most of the quatorzains of the time. Of his sixty-five, one which Wordsworth declared to be "above all, among modern writers," and of which Southey said, "I know not any poem in any language more beautifully imaginative," deserves to be quoted:

> In eddying course when leaves began to fly,
> And Autumn in her lap the store to strew,
> As mid wild scenes I chanced the Muse to woo,
> Thro' glens untrod and woods that frown'd on high,
> Two sleeping Nymphs with wonder mute I spy!
> And, lo, she's gone! — In robe of dark-green hue
> 'Twas Echo from her sister Silence flew,
> For quick the hunter's horn resounded to the sky!
> In shade affrighted Silence melts away.
> Not so her sister. — Hark! for onward still
> With far-heard step she takes her listening way,
> Bounding from rock to rock, and hill to hill.
> Ah, mark the merry Maid in mockful play
> With thousand mimic tones the laughing forest fill! [1]

but said nothing about several verbal borrowings, such as "with dangers compass'd round" (*ib.* 45, cf. *P. L.*, vii. 27). He imitated Milton's octosyllabics later in this same volume (p. 56) and his blank verse elsewhere. What particularly struck him in the Puritan quatorzains was their "rejection of flowery language," a feature that, coming at a critical period of his literary career, was never forgotten and seems to have affected all his poetry. Fifty years later he wrote in his *Autobiography* (1834, i. 5, and cf. 175), "On my arrival at Cambridge, October, 1780, I gave myself up to English poetry. I had, in studying Milton's noble Sonnets,—noble in defiance of Johnson,— convinced myself of the force and majesty of plain language; and I resolved never to be seduced into a departure from it." In his *Censura Literaria* (1808, vi. 415) he had said of these same sonnets, "For seven and twenty years they have been the objects of my admiration; and I do not like them the less because they are deficient in all the finical prettinesses of modern poetry." Yet in his 1835 edition of Milton (Boston, 1854, pp. 736–8) he frankly took "a less favourable view."

[1] See Wordsworth to A. Dyce, 1833, *Letters*, iii. 31; Brydges, *Autobiography*, ii. 262; cf. Leigh Hunt's *London Journal*, July 23, 1834, p. 134. The extra foot in the eighth and fourteenth lines of the poem is an unusual feature. Warton and Bampfylde, the only eighteenth-century sonneteers with whose work Brydges seems to have been acquainted when he began to write (*Poems*, 1807, p. 213), must also have influenced him, for his poems are much closer to theirs than to Milton's. In his *Autobiography* (i. 35) he writes, "I had not been three days at Cambridge before the little quarto pamphlet of *Sixteen Sonnets by John Bampfylde* was put into my hands, and I have never since forgotten them."

We have already seen how Cowper's enthusiasm for Milton led to his writing *The Task* and rendering Homer in a blank verse adapted from *Paradise Lost*. Another fruit of his devotion was a translation of the Italian and Latin poems of his favorite author. He began his version of the former (all but one of which are sonnets) in February, 1792, and finished it by March of the same year.[1] Cowper was over sixty at this time and, except for one published anonymously four years earlier, had never written a quatorzain. The translating seems to have interested him in the form, for we find him composing an original sonnet the following month (April 16, 1792), another in May, and a third in June; October brought another, the following May two more, and June still another.[2] None of these eight are strictly Petrarchan; but the couplet-ending, which is used in all but the first, probably came from Milton, since four of them, as well as all the translations, employ the same rime-scheme as three of Milton's Italian sonnets. All are addressed to friends, all begin with vocatives, all are serious, dignified, and inclined to be stately, although the finest, that to Mrs. Unwin, owes its beauty to the simple expression of deep and tender feeling. The legitimate pauses are usually observed, but run-over lines and internal pauses abound, and, together with inversions of the natural word-order, recall the Miltonic blank verse that Cowper had so long written. Two of the sonnets appear to be clearly, though not closely, patterned after two of Milton's.[3] The nature of the poems themselves, therefore, as well as the impulse which led to their composition, suggests that Cowper's sonnets afford another illustration of his debt to his "idol."

"I had just entered on my seventeenth year," wrote Coleridge, "when the sonnets of Mr. Bowles, twenty in number, and just then published . . . were first made known and presented to me. . . . My earliest acquaintances will not have forgotten the undisciplined eagerness and impetuous zeal with which I laboured to make prose-lytes, not only of my companions, but of all with whom I conversed, of whatever rank, and in whatever place. As my school finances did not permit me to purchase copies, I made, within less than a year and a half, more than forty transcriptions, as the best presents I could offer to those who had in any way won my regard. . . . My obliga-tions to Mr. Bowles were indeed important, and for radical good."

[1] See his letters to James Hurdis and Mrs. King, Feb. 21 and March 8, 1792.

[2] Bailey, in his edition of Cowper (1905, p. 445), prints one more, *To a Young Lady on her Birthday*, but says nothing about its date. It is Petrarchan, and recalls Milton's "Lady that in the prime of earliest youth."

[3] Compare that to Wilberforce with Milton's on Cromwell, and that to Dr. Austen with Milton's "Captain, or Colonel, or Knight in arms." See also p. 521, n. 3, below.

This passage from the *Biographia Literaria*,[1] and the faint memory of his quarrel with Byron over Pope, have preserved for Bowles a dubious sort of half-existence in the history of our literature, hardly a flattering position in view of the oft-expressed surprise that such thin, sentimental verses could have profoundly affected a great poet. This is unfair. Bowles's quiet sonnets, though not great and far from revolutionary, are natural in language, genuine if over-melancholy in feeling, easy and flowing without being diffuse, dignified without being stilted, and, with their pensive interpretations of nature, have a tender charm for persons who really read them. Poems like the following certainly do not suffer from a comparison with those of Coleridge, which they inspired:

> How sweet the tunefull bells' responsive peal!
> As when, at opening morn, the fragrant breeze
> Breathes on the trembling sense of pale disease,
> So piercing to my heart their force I feel!
> And hark! with lessening cadence now they fall!
> And now, along the white and level tide,
> They fling their melancholy music wide;
> Bidding me many a tender thought recall
> Of summer-days, and those delightful years
> When from an ancient tower, in life's fair prime,
> The mournful magic of their mingling chime
> First waked my wondering childhood into tears!
> But seeming now, when all those days are o'er,
> The sounds of joy once heard, and heard no more.

The circumstances under which Bowles composed his first volume were such as might easily have given birth to "an epoch-marking work." In 1785 or thereabouts, when fresh from college, he sought to forget an unfortunate love-affair by wandering through northern England, Scotland, and parts of the continent. At various picturesque spots on his journey, principally rivers, castles, and ruined abbeys, he composed sonnets. These, he afterwards declared, were thought out in the open air with no idea of publication, and were not even written down until three years later. "I confined myself to fourteen lines," he explained, "because fourteen lines seemed best adapted to unity of sentiment. I thought nothing about the strict

[1] Bohn ed., 6–7. In the same passage he speaks of his early favorite as "a poet, by whose works, year after year, I was so enthusiastically delighted and inspired." See also *ib.* 11–12; Main's *English Sonnets*, 362 n.; and Coleridge's sonnet to Bowles (*Poetical Works*, Globe ed., 40–41 and note). Wordsworth was so much impressed by Bowles's sonnets that he "kept his brother waiting on Westminster bridge until, seated in one of its recesses, he had read through the little quarto" (Coleridge, *Poetical Works*, p. xviii).

Italian model; the verses naturally flowed in unpremeditated harmony, as my ear directed." They were, however, considerably "corrected" before they were printed.[1]

Bowles's first publication included only fourteen sonnets, — not all he had written up to that time; but in the editions which rapidly followed each other more were added, until by 1805 there were thirty-two in print. Then, after a break of some twenty years during which none were composed, he wrote eighteen more. These later ones are nearer the Petrarchan rime-scheme than the earlier, and two of them follow it strictly; yet twenty-seven out of his total of fifty have the arrangement *a b b a c d d c e f f e g g;* the other sequences, of which there are almost twenty, tend towards the Petrarchan, though all but fourteen of the poems end with couplets. In the late as well as the early ones the structure is practically that of blank verse, with no regard for pauses or turn.

From the circumstances under which the earlier sonnets were composed, they might be expected to be unusually free from the influence of either contemporary or older writers; yet this seems not to have been the case. Things had changed greatly since Edwards's time: the sonnet had become a living form, and the verses which "naturally flowed" from Bowles's lips would almost invariably be like those of his contemporaries. His first volume, *Fourteen Sonnets, Elegiac and Descriptive, written during a Tour* (1789), probably owed its title to Bampfylde's *Sixteen Sonnets,* to which, as both books deal with nature, it may have been otherwise indebted. The year he published his sonnets Bowles devoted five stanzas to the memory of Thomas Russell, who had been "the gay companion" of his "stripling prime" at Winchester and again "by Isis' stream." [2] The quatorzains of the two friends are alike in their melancholy and in their fondness for nature, but Russell's are far more vigorous and lofty. As the two volumes were published the same year, and as the poems had in each case been written more than twelve months earlier, the young men could have known each other's work only in manuscript, if at all. Possibly they exchanged verses in school and college days; possibly neither knew the poems, or at least the sonnets, of the other, the similarities being in part temperamental and in part due to their acquaintance with Thomas Warton.

---

[1] These statements are derived principally from the prefaces to *Sonnets* (1805) and *Scenes and Shadows of Days Departed,* etc. (1837). In the *Scenes* Bowles for the first time makes it clear that there were two love-affairs, each of which inspired sonnets. On the whole subject, see the thesis on Bowles (Harvard, 1914) by Mr. Garland Greever, to whom I am indebted for looking up a number of matters in the British Museum.

[2] *Elegy written at the Hotwells,* stanzas 16–20.

Bowles could hardly have escaped Warton's influence. He had received much encouragement and direction in versifying from the poet's brother Joseph, his master at Winchester;[1] and, as he chose Trinity College, Oxford, because "Thomas Warton was residing there,"[2] he must have known and liked that genial scholar. There can be no question that in his formative years he knew Warton's sonnets, for they were published in 1777, while Bowles was a pupil at Winchester; and he must have admired them, since he wrote the same kind himself. Warton's poems are devoted mainly to nature, so are Bowles's; next to nature, Warton is principally concerned with the romantic and picturesque monuments of the past, and so is Bowles; several of Warton's sonnets are pensive, as are nearly all of Bowles's; Warton always writes in a dignified, elevated style, Bowles does the same; and, finally, Warton's sonnet to the river Lodon as certainly inspired Bowles's to the river Itchin as that in turn inspired Coleridge's to the river Otter.[3] Aside from the greater pensiveness of Bowles's poems, which is due to the circumstances under which they were composed, the only important difference between the work of the two men is one of expression, — the younger writer is more fluent, less archaic, less conventional; and it was precisely

[1] In lines 120–25 of his *Monody on Dr. Warton* Bowles tells us that his master led him to Milton's poems; therefore he must have been familiar with the sonnets at an early age. Two of his own deal with Milton, and in other pieces he borrows phrases (e. g., *To Burke*, last line, "Content, though poor, had we no other guard," cf. the last line of Milton's second sonnet to Skinner; *Elegy written at the Hotwells*, 43, "Some natural tears she drops, but wipes them soon," cf. *P. L.*, xii. 645; and see above, p. 257, n. 4); one of his early poems, *The Dying Slave*, imitates the close of *Comus;* and his blank verse, of which there is a good deal, is unmistakably derived from *Paradise Lost*. In their seriousness and directness his sonnets are Miltonic, but they lack the reserve, austerity, and vigor of the Puritan stanzas; they are sweeter, less compact, more flowing, and, though a number begin with vocatives, few are concerned with persons. They are the kind of poems that Bowles naturally wrote, and the kind he would probably have written even if he had been as ardent an admirer of his predecessor's sonnets as were Brydges and Miss Seward, whose work is, indeed, scarcely more Miltonic than his own.

[2] *Works* (ed. Gilfillan), vol. ii, p. xiii. Each of the Wartons stimulated his imagination, his love of ruins, his inclination towards melancholy poetry, and his other romantic tendencies.

[3] Warton's sonnet is given on p. 497 above. The other two poems express a similar feeling. Bowles asks why he feels pain at revisiting the river:

> Is it, that many a summer's day has past
> Since, in life's morn, I carolled on thy side!
> Is it, that oft since then my heart has sighed!

Coleridge writes,

> Dear native Brook! wild Streamlet of the West!
> How many various-fated years have past,
> What happy and what mournful hours, since last
> I skimmed the smooth thin stone along thy breast.

because of this natural and poetic voicing of genuine feeling that Bowles made so profound an impression on Coleridge.[1] Except in these respects his quatorzains can hardly be distinguished from many others of the period. Their importance does not lie in the introduction of new subjects into the sonnet or in a novel treatment of old ones, and not, as some have asserted, in their pensive melancholy, their "power to harmonise the moods of nature with those of the mind," or their combining introspection with outlook or description with sentiment in a new way.[2] In these matters Bowles had been anticipated by Warton, Brydges, Thomas Warwick,[3] Mrs. Smith, Miss Williams, and others; but he did dwell repeatedly, movingly, and naturally on themes which before 1789 sonneteers had seldom touched and only once or twice with success.

Coleridge was by no means Bowles's only admirer. The "Fourteen Sonnets" were reissued with additions the year they appeared, and by 1805 had passed through nine printings. Other volumes, to be sure, were enjoying equal or greater favor; but Bowles had the good fortune of appealing particularly to poets, with the result that few sonnets of the period immediately following escaped his influence. From 1790 to 1810 every picturesque spot visited by a bard — and all were bards in those days — received the tribute of a sonnet, no season passed without being made the subject of many quatorzains, and any ramble through the woods, any twilight, any lovely or depressing day, was likely to be eternized in fourteen lines of tender melancholy. It was largely because Bowles was not an innovator but a perfecter, because he hit the temper of the time by giving pleasant and natural expression to the mood of elegiac sentiment which already pervaded other forms of literature, that his poems came to be so popular.

Of the numerous forgotten effusions which sprang up under their influence and which in general show marked improvement over those of the two preceding decades, it is hardly necessary to speak, for

---

[1] See the *Biographia Literaria* (Bohn ed.), 11–12, and in particular the following sentence, "Of the then living poets Bowles and Cowper were, to the best of my knowledge, the first who combined natural thoughts with natural diction; the first who reconciled the heart with the head." As he did not know *The Task* "till many years afterwards" (*ib.* 12 n.), Bowles was for him "the first."

[2] See *Dict. Nat. Biog.*; and Saintsbury, in *Camb. Hist. Eng. Lit.*, English ed., xi. 178.

[3] Most of Warwick's sonnets, which were published in 1783, deal with nature, are somewhat melancholy in tone, and were written on picturesque spots during journeys. Like those of Bowles, they lament an absent sweetheart, picture castles and ruined abbeys, and one has a title that the later poet uses, *On Revisiting Oxford;* yet in expression they are more formal and stately, closer to Milton's and Warton's. Did Bowles know them?

Bowles's greatest significance undoubtedly lies in the inspiration he furnished to the lake poets and their friends. The term "inspiration" is used advisedly; for, though Coleridge published what he regarded as his best pieces under the caption "Sonnets attempted in the Manner of the Rev. W. L. Bowles," not many of them warrant that description. Few deal with places, most, unlike their models, being called forth either by events or by persons. The majority are melancholy, to be sure; but, as the sadness is analytical and more introspective and usually has nothing to do with nature (which plays an important part in only a ninth of the poems), it is in most cases different from Bowles's "lonely pang with dreamy joys combin'd." [1] In fact, if Coleridge had any eighteenth-century model at all, it would seem to have been Charlotte Smith, whose poems together with those of Bowles, he tells us, furnished the basis of his conception of the sonnet. His quatorzains are much better and less lugubrious than hers; but in their diction and loose formlessness, and, when they are melancholy, in their picturing the grief itself instead of nature or things, they recall the strains of the "Mistress of the Pensive Lyre." Like hers, too, they belong, not to the Miltonic but to the Hayley-Della Cruscan school. Even the thirteen "on eminent characters" are disfigured with expressions like "dewy light," "warbled strains," "soft anguish," "tear's ambrosial dew," and "temples with Hymettian flow'rets wreathed"; hence the title "effusions" (which they had till Lamb exclaimed, "Call [them] sonnets for God's sake" [2]) was entirely suitable.

Their "affectation of unaffectedness," their "puny pathos," "doleful egotism," and "elaborate and swelling language," were clear to Coleridge, for he wrote his Nehemiah Higginbottom sonnets to parody these defects in his own work, as well as in that of Lamb and Lloyd.[3] "The Sonnet," he admitted, "has been ever a favorite species of composition with me; but I am conscious that I have not succeeded in it. From a large number I have retained ten only, as not beneath mediocrity." [4] It is, indeed, something very like medi-

---

[1] Coleridge's sonnet on Bowles, first version, line 9. Mr. Arthur Symons very properly calls attention to the "moralising landscapes" in Coleridge's sonnets, but he errs in saying that they "are distinctly foreshadowed in those of Bowles" (*Romantic Movement in English Poetry*, 1909, p. 66). I do not remember them as a marked feature of any previous sonneteer's work.   [2] Letter to Coleridge, Dec. 2, 1796.

[3] Letter to Joseph Cottle, Nov., 1797, quoted in Globe edition of Coleridge, p. 599; *Biographia Literaria* (Bohn ed.), 12–13. "Cultivate simplicity, Coleridge," wrote Lamb, Nov. 8, 1796; and Coleridge himself owned to the "general turgidness" of his poems and their frequent deviations from "nature and simplicity" (*Poems*, 2d ed., 1797, preface; and letter to Thelwall, Dec. 17, 1796).

[4] "Introduction to the Sonnets," *Poems* (1797), 74.

ocrity — the unpardonable sin in art — which must be charged
against the poems; for most of them make that worst of all impressions, no impression at all. They lack vigor and feeling, compactness
and distinction of phrasing, as well as the ease and finished grace
which give charm to many lighter productions. Few of them, on
their poetic merits alone, are entitled to live; indeed, few have
ever been alive.

Coleridge needed not only the loftier conceptions of the sonnet
which better models would have given him, but the challenge offered
by the difficulties of the legitimate form. "Respecting the metre...",
he declared, "the Writer should consult his own convenience. —
Rhymes, many or few, or no rhymes at all — whatever the chastity
of his ear may prefer, whatever the rapid expression of his feelings
will permit." Of the Petrarchan form he was intolerant: "If there be
one species of composition more difficult and artificial than another,
it is an English Sonnet on the Italian Model. Adapted to the agita-
tions of a real passion! Express momentary bursts of feeling in it!
I should sooner expect to write pathetic *Axes* or *pour forth extempore
Eggs and Altarsi*" He defined the sonnet as "a small poem, in which
some lonely feeling is developed," and added, "Those Sonnets appear to me the most exquisite, in which moral Sentiments, Affec-
tions, or Feelings, are deduced from, and associated with, the scenery
of Nature." [1] Yet his practice by no means conformed to his theory.
One of his poems uses the Petrarchan arrangement of rimes, and
others come as near it as do those of Miss Seward at which he sneers;
he employs the Shakespearean system nine times, and unquestionably consulted some standard other than "his own convenience."
A considerable number of his pieces are without that development
of a lonely feeling which he declared indispensable, and still more of
them lack the association with the scenery of nature which he
stressed. These inconsistencies deepen the impression made by the
poems themselves, as well as by their astonishing "Introduction,"
that Coleridge had not thought his ideas on the subject through, and
this because he did not regard the form as one of much dignity or of
great possibilities, and therefore did not put his best efforts into it,
as Wordsworth did.

One of the forty copies that Coleridge made of Bowles's first volume he may well have given to his schoolmate, Charles Lamb, who
shared some of his friend's enthusiasm for the *Fourteen Sonnets*.
Lamb's own quatorzains, to be sure, seldom deal with nature or

---

[1] "Introduction to the Sonnets," *Poems* (1797), 71-3.

exhibit what he termed the "tender plaintiveness" of Bowles,[1] but
are more like Coleridge's when these are free from turgidity and
melancholy. As the two friends wrote sonnets together and discussed one another's productions freely, each undoubtedly affected
the work of the other. The "ewe lambs" of the gentle Elia, however,
show the beginning of a force which has since become very powerful, — that of Elizabethan literature, to which Lamb was devoted.
Not for many years had the English sonnet contained such lines as

> Methinks how dainty sweet it were, reclin'd. . . .

> The Lord of Life shakes off his drowsihed,
> And 'gins to sprinkle on the earth below
> Those rays that from his shaken locks do flow.

And surely Lamb had in mind the *Faerie Queene* (though not the
Amoretti, it should be observed) when he wrote,

> Was it some sweet device of Faery
> That mock'd my steps with many a lonely glade,
> And fancied wanderings with a fair-hair'd maid?[2]

Four of his sonnets are also Elizabethan in being love-poems. These
features, however, disappear from his later productions, which are
called forth by occasions or addressed to friends, and which, with
their frequent run-over lines, their simplicity and naturalness of expression, are much nearer to ordinary speech than any preceding
sonnets had been. A few of the thirty-five he wrote are refreshingly
playful and whimsical, and one or two have the Miltonic sweep, but
most are marked by quiet distinction, earnestness, and sincerity.
They had practically no effect on the development of the *genre*, for
they have never found many readers; yet Lamb was far more of an
innovator than writers like Bowles, whose influence has been great.

Intimately associated with Coleridge and Lamb in friendship and
in sonneteering was Charles Lloyd, another of the attractive young
poets who developed insanity in later years. To the volume the
three friends published together Lloyd contributed several poems,
which reveal such a fine sensitiveness to natural beauty and are so
little known that I am tempted to quote one:

---

[1] Letter to Coleridge, Oct. 28, 1796. Lamb left Christ's Hospital within two months
after Coleridge discovered Bowles; but to youthful enthusiasm two months is a long
time. He certainly admired Bowles at first (cf. his letters to Coleridge of June 8–10,
Nov. 14, and Dec. 10, 1796); he acknowledges taking one line from his sonnet *To a
Friend* (letter to Coleridge, May 24 or 31?, 1796), and may have been otherwise influenced by him, although Nov. 13, 1798, he wrote to Robert Lloyd of "the race of sonnet
writers and complainers, Bowles's and Charlotte Smiths, and all that tribe, who can
see no joys but what are past."

[2] The quotations are the opening lines of three of the sonnets.

SCOTLAND! when thinking on each heathy hill
O'er whose bleak breast the billowy vapours sweep,
While sullen winds imprison'd murmur deep
Mid' their dim caves, such thoughts my bosom fill,
I cannot chuse but sigh! Oft wandering wild
I've trac'd thy torrents to their haunted source,
Whence down some huge rock with fantastic course,
Their sheeted whiteness pouring, they beguil'd
The meek dishearten'd One, in solitude
Who sought relief. Beneath some aged tree
Thy white cots dimly seen yielded to me
Solace most sweet: nor seldom have I view'd
Their low thatch wishfully, and paus'd to bless
The uncultur'd children of lone Quietness! [1]

The pensive sentiment in the presence of nature which marks these lines and the best of their author's other one hundred and six quatorzains would point to Bowles, even if extracts from his poetry did not appear on two of Lloyd's title-pages and if several of the poems did not, like those of Bowles, describe a castle or other ruin, a lake or a river. Some of them, however, are closer to Lamb's, with which they were published. Many are injured by diffuseness and by the revelation of their author's weak, morbidly introspective personality. Although the eighth line is sometimes run-over and the arrangement of rimes Petrarchesque rather than Petrarchan, Lloyd held that Shakespearean quatorzains like Charlotte Smith's were not sonnets.[2]

Still another friend of Coleridge and Lamb was influenced by the *Fourteen Sonnets*. Soon after a third edition of the volume appeared, their author tells us, "two young gentlemen, strangers, one a particularly handsome and pleasing youth, . . . spoke in high commendation" of the work to the publisher and "expressed a desire to have some poems printed in the same type and form."[3] The young men were Robert Lovell and Robert Southey, and their volume, which came out the following year, 1795, resembled its predecessor in other respects than in type and form. It contained sixteen sonnets marked by the pensive sentiment, the fondness for ruins, the descriptions of nature harmonized with the writer's mood, that distinguish the work of Bowles, to which, indeed, it is closer than is Coleridge's. Southey himself made no secret of this obligation. Towards the close of his life he praised his fellow-poet's "sweet and unsophisticated style; upon which," he adds, "I endeavoured, now almost forty years ago, to form my own."[4] Although he composed sonnets

---

[1] *Poems by Coleridge, Lamb, and Lloyd* (1797), 170.   [2] *Nugae Canorae* (1819), 168.
[3] *Scenes and Shadows of Days Departed* (1837), p. xlv.
[4] Letter to Bowles, July 30, 1832. Cf. the preface to Southey's *Poetical Works*

at intervals throughout the forty years, most of those he wrote came before 1800. The later productions, though much better, are as a rule of the same type as the first, — quiet, pleasing descriptions expressed naturally, but, like Coleridge's, usually tagged with a moral. All show how much the province of the sonnet was widening; for six are vigorous attacks on the slave-trade, one is a humorous address to a roast goose, four are on love, and four seem to be parodies of the Della Cruscan effusions. Their arrangements of rimes, which are many and very irregular, seem to be dictated by convenience rather principle, and their run-over lines and disregard of the pauses and turns give the impression of blank verse. Of Lovell, who is said to have died the year after his poems appeared, almost nothing further is known than that Southey published three of his sonnets posthumously, one of which, like one of Warton's, is on Stonehenge.

With the work of Bowles and his followers the sonnet reaches a parting of the ways, and pauses for a moment between the type which was prevalent in the eighteenth century and that which was to predominate in the nineteenth. With Wordsworth it crosses the threshold and enters the new realm. Before following it into this lovelier and far better-known region, we may turn and look back over the road by which we have come.

From such a retrospect three classes of sonnets stand out, — the Miltonic, the Hayley-Smith-Williams type, and that used by Bowles, the last being a combination of the other two with particular emphasis on nature and melancholy. Widely as extreme instances of these types differ from one another, each class taken as a whole has much more in common with the other two than with the productions of the Elizabethans or the Italians. Nearly all are bound together and distinguished from the earlier quatorzains in being called forth by some actual happening, occasion, place, or person, instead of being spun largely out of the poet's inner consciousness. They are also united by their seriousness of purpose, and by their authors' intentions, however poorly carried out, to be direct, simple, dignified. Consequently, Capel Lofft could write in 1809: "No subject worthy

(1837), vol. i, p. ix: "I am conscious also of having derived much benefit at one time from Cowper, and more from Bowles; for which, and for the delight which his poems gave me at an age when we are most susceptible of such delight, my good friend [Bowles] . . . will allow me to make this grateful and cordial acknowledgement." As he tells us (*ib.* viii) that Warton was another of the poets on whose work he modelled his early verses, and as he took a particular interest in Bampfylde (see his *Vision of Judgement*, section xi, and p. 506 above), it is likely that these writers, whose sonnets resemble his own, also influenced him.

of poetry is so great and comprehensive, as not to have been with becoming dignity expressed in this form. . . . And it is the glory of the Sonnet to add that it has most rarely been disgraced by any unworthy subject."[1] Even Hayley, Polwhele, Mrs. Smith, Mrs. Robinson, and Miss Seward gave their best efforts to the form; they did not trifle with it. Their quatorzains are no more ridiculous and empty than everything else they wrote; they *tried* to say something, — the trouble was they had nothing to say. As for the Della Cruscans, it was not the sonnet that debauched them but they it, and it was far from being their favorite verse-form.

The attributes which the eighteenth-century quatorzains have in common seem to be derived from Milton, and from him also came the uses to which the form was put. With love, the chief concern of poetasters, it rarely dealt,[2] and until 1784 it was almost untouched by sentimentality. For a considerable time it was employed principally in addresses to persons; and, although this use waned as pensive description became the vogue, eighteen of Coleridge's effusions are "on eminent characters" or addressed to individuals. In this respect also Milton pointed the way, but his example was the more eagerly followed because other kinds of verse were largely given over to abstractions. The quatorzain was likewise popular for occasional poetry. For celebrating a visit to a friend or a beautiful spot, a birthday, the publication of a book, or similar events of general or merely personal interest, it became in the later eighteenth century the favorite form. With nature it had been concerned from the time of its revival; Gray, Mason, Warton, Polwhele, Bampfylde, Warwick, Brydges, and perhaps Russell and Jackson, as well as Miss Seward, Miss Williams, and Mrs. Smith, all dwelt upon the beauties of the country long before Bowles began to write. The increased attention given to nature, which after 1790 became the principal theme, is, however, not peculiar to the sonnet, but is characteristic of all the poetry of the time, even blank verse.

It might be supposed from the thousands of quatorzains written, from the praise bestowed upon the form, and from the partiality many evinced for it, that this style of verse was popular in the eighteenth century. To be sure, it never has been really popular, it is not now; all one would expect is that it should be admired by the lovers of good literature and recognized by poets and critics as one of our best verse-forms, that its position should no more be ques-

---

[1] Brydges, *Censura Literaria* (1809), x. 83.

[2] Aside from the forty-three in Mrs. Robinson's sequence, *Sappho and Phaon*, I have noted very few sonnets on love, but I have by no means examined all eighteenth-century quatorzains with this point in view.

tioned than that of blank verse. But in the eighteenth century the position of each was questioned, and the little lute of fourteen strings excited something of the same hostility, and in much the same quarters, as that roused by the organ-tones of the greater instrument. Dr. Johnson's critical bludgeon fell upon it several times. "Of the best" of Milton's sonnets, he wrote, "it can only be said that they are not bad, and perhaps only the eighth and the twenty-first are truly entitled to this slender commendation. The fabrick of a sonnet however adapted to the Italian language, has never succeeded in ours." When Hannah More "expressed a wonder that the poet who had written *Paradise Lost* should write such poor Sonnets," he remarked, "Milton, Madam, was a genius that could cut a Colossus from a rock; but could not carve heads upon cherry-stones." [1] Erasmus Darwin, grandfather of the evolutionist, "had in general no taste for Sonnets, and particularly disliked Milton's; [2] and John Pinkerton affirmed in 1782 that "the stated form and measure" of the quatorzain were "so disgustingly similar" that he believed "no man of genius would now write twenty in a life time." [3] About the same time George Steevens declared the sonnet to be a "metrical whim . . . composed in the highest strain of affectation, pedantry. circumlocution, and nonsense." [4]

From the reviews arose an almost unbroken chorus of condemnation. The *Critical* held Hugh Downman's attempts "to revive the antiquated sonnet" to be "convincing evidence" of his tendency towards affectation.[5] The *Monthly* declared: "The English language can boast of few good Sonnets. They are in general harsh, formal, and uncouth." [6] According to the *New London Magazine*, the quatorzain was in 1789 "in a state of almost rusticated barbarism, or refined absurdity," for "the metaphysic rubbish that . . . still appears under the title of Sonnets" seems "hard laboured, and rapidly sinking to the sable valley of oblivion";[7] and so late as 1803 the *Annual Review* asserted, "Sonnets . . . at best are but stiff diffi-

---

[1] "Milton," in *Lives* (ed. Hill), i. 169–70; Boswell's *Johnson* (ed. Hill), iv. 305. See also Johnson's *Dictionary*, "Sonnet."

[2] Anna Seward, *Memoirs of Dr. Darwin* (1804), 386.

[3] *Letters of Literature* (1785), 51. Ten years later, April 26, 1792, Cowper remarked to Lady Hesketh, "The Hills, I know, dislike sonnets. . . . For my own part I like them much, when they are on subjects proper to them; such, I mean, as are best expressed in a close sententious manner."

[4] Shakespeare's *Plays and Poems* (ed. James Boswell, 1821), xx. 358–9, note.

[5] xxvi. 198 (1768); cf. lvii. 6–7 (1784), and new arr., ii. 174 (1791). Yet in 1792 (new arr., v. 250) it speaks very well of a volume of sonnets.

[6] lxxi. 368 (1784); cf. lxxxi. 81, 366, and enl. ed., xviii. 429–30, xxiv. 17, xxix. 361–4, xxxvi. 145–6.

[7] v. 212.

cult trifles, and surely more remote from the simplicity which they often affect than any other class of poems in our language." [1] In 1786 the Chambers-Rees *Cyclopaedia* said that Milton's sonnet to Lawes, though one of his best, "shews how difficult and unnatural the construction of this species of poem is in the English language"; [2] and in 1802 Richard Mant, who, as editor of Thomas Warton's poems, should have been favorable to the form, called it "a species of poetry, foreign to the genius of the English language, and singularly liable to stiffness." [3] We know that at the beginning of the century Wordsworth held it "egregiously absurd," [4] and that in 1827, fearing others were of the same opinion, he admonished the critic to "scorn not the sonnet." Accordingly we are not surprised to find Sir Egerton Brydges saying in 1807, "It has been the fashion of late to despise Sonnets, more especially those, which, on account of the technical repetition, and contexture, of the rhymes, are called legitimate." [5] This last clause suggests that there were those who distinguished between sonnets, enjoying one type and disliking another. As to this discrimination there can be no question. It will be remembered that Coleridge, with whom the quatorzain had "been ever a favorite species of composition," found no words strong enough to express his contempt for the Petrarchan measure. Charlotte Smith wrote, "I am told, and I read it as the opinion of very good judges, that the legitimate Sonnet is illy calculated for our language." [6] This widely-held opinion Miss Seward characterized as an "unmeaning assertion of pedants"; yet she admitted that she often had to combat it, as well she might, for at least three of her friends entertained it, one of them holding the legitimate sonnet as her "supreme aversion." [7]

The reasons for such aversion are not far to seek. Poets found the Petrarchan form very difficult, and readers felt that too much was

[1] ii. 564. "C-T-O-" wrote to the *Gentleman's Magazine* in 1786 (lvi. 135), "Edwards's Sonnet upon a family picture, has as much merit as any Sonnet, perhaps, can be entitled to."

[2] Article, "Sonnet." This sentence was not in the 1728 and 1751 editions.

[3] Vol. i, p. cliv.

[4] See below, p. 529, n. 2.

[5] *Poems* (4th ed.), 213.

[6] Preface to *Elegiac Sonnets* (1784). The *Monthly Review* said the same in 1784, and again in 1785 and 1789 (lxxi. 368, lxxiii. 306, lxxxi. 366), as did Nathan Drake in 1798 (*Literary Hours*, 3d ed., 1804, i. 113-14). In 1802 the legitimate form was strongly opposed in the *Critical Review* (new arr., xxxiv. 393), as it had been in the *Universal Magazine* ten years earlier (xci. 409, 413); and in 1803 George Henderson wrote that the Petrarchan form was discarded by "almost the whole of those which have attained any popularity in the English" (*Petrarca*, p. xxx).

[7] *Letters*, i. 172, 186, 238, 261; ii. 255-60.

usually sacrificed for the sake of it, that it made the quatorzain — to use the adjectives most often hurled at it — unnatural, affected, artificial, obscure, harsh, formal, uncouth, and (in diction) antiquated and quaint.[1] Even Brydges, an enthusiastic imitator of Milton's "Petrarchian stanzas," recognized that he "was not able to conquer the stiffness, which this sort of metre generally causes," and praised Charlotte Smith's efforts for "that freedom and ease, which it is scarce possible to preserve while entangled by the complicated rules of the ancient sonnet."[2] In consequence of this general dissatisfaction, the preference for the Petrarchan model fell off steadily as the *genre* grew in popularity. This decline will be seen from the following table, which indicates very roughly the distribution of the eighteenth-century quatorzains that were published in books:[3]

	Petrarchan	Shakespearean	Spenserian	Irregular
1740–60 (20 years)	73	0	7	20
1760–80 " "	130	27	2	348
1780–90 (10 years)	234	154	7	448
1790–1800 " "	199	270	1	582
Total	636	451	17	1398

In at least one respect this table is misleading; for the first column contains only poems that conform to a strict, probably an over-strict, interpretation of the phrase "Petrarchan rime-scheme," one that would exclude a considerable number of the sonnets written by Milton and by Petrarch himself. Nor does it make any allowance for misunderstandings of the legitimate arrangement (such as that which throws sixty-seven of Miss Seward's quatorzains into the last column), or for any slight departure from it. Assuming that one-sixth of the irregular quatorzains were intended to be and in the main are legitimate, we should have about 870 Petrarchesque, as against 17 Spenserian, 450 Shakespearean, and 1165 irregular quatorzains.

[1] Two sorts of words impress the reader, — the inflated Latinic expressions, in which Miss Seward is the greatest offender ("sons of Phoebus deem My verse Aonian," she writes), and such antiquated words as "wont," "whilom," "what time," "erst," "yon," "massy," "approof," "ween," "sprent." See also p. 65 above.

[2] *Poems* (4th ed., 1807), 214, 213.

[3] This table is not, and could not well be made, accurate in detail. It does not include the considerable number of quatorzains that I have been unable to see or the hundreds that were published in magazines only. Furthermore, since all the poems of a single author are put in the period in which he began to write, some of those that are listed in the earlier periods really belong in the later. On the other hand, when the date of composition is unknown, as often happens, the poems are placed according to the time of printing, which may be long after; hence some of those listed in the later periods really belong in the earlier. This balancing of errors will, I hope, make the figures, relatively to one another, not far wrong, except for the correction to be noted in the text.

Aside from the exceedingly small number of Spenserian sonnets,[1] the most striking thing about these figures is the slowness with which the Shakespearean arrangement won favor. During the first forty years this rime-sequence is rarely found, and not until 1790 did the pieces employing it equal in number those using the Petrarchan. These facts are the more impressive because the Italian system is much the more difficult, because its difficulties loomed large to Charlotte Smith and her contemporaries, and because it was widely and severely criticized. The popularity of the Shakespearean arrangement in the last decade of the century was not due to the influence of Shakespeare, for his quatorzains were not admired at the time nor was their rime-scheme known by his name or justified by his practice. This particular structure seems, in fact, to have had no advocates and not to have been distinguished, by those who discussed the subject, from the irregular forms; but it had the dignity of conforming to *some* system and the advantage of being easy to write. All things considered, therefore, the legitimate arrangement was much more widely used than one would expect. In other matters of form there was less divergence; for by the constant use of run-over lines and internal pauses, as well as by the frequent neglect of the full stop and the turn between octave and sestet, most poets kept about as close to Milton's usage as they well could, apparently sharing the opinion of Miss Seward that the prosody of the sonnet should be practically that of blank verse.

In the course of a study like this, one comes naturally to assume that most persons of the period held definite and fairly vigorous opinions regarding the structure and rime-scheme of the sonnet. But such an assumption finds little warrant. There were, to be sure, those whose decided ideas regarding the poem and the arrangement of its rimes put them into one of four classes: that of Johnson and Darwin, who disliked all quatorzains; that of Hayley and Brydges, who admired any that were passable regardless of structure; that of Coleridge and Mrs. Smith, who were averse to the legitimate type but enjoyed the irregular, particularly if it inclined towards sentimental melancholy; and that of Miss Seward and other ardent Miltonians, who held a lofty conception of the poem and looked askance at any system except what they believed to be the Petrarchan. Yet it may be suspected that the great body of readers belonged to still another class, — those who had no attitude whatever, who neither

---

[1] Three of the Spenserian type were composed between 1755 and 1770 by Bishop Percy, author of the *Reliques* (see Miss Clarissa Rinaker on "Percy as a Sonneteer," *Modern Language Notes*, xxxv. 56–8).

knew nor cared anything about pauses or rime-schemes, to whom a sonnet was merely a rather stiff, dull poem of some twelve, fourteen, or sixteen lines.

Nor is this indifference hard to understand, for few eighteenth-century quatorzains would be likely to make a deep impression or to aid in establishing the form securely in the public favor. Of the three thousand or thereabouts that were produced hardly more than thirty deserve to live, for, although many have good lines or quatrains, few are good throughout. Furthermore, aside from Edwards's, less than fifty (scarcely any of which show real inspiration) were printed between 1700 and 1775; and many of the best — those of Russell, Bowles, Cowper, Coleridge, Southey, Lamb, and Lloyd — appeared after 1788, when they could have but slightly affected the eighteenth century. Besides, some of the choicest productions of the period, Russell's, Bampfylde's, and Lloyd's, which might have done not a little to help the reputation of the form, had a very limited circulation.[1] When, towards 1790, things were at last looking better and volumes of good sonnets were beginning to appear, the blight of Della Cruscanism struck the long-suffering quatorzain, bringing in its wake a new defamatory adjective, "trivial," which was so often dwelt upon that the other epithets tended to sink into the background. Throughout the century there had undoubtedly been persons who thought the poem a mere trifle, for Miss Seward and Wordsworth held this opinion at first;[2] but there is little evidence of such a view before 1790. After that, however, it is to be encountered frequently. On at least three occasions between 1797 and 1799 the *Monthly Review* spoke of the sonnet as a poem "of which the highest merit is elegant trifling," as one of "the lighter kinds of poetry" marked by "elegance of . . . language" and "harmony of . . . numbers" rather than by loftier qualities, and as "at best . . . a trifle."[3] In 1801 Alexander Thomson referred to "those who are inclined to consider the sonnet on a level, in laborious trifling, with the anagram and acrostich,"[4] a belief that seems to have been the accepted one so late as 1807, when Capel Lofft wrote,

[1] These facts probably explain William Belsham's omission of the sonnet from his discussion of verse-forms: *Essays*, 1789, essay xii (xxxiii in the 1799 edition).

[2] See Miss Seward's *Letters*, ii. 257; and below, p. 529, n. 2.

[3] Enlarged ed., xxiii. 460, xxiv. 17, xxix. 364. The *Annual Review* used almost the same words in 1803 (ii. 564), "Sonnets are at best stiff, difficult trifles." To this accusation George Henderson could answer only, "Yet to trifle with skill is no common art" (*Petrarca*, 1803, p. xxxii).

[4] Preface to his *Sonnets, Odes*, etc., quoted from *Crit. Rev.*, new arr., xxxvi. 110. Thomson added, "Amatory, descriptive, and sentimental subjects, have hitherto been almost the only topics on which the sonnet has been accustomed to dwell."

Long injur'd SONNET! whom the Crowd arraigns;
And as a mere frivolity disdains,
An empty toy of many a tinkling line;
Incapable of Great and High Design.[1]

The hostility that greeted the poem in some quarters, like the enthusiasm it aroused in others, can be understood only when we realize that its revival was one of those manifestations of the ferment termed romanticism which were being hailed by some and decried by others. Gray, Warton, Bowles, and Coleridge accepted the sonnet as instinctively as Johnson criticized it. The autocrat of letters disliked it just as he disliked the rhapsodies of Ossian, the short pieces of Milton, the odes of Gray and Warton, and all blank verse. The critical reviews, which looked askance at the sonnet, were also, it may be recalled, inclined to be hostile to unrimed poems, and pointed out with considerable justice the poor quality of most of the pieces written in both types of verse. And so, in general, it was the conservatives who were antagonistic to sonnets and the progressives who favored them; in other words, it was the old struggle for poetic freedom which was carried on throughout the eighteenth century. Significantly enough, among the persons using the form between 1740 and 1820 were all the poets of note (and many long since forgotten) who were inclined to romanticism, but none of those opposed to it.

This groping for freedom, life, and color which we name romanticism was in large measure responsible for the sudden reappearance of the sonnet in English. Presumably, it was this that led the anonymous contributor to the *London Magazine*, the Yorkes, Gray, Stillingfleet, and Edwards, independently but within a few years of one another, to employ an instrument covered with the dust and rust of nearly eighty years. These writers seem either to have come upon the sonnet accidentally or to have found it as they sought, perhaps unconsciously, for fresher and more varied measures. Different writers probably discovered it in different places, — Gray, for example, in Petrarch; but we know that the contributor to the *London Magazine*, the Yorkes, and Stillingfleet, not to mention Brydges, Cowper, and others who wrote later, got it from Milton. Nor can it be a mere coincidence that in the same years this search was leading the same men and others to Milton's octosyllabics, monody, masque, and unrimed stanza, which were then making their charm felt for the first time. Writers who were finding in these pieces a revelation of what poetry might be, could hardly fail to be stirred by the sonnets

[1] *La Corona*, sonnet xiv (in *Laura*, end of vol. v).

in the same volume, and, if they imitated the other poems, would be likely to copy these. In part, therefore, the revival of the sonnet was another phase of the *Allegro-Penseroso-Comus-Lycidas* movement; at any rate, without that movement, and without the general popularity of Milton and the admiration which his "Petrarchian stanzas" themselves aroused, the revival would probably not have come when it did or have enlisted in its service all the important and most of the minor poets of the time.

Furthermore, it would almost certainly have taken on another character. If the men who first interested themselves in the form, and many of those who adopted it later, had not been inspired directly by Milton, their productions would undoubtedly have been less desirable. Edwards's work, to be sure, may possibly represent the eighteenth-century quatorzain unaffected by that inspiration; but in view of the other literature of the time it seems more likely that effusions of the Smith-Polwhele-Hayley variety are what the century would have produced had it been left to itself. Although Milton's influence was towards the stiff and the unnatural, yet without his lofty example and the stimulus offered by the difficulties of the legitimate arrangement of rimes, which he used, the quatorzain would in all probability soon have deteriorated into lugubrious or prattling vapidity.

The number of eighteenth-century sonneteers who felt his influence was so considerable that a student of the subject remarked in 1803, "Milton has been studied and imitated by almost every one who has resorted to this kind of composition."[1] Not only do Charles Yorke, Hardinge, Brydges, Miss Seward, and others declare Milton to be their model, but in Warton's and Mason's case there is the evidence of other Miltonic poems, in Bampfylde's and Cary's that of borrowed phrases, and in Cowper's that of a recent translation of his "idol's" Italian sonnets. Were it worth while, similar evidence could be advanced regarding lesser men; but there is danger in this search for something tangible, definite, and beyond dispute, since it is apt

---

[1] Henderson, *Petrarca* (1803), p. xxiii. To be sure, there were those then, as there are to-day, who did not care for Milton's sonnets. Dr. Johnson and Erasmus Darwin, as we have seen, did not; and the *Critical Review*, which in 1768 spoke of them as 'failures' (xxvi. 198), thought sixteen years later that the loss of them "might be endured with patience and resignation" (lvii. 6). The *Monthly Review* said in 1795, " The failure of Milton in this species of poetry has often been mentioned and allowed" (enl. ed., xviii. 429; cf. xxiv. 17, xxix. 362, and first series, lxxxi. 81); yet on one occasion at least it spoke favorably of them (1783, lxviii. 46–7). "J. T." admitted in the *Universal Magazine* in 1792 that he read "as a task" the sonnets of the "great master of the epic lyre," and thought them far inferior to Charlotte Smith's (xci. 408–14, and cf. p. 503 above).

to blind us to the fact that Edwards's productions, which he says were not affected by Milton's, as well as Bowles's and Russell's, regarding the sources of which we know nothing, are nearer the Puritan stanzas than those of Miss Seward, Hardinge, and Brydges, who consciously adopted these poems as their model. Declarations like Miss Seward's and Brydges's are valuable principally as showing that poets did copy Milton's sonnets, and as warranting the belief that, if all of them had left autobiographies or volumes of letters, we should have more such confessions. But even if we did possess many more we should not have reached the most significant phase of the matter. An influence is likely to be most pervasive and vital when the writer is no longer conscious of its existence and the reader has difficulty in putting his finger on evidences of it; that is, when the manner and thought of the master have become so familiar to the disciple as to be used instinctively. This was not the case with the sonnet when it was first revived. At that time writers deliberately and somewhat painfully tried to follow in the steps of their guide; but in the last quarter of the century "the sonnet" had to a great extent come to mean "the Miltonic sonnet," and this even among persons who knew nothing and cared nothing about the poems that had wrought the change. Milton's innovations had become assimilated.

This survey of the eighteenth-century sonnet has been like the slow and laborious ascent of a thickly-wooded mountain. There have been not a few graceful ferns, shy flowers, dark brooks brawling under lichen-covered trees, and now and then a soul-cheering outlook on beauty; yet as a whole the ascent has been so steep and rocky and the view so restricted that when we come upon the sonnets of Wordsworth's first great years, particularly the stirring trumpet-calls for liberty, it is like stepping from a rough, gloomy path out upon a sunny summit affording prospects far and wide over great stretches of noble country with glimpses of the ocean beyond shimmering in a golden haze. So tremendous is the contrast and so inspiriting the sight that we stand before it bareheaded and speechless.

It is folly to pretend that Wordsworth's sonnets are an evolution from those of his immediate predecessors; he turned to other sources for his inspiration, his models, and his conception of the form. Between him and them is a great gulf fixed, which can be bridged only by his own personality. To be sure, since many of his quatorzains are devoted to nature, or were written on picturesque spots during journeys and thus deal with castles, abbeys, and ruins of past grandeur, they may be indebted to Warton and Bowles. Yet, as his other poems are on similar subjects, he probably chose his themes instinctively and would have used them if Bowles and the rest had never written. In his treatment of them he certainly owes nothing to his predecessors; for, instead of seeing his own sentimental melancholy writ large over hill and plain, he paints nature with epic breadth, emphasizing its significance not simply to himself but to all mankind as the great source of spiritual power. We know that he read and thought well of most of the sonneteers we have been considering, but it is doubtful if his work was appreciably affected by any of them. It was to Milton and Milton only that he was indebted.

We should know this from the poems themselves, but fortunately we have the additional testimony of his own words. "One afternoon in 1801," he tells us, — it was really May 21, 1802, — "my sister read to me the sonnets of Milton. I had long been well acquainted with them, but I was particularly struck on that occasion with the dignified simplicity and majestic harmony that runs through most of them — in character so totally different from the Italian, and still more so from Shakespeare's fine sonnets. I took fire, if I may be allowed to say so, and produced three sonnets the same afternoon, the first I ever wrote, except an irregular one at school. "[1] This event, so important in the history of the sonnet, seems, characteristically, to have been appreciated at its full value by the poet himself; for he referred to it nearly forty years later, and on another occasion said that this reading of Milton completely changed his attitude towards the form which he had previously thought "egregiously absurd."[2]

It was a memorable afternoon not simply because it gave Wordsworth a respect for quatorzains and started him writing them, but because for the remainder of the year he wrote almost nothing but

[1] Fenwick note, prefixed to "I grieved for Buonaparte" (*Poetical Works*, ed. Knight, ii. 323). Wordsworth had really written a number of sonnets before this time, at least three of which are preserved, — those that begin "Calm is all nature," "She wept. — Life's purple tide began to flow," "Sweet was the walk" (*ib.* iv. 28–30).

[2] In the advertisement to the collected volume of his sonnets, published in 1838, he said: "My admiration of some of the Sonnets of Milton, first tempted me to write in that form. The fact is ... mentioned ... as a public acknowledgment of one of the innumerable obligations, which, as a Poet and a Man, I am under to our great fellow-countryman." He wrote to Landor, April 20, 1822: "I used to think it [the sonnet] egregiously absurd, though the greatest poets since the revival of literature have written in it. Many years ago my sister happened to read to me the sonnets of Milton, which I could at that time repeat; but somehow or other I was singularly struck with the style of harmony, and the gravity, and republican austerity of those compositions."

sonnets, — and such sonnets! Included in the nineteen are those on Westminster Bridge, the extinction of the Venetian republic, Toussaint L'Ouverture, and Milton, as well as the ones that begin "Fair Star of evening, Splendour of the west," "It is a beauteous evening, calm and free," "Inland, within a hollow vale, I stood," "O Friend! I know not which way I must look," "Great men have been among us," "It is not to be thought of," and "When I have borne in memory." These poems, which Wordsworth rarely surpassed, not only were written under the immediate inspiration of Milton's but were obviously patterned after them. Their loftiness and nobility, their intensity of feeling, their directness, masculine vigor, and sonorous breadth, suggest as do those of no other writer the "soul-animating strains" that inspired them.

Furthermore, like his master but unlike most of his other predecessors, Wordsworth put into the sonnet his very life-blood, the noblest and deepest there was in him. In 1802, when he began to use the form, he was "opprest" and 'knew not which way he must look for comfort.' The cause of liberty to which he was passionately devoted seemed everywhere to be losing ground; England and France were rapidly drifting towards war, and he was torn between his love for each and between the disappointments, hopes, and fears that each caused him. At this crisis of his life, when he was shaken to his very foundations and many of his radical enthusiasms and theories were crumbling about him, it was the sonnet that he chose as an outlet, pouring into it the soul not only of his own difficulties but of the struggle that was convulsing all Europe. This was new. Since Milton "caught the sonnet from the dainty hand of love," no one had packed such intensity into it or devoted it to matters of such world-wide significance. It had, as we have seen, become to a great extent a personal poem, in which, even when picturing nature, the poet generally kept himself in the foreground. It was used principally for addresses to friends, for the expression of grief, and for the celebrating of occasions. For such purposes as these Wordsworth had made little use of verse, and, as he was repelled by the difficulties of the form, had composed few sonnets before 1800. His 'taking fire' at the reading of the Puritan stanzas was probably due to a sudden realization of the similarity of his situation to that described in some of them, to his admiration for the part Milton had played in the earlier crisis, and to a sense of the suitability of the sonnets of his favorite poet for expressing his own difficulties and fears. As the lines beginning "Milton! thou should'st be living at this hour" indicate, it was to the patriotism of the Latin secretary of the Commonwealth, and to the sonnet as his vehicle for voicing this patriotism, that Wordsworth turned in his hour of need.

In 1803, the year after his first great outburst of sonnet-writing, Wordsworth composed at least ten quatorzains, eight of which, including *To the Men of Kent, In the Pass of Killicranky*, and "These times strike monied worldlings with dismay," were on liberty. During 1804 and 1805 he wrote only one (aside from three translations), but in 1806 about twenty, among which are "Nuns fret not," the four that treat with lofty simplicity of "personal talk," and the great one, "The world is too much with us." Thereafter his average was almost ten a year, though none are credited to 1817–18 and nearly two hundred to 1819–21. This last group includes the ecclesiastical and river-Duddon sequences, the greater part of which were, as might be expected, still-born. The calm decision, executed with remorseless fidelity, to devote a cycle of sonnets to the history of the church of England with an account of its rites, shows how far the poet had travelled since he first poured out his whole heart in a few impassioned quatorzains. For his early ardor had soon died down: within five years of his catching fire Wordsworth's sonnets had become noticeably less sonorous and vigorous, had grown quieter, simpler, and more pedestrian, — in a word, less Miltonic and more Wordsworthian. This change was due in part to the natural loss of youthful imagination and vigor (a loss particularly marked in the lake poet), in part to the passing of the crisis of his life with the resulting decrease in the intensity of his feelings about current events, and in part to the weakening of the impulse that Milton had given him. But in no slight degree it came from his greater control over the tool he handled; for the facility he gained from writing sonnets so dulled the stimulus, the challenge, which the difficulties of the form had at first offered him, that he seems at last to have produced quatorzains on any occasion or none, and with as little effort as if he were dictating a letter. When he had thus ceased to exert himself over them, he found any difficulty they presented irksome, and as a result grew increasingly careless as to the arrangement of rimes, often violating the rules that he himself laid down. In the first six years of his sonnet activity, during which his best work was produced, thirty-seven of his octaves are legitimate, twenty have the three-rimed form, *a b b a a c c a*, and only one is irregular. From 1808 to 1821 one hundred and fifty-eight are legitimate, one hundred and thirty-three have the three rimes, and nine are irregular. From 1822 to 1846 sixty-one are legitimate, eighty-one use the three rimes, and the same number are irregular; but in the last six years of this period irregular forms occur in more than half of the poems. In his first great year Wordsworth did not employ the concluding couplet at all, and he allowed it but four times in the next five years; but thereafter in this matter, as in his octaves, he grew more and more lax, until from 1822 to 1846 the couplet-ending became a favorite with him.[1] Yet never, even when he was least careful, did he employ either the Shakespearean or the Spenserian form.[2] As regards run-over lines, internal pauses, and the failure to observe the prescribed pauses there was no change: throughout his life he conformed so closely to Milton's usage that many of his poems read like blank verse. The division into octave and sestet he usually kept, but in his early as well as his later work he often ran the eighth line into the ninth.

Such was his practice. His theory was in some respects quite different, being at once stricter and more liberal than would be supposed. "Wordsworth does not approve of closing the sonnet with a couplet," Crabb Robinson noted, "and he holds it to be absolutely a vice to have a sharp turning at the end with an epigrammatic point."[3] Yet he used the couplet-ending one hundred times. He also did not approve "of uniformly closing the second quatrain with a full stop, and of giving a turn to the thought in the terzines."[4] But as to the structure of the sonnet he confessed late in life to Alexander Dyce:[5]

Though I have written so many, I have scarcely made up my own mind upon the subject. It should seem that the sonnet, like every other legitimate composition, ought to have a beginning, a middle, and an end; in other words, to consist of three parts. . . . But the frame of metre adopted by the Italians . . . seems to be — if not arbitrary — best fitted to a division of the sense into two parts, of eight and six lines each. Milton, however, has not submitted to this; in the better half of his sonnets the sense does not close with the rhyme at the eighth line, but overflows into the second portion of the metre. Now it has struck me that this is not done merely to gratify the ear by variety and freedom of sound, but also to aid in giving that pervading sense of intense unity in which the excellence of

---

[1] For most of these details, as well as for other matters relating to the present discussion, I am indebted to Thomas Hutchinson's valuable "Note on the Wordsworthian Sonnet," in his reprint of Wordsworth's *Poems in Two Volumes* (1897), i. 208–26. The figures seem, however, not to total as they should or to agree with Mr. Hutchinson's other figures.

[2] He wrote one Shakespearean sonnet when at school, before the memorable afternoon in 1802; but, though he has one Spenserian octave, he seems never to have used the Spenserian form throughout.

[3] *Diary*, Jan. 26, 1836.　　　　[4] *Ib.*

[5] Undated letter of 1833, *Letters*, iii. 31–2.

the sonnet has always seemed to me mainly to consist. Instead of looking at this composition as a piece of architecture, making a whole out of three parts, I have been much in the habit of preferring the image of an orbicular body,—a sphere or a dew-drop. . . . I am well aware that a sonnet will often be found excellent, where the beginning, the middle, and the end are distinctly marked, and also where it is distinctly separated into *two* parts.

The clearest impression made by this letter is that of lack of clearness in its writer's mind. It confirms the notion one gets from the poems themselves, that Wordsworth had never given the structure of the sonnet sufficient attention to think through his ideas regarding it.[1] One would like some illustrations of the "sphere" form and of that with "three parts." Did the latter mean anything so definite as the divisions at the end of the first and second quatrains, or, as seems more likely, was it merely vague theorizing? He seems not to have noticed that, although the Miltonic sonnet "overflows into the second portion," it usually has a bipartite structure, and, like the majority of quatorzains (including most of Wordsworth's own), has a turn earlier or later, even if there is none at the ninth line. Clearly, he objected to the marked pause and turn between the octave and the sestet on the ground that they destroy the unity of the poem, and for this reason he favored the "orbicular" structure, presumably that of Milton's poems on Harry Vane and the Piemontese massacre, which move forward without a break. He would doubtless have been surprised to learn that a considerable body of his sonnets conform to the strict Italian rules, and that almost all of them fall into two clearly marked, even if irregular, parts. The explanation of this unintentional regularity is not far to seek. As the great difficulty of the sonnet lies in the rimes, it is to these that the poet must give most of his attention. Now if the first eight lines of his poem have certain rimes arranged in one way and the last six have other rimes arranged in another way, what is more natural than that, without regard to pauses or divisions, he should work out his two sets of rimes more or less separately, and that, as most short poems naturally fall into two parts, the division should come where the rimes change? Often, to be sure, the first part will fall short or will run over into the second, but it will quite as often end where its

[1] Astonishing as this is in one who put much of his best work into sonnets and who wrote on an average twelve a year for forty-four years, we must remember that we English-speaking people — poets, critics, and readers alike — usually maintain towards the structure and rules of the sonnet, as well as towards most matters of poetic form, an attitude of "superior" or ignorant indifference. The difficulty Wordsworth experienced in making up his mind he probably increased by trying to reconcile what he thought should be done with what he was in the habit of doing.

rimes end. This seems to be the explanation of Wordsworth's structure, — the sphere theory sometimes carried out, but more often modified unconsciously by the rimes into a bipartite arrangement, which frequently fulfils all the Italian rules.[1] If the explanation is correct, it affords a striking tribute to the reasonableness of the laws of the form.

That Milton and no one else is mentioned in this discussion of sonnet-structure suggests the source of Wordsworth's convictions in the matter. Yet this would be clear enough had he used no name, for the form he has in mind is found only in the work of Milton and his followers. In his comments on the *genre* he ignored Spenser, and usually even Shakespeare, of whose poems he did not entirely approve;[2] but he constantly quoted Milton's usage as authoritative. In another letter of 1833, for example, he wrote that he had used double rimes in his sonnets "much less in proportion than my great masters, especially Milton, who has two out of his eighteen with double rhymes."[3] He frankly imitated one of the "Petrarchian stanzas" of his master,[4] and took the best line of his fine *Afterthought* (to the Duddon series) from *Paradise Lost.*[5] Most of his poetic tributes to his favorite, furthermore, are in his quatorzains, — not only the famous "Milton! thou should'st be living at this hour" and the fine *Latitudinarianism,*[6] but the lines,

> We must be free or die, who speak the tongue
> That Shakespeare spake; the faith and morals hold
> Which Milton held.[7]

[1] Mr. Hutchinson notes (*Poems*, etc., i. 218) that in the 1807 volumes only seven have the sphere structure without pause or turn, whereas thirty-four have the regular Italian bipartite structure, and fifteen the bipartite structure but with the pause not in the regular place (though, as several of these fifteen have the pause without the turn, they are really not bipartite). This was approximately Wordsworth's usage throughout life.

[2] It will be remembered that in his account of 'taking fire' at Milton's sonnets (see p. 529 above) he spoke of Shakespeare's "fine sonnets." Yet he wrote to W. R. Hamilton, Nov. 22, 1831, "Shakespeare's sonnets . . . are not upon the Italian model, which Milton's are; they are merely quatrains with a couplet tacked to the end; and if they depended much on the versification, they would unavoidably be heavy."

[3] To Henry Taylor, *Letters*, iii. 33. Thirty years before he had written to his brother Richard: "Milton's sonnets . . . I think manly and dignified compositions, distinguished by simplicity and unity of object and aim, and undisfigured by false or vicious ornaments. . . . They have an energetic and varied flow of sound, crowding into narrow room more of the combined effect of rhyme and blank verse, than can be done by any other kind of verse I know of" (Knight's *Life*, i. 370).

[4] *On the Detraction which followed the Publication of a certain Poem* (cf. Milton's *On the Detraction which followed upon my writing certain Treatises*).

[5] "We feel that we are greater than we know" (cf. *P. L.*, viii. 282).

[6] Quoted on pp. 179–81 above.

[7] "It is not to be thought of that the Flood," 11–13.

In his "Great men have been among us" he mentions

> Young Vane, and others who called Milton friend;

and he closes his "Scorn not the Sonnet" with the lines,

> And, when a damp
> Fell round the path of Milton, in his hand
> The Thing became a trumpet; whence he blew
> Soul-animating strains — alas, too few!

Wordsworth performed a great service for the sonnet. The quality and quantity of his productions (there are five hundred twenty-three in all), combined with the commanding position their author came to occupy, have made them for nearly a hundred years the most widely read of all English quatorzains and have thus given them great influence. In his own day his most important contribution lay in freeing the *genre* from the sentimentality, melancholy, and triviality which were becoming fastened upon it. He re-dedicated it to the loftiest purpose and the most serious occasions, and in so doing secured for it some of the respect it had failed to win from many eighteenth-century readers.[1] He also helped to make it a favorite vehicle for nature poetry. Yet by no means all the credit is his; for the tendency of literature since 1800 has been steadily towards nature and away from sentimental melancholy, and even before this time the majority of sonnets, including many of those by Wordsworth's own friends, Coleridge, Southey, and Lamb, had not been pensive.[2] There can be no question, however, that then as now his

---

[1] Indirectly it is owing to Milton and Wordsworth that so many poets turned to the sonnet to express their feelings in regard to the recent war.

[2] The exacting and (as they seemed to him) arbitrary rules of the sonnet, and not, as Mr. Hutchinson believes (reprint of the 1807 *Poems*, i. 209–12), the sentimental melancholy of the contemporary quatorzain, were responsible for the poor opinion Wordsworth held of the *genre* in his earlier years. In the preface to his *Simonidea* Landor had observed "that the sonnet was a structure of verse incompatible with the excursive genius of our commanding language" (Forster's summary, in his life of Landor, 1869, ii. 8). It was in referring to this remark that Wordsworth said in a letter to its author: "You . . . depreciate that form of composition. I do not wonder at this. I used to think it egregiously absurd" (see above, p. 529, n. 2). Clearly, the *form* of the composition and not the contents of the poems was what each poet objected to. How far Wordsworth was from feeling contempt for the "green-sickness" of the eighteenth-century sonnets may be seen in his letter to Alexander Dyce (May 10, 1830, and cf. *Letters*, iii. 25, 31): "If a second edition of your *Specimens* should be called for, you might add from Helen Maria Williams the *Sonnet to the Moon*, and that to *Twilight;* and a few more from Charlotte Smith, particularly 'I love thee, mournful, sober-suited night.'" This shows, as does the strong impression Bowles's sonnets made upon him (see above, p. 511, n. 1), not only that he was fond of the very sonneteers upon whom Mr. Hutchinson says he turned his back, but that he particularly liked poems of the "deploring dumps" variety, for which, according to the same authority, he had a "hearty contempt."

quatorzains were an inspiration to many who used the form, and that for a century past they have been the strongest force in keeping it irregular in structure, lofty in tone, sincere, noble, and earnest in feeling, — in other words, in making it not simply a lute but a trumpet, an instrument for expressing the noblest and deepest things in man.

Notwithstanding the scorn Byron often expressed for the "great metaquizzical poet," it is quite possible that he owed to Wordsworth the inspiration of his best sonnets. In the summer of 1816 he was brought by Shelley (near whom he was living at Lake Geneva) to some appreciation of the lake poet's greatness, an appreciation reflected in the *Prisoner of Chillon*, the third canto of *Childe Harold*, and *Manfred*, all of which were written at this time or a little later. It may well be more than coincidence, therefore, that the sonnet on Chillon,

> Eternal Spirit of the chainless Mind!
> Brightest in dungeons, Liberty! thou art,

which was composed at this period, has much of the same ring as those Wordsworth had "dedicated to liberty" fourteen years earlier. Lines like the following, from two of Byron's other quatorzains, might have come from the same series:

> The lore
> Of mighty minds doth hallow in the core
> Of human hearts the ruin of a wall
> Where dwelt the wise and wondrous.

> To be the father of the fatherless,
> To stretch the hand from the throne's height, and raise
> *His* offspring, who expired in other days
> To make thy Sire's sway by a kingdom less, —
> *This* is to be a monarch.[1]

Some change must certainly have come over him, for two and a half years before composing his lines on Chillon he had written: "Redde some Italian, and wrote two Sonnets. . . . I will never write another. They are the most puling, petrifying, stupidly platonic compositions."[2] As these first two quatorzains are on love and are devoted largely to the beauty of the loved one, — in other words, as they are clearly patterned after the Italian poems which Byron had just read, — and as the later ones are on the Miltonic model, there can be little question that it was a strong impulse from without which changed his attitude towards the *genre* and inspired him to use it again. But, as so often with the Don Juan of literature, the impulse was short-

---

[1] *To Lake Leman*, 6–9; *To the Prince Regent*, 1–5.   [2] *Diary*, Dec. 18, 1813.

lived, and three years passed before another external suggestion led him to try the form again.[1]

Byron's six sonnets are Petrarchan, save that one has the three-rimed octave; all use run-over lines freely and in one case at the close of the octave. Yet, as the same rime-scheme is found in the early sonnets on the Italian model, and as the dignity, terseness, and vigor which characterize three of the poems mark most of Byron's serious verse, there is no evidence of any direct influence from Milton.[2]

One of Shelley's earliest sonnets is addressed to the "Poet of Nature," but neither this nor the later ones show any influence from Wordsworth. The restrictions of the Petrarchan type might have afforded an excellent condenser for the power that Shelley usually allowed to escape in beautiful but nebulous shapes; yet he did not submit to these restrictions, and perhaps for that reason wrote only three or four quatorzains of any great value. Though he translated Italian sonnets and used the terza and the ottava rima, the lawless indifference of romanticism, from which most of his verse suffers, led him habitually to disregard almost every rule of the form and to employ whatever arrangement of rimes came handy. Yet in spite of these defects *Ozymandias* is a deeply impressive poem, and *Political Greatness*, as will be seen from the opening lines, has a stateliness and weight which place it in the Miltonic class:

> Nor happiness, nor majesty, nor fame,
> Nor peace, nor strength, nor skill in arms or arts,
> Shepherd those herds whom tyranny makes tame;
> Verse echoes not one beating of their hearts,
> History is but the shadow of their shame.

The sonnets of Keats, like most of his work, will be better understood if they are studied in connection with those of Leigh Hunt. A volume of "Juvenilia" which Hunt published in 1801 contains six quatorzains, all in the Shakespearean form except that three do not end with couplets. The first is addressed to Sensibility, "soft pow'r"

> That warblest sweet thy lorn, romantic tale,
> Or by the mould'ring abbey lov'st to rove.

[1] On July 31, 1819, he composed one for the marriage of the Countess Rasponi, and twelve days later that to the Prince Regent.

[2] To be sure, Byron admired Milton; and as Shelley and his wife read *Paradise Lost* in 1816 (the summer they spent with Byron), and as a line in *Childe Harold* (canto iv, stanza xlvii, written a year later, "Thy wrongs should ring, and shall, from side to side") is taken from Milton's second sonnet to Cyriack Skinner, it is barely possible that Milton had something to do with the change in Byron's attitude towards the sonnet.

In another, *To Eve*, which shows the influence of Collins, the young bard exclaims,

> How sweet to wander thro' the dusky vale,
> When Philomela weeps her bleeding woes!

Such effusions clearly belong with those of Hayley, Miss Seward, Miss Williams, Mrs. Smith, and the Della Cruscans. In more mature years Hunt wrote over forty other sonnets, many of them winning and admirable in almost every way, and one to the Nile that is superb. Yet he never entirely rid himself of the somewhat sentimental prettiness of his early models, of expressions like "bosomy," "freshfulness," "a leafy rise, With farmy fields," "wilful blisses . . . kisses,"

> Delicious kisses put deliciously,
> A thousand, thousand, thousand, thousand times.[1]

His devotion to the Italians, the Elizabethans, and particularly to Spenser (who came to be his favorite poet), while it did not add to the virility of his poems, gave them a richness, a tender charm and grace, unknown to the eighteenth-century sonnet. As these qualities mark the quatorzains that Hunt produced immediately before and during the years when he was giving encouragement and direction to Keats, it is little wonder that the same characteristics appear in the sonnets of the younger poet.

Yet, as Mr. de Sélincourt has warned us, "it is uncritical to father upon Hunt all the vices of Keats's early work. For Hunt could never have gained the same sway over his mind had there not been a natural affinity between them." [2] His taste as a young man was not virile, but inclined toward excessive ornamentation of the wedding-cake variety; his early reading was largely in the sentimental poets of the eighteenth century ("Mrs. Tighe and Beattie," he tells us, "once delighted me"[3]), and he was without the intellectual discipline or the cultured surroundings and companionships which might have corrected these weaknesses. Since many of the Hayley-Williams-Smith-Tighe school were still alive and highly esteemed when he began to write, it is not strange that he followed them, as even Wordsworth did in his earliest work. Hunt, who began sonneteering when these writers were in their prime, did not so much hand a torch on to Keats as fan the one the younger man was already carrying.

---

[1] From the sonnets beginning, "The baffled spell" (lines 6, 13), "A steeple issuing" (1–2), "O lucky prison " (9, 11–13).

[2] Keats, *Poems* (2d ed., 1907), p. xxvii.

[3] Letter to George and Georgiana Keats, November, 1818 (*Letters*, ed. Forman, 1895, p. 249).

How closely akin the author of *Sleep and Poetry* was to the Della Cruscans may be seen in some lines from what appears to be his earliest sonnet, written in December, 1814, before he had met Hunt or was appreciably influenced by him:

> Thou thy griefs dost dress
> With a bright halo, shining beamily. . . .
> Still warble, dying swan! still tell the tale,
> The enchanting tale, the tale of pleasing woe.[1]

Nor is this sort of thing confined to his early verses. Passages like the following, written the one two years and the other five years later (the second being one of his last poems), show that he never entirely shook it off:

> Give me a golden pen, and let me lean
> On heap'd up flowers, in regions clear, and far;
> Bring me a tablet whiter than a star,
> Or hand of hymning angel, when 'tis seen
> The silver strings of heavenly harp atween:
> And let there glide by many a pearly car,
> Pink robes, and wavy hair, and diamond jar.
>
> The day is gone, and all its sweets are gone!
> Sweet voice, sweet lips, soft hand, and softer breast,
> Warm breath, tranced whisper, tender semi-tone,
> Bright eyes, accomplish'd shape, and lang'rous waist![2]

These lines, though better expressed, are not essentially different from what the Della Cruscans wrote, — this, for example:

> Dear balmy lips of her who holds my heart . . .
> Dear lips! — permit *my trembling lips* to press
> Your ripen'd softness, in a tender kiss:
> And, while my throbbing heart avows the bliss,
> Will you — (dear lips!) the eager stranger's bless?
>
> Her dark-brown tresses negligently flow
> In curls luxuriant, to her bending waist . . .
> Her cheeks — soft blushing, emulate the rose,
> Her witching smiles, the orient pearls disclose:
> And o'er her lips, the dew of Hybla strays.[3]

[1] *To Byron*, 7–8, 13–14. Compare the sonnet to Chatterton, and the three (the first of which begins, "Woman! when I behold thee") published in Keats's first volume but — probably because they were written earlier — not in the same part of the volume.

[2] *On Leaving some Friends*, 1–7; "The day is gone," 1–4; cf. the first three lines of *The Flowre and the Lefe*. Even in the sestet of "Bright star," the desire to "swoon to death" upon his "fair love's ripening breast" has an unpleasant suggestion of Hunt and the Della Cruscans.

[3] *Poetry of the World* (1788), ii. 123, 130.

The persistence of a modified Della Cruscanism in Keats's sonnets is due in no small part to the other great force at work upon them, the influence of the Elizabethans. His devotion to Spenser, who made him a poet and who affected almost everything he wrote, needs no comment here; yet it is worth noting that the *Amoretti* seem to have left him cold, since he never used their rime-scheme or apparently was otherwise influenced by them. For the greatest of the Elizabethan sonneteers, however, he had enthusiastic praise. "One of the three books I have with me," he wrote in 1817, "is Shakspeare's Poems: I never found so many beauties in the Sonnets — they seem to be full of fine things said unintentionally. . . . He has left nothing to say about nothing or anything." [1] This admiration for Shakespeare's quatorzains and for the *Faerie Queene* is reflected in the sensuous luxuriance of thought and expression which mark his own sonnets, in their grace and fluency, their frequent and ardent treatment of love, and in the rime-sequence of the later ones. Until his reading of Shakespeare's poems in November, 1817 (which led to the enthusiastic letter just quoted), he used the Petrarchan arrangement; thereafter, with a few exceptions, he employed only the Shakespearean. [2] As he rarely disregarded the pauses and turn, and as he was interested in Italian poetry, he may have derived his rime-scheme, and in part his conception of the sonnet, from Petrarch, Dante, and their countrymen. [3]

Notwithstanding the excellence of Keats's models, it is obvious that they were not of a kind to correct his tendency to lusciousness and over-ornamentation, which had been strengthened by the Della Cruscans and Hunt. Accordingly, though some of his greatest quatorzains have nobility of conception and dignity of expression as well as beauty, yet in the main they lack vigor, intensity, condensation, elevation of tone, and depth of thought. How it is that they were uninfluenced by the sonnets of Wordsworth, whom their author deeply admired, and of Milton, whose *Paradise Lost* transformed his other poetry, it is hard to say, unless the Della Cruscan-Italian-Elizabethan conceptions of the sonnet possessed him so completely

---

[1] Letter to J. H. Reynolds, Nov. 22, 1817. Keats's praise of Shakespeare's quatorzains is the earliest I recall from any sonneteer of the eighteenth or nineteenth century.

[2] Pointed out by Mr. de Sélincourt in his edition of Keats (pp. 543-4), which here, as in Chapter X above, has been of great assistance to me. Thirty-nine of the poet's sixty-one sonnets, according to Mr. de Sélincourt, are Petrarchan, three Petrarchan except for the final couplet, three experimental, and sixteen Shakespearean.

[3] Keats also translated twelve lines of a sonnet by Ronsard, whose "works," he wrote to Reynolds (Sept. 21 or 22, 1818), "have great beauties." This comment, and the fact that he was interested enough to translate the piece, show at least the kind of sonnet that attracted him.

that he did not admire, or, as is more probable, was disinclined to write, Miltonic sonnets.[1] At any rate, his significance in the development of the form lies in his reintroducing the Shakespearean quatorzain. It may be objected, to be sure, that the Elizabethan revival was in the air, that Hazlitt, Lamb, Hunt, and others were preaching and exemplifying it, and that Keats's sonnets had little immediate influence; but, at all events, he is the first writer since Drummond of Hawthornden to use in a considerable number of important poems the kind of quatorzain written by Shakespeare and his contemporaries. Strictly speaking, he did not revive the earlier type, but infused the amorous richness and splendor of the Elizabethans into the one used by Hayley, Charlotte Smith, the Della Cruscans, Coleridge, and Hunt, transforming it into what has ever since been one of the most popular kinds of sonnet.

Here we must pause; for to continue examining in this way all the more significant of the thousands of quatorzains written by Keats's contemporaries and successors would be a task epic in length if not in importance. Most of these later poems are far better than their predecessors, richer, more finished, weightier in meaning, and lovelier in expression. In fact, since Keats first heard Chapman speak out loud and bold, so many quatorzains have appeared that the world has been unable to read any considerable part of them or to remember even the best. Many, therefore, of real excellence, if not of purest ray serene, the dark unfathomed stacks of libraries bear. The sonnet has probably attained a higher level of general achievement in the past century, and given rise to a larger number of poems that come near to satisfying us, than has any other form. Yet most of these later quatorzains are less significant in the development of the *genre* than those we have been examining, for they belong in the main to one or another of the types we have already noted. With the awakening to the beauty of Shakespeare's poems, many have made use of the key wherewith he unlocked his heart, and as a result his disposition of the rimes has become more popular than any other. Similarly the growth of eclecticism and cosmopolitanism, of the knowledge and appreciation of other literatures, has greatly increased the admirers of Petrarch, Dante, and their countrymen, giving them an influence they never possessed in the eighteenth century. Indeed, the extensive use of Italian models, particularly by Rossetti and his ad-

---

[1] Mr. de Sélincourt thinks "there can be little doubt" that Keats's burlesque sonnet *To a Cat* was "intended as a parody of the Miltonic sonnet" (see his Keats, p. 557, and cf. 544); yet it is so poor a parody, catching so few of Milton's most obvious characteristics, that I cannot believe its author intended it as such. Mock-heroic it certainly is, and that, it seems to me, is all.

mirers, is the most significant modification introduced into the sonnet in the Victorian era. The example of the Italians and the
Elizabethans has revived sonnet-sequences, and has gone far towards giving the form back to "the dainty hand of love," which has
held many of the best quatorzains written in the last seventy-five
years. Yet nature, though by no means so prominent as it was in the
late eighteenth and early nineteenth centuries, is still a favorite
theme in this, as in all other poetic forms.

With the great increase in the number of good modern sonnets,
with the appreciation of those by the Elizabethans, Italians, French,
and others, and with the passing of the eighteenth-century enthusiasm for Milton, his "Petrarchian stanzas" have lost the preëminence
which they long enjoyed. Yet not a few of the bards who gild the
lapse of time from Keats's day to our own either have taken fire
from Milton's sonnets or have unconsciously modelled their own
upon his. One of the earliest of these men, Sir Aubrey de Vere, dedicated his one hundred fifty-two quatorzains in 1842 to Wordsworth,
"whose friendship," his son tells us, "he regarded as one of the chief
honours of his later life," and whose influence is clearly seen in the
subject-matter, spirit, and form of De Vere's own productions. Sir
Aubrey "valued the sonnet the more because its austere brevity, its
severity, and its majestic completeness fit it especially for the loftier
themes of song." [1] It is unnecessary to point out from whom this
conception of the quatorzain was ultimately derived, or how well it
is embodied in these lines:

> Godfrey, first Christian Captain! Bohemond!
> Tancred! and he, whose wayworn gabardine,
> And steel clad limbs, the throne of Constantine
> Pressed in the face of day, though thousands frowned!

> These iron-rifted cliffs, that o'er the deep,
> Wave-worn and thunder-scarred, enormous lower,
> Stand like the work of some primeval Power,
> Titan or Demiurgos, that would keep
> Firm ward for ever o'er the bastioned steep
> Of turret-crowned Beltard, or mightiest Moher. [2]

[1] Memoir by the younger Sir Aubrey, in his edition of his father's sonnets, 1875,
pp. xii–xiii. "For his earlier sonnets," adds the son, "he had found a model chiefly in
the Italian poets, especially Petrarch and Filicaja"; but it is difficult to trace any evidence of these writers in the poems published, some of which were written as early as
1817. They are grouped under the heads, "Religious and Moral," "On Character and
Events," "Descriptive," "Personal, Miscellaneous," "Historical," and "On the Lord's
Prayer."

[2] *Ib.* 58, 31: *The Crusaders*, no. 2; *The Cliffs*, no. 1.

The three hundred sonnets which the younger De Vere began to publish in 1842 are much like his father's, quite as good, and equally Miltonic:

> Allies! I deem that vision fair and brave
> Though dread which found in thee no dim-eyed seer. . . .
> The Tribes Barbaric o'er the Empire drave
> Launched from the terrible North; while froze for fear
> Cities high-walled, that tramp barbaric near.[1]

Wordsworth also left his mark on the numerous "toys of the Titans" composed by the corn-law poet, Ebenezer Elliott. These include a "cycle of revolutionary sonnets" fifty in number (*The Year of Seeds*, written in 1848), which attempted to improve on the rime-scheme, the bipartite structure, and other features of the legitimate form. Elliott appeals in three places to Milton's usage,[2] and seems to have been guided somewhat by it, though he lacks the condensation and power of the earlier poet. A few of his quatorzains recall those of Bowles.

It is an impressive but melancholy tribute to the wealth of good poetry contained in the nineteenth-century English sonnet that work of the noble, classic beauty of Sir John Hanmer's has been allowed to slip into an oblivion so deep that the Harvard Library copy of his sixty sonnets remained for nearly eighty years uncut. The quality of the poems may be judged from the following specimen, which is no better than many others, but in its lofty tone, its love of nature and of the past, its Petrarchan rime-scheme and general Miltonic cast, is typical of the entire volume:

> I saw two Columns, by a southern shore;
> One, standing in its Dorian majesty,
> Simple, and stern, and natural it might be;
> So blended with the hills the shape it wore.
> But some Cyclopean hand, ere time was hoar,
> Had reared it up to Neptune; and his sea
> Still bellows out beneath, memorially;
> Marking the moments' flight with tumbling roar.
> O'erthrown the other, of inferior race;
> Spiral and fretted, as a beechen bole,
> That thin green stems of ivy overlace;
> Between their dates did twenty ages roll;
> And still the first, with his Homeric grace,
> Stood scathless; lifting up the gazer's soul.[3]

---

[1] *To Thomas W. Allies* (in *Mediaeval Records*, 1893, p. 253).

[2] In the first poem of the "cycle," and in the preface and one sonnet ("Why should the tiny harp") of *Rhymed Rambles*.

[3] *Sonnets* (1840), no. vii.

None of the more eminent Victorians produced sonnets so closely akin to Milton's as are the twenty-five by Matthew Arnold. In spirit and in subject-matter these poems are much alike; all reveal the clear-eyed, resolute facing of life's problems, the fine breeding, restraint, and intellectuality of the fastidious scholar, dissatisfied with the life about him and yearning for the peace which his nature will not allow him to enjoy. The first eleven, however, are sharply distinguished from the later (Petrarchan) ones by their disregard for almost every law of the legitimate sonnet.[1] Arnold's antipathy to Puritanism chilled the enthusiasm he would otherwise have had for the most classic of English poets, and much that seems Miltonic in his quatorzains, whether written early or late, is probably due to their author's love for Greek poetry. This may also account for such inversions of the word-order as

> Was woe than Byron's woe more tragic far,

and for the pithy directness of such lines as

> *He saves the sheep, the goats he doth not save.*
> So rang Tertullian's sentence, on the side
> Of that unpitying Phrygian sect which cried:
> "Him can no fount of fresh forgiveness lave,
> "Who sins, once wash'd by the baptismal wave." [2]

Yet it is hard to believe that the following sonnet, with its quiet, impressive conclusion, and the similarity of its opening question and general tone to the second poem that Milton addressed to Cyriack Skinner, did not derive something from the utterances of the resolute Puritan fallen upon evil days:

> Who prop, thou ask'st, in these bad days, my mind? —
> He much, the old man, who, clearest-soul'd of men,
> Saw The Wide Prospect, and the Asian Fen,
> And Tmolus hill, and Smyrna bay, though blind.
> Much he, whose friendship I not long since won,
> That halting slave, who in Nicopolis
> Taught Arrian, when Vespasian's brutal son
> Clear'd Rome of what most shamed him. But be his
> My special thanks, whose even-balanced soul,
> From first youth tested up to extreme old age,
> Business could not make dull, nor passion wild;

---

[1] The *Austerity of Poetry*, which stands at the beginning of the later group, has a run-over line at the end of the octave and the turn comes at line twelve. Such sestet arrangements as *c d d e c e* and *c d c e d e* occur in the later sonnets, but none end with couplets.

[2] *A Picture at Newstead*, 14; *The Good Shepherd with the Kid*, 1–5.

Who saw life steadily, and saw it whole;
The mellow glory of the Attic stage,
Singer of sweet Colonus, and its child.[1]

In the first two volumes Tennyson published there are more sonnets than in all the rest combined; indeed, he never reprinted a number of the early ones. His comparative neglect of the form in later
life was not due to a poor opinion of it, for his last quatorzains are
more exalted than the first, and share, with *Ulysses*, the condensation and vigor which are none too prominent in his poetry. In
these respects, in the intensity and nobility of the spirit that ani-
mates it, as well as in the dignity of its style, the following address
to Montenegro ranks among the more notable of the Miltonic sonnets
that have appeared since Wordsworth's day:

> They rose to where their sovran eagle sails,
> They kept their faith, their freedom, on the height,
> Chaste, frugal, savage, arm'd by day and night
> Against the Turk; whose inroad nowhere scales
> Their headlong passes, but his footstep fails,
> And red with blood the Crescent reels from fight
> Before their dauntless hundreds, in prone flight
> By thousands down the crags and thro' the vales.
> O smallest among peoples! rough rock-throne
> Of Freedom! warriors beating back the swarm
> Of Turkish Islam for five hundred years,
> Great Tsernogora! never since thine own
> Black ridges drew the cloud and brake the storm
> Has breathed a race of mightier mountaineers.[2]

Any one who is surprised to find Miltonic sonnets among Tennyson's poems will be startled to encounter them among the brilliantly-
artificial and sensuously-exotic productions of Oscar Wilde's genius.
It is a genuine shock to meet, a few pages after the luscious richness
of the decadent *Charmides*, a sonnet to the austere Puritan poet,
ending,

> Dear God! is this the land
> Which bare a triple empire in her hand
> When Cromwell spake the word Democracy!

---

[1] *To a Friend.* Cf. Milton,

> What supports me, dost thou ask?
> The conscience, friend, to have lost them overplied.

As Arnold had a high regard for Wordsworth, he may have been influenced by the
sonnets of the lake poet, many of which are not unlike his own.

[2] This was first published in the *Nineteenth Century* for May, 1877. In its Petrarchan
rime-scheme and its preservation of the pause and turn between octave and sestet, it is
typical of the later quatorzains and unlike most of the earlier ones, several of which disregard almost every rule of the form. Those entitled *To Victor Hugo, Alexander, Buonaparte,* and *Poland* (the last three written early) are also of the Miltonic-Wordsworthian
variety.

Nor is this an isolated case; for on the opposite page is a sonnet *On the Massacre of the Christians in Bulgaria*, recalling Milton's on the Piemontese massacre, and, over the leaf, one that begins,

> Rome! what a scroll of History thine has been;
> In the first days thy sword republican
> Ruled the whole world for many an age's span:
> Then of the peoples wert thou royal Queen.

The influence of Milton is to be seen in the quatorzains of Cardinal Newman, the Earl of Beaconsfield, James Russell Lowell and his fellow-countryman Washington Allston,[1] in some of Swinburne's,[2] as well as in those of many other poets famous or forgotten. Nor should the noble sonnet on Milton by Ernest Myers, the best interpretation of the poet's character that we have in verse, be overlooked, or the work of other men still living. For if any one thinks that none but the dead have followed Milton he must have paid little heed to what was written during the recent war. One of the most striking features of this poetry, whether English or American, is the extent to which from the very beginning it made use of the sonnet. All the deepest, most intense feelings called forth by the struggle found a voice in the little instrument which in Milton's hands had become a trumpet. How direct, concentrated, and Miltonic many of the poems are, these lines *To the Hun* will show:

> Not for the lust of conquest do we blame
> Thy monstrous armies, nor the blinded rage
> That holds thee traitor to this gentler age,
> Nor yet for cities given to the flame;
> For changing Europe finds thy heart the same,
> And as of old thy bestial heritage.
> The Light is not for thee. The war we wage
> Is less on thee than on thy deathless shame.
> Lo! this is thy betrayal — that we know,
> Gazing on thee, how far Man's footsteps stray
> From the pure heights of love and brotherhood —
> How deep in undelivered night we go —
> How long on bitter paths we shall delay,
> Held by thy bruteship from the Gates of Good.[3]

It were folly to claim that every one who before or since 1914 has written sonnets of this kind was directly affected by the poet who

---

[1] The thirteen sonnets of Allston — one of them to Coleridge, whom he knew intimately in Rome — are appended to his *Lectures on Art* (ed. R. H. Dana, N. Y., 1850). Lowell's sonnet on Wendell Phillips has the Miltonic ring, as has Disraeli's on Wellington (printed in William Sharp's *Sonnets of this Century*, 1886, pp. 268-9).

[2] Particularly in some of his "Dirae" (*Songs of Two Nations*), which are notable for their directness and concentrated passion.

[3] George Sterling, in his *Binding of the Beast* (San Francisco, 1917).

first composed them. Some may have scarcely known his work, and only a few may have been inspired by his example to use the quatorzain for sterner, loftier purposes. The qualities, for example, that make the work of the younger De Vere seem Miltonic are probably due to the natural temper of his mind and to his study of Greek, for they are present in his other poetry. Milton may have had nothing directly to do with De Vere's belief that "a true sonnet is characterized by greatness, not prettiness ... it is in substance solidly simple";[1] yet ultimately this idea of the *genre* is derived from the Puritan stanzas which are the earliest, and perhaps still the greatest, exemplifications of it. The channel which let the mightier waters flow through the sonnet was dug by Milton, and, however little those who use these streams to-day may realize it, they are profiting by his originality and daring and are following his course. Even those who employ the form for lighter purposes and amorous themes copy him when, as often, they disregard the pauses and the turn or use run-over lines and internal pauses, — when, like most of the sonneteers of the last two centuries, they make their prosody practically that of blank verse. Furthermore, in so far as the poems have been held to the legitimate rime-scheme, the credit is in no slight degree due to Milton, who is also somewhat responsible for the many quatorzains that are addressed to persons and begin with proper names in the vocative.

Some of these obligations may be unimportant, others undesirable, but in one matter Milton has rendered vital service. The sonnet has always in all languages shown a tendency towards sweetness rather than strength, towards finish rather than thought, towards pretty trifling and absorption in the single theme, love. Not only does this hold of Elizabethan times and the late eighteenth century, but it is the popular conception of the form in our own day. The tendency, if it had not constantly been met by powerful forces of another kind, would have greatly narrowed the scope of the poem, would have made it monotonous, have lessened the esteem in which practically all modern English poets have held it, and have deprived us of much noble verse. Without the salutary influence of Milton and his followers the sonnet might have been devoted largely to what Johnson termed the carving of heads upon cherry-stones. This influence has been of the more permanent significance because, instead of being so decided as to suppress originality, it has only stimulated and given direction to it. Unlike the poems modelled upon the octosyllabics, those that have followed the sonnets are by no means slavish copies;

[1] Memoir prefixed to his edition of his father's sonnets, 1875, p. xiii.

they are like children, bearing their father's features but having their own tastes and wills and living their own lives. It is safe to say, then, not only that the sonnet was reborn under the influence of Milton and for many years kept subject almost solely to him, but that from the time of its rebirth, one hundred and fifty years ago, to the very present it has carried his impress as it has that of no other poet.

CHAPTER XX

THE INFLUENCE OF THE REMAINING POEMS

THE definite, tangible influence of Milton's other poems has been relatively slight. Not one of them has ever enjoyed a vogue comparable to that of the epic, the octosyllabics, or the sonnets; not one has furnished a pattern that other poets have used extensively. A mould was, to be sure, made from *Lycidas* by means of which some very chalky casts were turned out; but, as compared with the odes to abstractions, the sonnets, or the pieces in Miltonic blank verse, their number is negligible. This is not to minimize the inspiration that *Comus*, *Lycidas*, and *Samson Agonistes* have given to generations of readers and poets, the suggestions they have furnished, or the imponderable, often vague and unconscious, but none the less valuable influence they have exerted on the versification, language, imagery, and other aspects of the poet's art. But such things cannot be proved or their extent and importance estimated. All great art, like great action, makes impressions that cannot be calculated: it is only the more definite, and often more superficial, traces that we may hope to detect.

For this reason we cannot expect to separate the influence of *Paradise Regained* from that of *Paradise Lost*. Different as the two works are, it is impossible to tell, except by the subject-matter, whether a poet is following the later or the earlier one; and the subject-matter of *Paradise Regained* was little used, — never, I think, in a piece uninfluenced by *Paradise Lost*. From the almost universal preference for the epic and the remarkable frequency with which its phrases are borrowed, as well as from the expressive silence, or the occasionally-expressed indifference, in regard to its successor, the assumption seems warranted that *Paradise Regained* exerted a relatively unimportant influence, and that writers who employ the Miltonic style and diction derive them mainly from the account "Of man's first disobedience."

LYCIDAS

Lycidas, as has been said, did furnish the pattern for a number of poems, principally of the eighteenth century. I have found some thirty-five such, very few of which attracted any contemporary attention or are known to-day even to scholars. The features that impressed most of the imitators were that *Lycidas* is a pastoral on the death of a friend, that it is termed a "monody" (the English word appears to have been known in the eighteenth century only through Milton's use of it), that the lines vary in length and the rime-scheme is irregular, that several persons come to lament the dead, and that the piece ends with the departure of the shepherd who 'sings' the elegy. The expressions "Yet once more, O ye laurels," "Where were ye, Nymphs," "Alas! what boots it," and "Weep no more, woeful! shepherds . . . For Lycidas . . . is not dead," were apt to linger in the memory, as were the references to college days and the picture of the young poet's life in heaven.

The history of the monody movement is that of the *Allegro-Penseroso* vogue in miniature: it was of little account before 1747 or after 1800, and was at its height from 1770 to the end of the century. Although there are some borrowings from *Lycidas* in Robert Baron's *Cyprian Academy* (1647),[1] in the *Funeral Poem on Thomas Gunston* which Isaac Watts wrote during 1701, in Pope's *Windsor Forest* (1713), and in a few other pieces, the first poem to show any significant influence from it was *Colin's Despair, an Imitation of Milton's Lycidas*, one of Moses Browne's "Piscatory Eclogues" (1729). The piece is pastoral but not elegiac, and the "imitation" is limited to a varying line-length, an irregular rime-scheme, a somewhat similar ending, and a few verbal borrowings.[2]

In 1737 Richard West, whose death called forth Gray's sonnet, composed a *Monody on the Death of Queen Caroline*, which takes from *Lycidas* its lines of different length and its arrangement of rimes, as well as a number of its phrases.[3] Aside from these Miltonisms, to which may be added a passage reminiscent of *Allegro* and a line from the morning hymn of Adam and Eve curiously adapted to the queen's

---

[1] See above, p. 427.

[2] For example, "Yet, O ye *Muses*, let me once rehearse" (*Eclogues*, p. 74, cf. *Lycidas*, 1); "Begin, and not ungrateful be the Verse" (74, cf. *Lyc.*, 17); "swart Fairy-Bands" (84, cf. *Lyc.*, 138, and *Comus*, 436); "the rath Hind" (84, cf. *Lyc.*, 142). Note also "the spongy Air" (84, cf. *Comus*, 154) and "e'er the fled Cock rings his shrill Matin (84, cf. *Allegro*, 114). In later editions this eclogue is called *Renock's Despair*, and is much changed. For borrowings from the *Vacation Exercise, Lycidas, Allegro*, etc., in the other eclogues, see p. 426, n. 1, above. Browne prefixed to the volume a dedicatory poem to Bubb Dodington in Miltonic blank verse, and later wrote three other pieces in the measure (see below, Bibl. I, 1739, 1749, and App. B, 1739).

[3] "Mean time thy rural ditty was not mute" ("Dodsley's Miscellany," 1748, ii. 277, cf. *Lycidas*, 32); "oaten-flute" (277, cf. *Lyc.*, 33); "Return, sad muse" (278, cf. *Lyc.*, 132); "O honour'd flood! with reeds Pierian crown'd" (278, cf. *Lyc.*, 85–6); "And call thy chosen sons, and bid them bring" (279, cf. *Lyc.*, 134); "Ah me! what boots us" (279, cf. *Lyc.*, 64).

death, the monody is of interest to-day only because a quatrain from it suggested one of the finest stanzas in Gray's *Elegy*.[1]

West's lament was not published till 1748, six years after his death and one year after William Mason gave to the public his *Musaeus, a Monody to the Memory of Mr. Pope, in imitation of Milton's Lycidas*, which he had written in 1744. This effusion of one who came to be thought the

Harmonious Chief of Britain's living Choir,[2]

though not so flagrant an imitation as its author's *Il Bellicoso* and *Il Pacifico*, is of the Masonic order, since it copies every outstanding feature of Milton's elegy. The contents are curious; for, after the usual pastoral lament thickly sprinkled with phrases from *Lycidas*, and while "all pale th' expiring Poet *laid*," Chaucer, Spenser, and Milton come to comfort him. Chaucer speaks in a grotesque, ungrammatical jargon which shows how imperfectly Middle English was understood at the time; Spenser talks in a burlesque of his own language and meters; while Milton in blank verse praises the riming of the "heav'n-taught warbler! last and best Of all the train!" explaining that he himself had "aim'd to destroy" the "dire chains" of rime, "hopeless that Art could ease Their thraldom." "Thou cam'st," he exclaims,

and at thy magic touch the chains
Off dropt, and (passing strange!) soft-wreathed bands
Of flow'rs their place supply'd: which well the Muse
Might wear for choice, not force; obstruction none,
But loveliest ornament.

Milton is in the midst of an astounding adaptation of one of the finest passages in *Paradise Lost* to the praise of Pope's tinsel grotto, when the dying poet bids him cease, and, after speaking in heroic couplets the best lines in the monody, expires. Then follow the laments of nymphs and shepherds and an ending similar to that of *Lycidas*. Though revised by Gray,[3] praised by many, and printed

---

[1] Compare the last five lines of section iv with *Allegro*, 148–50 (for another use West made of the companion poems, see p. 453 above); and the first line of section v, "These are thy glorious deeds, almighty death," with *Paradise Lost*, v. 153–4. Lines 5–8 of section v,

Ah me! what boots us all our boasted power,
Our golden treasure, and our purple state?
They cannot ward th' inevitable hour,
Nor stay the fearful violence of fate,

prefigure Gray's *Elegy*, 33–6.

[2] Hayley, *Essay on Epic Poetry* (Dublin, 1782), 3. "That charming poet," Fanny Burney called him (*Diary*, May 8, 1771). [3] See above, p. 69, n. 4.

four times in two years, *Musaeus* is wretched stuff.[1] It has interest
only because it imitates *Lycidas* and because, by uniting two literary movements often thought hostile, the school of Pope and the
schools of Milton and Spenser, it illustrates how little the so-called
romanticists of the mid-eighteenth century revolted from neo-
classicism.

The pleasant relations that usually existed between these schools
is also shown in the case of George, Lord Lyttelton, the friend of Pope
and Thomson and the admirer of Milton. In 1747, the year in which
Musaeus appeared, Lyttelton won general praise with a "Monody"
on the death of his wife, the best poem the movement produced.
Inspired by the sincerity and depth of his grief for the woman whom
he had tenderly loved, he was able, while retaining the classical
allusions and something of the pastoral element, to be natural and
unhackneyed. He may have been somewhat influenced by Dryden's
great ode to the memory of Anne Killigrew, particularly since he
did not, like Milton and most of his imitators, begin every line flush
with the margin, but printed his monody as a Pindaric, varying the
indentation with the length of the line.   Yet there can be no question
of the debt to *Lycidas* here:

> Where were ye, Muses, when relentless Fate
> From these fond Arms your fair Disciple tore. . . .
> Nor then did *Pindus*, or *Castalia*'s Plain,
> Or *Aganippe*'s Fount your Steps detain,
> Nor in the *Thespian* Vallies did you play;
> > Nor then on *Mincio*'s Bank
> > Beset with Osiers dank,
> Nor where *Clitumnus* rolls his gentle Stream. . . .
> Now what avails it that in early Bloom,
> > When light, fantastic Toys
> > Are all her Sex's Joys,
> > With you she search'd the Wit of *Greece* and *Rome?* [2]

None of the succeeding monodies have sufficient esthetic value to
merit specific comment, and few are of interest on other grounds.
One was included in the volume of elegies on the Prince of Wales published in 1751 by the University of Cambridge; one was written for
the Seaton prize at the same university, and several were called forth
by the deaths of Gray, Garrick, Chatterton, Shenstone, and the

---

[1] For the surprisingly high opinion held of *Musaeus* in the eighteenth century, see
Mr. J. W. Draper's doctor's thesis on Mason, Harvard, 1920.

[2] *To the Memory of a Lady lately Deceased, a Monody* (1747), §§ vii–ix. The best lines
are not in the passage quoted, but in the last eight sections. The poem is parodied in
Smollett's *Burlesque Ode* in memory of a grandmother (*Plays and Poems*, 1777, pp.
248–9), which uses several phrases from *Lycidas*.

Warton brothers. A number of the authors are already familiar to us through their imitation of Milton's other poems, — Benjamin Stillingfleet the blue-stocking sonneteer, Robert Potter translator of the Greek dramatists, Michael Bruce author of the *Ode to the Cuckoo*, Anna Seward the Swan of Lichfield, Thomas Dermody the drink-curst Irish Chatterton,[1] besides W. L. Bowles, Thomas Warton, and Coleridge. The *Monody on the Death of Chatterton* which Coleridge wrote in 1790 is Miltonic not alone in title and in being an elegy on a dead poet, but in the arrangement of its rimes and the varying length of its lines. The most interesting, if not the only interesting, part of the piece comes near the end of the rewritten version, where the pantisocracy project is referred to:

> Wisely forgetful! O'er the ocean swell
> Sublime of Hope I seek the cottag'd dell
> Where Virtue calm with careless step may stray. . . .
> O Chatterton! that thou wert yet alive!
> Sure thou would'st spread the canvass to the gale,
> And love with us the tinkling team to drive
> O'er peaceful Freedom's undivided dale. . . .
> Where Susquehannah pours his untamed stream.[2]

Not every monody was Miltonic;[3] in fact, the term came to mean little more than an elegy which did not employ the quatrain with alternate rimes used in Gray's famous poem and in most of the numerous eighteenth-century laments. Yet monodies became sufficiently common to be recognized as a distinct species; for one section is devoted to them in Bell's *Classical Arrangement of Fugitive Poetry*, and Richard Cumberland warned fathers not to be "tickled into ecstacy" because their sons had

> hammer'd out a song,
> Or epigram, or monody perhaps
> On a dead greyhound, or a drown'd she-cat.[4]

They were also known well enough to be burlesqued in some lines *To a Gentleman who desired Proper Materials for a Monody:*

---

[1] Dermody composed his Miltonic *Corydon, a Monody*, when he was ten years old; before he was twelve he wrote a *Monody on the Death of Chatterton* and a translation of Milton's *Epitaphium Damonis*, neither of which apparently was ever published (see his *Life*, by J. G. Raymond, 1806, i. 6–9, ii. 342).

[2] In his poem *To a Friend . . . writing no more Poetry* (1796) he quotes the line, "Without the meed of one melodious tear" (cf. *Lycidas*, 14). His *Monody on a Tea-kettle* (written 1790) is intended to be humorous, but is not a burlesque. Lines 14–22 of his *Religious Musings* were clearly suggested by *Paradise Lost*, iv. 641–56. For his sonnets, see pp. 515–16 above.

[3] See p. 681 below.

[4] *Retrospection* (1811), lines 1090–93. In an "Essay on Elegiac Poetry" (*Poems*, 1802, i. 70) George Dyer has something to say of the monody as a literary form.

> Flowrets — wreaths — thy banks along —
> Silent eve — th' accustom'd song —
> Silver slipper'd — whilom — lore —
> Druid — Paynim — mountain hoar —
> Dulcet — eremite — what time . . .
> Let these be well together blended —
> Dodsley's your man — the poem's ended.[1]

More amusing than this parody is George Huddesford's diverting *Monody on the Death of Dick, an Academical Cat*, which is connected directly with *Lycidas* only through its title and the lines,

> Where were ye, Nymphs, — when to the silent coast
> Of gloomy Acheron DICK travell'd post? . . .
> For not on ISIS' classic shores ye stray'd. . . .
> Regardless of the meed that Fame bestows.[2]

Yet it may be that the picture of Lycidas in heaven is burlesqued in the account of Dick's occupations in the same place:

> There shall the worthies of the Whisker'd Race
> Elysian Mice o'er floors of sapphire chase,
> Midst beds of aromatic marum stray,
> Or raptur'd rove beside the Milky Way.[3]

Huddesford bubbles over with puns, from the motto on the title-page, "Micat inter omnes," through the reference to Caligula's horse, —which, when consul, could "silence Opposition with his Neigh," — to the cataract of words, "catacomb," "catechise," "categorical," "catarrhs," "catastrophe," "catalepsy." But the humor is varied, for we are told that Dick

> Taught the great Truth, to half his race unknown:
> "Cats are not kitten'd for themselves alone;
> But hold from Heav'n their delegated claws,
> Guardians of Larders, Liberty, and Laws.". . .
> Tho' much for Milk, more for Renown he mews,
> And nobler objects than his Tail pursues. . . .
> What mice descended, at each direful blow,
> To nibble brimstone in the realms below! . . .
> Unpill'd, unpoultic'd, unphlebotomiz'd![4]

Singularly enough, what seems to be the latest piece influenced by Milton's monody is another burlesque, one in which "Mary Jane, ex-munition worker, demobilized, speaks" of the aftermath of the

[1] *Poetical Calendar* (1763), v. 111.

[2] *Salmagundi* (1791), 131–2; with the last line compare *Lycidas*, 84, and *Comus*, 9. In the "thousand Cats . . . on sainted seats," one of which descends from his "throne" (p. 146), there is another reminiscence of the passage in *Comus* (line 11).

[3] *Ib.* 146.   [4] *Ib.* 133, 138–40.

world war.[1] In the century and a quarter between the disappearance of the "academical cat" and the demobilization of Mary Jane, the only close imitation of *Lycidas* I know of is that with which the Hon. Julian Fane won the chancellor's gold medal at Cambridge in 1850, *Monody on the Death of the Queen Dowager*.[2] But of course the influence of Milton's elegy in the past century was not limited to these belated survivors of the movement. For, although the monody as a *genre* may be said to have disappeared from our literature leaving no significant traces, the elegiac pastoral to which Milton gave new life still lives, and lives to the glory of English poetry. Just how much Shelley's *Adonais* and Arnold's *Thyrsis* owe to *Lycidas* it is impossible to say, but some inspiration and guidance at least; for, even if little in either piece can be pointed out as definitely Miltonic, nobody could have written a poem of the kind without thinking of *Lycidas*. Milton's irregular rime-scheme and varying length of lines have been adopted by many later writers, by Coventry Patmore, for example,[3] and by Milton's American editor William Vaughn Moody, whose poem on his dead mother's picture makes use of them.[4] In a few instances, as Tennyson's *Ode on the Death of the Duke of Wellington* (1852), Richard Le Gallienne's *Robert Louis Stevenson* (1895), and the *Cecil Rhodes* (1902) of Francis Thompson, who used the measure often, the meter of *Lycidas* is employed in elegies.[5] This meter is too unusual and the poem too well known for such resemblances to be dismissed as mere coincidences; yet one hesitates to say they are more.[6]

COMUS AND SAMSON AGONISTES

In view of the remarkable popularity of *Comus* on the stage and the success of Handel's admirable music for *Samson Agonistes*, it is surprising that Milton's dramas have exerted so little influence. The matter cannot be explained on the ground that no masques and dramas on the classic model were written, for such is not the case. The eighteenth-century masque was not like the Elizabethan or the

---

[1] Kathleen O'Brien, *Mary Jane*, etc., in *Littell's Living Age*, July 19, 1919, p. 188.

[2] *Poems which have obtained the Chancellor's Gold Medal in the University of Cambridge* (Camb., 1860), 293–300.

[3] In three pieces, *To the Unknown Eros*, *Amelia*, and *L'Allegro*.

[4] *The Daguerreotype*. Moody's *Ode in Time of Hesitation* and *The Brute* are in the same meter.

[5] Another instance is W. J. Lampton's *At Grover Cleveland's Grave*, which appeared in the New York *World*, presumably about July 1, 1908.

[6] There is probably some influence from the meter of *Lycidas* upon the irregular Pindaric ode which Lowell and many other nineteenth- and twentieth-century poets have used.

Jacobean, to be sure; it was a kind of light opera on the Italian model, consisting largely of songs and dances, a difference easily realized if the *Comus* that Milton wrote be compared with the adaptation of it that held the stage. *Samson Agonistes* would hardly be expected to find many imitators; for, though it has always won admiration, it has apparently never roused the enthusiasm of any large number of readers. *Comus*, on the other hand, was widely known. Through regular stage presentations it became more familiar to persons of a certain class than did Milton's non-dramatic writings, and through frequent amateur productions it was brought home to still another group. Its songs were in every mouth, and its phrases were sown thick in eighteenth-century poetry. Robert Baron plagiarized it as early as 1647;[1] the elder Warton and an anonymous writer imitated the invocation of Sabrina, and another poet copied the echo song;[2] one of the burlesque "Probationary Odes for the Laureatship" (1785) has the lines,

> Sweetest nymph, that liv'st unseen
> Within that lov'd recess;[3]

and in Bowles's *African* (or *Dying Slave*) the negroes chant,

> Now thy long, long task is done,
> Swiftly,. brother, wilt thou run.

Furthermore, the plan and contents of *Comus* did exert some influence on the drama of the time. In Gilbert West's *Institution of the Order of the Garter, a Dramatic Poem* (1742), a spirit descends and speaks these lines:

> From the gay realms of cloudless day I come,
> Where in the glitter of unnumber'd worlds,
> That like to isles of various magnitudes
> Float in the ocean of unbounded space;
> On my invisible aërial throne
> I sit, attended with a radiant band
> Of spirits immortal.[4]

The *Monthly Review* says that *Parthenia, or the Lost Shepherdess, an Arcadian Drama* (1764), is "a close imitation of Shakespear and Milton in the same species of poetry," and that *Midsummer Eve, or the Sowing of Hemp* (1793), is "an imitation, apparently, of the style of Comus, and of the Faithful Shepherdess; and it abounds with

---

[1] See pp. 427–8 above.   [2] See below, Bibl. III B, bef. 1745 w., 1787, 1788.
[3] *Ode XVII*, pt. ii.
[4] "Dodsley's Miscellany" (1748), ii. 151. Compare with this the opening of *Comus*, which is also faintly suggested by the descent and first words of the spirit (the "Genius of England") near the beginning of the poem (*ib.* 113).

beautiful lines, fanciful ideas, and plagiarisms." [1] These pastorals I have not seen; but I have read the *Sappho* which William Mason began as a masque and in 1778 completed as a "lyrical drama." *Sappho* contains a character named Lycidas, and a scene in which "the Naiad Arethusa rises from the stream, seated in a shell," and sings the song,

> See! from her translucent bed
> ARETHUSA brings thee aid.
> Lo! she sprinkles on thy breast
> Vial'd drops, by fingers chaste. . . .
> Thrice I lift my virgin hand,
> Thrice I shed the vapors bland.[2]

That ardent sympathizer with the French Revolution and friend of the lake poets, John Thelwall, whom we have met before,[3] published in 1801 a wild "dramatic romance," *The Fairy of the Lake*, in which, after he has let loose all the horrors of Scandinavian mythology, he makes the "Lady of the Lake" rise "on a Throne . . . in a car," by the "margent green," to speak and sing much as Sabrina does.[4] As the fairy disappears at the end of the play, Taliessin addresses her thus:

> May those fountains, Lady kind!
> Still their wonted channels find,
> Nor ever water-nymph neglect
> The silent tribute of respect,
> But, thro many a secret vein,
> Still the purer essence strain,
> And thy mystic urn supply,
> Never turbid, never dry.[5]

Much closer to *Comus* than Thelwall's extravagant work is *The Genii, a Masque* (1814), by Andrew Becket. In this piece, after the curtain has risen on "the Confine of a Wood" (which suggests *Comus*), the "Good Genius" enters and, as in *Comus*, delivers himself of a long speech explaining who he is and why he is there. His first words are,

---

[1] xxxii. 233; enl. ed., xii. 341–2.

[2] *Works* (1811), ii. 350. In the first of the "Letters" prefixed to the early editions of *Elfrida*, Mason says he has enlivened that drama "by various touches of pastoral description . . . a beauty so extremely striking in . . . *Comus* . . . *As You Like It* . . . and . . . *Philoctetes*" (*ib.* 178); and in his *Caractacus* he has the chorus sing, "Break off . . . I hear the sound Of steps profane" (*ib.* 100, cf. *Comus*, 91–2, 145–6.) Two of the choruses in E. B. Impey's *Sylphs* (1811) recall the octosyllabic passages in *Comus*.

[3] See above, pp. 300–301.

[4] *Poems chiefly written in Retirement* (1801), 32, 31.

[5] *Ib.* 91 (cf. *Comus*, 922–33, and in general 976 to the end).

> In that bright region of the middle air,
> Abode of chosen beings, who partake
> Of the celestial nature, — Genii call'd, —
> My proper station is.

Like Milton's attendant spirit, he contrasts life in the "ethereal space" with that in "the drear mazes of this nether world," breaks off with "But to my sacred duties," says he is waiting for a young nobleman, and refers to "these calm scenes of pure and simplest nature" which "meditative humour most affects"; then, after a lyric passage (which recalls the first speech of Comus) describing "Cynthias revels" and referring to a "violet-border'd stream," the spirit, upon the approach of his charge, explains that he must put on his "heavenly robe," his "sky-tinct vest," and for a time "remain unseen."[1] Becket's masque, like Milton's, abounds in octosyllabic passages, one of which closes the piece after the fashion of *Comus:*

> O youth! thou nearly mayst compare,
> With us, the denizens of air. . . .
> Those ranks thou'lt join — when thy freed soul,
> Through the vast space darts to its goal —
> Where virtue dwells, and to renown
> On earth acquir'd, presents the crown.

But for out-and-out, unblushing imitation of Milton's dramas we must turn to twentieth-century America, where, in 1905, Edwin T. Whiffen published a volume of dramatic poems, *Samson Marrying, Samson at Timnah, Samson Hybristes,* and *Samson Blinded.* These are all on the Greek model, with choruses that, like Milton's, are in lines of different length, without rimes (which are rare in the *Agonistes*), and "without regard had to Strophe, Antistrophe, or Epode." Two of the titles, furthermore, *Samson Marrying* and *Samson Hybristes,* seem clearly to have been taken from the list of dramas Milton drew up in 1642. Such borrowings are not surprising or objectionable; but what shall we say of these?

> A little onward lies the toilsome path
> For these faint step[s] of age,
> A little further on.[2]

> O miserable hope! is this the man,
> That mighty Samson far renowned?[3]

---

[1] Cf. *Comus*, 1-17, 37, 18, 41-2, 4, 386; 93 ff., 233, 82-92.

[2] Page 99; cf. *Samson Agonistes*, 1-2.

[3] Page 182; cf. *S. A.*, 340-41. Also cf. p. 57, "Can this indeed be he," etc., with *S. A.*, 124-6.

> Just are the ways of God,
> And justly ordained
> His purposes, though darkened oft by doubt
> What Heavenly disposition may allot.[1]

Or of this conclusion of *Samson at Timnah?*

> O glorious vengeance on our foes inflicted! . . .
> Come, friends, there seems not much for sorrow here,
> And lamentation. . . .
> All is best, though oft endured
> Our grievous ills with questioned doubt. . . .
> His high intent his purpose serves,
> With vindication full and fair event.[2]

Strangely enough, this appears to be the only influence worth mentioning that *Samson Agonistes* has exerted. Not a few plays on the Greek model have of course been written, but, aside from Whiffen's, none embody the distinctive features of Milton's work or seem indebted to it verbally, metrically, or structurally.[3] The idea of writing such a drama, as well as inspiration and vague, general guidance in composing it, may sometimes have come from Milton; for no writer would attempt so unusual a form without considering the only great example of it in English. William Mason, who composed two works "on the model of the ancient Greek tragedy," said frankly that *Samson* was "more simple and severe than Athens herself would have demanded. . . . Perhaps," his letter continues, "in your closet, and that of a few more, who unaffectedly admire genuine nature and antient simplicity, the Agonistes may hold a distinguished rank. Yet . . . unless one would be content with a very late and very learned posterity, Milton's conduct in this point should not be followed." [4]

---

[1] Page 183; cf. *S. A.*, 293–4, 1745–8.

[2] Pages 94–5; cf. *S. A.*, 1660, 1708–9, 1745–58. On page 100 Whiffen borrows from Milton's epic (iv. 32–7):

> O thou, that, with surpassing splendor adorned . . .
> To thee we call, O sun!

[3] Glover in his *Medea* (1761) tried regular unrimed lyrics that clearly owe nothing to Milton, and Dr. Frank Sayers employed unrimed choruses with lines of varying length in his *Dramatic Sketches of Northern Mythology* (1790); but the "Sketches" are otherwise very different from *Samson Agonistes*, "the Greek form of dramatic writing" being used merely because it afforded "in its choruses the most favourable opportunity for the display of mythological imagery" (introduction to *Moina*). His rejection of rime was part of a general theory (see p. 564 below) that presumably owed little to *Samson*, in which rime is used, though sparingly. Matthew Arnold also has unrimed lines of varying length in the choruses of his *Merope* and in many of the speeches of *Empedocles on Etna*. Of the English dramas that I have seen, the one most like *Samson Agonistes* is Andrew Becket's *Socrates* (1806).

[4] Letter ii, in *Works* (1811), ii. 181–2. Mason criticized *Samson* simply as a poor model for an acting play, but the cock-sure Southey showed his Midas ears in this com-

As this is almost the only point in which Mason did not follow Milton's conduct, his opinion is the more impressive.

THE TRANSLATION FROM HORACE

Milton's famous version of Horace's ode to Pyrrha, "rendered almost word for word, without rhyme, according to the Latin measure, as near as the language will permit," is probably better known to-day among Latin students than among the writers or readers of English verse. At least, the meter in which it is composed is rarely employed in modern poetry. But in the mid-eighteenth century, when new lyric forms were being sought and when almost every one translated Horace and was familiar with Milton, men turned to the measure more naturally. From 1700 to 1837 no fewer than eighty-three poems, and probably many more, were written in Milton's Horatian stanza,[1] which thus had a vogue almost as great, in proportion to the length and importance of the poem, as any of his other verse-forms enjoyed. It may be thought that the authors of some of these pieces took the unrimed stanza of two pentameter and two trimeter lines directly from Horace; but this was not so natural a thing to do as it appears to be, for rimes seemed indispensable to lyrics, and whoever used Horace's measure — Marvell, for example, in his *Horatian Ode upon Cromwell's Return from Ireland* — used rime. Then, too, before most of these writers could have derived the meter for themselves, it had been given some currency by several ardent admirers and consistent imitators of Milton's short pieces.

The credit for discovering the possibilities of the measure for lyric purposes does not belong to any one man. Milton in making his translation was trying, not to invent a new lyric form, but to see how closely he could follow Horace. Accordingly, he paid little heed to the unity of single lines and none to that of stanzas, printing and apparently conceiving his poem as sixteen continuous lines. The elder Thomas Warton was therefore something of a discoverer when, between 1744 and 1745, he employed the meter for an original poem.[2] To be sure, his *Ode to Taste*, an uninspired tribute to the "beauteous Arts of fair antiquity," is likewise not divided into stanzas; but the

ment: "Unrhymed lyrical measures had been tried by Milton with unhappy success. . . . There are parts in the choruses of the *Samson Agonistes*, wherein it is difficult to discover any principle of rhythm" (review of Sayers's works, *Quart. Rev.*, 1827, xxxv. 211).

[1] See Bibl. III c. Four of them, it will be noticed, were among the poems written at Oxford, in 1761–2, to celebrate the death of George II, the accession and marriage of George III, and the birth of the prince of Wales.

[2] Warton died in 1745, and the ode refers to the death of Pope, which took place in May, 1744. For Warton's other imitations of Milton, see pp. 461–2 above.

stanza conception is certainly present, as may be seen in these, the best lines:

> Or in some ruin'd Temple dost thou dwell
> Of ancient *Rome*, deserted of the World,
> Where prostrate lies in Dust
> The shapely Column's Height.

Warton passed on his metrical discovery to his two sons, the elder of whom, Joseph, included among the odes that he published in 1746 two in the meter of Milton's translation, one of which is "imitated from Horace."[1] Yet, as the poems are not attractive and are not printed with stanza divisions, they mark no advance over the father's work. Just when the younger Thomas Warton (the laureate and historian of English poetry) employed the measure in his renderings of two of Horace's odes is uncertain, but probably later than his brother, for in 1746 he was only eighteen years old. Both of his translations are divided into stanzas, and one is marked "after the manner of Milton," — which indicates where the family got the meter.

There is so little in any of these pieces to inspire imitation that the elder Warton's discovery would probably have interested few persons outside of the family if his elder son had not been a friend of William Collins. Writing to his brother Thomas sometime between May, 1745, and June, 1746, Joseph Warton remarked: "Collins met me in Surrey, at Guildford Races, when I wrote out for him my Odes, and he likewise communicated some of his to me: and being both in very high spirits, we took courage, resolved to join our forces, and to publish them immediately."[2] Perhaps it was through these odes which his friend "wrote out for him" that Collins's attention was drawn to the unrimed stanza; possibly he had already seen the *Ode to Taste* by Warton's father; or it may be that all three Wartons influenced his choice of the measure. At any rate, among the odes that he published in December, 1746, is one, *To Evening*, in the meter of Milton's translation from Horace. In its own field, that of the meditative lyric, this poem is hardly surpassed in all English literature, and certainly it has no equal — unless it be Smart's *Song to David* — among the lyrics of the hundred years that followed the dying-down of Restoration song. Without ceasing to be natural and tender, it achieves the classic finish and restraint, the finality, which is all too rare in English literature. And its beauty, we should observe, is due largely to the meter and to Collins's marvellous handling of it. If

---

[1] A third, *To Content*, is printed in Wooll's *Memoirs of Joseph Warton* (1806), 140–42. [2] *Ib.* 14 n.

rime were added, if the lines were made all of the same length, if they did not melt into one another as objects do in the evening, or if the rhythm were more obvious, the charm would be gone. Is it any wonder that discerning poets were quick to imitate stanzas like these when they came upon them amid the welter of eighteenth-century banalities?

> Whose numbers, stealing thro' thy dark'ning vale,
> May not unseemly with its stillness suit,
>   As, musing slow, I hail
>   Thy genial lov'd return! . . .
>
> And hamlets brown, and dim-discover'd spires,
> And hears their simple bell, and marks o'er all
>   Thy dewy fingers draw
>   The gradual dusky veil.[1]

It was unquestionably the *Ode to Evening* and not Milton's translation or anything the Wartons wrote that made the meter popular. The subjects of the later poems written in the measure make this clear, for not a few of them deal with nature and at least twelve are on morning, evening, or night. Moreover, several of them borrow phrases from Collins. Milton doubtless had some direct influence; for many who used his unrimed stanza, William Woty, Michael Bruce, Mrs. Barbauld, the Della Cruscans (Robert Merry and Mrs. Robinson), Richard Polwhele, Kirke White, Lamb's friend George Dyer, and Shelley, were affected by his other poems and almost certainly knew his translation from Horace. Besides, several of them followed Milton and the two older Wartons in not using stanza divisions. Yet, since poets seem to have been drawn to the meter primarily by their desire for new lyric forms, they are more likely to have found such a form in the *Ode to Evening* than in sixteen lines of a translation not divided into stanzas.

Only two or three of the later poems have any esthetic value. The Horatian measure has, like blank verse, the great drawback of being very easy to write and very hard to write well; and few of those who attempted it had sufficient metrical sensitiveness or taste to achieve success, even if they had tried harder than they did. Mrs. Barbauld's pleasing *Ode to Spring* (1773), which was clearly inspired by Collins, is, however, worth quoting from:

---

[1] Each of these stanzas, it will be observed, is closely connected with the one that precedes it, a circumstance which suggests the influence of Milton and the Wartons and perhaps indicates that as originally written the *Ode to Evening* was not divided into stanzas. The younger Thomas Warton tells us, in his edition of Milton's minor poems, 1785, p. 368, that Collins "had a design of writing many more Odes without rhyme."

> Now let me sit beneath the whitening thorn,
> And mark thy spreading tints steal o'er the dale;
> And watch with patient eye
> Thy fair unfolding charms.

John Keble's *Burial of the Dead* (written in 1823) and Sara Coleridge's "O sleep, my Babe" (1837) have found places in the *Oxford Book of Verse;*[1] but the truest poem in the meter since the *Ode to Evening* is by that inspired peasant, the half-starved, half-drunk, half-crazed John Clare. The thirty stanzas of his *Autumn* (1835) show the freshness, the deep love for nature, the keen observation, and the poetic gift that make all of Clare's best work attractive. He is far enough from the perfection and the magic of Collins; but not every writer can pen such a line as

> Ploughed lands, thin travelled with half-hungry sheep,

or draw such pictures as this of the cow-boy trilling his "frequent, unpremeditated song,"

> As on with plashy step, and clouted shoon,
> He roves, half indolent and self-employed,
> To rob the little birds
> Of hips and pendant haws,
>
> And sloes, dim covered as with dewy veils,
> And rambling bramble-berries, pulpy and sweet,
> Arching their prickly trails
> Half o'er the narrow lane.

Milton's translation affected a number of pieces that were not written in precisely the same meter, for it gave impetus to the movement towards unrimed lyrics which goes back to the Elizabethans or even farther.[2] Between 1698 and 1720 Samuel Say made free rimeless translations of two odes of Casimir and one of Horace, two of which (including that of Horace) resemble Milton's in employing unrimed quatrains with the last line in six syllables.[3] Inasmuch as Say wrote a discriminating essay "On the Numbers of Paradise Lost," used a modification of the *Nativity* stanza in one of his poems, and put

[1] For other poems by Keble and Miss Coleridge in the same meter, see Bibl. III c, 1823, 1827, 1837, and for one by Keble in the *Nativity* stanza, III D, 1827.

[2] See, for example, Spenser's sonnets (in Van der Noot's *Theatre*, 1569) and his iambics and hexameters (in the letters to Harvey); Sidney's "If mine eyes can speake " (in *Arcadia*, 1590, book i); Barnabe Barnes's elegy 21 and odes 18 and 20 (in *Parthenophil and Parthenophe*, 1593); Thomas Campion's *English Sapphic*, "Rose-checked Laura, come," and "Just beguiler" (in *Observations in the Art of English Poesie*, 1602); "A. W. 's" sapphics, phaleuciacks, epigram, and hexameters (in Francis Davison's *Poetical Rhapsody*, 1602).

[3] For these two, see Bibl. III c, *c.* 1701–20 w.

four of Horace's epistles into blank verse,[1] there can be little question as to how he came to discard rime in translating lyrics.[2]

A number of the opponents of "jingle" were, as we have seen, in favor of banishing it from all poetry,[3] but between Say's day and that of the Wartons they did nothing towards executing their purpose. Nor is there any reason to believe that the Wartons, Collins, and their followers felt any hostility to rime (which they used in nearly all their poems), or that they adopted the measure of Milton's translation except as an experiment in a new meter. Richard West, reacting against the free paraphrases of Dryden, Congreve, and Cowley, and "back'd by Milton's authority," was "entirely for a close translation" of Horace's odes;[4] but he said nothing against rime. Blake attacked it in the preface to *Jerusalem*, but used it in all his short pieces except the first seven of his earliest volume (1783). Nor did the movement against rime make much headway until 1790, when Frank Sayers published his *Dramatic Sketches of Northern Mythology*, a collection of short, superficial, sentimental pieces abounding in unrimed choral odes with lines of varying length. During the following year Sayers imitated the subject, meter, and contents of the *Ode to Evening* in his *Ode to Morning* and his *Ode to Night;* and two years later, in the course of a brief essay "Of English Metres" (a survey of earlier unrimed measures aside from blank verse), he remarked, "The measure used by Milton in his translation from Horace has been well received: it is adopted by Collins in his Ode to Evening, and by other modern poets, with success." [5]

The *Dramatic Sketches* was "the first book" that Southey "was ever master of money enough to order at a country bookseller's." [6] The volume made a profound impression on the young bard, who at that time had no decided poetic character of his own and was unusually susceptible to the influence of others, following one poet or group of poets after another in rapid succession. The principal result of the *Sketches* was seen a few years later in the strange mythology

---

[1] See above, p. 90, and below, pp. 566–7.

[2] Isaac Watts's *Day of Judgment* "attempted in English Sapphick" (*Horae Lyricae*, 1706, pp. 40–42), and the Rev. Dr. Shipley's lines written in 1738, *To the Memory of a Gentleman* ("Dodsley's Miscellany," 1758, v. 239–40), are unrimed odes that show no influence from Milton.

[3] See above, pp. 51–2.

[4] Letter to Walpole, June 1, 1736 (*Correspondence of Gray, Walpole*, etc., i. 79). An anonymous *Ode to Virtue*, "in blank lyric verse," appeared in 1767 (see *Crit. Rev.*, xxiv. 316).

[5] *Disquisitions Metaphysical and Literary* (1793), 132.

[6] Southey to William Taylor, Jan. 23, 1803 (J. W. Robberds, *Memoir of Taylor*, 1843, i. 447).

and the unrimed lines of different length which characterize *Thalaba* (1801); but between 1793 and 1799 Sayers's precepts and practice, strengthened by the influence of Collins,[1] led to Southey's composing some sixteen lyrics without rime. Three of these are in the meter of Milton's translation, and eight others employ slight variations of it.[2] Southey, therefore, made more use of the measure than did any other poet. Yet nothing that he wrote in it belongs — with Campion's "Rose-cheeked Laura," Collins's *Ode to Evening*, Lamb's *Old Familiar Faces*, Tennyson's "Tears, idle tears," the *Philomela* and some other pieces of Matthew Arnold, and Swinburne's *Sapphics* — among the few successful unrimed lyrics in English.

THE NATIVITY

In sharp contrast with the vogue enjoyed by the translation from Horace is the neglect which has befallen the *Nativity* ode. For, splendid as this stanza is and masterly as is Milton's handling of it, the meter has made almost no impress on English verse. Perhaps our writers, who do not take kindly to elaborate stanzas that are not of their own invention, have not cared to use this one; but more probably the idea of doing so has never occurred to most of them. No doubt if some one had led the way, if Gray, for instance, had adopted the meter in his *Elegy* or Collins in his *Ode to Evening*, it would have had a wide vogue. To be sure, both Gray and Collins did employ variations of it, but not in a way that would be likely to give it popularity. For the eight lines that Gray wrote in the *Nativity* meter he put into the least inspired of all his pieces, the *Ode for Music* (1769);[3] and Collins changed the stanza so much by omitting its last two lines that, even if his *Ode to Simplicity* (1746) had at-

---

[1] "Every one who has an ear for metre and a heart for poetry," Southey wrote in the preface to the 1837 edition of his works, "must have felt how perfectly the metre of Collins's *Ode to Evening* is in accordance with the imagery and the feeling." Although he thought Milton's translation "uncouth . . . in syntax as well as sound, and bearing no other resemblance to the Latin measure, which it was designed to imitate, than that it consists of two long and two short lines," he declared that it "presents the only example of a rhymeless stanza which can fairly be said to have become naturalized in our language" (review of Sayers's works, *Quart. Rev.*, 1827, xxxv. 211). For this reference, and for other matters relating to Southey's obligation to Sayers, I am indebted to William Haller's *Early Life of Southey* (N. Y., 1917), 77–86.

[2] See Bibl. III c, 1793–9 w. The other five are the *Battle of Pultowa*, the *Translation of a Greek Ode on Astronomy*, *The Huron's Address to the Dead*, *The Peruvian's Dirge over the Body of his Father*, *The Old Chikkasah to his Grandson*. Southey also wrote one unrimed poem in dactylics and one in sapphics. Thelwall printed eleven unrimed sapphics in his *Poetical Recreations*.

[3] Lines 27–34, which Milton speaks (see p. 459 above). Gray changed the seventh line of the *Nativity* stanza from tetrameter to pentameter.

tracted more attention, it would hardly have affected the vogue of
Milton's poem. As might be expected, Collins handled his measure
admirably, and in a poem to Simplicity he not unnaturally simplified
the somewhat complex meter of the *Nativity* ode. An additional
reason for thinking that he had the earlier poem in mind is his use of
four phrases suggested by the 1645 volume, one of which occurs in
the last of these lines:

> By all the honey'd store
> On Hybla's thymy shore,
> By all her blooms, and mingled murmurs dear,
> By her whose lovelorn woe
> In ev'ning musings slow
> Sooth'd sweetly sad Electra's poet's ear.[1]

In view of the close friendship between Collins and Joseph Warton
that led to their exchanging copies of their odes six months before
publication, there is undoubtedly a direct connection between the
Ode to Simplicity and Warton's odes *To Superstition* and *To a Gentleman upon his Travels thro' Italy.* Warton used the same meter as his
friend, except that his first, second, fourth, and fifth lines are tetrameter, instead of trimeter as in Collins and Milton, a change for the
worse. There can be little question as to the source of this passage:

> So by the Magi hail'd from far,
> When PHOEBUS mounts his early car,
> The shrieking ghosts to their dark charnels flock;
> The full-gorg'd wolves retreat, no more
> The prowling lionesses roar,
> But hasten with their prey to some deep-cavern'd rock.[2]

But it was not Collins, Warton, or Gray who first made use of
Milton's Christmas hymn. Robert Baron had taken several expressions from it as early as 1647;[3] the laureate Nahum Tate had paraphrased ten lines to make up his two stanzas *On Snow fall'n in
Autumn, and dissolv'd by the Sun;*[4] and about 1730 Samuel Say had

---

[1] Compare this with *Comus*, 526, and with line 13 of Milton's sonnet, "Captain, or
Colonel," etc.; also compare "trailing pall . . . decent maid In Attic robe" (lines 9–11)
with *Penseroso*, 97–8, 34–7, and "the meeting soul" (line 48) with *Allegro*, 138.

[2] *To Superstition*, stanza v (cf. *Nativity*, 22–3, 176–8, 232–4). The idea of the *Ode to
Superstition* is much the same as that of the *Nativity*, 173–236; and lines 13–14 mention
the sacrifice of infants to Moloch (cf. *Nativity*, 205–12).

[3] On Baron's plagiarism of Milton, see above, pp. 427–8. Bishop Thomas Ken's
verses *On the Nativity* (*Works*, 1721, i. 31–7), which he wrote before 1711, may owe
something to Milton's.

> [4] *Nature* now stript of all her *Summer-Dress*,
> And modestly surmizing, 'twere unmeet
> For each rude Eye to view her *Nakedness*;
> Around her *bare Limbs* wraps this *Snowy Sheet*.

used variations of it in his irregular metrical paraphrase of the ninety-seventh psalm. Say's tenth stanza, a very free rendering of "Zion heard and was glad," is the one that owes most to the *Nativity:*

> Thus, while Substantial Darkness shrouds
> The *Chamian* Heaven in Solid Clouds,
> And with black Wings o'er frighted *Mizraim* broods;
> In *Goshen's* favour'd Land
> Thy Chosen *Israel* stand,
> Enjoy the Sun's enlivening Ray,
> And wonder what Strange Night Usurps th' *Ægyptian* Day![1]

One anonymous eighteenth-century writer, besides copying whole lines from Milton's ode, adopted its stanza without change. His poem, *The Abolition of Catholicism*, "written on learning the arrival of the French at Rome in 1798," has passages as flagrantly Miltonic as this:

> Long absent Justice then
> Shall back return to men,
> With meas'ring look her scales and compass minding;
> And Peace, with myrtle wand,
> Shall take no fleeting stand,
> From either foot her turtle-wings unbinding;
> And orb a rainbow through the azure sky,
> In token that the tempest-clouds are now gone by.[2]

What seems to be a variation of the *Nativity* measure occurs in one of the splendid choruses of Shelley's *Hellas* (1822). The similarity is seen most clearly in these lines, the idea and cadence no less than the meter of which may be derived from Milton's poem:

> So fleet, so faint, so fair,
> The Powers of earth and air
> Fled from the folding-star of Bethlehem:
> Apollo, Pan, and Love,
> And even Olympian Jove
> Grew weak, for killing Truth had glared on them.[3]

> The wanton *Sun* the slight-wrought Shroud removes,
> T'embrace the naked Dame, whose fertile Womb
> Admits the lusty *Paramour's* warm Love's,
> And is made *big* with the fair *Spring* to come

(*Poems*, 1677, pp. 88–9; cf. *Nativity*, 32–42). This borrowing was called to my attention by Mr. B. C. Clough.

[1] Note also, in stanza vii, the meter and the reference to Dagon (cf. *Nativity*, 199), who is not mentioned in the psalm.

[2] *Mo. Mag.*, v. 368 (cf. *Nativity*, 141–3, 45–52). Compare also the first, second, and last stanzas with *Nativity*, 183, 189–96, 202, 214; and note "tears such as angels weep" (line 20, from *P. L.*, i. 620).

[3] Lines 229–34; cf. *Nativity*, 173–228, particularly 221–8.

None of the uncertainty that may be felt in regard to the source of Shelley's meter exists in the case of Jean Ingelow's *Song for the Night of Christ's Resurrection* (1867), for this is frankly labelled "a humble imitation" and is prefaced by a quotation from the *Nativity*. Moreover, Milton not only furnishes the stanza and suggests the subject and title, but contributes a simile as well as a few words and rimes.[1] His influence is felt most strongly in these lines:

> Or from the Morians' land
> See worshipped Nilus bland,
> Taking the silver road he gave the world,
> To wet his ancient shrine
> With waters held divine,
> And touch his temple steps with wavelets curled,
> And list, ere darkness change to gray,
> Old minstrel-throated Memnon chanting in the day.

Austin Dobson's *Miltonic Exercise*, "written, by request, for the celebration at Christ's College, Cambridge, July 10, 1908," was too obviously made to order to be significant, though it is interesting to see that Mr. Dobson employed the Collins-Warton adaptation of the *Nativity* meter.[2] The most convincing tribute to the beauty of the original measure is to be found in the use of it by so great a master of prosody and so fertile an inventor of new verse-forms as Swinburne. In his famous *Poems and Ballads* (first series, 1866) are some two hundred lines, *To Victor Hugo*, which employ it but change the last line from hexameter to pentameter. Here is one of the many admirable stanzas:

> Sunbeams and bays before
> Our master's servants wore,
> For these Apollo left in all men's lands;
> But far from these ere now
> And watched with jealous brow
> Lay the blind lightnings shut between God's hands,
> And only loosed on slaves and kings
> The terror of the tempest of their wings.

The excellence of this particular last line may seem to justify Swinburne's change, but a reading of the entire piece leads rather to the opposite conclusion; for he loses the crescendo at the close of the

---

[1] Some of the words are "eyn" (line 105, cf. *Nativity*, 223), "curtained" (114, of the setting moon, cf. *Nativity*, 229–30, of the rising sun), "oceán," riming with "began" (142, cf. *Nativity*, 66). The simile in next to the last stanza is like that in Milton's next to the last, besides beginning in the same way; and the first two lines of the last stanza of each poem have the same rimes, as well as similar ideas and phraseology.

[2] It is presumably by chance that the second stanza of Siegfried Sassoon's *Before the Battle* (*Old Huntsman*, N. Y., 1920, p. 75) is in the *Nativity* meter, with the seventh line omitted.

stanza, as well as the subtle "proportion of the rise in line-length from 6,10 to 8,12." [1] The poet himself could not have been satisfied with his innovation, for when he returned to the stanza three years later, in his *Eve of Revolution*,[2] he kept Milton's final hexameter. In this poem, however, he introduced another change by prefixing eight pentameter lines riming *a b a b a b a b*. Only a master is competent to criticize Swinburne's meters; but my own feeling is that the eight lines of uniform length which rime alternately do not combine happily with the eight of varying length — four of them very short — which rime irregularly. Most of the superb things in the poem, including the best of the twenty-seven stirring lines in praise of Milton,[3] seem to me to be in the non-Miltonic meter. Swinburne, however, liked the stanza well enough to use it twice again, — in the long *Song for the Centenary of Landor*, and in the *New-Year Ode to Victor Hugo*, where the lines in the *Nativity* measure contain some excellent poetry.

In his last book of poems, *A Channel Passage*, he tried still another variation, dropping the initial unaccented syllable in each of the first two lines and inserting after the fifth another line of three feet.[4] But this experiment seems to have pleased him no better, for in the same volume he twice returned to the original stanza,[5] which he had used three times previously.[6] As might be expected, the poems he wrote in the measure or in variations of it are free from the stiffness that mars some of Milton's lines, but they tend to be wordy and invertebrate, to gain suppleness and fluidity by sacrificing the dignity, the concentrated power, and the sonorous splendor of the earlier master. Yet does not the fact that he made use of some form of the meter no fewer than eleven times,[7] beginning with his first volume of poems and ending only with his last, — does not this fact constitute a rare tribute from one of the greatest singers of a great century to the prosodic genius of a college youth and to the Christmas hymn he composed nearly two hundred and fifty winters before?

[1] Saintsbury, *English Prosody*, ii. 210.

[2] Written in 1869; published in *Songs before Sunrise*, 1871.

[3] See stanzas 14–16. These lines make it practically certain that Swinburne derived his stanza from Milton. I have to thank Mr. Herbert Cory, recently assistant-professor of English at the University of California, for calling my attention, nearly fifteen years ago, to the indebtedness of two of these poems to the *Nativity* ode.

[4] In *High Oaks*, and its continuation, *Barking Hall*.

[5] In *Astræa Victrix*, and in section v of *Altar of Righteousness*.

[6] In *Blessed among Women* and *Insurrection in Candia* (*Songs before Sunrise*, 1871), and in the epodes in *Birthday of Victor Hugo* (*Songs of the Springtides*, 1880).

[7] See Bibl. III D, below.

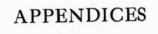

APPENDICES

APPENDICES

APPENDIX A

PARALLEL PASSAGES SHOWING EXPRESSIONS PROBABLY BORROWED FROM MILTON

POPE [1]

The birds, on ev'ry bloomy spray.	Pastorals, i. 23.
O Nightingale, that on yon bloomy spray.	*Nightingale sonnet, 1.*
Here the bright crocus and blue vi'let glow.	Ib. i. 31.
And glowing violets.	Odyssey, v. 94.
The glowing violet.	*Lycidas, 145.*
And ev'ry plant that drinks the morning dew.	Pastorals, ii. 32.
And every herb that sips the dew.	*Penseroso, 172.*
Rough satyrs dance.	Ib. ii. 50.
Rough Satyrs danced.	*Lycidas, 34.*
While lab'ring oxen, spent with toil and heat,	
In their loose traces from the field retreat.	Ib. iii. 61–2.
What time the labour'd ox	
In his loose traces from the furrow came.	*Comus, 291–2.*
Nor rivers winding through the vales below,	
So sweetly warble, or so smoothly flow.	Ib. iv. 3–4.
Fountains, and ye that warble, as ye flow.	*P. L. v. 195.*
In some still ev'ning, when the whisp'ring breeze	
Pants on the leaves, and dies upon the trees.	Ib. iv. 79–80.
Or usher'd with a shower still,	
When the gust hath blown his fill,	
Ending on the rustling leaves.	*Penseroso, 127–9.*
Crowned with tufted trees.	Windsor Forest, 27.
To happy Convents, bosom'd deep in vines.	Dunciad, iv. 301.
The tufted trees.	Odyssey, v. 513.
And spiry tops, the tufted trees above,	
Of Circe's palace bosom'd in the grove.	Odyssey, x. 175–6.
Towers and battlements it sees	
Bosom'd high in tufted trees.	*Allegro, 77–8.*
The weeping amber, or the balmy tree.	Windsor Forest, 30.
Groves whose rich trees wept odorous gums and balm.	*P. L. iv. 248.*
The yellow carp, in scales bedropped with gold.	Ib. 144.
Shew to the sun their waved coats dropt with gold. [Of fish.]	*P. L. vii 406.*

[1] Most of these parallels are selected from those given in the Elwin-Courthope edition of Pope, Gilbert Wakefield's edition of Pope's Homer, and Mary Leather's article, *Pope as a Student of Milton*, in *Englische Studien*, xxv. 398–410; some I have myself noted. None of the *Iliad* or *Odyssey* parallels can be explained by similarities between Homer and Milton; most of the passages, indeed, owe nothing to Homer but are original with Pope.

The gulphy Lee his sedgy tresses rears;
And sullen Mole, that hides his diving flood.　　Windsor Forest, 346–7.
Or gulfy Dun . . .
Or sullen Mole, that runneth underneath,
*　. . . . or of sedgy Lea.*　　*Vacation Exercise, 92–7.*

Or those green isles, where headlong Titan steeps
His hissing axle in th' Atlantic deeps.　　Ib. 387–8 (original reading).
And the gilded car of day
His glowing axle doth allay
In the steep Atlantic stream.　　*Comus, 95–7.*

Mean time the vig'rous dancers beat the ground.　　January and May, 353.
Come, knit hands, and beat the ground
In a light fantastic round.　　*Comus, 143–4.*

The dapper elves their moon-light sports pursue.　　Ib. 460.
The fairies . . . So featly tripped.　　Ib. 618–20.
Trip the pert faeries and the dapper elves.　　*Comus, 118.*

Full oft I drain'd the spicy nut-brown bowl.　　Wife of Bath, 214.
Then to the spicy nut-brown ale.　　*Allegro, 100.*

In air self-balanced hung the globe below.　　Temple of Fame, 13.
Let earth unbalanced from her orbit fly.　　Essay on Man, i. 251.
And Earth, self-balanced, on her centre hung.　　*P. L. vii. 242.*

On Doric pillars of white marble reared,
Crowned with an architrave of antique mold,
And sculpture rising on the roughened gold.　　Temple of Fame, 76–8.
With pomp of various architrave o'erlay'd.　　Odyssey, xxi. 46.
Doric pillars overlaid
With golden architrave; nor did there want
Cornice or frieze, with bossy sculptures graven.　　*P. L. i. 714–16.*

The growing tow'rs like exhalations rise.　　Temple of Fame, 91.
A fabric huge　Rose like an exhalation.　　*P. L. i. 710–11.*

Barbaric gold.　　Ib. 94.
Barbaric pearl and gold.　　*P. L. ii. 4.*

Wide vaults appear, and roofs of fretted gold.　　Ib. 138.
The roof was fretted gold.　　*P. L. i. 717.*

Ere warning Phoebus touched his trembling ears.　　Essay on Criticism, 131 (variant).
Phoebus replied, and touch'd my trembling ears.　　*Lycidas, 77.*

Amaranthine bow'rs.　　St. Cecilia, 76.
Blissful bowers　Of amaranthine shade.　　*P. L. xi. 77–8.*
(Of heaven in each case.)

And those love-darting eyes must roll no more.　　Elegy to an Unfortunate Lady, 34.
Love-darting eyes, or tresses like the morn.　　*Comus, 753.*

He from thick films shall purge the visual ray.　　Messiah, 39.
His visual ball.　　Odyssey, ix. 454.
Sharpen'd his visual ray.　　*P. L. iii. 620; cf. xi. 415.*
(The first case was pointed out by Pope.)

He wipes the tears for ever from our eyes.　　Messiah (1st ed.), 46.
All tears are wiped for ever from all eyes.　　Epilogue to Satires, i. 103.
And wipe the tears for ever from his eyes.　　*Lycidas, 181.*

In adamantine chains shall Death be bound.	Messiah, 47.
Arm'd in adamantine chains.	Song by Person of Quality, 18.
In War and Discord's adamantine chain.	Iliad, xiii. 452.
In adamantine chains.	*P. L. i. 48.*

For spirits, freed from mortal laws, with ease
Assume what sexes and what shapes they please.   Rape of the Lock, i. 69–70.
For Spirits, when they please,
Can either sex assume, or both . . .
        . . . . in what shape they choose.   *P. L. i. 423–8.*

Dipped in the richest tincture of the skies.   Ib. ii. 65.
And colours dipt in heaven . . .
Sky-tinctured grain.   *P. L. v. 283–5.*

Four knaves in garbs succinct.   Ib. iii. 41.
A Priest succinct in amice white.   Dunciad, iv. 549.
His vest succinct then girding round his waist.   Odyssey, xiv. 83.
        Aside they lay
Their garments, and succinct the victims slay.   Odyssey, xvii. 199–200.
His habit fit for speed succinct.   *P. L. iii. 643.*

Fate urged the shears, and cut the sylph in twain,
(But airy substance soon unites again).   Rape of the Lock, iii. 151–2.
    ("See Milton, lib. vi. 330, of Satan cut asunder by the Angel Michael": Pope's note.)

Snakes on rolling spires.   Ib. iv. 43.
[Satan] *erect Amidst his circling spires.*   *P. L. ix. 501–2.*

        While Time, with still career,
Wafts on his gentle wing his eightieth year.   Imitation of Martial, 1–2.
This subtle thief of life, this paltry time.   Horace's Epistles, II. ii. 76.
To whom Time bears me on his rapid wing.   Dunciad, iv. 6.
How soon hath Time, the subtle thief of youth,
Stolen on his wing my three-and-twentieth year! . . .
Toward which Time leads me.   Sonnet, *"How soon hath Time,"* 1–2, 12.

Ye grots and caverns, shagged with horrid thorn!   Eloisa to Abelard, 20.
So the rough rock had shagg'd Ulysses' hands.   Odyssey, v. 553.
By grots and caverns shagg'd with horrid shades.   *Comus, 429.*

I have not yet forgot myself to stone.   Eloisa to Abelard, 24.
Forget thyself to marble.   *Penseroso, 42.*

And the dim windows shed a solemn light.   Ib. 144.
And storied windows richly dight,
Casting a dim religious light.   *Penseroso, 159–60.*
        (Of a church in each case.)

But o'er the twilight groves.   Ib. 163.
Arched walks of twilight groves.   *Penseroso, 133.*

And wings of seraphs shed divine perfumes.   Ib. 218.
And shook his plumes, that heavenly fragrance fill'd
The circuit wide. [Said of an angel.]   *P. L. v. 286–7.*

Low-brow'd rocks hang nodding o'er the deeps.   Ib. 244.
Under ebon shades and low-brow'd rocks.   *Allegro, 8.*

Oblivion of low-thoughted care.   Ib. 298.
With low-thoughted care.   *Comus, 6.*

The chequer'd shade. — To Mr. Gay, 7.
In the chequer'd shade. — Dunciad, iv. 125.
In the chequer'd shade. — *Allegro, 96.*

Or in the golden cowslip's velvet head. — Lamentation of Glumdalclitch, 48.
O'er the cowslip's velvet head. — *Comus, 898.*

But vindicate the ways of God to man. — Essay on Man, i. 16.
And justify the ways of God to men. — *P. L. i. 26.*

Yonder argent fields above. [Of the firmament.] — Ib. i. 41.
Those argent fields. [Of the moon.] — *P. L. iii. 460.*

Favoured man by touch ethereal slain. — Ib. iii. 68.
With touch ethereal of Heaven's fiery rod. — *Samson, 549.*

Next his grim idol smeared with human blood. — Ib. iii. 266.
Dropping with Infants' blood, and Mothers' tears. — Dunciad, iv. 142.
First, Moloch, horrid king, besmear'd with blood
Of human sacrifice, and parents' tears . . .
Their children's cries unheard, that pass'd through fire
To his grim idol. — *P. L. i. 392-6.*
(The second case was pointed out by Pope.)

Ye little stars! hide your diminish'd rays. — Moral Essays, iii. 282.
All the stars   Hide their diminish'd heads. — *P. L. iv. 34-5.*

And bring all Paradise before your eye. — Ib. iv. 148.
And bring all Heaven before mine eyes. — *Penseroso, 166.*

To make men happy, and to keep them so. — Horace's Epistles, I. vi. 2.
What makes a nation happy, and keeps it so. — *P. R. iv. 362.*

To see themselves fall endlong into beasts. — Satires of Donne, iv. 167.
And downward fell into a grovelling swine. — *Comus, 53.*
(Of Circe's guests in each case.)

To wholesome solitude, the nurse of sense:
Where Contemplation prunes her ruffled wings. — Ib. iv. 185-6.
And Wisdom's self
Oft seeks to sweet retired solitude,
Where, with her best nurse, Contemplation,
She plumes her feathers, and lets grow her wings,
That . . . Were all-to ruffled. — *Comus, 375-80.*

And opes the temple of Eternity. — Epilogue to Satires, ii. 235.
That opes the palace of Eternity. — *Comus, 14.*

Daughter of Chaos and eternal Night. — Dunciad, i. 12.
Dread Chaos, and eternal Night. — Ib. iv. 2.
I sung of Chaos and eternal Night. — *P. L. iii. 18.*

Here pleas'd behold her mighty wings outspread. — Ib. i. 27.
With mighty wings outspread. — *P. L. i. 20.*

In clouded Majesty here Dulness shone. — Ib. i. 45.
The Moon,   Rising in clouded majesty. — *P. L. iv. 606-7.*
(Pointed out by Pope.)

He roll'd his eyes that witness'd huge dismay. — Ib. (1st ed.), i. 105.
Round he throws his baleful eyes,
That witness'd huge affliction and dismay. — *P. L. i. 56-7.*

High on a gorgeous seat, that far out-shone
Henley's gilt tub, or Fleckno's Irish throne,
Or that where on her Curls the Public pours,
All-bounteous, fragrant Grains and Golden show'rs,
Great Cibber sate.   Dunciad, ii. 1-5.
High on a throne, with stars of silver grac'd.   Iliad, xviii. 457.
High on a throne the king each stranger plac'd. Odyssey, xv. 147.
High on a throne of royal state, which far
Outshone the wealth of Ormus and of Ind,
Or where the gorgeous East with richest hand
Showers on her kings barbaric pearl and gold,
Satan exalted sat.   *P. L. ii. 1-5.*

So from the Sun's broad beam in shallow urns
Heav'n's twinkling Sparks draw light, and point their horns.   Dunciad, ii. 11-12.
Hither [to the sun], *as to their fountain, other stars*
Repairing, in their golden urns draw light,
And hence the morning planet gilds her horns.   *P. L. vii. 364-6.*

On feet and wings, and flies, and wades, and hops;
So lab'ring on, with shoulders, hands, and head.   Ib. ii. 64-5.
O'er hills, o'er dales, o'er crags, o'er rocks they go.   Iliad, xxiii. 141.
O'er bog or steep, through strait, rough, dense, or rare,
With head, hands, wings, or feet, pursues his way,
And swims, or sinks, or wades, or creeps, or flies.   *P. L. ii. 948-50.*
(The first case was pointed out by Pope.)

With arms expanded Bernard rows his state.   Dunciad, ii. 67.
Rows Her state with oary feet. [Of a swan.]   *P. L. vii. 439-40.*
(Pointed out by Pope.)

His papers light fly diverse, tost in air.   Ib. ii. 114.
The scatter'd Trojan bands   Fly diverse.   Iliad, xiv. 166-7; cf. xxi. 4.
Rolls diverse.   Odyssey, v. 469.
Then both [Sin and Death] . . .
Flew diverse . . . Tost up and down.   *P. L. x. 282-7; cf. iv. 234.*

In naked majesty Oldmixon stands.   Dunciad, ii. 283.
In naked majesty seem'd lords of all.   *P. L. iv. 290.*

Shaking the horrors of his sable brows.   Ib. ii. 327.
                    The wood,
Whose shady horrours on a rising brow
Wav'd high, and frown'd.   Odyssey, v. 613-15.
          This drear wood,
The nodding horror of whose shady brows.   *Comus, 37-8.*

As under seas Alpheus' secret sluice
Bears Pisa's off'rings to his Arethuse.   Dunciad, ii. 341-2.
Divine Alpheus, who, by secret sluice,
Stole under seas to meet his Arethuse.   *Arcades, 30-31.*

Smit with love of Poesy and Prate.   Ib. ii. 382.
Smit with the love of Sister Arts.   Epistle to Jervas, 13.
Smit with love of honourable deeds.   Iliad, i. 354.
Smit with the love of sacred song.   *P. L. iii. 29.*
(The first case was pointed out by Pope.)

Why should I sing, what bards the nightly Muse
Did slumb'ring visit?   Dunciad, ii. 421-2.
Of my celestial patroness, who deigns
Her nightly visitation unimplored,
And dictates to me slumbering.   *P. L. ix. 21-3.*

Where Brown and Mears unbar the gates of Light.   Ib. iii. 28.
Unbarr'd the gates of light.   *P. L. vi. 4.*
                (Pointed out by Pope.)

Behold the wonders of th' oblivious Lake.   Ib. iii. 44.
The oblivious pool.   *P. L. i. 266.*

For this our Queen unfolds to vision true
Thy mental eye, for thou hast much to view.   Ib. iii. 61-2.
                (Pointed out by Pope.[1])

Booth in his cloudy tabernacle shrin'd.   Ib. iii. 267.
She in a cloudy tabernacle   Sojourn'd.   *P. L. vii. 248-9.*

Of darkness visible so much be lent.   Ib. iv. 3.
No light, but rather darkness visible.   *P. L. i. 63.*

He, kingly, did but nod.   Ib. iv. 207.
He kingly from his state   Inclined not.   *P. L. xi. 249-50.*
                (Pointed out by Pope.)

It fled, I follow'd; now in hope, now pain;
It stopt, I stopt; it mov'd, I mov'd again.   Ib. iv. 427-8.
                I started back,
It started back; but pleased I soon return'd,
Pleased it return'd as soon.   *P. L. iv. 462-4.*
                (Pointed out by Pope.)

Let others creep by timid steps, and slow.   Ib. iv. 465.
Now far the last, with pensive pace and slow.   Odyssey, ix. 531.
Eurylochus, with pensive steps and slow.   Odyssey, x. 286.
Pensive and slow . . . The King arose.   Odyssey, xiii. 235-6.
They, hand in hand, with wandering steps and slow. *P. L. xii. 648.*
Satan had journey'd on, pensive and slow.   *P. L. iv. 173.*

At one bound o'erleaping all his laws.   Dunciad, iv. 477.
At one slight bound high overleap'd all bound.   *P. L. iv. 181.*

In amice white.   Ib. iv. 549.
In amice gray.   *P. R. iv. 427.*

Hurl'd headlong downward from th' etherial height. Iliad, i. 761.
And hurl them flaming, headlong to the ground.   Ib. viii. 495.
Hurl'd headlong flaming from the ethereal sky.   *P. L. i. 45.*

---

[1] Pope's note: "This has a resemblance to that passage in Milton, book xi. where the Angel —

> To noble sights from Adam's eye remov'd
> The film; then purg'd with Euphrasie and Rue
> The visual nerve — *For he had much to see.*

There is a general allusion in what follows to that whole episode." To quote from the arguments of the two poems, Settle "takes" Cibber "to a Mount of Vision, from whence he shows him the past triumphs of the Empire of Dulness, then the present, and lastly the future"; just as the angel leads Adam "up to a high hill" and "sets before him in vision what shall happen till the Flood."

From rank to rank she darts her ardent eyes.   Ib. ii. 525.
Thro' the thick files he darts his searching eyes.   Ib. iv. 235.
Thro' all the war   He darts his anxious eye.   Ib. xvii. 90-91.
He through the armed files   Darts his experienced eye.   *P. L. i. 567-8.*

Thick as autumnal leaves.   Ib. ii. 970.
Thick as autumnal leaves.   *P. L. i. 302.*

And Sangar's stream ran purple with their blood.   Ib. iii. 250.
While smooth Adonis from his native rock
Ran purple to the sea, supposed with blood.   *P. L. i. 450-51.*

He shook his hoary locks, and thus replied.   Ib. iv. 369.
The lord of thunders view'd, and stern bespoke.   Ib. v. 1093.
He shook his mitred locks, and stern bespake.   *Lycidas, 112.*

Thus they in heav'n.   Ib. v. 523.
Thus they in Heaven.   *P. L. iii. 416.*

[Mars] shakes a spear that casts a dreadful light.   Ib. v. 729.
[Death] *shook a dreadful dart.*   *P. L. ii. 672.*

Involve in clouds th' eternal gates of day.   Ib. v. 932.
Within thick clouds and dark tenfold involved.   *P. R. i. 41.*

Earth trembled as he strode.   Ib. vii. 256.
Hell trembled as he strode.   *P. L. ii. 676.*

Slow from his seat the rev'rend Priam rose:
His godlike aspect deep attention drew.   Ib. vii. 441-2.
With grave   Aspect he rose. . . . his look
Drew audience and attention still as night.   *P. L. ii. 300-308.*

As deep beneath th' infernal centre hurl'd,
As from that centre to th' ethereal world.   Ib. viii. 19-20.
As far removed from God and light of Heaven
As from the centre thrice to the utmost pole.   *P. L. i. 73-4.*
(Pointed out by Pope.)

And smil'd superiour on his best-belov'd.   Ib. viii. 48.
Smiling with superiour love.   Ib. xiv. 387.
Smiled with superior love.   *P. L. iv. 499.*
(A reference in each case to Jupiter's smiling on Juno or Minerva.)

Their strength he withers.   Ib. viii. 96.
That wither'd all their hearts.   Odyssey, xxii. 40.
That wither'd all their strength.   *P. L. vi. 850.*

Words, mix'd with sighs, thus bursting from his breast.   Iliad, ix. 22.
Words interwove with sighs found out their way.   *P. L. i. 621.*

And sweat laborious days.   Ib. ix. 431.
And live laborious days.   *Lycidas, 72.*

O friend! I hear some step of hostile feet,
Moving this way, or hast'ning to the fleet.   Ib. x. 405-6.
O friends, I hear the tread of nimble feet
Hasting this way.   *P. L. iv. 866-7.*

Stands collected in himself.   Ib. xi. 511.
Stood in himself collected.   *P. L. ix. 673.*

O'er his broad back his moony shield he threw.   Iliad, xi. 672.
His shield (a broad circumference) he bore.   Ib. xxi. 688.
And now his shoulders bear the massy shield.   Odyssey, xxii. 138.
His ponderous shield,
Ethereal temper, massy, large, and round,
Behind him cast. The broad circumference
Hung on his shoulders like the moon.   P. L. i. 284-7.

And threats his foll'wers with retorted eye.   Iliad, xi. 695.
And with retorted scorn his back he turn'd.   P. L. v. 906.

Flam'd in the front of heav'n.   Ib. xi. 871.
Flames in the forehead of the morning sky.   Lycidas, 171.
(Of the rising sun in each case.)

Now rushing in, the furious chief appears,
Gloomy as Night!   Ib. xii. 553-4.
He on his impious foes right onward drove,
Gloomy as night.   P. L. vi. 831-2.

Th' enormous monsters, rolling o'er the deep,
Gambol around him on the wat'ry way;
And heavy whales in awkward measures play.   Ib. xiii. 43-5.
Wallowing unwieldy, enormous in their gait,
Tempest the ocean. There leviathan,
Hugest of living creatures, on the deep.   P. L. vii. 411-13.
Bears, tigers, ounces, pards, Gamboll'd before them.   P. L. iv. 344-5.

Or pine, fit mast for some great admiral.   Ib. xiii. 494.
Or pine (fit mast for some great admiral).   Ib. xvi. 592.
The tallest pine
Hewn on Norwegian hills, to be the mast
Of some great ammiral.   P. L. i. 292-4.

Convok'd to council, weigh the sum of things.   Ib. xiii. 930.
Consulting on the sum of things.   P. L. vi. 673.

A shout, that tore heav'n's concave, and above.   Ib. xiii. 1060.
A shout that tore Hell's concave, and beyond.   P. L. i. 542.

The Goddess with the charming eyes
Glows with celestial red, and thus replies:
"Is this a scene for love?"   Ib. xiv. 373-5.
The Angel, with a smile that glow'd
Celestial rosy red, love's proper hue, Answer'd   P. L. viii. 618-20.

Veil'd in a mist of fragrance him they found.   Ib. xv. 174.
Veil'd in a cloud of fragrance, where she stood.   P. L. ix. 425.

Else had my wrath, heav'n's thrones all shaking round,
Burn'd to the bottom of the seas profound.   Ib. xv. 252-3.
Eternal wrath
Burn'd after them to the bottomless pit.   P. L. vi. 865-6.
(Pope says, "Milton has a thought very like it in his fourth book," and quotes
P. L. iv. 991 ff.)

Dire was the hiss of darts.   Ib. xv. 356.
Dire was the noise
Of conflict; overhead the dismal hiss
Of fiery darts.   P. L. vi. 211-13.

In heav'nly panoply divinely bright.
In brazen panoply [armor].
In arms they stood   Of golden panoply.
He, in celestial panoply all arm'd
Of radiant Urim, work divinely wrought.

Ib. xvii. 233.
Odyssey, xxii. 130; cf. xxiv. 577.
P. L. vi. 526-7.

P. L. vi. 760-61.

And Amatheia with her amber hair.
Thy amber-dropping hair.

Iliad, xviii. 64.
Comus, 863.

[Vulcan's tripods] instinct with spirit roll'd.
Forth rush'd . . . The chariot of Paternal Deity . . .
Itself instinct with spirit.

Ib. xviii. 442.

P. L. vi. 749-52.

Frequent and full.   [Of an assembly.]
Frequent and thick.   [Of fence-rails.]
Frequent and full.   [Of an assembly.]

Ib. xix. 48, xxiii. 38; Odyssey, xxiv. 482.
Odyssey, xiv. 17.
P. L. i. 797.

Like the red star, that from his flaming hair
Shakes down diseases, pestilence and war.
            And like a comet burn'd,
That fires the length of Ophiuchus huge
In the arctic sky, and from his horrid hair
Shakes pestilence and war.

Iliad, xix. 412-13.

P. L. ii. 708-11.

Smooth-gliding without step.
Smooth-sliding without step.

Ib. xx. 375.
P. L. viii. 302.

The huge dolphin tempesting the main.
    Bended dolphins play; part, huge of bulk . . .
Tempest the ocean.

Ib. xxi. 30.

P. L. vii. 410-12.

The waves flow after, wheresoe'er he wheels,
And gather fast, and murmur at his heels.
So when a peasant.
[Iris] Meteorous the face of Ocean sweeps,
Refulgent gliding o'er the sable deeps.
Gliding meteorous, as evening mist
Risen from a river o'er the marish glides,
And gathers ground fast at the labourer's heel.

Ib. xxi. 287-9.

Ib. xxiv. 101-2.

P. L. xii. 629-31.

He said, and stood, collected in his might.
Collecting all his might, dilated stood.

Ib. xxi. 675.
P. L. iv. 986.

Waves in mazy errours lost.
Rolling . . . With mazy error.
            (Of a stream in each case.)

Ib. xxiii. 178.
P. L. iv. 238-9.

Embracing rigid with implicit hands.
And fast beneath, in woolly curls inwove,
There cling implicit.
And bush with frizzled hair implicit.

Ib. xxiii. 823.

Odyssey, ix. 513-14.
P. L. vii. 323.

Now Twilight veil'd the glaring face of Day,
And clad the dusky fields in sober gray.
And twilight gray her ev'ning shade extends.
Now came still Evening on, and Twilight gray
Had in her sober livery all things clad.

Iliad, xxiv. 427-8.
Odyssey, iii. 422.

P. L. iv. 598-9.

There stands a rock, high eminent and steep.
Amid them stood the Tree of Life,   High eminent.

Odyssey, iii. 374.
P. L. iv. 218-19.

And stoops incumbent on the rolling deep.
Aloft, incumbent on the dusky air.

Ib. v. 63.
P. L. i. 226.

Some close design, or turn of womankind.	Odyssey, v. 224.
To work in close design, by fraud or guile.	*P. L. i. 646.*
Join Thy pleaded reason.	Ib. v. 454-5.
Approv'd His pleaded reason.	Ib. vii. 307-8.
Approved My pleaded reason.	*P. L. viii. 509-10.*
Since wide he wander'd on the wat'ry waste.	Ib. v. 497.
Wandering that watery desert.	*P. L. xi. 779.*
Wander'd this barren waste.	*P. R. i. 354.*
Where on the flow'ry herb as soft he lay.	Ib. v. 597.
Soft on the flowery herb I found me laid.	*P. L. viii. 254.*
In thick shelter of innum'rous boughs.	Ib. v. 606.
In this close dungeon of innumerous boughs.	*Comus, 349.*
The cool translucent springs.	Ib. vii. 231, x. 434.
The pure, translucent springs.	Ib. xvii. 105.
Thames' translucent wave.	On his Grotto, 1.
Under the glassy, cool, translucent wave.	*Comus, 861.*
Ever-during shade.	Odyssey, vii. 306.
Ever-during dark.	*P. L. iii. 45; cf. vii. 206.*

(Of eyesight in each case.)

Nor, till oblique he [Phoebus] slop'd his ev'ning ray.	Ib. vii. 372.
Oft till the star that rose at evening bright	
* . . . . had sloped his westering wheel.*	*Lycidas, 30–31.*
With sweet, reluctant, amorous delay.	Ib. ix. 32.
And sweet, reluctant, amorous delay.	*P. L. iv. 311.*
In shelter thick of horrid shade reclin'd.	Ib. ix. 219.
In thick shelter of black shades imbower'd.	*Comus, 62.*
Dusk with horrid shades.	*P. R. i. 296.*
Our groans the rocks remurmur'd to the main.	Ib. x. 60.
Their moans The vales redoubled to the hills.	*Piemont sonnet, 8–9.*
As huge in length extended lay the beast.	Ib. x. 206.
So stretch'd out huge in length the Arch-Fiend lay.	*P. L. i. 209.*
Darkness cover'd o'er The face of things.	Ib. x. 210–11, xiv. 510–11.
[The moon] *Shadowy sets off the face of things.*	*P. L. v. 43; cf. vii. 636.*
No more was seen the human form divine.	Ib. x. 278.
Not to me returns . . . or human face divine.	*P. L. iii. 41–4.*

This said, and scornful turning from the shore	
My haughty step, I stalk'd the valley o'er.	Ib. x. 325–6.
So spoke the wretch; but shunning farther fray,	
Turn'd his proud step, and left them.	Ib. xvii. 304–5.
So saying, his proud step he scornful turn'd.	*P. L. iv. 536.*

On his bloomy face
Youth smil'd celestial, with each op'ning grace.   Ib. x. 331–2.

In his face
Youth smiled celestial, and to every limb
Suitable grace diffused.   *P. L. iii. 637–9.*

There seek the Theban Bard, depriv'd of sight;	
Within, irradiate with prophetic light.	Ib. x. 582–3.
So much the rather thou, celestial Light,	
Shine inward, and the mind through all her powers	
Irradiate. [Of the blind Milton.]	*P. L. iii. 51–3.*

Behold the gloomy grot! whose cool recess.	Ib. xiii. 395.
Umbrageous grots and caves Of cool recess.	*P. L. iv. 257-8.*
And tilting o'er the bay the vessels ride.	Ib. xiv. 289.
Tilting on the tides	
Prepar'd to launch the freighted vessel rides.	Ib. xv. 507-8.
The floating vessel . . . Rode tilting o'er the waves.	*P. L. xi. 745-7.*
The osier-fringed bank.	Ib. xiv. 533.
By the rushy-fringèd bank,	
Where grows the willow and the osier dank.	*Comus, 890-91.*
Her sloping hills the mantling vines adorn.	Ib. xv. 444.
Under a green mantling vine,	
That crawls along the side of yon small hill.	*Comus, 294-5.*
O'er which the mantling vine . . . creeps Luxuriant.	*P. L. iv. 258-60.*
The bold emprize.	Ib. xxi. 308.
And bold emprise.	*P. L. xi. 642; Comus, 610.*
And all was riot, noise, and wild uproar.	Ib. xxi. 390.
Confusion heard his voice, and wild uproar.	*P. L. iii. 710; cf. ii. 541.*
A voice of loud lament thro' all the main	
Was heard.	Ib. xxiv. 67-8.
The resounding shore,	
A voice of weeping heard and loud lament.	*Nativity, 182-3.*
Arise (or ye for ever fall) arise!	Ib. xxiv. 497.
Awake, arise, or be for ever fall'n!	*P. L. i. 330.*

THOMSON [1]

All involved in smoke.	Spring, 129.
Stench-involved.	Autumn, 1206.
And leave a singèd bottom all involved	
With stench and smoke.	*P. L. i. 236-7.*
(Of earthquakes in the last two cases.)	
The nodding verdure of its brow.	Spring, 229.
The nodding horror of whose shady brows.	*Comus, 38.*
(Of woods in each case.)	
The first fresh dawn then waked the gladdened race	
Of uncorrupted man, nor blushed to see	
The sluggard sleep beneath its sacred beam;	
For their light slumbers gently fumed away.	Ib. 242-5.
Now Morn, her rosy steps in the eastern clime	
Advancing, sow'd the earth with orient pearl,	
When Adam waked, so custom'd; for his sleep	
Was aery light, from pure digestion bred.	*P. L. v. 1-4.*

[1] Most of these parallels were collected before Mr. G. C. Macaulay's life of Thomson appeared, and a number of them are not in his list (pp. 141-5). I am indebted to him, however, for six of those given above; and I think, as he does, that "the winter evening's occupations [*Winter*, 424-655] are partly suggested by Milton, those of the student, who holds 'high converse with the mighty dead' by *Il Penseroso*, and those of the village and the city by *L'Allegro*" (p. 144), but it is hardly practicable to quote two hundred lines to prove it. I have taken nothing from Mr. J. E. Wells's article in *Modern Language Notes*, xxiv. 60-61, though perhaps I should have included "where cowslips hang The dewy head" (*Spring*, 448-9; cf. *Lycidas*, 147).

Fruits and blossoms blushed
In social sweetness on the self-same bough.   Spring, 321-2.
    Goodliest trees, loaden with fairest fruit,
Blossoms and fruits at once of golden hue.   *P. L. iv. 147-8.*

Come with those downcast eyes, sedate and sweet,
Those looks demure that deeply pierce the soul.   Ib. 485-6.
Come, pensive Nun, devout and pure,
Sober, stedfast, and demure . . .
And looks commercing with the skies,
Thy rapt soul sitting in thine eyes . . . till
With a sad leaden downward cast
Thou fix them on the earth as fast.   *Penseroso, 31-44.*

The winding vale its lavish stores,   Irriguous, spreads.   Ib. 494-5.
The irriguous vale.   Autumn, 751.
Some irriguous valley spread her store.   *P. L. iv. 255.*

    The stately-sailing swan
Gives out his snowy plumage to the gale,
And, arching proud his neck, with oary feet
Bears forward fierce.   Spring, 778-81.
The boat light-skimming stretched its oary wings.   Autumn, 129.
    The swan, with arched neck
Between her white wings mantling proudly, rows
Her state with oary feet.   *P. L. vii. 438-40.*

    Sportive lambs,
This way and that convolved in friskful glee.   Spring, 836-7.
[Bees] Convolved   and agonizing in the dust.   Autumn, 1183.
Satan . . . writhed him to and fro convolved.   *P. L. vi. 327-8.*

With woods o'erhung, and shagged with mossy rocks.   Spring, 910.
    Scenes,
Of horrid prospect, shag the trackless plain.   Winter, 280-81.
By grots and caverns shagg'd with horrid shades.   *Comus, 429.*

And villages embosomed soft in trees.   Spring, 954.
Ancient seats, with venerable oaks   Embosomed high.   Liberty, v. 52-3.
Towers and battlements it sees
Bosom'd high in tufted trees.   *Allegro, 77-8.*

The rosy-bosomed Spring.   Spring, 1010.
Spring . . . and the rosy-bosom'd Hours.   *Comus, 985-6.*

Beside the brink   Of haunted stream.   Summer, 11-12.
Did ever poet image aught so fair,
Dreaming in whispering groves by the hoarse brook?   Isaac Newton, 119-20.
Such sights as youthful poets dream
On summer eves by haunted stream.   *Allegro, 129-30.*

The meek-eyed morn appears, mother of dews,
At first faint-gleaming in the dappled east.   Summer, 47-8.
Sent down the meek-eyed Peace.   *Nativity, 46.*
Till the dappled dawn doth rise.   *Allegro, 44.*

Prime cheerer, Light!
Of all material beings first and best!
Efflux divine!   Nature's resplendent robe,
Without whose vesting beauty all were wrapt
In unessential gloom; and thou, O Sun! . . . in whom . . .
Shines out thy Maker! may I sing of thee?   Ib. 90-96.
How shall I then attempt to sing of Him
Who, Light Himself, in uncreated light
Invested deep, dwells awfully retired.   Ib. 175-7.
Hail, holy Light, offspring of Heaven first-born!
Or of the Eternal coeternal beam
May I express thee unblamed? since God is light,
And never but in unapproached light
Dwelt from eternity, dwelt then in thee,
Bright effluence of bright essence increate!   *P. L. iii. 1-6.*
Unessential Night.   *P. L. ii. 439.*

While, round thy beaming car,
High-seen, the Seasons lead, in sprightly dance
Harmonious knit, the rosy-fingered hours.   Ib. 120-22.
[The moon] Leads on the gentle hours.   Spring, 1037.
Thy graces they, knit in harmonious dance.   Liberty, v. 684.
          While universal Pan,
Knit with the Graces and the Hours in dance,
Led on the eternal Spring.   *P. L. iv. 266-8.*

The unfruitful rock itself, impregned by thee.   Summer, 140.
When he [Jupiter] *impregns the clouds.*   *P. L. iv. 500.*

Half in a blush of clustering roses lost.   Ib. 205.
Half spied, so thick the roses bushing round.   *P. L. ix. 426.*
          ("Blushing" is the reading of the 1720 text.)

On the mingling boughs they sit embowered.   Ib. 228.
Oh! bear me then to vast embowering shades.   Autumn, 1030.
In thick shelter of black shades imbower'd.   *Comus, 62.*
The Etrurian shades   High over-arch'd embower.   *P. L. i. 303-4.*

The scenes where ancient bards . . .
Conversed with angels and immortal forms,
On gracious errands bent—to save the fall
Of virtue struggling on the brink of vice.   Summer, 523-7.
     (Perhaps suggested by the visit of Raphael to warn Adam and Eve: *P. L.*, book v.)

Here frequent, at the visionary hour,
When musing midnight reigns or silent noon,
Angelic harps are in full concert heard,
And voices chaunting from the wood-crown'd hill,
The deepening dale, or inmost sylvan glade.   Ib. 556-60.
          How often, from the steep
Of echoing hill or thicket, have we heard
Celestial voices to the midnight air . . .
With heavenly touch of instrumental sounds
In full harmonic number join'd.   *P. L. iv. 680-87.*

Where the bee . . . loads his little thigh.   Ib. 626-8.
While the bee with honied thigh.   *Penseroso, 142.*

Or lead me through the maze,
Embowering endless, of the Indian fig.   Summer, 670-71.
(A reference to *P. L.* ix. 1101-1110.)

Through the soft silence of the listening night.   Ib. 745.
Through the soft silence of the listening night.   *Upon the Circumcision, 5.*

The sober-suited songstress.   Ib. 746.
Civil-suited Morn.   *Penseroso, 122.*

Cool to the middle air.   Ib. 768.
Her wonted station in the middle air.   Ib. 1649.
As up the middle sky unseen they stole.   Autumn, 709.
Ruled the middle air.   *P. L. i. 516.*
Up to the middle region of thick air.   *P. R. ii. 117.*

Thro' gorgeous Ind.   Summer, 825.
Bring home of either Ind the gorgeous stores.   Castle of Indolence, II. xx. 6.
The gorgeous east.   Liberty, v. 27.
Outshone the wealth of Ormus and of Ind,
Or where the gorgeous East.   *P. L. ii. 2-3.*

In the farthest verge.   Summer, 944.
Her farthest verge.   *P. L. ii. 1038.*

The wonted roar is up.   Ib. 949.
The wonted roar was up.   *Comus, 549.*

The cheerful haunt of men.   Ib. 1072.
The cheerful haunt of men.   *Comus, 388.*

Thence nitre, sulphur, and the fiery spume
Of fat bitumen, steaming on the day . . .
. . . till, by the touch ethereal roused . . .
They furious spring.   Ib. 1108-16.
Deep under ground, materials dark and crude,
Of spiritous and fiery spume, till touch'd
With Heaven's ray, and temper'd, they shoot forth . . .
. . . sulphurous and nitrous foam.   *P. L. vi. 478-80, 512;* cf. *iv. 810-18.*
With touch ethereal of Heaven's fiery rod.   *Samson, 549.*

To close the face of things.   Ib. 1654.
Involve the face of things.   Winter, 57.
Shadowy sets off the face of things.   *P. L. v. 43;* cf. *vii. 636, xi. 712.*

Till by degrees the finished fabric rose.   Autumn, 83; cf. Liberty, iv. 1179, v. 376.
To it adjoined a rising fabric stands.   Lines on Marlefield, 15.
A fabric huge Rose like an exhalation.   *P. L. i. 710-11.*
(Of a building in each case.)

Frequent and full.   Autumn, 531.
Frequent and full.   *P. L. i. 797.*
(Of an assembly in each case.)

Even in the height of noon oppressed, the sun
Sheds, weak and blunt, his wide-refracted ray;
Whence glaring oft, with many a broadened orb,
He frights the nations.   Ib. 721-4.
       As when the sun new-risen
Looks through the horizontal misty air
Shorn of his beams, or from behind the moon,
In dim eclipse, disastrous twilight sheds
On half the nations, and with fear of change
Perplexes monarchs.   *P. L. i. 594-9.*

From Asian Taurus, from Imaus stretched
Athwart the roving Tartar's sullen bounds.   Ib. 783-4.
As when a vulture on Imaus bred,
Whose snowy ridge the roving Tartar bounds.   *P. L. iii. 431-2.*

      The congregated stores,
The crystal treasures of the liquid world.   Ib. 823-4.
Congregated clouds.   Winter, 55.
           The great receptacle
Of congregated waters he call'd seas.   *P. L. vii. 307-8.*

Infinite wings! till all the plume-dark air.   Autumn, 869.
The wing'd air dark'd with plumes.   *Comus, 730.*
           (Of birds in each case.)

With many a cool translucent brimming flood.   Ib. 888.
Under the glassy, cool, translucent wave.   *Comus, 861.*

To tread low-thoughted vice beneath their feet.   Ib. 967.
With low-thoughted care, Confined.   *Comus, 6-7.*

Oh! bear me then . . . To twilight groves.   Ib. 1030-31.
Me, Goddess, bring To arched walks of twilight groves.   *Penseroso, 132-3.*

      Meanwhile the moon . . .
Turned to the sun direct, her spotted disk
(Where mountains rise, umbrageous dales descend,
And caverns deep, as optic tube descries). . . .
Now through the passing cloud she seems to stoop.   Ib. 1088-96.
           The moon, whose orb
Through optic glass the Tuscan artist views . . .
Or in Valdarno, to descry new lands,
Rivers, or mountains, in her spotty globe.   *P. L. i. 287-91.*
And oft, as if her head she bow'd,
Stooping through a fleecy cloud. [Of the moon.]   *Penseroso, 71-2.*

      Armies in meet array,
Thronged with aerial spears and steeds of fire;
Till, the long lines of full-extended war
In bleeding fight commixed, the sanguine flood
Rolls a broad slaughter o'er the plains of heaven.   Ib. 1117-21.
As when, to warn proud cities, war appears
Waged in the troubled sky, and armies rush
To battle in the clouds; before each van
Prick forth the aery knights, and couch their spears,
Till thickest legions close; with feats of arms
From either end of Heaven the welkin burns.   *P. L. ii. 533-8.*
In dubious battle on the plains of Heaven.   *P. L. i. 104.*
(In the first two cases, of a battle in the clouds, which the people regard as a warning.)

Hurled Sheer from the black foundation.   Ib. 1205-6.
        Thrown by angry Jove
Sheer o'er the crystal battlements.   *P. L. i. 741-2.*

      Welcome, kindred glooms!
Cogenial horrors, hail!   Winter, 5-6.
Hail, horrors! hail, Infernal world!   *P. L. i. 250-1.*

The vivid Stars shine out, in radiant Files;
And boundless *Ether* glows, till the fair Moon
Shows her broad Visage, in the crimson'd East;
Now, stooping, seems to kiss the passing Cloud:
Now, o'er the pure *Cerulean*, rides sublime.
Wide the pale Deluge floats, with silver Waves.   Winter (1st ed.), 88-93.
         Now glow'd the firmament
With living sapphires; Hesperus, that led
The starry host, rode brightest, till the Moon,
Rising in clouded majesty, at length
Apparent queen, unveil'd her peerless light,
And o'er the dark her silver mantle threw.   P. L. iv. 604-9.

Descends the ethereal force, and with strong gust
Turns from its bottom the discoloured deep.   Winter, 156-7.
The outrageous flood.   Spring, 1071.
They view'd the vast immeasurable Abyss,
Outrageous as a sea, dark, wasteful, wild,
Up from the bottom turn'd by furious winds.   P. L. vii. 211-13.

And the thin Fabrick of the pillar'd Air.   Winter (1st ed.), 162.
His fabric of the heavens.   P. L. viii. 76.
The pillar'd firmament is rottenness.   Comus, 598.

         Till Nature's King, who oft
Amid tempestuous darkness dwells alone.   Winter, 197-8.
            How oft amidst
Thick clouds and dark doth Heaven's all-ruling Sire
Choose to reside.   P. L. ii. 263-5.

Then throng the busy shapes into his mind
Of covered pits, unfathomably deep.   Ib. 297-8.
A thousand shadows at her beck.   Summer, 1650.
         A thousand fantasies
Begin to throng into my memory,
Of calling shapes, and beckoning shadows dire.   Comus, 205-7.

Meantime the village rouses up the fire;
While, well attested, and as well believed,
Heard solemn, goes the goblin-story round,
Till superstitious horror creeps o'er all.   Winter, 617-20.
With stories told of many a feat . . .
And he, by friar's lantern led,
Tells how the drudging goblin sweat. . . .
Thus done the tales, to bed they creep.   Allegro, 101-15.

Or beauteous freakt with many a mingled hue.   Ib. 814.
The pansy freakt with jet.   Lycidas, 144.

The loud misrule   Of driving tempest.   Ib. 896-7.
The loud misrule   Of Chaos.   P. L. vii. 271-2.

Ill fares the bark, with trembling wretches charged,
That, tossed amid the floating fragments, moors
Beneath the shelter of an icy isle,
While night o'erwhelms the sea, and horror looks.   Ib. 1004-7.
The pilot of some small night-founder'd skiff
Deeming some island, oft, as seamen tell . . .
Moors by his side under the lee, while night
Invests the sea, and wished morn delays.   P. L. i. 204-8.

More to embroil the deep, Leviathan
And his unwieldy train in dreadful sport
Tempest the loosened brine.   Ib. 1014-16.
 The broad monsters of the foaming deep . . .
. . . . flounce and tumble in unwieldy joy.   Spring, 822-4.
Chaos . . . more embroils the fray.   *P. L. ii. 907-8.*
Wallowing unwieldy, enormous in their gait,
Tempest the ocean. There leviathan,
Hugest of living creatures, on the deep
Stretch'd like a promontory, sleeps or swims.   *P. L. vii. 411-14.*

On the whirlwind's wing   Riding sublime.   Hymn, 18-19.
He on the wings of Cherub rode sublime.   *P. L. vi. 771.*
     (Of the Deity in each case.)

As thick as idle motes in sunny ray.   Castle of Indolence, I. xxix. 2.
As thick and numberless
As the gay motes that people the sunbeams.   *Penseroso, 7-8.*
  (But cf. Chaucer's Wife of Bath's Tale, 12, "As thikke as motes in the sonne-
beem.")

When Dan Sol to slope his wheels began.   Ib. lviii. 3.
Till the star . . . had sloped his westering wheel.   *Lycidas, 30-31.*

His unpremeditated strain.   Ib. lxviii. 4.
My unpremeditated verse.   *P. L. ix. 24.*

With tottering step and slow.   Ib. lxxii. 5.
With wandering steps and slow.   *P. L. xii. 648.*

Bent on bold emprise.   Ib. II. xiv. 2.
I love thy courage yet, and bold emprise.   *Comus, 610.*

And tufted groves to shade the meadow-bed.   Ib. xxxvii. 8.
And casts a gleam over this tufted grove.   *Comus, 225;* cf. *Allegro, 78.*

With magic dust their eyne he tries to blind.   Ib. xli. 7.
   When once her eye
Hath met the virtue of this magic dust.   *Comus, 164-5.*

And o'er the nations shook her conquering dart.   Ib. l. 7.
And over them triumphant Death his dart   Shook.   *P. L. xi. 491-2;* cf. *ii. 672.*

All that boon nature could luxuriant pour.   Liberty, ii. 98.
Nature boon   Pour'd forth profuse.   *P. L. iv. 242-3.*

Barbaric gold.   Ib. ii. 444.
Barbaric pearl and gold.   *P. L. ii. 4.*

Let Arabia breathe   Her spicy gales.   Ib. v. 19-20.
Winds . . . from the spicy shore
Of Araby the Blest.   *P. L. iv. 161-3.*

In daring flight, above all modern wing.   Ib. v. 437.
Above the flight of Pegasean wing.   *P. L. vii. 4.*
    (Of the muse in each case.)

Wings [of a goddess],   Dipped in the colours of the heavenly bow. Ib. v. 549-50.
Wings [of an angel] . . . *with . . . colours dipt in heaven.   P. L. v. 277-83.*

    With her hand,
Celestial red, she touched my darken'd eyes. [Of a goddess.] Ib. v. 558-9.
To whom the Angel, with a smile that glow'd
Celestial rosy red.   *P. L. viii. 618-19.*

Now wrapt in some mysterious dream.   Solitude, 11.
And let some strange mysterious dream.   *Penseroso, 147.*

Thine is the balmy breath of morn.   Ib. 25.
Sweet is the breath of Morn.   *P. L. iv. 641.*

When meditation has her fill.   Ib. 44.
To meditate my rural minstrelsy,
Till fancy had her fill.   *Comus, 547-8.*

Till, to the forehead of our evening sky
Returned, the blazing wonder glares anew.   Isaac Newton, 79-80.
         And with new-spangled ore
Flames in the forehead of the morning sky.   *Lycidas, 170-71.*
      (Of the disappearance and return of a heavenly body in each case.)

The nibbling flock stray.   On Beauty, 13.
Where the nibbling flocks do stray.   *Allegro, 72.*

The morning springs, in thousand liveries drest.   Morning in the Country, 2.
The clouds in thousand liveries dight.   *Allegro, 62.*

Flowers of all hue, their queen the bashful rose.   Lines on Marlefield, 22.
Flowers of all hue, and without thorn the rose.   *P. L. iv. 256.*

YOUNG [1]

But chiefly thou, great Ruler! Lord of all!
Before whose throne archangels prostrate fall;
If at thy nod, from discord, and from night,
Sprang beauty, and yon sparkling worlds of light,
Exalt e'en me; all inward tumults quell;
The clouds and darkness of my mind dispel;
To my great subject thou my breast inspire,
And raise my lab'ring soul with equal fire.   Last Day, i (ii. 2).
And chiefly thou, O Spirit . . . what in me is dark
Illumine, what is low raise and support;
That to the highth of this great argument
I may assert Eternal Providence. . . .
In the beginning how the Heavens and Earth
Rose out of Chaos.   *P. L. i. 17-25, 9-10.*

And death might shake his threat'ning lance in vain.   Ib. i (ii. 5).
[Death] *shook a dreadful dart.*   *P. L. ii. 672; cf. xi. 491-2.*

And the grand rebel flaming downward hurl'd.   Ib. ii (ii. 18).
      Him [Satan] *the Almighty Power*
Hurl'd headlong flaming from the ethereal sky.   *P. L. i. 44-5.*

Less glorious, when of old th' eternal Son
From realms of night return'd with trophies won:
Thro' heaven's high gates, when he triumphant rode,
And shouting angels hail'd the victor God.   Ib. iii (ii. 27).
      (A reference to *P. L.* vi. 880-90.)

---

[1] Several of these parallels are pointed out in W. Thomas's *Le Poète Edward Young* (Paris, 1901), but I have not included all that M. Thomas notes. The figures in parentheses refer to the volume and page of the Aldine edition of Young (1852).

Down an abyss how dark, and how profound?
Down, down, (I still am falling, horrid pain!)
Ten thousand thousand fathoms still remain.   Ib. iii (ii. 29).
Then, from the crystal battlements of heaven,
Down, down, she hurls it thro' the dark profound,
Ten thousand thousand fathom.   Night Thoughts, ix (i. 235).
                    Thrown by angry Jove
Sheer o'er the crystal battlements.   *P. L. i. 741-2.*
            Plumb down he drops
Ten thousand fathom deep [in Chaos, an abyss dark and profound].   *P. L. ii. 933-4.*

The favour'd of their Judge, in triumph move
To take possession of their thrones above;
Satan's accurs'd desertion to supply,
And fill the vacant stations of the sky.   Last Day, iii (ii. 31).
        (This is the reason given for the creation of man in *P. L.* iii. 677-9 and vii.
        150-61.)

A lamp . . . sheds a quiv'ring melancholy gloom,
Which only shows the darkness of the room.   Force of Religion, ii (ii. 47).
                    Yet from those flames
No light, but rather darkness visible.   *P. L. i. 62-3.*

And glory, at one entrance, quite shut out.   Love of Fame, ii (ii. 76).
And wisdom at one entrance quite shut out.   *P. L. iii. 50.*
                        (Pointed out by Young.)

Till some god whispers in his tingling ear,
That fame's unwholesome taken without meat.   Ib. iv (ii. 92).
Phoebus replied, and touch'd my trembling ears:
"Fame is no plant that grows on mortal soil."   *Lycidas, 77-8.*

Naked in nothing should a woman be . . .
But yield her charms of mind with sweet delay.   Ib. vi (ii. 117).
Yielded with coy submission, modest pride,
And sweet, reluctant, amorous delay.   *P. L. iv. 310-11.*

Thus the majestic mother of mankind,
To her own charms most amiably blind,
On the green margin innocently stood,
And gaz'd indulgent on the crystal flood;
Survey'd the stranger in the painted wave,
And, smiling, prais'd the beauties which she gave.   Ib. vi (ii. 132-3).
Like Milton's Eve, when gazing on the lake,
Man makes the matchless image, man admires.   Night Thoughts, vi (i. 124).
        (Young refers in each case to Milton: cf. *P. L.* iv. 456-69.)

Intestine broils.   Night Thoughts, i (i. 8).
Intestine broils.   *P. L. ii. 1001.*

Rocks, desarts, frozen seas, and burning sands:
Wild haunts of monsters, poisons, stings, and death. Ib. i (i. 10).
Rocks, caves, lakes, fens, bogs, dens, and shades of death . . .
Where all life dies, death lives, and Nature breeds,
Perverse, all monstrous, all prodigious things.   *P. L. ii. 621-5.*

High-flusht, with insolence and wine.   Ib. ii (i. 27).
Flown with insolence and wine.   *P. L. i. 502.*
                    (Of a night orgy in each case.)

The wilderness of joy.   Night Thoughts, iii (i. 36).
A wilderness of joys.   Ib. viii (i. 187).
A wilderness of wonder.   Ib. ix (i. 276).
A wilderness of sweets.   *P. L. v. 294.*

   That husht Cimmerian vale,
Where darkness, brooding o'er unfinisht fates,
With raven wing incumbent, waits the day. Ib. iii (i. 43–4).
Where brooding Darkness spreads his jealous wings,
And the night-raven sings . . .
In dark Cimmerian desert ever dwell.   *Allegro, 6–10.*

Where am I rapt by this triumphant theme,
On Christian joy's exulting wing, above
Th' Aonian mount!   Ib. iv (i. 61).
But oh! I faint! my spirits fail! — Nor strange!
So long on wing, and in no middle clime!   Ib. ix (i. 290).
    My advent'rous song,
That with no middle flight intends to soar
Above the Aonian mount.   *P. L. i. 13–15.*

   Pavilion'd high he sits
In darkness from excessive splendour born,
By gods unseen, unless thro' lustre lost.   Ib. iv (i. 64).
Throned inaccessible, but when thou shadest
The full blaze of thy beams, and . . .
Dark with excessive bright thy skirts appear,
Yet dazzle Heaven, that brightest Seraphim
Approach not, but with both wings veil their eyes. *P. L. iii. 377–82.*
      (Of God in each case.)

As when a wretch, from thick, polluted air,
Darkness, and stench, and suffocating damps,
And dungeon-horrors, by kind fate, discharg'd
Climbs some fair eminence, where ether pure
Surrounds him, and Elysian prospects rise,
His heart exults, his spirits cast their load. Ib. iv (i. 69).
As one who, long in populous city pent,
Where houses thick and sewers annoy the air,
Forth issuing on a summer's morn to breathe
Among the pleasant villages and farms
Adjoin'd, from each thing met conceives delight. *P. L. ix. 445–9; cf. iii. 543–53.*

    Whence descends
Urania, my celestial guest! who deigns
Nightly to visit me, so mean.   Ib. v (i. 84).
Descend from Heaven, Urania.   *P. L. vii. 1.*
Of my celestial patroness, who deigns
Her nightly visitation unimplored.   *P. L. ix. 21–2.*

Smit with the pomp of lofty sentiments.   Ib. vii (i. 155).
Smit with the love of sacred song.   *P. L. iii. 29.*

Fall, how profound! like Lucifer's, the fall! . . .
   . . . . hurl'd headlong, hurl'd at once
To night! to nothing!   Ib. vii (i. 157).
[God] o'er heaven's battlements the felon [Lucifer] hurl'd
To groans, and chains, and darkness.   Ib. ix (i. 279).

Him [Satan] *the Almighty Power*
Hurl'd headlong flaming from the ethereal sky . . .
To bottomless perdition; there to dwell
In adamantine chains and penal fire.   P. L. i. 44–8.
                Thrown by angry Jove
Sheer o'er the crystal battlements.   P. L. i. 741–2.

And vindicate th' economy of heaven.   Ib. vii (i. 164).
And justify the ways of God to men.   P. L. i. 26.

Universal blank.   Ib. vii (i. 166).
A universal blank.   P. L. iii. 48.

'Midst upper, nether, and surrounding night.   Ib. vii (i. 166).
'Twixt upper, nether, and surrounding fires.   P. L. i. 346.

Witness, ye flames! th' Assyrian tyrant blew
To sevenfold rage.   Ib. vii (i. 171).
What if the breath that kindled those grim fires,
Awaked, should blow them into sevenfold rage,
And plunge us in the flames?   P. L. ii. 170–72.

A Christian dwells, like Uriel, in the sun.   Ib. vii (i. 178).
      (Young refers to Milton: cf. P. L. iii. 622–53.)

In ambient air.   Ib. viii (i. 186).
The ambient air.   P. L. vii. 89.

         Sudden as the spark
From smitten steel; from nitrous grain, the blaze.   Ib. ix (i. 231).
         As when a spark
Lights on a heap of nitrous powder . . .
     . . . . the smutty grain,
With sudden blaze diffused, inflames the air.   P. L. iv. 814–18.
      Sulphurous and nitrous foam
They found . . . and . . . reduced To blackest grain.   P. L. vi. 512–15.
      (Of gunpowder in each case.)

         The foe of God and man . . .
And rears his brazen front, with thunder scarr'd. . . .
Like meteors in a stormy sky, how roll
His baleful eyes!   Ib. ix (i. 233).
Above them all the Archangel; but his face
Deep scars of thunder had intrench'd.   P. L. i. 600–601.
Round he throws his baleful eyes.   P. L. i. 56.

         So, Cynthia (poets feign)
In shadows veil'd, soft sliding from her sphere.   Ib. ix (i. 241).
         Peace . . . came softly sliding
Down through the turning sphere.   Nativity, 46–8.

Sweet interchange of rays.   Ib. ix (i. 246).
Sweet interchange Of hill and valley.   P. L. ix. 115–16.

O what a confluence of ethereal fires,
From urns unnumber'd!   Ib. ix (i. 247).
Hither, as to their fountain, other stars
Repairing, in their golden urns draw light.   P. L. vii. 364–5.
      (Of stars in each case.)

[Angels] of various plume,
In heavenly liveries, distinctly clad,
Azure, green, purple, pearl, or downy gold,
Or all commix'd; they stand, with wings outspread,
List'ning.   Night Thoughts, ix (i. 251).
        [An angel's wings of] *downy gold*
And colours dipt in heaven.   *P. L. v. 282–3.*
        Those waved their limber fans
For wings, and smallest lineaments exact
In all the liveries deck'd of summer's pride,
With spots of gold and purple, azure and green.   *P. L. vii. 476–9.*

        The breastplate of the true High priest,
Ardent with gems oracular.   Ib. ix (i. 256).
Urim and Thummim, those oraculous gems
On Aaron's breast.   *P. R. iii. 14–15.*

Their dance perplex'd exhibits to the sight . . .
The circles intricate, and mystic maze.   Ib. ix (i. 259).
Mystical dance, which yonder starry sphere . . .
Resembles nearest, mazes intricate.   *P. L. v. 620–22.*
            (Of the stars in each case.)

What more than Atlantean shoulder props.   Ib. ix (i. 259).
With Atlantean shoulders fit to bear.   *P. L. ii. 306.*

What magic . . . these pond'rous orbs sustains?
Who would not think them hung in golden chains?   Ib. ix (i. 259).
And hangs creation, like a precious gem,
Though little, on the footstool of his throne!   Ib. ix (i. 270).
And fast by [heaven], *hanging in a golden chain,*
This pendent world, in bigness as a star.   *P. L. ii. 1051–2.*

Or has th' Almighty Father, with a breath,
Impregnated the womb of distant space?   Ib. ix (i. 271).
Dove-like sat'st brooding on the vast Abyss,
And madest it pregnant.   *P. L. i. 21–2.*

Chaos! of nature both the womb, and grave!   Ib. ix (i. 271).
        This wild Abyss [Chaos],
The womb of Nature, and perhaps her grave.   *P. L. ii. 910–11.*

His purple wing bedropp'd with eyes of gold.   Ib. ix (i. 284).
Their waved coats dropt with gold.   *P. L. vii. 406.*
And waves his purple wings.   *P. L. iv. 764.*

By second chaos; and eternal night.   Ib. ix (i. 289).
I sung of Chaos and eternal Night.   *P. L. iii. 18.*

Of matter multiform; or dense, or rare;
Opaque, or lucid; rapid, or at rest.   Ib. ix (i. 291).
O'er bog or steep, through strait, rough, dense, or rare.   *P. L. ii. 948.*

Where thou, from all eternity, hast dwelt.   Ib. ix (i. 293).
Dwelt from eternity.   *P. L. iii. 5.*
            (Of God in each case.)

THOMAS WARTON [1]

When chants the milk-maid at her balmy pail,	
And weary reapers whistle o'er the vale.	Triumph of Isis, 3-4.
While the ploughman, near at hand,	
Whistles o'er the furrow'd land,	
And the milkmaid singeth blithe.	Allegro, 63-5.
O'er Isis' willow-fringed banks I stray'd.	Ib. 6.
By the rushy-fringèd bank,	
Where grows the willow and the osier dank.	Comus, 890-1.
I fram'd the Doric lay.	Ib. 8.
O for the warblings of the Doric ote,	
That wept the youth deep-whelm'd in ocean's tide!	Elegy on Prince of Wales, 1-2.
And he, sweet master of the Doric oat.	King's Birthday, 1786, 27.
But now my oat proceeds. . . .	
With eager thought warbling his Doric lay.	Lycidas, 88, 189.
From her loose hair the dropping dew she press'd.	Triumph of Isis, 17.
The loose train of thy amber-dropping hair.	Comus, 863.
No more thy love-resounding sonnets suit	
To notes of pastoral pipe, or oaten flute.	Ib. 21-2.
Meanwhile the rural ditties were not mute,	
Temper'd to the oaten flute.	Lycidas, 32-3.
My Muse divine still keeps her wonted state,	
The mien erect, and high majestic gait.	Ib. 75-6 (original form).
That Albion still shall keep her wonted state.	New Year 1786, 90.
Come, but keep thy wonted state,	
With even step, and musing gait.	Penseroso, 37-8.
To hold short dalliance with the tuneful Nine.	Triumph of Isis, 98.
With her, as years successive glide,	
I'll hold divinest dalliance.	Approach of Summer, 336-7.
Held dalliance with his fair Egyptian spouse.	P. L. ix. 443.
Ye cloisters pale.	Triumph of Isis, 153.
The studious cloisters pale.	Penseroso, 156.
I see the sable-suited Prince advance.	Ib. 205.
Till civil-suited Morn appear.	Penseroso, 122.
Sat sable-vested Night.	P. L. ii. 962.
The sable-stolèd sorcerers bear his worshipp'd ark.	Nativity, 220.
She rests her weary feet, and plumes her wings.	Ib. 240.
Her painted wings Imagination plumes.	Sent to Mr. Upton, 26.
She plumes her feathers, and lets grow her wings.	Comus, 378.
To drop the sweeping pall of scepter'd pride.	Elegy on Prince of Wales, 14.
To throw the scepter'd pall of state aside.	Marriage of King, 72.
In sceptred pall come sweeping by.	Penseroso, 98.
With even step he walk'd, and constant hand.	Elegy on Prince of Wales, 21.
With even step, and musing gait.	Penseroso, 38.

[1] Most of these parallels, as well as many others that I have not included, are pointed out by Richard Mant in his edition of Warton's poems (Oxford, 1802).

Flam'd in the van of many a baron bold.   Death of George II, 54.
To mark the mouldering halls of barons bold.   Reynolds's Window, 13.
Whence Hardyknute, a baron bold.   Approach of Summer, 243.
Where throngs of knights and barons bold.   *Allegro, 119.*
       (But cf. Gray's Bard, 111, "Girt with many a Baron bold.")

While cunning Bards at ancient banquets sung
Of paynim foes defied, and trophies hung.   Marriage of King, 45–6.
And if aught else great bards beside
In sage and solemn tunes have sung,
Of turneys, and of trophies hung.   *Penseroso, 116–18.*

Entwine thy diadem with honour due.   Ib. 66.
The faded tomb, with honour due.   Grave of Arthur, 131.
If I give thee honour due.   *Allegro, 37.*

To tread with nymph-like step the conscious plain.   Marriage of King, 70.
If chance with nymph-like step fair virgin pass.   *P. L. ix. 452.*

Stream through the storied window's holy hue.   Birth of Prince of Wales, 50.
With rich reflection of the storied glass.   Vale-Royal Abbey, 16.
And storied windows richly dight,
Casting a dim religious light.   *Penseroso, 159–60.*

       (In each of these passages a colored glass window in a church is meant.
Warton also speaks of "the storied tapestry," Grave of Arthur, 15; and
"the stately-storied hall," Sonnet, Wilton-House, 10. The Epistle from
Hearn, which was probably written by Joseph Warton, has "saints in
storied windows.")

When stands th' embattled host in banner'd pride.   Birth of Prince of Wales, 54.
A banner'd host.   *P. L. ii. 885.*
That led the embattled Seraphim to war.   *P. L. i. 129;* cf. *vi. 16,* etc.

O'er deep embattled ears of corn.   Approach of Summer, 114.
Up stood the corny reed   Embattled.   *P. L. vii. 321–2.*
       (Warton also has "th' embattled sedge," Monody, 3; "embattled clouds,"
Pleasures of Melancholy, 294; "brows, imbattled high," King's Birth-
day 1790, 59.)

The tread majestic, and the beaming eye,
That lifted speaks its commerce with the sky.   Reynolds's Window, 57–8.
With even step, and musing gait,
And looks commercing with the skies.   *Penseroso, 38–9.*

There oft thou listen'st to the wild uproar.   Pleasures of Melancholy, 13.
Hell scarce holds the wild uproar.   *P. L. ii. 541.*

To ruin'd seats, to twilight cells and bow'rs,
Where thoughtful Melancholy loves to muse.   Ib. 19–20.
That musing Meditation most affects
The pensive secrecy of desert cell.   *Comus, 386–7.*

Pours her long-levell'd rule of streaming light.   Ib. 31.
With the level-streaming rays.   Approach of Summer, 121.
With thy long levell'd rule of streaming light.   *Comus, 340.*

Then, when the sullen shades of ev'ning close,
Where thro' the room a blindly-glimm'ring gleam
The dying embers scatter, far remote
From Mirth's mad shouts, that thro' th' illumin'd roof
Resound with festive echo, let me sit,
Blest with the lowly cricket's drowsy dirge.   Pleasures of Melancholy, 74–9.

Where glowing embers through the room
Teach light to counterfeit a gloom,
Far from all resort of mirth,
Save the cricket on the hearth.   *Penseroso, 79–82.*

   That like the dazzling spells
Of wily Comus cheat th' unweeting eye
With blear illusion, and persuade to drink
That charmed cup, which Reason's mintage fair
Unmoulds, and stamps the monster on the man. Ib. 85–9.
     Thus I hurl
My dazzling spells into the spongy air,
Of power to cheat the eye with blear illusion. . . .
By sly enticement gives his baneful cup,
With many murmurs mix'd, whose pleasing poison
The visage quite transforms of him that drinks,
And the inglorious likeness of a beast
Fixes instead, unmoulding reason's mintage. *Comus, 153–5, 525–9.*

The blest regent of the golden day.   Ib. 108.
Regent of day.   *P. L. vii. 371.*
       (Of the sun in each case.)

Yet not ungrateful is the morn's approach,
When dropping wet she comes, and clad in clouds. Ib. 135–6.
Till civil-suited Morn appear,
Not trick'd and frounced, as she was wont . . .
But kerchieft in a comely cloud . . .
Or usher'd with a shower still.   *Penseroso, 122–7.*

Rings not the high wood with enliven'd shouts
Of early hunter.   Ib. 150–51.
Oft listening how the hounds and horn
Cheerly rouse the slumbering Morn . . .
Through the high wood echoing shrill. *Allegro, 53–6.*

By frolic Zephyr's hand.   Ib. 190.
The frolic wind that breathes the spring, Zephyr. *Allegro, 18–19.*

The taper'd choir, at the late hour of pray'r,
Oft let me tread, while to th' according voice
The many-sounding organ peals on high,
The clear slow-dittied chaunt, or varied hymn,
Till all my soul is bath'd in ecstasies,
And lapp'd in Paradise.   Ib. 196–201.
There let the pealing organ blow
To the full-voiced choir below,
In service high and anthems clear,
As may with sweetness, through mine ear,
Dissolve me into ecstasies,
And bring all Heaven before mine eyes. *Penseroso, 161–6.*

The due clock swinging slow with sweepy sway. Ib. 209.
But when the curfeu's measur'd roar
Duly, the darkening valleys o'er,
Has echoed from the distant town.   The Hamlet, 27–9.
Oft, on a plat of rising ground,
I hear the far-off curfew sound,
Over some wide-water'd shore
Swinging slow with sullen roar.   *Penseroso, 73–6.*

Here palmy groves . . . here vine-clad hills
Lay forth their purple store.   Pleasures of Melancholy, 248–52.
Or palmy hillock; or the flowery lap
Of some irriguous valley spread her store. . . .
Lays forth her purple grape.   *P. L. iv. 254–9.*

Tho' thro' the blissful scenes Ilissus roll
His sage-inspiring flood.   Ib. 255–6.
                There Ilissus rolls
His whispering stream. Within the walls then view
The schools of ancient sages.   *P. R. iv. 249–51.*
                    (Of Athens in each case.)

But never let Euphrosyne beguile
With toys of wanton mirth my fixed mind.   Ib. 285–6.
In Heaven yclep'd Euphrosyne.   *Allegro, 12.*
How little you bested,
Or fill the fixed mind with all your toys!   *Penseroso, 3–4.*

And Bacchus, ivy-crown'd.   Ib. 291.
To ivy-crowned Bacchus bore.   *Allegro, 16.*

Yet are these joys that Melancholy gives.   Ib. 297.
These pleasures, Melancholy, give.   *Penseroso, 175.*

Of parting wings bedropt with gold.   Inscription in a Hermitage, 32.
Their waved coats dropt with gold.   *P. L. vii. 406.*
        (But cf. Pope's Windsor Forest, 144, "The yellow carp, in scales be-
        dropped with gold.")

To take my staff, and amice gray.   Ib. 38.
Came forth with pilgrim steps, in amice gray.   *P. R. iv. 427.*

Death stands prepar'd, but still delays, to strike. To Sleep, 16.
And over them triumphant Death his dart
Shook, but delay'd to strike.   *P. L. xi. 491–2.*

From the trim garden's thymy mound.   The Hamlet, 45 (original reading).
That in trim gardens takes his pleasure.   *Penseroso, 50.*

Massy proof. Vale-Royal Abbey, 64 (of a column); New Year 1786, 60 (of a bastion);
        New Year 1788, 1 (of a castle).
With antic pillars massy proof.   *Penseroso, 158.*
        (Warton also has "massy piles," Triumph of Isis, 151; "massy state,"
        Birth of Prince of Wales, 28; "massy pride," Reynolds's Window, 19;
        "massy cups" and "massy blade," Grave of Arthur, 11, 173; "massy
        pomp," King's Birthday 1788, 51; "massy maze," Sonnet, Stonehenge, 7.)

Yet partial as she sings.   Vale-Royal Abbey, 77.
Their song was partial.   *P. L. ii. 552.*

Then was loneliness to me
Best and true society.   Solitude at an Inn, 5–6.
For solitude sometimes is best society.   *P. L. ix. 249.*

Saw Cupid's stately maske come sweeping by.   Sent to Mr. Upton, 20.
Sometime let gorgeous Tragedy
In sceptred pall come sweeping by.   *Penseroso, 97–8.*

Lost in some melancholy fit.   Sent to a Friend, 26.
Wrapt in a pleasing fit of melancholy.   *Comus, 546.*

Where high o'er-arching trees embower.	Ib. 34.
Above th' embowering shade.	Monody, 10.
Where the Etrurian shades	
High over-arch'd embower.	*P. L. i. 303–4;* cf. *ix. 1038, Comus, 62.*

(Warton also has "in embow'ring woods" and "cave embower'd with mournful yew," Pleasures of Melancholy, 175, 281; "embowering elms," Inscription in a Hermitage, 4; "the hanging oak . . . Waves his imbowering head," Horace, III. xiii. 18–20; "the curling woodbine's shade imbow'rs," The Hamlet, 44; "with myrtle bower'd and jessamine" and "from bowering beech," Approach of Summer, 52, 169.)

In every rural sight or sound.	Sent to a Friend, 44.
Each rural sight, each rural sound.	*P. L. ix. 451.*

From the deep dell, where shaggy roots	
Fringe the rough brink with wreathed shoots,	
Th' unwilling Genius flies forlorn,	
His primrose chaplet rudely torn.	
With hollow shriek the Nymphs forsake	
The pathless copse and hedge-row brake.	Ib. 53–8.
With hollow shriek the steep of Delphos leaving. . . .	
From haunted spring, and dale	
Edged with poplar pale,	
The parting Genius is with sighing sent;	
With flower-inwoven tresses torn	
The Nymphs in twilight shade of tangled thickets mourn.	*Nativity, 178–88.*

The violet's unprinted head.	Ib. 68.
Thus I set my printless feet	
O'er the cowslip's velvet head.	*Comus, 897–8.*

Fair forms, in every wondrous wood,	
Or lightly tripp'd, or solemn stood.	Ib. 81–2.
Under the trees now tripp'd, now solemn stood,	
Nymphs of Diana's train, and Naiades.	*P. R. ii. 354–5.*

While gleaming o'er the crisped bowers.	Ib. 85.
Along the crisped shades and bowers.	*Comus, 984.*

The pine cerulean, never sere.	First of April, 66.
Ye myrtles brown, with ivy never sere.	*Lycidas, 2.*

A thousand tumbling rills inlay	
With silver veins the vale, or pass	
Redundant through the sparkling grass.	Ib. 92–4.
From a thousand petty rills,	
That tumble down the snowy hills.	*Comus, 926–7.*
Isles . . . inlay . . . the deep.	*Comus, 21–3.*
Amidst his circling spires, that on the grass	
Floated redundant. [Of a serpent.]	*P. L. ix. 502–3.*

Dim-figur'd on whose robe are shown.	Approach of Summer, 17.
His mantle hairy and his bonnet sedge,	
Inwrought with figures dim.	*Lycidas, 104–5.*

Thee April blithe, as long of yore.	Ib. 31.
Thee bright-hair'd Vesta long of yore.	*Penseroso, 23.*

With muskie nectar-trickling wing.	Ib. 33.
And west winds with musky wing.	*Comus, 989.*

Where a tall citron's shade imbrown'd
The soft lap of the fragrant ground.　　　　　Approach of Summer, 43–4.
　　　Where the unpierced shade
Imbrown'd the noon-tide bowers.　　　　　*P. L. iv. 245–6.*

You bloom'd a goddess debonnair.　　　　　Ib. 48.
Thou Goddess . . . So buxom, blithe, and debonair.　　*Allegro, 11, 24.*

Haste thee, nymph! and hand in hand,
With thee lead.　　　　　Ib. 57–8.
Haste thee, Nymph, and bring with thee.　　　*Allegro, 25.*

Bring fantastic-footed Joy.　　　　　Ib. 59.
On the light fantastic toe.　　　　　*Allegro, 34.*

His wattled cotes the shepherd plants.　　　Ib. 99.
The folded flocks, penn'd in their wattled cotes.　　*Comus, 344.*

Nor mastiff's bark from bosom'd cot.　　　Ib. 112.
Bosom'd high in tufted trees.　　　　　*Allegro, 78.*
　　　　　(In each case, of a dwelling half hidden by trees.)

The ruby chambers of the West.　　　　　Ib. 118.
His chamber in the east.　　　　　*Comus, 101.*
　　　　　(In connection with the sun in each case.)

Bathes my blithe heart in ecstasies.　　　Ib. 126.
Dissolve me into ecstasies.　　　　　*Penseroso, 165.*

Till Melancholy has her fill.　　　　　Ib. 136.
Wrapt in a pleasing fit of melancholy . . .
Till fancy had her fill.　　　　　*Comus, 546–8.*
　　　　　(Of an evening reverie in the woods in each case.)

But when the Sun, at noon-tide hour,
Sits throned in his highest tow'r.　　　　Ib. 139–40.
Sometimes towards Heaven and the full-blazing sun,
Which now sat high in his meridian tower.　　*P. L. iv. 29–30.*

To the tann'd haycock in the mead.　　　Ib. 142.
To the tann'd haycock in the mead.　　　*Allegro, 90.*

From bowering beech the mower blithe
With new-born vigour grasps the scythe.　　Ib. 169–70.
And the milkmaid singeth blithe,
And the mower whets his sithe.　　　　*Allegro, 65–6.*

But ever against restless heat.　　　　Ib. 173.
And ever, against eating cares.　　　　*Allegro, 135.*

Hangs nodding from the low-brow'd rock.　　Ib. 176.
Under ebon shades and low-brow'd rocks.　　*Allegro, 8.*
　　　(But cf. Pope's Eloisa to Abelard, 244, "Low-browed rocks hang nodding
　　　o'er the deeps.")

A rustic, wild, grotesque alcove,
Its side with mantling woodbines wove;
Cool as the cave where Clio dwells.　　　Ib. 181–3.
　　　　Whose hairy sides
With thicket overgrown, grotesque and wild. . . .
　　　. . . . . *caves*
Of cool recess, o'er which the mantling vine.　　*P. L. iv. 135–6, 257–8.*
A bank . . . interwove With . . . honeysuckle.　　*Comus, 543–5.*

On that hoar hill's aerial height.
From the side of some hoar hill.

Ib. 238.
Allegro, 55.

What open force, or secret guile.
Whether of open war or covert guile.

Ib. 253.
P. L. ii. 41.

Let not my due feet fail to climb.
Let my due feet never fail   To walk.

Ib. 257.
Penseroso, 155–6.

O beauteous, rural interchange!
The simple spire, and elmy grange!
            Sweet interchange
Of hill and valley, rivers, woods, and plains.

Ib. 267–8.

P. L. ix. 115–16.

Canst bid me carol wood-notes wild.
Warble his native wood-notes wild.

Ib. 274.
Allegro, 134.

With thee conversing, all the day.
With thee conversing I forget all time.

Ib. 283.
P. L. iv. 639.

I meditate my lightsome lay.
To meditate my rural minstrelsy.
And strictly meditate the thankless Muse.

Ib. 284.
Comus, 547.
Lycidas, 66.

In valleys, where mild whispers use.
Ye valleys low, where the mild whispers use.

Ib. 287.
Lycidas, 136.

For ever held in holy trance.
There held in holy passion still.

Ib. 338.
Penseroso, 41.

Thy brazen drums hoarse discord bray.
Arms on armour clashing bray'd   Horrible discord.

The Crusade, 24.
P. L. vi. 209–10.

And, rolling in terrific state,
On giant-wheels harsh thunders grate.
And on their hinges grate   Harsh thunder.

Ib. 71–2.
P. L. ii. 881–2.

Never yet in rime enroll'd,
Nor sung nor harp'd in hall or bower.
What never yet was heard in tale or song,
From old or modern bard, in hall or bower.

Grave of Arthur, 96–7.

Comus, 44–5.

A minstrel, sprung of Cornish line,
Who spoke of kings from old Locrine.
Virgin, daughter of Locrine,
Sprung of old Anchises' line.

Ib. 99–100.

Comus, 922–3.

The stoled fathers met the bier.
The sable-stolèd sorcerers bear his worshipp'd ark.

Ib. 120.
Nativity, 220.

He scorns awhile his bold emprise.
I love thy courage yet, and bold emprise.
Giants of mighty bone and bold emprise.

Ib. 164.
Comus, 610.
P. L. xi. 642.

(But cf. Faerie Queene, II. iii. 35, "Renowmd through many bold emprize.")

In vain to build the lofty rhyme.
Could build the genuine rime.
And build the lofty rhyme.

Ode for Music, 136.
The Suicide, 39.
Lycidas, 11.

            Hence he told
The banquet of Cambuscan bold.
        Left half told
The story of Cambuscan bold.

King's Birthday 1787, 9–10.

Penseroso, 109–10.

Here held his pomp, and trail'd the pall
Of triumph through the trophied hall;
And War was clad awhile in gorgeous weeds;
Amid the martial pageantries,
While Beauty's glance adjudg'd the prize,
And beam'd sweet influence on heroic deeds.   New Year 1788, 39–44.
Where throngs of knights and barons bold,
In weeds of peace, high triumphs hold,
With store of ladies, whose bright eyes
Rain influence, and judge the prize. . . .
And pomp, and feast, and revelry,
With masque and antique pageantry.   *Allegro, 119–28.*
Sometime let gorgeous Tragedy
In sceptred pall come sweeping by.   *Penseroso, 97–8.*

That, fraught with drops of precious cure.   King's Birthday 1790, 21.
Drops that from my fountain pure
I have kept of precious cure.   *Comus, 912–13.*

He rolls his eyes, that witness huge dismay.   Newmarket, 94.
Round he throws his baleful eyes,
That witness'd huge affliction and dismay.   *P. L. i. 56–7.*

Smit with the love of the laconic boot.   Ib. 107.
Smit with the love of sacred song.   *P. L. iii. 29.*

Where no crude surfeit, or intemperate joys
Of lawless Bacchus reign.   Oxford Ale, 9–10.
Where no crude surfeit reigns.   *Comus, 479.*

Of monumental oak.   Ib. 30.
Of pine, or monumental oak.   *Penseroso, 135.*

Quips and cranks, and wanton wiles,
That love to live within the one-curl'd Scratch,
With fun, and all the family of smiles.   Grizzle Wig, 18–20.
Quips, and Cranks, and wanton Wiles,
Nods and Becks, and wreathèd Smiles . . .
And love to live in dimple sleek.   *Allegro, 27–30.*

DICTION

Adamantine (Marriage of King, 22, Ode for Music, 36, New Year 1786, 37); cf. P. L.
    i. 48, ii. 646, etc. (nine times more, including "adamant" and "adamantean").
    Warton in two instances and Milton in four apply the word to arms.
Eden's *amaranthine* grove (Marriage of King, 58, and cf. Approach of Summer, 45,
    and New Year 1786, 7); cf. P. L. xi. 78, iii. 352.
In mantle *dank* (Complaint of Cherwell, 42); cf. Comus, 891, P. L. ix. 179, etc.
The *dimply* flood (Triumph of Isis, 15); cf. Comus, 119.
Flaunting ivy (Pleasures of Melancholy, 36); cf. Comus, 545.
Ivy's *gadding* spray (Inscription in a Hermitage, 24); cf. Lycidas, 40.
Honied flow'rs (The Hamlet, 43); cf. Lycidas, 140, Penseroso, 142.
Listed plain (Newmarket, 70); cf. Samson, 1087.
Morning's twilight-*tinctur'd* beam (The Hamlet, 5); cf. P. L. v. 285.
Shapes . . . *trick'd* by Fancy's pen (Vale-Royal Abbey, 82); cf. Penseroso, 123,
    Lycidas, 170.
Vi'let-woven couch (Pleasures of Melancholy, 189); cf. Comus, 233, Nativity, 187.

COWPER

When evening in her sober vest
Drew the grey curtain of the fading west.   Charity, 262-3.
Now came still Evening on, and Twilight gray
Had in her sober livery all things clad.   P. L. iv. 598-9.

Where covert guile and artifice abound.   Ib. 285.
Whether of open war or covert guile.   P. L. ii. 41.

These are thy glorious works, thou Source of good,
How dimly seen, how faintly understood!
Thine, and upheld by thy paternal care,
This universal frame, thus wondrous fair;
Thy power divine, and bounty beyond thought,
Adored and praised in all that thou hast wrought.   Retirement, 87-92.
These are thy glorious works, eternal Truth. . . .
Then these thy glorious works.   Hope, 742-50.
They are thy witnesses, who speak thy power
And goodness infinite. [Of created works as revealing God.] Task, v. 853-4.
These are thy glorious works, Parent of good,
Almighty! thine this universal frame,
Thus wondrous fair: thyself how wondrous then!
Unspeakable! who sitt'st above these Heavens
To us invisible, or dimly seen
In these thy lowest works; yet these declare
Thy goodness beyond thought, and power divine.   P. L. v. 153-9.

Delights unfelt before.   Retirement, 360.
Pangs unfelt before.   P. L. ii. 703.

When piping winds shall soon arise.   Mrs. Throckmorton's Bullfinch, 17.
While rocking winds are piping loud.   Penseroso, 126.

A massy slab, in fashion square or round.   Task, i. 21.
     Extended wide
In circuit, undetermined square or round.   P. L. ii. 1047-8.

     In the cushion fixed:
If cushion might be called what harder seemed.   Ib. i. 54-5.
     The other Shape,
If shape it might be call'd that shape had none.   P. L. ii. 666-7; cf. *i. 227-8.*
     (Similar parenthetical repetitions occur in The Task, i. 602-3, ii. 717,
754-5, v. 162-3, 871-2; Odyssey, ii. 449-50, 468-9.)

Nor rural sights alone, but rural sounds.   Ib. i. 181.
Each rural sight, each rural sound.   P. L. ix. 451.

At dewy eve.   Ib. i. 316.
From morn to eve his solitary task.   Ib. v. 44.
"From morn to eve I fell, a summer's day."   Iliad, i. 730.
     From morn
To noon he fell, from noon to dewy eve,
A summer's day.   P. L. i. 742-4.

And, armed himself in panoply complete
Of heavenly temper.   Task, ii. 345-6.
He, in celestial panoply all arm'd
Of radiant Urim.   P. L. vi. 760-61.

Bars and bolts
Grew rusty by disuse, and massy gates
Forgot their office, opening with a touch.   Task, ii. 745–7.
           Every bolt and bar
Of massy iron or solid rock with ease
Unfastens: on a sudden open fly.   P. L. ii. 877–9.

As one who, long in thickets and in brakes
Entangled, winds now this way and now that . . .
Or having long in miry ways been foiled
And sore discomfited, from slough to slough
Plunging, and half despairing of escape,
If chance at length he finds a greensward smooth
And faithful to the foot, his spirits rise,
He chirrups brisk his ear-erecting steed,
And winds his way with pleasure and with ease.   Ib. iii. 1–10.
As one who long detained on foreign shores
Pants to return.   Ib. v. 832–3.
As one who, long in populous city pent,
Where houses thick and sewers annoy the air,
Forth issuing on a summer's morn to breathe
Among the pleasant villages and farms
Adjoin'd, from each thing met conceives delight . . .
If chance with nymph-like step fair virgin pass,
What pleasing seem'd, for her now pleases more.   P. L. ix. 445–53.

Vernal airs breathe mild.   Ib. iii. 443.
Airs, vernal airs,   Breathing the smell of field.   P. L. iv. 264–5.

Overlaid with clear translucent glass.   Ib. iii. 485.
Under the glassy, cool, translucent wave.   Comus, 861.

The voluble and restless earth.   Ib. iii. 490.
This less volubil Earth.   P. L. iv. 594.

Much yet remains   Unsung.   Ib. iii. 605–6.
Half yet remains unsung.   P. L. vii. 21.

Fell Discord, arbitress of such debate,
Perched on the sign-post, holds with even hand
Her undecisive scales.   Ib. iv. 482–4.
           Chaos umpire sits,
And by decision more embroils the fray
By which he reigns; next him, high arbiter,
Chance governs all.   P. L. ii. 907–10.
     (Cf. *P. L.* ii. 960–67, where Discord is mentioned in connection with Chaos.)

Would I had fallen upon those happier days.   Ib. iv. 513.
Though fall'n on evil days.   P. L. vii. 25.

Leaving unconcerned
The cheerful haunts of man.   Ib. v. 41–2.
In nooks obscure, far from the ways of men.   Ib. vi. 842.
Exiled . . . from every cheerful haunt of man.   Iliad vi. 247–8.
Far from the cheerful haunt of men.   Comus, 388.
From the cheerful ways of men   Cut off.   P. L. iii. 46–7.

Half on wing   And half on foot.   Task, v. 62–3.
Half on foot,   Half flying.   P. L. ii. 941–2.

Arrowy sleet.   Ib. v. 140.
Sharp sleet of arrowy showers.   *P. R. iii. 324.*
    (But cf. Gray's Fatal Sisters, 3, "Iron-sleet of arrowy shower.")

Silently as a dream the fabric rose.   Ib. v. 144.
Anon out of the earth a fabric huge
Rose like an exhalation.   *P. L. i. 710–11.*
        (Of a palace in each case.)

        In that sickly, foul,
Opprobrious residence he finds them all.
Propense his heart to idols.   Ib. v. 583–5.
        For their dwelling-place
Accept this dark opprobrious den of shame.   *P. L. ii. 57–8.*
Hearts, propense enough before   To waver.   *Samson, 455–6.*

Ages of hopeless misery.   Ib. v. 607.
Ages of hopeless end.   *P. L. ii. 186.*
        (Of hell in each case.)

To gratulate the new-created earth.   Ib. v. 820.
To gratulate the sweet return of morn.   *P. R. iv. 438.*

        Wanders lost,
With intellects bemazed in endless doubt.   Ib. v. 847–8.
And found no end, in wandering mazes lost.   *P. L. ii. 561.*
        (Of religious doctrines in each case.)

        Pomona, Pales, Pan,
And Flora and Vertumnus.   Ib. vi. 233–4.
To Pales, or Pomona . . . when she fled Vertumnus. *P. L. ix. 393–5.*

[The effect of the fall of man upon the animals, as described in The Task, vi. 368–83,
was probably suggested by *Paradise Lost*, x. 710–14, xi. 182–90.]

Fixed motionless, and petrified with dread.   Ib. vi. 538.
In stony fetters fix'd and motionless.   *Comus, 819.*

Sheer o'er the craggy barrier.   Ib. vi. 554.
Sheer o'er the chariot front.   Iliad, xvi. 494.
Sheer o'er the crystal battlements.   *P. L. i. 742.*

The looms of Ormus, and the mines of Ind.   Task, vi. 806.
The wealth of Ormus and of Ind.   *P. L. ii. 2.*

And Saba's spicy groves.   Ib. vi. 807.
Sabaean odours from the spicy shore.   *P. L. iv. 162.*

From yonder withered spray.   To the Nightingale, 2.
O Nightingale, that on yon bloomy spray.   *Nightingale sonnet, 1.*
        (The riming word is "May" in each case.)

The grand consult dissolved.   Iliad, i. 385.
The great consult began.   *P. L. i. 798.*
The Stygian council thus dissolved.   *P. L. ii. 506.*

What word hath passed thy lips, Saturnian Jove,
Thou most severe!   Ib. i. 678–9.
What word hath pass'd thy lips, Jove most severe!   Ib. iv. 29, viii. 537, xviii. 446.
What words have pass'd thy lips, Adam severe!   *P. L. ix. 1144.*
        (Said by a woman to her husband in each case. Cowper has similar lines, ib.
        viii. 240–41, xiv. 97, Odyssey, i. 81.)

Writhing to and fro.	Iliad, ii. 321.
Convolved with pain he lay.	Ib. xiii. 752.
Then Satan first knew pain,	
And writhed him to and fro convolved.	*P. L. vi. 327–8.*

And twitch'd her fragrant robe.	Ib. iii. 458.
And twitch'd his mantle blue.	*Lycidas, 192.*

When through the adamantine gates he pass'd.	Ib. viii. 422; cf. ii. 324.
These adamantine gates.	*P. L. ii. 853;* cf. *436.*
(Of hell in each case.)	

Smooth-sliding streams.	Ib. xv. 328.
Smooth-sliding Mincius.	*Lycidas, 86.*

Tower'd city.	Ib. xv. 891.
Towered cities.	*Allegro, 117.*

With nimble steps and short.	Ib. xvi. 739.
With toilsome step and difficult.	On Finding Heel of a Shoe, 35.
With wandering steps and slow.	*P. L. xii. 648.*

Earthward he slopes again his westering wheels.	Odyssey, xi. 19.
Westering apace.	Iliad, xxiii. 195.
Toward Heaven's descent had sloped his westering wheel.	*Lycidas, 31.*

(Pointed out by Cowper in each place.)

DICTION

Covert (as a noun, Task, i. 233, Iliad, viii. 305); cf. P. L. iii. 39, iv. 693, etc.

Vapours *dank* (Task, i. 438, iii. 499); cf. P. L. vii. 441, ix. 179, etc.

Ever-during brass (Task, v. 710, Odyssey, xi. 704); cf. P. L. iii. 45, vii. 206.

Hedge-row shrubs (Retirement, 419, and cf. Task, i. 173); cf. Allegro, 58.

Horrent (Iliad, vii. 69, xiii. 413); cf. P. L. ii. 513. Of arms in each case.

Small *interval* between (Iliad, iii. 134, x. 191, xiii. 734, xvi. 557); cf. P. L. vi. 105. Of space between combatants in each case.

Intestine war (Mutual Forbearance, 48); cf. P. L. vi. 259, ii. 1001.

Massy (Task, i. 21, 59, ii. 746, Iliad, xiii. 620, 1007); cf. P. L. i. 285, 703, etc.

Misdeems (Task, iv. 685); cf. P. L. ix. 301, P. R. i. 424.

Nitrous air (Task, iii. 32); cf. P. L. iv. 815, vi. 512.

Oary barks (Iliad, ii. 193, xviii. 318, Odyssey, iii. 205); cf. P. L. vii. 440.

O'erleap (of barriers, Task, ii. 55, iii. 681, Table Talk, 302); cf. P. L. iv. 181, 583.

Shagg'd (Iliad, xv. 378); cf. Comus, 429.

Smit with (Task, v. 560); cf. P. L. iii. 29.

Speculative height (Task, i. 289, Jackdaw, 13); cf. P. L. xii. 588–9, P. R. iv. 236.

Tempest (as a verb, Iliad, xv. 168); cf. P. L. vii. 412. Pointed out by Cowper.

Tricked with flowers (Task, vi. 992); cf. Penseroso, 123, Lycidas, 170.

Unwieldy joy (Queen's Visit to London, 20); cf. P. L. iv. 345, vii. 411. Of sea-monsters in the first and third cases.

Well attired (of a plant, Task, vi. 168); cf. Lycidas, 146.

WORDSWORTH [1]

Toil, small as pigmies in the gulf profound.   Evening Walk, 163.
The cataract had borne him down
Into the gulf profound.   Idle Shepherd-Boys, 69–70.
Bishops and Priests, think what a gulf profound.   Eccl. Sonnets, III. xvi. 12.
A gulf profound as that Serbonian bog.   P. L. ii. 592.

The swan uplifts his chest, and backward flings
His neck, a varying arch, between his towering wings. . . .
Close by her mantling wings' embraces prest.   Evening Walk, 218–31.
Fair is the Swan, whose majesty, prevailing. . . .
Behold! the mantling spirit of reserve
Fashions his neck into a goodly curve;
An arch thrown back between luxuriant wings.   Dion (original form), 1–7.
        The swan, with arched neck
Between her white wings mantling proudly.   P. L. vii. 438–9; cf. v. 279.
      (Wordsworth also speaks of the "mantling" celandine, To the Small
      Celandine, 2d poem, 24; "mantling triumphs," Sonnet, "Grief, thou hast
      lost," 14; and "mantling ale," Duddon, xiii. 12.)

        Hear at morn
The hound, the horse's tread, and mellow horn.   Evening Walk, 244–5.
Oft listening how the hounds and horn
Cheerly rouse the slumbering Morn.   Allegro, 53–4.

Ah me! all light is mute amid the gloom,
The interlunar cavern of the tomb.   Ib. (1793 ed.), 267–8.
"As the moon   Hid in her vacant interlunar cave."   Prelude, vii. 283–4.
The Sun to me is dark
And silent as the Moon,
When she deserts the night,
Hid in her vacant interlunar cave.   Samson, 86–9.

The "parting Genius" sighs with hollow breath.   Desc. Sketches, 71.
The parting Genius is with sighing sent.   Nativity, 186.

Bosomed deep in chestnut groves.   Ib. 78.
Bosom'd high in tufted trees.   Allegro, 78.
      (Wordsworth uses "bosomed" three times more, twice in the sense of
      hidden by trees. "Embosom," "embosoming," and "embosomed" he
      uses nine times; cf. P. L. iii. 75, v. 597.)

And neighbouring moon, that coasts the vast profound,
Wheel pale and silent her diminish'd round.   Ib. (1793 ed.), 382–3.
       While overhead the moon . . .
Wheels her pale course.   P. L. i. 784–6.
A gulf profound.   P. L. ii. 592.
Round through the vast profundity obscure.   P. L. vii. 229.

Tinged like an angel's smile all rosy red.   Desc. Sketches, 475.
       Unveiling timidly a cheek
Suffused with blushes of celestial hue.   Eccl. Sonnets, II. xxii. 5–6.
To whom the Angel, with a smile that glow'd
Celestial rosy red, love's proper hue.   P. L. viii. 618–19.

---

[1] These parallels are nearly all taken from a collection of material regarding Wordsworth's debt to Milton, undertaken at Cornell University by Mrs. Alice M. Dunbar of Wilmington, Delaware, under the direction of Mr. Lane Cooper, who called my attention to the work. They are published here for the first time by the very kind consent of Mrs. Dunbar, whose list contains many more.

Dim religious groves embow'r.   Desc. Sketches (1793 ed.), 124.
Casting a dim religious light.   *Penseroso, 160.*
Etrurian shades   High over-arch'd embower.   *P. L. i. 303–4.*
   (Wordsworth also has ten cases of "embowering" and "embowered,"
   usually of trees.)

His larum-bell from village-tow'r to tow'r
Swing on th'astounded ear it's dull undying roar.   Ib. (1793 ed.), 778–9.
The solemn curfew swinging long and deep.   Evening Walk (1793 ed.), 318.
I hear the far-off curfew sound . . .
Swinging slow with sullen roar.   *Penseroso, 74–6.*

          Through his brain
At once the griding iron passage found.   Guilt and Sorrow, 492–3.
The griding sword with disconlinuous wound
Pass'd through him.   *P. L. vi. 329–30.*

When I behold the ruins of that face,
Those eyeballs dark — dark beyond hope of light.   Borderers, i. 135–6.
Nor appear'd   Less than Archangel ruin'd. . . .
. . . . Darken'd so, yet shone
Above them all the Archangel; but his face.   *P. L. i. 592–600.*
Oh dark, dark, dark, amid the blaze of noon,
Irrecoverably dark, total eclipse
Without all hope of day!   *Samson, 80–82.*

But, oh the heavy change!   Simon Lee, 25.
And, O the change!   Mother's Return, 53.
And partner of my loss. — O heavy change!   Excursion, iii. 669.
But, O the heavy change, now thou art gone!   *Lycidas, 37.*

Suffer my genial spirits to decay.   Tintern Abbey, 113.
So much I feel my genial spirits droop.   *Samson, 594.*

Could Father Adam open his eyes
And see this sight beneath the skies,
He'd wish to close them again.   Redbreast chasing the Butterfly, 12–14.
   (A reference, as Wordsworth pointed out, to *P. L.* xi. 185–90.)

Thou art . . . a thing "beneath our shoon."   To the Small Celandine (2), 49–50.
   · *The dull swain*
Treads on it daily with his clouted shoon.   *Comus, 634–5.*
         (Of a flower in each case.)

The beetle panoplied in gems and gold,
A mailèd angel on a battle-day.   Stanzas in "Castle of Indolence," 60–61.
Up rose the victor Angels, and to arms
The matin trumpet sung; in arms they stood
Of golden panoply, refulgent host. . . .
He, in celestial panoply all arm'd
Of radiant Urim, work divinely wrought.   *P. L. vi. 525–7, 760–1.*
Gems and gold.   *P. L. ii. 271, vi. 475.*
   (Wordsworth also has "whose panoply is not a thing put on"—"Who
   rises on the banks," 17; and "your scaly panoplies" — "The soaring
   lark," 23.)

To overleap   At will the crystal battlements . . .
O'er Limbo lake with aëry flight to steer,
And on the verge of Chaos hang in fear.   Departure from Grasmere, 5–12.

The "trumpery" that ascends in bare display —
Bulls, pardons, relics, cowls black, white, and grey —
Upwhirled, and flying o'er the ethereal plain
Fast bound for Limbo Lake.   Eccl. Sonnets, II. xxviii. 6–9.
At one slight bound high overleap'd all bound
Of hill or highest wall.   *P. L. iv. 181–2.*
Sheer o'er the crystal battlements.   *P. L. i. 742.*
Steers his flight.   *P. L. i. 225.*
Spread his aery flight.   *P. L. ii. 407.*
Into this wild Abyss [Chaos] *the wary Fiend*
Stood on the brink of Hell and look'd a while,
Pondering his voyage.   *P. L. ii. 917–19.*
                              Eremites and friars
White, black, and grey, with all their trumpery. . . .
Cowls, hoods, and habits, with their wearers, tost
And flutter'd into rags; then reliques, beads,
Indulgences, dispenses, pardons, bulls,
The sport of winds: all these, upwhirl'd aloft . . .
Into a limbo large and broad.   *P. L. iii. 474–5, 490–5.*

Stern Daughter of the Voice of God!   Ode to Duty, 1.
God so commanded, and left that command
Sole daughter of his voice.   *P. L. ix. 652–3.*

A watchful heart   Still couchant.   "When, to the attractions," 81–2.
Changes oft   His couchant watch.   *P. L. iv. 405–6.*
       (Wordsworth also speaks of a "couchant" lion, fawn, doe: To Enterprise,
       35; "Long has the dew," 5; White Doe, i. 203.)

Alas! what boots it? — who can hide?   The Waggoner, 702.
Alas! what boots the long laborious quest?   Tyrolese Sonnets, iv. 1.
"What boots," continued she, "to mourn?"   Egyptian Maid, 97.
What boots the sculptured tomb?   Excursion, vi. 615.
Alas! what boots it with uncessant care?   *Lycidas, 64.*

The gift of this adventurous song.   The Waggoner, 784.
Invoke thy aid to my advent'rous song.   *P. L. i. 13.*

The earth is all before me.   Prelude, i. 14.
The world was all before them.   *P. L. xii. 646.*

                    Immortal verse
Thoughtfully fitted to the Orphean lyre.   Ib. i. 232–3.
                    Raptures of the lyre;
And wisdom married to immortal verse.   Excursion, vii. 535–6.
Whose waves the Orphean lyre forbad to meet.   Source of the Danube, 9.
Where is the Orphean lyre, or Druid harp,
To accompany the verse?   To the Clouds, 60–61.
With other notes than to the Orphean lyre   I sung.   *P. L. iii. 17–18.*
Soft Lydian airs   Married to immortal verse.   *Allegro, 136–7.*

With crosses and with cyphers scribbled o'er.   Prelude, i. 511.
With centric and eccentric scribbled o'er.   *P. L. viii. 83.*

Hence life, and change, and beauty, solitude
More active even than "best society."   Ib. ii. 294–5.
Solitude to her   Is blithe society.   Characteristics of a Child, 12–13.
For solitude sometimes is best society.   *P. L. ix. 249.*

Her pealing organ was my neighbour too.   Prelude, iii. 57.
There let the pealing organ blow.   *Penseroso, 161.*

This is, in truth, heroic argument.
Argument   Not less but more heroic.

Prelude, iii. 184.
P. L. ix. 13–14; cf. 28–9.

Stood almost single . . .
Darkness before, and danger's voice behind.
In darkness, and with dangers compass'd round,
And solitude.

Ib. iii. 287–8.

P. L. vii. 27–8.

(Of Milton in each case.)

Grain-tinctured, drenched in empyrean light.
Sky-tinctured grain.

Ib. iv. 328.
P. L. v. 285.

Dews, vapours, and the melody of birds.
Walks, and the melody of birds.

Ib. iv. 331.
P. L. viii. 528.

Whether by native prose, or numerous verse.
In prose or numerous verse.

Ib. v. 200.
P. L. v. 150.

Her brood,   Though fledged and feathered.
Their brood . . . feather'd soon and fledge.

Ib. v. 246–7.
P. L. vii. 418–20.

(Of young fowl in each case.)

These mighty workmen of our later age,
Who, with a broad highway, have overbridged
The froward chaos of futurity.

Ib. v. 347–9.

(A reference to *P. L.* x. 249–320.)

A pensive sky, sad days, and piping winds.
While rocking winds are piping loud.

Ib. vi. 174.
Penseroso, 126.

That seemed another morn   Risen on mid noon.
Seems another morn   Risen on mid-noon.

Ib. vi. 197–8.
P. L. v. 310–11.

The mountains more by blackness visible
And their own size, than any outward light.
No light, but rather darkness visible.

Ib. vi. 714–15.
P. L. i. 63.

Lead his voice through many a maze.
The melting voice through mazes running.

Ib. vii. 555.
Allegro, 142.

Tract more exquisitely fair
Than that famed paradise of ten thousand trees,
Or Gehol's matchless gardens.
Spot more delicious than those gardens feign'd
Or of revived Adonis, or renown'd
Alcinous, host of old Laertes' son.

Ib. viii. 75–7.

P. L. ix. 439–41.

And boon nature's lavish help.
Of mountain-quiet and boon nature's grace.
But Nature boon
Pour'd forth profuse on hill, and dale, and plain.

Ib. viii. 81.
Eccl. Sonnets, I. i. 4.

P. L. iv. 242–3.

The curious traveller . . . sees, or thinks he sees.
Some belated peasant sees,   Or dreams he sees.

Prelude, viii. 560–65.
P. L. i. 783–4.

(Of the supernatural in each case.)

Such opposition as aroused
The mind of Adam, yet in Paradise
Though fallen from bliss, when in the East he saw
Darkness ere day's mid course, and morning light
More orient in the western cloud, that drew
O'er the blue firmament a radiant white,
Descending slow with something heavenly fraught.

Ib. viii. 658–64.

Why in the east
Darkness ere day's mid-course, and morning-light
More orient in yon western cloud, that draws
O'er the blue firmament a radiant white,
And slow descends, with something heavenly fraught? P. L. xi. 203–7.

And oft amid the "busy hum" I seemed. Ib. viii. 680.
And the busy hum of men. *Allegro, 118.*

Or crown of burning seraphs as they sit
In the empyrean. Ib. x. 522–3.
From the pure Empyrean when he [God] *sits.* P. L. iii. 57.
  (Wordsworth also uses "empyrean" twice as an adjective; Milton has
  it five times as a noun and once as an adjective.)

And thou, O flowery field Of Enna! Ib. xi. 419–20.
      Not that fair field
Of Enna, where Proserpin gathering flowers. P. L. iv. 268–9.

Not like a temple rich with pomp and gold. Ib. xiii. 229.
With gay religions full of pomp and gold. P. L. i. 372.

That broods Over the dark abyss. Ib. xiv. 71–2.
Dove-like sat'st brooding on the vast Abyss. P. L. i. 21.

Hence endless occupation for the Soul,
Whether discursive or intuitive. Ib. xiv. 119–20.
      Whence the soul
Reason receives, and reason is her being,
Discursive, or intuitive. P. L. v. 486–8.

And substitute a universe of death
For that which moves with light and life informed. Ib. xiv. 160–61.
A universe of death. P. L. ii. 622.
All alike inform'd With radiant light. P. L. iii. 593–4.

And sought *that* beauty, which, as Milton sings,
Hath terror in it. Ib. xiv. 245–6.
Not terrible, though terror be in love
And beauty. P. L. ix. 490–1.

Methought I saw the footsteps of a throne. Sonnet, "Methought I saw," 1.
Methought I saw my late espousèd saint. *Sonnet, "Methought I saw,"* 1.
      (But cf. Ralegh's sonnet on the Faerie Queene.)

His genius shook the buskined stage. Seat in Coleorton, 16.
Ennobled hath the buskin'd stage. *Penseroso, 102.*

Her duty is to stand and wait. White Doe, iv. 132.
They also serve who only stand and wait. Sonnet on his Blindness, 14.

But ere the Moon had sunk to rest
In her pale chambers of the west. Ib. iv. 223–4.
Pacing toward the other goal
Of his [the sun's] *chamber in the east.* Comus, 100–101.

With woollen cincture. Ib. vii. 57.
With feather'd cincture. P. L. ix. 1117.
      (Of clothing in each case. Wordsworth also has "encincture": Source
      of Danube, 8; Excursion, v. 159; Eccl. Sonnets, III. xli. 9.)

A hut, by tufted trees defended.   White Doe, vii. 142.
Upon a rising ground a grey church-tower,
Whose battlements were screened by tufted trees.   Excursion, v. 80–81.
[A chapel] tufted with an ivy grove.   Peter Bell, 855.
Towers and battlements it sees
Bosom'd high in tufted trees.   *Allegro, 77–8.*
On a plat of rising ground.   *Penseroso, 73.*

Dear Liberty! stern Nymph of soul untamed;
Sweet Nymph, O rightly of the mountains named!   Tyrolese Sonnets, ii. 2–3.
The mountain nymph, sweet Liberty.   *Allegro, 36.*

For they have learnt to open and to close
The ridges of grim war.   Spanish Guerillas, 3–4.
Expert . . . to . . . open when, and when to close
The ridges of grim war.   *P. L. vi. 233–6.*

Like the bright confines of another world.   View from Black Comb, 27.
Of those bright confines [heaven].   *P. L. ii. 395.*

I sing: — "fit audience let me find though few!"
So prayed, more gaining than he asked, the Bard —
In holiest mood. Urania, I shall need
Thy guidance, or a greater Muse, if such
Descend to earth or dwell in highest heaven!   Excursion, preface, 23–7.
Descend from Heaven, Urania. . . .
     . . . . Still govern thou my song,
Urania, and fit audience find, though few.   *P. L. vii. 1, 30–31.*

Under the covert of these clustering elms.   Ib. i. 51.
Under the covert of some ancient oak.   *P. R. i. 305;* cf. *ii. 262–3.*

That left half-told the preternatural tale.   Ib. i. 179.
That left half told The story.   *Penseroso, 109–10.*

     Commenced in pain,
In pain commenced, and ended without peace.   Ib. iv. 2–3.
     Though fall'n on evil days,
On evil days though fall'n, and evil tongues.   *P. L. vii. 25–6.*

Yet cease I not to struggle, and aspire.   Ib. iv. 126.
     Yet not the more
Cease I to wander where the Muses haunt.   *P. L. iii. 26–7.*

Who dwell on earth, yet breathe empyreal air.   Ib. iv. 231.
     I have presumed,
An earthly guest, and drawn empyreal air.   *P. L. vii. 13–14.*
     ("Empyreal air" occurs again in Epitaphs from Chiabrera, viii. 20, and
"empyreal" in five other places.)

Upon the breast of new-created earth
Man walked; and when and wheresoe'er he moved,
Alone or mated, solitude was not.
He heard, borne on the wind, the articulate voice
Of God; and Angels to his sight appeared
Crowning the glorious hills of paradise;
Or through the groves gliding like morning mist
Enkindled by the sun. He sate — and talked
With wingèd Messengers.   Ib. iv. 631–9.

(This appears to be a reference to God's talks with Adam and Eve, the visit of Raphael, Michael, etc., in *Paradise Lost*. Lines 634-7 seem to refer to the passages,

How often, from the steep
Of echoing hill or thicket, have we heard
Celestial voices!   P. L. iv. 680-82.

          For I descry
From yonder blazing cloud that veils the hill
One of the heavenly host.   P. L. xi. 228-30.
The Cherubim descended; on the ground
Gliding meteorous, as evening mist.   P. L. xii. 628-9; cf. *ix. 179-80.*)

Large and massy; for duration built;
With pillars crowded.   Ib. v. 145-6.
With antic pillars massy proof.   *Penseroso, 158.*

If to be weak is to be wretched — miserable,
As the lost Angel by a human voice
Hath mournfully pronounced.   Ib. v. 318-20.
Fall'n Cherub, to be weak is miserable.   P. L. i. 157.

"Unshaken, unseduced, unterrified."   Ib. vi. 260.
Unshaken, unseduced, unterrified.   P. L. v. 899.
    (Wordsworth's "Self-reviewed, self-catechised, self-punished, *ib.* vi. 386-7, seems made by analogy to this line of Milton's and similar ones: e. g., P. L. ii. 185, iii. 372-5, and particularly iii. 130, "self-tempted, self-depraved.")

That mixture of earth's mould.   Ib. vi. 273.
Can any mortal mixture of earth's mould.   *Comus, 244.*
                (Of a person in each case.)

Light . . . Whose sacred influence.   Ib. vii. 482-4.
The sacred influence Of light appears.   P. L. ii. 1034-5.

But each instinct with spirit.   Ib. vii. 509.
Itself instinct with spirit.   P. L. vi. 752.
    (Wordsworth also has "instinct with" music, freshness, malice, etc.: Morning Exercise, 29; Duddon, iii. 13; Eccl. Sonnets, I. vi. 2; etc.)

A many-windowed fabric huge.   Ib. viii. 169.
Strains that call forth upon empyreal ground
Immortal Fabrics, rising to the sound
Of penetrating harps and voices sweet.   Cathedral at Cologne, 12-14.
Rising like an exhalation.   The Waggoner, 689.
Anon out of the earth a fabric huge
Rose like an exhalation, with the sound
Of dulcet symphonies and voices sweet.   P. L. i. 710-12.
         (Of a building in every case but the third.)

Or lapse of liquid element.   Excursion, viii. 331.
The liquid lapse serene [of a river].   Duddon, xx. 4; cf. iv. 7.
And liquid lapse of murmuring streams.   P. L. viii. 263.
    (Wordsworth also speaks of the lapse of water in three other places: "Never enlivened," 14; Prelude, iv. 383; Excursion, iii. 93.)

Their human form divine.   Excursion, ix. 151.
Or flocks, or herds, or human face divine.   P. L. iii. 44.

They know if I be silent, morn or even.   Ib. ix. 750.
Witness if I be silent, morn or even.   P. L. v. 202.

Redundant are thy locks.   Laodamia, 59.
Graced with redundant hair, Iopas sings.   Aeneid, 121.
These redundant locks.   *Samson, 568.*
            (Virgil's word is "crinitus," long-haired.)

Thus was a Brother by a Brother saved;
With whom a crown (temptation that hath set
Discord in hearts of men till they have braved
Their nearest kin with deadly purpose met)
'Gainst duty weighed, and faithful love, did seem
A thing of no esteem.   Artegal and Elidure, 234–9.
Thus was a Brother sav'd by a Brother, to whom love of a
Crown, the thing that so often dazles, and vitiats mortal
men, for which, thousands of neerest blood have destroy'd
each other, was in respect of Brotherly dearness, a con-
temptible thing.   *History of Britain, book i.*

Bisect her orbèd shield.   "Who rises on the banks," 27.
Gripe fast his orbed shield.   *P. L. vi. 543.*

But with majestic lowliness endued.   Dion, 14.
With lowliness majestic.   *P. L. viii. 42.*

Your once sweet memory, studious walks and shades!   Ib. 44.
Her sweet recess . . . studious walks and shades.   *P. R. iv. 242–3.*

            Deaf was the Sea;
Her waves rolled on. . . .
Then Canute, rising from the invaded throne . . .
Said . . . "He only is a King, and he alone
Deserves the name (this truth the billows preach)
Whose everlasting laws, sea, earth, and heaven, obey."   Fact and Imagination, 6–14.
The Sea, as before, came rowling on. . . . Wherat the
King [Canute] *quickly riseing . . .* [said] *that none indeed*
deserv'd the name of a King, but he whose Eternal Laws
both Heav'n, Earth, and Sea obey.   *History of Britain, book vi.*

"A little onward lend thy guiding hand
To these dark steps, a little further on!"   "A little onward lend," 1–2.
A little onward lend thy guiding hand
To these dark steps, a little further on.   *Samson, 1–2.*

Thy nymph-like step swift bounding o'er the lawn.   Ib. 18.
If chance with nymph-like step fair virgin pass.   *P. L. ix. 452.*

Into the "abrupt abyss."   Ib. 31.
        (The quotation is apparently a confusion of "the vast Abyss," *P. L.* i. 21,
        and "the vast abrupt," ii. 409.)

Where ravens spread their plumy vans.   Ib. 32.
Who on their plumy vans received Him soft. [Of angels.] *P. R. iv. 583.*

What a vast abyss is there!   Ascent of Helvellyn, 10.
In the vast abyss.   Peter Bell, 44.
On the vast Abyss.   *P. L. i. 21.*
The vast immeasurable Abyss.   *P. L. vii. 211.*

To Niphates' top invited,
Whither spiteful Satan steered.   Ascent of Helvellyn, 29–30.
        (A reference to *P. L.* iii. 741–2.)

Of her [the bee's] laden thigh.
While the bee with honied thigh.

Vernal Ode, 115.
Penseroso, 142.

That Star, so proud of late, looked wan;
And reeled with visionary stir
In the blue depth, like Lucifer
Cast headlong to the pit!

Pilgrim's Dream, 53–6.

(A reference to *P. L.* i. 44–5.)

Time was when field and watery cove
With modulated echoes rang,
While choirs of fervent Angels sang
Their vespers in the grove.

Composed on an Evening of Beauty, 9–12.

How often, from the steep
Of echoing hill or thicket, have we heard
Celestial voices to the midnight air,
Sole, or responsive each to other's note,
Singing their great Creator!

P. L. iv. 680–4.

Or obvious hill.
Nor obvious hill.

"As the cold aspect," 3.
P. L. vi. 69.

A Book came forth of late, called PETER BELL;
Not negligent the style; — the matter? — good.

"On the Detraction which followed the Publication of a certain Poem," 1–2.

A Book was writ of late called Tetrachordon,
And woven close, both matter, form, and style.

"On the Detraction which followed upon my writing certain Treatises," 1–2.

Bold Spirit! who art free to rove
Among the starry courts of Jove.
Before the starry threshold of Jove's court
My mansion is. [Of the attendant Spirit.]

To Enterprise, 14–15.

Comus, 1–2.

The sweet Bird, misnamed the melancholy.
Sweet bird . . . Most musical, most melancholy!

Ib. 145.
Penseroso, 61–2.

(Of the nightingale in each case.)

We feel that we are greater than we know.
And feel that I am happier than I know.

After-thought (Duddon), 14.
P. L. viii. 282.

Shall lack not power the "meeting soul to pierce!"
Such as the meeting soul may pierce.

Tour on Continent, Dedication, 14.
Allegro, 138.

That Roland clove with huge two-handed sway.

Aix-la-Chapelle, 12.

The sword of Michael smote, and fell'd
Squadrons at once: with huge two-handed sway.

P. L. vi. 250–1.

Down the irriguous valley.
Some irriguous valley.

Our Lady of the Snow, 26.
P. L. iv. 255.

Thus after Man had fallen . . .
Throngs of celestial visages,
Darkening like water in the breeze,
A holy sadness shared.

Eclipse of the Sun, 55–60.

Soon as the unwelcome news
From Earth arrived at Heaven gate, displeased
All were who heard; dim sadness did not spare
That time celestial visages.

P. L. x. 21–4.

Bright Spirit, not with amaranth crowned.   Three Cottage Girls, 70.
Immortal amaranth.   Eccl. Sonnets, I. i. 14.
Their crowns inwove with amarant and gold:
Immortal amarant.   *P. L. iii. 352–3.*
  (Wordsworth also has "amaranthine flower" — "Weak is the will," 11;
 "amaranthine wreaths" — "When the soft hand," 50; "garlands . . .
 of amaranthine bloom"—"On to Iona," 13; "amaranthine crown"—
 "The vestal priestess," 7.)

Fetch, ye that post o'er seas and lands.   Elegiac Stanzas (Goddard), 44.
O whither with such eagerness of speed? . . .
. . . . thus post ye over vale and height
To rest?   To the Clouds, 4, 9–10.
  Thousands at his bidding speed,
And post o'er land and ocean without rest.   *Sonnet on his Blindness, 12–13.*

As the dread Voice that speaks from out the sea.   At Dover, 11.
The dread voice is past.   *Lycidas, 132.*

Springs from the ground the morn to gratulate.   Eccl. Sonnets, II. xiv. 2.
To gratulate the sweet return of morn.   *P. R. iv. 438.*
  (Of birds in each case. Wordsworth uses some form of "gratulate" in
 seven other cases — there are two other instances in Milton—and has
 "gratulant" once, perhaps by analogy to Milton's "congratulant,"
 P. L. x. 458.)

Not Iris, issuing from her cloudy shrine.   Ib. xxii. 9.
Met by the rainbow's form divine,
Issuing from her cloudy shrine.   The Triad, 84–5.
Transplanted from her cloudy shrine.   *P. L. vii. 360.*

Gales sweet as those that over Eden blew.   Eccl. Sonnets, II. xxiv. 14.
    Now gentle gales,
Fanning their odoriferous wings, dispense
Native perfumes, and whisper whence they stole
Those balmy spoils. [Describing Eden.]   *P. L. iv. 156–9.*

More sweet than odours caught by him who sails
Near spicy shores of Araby the blest.   Ib. xxxix. 9–10.
   As when to them who sail . . .
Sabaean odours from the spicy shore
Of Araby the Blest.   *P. L. iv. 159–63.*

Harp! could'st thou venture, on thy boldest string,
The faintest note to echo which the blast
Caught from the hand of Moses as it pass'd
O'er Sinai's top, or from the Shepherd-king,
Early awake, by Siloa's brook, to sing.   Ib. xlvi. 1–5.
Sing, Heavenly Muse, that on the secret top
Of Oreb, or of Sinai, didst inspire
That shepherd, who first taught the chosen seed . . .
  . . . . or, if Sion hill
Delight thee more, and Siloa's brook . . .
  . . . . my advent'rous song.   *P. L. i. 6–13.*

When Alpine Vales threw forth a suppliant cry,
The majesty of England interposed
And the sword stopped; the bleeding wounds were closed;
And Faith preserved her ancient purity.
How little boots that precedent of good!   Ib. III. vii. 1–5.

(Probably a reference to Milton's Piemontese sonnet, with a borrowing
    from it and one from *Lycidas*:

Even them who kept thy truth so pure of old.   Sonnet, *3.*
Alas! what boots it with uncessant care.   *Lycidas, 64.*)

Heart-thrilling strains, that cast, before the eye
Of the devout, a veil of ecstasy!   Ib. xliv. 13–14.
Dissolve me into ecstasies,
And bring all Heaven before mine eyes?   *Penseroso, 165–6.*
            (Of organ music in a church in each case.)

Down to their "dark opprobrious den."   To Lady Fleming (1), 83.
Accept this dark opprobrious den of shame.   *P. L. ii. 58.*

With "sober certainties" of love.   "O dearer far," 8.
Such sober certainty of waking bliss.   *Comus, 263.*

All summer-long the happy Eve
Of this fair Spot her flowers may bind.   Flower Garden, 19–20.
            (A reference to *P. L.* ix. 424–31.)

In the delight of moral prudence schooled.   Pillar of Trajan, 31.
Teachers best   Of moral prudence, with delight received.   *P. R. iv. 262–3.*

Or "the rathe primrose as it dies
Forsaken" in the shade!   To May, 59–60.
Bring the rathe primrose that forsaken dies.   *Lycidas, 142.*

Thanks not Heaven amiss.   Retirement, 14.
And thank the gods amiss.   *Comus, 177.*

In ten thousand dewy rays.   The Triad, 130.
Shot parallel to the Earth his dewy ray.   *P. L. v. 141.*

Even She whose Lydian airs inspire.   Power of Sound, 76.
Lap me in soft Lydian airs.   *Allegro, 136.*

                    The hymn
Of joy, that from her utmost walls
The six-days' Work, by flaming Seraphim
Transmits to Heaven.   Ib. 201–4.
        (This seems to be a reference to the hymns of the angels at the completion
        of God's "six days' work, a World," in *Paradise Lost*, vii. 557–634. The
        account in Genesis contains no hymns and no seraphim.)

Nor stopped, till in the dappling east
Appeared unwelcome dawn.   Russian Fugitive, 15–16.
Till the dappled dawn doth rise.   *Allegro, 44.*

And their necks play, involved in rings,
Like sinless snakes in Eden's happy land.   Egyptian Maid, 322–3.
            About them frisking play'd
All beasts of the earth, since wild. . . .
        . . . . close the serpent sly,
Insinuating, wove with Gordian twine
His braided train.   *P. L. iv. 340–49.*

With copious eulogy in prose or rhyme.   Elegiac Musings, 1.
Things unattempted yet in prose or rhyme.   *P. L. i. 16.*

Which moonlit elves, far seen by credulous eyes,
Enter in dance.   Place of Burial, 4–5.
                    Or faery elves,
Whose midnight revels, by a forest side
Or fountain, some belated peasant sees.   *P. L. i. 781–3.*

The sovereign Architect.   Cave of Staffa (1), 13.
The sovran Architect.   *P. L. v. 256.*
                    (Of God in each case.)

The pillared vestibule . . . the roof embowed.   Ib. (2), 5–6.
The high embowed roof,   With antic pillars.   *Penseroso, 157–8.*

He hath been an Elm without his Vine,
And her bright dower of clustering charities,
That, round his trunk and branches, might have clung
Enriching and adorning.   Death of Charles Lamb, 73–6.
                    Or they led the vine
To wed her elm; she, spoused, about him twines
Her marriageable arms, and with her brings
Her dower, the adopted clusters, to adorn
His barren leaves.   *P. L. v. 215–19.*

So pure, so fraught with knowledge and delight,
As to be likened in his Followers' minds
To that which our first Parents, ere the fall
From their high state da̍rkened the Earth with fear,
Held with all Kinds in Eden's blissful bowers.   Cuckoo at Laverna, 61–5.
                    (References to *P. L.* iv. 340–52.)

                    Intermingling with his dream . . .
To mock the *wandering* Voice beside some haunted stream.   Cuckoo-clock, 30–33.
Such sights as youthful poets dream
On summer eves by haunted stream.   *Allegro, 129–30.*

Intrenched your brows; ye gloried in each scar.   "Proud were ye, Mountains," 3.
                    But his face
Deep scars of thunder had intrench'd.   *P. L. i. 600–601.*

How look'd Achilles, their dread paramount.   Aeneid, 138.
The Word   (Thy Paramount, mighty Nature!).   "On to Iona," 4–5.
The head and mighty paramount of truths.   Excursion, vi. 85.
Midst came their mighty Paramount, and seem'd
Alone the antagonist of Heaven, nor less
Than Hell's dread Emperor.   *P. L. ii. 508–10.*

Through optic-glass discern.   Grace Darling, 36.
Through optic glass . . . views.   *P. L. i. 288;* cf. *iii. 590.*

Diction

The *adamantine* holds of truth (Prelude, v. 39); cf. P. L. i. 48, ii. 646, etc.
Towers *amain* (Desc. Sketches, 459; also blew *amain*, runs *amain*, etc., Prelude,
i. 334, x. 373, etc.); cf. Lycidas, 111, P. L. ii. 165, 1024, etc.
If willing *audience* fail not (Prelude, xi. 350), attentive *audience* (Excursion, iii.
600), how win Due *audience* ("The Baptist might have been," 3–4); cf. P. L.
ii. 308, v. 804, ix. 674, xii. 12.
Begirt with silver bells (Processions, 23), temporal shapes (Prelude, viii. 496),
battlements (Excursion, ii. 843–4); cf. P. L. i. 581, v. 868, P. R. ii. 213.

In the flower-*besprent* meadows (At Vallombrosa, 13), plains *Besprent* . . . with steeple-towers (Excursion, vi. 17–18); cf. Comus, 542.

Commerce with the summer night (Desc. Sketches, 578), the sun (Eccl. Sonnets, III. xlvi. 13), etc.; cf. Penseroso, 39.

Compeer (Prelude x. 199, Excursion viii. 581, ix. 431, etc.); cf. P. L. i. 127, iv. 974.

Up-coiling, and . . . *convolved* (Yew-trees, 18); cf. P. L. vi. 328.

Like a bird *Darkling* (Peter Bell, 344–5), *darkling* wren (Duddon, vii. 13), etc.; cf. P. L. iii. 38–9.

With *descant* soft (Redbreast, 41), the *descant* [bird-song], and the wind ("In desultory walk," 10); cf. P. L. iv. 603.

The *embattled* East ("O, for a kindling touch," 7), *embattled* House (Duddon, xxvii. 3), *embattled* hall (Eccl. Sonnets, II. vi. 6); cf. P. L. i. 129, vi. 16, etc.

Showed her *fulgent* head ("The Shepherd," 5), *fulgent* west (Gipsies, 14), *fulgent* eye ("The imperial Stature," 7), *fulgent* spectacle (Prelude, x. 526); cf. P. L. x. 449. — *Refulgent* cars (To Enterprise, 110), *refulgent* spectacle (Excursion, ix. 611); cf. P. L. vi. 527. — Bright *effulgence* (Vernal Ode, 11), solemn *effulgence* ("When the soft hand," 78), etc.; cf. P. L. iii. 388, v. 458, vi. 680.

The smooth *glozings* of the indulgent world (Excursion, vi. 1086); cf. P. L. iii. 93, Comus, 161.

A *griesly* sight (White Doe, 244), *griesly* object (Epistle to Beaumont, 130), etc.; cf. P. L. i. 670, ii. 704, etc.

A God, *incumbent* o'er her breast (Aeneid, 88), *incumbent* o'er the surface (Prelude, iv. 272), etc.; cf. P. L. i. 226.

She can so *inform* [= form within] The mind (Tintern Abbey, 125–6), *inform* The mind with . . . truth (Excursion, ix. 301–2), patriots *informed* with Apostolic light (Eccl. Sonnets, III. xv. 1), etc.; cf. P. L. iii. 593.

Natural *inlets* of just sentiment (Prelude, ix. 350); cf. Comus, 839.

While *jocund* June (Guilt and Sorrow, 413), with a *jocund* voice (Michael, 299), *jocund* din (Prelude, v. 379), etc.; cf. Allegro, 94, Comus, 173, 985, etc.

Massy (The Waggoner, 642, Peter Bell, 357, and eleven times more); cf. P. L. i. 285, 703, etc. (nine times more).

Ministrant To comfort (To John Wordsworth, 49–50); cf. P. L. x. 87, P. R. ii. 385.

One *oblivious* winter (Primrose of the Rock, 45), amid *oblivious* weeds (Eccl. Sonnets, I. xvii. 10), *oblivious* tendencies (Excursion, i. 928), etc.; cf. P. L. i. 266.

With *oozy* hair ("At early dawn," 8); cf. Lycidas, 175.

With *orient* rays ("Weak is the will," 8), beams of *orient* light ("While beams of," 1), *orient* gems (Excursion, iv. 568), etc.; cf. P. L. ii. 399, iii. 507, iv. 644, etc.

A *punctual* presence (Prelude, viii. 610); cf. P. L. viii. 23.

Girls — a happy *rout* (Ruth, 49), a *rout* . . . left Sir Walter's Hall (Hart-leap Well, 13), a *rout* Of giddy Bacchanals (Three Cottage Girls, 35–6), etc.; cf. P. L. i. 747, x. 534, etc.

Of their approach *Sagacious* (Prelude, viii. 224–5); cf. P. L. x. 281.

Sapient priests (Prelude, xi. 460), *sapient* Germany ("Alas, what boots," 8), *sapient* Art ("In desultory walk," 25); cf. P. L. ix. 442.

From *specular* towers ("Hope smiled," 9); cf. P. R. iv. 236, P. L. xii. 588–9.

She — a *statist* prudent (Vernal Ode, 101), Art thou a *Statist* in the van? (Poet's Epitaph, 1), modern *statists* (Prelude, xiii. 72); cf. P. R. iv. 354.

Anguish strayed from her *Tartarean* den (Vernal Ode, 130), *Tartarean* flags (Eccl. Sonnets, II. xxxvi. 12), *Tartarean* darkness (Excursion, iv. 297); cf. P. L. ii. 69, vii. 238.

Celestial with *terrene* (Eccl. Sonnets, II. xxv. 14); cf. P. L. vi. 78.

With *umbrage* wide (Evening Walk, 106), the pining *umbrage* (Yew-trees, 22), trees whose lofty *umbrage* (Brownie's Cell, 4), their leafy *umbrage* (Excursion. iv. 1067), etc.; cf. P. L. ix. 1087.

The *unapparent* face [of Napoleon] ("Haydon! let worthier judges," 9), acknowledged tie Though *unapparent* ("No more," 5–6), *unapparent* fount (Excursion, ix. 605); cf. P. L. vii. 103.

Some *unpremeditated* strains (Prelude, xiii. 353, cf. Excursion, ix. 556); cf. P. L. ix. 24.

The *unweeting* Child (Vaudracour and Julia, 208), *unweeting* that . . . the joy ("To public notice," 9); cf. Comus, 539, P. L. x. 335, 916, etc.

Push forth His arms, as swimmers *use* ("A little onward," 29–30); cf. Lycidas, 67, 136, etc.

Spread their plumy *vans* ("A little onward," 32), each wing a tiny *van* (Vernal Ode, 114); cf. P. R. iv. 583, P. L. ii. 927.

In *vermeil* colours (White Doe, ii. 12); cf. Comus, 752.

A *viewless* flight (Desc. Sketches, 69), the *viewless* winds (Prelude, v. 596), etc.; cf. Comus, 92, P. L. iii. 518, Passion, 50.

Volant spirit (In Lombardy, 13), *volant* tribe ("A volant Tribe," 1); cf. P. L. xi. 561.

O'er the pavement . . . *Welter* and flash ("Dogmatic Teachers," 11–12), if my spirit toss and *welter* (Inscriptions in Hermit's Cell, iv. 7), waves . . . *weltering*, die away (Evening Walk, 122); cf. Nativity, 124, Lycidas, 13, P. L. i. 78.

KEATS [1]

There saw the swan his neck of arched snow,
And oar'd himself along with majesty.
    The swan, with arched neck
Between her white wings mantling proudly, rows
Her state with oary feet.

Imitation of Spenser, 14–15.

P. L. vii. 438–40.

    Far different cares
Beckon me sternly from soft "Lydian airs."
And Lydian airs.
And ever, against eating cares,
Lap me in soft Lydian airs.

Epistle to G. F. Mathew, 17–18.
Vulgar Superstition, 7.

Allegro, 135–6.

To one who has been long in city pent,
'Tis very sweet to look into the fair
And open face of heaven.
As one who, long in populous city pent . . .
Forth issuing on a summer's morn to breathe
Among the pleasant villages and farms.

"To one who has," 1–3.

P. L. ix. 445–8.

How tiptoe Night holds back her dark-grey hood.
The grey-hooded Even.

Endymion, i. 831.
Comus, 188.

A mad-pursuing of the fog-born elf,
Whose flitting lantern, through rude nettle-briar,
Cheats us into a bog, into a fire.
    A wandering fire,
Compact of unctuous vapour . . .
Which oft, they say, some evil spirit attends . . .
Misleads the amazed night-wanderer from his way
To bogs and mires.
And he, by friar's lantern led.

Ib. ii. 277–9 (original form).

P. L. ix. 634–41.
Allegro, 104.

[1] These parallels (and much of the diction) were selected from those pointed out in De Sélincourt's edition of Keats.

After a thousand mazes overgone. Ib. ii. 387.
      (A classical construction perhaps suggested by
After the Tuscan mariners transform'd. *Comus, 48.*)

        And by her plainings drew
Immortal tear-drops down the thunderer's beard. Ib. ii. 475–6.
Drew iron tears down Pluto's cheek. *Penseroso, 107.*

        The unchariest muse
To embracements warm as theirs makes coy excuse. Ib. ii. 532–3.
Hence with denial vain and coy excuse;
So may some gentle Muse. *Lycidas, 18–19.*

To his capable ears   Silence was music. Ib. ii. 674–5.
Not capable her ear Of what was high. *P. L. viii. 49–50.*

Shell-winding Triton's bright-hair'd daughters. Ib. ii. 691.
By scaly Triton's winding shell. *Comus, 873.*

        And sculptures rude
In ponderous stone, developing the mood
Of ancient Nox; — then skeletons of man,
Of beast, behemoth, and leviathan,
And elephant, and eagle, and huge jaw
Of nameless monster. Ib. iii. 131–6.
Chaos and ancient Night. *P. L. ii. 970;* cf. *986.*
There leviathan, Hugest of living creatures. . . .
Behemoth, biggest born of earth. *P. L. vii. 412–13, 471.*

Into the dungeon core of that wild wood. Ib. iii. 565.
In this close dungeon of innumerous boughs. . . .
Within the navel of this hideous wood. *Comus, 349, 520.*

From vermeil lips. Ib. iv. 148.
A vermeil-tinctured lip. *Comus, 752.*

A lover would not tread
A cowslip on the head. Ib. iv. 167–8.
Thus I set my printless feet
O'er the cowslip's velvet head,
That bends not as I tread. *Comus, 897–9.*

And so I kept
Brimming the water-lily cups with tears. Ib. iv. 185–6.
And daffadillies fill their cups with tears. *Lycidas, 150.*

To the silver cymbals' ring. Ib. iv. 260.
In vain with cymbals' ring. *Nativity, 208.*

And all his priesthood moans. Ib. iv. 266.
And all their echoes mourn. *Lycidas, 41.*

Those winged steeds, with snorting nostrils bold
Snuff at its faint extreme. Ib. iv. 364–5.
Hyperion . . . still snuff'd the incense. Hyperion, i. 166–7.
With delight he snuff'd the smell. *P. L. x. 272.*

        Gone and past
Are cloudy phantasms. Caverns lone, farewel!
And air of visions, and the monstrous swell
Of visionary seas! No, never more
Shall airy voices cheat me to the shore. Endymion, iv. 650–4.
And thus in thousand hugest phantasies. Hyperion, ii. 13.

A thousand fantasies
Begin to throng into my memory,
Of calling shapes, and beckoning shadows dire,
And airy tongues that syllable men's names
On sands and shores and desert wildernesses.   *Comus, 205–9.*

And the grass, therewith besprent,
Wither'd at dew so sweet and virulent.   Lamia, i. 148–9.
Of knot-grass dew-besprent.   *Comus, 542.*

Cool'd a long age in the deep-delved earth.   Nightingale, 12.
Hid from the world in a low-delvèd tomb.   *Fair Infant, 32.*

Deep in forest drear.   Robin Hood, 18.
Of forests, and enchantments drear.   *Penseroso, 119.*

Far sunken from the healthy breath of morn.   Hyperion, i. 2.
Sweet is the breath of Morn.   *P. L. iv. 641.*

Am I to leave this haven of my rest,
This cradle of my glory, this soft clime,
This calm luxuriance of blissful light,
These crystalline pavilions, and pure fanes?   Ib. i. 235–8.
"Is this the region, this the soil, the clime,"
Said then the lost Archangel, "this the seat
That we must change for Heaven? this mournful gloom
For that celestial light?"   *P. L. i. 242–5.*

When the chill rain begins at shut of eve.   Ib. ii. 36.
Vanish'd unseasonably at shut of eve.   "The day is gone," 5.
At blushing shut of day.   Lamia, ii. 107.
Return'd at shut of evening flowers.   *P. L. ix. 278.*

Who cost her mother Tellus keener pangs.   Hyperion, ii. 54.
Which cost Ceres all that pain.   *P. L. iv. 271.*

With locks not oozy.   Ib. ii. 170.
His oozy locks he laves.   *Lycidas, 175.*

Too full of joy and soft delicious warmth.   Ib. ii. 266.
This soft ethereal frame.   Lamia, ii. 89 (rejected reading).
The soft delicious air. . . .
Their soft ethereal warmth.   *P. L. ii. 400, 601.*

In aid soft warble from the Dorian flute.   Hyperion, iii. 12.
The Dorian mood   Of flutes and soft recorders.   *P. L. i. 550–1.*

(By the touch
Of scent,) not far from roses. Turning round,
I saw an arbour with a drooping roof
Of trellis vines, and bells, and larger blooms,
Like floral censers, swinging light in air;
Before its wreathed doorway, on a mound
Of moss, was spread a feast of summer fruits,
Which, nearer seen, seem'd refuse of a meal
By angel tasted or our Mother Eve;
For empty shells were scatter'd on the grass,
And grape-stalks but half bare, and remnants more,
Sweet-smelling, whose pure kinds I could not know. . . .
Among the fragrant husks and berries crush'd
Upon the grass.   Fall of Hyperion, i. 23–34, 52–3.
(A reference to *P. L.* v. 298–395; note particularly,

Fruit of all kinds, in coat
Rough or smooth-rined, or bearded husk, or shell . . .
. . . . the grape . . . many a berry . . . then strews the ground
With rose and odours from the shrub unfumed. . . .
                    . . . . So to the sylvan lodge
They came, that like Pomona's arbour smiled,
With flowerets deck'd and fragrant smells. . . .
                    . . . . Raised of grassy turf
Their table was, and mossy seats had round. . . .   P. L. v. 341–9, 377–9, 391–2.)

The embossed roof, the silent massy range
Of columns.   Ib. i. 83–4.
And love the high embowed roof,
With antic pillars massy proof.   Penseroso, 157–8.

A power within me of enormous ken,
To see as a god sees.   Ib. i. 303–4.
At once, as far as Angels ken, he views.   P. L. i. 59.[1]

Which marries sweet sound with the grace of form.   Ib. i. 443.
Lap me in soft Lydian airs
Married to immortal verse.   Allegro, 136–7.

Mortal, that thou mayst understand aright,
I humanize my sayings to thine ear,
Making comparisons of earthly things.   Ib. ii. 1–3.
            And what surmounts the reach
Of human sense I shall delineate so,
By likening spiritual to corporal forms,
As may express them best.   P. L. v. 571–4.

When winds are all wist.   Song of Four Fairies, 98.
The winds, with wonder whist.   Nativity, 64.

        As the fabled fair Hesperian tree,
Bearing a fruit more precious!   Otho the Great, IV. i. 82–3.
But Beauty, like the fair Hesperian tree
Laden with blooming gold.   Comus, 393–4.
Trees . . . whose fruit, burnish'd with golden rind,
Hung amiable, Hesperian fables true.   P. L. iv. 248–50.

        As if Night's chariot-wheels
Were clogg'd in some thick cloud ? O, changeful Love,
Let not her steeds with drowsy-footed pace.   Ib. ii. 31–3.
Till an unusual stop of sudden silence
Gave respite to the drowsy-flighted steeds
That draw the litter of close-curtain'd Sleep.   Comus, 552–4.

Nods, becks, and hints.   Ib. V. iv. 32.
Nods and Becks, and wreathèd Smiles.   Allegro, 28.

In midmost Ind, beside Hydaspes cool. . . .
To Pigmio, of Imaus sovereign.   Cap and Bells, 1, 29.
As when a vulture on Imaus bred . . .
Of Ganges or Hydaspes, Indian streams.   P. L. iii. 431–6.

Of faeries stooping on their wings sublime.   Ib. 98.
        Or in the air sublime,
Upon the wing or in swift race contend.   P. L. ii. 528–9.
He on the wings of Cherub rode sublime.   P. L. vi. 771.

[1] This is not given by Mr. De Sélincourt.

Let the sweet mountain nymph thy favourite be,
With England's happiness proclaim Europa's Liberty.　On Peace, 8–9.
The mountain nymph, sweet Liberty.　　　　　　　*Allegro, 36.*

DICTION

I *admire* how crystal-smooth it felt (Endymion, iii. 383); cf. P. L. i. 690, ii. 677, etc.

To sit upon an *Alp* ("Happy is England," 7), upon that *alp* (End. i. 666); cf. P. L. ii. 620.

Feel *amain* (End. ii. 12; also gazed *amain*, drive *amain*, etc., Lamia, ii. 151, Cap and Bells, xxv. 9, etc.); cf. Lycidas, 111, P. L. ii. 165, 1024, etc.

I see, *astonied*, that (Hyperion, ii. 165); cf. P. L. ix. 890.

Begirt with ministring looks (End. i. 150); cf. P. L. i. 581, v. 868, P. R. ii. 213.

The whole mammoth-*brood* (of the Titans, Hyp. i. 164); cf. P. L. i. 510–11, 576, Samson, 1247.

Arcs, and broad-belting *colure* (Hyp. i. 274); cf. P. L. ix. 66.

Sly *compeers* (Cap and Bells, x. 7); cf. P. L. i. 127, iv. 974.

Curtain'd canopies (End. ii. 618), fragrant-*curtain'd* love ("The day is gone," 7); cf. Nativity, 230, Comus, 554.

A *darkling* way (Eve of St. Agnes, xl. 4), *darkling* I listen (Nightingale, 51); cf. P. L. iii. 39.

Knowledge *enormous* (Hyp. iii. 113); cf. P. L. v. 297.

My eternal *essence* (= myself, Hyp. i. 232), that puny *essence* (= Jove, ib. ii. 331); cf. P. L. i. 138, 425, ii. 215, iii. 6, ix. 166, etc.

Faded eyes (Hyp. i. 90); cf. P. L. i. 602.

Trees *Fledge* the . . . mountains (Ode to Psyche, 54–5), a *fledgy* sea-bird choir (Staffa, 41), the swan . . . on her *fledgy* breast (Otho, II. ii. 102); cf. P. L. iii. 627, vii. 420.

Eye of *gordian* snake (End. iii. 494), she [the snake] was a *gordian* shape (Lamia, i. 47); cf. P. L. iv. 347–8.

I *gratulate* you (Otho, I. i. 55); cf. Comus, 949, P. R. iv. 438.

Through . . . *griesly* gapes (End. ii. 629); cf. P. L. i. 670, ii. 704, etc.

Honied wings (End. ii. 997); cf. Penseroso, 142.　Of bees in each case.

That *inlet* to severe magnificence (Hyp. i. 211); cf. Comus, 839.

The *monstrous* sea (=peopled with monsters, End. iii. 69); cf. Lycidas, 158.

Thunder . . . Rumbles *reluctant* (Hyp. i. 60–61); cf. P. L. vi. 58, and Keats's note on it (De Sélincourt's ed., p. 497).

Of *sciential* brain (Lamia, i. 191); cf. P. L. ix. 837.

Who *'sdains* to yield to any (King Stephen, iii. 41), he *'sdeigned* the swine-head (Stanzas on Brown, ii. 4); cf. P. L. iv. 50.

The *slope* side of a suburb hill (Lamia, ii. 26), came *slope* upon the threshold of the west (Hyp. i. 204); cf. Comus, 98, P. L. iv. 261, 591.

Sovran voices (Hyp. iii. 115), her *sovran* shrine (Melancholy, iii. 6); cf. P. L. i. 246, 753, etc.

Turn'd, *syllabling* thus (Lamia, i. 244); cf. Comus, 208.

Herself, high-*thoughted* (Lamia, ii. 115), turn, sole-*thoughted*, to one Lady (Eve of St. Agnes, v. 6), one-*thoughted* . . . love ("I cry your mercy," 3); cf. Comus, 6.

APPENDIX B

POEMS IN NON-MILTONIC BLANK VERSE[1]

1667-1750

1680   ROSCOMMON, Earl of. Horace's Art of Poetry, made English, 1680.

1692   FLETCHER, THOMAS. Translations of parts of books ii–iv of the Aeneid (Poems on Several Occasions, 1692, pp. 120–32); Christ born, a pastoral (ib. 133–8).

1697-8   POPE, WALTER. The wish (1697); Moral and political fables, done into measured prose, etc. (1698).

1701-13 w. WATTS, ISAAC. A sight of Christ (Horae Lyricae, 1706, pp. 65–9); To Robert Atwood (ib. 146–52); To Sarissa (ib., 1709, pp. 174–8); True monarchy (ib. 188–90); True courage (ib. 191–3); Thoughts and meditations in a long sickness (Reliquiae Juveniles, 1734, pp. 172–83).

1702   TALBOT, G. On the vision, etc., a dialogue.—Prefixed to Matthew Smith's Vision, 1702.

1702-18   DENNIS, JOHN. The monument, a poem to William III (Select Works, 1718, i. 81–145); Battel of Ramellies (ib. 219–329); On the accession of King George (ib. 330–353); three translations, from the Bible and the Iliad (ib. ii. 468–71).

1706   D'URFEY, THOMAS. Loyalty's glory.—Stories, Moral and Comical, 1706, pp. 217–57.

1706 w. 1715 p. GROVE, HENRY. To Dr. Watts. —Works, 1747, iv. 391–2.

1708-11   ANON. [Short passages in] British Apollo, 1708–11, vol. i, nos. 50, 54, and supernumerary paper no. 7 (two pieces); vol. ii, nos. 11, 15, 18, 22, 25, 39, 49, 53, 74, 76, 83, 92, 108, 114, 115, and supernumerary paper no. 8 (two pieces); vol. iii, nos. 5, 13, 15, 18, 30, 55, 61; vol. iv, no. 5.

1713[2]   ANON. Joseph's discovery of himself to his brethren, imitated from Grotius. —Tate's Entire Set of the Monitors, 1713, vol. i, no. 8.

    ANON. Upon the crucifixion of our blessed Saviour.—Ib., no. 15, with a supplement in no. 17.

1716   MONCK, MARY. [Translations from Della Casa, Marini, and Tasso.]— Marinda, 1716, pp. 87, 89, 91, 97–107, 132–3.

1718   HINCHLIFFE, WILLIAM. To Sylvia, an epistle (Poems Amorous, Moral, and Divine, 1718, pp. 69–71); Upon Newton's Mathematical Principles, translated from Halley (ib. 171–7).

1719   RICHARDSON, JONATHAN. [A translation from Dante, and a short original piece, in Discourse on the Dignity, etc., of the Science of a Connoisseur.] —Works, new ed., 1792, pp. 184–6, 229.

1720   ANON. On Homer.—Mist's Weekly Journal, no. 105, pp. 625–6 (Dec. 3, 1720).

bef. 1721 w. PRIOR, MATTHEW. A prophecy.—Dialogues of the Dead, etc., ed. A. R. Waller, Camb., 1907, p. 318.

1725? w.   ARMSTRONG, JOHN. Imitations of Shakespeare: [Winter], Progne's dream, A storm. — Miscellanies, 1770, i. 147–63.

1726   THOMSON, JAMES. [A short translation from Virgil's Georgics.]—Winter, 2d ed., 1726, preface, pp. 17–18.

---

[1] For form and abbreviations, see the last paragraph on page 636 below.

[2] An American poem of this date is Richard Steere's *Earths Felicities, Heavens Allowances, a Blank Poem* (in *The Daniel Catcher*, Boston, 1713, pp. 55–73).

bef. 1729? CAREY, HENRY. The cypress-grove.—Poems on Several Occasions, 3d ed., 1729, pp. 118–19.

1729 ANON. Timon and Flavia.—Miscellaneous Poems, ed. James Ralph, 1729, pp. 43–52.
ANON. The courtier.—Ib. 73–9.
ANON. The lunatick.—Ib. 115–25.
ANON. Part of the third chapter of Job paraphras'd.—Ib. 208–11.

1729–39 ROWE, ELIZABETH. To the unknown God, in Letters Moral and Entertaining, 1729 (Works, 1796, i. 94–6); many short unnamed fragments (ib. 84–5, 93, 101, 104–5, 126, 220, 269, 300–1, ii. 30, 54–5, 110, and, "by another hand," i. 168, 176–7); parts of Pastor Fido translated (ib. iii. 160–62); Devout soliloquies, in blank verse (ib. 195–245); Paraphrase on Canticles, in blank verse (ib. 245–59).

1732 ANON. The happy savage.—Gent. Mag., ii. 718.

1739 BROWNE, MOSES. The power and presence of God: a version of Psalm 139.—Poems on Various Subjects, 1739, pp. 447–50.

c. 1740 w. 1849–84 p. GRAY, THOMAS. Dante, canto 33, dell' Inferno.—Works, ed. Gosse, 1884, i. 157–60.

1742 ANON. The muse's complaint to Strephon.—Scots Mag., iv. 166.
WINSTANLEY, JOHN. An address to the sepulchre of Prince George.—Poems, Dublin, 1742, pp. 69–71.

c. 1742 w. WARTON, JOSEPH. The dying Indian.—Biographical Memoirs, ed. Wooll, 1806, pp. 156–7.

bef. 1745 w. WARTON, THOMAS (the elder). A pastoral on the death of Bion, from Moschus.—Poems, 1748, pp. 197–208.

1746 HILL, AARON. Free thoughts upon faith (Works, 2d ed., 1754, iv. 217–42); Cleon to Lycidas, a time-piece (ib. 285–308). See also examples of various passions (joy, fear, etc.) in his "Essay on the Art of Acting" (ib. 377–84).

1746 w. 1777 p. ANON. (Miss A. CROSFIELD?). A description of the Castle hills, near Northallerton. — Town and Country Mag., ix. 605–6.

1747 ANON. An brutum sit machina?—Dodsley's Museum, 1747, iii. 380–84.

1748 WINGFIELD, RICHARD. To peace.—Gratulatio Academiae Cantabrigiensis de Reditu ... Georgii II, Camb., 1748, sign. B.

1750 STILLINGFLEET, BENJAMIN. Some thoughts occasioned by the late earthquakes, 1750.

APPENDIX C

LOCO–DESCRIPTIVE POEMS NOT KNOWN TO BE MILTONIC [1]

A. HILL–POEMS

1642 DENHAM, JOHN. Coopers hill, 1642.

1697 MANNING, FRANCIS. Greenwich-hill, 1697.

1711 w. MONCK, MARY. Moccoli [a villa on a hill near Florence].—Marinda, 1716, pp. 141–56.

1735 w. HARDINGE, NICHOLAS. [Two poems on Knoll Hills.] —J.Nichols's Illustrations of Literary History, 1817, i. 650–55.

1745 BARFORD, RICHARD. Knowls hill, in Essex, 1745. Not seen.

1746 w. 1777 p. ANON. (Miss A. CROSFIELD?) A description of the Castle hills, near Northallerton.—Town and Country Mag., ix. 605–6. (Blank verse.)

1747 RICH, E. P. Stinchcomb-hill, or the prospect, 1747.

1754 BOWDEN, SAMUEL. A description of Chedder-cliffs and Mendip-hills. — Poems, Bath, 1754, pp. 54–60.

1755 DUCK, STEPHEN. Caesar's camp, or St. George's hill, 1755.

1759 FORTESCUE, JAMES. Castle hill [two poems].—In Dissertations, Essays, etc., 1759. Not seen.

1769 LYTTELTON, GEORGE, Lord. Mount Edgecumbe.—Poetical Works, 1801, pp. 118–19. (Octosyllabics.)

c. 1770 w. 1777 p. ROSCOE, WILLIAM. Mount Pleasant. —Poetical Works, 1857, pp. 1–17.

1774 ANON. St. Thomas's mount, written by a gentleman in India, 2 cantos, 1774.—See Mo. Rev., i. 311–12.

MERCER, THOMAS. Arthur's seat.—Poems, Edin., 1774, pp. 1–41. (Octosyllabics.)

PYE, H. J. Faringdon hill, 2 books, Oxford, 1774.

1777 [2] ANON. The prospect from Malvern-hill, 1777.—See Crit. Rev., xliv. 475–7.

BEAVAN, EDWARD. Box-hill, 1777.—See ib., xliii. 158; no extract.

CRAWFORD, CHARLES. Richmond-hill.—Poems on Various Subjects, 3d ed., 1810, pp. 1–29.

HURN, W. Heath-hill, 1777.—See Crit. Rev., xliii. 233; no extract.

JORDAN, JOHN. Welcombe hills, 1777. Not seen.

P., T. (THOMAS PYE?). Witenham-hill, 1777?—Gent. Mag., xlviii. 129.

1781 MICKLE, W. J. Almada hill, an epistle from Lisbon, Oxford, 1781.

1784 N., T. One tree hill [Greenwich].—Univ. Mag., lxxiv. 266–7. (Octosyllabics.)

1785 HOBHOUSE, THOMAS. Kingsweston hill, 1785.

YEARSLEY, ANN. Clifton hill.—Poems, 1785, pp. 107–27.

1788 COTTER, G. S. Prospects, a descriptive poem, 4 books.—In Poems, Cork, 1788. Not seen.

1789 RUSHER, PHILIP. Crouch-hill, Banbury, 1789. Not seen.

---

[1] Unless otherwise designated, the poems are in heroic couplets. "No extract" means that no part of the poem appears in the review cited. A few unimportant loco-descriptive poems that show the influence of Milton but are not mentioned in Chapter XII above are listed in Bibliography I, under the years 1765, 1767, 1785, 1828, 1828 w., 1832, 1846, and Bibliography II, 1750, 1760, 1802.

[2] 1777. Astle, Daniel. A prospect from Barrow-hill, in Staffordshire, Birmingham, 1777.—See Mo. Rev., lviii. 308–9. (Prose.)

1794 [1] ANON. Llangunnor hill, a loco-descriptive poem, 1794.—See Mo. Rev., enl., xvi. 460–62. (Octosyllabics.)

1794? BIDLAKE, JOHN. Written at Mount Edgcumbe.—In Poems, 1794?; reprinted in W. H. K. Wright's West-Country Poets, 1896, pp. 38–40. (Octosyllabics.)

1796 DAVIS, T. Eastham hill, a loco-descriptive poem, Monmouth, 1796. Not seen.

1797 MACKAY, J. Quebec hill, or Canadian scenery, 2 parts, 1797.—See Mo. Rev., enl., xxiv. 210–12.

1798 BOWLES, W. L. St. Michael's mount, Salisbury, 1798.

1799 MAURICE, THOMAS. Grove-hill, 1799.

1800 CUNNINGHAM, PETER. St. Anne's hill, 3d ed., Chertsey, 1833. (Elegiac stanzas.)

1803 SHOEL, THOMAS. Mileshill [St. Michael's mount], 1803. Not seen.

1804 WOODLEY, GEORGE. Mount-Edgcumbe, Devonport, 1804. Not seen.

1807 MAURICE, THOMAS. Richmond hill, 1807.—See Mo. Rev., enl., lv. 132–8.

1808 SKURRAY, FRANCIS. Bidcombe hill, 1808. Not seen.

1811 HOGG, THOMAS. St. Michael's mount, 4 cantos, 1811.

REDDING, CYRUS. Mount Edgcumbe, 1811.—See Wright's West-Country Poets, 1896, p. 397.

TUCKER, W. J. Honiton-hill, Bath, 1811.—See ib. 457–8.

1812 PENTICROSS, WILLIAM. Witenham-hill, 1812. Not seen; may be the one noted under 1777 above.

1817 YEATMAN, H. F. Brent knoll, Sherborne, 1817. Not seen.

1821 THELWALL, JOHN. Shooter's hill.—Poetical Recreations, 1822, pp. 232–4. (Elegiac stanzas.)

B. OTHER POEMS

1679 w. 1745 p. ANON. Belvoir: a Pindaric ode upon Belvoir castle.—J. Nichols's History of Leicestershire, 1795, vol. ii, pt. i, app., 50–61. (Pindarics.)

1693 LEWIS, ——. Relation of a journey to Tunbridge Wells, with a description of the wells, 1693. Not seen.

1706 HARRISON, WILLIAM. Woodstock park.—Dodsley's Miscellany, 1758, v. 188–201.

1708 ANON. Windsor-castle, 1708.

1712 GOLDWIN, WILLIAM. A poetical description of Bristol, 1712. Not seen.

1713 POPE, ALEXANDER. Windsor forest, 1713.

1715 ANON. The country seat, a description of Langdon, near Plymouth, 1715. Not seen.

1718 ANON. Greenwich park, etc., inscribed to the duke of Montagu, 1718. Not seen.

JONES, SAMUEL. Whitby, 1718. Not seen.

bef.1723 p. WARD, JAMES. Phoenix park.—Miscellaneous Poems, published by Mr. Concanen, 1724, pp. 379–91.

1724 AMORY, THOMAS. A poem in the praises of Taunton, 1724. Not seen.

1726 HOWARD, LEONARD. Greenwich park.—Poetical Works, n. d., pp. 28–60.

1727 ANON. Description of Tunbridge, 1727. Not seen.

1727 w. PECK, FRANCIS. Belvoir castle.—J. Nichols's History of Leicestershire, 1795, vol. ii, pt. i, app., 61–6.

1731–8 BOYSE, SAMUEL. Loch Rian (Chalmers's English Poets, 1810, xiv. 533–4); The triumphs of nature (ib. 534–8); Nature (ib. 567–8); Retirement (ib. 576–9). The last three poems describe the parks at Stowe, Dalkeith, and Yester.

[1] The American poems, *Greenfield Hill* by Timothy Dwight (N. Y., 1794), *Beacon Hill* by S. W. Morton (Boston, 1797), and *Milton Hill* by H. M. Lisle (Boston, 1803), may also be noticed.

1732   ANON. Verses occasioned by seeing the palace, park, etc., of Dalkeith, Edin., 1732. Not seen.

1732-3   ARAM, PETER. Studley-park.—Thomas Gent's History of Rippon, York, 1733, pp. 1-28.

1733   DUICK, JOHN. Scarborough, 1733. Not seen; may be the poem in Gent. Mag., iv. 155-6.

1734   CHANDLER, MARY. A description of Bath, 7th ed., 1755.

1739   BROWNE, MOSES. A view of Scarborough, in four epistles.—Poems, 1739, pp. 205-26.

1747   ANON. Shrewsbury quarry, in imitation of Pope's Windsor-forest, Salop, 1747. (Not the same as under 1770 below.)

1748   ANON. Bath, 1748. Not seen.

1749   ANON. Bristol Wells, a poem for the year 1749, by a gentleman at the Wells, Bristol, 1749. Not seen.

    JONES, HENRY. Rath-Farnham. — Poems, 1749, pp. 44-50.

1749 w.   BROWNE, MOSES. Percy-lodge, seat of the duke of Somerset, 1755.—See Mo. Rev., xiv. 60-61. (Octosyllabics.)

1750?   ANON. A description of Bath, 1750(?). Not seen.

    ANON. Killarney, by an officer in the army, Dublin, 1750(?). Not seen.

1753   KIDDELL, HENRY. Tiverton, 1753.—See Mo. Rev., x. 78; no extract.

1755   DALTON, JOHN. A descriptive poem [on the mines near Whitehaven], 1755.

    MAXWELL, ARCHIBALD. Portsmouth, 2 books, 1755.—See Mo. Rev., xiii. 297; no extract.

c. 1755 w.   LANGHORNE, JOHN. Studley park.—Chalmers's English Poets, 1810, xvi. 416-19.

1758   HUCKELL, JOHN. Avon, 3 parts, Birmingham, 1758.

    POTTER, ROBERT. Holkham, 1758.

1760   MADDEN, W. B. Belle Isle, 1760.—See Crit. Rev., xi. 416; no extract.

1761   WILLIAMS, WILLIAM. An essay on Halifax, a poem in blank verse, Halifax, 1761. Not seen.

1763   NICHOLS, JOHN. Islington, 1763.—See Crit. Rev., xvi. 316.

    RITSO, GEORGE. Kew gardens, 1763. — See ib. 394-5.

1764   WILSON, JOHN. The Clyde, 1764.—See John Veitch's Feeling for Nature in Scottish Poetry, 1887, ii. 179-82.

    WOODHOUSE, JAMES. The Lessowes.—Poems on Sundry Occasions, 1764, pp. 38-109.

1765   ANON. Kimbolton-park, 1765.—See Mo. Rev., xxxiii. 240.

1766   JONES, HENRY. Vectis, the isle of Wight, 3 cantos, 1766.—See ib. xxxiv. 349-51.

    MICHELL, RICHARD. Hackwood-park, 1766.—See Crit. Rev., xxi. 318.

1767   ANON. The rise and progress of the present taste in planting parks, pleasure-grounds, etc., 1767 [treats of Kew, Kensington, and Stowe]. —See Mo. Rev., xxxvii. 139-44.

    JONES, HENRY. Clifton, 2 cantos, Bristol, 1767. Not seen.

1769   ANON. The prospect, a lyric essay, by Martin Scriblerus, jun., 1769.—See Crit. Rev., xxvii. 397. (Lines of eight and nine syllables, with alternate rime.)

    OGILVIE, JOHN. Paradise, 1769.

1770   JONES, HENRY. Shrewsbury quarry, etc., Shrewsbury, 1770.

1771   MAUDE, THOMAS. Wensleydale, or rural contemplations, 1771.

    SHERIDAN, R. B. The Bath picture, a ballad, 1771. Not seen.

1772   LESLIE, JOHN. Killarney (Dublin, 1772); Phoenix park (1772, see Crit. Rev., xxxv. 158, no extract).

1773   ANON. A description of Tunbridge.—Univ. Mag., lii. 266-7.

1773 w.   HILL, ROBERT. Greenwich-park.—Poems on Several Occasions, 1775, pp. 161-88.

1774   ELLIS, GEORGE. Bath, its beauties and amusements, Bath, 1774. Not seen.

1775   ANON. Bath and it's environs, 3 cantos, Bath, 1775.

1776   MAURICE, THOMAS. Netherby (Oxford, 1776); Hagley (Oxford, 1776).

      MUNDY, F. N. C. Needwood forest, Lichfield, 1776.—See Stebbing Shaw's History of Staffordshire, 1798, i. 68–70, second pagination. (Octosyllabics.)

      REEVE, JOSEPH. Ugbrooke park, 1776.—See Wright's West-Country Poets, 1896, p. 398.

1777   HUNTINGFORD, THOMAS. Nun's path [near Warminster], a descriptive poem, pt. 1, Salisbury, 1777. Not seen.

1778   HEARD, WILLIAM. A sentimental journey to Bath, Bristol, and their environs, a descriptive poem, 1778. Not seen.

1779 w.   WALTERS, DANIEL. Landough, a loco-descriptive poem.—John Walters's Poems, Oxford, 1780, pp. 135–42.

1782   MAUDE, THOMAS. Verbeia, or Wharfdale, York, 1782.—See Crit. Rev., lv. 257–60.

1783   DAVIES, EDWARD. Blaise castle, a prospective poem, Bristol, 1783. Not seen.

1784?   THOMAS, ANN. Shetland.—Probably in Poems, 1784: see Wright's West-Country Poets, 1896, p. 437.

1785   HADWEN, W. Rusland.—Univ. Mag., lxxvii. 152–3.

1786   ANON. Matlock, a farewell descriptive poem, 1786.—See Mo. Rev., lxxv. 313; no extract.

      COWLEY, HANNAH. The Scottish village, 1786. (Alternate rime.)

      RHODES, T. Dunstan park, or an evening walk, 1786.—See Crit. Rev., lxi. 234; no extract.

1787–9   MAVOR, WILLIAM. Blenheim (1787); A new description of Blenheim (1789, not seen).

1788   ANON. Chatsworth, 1788.—See Crit. Rev., lxvi. 488–9.

      WHALLEY, T. S. Mont Blanc, an irregular lyric poem, 1788.—See Gent. Mag., lviii. 146–7, 329–30. (Pindarics.)

1789   FERNYHOUGH, WILLIAM. Trentham park, 1789.—See Mo. Rev., enl., i. 336; no extract.

      WALKER, JOHN. A descriptive poem of the town and trade of Liverpool, Liverpool, 1789. Not seen.

1789 w. 1803 p.   WOODHOUSE, JAMES. Norbury park.—Life and Works, 1896, ii. 163–77.

1792   ANON. Stonehenge, 1792. Not seen.

1792 w.   SOTHEBY, WILLIAM. Llangollen.—Tour through Parts of Wales, 1794, pp. 103–120.

1793   ANON. Devon water.—The Bee, xv. 249 (June 19, 1793).

      ANON. The south downs, 1793.—See Mo. Rev., enl., xii. 166–9.

      CUMBERLAND, GEORGE. A poem on the landscapes of Great Britain, 1793.—See ib. 221–2.

      HAMPSON, WILLIAM. Duckinfield lodge, 2 cantos, 1793.—See Crit. Rev., new arr., xi. 347.

1794   LACY, WILLOUGHBY. The garden of Isleworth, 1794.—See ib. xiii. 354; no extract.

1796   DOIG, DAVID. Extracts from a poem on the prospect from Stirling castle, 1796.—See ib. xviii. 461–2.

      SEWARD, ANNA. Llangollen vale (Llangollen Vale, with other Poems, 1796, pp. 1–11, stanzas); Verses on Wrexham (ib. 12–14); Hoyle lake (ib. 15–21, elegiac stanzas).

1797   GISBORNE, JOHN. The vales of Wever, a loco-descriptive poem, 1797.—See Mo. Rev., enl., xxiv. 430–35. (Octosyllabics.)

1798   ATKINSON, JOSEPH. Killarney, 1798.—See ib. xxv. 472; no extract.

HOLFORD, MARGARET. Gresford vale, 1798.—See ib. 476. (Alternate rime.)

1800   BISSET, JAMES. A poetic survey round Birmingham, 1800.—See ib. xxxiii. 319–20.

1801   ANON. The vale of Trent, 1801.—See ib. xxxv. 110–111; no extract.

1803   WHITE, HENRY KIRKE. Clifton grove.—Remains, 5th ed., 1811, ii. 11–28.

1806   MUNNINGS, J. S. Cromer, a descriptive poem in blank verse, part i, 1806. Not seen.

TAPRELL, RICHARD. Barnstaple, 1806.—See Wright's West-Country Poets, 1896, pp. 434–5. (Blank verse.)

1808   SANSOM, JAMES. Greenwich, a poem descriptive and historical, 1808. Not seen.

1810   FREEMAN, ROWLAND. Regulbium, a poem, with an historical and descriptive account of the Roman station at Reculver, Canterbury, 1810. Not seen.

KENNEDY, JAMES. Glenochel, a descriptive poem, Glasgow, 1810. Not seen.

SMEDLEY, EDWARD. Erin, a geographical and descriptive poem, 1810. Not seen.

1811   DRUMMOND, W. H. The giants' causeway, 3 books, Belfast, 1811.

IRELAND, W. H. C. A poetic epistolary description of the city of York, York, 1811. Not seen.

1812   BRYSON, W. A. Sun-rise at Lough Erne (Poems, Dublin, 1812, pp. 90–1); Moon-light scene at Killarney (ib. 92–4). Hendecasyllabics, with alternate rime.

1814   MORGAN, WILLIAM. Long Ashton, a poem, in two parts, descriptive of the scenery of that village, etc., Bristol, 1814. Not seen.

1817   ANON. Tunbridge Wells, a descriptive poem, 1817. Not seen.

1817–21   CROLY, GEORGE. Paris in 1815, 2 parts, 1817–21. (Spenserian stanzas.)

1818   SHOEL, THOMAS. Glastonbury Tor, Sherborne, 1818. Not seen.

1819–20   WOODLEY, GEORGE. Cornubia [Cornwall], 5 cantos, 1819; Devonia [Devon], 5 cantos, 1820. Not seen.

1820 w. 1826–36 p. POLWHELE, RICHARD. Dartmoor.—Reminiscences, 1836, iii. 63–84.

1821   HEMANS, FELICIA D. Dartmoor, 1821.

1823   COTTLE, JOSEPH. Dartmoor, etc., 1823. Not seen.

1828   HOYLE, CHARLES. Killarney.—In his Three Days at Killarney, etc., 1828. Not seen.

APPENDIX D

RIMED TECHNICAL TREATISES

This is a list of poems that tell how to make or do something. It does not include translations of well-known classical works, or humorous poems that are technical in name only, such as The Art of Tickling-Trouts (anon., 1708); William King's Art of Cookery (1708); John Gay's Trivia, or the Art of Walking the Streets of London (1716), and Receipt for Stewing Veal (written 1726); The Art of Decyphering (anon., 1727); Horace's Art of Poetry Spiritualiz'd, or the Art of Priest-craft (anon., 1727?); William Dunkin's Art of Gate-passing, or the Mur-phaeid (1730) and Receipt for making a Doctor (written before 1765); James Miller's Harlequin Horace, or the Art of Modern Poetry (1731); Poeticorum Liber, a New Art of Poetry (anon., 1732); James Ralph's(?) Art of War (1740, Champion, i. 297–8); Thomas Tickell's Fragment on Hunting (written before 1740); A Receipt to make a Lord (anon., quoted from Common Sense in Horace Walpole's letter to Horace Mann, about July 1, 1742); A Recipe for an Asthma (anon., 1744, Norfolk Poetical Miscellany, i. 350–53); William Woty's Recipe to make a Man of Consequence (Shrubs of Parnassus, 1760, p. 145); William Upton's Dramatic Advice, or a Receipt for a New Play (Poems, 1788, pp. 50–52); C. V. Le Grice's Estianomy, or the Art of Stirring a Fire (in his Tineum, 1794); John Anstey's ("John Surrebutter's") Pleader's Guide (2 books, 1796); Joseph Fawcett's Art of Poetry (1797); G. S. Carey's Art of Imitation (Mo. Mirror, 1797, iv. 236–7); The Art of making Tea (anon., 1799); John Henham's Receipt to write Blank Verse (Mo. Mag., 1803, xvi. 339–40); John Taylor's Art of Acting (1827). Four other poems that I have not seen sound like genuine technical treatises, but may be humorous: Isaac Hallam's Cocker, or approv'd Rules for Breeding Game Fowl (1746), The Art of Preserving (anon., 1759), C. Grierson's Art of Printing (Dublin, 1764), Henry Jones's Inoculation, or Beauty's Triumph (Bath, 1768).

1673   EVELYN, JOHN (the younger). Of gardens, translated from Rapin, 1673. (Also translated by James Gardiner, 1706.) Not seen.

1682   BUCKINGHAM, Duke of. An essay upon poetry, 1682.

1683   SOAMES, WILLIAM. The art of poetry, translated from Boileau, 1683.

1684   ROSCOMMON, Earl of. An essay on translated verse, 1684.

1686   CHAMBERLAYNE, JOHN. A treasure of health, translated from Castor Durante, 1686. Not seen.

       TATE, NAHUM. Syphilis, translated from Fracastoro. — Appended to Dryden's Miscellany, 1693, part iii.

1697   ANON. The innocent epicure, or the art of angling, 1697.[1]

1700   HOPKINS, CHARLES. The art of love, 2 books, 1700.[2]

1704   ANON. A receipt to make an oat-meal pudding.—Dryden's Miscellany, 1704, v. 315.

        ANON. A receipt to make a sack-posset.—Ib. 316.

1710   ROWE, NICHOLAS. Paedotrophiae, or the art of bringing up children, from Sainte-Marthe, 1710. (Also translated by H. W. Tytler in 1797.)

        ROWE, NICHOLAS, and others. Callipaediae, or an art how to have handsome children, translated from Quillet, 1710. (Also translated anonymously in 1710, by W. Oldisworth in 1719, anonymously as Advice to New-married Persons in 1754, and as The Joys of Hymen, or the Conjugal Directory, in 1768.)

1711   POPE, ALEXANDER. An essay on criticism, 1711.

1713   GAY, JOHN. Rural sports, 1713.

        KING, WILLIAM. Apple-pye (Original Works, 1726, iii. 259–61); Hasty pudding (ib. 262).

1717   BREVAL, J. D. DE. The art of dress, 1717.

1719   B., J. The art of beauty, 1719. Not seen.

1722   DIAPER, WILLIAM, and JONES, JOHN. Oppian's Halieuticks, of the nature of fishes and fishing, Oxford, 1722.

1723   ANON. Silk worms, translated from Vida, 1723. (Also translated by S. Pullein, 1750.) Not seen.

1725–51   PITT, CHRISTOPHER. Vida's Art of Poetry, translated, 1725 (Chalmers's English Poets, 1810, xix. 633–51); Fragments of a rhapsody on the art of preaching, in imitation of some parts of Horace's Art of Poetry, 1751 (Poems, 1756, pp. 20–25).

1727   MARKLAND, ABRAHAM. Pteryplegia, or the art of shooting-flying, 1727.

1728   ANON. (JOHN LAURENCE?). Paradice regain'd, or the art of gardening, 1728.

1729   BRAMSTON, JAMES. The art of politicks, in imitation of Horace's Art of Poetry, 1729.

        JENYNS, SOAME. The art of dancing, 1729.

1735–8   DODSLEY, ROBERT. Beauty, or the art of charming, 1735; The art of preaching, in imitation of Horace's Art of Poetry, 1738.

1736   MAWER, JOHN. [First book of] Oppian's Cynegeticks, York, 1736.

1736–54   JEFFREYS, GEORGE. Vida's Chess, translated; Vaniere's Country Farm, books i, xiii, translated.—Miscellanies, 1754, pp. 137–63, 163–230. (Book xiv of Vaniere, on bees, was translated by Arthur Murphy in 1799, and book xv, on fish, by John Duncombe in 1809.)

1737   GREEN, MATTHEW. The spleen, 1737.

        STILLINGFLEET, BENJAMIN. An essay on conversation, 1737.

1738   MILLER, JAMES. Of politeness, 2d ed., 1738.

1740   DINSDALE, JOSHUA. The modern art of breeding bees, 1740. Not seen.

1741   ANON. The art of poetry, 1741. (Not a translation from Boileau or Horace.)

1742   ANON. The art of architecture, in imitation of Horace's Art of Poetry, 1742.

1746   HILL, AARON. The art of acting.—Works, 2d ed., 1754, iii. 387–408.

1747   LENNOX, CHARLOTTE. The art of coquettry.—Poems on Several Occasions, 1747, pp. 61–7.

1748   TRIPE, ANDREW. The small-pox, canto i, 1748. Not seen.

1753   FRANCKLIN, THOMAS. Translation, 1753.

---

[1] The anonymous *Art of Angling*, in W. Ruddiman's *Collection of Scarce Pieces* (Edin., 1773, pp. 269–334), gives no directions for fishing.

[2] This is not a translation of Ovid, though it imitates him at times.

1755   Coote, Robert. The compleat marksman, or the true art of shooting fly-ing, 1755. — See Scots Mag., xviii. 205–6. (Not the same as under 1727 above.)

Dalton, John. Some thoughts on building and planting.—A Descriptive Poem addressed to Two Ladies, 1755, pp. 29–35.

1758   Moore, Anthony. An essay on the art of preaching, 1758.—See Mo. Rev., xix. 585–6.

1759   Marriott, Thomas. Female conduct, an essay on the art of pleasing, 2 books, 1759.

1763   Elphinston, James. Education, 4 books, 1763.—See Mo. Rev., xxviii. 103–8.

1763 w. 1772 p. Jones, Sir William. Caissa, or the game at chess. — Works, 1807, x. 301–16.

1764   Anon. The cestus of Venus, or the art of charming, 1764.—See Mo. Rev., xxx. 68–9.

1767   Anon. The rise and progress of the present taste in planting parks, etc., 1767. — See ib. xxxvii. 139–44.

Langhorne, John. Precepts of conjugal happiness, 1767.

1768   Smith, James. The art of living in London, 2 cantos, 1768.

1770   Pratt, Ellis. The art of dressing the hair, Bath, 1770.

1777   Anon. The art of conversing, translated from Père André of Rouen, 1777. —See Mo. Rev., lvi. 480.

1778–84 Pye, H. J. The art of war, translated from Frederick the Great, 6 books, 1778; Shooting, 1784.

1783   Mason, William. Dufresnoy's Art of Painting, translated, York, 1783. (Dryden had translated it into prose in 1695.)

1785   Graham, Charles. On the arts of penmanship and engraving.—Univ. Mag., lxxvii. 38.

1789   Anon. The garden, or the art of laying out grounds, translated from Abbé de Lille, 1789.—See Mo. Rev., enl., v. 154–6. (Also translated by Mrs. Montolieu, 1798.)

1791   Thomson, Alexander. Whist, 12 cantos, 1791.

1794   Knight, R. P. The landscape, 3 books, 1794.

1796   Cooke, William. Conversation, 3 parts, 1796.—See Mo. Rev., enl., xxi. 111–12.

1798   Anon. Phthisiologia, a poem [on medicine] miscellaneously descriptive and didactical, 4 parts, 1798.—See Crit. Rev., new arr., xxvii. 96–7.

1810   Seward, Anna. Receipt for a sweet jar. — Poetical Works, Edin., 1810, i. 110–12.

1816   Anon. Vis medicatrix, a didactic poem, Bath, 1816. Not seen.

1819   Lathy, T. P. The angler, 10 cantos, 1819.

BIBLIOGRAPHIES

The following bibliographies are based primarily on an examination of every volume of English literature written between the middle of the seventeenth and nineteenth centuries which the Harvard Library possesses. A number of books not at Harvard I saw in the Boston libraries and the principal collections of England and Scotland. Several years later the list thus obtained was corrected and all the poems in it were re-examined to see if they continued to impress me as Miltonic. Numerous additions have been made from year to year, and the entire list has been verified by Miss Rowe.

There is no pretence to completeness, for if it were possible to go through the stacks of the British Museum as I went through those at Harvard many more titles would be added. Almost all such additions would, however, be works of slight importance, and, unless a considerable number of them belonged to the first half of the eighteenth century, they would probably give little information that cannot be deduced or conjectured from the present lists. It was for this reason that my systematic examination of the Harvard shelves stopped short of the Victorian age, and of 1806 in the case of magazines. I felt that additional titles of minor pieces written long after the Miltonic movement had passed its zenith would increase the bulk rather than the value of the book.

The bibliographies are not meant to include every poem showing any influence from Milton; pieces which merely borrow a few words or phrases, or which use the Miltonic style only in one or two short passages, are intentionally omitted. Of course there are many cases in which it is hard to draw the line, particularly in the work of men like Wordsworth and Southey, some of whose pieces certainly belong here while others almost certainly do not. I have leaned to the conservative side and have rejected many poems that others have called Miltonic. It should also be noticed that the fourth bibliography is not limited to *Miltonic* sonnets, and that it includes only those by authors who wrote sonnets before 1800 and published some in books.

In order that the growth of Milton's influence may easily be traced, the arrangement has been made chronological, but the scattered poems of an author can be brought together through the index. The undesignated date is that of publication. When the date of writing is known to be more than one or two years earlier than that of publication, it is given (marked "w.") followed by the earliest date of publication that I could find (marked "p."), unless this is the date of the volume cited. Titles have been condensed, and after the first occurrence in each bibliography the editor's name and the place of publication have been omitted. When the place of issue is London, as is usually the case, it has not been mentioned. The references are in every instance to the editions I have used.

BIBLIOGRAPHY I

POEMS INFLUENCED BY PARADISE LOST[1]

1685	ROSCOMMON, Earl of. An essay on translated verse, 2d ed., 1685.
1695	BLACKMORE, Sir RICHARD. Prince Arthur, an heroick poem, 10 books, 1695.
	DENNIS, JOHN. The court of death, a pindarique poem, 1695.
1697	BLACKMORE, Sir RICHARD. King Arthur, an heroick poem, 12 books, 1697.
1698 w.	SAY, SAMUEL. Epistles of Horace [four].—Poems on Several Occasions, 1745, pp. 1–26.
1701	PHILIPS, JOHN. Imitation of Milton [the Splendid Shilling].—A New Miscellany of Poems, ed. Charles Gildon, 1701, pp. 212–21.
1702	ANON. The vision.—Examen Miscellaneum [ed. Gildon?], 1702, pp. 44–64.
	SMITH, MATTHEW. The vision, or a prospect of death, heav'n and hell, 1702.
1703	BLACKMORE, Sir RICHARD. A hymn to the light of the world.—Collection of Poems, 1718, pp. 385–409.
1703–23 w. 1709–31 p.	TRAPP, JOSEPH. The works of Virgil, 2d ed., 3 vols., 1735.
1704	ADDISON, JOSEPH. Milton's style imitated, in a translation out of the third Aeneid.—Works, Bohn ed., 1890, i. 38–41.
	DENNIS, JOHN. Britannia triumphans, or a poem on the battel of Blenheim.—Select Works, 1718, i. 147–218.
	—— [Translations from Tasso's Jerusalem Delivered, in] Grounds of criticism in poetry.—Ib. ii. 436, 448–50.
1704?	ROWE, ELIZABETH. A description of hell, in imitation of Milton.—Works, 1739, i. 49–52.
	—— On heaven.—Ib. 52–5.
1705	BLACKMORE, Sir RICHARD. Eliza, an epick poem, 10 books, 1705.
	PHILIPS, JOHN. Bleinheim, 1705.
1705–6	DEFOE, DANIEL. Lines.—A Review of the Affairs of France, 1795, vol. i, supplement no. 5.
	—— A hymn to truth.—Ib., vol. ii, no. 1.
	—— On the fight at Ramellies.—Ib., vol. iii (1706), no. 61.
1706	ANON. Ramelies.—A. Harrach's John Philips, Kreuznach, 1906, pp. 111–21.
	DENNIS, JOHN. The battle of Ramillia, 5 books, 1706.
	PARIS, Mr. Ramillies, in imitation of Milton, 1706.
	PHILIPS, JOHN. Cerealia, an imitation of Milton, 1706.
1706 w. 1715 p.	STANDEN, JOSEPH. To Dr. Watts, on his Horae Lyricae.—Isaac Watts's Works, 1810, iv. 419–21.
1708	GAY, JOHN. Wine, 1709.
	PHILIPS, JOHN. Cyder, 2 books, 1708.
1708 w.	ROWE, THOMAS. Horace, book i, ode xii, imitated.—Original Poems, etc., 1738, appended to Miscellaneous Works of Elizabeth Rowe, 1739, ii. 245–8.
1708–11	ANON. [Short passages in] British Apollo, 1708–11, vol. i. nos. 50, 56, 78, 90, 99, 101, 105, 108, 111, quarterly paper no. 1, and supernumerary paper no. 8 (two pieces); vol. ii, nos. 3, 9 (two pieces), 14, 18, 19, 31, 55, 60, 61, 72, 90, 96, 104, 107, and supernumerary papers nos. 3, 4; vol. iii, nos. 17, 23, 127.

[1] All the poems in this bibliography are in blank verse, except those by Blackmore (1695, 1697, 1703, 1705), Dennis (1695), Smith (1702), Burges (1801), Palmer (1802), Cottle (1815), and Wordsworth (1822), all but a few lines of Roscommon (1685), and parts of the anonymous *Vision* (1702), of Fellows (1770), Thomson (1796), and Mrs. Flowerdew (1803).

1709   BELLAMY, DANIEL (the elder). Taffy's triumph, or a new translation of the Cambro-muo-machia, in imitation of Milton, 1709.

GROVE, HENRY. A thought on death.—Works, 1747, iv. 395.

"PHILO-MILTON." Milton's sublimity asserted, in a poem occasion'd by a late celebrated piece, entituled Cyder, 1709.

PRIOR, MATTHEW. The first hymn of Callimachus: to Jupiter.—Poems on Several Occasions, ed. Waller, Camb., 1905, pp. 196–9.

WATTS, ISAAC. The celebrated victory of the Poles over Osman.—Horae Lyricae, 1709, pp. 229–38.

—— To Mitio.—Ib. 261–79.

—— An elegiac thought on Mrs. Anne Warner.—Ib. 304–8.

bef.1710? w. ROWE, ELIZABETH. Part of the thirteenth book of Tasso's Jerusalem, translated.—Works, 1739, i. 147–50.

1711 w. 1724 p. NEEDLER, HENRY. [Poem proving the existence of God from the works of creation.]—Works, 2d ed., 1728, pp. 135–9.

—— To the memory of Favonia.—Ib. 198–200.

1712   FENTON, ELIJAH. Part of the fourteenth chapter of Isaiah, paraphras'd.— Poems on Several Occasions, 1717, pp. 37–40.

1713   FINCH, ANNE, Countess of Winchilsea. Fanscomb Barn, in imitation of Milton.—Miscellany Poems, 1713, pp. 58–65.

1713 w. 1724 p. THOMSON, JAMES. The works and wonders of almighty power.— Complete Poetical Works, ed. J. L. Robertson, 1908, pp. 483–4.

1713–26 BRADY, NICOLAS. Virgil's Aeneis, 4 vols. in one, 1716–26.

1714   ANON. Prae-existence, in imitation of Milton, 1714.

1715   ANON. The mouse-trap, done from the Latin in Milton's stile, 1715.

1717   FENTON, ELIJAH. The eleventh book of Homer's Odyssey, in Milton's style. —Poems on Several Occasions, 1717, pp. 85–127.

c. 1718 w. 1847 p. THOMSON, JAMES. Lisy's parting with her cat.—Works, 1908, pp. 511–13.

1719 [1]   PECK, FRANCIS. Sighs upon the death of Queen Anne, in imitation of Milton, 1719.

1720   "A GENTLEMAN OF TRINITY-COLLEGE IN CAMBRIDGE." An occasional poem.—Reasons for Abolishing Ceremony, by J. Swift, Jr., 1720, pp. 20–25.

1720?   ANON. (J. BULKELEY?). The last day, book i, 1720(?).

bef.1721 w. PRIOR, MATTHEW. Virgils Georgic 4 verse 511, translated.—Dialogues of the Dead, etc., ed. Waller, Camb., 1907, p. 334.

—— Prelude to a tale from Boccace.—Ib. 339–44.

1721   ANON. 'A description, in imitation of Milton.—Miscellaneous Collection of Poems, publish'd by T. M. Gent, Dublin, 1721, ii. 54–8.

PRIOR, MATTHEW. The second hymn of Callimachus: to Apollo.—Poems on Several Occasions, ed. Waller, 1905, pp. 200–204.

1721 w. 1793 p. MALLET, DAVID. The transfiguration, in imitation of Milton's style.— Europ. Mag., xxv. 52.

1723   BAKER, HENRY. An invocation of health, 1723.

NEWCOMB, THOMAS. The last judgment of men and angels, after the manner of Milton, 12 books, 1723.

1724   BROWN, N. The north-country wedding.—Miscellaneous Poems, published by Matthew Concanen, 1724, pp. 1–15.

—— The fire.—Ib. 16–21.

WARBURTON, WILLIAM. Pygmaio-geranomachia, or the battle of the cranes and pigmies, in imitation of Milton's style.—Tracts by Warburton, etc. [ed. Samuel Parr], 1789, pp. 56–62.

---

[1] bef. 1719 ANON. A description of the four last things, viz. death, judgment, hell, and heaven, in blank verse, 2 pts., 2d ed., 1719. Not seen.

1725   ANON. To Miss M-reton, in Milton's stile.—A New Miscellany of Poetry, from Bath, Tunbridge, etc., 1725, pp. 50-51.

1726   ANON. A verbal translation of part of the first Aeneid.—Miscellaneous Poems, published by D. Lewis, 1726, pp. 307-9.

THOMPSON, WILLIAM. A poetical paraphrase on part of the book of Job, in imitation of the style of Milton, 1726.

1726-30 THOMSON, JAMES. The seasons, 4 parts, 1730.

1727   BROOME, WILLIAM. Part of the tenth book of the Iliads of Homer, in the stile of Milton.—Poems on Several Occasions, 2d ed., 1739, pp. 101-30.

—— From the eleventh book of the Iliads of Homer, in the stile of Milton.—Ib. 176-84.

HARTE, WALTER. Psalm the civth, paraphrased.—Poems on Several Occasions, 1727, pp. 229-34.

—— Psalm the cviith, paraphrased.—Ib. 235-42.

PITT, CHRISTOPHER. The 139th psalm paraphras'd in Miltonick verse.—Poems and Translations, 1727, pp. 120-27.

RALPH, JAMES. The tempest, or the terrors of death, 1727.

SOMERVILE, WILLIAM. Hudibras and Milton reconciled.—Occasional Poems, Translations, etc., 1727, pp. 93-6.

THOMSON, JAMES. To the memory of Sir Isaac Newton.—Works, 1908, pp. 436-42.

1728   CURTEIS, THOMAS. Eirenodia.—R. Freeman's Kentish Poets, Canterbury, 1821, ii. 121-46.

GLOVER, RICHARD. A poem on Sir Isaac Newton.—Prefixed to Henry Pemberton's View of Newton's Philosophy, 1728.

LYTTELTON, GEORGE, Lord. Blenheim.—Poetical Works, 1801, pp. 26-33.

MALLET, DAVID. The excursion, 2 books, 1728.

RALPH, JAMES. Night, 4 books, 1728.

—— Sawney, an heroic poem occasion'd by the Dunciad, 1728.

bef. 1729? CAREY, HENRY. To Handel.—Poems on Several Occasions, 3d ed., 1729, pp. 108-9.

1729[1]   ANON. The loss of liberty, or fall of Rome, 1729.

BROWNE, MOSES. To George Dodington.—Piscatory Eclogues, 1729, dedication.

RALPH, JAMES. Zeuma, or the love of liberty, 3 books, 1729.

THOMSON, JAMES.(?) To the memory of Mr. Congreve.—Works, 1908, pp. 457-62.

—— Britannia.—Ib. 471-80.

1730-42 w. BLAIR, ROBERT. The grave, 1743.

c.1730-65w.DUNKIN, WILLIAM. The poetical mirror, 4 books.—Select Poetical Works, Dublin, 1769-70, i. 100-337.

—— The frosty winters of Ireland in 1739, 1740.—Ib. 430-43.

—— Notes to the Parson's Revels.—Ib. ii., sign. b 4.

—— Translation from Boetius.—Ib. 518-20.

1731   ANON. Isaiah, chap. lx.—A Miscellany of Poems, ed. J. Husbands, Oxford, 1731, pp. 1-8.

ANON. An epistle from Oxon.—Ib. 121-8.

ANON. To ——, on the death of J. Hill.—Ib. 134-40.

ANON. A hymn to the Creator.—Ib. 141-5.

ANON. From Oxford, to a friend.—Ib. 155-60.

ANON. Il penseroso.—Ib. 161-9.

ANON. Job, chap. the 3d.—Ib. 184-9.

ANON. The country.—Ib. 197-208.

ANON. A divine rhapsody, or morning hymn.—Ib. 255-62.

---

[1] 1729   ANON. The adventures of Telemachus, attempted in blank verse, books i-ii, 1729. Not seen.

1731   ANON. An evening hymn.—Ib. 266–70.

ANON. On Albanio's marrying the incomparable Monissa; in Miltonian verse.—New Miscellaneous Poems, 7th ed., 1731, pp. 180–88.

ANON. A paraphrase on the civth psalm, in imitation of Milton's style.—The Flower-Piece, 1731, pp. 205–9.

B——, J——. The templer's bill of complaint.—Ib. 119–29.

1732 [1]   ANON. A panegyrick on cuckoldom.—Lond. Mag., i. 202.

LAUDER, WILLIAM. A poem (Eucharistia) of H. Grotius on the holy sacrament, translated, Edin., 1732.

1732 w.   WOGAN, CHARLES. The psalms of David, paraphrased in Miltonic verse.—See Swift's Correspondence, ed. F. E. Ball, 1913, iv. 327–31 (Swift to Wogan, Aug. 2, 1732).

1733   ANON. Prize verses, no. xi: On her majesty and the bustoes in the royal grotto.—Gent. Mag., iii. 541.

LLOYD, JOHN. The blanket, in imitation of Milton, 1733.—See the Bee, iii. 1181 (Aug., 1733).

LONG, ROGER. "When o'er the sounding main to Belgia's coast."—Gratulatio Academiae Cantabrigiensis ... Annae Georgii II ... Filiae ... Nuptias celebrantis, Camb., 1733, pp. [3–6].

1734   ANON. Darius's feast, or the force of truth, 1734.

C., E. Gin, in Miltonick verse.—Lond. Mag., iii. 663.

THOMSON, JAMES. To Dr. De la Cour, in Ireland, on his "Prospect of Poetry."—Works, Aldine ed., 1847, i. 69–72.

1734–6   —— Liberty, 5 parts.—Works, 1908, pp. 309–421.

1735   BROWNE, ISAAC HAWKINS. Imitation iii.—A Pipe of Tobacco, in Imitation of Six Several Authors, 1736, pp. 13–15.

LILLY, WILLIAM. Psalm 8, in Miltonick verse.—Lond. Mag., iv. 683–4.

SOMERVILE, WILLIAM. The chace, 1735.

1736   ANON. The Christian hero.—Gent. Mag., vi. 343–7.

ARMSTRONG, JOHN. The oeconomy of love, 1736.

"ASTROPHIL." To Mr. Thomson on his excellent poems.—Gent. Mag., vi. 479.

"ENDYMION." An astronomical paradox.—Ib. 159–60.

—— Solution of the astronomical paradox.—Ib. 283.

WESLEY, SAMUEL (the younger). The dog, a Miltonick fragment.—Poems on Several Occasions, 1736, pp. 148–50.

—— The descriptive, a Miltonick, after the manner of the moderns.—Ib. 151–6.

1737   AKENSIDE, MARK. The poet.—Poetical Works, Aldine ed., 1835, pp. 282–7.

ANON. Albania, a poem addressed to the genius of Scotland.—Scottish Poetry of the Eighteenth Century, ed. G. Eyre-Todd, Glasgow, 1896, i. 82–6.

D., M. Animal oeconomy.—Gent. Mag., vii. 246.

GLOVER, RICHARD. Leonidas, 1737.

THOMSON, JAMES. To the memory of Lord Talbot.—Works, 1908, pp. 444–55.

1737 w. 1749 p. HOADLY, JOHN. Kambromyomachia, or the mouse-trap.—A Collection of Poems by Several Hands [Dodsley's Miscellany], 1758, v. 258–68.

1738   ANON. A hymn to the morning, attempted in Miltonic verse.—Lond. Mag., vii. 44.

—— A hymn to night, attempted in the same verse.—Ib. 44.

ANON. Written by a gentleman, a little inclin'd to melancholy.—Ib. 198–9.

ANON. An enigma.—Ib. 408–9.

---

[1] 1732 LOCKMAN, JOHN. [Voltaire's] Henriade, an epick poem, in ten cantos, translated into blank verse, 1732. Not seen.

1738 ANON. Verses wrote when smoaking some bad tobacco.—Gent. Mag., viii. 99–100.

"BRITANNICUS." The voice of liberty, a poem in Miltonic verse, occasion'd by the insults of the Spaniards, 1738.

"EUGENIO." A hymn to the Creator of the world.—Lond. Mag., vii. 509–10.

"A FRESHMAN OF CLARE-HALL." An elegy on the death of her majesty.— Ib. 253.

PRICE, HENRY. To Mr. [Moses] Browne.—Gent. Mag., viii. 651.

SHIPLEY, JONATHAN. On the death of Queen Caroline.—John Nichols's Select Collection of Poëms, 1782, viii. 109–11.

1738 w. EDWARDS, SAMUEL. The Copernican system.—Poetical Calendar, ed. Fawkes and Woty, 1763, iii. 67–77.

1739 ANON. On the declaration of war against Spain.—Gent. Mag., ix. 596–7.

BARTON, RICHARD. Fairy fort, or the pleasures of an acre.—Farrago, 1739, pp. 1–25.

—— The wicked man's reflections.—Ib. 119–21.

BROWNE, MOSES. To Mr. Thomson.—Poems on Various Subjects, 1739, pp. 266–8.

GLOVER, RICHARD. London, or the progress of commerce, 1739.

1739 w. DAVIES, SNEYD. Vacuna.—John Whaley's Collection of Poems, 1745, pp. 178–81.

—— Epithalamium.—Ib. 242–5.

1739–67 STRAHAN, ALEXANDER. The Aeneid, translated, 2 vols., 1767.—See Mo. Rev., ix. 1–11, xxxvii. 321–3.

1740 ANON. Liberty regain'd, in imitation of Milton, 1740.

ANON. On the resurrection, in imitation of Milton.—Appended to Francis Peck's New Memoirs of Milton, 1740.

DYER, JOHN. The ruins of Rome, 1740.

KING, WILLIAM. Milton's epistle to Pollio, from the Latin, 1740.

NEWCOMB, THOMAS. Part of Psalm cxlviii, after the manner of Milton.— Miscellaneous Collection of Poems, 1740, pp. 339–42.

PARKER, BENJAMIN. Money, in imitation of Milton.— See A. Boyer's Litterary State of Great-Britain for 1740 (appended to his Political State, etc.), p. 25.

RALPH, JAMES. (?) An essay on truth.—The Champion, 1741, ii. 63–70.

SOMERVILE, WILLIAM. Hobbinol, or the rural games, a burlesque, 1740.

c. 1740? w. DAVIES, SNEYD. Rhapsody, to Milton.—J. Whaley's Collection, 1745, pp. 182–6.

—— On J. W. ranging pamphlets.—Ib. 202–7.

—— To the Hon. and Rev. —— [Frederick Cornwallis].—Ib. 208–13.

—— A song of Deborah.—Ib. 217–24.

—— The nativity.—Ib. 225–8.

1740 w. 1744 p. WARTON, JOSEPH. The enthusiast, or the lover of nature.—Biographical Memoirs, etc., ed. J. Wooll, 1806, pp. 111–24.

1741 ANON. The country christning, from a Latin poem.—Lond. Mag., x. 44–5.

1742 [1] SOMERVILE, WILLIAM. Field sports, 1742.

WINSTANLEY, JOHN. An address from a youth his to father.—Poems, Dublin, 1742, pp. 283–6.

1742–6 YOUNG, EDWARD. The complaint, or night thoughts, 9 parts.—Poetical Works, Aldine ed., 1852, vol. i.

bef. 1743 w. SAY, SAMUEL. Fragment.—J. Nichols's Collection, 1780, vi. 43.

---

[1] bef. 1742 w. HINCHLIFFE, WILLIAM. [Translation of Telemachus, books i–ix, in manuscript.] In blank verse: Cibber's Lives, 1753, v. 25. Not seen.

1743   BRAMSTON, JAMES. The crooked sixpence, 1743.

1743 w. 1778 p. BROOKE, HENRY. Conrade.—Poetical Works, 3d ed., Dublin, 1792, iv. 391–414.

1744   AKENSIDE, MARK. The pleasures of imagination, 3 books, 1744.

ANON. Wrote at Ocriculum in Italy.—John Wesley's Collection of Moral and Sacred Poems, Bristol, 1744, ii. 191–3.

ARMSTRONG, JOHN. The art of preserving health, 1744.

PRICE, HENRY. On the loss of the victory.—Lond. Mag., xiii. 565.

1744? w.   DAVIES, SNEYD. To N. Hardinge.—Nichols's Illustrations, 1817, i. 647–50.

bef.1745 w. WARTON, THOMAS (the elder). To Baptista Turriano, from Fracastorius. —Poems on Several Occasions, 1748, pp. 76–91.

—— The song of Judith.—Ib. 122–7.

—— A paraphrase on the xiiith chapter of Isaiah.—Ib. 209–12.

—— A farewell to poetry.—Ib. 219–22.

1745 [1]   ANON. The Sunday-peasant, Dublin, 1745.

COOPER, JOHN GILBERT. The power of harmony, 2 books.—Poems on Several Subjects, 1764, pp. 79–120.

DAVIES, SNEYD. To C[harles] P[ratt], Esq.—J. Whaley's Collection, 1745, pp. 236–9.

—— A night thought.—Ib. 240–41.

—— To the Rev. T[imothy] T[homas], D.D.—Ib. 328–35.

HOBSON, THOMAS. Christianity, the light of the moral world, 1745.

THOMPSON, WILLIAM. Sickness, 1745.[2]

WARTON, THOMAS (the younger).? Five pastoral eclogues, 1745.

1745 w.   GIBBONS, THOMAS. A poem on the rebellion in 1745.—Juvenilia, 1750, pp. 244–59.

YOUNG, EDWARD. Reflections on the public situation of the kingdom.— Works, 1852, ii. 199–216.

c. 1745 w. CUMBERLAND, RICHARD. [Translation from Virgil's third Georgic.]— Memoirs, 1807, i. 83–7.

1746   ANON. A Bacchanalian rhapsody.—The Museum, or Literary and Historical Register [Dodsley's Museum], 1746, i. 336–9.

ANON. Advice to the fair sex.—Ib. ii. 223–4.

ANON. The nocturnal excursion of fancy.—Gent. Mag., xvi. 102–3.

"TOM SOBER." Small-beer.—Ib. 553.

1746 w. 1758 p. AKENSIDE, MARK. Hymn to the naiads.—Works, 1835, pp. 239–56.

1747   ANON. Pleasures of the night.—Lond. Mag., xvi. 239–40.

MALLET, DAVID. Amyntor and Theodora, or the hermit, 3 cantos, 1747.

R., R. The jealous lover's excuse.—Lond. Mag., xvi. 45.

S., G. Description of paradise, from Masenius.—Gent. Mag., xvii. 242.

STEPHENS, EDWARD. The dying heathen.—Miscellaneous Poems, Cirencester, 1747, pp. 43–5.

—— Universal praise.—Ib. 45–50.

WARTON, THOMAS (the younger). The pleasures of melancholy.—Poetical Works, ed. Mant, Oxford, 1802, i. 68–95.

1748   ANON. An inscription.—Dodsley's Miscellany, 1748, iii. 202.

ANON. Marriage.—Scots. Mag., x. 78–82.

ANON. The t——d. —Gent. Mag., xviii. 135.

ANON. Verses from the Jacobite Journal.—Ib. 135.

HAMILTON, WILLIAM, of Bangour. The flowers.—Poems and Songs, ed. J. Paterson, Edin., 1850, pp. 75–6.

---

[1] 1745   ANON. War, a poem in blank verse, 1745. Not seen.

[2] Thompson later removed two long passages from this work and printed them, as *Coresus and Callirhoe* and *On Mr. Pope's Works*, in his *Poems on Several Occasions*, Oxford, 1757, i. 85–102, 122–31.

1748   HAMILTON, WILLIAM, of Bangour.   Speech of Randolph [book ii of his MS. poem The Bruce].—Ib. 105-11.

—— Doves.—Ib. 112.

L., H. Paraphrase of the first psalm.—Univ. Mag., iii. 223.

LEAPOR, MARY. The fields of melancholy and chearfulness.—Poems upon Several Occasions, 1748, pp. 145-53.

"A SCHOLAR OF WINCHESTER SCHOOL." Poverty, in imitation of Mr. Philips's Splendid Shilling.—Gent. Mag., xviii. 88.

SHIELLS, ROBERT. Marriage, 1748.

TAPERELL, JOHN. Revenge.—Poems on Several Occasions, 2d ed., 1750, pp. 71-6.

1748 w. 1803 p. COWPER, WILLIAM. Verses on finding the heel of a shoe.—Poems, ed. J. C. Bailey, 1905, pp. 1-2.

1749   ANON. A hymn to the Author of the new year.—Scots Mag., xi. 20.

ANON. Panegyrick on a louse, in the stile of Milton.—Lond. Mag., xviii. 474.

ANON. Adam banish'd [translation of Grotius's Adamus Exul, act i].—Gent. Mag., xix. 67-9.

BROWNE, MOSES. Sunday thoughts.—See R. Freeman's Kentish Poets, Canterbury, 1821, ii. 168-75.

HAWKESWORTH, JOHN. God is love.—Gent. Mag., xix. 467.

JONES, HENRY. To Doctor Green.—Poems, 1749, pp. 20-22.

—— To a friend on his marriage.—Ib. 134-6.

ROLT, RICHARD. Cambria, 3 books, 2d ed., 1749.

—— A poem to Sir W. W. Wynne, 1749.

WILKS, Rev. Mr. The departure of a Christian; in Miltonic verse.—Newcastle General Mag., 1749, p. 101.

1750   ANON. The empty purse, a poem in Miltonics, 1750.

ANON. A rhapsody.—Scots Mag., xii. 264-5.

FREE, JOHN. Stigand, or the Antigallican, in Miltonic verse, 1750.

GIBBONS, THOMAS. On the death of several young acquaintance. — Juvenilia, 1750, pp. 146-8.

—— A morning-thought.—Ib. 148-50.

—— The distress and relief.—Ib. 153-6.

—— An elegiac poem, to Isaac Watts.—Ib. 173-98.

—— Psalm xxix.—Ib. 218-21.

—— The plague of locusts: Joel, chap. ii.—Ib. 234-7.

—— On the earthquake.—Ib. 238-41.

"PHILALETHES." Pandaemonium, inscrib'd to William Lauder, 1750.

SMART, CHRISTOPHER. On the eternity of the Supreme Being.—Cambridge Prize Poems, 1750-1806, Camb. 1817, i. 1-7.

WARTON, THOMAS (the younger). A panegyric on Oxford ale.—Works, 1802, ii. 181-8.

1750?   ARNOLD, CORNELIUS. Distress.—Poems on Several Occasions, 1757, pp. 139-49.

c. 1750 w. BROWN, JOHN, D. D. Fragment of a rhapsody, written at the lakes in Westmoreland.—Richard Cumberland's Odes, 1776, p. 5.

c. 1750 w. 1760 p. HAMILTON, WILLIAM, of Bangour. The parting of Hector and Andromache, from the Iliad.—Poems and Songs, 1850, pp. 165-7.

—— First scene of the Philoctetes of Sophocles.—Ib. 171-2.

1751   ANON. Il meditante.—Lond. Mag., xx. 603-4, xxi. 84-5.

ANON. Wisdom, 1751.

ARNOLD, CORNELIUS. Commerce, 1751.

"CLERICUS." The song of Deborah paraphrased.—The Student, Oxford, 1751, ii. 33-7.

DODD, WILLIAM. A day in vacation at college, a burlesque, 1751.

1751 DRAPER, W. H. The morning walk, 1751.

* PARSONS, PHIL. "Pensive and sad beneath the secret shade."—Academiae Cantabrigiensis Luctus in Obitum Frederici . . . Walliae Principis, Camb., 1751, Q2, verso.

HINCHLIFFE, JOHN. "If e'er the Muse could paint excess of woe."—Ib. V.

CARTER, GILBERT. "Enthron'd imperial on her gilded carr."—Ib. Cc, verso.

SHARP, J. "Why doth Britannia, clad in sable weed."—Ib. Ll2, verso.

LONG, ROGER. "Yes, I will weep for thy untimely fate."—Ib. Pp.

SMART, CHRISTOPHER. On the immensity of the Supreme Being.—Cambridge Prize Poems, i. 9–14.

STEPHENS, EDWARD. A poem on a violent storm, 1751.

STORMONT, DAVID, Lord Viscount. On Prince Frederick's death.—Nichols's Collection, 1782, viii. 195–9.

WHITEHEAD, WILLIAM. Hymn to the nymph of Bristol spring, 1751.

1751 w. HARRIS, JAMES. Concord.—Poetical Calendar, 1763, xii. 53–9.

1752 ¹ ANON. Life.—Escapes of a Poetical Genius, 1752, pp. 34–41.

—— Death.—Ib. 42–8.

ANON. The noctuary, or an address from the tombs, 1752.

"FANTOM." Solitude.—Scots Mag., xiv. 500.

SMART, CHRISTOPHER. On the omniscience of the Supreme Being.—Cambridge Prize Poems, i. 15–22.

—— The hop-garden, a georgic, 2 books.—Poems on Several Occasions, 1752, pp. 101–35.

1753 ² DODSLEY, ROBERT. Public virtue, 3 books: i, Agriculture, 3 cantos, 1753.

1753 w. SMART, CHRISTOPHER. On the power of the Supreme Being.—Cambridge Prize Poems, i. 23–8.

1754 ³ ANON. Ode on the death of Mr. Pelham, 1754.—See Scots Mag., xvi. 159.

ANON. The triumph of death, 1754.

BLACKLOCK, THOMAS. Elegy: To the memory of Constantia.—Poems, 3d ed., 1756, pp. 144–52.

—— A soliloquy.—Ib. 153–67.

FORTESCUE, JAMES. Pomery-hill, 1754.—See Gent. Mag., xxiv. 245.

GREY, RICHARD. Of the immortality of the soul, translated from I. H. Browne, 1754.

MILLER, JOHN. An idea of God, from Racine's Esther.—Poems on Several Occasions, 1754, pp. 206–7.

—— On love, a Miltonic essay.—Ib. 208–12.

PHILIPS, JOHN. (?) The fall of Chloe's piss–pot.—Lond. Mag., xxiii. 85–6.

WEEKES, NATHANIEL. Barbados, 1754.—See Mo. Rev., xi. 325–9.

WILLS, JAMES. De arte graphica, or the art of painting, translated from Dufresnoy, [2d ed.], 1765.

1754 w. BALLY, GEORGE. On the justice of the Supreme Being.—Cambridge Prize Poems, i. 29–45.

DODSLEY, ROBERT. Verses on arrival at the Leasowes.—Shenstone's Works, 1764, ii. 380–82.

* For convenience of reference, the titles in books which have signature letters instead of pagination are arranged as they occur in the volumes, and only the leaf on which the poem begins is indicated.

¹ 1752 ANON. Grace, 1752. In blank verse: Mo. Rev., vi. 240. Not seen.

² 1753 ANON. The vindication, or day-thoughts, occasioned by The Complaint, or Night-thoughts, 1753. In blank verse: ib. ix. 235–6. Not seen.

HARROD, WILLIAM. Sevenoke, 1753. In blank verse: ib. viii. 392. Not seen.

³ 1754 JONES, HENRY. The relief, or day-thoughts, occasioned by The Complaint, or Night-thoughts, 1754: see ib. x. 304. Not seen; may be in blank verse.

1755 [1]   ANON. From a clergyman to his friend.—Gent. Mag., xxv. 326.

ANON. On a late most terrible calamity.—Lond. Mag., xxiv. 624-5.

ANON. Religious conscience, in imitation of Young's Night Thoughts, 1755.—See Mo. Rev., xii. 509-10.

DANIEL, ——. Clackshugh, in Miltonic verse, 1755.

SCOTT, J. N. An essay towards a translation of Homer, 1755.—See Mo. Rev., xii. 355-70.

1755?   COMBERBACH, ROGER. Translation of an ode of Horace.—The Contest, 1755 (?): see Mo. Rev., xiii. 95-9.

—— [An "eclogue," or letter in verse to John Byrom.]—Byrom's Remains, ed. R. Parkinson, Chetham Soc., 1857, ii. 555-7.

1755 w.   EMILY, CHARLES. The praises of Isis.—A Collection of Poems by Several Hands [Pearch's Supplement to Dodsley], new ed., 1783, i. 26-38.

JEMMAT, CATHARINE. On the recovery of Lord Molesworth.—Miscellanies, 1771, pp. 19-20.

KEATE, GEORGE. Ancient and modern Rome, 1760.

SMART, CHRISTOPHER. On the goodness of the Supreme Being.—Cambridge Prize Poems, i. 47-52.

1755 w. 1785 p. LOVIBOND, EDWARD. On Lady Pomfret's presenting the university of Oxford with statues.—Chalmers's English Poets, xvi. 290-1.

c. 1755 w.   CUMBERLAND, RICHARD. [Fragment of an epic on India.]—Memoirs, 1807, i. 169-74.

1756 [2]   ANON. The old elm in Hurworth, Durham.—Gent. Mag., xxvi. 247-8.

ANON. The gout, a mock-heroic poem in imitation of the Splendid Shilling. —Ib. 584.

ANON. Sophronia, 5 books, 1756.

AVERAY, ROBERT. Britannia and the gods in council, a dramatic poem, 1756.—See Mo. Rev., xv. 84-5.

BALLY, GEORGE. On the wisdom of the Supreme Being.—Cambridge Prize Poems, i. 53-69.

DRUMMOND, THOMAS. Grotto of Calypso.—Poems Sacred to Religion, etc., 1756: see Mo. Rev., xv. 128-35.

—— Morning adoration.—Ib.

LEWIS, RICHARD ("PETER POUNCE"). The Robin-Hood society, a satire, 1756.

M., R. The dignity of knowledge.—Literary Magazine, or Universal Review, 1756, pp. 260-61.

REED, JOSEPH. A British philippic, 1756.

1756 w.   KEATE, GEORGE. The Helvetiad.—Poetical Works, 1781, i. 83-124.

STRATFORD, THOMAS. Four pastoral essays, Dublin, 1770.

1757   ANDREWS, ROBERT. Upon seeing a fair matron at the theatre, an ode.— Eidyllia, Edin., 1757, pp. 23-4.

—— Virtue's expostulation with the British poets, an ode.—Ib. 25-6.

—— To adversity, an ode.—Ib. 26-7.

—— Philocles, a monody.—Ib. 28-39.

—— The muses triumphant over Venus.—Ib. 40-45.

—— To Lord Shaftsbury's ghost, an ode.—Ib. 47.

ANON. Britain, 3 books, Edin., 1757.—See Crit. Rev., iv. 279-80.

ANON. The great shepherd, 3 parts, 1757.—See Mo. Rev., xvi. 400-402.

BALLY, GEORGE. The day of judgment.—Cambridge Prize Poems, i. 299-320.

---

[1] 1755   CLARKE, EDWARD. A letter to a friend in Italy, etc., 1755. In blank verse: Mo. Rev., xiii. 456. Not seen.

[2] 1756   GREENE, JOHN. Beauty, 1756. In blank verse: ib. xiv. 558-9. Not seen.

1757   BARNARD, EDWARD. The competitors.—Virtue the Source of Pleasure, 1757, pp. 17–21.
        DOBSON, WILLIAM. Anti-Lucretius, [from] Cardinal de Polignac, by the translator of Paradise Lost, 1757.
        DYER, JOHN. The fleece, 4 books, 1757.
        GLYNN, ROBERT. The day of judgment.—Cambridge Prize Poems, i. 71–82.
        HIGHMORE, SUSANNAH (Mrs. DUNCOMBE). Ambition, 1757.—See Crit. Rev., iii. 557.
        "WINDSOR." Upon a Birmingham halpenny.—Gent. Mag., xxvii. 325.

1757 w.   DAVIES, SNEYD. Caractacus.—J. Nichols's Illustrations, 1817, i. 668–71.

1757–64   NEWCOMB, THOMAS. Mr. Hervey's Meditations and Contemplations (after the manner of Dr. Young), 2 vols., 1764.—See Mo. Rev., xxx. 488.

1758   ANON. Euthemia, or the power of harmony, 1758.—See Crit. Rev., vi. 344–5.
        ANON. Isaiah xxiv.—Dodsley's Miscellany, 1758, v. 177–83.
        —— Isaiah xxxv.—Ib. 183–8.
        ANON. Reason, 1758.—See Crit. Rev., vi. 171–4.
        BALLY, GEORGE. The providence of the Supreme Being.—Cambridge Prize Poems, i. 83–96.
        BUSHE, AMYAS. Socrates, a dramatic poem, 5 acts, 1758.—See Crit. Rev., vi. 89–95.
        DOBSON, WILLIAM. The Prussian campaign, 1758.—See ib. 81–3.
        DODD, WILLIAM. Thoughts on the glorious epiphany of the Lord Jesus Christ, 1758.
        "RESTAURATUS." Verses in R. Drake's Essay on the Gout, 1758. — See Crit. Rev., vi. 493–4.
        WOTY, WILLIAM ("JEMMY COPYWELL"). Soliloquy on the approach of term.—Shrubs of Parnassus, 1760, pp. 14–16.
        —— The spouting-club.—Ib. 87–98.

1758 w.   PYE, Mrs. H. Philanthe.—Poems, 2d ed., 1772, pp. 41–4.

1758–9   FRANCKLIN, THOMAS. The tragedies of Sophocles, 2 vols., 1758–9.

1758–72   AKENSIDE, MARK. Inscriptions i–iv, vi–viii.—Works, 1835, pp. 257–62.

1759   ANON. The visitations of the Almighty, part i, 1759.—See Mo. Rev., xx. 17–20.
        COOPER, E. Bewdley, a descriptive poem, 2 books.—Collection of Elegiac Poesy, etc., 1760, pp. 53–77.
        FORTESCUE, JAMES. Contemplation.—In Dissertations, Essays, etc., 1759: see Mo. Rev., xxi. 293–4.
        GORDON, ALEXANDER. The Prussiad, an heroick poem, 1759.
        PORTEUS, BEILBY. Death.—Cambridge Prize Poems, i. 97–109.
        WOTY, WILLIAM. Pudding.—Shrubs of Parnassus, 1760, pp. 46–7.

1760   ANON. An essay on the evening and night.—Gent. Mag., xxx. 586–7.
        ANON. (JOHN PATRICK?). Quebec, in imitation of the Miltonic stile, 1760.—See Crit. Rev., x. 79.
        ANON. Verses to the king, 1760.—See Mo. Rev., xxiii. 411.
        HAMILTON, WILLIAM, of Bangour. To a gentleman going to travel.—Poems and Songs, 1850, pp. 94–101.
        HAYDEN, G. The birthday of Miss W.—Royal Female Mag., ii. 84–5.
        LANGHORNE, JOHN. Poem to Handel.—Poetical Works, 1766, i. 55–66.
        NEWCOMB, THOMAS. The retired penitent, a poetical version of one of Young's moral contemplations, 1760.—See Mo. Rev., xxiii. 330–31.
        WOTY, WILLIAM. A tankard of porter.—Shrubs of Parnassus, 1760, pp. 20–22.
        —— The corkscrew.—Ib. 26–8.
        —— The tobacco-stopper.—Ib. 36–8.

1760   WOTY, WILLIAM. The Caxon.—Ib. 51–4.
—— The moonlight night.—Ib. 59–61.
—— To independence.—Ib. 76–8.
—— Bagnigge-wells.—Ib. 107–11.
—— Hymn to the Deity.—Ib. 117–27.
—— The exhortation.—Poetical Works, 1770, ii. 51–5.

1760 w.   DODD, WILLIAM. Hymn to good-nature.—Poems, 1767, pp. 1–7.

DOWNMAN, HUGH. Address to peace.—Infancy, etc., 6th ed., Exeter, 1803, pp. 189–206.

1761 [1]   FAWKES, FRANCIS. A parody on a passage in Paradise Lost.—Original Poems and Translations, 1761, pp. 84–5.

SHEPHERD, RICHARD. The nuptials, a didactick poem, 3 books, 1761.

WOTY, WILLIAM. Campanalogia, in praise of ringing, 1761.

* BARRINGTON, SHUTE. "Genius of Britain! who with ancient Brute."—Pietas Universitatis Oxoniensis in Obitum . . . Georgii II et Gratulatio in . . . Georgii III Inaugurationem, Oxford, 1761, D.

NAPIER, GERARD. "If the rude Empire of wide-wasting Time."—Ib. E.

SHARP, WILLIAM. To the lord bishop of Sarum.—Ib. K2, verso.

BAGOT, LEWIS. "Now was still Time of Night."—Ib. 5L, verso.

GRENVILLE, JAMES. "Roll, Isis, roll your melancholy Stream." — Ib. T, verso.

CROSSE, RICHARD. "Hence empty Joys!"—Ib. Aa2, verso.

AWBREY, JOHN. "Profane not, Time."—Ib. Cc, verso.

FALCONER, J. "No more of festal Pomp."—Ib. Ff2.

VYSE, WILLIAM. "'Twas Silence all."—Ib. Hh, verso.

LOVELL, EDMUND. "'Twas Eve; Darkness came on."—Ib. Ii2.

BROADHEAD, H. T. "While every neighb'ring Land."—Ib. Kk, verso.

COURTENAY, HENRY. "Now strike the plaintive Lyre."—Ib. Kk2, verso.

STONE, FRANCIS. "Could fabled Phoebus, or th' Aonian Nine."—Ib. Oo2, verso.

JEKYLL, J. "Far from the Ken of those sad dreary Plains."—Ib. Qq2.

RUGELEY, GEORGE. "The Muse, that erst in soft Oblivion slept."—Ib. Rr.

LEIGH, THOMAS. "On Albion's topmost Cliff."—Ib. Zz, verso.

CLEAVER, W. "Haste on, ye Clouds."—Ib. Bbb.

FORSTER, NATHANIEL. "This, this is Virtue's Prize."—Ib. Eee2, verso.

CHILDREN, G "What now avails the splendid Boast of Arms."—Ib. Hhh2.

FORTESCUE, JAMES. "When Acclamations from each grateful Voice."—Ib. Kkk, verso.

FANSHAW, JOHN. "Let not unhallow'd sounds."—Epithalamia Oxoniensia, sive Gratulationes in . . . Georgii III . . . Nuptias, Oxford, 1761, D2, verso.

SPENCE, JOSEPH. "At length the gallant Navy from afar."—Ib. G.

THOMAS, EDWARD. "'Tis not the gaudy pageantry of state."—Ib. N, verso.

RATCLIFFE, HOUSTONNE. "The mitred Sage had now with reverence due." —Ib. T2.

REYNELL, W. H. "Not to the shepherd's hutt, and rural cell."—Ib. Z2, verso.

---

[1] 1761   DOYNE, PHILIP. The delivery of Jerusalem, translated into blank verse, 2 vols., Dublin, 1761. Not seen.

WILLIAMS, WILLIAM. An essay on Halifax [Yorkshire], in blank verse, Halifax, 1761. Not seen.

* For convenience of reference, the titles in books which have signature letters instead of pagination are arranged as they occur in the volumes, and only the leaf on which the poem begins is indicated.

1761   COURTENAY, HENRY. "Now from Germania's shore the chosen bark."—
        Ib. Ff2, verso.

        RUGELEY, GEORGE. "Still Britain sits amid surrounding waves."—Ib.
        Kk, verso.

        PEPYS, W. WELLER. "If yet, as Fame reports, the royal ear."—Ib. Nn,
        verso.

        LOVELL, EDMUND. "Visions of glory croud yon distant view."—Ib. Pp2,
        verso.

        PHELPS, RICHARD. To his royal highness the duke of York.—Ib. Qq2,
        verso.

        SNELL, POWELL. "Now was fair evening's hour."—Ib. Tt2.

        FORTESCUE, J. "Now Hymen in connubial bands unites."—Ib. Xx, verso.

        KEATE, WILLIAM. "How blest the self-directed peasant's choice."—
        Gratulatio Academiae Cantabrigiensis . . . Georgii III . . . Nuptias
        celebrantis, Camb. 1761, H2.

        EKINS, JEFFERY. "O Harcourt, in thy Prince's partial love."—Ib. Ii, verso.

1762 [1] ANON. The victory.—Scots Mag., xxiv. 263.

        DUNCAN, JOHN. An essay on happiness, 4 books, 1762.

        LANGHORNE, JOHN. The viceroy, 1762.

        LYTTELTON, GEORGE, Lord. On reading Miss Carter's poems.—Poetical
        Works, 1801, p. 117.

        PORTAL, ABRAHAM. Innocence, 2 books, 1762.

        WOTY, WILLIAM. The chimney-corner.—Works, 1770, ii. 115–31.

        * GRAHAM, ROBERT. "Must thou, Iberia! who in envied ease."—Gratu-
        latio Academiae Cantabrigiensis Natales . . . Georgii Walliae Principis . . .
        celebrantis, Camb., 1762, H.

        ZOUCH, THOMAS. "With wanton pride Ohio sweeps."—Ib. K, verso.

        TYSON, MICHAEL. "Breathe with soft melody."—Ib. U.

        MORGAN, NATHANIEL. "Spirit of Liberty."—Ib. Bb.

        HEY, JOHN. "Fair Hope, I thank thee!"—Ib. Cc2, verso.

        NORTH, BROWNLOW. To the queen.—Gratulatio Solennis Universitas
        Oxoniensis ob . . . Walliae Principem . . . Natum, Oxford, 1762, C.

        RUSSELL, JOHN. "Pure are the joys."—Ib. E2.

        SPENCE, JOSEPH. "Hail to the sacred day."—Ib. H2.

        FORTESCUE, JAMES. "From heaven again the roll descends."—Ib. I, verso.

        BAGOT, LEWIS. "Those votive strains, O Isis."—Ib. K2.

        COURTENAY, HENRY. "Again Britannia's bards."—Ib. O, verso.

        EARLE, W. B. "On that auspicious day."—Ib. U2.

        SYMMONS, JOHN. "All human things experience change."—Ib. Aa, verso.

        THOMAS, EDMUND. "Though distant far from Isis' honour'd banks."—Ib.
        Hh2.

        BUTT, GEORGE. "Time-honour'd Isis."—Ib. Kk2.

        SIBTHORP, HUMPHREY. "While by the side of Isis' sedgy stream."—Ib. Ll.

        BECKMAN, WILLIAM. "With joyous sound of gratulation due."—Ib. Nn,
        verso.

bef. 1763w. SHENSTONE, WILLIAM. Œconomy, addressed to young poets.—Works
        in Verse and Prose, 1764, i. 285–307.

        —— The ruin'd abby.—Ib. 308–21.

        —— Love and honour.—Ib. 321–32.

[1] 1762 OGDEN, JAMES. On the crucifixion and resurrection, 1762. In blank verse: Crit. Rev., xiii.
        363–4. Not seen.

* For the order, see above, p. 647, note.

1763   ANON. Liberty ["in imitation of Milton"], 1763.—See Crit. Rev., xvi. 240.

ANON. A poetical wreath of laurel and olive, 1763.—See ib. xv. 230–31.

ANON. Satires on the times, 2 parts, 1763.—See ib. xvi. 392–3.

ANON. The temple of Gnidus, from Montesquieu, 1763.—See ib. xv. 389–90.

ANON. The wedding ring.—Lond. Mag., xxxii. 608.

CALLANDER, JOHN. A hymn to the power of harmony, Edin., 1763.—See Crit. Rev., xviii. 320.

HEY, JOHN. The redemption.—Cambridge Prize Poems, i. 147–72.

KEATE, GEORGE. The Alps.—Works, 1781, ii. 51–84.

LLOYD, ROBERT. The death of Adam, from Klopstock, 3 acts, 1763.

MICKLE, W. J.(?) Providence, or Arandus and Emilec, 1763.—See Crit. Rev., xiv. 276–80.

NEWCOMB, THOMAS. The death of Abel [from Gessner], attempted in the stile of Milton, 1763.

PENNINGTON, Mrs. The copper farthing.—Poetical Calendar, 1763, x. 48–53.

THOMPSON, WILLIAM. Garden inscriptions, iv: In Milton's alcove.—Ib. viii. 100.

—— Garden inscriptions, xix: In an apple-tree, over Mr. Philips's Cyder.—Ib. 118.

WOTY, WILLIAM. The pin.—Works, 1770, i. 55–8.

ZOUCH, THOMAS. "'Tis false: not all the gay parade of power."—Gratulatio Acad. Cantab. in Pacem ... Restitutam, Camb., 1763, I.

c. 1763 w.   BRUCE, MICHAEL. The last day.—Works, ed. Grosart, Edin., 1865, pp. 157–75.

c. 1763? w.   LYTTELTON, GEORGE, Lord. Verses.—P. C. Yorke's Life of Philip Yorke, Earl of Hardwicke, Camb., 1913, ii. 524, 571; iii. 303.

1763–4   ANON. The Messiah: bk. i, The nativity; bk. ii, The temptation; bk. iii, The crucifixion; bk. iv, The resurrection. Camb., 1763–4.—See Crit. Rev., xvii. 318–20, 472; xviii. 320.

1764   ANON. On beneficence, 1764.—See Mo. Rev., xxx. 242–3.

CARR, JOHN. Filial piety, 1764.

GRAINGER, JAMES. The sugar-cane, 4 books, 1764.

H., W. The street.—Scots Mag., xxvi. 93–4.

HAWKINS, WILLIAM. The Aeneid [books i–vi], translated, 1764.[1]—See Crit. Rev., xvii. 424–9.

OGILVIE, JOHN. Providence, an allegorical poem, 3 books, 1764.

WHATELEY, MARY (Mrs. DARWALL). The pleasures of contemplation.—Original Poems, 1764: see Mo. Rev., xxx. 449.

1764 w.   LETTICE, JOHN. The conversion of St. Paul.—Cambridge Prize Poems, i. 173–82.

1765 [2]   ANON. Landscape: an August evening.—Scots Mag., xxvii. 154–5.

ANON. A rhapsody on leaving Bath.—Gent. Mag., xxxv. 431.

BRIDGES, THOMAS. The battle of the genii, 3 cantos, 1765.—See Mo. Rev., xxxii. 276–9.

COOPER, E. The elbow-chair, 1765.

FOSTER, MARK. Scarborough, Scarborough, 1765.— J. S. Fletcher's Picturesque Yorkshire, 1901, vi. 130–31.

HOLLIS, J. Morning. — Gent. Mag., xxxv. 527.

L., T. (THOMAS LETCHWORTH?). Miscellaneous reflections, or an evening's meditation, 1765.—See Mo. Rev., xxxii. 75.

---

1 The other six books were translated but not published.

2 1765   ANON. The advantages of repentance, a moral tale, 1765. In blank verse: Crit. Rev., xix. 152. Not seen.

ANON. The death of a friend, 1765. In blank verse: Mo. Rev., xxxiii. 85. Not seen.

1765   LETCHWORTH, THOMAS. A morning's meditation, 1765.—See Crit. Rev.,
            xix. 313.
            ZOUCH, THOMAS. The crucifixion.—Cambridge Prize Poems, i. 183–98.
1766 [1]   ANDREWS, ROBERT. The works of Virgil, Englished, Birmingham, 1766.
            ANON. The ocean, 1766.—See Crit. Rev., xxi. 151–2.
            MEEN, HENRY. Happiness, 1766.—See ib. xxii. 73.
1766?   ANON. Cooper's hill, address'd to Sir W. W. Wynne, 1766(?).—See ib. 380–
            81.
            BRUCE, MICHAEL. Lochleven.—Works, 1865, 176–97.
            NICHOLS, JOHN. Happiness.—Collection of Poems, 1782, viii. 144–6.
1766 w. 1774 p. RICHARDSON, WILLIAM. On the death of the earl and countess of
            Sutherland.—Poems, chiefly Rural, 3d ed., 1775, pp. 147–9.
1767   ANON. Health, 1767.—See Mo. Rev., xxxvii. 315–16.
            ANON. On the death of the marquis of Tavistock, 1767.—See ib. xxxvi.
            330–31.
            DODD, WILLIAM. On the death of Anthony Ellis.—Poems, 1767, pp. 71–3.
            JAGO, RICHARD. Edge-hill, 4 books, 1767.
            JENNER, CHARLES. The gift of tongues.—Cambridge Prize Poems, i.
            199–209.
            JONES, HENRY. Kew garden, 2 cantos, 1767.—See Crit. Rev., xxiv. 315–16.
            LANCASTER, NATHANIEL. Methodism triumphant, or the decisive battle
            between the old serpent and the modern saint, 1767.—See ib. xxv. 66–7.
            LANGLEY, SAMUEL. The Iliad, translated, book i, 1767.—See ib. xxiii. 36–41.
            SINGLETON, JOHN. A general description of the West-Indian islands, Bar-
            bados, 1767.
1768   ANON. Choheleth, or the royal preacher, 1768.
            ANON. The 30th psalm, paraphrased.—Court Miscellany, iv. 557–8.
            ANON. The tears of Neptune.—Gent. Mag., xxxviii. 439–40.
            J. An invocation to the gout.— Oxford Mag., i. 277.
            JENNER, CHARLES. The destruction of Nineveh.—Cambridge Prize Poems,
            i. 211–24.
            M., A. Verses on seeing a beautiful young lady.—Court Miscellany, iv. 614.
1768 w.   RICHARDSON, WILLIAM. Corsica.—Poems, chiefly Rural, 1774, pp. 67–78.
1768 w. 1785 p. LOVIBOND, EDWARD. Verses written after passing through Findon.—
            Chalmers's English Poets, xvi. 299.
1768? w. 1892 p. COWPER, WILLIAM.(?) A thunder storm.—Poetical Works, Oxford
            ed., pp. 626–8.
1769   ANON. Friendship, a poem, to which is added an ode, 1769.—See Crit. Rev.,
            xxviii. 300–302.
            ANON. A poetical address, in favour of the Corsicans, 1769.—See Mo. Rev.,
            xl. 250.
            ANON. Punch, a panegyric, attempted in the manner of Milton, 1769.
            ANON. On seeing the late comet.—Gent. Mag., xxxix. 551–2.
            HAZARD, JOSEPH. The conquest of Quebec, Oxford, 1769.—See Crit. Rev.,
            xxvii. 469–71.
            JONES, HENRY. The Arcana, or mystic gem, 2 cantos, Wolverhampton,
            1769.
1769 w.   AIKIN, A. L. (Mrs. BARBAULD). Corsica.—Poems, 1773, pp. 1–12.
1770   ANON. An idyllion.—Scots Mag., xxxii. 561–2.
            FELLOWS, JOHN. Grace triumphant, in nine dialogues, Birmingham, 1770.—
            Contains some Miltonic blank verse: see Mo. Rev., xliv. 89–90.
            HODSON, WILLIAM. Dedication of the temple of Solomon.—Cambridge
            Prize Poems, i. 225–40.

            [1] 1766   ANON. Dedication to Cavalier Marino's Cynthia and Daphne, 1766. In blank verse: Mo.
            Rev., xxxv. 322. Not seen.

1770   WOTY, WILLIAM. A mock invocation to genius.—Works, 1770, i. 1-7.
—— The looking-glass.—Ib. 59-63.
—— The pediculaiad, or buckram triumphant.—Ib. 142-59.
—— The moralist.—Ib. ii. 56-9.
—— To charity.—Ib. 78-81.
—— The death of Abel.—Ib. 132-44.
—— The old shoe.—Ib. 156-60.

1770 w. 1804 p. JONES, Sir WILLIAM. Britain discovered, an heroic poem in twelve, books [only "design" and two short fragments printed].—Works, 1807, ii. 429-54.

c. 1770 w. WALLACE, GEORGE. Prospects from hills in Fife, 1796.—See Scots Mag., lviii. 623-7.

1771   FELLOWS, JOHN. The Bromsgrove elegy on the death of George Whitefield, 1771.

FERGUSSON, ROBERT. A Saturday's expedition, in mock heroics.—Works 1851, pp. 179-84.

FOOT, JAMES. Penseroso, or the pensive philosopher, 6 books, 1771.

G——. Winter amusement.—Weekly Mag. or Edin. Amusement, xi. 180.

JEMMAT, CATHARINE. On seeing Mr. Mossop preform.—Miscellanies, 1771, pp. 10-12.
—— A morning reflection.—Ib. 17-18.
—— Retirement.—Ib. 72-3.
—— A paraphrase on the 104th psalm, in imitation of Milton's style.— Ib. 127-30.
—— Rural life.—Ib. 191-4.
—— The farmer.—Ib. 204-5.
—— An idea of God, translated from Racine.—Ib. 210-11.

LANGHORNE, JOHN. Fable x, The wilding and the broom.—Fables of Flora, 1771, pp. 57-61.

ROBERTS, W. H. A poetical epistle: [part i] on the existence of God; [part ii] on the attributes of God; [part iii] on the providence of God. 3 parts, 1771.

1771 w. LYTTELTON, THOMAS, Lord. The state of England in the year 2199.— Poems, 1780, pp. 7-16.

1772 [1]   ANON. A view of sundry regions of the earth.—Scots Mag., xxxiv. 38-9.

DAINTRY M. J. On music.—Town and Country Mag., iv. 553.

FERGUSSON, ROBERT. The town and country contrasted.—Works, ed. Grosart, 1851, pp. 173-5.
—— Fashion.—Ib. 191-3.
—— Good eating.—Ib. 214-18.

GIBBONS, THOMAS. Habakkuk, chapter iii.—The Christian Minister, 1772, pp. 90-95.
—— Hymn of Cleanthes to Jupiter.—Ib. 97-9.
—— Pythagoras's golden verses.—Ib. 99-104.
—— Casimire, book ii, ode 5.—Ib. 109-13.
—— To our Lord and Saviour Jesus Christ.—Ib. 118-21.
—— The sufferings of Christ.—Ib. 122-4.
—— God our Creator.—Ib. 161.

GIBSON, WILLIAM. Conscience.—Cambridge Prize Poems, i. 241-50.

1772-82 MASON, WILLIAM. The English garden, 4 books.—Works, 1811, i. 201-424.

---

[1] 1772 TRAPAUD, ELISHA. The oeconomy of happiness, 1772. In blank verse: Crit. Rev., xxxiv. 470. Not seen.

1773 [1]   AIKIN, A. L. (Mrs. BARBAULD). A summer evening's meditation.—Poems, 1773, pp. 131–8.

ANON. Soliloquy on the last shilling.—Gent. Mag., xliii. 294.

FERGUSSON, ROBERT. The Canongate play-house in ruins.—Works, 1851, pp. 205–8.

—— The bugs.—Ib. 230–34.

—— Tea.—Ib. 235–7.

—— An expedition to Fife, and the island of May.—Ib. 238–41.

—— To Dr. Samuel Johnson: food for a new edition of his dictionary.— Ib. 246–8.

LAYARD, C. P. Charity.—Cambridge Prize Poems, i. 251–66.

ROBERTS, W. H. A poetical epistle to Christopher Anstey, on the English poets, chiefly those who have written in blank verse, 1773.—See Crit. Rev., xxxv. 52–4.

c. 1773 w.   AIKIN, A. L. (Mrs. BARBAULD). [Character of John Mort.]—H. Toulmin's Short View of the Life of Mort, 1793, pp. 47–8.

1774   ANON. [A description of winter.]—Poems, 1774: see Crit. Rev., xxxvii. 395–6.

B., W. To Miss C——d, who lent the author Dodsley's Poems.—Gent. Mag., xliv. 135.

"MUSARUM AMICUS." Faith.—Town and Country Mag., vi. 271–2.

PRATT, S. J. ("COURTNEY MELMOTH"). The tears of genius, 1774.

"PYGMALION." The apple dumpling.—Town and Country Mag., vi. 271.

RICHARDSON, WILLIAM. Rowena.—Poems, chiefly Rural, 1774, pp. 47–8.

—— The fate of avarice.—Ib. 49–50.

—— The Naiad.—Ib. 51–3.

—— Runny mead.—Ib. 57–66.

—— On the death of a young lady.—Ib. 89–90.

—— The noble hermit.—Ib. 94–6.

—— The progress of melancholy.—Ib. 99–111.

ROBERTS, W. H. Judah restored, 6 books, 2 vols., 1774.

—— A poetical epistle to a young gentleman on leaving Eton.—Poems, 1774: see Crit. Rev., xxxvii. 213–14.

WHITEHEAD, WILLIAM. The sweepers.—Plays and Poems, 1774, ii. 239–43.

1774–6   BRYANT, JACOB. [Numerous short translations from classical writers.]— A New System, or an Analysis of Antient Mythology, 3d ed., 1807, 6 vols., *passim.*

DOWNMAN, HUGH. Infancy, or the management of children, 6 books.— Infancy, etc., 1803, pp. 1–186.

1775   ANON. The birth-place, in the manner of Young, 1775.—See Mo. Rev., lii. 356.

ANON. The cypress-tree, or moral reflections in a country churchyard, 1775.

F., D., Jun. Friendship.—Lond. Mag., xliv. 39–40.

HAYES, SAMUEL. Duelling.—Cambridge Prize Poems, i. 281–98.

LAYARD, C. P. Duelling.—Ib. 267–79.

MAURICE, THOMAS. The school-boy, in imitation of Mr. Philips's Splendid Shilling, Oxford, 1775.

PENROSE, THOMAS. The helmets.—Flights of Fancy, 1775, pp. 3–9.

1775–93   YOUDE, JOHN. The adventures of Telemachus, 3 vols., 1793.—See Mo. Rev., enl., xi. 105–6.

[1] 1773   CLARKE, JOHN. The adventures of Telemachus, translated, book i, 1773. In blank verse: Mo. Rev., xlix. 316. Not seen.

GREENE, E. B. Hero and Leander, from Musaeus, 1773. In blank verse: Crit. Rev., xxxvii. 315. Not seen.

1776 [1] B., E. Some additional lines recited at the Caractacan meeting.—Gent. Mag., xlvi. 427.

CRAWFORD, CHARLES. The first canto of the revolution, an epic poem, 1776.—See Crit. Rev., xli. 475–8.

HARDCASTLE, SANDFORD. Edgar. — Poetical Amusements at a Villa near Bath, ed. Lady A. R. Miller, 1776, ii. 14–22.

—— Benevolence.—Ib. 162–8.

JEPHSON, R. Extempore ludicrous Miltonic verses.—Asylum for Fugitive Pieces, 1799 [1789], iii. 266–7.

SCOTT, JOHN. Amwell, a descriptive poem, 1776.

1776 w. HAYES, SAMUEL. Prophecy.—Cambridge Prize Poems, ii. 1–19.

1777 ANON. Pursuit after happiness, 1777.

BEATSON, JOHN. Divine philanthropy, Leeds, 1777.—See Crit. Rev., xlvii. 156.

DODD, WILLIAM. Thoughts in prison, 5 parts, new ed., Bath, 1796.

HARDCASTLE, SANDFORD. Ancient and modern music compared.—Poetical Amusements, 1777, iii. 38–47.

HAYES, SAMUEL. Prayer.—Cambridge Prize Poems, ii. 21–38.

MAVOR, WILLIAM. An address to the Deity.—Parnassian Sprigs, 1777, pp. 17–24.

POTTER, ROBERT. The tragedies of Aeschylus, translated, Norwich, 1777.

SCHOMBERG, A. C. Bagley, a descriptive poem, Oxford, 1777.

1778 [2] ANON. Caledonia, 1778.—See Crit. Rev., xlvii. 311–12.

FELLOWS, JOHN. An elegiac poem on A. M. Toplady, 1778.—See ib. xlvi. 397.

HAYES, SAMUEL. The nativity of our Saviour.—Cambridge Prize Poems, ii. 39–53.

KELLET, ALEXANDER. Reason.—A Pocket of Prose and Verse, Bath, 1778: see Crit. Rev., xlvi. 457–60.

"LYSANDER." On the death of a friend.—Gent. Mag., xlviii. 232.

MAURICE, THOMAS. The Oxonian.—Poems, Epistolary, Lyric, and Elegiacal, 1800, pp. 32–40.

1778 w. JEPHSON, R. Burlesque Miltonic: extempore answer to an invitation.—Asylum for Fugitive Pieces, 1789, iii. 268–70.

bef. 1779 w. PENROSE, THOMAS. Address to the genius of Britain.—Poems, 1781, pp. 38–47.

—— Donnington castle.—Ib. 93–6.

1779 ANON. A ride and walk through Stourhead, 1779.—See Crit. Rev., xlix. 156.

ANON. The Anti-Palliseriad, or Britain's triumph over France, 1779.—See Mo. Rev., lx. 230.

CUNNINGHAM, PETER.(?) Leith hill [2d ed.], 1789.—See ib. lxxxi. 280.

FAWCETT, JOHN. The death of Eumenio, Leeds, 1779.

1779 w. 1802 p. ANON. Lines, written at Godstowe.—Europ. Mag., xli. 207–8.

1779 w. WARTON, JOSEPH. Verses written on passing through Hackwood park.—Biographical Memoirs, 1806, p. 168.

c. 1779 w. CRABBE, GEORGE. Midnight.—Poems, ed. A. W. Ward, Camb., 1905, i. 47–60.

1780 ANON. The churchyard, by a youth of eighteen.—Univ. Mag., lxvii. 37.

ANON. Paradise regain'd, or the battle of Adam and the Fox, an heroick poem, 1780.

HUGHES, THOMAS. The ascension.—Cambridge Prize Poems, ii. 55–66.

---

[1] 1776 ANON. The exhibition of fancy, 1776. In blank verse: Crit. Rev., xli. 404. Not seen.
ANON. The flight of freedom, 1776. In blank verse: ib. xlii. 231. Not seen.

[2] 1778 ANON. Academic trifles, a collection of poetical essays, 1778. Contains eight pieces in blank verse: ib. xlvi. 68. Not seen.

1780   HUNT, Mr. Habakkuck, chap. iii, in imitation of Milton: a college exercise.—Gent. Mag., l. 435.

LYTTELTON, THOMAS, Lord. An invitation to Miss Warb-rt-n.—Poems, 1780, pp. 28–9.

WALTERS, JOHN. The vision of Slander and Innocence.—Poems, Oxford, 1780, pp. 84–6.

1781   ANON. Ditis chorus, or hell broke loose, from Petronius Arbiter, 1781.—See Crit. Rev., liii. 67–8.

ANON. Verses on death of a youth.—Town and Country Mag., xiii. 46–7.

HERIOT, GEORGE. A descriptive poem, written in the West Indies, 1781.—See Crit. Rev., lii. 147.

LOFFT, CAPEL. Eudosia, or a poem on the universe, 1781.—See Mo. Rev., lxvi. 305–6.

PINKERTON, JOHN. Symphony i: On the music of poesy.—Rimes, 2d ed., 1782, pp. 57–64.

—— Symphony ii: Defeat of the opera.—Ib. 65–70.

SYMPSON, JOSEPH. The beauties of spring, 1781.—See Crit. Rev., lii. 201–3.

1781–3   POTTER, ROBERT. The tragedies of Euripides, translated, 2 vols., 1781–3.

1782 [1]   ANON. Address to health.—Verses on Several Occasions, 1782, pp. 79–81.

ANON. Enoch, book i, 1782.

BADCOCK, Mr. The hermitage.—Lond. Mag., li. 41.

MADAN, SPENCER. The call of the Gentiles.—Cambridge Prize Poems, ii. 107–17.

MORE, HANNAH. Introduction [to Sacred Dramas].—Works, 1830, i. 1–6.

ROGERS, CHARLES. The Inferno of Dante, translated, 1782.

STERLING, JOSEPH. The rhapsodist.—Poems, Dublin, 1782, pp. 3–26.

STEVENS, W. B. Retirement.—Poems, 1782, pp. 1–29.

WODHULL, MICHAEL. The nineteen tragedies and fragments of Euripides, translated, new ed., 3 vols., 1809.

1783 [2]   ROBERTS, WILLIAM. The sciences.—Poetical Attempts, 1783: see Crit. Rev., lvi. 71.

V. Imitations of three of our most celebrated poets: ii, An harvest scene; iii, "Look upon the Rainbow."—Gent. Mag., liii. 958–9.

bef. 1784 w. 1786 p. BOWDLER, JANE. On the new-year.—Poems and Essays, New York, 1811, pp. 39–49.

1784   ANON. Speech to the sun of the political hemisphere, by a fallen angel, 1784.—See Crit. Rev., lvii. 151–2.

BILLINGE, CHARLES. Charity.—Poems on Christian Charity, etc., Wolverhampton, 1784, pp. 7–29.

—— Contentment.—Ib. 31–51.

—— Hymn to Providence.—Ib. 53–4.

—— Melancholy.—Ib. 55–88.

HAYES, SAMUEL. Creation.—Cambridge Prize Poems, ii. 137–56.

LOFFT, CAPEL. The first and second Georgic, 1784.—See Mo. Rev., lxxii. 345–8.

V. On the dark, still, dry, warm weather.—Gent. Mag., liv. 287.

1784?   STRATFORD, THOMAS. The first book of Fontenoy, a poem in nine books, 1784(?).—See Mo. Rev., lxxi. 95–8.

1784 w. 1824 p. COWPER, WILLIAM. To the immortal memory of the halibut on which I dined.—Poems, ed. Bailey, 1905, pp. 440–41.

[1] 1782   MUGLISTON, WILLIAM. A contemplative walk, 1782. In blank verse: Crit. Rev., liv. 478–9. Not seen.

ROBERTS, WILLIAM. Thoughts upon creation, 1782. In blank verse: Gent. Mag., 1842, ii. 578 n. Not seen.

[2] 1783   ANON. Ippopaidia, 1783. In blank verse: Crit. Rev., lv. 488. Not seen.

1784–91 w. COWPER, WILLIAM. The Iliad [and Odyssey], translated, 2 vols., 1791.
1785   ANON. To Mr. Hayley, on reading his tragedy of Russel.—Gent. Mag., lv. 214.

BOOKER, LUKE. An elegy.—Poems, Wolverhampton, 1785, i. 60–65.
—— To the all-present, yet unknown God.—Ib. ii. 15–18.
—— Clifton-grove.—Ib. 69–112.
COWPER, WILLIAM. The task, 6 books, 1785.
PRATT, S. J. Landscapes in verse.—Sympathy, etc., 1807, pp. 75–118.
SEWARD, ANNA. Colebrook dale.—Poetical Works, ed. W. Scott, Edin., 1810, ii. 314–19.
YEARSLEY, ANN. Night.—Poems on Several Occasions, 1785, pp. 1–15.
—— Address to friendship.—Ib. 79–85.
—— On Mrs. Montagu.—Ib. 101–6.

1785–9 POLWHELE, RICHARD. The English orator, 4 books, 1785–9.
1786   ANON. Description of Achilles' attacking the Trojan army, from Homer.—New Foundling Hospital for Wit, new ed., 1786, i. 248–50.
ANON. Nature, book i, Bristol, 1786.—See Mo. Rev., lxxiv. 564.
F., E. The praise of potatoes, a burlesque.—Asylum for Fugitive Pieces, 1786, ii. 128–30. (In the Edinburgh Magazine for July, 1786, it is signed "K. A.")
HEADLEY, HENRY. Invocation to melancholy.—Poetical Works, ed. T. Park, 1808, pp. 11–16.
—— To Cynthia.—Ib. 17.
KNIPE, ELIZA. Monody [on] Frederick II.—Europ. Mag., x. 290.
RICKMAN, T. C. The fallen cottage, Philadelphia (U. S. A.), 1793.
ROBINSON, Mr. The prize of Venus, or Killarney lake, 1786.—See Crit. Rev., lxi. 314–15.

1786? CARYSFORT, J. J. The revenge of Guendolen, 5 books.—Dramatic and Narrative Poems, 1810, ii. 1–155.
1787   ANON. Female virtues, 1787.—See Crit. Rev., lxiv. 225.
ANON. Monody on Sir James Hunter-Blair.—Scots Mag., xlix. 348.
ANON. The death of honour.—Europ. Mag., xii. 422.
BOOKER, LUKE. The highlanders, Stourbridge, 1787.
GLOVER, RICHARD. The Athenaid, 30 books, 1787.
GREENWOOD, WILLIAM. Poem written during a shooting excursion, Bath, 1787.—See Mo. Rev., lxxvii. 491–2.
H——o. The twelfth of August.—Scots Mag., xlix. 402.
L., C. Written at the seat of T. B. Hollis.—Gent. Mag., lvii. 72.
POLWHELE, RICHARD. Address to Thomas Pennant on his intended visit into Cornwall.—Poems, 1810, ii. 32–5.
"RAMBLE." Lines written [near] a gentleman's seat.—Europ. Mag., xii. 424.
"VICARIUS." Sketches of beauty, 6 books, Stockdale, 1787.—See Mo. Rev., lxxviii. 80.
WHITEHOUSE, JOHN. Elegy written near the ruins of a nunnery.—Poems, 1787, pp. 1–9.
—— A hymn of triumph.—Ib. 54–60.
—— Description of the grotto of Calypso, from Fénelon.—Ib. 72–5.
—— Mentor's reproof of Telemachus [from Fénelon].—Ib. 76.
—— The song of the nymphs [from Fénelon].—Ib. 77–9.
—— Inscription iii.—Ib. 98–9.
—— Inscription for the root-house.—Ib. 100.
—— Written in a rustic temple.—Ib. 104–6.
YEARSLEY, ANN. To sensibility.—Poems on Various Subjects, 1787: see New Annual Register, 1787, pp. [199–200].
—— To indifference.—Ib. [201–2].

1787 w.   DOWNMAN, HUGH. To independence.—Infancy, etc., 1803, pp. 219–23.
          POLWHELE, RICHARD. To a clergyman.—Sketches in Verse, 1796, p. 66.

1787–8   ROSCOE, WILLIAM. The wrongs of Africa, 2 parts, 1787–8.

1788 [1]   ANON. (JAMES CRIRIE?). Address to Loch Lomond, 1788.—See Mo. Rev.,
          lxxix. 365–7.
          CROWE, WILLIAM. Lewesdon hill, Oxford, 1788.
          HURDIS, JAMES. The village curate, 1788.
          POTTER, ROBERT. The tragedies of Sophocles, translated, new ed., 1820.
          TURNBULL, GAVIN. Evening.—Poetical Essays, Glasgow, 1788, pp. 89–99.
          WESTON, JOSEPH. The woodmen of Arden, translated from John Morfitt's
          Philotoxi Ardenae, Birmingham, 1788. — Records of the Woodmen of
          Arden, 1885, pp. 105–13.

1788 w.   SEWARD, ANNA. Remonstrance to Cowper.—Works, 1810, iii. 5–14.

1789 [2]   ANON. The college hero, from the Latin.—Gent. Mag., lix. 451–2.
          ANON. Gallick liberty, a poem occasioned by the revolution in France.—
          New Lond. Mag., v. 552.
          ANON. The vision, on the restoration of his majesty's health, 1789.—See
          Mo. Rev., lxxx. 554.
          GILBANK, WILLIAM. The day of Pentecost, or man restored, 12 books, 1789.
          —See Crit. Rev., lxvii. 351–4.
          HOMER, PHILIP. To the fritillary.—Gent. Mag., lix. 448.
          JAMIESON, JOHN. The sorrows of slavery, 1789.—See Crit. Rev., lxvii.
          468–9.
          REID, W. H. The panic, or a meditation on the plague.—Scots Mag., li.
          444.
          SWAIN, JOSEPH. Redemption, 8 books, Boston (U. S. A.), 1812.

1789 w. 1794? p. ROBERTS, JOHN. The deluge.—Cambridge Prize Poems, ii. 193–205.

1790   ANON. Sunday, 1790.—See Crit. Rev., lxx. 95.
          DEACON, D. The triumph of liberty.—Poems, Chesterfield, 1790, pp. 1–53.
          DUNSTER, CHARLES ("MARMADUKE MILTON"). St. James's street, 1790.
          HURDIS, JAMES. Adriano, 1790.
          —— Elmer and Ophelia.—Poems, 1790, pp. 1–59.
          —— Panthea.—Ib. 69–227.
          SOTHEBY, WILLIAM. A tour through parts of Wales, 2 books.—Poems, etc.,
          Bath, 1790, pp. 1–40.

1790 w.   DERMODY, THOMAS. The triumph of gratitude.—Life, with Original Poetry,
          by J. G. Raymond, 1806, i. 118–23.

1791   AIKIN, JOHN. Picturesque, in the manner of Cowper.—Poems, 1791, pp.
          52–7.
          —— Epistle to the Rev. W. Enfield.—Ib. 82–9.
          F., D. S. "Nigh where the Thames rolls on in silent pomp."—Europ.
          Mag., xix. 231–3.
          PHILPOT, CHARLES. Humility, a night thought.—Cambridge Prize Poems,
          ii. 219–34.
          "AN UNDER GRADUATE." The dictates of indignation, on the African
          slave trade, 1791.—See Crit. Rev., new arr., ii. 168–70.
          WILLIAMS, JOHN ("ANTHONY PASQUIN"). Shrove Tuesday, a satiric rhap-
          sody, 1791.

1791 w. 1803 p. COWPER, WILLIAM. The four ages, a brief fragment.—Poems, ed.
          Bailey, 1905, pp. 477–8.

---

[1] 1788   CANTON, G. The adventures of Telemachus, translated into blank verse, book i, 1788. Not
      seen.
[2] 1789   BOOKER, LUKE. Knowle hill (in Miscellaneous Poems, Stourbridge, 1789). In blank verse:
      Crit. Rev., new arr., x. 41. Not seen.

1791 w. 1804 p. COWPER, WILLIAM. Yardley oak.—Ib. 479–83.
1791 w. 1810 p. COWPER, WILLIAM, and HAYLEY, WILLIAM. Adam, translated from
    Andreini.—Life and Works of Cowper, ed. Southey, 1837, x. 239–387.
1791–2 w. 1808 p. COWPER, WILLIAM. Nature unimpaired by time [from Milton].—
    Poems, ed. Bailey, 1905, pp. 576–8.
—— On the Platonic idea [from Milton].—Ib. 578–9.
—— To his father [from Milton].—Ib. 579–82.
1792   ANON. A morning walk, 1792.—See Mo. Rev., enl., ix. 330–31.
    CUMBERLAND, RICHARD. Calvary, or the death of Christ, 8 books, 1792.
    LLOYD, DAVID. The voyage of life, 9 books, 1792.
    YOUNG, WILLIAM. Paraphrase on the first chapter of Genesis.—Univ. Mag.,
        xc. 449–50.
1792 w.   AIKIN, A. L. (Mrs. BARBAULD). To Dr. Priestley.—Works, 1825, i. 183–4.
    C-B-S, L-S-R. The icead.—Gent. Mag., lxii. 846–7.
1793 [1]   ANON. The genius of France, 1793.—See Mo. Rev., enl., xii. 102–3.
    ANON. An hymn.—Anthologia Hibernica, Dublin, 1793, i. 388–9.
    KETT, HENRY. Translation of Jortin's poem on the nature of the soul.—
        Juvenile Poems, Oxford, 1793, pp. 31–40.
—— Episode taken from a poem on the earthquake at Lisbon.—Ib. 46–9.
    ROBINSON, MARY. Sight.—Sight, etc., 1793, pp. 1–10.
—— Solitude.—Ib. 19–32.
    SMITH, CHARLOTTE. The emigrants, 2 books, 1793.
    THORN, R. J. Retirement, Bristol, 1793.—See Crit. Rev., new arr., x.
        467–8.
1793 w.   HARLEY, G. D. Lines written at West Cowes.—Poems, 1796, pp. 114–16.
    JONES, JOHN, bishop of Cork. Epistle to Archdeacon Moore.—R. Polwhele's
        Traditions and Recollections, 1826, i. 337–8.
1793 w. 1796–7 p. CROWE, WILLIAM. Verses to the duke of Portland. — Southey's
    Annual Anthology, Bristol, 1799, i. 112–14.
1793–1800 w. ROBINSON, MARY. The progress of liberty.—Poetical Works, 1806, iii.
    1–52.
c. 1793?–1828 w. SOUTHEY, ROBERT. Inscriptions, i–xlv. — Poetical Works, 1837, iii.
        103–78. Seven inscriptions were not reprinted: Poems, 1797, pp. 55, 59;
        Letters written in Spain and Portugal, Bristol, 1797, pp. 270, 469–70;
        Annual Anthology, 1799, i. 67, 181, 208.
1794   ANON. The curate's caution.—Gent. Mag., lxiv. 365–6.
    ANON. War, 1794.—See Mo. Rev., enl., xvi. 107–8.
    BERESFORD, JAMES. The Aeneid, translated, 1794.—See ib. xviii. 1–12.
    BURRELL, SOPHIA, Lady. The Thymbriad (from Xenophon's Cyropaedia),
        7 books, 1794.
    CARY, H. F. The mountain seat.—Gent. Mag., lxiv. 161–2.
    GISBORNE, THOMAS. Walks in a forest, 3d ed., 1797.
    HARRISON, ANTHONY. Apostrophe to Shakspeare. — The Infant Vision of
        Shakspeare, etc., 1794, pp. 9–10.
    HURDIS, JAMES. Tears of affection, 1794.
    I. On history.—Anthologia Hibernica, 1794, iii. 135–7.
    JENNINGS, JAMES. Lines written during a morning walk in August.—
        Europ. Mag., xxvi. 289.
    SCARISBING, F. S. Paraphrase upon the canticle, 'Benedicite, omnia opera
        Domini.'—Gent. Mag., lxiv. 257–8.
    THORN, R. J. Howe triumphant, or the glorious first of June, an heroic
        poem, 1794.—See Crit. Rev., new arr., xiii. 112.
    WARTON, JOHN. The complaint.—Poems, Salisbury, 1794, pp. 1–9.
—— The vision of Moses.—Ib. 71–6.

[1] 1793   ANON. Christmas, 1793. In blank verse: Crit. Rev., new arr., x. 229–30. Not seen.

1794 w. SOUTHEY, ROBERT. Botany-Bay eclogues.—Poems, 1797, pp. 77–82; Mo. Mag., 1798, v. 41–2.

WRANGHAM, FRANCIS. The restoration of the Jews.—Cambridge Prize Poems, ii. 235–50.

1794–6 w. POLWHELE, RICHARD. The thunder.—Sketches in Verse, 1796, pp. 33–4.

—— The pilchard-seine.—Ib. 38–41.

—— The village.—Ib. 45–7.

—— A winter evening scene.—Influence of Local Attachment, 1798, pp. 62–3.

—— A winter piece.—Ib. 73.

1795 ANON. A call to the country, 1795.—See Mo. Rev., enl., xviii. 91.

ANON. Mensa regum, or the table of kings, 1795.—See Crit. Rev., new arr., xvi. 355–7.

BELLAMY, THOMAS. The London theatres, 1795.

CORNHILL, SEWELL. The old serpentine temple of the Druids, Marlborough, 1795.

FAWCETT, JOSEPH. The art of war, 1795.

HUCKS, JOSEPH. Upon the ruins of Denbigh castle.—A Pedestrian Tour through North Wales, 1795, pp. 46–7.

HURDIS, JAMES. Poem upon a prospect of the marriage of the prince of Wales, 1795.—See Crit. Rev., new arr., xvii. 264–8.

LETTICE, JOHN. The immortality of the soul, translated from I. H. Browne, Camb., 1795.

—— [Translation of a passage from Claudian.]—Ib. 309–10.

SMYTH, PHILIP. The coffee-house, a characteristic poem, 1795.—See Crit. Rev., new arr., xiv. 232–3.

TROLLOPE, A. W. The destruction of Babylon.—Cambridge Prize Poems, ii. 251–61.

1795–7 COLE, THOMAS. The life of Hubert, a narrative, descriptive, and didactic poem, books i–iii, 1795–7.—See Mo. Rev., enl., xix. 136–9, xxv. 102–5.

1795–1814 w. 1814 p. WORDSWORTH, WILLIAM. The excursion.—Poetical Works, ed. W. Knight, 1896, vol. v.

c. 1795 w. OPIE, AMELIA. An evening walk at Cromer [in] 1795.—Southey's Annual Anthology, 1800, ii. 131–3.

c. 1795 w. 1802–97 p. LANDOR, W. S. The Phocaeans.—Poems, etc., ed. Crump, 1892, ii. 59–76; Letters and other Unpublished Writings, ed. Wheeler, 1897, pp. 136, 236–8; W. Bradley's Early Poems of Landor, a Study, 1914, pp. 113–21.

1796 BIDLAKE, JOHN. The sea, 2 books, 1796.

BISHOP, SAMUEL. The man of taste, in imitation of Milton.—Poetical Works, 1796: see Mo. Mirror, ii. 290–91.[1]

COURTIER, P. L. The pleasures of solitude.—Poems, 1796, pp. 95–114.

—— To the memory of Thomson.—Ib. 115–16.

—— Revolutions, 2 books, 1796.

FITCHETT, JOHN. Bewsey, Warrington, 1796.—See New Annual Register, 1796, pp. [167–8].

GRAHAM, CHARLES. To the memory of James Thomson.—Gent. Mag., lxvi. 1102–4.

HARLEY, G. D. Address.—Poems, 1796, pp. 9–11.

—— Night.—Ib. 26–107.

—— Elegy on a Newfoundland dog.—Ib. 120–33.

—— The cat.—Ib. 139–63.

—— Lines, written at an inn.—Ib. 166–9.

—— Leander.—Ib. 177–218 (error in pagination).

---

[1] Bishop's *Preacher* is also in blank verse, but whether Miltonic or not I do not know.

1796   HARLEY, G. D.   A legacy of love.—Ib. 219–95.
        LAMB, CHARLES.   The grandame.—Works, ed. Lucas, 1903, v. 5–6.
        —— The Sabbath bells.—Ib. 9.
        SEWARD, ANNA.   Philippic on a modern epic.—Works, 1810, iii. 67–9.
        SKENE, GEORGE.   Donald Bane, an heroic poem, 3 books, 1796.—See Mo.
            Rev., enl., xxiv. 49–56.
        SOUTHEY, ROBERT.   Joan of Arc, an epic poem, Bristol, 1796.
        THOMSON, ALEXANDER.   The paradise of taste, 1796.—Contains some
            Miltonic blank verse: see Crit. Rev., new arr., xix. 129–37.
        V., T. (THOMAS VIVIAN?).   Description of Pandora, from Hesiod's Works
            and Days.—Essays by a Society of Gentlemen at Exeter, 1796, pp.
            432–3 n.
        —— The shield of Hercules, from Hesiod.—Ib. 455–65.
        —— The shield of Achilles, from Homer.—Ib. 466–73.
        WILLIAMS, WILLIAM.   Redemption, book i, 1796.—See Mo. Rev., enl., xxi.
            226–7.

1797   AIKIN, A. L. (Mrs. BARBAULD).   Washing-day.—Works, 1825, i. 202–6.
        ANON.   The castle of Olmutz, 1797.—See Crit. Rev., new arr., xx. 103–4.
        ANON.   Lines on the failure of standing for a fellowship at college.—Gent.
            Mag., lxvii. 238.
        BOLLAND, WILLIAM.   Miracles.—Cambridge Prize Poems, ii. 263–76.
        BROWN, ROBERT.   The campaign, 2 books, 1797.—See Crit. Rev., new arr.,
            xxii. 472–3.
        CANNING, GEORGE, and FRERE, J. H.   Inscription for the door of the cell
            in Newgate, where Mrs. Brownrigg was confined.—Poetry of the Anti-
            Jacobin, ed. C. Edmonds, 2d ed., 1854, p. 16.
        DALLAS, R. C.   Kirkstall abbey.—Miscellaneous Writings, 1797, pp. 1–15.
        DONOGHUE, J.   Juvenile essays in poetry, 1797.—See Mo. Rev., enl., xxiii.
            457–8.
        GORTON, JOHN.   Adam's morning hymn, imitated from Milton.—Gent.
            Mag., lxvii. 965–6.
        GRAHAME, JAMES.   The rural calendar.—The Birds of Scotland, etc., Edin.,
            1806, pp. 120–61.
        JACKSON, JOHN.   Gils-land Wells.—Poems on Several Occasions, 1797: see
            Mo. Rev., enl., xxv. 237–8.
        N.   Address to an old pair of boots newly tapped.—Mo. Mag., iii. 140.
        SHARPE, JOHN.   The church, 1797.—See Crit. Rev., new arr., xxi. 460–63.
        SOUTHEY, ROBERT.   Retrospective musings.—Letters written in Spain and
            Portugal, 1797, pp. xvii–xx.
        —— [Lines on the widow of Villa Franca.]—Ib. 63–5.
        —— [Translations from Lope de Vega's Hermosura de Angelica.]—Ib. 135,
            137, 138–9, 141–2, 147–50, 152, 159.
        —— [Translations from Pedro de Tojal's Carlos Reduzido.]—Ib. 333–4,
            336–7, 338, 340–1, 343, 350.
        —— Written after visiting the convent of Arrabida.—Ib. 476–9.
        WILCOCKE, S. H.   Britannia, 1797.—See Mo. Rev., enl., xxiv. 454–7.

1797 w. AIKIN, A. L. (Mrs. BARBAULD).   To Coleridge.—Works, 1825, i. 209–11.
        SOUTHEY, ROBERT.   Recollections of a day's journey in Spain.—Works,
            1837, ii. 233–5.
        THELWALL, JOHN.   Lines written at Bridgewater.—Poems written in Re-
            tirement, Hereford, 1801, pp. 126–32.
        —— On leaving the bottoms of Glocestershire.—Ib. 136–9.
        —— Maria.—Ib. 142–4.

1797–1812 w. 1805–14 p. CARY, H. F.   The vision, or hell, purgatory, and paradise of
            Dante, translated, 2d ed., 3 vols., 1819.

bef. 1798 w. MARRIOTT, JOHN. The falling leaf.—A Short Account of John Marriott, etc., Doncaster, 1803, pp. 155–62.

—— The vanity of expecting happiness, from superiour acquirements.—Ib. 189–90.

1798   ANON. Matriculation, 1798.—See Crit. Rev., new arr., xxiv. 468–9.

BOOKER, LUKE. Malvern, a descriptive and historical poem, 3 books, Dudley, 1798.

BOWLES, W. L. On a beautiful spring.—Poetical Works, ed. G. Gilfillan, Edin., 1855, i. 98–9.

—— Coombe-Ellen.—Ib. 115–25.

COTTLE, JOSEPH. Malvern hills, 1798.

DYER, GEORGE. On taking leave of Arthur Aikin.—Poems, 1801, pp. 129–34.

—— Addressed to the society for establishing a literary fund.—Ib. 140–44.

FAWCETT, JOSEPH. To the sun; written in the spring.—Poems, 1798: see Mo. Rev., enl., xxviii. 274–5.

LANDOR, W. S. Gebir.—Works, etc., ed. Forster, 1876, vii. 3–41.

LOFFT, CAPEL. On seeing Mrs. Siddons in The Stranger.—Mo. Mag., v. 443.

POLWHELE, RICHARD. To Miss S——. Influence of Local Attachment, 1798, ii. 57–8.

1798 w.   BOLLAND, WILLIAM. The epiphany.—Cambridge Prize Poems, ii. 277–87.

ELLIOTT, EBENEZER. The vernal walk, 1801.—See Mo. Rev., enl., xxxv. 109–110.

c. 1798–1838 w. 1808–42 p. FITCHETT, JOHN. King Alfred [2d ed.], 6 vols., completed and edited by Robert Roscoe, 1841–2.

1799   BOOKER, LUKE. The hop-garden, a didactic poem, 2 books, Newport, 1799.

—— A sequel-poem to the Hop-Garden.—Ib. 75–106.

DYER, GEORGE. On visiting Fuseli's Milton gallery in Pall Mall.—Gent. Mag., lxix. 509–10.

HILDRETH, W. The Niliad, an epic poem in honour of the victory off the mouth of the Nile, 1799.—See Crit. Rev., new arr., xxv. 354–5.

LLOYD, CHARLES. Lines suggested by the fast, Birmingham, 1799.

M., J. Atys, or human weakness, 1799.—See Mo. Rev., enl., xxxiii. 428–9.

NASON, GEORGE. Aphono and Ethina, including the science of ethics, 3 cantos, Edin., 1799.—See ib. xxxii. 437–8.

THOMSON, ALEXANDER. Pictures, 6, 7, 9.—Pictures of Poetry, Edin., 1799: see Crit. Rev., new arr., xxvii. 260–68.

THORN, R. J. Lodon and Miranda, Bristol, 1799.—See ib. 110–12.

1799 w.   BOLLAND, WILLIAM. Saint Paul at Athens.—Cambridge Prize Poems, ii. 289–97.

SOUTHEY, ROBERT. Madoc, 1805.

1799 w. 1815 p. COWPER, WILLIAM. Virgil's Aeneid, viii. 18 ff.—Poems, ed. Bailey, 1905, pp. 625–34.

1799–1805 w. 1850 p. WORDSWORTH, WILLIAM. The prelude.—Poetical Works, 1896, iii. 121–380.

bef. 1800 w. WARTON, JOSEPH. Epistle from Thomas Hearne, antiquary.—Biographical Memoirs, 1806, pp. 159–60.

—— Verses on Dr. Burton's death.—Ib. 163.

—— Verses spoken to the king by Lord Shaftesbury.—Ib. 163–4.

1800   ANON. Kilda.—Gent. Mag., lxx. 977.

"AURISCO GERESTEO (FRA GLI ARCADI)." Speech of Napoleon in Kassandra Pseudomantis, 1800.—See Crit. Rev., new arr., xxxi. 470.

BROWN, JAMES. Britain preserved, 7 books, Edin., 1800.—See ib. 109–11.

CASE, WILLIAM. Gorthmund, a tale in the manner of Ossian.—Southey's Annual Anthology, ii. 91–5.

1800   CASE, WILLIAM. Owen's grave.—Ib. 186–8.
        CHAMBERLIN, MASON. Equanimity, 1800.—See Mo. Rev., enl., xxxiii.
            429-30.
        —— Harvest.—Ib.
        COTTLE, JOSEPH. Alfred, an epic poem, 24 books, 1800.
        DYER, GEORGE. Homer's statue [translated from the Anthologia pub-
            lished by H. Stephens].—Poems, 1801, pp. 53–5.
        HURDIS, JAMES. The favorite village, Bishopstone, 1800.
        MANT, RICHARD. Verses to the memory of Joseph Warton, Oxford, 1800.
        ROBINSON, MARY. The Italian peasantry.—Mo. Mag., ix. 260–61.
        SHERIVE, C. H. On leaving Bristol Wells.—Southey's Annual Anthology
            ii. 243–6.
        WHITEHOUSE, JOHN. Hymn to the earth, etc., from Stolberg, 1800.—See
            Crit. Rev., new arr., xxxi. 348–9.
        WORDSWORTH, WILLIAM. Inscription for St. Herbert's island [text of 1815].
            —Poetical Works, 1896, ii. 210–13.
        WRANGHAM, FRANCIS. The Holy Land.—Cambridge Prize Poems, ii. 299–
            314.
c. 1800 w. SEWARD, ANNA. A meditation.—Works, 1810, iii. 317–18.
        —— Address to the river in a landscape.—Ib. 334–7.
        SOTHEBY, WILLIAM. Extracts from a manuscript poem on the elements.—
            Italy and other Poems, 1828, pp. 247–308.
c. 1800 w. 1807 p. WHITE, HENRY KIRKE. Commencement of a poem on despair.—
            Remains, ed. Southey, 5th ed., 1811, i. 358–60.
c. 1800 w. 1888 p. WORDSWORTH, WILLIAM. The recluse, book i, part i: Home at
            Grasmere.—Poetical Works, 1896, viii. 235–57.
1801   ANON. The prostitute.—A Collection of Poems [ed. Joshua Edkins], Dublin,
            1801, pp. 28–31.
        BOADEN, JAMES. A rainy day, 1801.—See Crit. Rev., new arr., xxxv. 111–12.
        BROUGHTON, BRIAN. Six picturesque views in North Wales, with poetical
            reflections, 1801.—See Mo. Rev., enl., xliv. 41–4. (Four "views" had
            been published in 1798.)
        BURGES, JAMES BLAND. Richard the First, 18 books, 2 vols., 1801.—See
            ib. xxxvii. 287–91.
        CARLISLE, FREDERICK HOWARD, Earl of. Naworth castle.—Tragedies and
            Poems, 1801, pp. 297–8.
        CHAMBERLIN, MASON. Ocean, 1801.—See Mo. Rev., enl., xxxvi. 437–8.
        DYER, GEORGE. The madman.—Poems, 1801, pp. 19–22.
        —— On visiting the tomb of David Hume.—Ib. 56–60.
        —— Monody on the death of Robert Robinson.—Ib. 182–6.
        FOX, WILLIAM, Jr. La bagatella, or delineations of home scenery, a descrip-
            tive poem, 2 parts, 1801.—See Mo. Rev., enl., xxxviii. 188–90.
        HUNT, LEIGH. Christ's hospital.—Juvenilia, 4th ed., 1803, pp. 17–25.
        LARDNER, W. O. The college gibb, an heroic sketch.—A Collection of Poems
            [ed. Joshua Edkins], 1801, pp. 1–8.
        OGILVIE, JOHN. Britannia, a national epic poem, 20 books, Aberdeen, 1801.
        THELWALL, JOHN. Paternal tears [10 "effusions"].—Poems written in
            Retirement, 1801, pp. 145–63.
        THOMPSON, GILBERT. Select translations from the works of Homer and
            Horace, 1801.—See Crit. Rev., new arr., xxxvi. 107–8.
1801 w. 1804 p. HERBERT, WILLIAM. Croyland abbey.—Works, 1842, i. pt. ii.169–70.
        —— Written in Somersetshire.—Ib. 171–7.
1801 w.   SEWARD, ANNA. Consolation.—Works, 1810, iii. 351–6.
1801–21   THELWALL, JOHN. Specimens of the Hope of Albion, or Edwin of Northum-
            bria, an epic poem.—Poems written in Retirement, 1801, pp. 175–202;
            Poetical Recreations, 1822, pp. 117–24, 235–42.

1802   ANON. [" Fragment of "] The art of candle-making, a didactic poem in
          twenty books.—Europ. Mag., xlii. 424-6.

          ANON. Sketch of Bonaparte.—Mo. Mag., xiv. 53-4.

          COCKBURN, WILLIAM. St. Peter's denial of Christ.—Cambridge Prize
          Poems, ii. 315-26.

          DYER, GEORGE. To the memory of George Morgan.—Poems, 1802, i. 95-
          101.

          —— On the death of Gilbert Wakefield.—Ib. 102-9.

          LANDOR, W. S. Chrysaor.—Works, etc., ed. Forster, 1876, vii. 456-63.

          M. The crooked sixpence, in imitation of Philips's "Splendid Shilling."—
          Gent. Mag., lxxii. 446-7.

          PALMER, JOHN. The creation and fall of man, 1802.—See Mo. Rev., enl.,
          xl. 102.

          S., E. Inscription in a wood in Sussex.—Europ. Mag., xlii. 223.

1802 w.   SEWARD, ANNA. Farewell to the seat of Lady Eleanor Butler.—Works,
          1810, iii. 345-50.

1803   ALLEY, JEROME. The judge, 3 cantos, 1803.

          ANON. Bonaparte's soliloquy on the invasion of England, 1803.—See Crit.
          Rev., new arr., xxxviii. 471-2.

          BAYLEY, PETER. The delusions of love.—Poems, Philadelphia (U. S. A.),
          1804, pp. 165-94.

          BOWLES, W. L. On a landscape by Rubens.—Works, 1855, i. 142-50.

          CRIRIE, JAMES. Scottish scenery, or sketches of scenes in the highlands,
          1803.—See Mo. Rev., enl., xlvi. 14-20.[1]

          DOWNMAN, HUGH. On taking the Havannah.—Infancy, etc., 1803, pp.
          207-11.

          —— On genius.—Ib. 213-18.

          EDRIDGE, REBECCA. The lapse of time, Uxbridge, 1803.—See Crit. Rev.,
          new arr., xxxvii. 234-5.

          FLOWERDEW, Mrs. A. Poems on moral and religious subjects, 1803.—
          Contains some Miltonic blank verse: see Mo. Rev., enl., xliii. 438-9.

          HOLLOWAY, WILLIAM. Scenes of youth.—Scenes of Youth, etc., 1803, pp.
          1-99.

          KENNEY, JAMES. Society, 2 parts, 1803.—See Mo. Rev., enl., xliv. 32-3.

          LOWE, JOHN, Jr. [Lines from one of his poems.]—Ib. xli. 100-101.

          "A WRANGLER." Address to mathematics.—Gent. Mag., lxxiii. 548-9.

1803 w.   COCKBURN, WILLIAM. Christ raising the daughter of Jaïrus.—Cambridge
          Prize Poems, ii. 327-36.

1803 w. 1805 p. BRYDGES, EGERTON. Retirement.—Censura Literaria, 2d ed., 1815,
          x. 267-75.

1803 w. 1815 p. WORDSWORTH, WILLIAM. Yew-trees.—Poetical Works, 1896, ii. 369-
          74.

c. 1803-6 w. 1807- p. WHITE, HENRY KIRKE. "Yes, my stray steps have wander'd."—
          Remains, 1811, i. 189-91.

          —— Christmas-day.—Ib. ii. 119-21.

          —— Nelsoni mors.—Ib. 121-2.

          —— Time.—Ib. 147-71.

          —— The Christiad.—Ib. 173-93.

          —— "Drear winter! who dost knock."—Ib. iii (1822), 89-90.

1804   BLAKE, WILLIAM. Milton, 2 books, 1804.—Prophetic Books: Milton, ed.
          E. R. D. Maclagan and A. G. B. Russell, 1907.

          BOWLES, W. L. The spirit of discovery by sea.—Works, 1855, i. 225-94.

---

[1] At least one of the "sketches" seems to have been published before: cf. *ib.* 15-16 (description of
Loch Lomond) with the *Bee*, xv. 293 (June 26, 1793). This may be the same as the *Address to Loch Lomond*
(1788, above).

1804   BROWN, THOMAS. The bard.—Poems, 1804: see Mo. Rev., enl., xlvi. 203–4.
—— To my mother.—The Wanderer in Norway, etc., 2d ed., 1816, pp. 1–7.
—— Musings during a night-walk.—Ib. 143–60.
E—TT, E. Inscription ii.—Mo. Mag., xvii. 146.
GRAHAME, JAMES. The Sabbath, 1804.
HOWARD, NATHANIEL. Bickleigh vale.—Bickleigh Vale, etc., York, 1804, pp. 1–37.
—— An inscription for Lidford bridge.—Ib. 117–18.
IRELAND, W. H. ("CHARLES CLIFFORD"). The angler, book i, 1804.
STRANGE, T. A hint to Britain's arch enemy, Buonaparte, Henley, 1804.— See Mo. Rev., enl., xliii. 437.
TINDAL, WILLIAM. The evils and advantages of genius contrasted, 3 cantos, 1804.—See ib. xliv. 101.
WHITFIELD, HENRY. The Christmas holidays, 1804.[1]—See ib. xlvi. 324.
WRANGHAM, FRANCIS. The raising of Jaïrus' daughter, 1804.

1804 w.   HERBERT, WILLIAM. To the memory of Thomas Brigstock.—Works, 1842, vol. i. pt. ii. 177–80.
HOYLE, CHARLES. Moses viewing the promised land.—Cambridge Prize Poems, ii. 337–52.
THELWALL, JOHN. To Miss Bannatine.—Poetical Recreations, 1822, pp. 219–21.

1805   BARLOW, JOHN. Loss of the Earl of Abergavenny, East-Indiaman, Weymouth, 1805.
BOOKER, LUKE. Tobias, 3 parts, 1805.
BOUNDEN, JOSEPH. Fatal curiosity, or the vision of Silvester, 3 books, 1805.
GOOD, J. M. The nature of things, a didactic poem, from Lucretius, 2 vols., 1805.
PEERS, CHARLES. Christ's lamentation over Jerusalem.—Cambridge Prize Poems, ii. 353–63.
R., W. Effusions to an English marigold.—Europ. Mag., xlviii. 307–8.
THELWALL, JOHN. The trident of Albion, an epic effusion, Liverpool, 1805.

1805 w.   BROWN, THOMAS. The renovation of India, Edin., 1808.
1806   GRAHAME, JAMES. The birds of Scotland.—The Birds of Scotland, etc., 1806, pp. 1–86.
—— Biblical pictures.—Ib. 87–119.
"HAFIZ." December.—Gent. Mag., lxxvi. 1151–2.
HOYLE, CHARLES. Paul and Barnabas at Lystra. — Cambridge Prize Poems, ii. 365–78.
SHEPHERD, RICHARD. "Your caution, sacred Guide."—The New Boethius, 2d ed., 1808, pp. 105–7.
THELWALL, JOHN. Monody on Charles James Fox, 1806.
YORKE, PHILIP, Viscount Royston. Cassandra, from Lycophron, Camb., 1806.

1807   CUMBERLAND, RICHARD, and BURGES, J. B. The Exodiad, 1807.
FORD, THOMAS. A token of respect to the memory of Archbishop Markham. —Gent. Mag., lxxvii. 1049–50.
HOWARD, J. J. The Metamorphoses of Ovid, 2 vols., 1807.—See Mo. Rev., enl., liv. 426–8.
HOWARD, NATHANIEL. The Inferno of Dante, translated, 1807.
HOYLE, CHARLES. Exodus, an epic poem, 13 books, 1807.—See Edin. Rev., enl., xi. 362–70.
MASTERS, MARTIN KEDGWIN. The progress of love, Boston (U.S.A.), 1808.
SMITH, CHARLOTTE. Beachy head.—Beachy Head, etc., 1807, pp. 1–51.
SOTHEBY, WILLIAM. Saul, 2 parts, 1807.

---

[1] In the same volume is another poem in blank verse, called *Black Monday*.

1808 BAYLEY, CATHARINE. Medicine, in imitation of Thomson.—Europ. Mag., liv. 218.

CoTTLE. JOSEPH. The fall of Cambria, 25 books, 1808.

DEARE, J. R. The Georgics, translated, 1808.—See Quart. Rev., i. 69, 76–7.

NOBLE, THOMAS. Blackheath, a didactic and descriptive poem, 5 cantos, 1808.

—— Lucan's Pharsalia, i. 447 ff.—Lumena (appended to Blackheath), preface, p. iv.

—— Lines composed on the bench at Dartmouth Point.—Miscellaneous Poems (appended ib.), 49–57.

—— [Translation of a passage from "Orpheus."]—Argonautica of C. Valerius Flaccus (appended ib.), 110–112.

—— Translation of Horace, book i, ode i: To Maecenas.—Academic Letters, 1808, pp. 135–6.

—— Concluding address.—Ib. 174–6.

VINCENT, JOHN. Fowling, 5 books, 1808.—See W. H. K. Wright's West-Country Poets, 1896, pp. 459–60.

1809 BOWLES, W. L. Pictures from Theocritus: from idyl xxii.—Works, 1855, i. 159–61.

—— Southampton castle.—Ib. 164–6.

—— Cadland, Southampton river.—Ib. 180–82.

—— The sylph of summer.—Ib. 184–201.

—— Avenue in Savernake forest.—Ib. 215–16.

—— Sketch from Bowden hill.—Ib. 219–22.

GRAHAME, JAMES. Africa delivered.—Poems on the Abolition of the Slave Trade, by J. Montgomery, Grahame, and E. Benger, 1809, pp. 55–100.

—— British georgics, Edin., 1809.

1809 w. 1814 p. SOUTHEY, ROBERT. Roderick, the last of the Goths.—Works, 1838, vol. ix.

1810 CRAWFORD, CHARLES. The palace of superstition.—Poems on Various Subjects, 3d ed., 1810, pp. 157–79.

THELWALL, JOHN. [Translation from the Aeneid, i. 81 ff.]—Vestibule of Eloquence, 1810, pp. 112–13.

bef.1811 w. AIKIN, A. L. (Mrs. BARBAULD). Eternity.—Works, 1825, i. 230–31.

1811 WEBB, FRANCIS. Somerset, 1811.

1811 w. AIKIN, A. L. (Mrs. BARBAULD). On the king's illness.—Works, 1825, i. 263–5.

1812 DIBDIN, T. F. Bibliography, book i, 1812.

ELTON, C. A. Hesiod's Theogony, translated.—Remains of Hesiod, 1812, pp. 65–133.

—— Hesiod's Shield of Hercules.—Ib. 199–233.

HUME, JOSEPH. Inferno, from Dante, 1812.

IRELAND, W. H. Lines in imitation of Milton.—Neglected Genius, 1812, pp. 111–12.

1813 WALKER, W. S. From the ninth book of Klopstock's Messiah.—Poetical Remains, ed. J. Moultrie, 1852, pp. 178–9.

1814 ELTON, C. A. Specimens of the classic poets, from Homer to Tryphiodorus, translated, 1814: i. 13–60, 77–84, 164–5, 221–2, 267–72, 283–91, 297–344, 353–4, 415–16; ii. 51–65, 335–6; iii. 9–36, 203–36, 293–4, 315–27.

LICKBARROW, ISABELLA. To the muse.—Poetical Effusions, 1814, pp. 1–2.

—— A fragment on solitude.—Ib. 3–5.

—— Written early in spring.—Ib. 5–7.

—— On music.—Ib. 8–9.

—— The naiad's complaint.—Ib. 9–11.

—— The throne of winter.—Ib. 11–13.

—— On sleep.—Ib. 13–15.

1814 LICKBARROW, ISABELLA. On sensibility.—Ib. 15–17.
—— Written at the commencement of the year 1813.—Ib. 17–18.
—— Invocation to peace.—Ib. 19–20.
—— On seeing some children playing.—Ib. 20–22.

1815 COTTLE, JOSEPH. Messiah, 28 books, 1815.
TOWNSEND, GEORGE. Armageddon, books i–viii, 1815. — See Eclectic
Rev., new series, iv. 392–5.
WORDSWORTH, WILLIAM. Written on Black Comb.—Poetical Works, 1896,
iv. 281–2.

1815 w. AIKIN, A. L. (Mrs. BARBAULD). The first fire.—Works, 1825, i. 273–7.
1816 SHELLEY, P. B. Alastor.—Complete Poetical Works, ed. T. Hutchinson,
Oxford, 1904, pp. 15–33.

1816 w. POLLOK, ROBERT. Lines to Liza.—Life, by David Pollok, Edin., 1843, pp.
20–21.

1816 w. 1820 p. WORDSWORTH, WILLIAM. "A little onward lend thy guiding hand."—
Poetical Works, 1896, vi. 132–5.

1817 DRUMMOND, Sir WILLIAM. Odin, part i, 1817.
PENNIE, J. F. The royal minstrel, or the witcheries of Endor, an epic poem,
12 books [2d ed.], 1819.

1817 w. 1820 p. WORDSWORTH, WILLIAM. To Lycoris [second poem].—Poetical Works,
1896, vi. 149–52.

c. 1817? w. POLLOK, ROBERT. The distressed Christian to his soul.—Life, by David
Pollok, 1843, pp. 413–15.

1818 MILMAN, H. H. Samor, lord of the bright city, an heroic poem.—Poetical
Works, 1839, ii. 1–296.

1818–19 w. 1820 p. KEATS, JOHN. Hyperion, a fragment.—Poems, ed. E. de Sélincourt, 2d ed., 1907, pp. 207–27.

1819 w. 1856 p. —— The fall of Hyperion, a dream.—Ib. 229–40.

1819 w. SNART, CHARLES. The angler's day.—Appended to Observations on
Angling in the River Trent, 2d ed., Newark, 1819 (an unpublished manu-
script in the Fearing collection, Harvard Library).
DRUMMOND, W. H. Clontarf, 2 books, Dublin, 1822.
—— [Five] poetical sketches.—Ib. 65–83.

1820 DRAKE, NATHAN. [Translation from Tasso's Jerusalem Delivered.]—
Winter Nights, 1820, ii. 120–30.
WORDSWORTH, W. The haunted tree.—Poetical Works, 1896, vi. 199–201.

1820 w. 1870 p. SHELLEY, P. B. Fragment: Milton's spirit.—Poetical Works, 1904,
p. 705.

1820? w. 1903 p. —— Fragment: Pater omnipotens.—Ib.

1820–22 THELWALL, JOHN. Sympathy and poesy.—Poetical Recreations, 1822, pp.
14–18.
—— Sylvanus.—Ib. 77–84.
—— Thoughts and remembrances.—Ib. 86–90.
—— Hymn to Alauda.—Ib. 95–6.
—— The champion's address.—Ib. 128–31.
—— Ottar of roses.—Ib. 131–2.
—— On the approach of spring.—Ib. 132–3.

1821 BYRON, GEORGE GORDON. Cain, a mystery.—Poetical Works, ed. E. H.
Coleridge, 1905, pp. 624–52.
S., A. [From Lucan's Pharsalia.] —John Thelwall's Poetical Recreations,
1822, pp. 203–8.

1822 BOWLES, W. L. The grave of the last Saxon.—Works, 1855, ii. 77–141.
HERBERT, WILLIAM. The Guahiba.—Works, 1842, vol. i. pt. ii. 47–74.
WORDSWORTH, WILLIAM. Processions.—Poetical Works, 1896, vi. 363–71.

1822 w. POLLOK, ROBERT. [Lines composed while walking.] —Life, by David Pollok,
1843, pp. 139–49.

1823   PENNIE, J. F. Rogvald, an epic poem, 12 books, 1823.
        SWAN, CHARLES. The false one, 3 cantos.—Gaston, or the heir of Foiz,
            1823, pp. 133–228.

c. 1823–4w.? POLLOK, ROBERT. To melancholy.—Life, by David Pollok, 1843, pp.
            442–4.
        —— Liberty.—Ib. 450–53.

1825   AIKIN, A. L. (Mrs. BARBAULD). Inscription for an ice-house.—Works,
            1825, i. 188–9.
        —— The caterpillar.—Ib. 278–80.
        —— On the death of the Princess Charlotte.—Ib. 281–2.
        —— Fragment.—Ib. 311–12.
        GOMPERTZ, ISAAC. Devon, 1825.—See Wright's West-Country Poets,
            1896, p. 210.

1826   ANON. The Messiah, by Klopstock, translated, 2 vols., 1826.
        CARRINGTON, N. T. Dartmoor, a descriptive poem, 1826.
        PENNIE, J. F. The artist.—Death's Doings, ed. R. Dagley, 2d ed., 1827,
            ii. 53–8.

1826 w. WORDSWORTH, WILLIAM. Composed [on] a probability of being obliged to
            quit Rydal Mount.—Poetical Works, 1896, viii. 289–95.

1827   —— Address to Kilchurn castle.—Ib. ii. 400–403.
        POLLOK, ROBERT. The course of time, 10 books, 7th ed., Edin., 1828.

1827 w. MONTGOMERY, ROBERT. The crucifixion.—Poetical Works, 1854, pp.
            614–16.

1828   —— Shadows of death.—Ib. 547–59.
        —— A vision of heaven.—Ib. 560–62.
        —— A vision of hell.—Ib. 563–6.
        —— Universal prayer.—Ib. 567–73.
        BOWLES, W. L. Days departed, or Banwell hill, 1828.
        MOORE, WILLIAM. Carnbrea.—Poetic Effusions, 1828: see Wright's West-
            Country Poets, 344–5.

1828 w. SOUTHEY, ROBERT. Epistle to Allan Cunningham.—Works, 1837, iii.
            303–18.
        MONTGOMERY, ROBERT. London by midnight.—Works, 1854, pp. 593–5.

1830   —— Satan.—Ib. 323–85.
        —— Spirit of time.—Ib. 604–6.
        PHILLIPS, WILLIAM. Mount Sinai, 4 books, 1830.

1831   CAMPBELL, THOMAS. Lines on the view from St. Leonards.—Complete
            Poetical Works, ed. J. L. Robertson, Oxford, 1907, pp. 288–92.
        MOSBY, J. N. Mount Sion.—The Fall of Algiers, etc., Doncaster, 1831,
            pp. 359–418.
        VENABLES, G. S. The north-west passage.—Cambridge Prize Poems, new
            ed., 1847, pp. 241–9.

1831 w. 1835 p. WORDSWORTH, WILLIAM. Apology for the foregoing poems.—Poetical
            Works, 1896, vii. 309–10.

1832   BRYDGES, EGERTON. The lake of Geneva, 2 vols., Geneva, 1832.
        MONTGOMERY, ROBERT. The Messiah.—Works, 1854, pp. 453–532.

1833 w. ——The departed year.—Ib. 609–12.

1833   WALL, W. E. CHRIST crucified, an epic poem, 12 books, Oxford, 1833.

1834   ELLIOTT, EBENEZER. Great folks at home.—The Splendid Village, etc.,
            1834, i. 129–37.
        —— Wharncliffe.—Ib. 245–61.
        ROSCOE, W. S. Fragments of "The Contemplative Day."—Poems, 1834,
            pp. 128–58.
        —— From the Messiah of Klopstock.—Ib. 159–95.
        SMITH, WILLIAM. Solitude, 4 cantos, 1834.

1835   ALFORD, HENRY. The school of the heart.—The School of the Heart, etc., Cambridge, 1835, vol. ii.

DRUMMOND, W. H. The pleasures of benevolence, 1835.

MITFORD, JOHN. Lines to ——. Prefixed to Poetical Works of Matthew Prior, Aldine ed., 1835.

1835 w.   CAMPBELL, THOMAS. The dead eagle.—Works, 1907, pp. 300–303.

1837 w. 1842 p. WORDSWORTH, WILLIAM. Musings near Aquapendente.—Poetical Works, 1896, viii. 42–57.

1838   BOWLES, W. L. St. John in Patmos.—Works, 1855, ii. 143–220.

HERBERT, WILLIAM. Attila, king of the Huns, 12 books, 1838.

1838 w.   —— Time.—Works, 1842, vol. i. pt. ii. 167–9.

c. 1838?w. BOWLES, W. L. The ark.—Works, 1855, ii. 315–17.

—— On the death of Dr. Burgess.—Ib. 320–21.

1839   BAILEY, PHILIP JAMES. Festus, 50th anniversary ed., 1889.

1839 w.   MONTGOMERY, ROBERT. A dream of worlds.—Works, 1854, pp. 607–8.

1842   —— Luther.—Ib. 173–288.

1843   MOULTRIE, JOHN. The dream of life.—Poems, ed. D. Coleridge, 1876, i. 353–462.

1844   HAWKINS, THOMAS. The wars of Jehovah, in heaven, earth, and hell, 9 books, 1844.—See Quart. Rev., xc. 333, 352–5.

1845   HARRIS, W. R. Napoleon portrayed, an epic poem, 12 cantos, 1845.—See ib. 333, 345–8.

HENRY, JAMES. The Eneis, books i and ii, rendered into blank iambic, 1845.

bef.1846 w. WALKER, W. S. Fragment.—Remains, 1852, pp. xlviii–xlix.

—— To B. H. Kennedy.—Ib. 41–2.

—— Judas Maccabeus, in imitation of Milton.—Ib. 94–100.

—— Horace, i. 22, imitated.—Ib. 157–8.

—— Written at the close of a college examination.—Ib. 159.

—— Scene from Aeschylus.—Ib. 167–8.

—— Fragments from Ennius.—Ib. 169–72.

1846   HERBERT, WILLIAM. The Christian, book i.—Supplement to Works, 1846, pp. 1–33.

MONTGOMERY, ROBERT. Scarborough.—Works, 1854, pp. 581–4.

SEWELL, WILLIAM. The Georgics, literally and rhythmically translated, 1846.—See Quart. Rev., cx. 106–7.[1]

1848   AIRD, THOMAS. Frank Sylvan.—Poetical Works, 4th ed., Edin., 1863, pp. 17–34.

—— Monkwood.—Ib. 76–81.

1849   BURGES, GEORGE. The Aias of Sophocles, translated, 1849.

KENNEDY, RANN, and C. R. The works of Virgil, 1849.

1850   BAILEY, PHILIP JAMES. The angel world.—The Angel World, etc., Boston (U. S. A.), 1850, pp. 1–77.

1851   MONTGOMERY, ROBERT. Wordsworth.—Works, 1854, pp. 588–9.

1852   CLIFFORD, C. C. Prometheus chained [from Aeschylus], Oxford, 1852.

MOIR, D. M. The angler.—Poetical Works, ed. T. Aird, 1852, ii. 352–61.

—— The tombless man.—Ib. 361–71.

—— Hymn to the night wind.—Ib. 377–83.

1853   REYNOLDS, S. H. The ruins of Egyptian Thebes, Oxford, 1853.

1855   BAILEY, PHILIP JAMES. The mystic.—The Mystic, etc., 1855, pp. 1–62.

—— A spiritual legend.—Ib. 63–135.

HENDERSON, THULIA S. Olga, or Russia in the tenth century, 1855.

1855–9   SINGLETON, R. C. The works of Virgil, closely rendered into English rhythm, 2 vols., 1855–9.

---

[1] SEWELL, WILLIAM. Agamemnon, translated literally and rhythmically, 1846; also Odes and epodes of Horace, translated literally and rhythmically, 1850. Not seen; may be in blank verse.

1859–64   WRIGHT, I. C. The Iliad, translated, 2 vols., Camb., etc., 1861–5.
1861   KENNEDY, CHARLES RANN. The works of Virgil, 1861.
1862–4   DERBY, EDWARD STANLEY, Earl of. The Iliad, 2 vols., 1864.
1865   MILMAN, H. H. [Translation from Onomacritus?] —The Agamemnon of
          Aeschylus, etc., 1865, pp. 245–7.
          MUSGRAVE, GEORGE. The Odyssey, 2 vols., 1865.
          PLUMPTRE, E. H. The tragedies of Sophocles, 2 vols., 1865.
1865–73   SWANWICK, ANNA. The dramas of Aeschylus, 4th ed., 1890.
1866   BICKERSTETH, E. H. Yesterday, to-day, and for ever, 12 books, 4th ed.,
          1870.
1868   PLUMPTRE, E. H. The tragedies of Aeschylos, 2 vols., 1868.
1869   EDGINTON, G. W. The Odyssey, 2 vols., 1869.—See Westminster Rev.,
          new series, xxxvi. 644.
          MOON, G. W. Eden.—Eden and other poems, 2d ed., 1869, pp. 1–26.
          WITT, E. E. The fifth and ninth books of the Odyssey, 1869.
1871   KING, HENRY. The Metamorphoses of Ovid, Edin., 1871.
          RICKARDS, G. K. The Aeneid, books i–vi, Edin., 1871.
1872   RAVENSWORTH, Lord. The Aeneid, books vii–xii [book xi by G. K.
          Rickards], Edin., 1872.—See Lond. Quart. Rev., xl. 126–8.
1877–84   GREEN, W. C. The Iliad, with a verse translation, books i–xii, 1884.
1877–1908 MORSHEAD, E. D. A. [Aeschylus:] The house of Atreus (Agamemnon,
          Libation-bearers, and Furies), 2d ed., 1889; The suppliant maidens, the
          Persians, the Seven against Thebes, and the Prometheus bound, 1908.
1883   CAMPBELL, LEWIS. Sophocles, the seven plays, 1883.
          WHITELAW, ROBERT. Sophocles, translated, 1883.
1886   MYERS, ERNEST. The judgment of Prometheus.—Gathered Poems, 1904,
          pp. 3–15.
          —— The Olympic Hermes.—Ib. 41–6.
          THORNHILL, W. J. The Aeneid, freely translated, Dublin, 1886.
1889 w.   DE VERE, AUBREY. Death of Copernicus.—Mediaeval Records and Son-
          nets, 1893, pp. 195–211.
1890   CAMPBELL, LEWIS. Aeschylus, the seven plays, 1890.
1891   BRIDGES, ROBERT. Eden, a dramatic oratorio in three acts, 1891.
1893   RHOADES, JAMES. The Aeneid, books i–vi, 1893.
1896   RIDLEY, EDWARD. The Pharsalia of Lucan, 10 books, 1896.
1903   BAUGHAN, B. E. Reuben.—Reuben, etc., 1903, pp. 9–45.
          —— The two ships.—Ib. 67–70.
1904   BINYON, LAURENCE. The death of Adam.—The Death of Adam, etc., 1904,
          pp. 1–25.
1906   BLANE, WILLIAM. Creation.—The Silent Land, etc., 1906, pp. 89–123.
1908   DOUGHTY, CHARLES M. Adam cast forth, 1908.
          NOYES, ALFRED. The last of the Titans.—The Golden Hynde, etc., N. Y.,
          1908, pp. 54–66.
1915   PHILLIPS, STEPHEN. Armageddon, a modern epic drama, 1915.

BIBLIOGRAPHY II

POEMS INFLUENCED BY L'ALLEGRO AND IL PENSEROSO

1647   BARON, ROBERT. Erotopaignion, or the Cyprian academy, 1648.

1697?   HUGHES, JOHN. Horace, book i, ode xxii, in paraphrase.—Poems on Several Occasions, 1735, i. 113–15.

1699   ADDISON, JOSEPH. An ode for St. Cecilia's day.—Works, Bohn ed., vi. 534–5.

1702 w. 1709 p. HUGHES, JOHN. Horace, book ii, ode xvi, in paraphrase.—Poems, 1735, i. 116–20.

1704 w.   —— A thought in a garden.—Ib. 171–3.

1714   PARNELL, THOMAS. A hymn to contentment.—Poems on Several Occasions, 1722, pp. 158–63.

1716   ROWE, NICHOLAS. Ode for the new year, 1716.

bef. 1718 w. PARNELL, THOMAS. Health, an eclogue.—Poems, 1722, pp. 116–21.

1718   HINCHLIFFE, WILLIAM. The seasons.—Collection of Poems, Amorous, Moral, etc., 1718, pp. 37–67.

bef. 1720 w. HUGHES, JOHN. The picture.—Poems, 1735, i. 74–6.

1723   BAKER, HENRY. An invocation of health, 1723.

1723 w. 1727 p. BROOME, WILLIAM. Melancholy, an ode.—Poems on Several Occasions, 2d ed., 1739, pp. 26–31.

1725 w. 1729 p. THOMSON, JAMES. Hymn on solitude.—Works, ed. Robertson, Oxford, 1908, pp. 429–30.

1726   DYER, JOHN. The country walk.—Miscellaneous Poems and Translations, ed. Richard Savage, 1726, pp. 48–57.

   —— Grongar hill.—Poems, 1761, pp. 9–16.

1729   HUGHES, JOHN. Supplement to Milton's Il Penseroso.—Poems, 1735, vol. i, p. lviii.

1731   ANON. Il penseroso.—A Miscellany of Poems, ed. J. Husbands, Oxford, 1731, pp. 161–9.

1732   DODSLEY, ROBERT. [Song in] An entertainment for the wedding of Governour Lowther.—The Muse in Livery, 1732, pp. 66, 72.

   GREEN, MATTHEW. The grotto.—A Collection of Poems by Several Hands [Dodsley's Miscellany], 1758, v. 159–68.

c. 1733? w. SWIFT, JONATHAN. Ode on science.—Works, ed. Walter Scott, 2d ed., Edin., 1824, xiv. 323–5.

1736   BROWNE, I. H. Imitation vi.—A Pipe of Tobacco, in Imitation of Six Several Authors, 1736, pp. 21–3.

   L., E. Contentment.—Gent. Mag., vi. 615.

   THOMSON, JAMES. "Come, gentle god."—Works, 1908, p. 424.

1738 w.   WEST, RICHARD. View from the thatcht house.—Correspondence of Gray, Walpole, West, etc., ed. P. Toynbee, Oxford, 1915, i. 191–5.

c. 1738 w. 1742 p. COLLINS, WILLIAM. Oriental eclogues: eclogue the first.—Poems, ed. W. C. Bronson, Boston (U. S. A.), 1898, pp. 12–13.

1739   AKENSIDE, MARK. Hymn to science.—Poetical Works, Aldine ed., 1835, pp. 293–6.

   HAMILTON, WILLIAM, of Bangour. Ode i, To fancy.—Poems and Songs, ed. J. Paterson, Edin., 1850, pp. 47–51.

   —— Ode ii.—Ib. 51–3.

   —— On the new year MDCCXXXIX.—Ib. 58–60.

c. 1739 w. 1747 p. HAMILTON, WILLIAM, of Bangour. Contemplation, or the triumph of love.—Ib. 34–47.

1740   JENNENS, CHARLES. Il moderato.—Georg Friedrich Händel's Werke, Leipzig, 1859, vi. 11–12 (of text).

1741   BROOKE, HENRY. Constantia, or the Man of Law's Tale.—George Ogle's Canterbury Tales of Chaucer Modernis'd, 1741, ii. 104–195.

1742 w.   WEST, RICHARD. Ode [to May].—Mason's Memoirs of Gray (prefixed to Gray's Poems, York, 1775), pp. 147–8.

1742 w. 1753 p. GRAY, THOMAS. Hymn to adversity.—English Poems, ed. D. C. Tovey, Camb., 1898, pp. 8–9.

1743?   MALLET, DAVID. A fragment.—Works, new ed., 1759, i. 49–53.

1744 w.   BLACKSTONE, Sir WILLIAM. The lawyer's farewel to his muse.—Dodsley's Miscellany, 1755, iv. 228–32.

1744 w. 1748 p. MASON, WILLIAM. Il pacifico.—Works, 1811, i. 166–71.

1744 w. 1771 p. —— Il bellicoso.—Ib. 158–65.

bef.1745 w. WARTON, THOMAS (the elder). Retirement.—Poems, 1748, pp. 13–16.
—— An ode, written in a grotto.—Ib. 115–18.
—— Ode to sleep.—Ib. 162–6.

1745   AKENSIDE, MARK. Ode vi, Hymn to cheerfulness.—Works, 1835, pp. 157–62.
ANON. Ode to May.—Lond. Mag., xiv. 252.
DAVIES, SNEYD. To the spring.—John Whaley's Collection of Poems, 1745, pp. 229–32.
DODSLEY, ROBERT. [Two airs in] Rex et pontifex.—Trifles, 1745, p. 12.

*c.*1745? w. CHAPONE, HESTER M. To health.—Works, 1807, iv. 152–4.
COWPER, WILLIAM, M.D. Il penseroso, an evening's contemplation in St. John's churchyard, Chester, 1767.

1746   ANON. A hymn to liberty, 1746.
ANON. Ode, occasion'd by his royal highness's victory.—Gent. Mag., xvi. 267.
ANON. To superstition, an ode.—The Museum, or Literary and Historical Register [Dodsley's Museum], 1746, i. 55–6.
ANON. Ode to pleasure.—Ib. ii. 50–51.
COLLINS, WILLIAM. Ode to fear.—Poems, 1898, pp. 36–9.
—— Ode on the poetical character.—Ib. 41–3.
—— The manners, an ode.—Ib. 56–8.
COOPER, J. G. The estimate of life, in three parts: i, Melpomene [the melancholy]; ii, Calliope [the cheerful]; iii, Terpsichore [the moderate].—Dodsley's Museum, 1746, i. 372–9.
HOADLY, BENJAMIN. The trophy, cantata vi: The religious.—Dodsley's Miscellany, 1748, iii. 264–5.
WARTON, JOSEPH. Ode i, To fancy.—Odes on Various Subjects, 1746, pp. 5–11.
—— Ode iii, To health.—Ib. 16–18.
—— Ode iv, To superstition.—Ib. 19–21.
—— Ode vi, Against despair.—Ib. 26–9.
—— Ode xi, To a lady who hates the country.—Ib. 38–40.
—— Ode xii, On the death of [his father].—Ib. 41–3.
—— Ode xiv, To solitude.—Ib. 46–7.

1747   "PHILO." Ode to hope.—Gent. Mag., xvii. 536.
1748   ANON. Advice to Mr. L——n, the dwarf fan-painter, 1748.
"CRAFTSMAN." Hymn to May.—Gent. Mag., xviii. 229.
FRANK, J. "Daughter of Him, at whose command."—Gratulatio Acad. Cantab. de Reditu . . . Georgii II post Pacem . . . Restitutam, Camb., 1748, Ee, verso.

1748   MASERES, F. "Janus, shut thy brazen gate."—Ib. V, verso.
              OTWAY, FR[ANCIS?]. "Come hither, all ye fair and gay."—Ib. Q, verso.

1748 w.   P., Rev.Mr. L'amoroso, in imitation of Milton's L'Allegro.—Poetical Calendar, ed. Fawkes and Woty, 1763, vii. 100–105.

1749   ANON. Epithalamic ode for music.—Scots Mag., xi. 494.

1750   A., S. Ode to piety.—The Student, or Oxford and Cambridge Monthly Miscellany, Oxford, 1750, i. 31–2.
              ANON. To fancy.—Ib. 113–14.
              ANON. Ode to taste.—Four Odes, 1750, pp. 17–32.
              COVENTRY, FRANCIS. Penshurst.—Dodsley's Miscellany, 1755, iv. 50–61.

1750 w. 1777 p. WARTON, THOMAS (the younger). Ode vii, Sent to a friend on his leaving a favourite village.—Works, ed. Mant, Oxford, 1802, i. 156–67.

c. 1750 w. MACPHERSON, JAMES. Death.—Poems of Ossian, Edin., 1805, ii. 443–61.

1751   "CHIMAERICUS OXONIENSIS." Ode to horror.—The Student, ii. 313–15.

1752   ANON. Another [ode].—Escapes of a Poetical Genius, 1752, pp. 19–20.
              ANON. Contemplation.—Lond. Mag., xxi. 188, 233–4, 283–4.
              ANON. Ode.—Ib. 332.
              H., Mr. Ode to fancy.—Ib. 377–8.
              SMART, CHRISTOPHER. The introduction: being two odes, the former on good-nature, the latter against ill-nature.—Poems on Several Occasions, 1752, pp. 1–6.
              —— Idleness: ode vii.—Ib. 19–20.

1752 w.   KEATE, GEORGE. A pastoral ode to echo.—Poetical Works, 1781, i. 53–5.

1753   ANON. Ode to health.—Scots Mag., xv. 76.
              ANON. A hymn to contentment, in imitation of Gray's Hymn to Adversity. —Ib. 518.
              ANON. Rus: an imitation of Milton's measure in L'Allegro and Il Penseroso. —Lond. Mag., xxii. 571–2.
              WARTON, THOMAS (the younger). Ode xi, On the approach of summer.— Works, 1802, ii. 1–37.
              WERGE, JOHN. Rural happiness.—Collection of Poems, Stamford, 1753, pp. 21–2.

1754   BLACKLOCK, THOMAS. To health, an ode.—Poems, 3d ed., 1756, pp. 73–4.
              BOWDEN, SAMUEL. Ode to echo. — Poems, Bath, 1754, pp. 42–3.
              MILLER, JOHN. To Mira.—Poems on Several Occasions, 1754, pp. 49–50.
              —— Ode composed for the Sober Society.—Ib. 139–44.

1755   ANON. St. Mungo's in Glasgow.—Scots Mag., xvii. 195.
              B–LL–E, Dr. Hymn to contentment. — Collection of Original Poems, by Samuel Derrick, 1755, pp. 180–81.
              FARMER, RICHARD. "Haste, young-eyed May!"—Carmina ad Nobilissimum Thomam Holles, Camb., 1755, pp. 27–8.
              GRAINGER, JAMES. Solitude, an ode.—Dodsley's Miscellany, 1755, iv. 233–43.
              HALL-STEVENSON, JOHN. Hymn to Miss Laurence in the pump-room at Bath, 1755.
              KIDDELL, H. The genius of Milton, an invocation.—Gent. Mag., xxv. 518.
              MARRIOTT, Sir JAMES. Ode to fancy.—Dodsley's Miscellany, 1755, iv. 294–300.
              MERRICK, JAMES. Ode to fancy.—Ib. 185–9.

1756   ANON. Epistles to Lorenzo, 1756.—See Mo. Rev., xvi. 226–30.
              ANON. Ode to melancholy.—Scots Mag., xviii. 75.

1757   WOTY, WILLIAM. On musick.—Shrubs of Parnassus, 1760, pp. 138–41.

1758   ANON. Ode to sleep.—Scots Mag., xx. 419–20.
              ANON. To peace.—Gent. Mag., xxviii. 329.
              ANON. Vacation.—Dodsley's Miscellany, 1758, vi. 148–54.

1758   LANGHORNE, JOHN. Le sociable, partly in the manner of Milton.—Poetical
            Works, ed. T. Park, 1806, ii. 5–6.
1759   AIRY, HARRIOT. Ode to truth.—Gent. Mag., xxix. 538.
            B., G. Ode to health.—Ib. 334.
            COLMAN, GEORGE, and LLOYD, ROBERT. Two odes: i, To obscurity; ii,
            To oblivion.—Colman's Prose on Several Occasions, 1787, ii. 273–83.
            WOTY, WILLIAM. Ode to friendship.—Shrubs of Parnassus, 1760, pp. 73–5.
1759 w.   DODD, WILLIAM. An ode occasioned by Lady N—d's being prevented from
            coming to Magdalen house.—Poems, 1767, pp. 148–52.
bef.1760 w. 1768 p. BROWNE, I. H. Ode to health.—A Collection of Poems in Four
            Volumes, by Several Hands [Pearch's Supplement to Dodsley], new ed.,
            1783, ii. 312–14.
1760   ANON. Spring; from the Italian.—Scots Mag., xxii. 89.
            ANON. Ode to sleep; intended as a chorus in a tragedy.—Ib. 315.
            COOPER, E. Hymn to learning.—A Collection of Elegiac Poesy, etc., 1760,
            pp. 85–8.
            GLASSE, J. Quantock-hill.—Lond. Mag., xxix. 316.
            STEELE, ANNE. Ode to content.—Works, Boston (U.S A.), 1808, i. 191–3.
            —— Solitude.—Ib. 283–5.
1760 w.   DODD, WILLIAM. Hymn to good-nature.—Poems, 1767, pp. 1–7.
1761   ANON. Ode to health.—Scots Mag., xxiii. 97.
            ANON. Ode to solitude.—Gent. Mag., xxxi. 38.
            ANON. A soliloquy in a thatch'd house.—Lond. Mag., xxx. 499.
            COOKE, JOHN. "Ill-boding Fears away."—Gratulatio Acad. Cantab. . . .
            Georgii III . . . Nuptias celebrantis, Camb., 1761, P.
            LANGHORNE, JOHN. Hymeneal.—Chalmers's English Poets, xvi. 461.
            —— A hymn to hope, 1761.
            "LIBRARY." To sleep.—Scots Mag., xxiii. 263.
            LLOYD, ROBERT. Arcadia, or the shepherd's wedding, a dramatic pastoral,
            1761.
            POOLEY, W. "Hence Melancholy, pensive maid."—Epithalamia Oxonien-
            sia, 1761, L2, verso.
            SCOTT, JAMES. On pleasure.—Odes on Several Subjects, Camb., 1761, pp.
            31–6.
            —— On despair.—Ib. 37–42.
            —— To wisdom.—Ib. 43–7.
            SHEPHERD, RICHARD. Ode x, To health.—Odes Descriptive and Allegorical,
            1761, pp. 32–8.
            —— Ode xi, To hope.—Ib. 39–46.
            THOMAS, B. "Hence to shades of blackest night."—Gratulatio Acad.
            Cantab., etc., 1761, Gg.
            TYSON, MICHAEL. "Hence pale Grief and anxious Care."—Ib. Y.
1761 w.   DOWNMAN, HUGH. Ode occasioned by the coronation.—Poems, 2d ed.,
            Exeter, 1790, pp. 50–59.
1762   CARTER, ELIZABETH. Ode to melancholy.—Poems on Several Occasions,
            1762, pp. 79–83.
            CHURCHILL, CHARLES. The ghost, 1762.
            EARLE, W. B. "Hither all ye fairy powers."—Gratulatio Solennis Univ.
            Oxon. ob . . . Walliae Principem . . . Natum, Oxford, 1762, U2, verso.
            FAWKES, FRANCIS. On occasion of the peace.—Chalmers's English Poets,
            xvi. 277–8.
            GROVE, WILLIAM. "Hail Euterpe, nymph divine."—Gratulatio Solennis
            Univ. Oxon., etc., 1762, X, verso.
            NOTT, SAMUEL. "Hither, swains! who, whistling blythe."—Ib. S, verso.
            OGILVIE, JOHN. Ode to sleep.—Poems on Several Subjects, 1762, pp. 23–8.

1762   OGILVIE, JOHN. Ode to evening.—Ib. 29–35.
            —— Ode to innocence.—Ib. 36–7.
            SCOTT, JAMES. Hymn to repentance.—Cambridge Prize Poems, i. 137–45.
1762 w.   SCOTT, JOHN, of Amwell. Ode to leisure.—Poetical Works, 1782, pp. 165–9;
            cf. Europ. Mag., xxxvi. 400.
1762 w. 1773 p. MORE, HANNAH. [Three songs and an ode in] The search after happi-
            ness.—Works, 1830, i. 261–3, 273–4, 287–8.
1763   ANON. Contemplation, an ode.—Poetical Calendar, 1763, vi. 7–8.
            ANON. Rodondo, or the state-jugglers, canto ii: Resignation.—Scots Mag.,
            xxv. 499–504.
            BROWN, Dr. JOHN. The cure of Saul, a sacred ode, 1763.
            D., J. Farewell to hope.—Poetical Calendar, x. 73–4.
            HARTIS, C. T. An ode.—Ib. vii. 106–8.
            HUDSON, Rev.Mr. Ode ii, To fancy.—Ib. vi. 26–9.
            PANTING, STEPHEN. Elegy iv, Midnight.—Ib. viii. 31–4.
            S., Dr. Ode on spring.—Scots Mag., xxv. 346–7.
            THOMPSON, WILLIAM. Garden inscriptions, i: In Il Spenseroso, on Spenser's
            Faerie Queene.—Poetical Calendar, viii. 97.
            TRAVIS, GEORGE. "Hence, monster, War! — hence to the wasted plains!"
            —Gratulatio Acad. Cantab. in Pacem . . . Restitutam, Camb.,
            1763, Y.
            TYSON, MICHAEL. "The gayly-gilded stream of light."—Ib. Z, verso.
1763 w.   LANGHORNE, JOHN. Inscription in a sequestered grotto.—Poetical Works,
            1789, p. 46.
bef.1764 w. LLOYD, ROBERT. To the moon.—Chalmers's English Poets, xv. 149–50.
1764   "CALEDONIUS." Ode to peace.—Scots Mag., xxvi. 96.
            —— Ode to mirth.—Ib. 394.
            "PROMETHEUS." Hymn to melancholy.—Lond. Mag., xxxiii. 101.
1764 w.   VICTOR, BENJAMIN. Ode xi, For the queen's birthday.—Original Letters,
            etc., 1776, iii. 138–41.
1765   ANON. Landscape: an August evening.—Scots Mag., xxvii. 154–5.
1766   ANON. Rural pleasure.—Lond. Mag., xxxv. 649.
            ANSTEY, CHRISTOPHER. Letter iii, The birth of fashion, a specimen of a
            modern ode.—New Bath Guide, 3d ed., 1766, pp. 22–8.
            —— Letter ix, A journal.—Ib. 61–8.
            FOWLER, B. To solitude, in imitation of Milton.—Gent. Mag., xxxvi. 427.
            JENNER, CHARLES. Ode to modesty.—Poems, Camb., 1766, pp. 24–5.
            M., J. Ode to content.—Lond. Mag., xxxv. 431.
1767   ANON. (Miss VANHOMRIGH?). Ode to spring.—Gent. Mag., xxxvii. 183.
            DODD, WILLIAM. The man of Southgate.—Poems, 1767, pp. 79–81.
            —— Ode to the marchioness of Granby.—Ib. 140–47.
1767 w.   DOWNMAN, HUGH. Sonnet i, "Hence Sickness."—Poems, 1790, p. 74.
1768?   —— Ode.—Ib. 101–3.
            —— Ode.—Ib. 103–6.
1768   H., Mr. Ode to taste.—Pearch's Supplement, 1783, i. 145–54.
1769   ANON. Ode to sleep.—Town and Country Mag., i. 104.
            GRAY, THOMAS. Ode for music.—English Poems, 1898, pp. 76–9.
            OGILVIE, JOHN. An Aeolian ode.—Poems on Several Subjects, 1769, ii.
            277–86.
1769 w.   WARTON, THOMAS (the younger). Ode iv, Solitude at an inn.—Works,
            1802, i. 140–41.
1770   ANON. Ode to solitude.—Lond. Mag., xxxix. 589.
            MARRIOTT, Dr. (Sir JAMES?). The valetudinarian, an ode.—Pearch's
            Supplement, 1783, iv. 1–8.
            "MUSAEUS." An ode.—Scots Mag., xxxii. 672.

1770   PARSONS, PHILIP. Inscription in an arbour.—Pearch's Supplement, 1783, iii. 277–8.

        WOTY, WILLIAM. On retirement.—Works, 1770, ii. 151–5.

1770 w. LYTTELTON, THOMAS, Lord. An irregular ode.—Poems, 1780, pp. 24–8.

        PRESTON, WILLIAM. The sirloin.—Poetical Works, Dublin, 1793, i. 185–93.

        —— The fire-side.—Ib. 195–7.

bef.1771 w. SMOLLETT, TOBIAS. Ode to mirth.—Plays and Poems, 1777, pp. 250–52.

        —— Ode to sleep.—Ib. 253–4.

1771   ANON. Ode to health.—Lond. Mag., xl. 654–5.

        FOOT, JAMES. Penseroso, or the pensive philosopher, 6 books, 1771.

        JEMMAT, CATHARINE. To Mr. Mason, on his Elfrida.—Miscellanies, 1771, pp. 156–8.

        PORDEN, W. The debauchee.—Town and Country Mag., iii. 158.

1772   ANON. Contentment.—Scots Mag., xxxiv. 38.

        ANON. Ode to peace.—Weekly Mag., or Edinburgh Amusement, xv. 179.

1773   AIKIN, A. L. (Mrs. BARBAULD). Hymn to content.—Poems, 1773, pp. 53–6.

        —— To wisdom.—Ib. 57–8.

        ANON. Ode on her majesty's birth-day.—Gent. Mag., xliii. 39.

        ANON. True picture of a debauchee.—Town and Country Mag., v. 48.

        ANON. "Hence ye unwholesome smells."—Ib. 437.

        FERGUSSON, ROBERT. Ode to hope.—Works, ed. Grosart, 1851, pp. 150–1.

        GREEN, HENRY. To content, an ode.—Lond. Mag., xlii. 459.

1774   ANON. Ode spoken by Lt. Col. Pennington, to the soldiers.—Scots Mag., xxxvi. 255.

        M., W. (WILLIAM MASON?). Mirth, a poem, in answer to Warton's Pleasures of Melancholy, 1774.

        RICHARDSON, WILLIAM. Hymn to virtue.—Poems, chiefly Rural, 1774, pp. 3–4.

        —— On winter.—Ib. 14–15.

        —— The relapse, an idyllion.—Ib. 22–3.

        —— Hymn to the muse.—Ib. 24–7.

        —— Hymn to health.—Ib. 28.

        —— To health, an idyllion.—Ib. 33–4.

        —— The invitation.—Ib. 36.

        —— Hymn to solitude.—Ib. 37–9.

        —— To mirth, an idyllion.—Ib. 40–41.

        S., H. To pleasure.—Town and Country Mag., vi. 270.

1775   ANON. The beauties of nature compared with those of art.—Poetical Amusements at a Villa near Bath, ed. Lady A. R. Miller, 3d ed., 1776, i. 118–22.

        ANON. The month of May.—Ib. 101–3.

        BAMPFYLDE, C. W. The month of April.—Ib. 47–9.

        BURGESS, ... The second opening of the Tusculum vase.—Ib. 89–93.

        C–SS–NS, ... Ode to the elegiac muse.—Ib. 139–42.

        G–V–L, Mrs. First of May.—Ib. 105–7.

        HALL, J. Ode to fancy.—Town and Country Mag., vii. 158.

        NUGENT, ROBERT. Epistle to Pollio.—Memoir by Claud Nugent, Chicago, etc., 1898, pp. 151–3.

        PENROSE, THOMAS. Madness.—Flights of Fancy, 1775, pp. 15–22.

        P–M–T–N, Lord Viscount. Beauty.—Poetical Amusements, 1776, i. 52–7.

1776   ANON. May-day.—Town and Country Mag., viii. 271.

        ANON. Ode to charity.—Poetical Amusements, 1776, ii. 27–31.

        ANON. To hope.—Ib. 79–81.

        ANON. Harmony.—Ib. 82–7.

        DAVIS, Miss. On the powers of harmony.—Ib. 95–7.

        GRAVES, RICHARD. On calumny.—Euphrosyne, 1776, pp. 110–12.

1777   ANON. The garrulous man, a parody upon L'Allegro of Milton, Bath, 1777.
ANON. Ode for the king's birthday.—Univ. Mag., lx. 322.
ANON. On the tyranny of custom.—Poetical Amusements, 1777, iii. 160–63.
"GOBLIN." Rhapsody to taste.—Gent. Mag., xlvii. 39.
RYAN, EVERHARD. The genealogy of winter.—Reliques of Genius, 1777:
see Mo. Rev., lvii. 231–2.
ST. JOHN, JOHN. Garrulity.—Poetical Amusements, 1777, iii. 63–9.
WHITEHEAD, WILLIAM. Ode for his majesty's birth-day.—Poems, York,
1788, iii. 93–5.

1777w.   MEYLER, WILLIAM. Ode to health.—Poetical Amusement on the Journey
of Life, Bath, 1806, pp. 106–9.

1778   LEMOINE, H. Ode to contemplation.—Lond. Mag., xlvii. 569–70.
1778 w.   SEWARD, ANNA. Ode to Euphrosyne.—Works, 1810, i. 161–4.
bef.1779 w. LANGHORNE, JOHN. Inscription in a temple of society.—Poetical Works,
1789, p. 45.
——— Song, "'Tis o'er, the pleasing prospect's o'er."—Ib. 66.
——— Hymn to the rising sun.—Ib. 164.

1779   ALVES, ROBERT. Malevolence, an ode.—Scots Mag., xli. 379.
ANON. Ode to distress.—Poetical Effusions, 1779, pp. 36–41.
MASON, WILLIAM. Ode xii, To the naval officers of Great Britain.—Works,
1811, i. 59–62.

1779 w.   GRANT, ANNE. Ode to Hygeia.—Poems, Edin., 1803, pp. 331–3.
1780   ANON. Apostrophe to peace.—Scots Mag., xlii. 607.
M. Ode to health.—Ib. 492.
WALTERS, JOHN. Song to the birds.—Poems, Oxford, 1780, pp. 91–6.

1781   ANON. The celestial beds, 1781.—See Crit. Rev., li. 473–4.
ANON. Ode to the genius of scandal, 1781.—See Mo. Rev., lxvi. 235–6.
FARREN, Miss. Song.—Univ. Mag., lxviii. 39.
JONES, Sir WILLIAM. The muse recalled, an ode.—Works, 1807, x. 381–8.
PINKERTON, JOHN. Ode ii, To peace.—Rimes, 2d ed., 1782, pp. 99–100.
——— Ode x, L'ozioso.—Ib. 130–42.
POTTER, ROBERT. Ode to sympathy.—Poetical Amusements, 1781, iv.
112–17.
——— Ode to health.—Ib. 118–23.
ROGERS, Miss. Thalia, or invocation of the comic muse.—Ib. 98–100.
SEWARD, ANNA. Invocation of the comic muse: prize poem at Bath-Easton.
—Works, 1810, ii. 22–4.

1782   ALVES, ROBERT. Ode to wisdom.—Poems, Edin., 1782, pp. 40–42.
——— Rural happiness, an ode.—Ib. 57–62.
ANON. To health.—Univ. Mag., lxx. 320.
ANON. Ode to melancholy.—J. Nichols's Collection of Poems, viii. 62–4.
PENNANT, THOMAS. Ode to indifference.—Ib. 229–30.
PINKERTON, JOHN. To laughter.—Two Dithyrambic Odes, 1782: see Crit.
Rev., liv. 234–5.
STEVENS, W. B. Ode to health.—Poems, 1782, pp. 30–35.

1783   ANON. Invocation to fancy.—Univ. Mag., lxxii. 103.
Y. Address to meditation.—Lond. Mag., enl., i. 130.

1784   BRADBURY, SAMUEL. Ode to virtue.—Gent. Mag., liv. 935.
HURN, WILLIAM. The blessings of peace, 1784.
ROBERTSON, DAVID. L'inamorato.—Poems, Edin., 1784: see Crit. Rev.,
lviii. 70.

1784 w.   BLAMIRE, SUSANNA. Address to health.—Poetical Works, Edin., 1842, pp.
72–7.
SMITH, Sir W. C.(?) Hymn to health.—The Anonymous, 1810, ii. 319–22.

bef.1785 w. HALL-STEVENSON, JOHN. Vacation.—Works, 1795: see Crit. Rev., new
arr., xviii. 319–21.

1785   ANON. To spring.—Univ. Mag., lxxvi. 156–7.
        ANON. No. vii, Irregular ode.—Probationary Odes for the Laureatship
            1785, pp. 30–34.
        BOSCAWEN, WILLIAM. No. xi, "By Michael Angelo Taylor."—Ib. 46–9.
        BRYDGES, EGERTON. Ode ii, Upon beginning the study of the law. —
            Sonnets, etc., 1785, pp. 20–22.
        —— Ode iv, To spring.—Ib. 26–31.
        BURGOYNE, General. No. xvii, Irregular ode for music.—Probationary
            Odes, 1785, pp. 73–83.
        ENYS, DOROTHY. Address to simplicity.—Gent. Mag., lv. 787.
        FITZPATRICK, RICHARD. No. xv, Pindaric.—Probationary Odes, 1785, pp.
            63–7.
        GREATHEED, BERTIE. Ode to duel.—The Florence Miscellany, Florence
            (Italy), 1785, pp. 103–4.
        —— Ode on apathy.—Ib. 129–31.
        HAYLEY, WILLIAM. Ode to Mr. Wright of Derby.—Poems and Plays, new
            ed., 1788, i. 141–7.
        MERRY, ROBERT. Ode to indolence.—The Florence Miscellany, 51–4.
        —— To Bacchus, dithyrambick.—Ib. 154–8.
        —— To Diana, dithyrambick.—Ib. 159–62.
        —— Il viaggio.—Ib. 196–202.
        —— La dimora.—Ib. 203–8.
        PRATT, S. J. Landscapes in verse.—Sympathy, etc., 1807, pp. 75–118.
        TICKELL, RICHARD. No. ix, Ode.—Probationary Odes, 1785, pp. 39–42.
1786   "A LADY." Address to simplicity.—Scots Mag., xlviii. 245.
        ANON. [Two travesties on Gray's Installation Ode.]—New Foundling
            Hospital for Wit, new ed., 1786, iv. 144–58.
        ANON. Inscription for a bench beneath a favourite tree.—Ib. vi. 42.
        GREVILLE, Mrs. A prayer to indifference.—Ib. 126–9.
        NUGENT, ROBERT. Epistle to the earl of Chesterfield.—Ib. i. 63–5.
        PARSONS, WILLIAM. Ode to sleep.—Univ. Mag., lxxix. 43.
1787   ANON. Ode to darkness.—Europ. Mag., xi. 286.
        "ARLEY." To ill-nature.—Poetry of the World, 1788, ii. 24–7.
        MERRY, ROBERT. Diversity.—British Album, Boston, 1793, pp. 224–40.
        "NERVA." Invocation to melancholy.—Europ. Mag., xi. 452.
        WHITEHOUSE, JOHN. Ode to superstition.—Poems, 1787, pp. 31–6.
        —— Ode to melancholy.—Ib. 47–51.
        YEARSLEY, ANN. Ode on the reconciliation between his majesty and the
            prince of Wales.—Univ. Mag., lxxx. 369–70.
1787 w. 1792 p. MAWBEY, JOSEPH. Ode, written at Tunbridge Wells.—Gent. Mag.,
            lxii. 748.
1788   ANON. Written on the near prospect of a place.—Europ. Mag., xiv. 224.
        C., G. Autumn.—Ib. 473.
        CARY, H. F. To inspiration.—Sonnets and Odes, 1788, pp. 41–5.
        DAVIES, EDWARD. Ode to the muse.—Vacunalia, 1788: see Crit. Rev., lxvi.
            230–31.
        MOODY, ELIZABETH. On youth.—Gent. Mag., lviii. 636.
        P., W. Ode to chearfulness.—Ib. 444–5.
        REID, W. H. Ode to reflexion.—Ib. 636.
        TURNBULL, GAVIN. Morning.—Poetical Essays, Glasgow, 1788, pp. 75–87.
        —— Evening.—Ib. 89–99.
        —— Ode i, To melancholy.—Ib. 151–2.
        —— Ode iv, To innocence.—Ib. 159–60.
1789   ANON. To peace.—New Lond. Mag., v. 646.
        BUTT, Dr.T. Ode to fun.—Gent. Mag., lix. 1034–5.

1789 "GLANVILLE." Ode to hope.—Poetry of the World, 1791, iii. 28–31.
  GRAVES, RICHARD. Ode on caprice.—Scots Mag., li. 342–3.

1790 ANON. Ode to superstition.—See New Annual Register, 1790, pp. [160–62].
  BENTLEY, ELIZABETH. Ode to content.—Gent. Mag., lx. 1167–8.

bef.1791 w. BLACKLOCK, THOMAS. Ode to Aurora.—Poems, Edin., 1793, pp. 200–201.
  ORAM, S. M. Ode to friendship.—Poems, 1794, pp. 24–8.

1791 ADNEY, THOMAS. Ode to health.—Europ. Mag., xx. 143–5.
  ANON. Hymn to humanity.—Univ. Mag., lxxxix. 391.
  ANON. On happiness, after the manner of Milton, translated.—The Bee,
   vi. 307 (Dec. 28, 1791).
  BLACKETT, MARY D. Ode to poetry.—Europ. Mag., xx. 224.
  HUDDESFORD, GEORGE. Illusions of fancy.—Salmagundi, 1791, pp. 1–19.
  —— Whitsuntide.—Ib. 65–7.
  —— Christmas.—Ib. 69–71.
  "JUVENTUS." Address to evening.—Gent. Mag., lxi. 68.
  L——D, T. Invocation to sympathy.—Ib. 260–61.
  MOORE, J. Ode to liberty.—Ib. 72.
  ROBINSON, MARY. Ode to the muse.—Poetical Works, 1806, i. 81–6.
  —— Ode to reflection.—Ib. 97–9.
  —— Ode to envy.—Ib. 100–103.
  —— Ode to health.—Ib. 104–8.
  —— Ode to melancholy.—Ib. 114–16.
  —— Ode to meditation.—Ib. 143–7.

1791 w. 1834 p. COLERIDGE, S. T. Music.—Complete Poetical Works, ed. E. H.
  Coleridge, Oxford, 1912, i. 28.

1792 "ALBERT." Verses written in midsummer. — Walker's Hibernian Mag.,
   Aug., 1792, p. 183.
  ANON. Clara (first song), in New songs in the opera The Prisoner.—Ib.,
   Nov., p. 472.
  ANON. Hymn to health.—Univ. Mag., xci. 370.
  DOWNMAN, HUGH. To candour.—Poems by Gentlemen of Devonshire and
   Cornwall, Bath, 1792, i. 30–31.
  DYER, GEORGE. To pity.—Poems, 1801, pp. 187–91.
  HOLE, Mr. [RICHARD?]. To melancholy. — Poems by Gentlemen of Devon-
   shire, etc., i. 86–94.
  Z., X. Address to the evening.—Walker's Hibernian Mag., Oct., 1792, p.
   376.

1792 w. SOUTHEY, ROBERT. To contemplation.—Works, 1837, ii. 132–4.

1792 w. 1895 p. COLERIDGE, S. T. To disappointment.—Works, 1912, i. 34.

1793 ANON. L'allegro.—The Looker-On, no. 53 (in British Essayists, Boston,
   U. S. A., 1857, xxxvi. 219–22).
  ANON. Invocation to patience. — Univ. Mag., xciii. 69.
  ANON. Invocation to praise.—Asylum for Fugitive Pieces, 1793, iv. 125–6.
  BURRELL, SOPHIA, Lady. L'allegro.—Poems, 1793, ii. 239.
  "EUSEBIUS." Ode to rage.—Univ. Mag., xcii. 289.
  ROBINSON, MARY. Ode to hope.—Works, 1806, i. 164–7.

bef.1794 w. BLAMIRE, SUSANNA. The farewell to affection.—Works, 1842, pp. 46–9.
  ——The recall to affection.—Ib. 49–51.
  —— Hope.—Ib. 148–53.

1794 ANON. Ode to sleep.—Univ. Mag., xcv. 119–20.
  "EUSEBIUS." Ode to envy.—Ib. xciv. 442–3.
  "HORATIO." Ode to despair.—Europ. Mag., xxvi. 437–8.
  LOCKE, Miss. The visionary.—Gent. Mag., lxiv. 67–8.

1795 MOORE, HENRY. Private life.—Poems, 1803, pp. 144–53.
  PORTER, ANNA MARIA. Address to summer.—Univ. Mag., xcvi. 369.

1796   "CASTOR." Ode to vengeance.—Europ. Mag., xxix. 201–2.
        COURTIER, PETER L. The triumph of freedom.—Poems, 1796, pp. 50–53.
        —— To night.—Ib. 56–61.
        D., D. W. Ode to hope.—Europ. Mag., xxx. 120.
        PERFECT, Dr. To solitude.—Gent. Mag., lxvi. 863–4.
        SHEPHERD, T. R. Ode to melancholy.—Ib. 600.
        W., ANNE MARIA. Lines on a young lady's recovery from illness.—Walker's
        Hibernian Mag., Sept., 1796, pp. 277–8.
1796 w. BOSCAWEN, WILLIAM. Ode iii, For the anniversary meeting of subscribers
        to the literary fund.—Poems, 1801, pp. 39–45.
1796 w. 1804 p. SMITH, E. F. Ode to melancholy.—Europ. Mag., xlix. 444–5.
1797   ANON. Address to melancholy.—Univ. Mag., c. 438–9.
        J., E. S. To despondency.—Scots Mag., lix. 841.
        PARK, THOMAS. The summer invitation.—Sonnets, etc., 1797, pp. 51–5.
        SMYTH, WILLIAM. Ode to mirth.—English Lyrics, 3d ed., 1806, pp. 39–45.
1798   "AN ENGLISH JACOBIN." Ode to Jacobinism.—Poetry of the Anti-Jacobin,
        ed. C. Edmonds, 2d ed., 1854, pp. 105–7.
        W., W. A. Ode to peace.—Hezekiah, King of Judah, 1798: see Mo. Rev.,
        enl., xxviii. 351.
bef.1800 w. WARTON, JOSEPH. The temple of love.—Biographical Memoirs, ed. J.
        Wooll, 1806, pp. 91–5.
1800   WAKEFIELD, GILBERT. Address to peace.—Mo. Mag., x. 438.
c. 1800 w. HARDINGE, GEORGE. To the winds.—Miscellaneous Works, 1818, ii. 173.
c. 1800 w. 1807 p. WHITE, HENRY KIRKE. Thanatos.—Remains, ed. Southey, 5th ed.,
        1811, i. 363–4.
        —— Athanatos.—Ib. 364–5.
1801   ANON. Il luttuoso ed il gaudioso, il giocoso ed il diligente, 1801.
        PRESTON, WILLIAM. Hymn to old age.—A Collection of Poems [ed. Joshua
        Edkins], Dublin, 1801, pp. 305–10.
        THELWALL, JOHN. [Songs in] The fairy of the lake.—Poems written in Re-
        tirement, Hereford, 1801, pp. 51–2.
bef.1802 w. MOORE, HENRY. A vernal ode.—Poems, 1803, pp. 1–5.
        —— A lyric rhapsody.—Ib. 6–10.
        —— Ode to religion.—Ib. 59–62.
        —— Invocation to melancholy.—Ib. 91–6.
        —— Ode to wisdom.—Ib. 97–101.
1802   B—, J—. Idyllium to mirth.—Gent. Mag., lxxii. 256.
        "SENNED." Greenwich park, or Whitsun Monday.—Europ. Mag., xli.
        385–7.
1803   HOLLOWAY, WILLIAM. Adieu and recal to poetry.—Scenes of Youth, etc.,
        1803, pp. 131–49.
        "SABINUS." Il romito, or the hermit.—Europ. Mag., xliv. 300–301.
        W., J. Peace of mind.—Ib. 136.
c. 1803–6 w. 1807– p. WHITE, HENRY KIRKE. Ode on disappointment.—Remains,
        1811, i. 35–8.
        —— To contemplation.—Ib. ii. 73–9.
        —— Ode to liberty.—Ib. iii. (1822), 114–16.
1804   DRAKE, NATHAN. To fancy.—Literary Hours, 3d ed., 1804, iii. 175–7.
        ELTON, C. A. The mistress.—Poems, 1804: see New Annual Register,
        1804, pp. [266–7].
        H—E, W. On melancholy.—Scots Mag., lxvi. 219.
        HOWARD, NATHANIEL. The rural evening.—Bickleigh Vale, etc., York,
        1804, pp. 52–6.
        —— To meditation; written near a Gothic church.—Ib. 72–3.
        —— To horror.—Ib. 110–14.

1804   RICHARDS, GEORGE. To autumn.—Poems, Oxford, 1804, ii. 33–6.
—— To prosperity.—Ib. 64–6.
1805   ANON. Ode to spring.—Gent. Mag., lxxv. 559–60.
RICHARDSON, WILLIAM. Address to meditation.—Poems and Plays, new ed., Edin., 1805, i. 11–13.
—— Hymn to melancholy. — Ib. 79–86.
—— Hymn to friendship. — Ib. 133–8.
c. 1805 w. STRUTHERS, JOHN. To content.—Poetical Works, 1850, ii. 185–7.
1806   ANON. Ode to war.—Gent. Mag., lxxvi. 750.
AUSTIN, W. Ode to amusement.—Europ. Mag., xlix. 373.
BECKET, ANDREW. [Choruses in] Socrates.—Dramatic and Prose Miscellanies, ed. W. Beattie, 1838, i. 272.
1807   FIELD, BARRON. La ciriegia, an austere imitation of Milton's L'Allegro.—The News, March 20, 1807.
1808   C. (JOSIAH CONDERS?). To forgetfulness.—The Associate Minstrels, 2d ed., 1813, pp. 179–84.
1809   —— To cheerfulness.—Ib. 168–74.
BOWLES, W. L. Inscription.—Poetical Works, ed. Gilfillan, Edin., 1855, i. 155–6.
1810 w. STRUTHERS, JOHN. Lines for the 25th of January, 1810.—Works, 1850, ii. 199–200.
1811   ——Stanzas for the anniversary of the birth of Burns.—The Winter Day, etc., Glasgow, 1811, pp. 93–6.
1812   DYER, GEORGE. On peace.—Poetics, 1812, i. 124–30.
1814   N., H. Ode to enthusiasm.—Mo. Mag., xxxvi. 522–3.
TWISS, HORACE. Fashion, a paraphrase of L'Allegro.—Posthumous Parodies, etc., 1814, pp. 3–12.
1818   BOWICK, JAMES. The genius of poetry, Montrose, 1818.
1820   KEATS, JOHN. Fancy.—Poems, ed. E. de Sélincourt, 2d ed., 1907, pp. 198–200.
1821   CLARE, JOHN. Solitude.—Poems, ed. A. Symons, 1908, pp. 75–84.
1822   WORDSWORTH, WILLIAM. To enterprise.—Poetical Works, ed. Knight, 1896, vi. 218–24.
1824   SHELLEY, P. B. To Jane: the invitation.—Poetical Works, ed. Hutchinson, Oxford, 1904, pp. 748–9.
1825   AIKIN, A. L. (Mrs. BARBAULD). Lines over a chimney-piece.—Works, 1825, i. 147.
1832   MOTHERWELL, WILLIAM. Melancholye.—Poetical Works, ed. James M'Conechy, Paisley, etc., 1881, pp. 67–70.

BIBLIOGRAPHY III

POEMS INFLUENCED BY THE REMAINING
WORKS OF MILTON [1]

A. POEMS INFLUENCED BY LYCIDAS

1729   BROWNE, MOSES. Eclogue v, Colin's despair, an imitation of Lycidas.— Piscatory Eclogues, 1729, pp. 74–86.

1737 w.[2] WEST, RICHARD. Monody on Queen Caroline.—Dodsley's Miscellany, 1748, ii. 276–81.

1744 w. 1747 p. MASON, WILLIAM. Musæus, a monody [on] Pope, in imitation of Lycidas.—Works, 1811, i. 1–15.

1747   LYTTELTON, GEORGE, Lord. To the memory of a lady lately deceased, a monody, 1747.

1751   IMAGE, JOHN. "Ah me! the luckless chime."—Acad. Cantab. Luctus in Obitum Frederici . . . Walliae Principis, Camb., 1751, X.

1753   WERGE, JOHN. An irregular ode on the death of Charles Broome.—Collection of Poems, Stamford, 1753, pp. 51–4.

1755   HALLIDAY, Dr. Brutus, a monody to the memory of [William] Bruce, 1755. —See Mo. Rev., xiv. 351–6.

1759[3] POTTER, ROBERT. Kymber, a monody, 1759.

1763   SCOTT, JAMES. The redemption, a monody, Camb., 1763.

1765 w. 1770 p. BRUCE, MICHAEL. Daphnis, a monody.—Works, ed. Grosart, Edin., 1865, pp. 230–34.

1767   SCOTT, JAMES. The vanity of human life, a monody, 1767.

c. 1769 w. SEWARD, ANNA. Monody on Mrs. Richard Vyse.—Works, Edin., 1810, i. 104–7.

1771 w. ANON. Ode on the death of Gray.—Works of Gray, with Memoirs by William Mason, 1827, pp. 434–5.

1774   ANON. Monody [on] Mr. Cholwell, in imitation of Lycidas, 1774.

1777   MAURICE, THOMAS. Monody [on] Elizabeth, duchess of Northumberland. —Poems, Epistolary, Lyric, etc., 1800, pp. 109–15.

        WARTON, THOMAS (the younger). Monody, written near Stratford upon Avon.—Works, ed. Mant, Oxford, 1802, i. 63–7.

1778   ANON. A monody (after the manner of Lycidas) on Mr. Linley, 1778.— See Crit. Rev., xlvi. 316.

1779   PRATT, S. J. The shadows of Shakespeare, a monody [on] Garrick, 2d ed., Bath, 1780 (?).

        SHERIDAN, ELIZABETH ("T. B."). On the death of my unfortunate brother. —Gent. Mag., xlix. 608; also lv. 56.

1785 w. DERMODY, THOMAS. Corydon, a monody.—Life, with Original Poetry, by J. G. Raymond, 1806, i. 6–9.

1786   DAMER, JOHN. Elegy on the death of a lady.—New Foundling Hospital for Wit, new ed., 1786, i. 254–8.

1790   "WARTOPHILUS." On Mr. [Thomas] Warton.—Gent. Mag., lx. 648–9.

1790 w. 1794 p. COLERIDGE, S. T. Monody on Chatterton.—Works, ed. E. H. Coleridge, Oxford, 1912, i. 13–15, 125–31.

---

[1] Except sonnets: cf. Bibliography IV.

[2] 1743–6 STILLINGFLEET, BENJAMIN. Monody [on] Lord Henry Spenser: MS. in the British Museum. Not seen.

[3] 1762 LAMBE, THOMAS. (?) Lycidas, a masque, 1762. Not seen.

1791 BOWLES, W. L. Monody, written at Matlock, Salisbury, 1791.
CARR, W. W. The muse, a monody [on] Shenstone.—Poems, 1791, pp. 1–28.
HUDDESFORD, GEORGE. Monody on Dick, an academical cat.—Salmagundi, 1791, pp. 129–47.

1792 "ALPIN." Eliza.—Europ. Mag., xxi. 69–70.

1798 ANON. Sidney, a monody, 1798.—See Crit. Rev., new arr., xxv. 230–31.

1800 BOWLES, W. L. Monody on Dr. Warton.—Works, ed. Gilfillan, Edin., 1855, i. 135–41.

1834 ROSCOE, W. S. Monody.—Poems, 1834, pp. 40–48.

1850 FANE, JULIAN. Monody on the queen dowager.—Poems which have obtained the Chancellor's Gold Medal, Camb., 1860, pp. 293–300.

1919 O'BRIEN, KATHLEEN. Mary Jane, ex-munition worker, demobilized, speaks.—Littell's Living Age, cccii. 188.

Monodies that owe little or nothing to Lycidas except the name were written by Edmund Smith (Thales, a Monody in imitation of Spenser, 1751, composed before 1710); Thomas Blacklock (Poems, 1754, pp. 107–124); Thomas Denton (1755, Dodsley's Miscellany, 1758, v. 226–38); anonymous writers, Scots Mag. (1758, 1815), xx. 20, lxxvii. 536, and Mo. Mirror (1797), iv. 108–9, 177–8; John Langhorne (1759–69, Chalmers's English Poets, xvi. 432, 458, 459); John Hoole (on Mrs. Woffington, 1760); anonymous authors (on George II, 1760, and the Duke of Cumberland, 1765); Cuthbert Shaw (on a "young lady," 1768, and to a nightingale, 1770); R. B. Sheridan and William Meyler (both on Garrick, 1779, and see Poetical Amusements near Bath, 1781, iv. 75–9); Anna Seward (on Garrick and André, 1781, Works, 1810, ii. 15–17, 68–88); G. D. Harley (on John Henderson of Covent Garden theater, 1786); "Della Crusca" (Poetry of the World, 1788, i. 76–9); Andrew M'Donald (Miscellaneous Works, 1791, pp. 52–4); "R. B. S[heridan?]" and W. H. Reid (1791, Scots Mag., liii. 339, 444–5), and "H." (on James Grahame, 1811, ib. lxxiii. 934); Joseph Cottle (on John Henderson of Bristol, in Cottle's Poems, Bristol, 1795); Richard Polwhele (Poetic Trifles, 1796, pp. 23–6); William Roscoe (1796, Currie's edition of Burns, 1800, i. 337–42); George Dyer (Poems, 1802, i. 110, ii. 229); John Leyden (1802, from the Arabic, Poetical Remains, 1819, pp. 233–9); John Thelwall (on the Princess Charlotte, 1817, Poetical Recreations, 1822, pp. 48–9), and a broadside on Princess Charlotte, signed "M." (1817); Mrs. Robinson (Works, 1806, i. 56, 246, iii. 53); Joseph Blackett (Kirke White's Remains, 1811, i. 311–14); W. H. Ireland (on William Cavendish, 1811); W. A. Bryson (Poems, Dublin, 1812, pp. 59–65); Byron (on Sheridan, 1816); John Taylor (1817 and 1821, Poems, 1827, ii. 225–6, 235); F. Mayne (Poems, Dover, 1818, pp. 5–13); William Beattie (on Campbell, 1844); Ebenezer Elliott (on Keats, in Elliott's Works, 1876, ii. 182–3). See also Bibl. I, 1757 (Andrews), 1786 (Knipe), 1787 (anon.), 1801 (Dyer), 1806 (Thelwall).

I have not seen Richard Rolt's monody on the Prince of Wales (1751), or the anonymous ones mentioned in the Critical Review, xxviii. 71 (1769), xxxi. 74 (1771), lvii. 153 (1784), or those on a young lady who died at Bath (Bath, 1778) and J. P. Kemble (1823), or T. Harral's on John Palmer (1798), Dennis Lawler's on the Duc d'Enghien (1804), Edward Rushton's on Burns (Rushton's Poems, 1806), Lady Champion de Crespigny's on Lord Collingwood (1810), Thomas Gent's on Sheridan (1816), C. A. Elton's on his two sons (The Brothers, 1820), James Davies's on an officer in the East India service (1844), "J. D.'s" on a brother (Halifax, undated), or William Beattie's on the death of his wife (1845).

B. POEMS INFLUENCED BY COMUS

1647 BARON, ROBERT. Erotopaignion, or the Cyprian academy, 1648.

1738 DALTON, JOHN. Comus [adapted by John Dalton], 3d ed., 1738.

1742 WEST, GILBERT. Instruction of the order of the garter, a dramatick poem. —Dodsley's Miscellany, 1748, ii. 107–68.

bef.1745 w. WARTON, THOMAS (the elder). Invocation to a water-nymph.—Poems, 1748, pp. 21–2.

1764   ANON. Parthenia, or the lost shepherdess, an Arcadian drama, 1764.—See Mo. Rev., xxxii. 233.

1778 w. MASON, WILLIAM. Sappho, a drama.—Poems, York, 1797, iii. 143–89.

1787   ANON. Ode to the nymph of the Bristol spring.—Europ. Mag., xi. 201.

1788   "CAMISIS." Ode to echo.—Ib. xiv. 128.

1793   ANON. Midsummer eve, or the sowing of hemp, 1793.—See Mo. Rev., enl., xii. 341–2.

1801   THELWALL, JOHN. [Songs in] The fairy of the lake.—Poems written in Retirement, Hereford, 1801, pp. 31–4, 90–92.

1811   IMPEY, E. B. [Choruses in] The sylphs.—Poems, 1811, pp. 104–7, 115–17.

1814   BECKET, ANDREW. The genii, attendants on the human race, a masque.— Dramatic and Prose Miscellanies, ed. W. Beattie, 1838, i. 183–218.

C. POEMS INFLUENCED BY THE TRANSLATION FROM HORACE

c.1701–20 w.[1] SAY, SAMUEL. To his harp, from Casimir.—Poems, 1745, pp. 47–8.
——— Horace, book iii, ode xvi, imitated.—Ib. 75–80.

1744–5 w. WARTON, THOMAS (the elder). Ode to taste.—Poems, 1748, pp. 180–83.

1746   COLLINS, WILLIAM. Ode to evening.—Poems, ed. Bronson, Boston (U.S.A.), 1898, pp. 53–5.
WARTON, JOSEPH. Ode viii, To a fountain, imitated from Horace.—Odes, 1746, pp. 32–3.
——— Ode xiii, On shooting.—Ib. 44–5.

1759   AIRY, HARRIOT. Ode to truth.—Gent. Mag., xxix. 538.

1759–60 WOTY, WILLIAM. Ode to content.—Shrubs of Parnassus, 1760, pp. 44–5.
——— Ode to friendship.—Ib. 73–5.
——— A summer's morning.—Ib. 104–6.
——— Ode to health.—Ib. 112–13.

1761   PHILIPPS, RICHARD. "Ye solemn Cloysters."—Pietas Univ. Oxon., 1761, 3L, verso.
VYSE, WILLIAM. "Midst the loud tumults."—Epithalamia Oxoniensia, 1761, Gg2.

1762   RAYNSFORD, RICHARD. "Hail, royal babe."—Gratulatio Solennis Univ. Oxon., 1762, 3I.
TERRY, MICHAEL. "Auspicious month."—Ib. Cc, verso.

1763   ANON. Ode to health.—Poetical Calendar, iv. 116–17.

1766 w. 1770 p. BRUCE, MICHAEL. Ode to a fountain.—Works, 1865, pp. 205–6.

1770   S—T, R—T. Ode to the morning.—Scots Mag., xxxii. 94.

1773   AIKIN, A. L. (Mrs. BARBAULD). Ode to spring.—Poems, 1773, pp. 97–100.

1776   K., G. Ode to morning. — Town and Country Mag., viii. 326.
WESTBY, S. Winter. — Ib. 101.

1780   KEMBLE, J. P. Ode to the memory of Mr. Inchbald.—Fugitive Pieces, 1780, pp. 34–6.

1782   ANON. Ode to health.—Univ. Mag., lxxi. 166.

c.1782 w. MARRIOTT, JOHN. Collins's Ode to Evening imitated.—A Short Account of John Marriott, etc., Doncaster, 1803, pp. 85–8.
——— Translation of Horace's twenty-second ode, in book i.—Ib. 89–90.

1783   ANON. Ode to the morning.—Univ. Mag., lxxii. 323.

1785   BOOKER, LUKE. Hymn to the moon.—Poems, Wolverhampton, 1785, i. 70–74.

---

[1] c. 1740 w. THOMAS, Captain LEWIS (?). Ode on Paradise Lost: see T. Warton's edition of Milton's minor poems, 1785, p. 368 n. Not seen.

1785   HEADLEY, HENRY. Ode to the memory of Chatterton.—Poetical Works, ed. Park, 1808, pp. 31–2.

MERRY, ROBERT. Ode to summer.—The Florence Miscellany, Florence (Italy), 1785, pp. 109–12.

—— Ode to winter.—Ib. 113–15.

c. 1785 w. ROBINSON, MARY. Ode to Della Crusca.—Poems, 1791, pp. 54–6.

1786   ANON. Ode to morning.—Europ. Mag., x. 55–6.

ANON. Ode to night.—Ib. 380–81.

ANON. On seeing an old man.—Gent. Mag., lvi. 65.

1787   MERRY, ROBERT. Ode to tranquillity.—Poetry of the World, 1788, i. 18–20.

WHITEHOUSE, JOHN. Ode to morning.—Poems, 1787, pp. 43–6.

bef.1790 w. WARTON, THOMAS (the younger). Horace, book iii, od. 13.—Works, 1802, i. 116.

—— Horace, book iii. od. 18, after the manner of Milton.—Ib. 117.

1790 w.   POLWHELE, RICHARD. Ode to the spirit of freshness.—Influence of Local Attachment, 1798, ii. 1–7.

1791 w.   SAYERS, FRANK. Ode to morning.—Poetical Works, 1830, pp. 156–8.

—— Ode to night.—Ib. 159–61.

1792   ANON. Ode to the Eolian harp.—Univ. Mag., xci. 60.

G. Ode to fancy.—Poems by Gentlemen of Devonshire and Cornwall, 1792, i. 71–7.

"PHILO-THOMSON." Ode to indolence.—Gent. Mag., lxii. 656.

1792 w.   OPIE, AMELIA. To twilight.—Southey's Annual Anthology, 1799, i. 202–4.

1793–9 w. 1795–1805 p. SOUTHEY, ROBERT. To hymen.—Works, 1837, ii. 145–7.

—— Written on the first of December [1793].—Ib. 148–9.

—— Written on the first of January [1794].—Ib. 150–52.

—— To recovery.—Ib. 159–60.

—— The destruction of Jerusalem.—Ib. 182–4.

—— The death of Wallace.—Ib. 185–6.

—— The Spanish Armada.—Ib. 187–8.

—— St. Bartholomew's day.—Ib. 189–90.

—— Song of the Araucans during a thunder storm.—Ib. 210–11.

—— Song of the Chikkasah widow.—Ib. 212–13.

—— To indolence.—Annual Anthology, 1799, i. 126–8.

1798   ANON. Translation of Horace, book iii, ode 3.—Mo. Mag., v. 208.

1798 w.   TAYLOR, WILLIAM. Ode on the death of Messrs. Shears of Dublin.—Memoir, ed. J. W. Robberds, 1843, i. 219–20.

1798–1803?w. 1803– p. WHITE, HENRY KIRKE. Ode, written on Whit-Monday.—Remains, 1811, i. 356–7.

—— The shipwreck'd solitary's song, to the night.—Ib. 371–3.

—— To an early primrose.—Ib. ii. 52.

—— Ode to the morning star.—Ib. iii (1822), 74–5.

1799   TAYLOR, WILLIAM. A topographical ode.—Southey's Annual Anthology, i. 1–9.

bef.1800 w. WARTON, JOSEPH. Ode to content.—Biographical Memoirs, ed. Wooll, 1806, pp. 140–42.

1801   HUNT, LEIGH. To friendship.—Juvenilia, 4th ed., 1803, pp. 116–18.

1802   DYER, GEORGE. To an enthusiast.—Poems, 1802, i. 9–13.

1804   ANON. To the oak [at Llangollen Vale].—Mo. Mirror, xviii. 342–3.

HOWARD, NATHANIEL. To want.—Bickleigh Vale, etc., York, 1804, pp. 47–51.

—— To a red-breast.—Ib. 61–3.

—— To the echo of a grotto.—Ib. 67–9.

S., F. Horace, ode xxxi, book i.—Poetical Register for 1804, 2d ed., 1806, p. 111.

1805   W. To the wind, at midnight.—Mo. Mirror, xix. 268–9.
1806   "A STRANGER." Autumn.—Ib. xxi. 130–31.
1807   C. (JOSIAH CONDERS?). To hope.—The Associate Minstrels, 2d ed., 1813, pp. 36–40.
1808   NOBLE, THOMAS. Translation of the thirty-first ode, first book of Horace. —Blackheath, etc., 1808, pp. 36–7 (second pagination).
1813   ANON. A song of freedom for the nineteenth century, translated from Stolberg.—Mo. Mag., xxxvi. pt. ii. 331–2.
         SHELLEY, P. B. To Harriet *****.—Poetical Works, ed. Hutchinson, Oxford, 1904, pp. 853–4.
1823 w. bef.1836 p. KEBLE, JOHN. Burial of the dead.—Miscellaneous Poems, 3d ed., Oxford, etc., 1870, pp. 15–18.
1827   —— Tuesday after Easter.—The Christian Year, Oxford, 1827, i. 125–7.
1835   CLARE, JOHN. Autumn.—Poems, ed. A. Symons, 1908, pp. 102–5.
1837   COLERIDGE, SARA. "O sleep my babe."—Phantasmion, N. Y., 1839, i. 151–2.
         —— "Ah, where lie now those locks that lately stream'd?"—Ib. ii. 192–3.
1907   GARNSEY, E. R. To Pyrrha [Horace, I. v].—Odes of Horace, 1907, p. 83.

D. POEMS INFLUENCED BY THE NATIVITY

1647   BARON, ROBERT. Erotopaignion, or the Cyprian academy, 1648.
c. 1730 w. SAY, SAMUEL. Psalm xcvii, in paraphrastic verse.—Poems, 1745, pp. 85–9.
1746   COLLINS, WILLIAM. Ode to simplicity.—Poems, 1898, pp. 39–41.
         WARTON, JOSEPH. Ode iv, To superstition.—Odes, 1746, pp. 19–21.
         —— Ode v, To a gentleman upon his travels thro' Italy.—Ib. 22–5.
1769   GRAY, THOMAS. Ode for music.—English Poems, ed. Tovey, Camb., 1898, pp. 76–9.
1775   "CLIO." Ode for the nativity. — Town and Country Mag., vii. 662–3.
1798   ANON. The abolition of catholicism.—Mo. Mag., v. 367–8.
1822   SHELLEY, P. B. Chorus.—Hellas, 1822, lines 197–238.
1827   KEBLE, JOHN. Second Sunday after Easter.—The Christian Year, 1827, i. 161–4.
1866–1904 SWINBURNE, A. C. To Victor Hugo.—Poems, 1904, i. 144–50.
         —— The eve of revolution.—Ib. ii. 10–26.
         —— Blessed among women.—Ib. 56–63.
         —— Ode on the insurrection in Candia.—Ib. 200–208.
         —— Birthday ode to Victor Hugo.—Ib. iii. 341–58.
         —— Song for the centenary of Landor.—Ib. v. 7–39.
         —— A new-year ode to Victor Hugo.—Ib. vi. 27–44.
         —— The altar of righteousness.—Ib. 301–20.
         —— The high oaks.—Ib. 326–30.
         —— Barking hall: a year after.—Ib. 331–3.
         —— Astraea victrix.—Ib. 389–92.
1867   INGELOW, JEAN. Song for the night of Christ's resurrection (a humble imitation).—A Story of Doom, etc., Boston (U.S.A.), 1867, pp. 204–11.
1908   DOBSON, AUSTIN. A Miltonic exercise.—De Libris, 1908, pp. 191–2.

SUMMARY

Paradise Lost	1239
L'Allegro and Il Penseroso	449
Remaining Works	150
Total	1838

BIBLIOGRAPHY IV

EIGHTEENTH-CENTURY SONNETS[1]

This is *not* a list of sonnets influenced by Milton (for such a list, see pages 696–7), but of all sonnets published between 1700 and 1800, as well as of all those by persons who began to write quatorzains before the end of the century.[2] Magazine sonnets are an exception, since they are included only when some of their authors' pieces appeared in books.[3] Unless otherwise indicated, each poem listed contains fourteen pentameter lines not riming in couplets.

Of the abbreviations, *trans.* = translation; *P.* = Petrarchan (only poems that rime *a b b a a b b a c d e c d e* or *-c d c d c d* are included under this head); *S.* = Shakespearean (*a b a b c d c d e f e f g g*); *Sp.* = Spenserian (*a b a b b c b c c d c d e e*); *Ir.* = Irregular, a designation used to cover any variation, however slight, from the other types but not intended as a reflection upon the poems, since Petrarch himself did not always use the system indicated by *P.* When the number or the kind of sonnets is not mentioned, it is because I have not seen the work.

bef.1701 w. SEDLEY, CHARLES. Miscellaneous Works, 1702, pp. 97, 100–101, 121–2, 144–5. *4 S.* (2 octosyllabic). Several other pieces have a similar rime-scheme but contain more or less than fourteen lines; two others of sonnet length are in couplets. None of the poems are called sonnets.

1705? KING, WILLIAM. Miscellanies in Prose and Verse, 1705 (?), pp. 491–2. *1 Ir.* (not called a sonnet; only six of the lines are pentameter).

bef.1715 w. MONCK, MARY. Marinda, 1716, pp. 25–7, 65, 71–5, 87–91, 122–3. *8 Ir. (trans.).* Called sonnets, but 1 is elegiac, 4 are in couplets, 3 in blank verse, 1 octosyllabic, 2 in more than fourteen lines.

1721 S., Mr. The Grove, 1721, pp. 163–4. *1 S.*

1741 w. YORKE, PHILIP, second earl of Hardwicke. H. Walpole's Catalogue of Royal and Noble Authors, ed. T. Park, 1806, iv. 400. *1 Ir.*

1742 w. 1775 p. GRAY, THOMAS. English Poems, ed. Tovey, Camb., 1898, p. 3. *1Ir.*

1743 w. YORKE, CHARLES. P. C. Yorke's Life of Philip Yorke, Earl of Hardwicke, Camb., 1913, i. 292, ii. 147. *2 Ir.*

1746 w. 1801– p. STILLINGFLEET, BENJAMIN. Literary Life and Select Works, ed. W. Coxe, 1811, ii. 159–68. *8 P.*

1746–55 w. 1748– p. EDWARDS, THOMAS. Canons of Criticism, 6th ed., 1758, pp. 1, 2, 3, and 18 prefatory, 260–61, 281–325; Nichols's Collection of Poems, 1782, vi. 103–5. *52: 44 P., 4 Sp., 4 Ir.*

---

[1] This bibliography owes a great deal both in accuracy and in completeness to the months of painstaking labor Miss Rowe has given to it.

[2] In case of the numerous sonnets of Wordsworth and Capel Lofft, however, only the three each wrote before 1800 are listed.

[3] These four may be regarded as significant on account of their early dates: *London Mag.*, 1737, vi. 448 (trans., eighteen lines, in couplets); 1738, vii. 356 ("in imitation of Milton's sonnets"); 1740, ix. 555 (trans.); 1741, x. 47 (trans., sixteen lines, in couplets).

1748   RODERICK, RICHARD. Collection of Poems by Several Hands [Dodsley's
             Miscellany], 1748, ii. 323.   *1 Ir. (trans.).*

1748–97w. 1764– p. MASON, WILLIAM. Works, 1811, vol. i, prefatory, and pp. 119–34.
             14: 12 P., 2 Ir.

1749– w.   HIGHMORE, SUSANNAH (Mrs. DUNCOMBE). R. Freeman's Kentish
             Poets, Canterbury, 1821, ii. 385–6; another sonnet is written in a
             Boston library copy of Edwards's Canons.   *4 (2 trans.): 2 P., 2 Ir.*

c.1750w. 1775– p. CHAPONE, HESTER M. Works, 1807, ii. 11–12, iv. 155, 193.   *3 Ir.
             (1 trans.).*

c.1750 w.   HALL, WILLIAM. Nichols's Literary Anecdotes, 1814, viii. 520.   *1 P.*

c.1750– w. 1755–77 p. WARTON, THOMAS (the younger). Works, ed. Mant, Oxford,
             1802, ii. 143–61.   *9: 5 P., 4 Ir.*

1755– w. 1764–71 p. PERCY, THOMAS. The Hermit of Warkworth, 1771, prefatory;
             Collection of Poems by Several Hands [Pearch's Supplement to
             Dodsley], new ed., 1783, iii. 298–300.   *3 Sp.*

bef.1757 w.   DUNCOMBE, JOHN. Freeman's Kentish Poets, 1821, ii. 379.   *1 P.*

1761w. 1770 p. C., Mr.   Pearch's Supplement, 1783, iv. 117.   *1 S.*

1762   CARTER, ELIZABETH. Poems on Several Occasions, 1762, p. 49.
             1 Ir. (trans.).

1763   ANON. Poetical Calendar, 1763, vii. 78–80, viii. 65, xi. 110.   *5 (4
             trans.): 1 S., 4 Ir. (1 in couplets).*

             THOMPSON, WILLIAM. Poetical Works, ed. T. Park, 1807, pp. 177–8.
             2 Sp.

1763–1800   HOOLE, JOHN. Tasso's Jerusalem Delivered, translated, 2d ed., 1764,
             vol. i, pp. xxxiii, xxxvi–vii; Metastasio's Dramas, translated, 1800,
             vol. i, pp. xix–xx; Ariosto's Orlando Furioso, translated, 1783, in
             Chalmers's English Poets, xxi. 34.   *4 Ir. (trans.).*

1764?   WALPOLE, HORACE. Castle of Otranto, 2d ed., 1765, p. iii.   *1 Ir.* (lines
             of four or three feet).

1764–76?   LANGHORNE, JOHN. Chalmers's English Poets, xvi. 430, 472–4; Mo.
             Rev., xxx. 123.   *12 (9 trans.): 4 P., 8 Ir.* (2 are in couplets, 5 in
             more or less than fourteen lines; 4 translations are from Petrarch,
             5 from Milton's Italian sonnets).

1766–70   SCOTT, JOHN, of Amwell. Poetical Works, 1782, pp. 313–17; Pearch's
             Supplement, 1783, iv. 112, 116.   *6 Ir.* (1 mainly in couplets).

1767   DODD, WILLIAM. Poems, 1767, pp. 82, 84.   *2 Ir.*

1767–96w. 1768?– p. DOWNMAN, HUGH. Poems, 2d ed., Exeter, 1790, pp. 74–9; Poems
             to Thespia, 2d ed., Exeter, 1791, pp. 141–73, 175; Poems by
             Gentlemen of Devonshire and Cornwall, Bath, 1792, i. 182; Essays
             by Gentlemen at Exeter, 1796, pp. 337–41, 549–51; Polwhele's
             Traditions and Recollections, 1826, i. 155–6, 203–4; three other
             sonnets are written in the Harvard copy of Poems to Thespia, and
             one in the Harvard Bampfylde MS.   *56: 1 P., 5 S., 50 Ir.* (5 in
             blank verse, 1 in couplets, 1 in thirteen lines).

c. 1767– w.   HUDDESFORD, GEORGE, and others. Wiccamical Chaplet, 1804, pp. 71,
             74–5, 80, 87–8.   *6: 4 P., 2 Ir.* (1 in blank verse, thirteen lines).[1]

1768   BOSWELL, JAMES. Account of Corsica, Glasgow, 1768, p. 214.   *1 Ir.*
             (trans., sixteen lines).

1769 w.   WOLCOT, JOHN ("PETER PINDAR"). Wrote some "descriptive son-
             nets": see Polwhele's Traditions and Recollections, 1826, i. 35.

1770– w. 1784– p. SEWARD, ANNA. Original Sonnets, 2d ed., 1799; Works, 1810,
             iii. 50, 314, 316; Asylum for Fugitive Pieces, 1786, ii. 139; Gent.
             Mag., 1789, lix. 743.   *105 (5 trans.): 38 P., 67 Ir.*

---

[1] Of the other sonnets in the volume, five are by Thomas Russell, four by Bampfylde, one each by Bowles,
Davenport, and Charlotte Smith.

1771– w.   CARR, W. W. Poems on Various Subjects, 1791, prefatory, and pp. 93–107. *14: 11 P., 3 Ir.* (1 partly octosyllabic).

1772   H., S. Conjugal Love, Camb., 1772. Contains sonnets: see Lofft's Laura, no. 912.

1772–94?   MICKLE, W. J. Chalmers's English Poets, xvii. 540, 554–5. *3 (2 trans.): 1 P., 2 Ir.*

1774   HENLEY, S. Nathaniel Tucker's Bermudian, 1774, prefatory. *1 Ir.*

1774 w.   COLLINS, JOHN. Letter to George Hardinge, 1777, p. 39. *1 Ir.*

1774–1805 w.   DUNSTER, CHARLES. Poems by Gentlemen of Devonshire and Cornwall, 1792, i. 183–5; S. E. Brydges's Censura Literaria, 1808, vi. 414–15; Gent. Mag., lxv. 328. *5 (1 trans.): 2 P., 3 Ir.* (1 in blank verse).

1776   ANON. Sonnets, 1776.

1776 w.   MORE, HANNAH. Memoirs, ed. W. Roberts, N. Y., 1836, i. 50. *1 Ir.* (sixteen lines).

1776–1818   BOOTHBY, Sir BROOKE. Sorrows, sacred to Penelope, 1796 (contains 24 sonnets, 5 of which, including 4 translations, are in Lofft's Laura and 7 others in Henderson's Petrarca); F. N. C. Mundy's Needwood Forest, Lichfield, 1776, app. *(1 P.);* George Hardinge's Miscellaneous Works, 1818, ii. 18 *(1 Ir.). 26* (most of them not seen).

1776– w.   CARTWRIGHT, EDMUND. Sonnets to Eminent Men, 1783 *(6 Ir.);* Letters and Sonnets, 1807; Armine and Elvira, 9th ed., 1804 (contains sonnets, see Mo. Rev., enl., xlvi. 216–17); Prince of Peace, etc., 1779 (contains 2 sonnets, see Mo. Rev., lx. 373–5). Five sonnets *(1 P., 4 Ir.)* are printed in Lofft's Laura.

1776–1816 w.   HARDINGE, GEORGE. Miscellaneous Works, 1818, ii. 3–28, 185, 436, 440, 442. *52 (24 trans.): 34 P., 18 Ir.* (All but two are called sonnets. Of the 18 irregular ones, 10 have more or less than fourteen lines and 2 are in lines of seven syllables; 4 are in couplets, — several other poems in fourteen lines and couplets, though not called sonnets, are in no way different from these four, — and 4 have a couplet-ending added to the regular Petrarchan rime-scheme.)

1777   ANON. Sonnets [20] and Odes, translated from Petrarch, 1777.
   SCHOMBERG, A. C. Bagley, Oxford, 1777, prefatory. *1 P.*

c.1777? w. 1804 p. JONES, Sir WILLIAM. Works, 1807, ii. 78 n. *1 P.*

1777– w.   ROSCOE, WILLIAM. Life of Lorenzo de' Medici, Liverpool, 1795, i. 113, 114, 261–2, 265, ii. 275; The Nurse, 3d ed., 1800, prefatory; Life of Leo X, Liverpool, 1805, i. 201, 210, 211 n., 282, iv. 207 n.; H. Roscoe's Life of Roscoe, 1833, i. 37, 166–7, 235–6, ii. 73, 82, 85, 222, 237–8, 301–2; W. W. Currie's Memoir of James Currie, 1831, i. 150. *21 (10 trans.): 6 P., 1 S., 14 Ir.*

1777– w. 1785– p. POLWHELE, RICHARD. Poems by Gentlemen of Devonshire, etc., 1792, ii. 194–203; Sketches in Verse, 1796, pp. 67–71, 74–80; Influence of Local Attachment, etc., new ed., 1798, ii. 55–8, 62–3, 67, 69–70, 73, 104–5, 108; Grecian Prospects, Helston, 1799, pp. i–ii; Poems, Truro, 1810, ii. 50–61, 73; Traditions and Recollections, 1826, i. 156, 176–7, ii. 635, 688–9, 699; Reminiscences, 1836, vol. i, pp. vi–vii, 15, vol. iii. 154–6, 163; P. L. Courtier's Pleasures of Solitude, etc., 3d ed., 1804, p. 7; S. J. Pratt's Harvest-Home, 1805, iii. 498–9; Europ. Mag., xxviii. 331. *60: 3 P., 17 S.* (3 octosyllabic), *40 Ir.* (5 in blank verse, 1 in Alexandrine couplets, 1 partly octosyllabic). Polwhele also wrote Pictures from Nature in Nineteen Sonnets, 2d ed., 1786(?); Poems, 1788, which include 20 sonnets; and Poetic Trifles, 1796, which contain sonnets (see Mo. Rev., enl., xxi. 463–4).

1777–89 w.   JACKSON, WILLIAM. Nichols's Collection, 1781, vii. 341–3; Freeman's Kentish Poets, 1821, ii. 403–8. *12 (3 trans.): 1 P., 4 S., 7 Ir.*

1778   "A GENTLEMAN OF OXFORD." Academic Trifles, 1778. Contains 2 sonnets in blank verse: see Crit. Rev., xlvi. 68.

    HOLMES, ROBERT. Alfred, with Six Sonnets, Oxford, 1778, pp. 21–8. *2 P., 4 Ir.*

    PEARCE, WILLIAM. The Haunts of Shakespeare, 1778, p. 26. *1 Ir.* ("collected from Shakespeare").

1778 w. 1789 p.   LETTICE, JOHN. Poetry of the World, 1791, iv. 5–6. *1 Ir.*

1778 w. bef.1821 p.   SIX, JAMES. Freeman's Kentish Poets, 1821, ii. 425–6. *3 P.*

1778–92   BAMPFYLDE, JOHN. Sixteen Sonnets, 1778. (Four of these and one new sonnet are printed in Poems by Gentlemen of Devonshire and Cornwall, 1792, i. 177–81; three more, apparently never printed, are in the Harvard Bampfylde MS.) *20: 4 P., 16 Ir.*

1779–1805w. 1781– p.   HAYLEY, WILLIAM. Poems and Plays, new ed., 1788, i. 161–71, iv. 29, 93, 189, 219, 221, v. 90, vi. 4; Triumph of Music, Chichester, 1804, pp. 21, 52, 72, 80–83, 85–91, 93–5, 97–9, 100, 101, 132–3, 145; Life of G. Romney, Chichester, 1809, pp. 99–100, 159–60, 235–6, 292; Memoirs, ed. J. Johnson, 1823, i. 427–8, ii. 12–13, 15–17, 22, 38, 43, 84, 94, 97, 102; Memoirs of T. A. Hayley, by J. Johnson, 1823, pp. 192–3, 211–12, 226, 250, 308, 324, 334–5, 425–6, 454–5, 471–2, 477–87, 492, 496–7; H. Roscoe's Life of William Roscoe, 1833, i. 244; Poetical Register for 1804, 2d ed., 1806, p. 377. *89 (5 trans.): 13 P., 76 Ir.* (Hayley's Essay on Sculpture, 1800, contains one or more sonnets: see Johnson, above, ii. 14).

1780   ANON. An Idle Hour's Amusement: Poems, Sonnets, etc., 1780.

c. 1780 w.   KETT, HENRY. Juvenile Poems, Oxford, 1793, pp. 16–27, 43–4. *14 Ir.*

1781   ANON. The Bevy of Beauties: [24] Sonnets, 1781.

    H., S. Nichols's Collection, 1781, vii. 343–4. *1 S.*

    PINKERTON, JOHN. Rimes, 2d ed., 1782, pp. 217–26. *5 Ir. (1 trans.).*

1781 w.   BRADFORD, A. M. Downman's Poems to Thespia, 1791, pp. 187–8. *1 Ir.*

    COLE, J. Ib. 189. *1 S.*

1781– w.   PRESTON, WILLIAM. Poetical Works, Dublin, 1793, vol. i, pp. v, 255–94. *27 (5 trans.): 9 P., 18 Ir.*

1782   ANON. W. Hayley's Essay on Poetry, 1782, p. 249. *2 (trans.): 1 P., 1 S.*

    BURNEY, CHARLES. General History of Music, 1782, ii. 334–5. *2 P. (trans.).*

    STERLING, JOSEPH. Poems, Dublin, 1782, pp. 2, 29, 109–119. *13: 6 S., 4 Sp., 3 Ir.*

1782–4   WARWICK, THOMAS. Abelard to Eloisa, 1783 (contains at least 13 sonnets, — see Mo. Rev., lxxii. 147–9, — most of which seem to be reprinted in Poems by Gentlemen of Devonshire and Cornwall, ii. 212–22); Univ. Mag., lxxi. 219, lxxiv. 395, lxxv. 334. At least *16 Ir. (2 trans.).*

1782–1823w. 1785– p.   BRYDGES, EGERTON. Poems, 4th ed., 1807, pp. 3–47; Censura Literaria, 1807–9, iii, prefatory, iv. 204–5, vi. 99, 402–3, 419; vii, pp. v–vi; x. 85; Five Sonnets to Wootton (Kent, 1819), pp. 3–7; Gnomica (Geneva, 1824), pp. 242–3, 295, 312–13. *65 (1 trans.): 15 P., 5 S., 45 Ir.*

1783–95   WILLIAMS, HELEN MARIA. Poems, 2d ed., 1791, i. 53–8, ii. 21–8; Paul and Virginia, translated, 1795, pp. 33, 53, 78, 91, 105, 113, 200, 202. *13: 8 P., 2 S., 3 Ir.* (The novel, Julia, 1790, also contains sonnets: see New Annual Reg., 1790, p. [179].)

1783–96 STEVENS, W. B. Stebbing Shaw's Staffordshire, 1798, i. 343–4; Gent. Mag., lvi. 427, lxvi. 421. *4 (1 trans.): 2 S., 2 Ir.* (1 in eighteen lines).

1784 LIPSCOMB, WILLIAM. Poems, [with] Translations of [23] Select Italian Sonnets, Oxford, 1784.

ROBERTSON, DAVID. Poems, Edin., 1784. Probably contains the irregular sonnet in Univ. Mag., lxxiv. 35.

1784–1803 SMITH, CHARLOTTE. Elegiac Sonnets, etc., 8th ed., 1797–1800, i. 1–59, ii. 1–33; Univ. Mag., lxxxiv. 331; Henderson's Petrarca, 1803, p. 52. *94: (5 trans.): 2 P., 40 S., 1 Sp., 51 Ir.*

1784–1810 TYTLER, A. F., Lord WOODHOUSLEE. Historical and Critical Essay on Petrarch, with a Translation of a few of his Sonnets, Edin., 1810, pp. 62–3 n., 107–8, 201–2, 255–69. *15 (trans.): 4 S., 11 Ir.* (1 in fifteen lines; 1 in twenty lines, seven of which have only six syllables each; 3 in blank verse).

1785 BLACK, JOHN. The Vale of Innocence, and Sonnets, Woodbridge, 1785. (Several sonnets by Black, some of later date, are printed in Lofft's Laura.)

GREATHEED, BERTIE. The Florence Miscellany, Florence (Italy), 1785, p. 80. *1 P.*

KNIGHT, SAMUEL. Elegies and Sonnets, 1785.

MERRY, ROBERT. The Florence Miscellany, 91. *1 P. (trans.).*

1785–96 PARSONS, WILLIAM. Ib. 31, 74, 89; Ode to a Boy at Eton, with three Sonnets, 1796, pp. 3, 19, 20; Europ. Mag., xxi. 222. *7 (2 trans.): 1 P., 3 S., 3 Ir.* (Parsons's Poetical Tour, 1787, also contains sonnets: see Crit. Rev., lxiv. 225.)

1785– w. DRUMMOND, G. H. Poems [= Verses Social and Domestic, Edin., 1802 ?]. Contains sonnets: see Lofft's Laura, nos. 222–3, 297.

1785?–1838w. 1788– p. BOWLES, W. L. Works, ed. Gilfillan, Edin., 1855, i. 7–31, ii. 145, 323, 324, 327, 328; Gent. Mag., new series, x. 44. *50: 2 P., 48 Ir.* (1 in thirteen lines, 2 in fifteen).

bef.1786 w. ANON. Jens Wolff's Sketches and Observations, 1801. *1 Ir.*: see Mo. Rev., enl., xl. 366–7.

1786 ANON. Asylum for Fugitive Pieces, 1786, ii. 24–9. *6 (1 trans.): 5 P., 1 Ir.*

HEADLEY, HENRY. Poetical Works, ed. T. Park, 1808, p. 23. *1 S.*

1786– w. PYE, H. J. Poems on Various Subjects, 1787, vol. i, pp. iii–iv; Verses on Several Subjects, 1802, pp. 71–3; S. J. Pratt's Harvest-Home, 1805, iii. 229, 233, 254; Lofft's Laura, no. 273; Gent. Mag., lxxv. 592. *8 (1 trans.): 6 P., 1 S., 1 Ir.*

1786–90 w. RANNIE (or RENNIE?), JOHN. Poems, 1789 (contains sonnets, see Crit. Rev., lxvii. 553); Poetry of the World, 1791, iii. 130; Europ. Mag., xvii. 232–3, xviii. 70–71, 220; Scots Mag., lii. 302; Edin. Mag., March, 1792, p. 460. *12: 11 S., 1 Ir.*

1786–92w. 1787– p. WORDSWORTH, WILLIAM. Poetical Works, ed. Knight, 1896, i. 3–4; viii. 209–10, 214–15. *3: 1 S., 2 Ir.* (As Wordsworth's 520 sonnets written after 1800 are of a later type, they are not included here.)

1786–1800w. 1789– p. ROBINSON, MARY. Works, 1806, iii. 63–126 (62, of which the 43 in the sequence "Sappho and Phaon, in a series of Legitimate Sonnets," and 3 others, are *P.*, 3 *S.*, the rest *Ir.*); Poems, 1791, pp. 172, 173, 174, 177, 179, 185; Memoirs, 1801, iii. 92; M. E. Robinson's Shrine of Bertha, 1794, i. 133; Univ. Mag., xciii. 300. *71: 46 P., 5 S., 20 Ir.*

1786–1833w. 1794– p. Coleridge, S. T. Works, ed. E. H. Coleridge, Oxford, 1912, i. 5,
9–10, 11–12, 16–17, 20, 21, 29, 37, 47–8, 71, 72–3, 79–90, 93, 152–5,
209–11, 236, 361–2, 392–3, 402–3, 429, 435, 447, 459–60, 490. *46 (1
trans.): 1 P., 9 S., 36 Ir.* (2 mainly in couplets, 1 mainly octosyllabic). The Bala Hill and Faded Flower sonnets (pp. 56, 70),
usually printed as Coleridge's, are counted as Southey's; "Pale
Roamer" (p. 71) is counted as Coleridge's; the two poems on pantisocracy (pp. 68–9), of uncertain authorship, are not counted
anywhere.

1787   B—o, J. Asylum for Fugitive Pieces, 1789, iii. 215. *1 Ir.* (sixteen
lines).
                CUNNINGHAM, PETER. Anna Seward's Letters, 1811, i. 291–2 n. *1 S.*

1787–8   ANON. (chiefly "BENEDICT"). Poetry of the World, 1788, ii. 122–32.
                11 Ir.

1787–93   REID, W. H. Poems (posthumous, date unknown). Probably includes
the following sonnets: Univ. Mag., lxxx. 264–5, lxxxi. 44, 208, 366,
lxxxii. 98, 211; Gent. Mag., lvii. 626, lix. 258, 353, 555, lx. 450, 555,
lxi. 759, 856, lxiii. 360; Scots. Mag., lii. 89; Europ. Mag., xviii. 223;
Literary Mag. and British Rev., August, 1790, p. 148. *21 (3 trans.):
7 S., 14 Ir.*

1787–1804   WHITEHOUSE, JOHN. Poems, 1787, pp. 81–9; Poetical Register for
1804, 2d ed., 1806, pp. 155, 159. *11: 4 P., 7 Ir.* (4 in couplets, 2 in
blank verse).

1787–1822   THELWALL, JOHN. Poems on Various Subjects, 1787, ii. 173; Poems
written in the Tower, 1795, pp. 1–12; Poems written in Retirement,
Hereford, 1801, p. 101; Poetical Recreations, 1822, pp. 44, 143,
184–5, 228–9. *20: 3 S., 17 Ir.* (1 in fifteen lines, 1 octosyllabic).

bef.1788 w.   RUSSELL, THOMAS. Sonnets, etc., Oxford, 1789, pp. 1–27. *23 (6 trans.):
9 P., 3 S., 11 Ir.*

1788   BROWN, JAMES. Original Poems, Sonnets, etc., 1788.
                DAY, J. William Upton's Poems on Several Occasions, 1788, pp. 187–
8. *1 S.*
                UPTON, WILLIAM. Poems on Several Occasions, 1788, pp. 62–3, 94–5,
112–13, 122–5, 222–5, 231–2. *8 S.* (1 octosyllabic).

1788–9   LISTER, THOMAS. Anna Seward's Letters, ii. 171, 279; H. Cary's
Memoir of H. F. Cary, 1847, i. 16; Gent. Mag., lix. 841. *4: 1 P.,
2 Ir., 1 not seen.*

1788–94   WESTON, JOSEPH. H. Cary's Memoir of H. F. Cary, i. 13–14; Gent.
Mag., lviii. 1008, lxi. 660, 760; Europ. Mag., xxvi. 366. *6 (1 trans.):
3 P., 3 Ir.* (May be included in the pieces that Weston published
with "Mrs. Pickering's" poems, 1794.)

1788–95   BELOE, WILLIAM. Poems, 1788, pp. 35–48; Miscellanies, 1795, i. 65–71.
                14 (2 trans.): 9 S., 5 Ir.

1788– w. 1794– p. PENN, JOHN. Poems, 1801, i. 38–42; ii. 245–9, 250, 253–7, 264–70,
275–82, 289–90. *25 (23 trans.): 16 P., 9 Ir.*

1788–93w. 1792– p. COWPER, WILLIAM. Poems, ed. J. C. Bailey, 1905, pp. 445, 459,
489–90, 492, 494–5, 499, 597–9. *14 (5 trans.): 1 P., 13 Ir.* (1 in
couplets).

1788–1823w.   PARK, THOMAS. Sonnets, etc., 1797, pp. i, 1–30; Anna Seward's
Original Sonnets, 1799, p. vii; Mo. Mirror, ix. 362, xv. 47, xix. 268,
xxii. 196; Poetical Register for 1804, 2d ed., 1806, p. 152; Park's
edition of T. Russell's Poems, 1808, prefatory; Kirke White's Remains, 1811, i. 304–5; Lofft's Laura, 1813, no. 291; S. E. Brydges's
Miscellaneous Articles, Kent, c. 1815 (2 sonnets, near the end);
Robert Bloomfield's Remains, 1824, i. 185–6. *43 (1 trans.): 3 P.,
10 S., 30 Ir.*

1788–1844 w.   CARY, H. F. Sonnets and Odes, 1788, pp. 7–34; Memoir, ed. H. Cary, 1847, i. 16, 23, 26, 30, 35, 37, 69, 96, ii. 6, 308–9; Gent. Mag., lix. 257, 553. In the prefatory life and the footnotes to the 1819 edition of his Dante are translations of 12 Italian sonnets, and in S. Waddington's Sonnets of Europe, 1886, pp. 87, 118, 137–9, are translations of one more Italian and 4 French sonnets. *58 (20 trans.)*: *36 P., 2 Sp., 20 Ir.* (Two translations from the Italian, mentioned in the Memoir, i. 109, I have not seen.)

1789   ANON. The Garland, 1789. Contains sonnets: see Mo. Rev., lxxx. 366.

ANON. Sonnets, 1789. Contains 60 sonnets, apparently Petrarchan: see Mo. Rev., lxxxi. 366.

GROOMBRIDGE, WILLIAM. Sonnets, Canterbury, 1789.

1789–92   EMETT, S. Poems by Gentlemen of Devonshire and Cornwall, 1792, i. 186–92, ii. 193. *8 S.*

1789 w.   FANSHAWE, C. M. Literary Remains, 1876, p. 79. *1 S.*

1789–94 w.   BURNS, ROBERT. Complete Works, Cambridge (U. S. A.) ed., pp. 144, 178, 179–80. *4 Ir.* (1 in couplets).

1789–1823w. 1791– p.   RADCLIFFE, ANN. Romance of the Forest, chs. iii, xviii (xvii in some editions); Mysteries of Udolpho, chs. i, viii (or ix), lii (or li); Poems, 1816, p. 115; Miscellaneous Poems, appended to St. Alban's Abbey, 1826, p. 231; Lofft's Laura, no. 365. *8: 3 S., 5 Ir.* (The novels contain eight or ten other poems of varying length and rime-scheme, which are usually termed sonnets.)

c.1789–1802w. 1789?– p.   DERMODY, THOMAS. Poems, 1800, pp. 3, 102–4, 109; Life, by J. G. Raymond, 1806, ii. 206–7, 209–10, 314–15; Mo. Mirror, ix. 236; Anthologia Hibernica, 1793, i. 225; Lofft's Laura, no. 953. *14: 7 S., 7 Ir.* (all called sonnets, but six are in more than fourteen lines).

1790   ANON. Sonnets to Eliza, 1790. Most of these have twenty or twenty-four lines, and are irregular in rime (see Crit. Rev., lxix. 591–2), but some may be true sonnets.

"JUNIA." Poetry of the World, 1791, iii. 181. *1 S.*

PEARSON, SUSANNA. Poems, Sheffield, 1790. Contains at least 3 sonnets: see Mo. Rev., enl., iv. 579; New Annual Reg., 1790, pp. [178–9]; Univ. Mag., lxxxix. 218.

SHILLITO, CHARLES. A Sonnet, supposed to have been written by Mary Queen of Scots, translated, 1790.

1790–91   ARMSTRONG, JOHN ("ALBERT"). Sonnets from Shakespeare, 1791. Contains 3 original sonnets (pp. 1, 44, 45) and 39 passages from Shakespeare's plays arranged in sonnet form. In the Boston Library copy are newspaper clippings of 3 more original sonnets. *45 S.*

1790–1803w. 1791– p.   SAYERS, FRANK. Poetical Works, 1830, pp. 1, 178–81, 183–5. *8: 2 P., 2 S., 4 Ir.*

1790–1817 w.   SOTHEBY, WILLIAM. Tour through Wales, etc., 1790, pp. 45–59; Saul, 1807, p. 95; Italy, etc., 1828, p. 220 (six other poems, pp. 221–2, 224, 311, 313–14, suggest the sonnet in their rime-scheme, but contain either too many or too few lines). *16: 1 P., 15 Ir.* (1 in sixteen lines, called sonnet).

1790–1822w. 1799– p.   OPIE, AMELIA. Poems, 1802 (contains at least 3 irregular sonnets, see Lofft's Laura, nos. 86, 290, 293); The Warrior's Return, etc., Phil., 1808, pp. 59–60, 105–6; Madeline, 1822, in Works, Phil., 1853, i. 51, 75; Brightwell's Memorials, Norwich, 1854, pp. 9, 39. At least *10: 5 S., 3 Ir., 2 not seen.*

1790–1826 w.   TAYLOR, JOHN. Verses on Various Occasions, 1795, pp. 46–9, 135–6; Poems on Various Subjects, 1827, i. 147–210, ii. 66, 253–7; Mrs. Robinson's Memoirs, 1801, iv. 162. *103: 74 P., 26 S., 3 Ir.*

c. 1790–1837   LLWYD, RICHARD. Poetical Works, 1837, pp. 71, 82, 93, 104, 117, 137, 161, 168, 182–3, 187, 247–8, 280, 285–6. *13: 2 S., 1 Sp., 10 Ir.* (mainly in couplets, 2 partly octosyllabic).

c. 1790 w. 1798 p. DRAKE, NATHAN. Literary Hours, 3d ed., 1804, i. 115–18. *4: 2 S., 2 Ir.* (Drake also prints, i. 78, 111, an anonymous irregular sonnet translated from Petrarch, and two from Lupercio, one of them in blank verse.)

c. 1790? w.   MANNERS, Lady. Poems, 2d ed., 1793, pp. 79–81, 84, 119, 121. *6: 5 S.* (3 octosyllabic), *1 Ir.*

c. 1790–1805 w. RODD, THOMAS. Sonnets, etc., 1814. *118: 14 P., 29 S., 75 Ir.*

c. 1790– w.   WRANGHAM, FRANCIS. Poems, 1795, pp. 55–6, 65–6, 100–102; A Few Sonnets from Petrarch, Kent, 1817 (40 trans., 1 orig.); Lofft's Laura, no. 527. *48 (41 trans.): 29 P., 2 S., 17 Ir.*

bef.1791 w.   ORAM, S. M. Poems, 1794, pp. 13–23. *11: 1 P., 2 S.* (1 anapestic), *8 Ir.*

1791   AIKIN, JOHN. Poems, 1791, pp. 75–8. *4 Ir.*

ANON. The Beauties of Mrs. Robinson, 1791, prefatory. See Crit. Rev., new arr., iii. 353.

BENTLEY, ELIZABETH. Poetical Compositions, Norwich, 1791. Contains sonnets: see Lofft's Laura, no. 727 (in couplets), no. 870 *(S.).*

M'DONALD, ANDREW. Miscellaneous Works, 1791, p. 145. *1 P.*

1791–1826   HOLE, RICHARD. H. Downman's Poems to Thespia, 1791, p. 203; R. Polwhele's Traditions and Recollections, 1826, i. 271–2. *1 Ir.*

1791?–1801   THOMSON, ALEXANDER. Sonnets, Odes, and Elegies, Edin., 1801. Contains 135 sonnets (see Mo. Mirror, xiii. 177–8), which may include one appended to his Whist (1791) and six adapted from Werter printed in his Essay on Novels (1793, see Crit. Rev., new arr., xi. 416–18).

1792   ANON. A Poem on a Voyage of Discovery, with Sonnets, 1792, pp. 35–46. *12: 1 P., 7 S., 4 Ir.*

F.   Poems by Gentlemen of Devonshire and Cornwall, 1792, i. 193–4. *2 (1 trans.): 1 S. 1 Ir.* (twelve lines).

FARRELL, SARAH. Charlotte, or a Sequel to the Sorrows of Werter, etc., Bath, 1792, pp. 61–2. *1 S.*

ROBERTSON, DAVID. Tour through the Isle of Man, 1794, p. 123. *1 S.*

SKELTON, ABRAHAM. The Temple of Friendship, York, 1792, pp. 29–30. *2 S.*

SWETE, JOHN. Poems by Gentlemen of Devonshire and Cornwall, 1792, ii. 205–9. *5 Ir.* (1 in twelve lines).

V.   Ib. 210. *1 Ir.*

WESTON, STEPHEN. Ib. 223. *1 Ir.*

Y.   Ib. 224. *1 S.* (octosyllabic).

1792?   ANON. Sonnets, Original and Translated, 1792(?).

1792 w.   G., R.   Polwhele's Traditions and Recollections, 1826, i. 291–2. *2: 1 S., 1 Ir.* (in couplets).

1792–1819   RICKMAN, T. C. Poetical Scraps, 2 vols., 1803 (probably includes the sonnets in Lofft's Laura,— *10 S., 6 Ir.*, one a translation); Life of Thomas Paine, 1819, dedicatory *(1 S.).*

bef.1793 w.   TICKELL, RICHARD. Mrs. Robinson's Memoirs, 1801, iv. 102. *1 Ir.*

1793   ANON. Asylum for Fugitive Pieces, 1793, iv. 145. *1 Ir.*

ANON. Sonnets by a Lady, 1793.

ANON. Sweets and Sorrows of Love, 1793. Contains sonnets: see Mo. Rev., enl., xv. 106.

KENDALL, WILLIAM. Poems, Exeter, 1793. Contains Petrarchan sonnets: see Crit. Rev., new arr., ix. 382–3.

LOGAN, MARIA. Poems on Several Occasions, York, 1793. Contains sonnets: see Lofft's Laura, no. 405.

1793   SCOTT, THOMAS. Poems, Paisley, 1793, pp. 310–12. *2: 1 S., 1 Ir.* (eighteen lines).

1793–1813   HOLCROFT, THOMAS. Asylum for Fugitive Pieces, 1793, iv. 183; Lofft's Laura, no. 285. *2 Ir.* (partly in couplets).

1793– w. 1819?–41 p.   MONTGOMERY, JAMES. Poetical Works, Boston, 1858, ii. 161–4, iii. 121–3, 196–7, iv. 347–52, v. 313; Lofft's Laura, vol. i, p. ccxxxiii. *16 (12 trans.): 4 P., 4 S., 8 Ir.*

1793–1805   MAVOR, WILLIAM. Poems, 1793, pp. 329–46; S. J. Pratt's Harvest-Home, 1805, iii. 292–6; Mo. Mirror, xvi. 84. *22 Ir.*

1794   BELLAMY, THOMAS. Miscellanies, 1794, ii. 130. *1 S.*

    BIDLAKE, JOHN. Poems, Plymouth, 1794. Contains sonnets: see Mo. Rev., enl., xvi. 261.

    HARRISON, ANTHONY. The Infant Vision of Shakspeare, etc., 1794, pp. 11–18, 21, 24. *10: 6 S., 4 Ir.* (2 in couplets, and only one with five feet in every line).

    IRWIN, EYLES. William Ouseley's Oriental Collections, 1797, i. 130; Gent. Mag., lxiv. 1035. *2 Ir. (1 trans.).*

    WILLIAMS, EDWARD. Poems, Lyric and Pastoral, 1794. Contains sonnets: see Mo. Rev., enl., xiii. 409.

    YOUNG, MARIA JULIA. Poems, 1798. Probably contains the sonnets in Univ. Mag., xcv. 375, and Gent. Mag., lxiv. 457.

1794 (1764?)   WHATELEY, MARY (Mrs. DARWALL). Poems on Several Occasions, Walsall, 1794. Contains sonnets: see Crit. Rev., new arr., xiv. 344–5.

1794–6   YEARSLEY, ANN. The Rural Lyre, 1796. Probably contains the 4 sonnets *(3 S., 1 Ir.)* in Europ. Mag., xxvi. 63, and Univ. Mag., xcviii. 360.

1794–9   JENNINGS, JAMES. Southey's Annual Anthology, i. 148–9; Europ. Mag., xxv. 54, 239, xxvi. 289, 366, xxviii. 198–9. *12: 3 S., 9 Ir.* (1 in couplets).

1794–1801   OLIPHANT, ROBERT. Mrs. Robinson's Memoirs, 1801, iv. 123, 157. *2: 1 S., 1 Ir.* (in couplets).

1794 w.   RUTT, J. T. Memorials, Bristol, 1845. Probably contains the irregular sonnet in Lofft's Laura, no. 825.

    V., R. (RICHARD VALPY?). S. J. Pratt's Harvest-Home, 1805, iii. 327. *1 S.*

1794– w.   WEST, JANE. Poems and Plays, 1799, i. 193–202, iii. 189–204; Tale of the Times, Alexandria, 1801, i. 240; The Mother, 1809, prefatory; Gent. Mag., lxx. 370, 465–6, 665. *29: 9 P., 6 S., 14 Ir.* (These may include the sonnets printed in her Gossip's Story, 1796: see Mo. Mirror, ii. 418–19.)

1794–1836   LAMB, CHARLES. Works, ed. Lucas, 1903, v. 3–4, 7–8, 14, 16, 40–42, 47, 54–7, 73–4, 77, 82–3, 90, 94, 101, 104, 105–6. *35: 4 S.* (1 in dactylic tetrameter), *31 Ir.* The first sonnet listed is counted also for Coleridge.

1794–1843 w.   SOUTHEY, ROBERT. Works, 1837, vol. ii, pp. xix, 55–8, 90–100, 117–20; Poems, by R. Lovell and R. Southey, Bath, 1795, pp. 57–62, 67–8, 71–2; Poems, 1797, pp. 110–11; Letters written in Spain and Portugal, Bristol, 1797, pp. 57–8, 120–21, 181–2, 231, 502–3; The Doctor, 1834–47, i. 53–4, vi. 340; Adamson's Memoirs of Camoens, 1820, i. 94, 105, 251, 256, 265; Lofft's Laura, no. 971. *56 (11 trans.): 5 S., 51 Ir.* (Includes the Faded Flower and Bala Hill sonnets.)

1795   ASHBURNHAM, WILLIAM. Elegiac Sonnets, etc., 1795. Contains at least 25 sonnets: see Mo. Rev., enl., xix. 222–3.

1795 w.   B., H. W. Southey's Annual Anthology, 1799, i. 135. *1 Ir.*

1795–1800   LOVELL, ROBERT. Poems by R. Lovell and R. Southey, Bath, 1795,
               pp. 63–6, 69–70; Southey's Annual Anthology, i. 146–7, ii. 160.
               9: 1 S., 8 Ir.

1795–1801   LE MESURIER, THOMAS, or HAMLEY, EDWARD (cf. below, 1796).
               Translations, chiefly from Petrarch and Metastasio, Oxford, 1795
               (contains translations of more than 24 Italian sonnets, see Mo. Rev.,
               enl., xviii. 429–33, British Museum catalogue, and Henderson's
               Petrarca, which prints 12 of them); Poems, chiefly Sonnets, by the
               Author of Translations from Petrarch, Metastasio, etc., 1801 (con-
               tains at least 37 sonnets, see Mo. Rev., xxxvi. 145–8).

1795–1820 w.   LLOYD, CHARLES. Poems on Various Subjects, Carlisle, 1795, pp. 3,
               7–21, 88–9; Poems on the Death of Priscilla Farmer, Bristol, 1796,
               pp. 7–17; Poems by Coleridge, Lamb, and Lloyd, 1797, pp. 169–78;
               Nugae Canorae, 1819, pp. iii, 183–252; Desultory Thoughts, 1821,
               pp. iii, 252; Southey's Annual Anthology, i. 140; Macready's
               Reminiscences, 1875, i. 164. *107 (8 trans.): 11 P., 18 S., 78 Ir.*

c. 1795?–1857 w. BRAY, E. A. Poems, 1799 (contains at least 2 sonnets, see Crit. Rev.,
               new arr., xxviii. 352–3); Literary Remains, 1859, i. 89–123, 214,
               222–3, ii. 45. *38 (2 trans.): 36 P., 2 S.*

1796   "ELIZA." Poems and Fugitive Pieces, 1796. Contains sonnets: see
               Lofft's Laura, no. 308.

               HAMLEY, EDWARD. Poems of Various Kinds, 1796. Contains "a
               series of sonnets formerly published": see Mo. Rev., enl., xx. 471,
               and cf. above, 1795–1801.

               HARROP, E. A. Original Miscellaneous Poems, 1796, pp. 19–20, 29–30,
               38–9, 42–3, 53–4, 76–7. *6: 1 S., 5 Ir.* (in couplets).

               JOHNSON, JOHN. Trifles in Verse, 1796. Contains at least 2 sonnets:
               see Mo. Rev., enl., xx. 347.

               ROBINSON, THOMAS. Sketches in Verse, 1796. Contains sonnets: see
               Crit. Rev., new arr., xxii. 474.

               "A STUDENT OF LINCOLN'S INN." Poems, Sonnets, etc., 1796.

c. 1796? w.   BERESFORD, BENJAMIN. Mrs. Robinson's Memoirs, 1801, iv. 156. *1 Ir.*
               COLOMBINE, PAUL. Ib. 161. *1 P.*

1796–7   BECKFORD, WILLIAM. Azemia, 1797, i. 119–120, ii. 9–10, 28–9. *3 Ir.*
               (Beckford's Modern Novel-writing, 1796, also contains sonnets: see
               his Memoirs, 1859, ii. 167. Over 30 Shakespearean sonnets by the
               William Beckford who wrote a history of Jamaica are printed in the
               Monthly Mirror from 1796 to 1805, and 3 more in Lofft's Laura.)

1796–9   CHEETHAM, R. F. Odes and Miscellanies, 1796, and Poems, 1798
               (contain sonnets, see Mo. Rev., enl., xxvi. 94, and Crit. Rev., new
               arr., xxvi. 230–32); Gent. Mag., lxvi. 774–5, lxix. 884 *(2 Ir.)*.

1796–1802   COURTIER, P. L. Poems, 1796, pp. 19–41; Pleasures of Solitude, etc.,
               3d ed., 1804, pp. 107, 136, 138. *24: 14 S., 10 Ir.*

               STRONG, E. K. (Mrs. CHARLES MATHEWS). Poems, Exeter, 1796, pp.
               23–8. *6: 2 S., 4 Ir.* (1 in couplets). Another volume, published at
               Doncaster, 1802, also contains sonnets (see Crit. Rev., new arr.,
               xxxvii. 474) and may include those in Europ. Mag., xxx. 207, Mo.
               Mirror, iii. 307, v. 368, and Lofft's Laura, no. 127.

1796–1804   GROVE, WILLIAM. Poetical Register for 1804, 2d ed., 1806, pp. 151,
               153, 380. *3 P.*

1796–1820   ANDERSON, ROBERT. Poetical Works, 1820, ii. 97–106; Europ. Mag.,
               xxix. 201, xxx. 55, 207, xxxii. 184, 185, 266, 344 (probably reprinted
               in his Poems, 1798). At least *19: 5 S., 14 Ir.* (1 in twelve lines).

1796–1805 w.   MEYLER, WILLIAM. Poetical Amusement on the Journey of Life,
               Bath, 1806, pp. 160–62, 206–7. *5: 2 S., 3 Ir.*

1796–1803? w. DAVENPORT, R. A. Henderson's Petrarca, 1803, pp. 182–3(?); Poetical Register for 1804, 2d ed., 1806, pp. 379, 381, 385. *5 Ir. (1 trans.).*

1796– w. 1801 p. HUNT, LEIGH. Juvenilia, 4th ed., 1803, pp. 51–2, 55–7, 59. *6 (1 trans.): 3 S., 3 Ir.* (At least 44 other original sonnets and 9 translations, written after 1800, are printed in Hunt's other works, but not all in any one edition.)

c. 1796– w. ROSCOE, W. S. Poems, 1834, pp. 14, 33–4, 72, 82–3, 94–5, 102–3. *10: 5 P., 5 Ir.*

1797 BETHAM, MATILDA. Elegies, etc., Ipswich, 1797. Contains sonnets: see Lofft's Laura, no. 193.

CARLISLE, FREDERICK HOWARD, Earl of. Poetry of the Anti-Jacobin, 2d ed., by C. Edmonds, 1854, p. 30. *1 P.*

DIBDIN, T. F. Poems, 1797. Contains at least 1 sonnet: see Mo. Mirror, iii. 353.

DONOGHUE, J. Juvenile Essays in Poetry, 1797. Contains at least 2 sonnets: see Mo. Rev., enl., xxiii. 457–8.

ROUGH, WILLIAM. Lorenzino di Medici, etc., 1797. Contains sonnets: see Crit. Rev., new arr., xxiii. 466–7.

SMITH, THOMAS. Poems, Manchester, 1797. Contains sonnets: see ib. xxvi. 349–50.

TOMLINS, E. S. and Sir T. E. Tributes of Affection, etc., 1797. Contains sonnets: see Mo. Rev., enl., xxiv. 214.

1798 ANON. Effusions of Fancy, 1798. Contains sonnets: see Crit. Rev., new arr., xxiii. 109.

FAWCETT, JOSEPH. Poems, 1798. Contains sonnets: see Mo. Rev., enl., xxviii. 272.

HOLFORD, MARGARET. Gresford Vale, etc., 1798. Contains sonnets: see ib. xxv. 476.

HUCKS, JOSEPH. Poems, 1798. Contains sonnets: see Crit. Rev., new arr., xxiii. 33–5.

HUGHES, H. Retribution, 1798. Contains sonnets: see ib. xxv. 112–13.

HUNTER, JOHN. Poems, 3d ed., 1805, pp. 219–27. *7 Ir.*

1798–1810 STOCKDALE, MARY R. Effusions of the Heart, 1798 (contains sonnets, see Crit. Rev., new arr., xxii. 352); Mirror of the Mind, 1810 (contains at least 38 sonnets, see Morning Post, Dec. 22, 1813).

1798–1819 LEYDEN, JOHN. Poetical Remains, 1819, pp. 12–17, 22–6, 114, 141, 223–4, 227–8, 254; Edin. Mag. or Lit. Misc., new series, xi. 467. *19 Ir. (6 trans.).*

1799 ANON. Original Sonnets, Elegiac, Ethic, and Erotic, Whitby, 1799.

F., S. Southey's Annual Anthology, i. 143–4. *2 Ir.*

JONES, JOHN. Amatory Odes, Epistles, and Sonnets, 1799.

MUNDY, F. N. C. Anna Seward's Letters, Edin., 1811, v. 217–18 n. *1 P.* (The Bibliotheca Staffordiensis, 1894, p. 321, mentions two manuscript sonnets.)

1799–1800 ANON. Southey's Annual Anthology, i. 134, 137, 139, 145; ii. 154, 161, 163. *7: 1 S., 6 Ir.*

CASE, WILLIAM. Ib. ii. 152–3. *2 P.*

HARLEY, G. D. Ballad Stories, Sonnets, etc., vol. i, Bath, 1799; Holyhead Sonnets, Bath, 1800.

1799–1800 w. LOFFT, CAPEL. Laura, 1814, nos. 31, 49, 51. *3: 1 S., 2 Ir.* (Besides these, the anthology contains over 300 more of Lofft's sonnets, written after 1800, most of them irregular and many of them translations.)

1799–1809 w. 1811? p. TIGHE, MARY ("Mrs. HENRY"). Psyche, with other Poems, 4th ed., 1812, pp. 1, 217–37, 268. *21 (1 trans.): 3 P., 1 S., 17 Ir.*

1799–1813   PRATT, S. J. Gleanings in England, 2d ed., 1801–03, i. 579, ii. 140, 174, 565–6, iii. 10–20; Lofft's Laura, no. 437. *16: 11 S.* (1 octosyllabic), *5 Ir.* (1 in eighteen lines).

bef.1800 w.[1]   MOORE, HENRY. Poems, 1803, pp. 127–34. *12 (1 trans.): 2 S.*, *10 Ir.* (1 octosyllabic).

bef.1800 w.?   FISHER, JOHN. The Valley of Llanherne, etc., 1801. Contains sonnets: see Henderson's Petrarca, 1803, pp. 179, 180.

1800   COLLIER, WILLIAM. Poems on Various Occasions [including Sonnets], with Translations, 1800. (16 of Collier's sonnets, 12 of them translations, are in Lofft's Laura.)
DIMOND, WILLIAM (the younger). Petrarchal Sonnets, etc., Bath, 1800. Contains at least 10 sonnets: see Mo. Rev., enl., xxxiii. 318–19.
SHERIVE, C. H. Southey's Annual Anthology, ii. 151. *1 Ir.*
T., J. W. Ib. 147. *1 Ir.*

1800–1814   BANNERMAN, ANNE. Poems, new ed., Edin., 1807, pp. 43–54, 67–74, 93–105; Lofft's Laura, no. 243. *28 (7 trans.): 14 S., 14 Ir.*

1800–1803 w.   FINCH, S. W. (Mrs. LOFFT). R. Bloomfield's Farmer's Boy, 3d ed., 1800, prefatory; Lofft's Laura, 1814, nos. 3, 4, 39, 41–5, 47–8, 52–61, 66–70, 73, 75, 94. *29 (2 trans.): 1 P., 6 S., 22 Ir.*
SYMMONS, CAROLINE. Poems, 1812. Probably includes the 6 sonnets *(3 P., 3 Ir.)* appended to F. Wrangham's Raising of Jaïrus' Daughter, 1804, pp. 21–3, 32–4.

1801   ANON. The Lamentation, in two parts, 1801. Contains sonnets: see Mo. Rev., enl., xxxvii. 9–10.

1802–22   WHITE, HENRY KIRKE. Remains, ed. Robert Southey, 5th ed., 1811–22, i. 373–4, ii. 53–6, 58–9, 101–14, 144, iii. 108, 112–13; Mo. Mirror, xiii. 343, xiv. 199. *27 (1 trans.): 7 S., 20 Ir.* (1 in blank verse, thirteen lines).

A. SONNETS IN IMITATION OF MILTON'S

1738[2]   ANON. A sonnet, in imitation of Milton's sonnets.—Lond. Mag., vii. 356.

1743 w.   YORKE, CHARLES. [Two sonnets] in imitation of Milton.—P. C. Yorke's Life of Philip Yorke, Camb., 1913, i. 292, ii. 147.

1747   ANON. Hope, a sonnet, written in the stile of Milton.—Lond. Mag., xvi. 382. (Consists of two elegiac stanzas.)

1786   R., M. H. P. Sonnet, in the manner of Milton.—Europ. Mag., ix. 53.

1791   T., W. A sonnet, in the manner of Milton.—Ib. xx. 220.
WESTON, JOSEPH. Allegorical sonnet, in imitation of Milton.—Gent. Mag., lxi. 660.

1792   "IULUS ALBA." To the nightingale.—Europ. Mag., xxi. 221.
WESTON, STEPHEN. Sonnet xxix.—Poems by Gentlemen of Devonshire and Cornwall, 1792, ii. 223.

1793   "NEMO." Burlesque imitation of Milton's famous sonnet written "on the intended Attack upon the City."—Gent. Mag., lxiii. 262.

---

[1] There is some reason to believe that the following persons who published sonnets may have begun writing before 1800: Peter Bayley, Thomas Brown, George Dyer, Mrs. B. Finch, Thomas Gent, William Crowe, Nathaniel Humfray, Thomas Noble, Mary Sewell, Viscount Strangford (translations), Theophilus Swift, Charles Hoyle. The anonymous anthology, *Sonnets of the Eighteenth Century* (1809), I have not seen.

[2] In 1714 an anonymous 42-line poem called *To Aristus, in Imitation of a Sonnet of Milton*, appeared in Steele's *Poetical Miscellanies*, 116–19.

1800 w. LOFFT, CAPEL. Imitation: To Miss Finch, on her birthday.—Laura, no. 51.

1802 ANON. Sonnet on a broken pair of snuffers, in imitation of Milton.—Europ. Mag., xli. 208.

"FLORIMEL." Sonnet.—Scots Mag., lxiv. 593.

1807 BRYDGES, EGERTON. Sonnet to the Rev. Cooper Willyams.—Poems, 4th ed., 1807, p. 24.

1820 WORDSWORTH, WILLIAM. On the detraction which followed the publication of a certain poem.—Poetical Works, 1896, vi. 212.

1827 TAYLOR, JOHN. An imitation [of Milton], on receiving an invitation from William Porden.—Poems, 1827, i. 188–9.

INDEX

INDEX

Figures in italics refer to pages in the appendices and bibliographies; figures in parentheses indicate the number of times authors are listed on the pages in question.